40th issue
40e édition
40.ª edición

1980 Year Book of Labour Statistics

Annuaire des statistiques du travail

Anuario de Estadísticas del Trabajo

International Labour Office   Geneva
Bureau international du Travail   Genève
Oficina Internacional del Trabajo   Ginebra

ISBN 92-2-002526-4 (hard cover; relié; empastado)
ISBN 92-2-002525-6 (limp cover; broché; en rústica)
ISSN 0084-3857

ILO publications can be obtained through major booksellers or ILO local offices in many countries, or direct from ILO Publications, International Labour Office, CH-1211 Geneva 22, Switzerland. A catalogue or list of new publications will be sent free of charge from the above address.

Les publications du BIT peuvent être obtenues dans les principales librairies ou les bureaux locaux du BIT dans de nombreux pays, ou sur demande adressée directement à Publications du BIT, Bureau international du Travail, CH-1211 Genève 22, Suisse, lequel enverra également sur demande un catalogue ou une liste des nouvelles publications.

Las publicaciones de la OIT pueden obtenerse en las principales librerías o en oficinas locales de la OIT en muchos países o pidiéndolas a: Publicaciones de la OIT, Oficina Internacional del Trabajo, CH-1211 Ginebra 22, Suiza, que también puede enviar a quienes lo soliciten un catálogo o una lista de nuevas publicaciones.

Price:
Hard cover: 100 Swiss frs.

Prix:
Relié: 100 fr. suisses

Precio:
Empastado: 100 frs. suizos

PRINTED IN SWITZERLAND   IMPRIMÉ EN SUISSE   IMPRESO EN SUIZA

Contents

Contents

Contents

Table des matières

Table des matières

Table des matières

Indice general

Indice general

Preface

The *Year Book of Labour Statistics, 1980,* presents a summary of the principal labour statistics for some 180 countries or territories. Whenever possible, the data cover the last ten years (1970-79) and, for some tables, one month or one period near the middle of 1980. Texts, headings and notes are given in English, French and Spanish, in order to enable as wide a use as possible of this publication.

Beginning with the present issue of the *Year Book,* employment data published in Chapter II, hitherto shown in the form of index-numbers, have been replaced by absolute figures; in addition, where possible, such data are shown for males and females separately. A new Table 6 B on employment in manufacturing, by major groups of industry, has also been introduced.

The presentation of the tables of the first two chapters has been changed as a result of the use of modern data processing technology; similar changes will be made to other tables in future editions of the *Year Book.*

The data published in the *Year Book* are drawn mainly from information sent to the Office by the national statistical services, or from official publications. The International Labour Office wishes to express its gratitude to the statistical services of the different countries for their valuable collaboration.

Arrangement of material

The various subjects are grouped in eight chapters, each with an introductory note briefly indicating the main characteristics of the different types of series published in the tables.

The countries appear by continent in accordance with the table " Order of arrangement of countries and territories " (see page XXI).

Base period of indices

For the series presented in the form of index numbers, a uniform base (1970 = 100) has been adopted in the *Year Book* in accordance with the practice followed by the statistical services of the United Nations and of the specialised agencies. When data are available only for periods after 1970, indices are shown in *italics,* usually with the first calendar year for which the figures are available as the base period. Whenever a series is interrupted and replaced by a new series the latter is linked to the former if the two series are sufficiently comparable or otherwise it is published on a new base; this break in continuity is indicated by a horizontal or vertical line separating the two series and by an explanatory footnote.

Classifications used in the " Year Book "

Data by division of economic activity, by industry or by occupational groups are arranged, as far as possible, according to international classifications, i.e. the *International Standard Industrial Classification of all Economic Activities* (ISIC) or the *International Standard Classification of Occupations* (ISCO).

In the tables where the industrial or occupational groups are shown under a digit system, the data relate to ISIC 1968 or ISCO 1968, as the case may be. Where there are no digits in the column headings, the data relate to national classifications unless identified as ISIC or ISCO 1958.

Whereas the differences between ISCO 1958 and ISCO 1968 at the level of detail shown in the Year Book (one-digit) are relatively minor, those between ISIC 1958 and ISIC 1968 are important, particularly as concerns service-type activities.

In ISIC 1968, for example, repair and installation of manufactured goods (previously in Manufacturing) and sanitary services (formerly with Electricity, Gas and Water) are included under "*Community, Social and Personal Services*"; real estate, insurance, banks and other financial institutions (previously under Commerce) now form a new major division "*Financing, Insurance, Real Estate and Business Services*"; restaurants and hotels (previously under

Services) are under "*Wholesale and Retail Trade, Restaurants and Hotels*".[1]

A third international classification used in the Year Book is that of *Status* (adopted in 1966), i.e. as employer, own-account worker, employee, unpaid family worker or member of producers' co-operative (for definitions, see introductory note, Chapter I).

Index

An Index at the end of the *Year Book* shows the countries and territories for which data are given in each table, with appropriate page references.

Sources

A list of the main national publications in which current labour statistics are issued is shown in the Appendix (see *References and Sources*, Part B).

Methodology

Basic information on the scope of the statistics, their definition and the methods of calculation used by the national statistical services in establishing the general series published in the *Year Book of Labour Statistics* and the *Bulletin of Labour Statistics* is given in the *Technical Guide* (Volume I: Consumer prices; Volume II: Employment — Unemployment — Hours of work — Wages).

This information complements the brief indications given in the footnotes to the tables and facilitates international comparison of the series.

A list of documents of the International Labour Office dealing with the statistical methodology recommended for the compilation of labour statistics is given in the Appendix (see *References and Sources*, Part A).

Other regular statistical publications

Bulletin of Labour Statistics

Monthly, quarterly or half-yearly data relating to the general series on employment, unemployment, hours of work, wages and consumer prices for the last three years are published in the *Bulletin of Labour Statistics*.

The second quarterly issue of the *Bulletin* also contains the results of an inquiry carried out annually by the ILO on the wages of adult wage earners in 41 occupations, monthly salaries and normal hours of work per week of employees in selected occupations, and retail prices of selected consumer goods, in October each year.

The *Bulletin* also features articles of interest to labour statisticians.

Labour Force Estimates and Projections

This publication provides, for the period 1950-2000, internationally comparable estimates and projections of total population, labour force and labour force participation rates by sex and age group for all countries and territories, major geographical areas, as well as for the world as a whole (for details see *References and Sources*, Part A).

Household Income and Expenditure Statistics

This publication presents, on a uniform basis, data on the level, composition and size distribution of household income and expenditure by social and occupational groups, size of households and geographical areas (for details, see *References and Sources*, Part A).

---

[1] For details, see United Nations: *International Standard Industrial Classification of All Economic Activities*, Series M., No. 4, Rev. 2, Part IV (New York, 1968).

Préface

L'*Annuaire des statistiques du travail, 1980*, présente, pour quelque 180 pays ou territoires, un résumé des principales statistiques du travail. Dans la mesure du possible, les données couvrent les dix dernières années (1970-79) et, pour certains tableaux, un mois ou une période proche du milieu de l'année 1980. Les textes, en-têtes et notes sont publiés en trois langues (anglais, français et espagnol), de manière à permettre une utilisation aussi large que possible de cet ouvrage.

A partir de la présente édition de l'*Annuaire*, les données sur l'emploi publiées, jusqu'ici, dans le chapitre II sous forme d'indices, ont été remplacées par des chiffres absolus; de plus, les données sont également présentées, dans la mesure du possible, pour les hommes et les femmes séparément. Un nouveau tableau 6 B fournissant les données de l'emploi dans les industries manufacturières, par classe d'industries, a également été introduit.

La présentation des tableaux des deux premiers chapitres a été modifiée grâce à l'utilisation d'une technique moderne de traitement des données; en ce qui concerne les autres tableaux, des modifications analogues seront faites dans les prochaines éditions de l'*Annuaire*.

Les données présentées dans l'*Annuaire* proviennent principalement de renseignements communiqués au Bureau par les services statistiques nationaux ou de publications officielles. Le Bureau international du Travail tient à exprimer sa gratitude aux services statistiques des différents pays pour leur précieuse collaboration.

Disposition des sujets traités

Les différents sujets traités dans cet *Annuaire* sont groupés en huit chapitres dont chacun comprend une note introductive où sont indiquées brièvement les principales caractéristiques des divers types de séries publiées dans les tableaux.

Les pays sont présentés par continent, selon la liste figurant au tableau « Ordre de présentation des pays et territoires » (voir p. XXI).

Période de base des indices

Pour les séries présentées sous forme de nombres-indices, une base uniforme (100 en 1970) a été adoptée dans l'*Annuaire*, conformément à la pratique suivie par les services statistiques des Nations Unies et des institutions spécialisées. Lorsque des données ne sont disponibles que pour des périodes postérieures à 1970, les indices, imprimés en *italique*, sont généralement présentés avec, pour période de base, la première année civile pour laquelle des chiffres sont disponibles. Lorsqu'une série est interrompue et remplacée par une nouvelle série, cette dernière est raccordée à la précédente dans la mesure où ces deux séries sont suffisamment comparables, ou publiée sur une nouvelle base dans le cas contraire; cette discontinuité dans l'homogénéité des séries est indiquée par un trait horizontal ou vertical séparant les deux séries et par une note explicative de bas de page.

Classifications utilisées dans l'« Annuaire »

Les données par branche d'activité économique, par classe d'industrie ou par groupe de professions sont, dans la mesure du possible, présentées selon les classifications internationales, soit respectivement, la *Classification internationale type, par industrie, de toutes les branches d'activité économique* (CITI) ou la *Classification internationale type des professions* (CITP).

Dans les tableaux où les groupes d'industries ou de professions sont présentés selon un système décimal, les données se rapportent à la CITI 1968 ou à la CITP 1968, selon les cas. Si aucun chiffre décimal n'est indiqué dans les têtières des colonnes, les données se rapportent à des classifications nationales à moins qu'elles ne soient identifiées comme étant des CITI ou CITP 1958.

Les différences entre la CITP 1958 et la CITP 1968, au niveau de détail (numéros de code à un chiffre) présenté dans l'*Annuaire*, sont relativement peu importantes; il n'en va pas de même, par contre, entre la CITI 1958 et la CITI 1968, notamment en ce qui concerne des activités liées à la prestation de services.

Dans la CITI 1968, par exemple, la réparation et l'installation de biens manufacturés (précédemment sous Industries manufacturières) ainsi que les services sanitaires (précédemment avec Electricité, gaz et eau) sont inclus dans « *Services fournis à la collectivité, services sociaux et services personnels* »; les affaires immobilières, les assurances, les banques et autres institutions financières (précédemment sous Commerce) forment maintenant une nouvelle branche d'activité économique: « *Banques, assurances, affaires immobilières et services fournis aux entreprises* »; les restaurants et les hôtels (précédemment sous Services) sont inclus dans « *Commerce de gros et de détail, restaurants et hôtels* » [1].

Une troisième classification internationale utilisée dans l'*Annuaire* porte sur la *Situation dans la profession* (adoptée en 1966), p. ex. personne travaillant à son propre compte, salarié, travailleur familial non rémunéré ou membre d'une coopérative de producteurs (pour définitions, voir Notes introductives, chapitre I).

Index

Un index présenté à la fin de l'*Annuaire* permet aux lecteurs de connaître les pays et territoires pour lesquels des données sont présentées dans chaque tableau, ainsi que la page où elles apparaissent.

Sources

Une liste des principales publications nationales dans lesquelles sont diffusées les statistiques courantes du travail est fournie dans l'Annexe (voir *Références et sources*, partie B).

---

[1] Pour détails, voir Nations Unies, *Classification internationale type, par industrie, de toutes les branches d'activité économique*, Série M, nº 4, Rév. 2, Partie IV (New York, 1968).

Méthodologie

Des renseignements de base sur la portée des statistiques, leur définition et les méthodes de calcul utilisées par les services statistiques nationaux lors de l'établissement des séries générales publiées dans l'*Annuaire des statistiques du travail* et le *Bulletin des statistiques du travail* sont présentés dans le *Guide technique* (volume I: Prix à la consommation; volume II: Emploi — Chômage — Durée du travail — Salaires).

Ces informations complètent les renseignements succincts qui figurent dans les notes de bas de page des tableaux et permettent une meilleure comparaison des séries sur le plan international.

Une liste des documents du Bureau international du Travail traitant des méthodes statistiques recommandées pour l'établissement des statistiques du travail est fournie dans l'Annexe (voir *Références et sources*, partie A).

Autres publications statistiques régulières

Bulletin des statistiques du travail

Des données mensuelles, trimestrielles ou semestrielles sur les séries générales relatives à l'emploi, au chômage, à la durée du travail, aux salaires et aux prix à la consommation sont publiées dans le *Bulletin des statistiques du travail* pour les trois dernières années.

Le deuxième fascicule trimestriel du *Bulletin* contient aussi les résultats d'une enquête menée annuellement par le BIT sur les salaires des ouvriers adultes dans 41 professions, les traitements mensuels et la durée du travail par semaine des employés dans certaines professions et les prix de détail de certains biens de consommation au mois d'octobre de chaque année.

Le *Bulletin* comprend également des articles intéressant les statisticiens du travail.

Evaluations et projections de la main-d'œuvre

Cette publication fournit, pour la période 1950-2000, des estimations et des projections, comparables sur le plan international, de la population totale, de la main-d'œuvre et des taux d'activité de la main-d'œuvre par sexe et par groupe d'âge pour tous les pays et territoires, les grandes divisions géographiques et pour l'ensemble du monde (pour détails, voir *Références et sources*, partie A).

Statistiques des revenus et des dépenses des ménages

Cet ouvrage présente sur une base uniformisée des données sur le niveau, la composition et la répartition des revenus et des dépenses des ménages, par groupes sociaux et professionnels, taille des ménages et zones géographiques (pour détails, voir *Références et sources*, partie A).

Prefacio

El *Anuario de Estadísticas del Trabajo*, *1980*, presenta, para unos 180 países y territorios, un resumen de las principales estadísticas del trabajo. En lo posible, los datos cubren los diez últimos años (1970-1979) y, para ciertos cuadros, un mes o un período próximo de la mitad del año 1980. Los textos, encabezamientos y notas son trilingües (inglés, francés y español), a fin de que esta publicación pueda ser utilizada con la mayor amplitud posible.

En las ediciones anteriores del *Anuario*, los datos sobre el empleo del capítulo II se presentaban en forma de números índices. A partir de la presente edición serán presentados como cifras absolutas y, en lo posible, por sexo. Además, se introducirá un nuevo cuadro: 6 B, el empleo en las industrias manufactureras por agrupaciones de industrias.

La presentación de los cuadros de los dos primeros capítulos ha cambiado, como consecuencia del uso de técnicas modernas de elaboración de datos. Se harán cambios similares en otros cuadros en las ediciones venideras del *Anuario*.

Los datos presentados en el *Anuario* provienen, en su mayor parte, de las informaciones comunicadas a la Oficina por los servicios estadísticos o de publicaciones oficiales de cada país. La Oficina Internacional del Trabajo expresa su gratitud a los servicios estadísticos de los diferentes países por su preciosa colaboración.

Disposición de los temas tratados

Los diferentes temas tratados en este *Anuario* se hallan agrupados en ocho capítulos, cada uno de los cuales comprende una nota de introducción que indica brevemente las principales características de las diversas clases de series publicadas en los cuadros.

Los países se presentan por continentes, según la lista que figura en el cuadro « Orden de presentación de los países y territorios » (véase pág. XXII).

Período de base de los índices

Para las series presentadas en forma de números índices, se ha adoptado en el *Anuario* una base uniforme (1970 = 100), de conformidad con la práctica seguida por los servicios estadísticos de las Naciones Unidas y de las instituciones especializadas. Cuando sólo se dispone de datos para períodos posteriores a 1970, los índices, impresos en *itálicas*, se presentan generalmente tomando como período de base el primer año civil para el cual se dispone de cifras. Cuando una serie queda interrumpida y se substituye por otra nueva, esta última serie se enlaza con la anterior en la medida en que esas dos series sean suficientemente comparables o, en caso contrario, se publica sobre una nueva base; esta discontinuidad de la homogeneidad de las series se indica por una raya horizontal o vertical entre las dos series y por una nota explicativa al pie de la página.

Clasificaciones utilizadas en el « Anuario »

Los datos por división de actividad económica, por industria o por grupo de ocupaciones se presentan, en la medida de lo posible, con arreglo a las clasificaciones internacionales, es decir, según la *Clasificación industrial internacional uniforme de todas las actividades económicas* (CIIU) y la *Clasificación internacional uniforme de ocupaciones* (CIUO), respectivamente.

En los cuadros en donde se presentan las industrias o las ocupaciones clasificadas mediante un sistema decimal, los datos se hallan relacionados con la CIIU de 1968 o con la CIUO del mismo año. Cuando no figuran cifras decimales en los encabezamientos de las columnas es porque se trata de clasificaciones nacionales, a no ser que se las identifique como de la CIIU de 1958 o de la CIUO de igual año.

Las diferencias entre la CIUO de 1958 y la CIUO de 1968, en lo que se refiere a detalles (cifras de un dígito) presentados en el *Anuario*, son relativamente de poca importancia. Por el contrario, las diferencias entre la CIIU de 1958 y la de 1968 son importantes, especialmente en lo que se refiere a las actividades vinculadas a la prestación de servicios.

En la CIIU de 1968, por ejemplo, la reparación e instalación de artículos manufacturados (antes en Industrias manufactureras) y los servicios sanitarios (antes con Electricidad, gas y agua) están incluidos en « *Servicios comunales, sociales y personales* »; los bienes inmuebles, seguros, bancos y otros establecimientos financieros (antes en Comercio) forman ahora una nueva gran división: *Establecimientos financieros, seguros, bienes inmuebles y servicios prestados a las empresas*; los restaurantes y hoteles (antes en Servicios) se encuentran ahora en « *Comercio al por mayor y al por menor y restaurantes y hoteles* » [1].

Una tercera clasificación internacional utilizada en el *Anuario* es según la *categoría de ocupación* (adoptada en 1966), es decir, empleador, trabajador por cuenta propia, trabajador familiar no remunerado o miembro de una cooperativa de productores (para definiciones, véase nota introductoria al capítulo I).

Indice

El índice, situado al fin del *Anuario*, señala los países y territorios que figuran en los datos presentados en cada cuadro y la página que contiene dichos datos.

Fuentes

En el apéndice figura una lista de las principales publicaciones nacionales en que aparecen las estadísticas ordinarias del trabajo (véase *Referencias y fuentes*, parte B).

---

[1] Para detalles, véase Naciones Unidas: *Clasificación industrial internacional uniforme de todas las actividades económicas*, Serie M, núm. 4, Rev. 2, Nueva York, 1969.

Metodología

En la *Guía Técnica* (Volumen I: Precios del consumo; Volumen II: Empleo — Desempleo — Horas de trabajo — Salarios) se presentan los datos básicos sobre el alcance de las estadísticas, su definición y los métodos de cálculo utilizados por los servicios estadísticos nacionales al establecer las series generales que se publican en el *Anuario de Estadísticas del Trabajo* y en el *Boletín de Estadísticas del Trabajo*.

Estas informaciones completan las informaciones sucintas que figuran en las notas de pie de página de los cuadros y permiten una mejor comparación de las series en el plano internacional.

En el apéndice figura una lista de los documentos de la Oficina Internacional del Trabajo sobre los métodos estadísticos recomendados para la compilación de las estadísticas del trabajo (véase *Referencias y fuentes*, parte A).

Otras publicaciones estadísticas regulares

Boletín de Estadísticas del Trabajo

En el *Boletín de Estadísticas del Trabajo* se presentan los datos mensuales, trimestrales y semestrales sobre las series generales del empleo, del desempleo, de las horas de trabajo, de los salarios y de los precios del consumo de los tres últimos años.

El fascículo del segundo trimestre del *Boletín* contiene también los resultados de una encuesta que efectúa cada año la OIT sobre los salarios de los obreros adultos en 41 profesiones, los sueldos mensuales y las horas normales de trabajo por semana de los empleados en ciertas profesiones y los precios al por menor de determinados bienes de consumo durante el mes de octubre de cada año.

En el *Boletín* se publican igualmente artículos que interesan a los estadígrafos del trabajo.

Evaluaciones y proyecciones de la mano de obra

Esta publicación proporciona, para el período 1950-2000, estimaciones y proyecciones, comparables internacionalmente, de la población total, de la mano de obra y tasas de actividad de la mano de obra, por sexo y grupo de edad, para todos los países y territorios, las grandes divisiones geográficas y también el mundo en su totalidad (para más detalles, véase *Referencias y fuentes*, parte A).

Estadísticas de ingresos y gastos de los hogares

En esta obra se presentan con una base uniforme datos sobre el nivel, la composición y la distribución de los ingresos y gastos de los hogares, por grupos sociales y profesionales, tamaño de los hogares y zonas geográficas (para más detalles, véase *Referencias y fuentes*, parte A).

Order of arrangement of countries and territories

Ordre de présentation des pays et territoires

Orden de presentación de los países y territorios

The countries and territories are listed by continent in the following order: Africa, America, Asia, Europe and Oceania. The designations employed are those in use on 30 June 1979 for statistical and other technical information.

The name of each country appears in English, French or Spanish when the national language of the country, or the language commonly used in it, is one of the three; in other cases the name of the country is given in the language used in official correspondence between the country in question and the ILO.

In the following table the name and order of listing of the countries appear under the heading " **Year Book** " with a reference number for each country. The table also comprises an index in which the countries are arranged in the alphabetical order of their names in each of the three languages; by using the reference numbers the reader can quickly find the name in English, French or Spanish of a country appearing under the heading " **Year Book** " or, starting from its name in any one of these languages, the country designation used in the *Year Book*.

Note : The designations employed (which reflect United Nations practice) and the presentation of the material in this publication do not imply the expression of any opinion whatsoever on the part of the International Labour Office concerning the legal status of any country, territory, city or area or of its authorities, or concerning the delimitation of its frontiers or boundaries ; where the designation " country " appears in the headings of tables, it covers countries, territories, cities or areas. Certain data which relate to the Federal Republic of Germany and the German Democratic Republic include the relevant data relating to Berlin for which separate data have not been supplied. This is without prejudice to any question of status which may be involved.

Les pays et territoires sont présentés par continent dans l'ordre: Afrique, Amérique, Asie, Europe et Océanie. Les désignations utilisées sont celles qui étaient en usage au 30 juin 1979 pour les données statistiques et les autres données techniques.

Le nom de chaque pays figure en français, en anglais ou en espagnol quand la langue nationale de ce pays ou celle qui y est communément utilisée est l'une de ces trois langues; dans les autres cas, le nom du pays figure dans la langue de correspondance officielle de ce pays avec le BIT.

Dans le tableau ci-après, la dénomination et l'ordre de présentation des pays figurent sous la rubrique « **Annuaire** » avec un numéro de référence pour chaque pays. Ce tableau comporte également un index où les pays sont disposés dans l'ordre alphabétique de leur dénomination dans chacune des trois langues; les numéros de référence permettent de retrouver rapidement la dénomination française, anglaise ou espagnole d'un pays figurant sous la rubrique « **Annuaire** » ou, inversement, de retrouver la dénomination d'un pays utilisée dans l'*Annuaire* en partant de sa dénomination dans l'une quelconque de ces langues.

Note : Les désignations utilisées dans cette publication (qui s'inspirent de la pratique des Nations Unies) et la présentation des données n'impliquent de la part du Bureau international du Travail aucune prise de position quant au statut juridique de tel ou tel pays, territoire, ville ou zone ou de ses autorités, ni quant au tracé de ses frontières ou limites ; l'appellation « pays » figurant dans certaines rubriques des tableaux désigne des pays, des territoires, des villes ou des zones. Certaines données se rapportant à la République fédérale d'Allemagne et à la République démocratique allemande comprennent, sans par là préjuger des questions de statut qui peuvent se poser à cet égard, les données relatives à Berlin, pour lequel des informations séparées n'ont pas été fournies.

Order of arrangement of countries and territories *(concl.)*

Ordre de présentation des pays et territoires *(fin)*

Orden de presentación de los países y territorios *(fin)*

Los países y territorios se presentan por continentes en este orden: Africa, América, Asia, Europa y Oceanía. Las designaciones empleadas son las vigentes en 30 de junio de 1979 para informaciones estadísticas y otras informaciones técnicas.

El nombre de cada país figura en español, francés o inglés, cuando su idioma nacional o de uso general es una de estas tres lenguas; en otros casos el nombre del país figura en la lengua que el país utiliza en su correspondencia oficial con la OIT.

En el cuadro siguiente, la denominación y el orden de presentación de los países figuran bajo la rúbrica « **Anuario** », que va acompañada de un número de referencia para cada país. Este cuadro comprende también un índice en que los países se hallan dispuestos en el orden alfabético de su denominación en cada una de las tres lenguas; los números de referencia permiten hallar rápidamente la denominación en español, francés o inglés de un país que figura en la rúbrica « **Anuario** » o, al contrario, hallar la denominación de un país que se utiliza en el *Anuario* partiendo de la denominación en una de estas tres lenguas.

Nota : Las designaciones empleadas en esta publicación (que se inspiran en la práctica seguida en las Naciones Unidas) y la forma en que aparecen presentados los datos no implican juicio alguno, por parte de la OIT, sobre la condición jurídica de ninguno de los países, territorios, ciudades o áreas citados o de sus autoridades, ni respecto de la delimitación de sus fronteras o límites ; con la palabra « país » que figura en los títulos de algunos cuadros se designa a países, territorios, ciudades o áreas. Ciertos datos relativos a la República Federal de Alemania y a la República Democrática Alemana comprenden los datos relativos a Berlín, respecto del cual no se han proporcionado cifras separadas. Tal presentación se hace sin perjuicio de las cuestiones de condición jurídica que puedan plantearse al respecto.

Order of arrangement of countries and territories
Ordre de présentation des pays et territoires
Orden de presentación de los países y territorios

Year Book Annuaire Anuario		Index — Indice		
		English	*Français*	*Español*
	AFRICA — AFRIQUE AFRICA			
		—	—	Alto Volta (15)
1	Algérie	Algeria	Algérie	Argelia
2	Bénin	Benin	Bénin	Benin
3	Botswana	Botswana	Botswana	Botswana
4	Burundi	Burundi	Burundi	Burundi
		—	—	Cabo Verde (6)
5	Cameroun	Cameroon	Cameroun	Camerún
6	Cap-Vert	Cape Verde Is.	Cap-Vert	*Cabo Verde*
7	République centrafricaine	Central African Republic	République centrafricaine	República Centroafricana
		Chad (40)	—	—
8	Congo	Congo	Congo	Congo
9	Côte-d'Ivoire	*Ivory Coast*	Côte-d'Ivoire	Costa de Marfil
		—		Chad (40)
10	Egypt	Egypt	Egypte	Egipto
11	Ethiopia	Ethiopia	Ethiopie	Etiopía
12	Gabon	Gabon	Gabon	Gabón
13	Gambia	Gambia	Gambie	Gambia
14	Ghana	Ghana	Ghana	Ghana
15	Haute-Volta	*Upper Volta*	Haute-Volta	*Alto Volta*
		Ivory Coast (9)	—	—
16	Kenya	Kenya	Kenya	Kenia
17	Lesotho	Lesotho	Lesotho	Lesotho
18	Liberia	Liberia	Libéria	Liberia
19	Libyan Arab Jamahiriya	Libyan Arab Jamahiriya	Jamahiriya arabe libyenne	Jamahiriya Arabe Libia
20	Madagascar	Madagascar	Madagascar	Madagascar
21	Malawi	Malawi	Malawi	Malawi
22	Mali	Mali	Mali	Malí
23	Maroc	*Morocco*	Maroc	Marruecos
		—	Maurice (25)	Mauricio (25)
24	Mauritanie	Mauritania	Mauritanie	Mauritania
25	Mauritius	Mauritius	*Maurice*	*Mauricio*
		Morocco (23)	—	—
26	Mozambique	Mozambique	Mozambique	Mozambique
27	Niger	Niger	Niger	Níger
28	Nigeria	Nigeria	Nigéria	Nigeria
		—	Ouganda (43)	—
29	Réunion	Réunion	Réunion	Reunión
30	Rwanda	Rwanda	Rwanda	Rwanda
31	St. Helena	St. Helena	Sainte-Hélène	Santa Elena
32	Sénégal	Senegal	Sénégal	Senegal
33	Seychelles	Seychelles	Seychelles	Seychelles
34	Sierra Leone	Sierra Leone	Sierra Leone	Sierra Leona
	Somalia	Somalia	Somalie	Somalia
35		—	Soudan (37)	
36	South Africa, Rep of	South Africa, Rep. of	République sud-africaine	República de Sudáfrica
37	Sudan	Sudan	*Soudan*	Sudán
38	Swaziland	Swaziland	Swaziland	Swazilandia

Order of arrangement of countries and territories
Ordre de présentation des pays et territoires
Orden de presentación de los países y territorios

Year Book / Annuaire / Anuario	Index — Indice		
	English	Français	Español
39	Tanzania:	Tanzania:	Tanzanie:	Tanzania:

Year Book / Annuaire / Anuario	English	Français	Español
39 **Tanzania:** Tanzania Tanganyika	Tanzania: Tanzania Tanganyika	Tanzanie: Tanzanie Tanganyika	Tanzania: Tanzania Tanganyika
40 **Tchad**	*Chad*	Tchad	*Chad*
41 **Togo**	Togo	Togo	Togo
42 **Tunisie**	Tunisia	Tunisie	Túnez
43 **Uganda**	Uganda	*Ouganda*	Uganda
	Upper Volta (15)	—	—
44 **Zaïre**	Zaire	Zaïre	Zaire
45 **Zambia**	Zambia	Zambie	Zambia
46 **Zimbabwe**	Zimbabwe	Zimbabwe	Zimbabwe
	AMERICA — AMÉRIQUE AMÉRICA		
47 **Antigua**	Antigua	Antigua	Antigua
	—	Antilles néerlandaises (77)	Antillas Neerlandesas (77)
48 **Argentina**	Argentina	Argentine	Argentina
49 **Bahamas**	Bahamas	Bahamas	Bahamas
50 **Barbados**	Barbados	Barbade	Barbados
51 **Belize**	Belize	Belize	Belize
52 **Bermuda**	Bermuda	Bermudes	Bermudas
53 **Bolivia**	Bolivia	Bolivie	Bolivia
54 **Brasil**	Brazil	Brésil	Brasil
55 **Canada**	Canada	Canada	Canadá
	Chile (59)	Chili (59)	—
56 **Colombia**	Colombia	Colombie	Colombia
57 **Costa Rica**	Costa Rica	Costa Rica	Costa Rica
58 **Cuba**	Cuba	Cuba	Cuba
59 **Chile**	*Chile*	*Chili*	Chile
60 **Dominica**	Dominica	Dominique	Dominica
61 **República Dominicana**	Dominican Republic	République dominicaine	República Dominicana
62 **Ecuador**	Ecuador	Equateur	Ecuador
63 **El Salvador**	El Salvador	El Salvador	El Salvador
64 **Falkland Is. (Malvinas)**	Falkland Is. (Malvinas)	*Iles Falkland (Malvinas)*	*Islas Malvinas (Falkland)*
	—	Etats-Unis (89)	Estados Unidos (89)
	—	Iles Falkland (Malvinas) (64)	—
	French Guiana (70)	—	—
	—	Grenade (66)	Granada (66)
65 **Greenland**	Greenland	Groenland	Groenlandia
66 **Grenada**	Grenada	*Grenade*	*Granada*
67 **Guadeloupe**	Guadeloupe	Guadeloupe	Guadalupe
68 **Guatemala**	Guatemala	Guatemala	Guatemala
	—	—	Guayana Francesa (70)
69 **Guyana**	Guyana	Guyane	Guyana
70 **Guyane française**	*French Guiana*	Guyane française	*Guayana Francesa*
71 **Haïti**	Haiti	Haïti	Haití
72 **Honduras**	Honduras	Honduras	Honduras
73 **Jamaica**	Jamaica	Jamaïque	Jamaica
	—	—	Islas Malvinas (Falkland) (64)
74 **Martinique**	Martinique	Martinique	Martinica

Order of arrangement of countries and territories
Ordre de présentation des pays et territoires
Orden de presentación de los países y territorios

Year Book Annuaire Anuario		Index — Indice		
		English	*Français*	*Español*
75	**México**	Mexico	Mexique	México
76	**Montserrat**	Montserrat	Montserrat	Montserrat
77	**Netherlands Antilles**	Netherlands Antilles	*Antilles néerlandaises*	*Antillas Neerlandesas*
78	**Nicaragua**	Nicaragua	Nicaragua	Nicaragua
79	**Panamá**	Panama	Panama	Panamá
80	**Paraguay**	Paraguay	Paraguay	Paraguay
81	**Perú**	Peru	Pérou	Perú
82	**Puerto Rico**	Puerto Rico	Porto Rico	Puerto Rico
83	**St. Kitts**	St. Kitts	Saint-Christophe	San Cristóbal
84	**St. Lucia**	St. Lucia	Sainte-Lucie	*Santa Lucía*
85	**Saint-Pierre-et-Miquelon**	St. Pierre and Miquelon	Saint-Pierre-et-Miquelon	San Pedro y Miquelón
86	**St. Vincent**	St. Vincent	Saint-Vincent	San Vincente
		—	—	Santa Lucía (84)
87	**Suriname**	Suriname	Suriname	Suriname
88	**Trinidad and Tobago**	Trinidad and Tobago	Trinité-et-Tobago	Trinidad y Tabago
89	**United States**	United States	*Etats-Unis*	*Estados Unidos*
90	**Uruguay**	Uruguay	Uruguay	Uruguay
91	**Venezuela**	Venezuela	Venezuela	Venezuela
92	**Virgin Is. (Brit.)**	Virgin Is. (Brit.)	Iles Vierges (brit.)	Islas Vírgenes (Brit.)
93	**Virgin Is. (US)**	Virgin Is. (US)	Iles Vierges (E-U)	Islas Vírgenes (EE.UU.)
	ASIA — ASIE ASIA			
94	**Afghanistan**	Afghanistan	Afghanistan	Afganistán
95	**Bahrain**	Bahrain	Bahrein	Bahrein
96	**Bangladesh**	Bangladesh	Bangladesh	Bangladesh
		—	Birmanie (98)	Birmania (98)
97	**Brunei**	Brunei	Brunéi	Brunéi
98	**Burma**	Burma	*Birmanie*	*Birmania*
		—	—	República de Corea (109)
99	**Cyprus**	Cyprus	Chypre	Chipre
		—	République de Corée (109)	—
		—	Emirats arabes unis (121)	Emiratos Arabes Unidos (121)
		—	—	Filipinas (116)
100	**Hong Kong**	Hong Kong	Hong-kong	Hong Kong
101	**India**	India	Inde	India
102	**Indonesia**	Indonesia	Indonésie	Indonesia
103	**Iran**	Iran	Iran	Irán
104	**Iraq**	Iraq	Iraq	Iraq
105	**Israel**	Israel	Israël	Israel
106	**Japan**	Japan	Japon	Japón
107	**Jordan**	Jordan	Jordanie	Jordania
108	**Kampuchea démocratique**	Democratic Kampuchea	Kampuchea démocratique	Kampuchea Democrática
109	**Korea, Rep. of**	Korea, Rep. of	*République de Corée*	*República de Corea*
110	**Kuwait**	Kuwait	Koweït	Kuwait
111	**République lao**	Lao Republic	République lao	República Lao
112	**Liban**	Lebanon	Liban	Líbano
113	**Malaysia:**	Malaysia:	Malaisie:	Malasia:
	Peninsular Malaysia	Peninsular Malaysia	Malaisie péninsulaire	Malasia Peninsular
	Sabah	Sabah	Sabah	Sabah
	Sarawak	Sarawak	Sarawak	Sarawak

Order of arrangement of countries and territories
Ordre de présentation des pays et territoires
Orden de presentación de los países y territorios

Year Book / Annuaire / Anuario		Index — Indice		
		English	Français	Español
114	**Nepal**	Nepal	Népal	Nepal
115	**Pakistan**	Pakistan	Pakistan	Pakistán
116	**Philippines**	Philippines	Philippines	*Filipinas*
117	**Singapore**	Singapore	Singapour	Singapur
		—	—	República Arabe Siria (119)
118	**Sri Lanka**	Sri Lanka	Sri Lanka	Sri Lanka
119	**République arabe syrienne**	Syrian Arab Republic	République arabe syrienne	*República Arabe Siria*
120	**Thailand**	Thailand	Thaïlande	Tailandia
121	**United Arab Emirates**	United Arab Emirates	*Emirats arabes unis*	*Emiratos Arabes Unidos*
122	**Viet Nam**	Viet Nam	Viet Nam	Viet Nam
123	**Yemen**	Yemen	Yémen	Yemen
124	**Yemen, Democratic**	Yemen, Democratic	Yémen, démocratique	Yemen, Democrático
	EUROPE — EUROPE EUROPA			
		—	Rép. dém. allemande (134)	Rep. Dem. Alemana (134)
		—	Allemagne, Rép. féd. d' (135)	Alemania, Rep. Fed. de (135)
125	**Austria**	Austria	Autriche	Austria
126	**Belgique**	Belgium	Belgique	Bélgica
127	**Bulgarie**	Bulgaria	Bulgarie	Bulgaria
128	**Czechoslovakia**	Czechoslovakia	*Tchécoslovaquie*	Checoslovaquia
129	**Denmark**	Denmark	Danemark	Dinamarca
130	**España**	*Spain*	Espagne	España
131	**Faeroe Is.**	Faeroe Is.	Iles Féroé	Islas Feroé
132	**Finland**	Finland	Finlande	Finlandia
133	**France**	France	France	Francia
134	**German Democratic Republic**	German Democratic Republic	*Rép. dém. allemande*	*Rep. Dem. Alemana*
135	**Germany, Fed. Rep. of**	Germany, Fed. Rep. of	*Allemagne, Rép. féd. d'*	*Alemania, Rep. Fed. de*
136	**Gibraltar**	Gibraltar	Gibraltar	Gibraltar
137	**Grèce**	Greece	Grèce	Grecia
138	**Hongrie**	Hungary	Hongrie	Hungría
		—	Irlande (140)	Irlanda (140)
139	**Iceland**	Iceland	Islande	Islandia
140	**Ireland**	Ireland	*Irlande*	*Irlanda*
141	**Isle of Man**	Isle of Man	*Ile de Man*	*Isla de Man*
142	**Italie**	Italy	Italie	Italia
143	**Luxembourg**	Luxembourg	Luxembourg	Luxemburgo
144	**Malta**	Malta	Malte	Malta
		—	Ile de Man (141)	Isla de Man (141)
145	**Netherlands**	Netherlands	*Pays-Bas*	*Países Bajos*
146	**Norway**	Norway	Norvège	Noruega
		—	Pays-Bas (145)	Países Bajos (145)
147	**Pologne**	Poland	Pologne	Polonia
148	**Portugal**	Portugal	Portugal	Portugal
		—	—	Reino Unido (153)
149	**Roumanie**	Romania	Roumanie	Rumania
		—	Royaume-Uni (153)	—
		—	Suède (151)	Suecia (151)
		Spain (130)	—	—
150	**Suisse**	*Switzerland*	Suisse	Suiza

Order of arrangement of countries and territories
Ordre de présentation des pays et territoires
Orden de presentación de los países y territorios

Year Book Annuaire Anuario		Index — Indice		
		English	*Français*	*Español*
151	**Sweden**	Sweden	*Suède*	*Suecia*
		Switzerland (150)	—	—
		—	Tchécoslovaquie (128)	—
152	**Turquie**	Turkey	Turquie	Turquía
153	**United Kingdom**	United Kingdom	*Royaume-Uni*	*Reino Unido*
154	**Yugoslavia**	Yugoslavia	Yougoslavie	Yugoslavia
	OCEANIA — OCÉANIE OCEANÍA			
155	**American Samoa**	American Samoa	*Samoa américaines*	*Samoa Americana*
156	**Australia**	Australia	Australie	Australia
157	**Cook Is.**	Cook Is.	Iles Cook	Islas Cook
158	**Fiji**	Fiji	Fidji	Fiji
		French Polynesia (165)	—	—
159	**Guam**	Guam	Guam	Guam
160	**Kiribati**	Kiribati	Kiribati	Kiribati
		—	Ile Nioué (162)	Isla Niue (162)
		New Caledonia (163)	—	Nueva Caledonia (163)
161	**New Zealand**	New Zealand	*Nouvelle-Zélande*	Nueva Zelandia
162	**Niue Is.**	Niue Is.	*Ile Nioué*	*Isla Niue*
163	**Nouvelle-Calédonie**	*New Caledonia*	Nouvelle-Calédonie	*Nueva Caledonia*
		—	Nouvelle-Zélande (161)	—
164	**Papua New Guinea**	Papua New Guinea	Papouasie-Nouvelle-Guinée	Papua-Nueva Guinea
165	**Polynésie française**	*French Polynesia*	Polynésie française	Polinesia Francesa
166	**Samoa**	Samoa	*Samoa*	*Samoa*
167	**Solomon Is.**	Solomon Is.	Iles Salomon	Islas Salomón
		—	Samoa	Samoa
168	**Tonga**	Tonga	*Tonga*	*Tonga*
		—	Samoa américaines (155)	Samoa Americana (155)
		—	Tonga (168)	Tonga (168)
169	**Vanuatu** [1]	Vanuatu	Vanuatu	Vanuatu
170	**URSS**	USSR	URSS	URSS
171	RSS de Biélorussie	Byelorussian SSR	RSS de Biélorussie	RSS de Bielorrusia
172	RSS d'Ukraine	Ukrainian SSR	RSS d'Ukraine	RSS de Ucrania

[1] Former New Hebrides.　　　　[1] *Précédemment Nouvelles Hébrides.*　　　　[1] Anteriormente Nuevas Hébridas.

Explanation of signs used in the tables

Explication des signes utilisés dans les tableaux

Explicación de los signos que figuran en los cuadros

    .   =   not applicable.
   ... =   not available.
   *   =   provisional.
   —   =   magnitude not zero but less than half of unit employed.
   ×   =   division of economic activity represented by only some of its constituent branches.
   —— or I = data placed before or after one of these two breaklines are not strictly comparable or a new series begins immediately after the line (see footnotes).

Indices in *italics* = indices based on a year other than **1970**.

In the tables, decimal figures are separated by a period.

    .   =   ne s'applique pas.
   ... =   pas disponible.
   *   =   provisoire.
   —   =   résultat inférieur à la moitié de l'unité retenue.
   ×   =   branche d'activité économique représentée seulement par quelques-unes des industries qui la constituent.
   —— ou I = les chiffres placés avant et après l'un de ces deux filets ne sont pas strictement comparables ou une nouvelle série commence immédiatement après le filet (voir les notes de bas de page).

Indices en *italique* = indices ayant comme base une année autre que **1970**.

Dans les tableaux, un point sépare les unités des décimales.

    .   =   no se aplica.
   ... =   no disponible.
   *   =   provisional.
   —   =   importancia numérica no nula, pero inferior a la mitad de la unidad empleada.
   ×   =   división de actividad económica representada solamente por algunas de las industrias que la constituyen.
   —— o I = las cifras que figuran antes y después de una de estas dos rayas no son estrictamente comparables o una nueva serie comienza inmediatamente después de la raya (véanse notas al pie de la página correspondiente).

Indices en *itálicas* = índices que no tienen por base el año **1970**.

En los cuadros, un punto separa las unidades de los decimales.

Total and economically active population

Population totale et population active

Población total
y población económicamente activa

Total and economically active population

The data presented in tables 1, 2 A, 2 B and 2 C on the *economically active* population, i.e. the total of *employed* persons and of *unemployed* persons have been drawn from the latest census or survey of the country concerned. [1]

National practices vary between countries as regards the treatment of such groups as armed forces, inmates of institutions, persons living on reservations, persons seeking work for the first time, seasonal workers and persons engaged in part-time economic activities. In some countries, all or part of these groups are included among the economically active while in other countries they are treated as inactive. However, in general, the data on economically active population do not include students, women occupied solely in domestic duties, retired persons, persons living entirely on their own means, and persons wholly dependent upon others.

The comparability of the data is hampered by the differences between countries—and even within a country—not only as regards details of the definitions used and groups covered, but also by differences in the methods of collection, classification and tabulation of the data. In particular, the extent to which family workers who assist in family enterprises are included among the enumerated economically active population, particularly females, varies considerably from one country to another. The

reference period is also an important factor of difference: in some countries census data on the economically active population according to *industry*, *occupation* or *status* (as employer, employee, etc.), refer to the actual position of each individual on the day of the census or survey or during a brief specific period such as the week immediately prior to the census or survey date, while in others the data recorded refer to the usual position of each person, generally without reference to any given period of time. Also, in some countries the statistics of the economically active population relate only to employed and unemployed persons above a specified age, in others there is no such age provision in the definition of economic activity. [2]

Table 1

Total and economically active population by sex and age group

This table shows the economically active population and its relation to the total population, by sex and age group.

In interpreting the crude activity rates, i.e. the ratios of the total economically active

---

[1] For further information on the source and coverage of the data, see page 14.

[2] For a review of the problems concerning definitions, methods of collection and classifications of data on total and economically active population, see United Nations: *Handbook of Population Census Methods*, Vol. II: *Economic Characteristics of the Population* (ST/STAT/ SER.F/5/Rev.1) (New York, 1958).

Note:

Commencing with the 1978 issue of the Year Book, *both for reasons of economy and in order to give prominence to fresh information, Tables 1, 2 A and 2 B no longer show data identical to that published in two or more previous issues. A Synoptic Table (see page 12) identifies the most recent issue of the* Year Book *containing information not repeated in the present edition.*

A new table (Table 2 C), introduced in the 1979 issue of the Year Book, *provides information on the distribution of economically active population according to type of work performed (occupational group) cross-classified by where work is performed (industry).*

population to the total population of all ages, it should be recalled that the sex-age structure of population, that is the proportions of population in each sex-age group (particularly those under 15 years of age), will affect the crude activity rate shown. The effects of differences in the definitions of the economically active population used in the various countries should also be taken into account. In particular, the activity rates for females are frequently not comparable internationally, since in many countries relatively large numbers of women assist on farms or in other family enterprises without pay, and there are differences from one country to another in the criteria adopted for determining the extent to which such workers are to be counted among the economically active. Activity rates for young people also should be compared with caution owing to variations among countries in the treatment of unpaid family workers, of persons seeking work for the first time, and of students engaged in part-time economic activities.

Tables 2 A, 2 B and 2 C

Structure of the economically active population

Tables 2 A and 2 B show the distribution of the economically active population, total and by sex, according to *status* (as employers, own-account workers, employees, etc.) cross-classified by *industry* (major division of economic activity) (table 2 A) and by *occupation* (major group) (table 2 B). Table 2 C (introduced in the 1979 issue of the *Year Book*) shows the total economically active population by *industry* cross-classified by *occupation*.

The international classification by *status* refers to "the status of an economically active individual with respect to his or her employment, that is, whether the person is (or was, if unemployed) an employer, own-account worker, employee, unpaid family worker, or a member of a producers' co-operative, as defined below:

(a) Employer : a person who operates his or her own economic enterprise or engages

independently in a profession or trade, and hires one or more employees.

(b) Own-account worker : a person who operates his or her own economic enterprise or engages independently in a profession or trade, and hires no employees.

(c) Employee : a person who works for a public or private employer and receives remuneration in wages, salary, commission, tips, piece-rates or pay in kind.

(d) Unpaid family worker : a person who works a specified minimum amount of time (at least one-third of normal working hours), without pay, in an economic enterprise operated by a related person living in the same household.

(e) Member of producers' co-operative : a person who is an active member of a producers' co-operative, regardless of the industry in which it is established.

(f) Persons not classifiable by status : experienced workers with status unknown or inadequately described and unemployed persons not previously employed." [1]

Many points of difference arise from country to country with regard to classification by *status*. In most countries managers and directors are classified as *employees*, but in a few cases they are grouped with *employers*. *Unpaid family workers* are nearly always counted among the economically active, but the figures are based on a number of different definitions or criteria. *Employers* and *own-account workers* are shown as one group since separate data for these categories are generally not available. In most countries, family workers who receive remuneration in wages, salary, commission, piece-rates or pay in kind are correctly classified as *employees* but in some countries they may still be included among family workers. Differences between countries with respect to classification by *status* are particularly pro-

[1] Definition of status adopted by the Statistical Commission of the United Nations (Fourteenth Session, October 1966). See ILO: *International Recommendations on Labour Statistics* (Geneva, 1976).

nounced with regard to the treatment of unemployed persons: in general unemployed persons with previous job experience are included with *employees*, but in some cases they and unemployed persons seeking work for the first time form the most important part of the group *Persons not classifiable by status*.

The classification according to *industry* (where work is performed) is fundamentally different from that according to *occupation* (type of work performed). In the first, all persons working in a given industry (major division of economic activity) are classed under the same industry, irrespective of their particular occupations. The classification according to *occupation*, on the other hand, brings together individuals working in similar occupations, irrespective of the industry in which the work is performed. As indicated in the tables, most countries have supplied data on the basis of the international standard classifications of industry (ISIC) and occupations (ISCO).[1] Where the data are given according to national classi-

fications, it should be borne in mind that the industrial and occupational classifications used by the different countries present many points of divergence. The actual content of industrial or occupational groups may differ from one country to another owing to variations in definitions and methods of tabulation. Classification into broad groups may also obscure fundamental differences in the industrial or occupational patterns of the various countries. Where the unemployed with previous job experience are not classified according to the industry or occupation in which they are usually, or were most recently engaged, they are frequently included under *Activities not adequately defined* (ISIC) or *Workers not classifiable by occupation* (ISCO).

It should be recalled that the purpose of international classification schemes is not to supersede national classifications but to provide a framework for the international comparison of national statistics. Many countries, particularly those developing classifications for the first time, or revising existing schemes, use international schemes as a central framework. As the data in Tables 2 A, 2 B and 2 C of this and previous issues of the *Year Book* attest, a large and ever increasing number of countries can and do rearrange national classifications to the international standard classification schemes.

---

[1] Abridged versions of the *International Standard Industrial Classification of All Economic Activities (ISIC-1968)* and the *International Standard Classification of Occupations (ISCO-1968)* are shown in the Appendix. For more complete versions, see ILO, *op. cit.* (Geneva, 1976).

Population totale et population active

Les données présentées dans les tableaux 1, 2 A, 2 B et 2 C sur la *population active*, c'est-à-dire le total des personnes *occupées* et des personnes *en chômage*, proviennent du dernier recensement ou de la dernière enquête effectuée par le pays concerné[1]. En ce qui concerne les membres des forces armées, les pensionnaires d'institutions, les personnes établies dans des réserves, les personnes qui cherchent pour la première fois un emploi, les travailleurs saisonniers et les personnes qui ont une activité à temps partiel, leur classement varie selon les pays: dans certains, ces groupes sont compris en totalité ou en partie dans la population active; dans d'autres, ils sont considérés comme inactifs. D'une façon générale cependant, les données sur la population active ne comprennent pas les étudiants, les femmes occupées exclusivement aux travaux de leur ménage, les retraités, les rentiers et les personnes entièrement à la charge d'autrui.

La comparabilité des données est affectée par les différences que présentent, selon les pays — et souvent pour un même pays —, non seulement les définitions utilisées et les groupes couverts, mais aussi les méthodes de rassemblement, de classification et de tabulation des don-

nées. Ainsi, la mesure dans laquelle les travailleurs familiaux aidant le chef de famille dans l'entreprise familiale sont compris dans la population active (féminine notamment) diffère très sensiblement d'un pays à un autre. Quant à la période de référence, elle est aussi un important élément de différence: dans certains pays, les données du recensement ou de l'enquête relatives à la population active selon l'*industrie*, la *profession* ou la *situation dans la profession* se rapportent à la situation effective de chaque individu le jour du recensement ou de l'enquête, ou pendant une brève période déterminée, telle que la semaine précédant immédiatement la date du recensement ou de l'enquête, tandis que, dans d'autres pays, les données recueillies ont trait à la situation habituelle de chaque personne, sans se rapporter à une période déterminée. De même, dans certains pays, les statistiques de la population active n'englobent que les personnes occupées et les chômeurs ayant dépassé un âge déterminé; alors que dans d'autres pays, une telle limite d'âge n'est pas prévue dans la définition de la population active[2].

---

[1] Pour de plus amples informations concernant la source et la portée des données, voir page 14.

[2] Pour l'étude des problèmes relatifs aux définitions, aux méthodes de rassemblement et à la classification des données sur la population active et la population totale, voir Nations Unies: *Manuel des méthodes de recensement de la population*, vol. II: *Caractéristiques économiques de la population* (ST/STAT/SER.F/5/Rev.1) (New York, 1958).

Note:

A partir de l'édition de 1978 de l'Annuaire, tant par souci d'économie que de manière à mettre en évidence les informations les plus récentes, les tableaux 1, 2 A et 2 B ne présentent plus de données ayant déjà été publiées, sans modification, dans au moins deux précédentes éditions. Un Tableau synoptique (voir page 12) permet d'identifier la plus récente édition de l'Annuaire contenant des informations non répétées dans la présente édition.

Un nouveau tableau (tableau 2 C), introduit dans l'édition 1979 de l'Annuaire, fournit une classification croisée des informations concernant la répartition de la population active totale distribuée selon le genre de travail effectué (groupe de professions) et la branche d'activité économique où ce travail est effectué (industrie).

Tableau 1

Population totale et population active par sexe et groupe d'âge

Ce tableau fournit des données sur la population active et son rapport à la population totale, par sexe et par groupe d'âge.

En analysant les taux d'activité brute, c'est-à-dire les rapports de la population active totale à la population totale pour tous les groupes d'âge, il faut rappeler que la structure de la population par sexe et groupe d'âge, c'est-à-dire les proportions de la population dans chaque groupe d'âge, selon le sexe (en particulier le groupe de moins de 15 ans) influencera le taux d'activité. Il convient aussi de tenir compte des différences que présente la définition de la population active selon les pays. Les taux d'activité des femmes, notamment, ne se prêtent souvent pas à des comparaisons internationales, car, dans beaucoup de pays, un nombre relativement élevé de femmes aident, sans rémunération, aux travaux de l'exploitation familiale, agricole ou autre, et il existe, entre les pays, des différences dans les critères utilisés pour déterminer dans quelle mesure cette catégorie de travailleuses doit être comptée dans la population active. Il convient aussi de se montrer prudent dans la comparaison des taux d'activité des jeunes gens, étant donné que les travailleurs familiaux non rémunérés, les personnes en quête d'emploi pour la première fois et les étudiants qui ont une activité à temps partiel ne sont pas comptés de la même manière dans les différents pays.

Tableaux 2 A, 2 B et 2 C

Structure de la population active

Les tableaux 2 A et 2 B montrent la répartition de la population active totale, par sexe, distribuée simultanément suivant la *situation dans la profession* (employeurs, personnes travaillant à leur propre compte, salariés, etc.), par *industrie* (branche d'activité économique) (tableau 2 A) et par *profession* (grand groupe) (tableau 2 B). Le tableau 2 C (introduit dans l'édition 1979 de l'*Annuaire*) présente une classification croisée des données de population active totale par *industrie* et par *profession*.

Selon la classification internationale, la *situation dans la profession* est « la situation d'une personne qui fait partie de la population active par rapport à son emploi actuel (ou antérieur, s'il est chômeur), c'est-à-dire: employeur, travailleur à son propre compte, salarié, travailleur familial non rémunéré ou membre d'une coopérative de producteurs. Chacun de ces groupes a été défini de la manière suivante:

a) *Employeur :* Personne qui exploite sa propre entreprise économique ou qui exerce pour son propre compte une profession ou un métier et qui emploie un ou plusieurs salariés;

b) *Personne travaillant à son propre compte :* Personne qui exploite sa propre entreprise économique ou qui exerce pour son propre compte une profession ou un métier, mais qui n'emploie aucun salarié;

c) *Salarié :* Personne qui travaille pour un employeur public ou privé et qui reçoit une rémunération sous forme de traitement, salaire, commission, pourboire, salaire aux pièces ou paiement en nature;

d) *Travailleur familial non rémunéré :* Personne qui accomplit sans rémunération un minimum donné de travail (un tiers au moins du nombre normal d'heures de travail) dans une entreprise exploitée par un parent vivant dans le même ménage;

e) *Membre d'une coopérative de producteurs :* Personne qui est membre actif d'une coopérative de producteurs, sans considération de la branche d'activité économique;

f) *Personnes inclassables selon la situation dans la profession :* Travailleurs expérimentés dont la situation exacte n'est pas connue, ou est mal définie, et chômeurs qui n'ont jamais travaillé. » [1]

---

[1] Définition de la situation dans la profession adoptée par la Commission statistique des Nations Unies (quatorzième session, octobre 1966). Voir BIT: *Recommandations internationales sur les statistiques du travail* (Genève, 1976).

La classification d'après la *situation dans la profession* présente de nombreuses différences d'un pays à un autre. Dans la plupart des pays, les directeurs et les administrateurs sont classés parmi les *salariés* alors que, dans quelques cas, ils sont rangés parmi les *employeurs*. Les *travailleurs familiaux non rémunérés* sont presque toujours compris dans la population active, mais les données se fondent sur des définitions et des critères différents. Les *employeurs* et les *personnes travaillant à leur propre compte* ont été groupés, car on ne dispose généralement pas de données distinctes sur ces deux groupes. Dans la plupart des pays, les travailleurs familiaux qui reçoivent une rémunération sous forme de salaire, traitement, commission, ou paiement aux pièces ou en nature sont correctement classés comme *salariés* mais, dans certains pays, ils peuvent encore être compris parmi les travailleurs familiaux. Les différences existant, entre les pays, dans les classifications par *situation dans la profession* sont particulièrement accusées en ce qui concerne les chômeurs: en général, les chômeurs ayant déjà occupé un emploi sont comptés avec les salariés; mais, dans certains cas, ils constituent, avec les personnes en quête d'un premier emploi, la majeure partie de la rubrique *Personnes inclassables selon la situation dans la profession*.

La classification d'après l'*industrie* (où le travail est effectué) est essentiellement différente de la classification par *profession* (genre de travail effectué). Dans la première, toutes les personnes travaillant dans une industrie (branche d'activité économique) donnée sont classées dans la même industrie quelle que soit leur profession individuelle. Par contre, dans la classification par *profession*, toutes les personnes travaillant dans des professions semblables sont réunies sans tenir compte de l'industrie à laquelle elles sont rattachées. Comme le montrent les tableaux, les données fournies par la plupart des pays reposent sur les classifications internationales types par industrie (CITI) et par professions (CITP) [1]. Il convient de ne pas oublier que lorsque les données fournies ont été rassemblées selon les classifications nationales des industries ou des groupes de professions, celles-ci présentent de nombreuses différences d'un pays à un autre. Le contenu réel des groupes dans lesquels sont rangées les industries et les professions peut varier selon les pays, en raison des différences dans les définitions et les méthodes de tabulation. De même, les classifications en larges divisions peuvent dissimuler des différences fondamentales dans la structure des industries ou des professions des divers pays. Les chômeurs ayant déjà occupé un emploi, qui ne sont pas classés par industries ou d'après leur profession — qu'il s'agisse de leur profession habituelle ou de celle qu'ils ont exercée en dernier lieu —, sont souvent compris dans *Activités mal désignées* (CITI) ou dans *Travailleurs ne pouvant être classés selon la profession* (CITP).

Il est bon de rappeler que les classifications internationales n'ont pas pour but de remplacer les classifications nationales mais de fournir un moyen de comparer les statistiques nationales sur le plan international. Beaucoup de pays et particulièrement ceux qui mettent sur pied des classifications pour la première fois ou qui révisent des classifications existantes se fondent sur les classifications internationales. Comme le montrent les données des tableaux 2 A, 2 B et 2 C de la présente édition et des éditions précédentes de l'*Annuaire*, un grand nombre de pays, sans cesse croissant, peuvent adapter — et adaptent d'ailleurs — leurs classifications nationales aux classifications internationales types.

---

[1] Des versions abrégées de la *Classification internationale type, par industrie, de toutes les branches d'activité économique (CITI-1968)* et la *Classification internationale type des professions (CITP-1968)* sont présentées dans l'Annexe. Pour des versions plus complètes, voir BIT, *op. cit.* (Genève, 1976).

Población total y población económicamente activa

En los cuadros 1, 2 A, 2 B y 2 C figuran los datos sobre la población *económicamente activa*, es decir, el total de personas *ocupadas* y de las que se encontraban *desempleadas*, provenientes del último censo de población o de la última encuesta efectuados por el país concerniente[1]. La práctica varía según los países en cuanto a la consideración que debe darse a grupos tales como las fuerzas armadas, las personas internadas en distintos establecimientos, los indígenas que viven en reservas, las personas que buscan trabajo por primera vez, los trabajadores estacionales y las personas ocupadas en actividades económicas a tiempo parcial. En algunos países, estos grupos son incluidos, totalmente o en parte, en la población económicamente activa, en tanto que en otros se los considera como población inactiva. En general, los datos sobre población económicamente activa no incluyen a los estudiantes, a las mujeres que se ocupan solamente de labores domésticas, a los pensionados, a los rentistas ni a las personas que dependen por completo de otras.

La comparabilidad de los datos se encuentra obstaculizada no sólo por las diferencias que existen de un país a otro — y a menudo para un mismo país — en lo que respecta a los detalles de las definiciones empleadas y de los grupos abarcados, sino igualmente por las diferencias en los métodos de recolección, clasifica-

ción y tabulación de los datos. En especial, el grado en que los trabajadores familiares, y particularmente las mujeres, que cooperan en la empresa familiar se encuentran incluidos en la población económicamente activa varía considerablemente de un país a otro. El período de referencia es también un importante factor de disparidad: en algunos países, los datos suministrados por el censo, relativos a la población económicamente activa según la *industria*, la *ocupación* o la *categoría de la ocupación* (como empleador, empleado, etc.), se refieren a la situación efectiva (o de hecho) de cada individuo en el día del censo o encuesta o durante un período breve y específico anterior a la fecha del censo o encuesta, por ejemplo, la semana precedente, en tanto que en otros países los datos obtenidos se refieren a la situación habitual de cada persona, en general sin referencia a un determinado período de tiempo. Asimismo, mientras que en ciertos países las estadísticas de población económicamente activa comprenden solamente a las personas empleadas y desempleadas que han sobrepasado cierta edad mínima, en otros no existen estipulaciones de edad en la definición de la actividad económica[2].

[1] Para más amplias informaciones sobre la fuente y el alcance de los datos, véase pág. 14.

[2] Para proceder a un estudio de los problemas relativos a las definiciones y a los métodos de obtención y clasificación de los datos sobre la población económicamente activa y la población total, véase Naciones Unidas: *Manual de métodos de censos de población*, vol. II: *Características económicas de la población* (ST/STAT/SER.F/5/Rev.1) (Nueva York, 1958).

Nota:

A partir de la edición de 1978 del Anuario, *por razones de economía y con el objeto de dar preeminencia a las informaciones más recientes, los cuadros 1, 2 A y 2 B ya no suministran datos aparecidos, sin modificación, en dos o más ediciones anteriores. Un Cuadro sinóptico (ver página 12) permite identificar la edición más reciente del* Anuario *conteniendo informaciones publicadas pero que no se repiten en la presente edición.*

El nuevo cuadro (cuadro 2 C), que apareció por primera vez en la edición de 1979 del Anuario, *presenta una clasificación cruzada de los datos sobre la distribución de la población económicamente activa según el tipo de trabajo efectuado (grupo de ocupaciones) y la rama de actividad económica en la que se efectúa dicho trabajo (industria).*

Cuadro 1

Población total y población económicamente activa por sexo y grupo de edad

Este cuadro muestra la población económicamente activa y su relación con la población total, por sexo y por grupo de edad.

Al interpretar las tasas brutas de actividad, es decir, la población económicamente activa total en porcentaje de la población total en todas las edades, convendría recordar que la estructura de la población por sexo y grupo de edad, o, lo que es lo mismo, las proporciones de la población en cada grupo de edad, según el sexo (en particular el grupo de menos de 15 años), influye en las tasas brutas de actividad. Debe tenerse igualmente en cuenta el efecto de las diferencias en las definiciones de la población económicamente activa utilizadas en los distintos países. La proporción de mujeres activas, en especial, no es, a menudo, comparable, ya que en muchos países un número relativamente grande de mujeres ayudan en el trabajo agrícola o en otras empresas de tipo familiar sin recibir remuneración, y porque el criterio adoptado para determinar la medida en que estas trabajadoras deben ser incluidas en la población económicamente activa varía de un país a otro. También las tasas de actividad correspondientes a los jóvenes deben compararse con precaución a causa de las diferencias que existen de país a país en la consideración del grupo de los trabajadores familiares no remunerados, de las personas que buscan trabajo por primera vez y de los estudiantes ocupados en actividades económicas a tiempo parcial.

Cuadros 2 A, 2 B y 2 C

Estructura de la población económicamente activa

Los cuadros 2 A y 2 B muestran la distribución de la población económicamente activa, total y por sexo, según la *categoría de ocupación* (es decir, según sean empleadores, trabajadores por cuenta propia, asalariados — obreros y empleados —, etcétera), clasificada según *la industria* (rama de actividad económica) (cuadro 2 A) y por *ocupación* (gran grupo) (cuadro 2 B). El cuadro 2 C presenta una clasificación cruzada de los datos de la población económicamente activa por industria y por ocupación.

Según la clasificación internacional, « la *categoría de ocupación* [1] denota la relación entre una persona económicamente activa y su empleo, es decir, que indica si la persona es (o ha sido, si está desempleada) empleador, trabajador por cuenta propia, empleado a sueldo o salario, trabajador familiar no remunerado o miembro de una cooperativa de producción, con arreglo a las definiciones siguientes:

a) *Empleador* es la persona que dirige su propia empresa económica o que ejerce por cuenta propia una profesión u oficio, y que tiene uno o más empleados a sueldo o salario.

b) *Trabajador por cuenta propia* es la persona que explota su propia empresa económica o que ejerce por cuenta propia una profesión u oficio, pero no tiene ningún empleado a sueldo o salario.

c) *Empleado a sueldo o salario* [2] es la persona que trabaja para un empleador público o privado y percibe una remuneración en forma de salario, sueldo, comisiones, propinas, pagos a destajo o pagos en especie.

d) *Trabajador familiar no remunerado* es la persona que realiza, sin remuneración, un mínimo dado de trabajo (por lo menos un tercio de la jornada normal de trabajo) en una empresa económica explotada por una persona emparentada con él que resida en el mismo hogar.

e) *Miembro de una cooperativa de producción* es la persona que es miembro activo de una cooperativa de producción, cualquiera sea la rama de actividad económica a que ésta se dedica.

f) *Personas no clasificadas según la categoría*: trabajadores cuya categoría no se conoce o se halla mal definida y personas desocupadas que nunca han trabajado » [3].

---

[1] La terminología de las Naciones Unidas y la de la OIT a veces difieren, y en este caso se ha denominado « categoría » a la situación en la ocupación.

[2] Obrero o empleado.

[3] Definiciones de los grupos adoptadas por la Comisión de Estadística de las Naciones Unidas (14.º período de sesiones, octubre de 1966). Véase OIT: *Recomendaciones internacionales sobre estadísticas del trabajo* (Ginebra, 1975).

La clasificación según la *categoría de ocupación* presenta numerosas diferencias de un país a otro. En la mayoría de los países se clasifica a los directores y gerentes como *empleados*, mientras que en otros se los agrega al grupo de los empleadores. Los *trabajadores familiares no remunerados* han sido casi siempre comprendidos en la población económicamente activa, pero las cifras se basan en definiciones y criterios diferentes. Los *empleadores* y los *trabajadores por cuenta propia* han sido incluidos en un mismo grupo, porque en general no existen datos separados disponibles para estas categorías de trabajadores. Los trabajadores familiares que reciben una remuneración en forma de sueldo, salario, comisión, o retribución en especie, o por tarea cumplida, se clasifican como *asalariados* en la mayor parte de los países, lo cual es correcto; algunos otros países, sin embargo, continúan incluyéndolos entre los trabajadores familiares. Las diferencias que ofrecen, de un país a otro, las clasificaciones según la *categoría de ocupación* se acentúan particularmente en lo que respecta al criterio observado en cuanto a las personas desempleadas. En general, los desempleados que habían tenido algún empleo se incluyen con los asalariados, pero en algunos casos constituyen, junto con los desempleados que buscan trabajo por primera vez, la mayor parte del grupo *Personas inclasificables según la situación en la ocupación.*

La clasificación según la *industria* en que se realiza el trabajo es fundamentalmente diferente de la clasificación según la *ocupación* (clase de trabajo realizado). En la primera, todas las personas ocupadas en una determinada industria (rama de la actividad económica) se clasifican dentro de ésta, sean cuales fueren sus ocupaciones individuales. Por el contrario, en la clasificación por *ocupaciones*, todas las personas que trabajan en ocupaciones similares se reúnen en un mismo grupo, independientemente de las industrias a las que se hallen vinculadas. Tal como se indica en los cuadros, la mayoría de los países han suministrado los datos basándose en las clasificaciones internacionales uniformes por industria (CIIU) y por ocupaciones (CIUO) [1]. Cuando los datos dados están basados en las clasificaciones nacionales, debe tenerse en cuenta que las clasificaciones por industrias y por ocupaciones utilizadas por los diferentes países presentan múltiples divergencias. La significación real de los grupos industriales o de ocupaciones puede variar de un país a otro en razón de las diferencias que existen en los sistemas de definiciones y en los métodos de tabulación. Asimismo, la clasificación en grandes grupos puede encubrir diferencias fundamentales en la estructura industrial o de las ocupaciones de los diversos países. Cuando los desempleados que habían tenido algún empleo no están clasificados según la industria o la ocupación en que trabajan habitualmente o en la que desempeñaron su última ocupación, a menudo están incluidos en *Actividades no bien especificadas (CIIU)* o en *Trabajadores que no pueden ser clasificados según la ocupación (CIUO).*

Sería conveniente recordar que al establecer las clasificaciones internacionales no se ha tenido el propósito de reemplazar las nacionales, sino el de ofrecer un sistema que permita la comparación internacional de las estadísticas de diferentes países. Son numerosos los países que fundan sus clasificaciones en los sistemas de las clasificaciones internacionales, en particular cuando revisan aquellas de que disponen o preparan una por la primera vez. La cantidad de países que pueden adaptar, y que ya han adaptado, sus clasificaciones nacionales a los sistemas de clasificación internacional aumenta considerablemente, como lo prueban los datos de los cuadros 2 A, 2 B y 2 C de la edición actual y de las precedentes del *Anuario.*

---

[1] Versiones abreviadas de la *Clasificación industrial internacional uniforme de todas las actividades económicas (CIIU-1968)* y la *Clasificación internacional uniforme de ocupaciones (CIUO-1968)* figuran en el apéndice. Para versiones más completas, véase OIT, *op. cit.* (Ginebra, 1976).

POPULATION

Synoptic table: Recent issues of the *Year Book* containing data not repeated in the present edition

Tableau synoptique: Récentes éditions de l'*Annuaire* contenant des données non répétées dans la présente édition

Cuadro sinóptico: Ediciones recientes del *Anuario* que contienen datos no repetidos en la presente edición

Country / Pays / País	Tables / Tableaux / Cuadros		
	1	2 A	2 B
AFRICA — AFRIQUE — AFRICA			
Algérie	1977	1977	1977
Angola	1977	.	.
Botswana	1977	.	.
Cap-Vert	1977	.	.
République centrafricaine	1977	.	.
Gabon	1977	.	.
Ghana	1977	.	1977
Lesotho	1977	.	.
Liberia	1979	(a)	.
Libyan Arab Jamahiriya	(a)	1979	1979
Maroc	1977	1977	1977
Mauritius:			
Mauritius	1977	1977	1977
Rodrigues	1977	.	.
Mozambique	1977	1977	.
Namibia	1977	.	.
Nigeria	1977	.	.
St. Helena	1977	.	.
Sénégal	1977	.	.
Seychelles	1979	1979	(a)
Sierra Leone	1977	.	.
South Africa, Rep. of	1977	1977	1977
Sudan	1977	1977	1977
Swaziland	1977	.	.
Tanzania:			
Tanganyika	1977	1977	.
Zanzibar	1977	1977	.
Tchad	1977	.	.
Togo	1977	.	.
Zambia	1979	1977	1977
AMERICA — AMÉRIQUE — AMÉRICA			
Antigua	1978	1977	1977
Bahamas	1978	1977	1977
Barbados	1979	1979	1979
Belize	1977	.	1977
Bermuda	1979	1977	1977
Brasil	1979	1979	1977
Cayman Is.	1977	.	.
Colombia	1977	1977	1977
Costa Rica	(a)	1977	1977
Cuba	1977	1977	1977
Chile	(a)	(a)	1979
Dominica	1977	.	.
Rep. Dominicana	(a)	1977	1977
Ecuador	1978	1978	1978
Grenada	1977	.	.
Guadeloupe	1979	1979	.
Guyana	(a)	1977	.
Haïti	1977	1977	(a)
Honduras	(a)	(a)	1978
Jamaica	(a)	(a)	1979
Martinique	1977	1977	1977
México	(a)	(a)	1979
Montserrat	(a)	1977	1977
Netherlands Antilles	1979	(a)	1977
Nicaragua	(a)	(a)	1977
Panamá	1977	1977	1977
Panama Canal Zone	1977	.	.
Paraguay	(a)	(a)	1978
Perú	(a)	(a)	1977
St. Kitts-Nevis	1977	.	.
St. Lucia	1977	.	.
Saint-Pierre-et-Miquelon	1979	(a)	(a)
St. Vincent	1977	.	.
Suriname	1977	.	.
Turks and Caicos Is.	1977	.	.
Venezuela	1979	(a)	1979
Virgin Is. (Brit.)	1977	1977	1977
Virgin Is. (US)	1977	.	.
ASIA — ASIE — ASIA			
Brunei	(a)	1977	1977
Cyprus	1979	1978	.
India	1977	1979	1979
Jordan	1979	.	.
Kampuchea démocratique	1977	.	.
Kuwait	1977	1977	1977
Liban	1977	1977	1977
Malaysia:			
Peninsular Malaysia	(a)	1977	1977
Sabah	1977	1977	1977
Sarawak	1977	1977	1977
Nepal	1977	1977	1977
Qatar	1977	.	.

(a) Data shown in the present edition.   (a) Données publiées dans la présente édition.   (a) Datos publicados en la presente edición.

Country *Pays* País	Tables *Tableaux* Cuadros		
	1	2 A	2 B
Sri Lanka	1977	1977	1977
Viet Nam	1977	.	.
Yemen, Democratic	1977	(a)	.
EUROPE — EUROPE — EUROPA			
Albanie	1977	.	.
Austria	1977	(a)	(a)
Belgique	1979	(a)	1977
Bulgarie	1978	1978	1979
Channel Is.	1977	1977	.
Czechoslovakia	1977	1977	1977
Denmark	(a)	(a)	1977
Faeroe Is.	(a)	(a)	1977
German Democratic Rep. . . .	1977	1977	.
Gibraltar	1977	1977	1977
Grèce	1977	1977	1977
Hongrie	(a)	(a)	1977
Italie	(a)	(a)	1978
Luxembourg	(a)	1977	1977
Malta	(a)	(a)	1977
Monaco	1977	1977	1977
Pologne	(a)	(a)	1977
Roumanie	1977	1977	1977

Country *Pays* País	Tables *Tableaux* Cuadros		
	1	2 A	2 B
Suisse	(a)	(a)	1977
United Kingdom	(a)	(a)	1977
Yugoslavia	(a)	1977	1977
OCEANIA — OCÉANIE OCEANÍA			
Christmas Is.	1977	.	.
Cocos Is.	1977	.	.
Fiji	1979	1979	(a)
Gilbert Is.	1977	.	.
Guam	1977	(a)	.
Nauru	1977	.	.
New Hebrides	1977	.	.
Niue Is.	1977	.	.
Norfolk Is.	1977	.	.
Nouvelle-Calédonie	1978	1978	1978
Pacific Is.	1977	.	.
Samoa	1979	(a)	(a)
Tokelau	1977	.	.
Tonga	1979	1979	(a)
URSS	(a)	1977	.
RSS de Biélorussie	1977	1977	.
RSS d'Ukraine	1977	1977	.

(a) Data shown in the present edition.   (a) *Données publiées dans la présente édition.*   *(a)* Datos publicados en la presente edición.

Sources and coverage of the data on total and economically active population

Sources et portée des données de population totale et de population active

Fuentes y alcance de los datos de población total y de población económicamente activa

Codes / *Codes* / Claves	Sources and coverage — *Sources et portée* — Fuentes y alcance
	Census — *Recensement* — Censo
C =	Complete count, final data *Tabulation complète, chiffres définitifs* Tabulación completa, cifras definitivas
Cs =	Sample tabulation, size not specified *Tabulation d'un échantillon, taille non spécifiée* Tabulación de una muestra, tamaño no especificado
C...% =	Sample tabulation, size specified *Tabulation d'un échantillon, taille spécifiée* Tabulación de una muestra, tamaño especificado
	Survey — *Enquête* — Encuesta
LFSS =	Labour force sample survey *Enquête par sondage sur la main-d'œuvre* Encuesta por muestra sobre la fuerza trabajadora
HS =	Household survey *Enquête auprès des ménages* Encuesta de hogares
	Others — *Autres* — Otros
OE =	Official estimates *Evaluations officielles* Estimaciones oficiales
* =	Provisional figures *Chiffres provisoires* Cifras provisionales
† =	See notes at the end of the Chapter *Voir notes à la fin du chapitre* Véanse notas al final del capítulo

REMARK: When the data refer to a *specific day*, the source is a census. If no day is cited, the source is either a survey or an official estimate.

REMARQUE: *Lorsque les données se réfèrent à* un jour déterminé, *la source est un recensement. Si le jour n'est pas indiqué, il s'agit soit d'une enquête soit d'évaluations officielles.*

OBSERVACIÓN: Cuando los datos se refieren a *un día especificado*, la fuente es un censo. Si el día no está indicado, se trata de una encuesta o de estimaciones oficiales.

1 Total and economically active population by sex and age group
Population totale et population active par sexe et groupe d'âge
Población total y población económicamente activa por sexo y grupo de edad

Country, source and scope Pays, source et portée País, fuente y alcance	Total			Males – Hommes – Hombres			Females – Femmes – Mujeres		
	Total population Population totale Población total	Active population Population active Población activa	Activity rate Taux d'activité Tasa de actividad %	Total population Population totale Población total	Active population Population active Población activa	Activity rate Taux d'activité Tasa de actividad %	Total population Population totale Población total	Active population Population active Población activa	Activity rate Taux d'activité Tasa de actividad %

AFRICA – AFRIQUE – AFRICA

Burundi (1979) OE

Total	4 083 000	1 882 000	46.1	1 943 000	876 000	45.1	2 140 000	1 006 000	47.0

Rép.-Unie du Cameroun (9–24.IV.76) C †

–15	1 878 618	174 504	9.3	966 675	96 678	10.0	911 943	77 826	8.5
15–19	687 891	278 352	40.5	335 324	153 476	45.8	352 567	124 876	35.4
20–24	550 541	337 012	61.2	252 827	204 817	81.0	297 714	132 195	44.4
25–29	495 316	335 589	67.8	222 434	206 235	92.7	272 882	129 354	47.4
30–44	1 180 445	863 614	73.2	543 839	520 915	95.8	636 606	342 699	53.8
45–49	294 715	233 307	79.2	145 654	138 838	95.3	149 061	94 469	63.4
50–54	236 132	178 946	75.8	116 995	109 272	93.4	119 137	69 674	58.5
55–59	177 997	135 616	76.2	90 785	81 861	90.2	87 212	53 755	61.6
60–64	150 795	99 291	65.8	75 546	63 415	83.9	75 249	35 876	47.7
65+	259 826	121 668	46.8	128 412	80 660	62.8	131 414	41 008	31.2
?	3 756	.	.	1 961	.	.	1 795	.	.
Total	5 916 032	2 757 899	46.6	2 880 452	1 656 167	57.5	3 035 580	1 101 732	36.3

Congo (7.II.74) C

–15	602 461	.	.	303 404	.	.	299 057	.	.
15–19	120 752	42 065	34.8	57 697	18 432	31.9	63 055	23 633	37.5
20–24	92 005	52 664	57.2	41 653	32 118	77.1	50 352	20 546	40.8
25–29	79 890	56 749	71.0	36 469	35 525	97.4	43 421	21 224	48.9
30–44	203 947	161 467	79.2	94 512	93 768	99.2	109 435	67 699	61.9
45–49	57 225	48 271	84.4	25 581	25 230	98.6	31 644	23 041	72.8
50–54	49 484	41 937	84.7	21 534	20 753	96.4	27 950	21 184	75.8
55–59	43 114	36 277	84.1	20 136	18 737	93.1	22 978	17 540	76.3
60–64	31 820	25 163	79.1	15 252	13 298	87.2	16 568	11 865	71.6
65+	32 772	18 821	57.4	14 871	10 128	68.1	17 901	8 693	48.6
?	6 320	3 853	61.0	2 890	2 044	70.7	3 430	1 809	52.7
Total	1 319 790	487 267	36.9	633 999	270 033	42.6	685 791	217 234	31.7

Côte-d'Ivoire (30.IV.75) C †

–15	2 983 227	262 938	8.8	1 537 716	144 338	9.4	1 445 511	118 600	8.2
15–59	3 452 748	2 423 234	70.2	1 790 353	1 655 727	92.5	1 662 395	767 507	46.2
60+	233 745	136 855	58.5	124 918	101 385	81.2	108 827	35 470	32.6
?	39 880	8 678	21.8	21 763	7 673	35.3	18 117	1 005	5.5
Total	6 709 600	2 831 705	42.2	3 474 750	1 909 123	54.9	3 234 850	922 582	28.5

Egypt (22–23.XI.76) C †

–15	14 599 095	1 423 324	9.7	7 536 103	1 138 018	15.1	7 062 992	285 306	4.0
15–19	3 981 508	1 159 438	29.1	2 135 971	1 064 849	49.9	1 845 537	94 589	5.1
20–24	3 065 641	1 275 460	41.6	1 509 410	1 082 106	71.7	1 556 231	193 354	12.4
25–29	2 675 063	1 367 903	51.1	1 315 311	1 221 149	92.8	1 359 752	146 754	10.8
30–44	6 044 511	3 098 066	51.3	2 984 281	2 915 419	97.7	3 060 230	182 647	6.0
45–49	1 523 443	799 046	52.5	786 948	773 033	98.2	736 495	26 013	3.5
50–54	1 456 394	716 573	49.2	716 531	693 343	96.8	739 863	23 230	3.1
55–59	890 633	467 449	52.5	480 058	456 169	95.0	410 575	11 280	2.7
60–64	967 176	377 591	39.0	478 259	366 849	76.7	488 917	10 742	2.2
65+	1 301 903	266 526	20.5	634 402	259 627	40.9	667 501	6 899	1.0
?	5 482	2 286	41.7	2 377	1 882	79.2	3 105	404	13.0
Total	36 510 849	11 037 093	30.2	18 579 651	10 053 547	54.1	17 931 198	983 546	5.5

ACTIVE POPULATION

1 Total and economically active population by sex and age group
Population totale et population active par sexe et groupe d'âge
Población total y población económicamente activa por sexo y grupo de edad

Country, source and scope Pays, source et portée País, fuente y alcance	Total			Males – Hommes – Hombres			Females – Femmes – Mujeres		
	Total population Population totale Población total	Active population Population active Población activa	Activity rate Taux d'activité Tasa de actividad %	Total population Population totale Población total	Active population Population active Población activa	Activity rate Taux d'activité Tasa de actividad %	Total population Population totale Población total	Active population Population active Población activa	Activity rate Taux d'activité Tasa de actividad %
Egypt (V.78) LFSS †									
–15	15 136 300	1 005 300	6.6	7 992 800	830 600	10.4	7 143 500	174 700	2.4
15–19	4 386 700	1 169 200	26.7	2 402 000	1 070 500	44.6	1 984 700	98 700	5.0
20–24	2 687 200	1 079 100	40.2	1 246 800	858 600	68.9	1 440 400	220 500	15.3
25–29	2 474 900	1 226 000	49.5	1 137 300	1 071 600	94.2	1 337 600	154 400	11.5
30–49	7 897 800	4 028 700	51.0	3 809 800	3 761 700	98.7	4 088 000	267 000	6.5
50–59	2 614 300	1 340 500	51.3	1 336 600	1 292 700	96.7	1 277 700	47 800	3.7
60–64	986 700	417 700	42.3	510 200	408 200	80.0	476 500	9 500	2.0
65+	1 390 700	476 800	34.3	728 200	337 400	46.3	662 500	139 400	21.0
Total	**37 574 600**	**10 743 300**	**28.6**	**19 163 700**	**9 631 300**	**50.3**	**18 410 900**	**1 112 000**	**6.0**
Ethiopia (1978) OE									
–15	12 690 500	1 529 800	12.1	6 459 500	941 500	14.6	6 231 000	588 300	9.4
15–19	3 044 300	2 097 800	68.9	1 562 800	1 209 100	77.4	1 481 500	888 700	60.0
20–24	2 573 700	1 968 800	76.5	1 324 600	1 176 500	88.8	1 249 100	792 300	63.4
25–29	2 250 300	1 760 500	78.2	1 160 900	1 070 400	92.2	1 089 400	690 100	63.3
30–44	4 940 800	3 981 700	80.6	2 500 500	2 430 300	97.2	2 440 300	1 551 400	63.6
45–49	1 087 700	827 100	76.0	535 800	525 200	98.0	551 900	301 900	54.7
50–54	867 300	645 900	74.5	431 600	417 700	96.8	435 700	228 200	52.4
55–59	661 100	449 100	67.9	312 500	297 900	95.3	348 600	151 200	43.4
60–64	499 600	309 100	61.9	238 100	215 100	90.3	261 500	94 000	35.9
65+	792 900	319 400	40.3	357 200	256 900	71.9	435 700	62 500	14.3
Total	**29 408 200**	**13 889 200**	**47.2**	**14 883 500**	**8 540 600**	**57.4**	**14 524 700**	**5 348 600**	**36.8**
Haute-Volta (1–7.XII.75) C * †									
–15	2 699 593	32 497	1.2	1 407 081	27 988	2.0	1 292 512	4 509	0.3
15–19	613 745	221 376	36.1	324 797	207 178	63.8	288 948	14 198	4.9
20–29	1 000 224	347 189	34.7	486 881	335 450	68.9	513 343	11 739	2.3
30–59	1 486 555	645 732	43.4	751 574	630 863	83.9	734 981	14 869	2.0
60+	337 656	159 272	47.2	182 114	156 244	85.8	155 542	3 028	1.9
?	9 735	2 089	21.5	5 036	1 995	39.6	4 699	94	2.0
Total	**6 147 508**	**1 408 155**	**22.9**	**3 157 483**	**1 359 718**	**43.1**	**2 990 025**	**48 437**	**1.6**
Libyan Arab Jamahiriya (31.VII.73) C †									
–15	1 096 763	4 752	0.4	560 122	2 702	0.5	536 641	2 050	0.4
15–19	183 923	25 278	13.7	96 112	22 000	22.9	87 811	3 278	3.7
20–24	162 488	67 529	41.6	85 974	62 081	72.2	76 514	5 448	7.1
25–29	152 501	83 447	54.7	82 429	77 855	94.5	70 072	5 592	8.0
30–44	345 183	204 507	59.2	197 310	193 220	97.9	147 873	11 287	7.6
45–49	83 817	49 799	59.4	48 007	46 547	97.0	35 810	3 252	9.1
50–54	59 486	34 152	57.4	33 587	31 865	94.9	25 899	2 287	8.8
55–59	40 649	22 095	54.4	22 836	20 696	90.6	17 813	1 399	7.9
60–64	36 620	16 189	44.2	19 024	15 358	80.7	17 596	831	4.7
65+	87 712	23 576	26.9	46 371	22 885	49.4	41 341	691	1.7
?	95	76	80.0	81	73	90.1	14	3	21.4
Total	**2 249 237**	**541 174**	**24.1**	**1 191 853**	**504 264**	**42.3**	**1 057 384**	**36 910**	**3.5**

1 Total and economically active population by sex and age group
Population totale et population active par sexe et groupe d'âge
Población total y población económicamente activa por sexo y grupo de edad

Country, source and scope Pays, source et portée País, fuente y alcance	Total			Males – Hommes – Hombres			Females – Femmes – Mujeres		
	Total population Population totale Población total	Active population Population active Población activa	Activity rate Taux d'activité Tasa de actividad %	Total population Population totale Población total	Active population Population active Población activa	Activity rate Taux d'activité Tasa de actividad %	Total population Population totale Población total	Active population Population active Población activa	Activity rate Taux d'activité Tasa de actividad %
Madagascar (1975) OE									
Total	8 161 000	4 177 000	51.2	4 011 000	2 249 000	56.1	4 150 000	1 928 000	46.5
Malawi (1.X.77) C									
–15	2 476 077	100 365	4.1	1 231 042	54 686	4.4	1 245 035	45 679	3.7
15–19	540 834	222 546	41.1	260 816	99 858	38.3	280 018	122 688	43.8
20–24	448 952	307 394	68.5	194 803	153 093	78.6	254 149	154 301	60.7
25–44	1 223 483	984 018	80.4	575 174	547 569	95.2	648 309	436 449	67.3
45–54	365 507	305 234	83.5	171 090	164 287	96.0	194 417	140 947	72.5
55–64	235 103	192 002	81.7	113 524	107 076	94.3	121 579	84 926	69.9
65+	248 389	171 694	69.1	122 239	102 069	83.5	126 150	69 625	55.2
?	9 115	5 098	55.9	4 901	3 174	64.8	4 214	1 924	45.7
Total	5 547 460	2 288 351	41.3	2 673 589	1 231 812	46.1	2 873 871	1 056 539	36.8
Niger (1978) OE									
Total	4 978 000	2 530 000	50.8	2 482 000	1 252 000	50.4	2 496 000	1 278 000	51.2
Réunion (16.X.74) C *									
–15	203 116	.	.	101 347	.	.	101 769	.	.
15–19	54 903	6 035	11.0	26 740	5 219	19.5	28 163	816	2.9
20–29	68 009	28 438	41.8	32 209	24 156	75.0	35 800	4 282	12.0
30–49	93 141	65 628	70.5	45 396	37 985	83.7	47 745	27 643	57.9
50–59	29 074	8 054	27.7	13 866	7 012	50.6	15 208	1 042	6.9
60+	28 432	1 207	4.2	11 402	979	8.6	17 030	228	1.3
Total	476 675	109 362	22.9	230 960	75 351	32.6	245 715	34 011	13.8
St. Helena (31.X.76) C									
Total	5 147	1 940	37.7	2 514	1 338	53.2	2 633	602	22.9
Tunisie (VI.79) OE									
–15	2 648 000	.	.	1 350 900	.	.	1 297 100	.	.
15–19	717 200	331 400	46.2	368 200	230 100	62.5	349 000	101 300	29.0
20–24	593 900	321 200	54.1	300 600	242 600	80.7	293 300	78 600	26.8
25–29	425 300	243 800	57.3	206 000	197 400	95.8	219 300	46 400	21.2
30–44	866 500	475 200	54.8	415 000	407 600	98.2	451 500	67 600	15.0
45–49	261 200	145 000	55.5	130 400	126 600	97.1	130 800	18 400	14.1
50–54	211 800	115 400	54.5	108 100	102 000	94.4	103 700	13 400	12.9
55–59	164 000	82 700	50.4	85 800	73 800	86.0	78 200	8 900	11.4
60+	371 100	110 700	29.8	203 400	100 200	49.3	167 700	10 500	6.3
Total	6 259 000	1 825 400	29.2	3 168 400	1 480 300	46.7	3 090 600	345 100	11.2
AMERICA – AMERIQUE – AMERICA									
Argentina (VI.79) OE									
–15	7 618 000	148 000	1.9	3 865 000	85 000	2.2	3 753 000	63 000	1.7
15–19	2 341 000	921 000	39.3	1 190 000	583 000	49.0	1 151 000	338 000	29.4
20–24	2 236 000	1 435 000	64.2	1 133 000	906 000	80.0	1 103 000	529 000	48.0
25–29	2 019 000	1 377 000	68.2	1 022 000	978 000	95.7	997 000	399 000	40.0
30–44	5 059 000	3 386 000	66.9	2 545 000	2 500 000	98.2	2 514 000	886 000	35.2
45–49	1 610 000	1 026 000	63.7	807 000	777 000	96.3	803 000	249 000	31.0
50–54	1 445 000	853 000	59.0	715 000	656 000	91.7	730 000	197 000	27.0
55–59	1 221 000	607 000	49.7	595 000	472 000	79.3	626 000	135 000	21.6
60–64	1 050 000	326 000	31.0	503 000	244 000	48.5	547 000	82 000	15.0
65+	2 130 000	258 000	12.1	969 000	208 000	21.5	1 161 000	50 000	4.3
Total	26 729 000	10 337 000	38.7	13 344 000	7 409 000	55.5	13 385 000	2 928 000	21.9

1 Total and economically active population by sex and age group
Population totale et population active par sexe et groupe d'âge
Población total y población económicamente activa por sexo y grupo de edad

Country, source and scope / Pays, source et portée / País, fuente y alcance	Total — Total population / Population totale / Población total	Active population / Population active / Población activa	Activity rate / Taux d'activité / Tasa de actividad %	Males – Hommes – Hombres — Total population / Population totale / Población total	Active population / Population active / Población activa	Activity rate / Taux d'activité / Tasa de actividad %	Females – Femmes – Mujeres — Total population / Population totale / Población total	Active population / Population active / Población activa	Activity rate / Taux d'activité / Tasa de actividad %
Bolivia (29.IX.76) C									
–15	1 913 331	71 636	3.7	970 161	44 894	4.6	943 170	26 742	2.8
15–19	496 556	191 173	38.5	247 639	136 138	55.0	248 917	55 035	22.1
20–24	407 948	219 152	53.7	198 700	166 513	83.8	209 248	52 639	25.2
25–29	343 195	203 112	59.2	167 060	158 296	94.8	176 135	44 816	25.4
30–44	709 676	422 046	59.5	342 781	337 227	98.4	366 895	84 819	23.1
45–49	196 327	116 747	59.5	95 821	94 140	98.2	100 506	22 607	22.5
50–54	142 061	80 670	56.8	67 142	65 248	97.2	74 919	15 422	20.6
55–59	111 679	61 425	55.0	53 346	50 558	94.8	58 333	10 867	18.6
60–64	99 013	50 141	50.6	45 980	41 258	89.7	53 033	8 883	16.7
65+	193 700	85 289	44.0	87 399	70 347	80.5	106 301	14 942	14.1
Total	**4 613 486**	**1 501 391**	**32.5**	**2 276 029**	**1 164 619**	**51.2**	**2 337 457**	**336 772**	**14.4**
Canada (1978) LFSS †									
Total	**23 483 000**	**10 963 000**	**46.7**	**11 675 000**	**6 726 000**	**57.6**	**11 808 000**	**4 237 000**	**35.9**
Costa Rica (VII.79) HS									
–15	694 151	.	.	354 783	.	.	339 368	.	.
15–19	445 365	149 367	33.5	224 645	109 646	48.8	220 720	39 721	18.0
20–44	693 387	442 468	63.8	335 632	316 361	94.3	357 755	126 107	35.2
45–64	240 582	130 351	54.2	119 109	106 942	89.8	121 473	23 409	19.3
65+	90 703	19 917	22.0	45 248	17 938	39.6	45 455	1 979	4.4
?	1 733	1 283	74.0	929	859	92.5	804	424	52.7
Total	**2 165 921**	**743 386**	**34.3**	**1 080 346**	**551 746**	**51.1**	**1 085 575**	**191 640**	**17.7**
Chile (III.80) LFSS									
Total	**11 057 300**	**3 697 800**	**33.4**	**5 375 300**	**...**	.	**5 682 000**	**...**	.
República Dominicana (VII.79) OE									
–15	2 508 410	135 017	5.4	1 263 566	99 872	7.9	1 244 844	35 145	2.8
15–19	588 267	215 535	36.6	279 038	159 431	57.1	309 229	56 104	18.1
20–24	432 626	228 192	52.7	205 330	168 794	82.2	227 296	59 398	26.1
25–29	321 832	184 242	57.2	152 681	136 285	89.3	169 151	47 957	28.4
30–44	778 106	461 306	59.3	392 232	341 228	87.0	385 874	120 078	31.1
45–49	160 884	96 692	60.1	84 238	71 523	84.9	76 646	25 169	32.8
50–54	142 414	86 495	60.7	76 340	63 980	83.8	66 074	22 515	34.1
55+	342 871	184 593	53.8	179 005	136 543	76.3	163 866	48 050	29.3
Total	**5 275 410**	**1 592 072**	**30.2**	**2 632 430**	**1 177 656**	**44.7**	**2 642 980**	**414 416**	**15.7**
El Salvador (II–IX.78) HS									
–15	1 919 581	65 379	3.4	966 703	49 104	5.1	952 878	16 275	1.7
15–19	460 521	195 890	42.5	227 264	136 005	59.8	233 257	59 885	25.7
20–24	332 552	203 560	61.2	152 040	134 502	88.5	180 512	69 058	38.3
25–29	260 743	174 491	66.9	126 109	117 928	93.5	134 634	56 563	42.0
30–44	621 670	416 609	67.0	287 733	274 367	95.4	333 937	142 242	42.6
45–59	150 440	99 157	65.9	70 006	66 544	95.1	80 434	32 613	40.5
60–64	351 904	209 220	59.5	167 071	148 438	88.8	184 833	60 782	32.9
65+	187 522	66 056	35.2	83 305	50 717	60.9	104 217	15 339	14.7
Total	**4 284 933**	**1 430 362**	**33.4**	**2 080 231**	**977 605**	**47.0**	**2 204 702**	**452 757**	**20.5**

1 Total and economically active population by sex and age group
Population totale et population active par sexe et groupe d'âge
Población total y población económicamente activa por sexo y grupo de edad

Country, source and scope Pays, source et portée País, fuente y alcance	Total			Males – Hommes – Hombres			Females – Femmes – Mujeres		
	Total population Population totale Población total	Active population Population active Población activa	Activity rate Taux d'activité Tasa de actividad %	Total population Population totale Población total	Active population Population active Población activa	Activity rate Taux d'activité Tasa de actividad %	Total population Population totale Población total	Active population Population active Población activa	Activity rate Taux d'activité Tasa de actividad %
Greenland (26.X.76) C									
-14	15 973	.	.	8 250	.	.	7 723	.	.
14–19	6 846	2 315	33.8	3 498	1 499	42.9	3 348	816	24.4
20–24	4 381	3 120	71.2	2 323	1 862	80.2	2 058	1 258	61.1
25–29	4 208	3 283	78.0	2 452	2 181	88.9	1 756	1 102	62.8
30–44	10 725	8 641	80.6	6 521	5 969	91.5	4 204	2 672	63.6
45–49	2 251	1 719	76.4	1 230	1 127	91.6	1 021	592	58.0
50–54	1 547	1 127	72.9	844	779	92.3	703	348	49.5
55–59	1 171	677	57.8	608	470	77.3	563	207	36.8
60+	2 528	496	19.6	1 130	347	30.7	1 398	149	10.7
Total	**49 630**	**21 378**	*43.1*	**26 856**	**14 234**	*53.0*	**22 774**	**7 144**	*31.4*
Guatemala (1979) OE * †									
-15	2 999 705	108 545	3.6	1 527 914	94 338	6.2	1 471 791	14 207	1.0
15–19	738 315	300 756	40.7	374 988	247 492	66.0	363 327	53 264	14.7
20–24	637 618	343 194	53.8	323 514	286 310	88.5	314 104	56 884	18.1
25–29	543 437	302 117	55.6	275 735	260 570	94.5	267 702	41 547	15.5
30–44	1 087 556	599 042	55.1	550 983	523 525	95.0	536 573	75 517	14.1
45–49	260 925	141 213	54.1	131 437	123 551	94.0	129 488	17 662	13.6
50–54	223 689	116 781	52.2	112 114	104 266	93.0	111 575	12 515	11.2
55–59	170 793	88 036	51.5	84 962	78 165	92.0	85 831	9 871	11.5
60–64	124 305	58 954	47.4	61 521	52 600	85.5	62 784	6 354	10.1
65+	219 677	79 004	36.0	107 226	71 841	67.0	112 541	7 163	6.4
Total	**7 006 020**	**2 137 642**	*30.5*	**3 550 394**	**1 842 658**	*51.9*	**3 455 626**	**294 984**	*8.5*
Guyana (7.IV.70) C									
-20	410 225	28 398	6.9	205 839	21 942	10.7	204 386	6 456	3.2
20–24	56 087	31 301	55.8	27 380	24 151	88.2	28 707	7 150	24.9
25–29	39 636	21 914	55.3	19 277	17 926	93.0	20 359	3 988	19.6
30–44	93 257	52 262	56.0	45 633	42 897	94.0	47 624	9 365	19.7
45–49	24 557	14 234	58.0	12 498	11 582	92.7	12 059	2 652	22.0
50–54	19 991	10 998	55.0	10 105	9 003	89.1	9 886	1 995	20.2
55–59	18 241	9 334	51.2	9 483	7 774	82.0	8 758	1 560	17.8
60–64	12 786	4 651	36.4	6 479	3 895	60.1	6 307	756	12.0
65+	25 043	4 072	16.3	11 133	3 365	30.2	13 910	707	5.1
Total	**699 823**	**177 164**	*25.3*	**347 827**	**142 535**	*41.0*	**351 996**	**34 629**	*9.8*
Guyane française (X.76) OE									
Total	**57 500**	**21 440**	*37.3*	...	**12 890**	.	...	**8 550**	.
Honduras (1979) OE									
-15	1 708 177	70 560	4.1	858 109	64 446	7.5	850 678	6 114	0.7
15–19	376 119	166 407	44.2	189 441	138 178	72.9	186 678	28 229	15.1
20–24	302 001	169 004	56.0	152 098	135 922	89.4	149 903	33 082	22.1
25–29	242 371	140 569	58.0	122 057	115 014	94.2	120 314	25 555	21.2
30–44	489 028	279 393	57.1	245 207	234 261	95.5	243 821	45 132	18.5
45–49	115 886	64 032	55.3	57 994	55 232	95.2	57 892	8 800	15.2
50–54	96 522	51 825	53.7	48 253	45 154	93.6	48 269	6 671	13.8
55–59	77 700	40 326	51.9	38 684	35 328	91.3	39 016	4 998	12.8
60–64	59 556	28 454	47.8	29 331	25 253	86.1	30 225	3 201	10.6
65+	96 463	33 863	35.1	45 741	30 565	66.8	50 722	3 298	6.5
Total	**3 563 823**	**1 044 433**	*29.3*	**1 786 915**	**879 353**	*49.2*	**1 776 908**	**165 080**	*9.3*

ACTIVE POPULATION

1 Total and economically active population by sex and age group
Population totale et population active par sexe et groupe d'âge
Población total y población económicamente activa por sexo y grupo de edad

Country, source and scope / Pays, source et portée / País, fuente y alcance	Total			Males – Hommes – Hombres			Females – Femmes – Mujeres		
	Total population / Population totale / Población total	Active population / Population active / Población activa	Activity rate / Taux d'activité / Tasa de actividad %	Total population / Population totale / Población total	Active population / Population active / Población activa	Activity rate / Taux d'activité / Tasa de actividad %	Total population / Population totale / Población total	Active population / Population active / Población activa	Activity rate / Taux d'activité / Tasa de actividad %
Jamaica (1978) LFSS									
-14	809 100	.	.	412 950	.	.	396 150	.	.
14–19	303 500	120 050	39.6	151 550	68 250	45.0	151 950	51 800	34.1
20–24	166 900	146 350	87.7	77 350	72 800	94.1	89 550	73 550	82.1
25–34	228 250	208 850	91.5	113 850	110 450	97.0	114 400	98 400	86.0
35–44	170 950	156 200	91.4	79 450	77 550	97.6	91 500	78 650	86.0
45–54	153 000	134 950	88.2	72 950	70 700	96.9	80 050	64 250	80.3
55–64	133 250	101 650	76.3	62 000	56 350	90.9	71 250	45 300	63.6
65+	151 150	70 900	46.9	70 200	46 050	65.6	80 950	24 850	30.7
Total	**2 116 100**	**938 950**	**44.4**	**1 040 300**	**502 150**	**48.3**	**1 075 800**	**436 800**	**40.6**
México (VI.79) OE									
-15	32 043 355	494 727	1.5	16 322 674	340 090	2.1	15 720 681	154 637	1.0
15–19	7 474 040	2 828 551	37.8	3 804 537	1 646 604	43.3	3 669 503	1 181 947	32.2
20–24	6 143 815	3 561 625	58.0	3 127 144	2 369 437	75.8	3 016 671	1 192 188	39.5
25–29	4 963 106	2 892 171	58.3	2 516 365	2 259 444	89.8	2 446 741	632 727	25.9
30–44	10 003 034	5 713 960	57.1	5 022 375	4 719 107	94.0	4 980 659	994 853	20.0
45–49	2 261 372	1 261 367	55.8	1 121 640	1 051 201	93.7	1 139 732	210 166	18.4
50–54	1 821 762	978 290	53.7	894 405	817 486	91.4	927 357	160 804	17.3
55–59	1 382 254	700 405	50.7	671 388	594 984	88.6	710 866	105 421	14.8
60–64	1 026 151	472 561	46.1	493 557	404 815	82.0	532 594	67 746	12.7
65+	2 262 215	747 038	33.0	1 061 625	640 024	60.3	1 200 590	107 014	8.9
Total	**69 381 104**	**19 650 695**	**28.3**	**35 035 710**	**14 843 192**	**42.4**	**34 345 394**	**4 807 503**	**14.0**
Montserrat (VI.78) OE									
Total	**11 252**	**4 218**	**37.5**	**5 250**	**2 672**	**50.9**	**6 002**	**1 546**	**25.8**
Nicaragua (VI.77) OE †									
-15	1 104 082	53 343	4.8	558 325	43 449	7.8	545 757	9 894	1.8
15–24	468 053	220 041	47.0	221 177	151 445	68.5	246 876	68 596	27.8
25–34	272 788	170 799	62.6	130 627	114 692	87.8	142 161	56 107	39.5
35–44	188 437	120 420	63.9	90 917	82 558	90.8	97 520	37 862	38.8
45+	291 567	150 088	51.5	139 040	108 865	78.3	152 527	41 223	27.0
Total	**2 324 927**	**714 691**	**30.7**	**1 140 086**	**501 009**	**43.9**	**1 184 841**	**213 682**	**18.0**
Paraguay (1980) OE									
Total	**3 061 824**	**1 111 442**	**36.3**	**1 529 649**	**793 570**	**51.9**	**1 532 175**	**317 872**	**20.7**
Perú (VI.80) OE									
-15	7 607 900	.	.	3 833 600	.	.	3 774 300	.	.
15–19	1 930 700	563 200	29.2	973 700	357 400	36.7	957 000	205 800	21.5
20–24	1 629 700	929 400	57.0	819 300	638 500	77.9	810 400	290 900	35.9
25–29	1 334 700	877 000	65.7	669 500	627 100	93.7	665 200	249 900	37.6
30–44	2 733 100	1 842 000	67.4	1 366 800	1 339 000	98.0	1 366 300	503 000	36.8
45–49	641 700	425 900	66.4	319 700	311 200	97.3	322 000	114 700	35.6
50–54	533 300	338 900	63.5	264 900	253 300	95.6	268 400	85 600	31.9
55–59	429 400	256 300	59.7	212 500	194 300	91.4	216 900	62 000	28.6
60–64	328 700	166 300	50.6	161 300	131 700	81.6	167 400	34 600	20.7
65+	610 300	214 500	35.1	289 700	167 000	57.6	320 600	47 500	14.8
Total	**17 779 500**	**5 613 500**	**31.6**	**8 911 000**	**4 019 500**	**45.1**	**8 868 500**	**1 594 000**	**18.0**

1 Total and economically active population by sex and age group
Population totale et population active par sexe et groupe d'âge
Población total y población económicamente activa por sexo y grupo de edad

Country, source and scope Pays, source et portée País, fuente y alcance	Total			Males – Hommes – Hombres			Females – Femmes – Mujeres		
	Total population Population totale Población total	Active population Population active Población activa	Activity rate Taux d'activité Tasa de actividad %	Total population Population totale Población total	Active population Population active Población activa	Activity rate Taux d'activité Tasa de actividad %	Total population Population totale Población total	Active population Population active Población activa	Activity rate Taux d'activité Tasa de actividad %
Puerto Rico (IV.80) LFSS									
–20	1 499 694	55 978	3.7	766 228	38 358	5.0	733 466	17 620	2.4
20–24	290 980	153 125	52.6	136 539	92 067	67.4	154 441	61 058	39.5
25–34	456 817	292 237	64.0	206 923	179 400	86.7	249 894	112 837	45.2
35–44	391 855	240 311	61.3	182 587	155 888	85.4	209 268	84 423	40.3
45–54	315 912	160 100	50.7	148 114	111 159	75.0	167 798	48 941	29.2
55–64	253 426	82 679	32.6	120 070	64 448	53.7	133 356	18 231	13.7
65+	287 833	27 901	9.7	136 609	24 047	17.6	151 224	3 854	2.5
Total	**3 496 517**	**1 012 331**	29.0	**1 697 070**	**665 367**	39.2	**1 799 447**	**346 964**	19.3
Trinidad and Tobago (I–VI.78) LFSS									
Total	**1 132 700**	**439 000**	38.8	**575 700**	**306 500**	53.2	**557 000**	**132 500**	23.8
United States (1979) LFSS †									
–16	50 212 000	.	.	25 639 000	.	.	24 574 000	.	.
16–19	20 862 000	9 813 000	47.0	10 580 000	5 309 000	50.2	10 281 000	4 504 000	43.8
20–24	20 527 000	16 083 000	78.4	10 254 000	8 983 000	87.6	10 273 000	7 100 000	69.1
25–29	18 342 000	14 666 000	80.0	9 091 000	8 600 000	94.6	9 251 000	6 066 000	65.6
30–44	41 596 000	32 693 000	78.6	20 374 000	19 417 000	95.3	21 222 000	13 276 000	62.6
45–49	11 217 000	8 511 000	75.9	5 471 000	5 061 000	92.5	5 746 000	3 450 000	60.0
50–54	11 734 000	8 438 000	71.9	5 666 000	5 027 000	88.7	6 068 000	3 411 000	56.2
55–59	11 367 000	7 272 000	64.0	5 428 000	4 404 000	81.1	5 939 000	2 868 000	48.3
60–64	9 585 000	4 448 000	46.4	4 487 000	2 737 000	61.0	5 098 000	1 711 000	33.6
65+	24 658 000	3 073 000	12.5	10 017 000	1 928 000	19.2	14 641 000	1 145 000	7.8
Total	**220 099 000**	**104 996 000**	47.7	**107 006 000**	**61 466 000**	57.4	**113 093 000**	**43 531 000**	38.5
Uruguay (21.V.75) C									
–15	752 588	13 505	1.8	382 224	9 889	2.6	370 364	3 616	1.0
15–19	236 137	104 865	44.4	118 085	72 750	61.6	118 052	32 115	27.2
20–24	203 780	133 346	65.4	100 121	89 673	89.6	103 659	43 673	42.1
25–29	188 858	128 291	67.9	92 746	88 070	95.0	96 112	40 221	41.8
30–44	536 965	363 560	67.7	263 922	255 567	96.8	273 043	107 993	39.6
45–49	178 607	115 379	64.6	88 227	83 646	94.8	90 380	31 733	35.1
50–54	159 200	94 763	59.5	78 888	71 137	90.2	80 312	23 626	29.4
55–59	132 662	67 179	50.6	65 074	52 598	80.8	67 588	14 581	21.6
60–64	126 816	43 375	34.2	60 261	35 329	58.6	66 555	8 046	12.1
65+	272 816	30 336	11.1	119 864	24 925	20.8	152 952	5 411	3.5
Total	**2 788 429**	**1 094 599**	39.3	**1 369 412**	**783 584**	57.2	**1 419 017**	**311 015**	21.9
ASIA – ASIE – ASIA									
Afghanistan (1978) OE									
Total	**15 108 000**	**3 724 100**	24.6	**7 834 820**	...	.	**7 273 180**	...	.

1 Total and economically active population by sex and age group
Population totale et population active par sexe et groupe d'âge
Población total y población económicamente activa por sexo y grupo de edad

Country, source and scope / Pays, source et portée / País, fuente y alcance	Total			Males – Hommes – Hombres			Females – Femmes – Mujeres		
	Total population / Population totale / Población total	Active population / Population active / Población activa	Activity rate / Taux d'activité / Tasa de actividad %	Total population / Population totale / Población total	Active population / Population active / Población activa	Activity rate / Taux d'activité / Tasa de actividad %	Total population / Population totale / Población total	Active population / Population active / Población activa	Activity rate / Taux d'activité / Tasa de actividad %
Bahrain (IV.79) OE									
−20	147 700	5 600	3.8	76 200	3 800	5.0	71 500	1 800	2.5
20–29	88 400	64 500	73.0	59 400	56 000	94.3	29 000	8 500	29.3
30–39	54 600	33 200	60.8	37 200	31 500	84.7	17 400	1 700	9.8
40–49	32 600	15 400	47.2	20 100	15 000	74.6	12 500	400	3.2
50+	41 700	16 200	38.8	26 000	16 000	61.5	15 700	200	1.3
Total	**365 000**	**134 900**	37.0	**218 900**	**122 300**	55.9	**146 100**	**12 600**	8.6
Bangladesh (1.III.74) C									
−15	34 371 965	2 353 360	6.8	17 600 997	2 087 078	11.9	16 770 968	266 282	1.6
15–19	5 918 320	2 264 457	38.3	3 153 750	2 138 842	67.8	2 764 570	125 615	4.5
20–24	4 911 695	2 109 029	42.9	2 416 167	2 030 476	84.0	2 495 528	78 553	3.1
25–34	8 928 717	4 380 984	49.1	4 389 244	4 253 670	96.9	4 539 473	127 314	2.8
35–44	7 072 950	3 846 712	54.4	3 779 315	3 739 451	98.9	3 293 635	107 261	3.3
45–54	4 865 434	2 699 766	55.5	2 662 987	2 619 313	98.4	2 202 447	80 453	3.7
55–64	3 034 510	1 678 484	55.3	1 695 299	1 625 108	95.9	1 339 211	53 376	4.0
65+	2 374 322	1 189 800	50.1	1 372 986	1 156 659	84.2	1 001 336	33 141	3.3
Total	**71 477 913**	**20 522 592**	28.7	**37 070 745**	**19 650 597**	53.0	**34 407 168**	**871 995**	2.5
Brunei (VI.78) OE									
−15	73 500	.	.	37 970	.	.	35 530	.	.
15–19	20 090	4 500	22.4	10 950	3 500	32.0	9 140	1 000	10.9
20–24	21 760	14 140	65.0	13 590	11 690	86.0	8 170	2 450	30.0
25–29	18 180	12 920	71.1	11 720	11 370	97.0	6 460	1 550	24.0
30–44	33 760	23 360	69.2	21 730	21 080	97.0	12 030	2 280	19.0
45–49	8 860	6 450	72.8	6 070	5 890	97.0	2 790	560	20.1
50–54	8 550	6 380	74.6	6 290	5 910	94.0	2 260	470	20.8
55–59	6 670	4 700	70.5	4 900	4 310	88.0	1 770	390	22.0
60–64	3 340	2 010	60.2	2 270	1 820	80.2	1 070	190	17.8
65+	6 060	2 330	38.4	3 530	2 050	58.1	2 530	280	11.1
?	490	.	.	440	.	.	50	.	.
Total	**201 260**	**76 790**	38.2	**119 460**	**67 620**	56.6	**81 800**	**9 170**	11.2
Hong Kong (IX.79) LFSS †									
−15	1 256 200	4 100	0.3	658 100	1 500	0.2	598 100	2 600	0.4
15–19	577 800	235 800	40.8	295 200	118 900	40.3	282 600	116 900	41.4
20–24	510 800	429 800	84.1	261 700	232 900	89.0	249 100	196 800	79.0
25–29	421 700	331 900	78.7	217 500	214 400	98.6	204 300	117 500	57.5
30–44	784 700	576 500	73.5	428 000	422 300	98.7	356 700	154 200	43.2
45–49	263 800	190 100	72.1	141 500	138 100	97.6	122 300	52 000	42.5
50–54	257 200	169 400	65.9	132 200	124 200	93.9	125 000	45 300	36.2
55–59	197 300	115 700	58.6	101 600	84 000	82.7	95 700	31 800	33.2
60–64	174 200	77 900	44.7	85 100	54 300	63.8	89 100	23 600	26.5
65+	320 000	63 300	19.8	123 000	41 900	34.1	197 000	21 300	10.8
Total	**4 763 700**	**2 194 500**	46.1	**2 443 900**	**1 432 500**	58.6	**2 319 800**	**762 000**	32.8

1 Total and economically active population by sex and age group
Population totale et population active par sexe et groupe d'âge
Población total y población económicamente activa por sexo y grupo de edad

Country, source and scope Pays, source et portée País, fuente y alcance	Total			Males – Hommes – Hombres			Females – Femmes – Mujeres		
	Total population Population totale Población total	Active population Population active Población activa	Activity rate Taux d'activité Tasa de actividad %	Total population Population totale Población total	Active population Population active Población activa	Activity rate Taux d'activité Tasa de actividad %	Total population Population totale Población total	Active population Population active Población activa	Activity rate Taux d'activité Tasa de actividad %
Indonesia (1976) LFSS									
–15	53 084 849	3 716 589	7.0	27 034 333	2 105 841	7.8	26 050 516	1 610 748	6.2
15–19	13 530 231	7 506 114	55.5	6 592 412	4 367 030	66.2	6 937 819	3 139 084	45.2
20–24	9 882 024	6 677 983	67.6	4 771 069	4 207 711	88.2	5 110 955	2 470 272	48.3
25–29	8 281 979	5 903 117	71.3	3 853 012	3 728 626	96.8	4 428 967	2 174 491	49.1
30–44	22 107 429	17 101 835	77.4	10 679 003	10 542 691	98.7	11 428 426	6 559 144	57.4
45–49	5 586 465	4 487 090	80.3	2 875 215	2 802 538	97.5	2 711 250	1 684 552	62.1
50–54	4 272 766	3 335 683	78.1	2 080 599	2 002 531	96.2	2 192 167	1 333 152	60.8
55–59	3 172 968	2 317 658	73.0	1 582 616	1 462 851	92.4	1 590 352	854 807	53.7
60–64	2 506 552	1 666 497	66.5	1 188 813	1 037 192	87.2	1 317 739	629 305	47.8
65+	3 624 763	1 764 846	48.7	1 671 796	1 161 419	69.5	1 952 967	603 427	30.9
?	43 155	12 873	29.8	28 415	10 799	38.0	14 740	2 074	14.1
Total	**126 093 181**	**54 490 285**	**43.2**	**62 357 283**	**33 429 229**	**53.6**	**63 735 898**	**21 061 056**	**33.0**
Iran (XI.76) C5%									
–15	14 958 029	606 048	4.1	7 787 215	386 035	5.0	7 170 814	220 013	3.1
15–19	3 609 084	1 228 770	34.0	1 821 891	948 730	52.1	1 787 193	280 040	15.7
20–24	2 808 756	1 415 720	50.4	1 355 584	1 155 242	85.2	1 453 172	260 478	17.9
25–29	2 105 726	1 141 453	54.2	1 009 213	960 579	95.2	1 096 513	180 874	16.5
30–44	4 992 716	2 811 605	56.3	2 554 325	2 500 189	97.9	2 438 391	311 416	12.8
45–49	1 388 549	794 547	57.2	752 743	722 991	96.0	635 806	71 556	11.3
50–54	1 325 800	734 085	55.4	728 486	673 641	92.5	597 314	60 444	10.1
55–59	706 827	369 655	52.3	398 077	344 461	86.5	308 750	25 194	8.2
60–64	581 199	252 578	43.5	303 003	233 909	77.2	278 196	18 669	6.7
65+	1 185 490	378 047	31.9	626 642	354 463	56.6	558 848	23 584	4.2
Total	**33 662 176**	**9 732 508**	**28.9**	**17 337 179**	**8 280 240**	**47.8**	**16 324 997**	**1 452 268**	**8.9**
Iraq (17.X.77) C									
–15	5 867 646	165 318	2.8	3 051 834	93 161	3.1	2 815 812	72 157	2.6
15–19	1 010 261	251 409	24.9	488 306	194 703	39.9	521 955	56 706	10.9
20–24	1 116 376	591 035	52.9	602 362	511 615	84.9	514 014	79 420	15.5
25–29	810 939	482 348	59.5	422 793	408 637	96.7	388 146	73 711	19.0
30–44	1 478 271	878 663	59.4	762 197	736 454	96.6	716 074	142 209	19.9
45–49	418 225	235 278	56.3	214 064	197 308	92.2	204 161	37 970	18.6
50–54	321 123	165 317	51.5	153 403	134 606	87.7	167 720	30 711	18.3
55–59	244 378	121 019	49.5	121 602	100 786	82.9	122 776	20 233	16.5
60–64	221 427	98 507	44.5	113 053	84 463	74.7	108 374	14 044	13.0
65+	477 055	141 192	29.6	230 847	124 670	54.0	246 208	16 522	6.7
?	34 796	3 853	11.1	22 437	3 158	14.1	12 359	695	5.6
Total	**12 000 497**	**3 133 939**	**26.1**	**6 182 898**	**2 589 561**	**41.9**	**5 817 599**	**544 378**	**9.4**
Israel (1979) LFSS †									
–14	1 190 500	.	.	611 100	.	.	579 400	.	.
14–17	268 100	35 300	13.2	138 100	21 400	15.5	130 000	13 900	10.7
18–24	464 300	188 500	40.6	236 800	95 100	40.2	227 500	93 400	41.1
25–34	595 900	407 000	68.3	298 700	254 700	85.3	297 300	152 300	51.2
35–44	348 600	240 000	68.8	171 800	156 700	91.2	176 800	83 300	47.1
45–54	324 800	208 400	64.2	153 200	138 400	90.3	171 700	70 000	40.8
55–64	272 200	142 800	52.5	130 000	107 400	82.6	142 200	35 400	24.9
65+	321 900	55 600	17.3	153 300	45 300	29.5	168 600	10 300	6.1
Total	**3 786 400**	**1 277 800**	**33.7**	**1 892 900**	**819 200**	**43.3**	**1 893 500**	**458 600**	**24.2**

ACTIVE POPULATION

1 Total and economically active population by sex and age group
Population totale et population active par sexe et groupe d'âge
Población total y población económicamente activa por sexo y grupo de edad

Country, source and scope Pays, source et portée País, fuente y alcance	Total			Males – Hommes – Hombres			Females – Femmes – Mujeres		
	Total population Population totale Población total	Active population Population active Población activa	Activity rate Taux d'activité Tasa de actividad %	Total population Population totale Población total	Active population Population active Población activa	Activity rate Taux d'activité Tasa de actividad %	Total population Population totale Población total	Active population Population active Población activa	Activity rate Taux d'activité Tasa de actividad %
Japan (1979) LFSS †									
-15	27 660 000	.	.	14 190 000	.	.	13 470 000	.	.
15-19	8 070 000	1 470 000	18.2	4 120 000	740 000	18.0	3 940 000	730 000	18.5
20-24	8 000 000	5 590 000	69.9	4 050 000	2 840 000	70.1	3 950 000	2 760 000	69.9
25-29	9 530 000	7 000 000	73.5	4 780 000	4 670 000	97.7	4 750 000	2 330 000	49.1
30-44	27 820 000	21 290 000	76.5	13 920 000	13 560 000	97.4	13 900 000	7 740 000	55.7
45-49	7 980 000	6 410 000	80.3	3 990 000	3 870 000	97.0	3 990 000	2 550 000	63.9
50-54	7 040 000	5 390 000	76.6	3 460 000	3 280 000	94.8	3 590 000	2 110 000	58.8
55-59	5 400 000	3 670 000	68.0	2 370 000	2 150 000	90.7	3 030 000	1 520 000	50.2
60-64	4 320 000	2 430 000	56.3	1 910 000	1 480 000	77.5	2 410 000	940 000	39.0
65+	10 310 000	2 710 000	26.3	4 390 000	1 790 000	40.8	5 920 000	920 000	15.5
Total	**116 130 000**	**55 960 000**	**48.2**	**57 180 000**	**34 370 000**	60.1	**58 950 000**	**21 600 000**	36.6
Korea, Republic of (1.X.75) C †									
-15	13 208 388	190 784	1.4	6 840 674	88 514	1.3	6 367 714	102 270	1.6
15-19	4 146 912	1 937 191	46.7	2 124 156	976 698	46.0	2 022 756	960 493	47.5
20-24	3 123 126	1 774 562	56.8	1 611 767	923 999	57.3	1 511 359	850 563	56.3
25-29	2 507 450	1 609 521	64.2	1 271 743	1 169 689	92.0	1 235 707	439 832	35.6
30-44	6 213 535	4 608 297	74.2	3 128 185	3 070 600	98.2	3 085 350	1 537 697	49.8
45-49	1 398 820	1 082 175	77.4	649 961	632 290	97.3	748 859	449 885	60.1
50-54	1 197 379	903 402	75.4	576 664	546 172	94.7	620 715	357 230	57.6
55-59	939 205	634 092	67.5	449 224	382 111	85.1	489 981	251 981	51.4
60-64	737 552	359 881	48.8	334 479	226 859	67.8	403 073	133 022	33.0
65+	1 206 599	250 699	20.8	458 387	158 912	34.7	748 212	91 787	12.3
?	6	.	.	6	.	.	.	.	.
Total	**34 678 972**	**13 350 604**	**38.5**	**17 445 246**	**8 175 844**	46.9	**17 233 726**	**5 174 760**	30.0
" " " " (1979) LFSS †									
Total	**37 604 806**	**14 206 000**	37.8	**18 961 815**	**8 820 000**	46.5	**18 642 991**	**5 386 000**	28.9
Peninsular Malaysia (1976) LFSS †									
-15	4 269 703	.	.	2 177 756	.	.	2 091 947	.	.
15-19	1 273 636	569 470	44.7	647 344	338 894	52.4	626 292	230 576	36.8
20-24	1 064 240	775 423	72.9	532 430	487 746	91.6	531 810	287 677	54.1
25-29	825 960	593 945	71.9	411 531	403 924	98.2	414 429	190 021	45.9
30-44	1 593 817	1 186 234	74.4	795 437	785 693	98.8	798 380	400 541	50.2
45-49	380 448	284 591	74.8	189 577	185 452	97.8	190 871	99 139	51.9
50-54	314 396	223 947	71.2	154 225	146 881	95.2	160 171	77 066	48.1
55-59	271 594	161 885	59.6	134 317	111 492	83.0	137 277	50 393	36.7
60+	620 675	106 456	17.2	311 513	75 732	24.3	309 162	30 724	9.9
Total	**10 614 469**	**3 901 951**	**36.8**	**5 354 130**	**2 535 814**	47.4	**5 260 339**	**1 366 137**	26.0
Pakistan (I.80) LFSS †									
-15	35 102 000	1 878 000	5.4	18 544 000	1 738 000	9.4	16 558 000	140 000	0.8
15-19	6 685 000	2 517 000	37.7	3 631 000	2 345 000	64.6	3 054 000	172 000	5.6
20-24	5 361 000	2 602 000	48.5	2 751 000	2 431 000	88.4	2 610 000	171 000	6.6
25-29	4 956 000	2 532 000	51.1	2 447 000	2 353 000	96.2	2 509 000	179 000	7.1
30-44	12 521 000	6 717 000	53.6	6 304 000	6 179 000	98.0	6 217 000	538 000	8.7
45-49	3 491 000	1 917 000	54.9	1 831 000	1 784 000	97.4	1 660 000	133 000	8.0
50-54	2 938 000	1 667 000	56.7	1 644 000	1 574 000	95.7	1 294 000	93 000	7.2
55-59	1 831 000	951 000	51.9	974 000	896 000	92.0	857 000	55 000	6.4
60-64	2 064 000	1 122 000	54.4	1 231 000	1 067 000	86.7	833 000	55 000	6.6
65+	2 969 000	1 083 000	36.5	1 768 000	1 053 000	59.6	1 201 000	30 000	2.5
Total	**77 918 000**	**22 986 000**	**29.5**	**41 125 000**	**21 420 000**	52.1	**36 793 000**	**1 566 000**	4.3

1

Total and economically active population by sex and age group
Population totale et population active par sexe et groupe d'âge
Población total y población económicamente activa por sexo y grupo de edad

Country, source and scope / Pays, source et portée / País, fuente y alcance	Total			Males – Hommes – Hombres			Females – Femmes – Mujeres		
	Total population / Population totale / Población total	Active population / Population active / Población activa	Activity rate / Taux d'activité / Tasa de actividad %	Total population / Population totale / Población total	Active population / Population active / Población activa	Activity rate / Taux d'activité / Tasa de actividad %	Total population / Population totale / Población total	Active population / Population active / Población activa	Activity rate / Taux d'activité / Tasa de actividad %
Philippines (1.V.75) C									
−15	18 493 255	547 422	3.0	9 469 348	336 297	3.6	9 023 907	211 125	2.3
15−19	4 950 580	1 957 171	39.5	2 454 432	1 172 017	47.8	2 496 148	785 154	31.5
20−24	3 837 688	2 229 780	58.1	1 893 903	1 512 825	79.9	1 943 785	716 955	36.9
25−29	2 982 466	1 867 684	62.6	1 491 032	1 393 411	93.5	1 491 434	474 273	31.8
30−44	6 268 907	3 841 271	61.3	3 150 395	3 052 101	96.9	3 118 512	789 170	25.3
45−49	1 478 256	901 156	61.0	751 499	719 727	95.8	726 757	181 429	25.0
50−54	1 151 010	678 209	58.9	582 036	544 173	93.5	568 974	134 036	23.6
55−59	914 420	523 052	57.2	469 678	426 171	90.7	444 742	96 881	21.8
60−64	791 910	419 243	52.9	408 277	343 942	84.2	383 633	75 301	19.6
65+	1 202 168	461 175	38.4	605 624	379 083	62.6	596 544	82 092	13.8
Total	**42 070 660**	**13 426 163**	**31.9**	**21 276 224**	**9 879 747**	**46.4**	**20 794 436**	**3 546 416**	**17.1**
Singapore (VI.79) LFSS †									
−15	647 417	3 182	0.5	338 424	1 685	0.5	308 994	1 497	0.5
15−19	306 457	133 481	43.6	155 236	68 259	44.0	151 222	65 222	43.1
20−24	290 422	244 604	84.2	149 537	136 725	91.4	140 885	107 879	76.6
25−29	228 049	174 806	76.7	114 638	112 080	97.8	113 411	62 726	55.3
30−44	454 517	306 728	67.5	224 534	221 352	98.6	229 983	85 375	37.1
45−49	110 291	67 427	61.1	55 447	53 367	96.2	54 844	14 059	25.6
50−54	94 194	54 262	57.6	49 665	45 693	92.0	44 528	8 569	19.2
55−59	69 111	32 632	47.2	36 001	27 266	75.7	33 110	5 366	16.2
60−64	61 791	21 027	34.0	30 885	17 158	55.6	30 906	3 868	12.5
65+	100 454	18 178	18.1	46 712	14 122	30.2	53 743	4 056	7.5
Total	**2 362 704**	**1 056 325**	**44.7**	**1 201 079**	**697 707**	**58.1**	**1 161 625**	**358 618**	**30.9**
République arabe syrienne (IX.79) LFSS									
−15	4 118 721	89 354	2.2	2 110 279	49 401	2.3	2 008 442	39 953	2.0
15−19	992 985	287 566	29.0	507 871	221 330	43.6	485 114	66 236	13.7
20−24	706 301	295 560	41.8	345 641	231 877	67.1	360 660	63 683	17.7
25−29	539 665	298 646	55.3	274 397	257 850	94.0	265 268	40 796	15.4
30−44	1 157 876	634 293	54.8	567 111	557 776	98.4	590 765	76 517	13.0
45−49	307 027	169 951	55.4	157 756	150 388	95.3	149 271	19 563	13.1
50−54	270 940	151 146	55.8	138 880	130 725	94.1	132 060	20 421	15.5
55−59	180 141	93 926	52.1	99 776	86 978	87.2	80 365	6 948	8.6
60−64	141 414	64 855	45.9	79 157	61 228	77.4	62 257	3 627	5.8
65+	308 359	88 930	28.8	166 009	83 821	50.5	142 350	5 109	3.6
Total	**8 723 429**	**2 174 227**	**24.9**	**4 446 877**	**1 831 374**	**41.2**	**4 276 552**	**342 853**	**8.0**
Thailand (VII−IX.78) LFSS †									
−15	20 054 800	1 358 400	6.8	10 247 200	638 800	6.2	9 807 600	719 600	7.3
15−19	4 846 400	3 403 500	70.2	2 412 900	1 703 500	70.6	2 433 500	1 700 000	69.9
20−24	3 621 100	3 077 600	85.0	1 800 700	1 598 800	88.8	1 820 400	1 478 800	81.2
25−29	3 178 500	2 875 200	90.5	1 578 600	1 539 400	97.5	1 599 900	1 335 800	83.5
30−39	5 381 500	4 971 300	92.4	2 696 500	2 662 400	98.7	2 685 000	2 308 900	86.0
40−49	3 588 700	3 299 800	91.9	1 811 500	1 783 400	98.4	1 777 200	1 516 400	85.3
50−59	2 290 700	1 938 600	84.6	1 133 700	1 073 500	94.7	1 157 000	865 100	74.8
60+	2 256 500	968 900	42.9	1 037 900	614 500	59.2	1 218 600	354 400	29.1
Total	**45 218 200**	**21 893 300**	**48.4**	**22 719 000**	**11 614 300**	**51.1**	**22 499 200**	**10 279 000**	**45.7**

ACTIVE POPULATION

1 Total and economically active population by sex and age group
Population totale et population active par sexe et groupe d'âge
Población total y población económicamente activa por sexo y grupo de edad

Country, source and scope	Total			Males – Hommes – Hombres			Females – Femmes – Mujeres		
Pays, source et portée País, fuente y alcance	Total population Population totale Población total	Active population Population active Población activa	Activity rate Taux d'activité Tasa de actividad %	Total population Population totale Población total	Active population Population active Población activa	Activity rate Taux d'activité Tasa de actividad %	Total population Population totale Población total	Active population Population active Población activa	Activity rate Taux d'activité Tasa de actividad %

EUROPE – EUROPE – EUROPA

Denmark (X.79) LFSS †

-15	1 081 431	.	.	553 432	.	.	527 999	.	.
15–19	387 713	154 379	39.8	197 531	89 719	45.4	190 182	64 660	34.0
20–24	371 017	308 209	83.1	190 819	162 375	85.1	180 198	145 834	80.9
25–29	375 692	337 942	90.0	191 372	179 499	93.8	184 320	158 443	86.0
30–44	1 072 482	972 698	90.7	547 431	534 158	97.6	525 051	438 540	83.5
45–49	273 670	235 475	86.0	135 866	130 593	96.1	137 804	104 882	76.1
50–54	272 989	218 263	80.0	134 996	125 936	93.3	137 993	92 327	66.9
55–59	293 047	211 781	72.3	142 093	129 030	90.8	150 954	82 751	54.8
60–64	255 146	119 035	46.7	122 792	76 074	62.0	132 354	42 961	32.5
65+	734 990	69 119	9.4	310 734	50 673	16.3	424 256	18 446	4.3
Total	**5 118 177**	**2 626 901**	**51.3**	**2 527 066**	**1 478 057**	**58.5**	**2 591 111**	**1 148 844**	**44.3**

España (X–XII.79) LFSS

-15	9 692 600	65 300	0.7	4 966 200	36 300	0.7	4 726 400	29 000	0.6
15–19	3 170 300	1 440 000	45.4	1 620 900	826 600	51.0	1 549 400	613 400	39.6
20–24	2 957 500	1 580 100	53.4	1 496 300	879 400	58.8	1 461 200	700 700	48.0
25–29	2 538 400	1 342 600	52.9	1 285 200	926 500	72.1	1 253 200	416 100	33.2
30–44	6 759 200	3 906 000	57.8	3 369 400	2 962 000	87.9	3 389 800	944 000	27.8
45–49	2 371 200	1 450 100	61.2	1 167 000	1 102 000	94.4	1 204 200	348 100	28.9
50–54	2 205 900	1 339 700	60.7	1 078 300	1 022 400	94.8	1 127 600	317 300	28.1
55–59	1 963 900	1 163 500	59.2	941 600	896 700	95.2	1 022 300	266 800	26.1
60–64	1 553 900	640 400	41.2	706 200	481 200	68.1	847 700	159 200	18.8
65+	4 029 000	373 800	9.3	1 642 000	246 400	15.0	2 387 000	127 400	5.3
Total	**37 241 900**	**13 301 500**	**35.7**	**18 273 100**	**9 379 500**	**51.3**	**18 968 800**	**3 922 000**	**20.7**

Faeroe Islands (22.IX.77) C

-14	11 588	.	.	5 964	.	.	5 624	.	.
14–19	4 576	2 109	46.1	2 397	1 261	52.6	2 179	848	38.9
20–24	3 094	2 364	76.4	1 671	1 481	88.6	1 423	883	62.1
25–29	3 207	2 256	70.3	1 739	1 631	93.8	1 468	625	42.6
30–44	7 272	5 138	70.7	4 055	3 964	97.8	3 217	1 174	36.5
45–49	2 122	1 442	68.0	1 120	1 090	97.3	1 002	352	35.1
50–54	2 114	1 314	62.2	1 042	992	95.2	1 072	322	30.0
55–59	2 105	1 281	60.9	1 093	986	90.2	1 012	295	29.2
60–64	1 835	931	50.7	936	758	81.0	899	173	19.2
65+	4 056	750	18.5	1 980	645	32.6	2 076	105	5.1
Total	**41 969**	**17 585**	**41.9**	**21 997**	**12 808**	**58.2**	**19 972**	**4 777**	**23.9**

Finland (1979) LFSS †

-14	989 786	.	.	505 890	.	.	483 896	.	.
14–19	385 677	123 000	31.9	196 867	71 000	36.1	188 810	52 000	27.5
20–24	394 116	289 000	73.3	201 673	157 000	77.8	192 443	132 000	68.6
25–29	419 225	353 000	84.2	216 359	196 000	90.6	202 866	157 000	77.4
30–44	1 000 319	901 000	90.1	510 249	490 000	96.0	490 070	411 000	83.9
45–49	277 222	232 000	83.7	137 908	120 000	87.0	139 314	112 000	80.4
50–54	276 817	202 000	73.0	132 909	105 000	79.0	143 908	97 000	67.4
55–59	244 946	137 000	55.9	107 435	67 000	62.4	137 511	70 000	50.9
60–64	215 630	58 000	26.9	89 896	29 000	32.3	125 734	29 000	23.1
65+	554 350	13 000	2.3	201 604	7 000	3.5	352 746	6 000	1.7
Total	**4 758 088**	**2 308 000**	**48.5**	**2 300 790**	**1 242 000**	**54.0**	**2 457 298**	**1 066 000**	**43.4**

1 Total and economically active population by sex and age group
Population totale et population active par sexe et groupe d'âge
Población total y población económicamente activa por sexo y grupo de edad

Country, source and scope / Pays, source et portée / País, fuente y alcance	Total			Males – Hommes – Hombres			Females – Femmes – Mujeres		
	Total population / Population totale / Población total	Active population / Population active / Población activa	Activity rate / Taux d'activité / Tasa de actividad %	Total population / Population totale / Población total	Active population / Population active / Población activa	Activity rate / Taux d'activité / Tasa de actividad %	Total population / Population totale / Población total	Active population / Population active / Población activa	Activity rate / Taux d'activité / Tasa de actividad %
France (III.79) LFSS									
−15	11 387 700	.	.	5 824 500	.	.	5 563 200	.	.
15–19	4 286 700	911 700	21.3	2 186 800	544 700	24.9	2 099 900	367 000	17.5
20–24	4 219 300	3 136 700	74.3	2 141 800	1 726 300	80.6	2 077 500	1 410 400	67.9
25–29	4 261 900	3 480 800	81.7	2 169 700	2 055 200	94.7	2 092 200	1 425 600	68.1
30–44	10 168 400	7 951 100	78.2	5 249 400	5 092 400	97.0	4 919 000	2 858 700	58.1
45–49	3 280 100	2 431 300	74.1	1 652 400	1 566 500	94.8	1 627 700	864 800	53.1
50–54	3 200 100	2 250 000	70.3	1 583 500	1 453 700	91.8	1 616 600	796 300	49.3
55–59	3 104 600	1 922 800	61.9	1 493 200	1 208 000	80.9	1 611 400	714 800	44.4
60–64	1 628 900	525 100	32.2	763 500	331 700	43.4	865 400	193 400	22.3
65+	7 873 000	390 200	5.0	3 103 500	211 400	6.8	4 769 500	178 800	3.7
Total	**53 410 700**	**22 999 700**	**43.1**	**26 168 300**	**14 189 900**	**54.2**	**27 242 400**	**8 809 800**	**32.3**
Germany, Fed. Rep. of (IV.79) LFSS †									
−15	11 796 000	.	.	6 040 000	.	.	5 756 000	.	.
15–19	5 103 000	2 509 000	49.2	2 631 000	1 367 000	52.0	2 472 000	1 142 000	46.2
20–24	4 221 000	3 178 000	75.3	2 166 000	1 755 000	81.0	2 055 000	1 423 000	69.2
25–29	3 998 000	3 022 000	75.6	2 010 000	1 813 000	90.2	1 988 000	1 209 000	60.8
30–44	13 000 000	9 968 000	76.7	6 662 000	6 527 000	98.0	6 338 000	3 441 000	54.3
45–49	3 825 000	2 841 000	74.3	1 941 000	1 875 000	96.6	1 884 000	966 000	51.3
50–54	3 844 000	2 621 000	68.2	1 787 000	1 661 000	92.9	2 057 000	960 000	46.7
55–59	3 655 000	2 062 000	56.4	1 503 000	1 236 000	82.2	2 152 000	825 000	38.3
60–64	2 380 000	539 000	22.6	954 000	377 000	39.5	1 426 000	162 000	11.4
65+	9 494 000	459 000	4.8	3 527 000	273 000	7.7	5 967 000	186 000	3.1
Total	**61 315 000**	**27 199 000**	**44.4**	**29 221 000**	**16 884 000**	**57.8**	**32 095 000**	**10 315 000**	**32.1**
Hongrie (I.79) OE									
Total	**10 688 000**	**5 081 000**	**47.5**	**5 186 000**	**2 819 900**	**54.4**	**5 502 000**	**2 261 100**	**41.1**
Iceland (XII.79) OE									
−15	62 079	.	.	31 822	.	.	30 257	.	.
15–19	22 629	13 578	60.0	11 538	6 923	60.0	11 091	6 655	60.0
20–24	21 361	18 094	84.7	10 984	9 856	89.7	10 377	8 238	79.4
25–29	18 525	16 101	86.9	9 641	9 352	97.0	8 884	6 749	76.0
30–44	39 361	32 971	83.8	20 069	19 467	97.0	19 292	13 504	70.0
45–49	11 297	9 444	83.6	5 692	5 521	97.0	5 605	3 923	70.0
50–54	10 686	8 575	80.2	5 431	5 159	95.0	5 255	3 416	65.0
55–59	9 810	7 238	73.8	4 893	4 648	95.0	4 917	2 590	52.7
60–64	8 182	5 886	71.9	3 991	3 791	95.0	4 191	2 095	50.0
65+	22 409	4 685	20.9	10 091	3 330	33.0	12 318	1 355	11.0
Total	**226 339**	**116 572**	**51.5**	**114 152**	**68 047**	**59.6**	**112 187**	**48 525**	**43.3**
Ireland (IV.77) LFSS †									
Total	**3 269 000**	**1 143 900**	**35.0**	**1 644 000**	**834 800**	**50.8**	**1 625 000**	**309 100**	**19.0**
Italie (1979) LFSS †									
−14	11 864 000	.	.	6 042 000	.	.	5 821 000	.	.
14–19	5 353 000	1 651 000	30.8	2 709 000	895 000	33.0	2 644 000	756 000	28.6
20–24	3 772 000	2 390 000	63.4	1 845 000	1 322 000	71.7	1 927 000	1 068 000	55.4
25–29	3 686 000	2 679 000	72.7	1 783 000	1 671 000	93.7	1 904 000	1 008 000	52.9
30–39	7 758 000	5 508 000	71.0	3 814 000	3 756 000	98.5	3 944 000	1 751 000	44.4
40–49	7 505 000	5 032 000	67.0	3 693 000	3 588 000	97.2	3 812 000	1 443 000	37.9
50–59	7 030 000	3 785 000	53.8	3 390 000	2 810 000	82.9	3 640 000	975 000	26.8
60–64	2 193 000	512 000	23.3	1 041 000	391 000	37.6	1 152 000	121 000	10.5
65+	6 855 000	518 000	7.6	3 002 000	377 000	12.6	3 854 000	140 000	3.6
Total	**56 610 000**	**22 313 000**	**39.4**	**27 518 000**	**14 933 000**	**54.3**	**29 091 000**	**7 380 000**	**25.4**

1 Total and economically active population by sex and age group
Population totale et population active par sexe et groupe d'âge
Población total y población económicamente activa por sexo y grupo de edad

Country, source and scope / Pays, source et portée / País, fuente y alcance	Total			Males – Hommes – Hombres			Females – Femmes – Mujeres		
	Total population / Population totale / Población total	Active population / Population active / Población activa	Activity rate / Taux d'activité / Tasa de actividad %	Total population / Population totale / Población total	Active population / Population active / Población activa	Activity rate / Taux d'activité / Tasa de actividad %	Total population / Population totale / Población total	Active population / Population active / Población activa	Activity rate / Taux d'activité / Tasa de actividad %
Luxembourg (X.78) OE									
−15	70 500	.	.	36 000	.	.	34 500	.	.
15–19	28 000	14 000	50.0	14 000	7 000	50.0	14 000	7 000	50.0
20–24	28 500	21 500	75.4	14 000	11 500	82.1	14 500	10 000	69.0
25–29	28 500	21 000	73.7	14 500	13 500	93.1	14 000	7 500	53.6
30–44	75 000	50 000	66.7	39 000	38 000	97.4	36 000	12 000	33.3
45–49	25 500	15 500	60.8	13 000	12 500	96.2	12 500	3 000	24.0
50–54	22 500	12 000	53.3	11 000	10 000	90.9	11 500	2 000	17.4
55–59	19 000	7 000	36.8	8 500	5 000	58.8	10 500	2 000	19.0
60–64	16 000	3 500	21.9	7 500	2 500	33.3	8 500	1 000	11.8
65+	48 500	2 000	4.1	19 500	1 500	7.7	29 000	500	1.7
Total	**362 000**	**146 500**	40.5	**177 000**	**101 500**	57.3	**185 000**	**45 000**	24.3
Malta (XII.79) OE									
Total	**311 421**	**122 556**	39.4	**150 872**	**90 461**	60.0	**160 549**	**32 095**	20.0
Netherlands (I.79) OE †									
−15	3 248 000	.	.	1 662 200	.	.	1 585 800	.	.
15–19	1 231 100	319 800	26.0	629 000	150 300	23.9	602 200	169 500	28.1
20–24	1 170 000	844 800	72.2	596 400	458 800	76.9	573 700	386 000	67.3
25–29	1 146 700	781 900	68.2	588 200	547 900	93.1	558 500	234 000	41.9
30–44	2 828 500	1 867 800	66.0	1 463 000	1 406 600	96.1	1 365 500	461 200	33.8
45–49	765 600	456 800	59.7	385 200	347 700	90.3	380 400	109 100	28.7
50–54	727 400	398 600	54.8	355 700	305 300	85.8	371 700	93 300	25.1
55–59	701 300	328 300	46.8	336 800	265 900	78.9	364 500	62 400	17.1
60–64	587 800	197 500	33.6	275 400	164 800	59.8	312 400	32 700	10.5
65+	1 579 100	35 700	2.3	654 400	28 800	4.4	924 800	6 900	0.7
Total	**13 985 600**	**5 232 300**	37.4	**6 946 300**	**3 676 600**	52.9	**7 039 200**	**1 555 700**	22.1
Norway (1978) LFSS †									
Total	**4 059 000**	**1 888 000**	46.5	**2 013 000**	**1 130 000**	56.1	**2 046 000**	**758 000**	37.0
Pologne (7.XII.78) C									
−15	8 367 332	.	.	4 279 387	.	.	4 087 945	.	.
15–19	2 943 605	748 979	25.4	1 516 894	443 744	29.3	1 426 711	305 235	21.4
20–24	3 418 932	2 587 613	75.7	1 743 452	1 441 351	82.7	1 675 480	1 146 262	68.4
25–29	3 256 631	2 794 765	85.8	1 650 994	1 588 483	96.2	1 605 637	1 206 282	75.1
30–44	6 476 909	5 742 103	88.7	3 229 519	3 102 831	96.1	3 247 390	2 639 272	81.3
45–49	2 227 128	1 897 246	85.2	1 095 452	1 008 987	92.1	1 131 676	888 259	78.5
50–54	2 054 412	1 618 493	78.8	953 240	830 123	87.1	1 101 172	788 370	71.6
55–59	1 651 464	1 132 473	68.6	743 806	606 495	81.5	907 658	525 978	57.9
60–64	1 082 849	521 713	48.2	467 744	291 832	62.4	615 105	229 881	37.4
65+	3 563 586	906 377	25.4	1 389 880	485 668	34.9	2 173 706	420 709	19.4
?	18 602	12 364	66.5	9 219	6 731	73.0	9 383	5 633	60.0
Total	**35 061 450**	**17 962 126**	51.2	**17 079 587**	**9 806 245**	57.4	**17 981 863**	**8 155 881**	45.4

1 Total and economically active population by sex and age group
Population totale et population active par sexe et groupe d'âge
Población total y población económicamente activa por sexo y grupo de edad

Country, source and scope	Total			Males – Hommes – Hombres			Females – Femmes – Mujeres		
Pays, source et portée	Total population	Active population	Activity rate	Total population	Active population	Activity rate	Total population	Active population	Activity rate
País, fuente y alcance	Population totale	Population active	Taux d'activité	Population totale	Population active	Taux d'activité	Population totale	Population active	Taux d'activité
	Población total	Población activa	Tasa de actividad %	Población total	Población activa	Tasa de actividad %	Población total	Población activa	Tasa de actividad %
Portugal (VII–XII.79) LFSS †									
–15	2 566 000	102 000	4.0	1 318 000	60 000	4.6	1 248 000	42 000	3.4
15–19	813 000	505 000	62.1	411 000	279 000	67.9	402 000	226 000	56.2
20–24	814 000	650 000	79.9	404 000	359 000	88.9	410 000	291 000	71.0
25–29	598 000	491 000	82.1	277 000	266 000	96.0	321 000	225 000	70.1
30–44	1 643 000	1 223 000	74.4	733 000	708 000	96.6	910 000	515 000	56.6
45–49	603 000	415 000	68.8	283 000	267 000	94.3	320 000	148 000	46.3
50–54	485 000	303 000	62.5	215 000	192 000	89.3	270 000	111 000	41.1
55–59	463 000	269 000	58.1	222 000	182 000	82.0	241 000	87 000	36.1
60–64	420 000	196 000	46.7	192 000	131 000	68.2	228 000	65 000	28.5
65+	927 000	165 000	17.8	365 000	113 000	31.0	562 000	52 000	9.3
Total	**9 338 000**	**4 328 000**	46.3	**4 426 000**	**2 566 000**	58.0	**4 912 000**	**1 762 000**	35.9
Suisse (1979) OE *									
Total	**6 297 600**	**2 973 300**	47.2	**3 065 900**	**1 938 300**	63.2	**3 231 700**	**1 035 000**	32.0
Sweden (1978) LFSS †									
Total	**8 275 000**	**4 209 000**	50.9	**4 107 000**	**2 346 000**	57.1	**4 168 000**	**1 863 000**	44.7
United Kingdom (VI.78) OE †									
Total	**55 902 000**	**26 328 000**	47.1	**27 234 000**	**16 186 000**	59.4	**28 668 000**	**10 142 000**	35.4
Yugoslavia (1978) OE									
–15	5 470 619	41 270	0.8	2 811 547	14 977	0.5	2 659 072	26 293	1.0
15–24	3 820 805	1 913 099	50.1	1 950 986	1 088 247	55.8	1 869 819	824 852	44.1
25–49	7 810 182	5 636 534	72.2	3 924 551	3 701 590	94.3	3 885 631	1 934 944	49.8
50–64	2 833 005	1 219 339	43.0	1 264 489	814 005	64.4	1 568 516	405 334	25.8
65+	2 039 197	514 100	25.2	869 256	355 489	40.9	1 169 941	158 611	13.6
Total	**21 973 808**	**9 324 342**	42.4	**10 820 829**	**5 974 308**	55.2	**11 152 979**	**3 350 034**	30.0

OCEANIA – OCEANIE – OCEANIA

American Samoa (1974) OE									
–15	13 096			6 808			6 288		
15–19	3 146	379	12.0	1 505	143	9.5	1 641	236	14.4
20–24	2 287	1 137	49.7	951	559	58.8	1 336	578	43.3
25–29	2 071	1 293	62.4	1 006	774	76.9	1 065	519	48.7
30–44	4 531	3 218	71.0	2 409	2 152	89.3	2 122	1 066	50.2
45–49	1 160	795	68.5	568	522	91.9	592	273	46.1
50–54	857	572	66.7	431	414	96.1	426	158	37.1
55–59	754	469	62.2	418	371	88.8	336	98	29.2
60+	1 201	648	54.0	596	467	78.4	605	181	29.9
?	87	37	42.5	55	26	47.3	32	11	34.4
Total	**29 190**	**8 548**	29.3	**14 747**	**5 428**	36.8	**14 443**	**3 120**	21.6

29

ACTIVE POPULATION

1 Total and economically active population by sex and age group
Population totale et population active par sexe et groupe d'âge
Población total y población económicamente activa por sexo y grupo de edad

Country, source and scope / Pays, source et portée / País, fuente y alcance	Total			Males – Hommes – Hombres			Females – Femmes – Mujeres		
	Total population / Population totale / Población total	Active population / Population active / Población activa	Activity rate / Taux d'activité / Tasa de actividad %	Total population / Population totale / Población total	Active population / Population active / Población activa	Activity rate / Taux d'activité / Tasa de actividad %	Total population / Population totale / Población total	Active population / Population active / Población activa	Activity rate / Taux d'activité / Tasa de actividad %
Australia (30.VI.76) CS †									
–15	3 690 346	.	.	1 890 486	.	.	1 799 861	.	.
15–19	1 216 576	647 038	53.2	620 938	347 537	56.0	595 637	299 501	50.3
20–24	1 111 593	858 799	77.3	559 078	499 899	89.4	552 515	358 900	65.0
25–29	1 134 737	826 891	72.9	572 007	545 716	95.4	562 730	281 175	50.0
30–44	2 484 750	1 886 575	75.9	1 271 067	1 221 241	96.1	1 213 682	665 334	54.8
45–49	768 128	580 073	75.5	396 609	374 861	94.5	371 518	205 212	55.2
50–54	743 778	515 510	69.3	376 501	345 930	91.9	367 277	169 581	46.2
55–59	623 860	379 331	60.8	309 000	268 622	86.9	314 860	110 709	35.2
60–64	565 745	239 524	42.3	272 256	186 210	68.4	293 489	53 314	18.2
65+	1 208 983	121 266	10.0	507 027	85 316	16.8	701 956	35 950	5.1
Total	**13 548 467**	**6 054 996**	**44.7**	**6 774 955**	**3 875 323**	**57.2**	**6 773 512**	**2 179 673**	**32.2**
" " " " (VI–VIII.78) LFSS									
Total	**14 249 000**	**6 435 000**	**45.2**	**7 140 000**	**4 120 000**	**57.7**	**7 109 000**	**2 315 000**	**32.6**
Cook Islands (1.XII.76) C									
–15	9 023	.	.	4 687	.	.	4 336	.	.
15–19	2 085	1 027	49.3	1 006	617	61.3	1 019	410	40.2
20–24	1 042	734	70.4	493	476	96.6	549	258	47.0.
25–29	879	628	71.4	433	426	98.4	446	202	45.3
30–44	2 340	1 634	69.8	1 148	1 142	99.5	1 192	492	41.3
45–49	625	412	65.9	330	328	99.4	295	84	28.5
50–54	580	347	59.8	312	301	96.5	268	46	17.2
55–59	464	262	56.5	259	244	94.2	205	18	8.8
60–64	374	187	50.0	197	171	86.8	177	16	9.0
65+	716	153	21.4	369	145	39.3	347	8	2.3
Total	**18 128**	**5 384**	**29.7**	**9 294**	**3 850**	**41.4**	**8 834**	**1 534**	**17.4**
New Zealand (III.78) OE †									
–15	892 910	.	.	456 900	.	.	436 010	.	.
15–19	316 150	165 300	52.3	161 840	89 160	55.1	154 310	76 140	49.3
20–24	260 240	197 010	75.7	132 910	120 330	90.5	127 330	76 680	60.2
25–29	242 430	163 990	67.6	121 320	118 190	97.4	121 110	45 800	37.8
30–44	561 620	403 440	71.8	284 440	279 850	98.4	277 180	123 590	44.6
45–49	155 670	114 980	73.9	79 630	77 800	97.7	76 040	37 180	48.9
50–54	158 190	110 190	69.7	80 890	77 480	95.8	77 300	32 710	42.3
55–59	141 120	84 080	59.6	69 000	62 460	90.5	72 120	21 620	30.0
60–64	125 350	42 610	34.0	59 810	33 660	56.3	65 540	8 950	13.7
65+	292 170	23 260	8.0	125 100	18 840	15.1	167 070	4 420	2.6
Total	**3 145 850**	**1 304 860**	**41.5**	**1 571 840**	**877 770**	**55.8**	**1 574 010**	**427 090**	**27.1**
Polynésie française (29.IV.77) C									
–20	72 605	4 219	5.8	37 324	3 114	8.3	35 281	1 105	3.1
20–59	58 110	37 185	52.9	31 341	26 271	83.8	26 769	10 914	40.8
60+	6 667	1 654	24.8	3 503	1 363	38.9	3 164	291	9.2
Total	**137 382**	**43 058**	**31.3**	**72 168**	**30 748**	**42.6**	**65 214**	**12 310**	**18.9**

1 Total and economically active population by sex and age group
Population totale et population active par sexe et groupe d'âge
Población total y población económicamente activa por sexo y grupo de edad

Country, source and scope Pays, source et portée País, fuente y alcance	Total			Males – Hommes – Hombres			Females – Femmes – Mujeres		
	Total population Population totale Población total	Active population Population active Población activa	Activity rate Taux d'activité Tasa de actividad %	Total population Population totale Población total	Active population Population active Población activa	Activity rate Taux d'activité Tasa de actividad %	Total population Population totale Población total	Active population Population active Población activa	Activity rate Taux d'activité Tasa de actividad %
USSR – URSS – URSS									
U R S S (17.I.79) C †									
Total	262 436 227	134 860 000	51.4	122 328 833	...	.	140 107 394	...	.

31

2 Structure of the economically active population
Structure de la population active
Estructura de la población económicamente activa

Industry (Major divisions of economic activity)	Total				Employers and own-account workers / Employeurs et personnes travaillant à leur propre compte / Empleadores y trabajadores por cuenta propia			Employees / Salariés / Empleados a sueldo o salario		
	Total	%	Males Hommes Hombres	Females Femmes Mujeres	Total	Males Hommes Hombres	Females Femmes Mujeres	Total	Males Hommes Hombres	Females Femmes Mujeres
AFRICA										
Rép.-Unie du Cameroun (9–24.IV.76) C †										
1. Agriculture, hunting, forestry & fishing	2 034 974	*73.8*	1 073 264	961 710	...	...	...	...	...	...
2. Mining & quarrying	1 258	–	1 188	70	...	...	...	...	...	...
3. Manufacturing	122 411	*4.5*	96 577	25 834	...	...	...	...	...	...
4. Electr., gas & water	2 471	*0.1*	2 366	105	...	...	...	...	...	...
5. Construction	46 779	*1.7*	46 065	714	...	...	...	...	...	...
6. Wholesale/retail trade, restaurants & hotels	108 042	*3.9*	80 862	27 180	...	...	...	...	...	...
7. Transport, storage & communication	36 259	*1.3*	35 541	718	...	...	...	...	...	...
8. Financing, insur., real estate & business serv.	6 039	*0.2*	5 224	815	...	...	...	...	...	...
9. Community, social & personal services	205 487	*7.5*	178 937	26 550	...	...	...	...	...	...
0. Not adequately defined	71 134	*2.5*	48 093	23 041	...	...	...	...	...	...
–. Persons seeking work for the first time	123 045	*4.5*	88 050	34 995	.	.	.	.	.	.
Total	**2 757 899**	*100.0*	**1 656 167**	**1 101 732**	**1 657 632**	**1 011 540**	**646 092**	**392 523**	**353 775**	**38 748**
Egypt (22–23.XI.76) C †										
1. Agriculture, hunting, forestry & fishing	4 878 623	*44.2*	4 723 059	155 564	1 872 873	1 850 469	22 404	2 433 576	2 351 057	82 519
2. Mining & quarrying	33 402	*0.3*	31 949	1 453	755	699	56	30 940	29 718	1 222
3. Manufacturing	1 366 642	*12.4*	1 277 033	89 609	204 772	192 269	12 503	1 142 064	1 066 653	75 411
4. Electr., gas & water	61 681	*0.5*	57 086	4 595	.	.	.	61 681	57 086	4 595
5. Construction	423 757	*3.9*	416 777	6 980	81 594	81 320	274	284 620	278 300	6 320
6. Wholesale/retail trade, restaurants & hotels	856 531	*7.7*	807 795	48 736	516 285	494 078	22 207	316 486	291 553	24 933
7. Transport, storage & communication	479 373	*4.4*	463 536	15 837	77 895	77 654	241	397 281	381 802	15 479
8. Financing, insur., real estate & business serv.	87 807	*0.8*	71 304	16 503	3 381	3 252	129	83 574	67 413	16 161
9. Community, social & personal services	1 859 954	*16.8*	1 532 660	327 294	107 668	105 792	1 876	1 744 612	1 420 356	324 256
0. Not adequately defined	182 179	*1.7*	151 292	30 887	19 849	14 725	5 124	106 520	88 896	17 624
–. Persons seeking work for the first time	807 144	*7.3*	521 056	286 088	.	.	.	.	.	.
Total	**11 037 093**	*100.0*	**10 053 547**	**983 546**	**2 885 072**	**2 820 258**	**64 814**	**6 601 354**	**6 032 834**	**568 520**
" " " " (V.78) LFSS †										
1. Agriculture, hunting, forestry & fishing	3 976 700	*40.6*	3 885 300	91 400	...	...	. ...	...	...	...
2. Mining & quarrying	35 700	*0.3*	32 600	3 100	...	...	...	...	...	...
3. Manufacturing	1 430 300	*14.6*	1 350 600	79 700	...	...	...	...	...	...
4. Electr., gas & water	68 900	*0.7*	63 600	5 300	...	...	...	...	...	...
5. Construction	385 800	*4.0*	380 800	5 000	...	...	...	...	...	...
6. Wholesale/retail trade, restaurants & hotels	913 100	*9.3*	865 300	47 800	. ...	...	...	...	...	...
7. Transport, storage & communication	467 500	*4.7*	448 800	18 700	...	...	...	...	...	...
8. Financing, insur., real estate & business serv.	107 000	*1.1*	90 500	16 500	...	...	...	...	...	...
9. Community, social & personal services	1 786 100	*18.3*	1 453 400	332 700	...	...	...	...	...	...
0. Not adequately defined	631 400	*6.4*	373 100	258 300	...	...	...	...	...	...
Total	**9 802 500**	*100.0*	**8 944 000**	**858 500**	**3 060 400**	**2 862 500**	**197 900**	**4 946 900**	**4 447 900**	**499 000**

A By industry, by status and by sex
Par industrie, selon la situation dans la profession et par sexe
Por industria, según la categoría de ocupación y por sexo

Unpaid family workers Travailleurs familiaux non rémunérés Trabajadores familiares no remunerados			Not classifiable by status Inclassables selon la situation Inclasificables según la categoría			Industrie (Branches d'activité économique)	Industria (Grandes divisiones de actividad económica)
Total	Males Hommes Hombres	Females Femmes Mujeres	Total	Males Hommes Hombres	Females Femmes Mujeres		

AFRIQUE – AFRICA

						Industrie	Industria
...	...	...	...	...	...	1. Agriculture, chasse, sylvi-culture et pêche	1. Agricultura, caza, silvi-cultura y pesca
...	...	...	...	...	...	2. Industries extractives	2. Minas y canteras
...	...	...	...	...	...	3. Industries manufacturières	3. Industrias manufactureras
...	...	...	...	...	...	4. Electricité, gaz et eau	4. Electricidad, gas y agua
...	...	...	...	...	...	5. Construction	5. Construcción
						6. Commerce (gros et détail); restaurants, hôtels	6. Comercio (por mayor y por me-nor); restaurantes, hoteles
...	...	...	...	...	...	7. Transports, entrepôts et commu-nications	7. Transportes, almacenamiento y comunicaciones
						8. Banques, assur., affaires imm., services aux entreprises	8. Bancos, seguros, bienes in-muebles, serv. para empresas
...	...	...	...	...	...	9. Services à la collectivité, services sociaux et personnels	9. Servicios comunales, sociales y personales
...	...	...	...	...	...	0. Activités mal désignées	0. Actividades no bien especif.
.	.	.	123 045	88 050	34 995	–. Personnes en quête d'emploi pour la première fois	–. Personas en busca de trabajo por primera vez
512 946	**152 781**	**360 165**	**194 798**	**138 071**	**56 727**	**Total**	**Total**
560 082	509 954	50 128	12 092	11 579	513	1. Agriculture, chasse, sylvi-culture et pêche	1. Agricultura, caza, silvi-cultura y pesca
266	234	32	1 441	1 298	143	2. Industries extractives	2. Minas y canteras
11 804	10 881	923	8 002	7 230	772	3. Industries manufacturières	3. Industrias manufactureras
.	.	.	.	.	.	4. Electricité, gaz et eau	4. Electricidad, gas y agua
2 470	2 367	103	55 073	54 790	283	5. Construction	5. Construcción
20 363	18 981	1 382	3 397	3 183	214	6. Commerce (gros et détail); restaurants, hôtels	6. Comercio (por mayor y por me-nor); restaurantes, hoteles
3 071	2 971	100	1 126	1 109	17	7. Transports, entrepôts et commu-nications	7. Transportes, almacenamiento y comunicaciones
47	45	2	805	594	211	8. Banques, assur., affaires imm., services aux entreprises	8. Bancos, seguros, bienes in-muebles, serv. para empresas
4 370	4 116	254	3 304	2 396	908	9. Services à la collectivité, services sociaux et personnels	9. Servicios comunales, sociales y personales
14 138	11 663	2 475	41 672	36 008	5 664	0. Activités mal désignées	0. Actividades no bien especif.
.	.	.	807 144	521 056	286 088	–. Personnes en quête d'emploi pour la première fois	–. Personas en busca de trabajo por primera vez
616 611	**561 212**	**55 399**	**934 056**	**639 243**	**294 813**	**Total**	**Total**
...	...	...	...	...	...	1. Agriculture, chasse, sylvi-culture et pêche	1. Agricultura, caza, silvi-cultura y pesca
...	...	...	...	...	...	2. Industries extractives	2. Minas y canteras
...	...	...	...	...	...	3. Industries manufacturières	3. Industrias manufactureras
...	...	...	...	...	...	4. Electricité, gaz et eau	4. Electricidad, gas y agua
...	...	...	...	...	...	5. Construction	5. Construcción
...	...	...	...	...	...	6. Commerce (gros et détail); restaurants, hôtels	6. Comercio (por mayor y por me-nor); restaurantes, hoteles
...	...	...	...	...	...	7. Transports, entrepôts et commu-nications	7. Transportes, almacenamiento y comunicaciones
...	...	...	...	...	...	8. Banques, assur., affaires imm., services aux entreprises	8. Bancos, seguros, bienes in-muebles, serv. para empresas
...	...	...	...	...	...	9. Services à la collectivité, services sociaux et personnels	9. Servicios comunales, sociales y personales
...	...	...	...	...	...	0. Activités mal désignées	0. Actividades no bien especif.
1 440 700	**1 394 300**	**46 400**	**354 500**	**239 300**	**115 200**	**Total**	**Total**

2 Structure of the economically active population
Structure de la population active
Estructura de la población económicamente activa

Industry (Major divisions of economic activity)	Total				Employers and own-account workers / Employeurs et personnes travaillant à leur propre compte / Empleadores y trabajadores por cuenta propia			Employees / Salariés / Empleados a sueldo o salario		
	Total	%	Males Hommes Hombres	Females Femmes Mujeres	Total	Males Hommes Hombres	Females Femmes Mujeres	Total	Males Hommes Hombres	Females Femmes Mujeres
Liberia (1.II.74) C										
1. Agriculture, hunting, forestry & fishing	310 023	71.6	212 577	97 446	...	...	...	...	...	...
2. Mining & quarrying	22 129	5.1	21 414	715	...	...	...	...	...	...
3. Manufacturing	5 604	1.3	5 331	273	...	...	...	...	...	...
4. Electr., gas & water	208	0.1	202	6	...	...	...	...	...	...
5. Construction	4 101	0.9	4 019	82	...	...	...	...	...	...
6. Wholesale/retail trade, restaurants & hotels	16 282	3.8	11 728	4 554	...	...	...	...	...	...
7. Transport, storage & communication	6 380	1.5	6 248	132	...	...	...	...	...	...
8. Financing, insur., real estate & business serv.	1 413	0.3	1 226	187	...	...	...	...	...	...
9. Community, social & personal services	43 232	10.0	36 626	6 606	...	...	...	...	...	...
–. Persons seeking work for the first time	23 499	5.4	17 476	6 023	.	.	.	.	.	.
Total	**432 871**	100.0	**316 847**	**116 024**	...	...	...	...	...	...
Malawi (1.X.77) C										
1. Agriculture, hunting, forestry & fishing	1 932 122	84.4	936 099	996 023	...	...	...	...	...	...
2. Mining & quarrying	2 174	0.1	2 140	34	...	...	...	...	...	...
3. Manufacturing	82 391	3.6	67 723	14 668	...	...	...	...	...	...
4. Electr., gas & water	4 213	0.2	4 003	210	...	...	...	...	...	...
5. Construction	47 452	2.1	44 985	2 467	...	...	...	...	...	...
6. Wholesale/retail trade, restaurants & hotels	62 608	2.7	50 150	12 458	...	...	...	...	...	...
7. Transport, storage & communication	23 400	1.0	22 776	624	...	...	...	...	...	...
8. Financing, insur., real estate & business serv.	4 494	0.2	3 824	670	...	...	...	...	...	...
9. Community, social & personal services	82 523	3.6	67 170	15 353	...	...	...	...	...	...
0. Not adequately defined	46 974	2.1	32 942	14 032	...	...	...	...	...	...
Total	**2 288 351**	100.0	**1 231 812**	**1 056 539**	**1 827 969**	**825 455**	**1 002 514**	**406 520**	**368 356**	**38 164**
Tunisie (8.V.75) C										
1. Agriculture, hunting, forestry & fishing	526 030	32.4	456 620	69 410	230 950	219 960	10 990	200 600	188 330	12 270
2. Mining & quarrying	27 210	1.7	26 780	430	1 660	1 620	40	25 320	24 990	330
3. Manufacturing	240 640	14.8	115 820	124 820	86 590	18 910	67 680	133 370	94 610	38 760
4. Electr., gas & water	11 680	0.8	11 160	520	200	170	30	11 410	10 920	490
5. Construction	140 740	8.6	139 560	1 180	14 030	13 910	120	124 110	123 130	980
6. Wholesale/retail trade, restaurants & hotels	119 570	7.4	112 350	7 220	47 810	47 000	810	68 340	62 270	6 070
7. Transport, storage & communication	57 380	3.6	54 530	2 850	7 030	6 850	180	49 700	47 100	2 600
8. Financing, insur., real estate & business serv.	7 770	0.4	5 860	1 910	380	340	40	7 340	5 480	1 860
9. Community, social & personal services	217 730	13.5	169 930	47 800	12 410	11 450	960	202 200	156 620	45 580
0. Not adequately defined	153 950	9.5	133 940	20 010	5 440	4 950	490	47 840	44 400	3 440
–. Persons seeking work for the first time	119 120	7.3	91 760	27 360	...	...	...	...	...	...
Total	**1 621 820**	100.0	**1 318 310**	**303 510**	**406 500**	**325 160**	**81 340**	**870 230**	**757 850**	**112 380**

A — By industry, by status and by sex
Par industrie, selon la situation dans la profession et par sexe
Por industria, según la categoría de ocupación y por sexo

Unpaid family workers / Travailleurs familiaux non rémunérés / Trabajadores familiares no remunerados			Not classifiable by status / Inclassables selon la situation / Inclasificables según la categoría			Industrie (Branches d'activité économique)	Industria (Grandes divisiones de actividad económica)
Total	Males / Hommes / Hombres	Females / Femmes / Mujeres	Total	Males / Hommes / Hombres	Females / Femmes / Mujeres		
...	...	...	...	...	...	1. Agriculture, chasse, sylviculture et pêche	1. Agricultura, caza, silvicultura y pesca
...	...	...	...	...	...	2. Industries extractives	2. Minas y canteras
...	...	...	...	...	...	3. Industries manufacturières	3. Industrias manufactureras
...	...	...	...	...	...	4. Electricité, gaz et eau	4. Electricidad, gas y agua
...	...	...	...	...	...	5. Construction	5. Construcción
...	...	...	...	...	...	6. Commerce (gros et détail); restaurants, hôtels	6. Comercio (por mayor y por menor); restaurantes, hoteles
...	...	...	...	...	...	7. Transports, entrepôts et communications	7. Transportes, almacenamiento y comunicaciones
...	...	...	...	...	...	8. Banques, assur., affaires imm., services aux entreprises	8. Bancos, seguros, bienes inmuebles, serv. para empresas
...	...	...	...	...	...	9. Services à la collectivité, services sociaux et personnels	9. Servicios comunales, sociales y personales
.	.	.	23 499	17 476	6 023	–. Personnes en quête d'emploi pour la première fois	–. Personas en busca de trabajo por primera vez
...	...	...	**23 499**	**17 476**	**6 023**	**Total**	**Total**
...	...	...	...	...	...	1. Agriculture, chasse, sylviculture et pêche	1. Agricultura, caza, silvicultura y pesca
...	...	...	...	...	...	2. Industries extractives	2. Minas y canteras
...	...	...	...	...	...	3. Industries manufacturières	3. Industrias manufactureras
...	...	...	...	...	...	4. Electricité, gaz et eau	4. Electricidad, gas y agua
...	...	...	...	...	...	5. Construction	5. Construcción
...	...	...	...	...	...	6. Commerce (gros et détail); restaurants, hôtels	6. Comercio (por mayor y por menor); restaurantes, hoteles
...	...	...	...	...	...	7. Transports, entrepôts et communications	7. Transportes, almacenamiento y comunicaciones
...	...	...	...	...	...	8. Banques, assur., affaires imm., services aux entreprises	8. Bancos, seguros, bienes inmuebles, serv. para empresas
...	...	...	...	...	...	9. Services à la collectivité, services sociaux et personnels	9. Servicios comunales, sociales y personales
...	...	...	...	...	...	0. Activités mal désignées	0. Actividades no bien especif.
7 233	**3 638**	**3 595**	**46 629**	**34 363**	**12 266**	**Total**	**Total**
89 320	44 320	45 000	5 160	4 010	1 150	1. Agriculture, chasse, sylviculture et pêche	1. Agricultura, caza, silvicultura y pesca
160	100	60	70	70	...	2. Industries extractives	2. Minas y canteras
15 990	980	15 010	4 690	1 320	3 370	3. Industries manufacturières	3. Industrias manufactureras
10	10	...	60	60	...	4. Electricité, gaz et eau	4. Electricidad, gas y agua
640	570	70	1 960	1 950	10	5. Construction	5. Construcción
2 520	2 280	240	900	810	90	6. Commerce (gros et détail); restaurants, hôtels	6. Comercio (por mayor y por menor); restaurantes, hoteles
330	270	60	320	310	10	7. Transports, entrepôts et communications	7. Transportes, almacenamiento y comunicaciones
10	...	10	40	30	10	8. Banques, assur., affaires imm., services aux entreprises	8. Bancos, seguros, bienes inmuebles, serv. para empresas
1 100	470	630	2 040	1 410	630	9. Services à la collectivité, services sociaux et personnels	9. Servicios comunales, sociales y personales
1 820	980	840	98 830	83 590	15 240	0. Activités mal désignées	0. Actividades no bien especif.
...	...	...	119 120	91 760	27 360	–. Personnes en quête d'emploi pour la première fois	–. Personas en busca de trabajo por primera vez
111 900	**49 980**	**61 920**	**233 190**	**185 320**	**47 870**	**Total**	**Total**

2 Structure of the economically active population
Structure de la population active
Estructura de la población económicamente activa

Industry (Major divisions of economic activity)	Total				Employers and own-account workers Employeurs et personnes travaillant à leur propre compte Empleadores y trabajadores por cuenta propia			Employees Salariés Empleados a sueldo o salario		
	Total	%	Males Hommes Hombres	Females Femmes Mujeres	Total	Males Hommes Hombres	Females Femmes Mujeres	Total	Males Hommes Hombres	Females Femmes Mujeres
AMERICA										
Bolivia (29.IX.76) C										
1. Agriculture, hunting, forestry & fishing	693 049	46.2	604 078	88 971	481 176	440 206	40 970	85 451	82 310	3 141
2. Mining & quarrying	60 599	4.0	57 194	3 405	5 541	5 186	355	54 782	51 749	3 033
3. Manufacturing	145 404	9.7	88 978	56 426	77 592	35 019	42 573	60 393	52 244	8 149
4. Electr., gas & water	2 143	0.1	1 987	156	44	42	2	2 090	1 937	153
5. Construction	82 447	5.5	81 918	529	23 099	23 033	66	58 533	58 084	449
6. Wholesale/retail trade, restaurants & hotels	106 862	7.1	49 650	57 212	87 644	37 385	50 259	17 414	11 668	5 746
7. Transport, storage & communication	55 972	3.8	54 250	1 722	18 718	18 626	92	36 206	34 586	1 620
8. Financing, insur., real estate & business serv.	12 941	0.8	10 627	2 314	3 163	2 963	200	9 676	7 574	2 102
9. Community, social & personal services	281 911	18.8	165 688	116 223	33 049	27 284	5 765	242 711	133 273	109 438
0. Not adequately defined	53 600	3.6	44 963	8 637	3 569	2 781	788	5 769	4 787	982
–. Persons seeking work for the first time	6 463	0.4	5 286	1 177	.	.	.	.	.	.
Total	**1 501 391**	100.0	**1 164 619**	**336 772**	**733 595**	**592 525**	**141 070**	**573 025**	**438 212**	**134 813**
Canada (IV.80) LFSS †										
1. Agriculture, hunting, forestry & fishing	563 000	5.0	432 000	131 000	276 000	255 000	21 000	215 000	156 000	58 000
2. Mining & quarrying	179 000	1.6	159 000	21 000	–	–	–	179 000	158 000	21 000
3. Manufacturing	2 062 000	18.2	1 495 000	567 000	23 000	19 000	5 000	2 038 000	1 476 000	562 000
4. Electr., gas & water	122 000	1.1	108 000	14 000	–	–	–	122 000	108 000	14 000
5. Construction	562 000	5.0	512 000	51 000	89 000	88 000	–	470 000	424 000	46 000
6. Wholesale/retail trade, restaurants & hotels	1 784 000	15.8	1 019 000	765 000	160 000	108 000	52 000	1 606 000	910 000	696 000
7. Transport, storage & communication	750 000	6.6	582 000	168 000	38 000	35 000	3 000	711 000	547 000	164 000
8. Financing, insur., real estate & business serv.	599 000	5.3	256 000	343 000	21 000	17 000	4 000	578 000	238 000	339 000
9. Community, social & personal services	3 730 000	33.1	1 651 000	2 079 000	335 000	141 000	194 000	3 385 000	1 510 000	1 875 000
–. Persons seeking work for the first time	65 000	0.6	19 000	46 000	.	.	.	.	.	.
–. Other unemployed	872 000	7.7	525 000	347 000	30 000	19 000	11 000	841 000	507 000	334 000
Total	**11 291 000**	100.0	**6 759 000**	**4 532 000**	**973 000**	**684 000**	**289 000**	**10 143 000**	**6 033 000**	**4 110 000**
Chile (III.80) LFSS †										
–. Agriculture, forestry, hunting & fishing	587 600	15.9	...	...	...	...	...	...	...	...
–. Mining & quarrying	78 300	2.1	...	...	...	...	...	...	...	...
–. Manufacturing	598 700	16.2	...	...	...	...	...	...	...	...
–. Construction	192 700	5.2	...	...	...	...	...	...	...	...
–. Electr., gas, water & sanitary serv.;transp., storage & communication	232 700	6.3	...	...	...	...	...	...	...	...
–. Commerce	516 500	14.0	...	...	...	...	...	...	...	...
–. Services	1 040 300	28.1	...	...	...	...	...	...	...	...
–. Not adeq. described	6 800	0.2	...	...	...	...	...	...	...	...
–. Persons seeking work for the first time	143 300	3.9	.	.	.	.	.	.	.	...
–. Other unemployed	300 900	8.1	...	...	...	...	...	...	...	...
Total	**3 697 800**	100.0	...	...	...	...	...	...	...	...

A — By industry, by status and by sex
Par industrie, selon la situation dans la profession et par sexe
Por industria, según la categoría de ocupación y por sexo

Unpaid family workers / Travailleurs familiaux non rémunérés / Trabajadores familiares no remunerados			Not classifiable by status / Inclassables selon la situation / Inclasificables según la categoría			Industrie (Branches d'activité économique)	Industria (Grandes divisiones de actividad económica)
Total	Males Hommes Hombres	Females Femmes Mujeres	Total	Males Hommes Hombres	Females Femmes Mujeres		

AMERIQUE – AMERICA

Total	Males	Females	Total	Males	Females	Industrie	Industria
123 869	79 331	44 538	2 553	2 231	322	1. Agriculture, chasse, sylviculture et pêche	1. Agricultura, caza, silvicultura y pesca
67	60	7	209	199	10	2. Industries extractives	2. Minas y canteras
6 412	1 047	5 365	1 007	668	339	3. Industries manufacturières	3. Industrias manufactureras
3	2	1	6	6	.	4. Electricité, gaz et eau	4. Electricidad, gas y agua
370	359	11	445	442	3	5. Construction	5. Construcción
1 537	475	1 062	267	122	145	6. Commerce (gros et détail); restaurants, hôtels	6. Comercio (por mayor y por menor); restaurantes, hoteles
339	336	3	709	702	7	7. Transports, entrepôts et communications	7. Transportes, almacenamiento y comunicaciones
17	13	4	85	77	8	8. Banques, assur., affaires imm., services aux entreprises	8. Bancos, seguros, bienes inmuebles, serv. para empresas
3 797	3 264	533	2 354	1 867	487	9. Services à la collectivité, services sociaux et personnels	9. Servicios comunales, sociales y personales
853	624	229	43 409	36 771	6 638	0. Activités mal désignées	0. Actividades no bien especif.
.	.	.	6 463	5 286	1 177	–. Personnes en quête d'emploi pour la première fois	–. Personas en busca de trabajo por primera vez
137 264	**85 511**	**51 753**	**57 507**	**48 371**	**9 136**	**Total**	**Total**

Total	Males	Females	Total	Males	Females	Industrie	Industria
72 000	20 000	52 000	.	.	.	1. Agriculture, chasse, sylviculture et pêche	1. Agricultura, caza, silvicultura y pesca
–	–	–	.	.	.	2. Industries extractives	2. Minas y canteras
–	–	–	.	.	.	3. Industries manufacturières	3. Industrias manufactureras
–	–	–	.	.	.	4. Electricité, gaz et eau	4. Electricidad, gas y agua
–	–	–	.	.	.	5. Construction	5. Construcción
18 000	–	17 000	.	.	.	6. Commerce (gros et détail); restaurants, hôtels	6. Comercio (por mayor y por menor); restaurantes, hoteles
–	–	–	.	.	.	7. Transports, entrepôts et communications	7. Transportes, almacenamiento y comunicaciones
–	–	–	.	.	.	8. Banques, assur., affaires imm., services aux entreprises	8. Bancos, seguros, bienes inmuebles, serv. para empresas
11 000	–	10 000	.	.	.	9. Services à la collectivité, services sociaux et personnels	9. Servicios comunales, sociales y personales
.	.	.	65 000	19 000	46 000	–. Personnes en quête d'emploi pour la première fois	–. Personas en busca de trabajo por primera vez
–	.	.	.	.	.	–. Autres chômeurs	–. Otros desempleados
110 000	**23 000**	**87 000**	**65 000**	**19 000**	**46 000**	**Total**	**Total**

Total	Males	Females	Total	Males	Females	Industrie	Industria
...	...	...	...	...	...	–. Agriculture, sylviculture, chasse et pêche	–. Agricultura, silvicultura, caza y pesca
...	...	...	...	...	...	–. Industries extractives	–. Minas y canteras
...	...	...	...	...	...	–. Industries manufacturières	–. Industrias manufactureras
...	...	...	...	...	...	–. Construction	–. Construcción
						–. Electr., gaz, eau et serv. sanitaires; transports, entrepôts et communications	–. Electr., gas, agua y serv. sanitarios; transp., almacenaje y comunicaciones
...	...	...	...	...	...	–. Comm., banq., assur., aff. imm.	–. Comercio
...	...	...	...	...	...	–. Services	–. Servicios
...	...	...	...	...	...	–. Activités mal désignées	–. Actividades no bien especif.
						–. Personnes en quête d'emploi pour la première fois	–. Personas en busca de trabajo por primera vez
.	.	.	.	.	.	–. Autres chômeurs	–. Otros desempleados
...	...	...	...	...	...	**Total**	**Total**

ACTIVE POPULATION

2 Structure of the economically active population
Structure de la population active
Estructura de la población económicamente activa

Industry (Major divisions of economic activity)	Total				Employers and own-account workers / Employeurs et personnes travaillant à leur propre compte / Empleadores y trabajadores por cuenta propia			Employees / Salariés / Empleados a sueldo o salario		
	Total	%	Males Hommes Hombres	Females Femmes Mujeres	Total	Males Hommes Hombres	Females Femmes Mujeres	Total	Males Hommes Hombres	Females Femmes Mujeres
El Salvador (II–IX.78) HS										
1. Agriculture, hunting, forestry & fishing	586 772	41.0	525 551	61 221	165 151	162 255	2 896	322 898	269 909	52 989
2. Mining & quarrying	4 197	0.3	4 197	.	.	.	.	3 954	3 954	.
3. Manufacturing	203 079	14.2	108 733	94 346	57 994	17 849	40 145	130 241	85 755	44 486
4. Electr., gas & water	6 941	0.5	6 537	404	644	644	.	6 297	5 893	404
5. Construction	77 496	5.4	77 159	337	1 693	1 693	.	72 217	71 880	337
6. Wholesale/retail trade, restaurants & hotels	222 347	15.6	68 257	154 090	153 273	39 227	114 046	48 229	24 986	23 243
7. Transport, storage & communication	54 223	3.8	52 048	2 175	9 189	9 001	188	44 242	42 334	1 908
8. Financing, insur., real estate & business serv.	13 514	0.9	10 046	3 468	86	86	.	13 349	9 881	3 468
9. Community, social & personal services	252 481	17.6	120 310	132 171	15 771	11 938	3 833	234 251	106 843	127 408
0. Not adequately defined	880	0.1	603	277	102	.	102	778	603	175
–. Persons seeking work for the first time	8 432	0.6	4 164	4 268	.	.	.	.	.	.
Total	**1 430 362**	**100.0**	**977 605**	**452 757**	**403 903**	**242 693**	**161 210**	**876 456**	**622 038**	**254 418**
Greenland (26.X.76) C										
1. Agriculture, hunting, forestry & fishing	3 221	15.1	3 206	15	2 016	2 012	4	239	238	1
2. Mining & quarrying	318	1.5	310	8	2	2	.	316	308	8
3. Manufacturing	2 705	12.6	1 576	1 129	36	34	2	2 666	1 542	1 124
4. Electr., gas & water	246	1.2	242	4	.	.	.	246	242	4
5. Construction	3 124	14.6	3 017	107	285	285	.	2 826	2 732	94
6. Wholesale/retail trade, restaurants & hotels	2 686	12.5	1 392	1 294	130	107	23	2 514	1 283	1 231
7. Transport, storage & communication	1 842	8.7	1 633	209	123	121	2	1 715	1 512	203
8. Financing, insur., real estate & business serv.	343	1.6	209	134	18	17	1	324	192	132
9. Community, social & personal services	6 305	29.4	2 277	4 028	84	59	25	6 216	2 218	3 998
0. Not adequately defined	588	2.8	372	216	6	6	.	582	366	216
Total	**21 378**	**100.0**	**14 234**	**7 144**	**2 700**	**2 643**	**57**	**17 644**	**10 633**	**7 011**
Guatemala (1979) OE * †										
–. Agriculture, forestry, hunting & fishing	1 222 709	57.2	1 205 121	17 588	570 773	569 185	1 588	440 108	427 943	12 165
–. Mining & quarrying	2 612	0.1	2 580	32	414	408	6	2 123	2 097	26
–. Manufacturing	292 685	13.7	228 898	63 787	122 241	85 097	37 144	152 554	132 006	20 548
–. Construction	88 324	4.1	88 067	257	19 373	19 373	.	66 701	66 450	251
–. Electricity, gas, water & sanitary services	5 731	0.3	5 572	159	568	568	.	5 126	4 969	157
–. Commerce	158 522	7.4	107 908	50 614	98 175	65 732	32 443	53 795	37 598	16 197
–. Transport, storage & communication	54 452	2.6	53 195	1 257	10 910	10 781	129	42 833	41 721	1 112
–. Services	267 304	12.5	116 179	151 125	23 205	13 966	9 239	241 868	101 364	140 504
–. Not adequately defined & persons seeking work for the first time	45 303	2.1	35 138	10 165	3 672	3 104	568	20 792	15 478	5 314
Total	**2 137 642**	**100.0**	**1 842 658**	**294 984**	**849 331**	**768 214**	**81 117**	**1 025 900**	**829 626**	**196 274**

A By industry, by status and by sex
Par industrie, selon la situation dans la profession et par sexe
Por industria, según la categoría de ocupación y por sexo

Unpaid family workers / Travailleurs familiaux non rémunérés / Trabajadores familiares no remunerados			Not classifiable by status / Inclassables selon la situation / Inclasificables según la categoría			Industrie (Branches d'activité économique)	Industria (Grandes divisiones de actividad económica)
Total	Males Hommes Hombres	Females Femmes Mujeres	Total	Males Hommes Hombres	Females Femmes Mujeres		
98 723	93 387	5 336	.	.	.	1. Agriculture, chasse, sylvi- culture et pêche	1. Agricultura, caza, silvi- cultura y pesca
243	243	.	.	.	.	2. Industries extractives	2. Minas y canteras
14 844	5 129	9 715	.	.	.	3. Industries manufacturières	3. Industrias manufactureras
.	.	.	.	.	.	4. Electricité, gaz et eau	4. Electricidad, gas y agua
3 586	3 586	.	.	.	.	5. Construction	5. Construcción
20 845	4 044	16 801	.	.	.	6. Commerce (gros et détail); restaurants, hôtels	6. Comercio (por mayor y por me- nor); restaurantes, hoteles
792	713	79	.	.	.	7. Transports, entrepôts et commu- nications	7. Transportes, almacenamiento y comunicaciones
79	79	.	.	.	.	8. Banques, assur., affaires imm., services aux entreprises	8. Bancos, seguros, bienes in- muebles, serv. para empresas
2 459	1 529	930	.	.	.	9. Services à la collectivité, services sociaux et personnels	9. Servicios comunales, sociales y personales
.	.	.	.	.	.	0. Activités mal désignées	0. Actividades no bien especif.
.	.	.	8 432	4 164	4 268	–. Personnes en quête d'emploi pour la première fois	–. Personas en busca de trabajo por primera vez
141 571	**108 710**	**32 861**	**8 432**	**4 164**	**4 268**	**Total**	**Total**
9	.	9	957	956	1	1. Agriculture, chasse, sylvi- culture et pêche	1. Agricultura, caza, silvi- cultura y pesca
.	.	.	.	.	.	2. Industries extractives	2. Minas y canteras
3	.	3	.	.	.	3. Industries manufacturières	3. Industrias manufactureras
.	.	.	.	.	.	4. Electricité, gaz et eau	4. Electricidad, gas y agua
13	.	13	.	.	.	5. Construction	5. Construcción
42	2	40	.	.	.	6. Commerce (gros et détail); restaurants, hôtels	6. Comercio (por mayor y por me- nor); restaurantes, hoteles
4	.	4	.	.	.	7. Transports, entrepôts et commu- nications	7. Transportes, almacenamiento y comunicaciones
1	.	1	.	.	.	8. Banques, assur., affaires imm., services aux entreprises	8. Bancos, seguros, bienes in- muebles, serv. para empresas
5	.	5	.	.	.	9. Services à la collectivité, services sociaux et personnels	9. Servicios comunales, sociales y personales
.	.	.	.	.	.	0. Activités mal désignées	0. Actividades no bien especif.
77	**2**	**75**	**957**	**956**	**1**	**Total**	**Total**
210 859	207 042	3 817	969	951	18	–. Agriculture, sylviculture, chasse et pêche	–. Agricultura, silvicultura, caza y pesca
71	71	.	4	4	.	–. Industries extractives	–. Minas y canteras
16 939	10 992	5 947	951	803	148	–. Industries manufacturières	–. Industrias manufactureras
1 914	1 908	6	336	336	.	–. Construction	–. Construcción
34	33	1	3	2	1	–. Electricité, gaz, eau et services sanitaires	–. Electricidad, gas, agua y servicios sanitarios
6 332	4 422	1 910	220	156	64	–. Comm., banq., assur., aff. imm.	–. Comercio
570	556	14	139	137	2	–. Transports, entrepôts et commu- nications	–. Transportes, almacenamiento y comunicaciones
1 617	476	1 141	614	373	241	–. Services	–. Servicios
783	630	153	20 056	15 296	4 130	–. Activités mal désignées et per- sonnes en quête d'emploi pour l première fois.	–. Actividades no bien especifi- cadas; personas en busca de trabajo por primera vez
239 119	**226 130**	**12 989**	**23 292**	**18 688**	**4 604**	**Total**	**Total**

2 Structure of the economically active population
Structure de la population active
Estructura de la población económicamente activa

Industry (Major divisions of economic activity)	Total				Employers and own-account workers / Employeurs et personnes travaillant à leur propre compte / Empleadores y trabajadores por cuenta propia			Employees / Salariés / Empleados a sueldo o salario		
	Total	%	Males Hommes Hombres	Females Femmes Mujeres	Total	Males Hommes Hombres	Females Femmes Mujeres	Total	Males Hommes Hombres	Females Femmes Mujeres
Guyane française (16.X.74) C										
1. Agriculture, hunting, forestry & fishing	3 241	15.5	2 215	1 026	...	...	...	...	...	...
2. Mining & quarrying	140	0.7	137	3	...	...	...	...	...	...
3. Manufacturing	1 669	8.0	1 344	325	...	...	...	...	...	...
4. Electr., gas & water	359	1.7	299	60	...	...	...	...	...	...
5. Construction	2 000	9.5	1 885	115	...	...	...	...	...	...
6. Wholesale/retail trade, restaurants & hotels	2 673	12.8	1 419	1 254	...	...	...	...	...	...
7. Transport, storage & communication	848	4.1	748	100	...	...	...	...	...	...
8. Financing, insur., real estate & business serv.	317	1.5	170	147	...	...	...	...	...	...
9. Community, social & personal services	7 482	35.8	3 927	3 555	...	...	...	...	...	...
0. Not adequately defined	2 006	9.6	1 039	967	...	...	...	...	...	...
-. Persons seeking work for the first time	168	0.8	116	52	.	.	.	.	.	.
Total	**20 903**	**100.0**	**13 299**	**7 604**	...	...	...	...	...	...
Honduras (1977) OE										
1. Agriculture, hunting, forestry & fishing	590 554	60.8	579 258	11 296	240 392	238 369	2 023	174 001	167 164	6 837
2. Mining & quarrying	3 009	0.4	2 958	51	204	201	3	2 709	2 662	47
3. Manufacturing	115 296	11.8	74 097	41 199	36 170	11 078	25 092	65 470	55 953	9 517
4. Electr., gas & water	3 300	0.4	3 062	238	13	13	.	3 280	3 042	238
5. Construction	32 124	3.3	31 807	317	6 798	6 795	3	23 846	23 536	310
6. Wholesale/retail trade, restaurants & hotels	78 514	8.1	48 453	30 061	30 993	18 534	12 459	35 570	22 506	13 064
7. Transport, storage & communication	27 562	2.8	26 155	1 407	205	203	2	27 105	25 719	1 386
8. Financing, insur., real estate & business serv.	8 152	0.9	5 998	2 154	512	495	17	7 222	5 095	2 127
9. Community, social & personal services	111 997	11.5	48 627	63 370	7 642	5 317	2 325	101 803	41 100	60 703
Total	**970 508**	**100.0**	**820 415**	**150 093**	**322 929**	**281 005**	**41 924**	**441 006**	**346 777**	**94 229**
Jamaica (1978) LFSS †										
-. Agriculture, forestry, hunting & fishing	273 600	29.1	196 800	76 800	...	...	...	...	...	...
-. Mining & quarrying	6 600	0.7	5 750	850	...	...	...	...	...	...
-. Manufacturing	98 950	10.6	69 400	29 550	...	...	...	...	...	...
-. Construction; transp., storage & communic.	33 500	3.5	24 950	8 550	...	...	...	...	...	...
-. Electricity, gas, water & sanitary services	48 150	5.2	46 400	1 750	...	...	...	...	...	...
-. Commerce	108 800	11.6	37 300	71 500	...	...	...	...	...	...
-. Services	288 500	30.7	97 600	190 900	...	...	...	...	...	...
-. Not adeq. described	5 950	0.6	3 850	2 100	...	...	...	...	...	...
-. Persons seeking work for the first time	74 900	8.0	20 100	54 800	.	.	.	.	.	.
Total	**938 950**	**100.0**	**502 150**	**436 800**	...	...	...	...	...	...

A By industry, by status and by sex
Par industrie, selon la situation dans la profession et par sexe
Por industria, según la categoría de ocupación y por sexo

Unpaid family workers / Travailleurs familiaux non rémunérés / Trabajadores familiares no remunerados			Not classifiable by status / Inclassables selon la situation / Inclasificables según la categoría			Industrie (Branches d'activité économique)	Industria (Grandes divisiones de actividad económica)
Total	Males Hommes Hombres	Females Femmes Mujeres	Total	Males Hommes Hombres	Females Femmes Mujeres		
...	...	...	...	...	...	1. Agriculture, chasse, sylvi- culture et pêche	1. Agricultura, caza, silvi- cultura y pesca
...	...	...	...	...	...	2. Industries extractives	2. Minas y canteras
...	...	...	...	...	...	3. Industries manufacturières	3. Industrias manufactureras
...	...	...	...	...	...	4. Electricité, gaz et eau	4. Electricidad, gas y agua
...	...	...	...	...	...	5. Construction	5. Construcción
...	...	...	...	...	...	6. Commerce (gros et détail); restaurants, hôtels	6. Comercio (por mayor y por me- nor); restaurantes, hoteles
...	...	...	...	...	...	7. Transports, entrepôts et commu- nications	7. Transportes, almacenamiento y comunicaciones
...	...	...	...	...	...	8. Banques, assur., affaires imm., services aux entreprises	8. Bancos, seguros, bienes in- muebles, serv. para empresas
...	...	...	...	...	...	9. Services à la collectivité, services sociaux et personnels	9. Servicios comunales, sociales y personales
...	...	...	...	...	...	0. Activités mal désignées	0. Actividades no bien especif.
.	.	.	.	.	.	–. Personnes en quête d'emploi pour la première fois	–. Personas en busca de trabajo por primera vez
...	...	...	...	...	...	**Total**	**Total**
131 031	128 899	2 132	45 130	44 826	304	1. Agriculture, chasse, sylvi- culture et pêche	1. Agricultura, caza, silvi- cultura y pesca
37	37	.	59	58	1	2. Industries extractives	2. Minas y canteras
6 555	2 318	4 237	7 101	4 748	2 353	3. Industries manufacturières	3. Industrias manufactureras
4	4	.	3	3	.	4. Electricité, gaz et eau	4. Electricidad, gas y agua
407	406	1	1 073	1 070	3	5. Construction	5. Construcción
2 942	1 391	1 551	9 009	6 022	2 987	6. Commerce (gros et détail); restaurants, hôtels	6. Comercio (por mayor y por me- nor); restaurantes, hoteles
51	44	7	201	189	12	7. Transports, entrepôts et commu- nications	7. Transportes, almacenamiento y comunicaciones
6	3	3	412	405	7	8. Banques, assur., affaires imm., services aux entreprises	8. Bancos, seguros, bienes in- muebles, serv. para empresas
406	312	94	2 146	1 898	248	9. Services à la collectivité, services sociaux et personnels	9. Servicios comunales, sociales y personales
141 439	**133 414**	**8 025**	**65 134**	**59 219**	**5 915**	**Total**	**Total**
...	...	...	...	...	...	–. Agriculture, sylviculture, chasse et pêche	–. Agricultura, silvicultura, caza y pesca
...	...	...	...	...	...	–. Industries extractives	–. Minas y canteras
...	...	...	...	...	...	–. Industries manufacturières	–. Industrias manufactureras
...	...	...	...	...	...	–. Construction; transp., entre- pôts et communications	–. Construcción; transp., alma- cenamiento y comunicaciones
...	...	...	...	...	...	–. Electricité, gaz, eau et services sanitaires	–. Electricidad, gas, agua y servicios sanitarios
...	...	...	...	...	...	–. Comm., banq., assur., aff. imm.	–. Comercio
...	...	...	...	...	...	–. Services	–. Servicios
...	...	...	...	...	...	–. Activités mal désignées	–. Actividades no bien especif.
.	.	.	.	.	.	–. Personnes en quête d'emploi pour la première fois	–. Personas en busca de trabajo por primera vez
...	...	...	...	...	...	**Total**	**Total**

2 Structure of the economically active population
Structure de la population active
Estructura de la población económicamente activa

Industry (Major divisions of economic activity)	Total				Employers and own-account workers / Employeurs et personnes travaillant à leur propre compte / Empleadores y trabajadores por cuenta propia			Employees / Salariés / Empleados a sueldo o salario		
	Total	%	Males Hommes Hombres	Females Femmes Mujeres	Total	Males Hommes Hombres	Females Femmes Mujeres	Total	Males Hommes Hombres	Females Femmes Mujeres
México (VI.79) OE †										
−. Agriculture, forestry, hunting & fishing	7 885 824	40.1	7 188 558	697 266	...	...	...	...	...	...
−. Mining & quarrying	288 865	1.5	250 850	38 015	...	...	...	...	...	...
−. Manufacturing	3 574 461	18.2	2 567 872	1 006 589	...	...	...	...	...	...
−. Construction	909 827	4.6	843 093	66 734	...	...	...	...	...	...
−. Electricity, gas, water & sanitary services	82 533	0.4	69 763	12 770	...	...	...	...	...	...
−. Commerce	1 974 895	10.1	1 285 420	689 475	...	...	...	...	...	...
−. Transport, storage & communication	581 661	2.9	528 418	53 243	...	...	...	...	...	...
−. Services	4 352 629	22.2	2 109 218	2 243 411	...	...	...	...	...	...
Total	**19 650 695**	**100.0**	**14 843 192**	**4 807 503**	...	...	...	...	...	...
Netherlands Antilles (I.79) OE										
1. Agriculture, hunting, forestry & fishing	680	0.7	637	43	...	...	...	...	...	...
2. Mining & quarrying	389	0.4	376	13	...	...	...	...	...	...
3. Manufacturing	11 455	12.2	9 096	2 359	...	...	...	...	...	...
4. Electr., gas & water	1 370	1.4	1 279	91	...	...	...	...	...	...
5. Construction	6 430	6.8	6 047	383	...	...	...	...	...	...
6. Wholesale/retail trade, restaurants & hotels	22 420	23.7	11 591	10 829	...	...	...	...	...	...
7. Transport, storage & communication	5 995	6.4	4 697	1 298	...	...	...	...	...	...
8. Financing, insur., real estate & business serv.	4 610	4.9	2 708	1 902	...	...	...	...	...	...
9. Community, social & personal services	23 456	24.8	13 605	9 851	...	...	...	...	...	...
0. Not adequately defined	6 711	7.1	6 125	586	...	...	...	...	...	...
−. Unemployed	10 982	11.6	5 930	5 052	...	...	...	...	...	...
Total	**94 498**	**100.0**	**62 091**	**32 407**	...	...	...	...	...	...
Nicaragua (VI.77) OE										
1. Agriculture, hunting, forestry & fishing	300 169	42.0	266 856	33 313	...	...	...	...	...	...
2. Mining & quarrying	475	0.1	475	.	...	...	...	...	...	...
3. Manufacturing	115 313	16.1	72 287	43 026	...	...	...	...	...	...
4. Electr., gas & water	4 120	0.6	3 606	514	...	...	...	...	...	...
5. Construction	34 100	4.7	33 486	614	...	...	...	...	...	...
6. Wholesale/retail trade, restaurants & hotels	94 517	13.3	38 434	56 083	...	...	...	...	...	...
7. Transport, storage & communication	21 036	2.9	19 676	1 360	...	...	...	...	...	...
8. Financing, insur., real estate & business serv.	10 941	1.5	7 686	3 255	...	...	...	...	...	...
9. Community, social & personal services	130 041	18.2	56 430	73 611	...	...	...	...	...	...
0. Not adequately defined	3 979	0.6	2 073	1 906	...	...	...	...	...	...
Total	**714 691**	**100.0**	**501 009**	**213 682**	...	...	...	...	...	...

A By industry, by status and by sex
Par industrie, selon la situation dans la profession et par sexe
Por industria, según la categoría de ocupación y por sexo

Unpaid family workers / Travailleurs familiaux non rémunérés / Trabajadores familiares no remunerados			Not classifiable by status / Inclassables selon la situation / Inclasificables según la categoría			Industrie (Branches d'activité économique)	Industria (Grandes divisiones de actividad económica)
Total	Males Hommes Hombres	Females Femmes Mujeres	Total	Males Hommes Hombres	Females Femmes Mujeres		
...	...	...	...	...	...	–. Agriculture, sylviculture, chasse et pêche	–. Agricultura, silvicultura, caza y pesca
...	...	...	...	...	...	–. Industries extractives	–. Minas y canteras
...	...	...	...	...	...	–. Industries manufacturières	–. Industrias manufactureras
...	...	...	...	...	...	–. Construction	–. Construcción
...	...	...	...	...	...	–. Electricité, gaz, eau et services sanitaires	–. Electricidad, gas, agua y servicios sanitarios
...	...	...	...	...	...	–. Comm., banq., assur., aff. imm.	–. Comercio
...	...	...	...	...	...	–. Transports, entrepôts et communications	–. Transportes, almacenamiento y comunicaciones
...	...	...	...	...	...	–. Services	–. Servicios
...	...	...	...	...	...	**Total**	**Total**
...	...	...	...	...	...	1. Agriculture, chasse, sylviculture et pêche	1. Agricultura, caza, silvicultura y pesca
...	...	...	...	...	...	2. Industries extractives	2. Minas y canteras
...	...	...	...	...	...	3. Industries manufacturières	3. Industrias manufactureras
...	...	...	...	...	...	4. Electricité, gaz et eau	4. Electricidad, gas y agua
...	...	...	...	...	...	5. Construction	5. Construcción
...	...	...	...	...	...	6. Commerce (gros et détail); restaurants, hôtels	6. Comercio (por mayor y por menor); restaurantes, hoteles
...	...	...	...	...	...	7. Transports, entrepôts et communications	7. Transportes, almacenamiento y comunicaciones
...	...	...	...	...	...	8. Banques, assur., affaires imm., services aux entreprises	8. Bancos, seguros, bienes inmuebles, serv. para empresas
...	...	...	...	...	...	9. Services à la collectivité, services sociaux et personnels	9. Servicios comunales, sociales y personales
...	...	...	...	...	...	0. Activités mal désignées	0. Actividades no bien especif.
...	...	...	...	...	...	–. Chômeurs	–. Desempleados
...	...	...	...	...	...	**Total**	**Total**
...	...	...	...	...	...	1. Agriculture, chasse, sylviculture et pêche	1. Agricultura, caza, silvicultura y pesca
...	...	...	...	...	...	2. Industries extractives	2. Minas y canteras
...	...	...	...	...	...	3. Industries manufacturières	3. Industrias manufactureras
...	...	...	...	...	...	4. Electricité, gaz et eau	4. Electricidad, gas y agua
...	...	...	...	...	...	5. Construction	5. Construcción
...	...	...	...	...	...	6. Commerce (gros et détail); restaurants, hôtels	6. Comercio (por mayor y por menor); restaurantes, hoteles
...	...	...	...	...	...	7. Transports, entrepôts et communications	7. Transportes, almacenamiento y comunicaciones
...	...	...	...	...	...	8. Banques, assur., affaires imm., services aux entreprises	8. Bancos, seguros, bienes inmuebles, serv. para empresas
...	...	...	...	...	...	9. Services à la collectivité, services sociaux et personnels	9. Servicios comunales, sociales y personales
...	...	...	...	...	...	0. Activités mal désignées	0. Actividades no bien especif.
...	...	...	...	...	...	**Total**	**Total**

2 Structure of the economically active population
Structure de la population active
Estructura de la población económicamente activa

Industry (Major divisions of economic activity)	Total				Employers and own-account workers / Employeurs et personnes travaillant à leur propre compte / Empleadores y trabajadores por cuenta propia			Employees / Salariés / Empleados a sueldo o salario		
	Total	%	Males Hommes Hombres	Females Femmes Mujeres	Total	Males Hommes Hombres	Females Femmes Mujeres	Total	Males Hommes Hombres	Females Femmes Mujeres
Paraguay (1980) OE										
1/2. Agriculture, hunting, forestry & fishing; mining & quarrying	483 366	43.5	425 144	58 222	...	...	...	...	...	...
3. Manufacturing	196 503	17.7	119 908	76 595	...	...	...	...	...	...
4,7. Electr., gas & water; transport, storage & communication	41 568	3.7	38 647	2 921	...	...	...	...	...	...
5. Construction	62 352	5.6	62 035	317	...	...	...	...	...	...
6. Wholesale/retail trade, restaurants & hotels	146 377	13.2	63 335	83 042	...	...	...	...	...	...
8. Financing, insur., real estate & business serv.	17 338	1.5	13 301	4 037	...	...	...	...	...	...
9. Community, social & personal services	163 604	14.8	70 866	92 738	...	...	...	...	...	...
0. Not adequately defined	334	–	334	.	...	...	...	...	...	...
Total	**1 111 442**	100.0	**793 570**	**317 872**	...	...	...	...	...	...
Perú (VI.80) OE										
1. Agriculture, hunting, forestry & fishing	2 248 000	40.0	...	...	1 575 800	...	...	410 500	...	...
2. Mining & quarrying	67 300	1.2	...	...	1 900	...	...	65 000	...	...
3. Manufacturing	708 700	12.7	...	...	226 100	...	...	462 300	...	...
4. Electr., gas & water	12 200	0.2	...	...	.	.	.	12 200	...	...
5. Construction	240 400	4.3	...	...	50 500	...	...	189 200	.	.
6. Wholesale/retail trade, restaurants & hotels	846 500	15.0	...	...	560 400	...	...	230 700		
7. Transport, storage & communication	260 700	4.7	...	...	91 100	...	...	164 500		
8. Financing, insur., real estate & business serv.	94 500	1.7	...	...	13 300	...	...	80 900		
9. Community, social & personal services	1 135 200	20.2	...	...	203 400	...	...	920 700		
Total	**5 613 500**	100.0	...	...	**2 722 500**	...	...	**2 536 000**	...	...
Puerto Rico (IV.80) LFSS †										
1. Agriculture, hunting, forestry & fishing	65 400	6.5	63 600	1 800	23 400	23 200	–	39 500	38 100	1 400
2. Mining & quarrying	1 600	0.1	1 400	–	–	–	–	1 600	1 400	–
3. Manufacturing	198 200	19.6	111 300	87 000	4 000	3 800	–	193 600	107 500	86 100
4. Electr., gas & water	14 700	1.4	13 300	1 400	–	–	–	14 700	13 300	1 400
5. Construction	76 200	7.6	75 000	1 200	7 500	7 400	–	68 700	67 700	1 000
6. Wholesale/retail trade, restaurants & hotels	171 700	16.9	124 200	47 500	48 800	41 800	7 000	115 500	81 500	34 000
7. Transport, storage & communication	41 300	4.1	36 200	5 000	15 700	15 600	–	25 400	20 600	4 800
8. Financing, insur., real estate & business serv.	23 600	2.3	14 100	9 400	1 000	500	500	22 700	13 600	9 200
9. Community, social & personal services	403 100	39.9	217 200	186 000	34 000	26 800	7 100	367 900	189 900	178 000
0. Not adequately defined	16 400	1.6	9 000	7 500	...	...	...	...	...	...
Total	**1 012 300**	100.0	**665 400**	**347 000**	**134 300**	**119 200**	**15 100**	**849 700**	**533 600**	**316 100**

A — By industry, by status and by sex
Par industrie, selon la situation dans la profession et par sexe
Por industria, según la categoría de ocupación y por sexo

Unpaid family workers Travailleurs familiaux non rémunérés Trabajadores familiares no remunerados			Not classifiable by status Inclassables selon la situation Inclasificables según la categoría			Industrie (Branches d'activité économique)	Industria (Grandes divisiones de actividad económica)
Total	Males Hommes Hombres	Females Femmes Mujeres	Total	Males Hommes Hombres	Females Femmes Mujeres		
...	...	...	...	...	...	1/2. Agriculture, chasse, sylviculture et pêche; industries extractives	1/2. Agricultura, caza, silvicultura y pesca; minas y canteras
						3. Industries manufacturières	3. Industrias manufactureras
...	...	...	...	...	...	4,7. Electricité, gaz et eau; transports, entrepôts et communications	4,7. Electricidad, gas y agua; transportes, almacenamiento y comunicaciones
...	...	...	...	...	...	5. Construction	5. Construcción
...	...	...	...	...	...	6. Commerce (gros et détail); restaurants, hôtels	6. Comercio (por mayor y por menor); restaurantes, hoteles
						8. Banques, assur., affaires imm., services aux entreprises	8. Bancos, seguros, bienes inmuebles, serv. para empresas
...	...	...	...	...	...	9. Services à la collectivité, services sociaux et personnels	9. Servicios comunales, sociales y personales
...	...	...	...	...	...	0. Activités mal désignées	0. Actividades no bien especif.
...	...	...	...	...	...	**Total**	**Total**
261 700	...	...	.	.	.	1. Agriculture, chasse, sylviculture et pêche	1. Agricultura, caza, silvicultura y pesca
400	...	...	.	.	.	2. Industries extractives	2. Minas y canteras
20 300	...	...	.	.	.	3. Industries manufacturières	3. Industrias manufactureras
.	.	.	.	.	.	4. Electricité, gaz et eau	4. Electricidad, gas y agua
700	...	...	.	.	.	5. Construction	5. Construcción
55 400	...	...	.	.	.	6. Commerce (gros et détail); restaurants, hôtels	6. Comercio (por mayor y por menor); restaurantes, hoteles
5 100	...	...	.	.	.	7. Transports, entrepôts et communications	7. Transportes, almacenamiento y comunicaciones
300	...	...	.	.	.	8. Banques, assur., affaires imm., services aux entreprises	8. Bancos, seguros, bienes inmuebles, serv. para empresas
11 100	...	...	.	.	.	9. Services à la collectivité, services sociaux et personnels	9. Servicios comunales, sociales y personales
355 000	...	...	.	.	.	**Total**	**Total**
2 500	2 300	–	...	...	...	1. Agriculture, chasse, sylviculture et pêche	1. Agricultura, caza, silvicultura y pesca
–	–	–	...	...	...	2. Industries extractives	2. Minas y canteras
–	–	–	...	...	...	3. Industries manufacturières	3. Industrias manufactureras
–	–	–	...	...	...	4. Electricité, gaz et eau	4. Electricidad, gas y agua
–	–	–	...	...	...	5. Construction	5. Construcción
7 400	1 000	6 500	...	...	...	6. Commerce (gros et détail); restaurants, hôtels	6. Comercio (por mayor y por menor); restaurantes, hoteles
–	–	–	...	...	...	7. Transports, entrepôts et communications	7. Transportes, almacenamiento y comunicaciones
–	–	–	...	...	...	8. Banques, assur., affaires imm., services aux entreprises	8. Bancos, seguros, bienes inmuebles, serv. para empresas
1 300	–	1 000	...	...	...	9. Services à la collectivité, services sociaux et personnels	9. Servicios comunales, sociales y personales
...	...	...	16 400	9 000	7 500	0. Activités mal désignées	0. Actividades no bien especif.
11 900	**3 600**	**8 300**	**16 400**	**9 000**	**7 500**	**Total**	**Total**

2 Structure of the economically active population
Structure de la population active
Estructura de la población económicamente activa

Industry (Major divisions of economic activity)	Total				Employers and own-account workers / Employeurs et personnes travaillant à leur propre compte / Empleadores y trabajadores por cuenta propia			Employees / Salariés / Empleados a sueldo o salario		
	Total	%	Males Hommes Hombres	Females Femmes Mujeres	Total	Males Hommes Hombres	Females Femmes Mujeres	Total	Males Hommes Hombres	Females Femmes Mujeres
Saint-Pierre-et-Miquelon (18.II.74) C										
1. Agriculture, hunting, forestry & fishing	126	5.9	126	.	53	53	.	73	73	.
3. Manufacturing	193	8.9	154	39	.	.	.	191	152	39
4. Electr., gas & water	17	0.8	16	1	.	.	.	17	16	1
5. Construction	341	15.8	335	6	41	41	.	296	290	6
6. Wholesale/retail trade, restaurants & hotels	403	18.8	236	167	136	78	58	262	154	108
7. Transport, storage & communication	240	11.1	237	3	29	29	.	210	208	2
8. Financing, insur., real estate & business serv.	26	1.2	16	10	1	1	.	24	14	10
9. Community, social & personal services	739	34.3	422	317	19	10	9	720	412	308
0. Not adequately defined	61	2.9	56	5	2	2	.	58	54	4
-. Persons seeking work for the first time	7	0.3	6	1	.	.	.	.	.	.
Total	**2 153**	100.0	**1 604**	**549**	**281**	**214**	**67**	**1 851**	**1 373**	**478**
Trinidad and Tobago (I–VI.78) LFSS †										
-. Agriculture, forestry, hunting & fishing	53 500	12.2	41 200	12 300	...	...	...	...	...	...
-. Mining & quarrying & manufacturing	80 900	18.4	62 400	18 500	...	...	...	...	...	...
-. Construction; electr., gas, water & san. serv.	90 100	20.5	76 400	13 700	...	...	...	...	...	...
-. Commerce	70 900	16.2	36 300	34 500	...	...	...	...	...	...
-. Transport, storage & communication	31 900	7.3	28 300	3 500	...	...	...	...	...	...
-. Services	103 500	23.5	58 600	44 800	...	...	...	...	...	...
-. Not adeq. described	1 500	0.4	900	600	...	...	...	...	...	...
-. Persons seeking work for the first time	6 800	1.5	2 300	4 500	.	.	.	.	.	.
Total	**439 000**	100.0	**306 500**	**132 500**	**61 600**	**43 800**	**17 700**	**352 500**	**250 900**	**101 600**
United States (1979) LFSS †										
1. Agriculture, hunting, forestry & fishing	3 618 000	3.4	2 883 000	735 000	1 625 000	1 457 000	169 000	1 687 000	1 328 000	359 000
2. Mining & quarrying	910 000	0.9	802 000	105 000	21 000	20 000	–	887 000	782 000	104 000
3. Manufacturing	23 416 000	22.3	15 994 000	7 422 000	338 000	278 000	60 000	23 048 000	15 712 000	7 336 000
4. Electr., gas & water	1 361 000	1.3	1 150 000	209 000	12 000	10 000	1 000	1 348 000	1 140 000	207 000
5. Construction	6 871 000	6.6	6 379 000	495 000	1 156 000	1 129 000	27 000	5 666 000	5 245 000	423 000
6. Wholesale/retail trade, restaurants & hotels	20 926 000	19.9	11 186 000	9 740 000	1 846 000	1 178 000	668 000	18 869 000	9 988 000	8 881 000
7. Transport, storage & communication	5 277 000	5.0	3 855 000	1 423 000	263 000	245 000	19 000	5 001 000	3 610 000	1 392 000
8. Financing, insur., real estate & business serv.	8 297 000	7.9	3 781 000	4 515 000	701 000	466 000	234 000	7 560 000	3 313 000	4 247 000
9. Community, social & personal services	31 434 000	30.0	13 145 000	18 289 000	2 371 000	1 418 000	953 000	28 953 000	11 717 000	17 236 000
-. Persons seeking work for the first time	798 000	0.7	343 000	455 000						
-. Armed forces	2 088 000	2.0	1 949 000	139 000	.	.	.	2 088 000	1 949 000	139 000
Total	**104 996 000**	100.0	**61 466 000**	**43 531 000**	**8 333 000**	**6 201 000**	**2 131 000**	**95 108 000**	**54 784 000**	**40 324 000**

A By industry, by status and by sex
Par industrie, selon la situation dans la profession et par sexe
Por industria, según la categoría de ocupación y por sexo

Unpaid family workers / Travailleurs familiaux non rémunérés / Trabajadores familiares no remunerados			Not classifiable by status / Inclassables selon la situation / Inclasificables según la categoría			Industrie (Branches d'activité économique)	Industria (Grandes divisiones de actividad económica)
Total	Males / Hommes / Hombres	Females / Femmes / Mujeres	Total	Males / Hommes / Hombres	Females / Femmes / Mujeres		
.	.	.	.	.	.	1. Agriculture, chasse, sylviculture et pêche	1. Agricultura, caza, silvicultura y pesca
2	2	.	.	.	.	3. Industries manufacturières	3. Industrias manufactureras
.	.	.	.	.	.	4. Electricité, gaz et eau	4. Electricidad, gas y agua
4	4	.	.	.	.	5. Construction	5. Construcción
5	4	1	.	.	.	6. Commerce (gros et détail); restaurants, hôtels	6. Comercio (por mayor y por menor); restaurantes, hoteles
1	.	1	.	.	.	7. Transports, entrepôts et communications	7. Transportes, almacenamiento y comunicaciones
1	1	.	.	.	.	8. Banques, assur., affaires imm., services aux entreprises	8. Bancos, seguros, bienes inmuebles, serv. para empresas
1	.	1	.	.	.	9. Services à la collectivité, services sociaux et personnels	9. Servicios comunales, sociales y personales
.	.	.	.	.	.	0. Activités mal désignées	0. Actividades no bien especif.
.	.	.	7	6	1	-. Personnes en quête d'emploi pour la première fois	-. Personas en busca de trabajo por primera vez
14	**11**	**3**	**7**	**6**	**1**	**Total**	**Total**
...	...	...	...	...	...	-. Agriculture, sylviculture, chasse et pêche	-. Agricultura, silvicultura, caza y pesca
...	...	...	...	...	...	-. Industries extractives et industries manufacturières	-. Minas y canteras; industrias manufactureras
...	...	...	...	...	...	-. Construction; electricité, gaz, eau et services sanitaires	-. Construcción; electr., gas, agua y serv. sanitarios
...	...	...	...	...	...	-. Comm., banq., assur., aff. imm.	-. Comercio
...	...	...	...	...	...	-. Transports, entrepôts et communications	-. Transportes, almacenamiento y comunicaciones
...	...	...	...	...	...	-. Services	-. Servicios
...	...	...	...	...	...	-. Activités mal désignées	-. Actividades no bien especif.
.	.	.	6 800	2 300	4 500	-. Personnes en quête d'emploi pour la première fois	-. Personas en busca de trabajo por primera vez
17 100	**9 000**	**8 100**	**7 800**	**2 800**	**5 000**	**Total**	**Total**
306 000	98 000	207 000	.	.	.	1. Agriculture, chasse, sylviculture et pêche	1. Agricultura, caza, silvicultura y pesca
2 000	–	1 000	.	.	.	2. Industries extractives	2. Minas y canteras
30 000	4 000	26 000	.	.	.	3. Industries manufacturières	3. Industrias manufactureras
1 000	–	1 000	.	.	.	4. Electricité, gaz et eau	4. Electricidad, gas y agua
49 000	5 000	45 000	.	.	.	5. Construction	5. Construcción
211 000	20 000	191 000	.	.	.	6. Commerce (gros et détail); restaurants, hôtels	6. Comercio (por mayor y por menor); restaurantes, hoteles
13 000	1 000	12 000	.	.	.	7. Transports, entrepôts et communications	7. Transportes, almacenamiento y comunicaciones
36 000	2 000	34 000	.	.	.	8. Banques, assur., affaires imm., services aux entreprises	8. Bancos, seguros, bienes inmuebles, serv. para empresas
110 000	10 000	100 000	.	.	.	9. Services à la collectivité, services sociaux et personnels	9. Servicios comunales, sociales y personales
.	.	.	798 000	343 000	455 000	-. Personnes en quête d'emploi pour la première fois	-. Personas en busca de trabajo por primera vez
.	.	.	.	.	.	-. Forces armées	-. Fuerzas armadas
758 000	**140 000**	**617 000**	**798 000**	**343 000**	**455 000**	**Total**	**Total**

2 Structure of the economically active population
Structure de la population active
Estructura de la población económicamente activa

Industry (Major divisions of economic activity)	Total				Employers and own-account workers Employeurs et personnes travaillant à leur propre compte Empleadores y trabajadores por cuenta propia			Employees Salariés Empleados a sueldo o salario		
	Total	%	Males Hommes Hombres	Females Femmes Mujeres	Total	Males Hommes Hombres	Females Femmes Mujeres	Total	Males Hommes Hombres	Females Femmes Mujeres
Uruguay (21.V.75) C †										
1. Agriculture, hunting, forestry & fishing	174 871	16.0	164 811	10 060	70 762	67 624	3 138	88 862	85 054	3 808
2. Mining & quarrying	2 159	0.2	2 112	47	358	352	6	1 781	1 742	39
3. Manufacturing	205 943	18.8	141 602	64 341	45 872	22 637	23 235	158 095	117 856	40 239
4. Electr., gas & water	16 206	1.5	14 594	1 612	.	.	.	16 206	14 594	1 612
5. Construction	59 428	5.4	58 744	684	15 437	15 379	58	43 479	42 863	616
6. Wholesale/retail trade, restaurants & hotels	134 509	12.3	98 635	35 874	58 575	45 128	13 447	72 349	51 963	20 386
7. Transport, storage & communication	53 728	4.9	48 969	4 759	10 889	10 718	171	42 456	37 904	4 552
8. Financing, insur., real estate & business serv.	29 461	2.7	22 636	6 825	6 655	5 237	1 418	22 625	17 302	5 323
9. Community, social & personal services	316 078	28.9	161 595	154 483	36 696	22 312	14 384	276 208	137 814	138 394
0. Not adequately defined	85 085	7.7	60 666	24 419	15 539	12 089	3 450	37 136	26 795	10 341
–. Persons seeking work for the first time	17 131	1.6	9 220	7 911	.	.	.	.	.	.
Total	**1 094 599**	**100.0**	**783 584**	**311 015**	**260 783**	**201 476**	**59 307**	**759 197**	**533 887**	**225 310**
Venezuela (VII–XII.78) HS										
1. Agriculture, hunting, forestry & fishing	948 625	19.0	900 494	48 131	218 442	208 782	9 660	640 041	609 533	30 508
2. Mining & quarrying	49 031	1.0	45 132	3 899	337	337	.	48 694	44 795	3 899
3. Manufacturing	778 318	15.7	522 957	255 361	89 007	28 551	60 456	677 862	489 954	187 908
4. Electr., gas & water	46 927	0.9	40 632	6 295	123	123	.	46 714	40 509	6 205
5. Construction	420 330	8.4	411 311	9 019	49 619	49 476	143	369 205	360 424	8 781
6. Wholesale/retail trade, restaurants & hotels	978 221	19.7	646 693	331 528	239 317	158 550	80 767	696 683	473 415	223 268
7. Transport, storage & communication	395 280	7.9	371 400	23 880	112 221	110 908	1 313	281 858	259 431	22 427
8. Financing, insur., real estate & business serv.	187 356	3.8	124 404	62 952	16 207	13 899	2 308	170 540	110 229	60 311
9. Community, social & personal services	1 138 203	22.8	550 084	588 119	75 075	36 063	39 012	1 059 899	512 812	547 087
0. Not adequately defined	9 483	0.2	6 813	2 670	261	.	261	3 024	2 271	753
–. Persons seeking work for the first time	28 795	0.6	16 092	12 703	.	.	.	.	.	.
Total	**4 980 569**	**100.0**	**3 636 012**	**1 344 557**	**800 609**	**606 689**	**193 920**	**3 994 520**	**2 903 373**	**1 091 147**

ASIA

Bahrain (IV.79) OE †										
1. Agriculture, hunting, forestry & fishing	4 600	3.4	4 400	200	...	...	...	...	...	...
2. Mining & quarrying	4 200	3.1	3 900	300	...	...	...	...	...	...
3. Manufacturing	12 200	9.1	11 700	500	...	...	...	...	...	...
4. Electr., gas & water	2 000	1.4	1 800	200	...	...	...	...	...	...
5. Construction	33 600	25.0	33 000	600	...	...	...	...	...	...
6. Wholesale/retail trade, restaurants & hotels	16 500	12.2	15 500	1 000	...	...	...	...	...	...
7. Transport, storage & communication	14 600	10.8	13 700	900	...	...	...	...	...	...
8. Financing, insur., real estate & business serv.	4 600	3.4	3 900	700	...	...	...	...	...	...
9. Community, social & personal services	39 000	28.9	31 000	8 000	...	...	...	...	...	...
0. Not adequately defined	3 600	2.7	3 400	200	...	...	...	...	...	...
Total	**134 900**	**100.0**	**122 300**	**12 600**	...	...	...	...	...	...

A — By industry, by status and by sex
Par industrie, selon la situation dans la profession et par sexe
Por industria, según la categoría de ocupación y por sexo

	Unpaid family workers / Travailleurs familiaux non rémunérés / Trabajadores familiares no remunerados			Not classifiable by status / Inclassables selon la situation / Inclasificables según la categoría			Industrie (Branches d'activité économique)	Industria (Grandes divisiones de actividad económica)
	Total	Males Hommes Hombres	Females Femmes Mujeres	Total	Males Hommes Hombres	Females Femmes Mujeres		
1	14 858	11 776	3 082	389	357	32	1. Agriculture, chasse, sylviculture et pêche	1. Agricultura, caza, silvicultura y pesca
2	10	8	2	10	10	.	2. Industries extractives	2. Minas y canteras
3	1 136	583	553	840	526	314	3. Industries manufacturières	3. Industrias manufactureras
4	.	.	.	.	.	.	4. Electricité, gaz et eau	4. Electricidad, gas y agua
5	179	172	7	333	330	3	5. Construction	5. Construcción
6	3 085	1 189	1 896	500	355	145	6. Commerce (gros et détail); restaurants, hôtels	6. Comercio (por mayor y por menor); restaurantes, hoteles
7	187	164	23	196	183	13	7. Transports, entrepôts et communications	7. Transportes, almacenamiento y comunicaciones
8	64	17	47	117	80	37	8. Banques, assur., affaires imm., services aux entreprises	8. Bancos, seguros, bienes inmuebles, serv. para empresas
9	489	280	209	2 685	1 189	1 496	9. Services à la collectivité, services sociaux et personnels	9. Servicios comunales, sociales y personales
0	2 055	1 202	853	30 355	20 580	9 775	0. Activités mal désignées	0. Actividades no bien especif.
–	.	.	.	17 131	9 220	7 911	–. Personnes en quête d'emploi pour la première fois	–. Personas en busca de trabajo por primera vez
Total	**22 063**	**15 391**	**6 672**	**52 556**	**32 830**	**19 726**	**Total**	**Total**
1	90 142	82 179	7 963	...	...	...	1. Agriculture, chasse, sylviculture et pêche	1. Agricultura, caza, silvicultura y pesca
2	.	.	.	...	...	...	2. Industries extractives	2. Minas y canteras
3	11 449	4 452	6 997	...	...	...	3. Industries manufacturières	3. Industrias manufactureras
4	90	.	90	...	...	...	4. Electricité, gaz et eau	4. Electricidad, gas y agua
5	1 506	1 411	95	...	...	...	5. Construction	5. Construcción
6	42 221	14 728	27 493	...	...	...	6. Commerce (gros et détail); restaurants, hôtels	6. Comercio (por mayor y por menor); restaurantes, hoteles
7	1 201	1 061	140	...	...	...	7. Transports, entrepôts et communications	7. Transportes, almacenamiento y comunicaciones
8	609	276	333	...	...	...	8. Banques, assur., affaires imm., services aux entreprises	8. Bancos, seguros, bienes inmuebles, serv. para empresas
9	3 229	1 209	2 020	...	...	...	9. Services à la collectivité, services sociaux et personnels	9. Servicios comunales, sociales y personales
0	150	.	150	6 048	4 542	1 506	0. Activités mal désignées	0. Actividades no bien especif.
–	.	.	.	28 795	16 092	12 703	–. Personnes en quête d'emploi pour la première fois	–. Personas en busca de trabajo por primera vez
Total	**150 597**	**105 316**	**45 281**	**34 843**	**20 634**	**14 209**	**Total**	**Total**

ASIE – ASIA

							Industrie	Industria
1	...	...	...	...	...	...	1. Agriculture, chasse, sylviculture et pêche	1. Agricultura, caza, silvicultura y pesca
2	...	...	...	...	...	...	2. Industries extractives	2. Minas y canteras
3	...	...	...	...	...	...	3. Industries manufacturières	3. Industrias manufactureras
4	...	...	...	...	...	...	4. Electricité, gaz et eau	4. Electricidad, gas y agua
5	...	...	...	...	...	...	5. Construction	5. Construcción
6	...	...	...	...	...	...	6. Commerce (gros et détail); restaurants, hôtels	6. Comercio (por mayor y por menor); restaurantes, hoteles
7	...	...	...	...	...	...	7. Transports, entrepôts et communications	7. Transportes, almacenamiento y comunicaciones
8	...	...	...	...	...	...	8. Banques, assur., affaires imm., services aux entreprises	8. Bancos, seguros, bienes inmuebles, serv. para empresas
9	...	...	...	...	...	...	9. Services à la collectivité, services sociaux et personnels	9. Servicios comunales, sociales y personales
0	...	...	...	...	...	...	0. Activités mal désignées	0. Actividades no bien especif.
Total	...	...	...	...	...	...	**Total**	**Total**

2 Structure of the economically active population
Structure de la population active
Estructura de la población económicamente activa

Industry (Major divisions of economic activity)	Total				Employers and own-account workers / Employeurs et personnes travaillant à leur propre compte / Empleadores y trabajadores por cuenta propia			Employees / Salariés / Empleados a sueldo o salario		
	Total	%	Males Hommes Hombres	Females Femmes Mujeres	Total	Males Hommes Hombres	Females Femmes Mujeres	Total	Males Hommes Hombres	Females Femmes Mujeres
Bangladesh (1.III.74) C †										
1. Agriculture, hunting, forestry & fishing	15 822 878	77.1	15 212 622	610 256	...	...	...	...	...	...
2. Mining & quarrying	1 922	–	1 900	22	...	...	...	...	...	...
3. Manufacturing	946 126	4.6	909 829	36 297	...	...	...	...	...	...
4. Electr., gas & water	7 543	0.1	7 401	142	...	...	...	...	...	...
5. Construction	32 886	0.1	32 417	469	...	...	...	...	...	...
6. Wholesale/retail trade, restaurants & hotels	770 907	3.8	762 168	8 739	...	...	...	...	...	...
7. Transport, storage & communication	320 015	1.5	318 448	1 567	...	...	...	...	...	...
8. Financing, insur., real estate & business serv.	55 567	0.3	55 000	567	...	...	...	...	...	...
9. Community, social & personal services	2 060 018	10.0	1 877 663	182 355	...	...	...	...	...	...
0. Not adequately defined	504 730	2.5	473 149	31 581	...	...	...	...	...	...
Total	**20 522 592**	100.0	**19 650 597**	**871 995**	...	...	...	...	...	...
Burma (1978–79) OE										
1. Agriculture, hunting, forestry & fishing	8 697 000	64.7	...	...	...	...	...	...	...	...
2. Mining & quarrying	68 000	0.5	...	...	...	...	...	...	...	...
3. Manufacturing	968 000	7.2	...	...	...	...	...	...	...	...
4. Electr., gas & water	15 000	0.1	...	...	...	...	...	...	...	...
5. Construction	189 000	1.4	...	...	...	...	...	...	...	...
6. Wholesale/retail trade, restaurants & hotels	1 239 000	9.2	...	...	...	...	...	...	...	...
7. Transport, storage & communication	430 000	3.2	...	...	...	...	...	...	...	...
8/9. Major divisions 8 & 9	760 000	5.7	...	...	...	...	...	...	...	...
0. Not adequately defined	569 000	4.2	...	...	...	...	...	...	...	...
–. Unemployed	512 000	3.8	...	...	...	...	...	...	...	...
Total	**13 447 000**	100.0	...	...	...	...	...	...	...	...
Hong Kong (IX.79) LFSS †										
1. Agriculture, hunting, forestry & fishing	26 700	1.2	20 100	6 700	18 300	...	...	4 500	...	...
2. Mining & quarrying	500	–	500	.	200	...	...	300	...	...
3. Manufacturing	933 800	42.6	510 000	423 800	56 900	...	...	846 200	...	...
4. Electr., gas & water	11 000	0.5	9 900	1 100	.	.	.	10 900	...	...
5. Construction	150 300	6.8	140 600	9 600	6 600	...	...	135 800	...	...
6. Wholesale/retail trade, restaurants & hotels	434 500	19.8	314 500	120 100	103 900	...	...	304 200	...	...
7. Transport, storage & communication	154 700	7.1	141 800	12 900	18 900	...	...	129 200	...	...
8. Financing, insur., real estate & business serv.	91 600	4.2	55 600	36 000	4 400	...	...	86 500	...	...
9. Community, social & personal services	365 400	16.6	222 800	142 600	23 200	...	...	337 200	...	...
0. Not adequately defined	600	–	600	.	300	...	...	200	...	...
–. Unemployed	25 400	1.2	16 200	9 200	...	...	...	...	...	...
Total	**2 194 500**	100.0	**1 432 500**	**762 000**	**232 600**	**199 100**	**33 400**	**1 854 900**	**1 172 300**	**682 600**

A By industry, by status and by sex
Par industrie, selon la situation dans la profession et par sexe
Por industria, según la categoría de ocupación y por sexo

Unpaid family workers / Travailleurs familiaux non rémunérés / Trabajadores familiares no remunerados			Not classifiable by status / Inclassables selon la situation / Inclasificables según la categoría			Industrie (Branches d'activité économique)	Industria (Grandes divisiones de actividad económica)
Total	Males Hommes Hombres	Females Femmes Mujeres	Total	Males Hommes Hombres	Females Femmes Mujeres		
...	...	...	...	...	...	1. Agriculture, chasse, sylvi- culture et pêche	1. Agricultura, caza, silvi- cultura y pesca
...	...	...	...	...	...	2. Industries extractives	2. Minas y canteras
...	...	...	...	...	...	3. Industries manufacturières	3. Industrias manufactureras
...	...	...	...	...	...	4. Electricité, gaz et eau	4. Electricidad, gas y agua
...	...	...	...	...	...	5. Construction	5. Construcción
...	...	...	...	...	...	6. Commerce (gros et détail); restaurants, hôtels	6. Comercio (por mayor y por me- nor); restaurantes, hoteles
						7. Transports, entrepôts et commu- nications	7. Transportes, almacenamiento y comunicaciones
						8. Banques, assur., affaires imm., services aux entreprises	8. Bancos, seguros, bienes in- muebles, serv. para empresas
...	...	...	...	...	...	9. Services à la collectivité, services sociaux et personnels	9. Servicios comunales, sociales y personales
						0. Activités mal désignées	0. Actividades no bien especif.
...	...	...	...	...	...	**Total**	**Total**
...	...	...	...	...	...	1. Agriculture, chasse, sylvi- culture et pêche	1. Agricultura, caza, silvi- cultura y pesca
...	...	...	...	...	...	2. Industries extractives	2. Minas y canteras
...	...	...	...	...	...	3. Industries manufacturières	3. Industrias manufactureras
...	...	...	...	...	...	4. Electricité, gaz et eau	4. Electricidad, gas y agua
...	...	...	...	...	...	5. Construction	5. Construcción
...	...	...	...	...	...	6. Commerce (gros et détail); restaurants, hôtels	6. Comercio (por mayor y por me- nor); restaurantes, hoteles
						7. Transports, entrepôts et commu- nications	7. Transportes, almacenamiento y comunicaciones
...	...	...	...	...	...	8/9. Branches 8 et 9	8/9. Grandes divisiones 8 y 9
...	...	...	...	...	...	0. Activités mal désignées	0. Actividades no bien especif.
...	...	...	...	...	...	-. Chômeurs	-. Desempleados
...	...	...	...	...	...	**Total**	**Total**
3 300	...	...	600	...	...	1. Agriculture, chasse, sylvi- culture et pêche	1. Agricultura, caza, silvi- cultura y pesca
						2. Industries extractives	2. Minas y canteras
8 800	...	...	21 900	...	...	3. Industries manufacturières	3. Industrias manufactureras
			100	...	...	4. Electricité, gaz et eau	4. Electricidad, gas y agua
400	...	...	7 500	...	...	5. Construction	5. Construcción
17 800	...	...	8 600	...	...	6. Commerce (gros et détail); restaurants, hôtels	6. Comercio (por mayor y por me- nor); restaurantes, hoteles
600	...	...	6 000	...	...	7. Transports, entrepôts et commu- nications	7. Transportes, almacenamiento y comunicaciones
200	...	...	600	...	...	8. Banques, assur., affaires imm., services aux entreprises	8. Bancos, seguros, bienes in- muebles, serv. para empresas
1 200	...	...	4 000	...	...	9. Services à la collectivité, services sociaux et personnels	9. Servicios comunales, sociales y personales
			100	...	...	0. Activités mal désignées	0. Actividades no bien especif.
...	...	...	25 400	16 200	9 200	-. Chômeurs	-. Desempleados
32 400	**8 600**	**23 800**	**74 600**	**52 400**	**22 200**	**Total**	**Total**

2 Structure of the economically active population
Structure de la population active
Estructura de la población económicamente activa

Industry (Major divisions of economic activity)	Total				Employers and own-account workers / Employeurs et personnes travaillant à leur propre compte / Empleadores y trabajadores por cuenta propia			Employees / Salariés / Empleados a sueldo o salario		
	Total	%	Males Hommes Hombres	Females Femmes Mujeres	Total	Males Hommes Hombres	Females Femmes Mujeres	Total	Males Hombres Hombres	Females Femmes Mujeres
Indonesia (1976) LFSS										
1. Agriculture, hunting, forestry & fishing	35 257 780	64.7	21 355 648	13 902 132	15 117 411	12 441 827	2 675 584	6 071 356	3 327 055	2 744 301
2. Mining & quarrying	43 932	0.1	40 344	3 588	15 847	15 675	172	22 729	20 820	1 909
3. Manufacturing	3 560 066	6.5	1 882 737	1 677 329	1 152 586	601 538	551 048	1 599 371	1 079 621	519 750
4. Electr., gas & water	34 194	0.1	32 649	1 545	962	864	98	32 445	31 785	660
5. Construction	1 097 913	2.0	1 067 013	30 900	119 680	114 233	5 447	961 950	937 224	24 726
6. Wholesale/retail trade, restaurants & hotels	6 253 171	11.5	3 244 111	3 009 060	4 907 447	2 570 533	2 336 914	471 387	375 562	95 825
7. Transport, storage & communication	1 111 857	2.0	1 093 724	18 133	313 714	310 996	2 718	776 743	763 225	13 518
8. Financing, insur., real estate & business serv.	74 269	0.1	63 917	10 352	6 910	6 423	487	65 804	55 950	9 854
9. Community, social & personal services	5 156 975	9.5	3 534 145	1 622 830	762 119	519 821	242 298	4 188 389	2 920 030	1 268 359
0. Not adequately defined	853 511	1.6	480 131	373 380	20 221	15 811	4 410	182 905	136 470	46 435
–. Unemployed	1 046 617	1.9	634 810	411 807	...	...	...	...	...	...
Total	**54 490 285**	**100.0**	**33 429 229**	**21 061 056**	**22 416 897**	**16 597 721**	**5 819 176**	**14 373 079**	**9 647 742**	**4 725 337**
Iran (IX.76) C5%										
1. Agriculture, hunting, forestry & fishing	3 613 944	37.1	3 186 222	427 722	1 736 838	1 718 938	17 900	671 269	593 768	77 501
2. Mining & quarrying	94 311	1.0	90 256	4 055	1 380	1 360	20	92 290	88 295	3 995
3. Manufacturing	1 672 393	17.2	1 036 822	635 571	375 185	258 497	116 688	893 534	718 416	175 118
4. Electr., gas & water	61 641	0.6	59 878	1 763	600	600	.	60 857	59 094	1 763
5. Construction	1 192 441	12.3	1 184 291	8 150	148 986	148 566	420	1 020 524	1 013 136	7 388
6. Wholesale/retail trade, restaurants & hotels	669 590	6.9	655 527	14 063	477 657	472 995	4 662	175 560	167 639	7 921
7. Transport, storage & communication	435 288	4.4	426 662	8 626	158 130	157 830	300	272 553	264 408	8 145
8. Financing, insur., real estate & business serv.	100 849	1.1	91 078	9 771	15 770	15 590	180	84 596	75 045	9 551
9. Community, social & personal services	1 544 686	15.8	1 256 838	287 848	109 071	101 029	8 042	1 425 177	1 148 536	276 641
0. Not adequately defined	109 108	1.2	89 477	19 631	6 263	5 663	600	38 498	34 813	3 685
–. Persons seeking work for the first time	238 257	2.4	203 189	35 068	.	.	.	.	.	.
Total	**9 732 508**	**100.0**	**8 280 240**	**1 452 268**	**3 029 880**	**2 881 068**	**148 812**	**4 734 858**	**4 163 150**	**571 708**
Iraq (17.X.77) C *										
1. Agriculture, hunting, forestry & fishing	943 890	30.1	591 066	352 824	...	...	...	...	...	...
2. Mining & quarrying	36 835	1.2	34 716	2 119	...	...	...	...	...	...
3. Manufacturing	284 395	9.1	235 777	48 618	...	...	...	...	...	...
4. Electr., gas & water	23 190	0.7	22 241	949	...	...	...	...	...	...
5. Construction	321 696	10.3	316 560	5 136	...	...	...	...	...	...
6. Wholesale/retail trade, restaurants & hotels	224 104	7.1	207 949	16 155	...	...	...	...	...	...
7. Transport, storage & communication	177 799	5.7	172 814	4 985	...	...	...	...	...	...
8. Financing, insur., real estate & business serv.	31 089	1.0	26 023	5 066	...	...	...	...	...	...
9. Community, social & personal services	957 979	30.6	871 879	86 100	...	...	...	...	...	...
0. Not adequately defined	58 237	1.8	46 258	11 979	...	...	...	...	...	...
–. Unemployed	74 725	2.4	64 278	10 447	...	...	...	...	...	...
Total	**3 133 939**	**100.0**	**2 589 561**	**544 378**	...	...	...	...	...	...

A By industry, by status and by sex
Par industrie, selon la situation dans la profession et par sexe
Por industria, según la categoría de ocupación y por sexo

Unpaid family workers / Travailleurs familiaux non rémunérés / Trabajadores familiares no remunerados			Not classifiable by status / Inclassables selon la situation / Inclasificables según la categoría			Industrie (Branches d'activité économique)	Industria (Grandes divisiones de actividad económica)
Total	Males Hommes Hombres	Females Femmes Mujeres	Total	Males Hommes Hombres	Females Femmes Mujeres		
14 039 285	5 568 665	8 470 620	29 728	18 101	11 627	1. Agriculture, chasse, sylviculture et pêche	1. Agricultura, caza, silvicultura y pesca
5 356	3 849	1 507	.	.	.	2. Industries extractives	2. Minas y canteras
805 372	201 045	604 327	2 737	533	2 204	3. Industries manufacturières	3. Industrias manufactureras
787	.	787	.	.	.	4. Electricité, gaz et eau	4. Electricidad, gas y agua
14 595	13 868	727	1 688	1 688	.	5. Construction	5. Construcción
866 395	292 707	573 688	7 942	5 309	2 633	6. Commerce (gros et détail); restaurants, hôtels	6. Comercio (por mayor y por menor); restaurantes, hoteles
21 400	19 503	1 897	.	.	.	7. Transports, entrepôts et communications	7. Transportes, almacenamiento y comunicaciones
23	12	11	1 532	1 532	.	8. Banques, assur., affaires imm., services aux entreprises	8. Bancos, seguros, bienes inmuebles, serv. para empresas
198 058	91 654	106 404	8 409	2 640	5 769	9. Services à la collectivité, services sociaux et personnels	9. Servicios comunales, sociales y personales
35 948	8 729	27 219	614 437	319 121	295 316	0. Activités mal désignées	0. Actividades no bien especif.
...	...	...	1 046 617	634 810	411 807	-. Chômeurs	-. Desempleados
15 987 219	**6 200 032**	**9 787 187**	**1 713 090**	**983 734**	**729 356**	**Total**	**Total**
569 292	441 952	177 340	636 545	431 564	204 981	1. Agriculture, chasse, sylviculture et pêche	1. Agricultura, caza, silvicultura y pesca
160	140	20	481	461	20	2. Industries extractives	2. Minas y canteras
390 148	49 107	341 041	13 526	10 802	2 724	3. Industries manufacturières	3. Industrias manufactureras
.	.	.	184	184	.	4. Electricité, gaz et eau	4. Electricidad, gas y agua
6 121	5 981	140	16 810	16 608	202	5. Construction	5. Construcción
12 163	11 003	1 160	4 210	3 890	320	6. Commerce (gros et détail); restaurants, hôtels	6. Comercio (por mayor y por menor); restaurantes, hoteles
2 340	2 200	140	2 265	2 224	41	7. Transports, entrepôts et communications	7. Transportes, almacenamiento y comunicaciones
41	41	.	442	402	40	8. Banques, assur., affaires imm., services aux entreprises	8. Bancos, seguros, bienes inmuebles, serv. para empresas
3 268	2 123	1 145	7 170	5 150	2 020	9. Services à la collectivité, services sociaux et personnels	9. Servicios comunales, sociales y personales
1 101	441	660	63 246	48 560	14 686	0. Activités mal désignées	0. Actividades no bien especif.
.	.	.	238 257	203 189	35 068	-. Personnes en quête d'emploi pour la première fois	-. Personas en busca de trabajo por primera vez
984 634	**512 988**	**471 646**	**983 136**	**723 034**	**260 102**	**Total**	**Total**
...	...	...	...	...	...	1. Agriculture, chasse, sylviculture et pêche	1. Agricultura, caza, silvicultura y pesca
...	...	...	...	...	...	2. Industries extractives	2. Minas y canteras
...	...	...	...	...	...	3. Industries manufacturières	3. Industrias manufactureras
...	...	...	...	...	...	4. Electricité, gaz et eau	4. Electricidad, gas y agua
...	...	...	...	...	...	5. Construction	5. Construcción
...	...	...	...	...	...	6. Commerce (gros et détail); restaurants, hôtels	6. Comercio (por mayor y por menor); restaurantes, hoteles
...	...	...	...	...	...	7. Transports, entrepôts et communications	7. Transportes, almacenamiento y comunicaciones
...	...	...	...	...	...	8. Banques, assur., affaires imm., services aux entreprises	8. Bancos, seguros, bienes inmuebles, serv. para empresas
...	...	...	...	...	...	9. Services à la collectivité, services sociaux et personnels	9. Servicios comunales, sociales y personales
...	...	...	...	...	...	0. Activités mal désignées	0. Actividades no bien especif.
...	...	...	...	...	...	-. Chômeurs	-. Desempleados
...	...	...	...	...	...	**Total**	**Total**

2 Structure of the economically active population
Structure de la population active
Estructura de la población económicamente activa

Industry (Major divisions of economic activity)	Total				Employers and own-account workers / Employeurs et personnes travaillant à leur propre compte / Empleadores y trabajadores por cuenta propia			Employees / Salariés / Empleados a sueldo o salario		
	Total	%	Males Hommes Hombres	Females Femmes Mujeres	Total	Males Hommes Hombres	Females Femmes Mujeres	Total	Males Hommes Hombres	Females Femmes Mujeres
Israel (1979) LFSS †										
1. Agriculture, hunting, forestry & fishing	72 700	5.7	55 500	17 200	44 000	37 700	6 300	17 900	14 400	3 500
2/3. Mining & quarrying, manufacturing	303 000	23.7	231 300	71 700	43 900	36 700	7 200	252 000	190 200	61 800
4. Electr., gas & water	11 600	0.9	9 900	1 700	200	200	–	11 200	9 500	1 700
5. Construction	84 300	6.6	79 500	4 800	19 800	19 600	200	61 700	57 300	4 400
6. Wholesale/retail trade, restaurants & hotels	147 200	11.5	97 200	50 000	54 600	44 600	10 000	79 300	49 800	29 500
7. Transport, storage & communication	85 700	6.7	71 200	14 500	24 400	20 800	3 600	59 600	49 200	10 400
8. Financing, insur., real estate & business serv.	98 200	7.7	51 700	46 500	16 100	13 000	3 100	79 100	37 900	41 200
9. Community, social & personal services	443 900	34.8	207 300	236 600	48 600	25 500	23 100	388 600	179 300	209 300
0. Not adequately defined	13 400	1.0	8 600	4 800	1 800	1 300	500	10 800	6 700	4 100
–. Persons seeking work for the first time	17 900	1.4	7 200	10 700	.	.	.	.	.	.
Total	**1 277 800**	100.0	**819 200**	**458 600**	**253 600**	**199 500**	**54 200**	**960 000**	**594 000**	**366 000**
Japan (1.X.75) C20% †										
1. Agriculture, hunting, forestry & fishing	7 369 215	13.6	3 761 985	3 607 230	3 233 540	2 672 185	561 360	467 160	378 605	88 555
2. Mining & quarrying	137 535	0.2	122 045	15 490	4 910	4 820	90	130 295	116 025	14 270
3. Manufacturing	13 158 010	24.3	8 681 090	4 476 920	1 236 730	775 800	460 935	11 237 285	7 752 670	3 484 615
4. Electr., gas & water	321 845	0.6	283 625	38 225	.	.	.	321 845	283 620	38 225
5. Construction	4 751 620	8.7	4 191 160	560 460	852 585	849 655	2 930	3 672 460	3 236 445	436 015
6. Wholesale/retail trade, restaurants & hotels	11 874 915	21.9	6 525 610	5 349 305	2 364 725	1 667 670	697 060	7 740 135	4 542 100	3 198 035
7. Transport, storage & communication	3 371 190	6.2	2 973 805	397 390	135 800	133 925	1 875	3 205 300	2 832 095	373 200
8. Financing, insur., real estate & business serv.	3 008 175	5.6	1 811 865	1 196 305	225 380	182 805	42 565	2 724 130	1 621 195	1 102 920
9. Community, social & personal services	8 962 500	16.5	5 008 780	3 953 725	1 255 060	673 795	581 270	7 304 450	4 263 700	3 040 750
0. Not adequately defined	60 420	0.1	19 740	40 680	17 515	1 780	15 735	27 165	16 000	11 165
–. Unemployed	1 249 290	2.3	890 615	358 680	...	...	...	...	...	...
Total	**54 264 725**	100.0	**34 270 320**	**19 994 405**	**9 326 240**	**6 962 425**	**2 363 815**	**36 830 210**	**25 042 470**	**11 787 740**
" " " " (1979) LFSS †										
1. Agriculture, hunting, forestry & fishing	6 130 000	11.0	3 110 000	3 020 000	2 880 000	22 700 000	610 000	440 000	330 000	110 000
2. Mining & quarrying	120 000	0.2	110 000	20 000	.	.	.	120 000	100 000	10 000
3. Manufacturing	13 330 000	23.8	8 240 000	5 080 000	1 540 000	750 000	790 000	11 070 000	7 340 000	3 730 000
4. Electr., gas & water	330 000	0.6	280 000	50 000	.	.	.	330 000	280 000	50 000
5. Construction	5 360 000	9.6	4 620 000	740 000	910 000	900 000	–	4 170 000	3 600 000	570 000
6. Wholesale/retail trade, restaurants & hotels	12 280 000	21.9	6 630 000	5 650 000	2 460 000	1 710 000	750 000	7 950 000	4 600 000	3 350 000
7. Transport, storage & communication	3 490 000	6.2	3 080 000	400 000	150 000	150 000	–	3 310 000	2 930 000	380 000
8. Financing, insur., real estate & business serv.	3 120 000	5.6	1 790 000	1 330 000	220 000	130 000	90 000	2 840 000	1 650 000	1 190 000
9. Community, social & personal services	10 540 000	18.8	5 700 000	4 850 000	1 510 000	810 000	700 000	8 510 000	4 810 000	3 710 000
0. Not adequately defined	110 000	0.2	70 000	40 000	–	–	–	20 000	20 000	10 000
–. Unemployed	1 170 000	2.1	740 000	430 000	...	...	...	...	...	...
Total	**55 960 000**	100.0	**34 370 000**	**21 600 000**	**9 670 000**	**6 720 000**	**2 940 000**	**38 760 000**	**25 660 000**	**13 100 000**

A By industry, by status and by sex
Par industrie, selon la situation dans la profession et par sexe
Por industria, según la categoría de ocupación y por sexo

Unpaid family workers / Travailleurs familiaux non rémunérés / Trabajadores familiares no remunerados			Not classifiable by status / Inclassables selon la situation / Inclasificables según la categoría			Industrie (Branches d'activité économique)	Industria (Grandes divisiones de actividad económica)
Total	Males Hommes Hombres	Females Femmes Mujeres	Total	Males Hommes Hombres	Females Femmes Mujeres		
10 300	3 000	7 300	500	400	100	1. Agriculture, chasse, sylviculture et pêche	1. Agricultura, caza, silvicultura y pesca
2 400	700	1 700	4 700	3 700	1 000	2/3. Industries extractives et industries manufacturières	2/3. Minas y canteras, industrias manufactureras
–	–	–	200	200	–	4. Electricité, gaz et eau	4. Electricidad, gas y agua
600	500	100	2 200	2 100	100	5. Construction	5. Construcción
10 900	1 500	9 400	2 400	1 300	1 100	6. Commerce (gros et détail); restaurants, hôtels	6. Comercio (por mayor y por menor); restaurantes, hoteles
400	100	300	1 300	1 100	200	7. Transports, entrepôts et communications	7. Transportes, almacenamiento y comunicaciones
1 300	–	1 300	1 700	800	900	8. Banques, assur., affaires imm., services aux entreprises	8. Bancos, seguros, bienes inmuebles, serv. para empresas
1 500	200	1 300	5 200	2 300	2 900	9. Services à la collectivité, services sociaux et personnels	9. Servicios comunales, sociales y personales
–	–	–	800	600	200	0. Activités mal désignées	0. Actividades no bien especif.
.	.	.	17 900	7 200	10 700	–. Personnes en quête d'emploi pour la première fois	–. Personas en busca de trabajo por primera vez
27 400	**6 000**	**21 400**	**37 000**	**19 700**	**17 300**	**Total**	**Total**

Unpaid family workers			Not classifiable by status			Industrie	Industria
Total	Males	Females	Total	Males	Females		
3 668 520	711 200	2 957 320	...	...	...	1. Agriculture, chasse, sylviculture et pêche	1. Agricultura, caza, silvicultura y pesca
2 335	1 200	1 135	...	...	...	2. Industries extractives	2. Minas y canteras
683 995	152 625	531 370	...	...	...	3. Industries manufacturières	3. Industrias manufactureras
.	.	.	.	.	.	4. Electricité, gaz et eau	4. Electricidad, gas y agua
226 570	105 060	121 515	...	...	...	5. Construction	5. Construcción
1 770 050	315 830	1 454 220	...	...	...	6. Commerce (gros et détail); restaurants, hôtels	6. Comercio (por mayor y por menor); restaurantes, hoteles
30 095	7 785	22 310	...	...	...	7. Transports, entrepôts et communications	7. Transportes, almacenamiento y comunicaciones
58 665	7 850	50 815	...	...	...	8. Banques, assur., affaires imm., services aux entreprises	8. Bancos, seguros, bienes inmuebles, serv. para empresas
403 005	71 300	331 710	...	...	...	9. Services à la collectivité, services sociaux et personnels	9. Servicios comunales, sociales y personales
8 615	225	8 390	7 125	1 735	5 390	0. Activités mal désignées	0. Actividades no bien especif.
...	...	...	1 249 290	890 615	358 680	–. Chômeurs	–. Desempleados
6 851 855	**1 373 075**	**5 478 780**	**1 256 415**	**892 350**	**364 070**	**Total**	**Total**

Unpaid family workers			Not classifiable by status			Industrie	Industria
Total	Males	Females	Total	Males	Females		
2 810 000	500 000	2 300 000	...	...	...	1. Agriculture, chasse, sylviculture et pêche	1. Agricultura, caza, silvicultura y pesca
–	–	–	...	...	...	2. Industries extractives	2. Minas y canteras
710 000	150 000	570 000	...	...	...	3. Industries manufacturières	3. Industrias manufactureras
.	.	.	...	...	...	4. Electricité, gaz et eau	4. Electricidad, gas y agua
280 000	120 000	170 000	...	...	...	5. Construction	5. Construcción
1 860 000	310 000	1 550 000	...	...	...	6. Commerce (gros et détail); restaurants, hôtels	6. Comercio (por mayor y por menor); restaurantes, hoteles
30 000	–	20 000	...	...	...	7. Transports, entrepôts et communications	7. Transportes, almacenamiento y comunicaciones
50 000	10 000	50 000	...	...	...	8. Banques, assur., affaires imm., services aux entreprises	8. Bancos, seguros, bienes inmuebles, serv. para empresas
520 000	80 000	440 000	...	...	...	9. Services à la collectivité, services sociaux et personnels	9. Servicios comunales, sociales y personales
–	–	–	80 000	50 000	30 000	0. Activités mal désignées	0. Actividades no bien especif.
...	...	...	1 170 000	740 000	430 000	–. Chômeurs	–. Desempleados
6 270 000	**1 180 000**	**5 090 000**	**1 260 000**	**800 000**	**460 000**	**Total**	**Total**

2 Structure of the economically active population
Structure de la population active
Estructura de la población económicamente activa

Industry (Major divisions of economic activity)	Total				Employers and own-account workers / Employeurs et personnes travaillant à leur propre compte / Empleadores y trabajadores por cuenta propia			Employees / Salariés / Empleados a sueldo o salario		
	Total	%	Males Hommes Hombres	Females Femmes Mujeres	Total	Males Hommes Hombres	Females Femmes Mujeres	Total	Males Hommes Hombres	Females Femmes Mujeres
Korea,Republic of (1.X.75) C †										
1. Agriculture, hunting, forestry & fishing	6 208 478	46.5	3 281 076	2 927 402	2 399 527	1 981 543	417 984	562 581	391 372	171 209
2. Mining & quarrying	93 059	0.7	89 434	3 625	3 552	3 477	75	88 856	85 530	3 326
3. Manufacturing	2 211 181	16.6	1 376 625	834 556	260 149	194 278	65 871	1 871 252	1 153 062	718 190
4. Electr., gas & water	34 952	0.2	31 658	3 294	1 873	1 776	97	32 980	29 842	3 138
5. Construction	484 351	3.7	459 057	25 294	40 982	40 130	852	438 286	415 403	22 883
6. Wholesale/retail trade, restaurants & hotels	1 694 231	12.6	979 280	714 951	986 823	652 021	334 802	468 879	277 622	191 257
7. Transport, storage & communication	431 816	3.3	386 463	45 353	43 156	42 467	689	386 295	341 924	44 371
8. Financing, insur., real estate & business serv.	150 772	1.1	117 673	33 099	36 408	34 629	1 779	112 836	81 992	30 844
9. Community, social & personal services	1 372 873	10.3	980 273	392 600	133 768	103 934	29 834	1 202 505	856 730	345 775
0. Not adequately defined	328	–	172	156	.	.	.	128	96	32
-. Unemployed	668 563	5.0	474 133	194 430	...	...	...	...	...	...
Total	**13 350 604**	*100.0*	**8 175 844**	**5 174 760**	**3 906 238**	**3 054 255**	**851 983**	**5 164 598**	**3 633 573**	**1 531 025**
" " " " (1979) LFSS †										
1. Agriculture, hunting, forestry & fishing	4 887 000	34.4	2 709 000	2 178 000	2 267 000	1 830 000	437 000	615 000	358 000	257 000
2. Mining & quarrying	111 000	0.8	102 000	9 000	4 000	4 000	.	106 000	97 000	9 000
3. Manufacturing	3 126 000	22.0	1 888 000	1 238 000	494 000	298 000	196 000	2 524 000	1 555 000	969 000
4. Electr., gas & water	46 000	0.3	40 000	6 000	2 000	2 000	.	44 000	38 000	6 000
5. Construction	836 000	5.9	772 000	64 000	48 000	47 000	1 000	784 000	723 000	61 000
6. Wholesale/retail trade, restaurants & hotels	2 304 000	16.2	1 176 000	1 128 000	1 380 000	832 000	548 000	499 000	280 000	219 000
7. Transport, storage & communication	610 000	4.3	554 000	56 000	83 000	81 000	2 000	525 000	471 000	54 000
8. Financing, insur., real estate & business serv.	259 000	1.8	182 000	77 000	74 000	71 000	3 000	183 000	110 000	73 000
9. Community, social & personal services	1 485 000	10.5	986 000	499 000	221 000	132 000	89 000	1 239 000	848 000	391 000
-. Unemployed	542 000	3.8	411 000	131 000	...	...	...	...	...	...
Total	**14 206 000**	*100.0*	**8 820 000**	**5 386 000**	**4 573 000**	**3 297 000**	**1 276 000**	**6 519 000**	**4 480 000**	**2 039 000**
Pakistan (I.80) LFSS †										
1. Agriculture, hunting, forestry & fishing	12 383 000	53.9	...	...	6 346 000	...	...	988 000	...	...
2. Mining & quarrying	34 000	0.1	...	...	6 000	...	...	25 000	...	...
3. Manufacturing	3 080 000	13.4	...	...	1 354 000	...	...	1 185 000	...	...
4. Electr., gas & water	111 000	0.5	...	...	4 000	...	...	106 000	...	...
5. Construction	946 000	4.1	...	...	535 000	...	...	366 000	...	...
6. Wholesale/retail trade, restaurants & hotels	2 506 000	10.9	...	...	1 820 000	...	...	299 000	...	...
7. Transport, storage & communication	1 100 000	4.8	...	...	473 000	...	...	550 000	...	...
8. Financing, insur., real estate & business serv.	151 000	0.7	...	...	36 000	...	...	112 000	...	...
9. Community, social & personal services	2 210 000	9.6	...	...	637 000	...	...	1 421 000	...	...
0. Not adequately defined	75 000	0.3	...	...	40 000	...	...	22 000	...	...
-. Unemployed	390 000	1.7	...	...	...	...	...	...	...	...
Total	**22 986 000**	*100.0*	...	...	**11 251 000**	...	...	**5 074 000**	...	...

A By industry, by status and by sex
Par industrie, selon la situation dans la profession et par sexe
Por industria, según la categoría de ocupación y por sexo

Unpaid family workers / Travailleurs familiaux non rémunérés / Trabajadores familiares no remunerados			Not classifiable by status / Inclassables selon la situation / Inclasificables según la categoría			Industrie (Branches d'activité économique)	Industria (Grandes divisiones de actividad económica)
Total	Males / Hommes / Hombres	Females / Femmes / Mujeres	Total	Males / Hommes / Hombres	Females / Femmes / Mujeres		
3 246 298	908 161	2 338 137	72	.	72	1. Agriculture, chasse, sylviculture et pêche	1. Agricultura, caza, silvicultura y pesca
651	427	224	.	.	.	2. Industries extractives	2. Minas y canteras
79 682	29 284	50 398	98	1	97	3. Industries manufacturières	3. Industrias manufactureras
99	40	59	.	.	.	4. Electricité, gaz et eau	4. Electricidad, gas y agua
5 035	3 524	1 511	48	.	48	5. Construction	5. Construcción
238 454	49 589	188 865	75	48	27	6. Commerce (gros et détail); restaurants, hôtels	6. Comercio (por mayor y por menor); restaurantes, hoteles
2 365	2 072	293	.	.	.	7. Transports, entrepôts et communications	7. Transportes, almacenamiento y comunicaciones
1 480	1 052	428	48	.	48	8. Banques, assur., affaires imm., services aux entreprises	8. Bancos, seguros, bienes inmuebles, serv. para empresas
36 241	19 499	16 742	359	110	249	9. Services à la collectivité, services sociaux et personnels	9. Servicios comunales, sociales y personales
27	27	.	173	49	124	0. Activités mal désignées	0. Actividades no bien especif.
...	...	...	668 563	474 133	194 430	-. Chômeurs	-. Desempleados
3 610 332	**1 013 675**	**2 596 657**	**669 436**	**474 341**	**195 095**	**Total**	**Total**

Total	Males / Hommes / Hombres	Females / Femmes / Mujeres	Total	Males / Hommes / Hombres	Females / Femmes / Mujeres	Industrie	Industria
2 005 000	521 000	1 484 000	...	...	...	1. Agriculture, chasse, sylviculture et pêche	1. Agricultura, caza, silvicultura y pesca
1 000	1 000	.	...	...	...	2. Industries extractives	2. Minas y canteras
108 000	35 000	73 000	...	...	...	3. Industries manufacturières	3. Industrias manufactureras
.	.	.	...	...	...	4. Electricité, gaz et eau	4. Electricidad, gas y agua
4 000	2 000	2 000	...	...	...	5. Construction	5. Construcción
425 000	64 000	361 000	...	...	...	6. Commerce (gros et détail); restaurants, hôtels	6. Comercio (por mayor y por menor); restaurantes, hoteles
2 000	2 000	.	...	...	...	7. Transports, entrepôts et communications	7. Transportes, almacenamiento y comunicaciones
2 000	1 000	1 000	...	...	...	8. Banques, assur., affaires imm., services aux entreprises	8. Bancos, seguros, bienes inmuebles, serv. para empresas
25 000	6 000	19 000	...	...	...	9. Services à la collectivité, services sociaux et personnels	9. Servicios comunales, sociales y personales
...	...	...	542 000	411 000	131 000	-. Chômeurs	-. Desempleados
2 572 000	**632 000**	**1 940 000**	**542 000**	**411 000**	**131 000**	**Total**	**Total**

Total	Males / Hommes / Hombres	Females / Femmes / Mujeres	Total	Males / Hommes / Hombres	Females / Femmes / Mujeres	Industrie	Industria
5 049 000	...	...				1. Agriculture, chasse, sylviculture et pêche	1. Agricultura, caza, silvicultura y pesca
3 000	...	...	.	.	.	2. Industries extractives	2. Minas y canteras
541 000	...	...	.	.	.	3. Industries manufacturières	3. Industrias manufactureras
1 000	...	...	.	.	.	4. Electricité, gaz et eau	4. Electricidad, gas y agua
45 000	...	...	.	.	.	5. Construction	5. Construcción
387 000	...	...				6. Commerce (gros et détail); restaurants, hôtels	6. Comercio (por mayor y por menor); restaurantes, hoteles
77 000	...	...				7. Transports, entrepôts et communications	7. Transportes, almacenamiento y comunicaciones
3 000	...	...				8. Banques, assur., affaires imm., services aux entreprises	8. Bancos, seguros, bienes inmuebles, serv. para empresas
152 000	...	...	.	.	.	9. Services à la collectivité, services sociaux et personnels	9. Servicios comunales, sociales y personales
13 000	...	...	.	.	.	0. Activités mal désignées	0. Actividades no bien especif.
...	...	...	390 000	...	...	-. Chômeurs	-. Desempleados
6 271 000	...	...	**390 000**	...	...	**Total**	**Total**

2 Structure of the economically active population
Structure de la population active
Estructura de la población económicamente activa

Industry (Major divisions of economic activity)	Total				Employers and own-account workers / Employeurs et personnes travaillant à leur propre compte / Empleadores y trabajadores por cuenta propia			Employees / Salariés / Empleados a sueldo o salario		
	Total	%	Males Hommes Hombres	Females Femmes Mujeres	Total	Males Hommes Hombres	Females Femmes Mujeres	Total	Males Hommes Hombres	Females Femmes Mujeres
Philippines (X–XII.77) LFSS †										
–. Agriculture, forestry, hunting & fishing	7 308 000	48.7	5 954 000	1 357 000	4 006 000	3 725 000	280 000	1 434 000	1 122 000	312 000
–. Mining & quarrying	72 000	0.5	69 000	4 000	3 000	3 000	–	66 000	63 000	3 000
–. Manufacturing	1 561 000	10.4	876 000	685 000	451 000	164 000	287 000	1 043 000	699 000	344 000
–. Construction	492 000	3.3	482 000	9 000	30 000	30 000	–	461 000	451 000	9 000
–. Electricity, gas, water & sanitary services	56 000	0.4	47 000	9 000	5 000	3 000	2 000	51 000	44 000	7 000
–. Commerce	1 384 000	9.2	532 000	852 000	938 000	353 000	586 000	314 000	153 000	161 000
–. Transport, storage & communication	654 000	4.4	622 000	32 000	95 000	93 000	2 000	552 000	523 000	29 000
–. Services	2 672 000	17.8	1 333 000	1 337 000	229 000	142 000	88 000	2 407 000	1 183 000	1 224 000
–. Not adeq. described	125 000	0.8	94 000	31 000	18 000	13 000	5 000	88 000	68 000	19 000
–. Persons seeking work for the first time	275 000	1.9	111 000	163 000	.	.	.	.	.	.
–. Other unemployed	396 000	2.6	156 000	240 000	43 000	17 000	26 000	245 000	103 000	142 000
Total	**14 994 000**	100.0	**10 277 000**	**4 716 000**	**5 817 000**	**4 543 000**	**1 275 000**	**6 660 000**	**4 410 000**	**2 250 000**
Singapore (VI.79) LFSS †										
1. Agriculture, hunting, forestry & fishing	15 182	1.4	10 857	4 326	6 947	5 907	1 040	3 494	2 912	582
2. Mining & quarrying	1 518	0.2	1 227	291	124	124	.	1 393	1 102	291
3. Manufacturing	294 685	27.9	162 328	132 358	18 759	12 999	5 761	273 617	148 476	125 141
4. Electr., gas & water	9 817	0.9	8 756	1 061	125	125	.	9 692	8 631	1 061
5. Construction	54 345	5.2	49 686	4 659	6 156	6 073	84	47 981	43 468	4 513
6. Wholesale/retail trade, restaurants & hotels	237 346	22.4	153 946	83 400	68 841	57 589	11 251	144 025	85 958	58 068
7. Transport, storage & communication	118 902	11.3	101 743	17 158	18 843	18 759	83	99 788	82 796	16 992
8. Financing, insur., real estate & business serv.	72 044	6.8	42 698	29 346	4 784	4 513	270	67 115	38 164	28 951
9. Community, social & personal services	216 444	20.5	145 232	71 212	10 711	8 111	2 600	205 130	136 871	68 259
0. Not adequately defined	749	0.1	686	62	42	42	.	707	645	62
–. Persons seeking work for the first time	10 981	1.0	4 305	6 676	.	.	.	.	.	.
–. Other unemployed	24 313	2.3	16 243	8 070	...	...	...	...	...	...
Total	**1 056 325**	100.0	**697 707**	**358 618**	**135 331**	**114 243**	**21 089**	**852 943**	**549 023**	**303 920**
République arabe syrienne (IX.79) LFSS										
1. Agriculture, hunting, forestry & fishing	692 552	31.9	492 745	199 807	...	...	...	...	...	...
2. Mining & quarrying	495	–	.	495	...	...	...	...	...	...
3. Manufacturing	338 792	15.6	298 212	40 580	...	...	...	...	...	...
4. Electr., gas & water	31 948	1.4	30 151	1 797	...	...	...	...	...	...
5. Construction	297 848	13.7	293 690	4 158	...	...	...	...	...	...
6. Wholesale/retail trade, restaurants & hotels	221 087	10.2	215 902	5 185	...	...	...	...	...	...
7. Transport, storage & communication	97 836	4.5	95 937	1 899	...	...	...	...	...	...
8. Financing, insur., real estate & business serv.	21 749	1.0	18 871	2 878	...	...	...	...	...	...
9. Community, social & personal services	422 189	19.4	347 424	74 765	...	...	...	...	...	...
–. Persons seeking work for the first time	49 731	2.3	38 442	11 289	.	.	.	.	.	.
Total	**2 174 227**	100.0	**1 831 374**	**342 853**	...	...	...	...	...	...

A — By industry, by status and by sex / Par industrie, selon la situation dans la profession et par sexe / Por industria, según la categoría de ocupación y por sexo

Unpaid family workers / Travailleurs familiaux non rémunérés / Trabajadores familiares no remunerados			Not classifiable by status / Inclassables selon la situation / Inclasificables según la categoría			Industrie (Branches d'activité économique)	Industria (Grandes divisiones de actividad económica)
Total	Males Hommes Hombres	Females Femmes Mujeres	Total	Males Hommes Hombres	Females Femmes Mujeres		
1 848 000	1 090 000	759 000	20 000	17 000	3 000	−. Agriculture, sylviculture, chasse et pêche	−. Agricultura, silvicultura, caza y pesca
3 000	2 000	1 000	–	–	–	−. Industries extractives	−. Minas y canteras
64 000	12 000	52 000	3 000	1 000	2 000	−. Industries manufacturières	−. Industrias manufactureras
–	–	–	1 000	1 000	–	−. Construction	−. Construcción
–	–	–	...	...	...	−. Electricité, gaz, eau et services sanitaires	−. Electricidad, gas, agua y servicios sanitarios
131 000	25 000	105 000	1 000	1 000	–	−. Comm., banq., assur., aff. imm.	−. Comercio
5 000	4 000	1 000	2 000	2 000	–	−. Transports, entrepôts et communications	−. Transportes, almacenamiento y comunicaciones
24 000	4 000	20 000	11 000	4 000	7 000	−. Services	−. Servicios
6 000	6 000	–	13 000	7 000	7 000	−. Activités mal désignées	−. Actividades no bien especif.
.	.	.	275 000	111 000	163 000	−. Personnes en quête d'emploi pour la première fois	−. Personas en busca de trabajo por primera vez
89 000	28 000	61 000	20 000	8 000	11 000	−. Autres chômeurs	−. Otros desempleados
2 170 000	**1 172 000**	**998 000**	**348 000**	**152 000**	**193 000**	**Total**	**Total**
4 742	2 038	2 704	...	...	...	1. Agriculture, chasse, sylviculture et pêche	1. Agricultura, caza, silvicultura y pesca
2 309	853	1 456	...	...	...	2. Industries extractives	2. Minas y canteras
.	.	.	...	...	...	3. Industries manufacturières	3. Industrias manufactureras
208	146	62	...	...	...	4. Electricité, gaz et eau	4. Electricidad, gas y agua
.	.	.	...	...	...	5. Construction	5. Construcción
24 479	10 399	14 080				6. Commerce (gros et détail); restaurants, hôtels	6. Comercio (por mayor y por menor); restaurantes, hoteles
270	187	83	...	...	...	7. Transports, entrepôts et communications	7. Transportes, almacenamiento y comunicaciones
146	21	125	...	...	...	8. Banques, assur., affaires imm., services aux entreprises	8. Bancos, seguros, bienes inmuebles, serv. para empresas
603	250	354	...	...	...	9. Services à la collectivité, services sociaux et personnels	9. Servicios comunales, sociales y personales
.	.	.	...	...	...	0. Activités mal désignées	0. Actividades no bien especif.
.	.	.	10 981	4 305	6 676	−. Personnes en quête d'emploi pour la première fois	−. Personas en busca de trabajo por primera vez
...	...	...	24 313	16 243	8 070	−. Autres chômeurs	−. Otros desempleados
32 757	**13 893**	**18 864**	**35 294**	**20 548**	**14 746**	**Total**	**Total**
...	...	...	...	...	...	1. Agriculture, chasse, sylviculture et pêche	1. Agricultura, caza, silvicultura y pesca
...	...	...	...	...	...	2. Industries extractives	2. Minas y canteras
...	...	...	...	...	...	3. Industries manufacturières	3. Industrias manufactureras
...	...	...	...	...	...	4. Electricité, gaz et eau	4. Electricidad, gas y agua
...	...	...	...	...	...	5. Construction	5. Construcción
...	...	...	...	...	...	6. Commerce (gros et détail); restaurants, hôtels	6. Comercio (por mayor y por menor); restaurantes, hoteles
...	...	...	...	...	...	7. Transports, entrepôts et communications	7. Transportes, almacenamiento y comunicaciones
...	...	...	...	...	...	8. Banques, assur., affaires imm., services aux entreprises	8. Bancos, seguros, bienes inmuebles, serv. para empresas
...	...	...	...	...	...	9. Services à la collectivité, services sociaux et personnels	9. Servicios comunales, sociales y personales
.	.	.	.	.	.	−. Personnes en quête d'emploi pour la première fois	−. Personas en busca de trabajo por primera vez
...	...	...	...	...	...	**Total**	**Total**

ACTIVE POPULATION

2 Structure of the economically active population
Structure de la population active
Estructura de la población económicamente activa

Industry (Major divisions of economic activity)	Total				Employers and own-account workers Employeurs et personnes travaillant à leur propre compte Empleadores y trabajadores por cuenta propia			Employees Salariés Empleados a sueldo o salario		
	Total	%	Males Hommes Hombres	Females Femmes Mujeres	Total	Males Hommes Hombres	Females Femmes Mujeres	Total	Males Hommes Hombres	Females Femmes Mujeres
Thailand (VII–IX.78) LFSS †										
–. Agriculture, forestry, hunting & fishing	16 017 000	73.2	8 183 900	7 833 100	5 247 900	4 311 000	936 900	1 042 900	536 300	506 600
–. Mining & quarrying	29 600	0.1	23 300	6 300	3 700	3 700	.	12 700	12 500	200
–. Manufacturing	1 476 500	6.7	858 400	618 100	337 400	207 500	129 900	931 900	580 700	351 200
–. Construction	312 500	1.5	270 800	41 700	43 100	42 600	500	263 900	224 100	39 800
–. Electricity, gas, water & sanitary services	58 000	0.2	50 100	7 900	100	100	.	57 900	50 000	7 900
–. Commerce	1 638 600	7.5	772 000	866 600	765 900	380 800	385 100	397 300	281 500	115 800
–. Transport, storage & communication	386 900	1.8	363 200	23 700	164 000	161 900	2 100	210 800	193 400	17 400
–. Services	1 811 700	8.3	985 200	826 500	262 800	112 100	150 700	1 391 700	838 100	553 600
–. Not adeq. described	5 700	–	2 700	3 000	...	...	...	...	...	...
–. Persons seeking work for the first time	100 900	0.4	61 800	39 100	.	.	.	.	.	.
–. Other unemployed	55 900	0.3	42 900	13 000	...	...	...	...	...	...
Total	**21 893 300**	*100.0*	**11 614 300**	**10 279 000**	**6 824 900**	**5 219 700**	**1 605 200**	**4 309 100**	**2 716 600**	**1 592 500**
United Arab Emirates (1975) OE										
1. Agriculture, hunting, forestry & fishing	13 569	4.6	13 528	41	...	...	...	...	...	...
2. Mining & quarrying	6 868	2.3	6 679	189	...	...	...	...	...	...
3. Manufacturing	17 265	5.8	17 163	102	...	...	...	...	...	...
4. Electr., gas & water	6 264	2.1	6 242	22	...	...	...	...	...	...
5. Construction	93 870	31.7	93 635	235	...	...	...	...	...	...
6. Wholesale/retail trade, restaurants & hotels	37 716	12.7	37 280	436	...	...	...	...	...	...
7. Transport, storage & communication	23 601	8.0	23 283	318	...	...	...	...	...	...
8. Financing, insur., real estate & business serv.	5 997	2.0	5 459	538	...	...	...	...	...	...
9. Community, social & personal services	86 788	29.3	79 142	7 646	...	...	...	...	...	...
0. Not adequately defined	588	0.2	576	12	...	...	...	...	...	...
–. Persons seeking work for the first time	3 990	1.3	3 568	422	...	...	...	...	...	...
Total	**296 516**	*100.0*	**286 555**	**9 961**	**26 824**	**26 580**	**244**	**264 642**	**255 413**	**9 229**
Yemen, Democratic (14.V.73) C										
1. Agriculture, hunting, forestry & fishing	166 132	40.5	118 546	47 586	...	...	...	...	...	...
2. Mining & quarrying	2 037	0.5	2 037	.	...	...	...	...	...	...
3. Manufacturing	14 439	3.6	12 487	1 952	...	...	...	...	...	...
4. Electr., gas & water	2 870	0.7	2 839	31	...	...	...	...	...	...
5. Construction	15 327	3.7	15 327	.	...	...	...	...	...	...
6. Wholesale/retail trade, restaurants & hotels	25 509	6.2	25 293	216	...	...	...	...	...	...
7. Transport, storage & communication	13 299	3.3	13 238	61	...	...	...	...	...	...
8. Financing, insur., real estate & business serv.	485	0.1	443	42	...	...	...	...	...	...
9. Community, social & personal services	79 588	19.4	74 928	4 660	...	...	...	...	...	...
0. Not adequately defined	18 534	4.5	13 223	5 311	...	...	...	...	...	...
–. Unemployed	71 522	17.5	55 593	15 929	...	...	...	...	...	...
Total	**409 742**	*100.0*	**333 954**	**75 788**	**122 189**	**103 025**	**19 164**	**140 123**	**134 668**	**5 455**

A By industry, by status and by sex
Par industrie, selon la situation dans la profession et par sexe
Por industria, según la categoría de ocupación y por sexo

Unpaid family workers / Travailleurs familiaux non rémunérés / Trabajadores familiares no remunerados			Not classifiable by status / Inclassables selon la situation / Inclasificables según la categoría			Industrie (Branches d'activité économique)	Industria (Grandes divisiones de actividad económica)
Total	Males Hommes Hombres	Females Femmes Mujeres	Total	Males Hommes Hombres	Females Femmes Mujeres		
9 726 200	3 336 600	6 389 600	...	...	...	–. Agriculture, sylviculture, chasse et pêche	–. Agricultura, silvicultura, caza y pesca
13 200	7 100	6 100	...	...	...	–. Industries extractives	–. Minas y canteras
207 200	70 200	137 000	...	...	...	–. Industries manufacturières	–. Industrias manufactureras
5 500	4 100	1 400	...	...	...	–. Construction	–. Construcción
						–. Electricité, gaz, eau et services sanitaires	–. Electricidad, gas, agua y servicios sanitarios
475 400	109 700	365 700	...	...	...	–. Comm., banq., assur., aff. imm.	–. Comercio
12 100	7 900	4 200	...	...	...	–. Transports, entrepôts et communications	–. Transportes, almacenamiento y comunicaciones
157 200	35 000	122 200	...	...	...	–. Services	–. Servicios
...	...	...	5 700	2 700	3 000	–. Activités mal désignées	–. Actividades no bien especif.
.	.	.	100 900	61 800	39 100	–. Personnes en quête d'emploi pour la première fois	–. Personas en busca de trabajo por primera vez
...	...	...	55 900	42 900	13 000	–. Autres chômeurs	–. Otros desempleados
10 596 800	**3 570 600**	**7 026 200**	**162 500**	**107 400**	**55 100**	**Total**	**Total**
...	...	...	...	...	...	1. Agriculture, chasse, sylviculture et pêche	1. Agricultura, caza, silvicultura y pesca
...	...	...	...	...	...	2. Industries extractives	2. Minas y canteras
...	...	...	...	...	...	3. Industries manufacturières	3. Industrias manufactureras
...	...	...	...	...	...	4. Electricité, gaz et eau	4. Electricidad, gas y agua
...	...	...	...	...	...	5. Construction	5. Construcción
...	...	...	...	...	...	6. Commerce (gros et détail); restaurants, hôtels	6. Comercio (por mayor y por menor); restaurantes, hoteles
...	...	...	...	...	...	7. Transports, entrepôts et communications	7. Transportes, almacenamiento y comunicaciones
...	...	...	...	...	...	8. Banques, assur., affaires imm., services aux entreprises	8. Bancos, seguros, bienes inmuebles, serv. para empresas
...	...	...	...	...	...	9. Services à la collectivité, services sociaux et personnels	9. Servicios comunales, sociales y personales
...	...	...	...	...	...	0. Activités mal désignées	0. Actividades no bien especif.
...	...	...	...	...	...	–. Personnes en quête d'emploi pour la première fois	–. Personas en busca de trabajo por primera vez
617	**563**	**54**	**4 433**	**3 999**	**434**	**Total**	**Total**
...	...	...	...	...	...	1. Agriculture, chasse, sylviculture et pêche	1. Agricultura, caza, silvicultura y pesca
...	...	...	...	...	...	2. Industries extractives	2. Minas y canteras
...	...	...	...	...	...	3. Industries manufacturières	3. Industrias manufactureras
...	...	...	...	...	...	4. Electricité, gaz et eau	4. Electricidad, gas y agua
...	...	...	...	...	...	5. Construction	5. Construcción
...	...	...	...	...	...	6. Commerce (gros et détail); restaurants, hôtels	6. Comercio (por mayor y por menor); restaurantes, hoteles
...	...	...	...	...	...	7. Transports, entrepôts et communications	7. Transportes, almacenamiento y comunicaciones
...	...	...	...	...	...	8. Banques, assur., affaires imm., services aux entreprises	8. Bancos, seguros, bienes inmuebles, serv. para empresas
...	...	...	...	...	...	9. Services à la collectivité, services sociaux et personnels	9. Servicios comunales, sociales y personales
...	...	...	...	...	...	0. Activités mal désignées	0. Actividades no bien especif.
...	...	...	...	...	...	–. Chômeurs	–. Desempleados
61 734	**31 284**	**30 450**	**85 696**	**64 977**	**20 719**	**Total**	**Total**

2 Structure of the economically active population
Structure de la population active
Estructura de la población económicamente activa

Industry (Major divisions of economic activity)	Total				Employers and own-account workers Employeurs et personnes travaillant à leur propre compte Empleadores y trabajadores por cuenta propia			Employees Salariés Empleados a sueldo o salario		
	Total	%	Males Hommes Hombres	Females Femmes Mujeres	Total	Males Hommes Hombres	Females Femmes Mujeres	Total	Males Hommes Hombres	Females Femmes Mujeres

EUROPE

Austria (1979) LFSS †

1. Agriculture, hunting, forestry & fishing	327 000	10.6	166 000	161 000	285 000	137 000	148 000	42 000	29 000	13 000
2. Mining & quarrying	19 000	0.6	18 000	1 000	1 000	1 000	–	18 000	17 000	1 000
3. Manufacturing	920 000	29.7	650 000	270 000	50 000	40 000	10 000	870 000	610 000	260 000
4. Electr., gas & water	39 000	1.3	32 000	7 000	–	–	–	39 000	32 000	7 000
5. Construction	285 000	9.2	264 000	21 000	18 000	15 000	3 000	267 000	249 000	18 000
6. Wholesale/retail trade, restaurants & hotels	533 000	17.2	220 000	313 000	113 000	56 000	57 000	420 000	164 000	256 000
7. Transport, storage & communication	197 000	6.4	165 000	32 000	13 000	11 000	2 000	184 000	154 000	30 000
8. Financing, insur., real estate & business serv.	158 000	5.1	85 000	73 000	16 000	12 000	4 000	142 000	73 000	69 000
9. Community, social & personal services	606 000	19.6	291 000	315 000	32 000	21 000	11 000	574 000	270 000	304 000
0. Not adequately defined	10 000	0.3	5 000	5 000	–	–	–	10 000	5 000	5 000
Total	**3 094 000**	*100.0*	**1 896 000**	**1 198 000**	**528 000**	**293 000**	**235 000**	**2 566 000**	**1 603 000**	**963 000**

Belgique (VI.78) OE †

1. Agriculture, hunting, forestry & fishing	118 467	2.9	93 084	25 383	85 014	74 392	10 622	12 174	10 788	1 386
2. Mining & quarrying	30 301	0.7	29 790	511	275	260	15	30 001	29 515	486
3. Manufacturing	1 001 132	24.6	756 697	244 435	48 344	44 523	3 821	941 573	708 359	233 214
4. Electr., gas & water	33 280	0.8	31 039	2 241	124	119	5	33 156	30 920	2 236
5. Construction	296 275	7.3	285 631	10 644	42 063	41 264	799	249 450	241 297	8 153
6. Wholesale/retail trade, restaurants & hotels	700 050	17.1	386 842	313 208	205 305	127 531	77 774	423 855	248 569	175 286
7. Transport, storage & communication	268 683	6.6	234 715	33 968	12 328	11 637	691	251 582	221 796	29 786
8. Financing, insur., real estate & business serv.	237 852	5.8	145 256	92 596	33 015	27 030	5 985	199 681	117 665	82 016
9. Community, social & personal services	1 084 700	26.6	504 346	580 354	60 472	38 923	21 549	1 008 446	463 587	544 859
0. Not adequately defined	3 954	0.1	2 587	1 367	.	.	.	.	.	.
–. Unemployed	278 587	6.9	108 107	170 480	...	...	...	...	...	...
–. Armed forces	26 149	0.6	26 149		.	.	.	.	.	.
Total	**4 079 430**	*100.0*	**2 604 243**	**1 475 187**	**486 940**	**365 679**	**121 261**	**3 149 918**	**2 072 496**	**1 077 422**

Denmark (X.79) LFSS †

1. Agriculture, hunting, forestry & fishing	208 371	7.9	148 969	59 042	108 587	104 137	4 450	51 730	44 832	6 897
2. Mining & quarrying	1 228	0.1	823	405	245	245	.	983	578	405
3. Manufacturing	560 874	21.3	394 245	166 629	30 870	28 328	2 542	521 363	365 917	155 446
4. Electr., gas & water	17 210	0.7	15 383	1 827	128	128	.	17 082	15 255	1 827
5. Construction	206 639	7.9	186 412	20 227	33 262	32 873	389	165 780	153 539	12 241
6. Wholesale/retail trade, restaurants & hotels	352 350	13.4	181 014	171 336	62 904	51 353	11 551	269 205	129 661	139 544
7. Transport, storage & communication	174 399	6.6	131 832	42 567	15 589	14 711	878	154 781	117 121	37 660
8. Financing, insur., real estate & business serv.	182 603	7.0	94 876	87 727	19 672	17 221	2 451	160 300	77 655	82 645
9. Community, social & personal services	874 462	33.2	303 549	570 913	33 939	22 804	11 135	834 191	280 745	553 446
0. Not adequately defined	48 763	1.9	20 953	27 810	.	.	.	48 763	20 953	27 810
Total	**2 626 901**	*100.0*	**1 478 057**	**1 148 844**	**305 197**	**271 801**	**33 396**	**2 224 177**	**1 206 256**	**1 017 921**

By industry, by status and by sex
Par industrie, selon la situation dans la profession et par sexe
Por industria, según la categoría de ocupación y por sexo

Unpaid family workers / Travailleurs familiaux non rémunérés / Trabajadores familiares no remunerados			Not classifiable by status / Inclassables selon la situation / Inclasificables según la categoría			Industrie (Branches d'activité économique)	Industria (Grandes divisiones de actividad económica)
Total	Males Hommes Hombres	Females Femmes Mujeres	Total	Males Hommes Hombres	Females Femmes Mujeres		

EUROPE – EUROPA

Total	Males	Females	Total	Males	Females	Industrie	Industria
...	...	...	.	.	.	1. Agriculture, chasse, sylviculture et pêche	1. Agricultura, caza, silvicultura y pesca
...	...	...	.	.	.	2. Industries extractives	2. Minas y canteras
...	...	...	.	.	.	3. Industries manufacturières	3. Industrias manufactureras
...	...	...	.	.	.	4. Electricité, gaz et eau	4. Electricidad, gas y agua
...	...	...	.	.	.	5. Construction	5. Construcción
						6. Commerce (gros et détail); restaurants, hôtels	6. Comercio (por mayor y por menor); restaurantes, hoteles
...	...	...	.	.	.	7. Transports, entrepôts et communications	7. Transportes, almacenamiento y comunicaciones
...	...	...	.	.	.	8. Banques, assur., affaires imm., services aux entreprises	8. Bancos, seguros, bienes inmuebles, serv. para empresas
...	...	...	.	.	.	9. Services à la collectivité, services sociaux et personnels	9. Servicios comunales, sociales y personales
...	...	...	.	.	.	0. Activités mal désignées	0. Actividades no bien especif.
...	...	...	.	.	.	**Total**	**Total**
21 279	7 904	13 375	...	...	...	1. Agriculture, chasse, sylviculture et pêche	1. Agricultura, caza, silvicultura y pesca
25	15	10	...	...	...	2. Industries extractives	2. Minas y canteras
11 215	3 815	7 400	...	...	...	3. Industries manufacturières	3. Industrias manufactureras
.	.	.	...	...	...	4. Electricité, gaz et eau	4. Electricidad, gas y agua
4 762	3 070	1 692	...	...	...	5. Construction	5. Construcción
70 890	10 742	60 148	...	...	...	6. Commerce (gros et détail); restaurants, hôtels	6. Comercio (por mayor y por menor); restaurantes, hoteles
4 773	1 282	3 491	...	...	...	7. Transports, entrepôts et communications	7. Transportes, almacenamiento y comunicaciones
5 156	561	4 595	...	...	...	8. Banques, assur., affaires imm., services aux entreprises	8. Bancos, seguros, bienes inmuebles, serv. para empresas
15 782	1 836	13 946	...	...	...	9. Services à la collectivité, services sociaux et personnels	9. Servicios comunales, sociales y personales
.	.	.	3 954	2 587	1 367	0. Activités mal désignées	0. Actividades no bien especif.
...	...	...	278 587	108 107	170 480	–. Chômeurs	–. Desempleados
.	.	.	26 149	26 149	.	–. Forces armées	–. Fuerzas armadas
133 882	**29 225**	**104 657**	**308 690**	**136 843**	**171 847**	**Total**	**Total**
48 055	.	48 055	.	.	.	1. Agriculture, chasse, sylviculture et pêche	1. Agricultura, caza, silvicultura y pesca
.	.	.	.	.	.	2. Industries extractives	2. Minas y canteras
8 641	.	8 641	.	.	.	3. Industries manufacturières	3. Industrias manufactureras
.	.	.	.	.	.	4. Electricité, gaz et eau	4. Electricidad, gas y agua
7 597	.	7 597	.	.	.	5. Construction	5. Construcción
20 241	.	20 241	.	.	.	6. Commerce (gros et détail); restaurants, hôtels	6. Comercio (por mayor y por menor); restaurantes, hoteles
4 029	.	4 029	.	.	.	7. Transports, entrepôts et communications	7. Transportes, almacenamiento y comunicaciones
2 631	.	2 631	.	.	.	8. Banques, assur., affaires imm., services aux entreprises	8. Bancos, seguros, bienes inmuebles, serv. para empresas
6 332	.	6 332	.	.	.	9. Services à la collectivité, services sociaux et personnels	9. Servicios comunales, sociales y personales
.	.	.	.	.	.	0. Activités mal désignées	0. Actividades no bien especif.
97 527	.	**97 527**	.	.	.	**Total**	**Total**

2 Structure of the economically active population
Structure de la population active
Estructura de la población económicamente activa

Industry (Major divisions of economic activity)	Total				Employers and own-account workers / Employeurs et personnes travaillant à leur propre compte / Empleadores y trabajadores por cuenta propia			Employees / Salariés / Empleados a sueldo o salario		
	Total	%	Males Hommes Hombres	Females Femmes Mujeres	Total	Males Hommes Hombres	Females Femmes Mujeres	Total	Males Hommes Hombres	Females Femmes Mujeres
España (X–XII.79) LFSS †										
1. Agriculture, hunting, forestry & fishing	2 314 300	17.4	1 667 200	647 100	1 056 700	884 800	171 900	650 200	573 900	76 300
2. Mining & quarrying	340 000	2.6	306 900	33 100	9 900	9 200	700	329 000	296 900	32 100
3. Manufacturing	2 801 600	21.0	2 090 300	711 300	267 800	204 000	63 800	2 472 400	1 859 600	612 800
4. Electr., gas & water	74 300	0.6	70 100	4 200	700	500	200	73 300	69 500	3 800
5. Construction	1 087 200	8.1	1 066 700	20 500	175 100	174 600	500	897 000	878 600	18 400
6. Wholesale/retail trade, restaurants & hotels	2 320 300	17.5	1 448 700	871 600	749 500	515 100	234 400	1 265 500	865 500	400 000
7. Transport, storage & communication	684 500	5.1	631 300	53 200	149 700	149 600	100	522 900	471 700	51 200
8. Financing, insur., real estate & business serv.	407 600	3.1	320 300	87 300	40 400	39 300	1 100	360 700	278 600	82 100
9. Community, social & personal services	1 923 200	14.5	886 100	1 037 100	114 100	64 200	49 900	1 789 600	817 200	972 400
–. Unemployed	1 348 500	10.1	891 900	456 600	...	...	...	...	...	...
Total	13 301 500	100.0	9 379 500	3 922 000	2 563 900	2 041 300	522 600	8 360 600	6 111 500	2 249 100
Faeroe Islands (22.IX.77) C †										
1. Agriculture, hunting, forestry & fishing	3 314	18.8	3 275	39	508	475	33	2 806	2 800	6
2. Mining & quarrying	98	0.6	98	.	3	3	.	95	95	.
3. Manufacturing	3 621	20.6	2 795	826	301	267	34	3 319	2 527	792
4. Electr., gas & water	135	0.8	128	7	.	.	.	135	128	7
5. Construction	1 952	11.1	1 913	39	358	341	17	1 593	1 571	22
6. Wholesale/retail trade, restaurants & hotels	2 091	11.9	1 018	1 073	607	390	217	1 484	628	856
7. Transport, storage & communication	1 944	11.0	1 697	247	123	118	5	1 820	1 579	241
8. Financing, insur., real estate & business serv.	339	1.9	170	169	3	3	.	336	167	169
9. Community, social & personal services	3 530	20.1	1 376	2 154	190	119	71	3 339	1 256	2 083
0. Not adequately defined	561	3.2	338	223	2	2	.	220	152	68
Total	17 585	100.0	12 808	4 777	2 095	1 718	377	15 147	10 903	4 244
Finland (1979) LFSS †										
1. Agriculture, hunting, forestry & fishing	250 000	11.0	148 000	102 000	...	...	...	...	...	...
2. Mining & quarrying	9 000	0.4	8 000	1 000	...	...	...	...	...	...
3. Manufacturing	547 000	24.1	347 000	200 000	...	...	...	...	...	...
4. Electr., gas & water	25 000	1.1	21 000	4 000	...	...	...	...	...	...
5. Construction	150 000	6.6	136 000	14 000	...	...	...	...	...	...
6. Wholesale/retail trade, restaurants & hotels	305 000	13.4	123 000	182 000	...	...	...	...	...	...
7. Transport, storage & communication	166 000	7.3	118 000	48 000	...	...	...	...	...	...
8. Financing, insur., real estate & business serv.	120 000	5.3	46 000	74 000	...	...	...	...	...	...
9. Community, social & personal services	544 000	23.9	172 000	372 000	...	...	...	...	...	...
0. Not adequately defined	18 000	0.8	9 000	9 000	...	...	...	...	...	...
–. Unemployed	139 000	6.1	79 000	60 000	...	...	...	...	...	...
Total	2 273 000	100.0	1 207 000	1 066 000	...	...	...	...	...	...

A — By industry, by status and by sex
Par industrie, selon la situation dans la profession et par sexe
Por industria, según la categoría de ocupación y por sexo

Unpaid family workers / Travailleurs familiaux non rémunérés / Trabajadores familiares no remunerados			Not classifiable by status / Inclassables selon la situation / Inclasificables según la categoría			Industrie (Branches d'activité économique)	Industria (Grandes divisiones de actividad económica)
Total	Males Hommes Hombres	Females Femmes Mujeres	Total	Males Hommes Hombres	Females Femmes Mujeres		
593 600	199 200	394 400	13 800	9 300	4 500	1. Agriculture, chasse, sylviculture et pêche	1. Agricultura, caza, silvicultura y pesca
900	600	300	200	200	.	2. Industries extractives	2. Minas y canteras
56 500	23 200	33 300	4 900	3 500	1 400	3. Industries manufacturières	3. Industrias manufactureras
200	.	200	100	100	.	4. Electricité, gaz et eau	4. Electricidad, gas y agua
13 600	12 100	1 500	1 500	1 400	100	5. Construction	5. Construcción
303 300	67 600	235 700	2 000	500	1 500	6. Commerce (gros et détail); restaurants, hôtels	6. Comercio (por mayor y por menor); restaurantes, hoteles
9 000	7 200	1 800	2 900	2 800	100	7. Transports, entrepôts et communications	7. Transportes, almacenamiento y comunicaciones
5 500	1 400	4 100	1 000	1 000		8. Banques, assur., affaires imm., services aux entreprises	8. Bancos, seguros, bienes inmuebles, serv. para empresas
14 500	3 400	11 100	5 000	1 300	3 700	9. Services à la collectivité, services sociaux et personnels	9. Servicios comunales, sociales y personales
...	...	...	1 348 500	891 900	456 600	-. Chômeurs	-. Desempleados
997 100	**314 700**	**682 400**	**1 379 900**	**912 000**	**467 900**	**Total**	**Total**
...	...	...	...	...	...	1. Agriculture, chasse, sylviculture et pêche	1. Agricultura, caza, silvicultura y pesca
...	...	...	...	...	...	2. Industries extractives	2. Minas y canteras
...	...	...	1	1	.	3. Industries manufacturières	3. Industrias manufactureras
...	...	...	...	...	...	4. Electricité, gaz et eau	4. Electricidad, gas y agua
...	...	...	1	1	.	5. Construction	5. Construcción
...	...	...	...	...	...	6. Commerce (gros et détail); restaurants, hôtels	6. Comercio (por mayor y por menor); restaurantes, hoteles
...	...	...	1	...	1	7. Transports, entrepôts et communications	7. Transportes, almacenamiento y comunicaciones
...	...	...	...	...	...	8. Banques, assur., affaires imm., services aux entreprises	8. Bancos, seguros, bienes inmuebles, serv. para empresas
...	...	...	1	1	...	9. Services à la collectivité, services sociaux et personnels	9. Servicios comunales, sociales y personales
...	...	...	339	184	155	0. Activités mal désignées	0. Actividades no bien especif.
...	...	...	**343**	**187**	**156**	**Total**	**Total**
...	...	...	...	...	...	1. Agriculture, chasse, sylviculture et pêche	1. Agricultura, caza, silvicultura y pesca
...	...	...	...	...	...	2. Industries extractives	2. Minas y canteras
...	...	...	...	...	...	3. Industries manufacturières	3. Industrias manufactureras
...	...	...	...	...	...	4. Electricité, gaz et eau	4. Electricidad, gas y agua
...	...	...	...	...	...	5. Construction	5. Construcción
...	...	...	...	...	...	6. Commerce (gros et détail); restaurants, hôtels	6. Comercio (por mayor y por menor); restaurantes, hoteles
...	...	...	...	...	...	7. Transports, entrepôts et communications	7. Transportes, almacenamiento y comunicaciones
...	...	...	...	...	...	8. Banques, assur., affaires imm., services aux entreprises	8. Bancos, seguros, bienes inmuebles, serv. para empresas
...	...	...	...	...	...	9. Services à la collectivité, services sociaux et personnels	9. Servicios comunales, sociales y personales
...	...	...	...	...	...	0. Activités mal désignées	0. Actividades no bien especif.
...	...	...	...	...	...	-. Chômeurs	-. Desempleados
...	...	...	...	...	...	**Total**	**Total**

ACTIVE POPULATION

2 Structure of the economically active population
Structure de la population active
Estructura de la población económicamente activa

Industry (Major divisions of economic activity)	Total				Employers and own-account workers / Employeurs et personnes travaillant à leur propre compte / Empleadores y trabajadores por cuenta propia			Employees / Salariés / Empleados a sueldo o salario		
	Total	%	Males Hommes Hombres	Females Femmes Mujeres	Total	Males Hommes Hombres	Females Femmes Mujeres	Total	Males Hommes Hombres	Females Femmes Mujeres
France (1979) OE †										
1. Agriculture, hunting, forestry & fishing	1 866 800	8.2	...	...	1 497 900	...	...	368 900	...	...
2. Mining & quarrying	149 800	0.7	...	...	4 400	...	...	145 400	...	...
3. Manufacturing	5 496 100	24.1	...	...	263 000	...	...	5 233 100	...	...
4. Electr., gas & water	182 600	0.8	...	...	800	...	...	181 800	...	...
5. Construction	1 820 000	8.0	...	...	315 300	...	...	1 504 500	...	...
6. Wholesale/retail trade, restaurants & hotels	3 373 500	14.8	...	...	840 400	...	...	2 533 100	...	...
7. Transport, storage & communication	1 334 300	5.9	...	...	55 000	...	...	1 279 300	...	...
8. Financing, insur., real estate & business serv.	1 491 900	6.5	...	...	145 800	...	...	1 346 100	...	...
9. Community, social & personal services	5 688 600	25.0	...	...	485 700	...	...	5 202 900	...	...
–. Unemployed	1 357 400	6.0	569 900	787 500	...	...	...	...	...	...
Total	**22 761 000**	100.0	...	...	**3 608 500**	...	...	**17 795 100**	...	...
Germany, Fed. Rep. of (1979) OE †										
1. Agriculture, hunting, forestry & fishing	1 553 000	5.9	752 000	801 000	544 000	474 000	70 000	264 000	184 000	80 000
2. Mining & quarrying	336 000	1.2	316 000	20 000	6 000	5 000	1 000	330 000	311 000	19 000
3. Manufacturing	9 058 000	34.3	6 233 000	2 825 000	397 000	339 000	58 000	8 594 000	5 891 000	2 703 000
4. Electr., gas & water	221 000	0.9	194 000	27 000	–	–	–	221 000	194 000	27 000
5. Construction	1 931 000	7.3	1 770 000	161 000	175 000	169 000	6 000	1 733 000	1 599 000	134 000
6. Wholesale/retail trade, restaurants & hotels	3 782 000	14.3	1 674 000	2 108 000	682 000	467 000	215 000	2 898 000	1 187 000	1 711 000
7. Transport, storage & communication	1 523 000	5.7	1 237 000	286 000	90 000	80 000	10 000	1 422 000	1 156 000	266 000
8. Financing, insur., real estate & business serv.	1 405 000	5.4	762 000	643 000	191 000	166 000	25 000	1 189 000	594 000	595 000
9. Community, social & personal services	6 423 000	24.3	3 407 000	3 016 000	352 000	235 000	117 000	6 011 000	3 168 000	2 843 000
–. Not adequately defined & persons seeking work for the first time	192 000	0.7	96 000	96 000	.	.	.	192 000	96 000	96 000
Total	**26 424 000**	100.0	**16 441 000**	**9 983 000**	**2 437 000**	**1 935 000**	**502 000**	**22 854 000**	**14 380 000**	**8 474 000**
Hongrie (I.79) OE †										
1. Agriculture, hunting, forestry & fishing	1 104 800	21.7	669 800	435 000	32 700	24 900	7 800	431 300	297 100	134 200
2–4. Min./quarrying; manuf.; electr., gas & water	1 733 900	34.2	958 100	775 800	30 000	20 900	9 100	1 501 400	868 100	633 300
5. Construction	413 200	8.1	340 800	72 400	17 900	17 400	500	350 800	286 300	64 500
6. Wholesale/retail trade, restaurants & hotels	485 100	9.5	175 100	310 000	10 900	3 700	7 200	471 700	170 600	301 100
7. Transport, storage & communication	408 700	8.1	309 700	99 000	5 400	5 100	300	402 400	303 700	98 700
8–0. Major div. 8, 9 & 0	935 300	18.4	366 400	568 900	12 200	5 600	6 600	900 800	354 900	545 900
Total	**5 081 000**	100.0	**2 819 900**	**2 261 100**	**109 100**	**77 600**	**31 500**	**4 058 400**	**2 280 700**	**1 777 700**

A By industry, by status and by sex
Par industrie, selon la situation dans la profession et par sexe
Por industria, según la categoría de ocupación y por sexo

Unpaid family workers / Travailleurs familiaux non rémunérés / Trabajadores familiares no remunerados			Not classifiable by status / Inclassables selon la situation / Inclasificables según la categoría			Industrie (Branches d'activité économique)	Industria (Grandes divisiones de actividad económica)
Total	Males Hommes Hombres	Females Femmes Mujeres	Total	Males Hommes Hombres	Females Femmes Mujeres		
...	...	...	...	...	...	1. Agriculture, chasse, sylvi-culture et pêche	1. Agricultura, caza, silvi-cultura y pesca
...	...	...	...	...	...	2. Industries extractives	2. Minas y canteras
...	...	...	...	...	...	3. Industries manufacturières	3. Industrias manufactureras
...	...	...	...	...	...	4. Electricité, gaz et eau	4. Electricidad, gas y agua
...	...	...	...	...	...	5. Construction	5. Construcción
...	...	...	...	...	...	6. Commerce (gros et détail); restaurants, hôtels	6. Comercio (por mayor y por menor); restaurantes, hoteles
...	...	...	...	...	...	7. Transports, entrepôts et communications	7. Transportes, almacenamiento y comunicaciones
...	...	...	...	...	...	8. Banques, assur., affaires imm., services aux entreprises	8. Bancos, seguros, bienes inmuebles, serv. para empresas
...	...	...	...	...	...	9. Services à la collectivité, services sociaux et personnels	9. Servicios comunales, sociales y personales
...	...	...	1 357 400	569 900	787 500	–. Chômeurs	–. Desempleados
...	...	...	1 357 400	569 900	787 500	**Total**	**Total**
745 000	94 000	651 000	...	...	...	1. Agriculture, chasse, sylvi-culture et pêche	1. Agricultura, caza, silvi-cultura y pesca
–	–	–	...	...	...	2. Industries extractives	2. Minas y canteras
67 000	3 000	64 000	...	...	...	3. Industries manufacturières	3. Industrias manufactureras
–	–	–	...	...	...	4. Electricité, gaz et eau	4. Electricidad, gas y agua
23 000	2 000	21 000	...	...	...	5. Construction	5. Construcción
202 000	20 000	182 000	...	...	...	6. Commerce (gros et détail); restaurants, hôtels	6. Comercio (por mayor y por menor); restaurantes, hoteles
11 000	1 000	10 000	...	...	...	7. Transports, entrepôts et communications	7. Transportes, almacenamiento y comunicaciones
25 000	2 000	23 000	...	...	...	8. Banques, assur., affaires imm., services aux entreprises	8. Bancos, seguros, bienes inmuebles, serv. para empresas
60 000	4 000	56 000	...	...	...	9. Services à la collectivité, services sociaux et personnels	9. Servicios comunales, sociales y personales
.	.	.	...	...	...	–. Activités mal désignées et personnes en quête d'emploi pour l première fois.	–. Actividades no bien especificadas; personas en busca de trabajo por primera vez
1 133 000	126 000	1 007 000	...	...	...	**Total**	**Total**
129 300	5 400	123 900	511 500	342 400	169 100	1. Agriculture, chasse, sylvi-culture et pêche	1. Agricultura, caza, silvi-cultura y pesca
2 900	800	2 100	199 600	68 300	131 300	2-4. Industries extract.; industries manuf.; électricité, gaz et eau	2-4. Minas y canteras; industrias manufact.; electr., gas y agua
700	400	300	43 800	36 700	7 100	5. Construction	5. Construcción
1 800	500	1 300	700	300	400	6. Commerce (gros et détail); restaurants, hôtels	6. Comercio (por mayor y por menor); restaurantes, hoteles
500	500	–	400	400	.	7. Transports, entrepôts et communications	7. Transportes, almacenamiento y comunicaciones
2 300	900	1 400	20 000	5 000	15 000	8-0. Branches 8, 9 et 0	8-0. Grandes divisiones 8, 9 y 0
137 500	8 500	129 000	776 000	453 100	322 900	**Total**	**Total**

2 Structure of the economically active population
Structure de la population active
Estructura de la población económicamente activa

Industry (Major divisions of economic activity)	Total				Employers and own-account workers Employeurs et personnes travaillant à leur propre compte Empleadores y trabajadores por cuenta propia			Employees Salariés Empleados a sueldo o salario		
	Total	%	Males Hommes Hombres	Females Femmes Mujeres	Total	Males Hommes Hombres	Females Femmes Mujeres	Total	Males Hommes Hombres	Females Femmes Mujeres
Ireland (IV.77) LFSS †										
1. Agriculture, hunting, forestry & fishing	217 500	19.0	199 100	18 400	161 200	152 200	8 900	26 200	24 800	1 300
2. Mining & quarrying	8 000	0.7	7 600	400	–	–	–	7 800	7 500	300
3. Manufacturing	220 000	19.2	159 900	60 100	10 000	9 000	1 000	210 100	150 800	59 400
4. Electr., gas & water	12 200	1.1	10 800	1 400	.	.	.	12 200	10 800	1 400
5. Construction	85 300	7.5	82 900	2 400	13 600	13 500	–	71 400	69 100	2 300
6. Wholesale/retail trade, restaurants & hotels	152 300	13.3	101 900	50 400	37 800	28 500	9 300	109 500	72 300	37 200
7. Transport, storage & communication	65 000	5.7	53 100	11 900	4 500	4 500	–	60 300	48 500	11 800
8. Financing, insur., real estate & business serv.	29 100	2.5	16 400	12 700	1 700	1 600	–	27 300	14 800	12 500
9. Community, social & personal services	234 700	20.5	105 500	129 200	15 100	10 800	4 300	218 400	94 300	124 100
0. Not adequately defined	3 200	0.3	1 800	1 400	300	300	–	2 900	1 500	1 300
–. Unemployed	100 600	8.8	79 800	20 800	...	...	...	...	...	...
–. Armed forces	16 100	1.4	16 100	.	.	.	.	16 100	16 100	.
Total	**1 143 900**	**100.0**	**834 800**	**309 100**	**244 200**	**220 400**	**23 500**	**762 000**	**510 700**	**251 400**
Italie (1979) LFSS †										
–. Agriculture, forestry, hunting & fishing	3 012 000	13.5	1 909 000	1 103 000	1 442 000	1 088 000	354 000	1 114 000	684 000	430 000
–. Mining & quarrying & manufacturing	5 413 000	24.3	3 729 000	1 684 000	566 000	438 000	128 000	4 754 000	3 251 000	1 503 000
–. Construction	2 021 000	9.0	1 966 000	16 000	392 000	389 000	3 000	1 607 000	1 561 000	46 000
–. Electricity, gas, water & sanitary services	212 000	1.0	196 000	16 000	17 000	16 000	1 000	195 000	180 000	15 000
–. Commerce	3 767 000	16.8	2 552 000	1 214 000	1 635 000	1 224 000	411 000	1 687 000	1 189 000	499 000
–. Transport, storage & communication	1 128 000	5.1	1 012 000	116 000	158 000	156 000	2 000	961 000	851 000	110 000
–. Services	5 063 000	22.7	2 839 000	2 224 000	492 000	362 000	129 000	4 530 000	2 460 000	2 070 000
–. Persons seeking work for the first time	866 000	3.9	413 000	453 000	.	.	.	.	.	.
–. Other unemployed	831 000	3.7	317 000	515 000	...	...	...	...	...	...
Total	**22 313 000**	**100.0**	**14 933 000**	**7 380 000**	**4 703 000**	**3 672 000**	**1 031 000**	**14 849 000**	**10 176 000**	**4 674 000**
Malta (XII.79) OE †										
1. Agriculture, hunting, forestry & fishing	7 271	5.9	6 483	788	6 397	5 764	633	874	719	155
2. Mining & quarrying	868	0.7	829	39	87	87	.	781	742	39
3. Manufacturing	39 454	32.2	24 276	15 178	2 384	2 204	180	37 070	22 072	14 998
4. Electr., gas & water	1 106	0.9	1 075	31	.	.	.	1 106	1 075	31
5. Construction	4 867	4.0	4 823	44	1 876	1 873	3	2 991	2 950	41
6. Wholesale/retail trade, restaurants & hotels	19 745	16.1	14 011	5 734	6 468	4 541	1 927	13 277	9 470	3 807
7. Transport, storage & communication	7 739	6.3	6 884	855	1 406	1 400	6	6 333	5 484	849
8. Financing, insur., real estate & business serv.	2 439	2.0	1 567	872	56	50	6	2 383	1 517	866
9. Community, social & personal services	7 847	6.4	4 015	3 832	1 378	863	515	6 469	3 152	3 317
0. Not adequately defined	27 926	22.8	23 504	4 422	.	.	.	27 926	23 504	4 422
–. Unemployed	3 294	2.7	2 994	300	...	...	...	...	...	...
Total	**122 556**	**100.0**	**90 461**	**32 095**	**20 052**	**16 782**	**3 270**	**99 210**	**70 685**	**28 525**

A By industry, by status and by sex
Par industrie, selon la situation dans la profession et par sexe
Por industria, según la categoría de ocupación y por sexo

Unpaid family workers / Travailleurs familiaux non rémunérés / Trabajadores familiares no remunerados			Not classifiable by status / Inclassables selon la situation / Inclasificables según la categoría			Industrie (Branches d'activité économique)	Industria (Grandes divisiones de actividad económica)
Total	Males Hommes Hombres	Females Femmes Mujeres	Total	Males Hommes Hombres	Females Femmes Mujeres		
30 100	22 000	8 200	...	...	...	1. Agriculture, chasse, sylviculture et pêche	1. Agricultura, caza, silvicultura y pesca
–	–	–	...	...	...	2. Industries extractives	2. Minas y canteras
–	–	–	...	...	...	3. Industries manufacturières	3. Industrias manufactureras
.	.	.	...	...	...	4. Electricité, gaz et eau	4. Electricidad, gas y agua
–	–	–	...	...	...	5. Construction	5. Construcción
4 800	1 000	3 800	...	...	...	6. Commerce (gros et détail); restaurants, hôtels	6. Comercio (por mayor y por menor); restaurantes, hoteles
–	–	–	...	...	...	7. Transports, entrepôts et communications	7. Transportes, almacenamiento y comunicaciones
						8. Banques, assur., affaires imm., services aux entreprises	8. Bancos, seguros, bienes inmuebles, serv. para empresas
1 000	–	800	...	...	...	9. Services à la collectivité, services sociaux et personnels	9. Servicios comunales, sociales y personales
.	.	.				0. Activités mal désignées	0. Actividades no bien especif.
...	...	...	100 600	79 800	20 800	–. Chômeurs	–. Desempleados
			...	...	...	–. Forces armées	–. Fuerzas armadas
35 900	**23 000**	**12 800**	**100 600**	**79 800**	**20 800**	**Total**	**Total**
456 000	137 000	319 000	...	...	...	–. Agriculture, sylviculture, chasse et pêche	–. Agricultura, silvicultura, caza y pesca
92 000	39 000	53 000	...	...	...	–. Industries extractives et industries manufacturières	–. Minas y canteras; industrias manufactureras
21 000	17 000	4 000	...	...	...	–. Construction	–. Construcción
1 000	1 000	–				–. Electricité, gaz, eau et services sanitaires	–. Electricidad, gas, agua y servicios sanitarios
444 000	140 000	304 000	...	...	...	–. Comm., banq., assur., aff. imm.	–. Comercio
9 000	6 000	3 000				–. Transports, entrepôts et communications	–. Transportes, almacenamiento y comunicaciones
40 000	16 000	24 000	...	...	...	–. Services	–. Servicios
.	.	.	866 000	413 000	453 000	–. Personnes en quête d'emploi pour la première fois	–. Personas en busca de trabajo por primera vez
...	...	...	831 000	317 000	515 000	–. Autres chômeurs	–. Otros desempleados
1 063 000	**355 000**	**708 000**	**1 698 000**	**730 000**	**968 000**	**Total**	**Total**
...	...	...	...	...	...	1. Agriculture, chasse, sylviculture et pêche	1. Agricultura, caza, silvicultura y pesca
...	...	...	...	...	...	2. Industries extractives	2. Minas y canteras
...	...	...	...	...	...	3. Industries manufacturières	3. Industrias manufactureras
...	...	...	...	...	...	4. Electricité, gaz et eau	4. Electricidad, gas y agua
...	...	...	...	...	...	5. Construction	5. Construcción
...	...	...	...	...	...	6. Commerce (gros et détail); restaurants, hôtels	6. Comercio (por mayor y por menor); restaurantes, hoteles
...	...	...	...	...	...	7. Transports, entrepôts et communications	7. Transportes, almacenamiento y comunicaciones
...	...	...	...	...	...	8. Banques, assur., affaires imm., services aux entreprises	8. Bancos, seguros, bienes inmuebles, serv. para empresas
...	...	...	...	...	...	9. Services à la collectivité, services sociaux et personnels	9. Servicios comunales, sociales y personales
...	...	...				0. Activités mal désignées	0. Actividades no bien especif.
...	...	...	3 294	2 994	300	–. Chômeurs	–. Desempleados
...	**...**	**...**	**3 294**	**2 994**	**300**	**Total**	**Total**

2 Structure of the economically active population
Structure de la population active
Estructura de la población económicamente activa

Industry (Major divisions of economic activity)	Total				Employers and own-account workers / Employeurs et personnes travaillant à leur propre compte / Empleadores y trabajadores por cuenta propia			Employees / Salariés / Empleados a sueldo o salario		
	Total	%	Males Hommes Hombres	Females Femmes Mujeres	Total	Males Hommes Hombres	Females Femmes Mujeres	Total	Males Hommes Hombres	Females Femmes Mujeres
Netherlands (III–V.77) LFSS †										
1. Agriculture, hunting, forestry & fishing	281 000	5.6	234 000	46 000	150 000	142 000	8 000	93 000	83 000	9 000
2. Mining & quarrying	9 000	0.1	8 000	1 000	–	–	–	9 000	8 000	1 000
3. Manufacturing	1 114 000	22.1	954 000	159 000	31 000	28 000	3 000	1 077 000	926 000	152 000
4. Electr., gas & water	45 000	0.8	43 000	3 000	–	–	–	45 000	43 000	3 000
5. Construction	500 000	9.9	477 000	23 000	40 000	39 000	1 000	455 000	437 000	18 000
6. Wholesale/retail trade, restaurants & hotels	767 000	15.2	473 000	294 000	148 000	119 000	29 000	575 000	352 000	222 000
7. Transport, storage & communication	310 000	6.1	275 000	36 000	12 000	12 000	–	296 000	262 000	33 000
8. Financing, insur., real estate & business serv.	345 000	6.8	231 000	114 000	26 000	23 000	3 000	316 000	208 000	108 000
9. Community, social & personal services	1 423 000	28.2	781 000	642 000	63 000	47 000	16 000	1 349 000	733 000	616 000
0. Not adequately defined	11 000	0.2	7 000	3 000	1 000	1 000	–	10 000	7 000	3 000
–. Unemployed	252 000	5.0	...	...	...	...	...	...	...	...
Total	**5 058 000**	100.0	**3 484 000**	**1 322 000**	**471 000**	**411 000**	**60 000**	**4 224 000**	**3 059 000**	**1 166 000**
Norway (1979) LFSS †										
1. Agriculture, hunting, forestry & fishing	160 000	8.4	111 000	49 000	79 000	70 000	9 000	37 000	31 000	6 000
2–4. Min./quarrying; manuf.; electr., gas & water	411 000	21.5	314 000	98 000	12 000	10 000	2 000	398 000	303 000	95 000
5. Construction	150 000	7.9	142 000	9 000	25 000	25 000	–	124 000	116 000	8 000
6. Wholesale/retail trade, restaurants & hotels	316 000	16.5	147 000	169 000	26 000	18 000	8 000	283 000	128 000	155 000
7. Transport, storage & communication	172 000	9.0	135 000	36 000	14 000	14 000	–	157 000	121 000	36 000
8. Financing, insur., real estate & business serv.	110 000	5.8	60 000	48 000	9 000	8 000	1 000	101 000	53 000	48 000
9. Community, social & personal services	547 000	28.6	197 000	350 000	27 000	14 000	13 000	518 000	183 000	335 000
0. Not adequately defined	4 000	0.3	3 000	1 000	...	...	...	2 000	2 000	–
–. Unemployed	38 000	1.9	18 000	19 000	...	...	...	...	...	...
Total	**1 909 000**	100.0	**1 128 000**	**781 000**	**191 000**	**158 000**	**33 000**	**1 619 000**	**937 000**	**682 000**
Pologne (7 XII.78) C †										
–. Agriculture, hunting, forestry & fishing (excl. sea fishing)	5 419 194	30.2	2 758 802	2 660 392	2 098 726	1 377 550	721 176	1 044 843	770 509	274 334
–. Coal mining	413 257	2.3	365 806	47 451	.	.	.	413 257	365 806	47 451
–. Other mining & quarrying, manufacturing, gas product. & sea fishing	4 826 707	26.8	2 813 794	2 012 913	115 158	94 373	20 785	4 695 990	2 713 059	1 982 931
–. Electricity & water	130 274	0.8	101 021	29 253	.	.	.	130 274	101 021	29 253
–. Construction	1 481 525	8.2	1 228 826	252 699	47 515	47 014	501	1 431 458	1 180 021	251 437
–. Wholesale/retail trade, restaurants	1 374 021	7.7	384 077	989 944	19 903	8 872	11 031	1 348 693	373 382	975 311
–. Transport, storage & communication	1 220 443	6.8	928 491	291 952	58 926	58 316	610	1 161 071	869 855	291 216
–. Financing, insur., real estate & services (incl. hotels)	3 096 705	17.2	1 225 428	1 871 277	23 894	14 011	9 883	3 070 672	1 210 842	1 859 830
Total	**17 962 126**	100.0	**9 806 245**	**8 155 881**	**2 364 122**	**1 600 136**	**763 986**	**13 296 258**	**7 584 495**	**5 711 763**

A By industry, by status and by sex
Par industrie, selon la situation dans la profession et par sexe
Por industria, según la categoría de ocupación y por sexo

Unpaid family workers / Travailleurs familiaux non rémunérés / Trabajadores familiares no remunerados			Not classifiable by status / Inclassables selon la situation / Inclasificables según la categoría			Industrie (Branches d'activité économique)	Industria (Grandes divisiones de actividad económica)
Total	Males / Hommes / Hombres	Females / Femmes / Mujeres	Total	Males / Hommes / Hombres	Females / Femmes / Mujeres		
38 000	9 000	29 000	...	...	...	1. Agriculture, chasse, sylviculture et pêche	1. Agricultura, caza, silvicultura y pesca
–	–	–	...	...	...	2. Industries extractives	2. Minas y canteras
7 000	1 000	6 000	...	...	...	3. Industries manufacturières	3. Industrias manufactureras
–	–	–	...	...	...	4. Electricité, gaz et eau	4. Electricidad, gas y agua
5 000	1 000	4 000	...	...	...	5. Construction	5. Construcción
45 000	3 000	42 000	...	...	...	6. Commerce (gros et détail); restaurants, hôtels	6. Comercio (por mayor y por menor); restaurantes, hoteles
2 000	–	2 000	...	...	...	7. Transports, entrepôts et communications	7. Transportes, almacenamiento y comunicaciones
3 000	–	3 000	...	...	...	8. Banques, assur., affaires imm., services aux entreprises	8. Bancos, seguros, bienes inmuebles, serv. para empresas
11 000	–	10 000	...	...	...	9. Services à la collectivité, services sociaux et personnels	9. Servicios comunales, sociales y personales
–	–	–	...	...	...	0. Activités mal désignées	0. Actividades no bien especif.
...	...	...	...	...	...	-. Chômeurs	-. Desempleados
111 000	**14 000**	**97 000**	**252 000**	...	...	**Total**	**Total**

Total	Males / Hommes / Hombres	Females / Femmes / Mujeres	Total	Males / Hommes / Hombres	Females / Femmes / Mujeres	Industrie	Industria
44 000	10 000	34 000	...	...	...	1. Agriculture, chasse, sylviculture et pêche	1. Agricultura, caza, silvicultura y pesca
1 000	–	1 000	...	...	...	2-4. Industries extract.; industries manuf.; électricité, gaz et eau	2-4. Minas y canteras; industrias manufact.; electr., gas y agua
–	–	–	...	...	...	5. Construction	5. Construcción
7 000	1 000	6 000	...	...	...	6. Commerce (gros et détail); restaurants, hôtels	6. Comercio (por mayor y por menor); restaurantes, hoteles
1 000	–	1 000	...	...	...	7. Transports, entrepôts et communications	7. Transportes, almacenamiento y comunicaciones
–	–	–	...	...	...	8. Banques, assur., affaires imm., services aux entreprises	8. Bancos, seguros, bienes inmuebles, serv. para empresas
2 000	–	2 000	...	...	...	9. Services à la collectivité, services sociaux et personnels	9. Servicios comunales, sociales y personales
2 000	1 000	1 000	...	...	...	0. Activités mal désignées	0. Actividades no bien especif.
...	...	...	38 000	18 000	19 000	-. Chômeurs	-. Desempleados
57 000	**12 000**	**45 000**	**38 000**	**18 000**	**19 000**	**Total**	**Total**

Total	Males / Hommes / Hombres	Females / Femmes / Mujeres	Total	Males / Hommes / Hombres	Females / Femmes / Mujeres	Industrie	Industria
2 154 316	516 854	1 637 462	121 309	93 889	27 420	-. Agriculture, chasse, sylviculture et pêche (non compris la pêche maritime)	-. Agricultura, caza, silvicultura y pesca (excl. la pesca marítima)
.	.	.	.	.	.	-. Mines de charbon	-. Minas de carbón
15 559	6 362	9 197	.	.	.	-. Autres industries extract., ind. manufacturières, production de gaz et pêche maritime	-. Otras minas y canteras, ind. manufactureras, prod. del gas y pesca marítima
2 552	1 791	761	.	.	.	-. Electricité et eau	-. Electricidad y agua
.	.	.	.	.	.	-. Construction	-. Construcción
5 425	1 823	3 602	.	.	.	-. Commerce (gros et détail), restaurants	-. Comercio (por mayor y por menor), restaurantes
446	320	126	.	.	.	-. Transports, entrepôts et communications	-. Transportes, almacenamiento y comunicaciones
2 139	575	1 564	.	.	.	-. Banques, assurances, affaires immobilières, services (y compris hôtels)	-. Bancos, seguros, bienes inmuebles y servicios (incl. hoteles)
2 180 437	**527 725**	**1 652 712**	**121 309**	**93 889**	**27 420**	**Total**	**Total**

2 Structure of the economically active population
Structure de la population active
Estructura de la población económicamente activa

Industry (Major divisions of economic activity)	Total				Employers and own-account workers Employeurs et personnes travaillant à leur propre compte Empleadores y trabajadores por cuenta propia			Employees Salariés Empleados a sueldo o salario		
	Total	%	Males Hommes Hombres	Females Femmes Mujeres	Total	Males Hommes Hombres	Females Femmes Mujeres	Total	Males Hommes Hombres	Females Femmes Mujeres
Portugal (VII–XII.79) LFSS †										
1. Agriculture, hunting, forestry & fishing	1 186 000	27.4	589 000	597 000	401 000	319 000	82 000	248 000	154 000	94 000
2. Mining & quarrying	21 000	0.5	20 000	1 000	1 000	1 000	–	20 000	19 000	1 000
3. Manufacturing	1 064 000	24.6	649 000	415 000	88 000	53 000	35 000	941 000	582 000	359 000
4. Electr., gas & water	13 000	0.3	13 000	.	.	.	.	13 000	13 000	.
5. Construction	342 000	7.9	335 000	7 000	24 000	24 000	–	311 000	306 000	5 000
6. Wholesale/retail trade, restaurants & hotels	489 000	11.3	294 000	195 000	148 000	104 000	44 000	273 000	171 000	102 000
7. Transport, storage & communication	164 000	3.8	137 000	27 000	11 000	11 000	–	150 000	123 000	27 000
8. Financing, insur., real estate & business serv.	78 000	1.8	52 000	26 000	6 000	6 000	–	70 000	44 000	26 000
9. Community, social & personal services	678 000	15.6	326 000	352 000	35 000	30 000	5 000	636 000	288 000	348 000
0. Not adequately defined	10 000	0.3	10 000	–	...	...	...	...	...	...
–. Persons seeking work for the first time	198 000	4.5	63 000	135 000	.	.	.	.	.	.
–. Armed forces	77 000	1.8	77 000	.	.	.	.	77 000	77 000	.
Total	4 328 000	100.0	2 566 000	1 762 000	725 000	557 000	168 000	2 743 000	1 777 000	966 000
Suisse (1979) OE *										
1. Agriculture, hunting, forestry & fishing	220 400	7.4	...	...	...	...	...	...	...	...
2. Mining & quarrying	5 300	0.2	...	...	...	...	...	...	...	...
3. Manufacturing	955 700	32.1	...	...	...	...	...	...	...	...
4. Electr., gas & water	28 800	1.0	...	...	...	...	...	...	...	...
5. Construction	182 900	6.2	...	...	...	...	...	...	...	...
6. Wholesale/retail trade, restaurants & hotels	578 000	19.4	...	...	...	...	...	...	...	...
7. Transport, storage & communication	179 100	6.0	...	...	...	...	...	...	...	...
8. Financing, insur., real estate & business serv.	236 000	8.0	...	...	...	...	...	...	...	...
9. Community, social & personal services	575 700	19.3	...	...	...	...	...	...	...	...
–. Unemployed	11 400	0.4	6 500	4 900	...	...	...	...	...	...
Total	2 973 300	100.0	1 938 300	1 035 000	...	...	...	...	...	...
Sweden (1979) LFSS †										
1. Agriculture, hunting, forestry & fishing	242 000	5.7	181 000	61 100	134 500	104 900	29 700	87 100	72 200	14 900
2. Mining & quarrying	15 200	0.3	13 600	1 600	300	300	–	14 900	13 300	1 600
3. Manufacturing	1 026 400	24.1	749 900	276 400	20 800	16 100	4 700	1 005 100	733 900	271 200
4. Electr., gas & water	34 300	0.8	29 600	4 800	–	–	–	34 300	29 600	4 800
5. Construction	284 000	6.6	258 500	25 500	30 200	28 700	1 600	253 300	229 700	23 500
6. Wholesale/retail trade, restaurants & hotels	576 400	13.5	280 200	296 200	47 700	28 900	18 800	527 200	250 900	276 300
7. Transport, storage & communication	289 900	6.8	210 800	79 100	23 900	21 600	2 300	265 100	189 100	76 000
8. Financing, insur., real estate & business serv.	266 900	6.3	149 200	117 600	13 100	11 000	2 100	253 400	138 200	115 200
9. Community, social & personal services	1 444 400	33.8	441 900	1 002 500	41 600	25 500	16 200	1 402 300	416 400	985 900
–. Unemployed	88 000	2.1	44 000	44 000	...	...	...	...	...	...
Total	4 267 600	100.0	2 359 000	1 908 600	312 300	237 000	75 400	3 842 800	2 073 300	1 769 500

A — By industry, by status and by sex
Par industrie, selon la situation dans la profession et par sexe
Por industria, según la categoría de ocupación y por sexo

Unpaid family workers / Travailleurs familiaux non rémunérés / Trabajadores familiares no remunerados			Not classifiable by status / Inclassables selon la situation / Inclasificables según la categoría			Industrie (Branches d'activité économique)	Industria (Grandes divisiones de actividad económica)
Total	Males Hommes Hombres	Females Femmes Mujeres	Total	Males Hommes Hombres	Females Femmes Mujeres		
519 000	104 000	415 000	14 000	7 000	7 000	1. Agriculture, chasse, sylviculture et pêche	1. Agricultura, caza, silvicultura y pesca
–	–	–	–	–	–	2. Industries extractives	2. Minas y canteras
18 000	8 000	10 000	13 000	3 000	10 000	3. Industries manufacturières	3. Industrias manufactureras
1 000	1 000	.	.	.	.	4. Electricité, gaz et eau	4. Electricidad, gas y agua
1 000	1 000	–	3 000	3 000	–	5. Construction	5. Construcción
56 000	10 000	46 000	8 000	6 000	2 000	6. Commerce (gros et détail); restaurants, hôtels	6. Comercio (por mayor y por menor); restaurantes, hoteles
1 000	–	1 000	–	–	–	7. Transports, entrepôts et communications	7. Transportes, almacenamiento y comunicaciones
–	–	–	–	–	–	8. Banques, assur., affaires imm., services aux entreprises	8. Bancos, seguros, bienes inmuebles, serv. para empresas
6 000	4 000	2 000	1 000	1 000	–	9. Services à la collectivité, services sociaux et personnels	9. Servicios comunales, sociales y personales
...	...	.	10 000	10 000	–	0. Activités mal désignées	0. Actividades no bien especif.
.	.	.	198 000	63 000	135 000	–. Personnes en quête d'emploi pour la première fois	–. Personas en busca de trabajo por primera vez
.	.	.	.	.	.	–. Forces armées	–. Fuerzas armadas
606 000	**131 000**	**475 000**	**246 000**	**93 000**	**153 000**	**Total**	**Total**
...	...	...	...	...	...	1. Agriculture, chasse, sylviculture et pêche	1. Agricultura, caza, silvicultura y pesca
...	...	...	...	...	...	2. Industries extractives	2. Minas y canteras
...	...	...	...	...	...	3. Industries manufacturières	3. Industrias manufactureras
...	...	...	...	...	...	4. Electricité, gaz et eau	4. Electricidad, gas y agua
...	...	...	...	...	...	5. Construction	5. Construcción
...	...	...	...	...	...	6. Commerce (gros et détail); restaurants, hôtels	6. Comercio (por mayor y por menor); restaurantes, hoteles
...	...	...	...	...	...	7. Transports, entrepôts et communications	7. Transportes, almacenamiento y comunicaciones
...	...	...	...	...	...	8. Banques, assur., affaires imm., services aux entreprises	8. Bancos, seguros, bienes inmuebles, serv. para empresas
...	...	...	...	...	...	9. Services à la collectivité, services sociaux et personnels	9. Servicios comunales, sociales y personales
...	...	...	11 400	6 500	4 900	–. Chômeurs	–. Desempleados
...	...	...	**11 400**	**6 500**	**4 900**	**Total**	**Total**
20 500	3 900	16 500	...	...	...	1. Agriculture, chasse, sylviculture et pêche	1. Agricultura, caza, silvicultura y pesca
–	–	–	...	...	...	2. Industries extractives	2. Minas y canteras
500	–	500	...	...	...	3. Industries manufacturières	3. Industrias manufactureras
–	–	–	...	...	...	4. Electricité, gaz et eau	4. Electricidad, gas y agua
500	100	400	...	...	...	5. Construction	5. Construcción
1 500	400	1 200	...	...	...	6. Commerce (gros et détail); restaurants, hôtels	6. Comercio (por mayor y por menor); restaurantes, hoteles
800	100	800	...	...	...	7. Transports, entrepôts et communications	7. Transportes, almacenamiento y comunicaciones
300	–	300	...	...	...	8. Banques, assur., affaires imm., services aux entreprises	8. Bancos, seguros, bienes inmuebles, serv. para empresas
500	100	400	...	...	...	9. Services à la collectivité, services sociaux et personnels	9. Servicios comunales, sociales y personales
...	...	...	88 000	44 000	44 000	–. Chômeurs	–. Desempleados
24 600	**4 500**	**20 100**	**88 000**	**44 000**	**44 000**	**Total**	**Total**

2 Structure of the economically active population
Structure de la population active
Estructura de la población económicamente activa

Industry (Major divisions of economic activity)	Total				Employers and own-account workers / Employeurs et personnes travaillant à leur propre compte / Empleadores y trabajadores por cuenta propia			Employees / Salariés / Empleados a sueldo o salario		
	Total	%	Males Hommes Hombres	Females Femmes Mujeres	Total	Males Hommes Hombres	Females Femmes Mujeres	Total	Males Hommes Hombres	Females Femmes Mujeres
United Kingdom (VI.77) OE †										
1. Agriculture, hunting, forestry & fishing	656 000	2.5	531 000	125 000	...	...	...	...	...	...
2. Mining & quarrying	351 000	1.3	336 000	15 000	...	...	...	...	...	...
3. Manufacturing	7 413 000	28.2	5 243 000	2 170 000	...	...	...	...	...	...
4. Electr., gas & water	347 000	1.4	282 000	65 000	...	...	...	...	...	...
5. Construction	1 656 000	6.3	1 549 000	107 000	...	...	...	...	...	...
6. Wholesale/retail trade, restaurants & hotels	4 180 000	15.9	1 895 000	2 285 000	...	...	...	...	...	...
7. Transport, storage & communication	1 546 000	5.8	1 283 000	263 000	...	...	...	...	...	...
8. Financing, insur., real estate & business serv.	1 444 000	5.5	715 000	729 000	...	...	...	...	...	...
9. Community, social & personal services	6 912 000	26.3	3 044 000	3 868 000	...	...	...	...	...	...
–. Unemployed	1 450 000	5.6	1 051 000	399 000	...	...	...	...	...	...
–. Armed forces	327 000	1.2	313 000	14 000	...	...	...	...	...	...
Total	**26 282 000**	100.0	**16 242 000**	**10 040 000**	**1 886 000**	**1 514 000**	**372 000**	**22 946 000**	**13 677 000**	**9 269 000**
OCEANIA										
Australia (30.VI.76) CS †										
1. Agriculture, hunting, forestry & fishing	404 579	6.7	274 669	129 910	...	...	...	...	...	...
2. Mining & quarrying	72 688	1.2	67 373	5 315	...	...	...	...	...	...
3. Manufacturing	1 138 531	18.8	847 764	290 767	...	...	...	...	...	...
4. Electr., gas & water	103 009	1.7	95 102	7 907	...	...	...	...	...	...
5. Construction	429 682	7.1	391 244	38 438	...	...	...	...	...	...
6. Wholesale/retail trade, restaurants & hotels	1 044 471	17.2	622 564	421 907	...	...	...	...	...	...
7. Transport, storage & communication	399 749	6.6	331 349	68 400	...	...	...	...	...	...
8. Financing, insur., real estate & business serv.	417 861	6.9	230 937	186 925	...	...	...	...	...	...
9. Community, social & personal services	1 386 087	22.9	651 700	734 386	...	...	...	...	...	...
0. Not adequately defined	391 513	6.5	204 913	186 600	...	...	...	...	...	...
–. Unemployed	266 826	4.4	157 708	109 118	...	...	...	...	...	...
Total	**6 054 996**	100.0	**3 875 323**	**2 179 673**	**801 956**	**561 276**	**240 680**	**4 901 416**	**3 139 222**	**1 762 194**
" " " " (VIII.78) LFSS †										
1. Agriculture, hunting, forestry & fishing	377 000	5.9	296 000	81 000	...	...	...	...	...	...
2. Mining & quarrying	80 000	1.2	74 000	5 000	...	...	...	...	...	...
3. Manufacturing	1 194 000	18.6	883 000	311 000	...	...	...	...	...	...
4. Electr., gas & water	106 000	1.6	97 000	9 000	...	...	...	...	...	...
5. Construction	485 000	7.5	441 000	44 000	...	...	...	...	...	...
6. Wholesale/retail trade, restaurants & hotels	1 239 000	19.3	729 000	510 000						
7. Transport, storage & communication	456 000	7.1	379 000	77 000	...	...	...	...	...	...
8. Financing, insur., real estate & business serv.	466 000	7.2	247 000	219 000	...	...	...	...	...	...
9. Community, social & personal services	1 567 000	24.4	686 000	881 000	...	...	...	...	...	...
–. Unemployed	396 000	6.1	222 000	174 000	...	...	...	...	...	...
–. Armed forces	70 000	1.1	66 000	4 000	.	.	.	70 000	66 000	4 000
Total	**6 435 000**	100.0	**4 120 000**	**2 315 000**	**921 000**	**666 000**	**255 000**	**5 093 000**	**3 222 000**	**1 871 000**

A By industry, by status and by sex
Par industrie, selon la situation dans la profession et par sexe
Por industria, según la categoría de ocupación y por sexo

Unpaid family workers / Travailleurs familiaux non rémunérés / Trabajadores familiares no remunerados			Not classifiable by status / Inclassables selon la situation / Inclasificables según la categoría			Industrie (Branches d'activité économique)	Industria (Grandes divisiones de actividad económica)
Total	Males Hommes Hombres	Females Femmes Mujeres	Total	Males Hommes Hombres	Females Femmes Mujeres		
...	...	...	...	...	...	1. Agriculture, chasse, sylviculture et pêche	1. Agricultura, caza, silvicultura y pesca
...	...	...	...	...	...	2. Industries extractives	2. Minas y canteras
...	...	...	...	...	...	3. Industries manufacturières	3. Industrias manufactureras
...	...	...	...	...	...	4. Electricité, gaz et eau	4. Electricidad, gas y agua
...	...	...	...	...	...	5. Construction	5. Construcción
...	...	...	...	...	...	6. Commerce (gros et détail); restaurants, hôtels	6. Comercio (por mayor y por menor); restaurantes, hoteles
...	...	...	...	...	...	7. Transports, entrepôts et communications	7. Transportes, almacenamiento y comunicaciones
...	...	...	...	...	...	8. Banques, assur., affaires imm., services aux entreprises	8. Bancos, seguros, bienes inmuebles, serv. para empresas
...	...	...	1 450 000	1 051 000	399 000	9. Services à la collectivité, services sociaux et personnels	9. Servicios comunales, sociales y personales
...	...	...	...	...	...	–. Chômeurs	–. Desempleados
						–. Forces armées	–. Fuerzas armadas
...	...	...	1 450 000	1 051 000	399 000	**Total**	**Total**

OCEANIE – OCEANIA

Total	Males Hommes Hombres	Females Femmes Mujeres	Total	Males Hommes Hombres	Females Femmes Mujeres	Industrie	Industria
...	...	...	...	...	...	1. Agriculture, chasse, sylviculture et pêche	1. Agricultura, caza, silvicultura y pesca
...	...	...	...	...	...	2. Industries extractives	2. Minas y canteras
...	...	...	...	...	...	3. Industries manufacturières	3. Industrias manufactureras
...	...	...	...	...	...	4. Electricité, gaz et eau	4. Electricidad, gas y agua
...	...	...	...	...	...	5. Construction	5. Construcción
...	...	...	...	...	...	6. Commerce (gros et détail); restaurants, hôtels	6. Comercio (por mayor y por menor); restaurantes, hoteles
...	...	...	...	...	...	7. Transports, entrepôts et communications	7. Transportes, almacenamiento y comunicaciones
...	...	...	...	...	...	8. Banques, assur., affaires imm., services aux entreprises	8. Bancos, seguros, bienes inmuebles, serv. para empresas
...	...	...	...	...	...	9. Services à la collectivité, services sociaux et personnels	9. Servicios comunales, sociales y personales
...	...	...	...	...	...	0. Activités mal désignées	0. Actividades no bien especif.
...	...	...	...	...	...	–. Chômeurs	–. Desempleados
84 784	**17 109**	**67 675**	**266 826**	**157 708**	**109 118**	**Total**	**Total**

Total	Males Hommes Hombres	Females Femmes Mujeres	Total	Males Hommes Hombres	Females Femmes Mujeres	Industrie	Industria
...	...	...	...	...	...	1. Agriculture, chasse, sylviculture et pêche	1. Agricultura, caza, silvicultura y pesca
...	...	...	...	...	...	2. Industries extractives	2. Minas y canteras
...	...	...	...	...	...	3. Industries manufacturières	3. Industrias manufactureras
...	...	...	...	...	...	4. Electricité, gaz et eau	4. Electricidad, gas y agua
...	...	...	...	...	...	5. Construction	5. Construcción
...	...	...	...	...	...	6. Commerce (gros et détail); restaurants, hôtels	6. Comercio (por mayor y por menor); restaurantes, hoteles
...	...	...	...	...	...	7. Transports, entrepôts et communications	7. Transportes, almacenamiento y comunicaciones
...	...	...	...	...	...	8. Banques, assur., affaires imm., services aux entreprises	8. Bancos, seguros, bienes inmuebles, serv. para empresas
...	...	...	...	...	...	9. Services à la collectivité, services sociaux et personnels	9. Servicios comunales, sociales y personales
...	...	...	396 000	222 000	174 000	–. Chômeurs	–. Desempleados
.	.	.	.	.	.	–. Forces armées	–. Fuerzas armadas
26 000	**11 000**	**15 000**	**396 000**	**222 000**	**174 000**	**Total**	**Total**

2 Structure of the economically active population
Structure de la population active
Estructura de la población económicamente activa

Industry (Major divisions of economic activity)	Total				Employers and own-account workers Employeurs et personnes travaillant à leur propre compte Empleadores y trabajadores por cuenta propia			Employees Salariés Empleados a sueldo o salario		
	Total	%	Males Hommes Hombres	Females Femmes Mujeres	Total	Males Hommes Hombres	Females Femmes Mujeres	Total	Males Hommes Hombres	Females Femmes Mujeres
Cook Islands (1.XII.76) C										
1. Agriculture, hunting, forestry & fishing	1 175	21.8	1 153	22	727	721	6	289	284	5
2. Mining & quarrying	11	0.2	11	.	.	.	.	11	11	.
3. Manufacturing	520	9.7	206	314	52	10	42	465	193	272
4. Electr., gas & water	81	1.5	76	5	2	2	.	79	74	5
5. Construction	275	5.1	266	9	21	21	.	250	241	9
6. Wholesale/retail trade, restaurants & hotels	495	9.2	230	265	80	49	31	409	179	230
7. Transport, storage & communication	437	8.1	393	44	12	9	3	425	384	41
8. Financing, insur., real estate & business serv.	39	0.7	21	18	3	3	.	36	18	18
9. Community, social & personal services	1 765	32.8	1 165	600	23	18	5	1 739	1 144	595
0. Not adequately defined	586	10.9	329	257	12	9	3	13	12	1
Total	**5 384**	100.0	**3 850**	**1 534**	**932**	**842**	**90**	**3 716**	**2 540**	**1 176**
Guam (XII.79) LFSS †										
1. Agriculture, hunting, forestry & fishing	100	0.3	...	...	...	...	...	...	...	...
2/3. Mining & quarrying, manufacturing	1 200	3.4	...	...	...	...	...	...	...	...
4,7. Electr., gas & water; transport, storage & communication	2 700	7.5	...	...	...	...	...	...	...	...
5. Construction	2 900	8.2	...	...	...	...	...	...	...	...
6. Wholesale/retail trade, restaurants & hotels	7 000	19.7	...	...	...	...	...	...	...	...
8. Financing, insur., real estate & business serv.	1 200	3.4	...	...	...	...	...	...	...	...
9. Community, social & personal services	18 200	51.1	...	...	...	...	...	...	...	...
–. Unemployed	2 260	6.4	930	1 330	...	...	...	...	...	...
Total	**35 560**	100.0	...	...	...	...	...	...	...	...
New Zealand (23.III.76) C †										
1. Agriculture, hunting, forestry & fishing	128 900	10.1	105 697	23 203	68 851	59 578	9 273	56 736	44 797	11 939
2. Mining & quarrying	5 059	0.4	4 839	220	180	176	4	4 828	4 612	216
3. Manufacturing	305 724	24.1	223 721	82 003	10 258	8 292	1 966	292 231	213 432	78 799
4. Electr., gas & water	15 329	1.2	13 768	1 561	25	25	.	15 253	13 704	1 549
5. Construction	112 137	8.8	107 295	4 842	28 131	27 854	277	82 556	78 153	4 403
6. Wholesale/retail trade, restaurants & hotels	216 122	17.0	123 259	92 863	31 352	20 640	10 712	181 342	101 440	79 902
7. Transport, storage & communication	111 287	8.7	87 764	23 523	5 967	5 580	387	104 541	81 670	22 871
8. Financing, insur., real estate & business serv.	79 792	6.3	44 888	34 904	10 939	10 196	743	68 227	34 460	33 767
9. Community, social & personal services	263 249	20.7	132 599	130 650	16 768	13 328	3 440	243 656	118 361	125 295
0. Not adequately defined	30 441	2.4	19 557	10 884	2 527	2 069	458	13 800	8 697	5 103
–. Persons seeking work for the first time	4 293	0.3	1 711	2 582	.	.	.	.	.	.
Total	**1 272 333**	100.0	**865 098**	**407 235**	**174 998**	**147 738**	**27 260**	**1 063 170**	**699 326**	**363 844**

A By industry, by status and by sex
Par industrie, selon la situation dans la profession et par sexe
Por industria, según la categoría de ocupación y por sexo

Unpaid family workers / Travailleurs familiaux non rémunérés / Trabajadores familiares no remunerados			Not classifiable by status / Inclassables selon la situation / Inclasificables según la categoría			Industrie (Branches d'activité économique)	Industria (Grandes divisiones de actividad económica)
Total	Males Hommes Hombres	Females Femmes Mujeres	Total	Males Hommes Hombres	Females Femmes Mujeres		
159	148	11	...	...	...	1. Agriculture, chasse, sylviculture et pêche	1. Agricultura, caza, silvicultura y pesca
3	3	.	...	...	...	2. Industries extractives	2. Minas y canteras
			...	...	...	3. Industries manufacturières	3. Industrias manufactureras
4	4	.	...	...	...	4. Electricité, gaz et eau	4. Electricidad, gas y agua
			...	...	...	5. Construction	5. Construcción
6	2	4	...	...	...	6. Commerce (gros et détail); restaurants, hôtels	6. Comercio (por mayor y por menor); restaurantes, hoteles
			...	...	...	7. Transports, entrepôts et communications	7. Transportes, almacenamiento y comunicaciones
			...	...	...	8. Banques, assur., affaires imm., services aux entreprises	8. Bancos, seguros, bienes inmuebles, serv. para empresas
3	3	.				9. Services à la collectivité, services sociaux et personnels	9. Servicios comunales, sociales y personales
300	156	144	261	152	109	0. Activités mal désignées	0. Actividades no bien especif.
475	**316**	**159**	**261**	**152**	**109**	**Total**	**Total**
...	...	...	...	...	...	1. Agriculture, chasse, sylviculture et pêche	1. Agricultura, caza, silvicultura y pesca
...	...	...	...	...	...	2/3. Industries extractives et industries manufacturières	2/3. Minas y canteras, industrias manufactureras
...	...	...	...	...	...	4,7. Electricité, gaz et eau; transports, entrepôts et communications	4,7. Electricidad, gas y agua; transportes, almacenamiento y comunicaciones
...	...	...	...	...	...	5. Construction	5. Construcción
...	...	...	...	...	...	6. Commerce (gros et détail); restaurants, hôtels	6. Comercio (por mayor y por menor); restaurantes, hoteles
...	...	...	...	...	...	8. Banques, assur., affaires imm., services aux entreprises	8. Bancos, seguros, bienes inmuebles, serv. para empresas
...	...	...	...	...	...	9. Services à la collectivité, services sociaux et personnels	9. Servicios comunales, sociales y personales
...	...	...	2 260	930	1 330	-. Chômeurs	-. Desempleados
...	...	...	**2 260**	**930**	**1 330**	**Total**	**Total**
2 208	484	1 724	1 105	838	267	1. Agriculture, chasse, sylviculture et pêche	1. Agricultura, caza, silvicultura y pesca
.	.	.	51	51	.	2. Industries extractives	2. Minas y canteras
130	14	116	3 105	1 983	1 122	3. Industries manufacturières	3. Industrias manufactureras
2	.	2	49	39	10	4. Electricité, gaz et eau	4. Electricidad, gas y agua
129	13	116	1 321	1 275	46	5. Construction	5. Construcción
1 021	105	916	2 407	1 074	1 333	6. Commerce (gros et détail); restaurants, hôtels	6. Comercio (por mayor y por menor); restaurantes, hoteles
54	2	52	725	512	213	7. Transports, entrepôts et communications	7. Transportes, almacenamiento y comunicaciones
36	2	34	590	230	360	8. Banques, assur., affaires imm., services aux entreprises	8. Bancos, seguros, bienes inmuebles, serv. para empresas
213	20	193	2 612	890	1 722	9. Services à la collectivité, services sociaux et personnels	9. Servicios comunales, sociales y personales
82	30	52	14 032	8 761	5 271	0. Activités mal désignées	0. Actividades no bien especif.
.	.	.	4 293	1 711	2 582	-. Personnes en quête d'emploi pour la première fois	-. Personas en busca de trabajo por primera vez
3 875	**670**	**3 205**	**30 290**	**17 364**	**12 926**	**Total**	**Total**

2 Structure of the economically active population
Structure de la population active
Estructura de la población económicamente activa

Industry (Major divisions of economic activity)	Total				Employers and own-account workers Employeurs et personnes travaillant à leur propre compte Empleadores y trabajadores por cuenta propia			Employees Salariés Empleados a sueldo o salario		
	Total	%	Males Hommes Hombres	Females Femmes Mujeres	Total	Males Hommes Hombres	Females Femmes Mujeres	Total	Males Hommes Hombres	Females Femmes Mujeres
Samoa (3.XI.76) C										
1. Agriculture, hunting, forestry & fishing	23 373	61.1	21 782	1 591	729	653	76	2 082	1 630	452
2. Mining & quarrying	7	–	6	1	.	.	.	7	6	1
3. Manufacturing	712	1.9	514	198	23	16	7	689	498	191
4. Electr., gas & water	468	1.2	453	15	10	10	.	458	443	15
5. Construction	1 813	4.8	1 791	22	46	46	.	1 765	1 743	22
6. Wholesale/retail trade, restaurants & hotels	2 407	6.2	1 294	1 113	403	204	199	1 999	1 085	914
7. Transport, storage & communication	2 058	5.4	1 864	194	164	161	3	1 891	1 700	191
8. Financing, insur., real estate & business serv.	322	0.9	168	154	3	3	.	319	165	154
9. Community, social & personal services	6 893	18.0	3 835	3 058	73	63	10	6 812	3 766	3 046
0. Not adequately defined	151	0.4	131	20	.	.	.	13	10	3
–. Unemployed	45	0.1	29	16	1	1	.	34	23	11
Total	**38 249**	**100.0**	**31 867**	**6 382**	**1 452**	**1 157**	**295**	**16 069**	**11 069**	**5 000**

A By industry, by status and by sex
Par industrie, selon la situation dans la profession et par sexe
Por industria, según la categoría de ocupación y por sexo

Unpaid family workers / Travailleurs familiaux non rémunérés / Trabajadores familiares no remunerados			Not classifiable by status / Inclassables selon la situation / Inclasificables según la categoría			Industrie (Branches d'activité économique)	Industria (Grandes divisiones de actividad económica)
Total	Males Hommes Hombres	Females Femmes Mujeres	Total	Males Hommes Hombres	Females Femmes Mujeres		
20 559	19 497	1 062	3	2	1	1. Agriculture, chasse, sylviculture et pêche	1. Agricultura, caza, silvicultura y pesca
.	.	.	...	...	...	2. Industries extractives	2. Minas y canteras
			...	...	...	3. Industries manufacturières	3. Industrias manufactureras
2	2	.	...	...	...	4. Electricité, gaz et eau	4. Electricidad, gas y agua
						5. Construction	5. Construcción
5	5		...	...	...	6. Commerce (gros et détail); restaurants, hôtels	6. Comercio (por mayor y por menor); restaurantes, hoteles
3	3	.	...	...	...	7. Transports, entrepôts et communications	7. Transportes, almacenamiento y comunicaciones
.	.	.	...	...	...	8. Banques, assur., affaires imm., services aux entreprises	8. Bancos, seguros, bienes inmuebles, serv. para empresas
8	6	2	...	...	...	9. Services à la collectivité, services sociaux et personnels	9. Servicios comunales, sociales y personales
121	115	6	17	6	11	0. Activités mal désignées	0. Actividades no bien especif.
5	4	1	5	1	4	-. Chômeurs	-. Desempleados
20 703	**19 632**	**1 071**	**25**	**9**	**16**	**Total**	**Total**

2 Structure of the economically active population
Structure de la population active
Estructura de la población económicamente activa

Occupation (Major groups)	Total				Employers and own-account workers / Employeurs et personnes travaillant à leur propre compte / Empleadores y trabajadores por cuenta propia			Employees / Salariés / Empleados a sueldo o salario		
	Total	%	Males Hommes Hombres	Females Femmes Mujeres	Total	Males Hommes Hombres	Females Femmes Mujeres	Total	Males Hommes Hombres	Females Femmes Mujeres

AFRICA

Rép.-Unie du Cameroun (9–24.IV.76) C †

0/1. Professional, technical & related workers	66 973	2.4	55 070	11 903	...	...	...	...	...	...
2. Administrative & managerial workers	2 699	0.1	2 535	164	...	...	...	...	...	...
3. Clerical & related workers	52 060	1.9	43 356	8 704	...	...	...	...	...	...
4. Sales workers	88 649	3.2	62 016	26 633	...	...	...	...	...	...
5. Service workers	54 755	2.0	44 313	10 442	...	...	...	...	...	...
6. Agric., animal husbandry & forestry workers, fishermen & hunters	2 032 136	73.7	1 070 183	961 953	...	...	...	...	...	...
7–9. Prod./related workers, transport equipment operators & labourers	311 035	11.3	275 255	35 780	...	...	...	...	...	...
X. Workers not classifiable by occupation	26 547	0.9	15 389	11 158	...	...	...	...	...	...
–. Persons seeking work for the first time	123 045	4.5	88 050	34 995	.	.	.	.	.	.
Total	**2 757 899**	*100.0*	**1 656 167**	**1 101 732**	**1 657 632**	**1 011 540**	**646 092**	**392 523**	**353 775**	**38 748**

Egypt (22–23.XI.76) C †

0/1. Professional, technical & related workers	719 307	7.5	538 901	180 406	16 160	15 439	721	699 130	519 949	179 181
2. Administrative & managerial workers	107 541	1.1	95 563	11 978	7 832	7 748	84	99 066	87 216	11 850
3. Clerical & related workers	700 950	7.3	565 886	135 064	.	.	.	698 701	564 071	134 630
4. Sales workers	628 368	6.5	595 392	32 976	452 668	431 700	20 968	173 192	161 302	11 890
5. Service workers	814 545	8.5	751 232	63 313	95 826	94 104	1 722	716 280	654 931	61 349
6. Agric., animal husbandry & forestry workers, fishermen & hunters	4 033 281	42.0	3 952 451	80 830	1 844 867	1 823 568	21 299	2 179 253	2 119 874	59 379
7–9. Prod./related workers, transport equipment operators & labourers	2 052 506	21.3	1 994 505	58 001	407 918	395 955	11 963	1 583 075	1 537 557	45 518
–. Not classif. by occup. & persons seeking work for the first time	557 271	5.8	421 599	135 672	23 384	17 969	5 415	123 257	101 719	21 538
Total	**9 613 769**	*100.0*	**8 915 529**	**698 240**	**2 848 655**	**2 786 483**	**62 172**	**6 271 954**	**5 746 619**	**525 335**

" " " " (V.78) LFSS †

0/1. Professional, technical & related workers	945 700	9.6	697 400	248 300	...	...	...	...	...	...
2. Administrative & managerial workers	158 400	1.7	141 500	16 900	...	...	...	...	...	...
3. Clerical & related workers	714 200	7.2	559 700	154 500	...	...	...	...	...	...
4. Sales workers	707 900	7.3	676 200	31 700	...	...	...	...	...	...
5. Service workers	801 600	8.1	736 600	65 000	...	...	...	...	...	...
6. Agric., animal husbandry & forestry workers, fishermen & hunters	3 878 900	39.6	3 791 200	87 700						
7–9. Prod./related workers, transport equipment operators & labourers	2 177 900	22.2	2 120 100	57 800	...	...	...	...	...	...
X. Workers not classifiable by occupation	417 900	4.3	221 300	196 600	...	...	...	...	...	...
Total	**9 802 500**	*100.0*	**8 944 000**	**858 500**	**3 060 400**	**2 862 500**	**197 900**	**4 946 900**	**4 447 900**	**499 000**

B
By occupational group, by status and by sex
Par groupe de professions, selon la situation dans la profession et par sexe
Por grupo de ocupación, según la categoría de ocupación y por sexo

AFRIQUE – AFRICA

Unpaid family workers / Travailleurs familiaux non rémunérés / Trabajadores familiares no remunerados			Not classifiable by status / Inclassables selon la situation / Inclasificables según la categoría			Profession (Grands groupes)	Ocupación (Grandes grupos)
Total	Males Hommes Hombres	Females Femmes Mujeres	Total	Males Hommes Hombres	Females Femmes Mujeres		
...	...		...	...	...	0/1. Personnel des prof. scientif., techn., libérales et assimilées	0/1. Profesionales, técnicos y trabajadores asimilados
...	...		...	...	...	2. Directeurs et cadres administratifs supérieurs	2. Directores y funcionarios públicos superiores
...	...	...	...	...	...	3. Personnel administratif et travailleurs assimilés	3. Personal administrativo y trabajadores asimilados
...	...	...	...	...	...	4. Pers. commercial et vendeurs	4. Comerciantes y vendedores
						5. Travailleurs des services	5. Trabajadores de los servicios
...	...		...	...	...	6. Agriculteurs, éleveurs, forestiers, pêcheurs et chasseurs	6. Trabajadores agrícolas y forestales, pescadores y cazadores
...	...		...	...	...	7–9. Ouvriers et manœuvres non agricoles et conducteurs d'engins de transport	7–9. Obreros no agrícolas, conductores de máquinas y vehíc. de transporte y trab. asimilados
...	...		...	...	...	X. Travailleurs ne pouvant être classés selon la profession	X. Trab. que no pueden ser clasificados según la ocupación
.	.	.	123 045	88 050	34 995	–. Personnes en quête d'emploi pour la première fois	–. Personas en busca de trabajo por primera vez
512 946	**152 781**	**360 165**	**194 798**	**138 071**	**56 727**	**Total**	**Total**
...	...	...	4 017	3 513	504	0/1. Personnel des prof. scientif., techn., libérales et assimilées	0/1. Profesionales, técnicos y trabajadores asimilados
...	...	...	643	599	44	2. Directeurs et cadres administratifs supérieurs	2. Directores y funcionarios públicos superiores
...	...	...	2 249	1 815	434	3. Personnel administratif et travailleurs assimilés	3. Personal administrativo y trabajadores asimilados
...	...	...	2 508	2 390	118	4. Pers. commercial et vendeurs	4. Comerciantes y vendedores
...	...	...	2 439	2 197	242	5. Travailleurs des services	5. Trabajadores de los servicios
...	...	...	9 161	9 009	152	6. Agriculteurs, éleveurs, forestiers, pêcheurs et chasseurs	6. Trabajadores agrícolas y forestales, pescadores y cazadores
...	...	...	61 513	60 993	520	7–9. Ouvriers et manœuvres non agricoles et conducteurs d'engins de transport	7–9. Obreros no agrícolas, conductores de máquinas y vehíc. de transporte y trab. asimilados
...	...	...	410 630	301 911	108 719	–. Inclassables selon la professio et personnes en quête d'emploi pour la première fois	–. Inclasificables según la ocupación y pers. en busca de trabajo por primera vez
...	...	...	**493 160**	**382 427**	**110 733**	**Total**	**Total**
...	...		...	...	...	0/1. Personnel des prof. scientif., techn., libérales et assimilées	0/1. Profesionales, técnicos y trabajadores asimilados
...	...		...	...	...	2. Directeurs et cadres administratifs supérieurs	2. Directores y funcionarios públicos superiores
...	...	...	...	...	...	3. Personnel administratif et travailleurs assimilés	3. Personal administrativo y trabajadores asimilados
...	...	...	...	...	...	4. Pers. commercial et vendeurs	4. Comerciantes y vendedores
						5. Travailleurs des services	5. Trabajadores de los servicios
...	...		...	...	...	6. Agriculteurs, éleveurs, forestiers, pêcheurs et chasseurs	6. Trabajadores agrícolas y forestales, pescadores y cazadores
...	...		...	...	...	7–9. Ouvriers et manœuvres non agricoles et conducteurs d'engins de transport	7–9. Obreros no agrícolas, conductores de máquinas y vehíc. de transporte y trab. asimilados
...	...		...	...	...	X. Travailleurs ne pouvant être classés selon la profession	X. Trab. que no pueden ser clasificados según la ocupación
1 440 700	**1 394 300**	**46 400**	**354 500**	**239 300**	**115 200**	**Total**	**Total**

2 Structure of the economically active population
Structure de la population active
Estructura de la población económicamente activa

Occupation (Major groups)	Total				Employers and own-account workers / Employeurs et personnes travaillant à leur propre compte / Empleadores y trabajadores por cuenta propia			Employees / Salariés / Empleados a sueldo o salario		
	Total	%	Males Hommes Hombres	Females Femmes Mujeres	Total	Males Hommes Hombres	Females Femmes Mujeres	Total	Males Hommes Hombres	Females Femmes Mujeres
Malawi (1.X.77) C †										
0/1. Professional, technical & related workers	30 454	1.3	22 630	7 824	2 296	1 606	690	27 684	20 695	6 989
2. Administrative & managerial workers	2 207	0.1	2 074	133	127	117	10	2 056	1 935	121
3. Clerical & related workers	30 134	1.3	26 116	4 018	263	221	42	29 171	25 357	3 814
4. Sales workers	53 792	2.4	43 133	10 659	37 058	29 849	7 209	13 662	11 704	1 958
5. Service workers	46 955	2.0	38 087	8 868	1 380	1 005	375	44 343	36 148	8 195
6. Agric., animal husbandry & forestry workers, fishermen & hunters	1 901 994	83.2	907 885	994 109	1 742 069	759 866	982 203	156 208	145 056	11 152
7-9. Prod./related workers, transport equipment operators & labourers	178 401	7.8	161 133	17 268	43 332	31 902	11 430	131 223	125 822	5 401
X. Workers not classifiable by occupation	44 414	1.9	30 754	13 660	1 444	889	555	2 173	1 639	534
Total	**2 288 351**	100.0	**1 231 812**	**1 056 539**	**1 827 969**	**825 455**	**1 002 514**	**406 520**	**368 356**	**38 164**
Seychelles (VIII.77) C †										
0/1. Professional, technical & related workers	1 790	6.9	745	1 045	138	...	...	1 616	...	...
2. Administrative & managerial workers	552	2.1	436	116	201	...	...	338	...	...
3. Clerical & related workers	1 062	4.1	381	681	18	...	...	997	...	...
4. Sales workers	1 227	4.7	753	474	459	...	...	700	...	...
5. Service workers	7 155	27.6	2 392	4 763	120	...	...	6 150	...	...
6. Agric., animal husbandry & forestry workers, fishermen & hunters	4 691	18.1	3 463	1 228	980	...	...	3 535	...	...
7-9. Prod./related workers, transport equipment operators & labourers	8 616	33.2	7 743	873	1 150	...	...	6 885	...	...
X. Workers not classifiable by occupation	90	0.4	53	37	11	...	...	41	...	...
–. Persons seeking work for the first time	764	2.9	396	368	.	.	.	.	.	.
Total	**25 947**	100.0	**16 362**	**9 585**	**3 077**	**2 378**	**699**	**20 262**	**12 717**	**7 545**
Tunisie (8.V.75) C										
0/1. Professional, technical & related workers	72 090	4.4	56 090	16 000	3 720	3 400	320	67 560	52 090	15 470
2. Administrative & managerial workers	4 700	0.3	4 470	230	400	380	20	4 240	4 040	200
3. Clerical & related workers	85 790	5.3	68 630	17 160	960	810	150	83 080	66 620	16 460
4. Sales workers	74 620	4.6	72 040	2 580	44 830	44 190	640	26 590	24 940	1 650
5. Service workers	93 940	5.8	67 230	26 710	6 190	5 340	850	85 230	60 730	24 500
6. Agric., animal husbandry & forestry workers, fishermen & hunters	525 700	32.4	456 420	69 280	230 550	219 610	10 940	197 240	185 170	12 070
7-9. Prod./related workers, transport equipment operators & labourers	545 980	33.7	415 650	130 330	118 180	50 030	68 150	381 260	341 160	40 100
X. Workers not classifiable by occupation	99 880	6.2	86 020	13 860	1 670	1 400	270	25 030	23 100	1 930
–. Persons seeking work for the first time	119 120	7.3	91 760	27 360	.	.	.	.	.	.
Total	**1 621 820**	100.0	**1 318 310**	**303 510**	**406 500**	**325 160**	**81 340**	**870 230**	**757 850**	**112 380**

B By occupational group, by status and by sex
Par groupe de professions, selon la situation dans la profession et par sexe
Por grupo de ocupación, según la categoría de ocupación y por sexo

Unpaid family workers Travailleurs familiaux non rémunérés Trabajadores familiares no remunerados			Not classifiable by status Inclassables selon la situation Inclasificables según la categoría			Profession (Grands groupes)	Ocupación (Grandes grupos)
Total	Males Hommes Hombres	Females Femmes Mujeres	Total	Males Hommes Hombres	Females Femmes Mujeres		
39	24	15	435	305	130	0/1. Personnel des prof. scientif., techn., libérales et assimilées	0/1. Profesionales, técnicos y trabajadores asimilados
6	6	.	18	16	2	2. Directeurs et cadres administratifs supérieurs	2. Directores y funcionarios públicos superiores
43	22	21	657	516	141	3. Personnel administratif et travailleurs assimilés	3. Personal administrativo y trabajadores asimilados
2 651	1 237	1 414	421	343	78	4. Pers. commercial et vendeurs	4. Comerciantes y vendedores
282	93	189	950	841	109	5. Travailleurs des services	5. Trabajadores de los servicios
1 120	916	204	2 597	2 047	550	6. Agriculteurs, éleveurs, forestiers, pêcheurs et chasseurs	6. Trabajadores agrícolas y forestales, pescadores y cazadores
810	469	341	3 036	2 940	96	7-9. Ouvriers et manœuvres non agricoles et conducteurs d'engins de transport	7-9. Obreros no agrícolas, conductores de máquinas y vehíc. de transporte y trab. asimilados
2 282	871	1 411	38 515	27 355	11 160	X. Travailleurs ne pouvant être classés selon la profession	X. Trab. que no pueden ser clasificados según la ocupación
7 233	**3 638**	**3 595**	**46 629**	**34 363**	**12 266**	**Total**	**Total**
.	.	.	36	4	32	0/1. Personnel des prof. scientif., techn., libérales et assimilées	0/1. Profesionales, técnicos y trabajadores asimilados
.	.	.	13	8	5	2. Directeurs et cadres administratifs supérieurs	2. Directores y funcionarios públicos superiores
.	.	.	47	20	27	3. Personnel administratif et travailleurs assimilés	3. Personal administrativo y trabajadores asimilados
.	.	.	68	33	35	4. Pers. commercial et vendeurs	4. Comerciantes y vendedores
.	.	.	885	150	735	5. Travailleurs des services	5. Trabajadores de los servicios
.	.	.	176	120	56	6. Agriculteurs, éleveurs, forestiers, pêcheurs et chasseurs	6. Trabajadores agrícolas y forestales, pescadores y cazadores
.	.	.	581	517	64	7-9. Ouvriers et manœuvres non agricoles et conducteurs d'engins de transport	7-9. Obreros no agrícolas, conductores de máquinas y vehíc. de transporte y trab. asimilados
.	.	.	38	19	19	X. Travailleurs ne pouvant être classés selon la profession	X. Trab. que no pueden ser clasificados según la ocupación
.	.	.	764	396	368	-. Personnes en quête d'emploi pour la première fois	-. Personas en busca de trabajo por primera vez
.	.	.	**2 608**	**1 267**	**1 341**	**Total**	**Total**
540	390	150	270	210	60	0/1. Personnel des prof. scientif., techn., libérales et assimilées	0/1. Profesionales, técnicos y trabajadores asimilados
30	20	10	30	30	.	2. Directeurs et cadres administratifs supérieurs	2. Directores y funcionarios públicos superiores
740	500	240	1 010	700	310	3. Personnel administratif et travailleurs assimilés	3. Personal administrativo y trabajadores asimilados
2 760	2 510	250	440	400	40	4. Pers. commercial et vendeurs	4. Comerciantes y vendedores
1 880	770	1 110	640	390	250	5. Travailleurs des services	5. Trabajadores de los servicios
72 740	31 660	41 080	25 170	19 980	5 190	6. Agriculteurs, éleveurs, forestiers, pêcheurs et chasseurs	6. Trabajadores agrícolas y forestales, pescadores y cazadores
31 390	13 150	18 240	15 150	11 310	3 840	7-9. Ouvriers et manœuvres non agricoles et conducteurs d'engins de transport	7-9. Obreros no agrícolas, conductores de máquinas y vehíc. de transporte y trab. asimilados
1 820	980	840	71 360	60 540	10 820	X. Travailleurs ne pouvant être classés selon la profession	X. Trab. que no pueden ser clasificados según la ocupación
.	.	.	119 120	91 760	27 360	-. Personnes en quête d'emploi pour la première fois	-. Personas en busca de trabajo por primera vez
111 900	**49 980**	**61 920**	**233 190**	**185 320**	**47 870**	**Total**	**Total**

2 Structure of the economically active population
Structure de la population active
Estructura de la población económicamente activa

Occupation (Major groups)	Total				Employers and own-account workers Employeurs et personnes travaillant à leur propre compte Empleadores y trabajadores por cuenta propia			Employees Salariés Empleados a sueldo o salario		
	Total	%	Males Hommes Hombres	Females Femmes Mujeres	Total	Males Hommes Hombres	Females Femmes Mujeres	Total	Males Hommes Hombres	Females Femmes Mujeres

AMERICA

Bolivia (29.IX.76) C †

Occupation	Total	%	Males	Females	Total	Males	Females	Total	Males	Females
–. Professional, technical & related workers	85 500	5.7	50 183	35 317	10 876	9 607	1 269	73 941	40 081	33 860
–. Administrative, executive & managerial workers	9 092	0.6	7 488	1 604	4 533	3 405	1 128	4 416	4 009	407
–. Clerical workers	59 609	4.0	41 020	18 589	1 153	928	225	58 143	39 902	18 241
–. Sales workers	91 385	6.1	41 248	50 137	79 722	33 885	45 837	10 090	6 831	3 259
–. Farmers, fishermen, hunters, loggers & related workers	697 140	46.4	607 950	89 190	481 414	440 334	41 080	87 905	84 791	3 114
–. Miners, quarrymen & related workers	370 535	24.7	310 073	60 462	142 262	97 783	44 479	217 424	207 355	10 069
–. Service, sport & recreation workers	128 595	8.5	57 153	71 442	9 831	3 671	6 160	114 707	50 061	64 646
–. Workers not classifiable by occupation	53 072	3.6	44 218	8 854	3 804	2 912	892	6 399	5 182	1 217
–. Persons seeking work for the first time	6 463	0.4	5 286	1 177	.	.	.	.	.	.
Total	**1 501 391**	*100.0*	**1 164 619**	**336 772**	**733 595**	**592 525**	**141 070**	**573 025**	**438 212**	**134 813**

Canada (IV.80) LFSS †

Occupation	Total	%	Males	Females	Total	Males	Females	Total	Males	Females
0/1. Professional, technical & related workers	1 597 000	14.1	797 000	797 000	100 000	71 000	30 000	1 494 000	727 000	767 000
2. Administrative & managerial workers	763 000	6.8	572 000	191 000	12 000	9 000	4 000	751 000	564 000	187 000
3. Clerical & related workers	1 839 000	16.3	404 000	1 436 000	35 000	4 000	32 000	1 804 000	400 000	1 404 000
4. Sales workers	1 102 000	9.7	675 000	427 000	155 000	95 000	61 000	946 000	580 000	366 000
5. Service workers	1 377 000	12.2	636 000	741 000	201 000	49 000	152 000	1 176 000	587 000	589 000
6. Agric., animal husbandry & forestry workers, fishermen & hunters	592 000	5.3	471 000	116 000	348 000	281 000	67 000	240 000	191 000	49 000
7–9. Prod./related workers, transport equipment operators & labourers	3 083 000	27.3	2 658 000	423 000	194 000	177 000	17 000	2 887 000	2 481 000	406 000
–. Persons seeking work for the first time	65 000	0.6	19 000	46 000	.	.	.	.	.	.
–. Other unemployed	872 000	7.7	525 000	347 000	32 000	19 000	13 000	841 000	507 000	334 000
Total	**11 291 000**	*100.0*	**6 759 000**	**4 532 000**	**1 083 000**	**707 000**	**376 000**	**10 143 000**	**6 033 000**	**4 110 000**

El Salvador (II–IX.78) HS

Occupation	Total	%	Males	Females	Total	Males	Females	Total	Males	Females
0/1. Professional, technical & related workers	66 031	4.6	39 833	26 198	6 512	5 227	1 285	59 220	34 374	24 846
2. Administrative & managerial workers	6 806	0.5	5 773	1 033	446	360	86	6 188	5 327	861
3. Clerical & related workers	75 516	5.3	44 254	31 262	172	.	172	74 813	43 927	30 886
4. Sales workers	203 860	14.2	61 013	142 847	150 908	38 966	111 942	33 225	18 020	15 205
5. Service workers	131 302	9.2	38 418	92 884	5 224	1 897	3 327	124 558	35 990	88 568
6. Agric., animal husbandry & forestry workers, fishermen & hunters	580 121	40.6	518 757	61 364	164 994	162 098	2 896	316 325	263 193	53 132
7–9. Prod./related workers, transport equipment operators & labourers	357 439	25.0	264 726	92 713	75 545	34 145	41 400	261 460	220 540	40 920
X. Workers not classifiable by occupation	855	–	667	188	102	.	102	667	667	.
–. Persons seeking work for the first time	8 432	0.6	4 164	4 268	.	.	.	.	.	.
Total	**1 430 362**	*100.0*	**977 605**	**452 757**	**403 903**	**242 693**	**161 210**	**876 456**	**622 038**	**254 418**

B By occupational group, by status and by sex
Par groupe de professions, selon la situation dans la profession et par sexe
Por grupo de ocupación, según la categoría de ocupación y por sexo

Unpaid family workers / Travailleurs familiaux non rémunérés / Trabajadores familiares no remunerados			Not classifiable by status / Inclassables selon la situation / Inclasificables según la categoría			Profession (Grands groupes)	Ocupación (Grandes grupos)
Total	Males Hommes Hombres	Females Femmes Mujeres	Total	Males Hommes Hombres	Females Femmes Mujeres		

AMERIQUE – AMERICA

Total	Males	Females	Total	Males	Females	Profession	Ocupación
204	107	97	479	388	91	–. Personnes exerçant une prof. libérale, techn. et assimilés	–. Trabajadores profesionales, técnicos y trab. asimilados
72	24	48	71	50	21	–. Directeurs et cadres adminis-tratifs supérieurs	–. Administradores, gerentes y directores
80	31	49	233	159	74	–. Employés de bureau	–. Empleados de oficina
1 290	377	913	283	155	128	–. Vendeurs	–. Vendedores
124 008	79 387	44 621	3 813	3 438	375	–. Agriculteurs, pêcheurs, chasseurs, forestiers et travailleurs assimilés	–. Agricultores, pescadores, cazadores, trab. forestales y asimilados
7 626	2 122	5 504	3 223	2 813	410	–. Mineurs, carriers, et travailleurs assimilés	–. Mineros, canteros y trabajadores asimilados
3 108	2 812	296	949	609	340	–. Trav. des services, sports et activités récréatives	–. Trab. de los servicios, los deportes y las diversiones
876	651	225	41 993	35 473	6 520	–. Travailleurs ne pouvant être classés selon la profession	–. Trab. que no pueden ser cla-sificados según la ocupación
.	.	.	6 463	5 286	1 177	–. Personnes en quête d'emploi pour la première fois	–. Personas en busca de trabajo por primera vez
137 264	**85 511**	**51 753**	**57 507**	**48 371**	**9 136**	**Total**	**Total**
...	...	...	.	.	.	0/1. Personnel des prof. scientif., techn., libérales et assimilées	0/1. Profesionales, técnicos y tra-bajadores asimilados
...	...	...	.	.	.	2. Directeurs et cadres adminis-tratifs supérieurs	2. Directores y funcionarios públicos superiores
						3. Personnel administratif et travailleurs assimilés	3. Personal administrativo y tra-bajadores asimilados
...	...	...	.	.	.	4. Pers. commercial et vendeurs	4. Comerciantes y vendedores
...	...	...	.	.	.	5. Travailleurs des services	5. Trabajadores de los servicios
						6. Agriculteurs, éleveurs, forestiers, pêcheurs et chasseurs	6. Trabajadores agrícolas y forestales, pescadores y cazadores
...	...	...	.	.	.	7-9. Ouvriers et manœuvres non agricoles et conducteurs d'engins de transport	7-9. Obreros no agrícolas, conduc-tores de máquinas y vehíc. de transporte y trab. asimilados
.	.	.	65 000	19 000	46 000	–. Personnes en quête d'emploi pour la première fois	–. Personas en busca de trabajo por primera vez
...	...	...	.	.	.	–. Autres chômeurs	–. Otros desempleados
...	...	...	**65 000**	**19 000**	**46 000**	**Total**	**Total**
299	232	67	.	.	.	0/1. Personnel des prof. scientif., techn., libérales et assimilées	0/1. Profesionales, técnicos y tra-bajadores asimilados
172	86	86	.	.	.	2. Directeurs et cadres adminis-tratifs supérieurs	2. Directores y funcionarios públicos superiores
531	327	204	.	.	.	3. Personnel administratif et travailleurs assimilés	3. Personal administrativo y tra-bajadores asimilados
19 727	4 027	15 700	.	.	.	4. Pers. commercial et vendeurs	4. Comerciantes y vendedores
1 520	531	989	.	.	.	5. Travailleurs des services	5. Trabajadores de los servicios
98 802	93 466	5 336	.	.	.	6. Agriculteurs, éleveurs, forestiers, pêcheurs et chasseurs	6. Trabajadores agrícolas y forestales, pescadores y cazadores
20 434	10 041	10 393	.	.	.	7-9. Ouvriers et manœuvres non agricoles et conducteurs d'engins de transport	7-9. Obreros no agrícolas, conduc-tores de máquinas y vehíc. de transporte y trab. asimilados
86	.	86	.	.	.	X. Travailleurs ne pouvant être classés selon la profession	X. Trab. que no pueden ser cla-sificados según la ocupación
.	.	.	8 432	4 164	4 268	–. Personnes en quête d'emploi pour la première fois	–. Personas en busca de trabajo por primera vez
141 571	**108 710**	**32 861**	**8 432**	**4 164**	**4 268**	**Total**	**Total**

2 Structure of the economically active population
Structure de la population active
Estructura de la población económicamente activa

Occupation (Major groups)	Total				Employers and own-account workers / Employeurs et personnes travaillant à leur propre compte / Empleadores y trabajadores por cuenta propia			Employees / Salariés / Empleados a sueldo o salario		
	Total	%	Males Hommes Hombres	Females Femmes Mujeres	Total	Males Hommes Hombres	Females Femmes Mujeres	Total	Males Hommes Hombres	Females Femmes Mujeres
Guatemala (1979) OE * †										
0/1. Professional, technical & related workers	77 966	3.6	46 500	31 466	9 200	7 519	1 681	68 131	38 558	29 573
2. Administrative & managerial workers	23 044	1.1	18 771	4 273	10 173	7 042	3 131	12 695	11 610	1 085
3. Clerical & related workers	57 111	2.7	37 762	19 349	1 120	882	238	55 548	36 643	18 905
4. Sales workers	132 488	6.2	86 350	46 138	94 367	61 964	32 403	31 924	20 174	11 750
5. Service workers	194 586	9.1	77 891	116 695	11 011	5 892	5 119	161 753	55 457	106 296
6. Agric., animal husbandry & forestry workers, fishermen & hunters	1 211 383	56.7	1 196 013	15 370	572 104	570 595	1 509	427 037	416 989	10 048
7–9. Prod./related workers, transport equipment operators & labourers	390 639	18.2	332 456	58 183	148 582	111 722	36 860	222 473	207 176	15 297
X. Workers not classifiable by occupation	50 425	2.4	46 915	3 510	2 774	2 598	176	46 339	43 019	3 320
Total	**2 137 642**	**100.0**	**1 842 658**	**294 984**	**849 331**	**768 214**	**81 117**	**1 025 900**	**829 626**	**196 274**
Haïti (31.VIII.71) C †										
0/1. Professional, technical & related workers	22 733	1.0	14 358	8 375	...	...	...	...	...	...
2. Administrative & managerial workers	253	–	235	18	...	...	...	...	...	...
3. Clerical & related workers	11 788	0.5	8 670	3 118	...	...	...	...	...	...
4. Sales workers	194 138	8.6	18 986	175 152	...	...	...	...	...	...
5. Service workers	119 264	5.2	35 754	83 510	...	...	...	...	...	...
6. Agric., animal husbandry & forestry workers, fishermen & hunters	1 430 984	63.0	881 681	549 303	...	...	...	...	...	...
7–9. Prod./related workers, transport equipment operators & labourers	163 421	7.2	93 443	69 978	...	...	...	...	...	...
X. Workers not classifiable by occupation	1 850	0.1	1 091	759	...	...	...	...	...	...
–. Unemployed	323 082	14.2	137 624	185 458	...	...	...	...	...	...
–. Armed forces	4 569	0.2	4 536	33	...	...	...	...	...	...
Total	**2 272 082**	**100.0**	**1 196 378**	**1 075 704**	...	...	...	...	...	...
Puerto Rico (IV.80) LFSS †										
0/1. Professional, technical & related workers	123 900	12.2	57 000	66 900	7 800	6 500	1 300	115 600	50 500	65 100
2. Administrative & managerial workers	91 900	9.1	75 600	16 300	44 900	39 200	5 700	46 700	36 400	10 300
3. Clerical & related workers	130 000	12.9	43 700	86 300	–	–	–	128 400	43 400	85 000
4. Sales workers	58 900	5.8	39 000	19 900	9 700	7 500	2 200	43 800	30 900	12 900
5. Service workers	135 200	13.3	68 400	66 800	6 200	2 200	4 100	127 900	66 200	61 700
6. Agric., animal husbandry & forestry workers, fishermen & hunters	61 300	6.1	59 900	1 400	21 800	21 600	–	37 700	36 500	1 200
7–9. Prod./related workers, transport equipment operators & labourers	394 700	39.0	312 900	81 900	43 600	42 000	1 600	349 600	269 700	79 900
X. Workers not classifiable by occupation	16 400	1.6	9 000	7 500	...	...	...	...	...	...
Total	**1 012 300**	**100.0**	**665 400**	**347 000**	**134 300**	**119 200**	**15 100**	**849 700**	**533 600**	**316 100**

B By occupational group, by status and by sex
Par groupe de professions, selon la situation dans la profession et par sexe
Por grupo de ocupación, según la categoría de ocupación y por sexo

Unpaid family workers / Travailleurs familiaux non rémunérés / Trabajadores familiares no remunerados			Not classifiable by status / Inclassables selon la situation / Inclasificables según la categoría			Profession (Grands groupes)	Ocupación (Grandes grupos)
Total	Males Hommes Hombres	Females Femmes Mujeres	Total	Males Hommes Hombres	Females Femmes Mujeres		
286	146	140	349	277	72	0/1. Personnel des prof. scientif., techn., libérales et assimilées	0/1. Profesionales, técnicos y trabajadores asimilados
119	65	54	57	54	3	2. Directeurs et cadres administratifs supérieurs	2. Directores y funcionarios públicos superiores
295	133	162	148	104	44	3. Personnel administratif et travailleurs assimilés	3. Personal administrativo y trabajadores asimilados
5 987	4 066	1 921	210	146	64	4. Pers. commercial et vendeurs	4. Comerciantes y vendedores
1 852	822	1 030	19 970	15 720	4 250	5. Travailleurs des services	5. Trabajadores de los servicios
211 267	207 472	3 795	975	957	18	6. Agriculteurs, éleveurs, forestiers, pêcheurs et chasseurs	6. Trabajadores agrícolas y forestales, pescadores y cazadores
18 139	12 261	5 878	1 445	1 297	148	7–9. Ouvriers et manœuvres non agricoles et conducteurs d'engins de transport	7–9. Obreros no agrícolas, conductores de máquinas y vehíc. de transporte y trab. asimilados
1 174	1 165	9	138	133	5	X. Travailleurs ne pouvant être classés selon la profession	X. Trab. que no pueden ser clasificados según la ocupación
239 119	**226 130**	**12 989**	**23 292**	**18 688**	**4 604**	**Total**	**Total**
...	...	...	...	...	...	0/1. Personnel des prof. scientif., techn., libérales et assimilées	0/1. Profesionales, técnicos y trabajadores asimilados
...	...	...	...	...	...	2. Directeurs et cadres administratifs supérieurs	2. Directores y funcionarios públicos superiores
...	...	...	...	...	...	3. Personnel administratif et travailleurs assimilés	3. Personal administrativo y trabajadores asimilados
...	...	...	...	...	...	4. Pers. commercial et vendeurs	4. Comerciantes y vendedores
...	...	...	...	...	...	5. Travailleurs des services	5. Trabajadores de los servicios
...	...	...	...	...	...	6. Agriculteurs, éleveurs, forestiers, pêcheurs et chasseurs	6. Trabajadores agrícolas y forestales, pescadores y cazadores
...	...	...	...	...	...	7–9. Ouvriers et manœuvres non agricoles et conducteurs d'engins de transport	7–9. Obreros no agrícolas, conductores de máquinas y vehíc. de transporte y trab. asimilados
...	...	...	...	...	...	X. Travailleurs ne pouvant être classés selon la profession	X. Trab. que no pueden ser clasificados según la ocupación
...	...	...	...	...	...	–. Chômeurs	–. Desempleados
...	...	...	...	...	...	–. Forces armées	–. Fuerzas armadas
...	...	...	...	...	...	**Total**	**Total**
–	–	–	...	...	...	0/1. Personnel des prof. scientif., techn., libérales et assimilées	0/1. Profesionales, técnicos y trabajadores asimilados
–	–	–	...	...	...	2. Directeurs et cadres administratifs supérieurs	2. Directores y funcionarios públicos superiores
1 300	–	1 200	...	...	...	3. Personnel administratif et travailleurs assimilés	3. Personal administrativo y trabajadores asimilados
5 400	600	4 800	...	...	...	4. Pers. commercial et vendeurs	4. Comerciantes y vendedores
1 000	–	1 000	...	...	...	5. Travailleurs des services	5. Trabajadores de los servicios
1 900	1 700	–	...	...	...	6. Agriculteurs, éleveurs, forestiers, pêcheurs et chasseurs	6. Trabajadores agrícolas y forestales, pescadores y cazadores
1 600	1 200	500	...	...	...	7–9. Ouvriers et manœuvres non agricoles et conducteurs d'engins de transport	7–9. Obreros no agrícolas, conductores de máquinas y vehíc. de transporte y trab. asimilados
...	...	...	16 400	9 000	7 500	X. Travailleurs ne pouvant être classés selon la profession	X. Trab. que no pueden ser clasificados según la ocupación
11 900	**3 600**	**8 300**	**16 400**	**9 000**	**7 500**	**Total**	**Total**

2 Structure of the economically active population
Structure de la population active
Estructura de la población económicamente activa

Occupation (Major groups)	Total				Employers and own-account workers / Employeurs et personnes travaillant à leur propre compte / Empleadores y trabajadores por cuenta propia			Employees / Salariés / Empleados a sueldo o salario		
	Total	%	Males Hommes Hombres	Females Femmes Mujeres	Total	Males Hommes Hombres	Females Femmes Mujeres	Total	Males Hommes Hombres	Females Femmes Mujeres
Saint-Pierre-et-Miquelon (II.74) C *										
0/1. Professional, technical & related workers	411	19.1	175	236	...	...	...	...	...	...
2/3. Admin. & managerial workers / clerical & related workers	282	13.1	172	110	...	...	...	...	...	...
4. Sales workers	327	15.2	184	143	...	...	...	...	...	...
5. Service workers	43	2.0	42	1	...	...	...	...	...	...
6. Agric., animal husbandry & forestry workers, fishermen & hunters	166	7.7	166	.	...	...	...	...	...	...
7–9. Prod./related workers, transport equipment operators & labourers	838	38.9	781	57	...	...	...	...	...	...
X. Workers not classifiable by occupation	45	2.1	44	1	...	...	...	...	...	...
–. Persons seeking work for the first time	7	0.3	6	1	.	.	.	.	.	.
–. Armed forces	34	1.6	34	.	.	.	.	.	.	.
Total	**2 153**	*100.0*	**1 604**	**549**	**281**	**214**	**67**	**1 851**	**1 373**	**478**
Trinidad and Tobago (I–VI.78) LFSS †										
0/1. Professional, technical & related workers	33 000	7.5	18 800	14 200	...	...	...	...	...	...
2/3. Admin. & managerial workers / clerical & related workers	54 500	12.4	26 800	27 700	...	...	...	...	...	...
4. Sales workers	37 900	8.7	19 300	18 600	...	...	...	...	...	...
5. Service workers	55 200	12.5	26 000	29 200	...	...	...	...	...	...
6. Agric., animal husbandry & forestry workers, fishermen & hunters	49 400	11.3	37 700	11 700	...	...	...	...	...	...
7–9. Prod./related workers, transport equipment operators & labourers	200 600	45.7	174 500	26 100	...	...	...	...	...	...
X. Workers not classifiable by occupation	1 500	0.3	1 100	500	...	...	...	...	...	...
–. Persons seeking work for the first time	6 800	1.6	2 300	4 500	.	.	.	.	.	.
Total	**439 000**	*100.0*	**306 500**	**132 500**	**61 600**	**43 800**	**17 700·**	**352 500**	**250 900**	**101 600**
United States (1979) LFSS †										
0/1. Professional, technical & related workers	15 423 000	14.7	8 683 000	6 740 000	1 175 000	868 000	307 000	13 865 000	7 661 000	6 204 000
2. Administrative & managerial workers	10 741 000	10.2	8 065 000	2 676 000	1 757 000	1 370 000	387 000	8 732 000	6 558 000	2 174 000
3. Clerical & related workers	18 466 000	17.6	3 599 000	14 866 000	229 000	44 000	185 000	17 128 000	3 415 000	13 713 000
4. Sales workers	6 416 000	6.1	3 481 000	2 935 000	815 000	486 000	330 000	5 289 000	2 892 000	2 397 000
5. Service workers	13 814 000	13.2	5 165 000	8 649 000	770 000	186 000	583 000	12 017 000	4 631 000	7 387 000
6. Agric., animal husbandry & forestry workers, fishermen & hunters	2 809 000	2.6	2 285 000	524 000	1 413 000	1 279 000	134 000	1 004 000	841 000	163 000
7–9. Prod./related workers, transport equipment operators & labourers	34 442 000	32.9	27 896 000	6 546 000	2 074 000	1 899 000	175 000	29 917 000	24 230 000	5 687 000
–. Persons seeking work for the first time	798 000	0.7	343 000	455 000	.	.	.			
–. Armed forces	2 088 000	2.0	1 949 000	139 000	.	.	.	2 088 000	1 949 000	139 000
Total	**104 996 000**	*100.0*	**61 466 000**	**43 531 000**	**8 233 000**	**6 132 000**	**2 101 000**	**90 040 000**	**52 177 000**	**37 864 000**

B By occupational group, by status and by sex
Par groupe de professions, selon la situation dans la profession et par sexe
Por grupo de ocupación, según la categoría de ocupación y por sexo

Unpaid family workers / Travailleurs familiaux non rémunérés / Trabajadores familiares no remunerados			Not classifiable by status / Inclassables selon la situation / Inclasificables según la categoría			Profession (Grands groupes)	Ocupación (Grandes grupos)
Total	Males Hommes Hombres	Females Femmes Mujeres	Total	Males Hommes Hombres	Females Femmes Mujeres		
...	...	...	...	...	...	0/1. Personnel des prof. scientif., techn., libérales et assimilées	0/1. Profesionales, técnicos y trabajadores asimilados
						2/3. Directeurs et cadres admin. supér. / personnel admin. et travailleurs assimilés	2/3. Directores y funcionarios públicos super. / pers. admin. y trabajadores asimilados
...	...	...	...	...	...	4. Pers. commercial et vendeurs	4. Comerciantes y vendedores
...	...	...	...	...	...	5. Travailleurs des services	5. Trabajadores de los servicios
						6. Agriculteurs, éleveurs, forestiers, pêcheurs et chasseurs	6. Trabajadores agrícolas y forestales, pescadores y cazadores
...					...	7-9. Ouvriers et manœuvres non agricoles et conducteurs d'engins de transport	7-9. Obreros no agrícolas, conductores de máquinas y vehíc. de transporte y trab. asimilados
...				...	...	X. Travailleurs ne pouvant être classés selon la profession	X. Trab. que no pueden ser clasificados según la ocupación
...			...			-. Personnes en quête d'emploi pour la première fois	-. Personas en busca de trabajo por primera vez
.	.	.	.	.	.	-. Forces armées	-. Fuerzas armadas
14	**11**	**3**	**7**	**6**	**1**	**Total**	**Total**

Total	Males	Females	Total	Males	Females	Profession (Grands groupes)	Ocupación (Grandes grupos)
...	...	...	...	...	...	0/1. Personnel des prof. scientif., techn., libérales et assimilées	0/1. Profesionales, técnicos y trabajadores asimilados
						2/3. Directeurs et cadres admin. supér. / personnel admin. et travailleurs assimilés	2/3. Directores y funcionarios públicos super. / pers. admin. y trabajadores asimilados
...	...	...	...	...	...	4. Pers. commercial et vendeurs	4. Comerciantes y vendedores
...	...	...	...	...	...	5. Travailleurs des services	5. Trabajadores de los servicios
						6. Agriculteurs, éleveurs, forestiers, pêcheurs et chasseurs	6. Trabajadores agrícolas y forestales, pescadores y cazadores
...	...	...	...	...	...	7-9. Ouvriers et manœuvres non agricoles et conducteurs d'engins de transport	7-9. Obreros no agrícolas, conductores de máquinas y vehíc. de transporte y trab. asimilados
...			...	...	...	X. Travailleurs ne pouvant être classés selon la profession	X. Trab. que no pueden ser clasificados según la ocupación
.	.	.	6 800	2 300	4 500	-. Personnes en quête d'emploi pour la première fois	-. Personas en busca de trabajo por primera vez
17 100	**9 000**	**8 100**	**7 800**	**2 800**	**5 000**	**Total**	**Total**

Total	Males	Females	Total	Males	Females	Profession (Grands groupes)	Ocupación (Grandes grupos)
10 000	2 000	8 000	373 000	152 000	221 000	0/1. Personnel des prof. scientif., techn., libérales et assimilées	0/1. Profesionales, técnicos y trabajadores asimilados
27 000	3 000	24 000	225 000	135 000	90 000	2. Directeurs et cadres administratifs supérieurs	2. Directores y funcionarios públicos superiores
256 000	2 000	254 000	853 000	138 000	714 000	3. Personnel administratif et travailleurs assimilés	3. Personal administrativo y trabajadores asimilados
59 000	6 000	53 000	252 000	97 000	156 000	4. Pers. commercial et vendeurs	4. Comerciantes y vendedores
47 000	6 000	41 000	980 000	342 000	638 000	5. Travailleurs des services	5. Trabajadores de los servicios
286 000	97 000	189 000	106 000	69 000	37 000	6. Agriculteurs, éleveurs, forestiers, pêcheurs et chasseurs	6. Trabajadores agrícolas y forestales, pescadores y cazadores
74 000	25 000	49 000	2 377 000	1 742 000	634 000	7-9. Ouvriers et manœuvres non agricoles et conducteurs d'engins de transport	7-9. Obreros no agrícolas, conductores de máquinas y vehíc. de transporte y trab. asimilados
.	.	.	798 000	343 000	455 000	-. Personnes en quête d'emploi pour la première fois	-. Personas en busca de trabajo por primera vez
						-. Forces armées	-. Fuerzas armadas
759 000	**141 000**	**618 000**	**5 964 000**	**3 018 000**	**2 945 000**	**Total**	**Total**

2 Structure of the economically active population
Structure de la population active
Estructura de la población económicamente activa

Occupation (Major groups)	Total				Employers and own-account workers / Employeurs et personnes travaillant à leur propre compte / Empleadores y trabajadores por cuenta propia			Employees / Salariés / Empleados a sueldo o salario		
	Total	%	Males Hommes Hombres	Females Femmes Mujeres	Total	Males Hommes Hombres	Females Femmes Mujeres	Total	Males Hommes Hombres	Females Femmes Mujeres
Uruguay (21.V.75) C †										
0/1. Professional, technical & related workers	79 699	7.3	33 725	45 974	15 686	9 417	6 269	61 202	22 945	38 257
2. Administrative & managerial workers	14 237	1.3	12 294	1 943	7 642	6 622	1 020	6 494	5 611	883
3. Clerical & related workers	118 270	10.8	78 154	40 116	1 996	1 607	389	115 580	76 236	39 344
4. Sales workers	105 270	9.6	76 264	29 006	59 779	46 465	13 314	42 257	28 542	13 715
5. Service workers	156 016	14.3	58 043	97 973	13 883	4 535	9 348	141 361	53 206	88 155
6. Agric., animal husbandry & forestry workers, fishermen & hunters	172 214	15.7	164 783	7 431	70 790	67 724	3 066	86 499	85 108	1 391
7–9. Prod./related workers, transport equipment operators & labourers	316 023	28.9	260 776	55 247	77 319	54 560	22 759	235 489	203 710	31 779
X. Workers not classifiable by occupation	85 913	7.8	61 823	24 090	13 688	10 546	3 142	40 489	30 027	10 462
–. Persons seeking work for the first time	17 131	1.6	9 220	7 911	.	.	.	.	.	.
–. Armed forces	29 826	2.7	28 502	1 324				29 826	28 502	1 324
Total	**1 094 599**	*100.0*	**783 584**	**311 015**	**260 783**	**201 476**	**59 307**	**759 197**	**533 887**	**225 310**
ASIA										
Bahrain (IV.79) OE †										
0/1. Professional, technical & related workers	14 700	10.9	10 500	4 200	...	...	...	...	...	...
2. Administrative & managerial workers	4 900	3.6	4 800	100	...	...	...	...	...	...
3. Clerical & related workers	16 200	12.0	12 800	3 400	...	...	...	...	...	...
4. Sales workers	10 800	8.0	10 200	600	...	...	...	...	...	...
5. Service workers	14 700	10.9	11 200	3 500	...	...	...	...	...	...
6. Agric., animal husbandry & forestry workers, fishermen & hunters	4 600	3.5	4 400	200	...	...	...	...	...	...
7–9. Prod./related workers, transport equipment operators & labourers	65 400	48.4	65 000	400	...	...	...	...	...	...
X. Workers not classifiable by occupation	3 600	2.7	3 400	200	...	...	...	...	...	...
Total	**134 900**	*100.0*	**122 300**	**12 600**	...	...	...	...	...	...
Bangladesh (1.III.74) C †										
0/1. Professional, technical & related workers	375 092	1.8	352 926	22 166	...	...	...	...	...	...
2. Administrative & managerial workers	30 841	0.2	30 389	452	...	...	...	...	...	...
3. Clerical & related workers	208 495	1.0	206 245	2 250	...	...	...	...	...	...
4. Sales workers	934 307	4.5	923 033	11 274	...	...	...	...	...	...
5. Service workers	386 151	1.9	296 783	89 368	...	...	...	...	...	...
6. Agric., animal husbandry & forestry workers, fishermen & hunters	15 837 883	77.2	15 229 075	608 808	...	...	...	...	...	...
7–9. Prod./related workers, transport equipment operators & labourers	2 247 173	11.0	2 140 984	106 189	...	...	...	...	...	...
X. Workers not classifiable by occupation	502 650	2.4	471 162	31 488	...	...	...	...	...	...
Total	**20 522 592**	*100.0*	**19 650 597**	**871 995**	...	...	...	...	...	...

B By occupational group, by status and by sex
Par groupe de professions, selon la situation dans la profession et par sexe
Por grupo de ocupación, según la categoría de ocupación y por sexo

Unpaid family workers Travailleurs familiaux non rémunérés Trabajadores familiares no remunerados			Not classifiable by status Inclassables selon la situation Inclasificables según la categoría			Profession (Grands groupes)	Ocupación (Grandes grupos)
Total	Males Hommes Hombres	Females Femmes Mujeres	Total	Males Hommes Hombres	Females Femmes Mujeres		
108	51	57	2 703	1 312	1 391	0/1. Personnel des prof. scientif., techn., libérales et assimilées	0/1. Profesionales, técnicos y trabajadores asimilados
38	14	24	63	47	16	2. Directeurs et cadres administratifs supérieurs	2. Directores y funcionarios públicos superiores
310	91	219	384	220	164	3. Personnel administratif et travailleurs assimilés	3. Personal administrativo y trabajadores asimilados
2 923	1 041	1 882	311	216	95	4. Pers. commercial et vendeurs	4. Comerciantes y vendedores
409	154	255	363	148	215	5. Travailleurs des services	5. Trabajadores de los servicios
14 581	11 629	2 952	344	322	22	6. Agriculteurs, éleveurs, forestiers, pêcheurs et chasseurs	6. Trabajadores agrícolas y forestales, pescadores y cazadores
1 631	1 232	399	1 584	1 274	310	7-9. Ouvriers et manœuvres non agricoles et conducteurs d'engins de transport	7-9. Obreros no agrícolas, conductores de máquinas y vehíc. de transporte y trab. asimilados
2 063	1 179	884	29 673	20 071	9 602	X. Travailleurs ne pouvant être classés selon la profession	X. Trab. que no pueden ser clasificados según la ocupación
.	.	.	17 131	9 220	7 911	–. Personnes en quête d'emploi pour la première fois	–. Personas en busca de trabajo por primera vez
						–. Forces armées	–. Fuerzas armadas
22 063	**15 391**	**6 672**	**52 556**	**32 830**	**19 726**	**Total**	**Total**

ASIE – ASIA

						0/1. Personnel des prof. scientif., techn., libérales et assimilées	0/1. Profesionales, técnicos y trabajadores asimilados
...	...	...	...	...	...	2. Directeurs et cadres administratifs supérieurs	2. Directores y funcionarios públicos superiores
...	...	...	...	...	...	3. Personnel administratif et travailleurs assimilés	3. Personal administrativo y trabajadores asimilados
...	...	...	...	...	...	4. Pers. commercial et vendeurs	4. Comerciantes y vendedores
...	...	...	...	...	...	5. Travailleurs des services	5. Trabajadores de los servicios
						6. Agriculteurs, éleveurs, forestiers, pêcheurs et chasseurs	6. Trabajadores agrícolas y forestales, pescadores y cazadores
...	...	...	...	...	...	7-9. Ouvriers et manœuvres non agricoles et conducteurs d'engins de transport	7-9. Obreros no agrícolas, conductores de máquinas y vehíc. de transporte y trab. asimilados
...	...	...	...	...	...	X. Travailleurs ne pouvant être classés selon la profession	X. Trab. que no pueden ser clasificados según la ocupación
...	...	...	...	...	...	**Total**	**Total**
...	...	...	...	...	...	0/1. Personnel des prof. scientif., techn., libérales et assimilées	0/1. Profesionales, técnicos y trabajadores asimilados
						2. Directeurs et cadres administratifs supérieurs	2. Directores y funcionarios públicos superiores
						3. Personnel administratif et travailleurs assimilés	3. Personal administrativo y trabajadores asimilados
...	...	...	...	...	...	4. Pers. commercial et vendeurs	4. Comerciantes y vendedores
...	...	...	...	...	...	5. Travailleurs des services	5. Trabajadores de los servicios
						6. Agriculteurs, éleveurs, forestiers, pêcheurs et chasseurs	6. Trabajadores agrícolas y forestales, pescadores y cazadores
...	...	...	...	...	...	7-9. Ouvriers et manœuvres non agricoles et conducteurs d'engins de transport	7-9. Obreros no agrícolas, conductores de máquinas y vehíc. de transporte y trab. asimilados
...	...	...	...	...	...	X. Travailleurs ne pouvant être classés selon la profession	X. Trab. que no pueden ser clasificados según la ocupación
...	...	...	...	...	...	**Total**	**Total**

2 Structure of the economically active population
Structure de la population active
Estructura de la población económicamente activa

Occupation (Major groups)	Total				Employers and own-account workers Employeurs et personnes travaillant à leur propre compte Empleadores y trabajadores por cuenta propia			Employees Salariés Empleados a sueldo o salario		
	Total	%	Males Hommes Hombres	Females Femmes Mujeres	Total	Males Hommes Hombres	Females Femmes Mujeres	Total	Males Hommes Hombres	Females Femmes Mujeres
Hong Kong (IX.79) LFSS †										
0/1. Professional, technical & related workers	140 200	6.4	79 700	60 400	10 100	...	...	127 900	...	...
2. Administrative & managerial workers	52 400	2.4	47 700	4 800	26 300	...	...	25 700	...	...
3. Clerical & related workers	266 100	12.1	137 800	128 400	600	...	...	260 800	...	...
4. Sales workers	228 800	10.4	173 400	55 400	112 200	...	...	98 800	...	...
5. Service workers	343 700	15.7	231 000	112 600	9 900	...	...	323 100	...	...
6. Agric., animal husbandry & forestry workers, fishermen & hunters	29 000	1.3	22 400	6 600	18 300	...	...	6 800	...	...
7-9. Prod./related workers, transport equipment operators & labourers	1 103 900	50.3	720 400	383 500	54 400	...	...	1 008 100	...	...
X. Workers not classifiable by occupation	4 900	0.2	3 700	1 100	800	...	...	3 700	...	...
–. Persons seeking work for the first time	25 400	1.2	16 200	9 200	...	...	...	...	...	...
Total	**2 194 500**	*100.0*	**1 432 500**	**762 000**	**232 600**	**199 100**	**33 400**	**1 854 900**	**1 172 300**	**682 600**
Indonesia (1976) LFSS										
0/1. Professional, technical & related workers	1 012 434	1.9	675 107	337 327	86 058	51 748	34 310	905 331	608 658	296 673
2. Administrative & managerial workers	77 496	0.1	73 189	4 307	13 441	12 920	521	63 687	60 055	3 632
3. Clerical & related workers	1 598 791	2.9	1 419 754	179 037	11 287	10 942	345	1 581 160	1 404 485	176 675
4. Sales workers	6 125 598	11.3	3 166 632	2 958 966	4 909 989	2 589 461	2 320 528	365 060	279 957	85 103
5. Service workers	2 200 138	4.0	1 231 635	968 503	166 401	106 304	60 097	1 924 948	1 090 651	834 297
6. Agric., animal husbandry & forestry workers, fishermen & hunters	35 027 949	64.3	21 195 910	13 832 039	15 109 184	12 437 848	2 671 336	5 864 925	3 176 196	2 688 729
7-9. Prod./related workers, transport equipment operators & labourers	6 344 942	11.6	4 321 732	2 023 210	2 092 986	1 365 275	727 711	3 307 599	2 679 964	627 635
X. Workers not classifiable by occupation	1 056 320	2.0	710 460	345 860	27 551	23 223	4 328	360 369	347 776	12 593
–. Unemployed	1 046 617	1.9	634 810	411 807	...	...	...	...	...	...
Total	**54 490 285**	*100.0*	**33 429 229**	**21 061 056**	**22 416 897**	**16 597 721**	**5 819 176**	**14 373 079**	**9 647 742**	**4 725 337**
Iran (XI.76) C5% †										
0/1. Professional, technical & related workers	537 877	5.5	349 626	188 251	42 123	40 298	1 825	492 667	307 174	185 493
2. Administrative & managerial workers	48 112	0.5	46 426	1 686	12 866	12 786	80	34 906	33 360	1 546
3. Clerical & related workers	450 446	4.6	384 660	65 786	7 846	7 646	200	439 656	374 446	65 210
4. Sales workers	598 284	6.2	590 125	8 159	462 099	457 799	4 300	121 719	119 060	2 659
5. Service workers	427 255	4.4	362 351	64 904	57 460	50 957	6 503	363 398	306 985	56 413
6. Agric., animal husbandry & forestry workers, fishermen & hunters	3 605 238	37.0	3 178 717	426 521	1 735 977	1 718 137	17 840	664 279	587 478	76 801
7-9. Prod./related workers, transport equipment operators & labourers	3 326 859	34.2	2 688 541	638 318	705 506	588 042	117 464	2 189 194	2 013 016	176 178
X. Workers not classifiable by occupation	500 180	5.2	476 605	23 575	6 003	5 403	600	429 039	421 631	7 408
–. Persons seeking work for the first time	238 257	2.4	203 189	35 068	.	.	.	.	.	.
Total	**9 732 508**	*100.0*	**8 280 240**	**1 452 268**	**3 029 880**	**2 881 068**	**148 812**	**4 734 858**	**4 163 150**	**571 708**

B By occupational group, by status and by sex
Par groupe de professions, selon la situation dans la profession et par sexe
Por grupo de ocupación, según la categoría de ocupación y por sexo

Unpaid family workers / Travailleurs familiaux non rémunérés / Trabajadores familiares no remunerados			Not classifiable by status / Inclassables selon la situation / Inclasificables según la categoría			Profession (Grands groupes)	Ocupación (Grandes grupos)
Total	Males Hommes Hombres	Females Femmes Mujeres	Total	Males Hommes Hombres	Females Femmes Mujeres		
600	...	...	1 600	...	...	0/1. Personnel des prof. scientif., techn., libérales et assimilées	0/1. Profesionales, técnicos y trabajadores asimilados
200	...	...	300	...	...	2. Directeurs et cadres administratifs supérieurs	2. Directores y funcionarios públicos superiores
800	...	...	4 000	...	...	3. Personnel administratif et travailleurs assimilés	3. Personal administrativo y trabajadores asimilados
15 000	...	...	2 800	...	...	4. Pers. commercial et vendeurs	4. Comerciantes y vendedores
3 100	...	...	7 500	...	...	5. Travailleurs des services	5. Trabajadores de los servicios
3 300	...	...	600	...	...	6. Agriculteurs, éleveurs, forestiers, pêcheurs et chasseurs	6. Trabajadores agrícolas y forestales, pescadores y cazadores
9 300	...	...	32 200	...	...	7-9. Ouvriers et manœuvres non agricoles et conducteurs d'engins de transport	7-9. Obreros no agrícolas, conductores de máquinas y vehíc. de transporte y trab. asimilados
100	...	...	200	...	...	X. Travailleurs ne pouvant être classés selon la profession	X. Trab. que no pueden ser clasificados según la ocupación
...	...	...	25 400	...	...	-. Personnes en quête d'emploi pour la première fois	-. Personas en busca de trabajo por primera vez
32 400	**8 600**	**23 800**	**74 600**	**52 400**	**22 200**	**Total**	**Total**
19 024	13 313	5 711	2 021	1 388	633	0/1. Personnel des prof. scientif., techn., libérales et assimilées	0/1. Profesionales, técnicos y trabajadores asimilados
368	214	154	.	.	.	2. Directeurs et cadres administratifs supérieurs	2. Directores y funcionarios públicos superiores
5 483	3 466	2 017	861	861	.	3. Personnel administratif et travailleurs assimilés	3. Personal administrativo y trabajadores asimilados
841 372	290 670	550 702	9 177	6 544	2 633	4. Pers. commercial et vendeurs	4. Comerciantes y vendedores
102 698	33 725	68 973	6 091	955	5 136	5. Travailleurs des services	5. Trabajadores de los servicios
14 024 112	5 563 765	8 460 347	29 728	18 101	11 627	6. Agriculteurs, éleveurs, forestiers, pêcheurs et chasseurs	6. Trabajadores agrícolas y forestales, pescadores y cazadores
940 199	274 539	665 660	4 158	1 954	2 204	7-9. Ouvriers et manœuvres non agricoles et conducteurs d'engins de transport	7-9. Obreros no agrícolas, conductores de máquinas y vehíc. de transporte y trab. asimilados
53 963	20 340	33 623	614 437	319 121	295 316	X. Travailleurs ne pouvant être classés selon la profession	X. Trab. que no pueden ser clasificados según la ocupación
...	...	...	1 046 617	634 810	411 807	-. Chômeurs	-. Desempleados
15 987 219	**6 200 032**	**9 787 187**	**1 713 090**	**983 734**	**729 356**	**Total**	**Total**
358	278	80	2 729	1 876	853	0/1. Personnel des prof. scientif., techn., libérales et assimilées	0/1. Profesionales, técnicos y trabajadores asimilados
.	.	.	340	280	60	2. Directeurs et cadres administratifs supérieurs	2. Directores y funcionarios públicos superiores
1 080	1 000	80	1 864	1 568	296	3. Personnel administratif et travailleurs assimilés	3. Personal administrativo y trabajadores asimilados
10 862	9 942	920	3 604	3 324	280	4. Pers. commercial et vendeurs	4. Comerciantes y vendedores
3 671	2 366	1 305	2 726	2 043	683	5. Travailleurs des services	5. Trabajadores de los servicios
568 392	441 592	126 800	636 590	431 510	205 080	6. Agriculteurs, éleveurs, forestiers, pêcheurs et chasseurs	6. Trabajadores agrícolas y forestales, pescadores y cazadores
399 090	57 369	341 721	33 069	30 114	2 955	7-9. Ouvriers et manœuvres non agricoles et conducteurs d'engins de transport	7-9. Obreros no agrícolas, conductores de máquinas y vehíc. de transporte y trab. asimilados
1 181	441	740	63 957	49 130	14 827	X. Travailleurs ne pouvant être classés selon la profession	X. Trab. que no pueden ser clasificados según la ocupación
.	.	.	238 257	203 189	35 068	-. Personnes en quête d'emploi pour la première fois	-. Personas en busca de trabajo por primera vez
984 634	**512 488**	**471 646**	**983 136**	**723 034**	**260 102**	**Total**	**Total**

2 Structure of the economically active population
Structure de la population active
Estructura de la población económicamente activa

Occupation (Major groups)	Total				Employers and own-account workers / Employeurs et personnes travaillant à leur propre compte / Empleadores y trabajadores por cuenta propia			Employees / Salariés / Empleados a sueldo o salario		
	Total	%	Males Hommes Hombres	Females Femmes Mujeres	Total	Males Hommes Hombres	Females Femmes Mujeres	Total	Males Hommes Hombres	Females Femmes Mujeres
Israel (1979) LFSS †										
0/1. Professional, technical & related workers	274 200	21.5	132 800	141 400	36 000	19 200	16 800	236 300	112 800	123 500
2. Administrative & managerial workers	48 300	3.7	44 000	4 300	13 900	13 100	800	34 200	30 700	3 500
3. Clerical & related workers	222 200	17.4	93 100	129 100	13 300	5 600	7 700	205 500	86 400	119 100
4. Sales workers	93 600	7.4	65 500	28 100	57 800	42 900	14 900	34 500	21 900	12 600
5. Service workers	136 700	10.7	59 300	77 400	24 900	10 800	14 100	109 200	47 400	61 800
6. Agric., animal husbandry & forestry workers, fishermen & hunters	69 400	5.4	54 700	14 700	50 300	38 300	12 000	18 500	15 900	2 600
7–9. Prod./related workers, transport equipment operators & labourers	391 900	30.7	344 100	47 800	82 700	74 100	8 600	300 900	262 500	38 400
X. Workers not classifiable by occupation	23 600	1.8	18 400	5 200	1 900	1 400	500	20 900	16 400	4 500
–. Persons seeking work for the first time	17 900	1.4	7 200	10 700						
Total	**1 277 800**	100.0	**819 200**	**458 600**	**280 800**	**205 400**	**75 400**	**960 000**	**594 000**	**366 000**
Japan (1.X.75) C20% †										
0/1. Professional, technical & related workers	4 438 600	8.2	2 782 840	1 655 765	597 105	435 500	161 605	3 771 580	2 328 395	1 443 190
2. Administrative & managerial workers	2 251 995	4.1	2 129 915	122 075	100 335	92 290	8 050	2 151 040	2 037 220	113 820
3. Clerical & related workers	9 197 710	17.0	4 548 650	4 649 065	55 170	28 150	27 015	8 661 945	4 500 935	4 161 010
4. Sales workers	6 824 680	12.6	4 192 590	2 632 085	1 590 845	1 171 095	419 750	4 097 730	2 824 855	1 272 865
5. Service workers	4 682 460	8.6	2 167 515	2 514 950	980 970	509 485	471 485	3 174 600	1 572 900	1 601 705
6. Agric., animal husbandry & forestry workers, fishermen & hunters	7 290 080	13.4	3 712 275	3 577 805	3 227 020	2 666 030	560 990	410 180	336 895	73 285
7–9. Prod./related workers, transport equipment operators & labourers	18 269 480	33.7	13 826 185	4 443 295	2 757 280	2 058 100	699 185	14 535 965	11 425 270	3 110 695
X. Workers not classifiable by occupation	60 420	0.1	19 740	40 680	17 515	1 780	15 735	27 165	16 000	11 165
–. Unemployed	1 249 290	2.3	890 615	358 680	...	...	...	...	...	...
Total	**54 264 725**	100.0	**34 270 320**	**19 994 405**	**9 326 245**	**6 962 425**	**2 363 815**	**36 830 210**	**25 042 470**	**11 787 740**
" " " " (1979) LFSS †										
0/1. Professional, technical & related workers	4 260 000	7.6	2 270 000	1 990 000	660 000	440 000	220 000	3 520 000	1 810 000	1 710 000
2. Administrative & managerial workers	2 170 000	3.9	2 060 000	120 000	20 000	20 000	–	2 150 000	2 040 000	110 000
3. Clerical & related workers	8 980 000	16.0	4 240 000	4 730 000	70 000	40 000	40 000	8 440 000	4 190 000	4 250 000
4. Sales workers	7 840 000	14.0	4 810 000	3 030 000	1 880 000	1 340 000	540 000	4 760 000	3 280 000	1 490 000
5. Service workers	4 970 000	8.9	2 250 000	2 720 000	980 000	510 000	470 000	3 360 000	1 640 000	1 710 000
6. Agric., animal husbandry & forestry workers, fishermen & hunters	6 050 000	10.8	3 050 000	3 000 000	2 870 000	2 260 000	610 000	380 000	290 000	90 000
7–9. Prod./related workers, transport equipment operators & labourers	20 410 000	36.5	14 870 000	5 540 000	3 170 000	2 110 000	1 060 000	16 120 000	12 400 000	3 730 000
X. Workers not classifiable by occupation	110 000	0.2	80 000	40 000	–	–	–	30 000	20 000	10 000
–. Unemployed	1 170 000	2.1	740 000	430 000	...	...	...	...	...	...
Total	**55 960 000**	100.0	**34 370 000**	**21 600 000**	**9 670 000**	**6 720 000**	**2 940 000**	**38 760 000**	**25 660 000**	**13 100 000**

B

By occupational group, by status and by sex
Par groupe de professions, selon la situation dans la profession et par sexe
Por grupo de ocupación, según la categoría de ocupación y por sexo

Unpaid family workers / Travailleurs familiaux non rémunérés / Trabajadores familiares no remunerados			Not classifiable by status / Inclassables selon la situation / Inclasificables según la categoría			Profession (Grands groupes)	Ocupación (Grandes grupos)
Total	Males Hommes Hombres	Females Femmes Mujeres	Total	Males Hommes Hombres	Females Femmes Mujeres		
...	...	...	1 900	800	1 100	0/1. Personnel des prof. scientif., techn., libérales et assimilées	0/1. Profesionales, técnicos y trabajadores asimilados
...	...	...	200	200	–	2. Directeurs et cadres administratifs supérieurs	2. Directores y funcionarios públicos superiores
...	...	...	3 400	1 100	2 300	3. Personnel administratif et travailleurs assimilés	3. Personal administrativo y trabajadores asimilados
...	...	...	1 300	700	600	4. Pers. commercial et vendeurs	4. Comerciantes y vendedores
...	...	...	2 600	1 100	1 500	5. Travailleurs des services	5. Trabajadores de los servicios
...	...	...	600	500	100	6. Agriculteurs, éleveurs, forestiers, pêcheurs et chasseurs	6. Trabajadores agrícolas y forestales, pescadores y cazadores
...	...	...	8 300	7 500	800	7–9. Ouvriers et manœuvres non agricoles et conducteurs d'engins de transport	7–9. Obreros no agrícolas, conductores de máquinas y vehíc. de transporte y trab. asimilados
...	...	...	800	600	200	X. Travailleurs ne pouvant être classés selon la profession	X. Trab. que no pueden ser clasificados según la ocupación
...	...	...	17 900	7 200	10 700	–. Personnes en quête d'emploi pour la première fois	–. Personas en busca de trabajo por primera vez
...	...	...	**37 000**	**19 700**	**17 300**	**Total**	**Total**
69 920	18 945	50 975	...	...	...	0/1. Personnel des prof. scientif., techn., libérales et assimilées	0/1. Profesionales, técnicos y trabajadores asimilados
615	405	210	...	...	...	2. Directeurs et cadres administratifs supérieurs	2. Directores y funcionarios públicos superiores
480 590	19 565	461 030	...	...	...	3. Personnel administratif et travailleurs assimilés	3. Personal administrativo y trabajadores asimilados
1 136 110	196 635	939 475	...	...	...	4. Pers. commercial et vendeurs	4. Comerciantes y vendedores
526 890	85 135	441 755	...	...	...	5. Travailleurs des services	5. Trabajadores de los servicios
3 652 885	709 355	2 943 530	...	...	...	6. Agriculteurs, éleveurs, forestiers, pêcheurs et chasseurs	6. Trabajadores agrícolas y forestales, pescadores y cazadores
976 230	342 815	633 420	...	...	...	7–9. Ouvriers et manœuvres non agricoles et conducteurs d'engins de transport	7–9. Obreros no agrícolas, conductores de máquinas y vehíc. de transporte y trab. asimilados
8 615	225	8 390	7 125	1 735	5 390	X. Travailleurs ne pouvant être classés selon la profession	X. Trab. que no pueden ser clasificados según la ocupación
...	...	...	1 249 290	890 615	358 680	–. Chômeurs	–. Desempleados
6 851 855	**1 373 075**	**5 478 780**	**1 256 415**	**892 350**	**364 070**	**Total**	**Total**
70 000	20 000	60 000	...	...	...	0/1. Personnel des prof. scientif., techn., libérales et assimilées	0/1. Profesionales, técnicos y trabajadores asimilados
–	–	–	...	...	...	2. Directeurs et cadres administratifs supérieurs	2. Directores y funcionarios públicos superiores
470 000	20 000	450 000	...	...	...	3. Personnel administratif et travailleurs assimilés	3. Personal administrativo y trabajadores asimilados
1 200 000	190 000	1 000 000	...	...	...	4. Pers. commercial et vendeurs	4. Comerciantes y vendedores
630 000	90 000	530 000	...	...	...	5. Travailleurs des services	5. Trabajadores de los servicios
2 800 000	510 000	2 290 000	...	...	...	6. Agriculteurs, éleveurs, forestiers, pêcheurs et chasseurs	6. Trabajadores agrícolas y forestales, pescadores y cazadores
1 100 000	350 000	760 000	10 000	10 000		7–9. Ouvriers et manœuvres non agricoles et conducteurs d'engins de transport	7–9. Obreros no agrícolas, conductores de máquinas y vehíc. de transporte y trab. asimilados
–	–	–	80 000	50 000	30 000	X. Travailleurs ne pouvant être classés selon la profession	X. Trab. que no pueden ser clasificados según la ocupación
...	...	...	1 170 000	740 000	430 000	–. Chômeurs	–. Desempleados
6 270 000	**1 180 000**	**5 090 000**	**1 260 000**	**800 000**	**460 000**	**Total**	**Total**

2 Structure of the economically active population
Structure de la population active
Estructura de la población económicamente activa

Occupation (Major groups)	Total				Employers and own-account workers / Employeurs et personnes travaillant à leur propre compte / Empleadores y trabajadores por cuenta propia			Employees / Salariés / Empleados a sueldo o salario		
	Total	%	Males Hommes Hombres	Females Femmes Mujeres	Total	Males Hommes Hombres	Females Femmes Mujeres	Total	Males Hommes Hombres	Females Femmes Mujeres
Korea, Republic of (1.X.75) C †										
0/1. Professional, technical & related workers	417 423	3.1	312 027	105 396	54 916	46 996	7 920	353 178	261 592	91 586
2. Administrative & managerial workers	102 327	0.8	98 531	3 796	62 665	60 054	2 611	39 662	38 477	1 185
3. Clerical & related workers	844 210	6.3	647 455	196 755	15 330	13 441	1 889	823 311	631 018	192 293
4. Sales workers	1 317 122	9.9	842 263	474 859	853 291	604 944	248 347	272 240	194 143	78 097
5. Service workers	815 791	6.1	350 452	465 339	211 050	101 947	109 103	544 913	239 306	305 607
6. Agric., animal husbandry & forestry workers, fishermen & hunters	6 190 008	46.4	3 264 069	2 925 939	2 398 049	1 980 202	417 847	545 307	375 443	169 864
7-9. Prod./related workers, transport equipment operators & labourers	2 890 668	21.6	2 083 206	807 462	310 708	246 442	64 266	2 492 587	1 800 841	691 746
X. Workers not classifiable by occupation	104 492	0.8	103 708	784	229	229	.	93 400	92 753	647
-. Unemployed	668 563	5.0	474 133	194 430	...	...	...	...	...	...
Total	**13 350 604**	*100.0*	**8 175 844**	**5 174 760**	**3 906 238**	**3 054 255**	**851 983**	**5 164 598**	**3 633 573**	**1 531 025**
" " " " (1979) LFSS †										
0/1. Professional, technical & related workers	531 000	3.7	359 000	172 000	88 000	48 000	40 000	438 000	309 000	129 000
2. Administrative & managerial workers	160 000	1.2	150 000	10 000	123 000	114 000	9 000	36 000	36 000	–
3. Clerical & related workers	1 196 000	8.4	830 000	366 000	17 000	16 000	1 000	1 166 000	809 000	357 000
4. Sales workers	1 806 000	12.7	1 022 000	784 000	2 205 000	791 000	414 000	273 000	182 000	91 000
5. Service workers	981 000	6.9	429 000	552 000	291 000	131 000	160 000	587 000	285 000	302 000
6. Agric., animal husbandry & forestry workers, fishermen & hunters	4 883 000	34.4	2 704 000	2 179 000	2 265 000	1 828 000	437 000	613 000	355 000	258 000
7-9. Prod./related workers, transport equipment operators & labourers	4 107 000	28.9	2 915 000	1 192 000	584 000	369 000	215 000	3 406 000	2 504 000	902 000
-. Unemployed	542 000	3.8	411 000	131 000	...	...	...	...	...	...
Total	**14 206 000**	*100.0*	**8 820 000**	**5 386 000**	**4 573 000**	**3 297 000**	**1 276 000**	**6 519 000**	**4 480 000**	**2 039 000**
Pakistan (I.80) LFSS †										
0/1. Professional, technical & related workers	680 000	3.0	...	...	156 000	...	...	506 000	...	...
2. Administrative & managerial workers	160 000	0.7	...	...	73 000	...	...	77 000	...	...
3. Clerical & related workers	607 000	2.6	...	...	14 000	...	...	590 000	...	...
4. Sales workers	2 255 000	9.8	...	...	1 701 000	...	...	203 000	...	...
5. Service workers	1 012 000	4.4	...	...	334 000	...	...	557 000	...	...
6. Agric., animal husbandry & forestry workers, fishermen & hunters	12 360 000	53.8	...	...	6 341 000	...	...	970 000	...	...
7-9. Prod./related workers, transport equipment operators & labourers	5 495 000	23.9	...	...	2 620 000	...	...	2 159 000	...	...
X. Workers not classifiable by occupation	27 000	0.1	...	...	12 000	...	...	14 000	...	...
-. Unemployed	390 000	1.7	...	...	...	...	...	...	...	...
Total	**22 986 000**	*100.0*	...	...	**11 251 000**	...	...	**5 076 000**	...	...

B By occupational group, by status and by sex
Par groupe de professions, selon la situation dans la profession et par sexe
Por grupo de ocupación, según la categoría de ocupación y por sexo

Unpaid family workers / Travailleurs familiaux non rémunérés / Trabajadores familiares no remunerados			Not classifiable by status / Inclassables selon la situation / Inclasificables según la categoría			Profession (Grands groupes)	Ocupación (Grandes grupos)
Total	Males Hommes Hombres	Females Femmes Mujeres	Total	Males Hommes Hombres	Females Femmes Mujeres		
9 229	3 342	5 887	100	97	3	0/1. Personnel des prof. scientif., techn., libérales et assimilées	0/1. Profesionales, técnicos y trabajadores asimilados
.	.	.	.	.	.	2. Directeurs et cadres administratifs supérieurs	2. Directores y funcionarios públicos superiores
5 569	2 996	2 573	.	.	.	3. Personnel administratif et travailleurs assimilés	3. Personal administrativo y trabajadores asimilados
191 468	43 128	148 340	123	48	75	4. Pers. commercial et vendeurs	4. Comerciantes y vendedores
59 626	9 195	50 431	202	4	198	5. Travailleurs des services	5. Trabajadores de los servicios
3 246 580	908 424	2 338 156	72	.	72	6. Agriculteurs, éleveurs, forestiers, pêcheurs et chasseurs	6. Trabajadores agrícolas y forestales, pescadores y cazadores
87 179	35 922	51 257	194	1	193	7–9. Ouvriers et manœuvres non agricoles et conducteurs d'engins de transport	7–9. Obreros no agrícolas, conductores de máquinas y vehíc. de transporte y trab. asimilados
10 681	10 668	13	182	58	124	X. Travailleurs ne pouvant être classés selon la profession	X. Trab. que no pueden ser clasificados según la ocupación
...	...	...	668 563	474 133	194 430	–. Chômeurs	–. Desempleados
3 610 332	**1 013 675**	**2 596 657**	**669 436**	**474 341**	**195 095**	**Total**	**Total**
5 000	2 000	3 000	...	...	...	0/1. Personnel des prof. scientif., techn., libérales et assimilées	0/1. Profesionales, técnicos y trabajadores asimilados
1 000	–	1 000	...	...	...	2. Directeurs et cadres administratifs supérieurs	2. Directores y funcionarios públicos superiores
13 000	5 000	8 000	...	...	...	3. Personnel administratif et travailleurs assimilés	3. Personal administrativo y trabajadores asimilados
328 000	49 000	279 000	...	...	...	4. Pers. commercial et vendeurs	4. Comerciantes y vendedores
103 000	13 000	90 000	...	...	...	5. Travailleurs des services	5. Trabajadores de los servicios
2 005 000	521 000	1 484 000	...	...	...	6. Agriculteurs, éleveurs, forestiers, pêcheurs et chasseurs	6. Trabajadores agrícolas y forestales, pescadores y cazadores
117 000	42 000	75 000	...	...	...	7–9. Ouvriers et manœuvres non agricoles et conducteurs d'engins de transport	7–9. Obreros no agrícolas, conductores de máquinas y vehíc. de transporte y trab. asimilados
...	...	...	542 000	411 000	131 000	–. Chômeurs	–. Desempleados
2 572 000	**632 000**	**1 940 000**	**542 000**	**411 000**	**131 000**	**Total**	**Total**
18 000	...	...	...	...	...	0/1. Personnel des prof. scientif., techn., libérales et assimilées	0/1. Profesionales, técnicos y trabajadores asimilados
10 000	...	...	...	...	...	2. Directeurs et cadres administratifs supérieurs	2. Directores y funcionarios públicos superiores
3 000	...	...	...	...	...	3. Personnel administratif et travailleurs assimilés	3. Personal administrativo y trabajadores asimilados
351 000	...	...	...	...	...	4. Pers. commercial et vendeurs	4. Comerciantes y vendedores
121 000	...	...	...	...	...	5. Travailleurs des services	5. Trabajadores de los servicios
5 049 000	...	...	...	...	...	6. Agriculteurs, éleveurs, forestiers, pêcheurs et chasseurs	6. Trabajadores agrícolas y forestales, pescadores y cazadores
716 000	...	...	...	...	...	7–9. Ouvriers et manœuvres non agricoles et conducteurs d'engins de transport	7–9. Obreros no agrícolas, conductores de máquinas y vehíc. de transporte y trab. asimilados
1 000	...	...	...	...	...	X. Travailleurs ne pouvant être classés selon la profession	X. Trab. que no pueden ser clasificados según la ocupación
...	...	...	...	...	...	–. Chômeurs	–. Desempleados
6 269 000	**...**	**...**	**390 000**	**...**	**...**	**Total**	**Total**

2 Structure of the economically active population
Structure de la population active
Estructura de la población económicamente activa

Occupation (Major groups)	Total				Employers and own-account workers Employeurs et personnes travaillant à leur propre compte Empleadores y trabajadores por cuenta propia			Employees Salariés Empleados a sueldo o salario		
	Total	%	Males Hommes Hombres	Females Femmes Mujeres	Total	Males Hommes Hombres	Females Femmes Mujeres	Total	Males Hommes Hombres	Females Femmes Mujeres
Philippines (X–XII.77) LFSS †										
0/1. Professional, technical & related workers	930 000	6.2	408 000	522 000	54 000	42 000	12 000	867 000	361 000	505 000
2. Administrative & managerial workers	105 000	0.7	89 000	16 000	36 000	31 000	6 000	68 000	58 000	10 000
3. Clerical & related workers	661 000	4.4	389 000	272 000	3 000	2 000	1 000	657 000	385 000	271 000
4. Sales workers	1 421 000	9.5	558 000	863 000	958 000	353 000	604 000	329 000	174 000	154 000
5. Service workers	1 086 000	7.2	473 000	613 000	99 000	39 000	60 000	959 000	430 000	529 000
6. Agric., animal husbandry & forestry workers, fishermen & hunters	7 234 000	48.3	5 903 000	1 331 000	4 006 000	3 727 000	279 000	1 371 000	1 072 000	299 000
7–9. Prod./related workers, transport equipment operators & labourers	2 810 000	18.7	2 145 000	664 000	611 000	329 000	283 000	2 116 000	1 789 000	327 000
X. Workers not classifiable by occupation	77 000	0.5	45 000	32 000	6 000	2 000	4 000	50 000	37 000	13 000
–. Persons seeking work for the first time	275 000	1.9	111 000	163 000	.	.	.	.	.	.
–. Other unemployed	396 000	2.6	156 000	240 000	43 000	17 000	26 000	245 000	103 000	142 000
Total	**14 994 000**	*100.0*	**10 277 000**	**4 716 000**	**5 817 000**	**4 543 000**	**1 275 000**	**6 660 000**	**4 410 000**	**2 250 000**
Singapore (VI.79) LFSS †										
0/1. Professional, technical & related workers	87 601	8.3	54 823	32 777	4 471	3 473	998	83 004	51 329	31 675
2. Administrative & managerial workers	28 244	2.7	26 455	1 789	16 430	15 828	603	11 751	10 607	1 144
3. Clerical & related workers	161 496	15.3	71 399	90 097	291	208	83	160 622	71 025	89 597
4. Sales workers	155 963	14.7	111 498	44 466	64 661	54 054	10 607	68 966	47 939	21 027
5. Service workers	113 494	10.8	65 451	48 043	6 863	4 701	2 163	104 468	59 898	44 570
6. Agric., animal husbandry & forestry workers, fishermen & hunters	18 177	1.7	13 248	4 929	7 009	5 948	1 061	6 427	5 262	1 165
7–9. Prod./related workers, transport equipment operators & labourers	394 536	37.3	273 326	121 210	35 564	29 990	5 574	356 226	242 046	114 180
X. Workers not classifiable by occupation	61 520	5.9	60 959	562	42	42	.	61 479	60 917	562
–. Other unemployed	24 313	2.3	16 243	8 070	...	...	...	...	...	...
Total	**1 056 325**	*100.0*	**697 707**	**358 618**	**135 331**	**114 243**	**21 089**	**852 943**	**549 023**	**303 920**
République arabe syrienne (IX.79) LFSS										
0/1. Professional, technical & related workers	199 807	9.2	147 090	52 717	...	...	...	...	...	...
2. Administrative & managerial workers	12 459	0.6	11 760	699	...	...	...	...	...	...
3. Clerical & related workers	160 801	7.4	137 196	23 605	...	...	...	...	...	...
4. Sales workers	195 357	8.9	192 891	2 466	...	...	...	...	...	...
5. Service workers	57 774	2.7	51 373	6 401	...	...	...	...	...	...
6. Agric., animal husbandry & forestry workers, fishermen & hunters	683 152	31.4	482 700	200 452	...	...	...	...	...	...
7–9. Prod./related workers, transport equipment operators & labourers	815 146	37.5	769 922	45 224	...	...	...	...	...	...
–. Persons seeking work for the first time	49 731	2.3	38 442	11 289	.	.	.	.	.	.
Total	**2 174 227**	*100.0*	**1 831 374**	**342 853**	...	...	...	...	...	...

B By occupational group, by status and by sex
Par groupe de professions, selon la situation dans la profession et par sexe
Por grupo de ocupación, según la categoría de ocupación y por sexo

Unpaid family workers / Travailleurs familiaux non rémunérés / Trabajadores familiares no remunerados			Not classifiable by status / Inclassables selon la situation / Inclasificables según la categoría			Profession (Grands groupes)	Ocupación (Grandes grupos)
Total	Males Hommes Hombres	Females Femmes Mujeres	Total	Males Hommes Hombres	Females Femmes Mujeres		
2 000	1 000	1 000	6 000	3 000	3 000	0/1. Personnel des prof. scientif., techn., libérales et assimilées	0/1. Profesionales, técnicos y trabajadores asimilados
–	–	–	–	–	–	2. Directeurs et cadres adminis- tratifs supérieurs	2. Directores y funcionarios públicos superiores
–	–	–	1 000	1 000	–	3. Personnel administratif et travailleurs assimilés	3. Personal administrativo y trabajadores asimilados
133 000	29 000	103 000	2 000	1 000	1 000	4. Pers. commercial et vendeurs	4. Comerciantes y vendedores
23 000	4 000	19 000	6 000	2 000	4 000	5. Travailleurs des services	5. Trabajadores de los servicios
1 832 000	1 084 000	748 000	25 000	20 000	5 000	6. Agriculteurs, éleveurs, forestiers, pêcheurs et chasseurs	6. Trabajadores agrícolas y forestales, pescadores y cazadores
76 000	23 000	53 000	7 000	4 000	2 000	7–9. Ouvriers et manœuvres non agricoles et conducteurs d'engins de transport	7–9. Obreros no agrícolas, conductores de máquinas y trab. de transporte y trab. asimilados
15 000	3 000	12 000	6 000	2 000	4 000	X. Travailleurs ne pouvant être classés selon la profession	X. Trab. que no pueden ser clasificados según la ocupación
			275 000	111 000	163 000	–. Personnes en quête d'emploi pour la première fois	–. Personas en busca de trabajo por primera vez
89 000	28 000	61 000	20 000	8 000	11 000	–. Autres chômeurs	–. Otros desempleados
2 170 000	**1 172 000**	**998 000**	**348 000**	**152 000**	**193 000**	**Total**	**Total**
125	21	104	.	.	.	0/1. Personnel des prof. scientif., techn., libérales et assimilées	0/1. Profesionales, técnicos y trabajadores asimilados
62	21	42	.	.	.	2. Directeurs et cadres adminis- tratifs supérieurs	2. Directores y funcionarios públicos superiores
582	166	416	.	.	.	3. Personnel administratif et travailleurs assimilés	3. Personal administrativo y trabajadores asimilados
22 337	9 505	12 832	.	.	.	4. Pers. commercial et vendeurs	4. Comerciantes y vendedores
2 163	853	1 310	.	.	.	5. Travailleurs des services	5. Trabajadores de los servicios
4 742	2 038	2 704	.	.	.	6. Agriculteurs, éleveurs, forestiers, pêcheurs et chasseurs	6. Trabajadores agrícolas y forestales, pescadores y cazadores
2 745	1 289	1 456	.	.	.	7–9. Ouvriers et manœuvres non agricoles et conducteurs d'engins de transport	7–9. Obreros no agrícolas, conductores de máquinas y vehíc. de transporte y trab. asimilados
...	...	...	24 313	16 243	8 070	X. Travailleurs ne pouvant être classés selon la profession / –. Autres chômeurs	X. Trab. que no pueden ser clasificados según la ocupación / –. Otros desempleados
32 757	**13 893**	**18 864**	**35 294**	**20 548**	**14 746**	**Total**	**Total**
...	...	...	...	...	...	0/1. Personnel des prof. scientif., techn., libérales et assimilées	0/1. Profesionales, técnicos y trabajadores asimilados
...	...	...	...	...	...	2. Directeurs et cadres adminis- tratifs supérieurs	2. Directores y funcionarios públicos superiores
...	...	...	...	...	...	3. Personnel administratif et travailleurs assimilés	3. Personal administrativo y trabajadores asimilados
...	...	...	...	...	...	4. Pers. commercial et vendeurs	4. Comerciantes y vendedores
...	...	...	...	...	...	5. Travailleurs des services	5. Trabajadores de los servicios
...	...	...	...	...	...	6. Agriculteurs, éleveurs, forestiers, pêcheurs et chasseurs	6. Trabajadores agrícolas y forestales, pescadores y cazadores
...	...	...	...	...	...	7–9. Ouvriers et manœuvres non agricoles et conducteurs d'engins de transport	7–9. Obreros no agrícolas, conductores de máquinas y vehíc. de transporte y trab. asimilados
.	.	.	.	.	.	–. Personnes en quête d'emploi pour la première fois	–. Personas en busca de trabajo por primera vez
...	...	...	...	...	...	**Total**	**Total**

2 Structure of the economically active population
Structure de la population active
Estructura de la población económicamente activa

Occupation (Major groups)	Total				Employers and own-account workers / Employeurs et personnes travaillant à leur propre compte / Empleadores y trabajadores por cuenta propia			Employees / Salariés / Empleados a sueldo o salario		
	Total	%	Males Hommes Hombres	Females Femmes Mujeres	Total	Males Hommes Hombres	Females Femmes Mujeres	Total	Males Hommes Hombres	Females Femmes Mujeres
Thailand (VII–IX.78) LFSS †										
0/1. Professional, technical & related workers	488 200	2.2	263 900	224 300	18 100	13 100	5 000	467 100	249 700	217 400
2. Administrative & managerial workers	211 100	1.0	176 200	34 900	85 400	75 600	9 800	125 700	100 600	25 100
3. Clerical & related workers	334 000	1.5	188 300	145 700	1 100	900	200	317 500	185 000	132 500
4. Sales workers	1 660 900	7.6	666 100	994 800	892 200	414 000	478 200	163 000	116 000	47 000
5. Service workers	603 800	2.8	340 500	263 300	72 000	28 300	43 700	516 600	308 200	208 400
6. Agric., animal husbandry & forestry workers, fishermen & hunters	16 026 700	73.2	8 195 100	7 831 600	5 249 600	4 313 200	936 400	1 043 400	541 900	501 500
7–9. Prod./related workers, transport equipment operators & labourers	2 405 400	11.0	1 676 100	729 300	506 500	374 600	131 900	1 675 200	1 214 600	460 600
X. Workers not classifiable by occupation	6 400	–	3 400	3 000	.	.	.	600	600	
–. Persons seeking work for the first time	100 900	0.4	61 800	39 100	.	.	.	.	.	.
–. Other unemployed	55 900	0.3	42 900	13 000	...	...	...	...	...	...
Total	**21 893 300**	*100.0*	**11 614 300**	**10 279 000**	**6 824 900**	**5 219 700**	**1 605 200**	**4 309 100**	**2 716 600**	**1 592 500**
United Arab Emirates (1975) OE										
0/1. Professional, technical & related workers	22 026	7.4	17 703	4 323	...	...	...	...	...	...
2. Administrative & managerial workers	5 840	2.0	5 800	40	...	...	...	...	...	...
3. Clerical & related workers	31 373	10.6	29 398	1 975	...	...	...	...	...	...
4. Sales workers	18 080	6.1	17 942	138	...	...	...	...	...	...
5. Service workers	46 688	15.7	43 788	2 900	...	...	...	...	...	...
6. Agric., animal husbandry & forestry workers, fishermen & hunters	13 732	4.7	13 694	38	...	...	...	...	...	...
7–9. Prod./related workers, transport equipment operators & labourers	154 213	52.0	154 098	115	...	...	...	...	...	...
X. Workers not classifiable by occupation	574	0.2	564	10	...	...	...	...	...	...
–. Persons seeking work for the first time	3 990	1.3	3 568	422	...	...	...	...	...	...
Total	**296 516**	*100.0*	**286 555**	**9 961**	...	...	...	...	...	...
EUROPE										
Austria (1979) LFSS †										
0/1. Professional, technical & related workers	114 000	3.7	106 000	8 000	10 000	10 000	–	104 000	96 000	8 000
2/3. Admin. & managerial workers / clerical & related workers	632 000	20.4	314 000	318 000	39 000	23 000	16 000	593 000	291 000	302 000
4. Sales workers	267 000	8.6	109 000	158 000	59 000	31 000	28 000	208 000	78 000	130 000
5. Service workers	507 000	16.4	159 000	348 000	71 000	35 000	36 000	436 000	124 000	312 000
6. Agric., animal husbandry & forestry workers, fishermen & hunters	325 000	10.5	164 000	161 000	284 000	136 000	148 000	41 000	28 000	13 000
7–9. Prod./related workers, transport equipment operators & labourers	1 230 000	39.8	1 029 000	201 000	65 000	58 000	7 000	1 165 000	971 000	194 000
X. Workers not classifiable by occupation	8 000	0.2	4 000	4 000	–	–	–	8 000	4 000	4 000
–. Armed forces	11 000	0.4	11 000	.	.	.	.	11 000	11 000	
Total	**3 094 000**	*100.0*	**1 896 000**	**1 198 000**	**528 000**	**293 000**	**235 000**	**2 566 000**	**1 603 000**	**963 000**

B By occupational group, by status and by sex
Par groupe de professions, selon la situation dans la profession et par sexe
Por grupo de ocupación, según la categoría de ocupación y por sexo

Unpaid family workers / Travailleurs familiaux non rémunérés / Trabajadores familiares no remunerados			Not classifiable by status / Inclassables selon la situation / Inclasificables según la categoría			Profession (Grands groupes)	Ocupación (Grandes grupos)
Total	Males Hommes Hombres	Females Femmes Mujeres	Total	Males Hommes Hombres	Females Femmes Mujeres		
3 000	1 100	1 900	...	...	...	0/1. Personnel des prof. scientif., techn., libérales et assimilées	0/1. Profesionales, técnicos y trabajadores asimilados
.	.	.	...	...	...	2. Directeurs et cadres administratifs supérieurs	2. Directores y funcionarios públicos superiores
15 400	2 400	13 000	...	...	...	3. Personnel administratif et travailleurs assimilés	3. Personal administrativo y trabajadores asimilados
605 700	136 100	469 600	...	...	...	4. Pers. commercial et vendeurs	4. Comerciantes y vendedores
15 200	4 000	11 200	...	...	...	5. Travailleurs des services	5. Trabajadores de los servicios
9 733 700	3 340 000	6 393 700	...	...	...	6. Agriculteurs, éleveurs, forestiers, pêcheurs et chasseurs	6. Trabajadores agrícolas y forestales, pescadores y cazadores
223 700	86 900	136 800	...	...	...	7–9. Ouvriers et manœuvres non agricoles et conducteurs d'engins de transport	7–9. Obreros no agrícolas, conductores de máquinas y vehíc. de transporte y trab. asimilados
100	100	.	5 700	2 700	3 000	X. Travailleurs ne pouvant être classés selon la profession	X. Trab. que no pueden ser clasificados según la ocupación
.	.	.	100 900	61 800	39 100	–. Personnes en quête d'emploi pour la première fois	–. Personas en busca de trabajo por primera vez
...	...	...	55 900	42 900	13 000	–. Autres chômeurs	–. Otros desempleados
10 596 800	**3 570 600**	**7 026 200**	**162 500**	**107 400**	**55 100**	**Total**	**Total**
...	...	...	...	...	...	0/1. Personnel des prof. scientif., techn., libérales et assimilées	0/1. Profesionales, técnicos y trabajadores asimilados
...	...	...	...	...	...	2. Directeurs et cadres administratifs supérieurs	2. Directores y funcionarios públicos superiores
...	...	...	...	...	...	3. Personnel administratif et travailleurs assimilés	3. Personal administrativo y trabajadores asimilados
...	...	...	...	...	...	4. Pers. commercial et vendeurs	4. Comerciantes y vendedores
...	...	...	...	...	...	5. Travailleurs des services	5. Trabajadores de los servicios
						6. Agriculteurs, éleveurs, forestiers, pêcheurs et chasseurs	6. Trabajadores agrícolas y forestales, pescadores y cazadores
...	...	...	...	...	...	7–9. Ouvriers et manœuvres non agricoles et conducteurs d'engins de transport	7–9. Obreros no agrícolas, conductores de máquinas y vehíc. de transporte y trab. asimilados
...	...	...	...	...	...	X. Travailleurs ne pouvant être classés selon la profession	X. Trab. que no pueden ser clasificados según la ocupación
...	...	...	...	...	...	–. Personnes en quête d'emploi pour la première fois	–. Personas en busca de trabajo por primera vez
...	...	...	...	...	...	**Total**	**Total**

EUROPE – EUROPA

...	...	...	.	.	.	0/1. Personnel des prof. scientif., techn., libérales et assimilées	0/1. Profesionales, técnicos y trabajadores asimilados
						2/3. Directeurs et cadres admin. supér. / personnel admin. et travailleurs assimilés	2/3. Directores y funcionarios públicos super. / pers. admin. y trabajadores asimilados
...	...	...	.	.	.	4. Pers. commercial et vendeurs	4. Comerciantes y vendedores
...	...	...	.	.	.	5. Travailleurs des services	5. Trabajadores de los servicios
						6. Agriculteurs, éleveurs, forestiers, pêcheurs et chasseurs	6. Trabajadores agrícolas y forestales, pescadores y cazadores
...	...	...	.	.	.	7–9. Ouvriers et manœuvres non agricoles et conducteurs d'engins de transport	7–9. Obreros no agrícolas, conductores de máquinas y vehíc. de transporte y trab. asimilados
.	.	.	.	.	.	X. Travailleurs ne pouvant être classés selon la profession	X. Trab. que no pueden ser clasificados según la ocupación
						–. Forces armées	–. Fuerzas armadas
...	...	...	.	.	.	**Total**	**Total**

2 Structure of the economically active population
Structure de la population active
Estructura de la población económicamente activa

Occupation (Major groups)	Total				Employers and own-account workers / Employeurs et personnes travaillant à leur propre compte / Empleadores y trabajadores por cuenta propia			Employees / Salariés / Empleados a sueldo o salario		
	Total	%	Males Hommes Hombres	Females Femmes Mujeres	Total	Males Hommes Hombres	Females Femmes Mujeres	Total	Males Hommes Hombres	Females Femmes Mujeres
España (X–XII.79) LFSS †										
0/1. Professional, technical & related workers	778 300	5.9	498 100	280 200	97 000	77 700	19 300	674 100	415 900	258 200
2. Administrative & managerial workers	182 400	1.3	176 700	5 700	103 300	100 500	2 800	78 900	76 000	2 900
3. Clerical & related workers	1 224 100	9.2	763 500	460 600	.	.	.	1 191 000	753 100	437 900
4. Sales workers	1 217 700	9.2	693 400	524 300	489 400	311 000	178 400	541 800	347 800	194 000
5. Service workers	1 445 600	10.8	582 300	863 300	195 100	122 900	72 200	1 155 200	439 100	716 100
6. Agric., animal husbandry & forestry workers, fishermen & hunters	2 326 900	17.5	1 678 600	648 300	1 072 100	897 000	175 100	643 400	571 300	72 100
7–9. Prod./related workers, transport equipment operators & labourers	4 671 400	35.2	3 989 300	682 100	606 500	532 200	74 300	3 970 100	3 402 600	567 500
X. Workers not classifiable by occupation	1 200	–	300	900	500	.	500	700	300	400
–. Unemployed	1 348 500	10.1	891 900	456 600	...	...	...	...	...	...
–. Armed forces	105 400	0.8	105 400	.	.	.	.	105 400	105 400	.
Total	**13 301 500**	**100.0**	**9 379 500**	**3 922 000**	**2 563 900**	**2 041 300**	**522 600**	**8 360 600**	**6 111 500**	**2 249 100**
France (20.II.75) C5% †										
0/1. Professional, technical & related workers	3 365 500	15.5	1 872 200	1 493 300	368 100	233 300	134 800	2 989 200	1 637 500	1 351 700
2. Administrative & managerial workers	709 300	3.2	593 200	116 100	151 000	133 200	17 800	556 400	459 500	96 900
3. Clerical & related workers	3 059 000	14.1	1 020 900	2 038 100	7 300	3 500	3 800	3 020 900	1 016 400	2 004 500
4. Sales workers	1 579 000	7.2	795 000	784 000	564 500	331 700	232 800	888 500	452 300	436 200
5. Service workers	1 730 300	8.0	575 800	1 154 500	210 300	102 500	107 800	1 485 600	468 100	1 017 500
6. Agric., animal husbandry & forestry workers, fishermen & hunters	2 099 400	9.6	1 488 800	610 600	1 160 500	971 100	189 400	432 100	388 500	43 600
7–9. Prod./related workers, transport equipment operators & labourers	7 858 500	36.1	6 488 700	1 369 800	576 500	546 000	30 500	7 254 700	5 928 700	1 326 000
X. Workers not classifiable by occupation	299 000	1.4	198 300	100 700	1 000	800	200	292 500	193 900	98 600
–. Unemployed	830 900	3.8	374 500	456 400	...	...	...	...	...	...
–. Armed forces	244 000	1.1	235 300	8 700	.	.	.	244 000	235 300	8 700
Total	**21 774 900**	**100.0**	**13 642 700**	**8 132 200**	**3 039 200**	**2 322 100**	**717 100**	**17 163 900**	**10 780 200**	**6 383 700**
Germany, Fed. Rep. of (IV.78) LFSS †										
0/1. Professional, technical & related workers	3 451 000	12.8	2 143 000	1 308 000	322 000	263 000	59 000	3 119 000	1 878 000	1 241 000
2. Administrative & managerial workers	837 000	3.1	697 000	140 000	141 000	114 000	28 000	691 000	582 000	108 000
3. Clerical & related workers	5 095 000	18.9	2 158 000	2 938 000	41 000	25 000	16 000	4 970 000	2 130 000	2 840 000
4. Sales workers	2 291 000	8.5	1 038 000	1 252 000	531 000	370 000	161 000	1 676 000	661 000	1 015 000
5. Service workers	2 909 000	10.8	1 307 000	1 602 000	230 000	125 000	105 000	2 618 000	1 175 000	1 442 000
6. Agric., animal husbandry & forestry workers, fishermen & hunters	1 541 000	5.7	778 000	763 000	523 000	449 000	73 000	285 000	213 000	72 000
7–9. Prod./related workers, transport equipment operators & labourers	9 531 000	35.4	8 000 000	1 531 000	466 000	434 000	32 000	9 045 000	7 558 000	1 487 000
X. Workers not classifiable by occupation	367 000	1.3	206 000	162 000	37 000	28 000	9 000	278 000	173 000	105 000
–. Unemployed	931 000	3.5	467 000	464 000	...	...	...	...	...	...
Total	**26 952 000**	**100.0**	**16 793 000**	**10 159 000**	**2 291 000**	**1 809 000**	**482 000**	**22 681 000**	**14 371 000**	**8 310 000**

B By occupational group, by status and by sex
Par groupe de professions, selon la situation dans la profession et par sexe
Por grupo de ocupación, según la categoría de ocupación y por sexo

Unpaid family workers / Travailleurs familiaux non rémunérés / Trabajadores familiares no remunerados			Not classifiable by status / Inclassables selon la situation / Inclasificables según la categoría			Profession (Grands groupes)	Ocupación (Grandes grupos)
Total	Males Hommes Hombres	Females Femmes Mujeres	Total	Males Hommes Hombres	Females Femmes Mujeres		
5 400	3 200	2 200	1 800	1 300	500	0/1. Personnel des prof. scientif., techn., libérales et assimilées	0/1. Profesionales, técnicos y trabajadores asimilados
.	.	.	200	200	.	2. Directeurs et cadres administratifs supérieurs	2. Directores y funcionarios públicos superiores
31 400	9 500	21 900	1 700	900	800	3. Personnel administratif et travailleurs assimilés	3. Personal administrativo y trabajadores asimilados
184 000	33 700	150 300	2 500	900	1 600	4. Pers. commercial et vendeurs	4. Comerciantes y vendedores
91 400	19 100	72 300	3 900	1 200	2 700	5. Travailleurs des services	5. Trabajadores de los servicios
597 500	201 000	396 500	13 900	9 300	4 600	6. Agriculteurs, éleveurs, forestiers, pêcheurs et chasseurs	6. Trabajadores agrícolas y forestales, pescadores y cazadores
87 400	48 200	39 200	7 400	6 300	1 100	7-9. Ouvriers et manœuvres non agricoles et conducteurs d'engins de transport	7-9. Obreros no agrícolas, conductores de máquinas y vehíc. de transporte y trab. asimilados
.	.	.	.	.	.	X. Travailleurs ne pouvant être classés selon la profession	X. Trab. que no pueden ser clasificados según la ocupación
...	...	...	1 348 500	891 900	456 600	-. Chômeurs	-. Desempleados
.	.	.	.	.	.	-. Forces armées	-. Fuerzas armadas
997 100	**314 700**	**682 400**	**1 379 900**	**912 000**	**467 900**	**Total**	**Total**
8 200	1 400	6 800	...	...	...	0/1. Personnel des prof. scientif., techn., libérales et assimilées	0/1. Profesionales, técnicos y trabajadores asimilados
1 900	500	1 400	...	...	...	2. Directeurs et cadres administratifs supérieurs	2. Directores y funcionarios públicos superiores
30 700	900	29 800	...	...	...	3. Personnel administratif et travailleurs assimilés	3. Personal administrativo y trabajadores asimilados
126 000	11 000	115 000	...	...	...	4. Pers. commercial et vendeurs	4. Comerciantes y vendedores
34 400	5 200	29 200	...	...	...	5. Travailleurs des services	5. Trabajadores de los servicios
506 800	129 200	377 600	...	...	...	6. Agriculteurs, éleveurs, forestiers, pêcheurs et chasseurs	6. Trabajadores agrícolas y forestales, pescadores y cazadores
27 300	14 000	13 300	...	...	...	7-9. Ouvriers et manœuvres non agricoles et conducteurs d'engins de transport	7-9. Obreros no agrícolas, conductores de máquinas y vehíc. de transporte y trab. asimilados
1 400	400	1 000	4 200	3 300	900	X. Travailleurs ne pouvant être classés selon la profession	X. Trab. que no pueden ser clasificados según la ocupación
...	...	...	830 900	374 500	456 400	-. Chômeurs	-. Desempleados
.	.	.	.	.	.	-. Forces armées	-. Fuerzas armadas
736 700	**162 600**	**574 100**	**835 000**	**377 700**	**457 300**	**Total**	**Total**
9 000	–	7 000	...	...	...	0/1. Personnel des prof. scientif., techn., libérales et assimilées	0/1. Profesionales, técnicos y trabajadores asimilados
–	–	–	...	...	...	2. Directeurs et cadres administratifs supérieurs	2. Directores y funcionarios públicos superiores
84 000	–	82 000	...	...	...	3. Personnel administratif et travailleurs assimilés	3. Personal administrativo y trabajadores asimilados
84 000	7 000	77 000	...	...	...	4. Pers. commercial et vendeurs	4. Comerciantes y vendedores
61 000	6 000	55 000	...	...	...	5. Travailleurs des services	5. Trabajadores de los servicios
734 000	116 000	618 000	...	...	...	6. Agriculteurs, éleveurs, forestiers, pêcheurs et chasseurs	6. Trabajadores agrícolas y forestales, pescadores y cazadores
20 000	8 000	13 000	...	...	...	7-9. Ouvriers et manœuvres non agricoles et conducteurs d'engins de transport	7-9. Obreros no agrícolas, conductores de máquinas y vehíc. de transporte y trab. asimilados
52 000	–	47 000	...	...	...	X. Travailleurs ne pouvant être classés selon la profession	X. Trab. que no pueden ser clasificados según la ocupación
...	...	...	931 000	467 000	464 000	-. Chômeurs	-. Desempleados
1 049 000	**147 000**	**903 000**	**931 000**	**467 000**	**464 000**	**Total**	**Total**

ACTIVE POPULATION

2 Structure of the economically active population
Structure de la population active
Estructura de la población económicamente activa

Occupation (Major groups)	Total				Employers and own-account workers / Employeurs et personnes travaillant à leur propre compte / Empleadores y trabajadores por cuenta propia			Employees / Salariés / Empleados a sueldo o salario		
	Total	%	Males Hommes Hombres	Females Femmes Mujeres	Total	Males Hommes Hombres	Females Femmes Mujeres	Total	Males Hommes Hombres	Females Femmes Mujeres
Ireland (IV.77) LFSS †										
0/1. Professional, technical & related workers	128 700	11.3	66 100	62 700	10 000	8 000	2 000	118 700	58 100	60 600
2. Administrative & managerial workers	27 300	2.3	25 100	2 300	2 100	1 900	–	25 200	23 100	2 100
3. Clerical & related workers	111 800	9.8	34 700	77 100	–	–	–	111 000	34 500	76 600
4. Sales workers	108 500	9.5	71 400	37 100	35 500	26 600	8 900	68 200	43 900	24 400
5. Service workers	71 100	6.2	30 100	41 000	7 000	4 200	2 700	63 400	25 600	37 800
6. Agric., animal husbandry & forestry workers, fishermen & hunters	219 700	19.2	201 700	18 000	161 200	152 300	8 900	28 400	27 400	1 000
7–9. Prod./related workers, transport equipment operators & labourers	359 000	31.4	309 300	49 700	28 100	27 100	1 000	330 000	281 500	48 500
X. Workers not classifiable by occupation	17 200	1.5	16 700	–	–	–	–	17 100	16 600	–
–. Unemployed	100 600	8.8	79 800	20 800	...	...	...	...	...	...
Total	**1 143 900**	*100.0*	**834 800**	**309 100**	**243 900**	**220 100**	**23 500**	**762 000**	**510 700**	**251 000**
Netherlands (III–V.77) LFSS †										
0/1. Professional, technical & related workers	820 000	16.2	537 000	283 000	49 000	37 000	12 000	771 000	500 000	271 000
2. Administrative & managerial workers	118 000	2.3	111 000	8 000	26 000	24 000	2 000	93 000	87 000	6 000
3. Clerical & related workers	891 000	17.7	506 000	386 000	23 000	3 000	20 000	868 000	503 000	366 000
4. Sales workers	493 000	9.7	313 000	180 000	159 000	104 000	55 000	334 000	209 000	125 000
5. Service workers	501 000	9.9	177 000	324 000	56 000	31 000	25 000	445 000	146 000	299 000
6. Agric., animal husbandry & forestry workers, fishermen & hunters	289 000	5.7	246 000	43 000	186 000	151 000	35 000	103 000	95 000	8 000
7–9. Prod./related workers, transport equipment operators & labourers	1 573 000	31.1	1 482 000	91 000	81 000	75 000	6 000	1 492 000	1 407 000	85 000
X. Workers not classifiable by occupation	28 000	0.6	22 000	6 000	.	.	.	28 000	22 000	6 000
–. Unemployed	252 000	5.0	...	...	...	...	...	...	...	...
–. Armed forces	91 000	1.8	91 000	.	.	.	.	91 000	91 000	.
Total	**5 058 000**	*100.0*	**3 484 000**	**1 322 000**	**580 000**	**425 000**	**155 000**	**4 224 000**	**3 059 000**	**1 166 000**
Norway (1979) LFSS †										
0/1. Professional, technical & related workers	351 000	18.4	175 000	176 000	18 000	14 000	4 000	332 000	161 000	171 000
2. Administrative & managerial workers	94 000	4.9	77 000	16 000	9 000	7 000	2 000	85 000	70 000	15 000
3. Clerical & related workers	204 000	10.7	57 000	147 000	2 000	1 000	1 000	199 000	56 000	143 000
4. Sales workers	173 000	9.1	80 000	94 000	18 000	13 000	5 000	150 000	66 000	84 000
5. Service workers	239 000	12.5	50 000	191 000	13 000	3 000	10 000	224 000	46 000	178 000
6. Agric., animal husbandry & forestry workers, fishermen & hunters	157 000	8.2	108 000	49 000	79 000	70 000	9 000	34 000	28 000	6 000
7–9. Prod./related workers, transport equipment operators & labourers	639 000	33.5	552 000	87 000	51 000	49 000	2 000	585 000	500 000	85 000
X. Workers not classifiable by occupation	11 000	0.6	11 000	–	1 000	1 000	–	10 000	10 000	–
–. Unemployed	38 000	1.9	18 000	19 000	...	...	...	...	...	...
Total	**1 909 000**	*100.0*	**1 128 000**	**781 000**	**191 000**	**158 000**	**33 000**	**1 619 000**	**937 000**	**682 000**

B — By occupational group, by status and by sex
Par groupe de professions, selon la situation dans la profession et par sexe
Por grupo de ocupación, según la categoría de ocupación y por sexo

Unpaid family workers / Travailleurs familiaux non rémunérés / Trabajadores familiares no remunerados			Not classifiable by status / Inclassables selon la situation / Inclasificables según la categoría			Profession (Grands groupes)	Ocupación (Grandes grupos)
Total	Males / Hommes / Hombres	Females / Femmes / Mujeres	Total	Males / Hommes / Hombres	Females / Femmes / Mujeres		

Total	Males	Females	Total	Males	Females	Profession (Grands groupes)	Ocupación (Grandes grupos)
–	–	–	...	...	...	0/1. Personnel des prof. scientif., techn., libérales et assimilées	0/1. Profesionales, técnicos y trabajadores asimilados
–	–	–	...	...	...	2. Directeurs et cadres administratifs supérieurs	2. Directores y funcionarios públicos superiores
–	–	–	...	...	...	3. Personnel administratif et travailleurs assimilés	3. Personal administrativo y trabajadores asimilados
4 700	1 000	3 800	...	...	...	4. Pers. commercial et vendeurs	4. Comerciantes y vendedores
–	–	–	...	...	...	5. Travailleurs des services	5. Trabajadores de los servicios
30 100	22 000	8 100			...	6. Agriculteurs, éleveurs, forestiers, pêcheurs et chasseurs	6. Trabajadores agrícolas y forestales, pescadores y cazadores
						7–9. Ouvriers et manœuvres non agricoles et conducteurs d'engins de transport	7–9. Obreros no agrícolas, conductores de máquinas y vehíc. de transporte y trab. asimilados
–	–	–	...	...	...	X. Travailleurs ne pouvant être classés selon la profession	X. Trab. que no pueden ser clasificados según la ocupación
...	...	...	100 600	79 800	20 800	–. Chômeurs	–. Desempleados
34 800	**23 000**	**11 900**	**100 600**	**79 800**	**20 800**	**Total**	**Total**

Total	Males	Females	Total	Males	Females	Profession (Grands groupes)	Ocupación (Grandes grupos)
...	...	...	...	...	...	0/1. Personnel des prof. scientif., techn., libérales et assimilées	0/1. Profesionales, técnicos y trabajadores asimilados
...	...	...	...	...	...	2. Directeurs et cadres administratifs supérieurs	2. Directores y funcionarios públicos superiores
...	...	...	...	...	...	3. Personnel administratif et travailleurs assimilés	3. Personal administrativo y trabajadores asimilados
...	...	...	...	...	...	4. Pers. commercial et vendeurs	4. Comerciantes y vendedores
...	...	...	...	...	...	5. Travailleurs des services	5. Trabajadores de los servicios
...	...	...	...	...	...	6. Agriculteurs, éleveurs, forestiers, pêcheurs et chasseurs	6. Trabajadores agrícolas y forestales, pescadores y cazadores
...	...	...	...	...	...	7–9. Ouvriers et manœuvres non agricoles et conducteurs d'engins de transport	7–9. Obreros no agrícolas, conductores de máquinas y vehíc. de transporte y trab. asimilados
...	...	...	...	...	...	X. Travailleurs ne pouvant être classés selon la profession	X. Trab. que no pueden ser clasificados según la ocupación
.	.	...	252 000	...	...	–. Chômeurs	–. Desempleados
.	.	.	.	.	.	–. Forces armées	–. Fuerzas armadas
...	**...**	**...**	**252 000**	**...**	**...**	**Total**	**Total**

Total	Males	Females	Total	Males	Females	Profession (Grands groupes)	Ocupación (Grandes grupos)
1 000	–	1 000	...	...	...	0/1. Personnel des prof. scientif., techn., libérales et assimilées	0/1. Profesionales, técnicos y trabajadores asimilados
–	–	–	...	...	...	2. Directeurs et cadres administratifs supérieurs	2. Directores y funcionarios públicos superiores
3 000	–	3 000	...	...	...	3. Personnel administratif et travailleurs assimilés	3. Personal administrativo y trabajadores asimilados
5 000	1 000	4 000	...	...	...	4. Pers. commercial et vendeurs	4. Comerciantes y vendedores
2 000	–	2 000	...	...	...	5. Travailleurs des services	5. Trabajadores de los servicios
44 000	10 000	34 000	...	...	...	6. Agriculteurs, éleveurs, forestiers, pêcheurs et chasseurs	6. Trabajadores agrícolas y forestales, pescadores y cazadores
2 000	1 000	1 000	...	...	...	7–9. Ouvriers et manœuvres non agricoles et conducteurs d'engins de transport	7–9. Obreros no agrícolas, conductores de máquinas y vehíc. de transporte y trab. asimilados
–	–	–	...	...	...	X. Travailleurs ne pouvant être classés selon la profession	X. Trab. que no pueden ser clasificados según la ocupación
...	...	...	38 000	18 000	19 000	–. Chômeurs	–. Desempleados
57 000	**12 000**	**45 000**	**38 000**	**18 000**	**19 000**	**Total**	**Total**

2 Structure of the economically active population
Structure de la population active
Estructura de la población económicamente activa

Occupation (Major groups)	Total				Employers and own-account workers / Employeurs et personnes travaillant à leur propre compte / Empleadores y trabajadores por cuenta propia			Employees / Salariés / Empleados a sueldo o salario		
	Total	%	Males Hommes Hombres	Females Femmes Mujeres	Total	Males Hommes Hombres	Females Femmes Mujeres	Total	Males Hommes Hombres	Females Femmes Mujeres
Portugal (VII–XII.79) LFSS †										
0/1. Professional, technical & related workers	212 000	4.9	93 000	119 000	...	...	...	...	...	...
2. Administrative & managerial workers	59 000	1.4	50 000	9 000	...	...	...	...	...	...
3. Clerical & related workers	405 000	9.3	228 000	177 000	...	...	...	...	...	...
4. Sales workers	306 000	7.1	180 000	126 000	...	...	...	...	...	...
5. Service workers	385 000	8.9	149 000	236 000	...	...	...	...	...	...
6. Agric., animal husbandry & forestry workers, fishermen & hunters	1 179 000	27.2	584 000	595 000	...	...	...	...	...	...
7–9. Prod./related workers, transport equipment operators & labourers	1 498 000	34.6	1 133 000	365 000	...	...	...	...	...	...
X. Workers not classifiable by occupation	10 000	0.3	9 000	1 000	...	...	...	...	...	...
–. Persons seeking work for the first time	198 000	4.5	63 000	135 000	.	.	.	.	.	.
–. Armed forces	77 000	1.8	77 000	.	.	.	.	.	.	.
Total	**4 328 000**	**100.0**	**2 566 000**	**1 762 000**	...	...	...	...	...	...
Sweden (1979) LFSS †										
0/1. Professional, technical & related workers	1 069 800	25.1	514 600	555 200	25 500	18 400	7 100	1 044 300	496 300	548 000
2. Administrative & managerial workers	97 600	2.3	81 700	15 900	2 400	2 000	300	95 200	79 700	15 500
3. Clerical & related workers	508 300	11.9	107 400	400 900	6 500	1 400	5 100	500 700	106 000	394 700
4. Sales workers	342 500	8.0	179 900	162 600	41 900	25 800	16 100	298 800	153 900	144 900
5. Service workers	575 800	13.5	136 700	439 100	21 600	9 400	12 200	554 000	127 300	426 700
6. Agric., animal husbandry & forestry workers, fishermen & hunters	240 800	5.6	182 800	58 000	130 000	101 000	29 000	90 700	78 100	12 600
7–9. Prod./related workers, transport equipment operators & labourers	1 344 500	31.5	1 111 500	233 100	84 500	78 900	5 500	1 258 800	1 031 800	227 000
–. Unemployed	88 000	2.1	44 000	44 000	...	...	...	...	...	...
Total	**4 267 600**	**100.0**	**2 359 000**	**1 908 600**	**312 300**	**237 000**	**75 400**	**3 842 800**	**2 073 300**	**1 769 500**

OCEANIA

Occupation (Major groups)	Total	%	Males	Females	Total	Males	Females	Total	Males	Females
Australia (30.VI.76) C †										
0/1. Professional, technical & related workers	683 613	11.3	372 938	310 675	50 424	42 984	7 440	631 527	329 436	302 091
2. Administrative & managerial workers	381 329	6.3	325 191	56 139	114 000	89 279	24 721	266 855	235 670	31 185
3. Clerical & related workers	954 880	15.8	311 871	643 009	50 134	1 460	48 674	898 221	310 217	589 004
4. Sales workers	448 809	7.4	220 522	228 286	70 507	22 564	47 943	352 062	175 022	177 040
5. Service workers	452 755	7.4	171 434	281 322	30 516	16 892	13 624	419 750	154 107	265 643
6. Agric., animal husbandry & forestry workers, fishermen & hunters	430 838	7.2	304 005	126 833	263 088	179 448	83 640	132 357	116 827	15 530
7–9. Prod./related workers, transport equipment operators & labourers	2 058 637	34.0	1 796 688	261 949	192 551	182 756	9 795	1 862 902	1 611 580	251 322
X. Workers not classifiable by occupation	61 215	1.0	57 913	3 302	8 691	3 852	4 839	276 520	148 448	128 072
–. Unemployed	266 826	4.4	157 708	109 118	...	...	...	...	...	...
–. Armed forces	61 214	1.0	57 912	3 302	.	.	.	61 214	57 912	3 302
Total	**6 054 996**	**100.0**	**3 875 323**	**2 179 673**	**801 956**	**561 276**	**240 680**	**4 901 416**	**3 139 222**	**1 762 194**

B By occupational group, by status and by sex
Par groupe de professions, selon la situation dans la profession et par sexe
Por grupo de ocupación, según la categoría de ocupación y por sexo

Unpaid family workers Travailleurs familiaux non rémunérés Trabajadores familiares no remunerados			Not classifiable by status Inclassables selon la situation Inclasificables según la categoría			Profession (Grands groupes)	Ocupación (Grandes grupos)
Total	Males Hommes Hombres	Females Femmes Mujeres	Total	Males Hommes Hombres	Females Femmes Mujeres		
...	...	...	...	...	...	0/1. Personnel des prof. scientif., techn., libérales et assimilées	0/1. Profesionales, técnicos y trabajadores asimilados
...	...	...	...	...	...	2. Directeurs et cadres administratifs supérieurs	2. Directores y funcionarios públicos superiores
...	...	...	...	...	...	3. Personnel administratif et travailleurs assimilés	3. Personal administrativo y trabajadores asimilados
...	...	...	...	...	...	4. Pers. commercial et vendeurs	4. Comerciantes y vendedores
...	...	...	...	...	...	5. Travailleurs des services	5. Trabajadores de los servicios
...	...	...	...	...	...	6. Agriculteurs, éleveurs, forestiers, pêcheurs et chasseurs	6. Trabajadores agrícolas y forestales, pescadores y cazadores
						7–9. Ouvriers et manœuvres non agricoles et conducteurs d'engins de transport	7–9. Obreros no agrícolas, conductores de máquinas y vehíc. de transporte y trab. asimilados
...	...	...	...	...	...	X. Travailleurs ne pouvant être classés selon la profession	X. Trab. que no pueden ser clasificados según la ocupación
.	.	.	.	.	.	–. Personnes en quête d'emploi pour la première fois	–. Personas en busca de trabajo por primera vez
.	.	.	.	.	.	–. Forces armées	–. Fuerzas armadas
...	...	...	...	...	...	**Total**	**Total**
100	–	100	...	...	...	0/1. Personnel des prof. scientif., techn., libérales et assimilées	0/1. Profesionales, técnicos y trabajadores asimilados
–	–	–	...	...	...	2. Directeurs et cadres administratifs supérieurs	2. Directores y funcionarios públicos superiores
1 100	–	1 100	...	...	...	3. Personnel administratif et travailleurs assimilés	3. Personal administrativo y trabajadores asimilados
1 800	200	1 600	...	...	...	4. Pers. commercial et vendeurs	4. Comerciantes y vendedores
300	–	200	...	...	...	5. Travailleurs des services	5. Trabajadores de los servicios
20 200	3 700	16 400	...	...	...	6. Agriculteurs, éleveurs, forestiers, pêcheurs et chasseurs	6. Trabajadores agrícolas y forestales, pescadores y cazadores
1 200	600	600				7–9. Ouvriers et manœuvres non agricoles et conducteurs d'engins de transport	7–9. Obreros no agrícolas, conductores de máquinas y vehíc. de transporte y trab. asimilados
...	...	...	88 000	44 000	44 000	–. Chômeurs	–. Desempleados
24 600	**4 500**	**20 100**	**88 000**	**44 000**	**44 000**	**Total**	**Total**

OCEANIE – OCEANIA

Unpaid family workers			Not classifiable by status			Profession (Grands groupes)	Ocupación (Grandes grupos)
1 660	517	1 143	...	...	...	0/1. Personnel des prof. scientif., techn., libérales et assimilées	0/1. Profesionales, técnicos y trabajadores asimilados
472	241	231	...	...	...	2. Directeurs et cadres administratifs supérieurs	2. Directores y funcionarios públicos superiores
6 522	193	6 329	...	...	...	3. Personnel administratif et travailleurs assimilés	3. Personal administrativo y trabajadores asimilados
4 197	895	3 302	...	...	...	4. Pers. commercial et vendeurs	4. Comerciantes y vendedores
2 496	434	2 052	...	...	...	5. Travailleurs des services	5. Trabajadores de los servicios
35 391	7 730	27 661	...	...	...	6. Agriculteurs, éleveurs, forestiers, pêcheurs et chasseurs	6. Trabajadores agrícolas y forestales, pescadores y cazadores
3 180	2 350	830	...	...	...	7–9. Ouvriers et manœuvres non agricoles et conducteurs d'engins de transport	7–9. Obreros no agrícolas, conductores de máquinas y vehíc. de transporte y trab. asimilados
30 876	4 750	26 126	...	...	...	X. Travailleurs ne pouvant être classés selon la profession	X. Trab. que no pueden ser clasificados según la ocupación
...	...	...	266 826	157 708	109 118	–. Chômeurs	–. Desempleados
.	.	.	.	.	.	–. Forces armées	–. Fuerzas armadas
84 784	**17 109**	**67 675**	**266 826**	**157 708**	**109 118**	**Total**	**Total**

2 Structure of the economically active population
Structure de la population active
Estructura de la población económicamente activa

Occupation (Major groups)	Total				Employers and own-account workers / Employeurs et personnes travaillant à leur propre compte / Empleadores y trabajadores por cuenta propia			Employees / Salariés / Empleados a sueldo o salario		
	Total	%	Males Hommes Hombres	Females Femmes Mujeres	Total	Males Hommes Hombres	Females Femmes Mujeres	Total	Males Hommes Hombres	Females Femmes Mujeres
Australia (V.80) LFSS										
0/1. Professional, technical & related workers	870 500	13.1	473 800	396 700	...	...	...	...	...	...
2. Administrative & managerial workers	410 100	6.2	350 200	60 000	...	...	...	...	...	...
3. Clerical & related workers	1 056 500	15.8	316 400	740 100	...	...	...	...	...	...
4. Sales workers	572 500	8.6	266 600	305 900	...	...	...	...	...	...
5. Service workers	609 100	9.2	228 200	380 900	...	...	...	...	...	...
6. Agric., animal husbandry & forestry workers, fishermen & hunters	445 100	6.7	356 100	89 000	...	...	...	...	...	...
7-9. Prod./related workers, transport equipment operators & labourers	2 273 900	34.2	1 989 900	284 000	...	...	...	...	...	...
-. Unemployed	413 600	6.2	219 900	193 700	...	...	...	...	...	...
Total	**6 651 400**	100.0	**4 201 100**	**2 450 300**	...	...	...	...	...	...
Cook Islands (1.XII.76) C										
0/1. Professional, technical & related workers	882	16.4	510	372	20	15	5	862	495	367
2. Administrative & managerial workers	187	3.5	165	22	18	13	5	169	152	17
3. Clerical & related workers	511	9.4	281	230	10	5	5	500	275	225
4. Sales workers	279	5.2	126	153	77	51	26	196	72	124
5. Service workers	410	7.6	237	173	6	3	3	400	232	168
6. Agric., animal husbandry & forestry workers, fishermen & hunters	1 117	20.8	1 101	16	726	718	8	232	232	.
7-9. Prod./related workers, transport equipment operators & labourers	1 425	26.5	1 116	309	67	30	37	1 354	1 082	272
X. Workers not classifiable by occupation	573	10.6	314	259	8	7	1	3	.	3
Total	**5 384**	100.0	**3 850**	**1 534**	**932**	**842**	**90**	**3 716**	**2 540**	**1 176**
Fiji (13.IX.76) C †										
0/1. Professional, technical & related workers	12 649	7.2	7 817	4 772	413	355	58	12 017	7 583	4 634
2. Administrative & managerial workers	1 656	0.9	1 529	127	363	333	30	1 277	1 183	94
3. Clerical & related workers	11 462	6.6	6 896	4 566	106	78	28	11 245	6 755	4 490
4. Sales workers	9 222	5.2	7 124	2 098	3 612	2 862	750	4 956	3 835	1 121
5. Service workers	11 429	6.5	6 303	5 126	349	283	66	10 913	5 966	4 947
6. Agric., animal husbandry & forestry workers, fishermen & hunters	76 444	43.5	69 849	6 595	49 114	45 275	3 839	14 808	14 406	402
7-9. Prod./related workers, transport equipment operators & labourers	38 680	22.0	36 979	1 701	4 313	3 891	422	33 556	32 397	1 159
-. Workers not classifiable by occupation & unemployed	14 243	8.1	9 758	4 485	411	355	56	1 741	1 440	301
Total	**175 785**	100.0	**146 315**	**29 470**	**58 681**	**53 432**	**5 249**	**90 513**	**73 365**	**17 148**

B By occupational group, by status and by sex
Par groupe de professions, selon la situation dans la profession et par sexe
Por grupo de ocupación, según la categoría de ocupación y por sexo

Unpaid family workers — Travailleurs familiaux non rémunérés — Trabajadores familiares no remunerados			Not classifiable by status — Inclassables selon la situation — Inclasificables según la categoría			Profession (Grands groupes)	Ocupación (Grandes grupos)
Total	Males / Hommes / Hombres	Females / Femmes / Mujeres	Total	Males / Hommes / Hombres	Females / Femmes / Mujeres		
...	...	...	...	...	...	0/1. Personnel des prof. scientif., techn., libérales et assimilées	0/1. Profesionales, técnicos y trabajadores asimilados
...	...	...	...	...	...	2. Directeurs et cadres administratifs supérieurs	2. Directores y funcionarios públicos superiores
...	...	...	...	...	...	3. Personnel administratif et travailleurs assimilés	3. Personal administrativo y trabajadores asimilados
...	...	...	...	...	...	4. Pers. commercial et vendeurs	4. Comerciantes y vendedores
...	...	...	...	...	...	5. Travailleurs des services	5. Trabajadores de los servicios
						6. Agriculteurs, éleveurs, forestiers, pêcheurs et chasseurs	6. Trabajadores agrícolas y forestales, pescadores y cazadores
...	...	...	...	...	...	7-9. Ouvriers et manœuvres non agricoles et conducteurs d'engins de transport	7-9. Obreros no agrícolas, conductores de máquinas y vehíc. de transporte y trab. asimilados
...	...	...	...	...	...	-. Chômeurs	-. Desempleados
...	**...**	**...**	**...**	**...**	**...**	**Total**	**Total**
·	·	·	...	...	...	0/1. Personnel des prof. scientif., techn., libérales et assimilées	0/1. Profesionales, técnicos y trabajadores asimilados
·	·	·	...	...	...	2. Directeurs et cadres administratifs supérieurs	2. Directores y funcionarios públicos superiores
1	1	.	...	...	...	3. Personnel administratif et travailleurs assimilés	3. Personal administrativo y trabajadores asimilados
6	3	3	...	...	...	4. Pers. commercial et vendeurs	4. Comerciantes y vendedores
4	2	2	...	...	...	5. Travailleurs des services	5. Trabajadores de los servicios
159	151	8	...	...	...	6. Agriculteurs, éleveurs, forestiers, pêcheurs et chasseurs	6. Trabajadores agrícolas y forestales, pescadores y cazadores
4	4	.	...	...	...	7-9. Ouvriers et manœuvres non agricoles et conducteurs d'engins de transport	7-9. Obreros no agrícolas, conductores de máquinas y vehíc. de transporte y trab. asimilados
301	155	146	261	152	109	X. Travailleurs ne pouvant être classés selon la profession	X. Trab. que no pueden ser clasificados según la ocupación
475	**316**	**159**	**261**	**152**	**109**	**Total**	**Total**
102	63	39	117	76	41	0/1. Personnel des prof. scientif., techn., libérales et assimilées	0/1. Profesionales, técnicos y trabajadores asimilados
9	9	.	7	4	3	2. Directeurs et cadres administratifs supérieurs	2. Directores y funcionarios públicos superiores
38	20	18	73	43	30	3. Personnel administratif et travailleurs assimilés	3. Personal administrativo y trabajadores asimilados
611	402	209	43	25	18	4. Pers. commercial et vendeurs	4. Comerciantes y vendedores
83	27	56	84	27	57	5. Travailleurs des services	5. Trabajadores de los servicios
12 161	9 837	2 324	361	331	30	6. Agriculteurs, éleveurs, forestiers, pêcheurs et chasseurs	6. Trabajadores agrícolas y forestales, pescadores y cazadores
566	452	114	245	239	6	7-9. Ouvriers et manœuvres non agricoles et conducteurs d'engins de transport	7-9. Obreros no agrícolas, conductores de máquinas y vehíc. de transporte y trab. asimilados
106	54	52	11 985	7 909	4 076	-. Travailleurs ne pouvant être classés selon la profession et chômeurs	-. Trab. que no pueden ser clasificados según la ocupación y desempleados
13 676	**10 864**	**2 812**	**12 915**	**8 654**	**4 261**	**Total**	**Total**

2 Structure of the economically active population
Structure de la population active
Estructura de la población económicamente activa

Occupation (Major groups)	Total				Employers and own-account workers Employeurs et personnes travaillant à leur propre compte Empleadores y trabajadores por cuenta propia			Employees Salariés Empleados a sueldo o salario		
	Total	%	Males Hommes Hombres	Females Femmes Mujeres	Total	Males Hommes Hombres	Females Femmes Mujeres	Total	Males Hommes Hombres	Females Femmes Mujeres
New Zealand (23.III.76) C †										
0/1. Professional, technical & related workers	178 821	14.1	104 857	73 964	15 419	13 689	1 730	161 622	90 474	71 148
2. Administrative & managerial workers	40 908	3.2	38 035	2 873	3 563	3 075	488	37 208	34 858	2 350
3. Clerical & related workers	205 918	16.2	70 019	135 899	1 792	703	1 089	201 412	68 935	132 477
4. Sales workers	125 280	9.8	77 618	47 662	25 065	17 178	7 887	98 186	59 831	38 355
5. Service workers	84 619	6.7	35 725	48 894	10 344	5 852	4 492	72 385	29 292	43 093
6. Agric., animal husbandry & forestry workers, fishermen & hunters	130 690	10.2	108 650	22 040	69 603	60 292	9 311	57 759	46 975	10 784
7-9. Prod./related workers, transport equipment operators & labourers	468 836	36.9	403 071	65 765	47 726	45 682	2 044	414 228	351 875	62 353
X. Workers not classifiable by occupation	21 606	1.7	14 786	6 820	1 486	1 267	219	9 008	6 460	2 548
–. Persons seeking work for the first time	4 293	0.3	1 711	2 582	.	.	.	.	.	.
–. Armed forces	11 362	0.9	10 626	736	.	.	.	11 362	10 626	736
Total	**1 272 333**	**100.0**	**865 098**	**407 235**	**174 998**	**147 738**	**27 260**	**1 063 170**	**699 326**	**363 844**
Samoa (3.XI.76) C										
0/1. Professional, technical & related workers	4 312	11.3	2 241	2 071	34	30	4	4 268	2 203	2 065
2. Administrative & managerial workers	225	0.6	201	24	5	5	.	220	196	24
3. Clerical & related workers	2 175	5.6	1 308	867	11	8	3	2 163	1 299	864
4. Sales workers	1 444	3.8	678	766	397	201	196	1 044	474	570
5. Service workers	1 470	3.9	715	755	13	9	4	1 454	703	751
6. Agric., animal husbandry & forestry workers, fishermen & hunters	23 082	60.3	21 545	1 537	726	651	75	1 800	1 401	399
7-9. Prod./related workers, transport equipment operators & labourers	5 475	14.3	5 141	334	265	252	13	5 082	4 767	315
X. Workers not classifiable by occupation	21	0.1	9	12	.	.	.	5	3	2
–. Unemployed	45	0.1	29	16	1	1	.	33	23	10
Total	**38 249**	**100.0**	**31 867**	**6 382**	**1 452**	**1 157**	**295**	**16 069**	**11 069**	**5 000**
Tonga (30.XI.76) C †										
0/1. Professional, technical & related workers	2 452	11.4	1 536	916	62	59	3	2 223	1 379	844
2. Administrative & managerial workers	187	0.9	172	15	21	17	4	151	143	8
3. Clerical & related workers	1 062	5.0	655	407	7	6	1	1 026	632	394
4. Sales workers	549	2.5	291	258	146	118	28	356	160	196
5. Service workers	970	4.6	810	160	13	10	3	927	778	149
6. Agric., animal husbandry & forestry workers, fishermen & hunters	9 425	43.9	9 369	56	6 486	6 460	26	234	224	10
7-9. Prod./related workers, transport equipment operators & labourers	2 207	10.3	2 093	114	246	233	13	1 899	1 808	91
X. Workers not classifiable by occupation	1 774	8.3	957	817	22	21	1	315	269	46
–. Persons seeking work for the first time	2 809	13.1	2 194	615	...	...	...	...	...	...
Total	**21 435**	**100.0**	**18 077**	**3 358**	**7 003**	**6 924**	**79**	**7 131**	**5 393**	**1 738**

B By occupational group, by status and by sex
Par groupe de professions, selon la situation dans la profession et par sexe
Por grupo de ocupación, según la categoría de ocupación y por sexo

Unpaid family workers / Travailleurs familiaux non rémunérés / Trabajadores familiares no remunerados			Not classifiable by status / Inclassables selon la situation / Inclasificables según la categoría			Profession (Grands groupes)	Ocupación (Grandes grupos)
Total	Males Hommes Hombres	Females Femmes Mujeres	Total	Males Hommes Hombres	Females Femmes Mujeres		
36	5	31	1 744	689	1 055	0/1. Personnel des prof. scientif., techn., libérales et assimilées	0/1. Profesionales, técnicos y trabajadores asimilados
24	3	21	113	99	14	2. Directeurs et cadres administratifs supérieurs	2. Directores y funcionarios públicos superiores
407	3	404	2 307	378	1 929	3. Personnel administratif et travailleurs assimilés	3. Personal administrativo y trabajadores asimilados
720	64	656	1 309	545	764	4. Pers. commercial et vendeurs	4. Comerciantes y vendedores
237	23	214	1 653	558	1 095	5. Travailleurs des services	5. Trabajadores de los servicios
2 173	487	1 686	1 155	896	259	6. Agriculteurs, éleveurs, forestiers, pêcheurs et chasseurs	6. Trabajadores agrícolas y forestales, pescadores y cazadores
217	58	159	6 665	5 456	1 209	7–9. Ouvriers et manœuvres non agricoles et conducteurs d'engins de transport	7–9. Obreros no agrícolas, conductores de máquinas y vehíc. de transporte y trab. asimilados
61	27	34	11 051	7 032	4 019	X. Travailleurs ne pouvant être classés selon la profession	X. Trab. que no pueden ser clasificados según la ocupación
.	.	.	4 293	1 711	2 582	–. Personnes en quête d'emploi pour la première fois	–. Personas en busca de trabajo por primera vez
.	.	.	.	.	.	–. Forces armées	–. Fuerzas armadas
3 875	**670**	**3 205**	**30 290**	**17 364**	**12 926**	**Total**	**Total**
9	7	2	1	1	0	0/1. Personnel des prof. scientif., techn., libérales et assimilées	0/1. Profesionales, técnicos y trabajadores asimilados
.	.	.	...	...	...	2. Directeurs et cadres administratifs supérieurs	2. Directores y funcionarios públicos superiores
1	1	.	...	...	...	3. Personnel administratif et travailleurs assimilés	3. Personal administrativo y trabajadores asimilados
3	3	.	...	...	...	4. Pers. commercial et vendeurs	4. Comerciantes y vendedores
3	3	.	...	...	...	5. Travailleurs des services	5. Trabajadores de los servicios
20 554	19 492	1 062	2	1	1	6. Agriculteurs, éleveurs, forestiers, pêcheurs et chasseurs	6. Trabajadores agrícolas y forestales, pescadores y cazadores
128	122	6	...	...	...	7–9. Ouvriers et manœuvres non agricoles et conducteurs d'engins de transport	7–9. Obreros no agrícolas, conductores de máquinas y vehíc. de transporte y trab. asimilados
.	.	.	16	6	10	X. Travailleurs ne pouvant être classés selon la profession	X. Trab. que no pueden ser clasificados según la ocupación
5	4	1	6	1	5	–. Chômeurs	–. Desempleados
20 703	**19 632**	**1 071**	**25**	**9**	**16**	**Total**	**Total**
131	77	54	36	21	15	0/1. Personnel des prof. scientif., techn., libérales et assimilées	0/1. Profesionales, técnicos y trabajadores asimilados
1	.	1	14	12	2	2. Directeurs et cadres administratifs supérieurs	2. Directores y funcionarios públicos superiores
.	.	.	29	17	12	3. Personnel administratif et travailleurs assimilés	3. Personal administrativo y trabajadores asimilados
37	8	29	10	5	5	4. Pers. commercial et vendeurs	4. Comerciantes y vendedores
18	11	7	12	11	1	5. Travailleurs des services	5. Trabajadores de los servicios
2 576	2 557	19	129	128	1	6. Agriculteurs, éleveurs, forestiers, pêcheurs et chasseurs	6. Trabajadores agrícolas y forestales, pescadores y cazadores
36	31	5	26	21	5	7–9. Ouvriers et manœuvres non agricoles et conducteurs d'engins de transport	7–9. Obreros no agrícolas, conductores de máquinas y vehíc. de transporte y trab. asimilados
14	13	1	1 423	654	769	X. Travailleurs ne pouvant être classés selon la profession	X. Trab. que no pueden ser clasificados según la ocupación
...	...	...	2 809	2 194	615	–. Personnes en quête d'emploi pour la première fois	–. Personas en busca de trabajo por primera vez
2 813	**2 697**	**116**	**4 488**	**3 063**	**1 425**	**Total**	**Total**

2 Structure of the economically active population
Structure de la population active
Estructura de la población económicamente activa

Industry (Major divisions of economic activity)	Total	Occupation (Major groups) [a]						
		1	2	3	4	5	6	7/8/9
		Professional, technical & related workers	Administrative & managerial workers	Clerical & related workers	Sales workers	Service workers	Agriculture, animal husbandry & forestry workers, fishermen & hunters	Production & related workers, transport equipment operators & labourers

AFRICA

Egypt (22–23.XI.76) C †

1. Agriculture, hunting, forestry & fishing	4 089 252	18 546	3 356	20 623	1 185	17 921	3 981 931	23 032
2. Mining & quarrying	32 474	3 919	380	2 852	226	2 257	1 433	20 798
3. Manufacturing	1 297 342	75 117	10 449	94 847	6 804	51 245	4 389	1 045 054
4. Electr., gas & water	61 487	12 695	388	11 029	165	7 644	581	28 367
5. Construction	408 878	15 642	12 381	18 072	555	18 202	8 050	332 944
6. Wholesale/retail trade, restaurants & hotels	821 678	15 983	3 798	33 227	613 602	100 742	1 631	49 350
7. Transport, storage & communication	472 794	23 014	3 094	90 431	793	25 193	698	326 409
8. Financing, insur., real estate & business serv.	87 117	25 142	3 728	40 033	2 105	10 902	931	3 328
9. Community, social & personal services	1 816 151	525 119	68 549	383 788	2 301	576 169	31 059	217 042
0. Not adequately defined	151 210	4 130	1 418	6 048	632	4 270	2 578	6 182
–. Persons seeking work for the first time	375 386	.	.	.	.	.	.	.
Total	**9 613 769**	**719 307**	**107 541**	**700 950**	**628 368**	**814 545**	**4 033 281**	**2 052 506**

Libyan Arab Jamahiriya (31.VII.73) C

1. Agriculture, hunting, forestry & fishing	121 917	1 045	94	1 755	136	2 863	110 559	5 402
2. Mining & quarrying	11 560	1 219	178	1 938	82	1 246	19	6 734
3. Manufacturing	22 173	355	179	751	160	822	57	19 767
4. Electr., gas & water	9 944	569	30	1 395	22	1 035	9	6 822
5. Construction	88 973	2 434	2 191	1 567	170	2 405	135	79 831
6. Wholesale/retail trade, restaurants & hotels	37 469	602	190	1 562	28 493	3 385	177	2 990
7. Transport, storage & communication	43 619	821	194	5 522	130	2 562	183	34 049
8. Financing, insur., real estate & business serv.	6 277	1 110	212	3 394	83	918	18	501
9. Community, social & personal services	172 963	45 400	797	19 481	240	64 371	729	32 232
0. Not adequately defined	16 505	257	66	677	1 132	734	129	2 331
–. Persons seeking work for the first time	9 774	.	.	.	.	.	.	.
Total	**541 174**	**53 812**	**4 131**	**38 042**	**30 648**	**80 341**	**112 015**	**190 659**

Malawi (1.X.77) C

1. Agriculture, hunting, forestry & fishing	1 932 122	2 930	176	5 888	3 308	5 494	1 893 640	20 511
2. Mining & quarrying	2 174	36	2	84	8	100	17	1 920
3. Manufacturing	82 391	952	377	3 367	2 994	3 560	3 468	67 478
4. Electr., gas & water	4 213	357	31	484	152	270	36	2 836
5. Construction	47 452	650	111	1 382	168	1 140	187	43 742
6. Wholesale/retail trade, restaurants & hotels	62 608	392	228	2 041	44 762	6 355	804	7 838
7. Transport, storage & communication	23 400	979	154	5 221	271	1 106	89	15 461
8. Financing, insur., real estate & business serv.	4 494	570	192	2 127	217	219	123	1 019
9. Community, social & personal services	82 523	23 412	894	8 906	1 510	28 196	3 323	15 970
0. Not adequately defined	46 974	176	42	634	402	515	307	1 626
Total	**2 288 351**	**30 454**	**2 207**	**30 134**	**53 792**	**46 955**	**1 901 994**	**178 401**

C By industry and by occupational group
Par industrie et par groupe de professions
Por industria y por grupo de ocupación

X Workers not classifiable by occupation	Unemployed First-time job seekers	Members of the armed forces	Industrie (Branches d'activité économique)	Industria (Grandes divisiones de actividad económica)

X	Unemployed / First-time job seekers	Members of the armed forces	Industrie	Industria
22 658	.	.	1. Agriculture, chasse, sylvi- culture et pêche	1. Agricultura, caza, silvi- cultura y pesca
609	.	.	2. Industries extractives	2. Minas y canteras
9 437	.	.	3. Industries manufacturières	3. Industrias manufactureras
618	.	.	4. Electricité, gaz et eau	4. Electricidad, gas y agua
3 032	.	.	5. Construction	5. Construcción
3 345	.	.	6. Commerce (gros et détail); restaurants, hôtels	6. Comercio (por mayor y por menor); restaurantes, hoteles
3 162	.	.	7. Transports, entrepôts et commu- nications	7. Transportes, almacenamiento y comunicaciones
948	.	.	8. Banques, assur., affaires imm., services aux entreprises	8. Bancos, seguros, bienes in- muebles, serv. para empresas
12 124	.	.	9. Services à la collectivité, services sociaux et personnels	9. Servicios comunales, sociales y personales
125 952	.	.	0. Activités mal désignées	0. Actividades no bien especif.
.	375 386	.	–. Personnes en quête d'emploi pour la première fois	–. Personas en busca de trabajo por primera vez
181 885	**375 386**	.	**Total**	**Total**
63	.	.	1. Agriculture, chasse, sylvi- culture et pêche	1. Agricultura, caza, silvi- cultura y pesca
144	.	.	2. Industries extractives	2. Minas y canteras
82	.	.	3. Industries manufacturières	3. Industrias manufactureras
62	.	.	4. Electricité, gaz et eau	4. Electricidad, gas y agua
240	.	.	5. Construction	5. Construcción
70	.	.	6. Commerce (gros et détail); restaurants, hôtels	6. Comercio (por mayor y por menor); restaurantes, hoteles
158	.	.	7. Transports, entrepôts et commu- nications	7. Transportes, almacenamiento y comunicaciones
41	.	.	8. Banques, assur., affaires imm., services aux entreprises	8. Bancos, seguros, bienes in- muebles, serv. para empresas
9 713	.	.	9. Services à la collectivité, services sociaux et personnels	9. Servicios comunales, sociales y personales
11 179	.	.	0. Activités mal désignées	0. Actividades no bien especif.
.	9 774	.	–. Personnes en quête d'emploi pour la première fois	–. Personas en busca de trabajo por primera vez
21 752	**9 774**	.	**Total**	**Total**
175	.	.	1. Agriculture, chasse, sylvi- culture et pêche	1. Agricultura, caza, silvi- cultura y pesca
7	.	.	2. Industries extractives	2. Minas y canteras
195	.	.	3. Industries manufacturières	3. Industrias manufactureras
47	.	.	4. Electricité, gaz et eau	4. Electricidad, gas y agua
72	.	.	5. Construction	5. Construcción
188	.	.	6. Commerce (gros et détail); restaurants, hôtels	6. Comercio (por mayor y por menor); restaurantes, hoteles
119	.	.	7. Transports, entrepôts et commu- nications	7. Transportes, almacenamiento y comunicaciones
27	.	.	8. Banques, assur., affaires imm., services aux entreprises	8. Bancos, seguros, bienes in- muebles, serv. para empresas
312	.	.	9. Services à la collectivité, services sociaux et personnels	9. Servicios comunales, sociales y personales
43 272	.	.	0. Activités mal désignées	0. Actividades no bien especif.
44 414	.	.	**Total**	**Total**

(a) Les libellés en français des grands groupes de professions sont indiqués à la page suivante.

2 Structure of the economically active population
Structure de la population active
Estructura de la población económicamente activa

Industry (Major divisions of economic activity)	Total	Profession (Grands groupes) [a]						
		1	2	3	4	5	6	7/8/9
		Personnel des prof. scientif., techniques, libérales et assimilées	Directeurs et cadres administratifs supérieurs	Personnel administratif et travailleurs assimilés	Personnel commercial et vendeurs	Travailleurs des services	Agriculteurs, éleveurs, forestiers, pêcheurs et chasseurs	Ouvriers et manœuvres non agricoles et conducteurs d'engins de transport
Tunisie (8.V.75) C*								
1. Agriculture, hunting, forestry & fishing	526 030	830	110	2 000	410	2 400	510 560	8 820
2. Mining & quarrying	27 210	590	50	1 190	30	660	150	24 370
3. Manufacturing	240 640	2 250	740	6 030	1 640	2 260	410	224 720
4. Electr., gas & water	11 680	790	70	2 740	60	530	90	7 050
5. Construction	140 740	960	190	1 230	120	650	660	136 410
6. Wholesale/retail trade, restaurants & hotels	119 570	2 560	920	12 180	67 700	25 620	2 550	4 040
7. Transport, storage & communication	57 380	1 580	320	14 540	420	1 520	260	37 760
8. Financing, insur., real estate & business serv.	7 770	120	20	1 050	340	450	970	3 950
9. Community, social & personal services	217 730	60 890	1 960	39 290	670	58 100	6 540	41 590
0. Not adequately defined	153 950	1 520	320	5 540	3 230	1 750	3 510	57 270
–. Persons seeking work for the first time	119 120	.	.	.	.	.	.	.
Total	**1 621 820**	**72 090**	**4 700**	**85 790**	**74 620**	**93 940**	**525 700**	**545 980**
AMERICA								
Bolivia (29.IX.76) C								
1. Agriculture, hunting, forestry & fishing	693 049	570	153	206	178	196	689 608	1 431
2. Mining & quarrying	60 599	2 087	1 015	4 403	82	1 836	194	50 605
3. Manufacturing	145 404	1 330	1 293	2 777	1 229	803	892	135 817
4. Electr., gas & water	2 143	185	33	522	5	84	13	1 275
5. Construction	82 447	1 797	386	1 360	11	572	1 018	76 901
6. Wholesale/retail trade, restaurants & hotels	106 862	819	2 786	2 770	86 945	7 147	277	5 713
7. Transport, storage & communication	55 972	749	288	6 540	169	706	56	46 988
8. Financing, insur., real estate & business serv.	12 941	4 888	234	6 967	225	141	3	370
9. Community, social & personal services	281 911	72 519	2 811	33 619	2 130	116 486	2 827	49 282
0. Not adequately defined	53 600	556	93	445	411	624	2 252	2 153
–. Persons seeking work for the first time	6 463	.	.	.	.	.	.	.
Total	**1 501 391**	**85 500**	**9 092**	**59 609**	**91 385**	**128 595**	**697 140**	**370 535**
Brasil (1.IX.70) C25% †								
1. Agriculture, hunting, forestry & fishing	12 878 320	1 613	39 713	3 965	338	710	12 800 461	31 272
2–5. Major div. 2, 3, 4 & 5	4 314 325	115 914	121 396	335 669	110 650	13 959	19 690	3 595 370
6. Wholesale/retail trade, restaurants & hotels	2 150 053	14 259	57 272	179 673	1 801 103	1 551	1 607	94 388
7. Transport, storage & communication	1 580 735	517 627	19 227	69 507	6 193	2 466	787	961 710
8. Financing, insur., real estate & business serv.	628 277	113 677	8 666	418 005	61 868	1 491	1 844	22 080
9. Community, social & personal services	5 625 208	1 141 493	93 258	410 712	245 628	2 253 293	47 474	990 730
0. Not adequately defined	2 161 599	...	...	...	...	...	...	...
–. Persons seeking work for the first time	218 757	.	.	.	.	.	.	.
–. Armed forces	*448 559*	.	.	.	.	.	.	.
Total	**29 557 224**	**1 904 583**	**339 532**	**1 417 531**	**2 225 780**	**2 273 470**	**12 871 863**	**5 695 550**

[a] The English designation of major occupational groups is shown on the preceding page.

C By industry and by occupational group
Par industrie et par groupe de professions
Por industria y por grupo de ocupación

X	Chômeurs		Membres des forces armées	Industrie (Branches d'activité économique)	Industria (Grandes divisiones de actividad económica)
Travailleurs ne pouvant être classés selon la profession		en quête d'un premier emploi			

				1. Agriculture, chasse, sylvi-culture et pêche	1. Agricultura, caza, silvi-cultura y pesca
900	.	.	.	1. Agriculture, chasse, sylvi-culture et pêche	1. Agricultura, caza, silvi-cultura y pesca
170	.	.	.	2. Industries extractives	2. Minas y canteras
2 590	.	.	.	3. Industries manufacturières	3. Industrias manufactureras
350	.	.	.	4. Electricité, gaz et eau	4. Electricidad, gas y agua
520	.	.	.	5. Construction	5. Construcción
4 000	.	.	.	6. Commerce (gros et détail); restaurants, hôtels	6. Comercio (por mayor y por menor); restaurantes, hoteles
980	.	.	.	7. Transports, entrepôts et commu-nications	7. Transportes, almacenamiento y comunicaciones
870	.	.	.	8. Banques, assur., affaires imm., services aux entreprises	8. Bancos, seguros, bienes in-muebles, serv. para empresas
8 690	.	.	.	9. Services à la collectivité, services sociaux et personnels	9. Servicios comunales, sociales y personales
80 810	.	.	.	0. Activités mal désignées	0. Actividades no bien especif.
.	.	119 120	.	–. Personnes en quête d'emploi pour la première fois	–. Personas en busca de trabajo por primera vez
99 880	.	**119 120**	.	**Total**	**Total**

				1. Agriculture, chasse, sylvi-culture et pêche	1. Agricultura, caza, silvi-cultura y pesca
707	.	.	.	1. Agriculture, chasse, sylvi-culture et pêche	1. Agricultura, caza, silvi-cultura y pesca
377	.	.	.	2. Industries extractives	2. Minas y canteras
1 263	.	.	.	3. Industries manufacturières	3. Industrias manufactureras
26	.	.	.	4. Electricité, gaz et eau	4. Electricidad, gas y agua
402	.	.	.	5. Construction	5. Construcción
405	.	.	.	6. Commerce (gros et détail); restaurants, hôtels	6. Comercio (por mayor y por menor); restaurantes, hoteles
476	.	.	.	7. Transports, entrepôts et commu-nications	7. Transportes, almacenamiento y comunicaciones
113	.	.	.	8. Banques, assur., affaires imm., services aux entreprises	8. Bancos, seguros, bienes in-muebles, serv. para empresas
2 237	.	.	.	9. Services à la collectivité, services sociaux et personnels	9. Servicios comunales, sociales y personales
47 066	.	.	.	0. Activités mal désignées	0. Actividades no bien especif.
.	.	6 463	.	–. Personnes en quête d'emploi pour la première fois	–. Personas en busca de trabajo por primera vez
53 072	.	**6 463**	.	**Total**	**Total**

				1. Agriculture, chasse, sylvi-culture et pêche	1. Agricultura, caza, silvi-cultura y pesca
...	.	.	248	1. Agriculture, chasse, sylvi-culture et pêche	1. Agricultura, caza, silvi-cultura y pesca
...	.	.	1 677	2–5. Branches 2, 3, 4 et 5	2–5. Grandes div. 2, 3, 4 y 5
...	.	.	200	6. Commerce (gros et détail); restaurants, hôtels	6. Comercio (por mayor y por menor); restaurantes, hoteles
...	.	.	3 218	7. Transports, entrepôts et commu-nications	7. Transportes, almacenamiento y comunicaciones
...	.	.	596	8. Banques, assur., affaires imm., services aux entreprises	8. Bancos, seguros, bienes in-muebles, serv. para empresas
...	.	.	442 620	9. Services à la collectivité, services sociaux et personnels	9. Servicios comunales, sociales y personales
2 161 599	.	.	.	0. Activités mal désignées	0. Actividades no bien especif.
.	.	218 757	.	–. Personnes en quête d'emploi pour la première fois	–. Personas en busca de trabajo por primera vez
.	.	.	*448 559*	–. Forces armées	–. Fuerzas armadas
2 161 599	.	**218 757**	**448 559**	**Total**	**Total**

(a) La designación en español de los grandes grupos de ocupación figura en la página siguiente.

2 Structure of the economically active population
Structure de la population active
Estructura de la población económicamente activa

Industry (Major divisions of economic activity)	Total	Ocupación (Grandes grupos) [a]						
		1	2	3	4	5	6	7/8/9
		Profesionales técnicos y trabajadores asimilados	Directores y funcionarios públicos superiores	Personal administrativo y trabajadores	Comerciantes y vendedores	Trabajadores de los servicios	Trabajadores agrícolas, forestales, pescadores y cazadores	Obreros no agr. y conductores de máquinas y vehículos de transp. y trab. asimilados
Canada (IV.80) LFSS †								
1/2. Agriculture, hunting, forestry & fishing; mining & quarrying	805 000	47 000	.	34 000	–	9 000	558 000	92 000
3. Manufacturing	2 259 000	273 000	.	266 000	84 000	53 000	17 000	1 369 000
4,7. Electr., gas & water; transport, storage & communication	929 000	125 000	.	228 000	15 000	33 000	6 000	465 000
5. Construction	687 000	48 000	.	41 000	7 000	6 000	15 000	445 000
6. Wholesale/retail trade, restaurants & hotels	1 924 000	110 000	.	394 000	793 000	55 000	14 000	418 000
8. Financing, insur., real estate & business serv.	618 000	141 000	.	251 000	146 000	44 000	5 000	13 000
9. Community, social & personal services	4 005 000	1 614 000	.	624 000	55 000	1 178 000	34 000	224 000
–. Persons seeking work for the first time	65 000	.	.	.	.	.	.	.
–. Other unemployed	*872 000*	84 000	.	121 000	68 000	153 000	68 000	380 000
Total	**11 291 000**	**2 443 000**	.	**1 960 000**	**1 170 000**	**1 530 000**	**717 000**	**3 406 000**
República Dominicana (9.I.70) C								
1. Agriculture, hunting, forestry & fishing	502 029	848	184	504	184	533	497 599	1 165
2. Mining & quarrying	840	35	12	120	9	28	252	291
3. Manufacturing	97 456	1 172	555	5 803	914	1 702	2 278	83 121
4. Electr., gas & water	1 711	94	11	695	.	82		789
5. Construction	27 822	2 991	280	904	51	217	70	22 543
6. Wholesale/retail trade, restaurants & hotels	74 765	160	428	9 601	56 409	2 068	246	4 245
7. Transport, storage & communication	42 598	95	117	3 398	906	217	78	37 208
8. Financing, insur., real estate & business serv.	19 904	1 770	401	15 339	307	639	43	1 142
9. Community, social & personal services	147 227	25 495	1 361	28 873	236	49 960	368	27 135
0. Not adequately defined	193 116	987	476	14 505	665	2 775	3 196	52 634
Total	**1 107 468**	**33 647**	**3 825**	**79 742**	**59 681**	**58 221**	**504 130**	**230 273**
Ecuador (8.VI.74) C 10%								
1. Agriculture, hunting, forestry & fishing	896 897	1 128	5 579	435	568	1 311	883 033	4 478
2. Mining & quarrying	6 155	458	171	367	42	244	120	4 590
3. Manufacturing	226 265	3 210	3 395	3 969	2 972	1 560	3 035	206 627
4. Electr., gas & water	8 470	823	192	1 332	42	381	32	5 390
5. Construction	86 192	3 491	1 434	1 245	123	1 082	256	78 168
6. Wholesale/retail trade, restaurants & hotels	189 072	2 611	4 693	8 491	144 144	10 823	2 350	14 793
7. Transport, storage & communication	54 649	1 047	560	11 622	447	741	70	39 520
8. Financing, insur., real estate & business serv.	19 694	5 602	766	9 618	723	1 489	23	1 093
9. Community, social & personal services	329 553	77 914	2 004	31 215	2 116	116 215	2 843	76 421
0. Not adequately defined	92 933	4 226	550	5 188	439	1 944	251	4 597
–. Persons seeking work for the first time	30 748	.	.	.	.	.	.	.
Total	**1 940 628**	**100 510**	**19 344**	**73 482**	**151 616**	**135 790**	**892 013**	**435 677**

[a] Les libellés en français des grands groupes de professions sont indiqués à la page précédente.

C — By industry and by occupational group
Par industrie et par groupe de professions
Por industria y por grupo de ocupación

X — Trab. que no pueden ser clasificados según la ocupación	Desempleados	en busca de trabajo por primera vez	Miembros de las fuerzas armadas	Industrie (Branches d'activité économique)	Industria (Grandes divisiones de actividad económica)
.	62 000	.	.	1/2. Agriculture, chasse, sylviculture et pêche; industries extractives	1/2. Agricultura, caza, silvicultura y pesca; minas y canteras
.	196 000	.	.	3. Industries manufacturières	3. Industrias manufactureras
.	56 000	.	.	4,7. Electricité, gaz et eau; transports, entrepôts et communications	4,7. Electricidad, gas y agua; transportes, almacenamiento y comunicaciones
.	124 000	.	.	5. Construction	5. Construcción
.	140 000	.	.	6. Commerce (gros et détail); restaurants, hôtels	6. Comercio (por mayor y por menor); restaurantes, hoteles
.	19 000	.	.	8. Banques, assur., affaires imm., services aux entreprises	8. Bancos, seguros, bienes inmuebles, serv. para empresas
.	275 000	.	.	9. Services à la collectivité, services sociaux et personnels	9. Servicios comunales, sociales y personales
.		65 000	.	–. Personnes en quête d'emploi pour la première fois	–. Personas en busca de trabajo por primera vez
.		.	.	–. Autres chômeurs	–. Otros desempleados
.	*872 000*	**65 000**	.	**Total**	**Total**
1 012	.	.	.	1. Agriculture, chasse, sylviculture et pêche	1. Agricultura, caza, silvicultura y pesca
93	.	.	.	2. Industries extractives	2. Minas y canteras
1 888	.	.	23	3. Industries manufacturières	3. Industrias manufactureras
40	.	.	.	4. Electricité, gaz et eau	4. Electricidad, gas y agua
766	.	.	.	5. Construction	5. Construcción
1 585	.	.	23	6. Commerce (gros et détail); restaurants, hôtels	6. Comercio (por mayor y por menor); restaurantes, hoteles
530	.	.	49	7. Transports, entrepôts et communications	7. Transportes, almacenamiento y comunicaciones
242	.	.	21	8. Banques, assur., affaires imm., services aux entreprises	8. Bancos, seguros, bienes inmuebles, serv. para empresas
1 883	.	.	11 916	9. Services à la collectivité, services sociaux et personnels	9. Servicios comunales, sociales y personales
117 728	.	.	150	0. Activités mal désignées	0. Actividades no bien especif.
125 767	.	.	**12 182**	**Total**	**Total**
365	.	.	.	1. Agriculture, chasse, sylviculture et pêche	1. Agricultura, caza, silvicultura y pesca
163	.	.	.	2. Industries extractives	2. Minas y canteras
1 497	.	.	.	3. Industries manufacturières	3. Industrias manufactureras
278	.	.	.	4. Electricité, gaz et eau	4. Electricidad, gas y agua
393	.	.	.	5. Construction	5. Construcción
1 167	.	.	.	6. Commerce (gros et détail); restaurants, hôtels	6. Comercio (por mayor y por menor); restaurantes, hoteles
642	.	.	.	7. Transports, entrepôts et communications	7. Transportes, almacenamiento y comunicaciones
380	.	.	.	8. Banques, assur., affaires imm., services aux entreprises	8. Bancos, seguros, bienes inmuebles, serv. para empresas
20 825	.	.	.	9. Services à la collectivité, services sociaux et personnels	9. Servicios comunales, sociales y personales
75 738	.	.	.	0. Activités mal désignées	0. Actividades no bien especif.
.	.	30 748	.	–. Personnes en quête d'emploi pour la première fois	–. Personas en busca de trabajo por primera vez
101 448	.	**30 748**	.	**Total**	**Total**

(a) The English designation of major occupational groups is shown on the following page.

2 Structure of the economically active population
Structure de la population active
Estructura de la población económicamente activa

Industry (Major divisions of economic activity)	Total	Occupation (Major groups) [a]						
		1	2	3	4	5	6	7/8/9
		Professional, technical & related workers	Administrative & managerial workers	Clerical & related workers	Sales workers	Service workers	Agriculture, animal husbandry & forestry workers, fishermen & hunters	Production & related workers, transport equipment operators & labourers
El Salvador (II–IX.78) HS								
1. Agriculture, hunting, forestry & fishing	586 772	569	.	1 257	.	470	575 967	8 509
2. Mining & quarrying	4 197	.	.	67	.	.	.	4 130
3. Manufacturing	203 079	3 702	2 108	9 583	3 611	3 762	2 180	177 958
4. Electr., gas & water	6 941	513	.	1 013	86	392	.	4 937
5. Construction	77 496	1 452	86	1 135	89	902	158	73 674
6. Wholesale/retail trade, restaurants & hotels	222 347	1 438	1 222	9 260	197 535	7 824	.	5 068
7. Transport, storage & communication	54 223	274	172	12 008	141	280	130	41 218
8. Financing, insur., real estate & business serv.	13 514	3 545	439	6 933	853	1 314	.	430
9. Community, social & personal services	252 481	54 538	2 690	33 995	1 456	116 358	1 686	41 180
0. Not adequately defined	880	.	89	265	89	.	.	335
–. Persons seeking work for the first time	8 432	.	.	.	.	.	.	.
Total	**1 430 362**	**66 031**	**6 806**	**75 516**	**203 860**	**131 302**	**580 121**	**357 439**
Guatemala (26.III.73) C †								
–. Agriculture, forestry, hunting & fishing	884 100	1 522	287	2 194	376	2 147	863 605	10 440
–. Mining & quarrying	1 889	38	44	42	4	51	35	1 614
–. Manufacturing	211 631	3 144	2 872	3 896	3 553	2 087	6 881	185 045
–. Construction	63 864	1 317	1 018	1 106	32	942	104	43 478
–. Electricity, gas, water & sanitary services	4 144	314	102	498	24	259	40	2 514
–. Commerce	114 622	2 427	3 168	7 223	89 814	1 659	1 565	6 186
–. Transport, storage & communication	39 372	477	1 962	5 981	71	774	78	23 269
–. Services	193 279	45 408	6 667	14 971	1 491	111 624	3 192	7 531
–. Not adequately defined & persons seeking work for the first time	32 757	1 727	543	5 384	433	21 156	410	2 382
Total	**1 545 658**	**56 374**	**16 663**	**41 295**	**95 798**	**140 699**	**875 910**	**282 459**
" " " " (1979) OE * †								
–. Agriculture, forestry, hunting & fishing	1 222 709	2 105	397	3 034	520	2 969	1 194 364	14 439
–. Mining & quarrying	2 612	53	61	58	5	71	48	2 232
–. Manufacturing	292 685	4 348	3 972	5 388	4 914	2 886	9 516	255 917
–. Construction	88 324	1 821	1 408	1 530	44	1 303	144	60 130
–. Electricity, gas, water & sanitary services	5 731	434	141	689	33	358	55	3 477
–. Commerce	158 522	3 357	4 381	9 989	124 213	2 294	2 166	8 554
–. Transport, storage & communication	54 452	661	2 713	8 272	98	1 070	108	32 181
–. Services	267 304	62 799	9 220	20 705	2 062	154 376	4 415	10 415
–. Not adequately defined & persons seeking work for the first time	45 303	2 388	751	7 446	599	29 259	567	3 294
Total	**2 137 642**	**77 966**	**23 044**	**57 111**	**132 488**	**194 586**	**1 211 383**	**390 639**

[a] La designación en español de los grandes grupos de ocupación figura en la página precedente.

C   By industry and by occupational group
Par industrie et par groupe de professions
Por industria y por grupo de ocupación

X Workers not classifiable by occupation	Unemployed	First-time job seekers	Members of the armed forces	Industrie (Branches d'activité économique)	Industria (Grandes divisiones de actividad económica)
.	.	.	.	1. Agriculture, chasse, sylviculture et pêche	1. Agricultura, caza, silvicultura y pesca
.	.	.	.	2. Industries extractives	2. Minas y canteras
175	.	.	.	3. Industries manufacturières	3. Industrias manufactureras
.	.	.	.	4. Electricité, gaz et eau	4. Electricidad, gas y agua
.	.	.	.	5. Construction	5. Construcción
.	.	.	.	6. Commerce (gros et détail); restaurants, hôtels	6. Comercio (por mayor y por menor); restaurantes, hoteles
.	.	.	.	7. Transports, entrepôts et communications	7. Transportes, almacenamiento y comunicaciones
.	.	.	.	8. Banques, assur., affaires imm., services aux entreprises	8. Bancos, seguros, bienes inmuebles, serv. para empresas
578	.	.	.	9. Services à la collectivité, services sociaux et personnels	9. Servicios comunales, sociales y personales
102	.	.	.	0. Activités mal désignées	0. Actividades no bien especif.
.	.	8 432	.	–. Personnes en quête d'emploi pour la première fois	–. Personas en busca de trabajo por primera vez
855	.	**8 432**	.	**Total**	**Total**
3 529	.	.	.	–. Agriculture, sylviculture, chasse et pêche	–. Agricultura, silvicultura, caza y pesca
61	.	.	.	–. Industries extractives	–. Minas y canteras
4 153	.	.	.	–. Industries manufacturières	–. Industrias manufactureras
15 867	.	.	.	–. Construction	–. Construcción
393	.	.	.	–. Electricité, gaz, eau et services sanitaires	–. Electricidad, gas, agua y servicios sanitarios
2 580	.	.	.	–. Comm., banq., assur., aff. imm.	–. Comercio
6 760	.	.	.	–. Transports, entrepôts et communications	–. Transportes, almacenamiento y comunicaciones
2 395	.	.	.	–. Services	–. Servicios
722	.	.	.	–. Activités mal désignées et personnes en quête d'emploi pour l première fois.	–. Actividades no bien especificadas; personas en busca de trabajo por primera vez
36 460	.	.	.	**Total**	**Total**
4 881	.	.	.	–. Agriculture, sylviculture, chasse et pêche	–. Agricultura, silvicultura, caza y pesca
84	.	.	.	–. Industries extractives	–. Minas y canteras
5 744	.	.	.	–. Industries manufacturières	–. Industrias manufactureras
21 944	.	.	.	–. Construction	–. Construcción
544	.	.	.	–. Electricité, gaz, eau et services sanitaires	–. Electricidad, gas, agua y servicios sanitarios
3 568	.	.	.	–. Comm., banq., assur., aff. imm.	–. Comercio
9 349	.	.	.	–. Transports, entrepôts et communications	–. Transportes, almacenamiento y comunicaciones
3 312	.	.	.	–. Services	–. Servicios
999	.	.	.	–. Activités mal désignées et personnes en quête d'emploi pour l première fois.	–. Actividades no bien especificadas; personas en busca de trabajo por primera vez
50 425	.	.	.	**Total**	**Total**

(a) Les libellés en français des grands groupes de professions sont indiqués à la page suivante.

2 Structure of the economically active population
Structure de la population active
Estructura de la población económicamente activa

Industry (Major divisions of economic activity)	Total	Profession (Grands groupes) (a)						
		1 Personnel des prof. scientif., techniques, libérales et assimilées	2 Directeurs et cadres administratifs supérieurs	3 Personnel administratif et travailleurs assimilés	4 Personnel commercial et vendeurs	5 Travailleurs des services	6 Agriculteurs, éleveurs, forestiers, pêcheurs et chasseurs	7/8/9 Ouvriers et manœuvres non agricoles et conducteurs d'engins de transport
United States (1979) LFSS †								
1. Agriculture, hunting, forestry & fishing	3 618 000	120 000	42 000	97 000	7 000	13 000	2 703 000	471 000
2. Mining & quarrying	910 000	128 000	68 000	99 000	5 000	11 000	–	554 000
3. Manufacturing	23 416 000	2 375 000	1 563 000	2 648 000	502 000	435 000	–	14 614 000
4. Electr., gas & water	1 361 000	170 000	89 000	277 000	5 000	34 000	–	753 000
5. Construction	6 871 000	186 000	737 000	440 000	29 000	29 000	–	4 878 000
6. Wholesale/retail trade, restaurants & hotels	20 926 000	397 000	3 755 000	3 445 000	4 110 000	3 523 000	–	4 444 000
7. Transport, storage & communication	5 277 000	396 000	539 000	1 171 000	50 000	151 000	–	2 770 000
8. Financing, insur., real estate & business serv.	8 297 000	779 000	1 366 000	3 208 000	1 370 000	712 000	–	547 000
9. Community, social & personal services	31 434 000	10 497 000	2 358 000	6 229 000	83 000	7 928 000	–	3 033 000
–. Persons seeking work for the first time	798 000							
–. Other unemployed	5 167 000	373 000	225 000	853 000	252 000	979 000	106 000	2 377 000
–. Armed forces	2 088 000							
Total	**104 996 000**	**15 422 000**	**10 742 000**	**18 467 000**	**6 413 000**	**13 815 000**	**2 809 000**	**34 441 000**
ASIA								
Bahrain (VI.79) OE †								
1. Agriculture, hunting, forestry & fishing	4 600	100				.	4 500	
2. Mining & quarrying	4 200	800	100	500	100	100	.	2 600
3. Manufacturing	12 200	400	300	1 500	200	100	.	9 700
4. Electr., gas & water	2 000	100	100	300	.	.	.	1 500
5. Construction	33 600	1 200	1 200	2 700	200	300	.	28 000
6. Wholesale/retail trade, restaurants & hotels	16 500	500	1 100	1 000	9 900	1 800	.	2 200
7. Transport, storage & communication	14 600	1 800	500	1 500	300	2 400	.	8 100
8. Financing, insur., real estate & business serv.	4 600	1 800	1 000	1 200	.	200	.	400
9. Community, social & personal services	39 000	8 000	600	7 500	100	9 800	100	12 900
0. Not adequately defined	3 600	...	...	...	...	...	...	...
Total	**134 900**	**14 700**	**4 900**	**16 200**	**10 800**	**14 700**	**4 600**	**65 400**
Cyprus (V.78) LFSS †								
1. Agriculture, hunting, forestry & fishing	44 661	56	17	69	12	33	44 100	196
2. Mining & quarrying	1 992	89	48	154	1	36	1	1 627
3. Manufacturing	34 237	444	1 328	1 895	699	790	40	28 750
4. Electr., gas & water	1 344	180	19	450	1	61	.	599
5. Construction	17 749	754	167	860	17	138	3	15 516
6. Wholesale/retail trade, restaurants & hotels	26 036	300	117	3 177	12 456	6 504	34	2 961
7. Transport, storage & communication	8 072	158	270	2 578	32	264	.	4 617
8. Financing, insur., real estate & business serv.	5 124	877	566	3 150	296	85	.	78
9. Community, social & personal services	36 458	11 164	398	5 849	210	10 224	864	7 210
0. Not adequately defined	22 740	...	...	...	...	...	...	...
–. Persons seeking work for the first time	1 290							
Total	**199 703**	**14 022**	**2 930**	**18 182**	**13 724**	**18 135**	**45 042**	**61 554**

(a) The English designation of major occupational groups is shown on the preceding page.

C By industry and by occupational group
Par industrie et par groupe de professions
Por industria y por grupo de ocupación

X — Travailleurs ne pouvant être classés selon la profession	Chômeurs	en quête d'un premier emploi	Membres des forces armées	Industrie (Branches d'activité économique)	Industria (Grandes divisiones de actividad económica)
.	163 000	.	.	1. Agriculture, chasse, sylvi‑ culture et pêche	1. Agricultura, caza, silvi‑ cultura y pesca
.	44 000	.	.	2. Industries extractives	2. Minas y canteras
.	1 279 000	.	.	3. Industries manufacturières	3. Industrias manufactureras
.	32 000	.	.	4. Electricité, gaz et eau	4. Electricidad, gas y agua
.	573 000	.	.	5. Construction	5. Construcción
.	1 255 000	.	.	6. Commerce (gros et détail); restaurants, hôtels	6. Comercio (por mayor y por me‑ nor); restaurantes, hoteles
.	201 000	.	.	7. Transports, entrepôts et commu‑ nications	7. Transportes, almacenamiento y comunicaciones
.	318 000	.	.	8. Banques, assur., affaires imm., services aux entreprises	8. Bancos, seguros, bienes in‑ muebles, serv. para empresas
.	1 302 000	.	.	9. Services à la collectivité, services sociaux et personnels	9. Servicios comunales, sociales y personales
.	.	798 000	.	–. Personnes en quête d'emploi pour la première fois	–. Personas en busca de trabajo por primera vez
.	.	.	.	–. Autres chômeurs	–. Otros desempleados
.	.	.	2 088 000	–. Forces armées	–. Fuerzas armadas
.	*5 167 000*	**798 000**	**2 088 000**	**Total**	**Total**

X — Travailleurs ne pouvant être classés selon la profession	Chômeurs	en quête d'un premier emploi	Membres des forces armées	Industrie (Branches d'activité économique)	Industria (Grandes divisiones de actividad económica)
...	.	.	.	1. Agriculture, chasse, sylvi‑ culture et pêche	1. Agricultura, caza, silvi‑ cultura y pesca
...	.	.	.	2. Industries extractives	2. Minas y canteras
...	.	.	.	3. Industries manufacturières	3. Industrias manufactureras
...	.	.	.	4. Electricité, gaz et eau	4. Electricidad, gas y agua
...	.	.	.	5. Construction	5. Construcción
...	.	.	.	6. Commerce (gros et détail); restaurants, hôtels	6. Comercio (por mayor y por me‑ nor); restaurantes, hoteles
...	.	.	.	7. Transports, entrepôts et commu‑ nications	7. Transportes, almacenamiento y comunicaciones
...	.	.	.	8. Banques, assur., affaires imm., services aux entreprises	8. Bancos, seguros, bienes in‑ muebles, serv. para empresas
...	.	.	.	9. Services à la collectivité, services sociaux et personnels	9. Servicios comunales, sociales y personales
3 600	.	.	.	0. Activités mal désignées	0. Actividades no bien especif.
3 600	.	.	.	**Total**	**Total**

X — Travailleurs ne pouvant être classés selon la profession	Chômeurs	en quête d'un premier emploi	Membres des forces armées	Industrie (Branches d'activité économique)	Industria (Grandes divisiones de actividad económica)
.	178	.	.	1. Agriculture, chasse, sylvi‑ culture et pêche	1. Agricultura, caza, silvi‑ cultura y pesca
.	36	.	.	2. Industries extractives	2. Minas y canteras
.	291	.	.	3. Industries manufacturières	3. Industrias manufactureras
.	34	.	.	4. Electricité, gaz et eau	4. Electricidad, gas y agua
.	294	.	.	5. Construction	5. Construcción
.	487	.	.	6. Commerce (gros et détail); restaurants, hôtels	6. Comercio (por mayor y por me‑ nor); restaurantes, hoteles
.	153	.	.	7. Transports, entrepôts et commu‑ nications	7. Transportes, almacenamiento y comunicaciones
.	72	.	.	8. Banques, assur., affaires imm., services aux entreprises	8. Bancos, seguros, bienes in‑ muebles, serv. para empresas
.	539	.	.	9. Services à la collectivité, services sociaux et personnels	9. Servicios comunales, sociales y personales
22 740	.	.	.	0. Activités mal désignées	0. Actividades no bien especif.
.	.	1 290	.	–. Personnes en quête d'emploi pour la première fois	–. Personas en busca de trabajo por primera vez
22 740	**2 084**	**1 290**	.	**Total**	**Total**

(a) La designación en español de los grandes grupos de ocupación figura en la página siguiente.

2 Structure of the economically active population
Structure de la population active
Estructura de la población económicamente activa

Industry (Major divisions of economic activity)	Total	Ocupación (Grandes grupos) [a]						
		1 Profesionales técnicos y trabajadores asimilados	2 Directores y funcionarios públicos superiores	3 Personal administrativo y trabajadores	4 Comerciantes y vendedores	5 Trabajadores de los servicios	6 Trabajadores agrícolas, forestales, pescadores y cazadores	7/8/9 Obreros no agr. y conductores de máquinas y vehículos de transp. y trab. asimilados
Hong Kong (IX.79) LFSS †								
1. Agriculture, hunting, forestry & fishing	26 700	–	–	–	100	200	26 300	200
2. Mining & quarrying	500	–	–	100	–	–	–	400
3. Manufacturing	933 800	11 400	22 100	53 700	25 100	46 500	100	774 400
4. Electr., gas & water	11 000	1 300	500	1 400	–	1 200	–	6 600
5. Construction	150 300	9 200	2 400	5 300	1 800	8 900	200	122 500
6. Wholesale/retail trade, restaurants & hotels	434 500	3 800	10 700	73 500	190 900	119 900	300	35 200
7. Transport, storage & communication	154 700	4 500	4 800	24 000	1 800	6 900	100	112 400
8. Financing, insur., real estate & business serv.	91 600	7 000	7 100	64 200	5 900	4 700	–	2 700
9. Community, social & personal services	365 400	102 900	4 900	43 900	3 300	155 200	2 100	49 400
0. Not adequately defined	600	100	–	100	–	100	–	200
–. Persons seeking work for the first time	25 400							
Total	**2 194 500**	**140 200**	**52 400**	**266 100**	**228 800**	**343 700**	**29 000**	**1 103 900**
Indonesia (1976) LFSS								
1. Agriculture, hunting, forestry & fishing	35 257 780	7 775	2 665	47 917	10 199	100 963	34 913 706	136 801
2. Mining & quarrying	43 932	2 424	.	10 076	147	1 830		29 455
3. Manufacturing	3 560 066	11 180	4 601	104 560	46 155	101 665	18 052	3 268 534
4. Electr., gas & water	34 194	1 483	.	16 743	.	952	98	13 974
5. Construction	1 097 913	8 126	9 949	26 683	9 938	35 505	1 750	1 002 150
6. Wholesale/retail trade, restaurants & hotels	6 253 171	2 772	7 085	70 109	5 938 902	94 452	20 438	117 402
7. Transport, storage & communication	1 111 857	5 736	7 603	189 081	14 341	117 880	1 521	768 574
8. Financing, insur., real estate & business serv.	74 269	2 437	3 804	54 402	9 180	1 544	.	2 902
9. Community, social & personal services	5 156 975	967 465	38 983	1 039 217	91 223	1 642 733	62 736	990 532
0. Not adequately defined	853 511	3 036	2 806	40 003	5 513	102 614	9 648	14 618
–. Unemployed	1 046 617	...	...	...	...	...	...	...
Total	**54 490 285**	**1 012 434**	**77 496**	**1 598 791**	**6 125 598**	**2 200 138**	**35 027 949**	**6 344 942**
Iran (XI.76) C5% †								
1. Agriculture, hunting, forestry & fishing	3 613 944	3 400	841	5 343	882	7 151	2 938 303	20 037
2. Mining & quarrying	94 311	8 025	1 160	15 271	940	8 121	442	59 001
3. Manufacturing	1 672 393	25 003	9 783	48 466	9 602	28 495	6 321	1 529 591
4. Electr., gas & water	61 641	5 950	1 220	16 046	440	6 902	1 360	29 058
5. Construction	1 192 441	31 634	8 979	15 430	1 753	12 150	1 110	1 104 689
6. Wholesale/retail trade, restaurants & hotels	669 590	5 345	2 441	17 610	560 051	65 738	1 761	11 094
7. Transport, storage & communication	435 288	12 041	4 305	91 508	1 502	17 291	1 020	303 832
8. Financing, insur., real estate & business serv.	100 849	14 088	2 323	58 742	14 569	6 687	220	3 138
9. Community, social & personal services	1 544 750	426 091	15 160	173 126	4 042	268 124	17 650	224 113
0. Not adequately defined	109 044	4 856	1 820	7 786	1 280	4 714	1 661	14 101
–. Persons seeking work for the first time	238 257							
–. Other unemployed	*705 357*	1 444	80	1 118	3 223	1 882	635 390	28 205
Total	**9 732 508**	**537 877**	**48 112**	**450 446**	**598 284**	**427 255**	**3 605 238**	**3 326 859**

[a] Les libellés en français des grands groupes de professions sont indiqués à la page précédente.

C By industry and by occupational group
Par industrie et par groupe de professions
Por industria y por grupo de ocupación

X — Trab. que no pueden ser clasificados según la ocupación	Desempleados	en busca de trabajo por primera vez	Miembros de las fuerzas armadas	Industrie (Branches d'activité économique)	Industria (Grandes divisiones de actividad económica)
–	.	.	.	1. Agriculture, chasse, sylviculture et pêche	1. Agricultura, caza, silvicultura y pesca
–	.	.	.	2. Industries extractives	2. Minas y canteras
600	.	–	.	3. Industries manufacturières	3. Industrias manufactureras
–	.	.	.	4. Electricité, gaz et eau	4. Electricidad, gas y agua
				5. Construction	5. Construcción
200	.	.	.	6. Commerce (gros et détail); restaurants, hôtels	6. Comercio (por mayor y por menor); restaurantes, hoteles
300	.	.	.	7. Transports, entrepôts et communications	7. Transportes, almacenamiento y comunicaciones
–	.	.	.	8. Banques, assur., affaires imm., services aux entreprises	8. Bancos, seguros, bienes inmuebles, serv. para empresas
3 700	.	.	.	9. Services à la collectivité, services sociaux et personnels	9. Servicios comunales, sociales y personales
100	.	.	.	0. Activités mal désignées	0. Actividades no bien especif.
.	.	25 400	.	–. Personnes en quête d'emploi pour la première fois	–. Personas en busca de trabajo por primera vez
4 900	.	**25 400**	.	**Total**	**Total**
37 754	...	.	.	1. Agriculture, chasse, sylviculture et pêche	1. Agricultura, caza, silvicultura y pesca
.	...	.	.	2. Industries extractives	2. Minas y canteras
5 319	...	.	.	3. Industries manufacturières	3. Industrias manufactureras
944	...	.	.	4. Electricité, gaz et eau	4. Electricidad, gas y agua
3 812	...	.	.	5. Construction	5. Construcción
2 011	...	.	.	6. Commerce (gros et détail); restaurants, hôtels	6. Comercio (por mayor y por menor); restaurantes, hoteles
7 121	...	.	.	7. Transports, entrepôts et communications	7. Transportes, almacenamiento y comunicaciones
.	...	.	.	8. Banques, assur., affaires imm., services aux entreprises	8. Bancos, seguros, bienes inmuebles, serv. para empresas
324 086	...	.	.	9. Services à la collectivité, services sociaux et personnels	9. Servicios comunales, sociales y personales
675 273	...	.	.	0. Activités mal désignées	0. Actividades no bien especif.
...	1 046 617	...	.	–. Chômeurs	–. Desempleados
1 056 320	**1 046 617**	...	.	**Total**	**Total**
2 584	635 403	.	.	1. Agriculture, chasse, sylviculture et pêche	1. Agricultura, caza, silvicultura y pesca
950	401	.	.	2. Industries extractives	2. Minas y canteras
4 335	10 797	.	.	3. Industries manufacturières	3. Industriàs manufactureras
505	160	.	.	4. Electricité, gaz et eau	4. Electricidad, gas y agua
1 321	15 375	.	.	5. Construction	5. Construcción
1 643	3 907	.	.	6. Commerce (gros et détail); restaurants, hôtels	6. Comercio (por mayor y por menor); restaurantes, hoteles
2 045	1 744	.	.	7. Transports, entrepôts et communications	7. Transportes, almacenamiento y comunicaciones
821	261	.	.	8. Banques, assur., affaires imm., services aux entreprises	8. Bancos, seguros, bienes inmuebles, serv. para empresas
412 635	3 819	.	.	9. Services à la collectivité, services sociaux et personnels	9. Servicios comunales, sociales y personales
39 336	33 490	.	.	0. Activités mal désignées	0. Actividades no bien especif.
.	.	238 257	.	–. Personnes en quête d'emploi pour la première fois	–. Personas en busca de trabajo por primera vez
34 015	.	.	.	–. Autres chômeurs	–. Otros desempleados
500 180	*705 357*	**238 257**	.	**Total**	**Total**

(a) The English designation of major occupational groups is shown on the following page.

2 Structure of the economically active population
Structure de la population active
Estructura de la población económicamente activa

Industry (Major divisions of economic activity)	Total	Occupation (Major groups) [a]						
		1 Professional, technical & related workers	2 Administrative & managerial workers	3 Clerical & related workers	4 Sales workers	5 Service workers	6 Agriculture, animal husbandry & forestry workers, fishermen & hunters	7/8/9 Production & related workers, transport equipment operators & labourers
Israel (1979) LFSS †								
1. Agriculture, hunting, forestry & fishing	72 700	800	700	5 100	400	800	60 500	2 400
2/3. Mining & quarrying, manufacturing	303 000	32 900	18 400	32 300	5 700	6 700	400	197 700
4. Electr., gas & water	11 600	2 200	400	2 800	200	400	–	5 200
5. Construction	84 300	3 300	4 300	5 700	300	600	100	67 600
6. Wholesale/retail trade, restaurants & hotels	147 200	4 700	4 200	20 800	75 900	24 900	400	13 200
7. Transport, storage & communication	85 700	4 400	2 800	23 300	1 900	4 800	100	46 700
8. Financing, insur., real estate & business serv.	98 200	23 600	7 800	52 700	5 800	3 800	–	2 400
9. Community, social & personal services	443 900	199 300	9 600	74 100	1 900	91 200	6 500	46 300
0. Not adequately defined	13 400	600	300	1 700	–	500	400	2 100
–. Persons seeking work for the first time	17 900	.	.	.	.	.	.	.
–. Other unemployed	*19 100*	2 100	–	3 400	1 200	2 800	900	8 000
Total	**1 277 800**	**274 200**	**48 300**	**222 200**	**93 600**	**136 700**	**69 400**	**391 900**
Japan (1979) LFSS †								
1. Agriculture, hunting, forestry & fishing	6 130 000	10 000	10 000	50 000	10 000	–	5 990 000	50 000
2. Mining & quarrying	120 000	–	–	10 000	–	–	–	100 000
3. Manufacturing	13 330 000	260 000	600 000	1 630 000	640 000	110 000	10 000	10 070 000
4. Electr., gas & water	330 000	10 000	10 000	150 000	10 000	–	–	150 000
5. Construction	5 360 000	80 000	270 000	620 000	100 000	30 000	–	4 260 000
6. Wholesale/retail trade, restaurants & hotels	12 280 000	100 000	550 000	1 750 000	6 230 000	1 960 000	–	1 690 000
7. Transport, storage & communication	3 490 000	30 000	160 000	900 000	60 000	60 000	–	2 270 000
8. Financing, insur., real estate & business serv.	3 120 000	120 000	250 000	1 480 000	660 000	280 000	20 000	310 000
9. Community, social & personal services	10 540 000	3 630 000	300 000	2 390 000	130 000	2 520 000	30 000	1 530 000
0. Not adequately defined	110 000	–	–	–	–	–	–	–
–. Unemployed	1 170 000	...	...	...	...	...	...	...
Total	**55 960 000**	**4 260 000**	**2 170 000**	**8 980 000**	**7 840 000**	**4 970 000**	**6 050 000**	**20 410 000**
Pakistan (I.80) LFSS †								
1. Agriculture, hunting, forestry & fishing	12 382 000	9 000	–	11 000	.	10 000	12 323 000	29 000
2. Mining & quarrying	33 000	–	–	2 000	–	–	2 000	29 000
3. Manufacturing	3 080 000	20 000	41 000	66 000	7 000	31 000	3 000	2 910 000
4. Electr., gas & water	111 000	10 000	–	20 000	–	9 000	2 000	70 000
5. Construction	949 000	9 000	35 000	14 000	.	16 000	.	875 000
6. Wholesale/retail trade, restaurants & hotels	2 506 000	2 000	14 000	29 000	2 226 000	137 000	5 000	93 000
7. Transport, storage & communication	1 100 000	11 000	16 000	147 000	2 000	41 000		881 000
8. Financing, insur., real estate & business serv.	151 000	25 000	25 000	61 000	15 000	18 000	.	7 000
9. Community, social & personal services	2 209 000	583 000	29 000	255 000	5 000	750 000	20 000	560 000
0. Not adequately defined	75 000	11 000	–	2 000	–	.	5 000	41 000
–. Unemployed	390 000	...	...	...	...	...	...	...
Total	**22 986 000**	**680 000**	**160 000**	**607 000**	**2 255 000**	**1 012 000**	**12 360 000**	**5 495 000**

[a] La designación en español de los grandes grupos de ocupación figura en la página precedente.

C By industry and by occupational group
Par industrie et par groupe de professions
Por industria y por grupo de ocupación

X Workers not classifiable by occupation	Unemployed	First-time job seekers	Members of the armed forces	Industrie (Branches d'activité économique)	Industria (Grandes divisiones de actividad económica)
1 100	500	.	.	1. Agriculture, chasse, sylvi-culture et pêche	1. Agricultura, caza, silvi-cultura y pesca
4 400	4 700	.	.	2/3. Industries extractives et industries manufacturières	2/3. Minas y canteras, industrias manufactureras
100	200	.	.	4. Electricité, gaz et eau	4. Electricidad, gas y agua
200	2 200	.	.	5. Construction	5. Construcción
300	2 400	.	.	6. Commerce (gros et détail); restaurants, hôtels	6. Comercio (por mayor y por menor); restaurantes, hoteles
500	1 300	.	.	7. Transports, entrepôts et communications	7. Transportes, almacenamiento y comunicaciones
200	1 700	.	.	8. Banques, assur., affaires imm., services aux entreprises	8. Bancos, seguros, bienes inmuebles, serv. para empresas
9 100	5 200	.	.	9. Services à la collectivité, services sociaux et personnels	9. Servicios comunales, sociales y personales
6 900	800	.	.	0. Activités mal désignées	0. Actividades no bien especif.
	.	17 900	.	-. Personnes en quête d'emploi pour la première fois	-. Personas en busca de trabajo por primera vez
700	.	.	.	-. Autres chômeurs	-. Otros desempleados
23 600	*19 100*	**17 900**	.	**Total**	**Total**
–	...	.	.	1. Agriculture, chasse, sylvi-culture et pêche	1. Agricultura, caza, silvi-cultura y pesca
–	...	.	.	2. Industries extractives	2. Minas y canteras
–	...	.	.	3. Industries manufacturières	3. Industrias manufactureras
–	...	.	.	4. Electricité, gaz et eau	4. Electricidad, gas y agua
–	...	.	.	5. Construction	5. Construcción
–	...	.	.	6. Commerce (gros et détail); restaurants, hôtels	6. Comercio (por mayor y por menor); restaurantes, hoteles
–	...	.	.	7. Transports, entrepôts et communications	7. Transportes, almacenamiento y comunicaciones
–	...	.	.	8. Banques, assur., affaires imm., services aux entreprises	8. Bancos, seguros, bienes inmuebles, serv. para empresas
–	...	.	.	9. Services à la collectivité, services sociaux et personnels	9. Servicios comunales, sociales y personales
100 000	...	.	.	0. Activités mal désignées	0. Actividades no bien especif.
...	1 170 000	...	.	-. Chômeurs	-. Desempleados
110 000	**1 170 000**	...	.	**Total**	**Total**
–	...	.	.	1. Agriculture, chasse, sylvi-culture et pêche	1. Agricultura, caza, silvi-cultura y pesca
–	...	.	.	2. Industries extractives	2. Minas y canteras
2 000	...	.	.	3. Industries manufacturières	3. Industrias manufactureras
–	...	.	.	4. Electricité, gaz et eau	4. Electricidad, gas y agua
–	...	.	.	5. Construction	5. Construcción
–	...	.	.	6. Commerce (gros et détail); restaurants, hôtels	6. Comercio (por mayor y por menor); restaurantes, hoteles
2 000	...	.	.	7. Transports, entrepôts et communications	7. Transportes, almacenamiento y comunicaciones
–	...	.	.	8. Banques, assur., affaires imm., services aux entreprises	8. Bancos, seguros, bienes inmuebles, serv. para empresas
7 000	...	.	.	9. Services à la collectivité, services sociaux et personnels	9. Servicios comunales, sociales y personales
16 000	...	.	.	0. Activités mal désignées	0. Actividades no bien especif.
...	390 000	...	.	-. Chômeurs	-. Desempleados
27 000	**390 000**	.	.	**Total**	**Total**

(a) Les libellés en français des grands groupes de professions sont indiqués à la page suivante.

ACTIVE POPULATION

2 Structure of the economically active population
Structure de la population active
Estructura de la población económicamente activa

Industry (Major divisions of economic activity)	Total	Profession (Grands groupes) (a)						
		1 Personnel des prof. scientif., techniques, libérales et assimilées	2 Directeurs et cadres administratifs supérieurs	3 Personnel administratif et travailleurs assimilés	4 Personnel commercial et vendeurs	5 Travailleurs des services	6 Agriculteurs, éleveurs, forestiers, pêcheurs et chasseurs	7/8/9 Ouvriers et manœuvres non agricoles et conducteurs d'engins de transport
Philippines (X–XII.77) LFSS †								
–. Agriculture, forestry, hunting & fishing	7 308 000	18 000	1 000	9 000	19 000	13 000	7 152 000	77 000
–. Mining & quarrying	72 000	5 000	1 000	4 000	–	1 000	–	61 000
–. Manufacturing	1 561 000	53 000	29 000	81 000	63 000	22 000	12 000	1 291 000
–. Construction	492 000	10 000	2 000	11 000	4 000	5 000	–	456 000
–. Electricity, gas, water & sanitary services	56 000	4 000	1 000	15 000	7 000	–		28 000
–. Commerce	1 384 000	6 000	6 000	35 000	1 256 000	15 000	26 000	35 000
–. Transport, storage & communication	654 000	12 000	11 000	107 000	1 000	16 000	4 000	499 000
–. Services	2 672 000	816 000	49 000	378 000	60 000	1 001 000	13 000	327 000
–. Not adeq. described	125 000	5 000	3 000	20 000	11 000	13 000	26 000	35 000
–. Persons seeking work for the first time	275 000	.	.	.	.	.	.	.
–. Other unemployed	396 000	16 600	400	20 700	55 500	42 500	149 300	102 100
Total	**14 994 000**	**946 600**	**105 400**	**681 700**	**1 476 500**	**1 128 500**	**7 383 300**	**2 912 100**
Singapore (VI.79) LFSS †								
1. Agriculture, hunting, forestry & fishing	15 182	21	83	291	21	354	13 643	770
2. Mining & quarrying	1 518	83	146	312	21	21	.	936
3. Manufacturing	294 685	15 848	11 917	24 022	3 556	5 844	83	233 394
4. Electr., gas & water	9 817	1 206	125	1 830	21	645	125	5 823
5. Construction	54 345	3 265	5 387	2 829	42	770	187	41 866
6. Wholesale/retail trade, restaurants & hotels	237 346	2 059	1 414	34 899	147 353	33 401	187	18 011
7. Transport, storage & communication	118 902	8 028	2 974	34 421	541	5 699	125	67 094
8. Financing, insur., real estate & business serv.	72 044	9 692	4 534	37 665	3 993	7 799	811	7 154
9. Community, social & personal services	216 444	47 398	1 622	25 186	416	58 962	3 016	19 051
0. Not adequately defined	749	.	42	42	.	.	.	437
–. Persons seeking work for the first time	10 981	.	.	.	.	.	.	.
–. Other unemployed	*24 313*	*1 123*	*270*	*3 910*	*2 683*	*2 683*	*187*	.
Total	**1 056 325**	**87 601**	**28 244**	**161 496**	**155 963**	**113 494**	**18 177**	**394 536**
Sri Lanka (9.X.71) C †								
1. Agriculture, hunting, forestry & fishing	1 828 977	1 904	475	6 852	2 154	13 712	1 765 114	58 011
2. Mining & quarrying	13 079	127	51	219	131	147	49	12 331
3. Manufacturing	339 405	4 519	2 075	11 291	10 284	4 697	5 583	299 250
4. Electr., gas & water	9 567	467	55	1 203	40	275	118	7 247
5. Construction	103 561	2 485	255	4 723	412	2 444	451	92 209
6. Wholesale/retail trade, restaurants & hotels	343 768	2 132	2 526	22 021	241 977	37 608	2 554	33 935
7. Transport, storage & communication	178 876	2 738	979	51 053	588	4 861	624	116 104
8. Financing, insur., real estate & business serv.	24 945	3 292	1 157	10 580	960	442	66	8 133
9. Community, social & personal services	492 780	156 507	4 464	61 822	5 082	126 923	5 088	116 236
0. Not adequately defined	313 917	4 317	1 880	16 380	10 739	6 869	2 487	202 935
–. Unemployed	839 264	…	…	…	…	…	…	…
Total	**4 488 139**	**178 488**	**13 917**	**186 144**	**272 367**	**197 978**	**1 782 134**	**926 391**

(a) The English designation of major occupational groups is shown on the preceding page.

126

C By industry and by occupational group
Par industrie et par groupe de professions
Por industria y por grupo de ocupación

X Travailleurs ne pouvant être classés selon la profession	Chômeurs	en quête d'un premier emploi	Membres des forces armées	Industrie (Branches d'activité économique)	Industria (Grandes divisiones de actividad económica)
18 000	...	.	.	–. Agriculture, sylviculture, chasse et pêche	–. Agricultura, silvicultura, caza y pesca
–	...	.	.	–. Industries extractives	–. Minas y canteras
9 000	...	.	.	–. Industries manufacturières	–. Industrias manufactureras
3 000	...	.	.	–. Construction	–. Construcción
–	...	.	.	–. Electricité, gaz, eau et services sanitaires	–. Electricidad, gas, agua y servicios sanitarios
4 000	...	.	.	–. Comm., banq., assur., aff. imm.	–. Comercio
4 000	...	.	.	–. Transports, entrepôts et communications	–. Transportes, almacenamiento y comunicaciones
26 000	...	.	.	–. Services	–. Servicios
12 000	...	.	.	–. Activités mal désignées	–. Actividades no bien especif.
.	.	275 000	.	–. Personnes en quête d'emploi pour la première fois	–. Personas en busca de trabajo por primera vez
9 200	396 000	.	.	–. Autres chômeurs	–. Otros desempleados
85 200	**396 000**	**275 000**	.	**Total**	**Total**
.	83	.	.	1. Agriculture, chasse, sylviculture et pêche	1. Agricultura, caza, silvicultura y pesca
.	21	.	.	2. Industries extractives	2. Minas y canteras
21	7 446	.	.	3. Industries manufacturières	3. Industrias manufactureras
42	125	.	.	4. Electricité, gaz et eau	4. Electricidad, gas y agua
.	1 851	.	.	5. Construction	5. Construcción
21	5 428	.	.	6. Commerce (gros et détail); restaurants, hôtels	6. Comercio (por mayor y por menor); restaurantes, hoteles
21	2 953	.	.	7. Transports, entrepôts et communications	7. Transportes, almacenamiento y comunicaciones
395	1 102	.	.	8. Banques, assur., affaires imm., services aux entreprises	8. Bancos, seguros, bienes inmuebles, serv. para empresas
60 792	5 158	.	.	9. Services à la collectivité, services sociaux et personnels	9. Servicios comunales, sociales y personales
229	146	.	.	0. Activités mal désignées	0. Actividades no bien especif.
.	.	10 981	.	–. Personnes en quête d'emploi pour la première fois	–. Personas en busca de trabajo por primera vez
2 163	.	.	.	–. Autres chômeurs	–. Otros desempleados
61 520	**24 313**	**10 981**	.	**Total**	**Total**
755	...	.	.	1. Agriculture, chasse, sylviculture et pêche	1. Agricultura, caza, silvicultura y pesca
24	...	.	.	2. Industries extractives	2. Minas y canteras
1 706	...	.	.	3. Industries manufacturières	3. Industrias manufactureras
162	...	.	.	4. Electricité, gaz et eau	4. Electricidad, gas y agua
582	...	.	.	5. Construction	5. Construcción
1 015	...	.	.	6. Commerce (gros et détail); restaurants, hôtels	6. Comercio (por mayor y por menor); restaurantes, hoteles
1 929	...	.	.	7. Transports, entrepôts et communications	7. Transportes, almacenamiento y comunicaciones
315	...	.	.	8. Banques, assur., affaires imm., services aux entreprises	8. Bancos, seguros, bienes inmuebles, serv. para empresas
16 658	...	.	.	9. Services à la collectivité, services sociaux et personnels	9. Servicios comunales, sociales y personales
68 310	...	.	.	0. Activités mal désignées	0. Actividades no bien especif.
...	839 264	...	.	–. Chômeurs	–. Desempleados
91 456	**839 264**	...	.	**Total**	**Total**

(a) La designación en español de los grandes grupos de ocupación figura en la página siguiente.

2 Structure of the economically active population
Structure de la population active
Estructura de la población económicamente activa

Industry (Major divisions of economic activity)	Total	Ocupación (Grandes grupos) [a]						
		1	2	3	4	5	6	7/8/9
		Profesionales técnicos y trabajadores asimilados	Directores y funcionarios públicos superiores	Personal administrativo y trabajadores	Comerciantes y vendedores	Trabajadores de los servicios	Trabajadores agrícolas, forestales, pescadores y cazadores	Obreros no agr. y conductores de máquinas y vehículos de transp. y trab. asimilados
Thailand (VII–IX.78) LFSS †								
–. Agriculture, forestry, hunting & fishing	16 017 000	200	400	2 000	.	2 900	15 997 300	14 200
–. Mining & quarrying	29 600	100	1 200	1 000	.	1 100	16 400	9 800
–. Manufacturing	1 476 500	13 500	27 000	57 400	500	27 400	300	1 350 400
–. Construction	312 500	2 800	16 500	9 600	.	500	100	283 000
–. Electricity, gas, water & sanitary services	58 000	1 300	3 400	12 300	100	3 100	.	37 800
–. Commerce	1 638 600	30 200	43 800	89 800	1 364 500	11 200	200	98 900
–. Transport, storage & communication	386 900	3 900	10 900	21 900	.	9 200	.	341 000
–. Services	1 811 700	436 200	107 900	140 000	295 800	548 400	13 000	270 400
–. Not adeq. described	5 700	...	...	...	...	...	...	...
–. Persons seeking work for the first time	100 900	.	.	.	.	.	.	.
–. Other unemployed	55 900	...	...	...	...	...	...	...
Total	**21 893 300**	**488 200**	**211 100**	**334 000**	**1 660 900**	**603 800**	**16 026 700**	**2 405 400**
EUROPE								
Czechoslovakia (1.XII.70) C †								
1. Agriculture, hunting, forestry & fishing	1 143 597	58 552	229	11 933	3 440	20 025	912 233	136 001
2–4. Min./quarrying; manuf.; electr., gas & water	2 754 666	460 638	11 224	106 047	39 580	107 859	488	2 024 926
5. Construction	598 000	136 233	2 933	22 376	7 241	20 573	184	407 788
6. Wholesale/retail trade, restaurants & hotels	632 011	69 116	474	33 207	250 148	150 438	167	127 553
7. Transport, storage & communication	491 686	72 057	1 534	110 142	8 679	21 518	15	277 258
8. Financing, insur., real estate & business serv.	66 492	38 773	2 974	15 902	1 427	3 919	9	3 312
9. Community, social & personal services	1 243 811	615 797	133 185	99 923	13 744	221 243	647	156 229
0. Not adequately defined	52 239	3 887	117	1 103	391	2 214	84	12 623
Total	**6 982 502**	**1 455 053**	**152 670**	**400 633**	**324 650**	**547 789**	**913 827**	**3 145 690**
Finland (I.I.76) C †								
1. Agriculture, hunting, forestry & fishing	318 088	3 461	284	1 295	361	525	309 428	2 249
2. Mining & quarrying	8 397	1 086	156	542	72	430	1	5 934
3. Manufacturing	543 806	54 089	14 866	45 221	13 104	22 009	1 172	386 952
4. Electr., gas & water	23 771	4 566	527	3 013	91	1 796	32	13 428
5. Construction	179 398	15 987	2 458	8 238	1 027	4 175	276	145 802
6. Wholesale/retail trade, restaurants & hotels	310 123	14 618	13 323	49 143	128 222	52 125	460	50 158
7. Transport, storage & communication	160 738	9 540	2 205	33 098	845	8 377	105	105 341
8. Financing, insur., real estate & business serv.	100 320	16 737	5 507	49 692	4 555	17 452	66	5 760
9. Community, social & personal services	444 342	197 703	13 195	56 510	3 804	118 938	4 055	39 147
0. Not adequately defined	32 191	940	308	1 143	2 076	1 195	164	8 504
Total	**2 121 174**	**318 727**	**52 829**	**247 895**	**154 157**	**227 022**	**315 759**	**763 275**

[a] Les libellés en français des grands groupes de professions sont indiqués à la page précédente.

C By industry and by occupational group
Par industrie et par groupe de professions
Por industria y por grupo de ocupación

X Trab. que no pueden ser clasificados según la ocupación	Desempleados en busca de trabajo por primera vez	Miembros de las fuerzas armadas	Industrie (Branches d'activité économique)	Industria (Grandes divisiones de actividad económica)
...	...	.	.	–. Agriculture, sylviculture, chasse et pêche	–. Agricultura, silvicultura, caza y pesca
...	...	.	.	–. Industries extractives	–. Minas y canteras
...	...	.	.	–. Industries manufacturières	–. Industrias manufactureras
...	...	.	.	–. Construction	–. Construcción
...	...	.	.	–. Electricité, gaz, eau et services sanitaires	–. Electricidad, gas, agua y servicios sanitarios
...	...	.	.	–. Comm., banq., assur., aff. imm.	–. Comercio
...	...	.	.	–. Transports, entrepôts et communications	–. Transportes, almacenamiento y comunicaciones
5 700	...	.	.	–. Services	–. Servicios
.	.	100 900	.	–. Activités mal désignées	–. Actividades no bien especif.
...	55 900	...	.	–. Personnes en quête d'emploi pour la première fois	–. Personas en busca de trabajo por primera vez
.	.	.	.	–. Autres chômeurs	–. Otros desempleados
6 400	**55 900**	**100 900**	**.**	**Total**	**Total**

EUROPE – EUROPA

1 184	.	.	.	1. Agriculture, chasse, sylviculture et pêche	1. Agricultura, caza, silvicultura y pesca
3 904	.	.	.	2–4. Industries extract.; industries manuf.; électricité, gaz et eau	2–4. Minas y canteras; industrias manufact.; electr., gas y agua
672	.	.	.	5. Construction	5. Construcción
908	.	.	.	6. Commerce (gros et détail); restaurants, hôtels	6. Comercio (por mayor y por menor); restaurantes, hoteles
483	.	.	.	7. Transports, entrepôts et communications	7. Transportes, almacenamiento y comunicaciones
176	.	.	.	8. Banques, assur., affaires imm., services aux entreprises	8. Bancos, seguros, bienes inmuebles, serv. para empresas
3 043	.	.	.	9. Services à la collectivité, services sociaux et personnels	9. Servicios comunales, sociales y personales
31 820	.	.	.	0. Activités mal désignées	0. Actividades no bien especif.
42 190	**.**	**.**	**.**	**Total**	**Total**

485	.	.	.	1. Agriculture, chasse, sylviculture et pêche	1. Agricultura, caza, silvicultura y pesca
176	.	.	.	2. Industries extractives	2. Minas y canteras
6 389	.	.	4	3. Industries manufacturières	3. Industrias manufactureras
318	.	.	.	4. Electricité, gaz et eau	4. Electricidad, gas y agua
1 435	.	.	.	5. Construction	5. Construcción
2 074	.	.	.	6. Commerce (gros et détail); restaurants, hôtels	6. Comercio (por mayor y por menor); restaurantes, hoteles
1 217	.	.	10	7. Transports, entrepôts et communications	7. Transportes, almacenamiento y comunicaciones
547	.	.	4	8. Banques, assur., affaires imm., services aux entreprises	8. Bancos, seguros, bienes inmuebles, serv. para empresas
3 288	.	.	7 702	9. Services à la collectivité, services sociaux et personnels	9. Servicios comunales, sociales y personales
17 850	.	.	11	0. Activités mal désignées	0. Actividades no bien especif.
33 779	**.**	**.**	**7 731**	**Total**	**Total**

(a) The English designation of major occupational groups is shown on the following page.

2 Structure of the economically active population
Structure de la population active
Estructura de la población económicamente activa

Industry (Major divisions of economic activity)	Total	Occupation (Major groups) [a]						
		1	2	3	4	5	6	7/8/9
		Professional, technical & related workers	Administrative & managerial workers	Clerical & related workers	Sales workers	Service workers	Agriculture, animal husbandry & forestry workers, fishermen & hunters	Production & related workers, transport equipment operators & labourers
Germany, Fed. Rep. of (IV.78) LFSS †								
1. Agriculture, hunting, forestry & fishing	1 519 000	9 000	–	14 000	9 000	–	1 445 000	28 000
2. Mining & quarrying	357 000	34 000	7 000	35 000	–	8 000	–	264 000
3. Manufacturing	8 801 000	762 000	235 000	1 436 000	381 000	195 000	13 000	5 675 000
4. Electr., gas & water	234 000	37 000	7 000	49 000	7 000	12 000	–	119 000
5. Construction	1 966 000	105 000	35 000	178 000	25 000	15 000	–	1 582 000
6. Wholesale/retail trade, restaurants & hotels	3 667 000	102 000	165 000	767 000	1 515 000	575 000	16 000	461 000
7. Transport, storage & communication	1 521 000	104 000	76 000	594 000	62 000	93 000	–	578 000
8. Financing, insur., real estate & business serv.	1 412 000	244 000	49 000	777 000	202 000	88 000	–	40 000
9. Community, social & personal services	6 345 000	2 046 000	255 000	1 202 000	81 000	1 911 000	61 000	737 000
0. Not adequately defined	199 000	9 000	5 000	44 000	6 000	7 000	–	47 000
–. Unemployed	931 000	...	...	...	...	...	...	...
Total	**26 952 000**	**3 451 000**	**837 000**	**5 095 000**	**2 291 000**	**2 909 000**	**1 541 000**	**9 531 000**
Ireland (IV.77) LFSS †								
1. Agriculture, hunting, forestry & fishing	224 400	800	–	700	–	–	215 100	500
2–4. Min./quarrying; manuf.; electr., gas & water	265 500	11 300	12 500	22 200	5 800	3 300	400	184 500
5. Construction	109 600	3 000	1 000	2 900	200	1 000	–	76 800
6–8. Major div. 6, 7 & 8	262 100	6 100	7 400	46 000	99 100	4 100	300	83 500
9. Community, social & personal services	251 300	107 500	6 300	40 100	3 400	62 700	3 900	14 000
–. Persons seeking work for the first time	15 000	.	.	.	.	.	.	.
–. Armed forces	16 100	.	.	.	.	.	.	.
Total	**1 143 900**	**128 700**	**27 300**	**111 800**	**108 500**	**71 100**	**219 700**	**359 000**
Netherlands (III–V.77) LFSS †								
1. Agriculture, hunting, forestry & fishing	281 000	2 000	1 000	4 000	1 000	1 000	265 000	7 000
2. Mining & quarrying	9 000	2 000	–	2 000	–	–	–	5 000
3. Manufacturing	1 114 000	97 000	44 000	149 000	48 000	26 000	7 000	727 000
4. Electr., gas & water	45 000	8 000	1 000	12 000	1 000	2 000	–	23 000
5. Construction	500 000	28 000	18 000	32 000	5 000	5 000	3 000	407 000
6. Wholesale/retail trade, restaurants & hotels	767 000	24 000	9 000	120 000	395 000	95 000	4 000	120 000
7. Transport, storage & communication	310 000	27 000	9 000	117 000	2 000	9 000	–	145 000
8. Financing, insur., real estate & business serv.	345 000	72 000	12 000	198 000	29 000	15 000	1 000	19 000
9. Community, social & personal services	1 332 000	560 000	24 000	255 000	12 000	348 000	9 000	118 000
0. Not adequately defined	11 000	...	...	...	...	...	...	...
–. Unemployed	252 000	...	...	...	...	...	...	...
–. Armed forces	91 000	.	.	.	.	.	.	.
Total	**5 058 000**	**820 000**	**118 000**	**891 000**	**493 000**	**501 000**	**289 000**	**1 573 000**

[a] La designación en español de los grandes grupos de ocupación figura en la página precedente.

C By industry and by occupational group
Par industrie et par groupe de professions
Por industria y por grupo de ocupación

X — Workers not classifiable by occupation	Unemployed	First-time job seekers	Members of the armed forces	Industrie (Branches d'activité économique)	Industria (Grandes divisiones de actividad económica)
7 000	...	.	.	1. Agriculture, chasse, sylviculture et pêche	1. Agricultura, caza, silvicultura y pesca
–	...	.	.	2. Industries extractives	2. Minas y canteras
106 000	...	.	.	3. Industries manufacturières	3. Industrias manufactureras
–	...	.	.	4. Electricité, gaz et eau	4. Electricidad, gas y agua
24 000	...	.	.	5. Construction	5. Construcción
67 000	...	.	.	6. Commerce (gros et détail); restaurants, hôtels	6. Comercio (por mayor y por menor); restaurantes, hoteles
13 000	...	.	.	7. Transports, entrepôts et communications	7. Transportes, almacenamiento y comunicaciones
11 000	...	.	.	8. Banques, assur., affaires imm., services aux entreprises	8. Bancos, seguros, bienes inmuebles, serv. para empresas
53 000	...	.	.	9. Services à la collectivité, services sociaux et personnels	9. Servicios comunales, sociales y personales
81 000	...	.	.	0. Activités mal désignées	0. Actividades no bien especif.
...	931 000	.	.	–. Chômeurs	–. Desempleados
367 000	**931 000**	.	.	**Total**	**Total**

X — Workers not classifiable by occupation	Unemployed	First-time job seekers	Members of the armed forces	Industrie (Branches d'activité économique)	Industria (Grandes divisiones de actividad económica)
500	6 900	.	.	1. Agriculture, chasse, sylviculture et pêche	1. Agricultura, caza, silvicultura y pesca
–	25 300	.	.	2-4. Industries extract.; industries manuf.; électricité, gaz et eau	2-4. Minas y canteras; industrias manufact.; electr., gas y agua
–	24 300	.	.	5. Construction	5. Construcción
–	15 700	.	.	6-8. Branches 6, 7 et 8	6-8. Grandes divisiones 6, 7 y 8
–	13 400	.	.	9. Services à la collectivité, services sociaux et personnels	9. Servicios comunales, sociales y personales
.	.	15 000	.	–. Personnes en quête d'emploi pour la première fois	–. Personas en busca de trabajo por primera vez
.	.	.	16 100	–. Forces armées	–. Fuerzas armadas
1 000	**85 600**	**15 000**	**16 100**	**Total**	**Total**

X — Workers not classifiable by occupation	Unemployed	First-time job seekers	Members of the armed forces	Industrie (Branches d'activité économique)	Industria (Grandes divisiones de actividad económica)
...	...	.	.	1. Agriculture, chasse, sylviculture et pêche	1. Agricultura, caza, silvicultura y pesca
...	...	.	.	2. Industries extractives	2. Minas y canteras
...	...	.	.	3. Industries manufacturières	3. Industrias manufactureras
...	...	.	.	4. Electricité, gaz et eau	4. Electricidad, gas y agua
...	...	.	.	5. Construction	5. Construcción
...	...	.	.	6. Commerce (gros et détail); restaurants, hôtels	6. Comercio (por mayor y por menor); restaurantes, hoteles
...	...	.	.	7. Transports, entrepôts et communications	7. Transportes, almacenamiento y comunicaciones
...	...	.	.	8. Banques, assur., affaires imm., services aux entreprises	8. Bancos, seguros, bienes inmuebles, serv. para empresas
...	...	.	.	9. Services à la collectivité, services sociaux et personnels	9. Servicios comunales, sociales y personales
11 000	...	.	.	0. Activités mal désignées	0. Actividades no bien especif.
...	252 000	...	.	–. Chômeurs	–. Desempleados
.	.	.	91 000	–. Forces armées	–. Fuerzas armadas
28 000	**252 000**	**...**	**91 000**	**Total**	**Total**

(a) Les libellés en français des grands groupes de professions sont indiqués à la page suivante.

2 Structure of the economically active population
Structure de la population active
Estructura de la población económicamente activa

Industry (Major divisions of economic activity)	Total	Profession (Grands groupes) [a]						
		1	2	3	4	5	6	7/8/9
		Personnel des prof. scientif., techniques, libérales et assimilées	Directeurs et cadres administratifs supérieurs	Personnel administratif et travailleurs assimilés	Personnel commercial et vendeurs	Travailleurs des services	Agriculteurs, éleveurs, forestiers, pêcheurs et chasseurs	Ouvriers et manœuvres non agricoles et conducteurs d'engins de transport
Norway (1979) LFSS †								
1. Agriculture, hunting, forestry & fishing	160 000	1 000	1 000	–	–	1 000	153 000	4 000
2–4. Min./quarrying; manuf.; electr., gas & water	411 000	34 000	18 000	34 000	13 000	14 000	1 000	298 000
5. Construction	150 000	9 000	3 000	8 000	1 000	3 000	–	126 000
6. Wholesale/retail trade, restaurants & hotels	316 000	14 000	24 000	43 000	151 000	43 000		41 000
7. Transport, storage & communication	172 000	6 000	7 000	17 000	–	12 000		129 000
8. Financing, insur., real estate & business serv.	110 000	25 000	12 000	53 000	6 000	8 000	–	5 000
9. Community, social & personal services	547 000	262 000	29 000	48 000	2 000	159 000	2 000	36 000
0. Not adequately defined	4 000	1 000	–	–	–	–	–	–
–. Unemployed	38 000	...	...	...	...	...	...	...
Total	**1 909 000**	**351 000**	**94 000**	**204 000**	**173 000**	**239 000**	**157 000**	**639 000**
Portugal (VII–XII.79) LFSS †								
1/2. Agriculture, hunting, forestry & fishing; mining & quarrying	1 205 000	–	–	2 000	–	2 000	1 164 000	28 000
3–5. Major div. 3, 4 & 5	1 414 000	24 000	31 000	88 000	19 000	33 000	2 000	1 196 000
6–9. Major div. 6, 7, 8 & 9	1 414 000	179 000	22 000	305 000	279 000	338 000	5 000	262 000
0. Not adequately defined	10 000	...	...	...	...	...	...	...
–. Persons seeking work for the first time	198 000							
–. Other unemployed	*146 000*	*7 000*	–	18 000	*12 000*	*24 000*	*7 000*	
–. Armed forces	77 000							
Total	**4 328 000**	**212 000**	**59 000**	**405 000**	**306 000**	**385 000**	**1 179 000**	**1 498 000**
Sweden (1.XI.75) C †								
1. Agriculture, hunting, forestry & fishing	243 025	3 776	1 106	3 759	986	2 468	223 398	7 415
2. Mining & quarrying	19 507	2 959	213	931	133	657	26	14 576
3. Manufacturing	1 049 161	152 146	17 789	88 771	40 690	27 872	1 092	719 277
4. Electr., gas & water	29 433	8 963	1 272	3 350	198	862	62	14 704
5. Construction	290 804	40 169	3 301	17 719	3 220	5 104	913	220 178
6. Wholesale/retail trade, restaurants & hotels	560 048	24 548	10 821	85 966	268 922	69 324	445	99 516
7. Transport, storage & communication	270 701	11 239	5 509	32 432	2 451	11 486	60	207 305
8. Financing, insur., real estate & business serv.	223 955	55 167	12 918	93 264	12 098	32 217	701	17 329
9. Community, social & personal services	1 154 882	548 874	38 829	118 877	7 021	335 577	3 107	78 739
0. Not adequately defined	8 935	1 282	73	529	842	379	21	1 560
Total	**3 850 451**	**849 123**	**91 831**	**445 598**	**336 561**	**485 946**	**229 825**	**1 380 599**

[a] The English designation of major occupational groups is shown on the preceding page.

C By industry and by occupational group
Par industrie et par groupe de professions
Por industria y por grupo de ocupación

X — Travailleurs ne pouvant être classés selon la profession	Chômeurs	en quête d'un premier emploi	Membres des forces armées	Industrie (Branches d'activité économique)	Industria (Grandes divisiones de actividad económica)
–	2 000	.	.	1. Agriculture, chasse, sylviculture et pêche	1. Agricultura, caza, silvicultura y pesca
–	7 000	.	.	2–4. Industries extract.; industries manuf.; électricité, gaz et eau	2–4. Minas y canteras; industrias manufact.; electr., gas y agua
–	3 000	.	.	5. Construction	5. Construcción
–	6 000	.	.	6. Commerce (gros et détail); restaurants, hôtels	6. Comercio (por mayor y por menor); restaurantes, hoteles
–	3 000	.	.	7. Transports, entrepôts et communications	7. Transportes, almacenamiento y comunicaciones
–	1 000	.	.	8. Banques, assur., affaires imm., services aux entreprises	8. Bancos, seguros, bienes inmuebles, serv. para empresas
9 000	6 000	.	.	9. Services à la collectivité, services sociaux et personnels	9. Servicios comunales, sociales y personales
2 000	10 000	.	.	0. Activités mal désignées	0. Actividades no bien especif.
...	*38 000*	....	.	–. Chômeurs	–. Desempleados
11 000	**38 000**	.	.	**Total**	**Total**
...	5 000	.	.	1/2. Agriculture, chasse, sylviculture et pêche; industries extractives	1/2. Agricultura, caza, silvicultura y pesca; minas y canteras
...	74 000	.	.	3–5. Branches 3, 4 et 5	2–5. Grandes divisiones 3, 4 y 5
...	58 000	.	.	6–9. Branches 6, 7, 8 et 9	6–9. Grandes div. 6, 7, 8 y 9
10 000	...	.	.	0. Activités mal désignées	0. Actividades no bien especif.
		198 000	.	–. Personnes en quête d'emploi pour la première fois	–. Personas en busca de trabajo por primera vez
–	*146 000*	.	.	–. Autres chômeurs	–. Otros desempleados
	.	.	77 000	–. Forces armées	–. Fuerzas armadas
10 000	*146 000*	**198 000**	**77 000**	**Total**	**Total**
117	.	.	.	1. Agriculture, chasse, sylviculture et pêche	1. Agricultura, caza, silvicultura y pesca
12	.	.	.	2. Industries extractives	2. Minas y canteras
1 081	.	.	443	3. Industries manufacturières	3. Industrias manufactureras
22	.	.	.	4. Electricité, gaz et eau	4. Electricidad, gas y agua
200	.	.	.	5. Construction	5. Construcción
506	.	.	.	6. Commerce (gros et détail); restaurants, hôtels	6. Comercio (por mayor y por menor); restaurantes, hoteles
219	.	.	.	7. Transports, entrepôts et communications	7. Transportes, almacenamiento y comunicaciones
261	.	.	.	8. Banques, assur., affaires imm., services aux entreprises	8. Bancos, seguros, bienes inmuebles, serv. para empresas
863	.	.	22 995	9. Services à la collectivité, services sociaux et personnels	9. Servicios comunales, sociales y personales
4 249	.	.	.	0. Activités mal désignées	0. Actividades no bien especif.
7 530	.	.	**23 438**	**Total**	**Total**

(a) La designación en español de los grandes grupos de ocupación figura en la página siguiente.

2 Structure of the economically active population
Structure de la population active
Estructura de la población económicamente activa

Industry (Major divisions of economic activity)	Total	Ocupación (Grandes grupos) [a]						
		1	2	3	4	5	6	7/8/9
		Profesionales técnicos y trabajadores asimilados	Directores y funcionarios públicos superiores	Personal administrativo y trabajadores	Comerciantes y vendedores	Trabajadores de los servicios	Trabajadores agrícolas, forestales, pescadores y cazadores	Obreros no agr. y conductores de máquinas y vehículos de transp. y trab. asimilados
Turquie (26.X.75) C1%								
1. Agriculture, hunting, forestry & fishing	10 482 966	16 402	600	4 901	2 800	8 600	10 418 862	30 801
2. Mining & quarrying	108 506	4 300	900	4 700	1 400	3 600	800	92 806
3. Manufacturing	1 243 567	39 302	15 101	20 502	16 701	16 401	9 000	1 126 560
4. Electr., gas & water	16 401	3 300	100	1 200	801	900	100	10 000
5. Construction	447 324	11 601	14 401	6 600	1 500	6 401	1 600	405 221
6. Wholesale/retail trade, restaurants & hotels	818 644	22 801	2 400	7 900	442 824	193 010	22 103	127 606
7. Transport, storage & communication	512 327	8 600	14 301	47 103	3 000	9 500	900	428 923
8. Financing, insur., real estate & business serv.	176 207	40 401	6 100	94 405	9 500	11 901	800	13 100
9. Community, social & personal services	1 866 002	501 828	15 701	292 516	6 100	285 816	11 801	752 240
0. Not adequately defined	677 436	112 206	7 800	29 301	32 002	27 201	10 000	458 926
Total	**16 349 380**	**760 741**	**77 404**	**509 128**	**516 628**	**563 330**	**10 475 966**	**3 446 183**
OCEANIA								
Fiji (13.IX.76) C								
1. Agriculture, hunting, forestry & fishing	76 886	95	49	107	201	63	74 660	1 472
2. Mining & quarrying	1 662	92	5	85	11	50	19	1 352
3. Manufacturing	13 039	446	245	929	478	274	595	9 806
4. Electr., gas & water	1 628	83	15	172	23	50	40	1 189
5. Construction	11 186	189	70	343	36	196	58	10 186
6. Wholesale/retail trade, restaurants & hotels	17 372	373	360	2 276	8 089	3 317	227	2 420
7. Transport, storage & communication	9 039	490	261	1 526	74	527	45	5 896
8. Financing, insur., real estate & business serv.	3 518	661	180	1 913	152	106	12	349
9. Community, social & personal services	29 134	10 188	464	4 042	154	6 818	768	5 861
–. Not adequately defined & persons seeking work for the first time	12 321	32	7	69	4	28	20	149
Total	**175 785**	**12 649**	**1 656**	**11 462**	**9 222**	**11 429**	**76 444**	**38 680**
New Zealand (23.III.76) C †								
1. Agriculture, hunting, forestry & fishing	128 900	1 454	410	1 130	153	498	122 286	2 894
2. Mining & quarrying	5 059	379	359	374	18	47	18	3 840
3. Manufacturing	305 724	16 188	17 904	29 545	9 999	3 659	1 593	224 770
4. Electr., gas & water	15 329	2 185	148	3 058	111	192	44	9 459
5. Construction	112 137	6 734	2 431	5 885	406	350	227	95 653
6. Wholesale/retail trade, restaurants & hotels	216 122	5 981	6 523	32 654	99 988	28 419	508	41 236
7. Transport, storage & communication	111 287	8 264	2 852	40 569	685	4 107	53	53 705
8. Financing, insur., real estate & business serv.	79 792	17 744	5 192	44 697	9 474	1 206	58	1 298
9. Community, social & personal services	251 887	119 251	4 313	45 318	2 222	45 255	5 685	28 868
0. Not adequately defined	30 441	641	776	2 688	2 224	886	218	7 113
–. Persons seeking work for the first time	4 293	.	.	.	.	.	.	.
–. Armed forces	11 362	.	.	.	.	.	.	.
Total	**1 272 333**	**178 821**	**40 908**	**205 918**	**125 280**	**84 619**	**130 690**	**468 836**

[a] Les libellés en français des grands groupes de professions sont indiqués à la page précédente.

C — By industry and by occupational group
Par industrie et par groupe de professions
Por industria y por grupo de ocupación

X — Trab. que no pueden ser clasificados según la ocupación	Desempleados — en busca de trabajo por primera vez	Miembros de las fuerzas armadas	Industrie (Branches d'activité économique)	Industria (Grandes divisiones de actividad económica)
.	.	.	.	1. Agriculture, chasse, sylviculture et pêche	1. Agricultura, caza, silvicultura y pesca
.	.	.	2. Industries extractives	2. Minas y canteras
.	.	.	3. Industries manufacturières	3. Industrias manufactureras
.	.	.	4. Electricité, gaz et eau	4. Electricidad, gas y agua
.	.	.	5. Construction	5. Construcción
.	.	.	6. Commerce (gros et détail); restaurants, hôtels	6. Comercio (por mayor y por menor); restaurantes, hoteles
.	.	.	7. Transports, entrepôts et communications	7. Transportes, almacenamiento y comunicaciones
.	.	.	8. Banques, assur., affaires imm., services aux entreprises	8. Bancos, seguros, bienes inmuebles, serv. para empresas
.	.	.	9. Services à la collectivité, services sociaux et personnels	9. Servicios comunales, sociales y personales
.	.	.	0. Activités mal désignées	0. Actividades no bien especif.
.	.	.	**Total**	**Total**

OCEANIE – OCEANIA

X — Trab. que no pueden ser clasificados según la ocupación	Desempleados — en busca de trabajo por primera vez	Miembros de las fuerzas armadas	Industrie (Branches d'activité économique)	Industria (Grandes divisiones de actividad económica)
222	17	.	1. Agriculture, chasse, sylviculture et pêche	1. Agricultura, caza, silvicultura y pesca
46	2	.	2. Industries extractives	2. Minas y canteras
263	3	.	3. Industries manufacturières	3. Industrias manufactureras
54	2	.	4. Electricité, gaz et eau	4. Electricidad, gas y agua
104	4	.	5. Construction	5. Construcción
302	8	.	6. Commerce (gros et détail); restaurants, hôtels	6. Comercio (por mayor y por menor); restaurantes, hoteles
216	4	.	7. Transports, entrepôts et communications	7. Transportes, almacenamiento y comunicaciones
142	3	.	8. Banques, assur., affaires imm., services aux entreprises	8. Bancos, seguros, bienes inmuebles, serv. para empresas
822	17	.	9. Services à la collectivité, services sociaux et personnels	9. Servicios comunales, sociales y personales
4 383	7 629	.	–. Activités mal désignées et personnes en quête d'emploi pour l première fois.	–. Actividades no bien especificadas; personas en busca de trabajo por primera vez
6 554	**7 689**	.	**Total**	**Total**

X — Trab. que no pueden ser clasificados según la ocupación	Desempleados — en busca de trabajo por primera vez	Miembros de las fuerzas armadas	Industrie (Branches d'activité économique)	Industria (Grandes divisiones de actividad económica)
75	.	.	1. Agriculture, chasse, sylviculture et pêche	1. Agricultura, caza, silvicultura y pesca
24	.	.	2. Industries extractives	2. Minas y canteras
2 066	.	.	3. Industries manufacturières	3. Industrias manufactureras
132	.	.	4. Electricité, gaz et eau	4. Electricidad, gas y agua
451	.	.	5. Construction	5. Construcción
813	.	.	6. Commerce (gros et détail); restaurants, hôtels	6. Comercio (por mayor y por menor); restaurantes, hoteles
1 052	.	.	7. Transports, entrepôts et communications	7. Transportes, almacenamiento y comunicaciones
123	.	.	8. Banques, assur., affaires imm., services aux entreprises	8. Bancos, seguros, bienes inmuebles, serv. para empresas
975	.	.	9. Services à la collectivité, services sociaux et personnels	9. Servicios comunales, sociales y personales
15 895	.	.	0. Activités mal désignées	0. Actividades no bien especif.
.	4 293	.	–. Personnes en quête d'emploi pour la première fois	–. Personas en busca de trabajo por primera vez
.	.	11 362	–. Forces armées	–. Fuerzas armadas
21 606	**4 293**	**11 362**	**Total**	**Total**

(a) The English designation of major occupational groups is shown on the following page.

135

2 Structure of the economically active population
Structure de la population active
Estructura de la población económicamente activa

Industry (Major divisions of economic activity)	Total	Occupation (Major groups) [a]						
		1 Professional, technical & related workers	2 Administrative & managerial workers	3 Clerical & related workers	4 Sales workers	5 Service workers	6 Agriculture, animal husbandry & forestry workers, fishermen & hunters	7/8/9 Production & related workers, transport equipment operators & labourers
Samoa (3.XI.76) C								
1. Agriculture, hunting, forestry & fishing	23 373	25	4	94	6	17	23 082	145
2. Mining & quarrying	7	1	.	1	.	.	.	4
3. Manufacturing	712	23	17	109	25	14	.	524
4. Electr., gas & water	468	58	3	32	1	3	.	371
5. Construction	1 813	19	5	38	1	20	.	1 730
6. Wholesale/retail trade, restaurants & hotels	2 407	53	26	350	1 372	264	.	342
7. Transport, storage & communication	2 058	118	13	399	5	41	.	1 481
8. Financing, insur., real estate & business serv.	322	37	11	253	4	7	.	10
9. Community, social & personal services	6 893	3 974	146	895	29	1 102	.	746
0. Not adequately defined	196	4	.	4	1	2	.	122
Total	**38 249**	**4 312**	**225**	**2 175**	**1 444**	**1 470**	**23 082**	**5 475**

[a] La designación en español de los grandes grupos de ocupación figura en la página precedente.

C By industry and by occupational group
Par industrie et par groupe de professions
Por industria y por grupo de ocupación

X Workers not classifiable by occupation	Unemployed First-time job seekers	Members of the armed forces	Industrie (Branches d'activité économique)	Industria (Grandes divisiones de actividad económica)
1	·	·	·	1. Agriculture, chasse, sylvi– culture et pêche	1. Agricultura, caza, silvi– cultura y pesca
·	·	·	·	2. Industries extractives	2. Minas y canteras
·	·	·	·	3. Industries manufacturières	3. Industrias manufactureras
·	·	·	·	4. Electricité, gaz et eau	4. Electricidad, gas y agua
·	·	·	·	5. Construction	5. Construcción
·	·	·	·	6. Commerce (gros et détail); restaurants, hôtels	6. Comercio (por mayor y por me– nor); restaurantes, hoteles
1	·	·	·	7. Transports, entrepôts et commu– nications	7. Transportes, almacenamiento y comunicaciones
·	·	·	·	8. Banques, assur., affaires imm., services aux entreprises	8. Bancos, seguros, bienes in– muebles, serv. para empresas
1	·	·	·	9. Services à la collectivité, services sociaux et personnels	9. Servicios comunales, sociales y personales
63	·	·	·	0. Activités mal désignées	0. Actividades no bien especif.
66	·	·	·	**Total**	**Total**

137

ACTIVE POPULATION

Notes to tables 1 to 2C   (indicated by the symbol †)
Notes relatives aux tableaux 1 à 2C   (indiquées par le symbole †)
Notas relativas a los cuadros 1 a 2C   (indicadas por medio del símbolo †)

AFRICA - AFRIQUE - AFRICA

Rép.- Unie du Cameroun

Tables 1, 2A, 2B

African population.

Tableaux 1, 2A, 2B

Population africaine.

Cuadros 1, 2A, 2B

Población africana.

Côte-d'Ivoire

Table 1

"De jure" population.

Economically active population figures do not include unpaid family workers.

Tableau 1

Population «de jure».

Les chiffres de la population active ne comprennent pas les travailleurs familiaux non rémunérés.

Cuadro 1

Población «de jure».

Las cifras de la población económicamente activa no incluyen a los trabajadores familiares no remunerados.

Egypt

Tables 1, 2A, 2B, 2C

Egyptian population.

1976: economically active population figures relate to persons 6 years of age and over (tables 1, 2A) and 15 years of age and over (tables 2B, 2C). Economically active population totals shown in table 1 include 83,431 persons (81,103 males and 2,328 females) whose distribution by age group is not available.

Tableaux 1, 2A, 2B, 2C

Population égyptienne.

1976: les chiffres de la population active se réfèrent aux personnes âgées de 6 ans et plus (tableaux 1, 2A) et de 15 ans et plus (tableaux 2B, 2C). Les totaux de population active figurant au tableau 1 comprennent 83 431 personnes (81 103 hommes et 2 328 femmes) dont la répartition par groupe d'âge n'est pas disponible.

Cuadros 1, 2A, 2B, 2C

Población egipcia.

1976: las cifras de la población económicamente activa se refieren a las personas de 6 años y más de edad (cuadros 1, 2A) y de 15 años y más de edad (cuadros 2B, 2C). Los totales de población económicamente activa que figuran en el cuadro 1 incluyen a 83 431 personas (81 103 hombres y 2 328 mujeres) cuya distribución por grupo de edad no está disponible.

Tables 1, 2A, 2B

1978: economically active population figures relate to persons 6 years of age and over (table 1) and 12 to 64 years of age (tables 2A, 2B).

Tableaux 1, 2A, 2B

1978: les chiffres de la population active se réfèrent aux personnes âgées de 6 ans et plus (tableau 1) et de 12 à 64 ans (tableaux 2A, 2B).

Cuadros 1, 2A, 2B

1978: las cifras de la población económicamente activa se refieren a las personas de 6 años y más de edad (cuadro 1) y de 12 a 64 años de edad (cuadros 2A, 2B).

Table 2A

1976: the group "Not classifiable by status" includes 850,625 unemployed (558,140 males and 292,485 females) and 83,431 persons whose status is unknown (81,103 males and 2,328 females).

Tableau 2A

1976: la rubrique «Inclassables selon la situation» comprend 850 625 chômeurs (558 140 hommes et 292 485 femmes) ainsi que 83 431 personnes dont la situation n'est pas définie (81 103 hommes et 2 328 femmes).

Cuadro 2A

1976: el grupo «Inclasificables según la categoría» incluye a 850 625 desempleados (558 140 hombres y 292 485 mujeres) así como a 83 431 personas cuya categoría no está definida (81 103 hombres y 2 328 mujeres).

Table 2B

1976: the occupational group "Not classifiable by occupation, etc." includes 375,386 persons seeking work for the first time (238,516 males and 136,870 females).

Tableau 2B

1976: le groupe de professions «Inclassables selon la profession, etc.» comprend 375 386 personnes en quête d'emploi pour la première fois (238 516 hommes et 136 870 femmes).

Cuadro 2B

1976: el grupo de ocupación «Inclasificables según la ocupación, etc.» incluye a 375 386 personas en busca de trabajo por primera vez (238 516 hombres y 136 870 mujeres).

Haute-Volta

Table 1

Economically active population figures do not include unemployed.

Tableau 1

Les chiffres de la population active ne comprennent pas les chômeurs.

Cuadro 1

Las cifras de la población económicamente activa no incluyen a los desempleados.

Libyan Arab Jamahiriya

Table 1

Economically active population figures by sex and age group do not include 9,774 persons seeking work for the first time (8,982 males and 792 females) who appear only in the totals.

Tableau 1

Les chiffres de la population active par sexe et groupe d'âge ne comprennent pas 9 774 personnes en quête d'emploi pour la première fois (8 982 hommes et 792 femmes) qui figurent uniquement dans les totaux.

Cuadro 1

Las cifras de la población económicamente activa por sexo y grupo de edad no incluyen a 9 774 personas en busca de trabajo por primera vez (8 982 hombres y 792 mujeres), que aparecen únicamente en los totales.

Malawi

Table 2B

The group "Not classifiable by status" relates to unemployed.

Tableau 2B

La rubrique «Inclassables selon la situation» se réfère aux chômeurs.

Cuadro 2B

El grupo «Inclasificables según la categoría» se refiere a los desempleados.

Notes to tables 1 to 2C (indicated by the symbol †)
Notes relatives aux tableaux 1 à 2C (indiquées par le symbole †)
Notas relativas a los cuadros 1 a 2C (indicadas por medio del símbolo †)

Seychelles

Table 2B

The group "Employers and own-account workers" includes unpaid family workers.

The group "Not classifiable by status" relates to unemployed.

Tableau 2B

La rubrique «Employeurs et personnes travaillant à leur propre compte» comprend les travailleurs familiaux non rémunérés.

La rubrique «Inclassables selon la situation» se réfère aux chômeurs.

Cuadro 2B

El grupo «Empleadores y trabajadores por cuenta propia» incluye a los trabajadores familiares no remunerados.

El grupo «Inclasificables según la categoría» se refiere a los desempleados.

AMERICA - AMERIQUE - AMERICA

Bolivia

Table 2B

1958 ISCO.

Tableau 2B

CITP de 1958.

Cuadro 2B

CIUO de 1958.

Brasil

Table 2C

Figures in italics show totals for persons already included in the component occupational and/or industrial group.

Tableau 2C

Les chiffres en italique indiquent les totaux de personnes déjà incluses dans les composantes des groupes de professions et/ou industriels.

Cuadro 2C

Las cifras en itálica indican los totales de personas ya incluidas dentro de las partes que componen los grupos de ocupaciones y/o industriales.

Canada

Tables 1, 2A, 2B, 2C

Excl. Yukon, Northwest Territories, armed forces and Indians living on reserves.

Tableaux 1, 2A, 2B, 2C

Non compris le Yukon, les territoires du Nord-Ouest, les forces armées et les Indiens vivant dans les réserves.

Cuadros 1, 2A, 2B, 2C

Excl. el Yukón, los Territorios del Noroeste, las fuerzas armadas y los indios que viven en las reservas.

Tables 2A, 2B, 2C

Figures of less than 4,000 are indicated by a dash. All figures are rounded off to the nearest 1,000; consequently, the totals shown may differ from the sum of the component parts.

Tableaux 2A, 2B, 2C

Les chiffres représentant moins de 4 000 personnes sont désignés par un tiret. Tous les nombres étant arrondis au multiple de 1 000 le plus proche, les totaux indiqués peuvent différer de la somme de leurs parties composantes.

Cuadros 2A, 2B, 2C

Las cifras inferiores a 4 000 personas están indicadas por un guión. Todas las cifras han sido redondeadas al múltiplo de 1 000 más próximo; en consecuencia, los totales indicados pueden diferir de la suma de las partes que la componen.

Table 2B

The group "Employers and own-account workers" includes unpaid family workers.

Tableau 2B

La rubrique «Employeurs et personnes travaillant à leur propre compte» comprend les travailleurs familiaux non rémunérés.

Cuadro 2B

El grupo «Empleadores y trabajadores por cuenta propia» incluye a los trabajadores familiares no remunerados.

Table 2C

The occupational group "0/1" includes data relating to the occupational group "2".

Figures in italics show totals for persons already included in the component occupational and/or industrial group.

Tableau 2C

Le groupe de professions «0/1» comprend les données relatives au groupe de professions «2».

Les chiffres en italique indiquent les totaux de personnes déjà incluses dans les composantes des groupes de professions et/ou industriels.

Cuadro 2C

El grupo de ocupación «0/1» incluye los datos relativos al grupo de ocupación «2».

Las cifras en itálica indican los totales de personas ya incluidas dentro de las partes que componen los grupos de ocupaciones y/o industriales.

Chile

Table 2A

1958 ISIC.

Tableau 2A

CITI de 1958.

Cuadro 2A

CIIU de 1958.

Guatemala

Tables 1, 2A, 2B, 2C

Excl. institutional households.

Tables 2A, 2C

1958 ISIC.

Tableaux 1, 2A, 2B, 2C

Non compris les ménages collectifs.

Tableaux 2A, 2C

CITI de 1958.

Cuadros 1, 2A, 2B, 2C

Excl. los hogares colectivos.

Cuadros 2A, 2C

CIIU de 1958.

ACTIVE POPULATION

Notes to tables 1 to 2C (indicated by the symbol †)
Notes relatives aux tableaux 1 à 2C (indiquées par le symbole †)
Notas relativas a los cuadros 1 a 2C (indicadas por medio del símbolo †)

Haïti

Table 2B

Data relate to persons 10 years of age and over (data previously published in tables 1 and 2A related to economically active persons 5 years of age and over).

Tableau 2B

Les données se réfèrent aux personnes âgées de 10 ans et plus (les données précédemment publiées dans les tableaux 1 et 2A se référaient à la population active âgée de 5 ans et plus).

Cuadro 2B

Los datos se refieren a las personas de 10 años y más de edad (los datos anteriormente publicados en los cuadros 1 y 2A se referían a la población económicamente activa de 5 años y más de edad).

Jamaica

Table 2A

1958 ISIC.

Tableau 2A

CITI de 1958.

Cuadro 2A

CIIU de 1958.

México

Table 2A

1958 ISIC.

Tableau 2A

CITI de 1958.

Cuadro 2A

CIIU de 1958.

Nicaragua

Tables 1, 2A

Economically active population figures do not include unemployed.

Tableaux 1, 2A

Les chiffres de la population active ne comprennent pas les chômeurs.

Cuadros 1, 2A

Las cifras de la población económicamente activa no incluyen a los desempleados.

Puerto Rico

Tables 2A, 2B

Figures of less than 1,000 are indicated by a dash; all figures are rounded off to the nearest 100; consequently, the totals shown may differ from the sum of the component parts.

Tableaux 2A, 2B

Les nombres représentant moins de 1 000 personnes sont désignés par un tiret; tous les nombres sont arrondis au multiple de 100 le plus proche; en conséquence, les totaux indiqués peuvent différer de la somme de leurs parties composantes.

Cuadros 2A, 2B

Las cifras inferiores a 1 000 personas están indicadas por un guión; todas las cifras han sido redondeadas al múltiplo de 100 más próximo; en consecuencia, los totales indicados pueden diferir de la suma de las partes que la componen.

Trinidad and Tobago

Tables 2A, 2B

All figures are rounded off to the nearest 100; consequently, the totals shown may differ from the sum of the component parts.

Tableaux 2A, 2B

Tous les nombres étant arrondis au multiple de 100 le plus proche, les totaux indiqués peuvent différer de la somme de leurs parties composantes.

Cuadros 2A, 2B

Todas las cifras han sido redondeadas al múltiplo de 100 más próximo; en consecuencia, los totales indicados pueden diferir de la suma de las partes que la componen.

Table 2A

1958 ISIC.

Tableau 2A

CITI de 1958.

Cuadro 2A

CIIU de 1958.

United States

Tables 1, 2A, 2B, 2C

Economically active population figures relate to persons 16 years of age and over.

All figures are rounded off to the nearest 1,000; consequently, the totals shown may differ from the sum of the component parts.

Tableaux 1, 2A, 2B, 2C

Les chiffres de la population active se réfèrent aux personnes âgées de 16 ans et plus.

Tous les nombres étant arrondis au multiple de 1 000 le plus proche, les totaux indiqués peuvent différer de la somme de leurs parties composantes.

Cuadros 1, 2A, 2B, 2C

Las cifras de la población económicamente activa se refieren a las personas de 16 años y más de edad.

Todas las cifras han sido redondeadas al múltiplo de 1 000 más próximo; en consecuencia, los totales indicados pueden diferir de la suma de las partes que la componen.

Table 1

Total population figures are based on mid-year estimates.

Tableau 1

Les chiffres de la population totale sont fondés sur des estimations au milieu de l'année.

Cuadro 1

Las cifras de la población total están basadas en estimaciones a mediados del año.

Table 2B

The group "Not classifiable by status" relates to unemployed.

Tableau 2B

La rubrique «Inclassables selon la situation» se réfère aux chômeurs.

Cuadro 2B

El grupo «Inclasificables según la categoría» se refiere a los desempleados.

Table 2C

Figures in italics show totals for persons already included in the component occupational and/or industrial group.

Tableau 2C

Les chiffres en italique indiquent les totaux de personnes déjà incluses dans les composantes des groupes de professions et/ou industriels.

Cuadro 2C

Las cifras en itálica indican los totales de personas ya incluidas dentro de las partes que componen los grupos de ocupaciones y/o industriales.

Notes to tables 1 to 2C (indicated by the symbol †)
Notes relatives aux tableaux 1 à 2C (indiquées par le symbole †)
Notas relativas a los cuadros 1 a 2C (indicadas por medio del símbolo †)

Uruguay

Tables 2A, 2B

The group "Employers and own-account workers" includes 3,742 members of producers' cooperatives (3,295 males and 447 females).

Tableaux 2A, 2B

La rubrique «Employeurs et personnes travaillant à leur propre compte» comprend 3 742 membres de coopératives de producteurs (3 295 hommes et 447 femmes).

Cuadros 2A, 2B

El grupo «Empleadores y trabajadores por cuenta propia» incluye a 3 742 miembros de cooperativas de producción (3 295 hombres y 447 mujeres).

ASIA - ASIE - ASIA

Bahrain

Tables 2A, 2B, 2C

The major division "Not adequately defined" and the occupational group "Workers not classifiable by occupation" include unemployed.

Tableaux 2A, 2B, 2C

La branche d'activité «Activités mal désignées» et le groupe de professions «Travailleurs ne pouvant être classés selon la profession» comprennent les chômeurs.

Cuadros 2A, 2B, 2C

La gran división «Actividades no bien especificadas» y el grupo de ocupación «Trabajadores que no pueden ser clasificados según la ocupación» incluyen a los desempleados.

Bangladesh

Tables 2A, 2B

The major division "Not adequately defined" and the occupational group "Workers not classifiable by occupation" include 502,706 unemployed (471,254 males and 31,452 females).

Tableaux 2A, 2B

La branche d'activité «Activités mal désignées» et le groupe de professions «Travailleurs ne pouvant être classés selon la profession» comprennent 502 706 chômeurs (471 254 hommes et 31 452 femmes).

Cuadros 2A, 2B

La gran división «Actividades no bien especificadas» y el grupo de ocupación «Trabajadores que no pueden ser clasificados según la ocupación» incluyen a 502 706 desempleados (471 254 hombres y 31 452 mujeres).

Cyprus

Table 2C

Incl. Cypriots working temporarily abroad.

Tableau 2C

Y compris les Chypriotes travaillant temporairement à l'étranger.

Cuadro 2C

Incl. los chipriotas que trabajan temporalmente en el extranjero.

Hong Kong

Tables 1, 2A, 2B, 2C

All figures are rounded off to the nearest 100; consequently, the totals shown may differ from the sum of the component parts.

Tableaux 1, 2A, 2B, 2C

Tous les nombres étant arrondis au multiple de 100 le plus proche, les totaux indiqués peuvent différer de la somme de leurs parties composantes.

Cuadros 1, 2A, 2B, 2C

Todas las cifras han sido redondeadas al múltiplo de 100 más próximo; en consecuencia, los totales indicados pueden diferir de la suma de las partes que la componen.

Iran

Tables 2A, 2B

The group "Not classifiable by status" includes 705,357 unemployed with previous job experience (492,734 males and 212,623 females). For the distribution of these unemployed according to their previous job experience by industry and occupational group, see table 2C.

Tableaux 2A, 2B

La rubrique «Inclassables selon la situation» comprend 705 357 chômeurs ayant déjà occupé un emploi (492 734 hommes et 212 623 femmes). Pour la répartition de ces chômeurs selon l'industrie et le groupe de professions où ils ont précédemment travaillé, voir tableau 2C.

Cuadros 2A, 2B

El grupo «Inclasificables según la categoría» incluye a 705 357 desempleados que han trabajado anteriormente (492 734 hombres y 212 623 mujeres). Para la distribución de estos desempleados según la industria y el grupo de ocupación en los cuales trabajaron anteriormente, véase cuadro 2C.

Table 2C

Figures in italics show totals for persons already included in the component occupational and/or industrial group.

Tableau 2C

Les chiffres en italique indiquent les totaux de personnes déjà incluses dans les composantes des groupes de professions et/ou industriels.

Cuadro 2C

Las cifras en itálica indican los totales de personas ya incluidas dentro de las partes que componen los grupos de ocupaciones y/o industriales.

ACTIVE POPULATION

Notes to tables 1 to 2C (indicated by the symbol †)
Notes relatives aux tableaux 1 à 2C (indiquées par le symbole †)
Notas relativas a los cuadros 1 a 2C (indicadas por medio del símbolo †)

Israel

Tables 1, 2A, 2B, 2C

Incl. data relating to certain territories under occupation by Israeli military forces since June 1967.

Economically active population figures do not include armed forces.

All figures are rounded off to the nearest 100; consequently, the totals shown may differ from the sum of the component parts.

Tables 2A, 2B

The group "Employers and own-account workers" includes members of producers' co-operatives and 59,800 members of communal farms (kibbutzim).

The group "Not classifiable by status" relates to unemployed.

Table 2B

The group "Employers and own-account workers" includes 27,400 unpaid family workers (6,000 males and 21,400 females).

Table 2C

Figures in italics show totals for persons already included in the component occupational and/or industrial group.

Tableaux 1, 2A, 2B, 2C

Y compris les données relatives à certains territoires occupés par les forces armées israéliennes depuis juin 1967.

Les chiffres de la population active ne comprennent pas les forces armées.

Tous les nombres étant arrondis au multiple de 100 le plus proche, les totaux indiqués peuvent différer de la somme de leurs parties composantes.

Tableaux 2A, 2B

La rubrique «Employeurs et personnes travaillant à leur propre compte» comprend les membres de coopératives de producteurs et 59 800 membres de fermes communautaires (kibboutzim).

La rubrique «Inclassables selon la situation» se réfère aux chômeurs.

Tableau 2B

La rubrique «Employeurs et personnes travaillant à leur propre compte» comprend 27 400 travailleurs familiaux non rémunérés (6 000 hommes et 21 400 femmes).

Tableau 2C

Les chiffres en italique indiquent les totaux de personnes déjà incluses dans les composantes des groupes de professions et/ou industriels.

Cuadros 1, 2A, 2B, 2C

Incl. los datos relativos a ciertos territorios ocupados por las fuerzas armadas israelíes desde junio de 1967.

Las cifras de la población económicamente activa no incluyen las fuerzas armadas.

Todas las cifras han sido redondeadas al múltiplo de 100 más próximo; en consecuencia, los totales indicados pueden diferir de la suma de las partes que la componen.

Cuadros 2A, 2B

El grupo «Empleadores y trabajadores por cuenta propia» incluye a los miembros de cooperativas de producción y a 59 800 miembros de granjas comunales (qibbuzim).

El grupo «Inclasificables según la categoría» se refiere a los desempleados.

Cuadro 2B

El grupo «Empleadores y trabajadores por cuenta propia» incluye a 27 400 trabajadores familiares no remunerados (6 000 hombres y 21 400 mujeres).

Cuadro 2C

Las cifras en itálica indican los totales de personas ya incluidas dentro de las partes que componen los grupos de ocupaciones y/o industriales.

Japan

Tables 1, 2A, 2B, 2C

1979: all figures are rounded off to the nearest 10,000; consequently, the totals shown may differ from the sum of the component parts.

Tables 2A, 2B

1975: all figures are rounded off to the nearest 5 or 0; consequently, the totals shown may differ from the sum of the component parts.

The group "Employees" includes members of producers' co-operatives.

The group "Unpaid family workers" includes paid and unpaid family workers.

Table 2A

1979: the major division "Community, social and personal services" includes hotels and business services

Tableaux 1, 2A, 2B, 2C

1979: tous les nombres étant arrondis au multiple de 10 000 le plus proche, les totaux indiqués peuvent différer de la somme de leurs parties composantes.

Tableaux 2A, 2B

1975: tous les nombres étant arrondis au multiple de 5 ou 0 le plus proche, les totaux indiqués peuvent différer de la somme de leurs parties composantes.

La rubrique «Salariés» comprend les membres de coopératives de producteurs.

La rubrique «Travailleurs familiaux non rémunérés» comprend les travailleurs familiaux rémunérés et non rémunérés.

Tableau 2A

1979: la branche d'activité «Services à la collectivité, services sociaux et personnels» comprend les hôtels et les services aux entreprises.

Cuadros 1, 2A, 2B, 2C

1979: todas las cifras han sido redondeadas al múltiplo de 10 000 más próximo; en consecuencia, los totales indicados pueden diferir de la suma de las partes que la componen.

Cuadros 2A, 2B

1975: todas las cifras han sido redondeadas al múltiplo de 5 o 0 más próximo: en consecuencia, los totales indicados pueden diferir de la suma de las partes que la componen.

El grupo «Empleados a sueldo o salario» incluye a los miembros de cooperativas de producción.

El grupo «Trabajadores familiares no remunerados» incluye a los trabajadores familiares remunerados y no remunerados.

Cuadro 2A

1979: la gran división «Servicios comunales, sociales y personales» incluye los hoteles y los servicios para las empresas.

Korea, Republic of

Tables 1, 2A, 2B

Excl. armed forces.

Tables 2A, 2B

1979: figures of less than 1,000 are indicated by a dash.

Tableaux 1, 2A, 2B

Non compris les forces armées.

Tableaux 2A, 2B

1979: les chiffres représentant moins de 1 000 personnes sont désignés par un tiret.

Cuadros 1, 2A, 2B

Excl. las fuerzas armadas.

Cuadros 2A, 2B

1979: las cifras inferiores a 1 000 personas están indicadas por un guión.

Notes to tables 1 to 2C (indicated by the symbol †)
Notes relatives aux tableaux 1 à 2C (indiquées par le symbole †)
Notas relativas a los cuadros 1 a 2C (indicadas por medio del símbolo †)

Peninsular Malaysia

Table 1

Total population figures are based on mid-year estimates.

Tableau 1

Les chiffres de la population totale sont fondés sur des estimations au milieu de l'année.

Cuadro 1

Las cifras de la población total están basadas en estimaciones a mediados del año.

Pakistan

Tables 1, 2A, 2B, 2C

Excl. Jammu and Kashmir (the final status of which has not yet been determined), Gilgit and Baltistan, Junagardh and Manavadar.

Tableaux 1, 2A, 2B, 2C

Non compris le Jammu et le Cachemire (dont le statut définitif n'a pas encore été déterminé), le Gilgit et Baltistan, le Junagardh et le Manavadar.

Cuadros 1, 2A, 2B, 2C

Excl. Jammu y Cachemira (para los cuales el estatuto definitivo no ha sido por ahora determinado), Gilgit y Baltistan, Junagardh y Manavadar.

Philippines

Tables 2A, 2B, 2C

Economically active population figures do not include armed forces and institutional households.

All figures are rounded off to the nearest 1,000; consequently, the totals shown may differ from the sum of the component parts.

Tables 2A, 2C

1958 ISIC.

Table 2C

Figures in italics show totals for persons already included in the component occupational and/or industrial group.

Tableaux 2A, 2B, 2C

Les chiffres de la population active ne comprennent ni les forces armées ni les ménages collectifs.

Tous les nombres étant arrondis au multiple de 1 000 le plus proche, les totaux indiqués peuvent différer de la somme de leurs parties composantes.

Tableaux 2A, 2C

CITI de 1958.

Tableau 2C

Les chiffres en italique indiquent les totaux de personnes déjà incluses dans les composantes des groupes de professions et/ou industriels.

Cuadros 2A, 2B, 2C

Las cifras de la población económicamente activa no incluyen las fuerzas armadas ni los hogares colectivos.

Todas las cifras han sido redondeadas al múltiplo de 1 000 más próximo; en consecuencia, los totales indicados pueden diferir de la suma de las partes que la componen.

Cuadros 2A, 2C

CIIU de 1958.

Cuadro 2C

Las cifras en itálica indican los totales de personas ya incluidas dentro de las partes que componen los grupos de ocupaciones y/o industriales.

Singapore

Tables 1, 2A, 2B, 2C

Due to independent estimation, the totals shown may differ from the sum of the component parts.

Table 2C

Figures in italics show totals for persons already included in the component occupational and/or industrial group.

Tableaux 1, 2A, 2B, 2C

En raison d'une estimation indépendante, les totaux indiqués peuvent différer de la somme de leurs parties composantes.

Tableau 2C

Les chiffres en italique indiquent les totaux de personnes déjà incluses dans les composantes des groupes de professions et/ou industriels.

Cuadros 1, 2A, 2B, 2C

En razón de una estimación independiente, los totales indicados pueden diferir de la suma de las partes que la componen.

Cuadro 2C

Las cifras en itálica indican los totales de personas ya incluidas dentro de las partes que componen los grupos de ocupaciones y/o industriales.

Sri Lanka

Table 2C

The group "Workers not classifiable by occupation" includes armed forces.

Tableau 2C

Le groupe «Travailleurs ne pouvant être classés selon la profession» comprend les forces armées.

Cuadro 2C

El grupo «Trabajadores que no pueden ser clasificados según la ocupación» incluye las fuerzas armadas.

Thailand

Tables 1, 2A, 2B, 2C

Economically active population figures do not include unpaid family workers who, during the survey week, worked less than 20 hours.

Tables 2A, 2C

1958 ISIC.

Tableaux 1, 2A, 2B, 2C

Les chiffres de la population active ne comprennent pas les travailleurs familiaux non rémunérés qui, au cours de la semaine de l'enquête, ont travaillé moins de 20 heures.

Tableaux 2A, 2C

CITI de 1958.

Cuadros 1, 2A, 2B, 2C

Las cifras de la población económicamente activa no incluyen a los trabajadores familiares no remunerados que durante la semana de la encuesta trabajaron menos de 20 horas.

Cuadros 2A, 2C

CIIU de 1958.

ACTIVE POPULATION

Notes to tables 1 to 2C (indicated by the symbol †)
Notes relatives aux tableaux 1 à 2C (indiquées par le symbole †)
Notas relativas a los cuadros 1 a 2C (indicadas por medio del símbolo †)

EUROPE - EUROPE - EUROPA

Austria

Tables 2A, 2B

Excl. institutional households.

Figures of less than 1,000 are indicated by a dash.

The group "Employers and own-account workers" includes unpaid family workers.

Tableaux 2A, 2B

Non compris les ménages collectifs.

Les chiffres représentant moins de 1 000 personnes sont désignés par un tiret.

La rubrique «Employeurs et personnes travaillant à leur propre compte» comprend les travailleurs familiaux non rémunérés.

Cuadros 2A, 2B

Excl. los hogares colectivos.

Las cifras inferiores a 1 000 personas están indicadas por un guión.

El grupo «Empleadores y trabajadores por cuenta propia» incluye a los trabajadores familiares no remunerados.

Belgique

Table 2A

The major division "Wholesale and retail trade, restaurants and hotels" includes repair services.

The major division "Not adequately defined" relates to workers in vocational training.

The group "Armed forces" relates to persons on compulsory military service.

Tableau 2A

La branche d'activité «Commerce de gros et de détail, restaurants et hôtels» comprend les services de réparation.

La branche d'activité «Activités mal désignées» se réfère aux travailleurs en formation professionnelle.

Le groupe «Forces armées» se réfère aux personnes effectuant leur service militaire obligatoire.

Cuadro 2A

La gran división «Comercio al por mayor y al por menor, restaurantes y hoteles» incluye los servicios de reparación.

La gran división «Actividades no bien especificadas» se refiere a los trabajadores en formación profesional.

El grupo «Fuerzas armadas» se refiere a las personas en servicio militar obligatorio.

Czechoslovakia

Table 2C

The total indicated for major divisions "2, 3 and 4" includes 203,550 persons engaged in major division "2", 2,466,848 persons engaged in major division "3" and 84,268 persons engaged in major division "4". A separate distribution of these persons by occupational group is not available.

Tableau 2C

Le total indiqué pour les branches d'activité «2, 3 et 4» comprend 203 550 personnes engagées dans la branche d'activité «2», 2 466 848 personnes engagées dans la branche d'activité «3» et 84 268 personnes engagées dans la branche d'activité «4». Une répartition séparée de ces personnes par groupe de professions n'est pas disponible.

Cuadro 2C

El total indicado para las grandes divisiones «2, 3 y 4» incluye a 203 550 personas que trabajan en la gran división «2», 2 466 848 personas que trabajan en la gran división «3» y 84 268 personas que trabajan en la gran división «4». Una distribución separada de estas personas por grupo de ocupación no está disponible.

Denmark

Tables 1, 2A

Economically active population figures relate to persons 15 to 74 years of age.

Tableaux 1, 2A

Les chiffres de la population active se réfèrent aux personnes âgées de 15 à 74 ans.

Cuadros 1, 2A

Las cifras de la población económicamente activa se refieren a las personas de 15 a 74 años de edad.

Table 2A

The group "Unpaid family workers" includes paid and unpaid family workers.

Tableau 2A

La rubrique «Travailleurs familiaux non rémunérés» comprend les travailleurs familiaux rémunérés et non rémunérés.

Cuadro 2A

El grupo «Trabajadores familiares no remunerados» incluye a los trabajadores familiares remunerados y no remunerados.

España

Table 2A

The major division "Mining and quarrying" includes the transformation of minerals.

The major division "Manufacturing" includes the extraction of fuels.

Tableau 2A

La branche d'activité «Industries extractives» comprend la transformation des minéraux.

La branche d'activité «Industries manufacturières» comprend l'extraction des combustibles.

Cuadro 2A

La gran división «Minas y canteras» incluye la transformación de minerales.

La gran división «Industrias manufactureras» incluye la extracción de combustible.

Faeroe Islands

Table 2A

The group "Employers and own-account workers" includes unpaid family workers.

Tableau 2A

La rubrique «Employeurs et personnes travaillant à leur propre compte» comprend les travailleurs familiaux non rémunérés.

Cuadro 2A

El grupo «Empleadores y trabajadores por cuenta propia» incluye a los trabajadores familiares no remunerados.

Notes to tables 1 to 2C (indicated by the symbol †)
Notes relatives aux tableaux 1 à 2C (indiquées par le symbole †)
Notas relativas a los cuadros 1 a 2C (indicadas por medio del símbolo †)

Finland

Tables 1, 2A, 2C

Economically active population figures relate to persons 15 to 74 years of age.

Tableaux 1, 2A, 2C

Les chiffres de la population active se réfèrent aux personnes âgées de 15 à 74 ans.

Cuadros 1, 2A, 2C

Las cifras de la población económicamente activa se refieren a las personas de 15 a 74 años de edad.

France

Table 2A

The group "Employers and own-account workers" includes unpaid family workers.

Excl. persons on compulsory military service.

Tableau 2A

La rubrique «Employeurs et personnes travaillant à leur propre compte» comprend les travailleurs familiaux non rémunérés.

Non compris les personnes effectuant leur service militaire obligatoire (militaires du contingent).

Cuadro 2A

El grupo «Empleadores y trabajadores por cuenta propia» incluye a los trabajadores familiares no remunerados.

Excl. las personas en servicio militar obligatorio.

Table 2B

All figures are rounded off to the nearest 100; consequently, the totals shown may differ from the sum of the component parts.

Tableau 2B

Tous les nombres étant arrondis au multiple de 100 le plus proche, les totaux indiqués peuvent différer de la somme de leurs parties composantes.

Cuadro 2B

Todas las cifras han sido redondeadas al múltiplo de 100 más próximo; en consecuencia, los totales indicados pueden diferir de la suma de las partes que la componen.

Germany, Fed. Rep. of

Tables 1, 2A, 2B, 2C

All figures are rounded off to the nearest 1,000; consequently, the totals shown may differ from the sum of the component parts.

Tableaux 1, 2A, 2B, 2C

Tous les nombres étant arrondis au multiple de 1 000 le plus proche, les totaux indiqués peuvent différer de la somme de leurs parties composantes.

Cuadros 1, 2A, 2B, 2C

Todas las cifras han sido redondeadas al múltiplo de 1 000 más próximo; en consecuencia, los totales indicados pueden diferir de la suma de las partes que la componen.

Tables 2A, 2C

Figures of less than 5,000 are indicated by a dash.

Tableaux 2A, 2C

Les chiffres représentant moins de 5 000 personnes sont désignés par un tiret.

Cuadros 2A, 2C

Las cifras inferiores a 5 000 personas están indicadas por un guión.

Hungary

Table 2A

The group "Not classifiable by status" relates to members of producers' co-operatives.

Tableau 2A

La rubrique «Inclassables selon la situation» se réfère aux membres de coopératives de producteurs.

Cuadro 2A

El grupo «Inclasificables según la categoría» se refiere a los miembros de cooperativas de producción.

Ireland

Tables 1, 2A, 2B, 2C

All figures are rounded off to the nearest 100; consequently, the totals shown may differ from the sum of the component parts.

Tableaux 1, 2A, 2B, 2C

Tous les nombres étant arrondis au multiple de 100 le plus proche, les totaux indiqués peuvent différer de la somme de leurs parties composantes.

Cuadros 1, 2A, 2B, 2C

Todas las cifras han sido redondeadas al múltiplo de 100 más próximo; en consecuencia, los totales indicados pueden diferir de la suma de las partes que la componen.

Tables 2A, 2C

The major division "Community, social and personal services" includes restaurants and hotels.

Tableaux 2A, 2C

La branche d'activité «Services à la collectivité, services sociaux et personnels» comprend les restaurants et hôtels.

Cuadros 2A, 2C

La gran división «Servicios comunales, sociales y personales» incluye los restaurantes y hoteles.

ACTIVE POPULATION

Notes to tables 1 to 2C   (indicated by the symbol †)
Notes relatives aux tableaux 1 à 2C   (indiquées par le symbole †)
Notas relativas a los cuadros 1 a 2C   (indicadas por medio del símbolo †)

Italie

Tables 1, 2A

Economically active population figures do not include persons on compulsory military service.

All figures are rounded off to the nearest 1,000; consequently, the totals shown may differ from the sum of the component parts.

Table 1

The age group "?" relates to permanent members of institutional households for whom a distribution by age group is not available.

Table 2A

1958 ISIC.

Malta

Table 2A

The group "Employers and own-account workers" includes unpaid family workers.

Netherlands

Table 1

All figures are rounded off to the nearest 100; consequently, the totals shown may differ from the sum of the component parts.

Tables 2A, 2B, 2C

All figures are rounded off to the nearest 1,000; consequently, the totals shown may differ from the sum of the component parts.

Tables 2A, 2B

Column "Total" includes 252,000 unemployed whose distribution by sex is not available.

Table 2B

The group "Employers and own-account workers" includes 111,000 unpaid family workers (14,000 males and 97,000 females).

Norway

Tables 1, 2A, 2B, 2C

Economically active population figures do not include persons on compulsory military service.

Tables 2A, 2B, 2C

Figures of less than 1,000 are indicated by a dash.

Table 2C

Figures in italics show totals for persons already included in the component occupational and/or industrial group.

Tableaux 1, 2A

Les chiffres de la population active ne comprennent pas les personnes effectuant leur service militaire obligatoire (militaires du contingent).

Tous les nombres étant arrondis au multiple de 1 000 le plus proche, les totaux indiqués peuvent différer de la somme de leurs parties composantes.

Tableau 1

Le groupe d'âge «?» se réfère aux membres permanents des ménages collectifs, dont la répartition par groupe d'âge n'est pas disponible.

Tableau 2A

CITI de 1958.

Tableau 2A

La rubrique «Employeurs et personnes travaillant à leur propre compte» comprend les travailleurs familiaux non rémunérés.

Tableau 1

Tous les nombres étant arrondis au multiple de 100 le plus proche, les totaux indiqués peuvent différer de la somme de leurs parties composantes.

Tableaux 2A, 2B, 2C

Tous les nombres étant arrondis au multiple de 1 000 le plus proche, les totaux indiqués peuvent différer de la somme de leurs parties composantes.

Tableaux 2A, 2B

La colonne «Total» comprend 252 000 chômeurs dont la répartition par sexe n'est pas disponible.

Tableau 2B

La rubrique «Employeurs et personnes travaillant à leur propre compte» comprend 111 000 travailleurs familiaux non rémunérés (14 000 hommes et 97 000 femmes).

Tableaux 1, 2A, 2B, 2C

Les chiffres de la population active ne comprennent pas les personnes effectuant leur service militaire obligatoire (militaires du contingent).

Tableaux 2A, 2B, 2C

Les chiffres représentant moins de 1 000 personnes sont désignés par un tiret.

Tableau 2C

Les chiffres en italique indiquent les totaux de personnes déjà incluses dans les composantes des groupes de professions et/ou industriels.

Cuadros 1, 2A

Las cifras de la población económicamente activa no incluyen a las personas en servicio militar obligatorio.

Todas las cifras han sido redondeadas al múltiplo de 1 000 más próximo; en consecuencia, los totales indicados pueden diferir de la suma de las partes que la componen.

Cuadro 1

El grupo de edad «?» se refiere a los miembros permanentes de los hogares colectivos, para los cuales una distribución por grupo de edad no está disponible.

Cuadro 2A

CIIU de 1958.

Cuadro 2A

El grupo «Empleadores y trabajadores por cuenta propia» incluye a los trabajadores familiares no remunerados.

Cuadro 1

Todas las cifras han sido redondeadas al múltiplo de 100 más próximo; en consecuencia, los totales indicados pueden diferir de la suma de las partes que la componen.

Cuadros 2A, 2B, 2C

Todas las cifras han sido redondeadas al múltiplo de 1 000 más próximo; en consecuencia, los totales indicados pueden diferir de la suma de las partes que la componen.

Cuadros 2A, 2B

La columna «Total» incluye a 252 000 desempleados cuya distribución por sexo no está disponible.

Cuadro 2B

El grupo «Empleadores y trabajadores por cuenta propia» incluye a 111 000 trabajadores familiares no remunerados (14 000 hombres y 97 000 mujeres).

Cuadros 1, 2A, 2B, 2C

Las cifras de la población económicamente activa no incluyen a las personas en servicio militar obligatorio.

Cuadros 2A, 2B, 2C

Las cifras inferiores a 1 000 personas están indicadas por un guión.

Cuadro 2C

Las cifras en itálica indican los totales de personas ya incluidas dentro de las partes que componen los grupos de ocupaciones y/o industriales.

Notes to tables 1 to 2C (indicated by the symbol †)
Notes relatives aux tableaux 1 à 2C (indiquées par le symbole †)
Notas relativas a los cuadros 1 a 2C (indicadas por medio del símbolo †)

Poland

Table 2A

National classification.

Tableau 2A

Classification nationale.

Cuadro 2A

Clasificación nacional.

Portugal

Tables 1, 2A, 2B, 2C

Due to independent estimation, the totals shown may differ from the sum of the component parts.

Table 2C

Figures in italics show totals for persons already included in the component occupational and/or industrial group.

Tableaux 1, 2A, 2B, 2C

En raison d'une estimation indépendante, les totaux indiqués peuvent différer de la somme de leurs parties composantes.

Tableau 2C

Les chiffres en italique indiquent les totaux de personnes déjà incluses dans les composantes des groupes de professions et/ou industriels.

Cuadros 1, 2A, 2B, 2C

En razón de una estimación independiente, los totales indicados pueden diferir de la suma de las partes que la componen.

Cuadro 2C

Las cifras en itálica indican los totales de personas ya incluidas dentro de las partes que componen los grupos de ocupaciones y/o industriales.

Suisse

Table 1

Total population figures are based on estimates at the beginning of the year.

Tableau 1

Les chiffres de la population totale sont fondés sur des estimations au début de l'année.

Cuadro 1

Las cifras de la población total están basadas en estimaciones al principio del año.

Sweden

Tables 1, 2A, 2B, 2C

Economically active population figures do not include persons on compulsory military service and persons seeking work for the first time.

Economically active population figures relate to persons 16 to 74 years of age who have worked at least one hour per week.

Tables 2A, 2B

All figures are rounded off to the nearest 100; consequently, the totals shown may differ from the sum of the component parts.

Tableaux 1, 2A, 2B, 2C

Les chiffres de la population active ne comprennent ni les personnes effectuant leur service militaire obligatoire (militaires du contingent) ni les personnes en quête d'emploi pour la première fois.

Les chiffres de la population active se réfèrent aux personnes âgées de 16 à 74 ans ayant travaillé au moins une heure par semaine.

Tableaux 2A, 2B

Tous les nombres étant arrondis au multiple de 100 le plus proche, les totaux indiqués peuvent différer de la somme de leurs parties composantes.

Cuadros 1, 2A, 2B, 2C

Las cifras de la población económicamente activa no incluyen a las personas en servicio militar obligatorio ni a las personas en busca de trabajo por primera vez.

Las cifras de la población económicamente activa se refieren a las personas de 16 a 74 años de edad que han trabajado por lo menos una hora por semana.

Cuadros 2A, 2B

Todas las cifras han sido redondeadas al múltiplo de 100 más próximo; en consecuencia, los totales indicados pueden diferir de la suma de las partes que la componen.

United Kingdom

Tables 1, 2A

"De jure" population.

Tableaux 1, 2A

Population «de jure».

Cuadros 1, 2A

Población «de jure».

OCEANIA - OCEANIE - OCEANIA

Australia

Tables 1, 2A, 2B

1976: due to independent estimation, the totals shown may differ from the sum of the component parts.

Table 2A

1978: all figures are rounded off to the nearest 1,000; consequently, the totals shown may differ from the sum of the component parts.

Tableaux 1, 2A, 2B

1976: en raison d'une estimation indépendante, les totaux indiqués peuvent différer de la somme de leurs parties composantes.

Tableau 2A

1978: tous les nombres étant arrondis au multiple de 1 000 le plus proche, les totaux indiqués peuvent différer de la somme de leurs parties composantes.

Cuadros 1, 2A, 2B

1976: en razón de una estimación independiente, los totales indicados pueden diferir de la suma de las partes que la componen.

Cuadro 2A

1978: todas las cifras han sido redondeadas al múltiplo de 1 000 más próximo; en consecuencia, los totales indicados pueden diferir de la suma de las partes que la componen.

ACTIVE POPULATION

Notes to tables 1 to 2C   (indicated by the symbol †)
Notes relatives aux tableaux 1 à 2C   (indiquées par le symbole †)
Notas relativas a los cuadros 1 a 2C   (indicadas por medio del símbolo †)

Fiji

Table 2B

The group "Employers and own-account workers" includes 28,214 agricultural members of producers' co-operatives (25,206 males and 3,008 females).

The group "Not classifiable by status" includes unemployed.

Tableau 2B

La rubrique «Employeurs et personnes travaillant à leur propre compte» comprend 28 214 membres de coopératives de producteurs agricoles (25 206 hommes et 3 008 femmes).

La rubrique «Inclassables selon la situation» comprend les chômeurs.

Cuadro 2B

El grupo «Empleadores y trabajadores por cuenta propia» incluye a 28 214 miembros de cooperativas de producción agrícola (25 206 hombres y 3 008 mujeres).

El grupo «Inclasificables según la categoría» incluye a los desempleados.

Guam

Table 2A

"De jure" population; excl. armed forces.

Tableau 2A

Population «de jure»; non compris les forces armées.

Cuadro 2A

Población «de jure»; excl. las fuerzas armadas.

New Zealand

Tables 1, 2A, 2B, 2C

Incl. Maoris; excl. armed forces overseas.

Economically active population figures relate to persons who have worked at least 20 hours per week.

Tableaux 1, 2A, 2B, 2C

Y compris les Maoris; non compris les forces armées stationnées outre-mer.

Les chiffres de la population active se réfèrent aux personnes ayant travaillé au moins 20 heures par semaine.

Cuadros 1, 2A, 2B, 2C

Incl. los maoríes; excl. las fuerzas armadas en ultramar.

Las cifras de la población económicamente activa se refieren a las personas que han trabajado por lo menos 20 horas a la semana.

Tonga

Table 2B

"De jure" population.

Tableau 2B

Population «de jure».

Cuadro 2B

Población «de jure».

USSR - URSS - URSS

URSS

Table 1

Economically active population figure is provisional.

Tableau 1

Le chiffre de la population active est provisoire.

Cuadro 1

La cifra de la población económicamente activa es provisional.

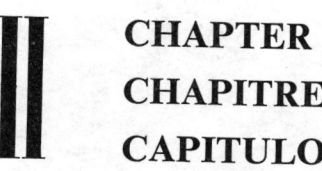

CHAPTER
CHAPITRE
CAPITULO

Employment

Emploi

Empleo

Employment

Employment is defined as follows in the Resolution concerning statistics of the labour force, employment and unemployment, adopted by the Eighth International Conference of Labour Statisticians (Geneva, 1954): [1]

"(1) Persons in employment consist of all persons above a specified age in the following categories:

(a) at work: persons who performed some work for pay or profit during a specified brief period, either one week or one day;

(b) with a job but not at work: persons who, having already worked in their present job, were temporarily absent during the specified period because of illness or injury, industrial dispute, vacation or other leave of absence, absence without leave, or temporary disorganisation of work due to such reasons as bad weather or mechanical breakdown.

(2) Employers and own-account workers should be included among the employed and may be classified as " at work " or " not at work " on the same basis as other employed persons.

(3) Unpaid family workers currently assisting in the operation of a business or farm are considered as employed if they worked for at least one-third of the normal working time during the specified period.

(4) The following categories of persons are *not* considered as employed:

(a) workers who during the specified period were on temporary or indefinite lay-off without pay;

(b) persons without jobs or businesses or farms who had arranged to start a new job or business or farm at a date subsequent to the period of reference;

(c) unpaid members of the family who worked for less than one-third of the normal working time during the specified period in a family business or farm."

For various reasons, national definitions of employment often differ from the recommended international standard definition. The differences reflect in large measure the variety of national practices in measuring employment.[2]

---

[1] See ILO: *International Recommendations on Labour Statistics* (Geneva, 1976).

[2] For the descriptions of the various national series, sources, scopes, definitions and methods of compilation used, etc., see ILO: *Technical Guide 1980* (description of general series published in the *Bulletin* and the *Year Book of Labour Statistics*), Vol. II, " Employment—Unemployment—Hours of Work—Wages " (Geneva, 1980).

In general, employment data are obtained from four main sources, namely, household sample surveys, establishment surveys, administrative records of social insurance schemes, or official national estimates.

The four main sources of employment statistics described below are identified in the tables by the codes I, II, III and IV:

Source I. *Labour force sample surveys.* These surveys are a source of regular information on the total civilian labour force (employed plus unemployed).

In general, Source I data on employed persons relate to all *status* groups (employers, own-account workers, employees, unpaid family workers, members of producers' co-operatives), and not only to employees (wage earners and salaried employees). The data generally relate to the total number of persons in employment during a specified brief period, either one week or one day. Usually, no distinction is made between persons employed full time and those working less than full time.

Source II. *Administrative records (Statistics of compulsory social insurance).* These data relate to the working population covered by sickness, accident or unemployment insurance schemes, or the like. The number of contributors or of contributions paid provides a measure of the number of insured persons in employment (unemployed persons being exempt from the obligation to pay contributions). Persons working a very short time or receiving a very low pay are sometimes excluded from these statistics. In addition to changes in the actual number of persons employed, employment statistics based on social insurance records may also reflect changes in coverage of particular industrial, occupational or status groups. More generally, the provisions relating to social insurance schemes determine the scope of the statistics derived from their operation.

Source III. *Establishments surveys.* These data show the number of workers on establishment payrolls for a specified payroll period or working day in this period. In general, there are two types of establishment statistics.

The first type covers *all establishments of a given importance*, e.g. those fulfilling certain conditions, such as having more than a certain number of employees, having an annual output of more than a certain value, etc. The data thus obtained may be subject to some bias owing to the exclusion of establishments which are below the minimum size fixed for the series; moreover, a shift of employment from small to large establishments will be reflected in a rising trend in the series; provided, however, that this minimum is small, the scope of such series is usually very wide and they furnish a close approximation of the fluctuations in employment.

The second type of statistics relate to a *sample of establishments*. The chief difficulty with such statistics is to ensure that the sample of establishments remains representative of the whole. For example, changes in industrial structure, the growth and decline of individual establishments, general population movements and pronounced changes in the levels of activity in some sectors of the economy tend to introduce a cumulative bias in this sample which may become apreciable after several years.

In certain countries where statistics of the first type *(all establishments of a given importance)* are available only at annual or longer intervals, they may be combined either by chaining or by interpolation with statistics of the second type *(samples of establishments)* which are available more frequently.

Source IV. *Official estimates*. These statistics are official estimates provided by national authorities. Such estimates are usually based on combined information drawn from one or more of the above sources (I, II and III).

Table 3

Structure of Employment

This table presents absolute figures on the distribution of the employed civilian labour force by major divisions of economic activity *(Industry)*. Data are arranged, so far as possible, according to the major divisions of economic activity of the *International Standard Industrial Classification of All Economic Activities (ISIC-1968)*, shown in the Appendix. In general, the scope of the statistics encompasses all *status* groups. However in certain cases, the figures may refer only to employees (wage earners and salaried employees).

Table 4

General Level of Employment

The employment series shown in this table refer to the number of employees (wage earners and salaried employees) in all major divisions of economic activity *(Industry)*. In certain cases, the statistics may also cover other *status* groups (employers, own-account workers, etc.). In addition, for certain series some component major divisions of economic activity such as "Major division 1. Agriculture, hunting, forestry and fishing" and "Major division 9. Community, social and personal services" may not be fully represented.

Table 5

Employment in Non-Agricultural Sectors

The data on employment shown in this table refer, in general, to the number of employees (wage earners and salaried employees) in all major divisions of economic activity other than "Major division 1. Agriculture, hunting, forestry and fishing." In certain cases, the statistics may also cover other *status* groups.

Table 6

Employment in Manufacturing

Part A of this table presents data on employment in manufacturing as a whole, that is, for all components of this major division of economic activity *(Industry)*.

Part B shows employment in manufacturing by major groups of industry.

Table 7

Employment in Mining and Quarrying

Table 8

Employment in Construction

Table 9

Employment in Transport, Storage and Communication

* * *

The number of persons employed (wage earners and salaried employees) in the major divisions of economic activity *(Industry)* given in tables 5, 6, 7, 8 and 9 usually form component parts of the corresponding general series in table 4.

New information:

Commencing with the present issue of the Year Book, *absolute figures are shown rather than indices. In addition, where possible, data are also presented for males and females separately.*

Emploi

L'emploi est défini de la manière suivante dans la résolution concernant les statistiques de la main-d'œuvre, de l'emploi et du chômage, adoptée par la huitième Conférence internationale des statisticiens du travail (Genève, 1954) [1]:

« (1) Les personnes pourvues d'un emploi sont toutes les personnes qui, ayant dépassé un âge spécifié, rentrent dans une des catégories suivantes:

a) personnes au travail: personnes qui ont effectué un travail rémunéré durant une courte période spécifiée, qui peut être soit une semaine, soit un jour;

b) personnes qui ont un emploi mais ne sont pas au travail: personnes qui, ayant déjà travaillé dans leur emploi actuel, en sont temporairement absentes durant la période spécifiée pour cause de maladie ou d'accident, conflit du travail, vacances ou autre forme de congés, absence volontaire ou empêchement temporaire de travailler dû à des causes telles que conditions climatiques défavorables ou incidents techniques.

(2) Les employeurs et les personnes travaillant à leur propre compte doivent rentrer dans la catégorie des personnes pourvues d'un emploi et peuvent être classées comme « étant au travail » ou « n'étant pas au travail », sur la même base que les autres personnes pourvues d'un emploi.

(3) Les travailleurs familiaux non rémunérés qui collaborent de façon habituelle au fonctionnement d'une exploitation agricole ou d'une entreprise sont considérés comme pourvus d'un emploi s'ils ont travaillé pendant une durée au moins égale au tiers de la durée normale du travail pendant la période spécifiée.

(4) Ne sont *pas* considérés comme personnes pourvues d'un emploi:

a) les travailleurs qui, durant la période spécifiée, sont mis à pied temporairement ou pour une durée indéfinie, sans rémunération;

b) les personnes qui n'ont ni emploi, ni exploitation agricole, ni entreprise, et qui ont pris leurs dispositions en vue de commencer à travailler dans un nouvel emploi ou d'ouvrir une exploitation agricole ou une entreprise à une date postérieure à la période de référence;

c) les membres de la famille non rémunérés qui ont travaillé dans l'entreprise ou l'exploitation familiale pendant une durée inférieure au tiers de la durée normale du travail pendant la période spécifiée. »

Pour des raisons diverses, les définitions nationales de l'emploi diffèrent souvent de la définition internationale type recommandée. Les différences sont dues, pour une grande part, aux diverses méthodes nationales utilisées dans la mesure de l'emploi [2].

Les données sur l'emploi sont, en général, obtenues à partir de quatre sources principales, à savoir: les enquêtes par sondage auprès des ménages, les enquêtes auprès des établissements, les registres administratifs provenant des régimes d'assurances sociales, ou d'évaluations officielles nationales.

Les quatre sources principales des statistiques de l'emploi décrites ci-après sont identifiées dans les tableaux par les codes I, II, III et IV:

Source I. Enquêtes par sondage sur la main-d'œuvre. Ces enquêtes constituent une source d'information régulière concernant la main-d'œuvre civile totale (personnes occupées plus chômeurs). En général, les données de la source I se rapportent aux personnesoc cupées appartenant à toutes les catégories de *situation dans la profession* (employeurs, travailleurs à leur propre compte, salariés, travailleurs familiaux non rémunérés, membres de coopératives de production), et pas seulement aux salariés (ouvriers et employés). Les données se rapportent en général au nombre total des personnes pourvues d'un emploi durant une courte période spécifiée, qui peut être soit une semaine, soit un jour. Aucune distinction n'est généralement faite entre les personnes travaillant à plein temps et celles qui travaillent à temps partiel.

Source II. (Statistiques d'assurances sociales obligatoires.) Ces statistiques concernent la population active couverte par l'assurance-maladie, accidents ou chômage, ou par un régime analogue. Le nombre des cotisants ou des cotisations versées fournit une mesure des effectifs assurés et occupés (les chômeurs étant dispensés

---

[1] Voir BIT: *Recommandations internationales sur les statistiques du travail* (Genève, 1975).

[2] Pour les descriptions des diverses séries nationales, sources, portées, définitions et méthodes de calcul utilisées, etc., voir BIT: *Guide technique 1980* (description des séries générales publiées dans le *Bulletin* et l'*Annuaire des statistiques du travail*), vol. II, « Emploi — Chômage — Durée du travail — Salaires » (Genève, 1980).

du paiement de leur cotisation). Les personnes travaillant durant une très courte période ou qui sont très peu rémunérées sont quelquefois omises de ces statistiques. Outre les changements intervenant dans le nombre effectif des personnes occupées, les statistiques de l'emploi fondées sur les archives des assurances sociales peuvent également refléter des modifications de portée pour certains groupes classés selon la branche d'activité économique, la profession ou la situation dans la profession. De façon plus générale, les dispositions relatives au régime d'assurances sociales déterminent la portée des statistiques tirées de son application.

Source III. *Enquêtes auprès des établissements.* Ces statistiques fournissent le nombre des travailleurs inscrits sur les bordereaux de salaires au cours d'un période de paie déterminée ou d'un jour de travail de cette période. En général, on distingue deux types d'enquêtes auprès des établissements:

Le premier type de statistiques englobe *tous les établissements d'une importance déterminée,* c'est-à-dire ceux qui répondent à certains critères (par exemple, les entreprises qui occupent plus d'un certain nombre d'ouvriers; celles dont la production annuelle est supérieure à une certaine valeur, etc.). Les données ainsi rassemblées peuvent être sujettes à des écarts systématiques provenant de l'élimination d'établissements qui n'atteignent pas la limite minimum fixée pour ces séries; de plus, un déplacement de l'emploi des petits établissements vers les grands établissements se traduira par une tendance à l'augmentation des séries. Toutefois, lorsque la limite minimum est fixée assez bas, la portée de telles séries est généralement très étendue et ces statistiques reflètent assez fidèlement les fluctuations de l'emploi.

Les statistiques du second type reposent sur un *échantillon d'établissements.* Dans de telles séries, la difficulté principale consiste à conserver aux établissements sélectionnés un carac-

tère représentatif. Par exemple, des variations de la structure industrielle, le développement ou le déclin d'établissements particuliers, le mouvement général de la population ou des changements marqués dans l'activité de certains secteurs économiques ont tendance à introduire un écart systématique cumulatif dans l'échantillon qui, au bout de quelques années, peut devenir sensible.

Dans certains pays où les statistiques du premier type (tous les établissements d'une importance déterminée) ne sont disponibles que tous les ans ou à des intervalles plus longs, celles-ci sont combinées soit par enchaînement, soit par interpolation, avec les statistiques du second type *(échantillon d'établissements)* plus fréquemment disponibles.

Source IV. *Evaluations officielles.* Ces statistiques sont des évaluations officielles fournies par les autorités nationales. De telles estimations sont généralement basées sur une combinaison d'informations tirées d'une ou plusieurs sources mentionnées ci-dessus (I, II et III).

Tableau 3

Structure de l'emploi

Ce tableau présente des chiffres absolus relatifs à la distribution par *industrie* (branche d'activité économique) de la main-d'œuvre civile occupée. Les données sont disposées, dans toute la mesure possible, selon les branches d'activité économique de la *Classification internationale type, par industrie, de toutes les branches d'activité économique (CITI-1968),* présentée dans l'Annexe. En général, la portée des statistiques englobe les personnes occupées appartenant à toutes les catégories de situation dans la profession. Cependant, dans certains cas, les chiffres ne représentent que les salariés (ouvriers et employés).

Tableau 4

Niveau général de l'emploi

Les séries de l'emploi présentées dans ce tableau correspondent au nombre de salariés (ouvriers et employés) dans toutes les branches d'activité économique *(industrie)*. Dans certains cas, les statistiques peuvent également couvrir d'autres groupes professionnels classés selon la situation dans la profession (employeurs, travailleurs à leur propre compte, etc.). En outre, il arrive que, pour certaines séries, les branches d'activité économique composantes (telles que: « Branche 1. Agriculture, chasse, sylviculture et pêche » et « Branche 9. Services fournis à la collectivité, services sociaux et services personnels ») ne soient pas toutes représentées.

Tableau 5

Emploi dans les secteurs non agricoles

Les données de l'emploi présentées dans ce tableau correspondent, en général, au nombre de salariés (ouvriers et employés) dans l'ensemble des branches d'activité économique à l'exception de la « Branche 1. Agriculture, chasse, sylviculture et pêche ». Dans certains cas, les statistiques peuvent également couvrir d'autres groupes professionnels classés selon la *situation dans la profession*.

Tableau 6

Emploi dans les industries manufacturières

La partie A de ce tableau présente les données de l'emploi dans l'ensemble des industries manufacturières, c'est-à-dire, pour l'ensemble des composantes de cette branche d'activité économique *(industrie)*.

La partie B de ce tableau fournit les données de l'emploi dans les industries manufacturières par classe d'industrie.

Tableau 7

Emploi dans les industries extractives

Tableau 8

Emploi dans la construction

Tableau 9

Emploi dans les transports, les entrepôts et les communications

* * *

Le nombre de personnes occupées (ouvriers et employés) dans les branches d'activité économique *(industrie)* fourni dans les tableaux 5, 6, 7, 8 et 9 forme en général des éléments constitutifs des séries générales du tableau 4.

Nouvelle information:

*A partir de la présente édition de l'*Annuaire, *les données sont présentées en chiffres absolus plutôt que sous forme d'indices. De plus, les données sont également présentées, dans la mesure du possible, pour les hommes et les femmes séparément.*

Empleo

El empleo se halla definido de la manera siguiente en la resolución sobre estadísticas de la fuerza del trabajo, del empleo y del desempleo adoptada por la octava Conferencia Internacional de Estadígrafos del Trabajo (Ginebra, 1954)[1]:

« 1) Las personas comprendidas en el empleo son todas aquellas que tengan más de cierta edad especificada y que estén dentro de las categorías siguientes:

a) que estén trabajando; es decir, las personas que realizan algún trabajo remunerado durante un breve período especificado, ya sea durante una semana o un día;

b) que tengan un empleo, pero que no estén trabajando, o sea, las personas que hayan trabajado ya en su empleo actual, pero que se hallen temporalmente ausentes del trabajo en el curso del período especificado debido a enfermedad o accidente, conflicto de trabajo, vacaciones u otra clase de permiso, ausencia sin permiso, interrupción del trabajo a causa de determinados motivos, como, por ejemplo, el mal tiempo o averías producidas en las máquinas.

2) Los empleadores y los trabajadores por cuenta propia deberían ser incluidos en la categoría de las personas con empleo y se podrían clasificar como « trabajando » o « sin trabajar » sobre la misma base que las demás personas empleadas.

3) Se considerará que los trabajadores familiares no remunerados que ordinariamente exploten o ayuden a explotar un negocio cualquiera o una explotación agrícola tienen un empleo si han trabajado por lo menos un tercio del tiempo normal de trabajo durante el período especificado.

4) *No* se considerarán como empleadas las personas comprendidas en las categorías siguientes:

a) los trabajadores que durante el período especificado hayan sido suspendidos temporal o indefinidamente, sin goce de remuneración;

b) las personas que no tengan ningún empleo o que no exploten un negocio cualquiera o una explotación agrícola, pero que hayan obtenido un nuevo empleo, negocio o explotación agrícola que haya de comenzar en una fecha subsiguiente al período de referencia;

c) los trabajadores familiares no remunerados que trabajen menos de un tercio del tiempo normal de trabajo durante el período especificado en un negocio o explotación agrícola familiar. »

Por diversas razones, las definiciones nacionales de empleo difieren a menudo de la definición internacional tipo recomendada. Las diferencias reflejan en gran medida la variedad de prácticas nacionales en lo que hace a la medición del empleo[2].

Para obtener los datos de empleo se recurre por lo regular a una de las cuatro fuentes principales, que son la encuesta por muestra de los hogares, la encuesta de establecimientos, los registros administrativos de los regímenes de seguridad social y las estimaciones nacionales oficiales.

A continuación se describe cada una de las cuatro fuentes principales de estadísticas de empleo (identificadas en los cuadros por las claves I, II, III y IV):

Fuente I. *Encuestas por muestra sobre la fuerza trabajadora.* Estas encuestas permiten reunir regularmente datos sobre el total de la fuerza de trabajo civil (empleados más desempleados).

En general, los datos de la fuente I se refieren a las personas empleadas en todas las *categorías ocupacionales* (empleadores, trabajadores por cuenta propia, asalariados, trabajadores familiares no remunerados, miembros de cooperativas de productores), y no sólo a los asalariados (obreros y empleados). Los datos se refieren generalmente al total de trabajadores ocupados por un breve período determinado, sea de una semana o de un día. Por lo general, no se hace ninguna distinción entre las personas ocupadas a horario completo y las que trabajan a horario reducido.

Fuente II. *Registros administrativos (Estadísticas del seguro social obligatorio).* Estos datos se refieren a la población activa que tiene un seguro de enfermedad, accidente o desempleo. El número de contribuyentes o de contribuciones pagadas sirve para determi-

[1] Véase OIT: *Recomendaciones internacionales sobre estadísticas del trabajo* (Ginebra, 1975).

[2] Para las descripciones de las diversas series nacionales, fuentes, alcance, definiciones y métodos de compilación utilizados, etc., véase OIT: *Guía Técnica 1980* (descripciones de las series generales publicadas en el *Boletín* y el *Anuario de Estadísticas del Trabajo*), vol. II, « Empleo — Desempleo — Horas de trabajo — Salarios » (Ginebra, 1980).

nar el número de personas ocupadas aseguradas (ya que los desempleados están exentos de pagar contribuciones). A veces se excluye de estas estadísticas a las personas que trabajan durante períodos muy breves o que reciben una remuneración muy baja. Además de los cambios en el número actual de personas ocupadas, las estadísticas del empleo basadas en los registros del seguro social pueden también reflejar cambios en el alcance de determinados grupos de actividades económicas, de ocupación o profesionales. Más generalmente, las disposiciones reglamentarias de los seguros sociales determinan el alcance de las estadísticas basadas en los datos de su funcionamiento.

Fuente III. *Encuestas de establecimientos*. Estas estadísticas indican el número de trabajadores que figuran en las nóminas de salarios de los establecimientos, correspondientes a un período de pago o a un día laboral específico dentro de dicho período, y también pueden proporcionar el total de horas trabajadas durante un período de pago determinado. En general, existen dos tipos de estadísticas de establecimientos.

El primer tipo se refiere a *todos los establecimientos de una importancia determinada*, es decir, a aquellos que responden a ciertos criterios, por ejemplo, establecimientos que ocupan más de cierto número de obreros, establecimientos cuya producción anual es superior a cierto valor, etc. Los datos obtenidos pueden estar sujetos a errores sistemáticos debidos a la eliminación de los establecimientos que no alcanzan los límites fijados como criterio mínimo de inclusión en la serie; además, el desplazamiento del empleo de los establecimientos pequeños hacia los grandes se reflejará en las series como una tendencia de crecimiento. Sin embargo, y a condición de que esos mínimos sean bajos, el alcance de estas series es generalmente muy amplio y refleja con bastante exactitud las fluctuaciones del empleo.

El segundo tipo de estadísticas se refiere a *muestras de establecimientos*. La principal difi-

cultad en dichas estadísticas consiste en mantener el carácter representativo de la muestra de establecimientos. Por ejemplo, los cambios en la estructura industrial, el crecimiento o la declinación de determinados establecimientos, el movimiento general de la población y otras modificaciones importantes del nivel de actividad de ciertos sectores de la economía tienden a introducir un error en la muestra que, al acumularse, puede llegar a ser apreciable al cabo de algunos años.

En ciertos países en que se dispone de estadísticas del primer tipo (establecimientos de determinada importancia) solamente a intervalos anuales o aun mayores, los datos pueden combinarse con estadísticas del segundo tipo *(muestras de establecimientos)* de las que se dispone con mayor frecuencia, utilizando el método de enlace o por interpolación.

Fuente IV. *Estimaciones oficiales*. Estas estadísticas son estimaciones oficiales provenientes de autoridades nacionales. Por lo general estas estimaciones se basan en informaciones combinadas extraídas de una o más de las fuentes ya mencionadas (I, II y III).

Cuadro 3

Estructura del empleo

Este cuadro presenta las cifras absolutas de la distribución por *industrias* (ramas de actividad económica) de la fuerza de trabajo civil ocupada. Los datos se clasifican, en la medida de lo posible, por ramas de actividad económica de la *Clasificación industrial internacional uniforme de todas las actividades económicas (CIIU-1968)*, presentada en el apéndice. Por lo general, las estadísticas abarcan todas las categorías ocupacionales; sin embargo, en ocasiones, las cifras pueden referirse solamente a los asalariados (obreros y empleados).

Cuadro 4

Nivel general del empleo

Las series del empleo que figuran en este cuadro se refieren al número de asalariados (obreros y empleados) en todas las ramas de la actividad económica *(industria)*. En ciertos casos, las estadísticas pueden comprender también otras *categorías de ocupación* (empleadores, trabajadores por cuenta propia, etc.). Además, en ciertas series, algunas ramas de actividad económica, tales como « Agricultura, caza, silvicultura y pesca » y « Gran División 9. Servicios comunales, sociales y personales », no se hallan todas representadas.

Cuadro 5

Empleo en los sectores no agrícolas

Los datos sobre el empleo que figuran en este cuadro se refieren, por lo general, al número de asalariados (obreros y empleados) en todas las ramas de la actividad económica, excepto la « Gran División 1. Agricultura, caza, silvicultura y pesca ». En algunos casos las estadísticas abarcan también otras *categorías de ocupación*.

Cuadro 6

Empleo en las industrias manufactureras

En la parte A de este cuadro figuran los datos sobre el empleo del conjunto de las industrias manufactureras, es decir, del conjunto de los componentes de esta rama de actividad económica *(industria)*. En la parte B figuran los datos sobre el empleo en las industrias manufactureras por agrupaciones de industria.

Cuadro 7

Empleo en minas y canteras

Cuadro 8

Empleo en la construcción

Cuadro 9

Empleo en los transportes, almacenaje y comunicaciones

* * *

El número de personas ocupadas (obreros y empleados) en las ramas de la actividad económica *(industria)* presentado en los cuadros 5, 6, 7, 8 y 9 por lo común forma parte de las series generales correspondientes del cuadro 4.

Nueva información:

A partir de la presente edición del Anuario, *los datos aparecen más bien como cifras absolutas que como índices. Además, en la medida de lo posible, van separados por sexo.*

3 Structure of employment
Structure de l'emploi
Estructura del empleo

Country Scope	Total	Major divisions of economic activity [a]									
		1 Agriculture, hunting, forestry and fishing	2 Mining, quarrying	3 Manu-facturing	4 Electricity, gas, water	5 Construction	6 Trade, restaurants and hotels	7 Transport, storage, communi-cation	8 Financing, insurance, real estate business services	9 Community, social and personal services	0 Activities not adequately defined
AFRICA – AFRIQUE – AFRICA											
Botswana		*Registered employees – Salariés inscrits – Asalariados registrados (Source – Fuente: III)*									
Total [1]											
1972	41.300	4.825	1.675	2.650	.	6.475	7.850	1.125	3.150	13.550	.
1973	46.950	4.625	3.525	2.850	0.325	7.225	8.600	1.350	3.275	15.175	.
1974	51.600	4.450	4.100	3.300	0.525	8.075	9.400	1.650	3.425	16.675	.
1975	57.325	4.250	4.525	3.850	0.650	9.000	10.250	1.975	2.000	20.825	.
1976	59.375	4.025	5.450	4.275	0.750	6.125	10.500	2.025	2.675	23.550	.
1977	62.700	4.250	5.500	4.150	0.950	6.900	10.000	1.850	2.425	26.675	.
1978	69.400	5.200	4.700	4.400	1.200	9.200	11.000	2.000	2.700	29.000	.
Male – Hommes – Hombres [1]											
1976	48.276	3.654	5.149	3.534	0.729	5.929	8.065	1.959	2.112	17.145	.
1977	49.030	3.910	5.280	3.500	.930	6.750	6.310	1.780	1.740	18.830	.
1978	54.405	4.655	4.470	3.800	1.180	8.970	7.000	1.910	2.020	20.400	.
Female – Femmes – Mujeres [1]											
1976	11.099	0.371	0.301	0.741	0.021	0.196	2.435	0.066	0.563	6.405	.
1977	13.680	0.340	0.230	0.660	0.020	0.140	3.700	0.060	0.700	7.840	.
1978	14.995	0.545	0.230	0.600	0.020	0.230	4.000	0.090	0.680	8.600	.
Burundi		*Employees – Salariés – Asalariados (Source – Fuente: IV)*									
Total [2]											
1972	28.891	12.889	0.260	2.245	0.300	1.945	1.863	0.924	0.755	7.488	0.222
1973	25.731	13.793	0.502	2.453	0.290	2.211	1.980	0.880	0.757	2.865	.
1974	25.805	13.495	0.697	2.543	0.270	2.087	2.076	0.906	0.744	2.987	.
1975	28.508	17.233	0.746	2.673	0.254	2.286	1.879	0.821	0.734	1.882	.
1976	27.265	17.176	0.511	2.539	0.254	1.920	1.811	0.731	0.816	1.507	.
1977	34.199	20.578	0.785	2.783	0.448	3.875	1.471	0.669	2.729	.	.
1978	33.381	19.951	1.270	2.771	0.510	4.207	1.553	0.973	1.027	.	.
1979	34.060	20.240	1.480	2.830	0.680	4.052	1.615	1.058	1.021	.	.
Rép.-Unie du Cameroun		*Registered employees – Salariés inscrits – Asalariados registrados (Source – Fuente: III)*									
Total											
1973	180.482	35.064	0.178	30.887	2.285	16.925	16.527	13.225	3.181	18.621	43.589
1974	187.831	37.102	0.182	33.489	2.845	18.182	19.001	16.342	3.216	19.849	37.623
1975	191.478	50.460	0.233	41.332	3.054	22.651	23.711	18.683	4.559	26.795	.
1976	203.821	56.832	0.153	47.371	3.125	21.263	25.837	18.839	3.466	26.935	.
1977	212.812	57.116	0.187	49.854	3.025	23.193	28.913	19.347	3.713	27.459	.
1978	224.670	61.215	0.191	50.116	3.663	25.740	29.386	20.815	4.003	29.541	.
1979	267.483	66.811	8.554	70.223	14.395	31.212	38.753	8.833	18.169	10.533	.
Côte-d'Ivoire		*Registered employees – Salariés inscrits – Asalariados registrados (Source – Fuente: III)*									
Total											
1972	302.74	125.15	1.45	39.23	9.10	22.35	16.70	25.60	3.11	53.20	6.85
1973	296.82	67.30	1.60	63.29	11.00	27.40	24.30	35.20	4.93	50.60	11.20
1974	321.54	70.10	1.66	70.33	12.00	29.20	26.00	38.00	6.05	55.00	13.20
1975	330.59	71.60	1.69	70.95	13.00	29.60	27.40	39.40	6.55	56.20	14.20

[a] Les libellés en français des branches d'activité économique sont indiqués à la page suivante.

[1] Aug. of each year. [2] Dec. of each year. [1] Août de chaque année. [2] Déc. de chaque année. [1] Agosto de cada año. [2] Dic. de cada año.

3 Structure of employment
Structure de l'emploi
Estructura del empleo

(Thousands – Milliers – Millares)

Pays Portée	Total	Branches d'activité économique [a] 1 Agriculture, chasse, sylviculture et pêche	2 Industries extractives	3 Industries manufacturières	4 Electricité, gaz, eau	5 Construction	6 Commerce, restaurants et hôtels	7 Transports, entrepôts, communications	8 Banques, assurances, aff. imm., serv. aux entreprises	9 Services à collectivité, services soc. et pers.	0 Activités mal désignées
Egypt [1]					*Civilian employment – Emploi civil – Empleo civil (Source – Fuente: I)*						
Total [2]											
1970	8 044.2	4 108.5	29.8	1 211.7	56.8	192.2	716.8	366.9		1 333.9	27.6
1971	8 252.5	4 469.5	7.2	1 030.2	25.8	193.2	797.4	323.1	83.2	1 268.7	54.2
1972	8 682.0	4 653.4	19.8	1 108.6	39.2	205.8	846.3	339.1	79.6	1 327.1	63.1
1973	8 567.3	4 399.3	15.4	1 208.4	43.8	242.3	833.3	353.1	87.5	1 357.9	26.3
1974	8 867.3	4 197.9	20.2	1 354.5	40.4	232.8	1 031.3	396.4	85.6	1 461.4	46.8
1975	9 030.7	4 423.6	13.1	1 295.8	46.0	247.3	841.3	419.5	83.3	1 557.5	103.3
1976	...	...	...	...	...	...	...	...		...	...
1977	9 198.2	4 189.9	19.9	1 353.4	52.4	334.3	914.8	428.0	107.5	1 798.0	...
1978	9 448.0	3 975.8	35.7	1 427.8	68.7	384.9	912.8	467.3	107.0	1 785.5	282.5
Male – Hommes – Hombres [2]											
1970	7 259.5	3 981.3	28.6	1 126.3	54.2	189.8	668.0	357.7	.	1 102.0	21.7
1971	7 714.5	4 322.2	7.1	963.2	24.9	190.0	742.6	314.2	73.7	1 040.4	36.2
1972	8 106.5	4 479.2	19.6	1 048.1	36.1	201.4	795.4	331.5	67.1	1 087.0	41.1
1973	8 100.8	4 289.1	15.2	1 146.5	40.9	239.2	791.0	341.2	77.9	1 141.8	18.0
1974	8 362.2	4 096.7	19.8	1 285.3	38.0	229.4	982.0	384.9	71.1	1 215.6	39.4
1975	8 482.7	4 321.9	12.1	1 229.9	42.5	243.3	794.3	405.6	71.3	1 299.3	62.5
1976	...	...	...	...	...	...	...	...	...	...	...
1977	8 572.3	4 062.6	19.7	1 284.2	46.7	329.0	868.7	412.5	87.5	1 461.4	.
1978	8 704.7	3 884.4	32.6	1 348.1	63.5	379.9	865.0	448.6	90.5	1 452.8	139.3
Female – Femmes – Mujeres [2]											
1970	514.7	127.2	1.2	85.4	2.7	2.4	48.8	9.2	.	231.9	5.9
1971	538.0	147.3	0.1	67.0	0.9	3.2	54.8	8.9	9.5	228.3	18.0
1972	575.5	174.2	0.2	60.5	3.1	4.4	50.9	7.6	12.5	240.1	22.0
1973	466.5	110.2	0.2	61.9	2.9	3.1	42.3	11.9	9.6	216.1	8.3
1974	505.1	101.2	0.4	69.2	2.4	3.4	49.3	11.5	14.5	245.8	7.4
1975	548.0	101.7	1.0	65.9	3.5	4.0	47.0	13.9	12.0	258.2	40.8
1976	...	...	...	...	...	...	...	...	...	...	...
1977	625.9	127.3	0.2	69.2	5.7	5.3	46.1	15.5	20.0	335.6	...
1978	743.3	91.4	3.1	79.7	5.2	5.0	47.8	18.7	16.5	332.7	143.2
Gabon [3]					*Insured persons – Personnes assurées – Personas aseguradas (Source – Fuente: II)*						
ISIC – CITI – CIIU 1958 Total				4	5		6			7	
1970	63.0	11.5	5.3	9.3	0.7	11.8	6.7	4.6	.	13.1	0.1
1971	65.0	11.2	6.1	9.2	1.1	6.1	11.5	5.1	.	14.7	–
1972	68.5	12.5	7.0	9.1	1.7	10.0	7.3	6.2	.	14.7	–
1973	...	...	...	...	...	...	...	...	.	...	...
1974	...	...	...	...	...	...	...	...	...	...	...
1975	113.2	15.9	7.1	11.9	2.3	37.8	11.2	8.5	.	18.0	0.5
1976	128.9	17.1	7.9	15.6	3.1	43.9	12.3	10.1	.	18.2	0.7
1977	138.6	18.8	6.7	17.1	4.7	40.7	12.6	15.8	.	21.0	1.2

[a] La designación en español de las grandes divisiones de actividad económica figura en la página siguiente. – The English designation of major divisions of economic activity is shown on the preceding page.

[1] Persons aged 12 to 64 years. [2] May of each year. [3] Excl. domestic services. [4] Incl. repair and installation services. [5] Incl. sanitary services. [6] Incl. financing, insurance and real estate; excl. restaurants and hotels. [7] Incl. restaurants and hotels; excl. repair and installation services and sanitary services.

[1] Personnes âgées de 12 à 64 ans. [2] Mai de chaque année. [3] Non compris les services domestiques. [4] Y compris les services de réparation et d'installation. [5] Y compris les services sanitaires. [6] Y compris les banques, les assurances et affaires immobilières; non compris les restaurants et hôtels. [7] Y compris les restaurants et hôtels; non compris les services de réparation et d'installation, et les services sanitaires.

[1] Personas de 12 a 64 años. [2] Mayo de cada año. [3] Excl. los servicios domésticos. [4] Incl. los servicios de reparación y de instalación. [5] Incl. los servicios de saneamiento. [6] Incl. establecimientos financieros, seguros y bienes inmuebles; excl. restaurantes y hoteles. [7] Incl. restaurantes y hoteles; excl. los servicios de reparación y de instalación y los servicios de saneamiento.

EMPLOYMENT

3 Structure of employment
Structure de l'emploi
Estructura del empleo

(Thousands – Milliers – Millares)

País / Alcance	Total	1 Agricultura, caza, silvicultura y pesca	2 Minas, canteras	3 Industrias manufactureras	4 Electricidad, gas, agua	5 Construcción	6 Comercio, restaurantes y hoteles	7 Transportes, almacenaje, comunicaciones	8 Bancos, seguros, bienes inm., serv. para empresas	9 Servicios comunales, sociales y personales	0 Actividades no bien especificadas

Grandes divisiones de actividad económica [a]

Gambia — Registered employees – Salariés inscrits – Asalariados registrados (Source – Fuente: III)

País / Alcance	Total	1	2	3	4	5	6	7	8	9	0
Total [1]											
1973	17.004	1.266	–	2.741	0.699	3.529	1.498	2.398	0.265	4.608	.
1974	18.114	0.966	–	2.594	0.693	4.182	1.816	2.800	0.307	4.756	.
1975	18.801	1.172	–	2.302	0.779	5.180	1.439	2.909	0.360	4.660	.
1976	19.148	1.047	–	1.694	0.562	3.873	2.117	3.381	0.371	6.103	.
Male – Hommes – Hombres [1]											
1974	16.137	0.854	–	2.035	0.679	4.035	1.668	2.732	0.259	3.875	.
1975	16.871	1.043	–	1.846	0.767	5.040	1.272	2.844	0.296	3.764	.
1976	17.336	0.940	–	1.625	0.548	3.855	1.917	3.272	0.300	4.879	.
Female – Femmes – Mujeres [1]											
1974	1.977	0.112	–	0.559	0.014	0.147	0.148	0.068	0.048	0.881	.
1975	1.930	0.130	–	0.456	0.012	0.140	0.167	0.065	0.068	0.896	.
1976	1.812	0.107	–	0.069	0.014	0.018	0.100	0.109	0.071	1.224	.

Kenya [2] — Registered employees – Salariés inscrits – Asalariados registrados (Source – Fuente: III)

País / Alcance	Total	1	2	3	4	5	6	7	8	9	0
Total [3]											
1972	719.8	246.9	3.2	84.8	5.1	37.6	47.6	45.3	17.5	231.8	–
1973	761.7	265.4	3.1	94.5	5.4	41.2	46.6	44.4	20.3	240.9	–
1974	826.3	261.1	3.9	101.3	5.6	44.5	57.0	46.3	21.9	284.5	–
1975	819.1	240.6	3.5	100.7	7.7	40.5	53.7	45.5	24.1	302.7	–
1976	857.5	243.0	3.9	108.8	8.6	47.1	60.2	47.7	25.4	312.8	–
1977	902.9	260.3	3.4	117.9	9.7	48.9	62.6	48.1	29.7	322.4	–
1978	911.6	243.0	2.5	130.1	9.3	55.3	62.5	50.9	32.0	325.9	–
1979	972.3	254.5	2.6	138.4	9.9	61.3	68.7	54.8	35.7	346.4	–
Male – Hommes – Hombres											
1977	748.2	207.7	3.3	106.1	9.3	46.7	55.7	45.0	24.8	249.5	–
1978	752.8	194.1	2.5	116.2	8.8	53.8	53.4	47.4	27.0	249.6	–
1979	807.1	208.9	2.6	126.9	9.4	59.1	59.4	51.0	30.2	259.5	–
Female – Femmes – Mujeres											
1977	154.7	52.6	–	11.8	0.3	2.2	6.9	3.1	4.8	72.9	–
1978	158.7	48.9	0.1	13.8	0.5	1.5	9.1	3.6	5.0	76.2	–
1979	165.2	45.6	0.1	11.6	0.6	2.2	9.3	3.7	5.4	86.9	–

Liberia — Registered employees – Salariés inscrits – Asalariados registrados (Source – Fuente: III)

País / Alcance	Total	1	2	3	4	5	6	7	8	9	0
Total											
1970	45.948	8.641	7.535	2.940	4.091	4.502	6.984	2.710	1.148	4.181	3.216
1971	46.116	8.673	7.566	2.955	4.107	4.522	7.013	2.723	1.128	4.200	3.229
1972	46.503	8.744	7.628	2.976	4.138	4.557	7.068	2.743	1.163	4.231	3.255
1973	43.464	8.173	7.128	2.782	3.868	4.259	6.607	2.564	1.086	3.955	3.042
1974	38.205	7.183	6.265	2.445	3.400	3.744	5.807	2.254	0.955	3.477	2.675
1975	46.882	10.563	7.928	2.030	1.470	4.128	8.039	6.380	1.773	4.230	0.341
1976	46.182	8.695	7.573	2.955	4.110	4.525	7.019	2.724	1.146	4.203	3.232
1977	40.304	18.138	6.611	1.471	1.367	1.694	7.628	1.013	2.318	0.064	–
1978	93.101	38.437	10.491	6.101	0.253	4.205	20.931	4.038	6.334	2.231	–
1979	126.464	33.440	10.376	13.214	1.012	2.188	28.620	5.529	1.738	13.625	16.722
Male – Hommes – Hombres											
1970	40.250	7.017	6.300	2.752	3.727	4.061	5.922	2.559	1.120	3.801	2.991
1971	40.378	7.043	6.316	2.766	3.742	4.079	5.948	2.563	1.100	3.818	3.003
1972	40.728	7.101	6.378	2.786	3.770	4.110	5.994	2.581	1.134	3.846	3.028
1973	38.063	6.637	5.960	2.609	3.564	3.842	5.693	2.413	1.059	3.596	2.830
1974	33.464	5.833	5.238	2.289	3.098	3.378	4.925	2.122	0.932	3.161	2.488
1975	39.136	9.354	6.328	1.998	1.143	3.263	5.098	6.066	1.585	3.985	0.316
1976	40.447	7.061	6.332	2.766	3.745	4.082	5.953	2.564	1.117	3.821	3.006
1977	34.149	14.729	5.527	1.377	1.246	1.528	6.469	0.954	2.260	0.059	–
1978	79.370	31.211	8.771	5.711	0.131	3.793	17.749	3.800	6.176	2.028	–
1979	86.922	26.752	9.116	11.434	0.632	1.602	18.508	4.561	1.198	3.975	9.144

[a] The English designation of major divisions of economic activity is shown on the following page. – Les libellés en français des branches d'activité économique sont indiqués à la page précédente.

[1] Third quarter of each year. [2] Excl. employment in rural areas (except for large enterprises) estimated at between 300,000 and 500,000 employees. [3] June of each year.

[1] Troisième trimestre de chaque année. [2] Non compris l'emploi dans les zones rurales (à l'exception des grandes entreprises) évalué entre 300 000 et 500 000 salariés. [3] Juin de chaque année.

[1] Tercer trimestre de cada año. [2] Excl. el empleo en las zonas rurales (con excepción de las grandes empresas), estimado entre 300 000 y 500 000 trabajadores. [3] Junio de cada año.

3 Structure of employment
Structure de l'emploi
Estructura del empleo

(Thousands – Milliers – Millares)

Country Scope	Total	Major divisions of economic activity [a]									
		1 Agriculture, hunting, forestry and fishing	2 Mining, quarrying	3 Manu-facturing	4 Electricity, gas, water	5 Construction	6 Trade, restaurants and hotels	7 Transport, storage, communication	8 Financing, insurance, real estate business services	9 Community, social and personal services	0 Activities not adequately defined
Liberia		*Registered employees – Salariés inscrits – Asalariados registrados (Source – Fuente: III)*									
Female – Femmes – Mujeres											
1970	5.698	1.624	1.235	0.180	0.364	0.441	1.062	0.159	0.028	0.380	0.225
1971	5.738	1.630	1.240	0.189	0.365	0.443	1.065	0.160	0.038	0.382	0.226
1972	5.775	1.643	1.250	0.190	0.368	0.447	1.074	0.162	0.029	0.385	0.227
1973	5.401	1.536	1.168	0.183	0.344	0.417	1.004	0.151	0.027	0.385	0.227
1974	4.741	1.350	1.027	0.156	0.302	0.366	0.882	0.132	0.023	0.359	0.212
1975	7.746	1.209	1.600	0.032	0.327	0.865	2.941	0.314	0.188	0.316	0.187
1976	5.735	1.634	1.241	0.189	0.365	0.443	1.066	0.160	0.029	0.245	0.025
1977	6.155	3.409	1.084	0.094	0.121	0.166	1.159	0.059	0.058	0.382	0.226
1978	13.731	7.226	1.720	0.390	0.022	0.412	3.182	0.238	0.338	0.005	–
1979	39.542	6.688	1.260	1.780	0.380	0.586	10.112	0.968	0.540	9.650	7.578
Libyan Arab Jamahiriya		*Civilian employment – Emploi civil – Empleo civil (Source – Fuente: IV)*									
Total											
1971	459.0	127.0	14.2	21.4	8.7	56.7	32.5	38.4	6.0	118.2	35.9
1972	488.0	127.7	14.4	22.9	9.1	66.6	35.7	41.7	6.1	124.2	39.6
1973	538.1	129.5	15.3	25.9	10.2	87.4	39.3	45.0	6.5	136.1	42.9
1974	607.2	131.4	16.3	29.3	11.5	118.1	44.0	48.8	7.0	149.6	51.2
1975	677.1	133.1	17.6	32.9	13.0	148.5	48.5	53.5	7.7	163.7	58.6
1976	732.7	141.2	18.5	37.4	13.9	167.8	52.0	57.9	8.1	175.8	60.1
1977	765.0	144.9	19.2	41.7	14.7	171.4	52.3	63.1	8.5	185.9	63.3
1978	773.2	147.9	20.4	47.4	15.8	164.3	47.5	67.5	9.1	191.2	62.1
Malawi [1]		*Registered employed – Effectif occupé – Efectivo ocupado (Source – Fuente: III)*									
Total											
1970	159.5	53.7	0.6	18.7	1.7	18.2	12.2	8.5	1.2	44.7	.
1971	173.0	57.3	0.6	21.8	2.1	17.5	13.8	9.0	1.4	49.5	.
1972	189.1	63.8	0.7	23.1	2.4	18.0	15.8	9.7	1.4	54.2	.
1973	215.1	76.4	0.7	25.6	2.8	21.1	18.4	10.4	1.8	57.9	.
1974	226.5	80.5	0.8	26.7	2.4	22.7	20.8	11.3	2.2	59.1	.
1975	246.1	94.8	0.8	31.3	2.6	21.0	19.8	11.9	2.6	61.3	.
1976	266.4	106.5	1.0	36.0	3.0	21.1	20.6	12.8	3.3	62.1	.
1977 [2]	▌308.9	▌154.7	▌0.6	▌33.5	▌2.8	▌23.2	▌25.2	▌16.6	▌6.7	▌45.6	.
1978	353.7	170.8	0.6	36.2	2.9	31.6	39.0	17.9	6.9	47.8	.
Male – Hommes – Hombres											
1970	146.5	47.4	0.6	18.1	1.7	18.2	11.5	8.4	1.0	39.6	.
1971	158.7	50.6	0.6	21.3	2.1	17.5	13.1	8.9	1.1	43.5	.
1972	173.8	56.2	0.7	22.3	2.4	18.0	14.9	9.5	1.2	48.6	.
1973	193.5	63.7	0.7	24.5	2.7	21.1	17.2	10.2	1.5	51.9	.
1974	203.1	66.5	0.8	25.8	2.3	22.7	19.3	11.1	1.9	52.7	.
1975	221.3	80.2	0.8	29.8	2.4	21.0	18.5	11.5	2.3	54.8	.
1976	239.4	90.9	1.0	34.4	2.8	21.0	18.2	12.5	2.9	55.7	.
1977 [2]	▌276.4	▌134.4	▌0.6	▌31.7	▌2.6	▌23.1	▌23.3	▌16.0	▌6.1	▌38.6	.
1978	312.7	147.6	0.6	34.4	2.7	31.4	33.3	16.9	6.1	39.7	.
Female – Femmes – Mujeres											
1970	13.0	6.3	.	0.6	.	–	0.7	0.1	0.2	5.1	.
1971	14.3	6.7	.	0.5	.	–	0.7	0.1	0.3	6.0	.
1972	15.3	7.6	.	0.8	.	–	0.9	0.2	0.2	5.6	.
1973	21.6	12.7	.	1.1	0.1	–	1.2	0.2	0.2	5.6	.
1974	23.4	14.0	.	0.9	0.1	–	1.2	0.2	0.3	6.4	.
1975	24.8	14.6	.	1.5	0.2	–	1.3	0.4	0.3	6.5	.
1976	27.0	15.6	.	1.6	0.2	0.1	2.4	0.3	0.4	6.4	.
1977 [2]	▌32.5	▌20.3	▌.	▌1.8	▌0.2	▌0.1	▌1.9	▌0.6	▌0.6	▌7.0	.
1978	41.0	23.2	.	1.8	0.2	0.2	5.7	1.0	0.8	8.1	.

[a] Les libellés en français des branches d'activité économique sont indiqués à la page suivante. – La designación en español de las grandes divisiones de actividad económica figura en la página precedente.

[1] Incl. working proprietors and unpaid family workers. [2] Prior to 1977: establishments with 20 or more persons employed; beginning 1977: sample of establishments and revised allocation of establishments in the industrial classification.

[1] Y compris les propriétaires–exploitants et les travailleurs familiaux non rémunérés. [2] Avant 1977: établissements occupant 20 personnes et plus; à partir de 1977: échantillon d'établissements et changements dans leur répartition industrielle.

[1] Incl. los empresarios propietarios y los trabajadores familiares no remunerados. [2] Antes de 1977: establecimientos con 20 y más trabajadores; a partir de 1977: muestra de establecimientos y cambios en la distribución industrial de los establecimientos.

EMPLOYMENT

3 Structure of employment
Structure de l'emploi
Estructura del empleo

(Thousands – Milliers – Millares)

Pays Portée	Total	Branches d'activité économique [(a)]									
		1	2	3	4	5	6	7	8	9	0
		Agriculture, chasse, sylviculture et pêche	Industries extractives	Industries manu-facturières	Electricité, gaz, eau	Construction	Commerce, restaurants et hôtels	Transports, entrepôts, communi-cations	Banques, assurances, aff. imm., serv. aux entreprises	Services à collectivité, services soc. et pers.	Activités mal désignées

Mauritius [1] — Registered employees – Salariés inscrits – Asalariados registrados (Source – Fuente: III)

Total
		[2]		[3]							
1970	130.249	60.561	0.160	7.821	1.294	2.332	3.715	5.242	1.479	47.645	–
1971	142.485	59.842	0.165	9.775	1.293	2.525	4.693	6.568	1.755	52.625	3.244
1972	148.179	61.924	0.146	11.576	1.338	3.311	5.353	6.886	1.955	49.287	6.403
1973	157.787	62.063	0.144	15.722	2.739	4.864	6.154	7.911	2.295	50.038	5.857
1974	167.218	63.049	0.152	20.813	2.918	5.430	6.275	9.074	2.582	49.734	7.191
1975	172.814	64.469	0.163	22.517	2.989	6.034	6.455	9.412	2.812	51.083	6.880
1976	184.539	64.182	0.153	29.348	3.093	7.253	7.817	9.932	3.220	52.888	6.653
1977	194.762	65.297	0.121	33.241	3.152	7.749	8.480	11.151	3.747	54.689	7.135
1978	198.435	60.767	0.198	33.077	3.601	9.765	9.280	10.487	4.368	58.821	8.071*
1979	197.816	59.466	0.148	33.052	3.983	8.980	9.716	8.278	4.327	61.199	6.667

Male – Hommes – Hombres
1970	104.602	44.091	0.118	6.304	1.243	2.300	3.157	5.154	1.186	41.049	–
1971	114.459	43.151	0.117	7.183	.1.240	2.491	3.980	6.453	1.403	45.202	3.239
1972	119.117	45.405	0.101	8.017	1.289	3.282	4.470	6.747	1.542	41.876	6.388
1973	125.533	45.752	0.097	9.367	2.662	4.829	5.103	7.705	1.792	42.391	5.835
1974	130.452	46.468	0.100	10.714	2.839	5.393	5.198	8.860	1.996	41.722	7.162
1975	134.003	47.590	0.107	11.551	2.905	5.993	5.353	9.147	2.144	42.373	6.840
1976	140.275	47.554	0.091	13.547	2.996	7.193	6.274	9.627	2.462	43.903	6.628
1977	145.508	47.617	0.063	14.753	3.030	7.661	6.739	10.821	2.865	44.857	7.102
1978	148.966	44.318	0.123	14.886	3.490	9.628	7.367	10.104	3.349	47.666	8.035
1979	146.005	43.634	0.067	15.306	3.861	8.849	7.624	7.863	3.237	48.933	6.631

Female – Femmes – Mujeres
1970	25.647	16.470	0.042	1.517	0.051	0.032	0.558	0.088	0.293	6.596	–
1971	28.026	16.691	0.048	2.592	0.053	0.034	0.713	0.115	0.352	7.423	0.005
1972	29.062	16.519	0.045	3.559	0.049	0.029	0.883	0.139	0.413	7.411	0.015
1973	32.254	16.311	0.047	6.355	0.077	0.035	1.051	0.206	0.503	7.647	0.022
1974	36.766	16.581	0.052	10.099	0.079	0.037	1.077	0.214	0.586	8.012	0.029
1975	38.811	16.879	0.056	10.966	0.084	0.041	1.102	0.265	0.668	8.710	0.040
1976	44.264	16.628	0.062	15.801	0.097	0.060	1.543	0.305	0.758	8.985	0.025
1977	49.254	17.680	0.058	18.488	0.122	0.088	1.741	0.330	0.882	9.832	0.033
1978	49.469	16.449	0.075	18.191	0.111	0.137	1.913	0.383	1.019	11.155	0.036
1979	51.811	15.832	0.081	19.746	0.122	0.131	2.092	0.415	1.090	12.266	0.036

Seychelles — Insured persons – Personnes assurées – Personas aseguradas (Source – Fuente: II)

Total
		[4]						[5]		[6]	
1973	13.709	1.697	.	0.432	.	3.353	1.716	0.851	.	5.660	.
1974	12.973	1.998	.	0.490	.	1.760	2.083	0.947	.	5.695	.
1975	13.758	2.092	.	0.581	.	1.364	2.587	0.979	.	6.185	.
1976	14.920	2.186	.	0.650	.	1.783	2.888	0.995	.	6.418	.
1977	16.009	2.159	.	0.657	.	2.086	2.938	1.230	.	6.939	.
1978	15.351	1.560	.	0.674	.	1.454	2.816	1.608	.	7.239	.

Sierra Leone — Registered employees – Salariés inscrits – Asalariados registrados (Source – Fuente: III)

Total [7]
1974	63.959	4.915	9.603	5.885	1.944	6.959	4.693	8.027	0.833	21.100	.
1975	61.297	4.931	4.686	5.840	1.978	7.549	4.592	8.823	0.927	21.971	.
1976	61.889	4.874	5.349	6.288	2.048	7.850	5.292	6.359	1.294	22.535	.
1977	61.328	5.145	5.258	6.018	1.999	7.803	5.211	5.854	1.247	22.793	.
1978	60.052	5.127	5.258	6.033	1.993	7.807	5.164	5.919	1.335	21.416	.
1979	67.932	5.695	5.248	7.680	1.807	8.470	5.384	7.397	1.798	24.453	.

[(a)] La designación en español de las grandes divisiones de actividad económica figura en la página siguiente. – The English designation of major divisions of economic activity is shown on the preceding page.

[1] Sep. of each year. [2] Incl. sugar and tea factories. [3] Excl. sugar and tea factories. [4] Excl. hunting. [5] Excl. storage. [6] Incl. financing, insurance, real estate and business services. [7] Dec. of each year.

[1] Sept. de chaque année. [2] Y compris les fabriques de sucre et de thé. [3] Non compris les fabriques de sucre et de thé. [4] Non compris la chasse. [5] Non compris les entrepôts. [6] Y compris les banques, les assurances, les affaires immobilières et les services aux entreprises. [7] Déc. de chaque année.

[1] Sept. de cada año. [2] Incl. las fábricas de azúcar y té. [3] Excl. las fábricas de azúcar y té. [4] Excl. caza. [5] Excl. almacenaje. [6] Incl. establecimientos financieros, seguros, bienes inmuebles y servicios para empresas. [7] Dic. de cada año.

3 Structure of employment
Structure de l'emploi
Estructura del empleo

(Thousands – Milliers – Millares)

País Alcance	Total	Grandes divisiones de actividad económica (a)									
		1 Agricultura, caza, silvicultura y pesca	2 Minas, canteras	3 Industrias manufactureras	4 Electricidad, gas, agua	5 Construcción	6 Comercio, restaurantes y hoteles	7 Transportes, almacenaje, comunicaciones	8 Bancos, seguros, bienes inm., serv. para empresas	9 Servicios comunales, sociales y personales	0 Actividades no bien especificadas

Swaziland — Registered employees – Salariés inscrits – Asalariados registrados (Source – Fuente: III)

País Alcance	Total	1	2	3	4	5	6	7	8	9	0
Total [1]											
1970	42.426	18.319	2.907	5.383	0.509	2.328	3.423	1.877	0.344	7.336	.
1971	47.051	20.840	2.926	5.837	0.518	2.537	3.842	2.050	0.427	8.074	.
1972	53.856	24.332	2.950	6.512	0.541	3.629	3.842	2.280	0.580	9.190	.
1973	57.032	23.655	2.924	7.360	0.592	3.950	4.002	2.688	0.581	11.280	.
1974	62.061	28.069	3.020	7.547	0.546	4.421	4.414	2.483	0.773	10.828	.
1975	64.405	28.407	3.079	8.998	0.405	3.341	4.519	2.540	1.187	11.929	.
1976	66.215	28.520	3.076	8.216	0.799	3.075	5.093	2.566	1.187	11.929	.
1976	66.215	28.520	3.076	8.216	0.799	3.075	5.093	2.566	1.147	13.724	.
1977	66.225	26.377	3.086	8.411	1.226	4.081	5.516	2.768	1.477	13.283	.
1978	71.256	27.152	2.607	8.743	1.208	7.909	5.589	2.934	1.456	13.658	.
Male – Hommes – Hombres [1]											
1970	35.068	15.269	2.827	5.017	0.493	2.293	2.499	1.756	0.220	4.694	.
1971	35.953	14.570	2.855	5.427	0.501	2.522	2.677	1.915	0.290	5.156	.
1972	42.609	18.660	2.877	5.788	0.517	3.614	2.701	2.128	0.403	5.921	.
1973	44.769	18.103	2.854	6.035	0.569	3.922	2.727	2.527	0.387	7.645	.
1974	48.746	21.168	2.953	6.348	0.516	4.388	2.934	2.318	0.540	7.311	.
1975	50.011	21.185	3.008	7.560	0.382	3.302	2.986	2.321	0.838	7.799	.
1976	47.559	18.686	3.013	6.831	0.767	3.027	3.248	2.376	0.774	8.837	.
1977	47.266	19.014	3.007	6.553	1.172	3.978	3.400	2.508	1.003	8.018	.
1978	54.017	20.993	2.567	6.543	1.138	7.762	3.382	2.631	0.924	8.077	.
Female – Femmes – Mujeres [1]											
1970	7.358	3.050	0.080	0.366	0.016	0.035	0.924	0.121	0.124	2.642	.
1971	11.098	6.270	0.071	0.410	0.017	0.015	1.165	0.135	0.137	2.878	.
1972	11.247	5.672	0.073	0.724	0.024	0.015	1.141	0.152	0.177	3.269	.
1973	12.263	5.552	0.070	1.325	0.023	0.028	1.275	0.161	0.194	3.635	.
1974	13.585	6.861	0.067	1.199	0.030	0.033	1.480	0.165	0.233	3.517	.
1975	14.394	6.592	0.071	1.438	0.023	0.039	1.533	0.219	0.349	4.130	.
1976	18.656	9.834	0.063	1.385	0.032	0.048	1.845	0.190	0.373	4.886	.
1977	17.572	7.363	0.079	1.858	0.054	0.103	2.116	0.260	0.474	5.265	.
1978	17.239	6.159	0.040	2.200	0.070	0.147	2.207	0.303	0.532	5.581	.

Tunisie — Civilian employment – Emploi civil – Empleo civil (Source – Fuente: IV)

País Alcance	Total	1	2	3	4	5	6	7	8	9	0
Total											
1975	1 366.5	508.9	26.6	235.2	11.5	128.4	116.6	56.0	7.7	213.3	62.3
1976	1 440.1	531.0	15.7	270.2	7.8	139.6	121.5	53.3	8.3	230.3	62.3
1977	1 480.0	533.0	16.0	289.0	8.0	147.0	126.0	55.0	8.5	235.5	62.0
1978	1 524.0	534.0	16.0	309.0	8.0	155.0	132.0	57.0	8.5	242.3	62.0
1978	1 524.0	534.0	16.0	309.0	8.0	155.0	132.0	57.0	8.7	242.3	62.0
1979	1 567.9	534.2	15.8	329.0	8.7	162.0	136.1	58.8	9.4	249.0	64.8
Male – Hommes – Hombres											
1975	1 105.9	439.9	26.2	112.0	11.0	127.3	109.5	53.2	5.8	165.9	55.1
1976	1 163.5	461.0	15.7	135.5	7.2	138.5	111.9	51.7	6.3	180.5	55.1
Female – Femmes – Mujeres											
1975	260.6	69.0	0.4	123.2	0.5	1.1	7.1	2.8	1.9	47.4	7.2
1976	276.6	70.0	–	134.7	0.6	1.1	9.6	1.6	2.0	49.7	7.2

(a) The English designation of major divisions of economic activity is shown on the following page. – Les libellés en français des branches d'activité économique sont indiqués à la page précédente.

[1] June of each year; prior to 1976: Sep.   [1] Juin de chaque année; avant 1976: sept.   [1] Junio de cada año; antes de 1976: sept.

3 Structure of employment
Structure de l'emploi
Estructura del empleo

(Thousands – Milliers – Millares)

Country Scope	Total	Major divisions of economic activity (a)									
		1 Agriculture, hunting, forestry and fishing	2 Mining, quarrying	3 Manu-facturing	4 Electricity, gas, water	5 Construction	6 Trade, restaurants and hotels	7 Transport, storage, communi-cation	8 Financing, insurance, real estate business services	9 Community, social and personal services	0 Activities not adequately defined

Zambia — Registered employees – Salariés inscrits – Asalariados registrados (Source – Fuente: III)

Total [1]

										[2]	
1971	365.55	39.32	58.16	42.02	4.04	65.88	37.93	22.58	10.56	85.06	.
1972	367.93	31.14	60.65	43.30	4.53	72.32	33.69	25.04	14.31	82.95	.
1973	373.44	31.73	61.74	43.60	4.68	70.49	34.86	24.21	15.01	87.12	.
1974	384.89	33.61	65.11	44.07	4.75	70.58	35.58	22.15	16.45	92.59	.
1975	393.49	36.10	64.75	44.33	5.13	71.75	32.96	22.05	18.70	97.72	.
1976	368.47	32.50	64.58	41.66	5.41	50.27	36.10	21.08	18.90	97.97	.
1977 [3]	372.50	32.50	68.10	40.80	5.50	45.40	38.80	21.30	19.50	100.60	.

Male – Hommes – Hombres [4]

| 1975 | 374.08 | 35.23 | 63.79 | 42.10 | 4.71 | 73.10 | 34.13 | 21.31 | 15.92 | 83.79 | . |
| 1976 | 352.87 | 32.23 | 63.62 | 41.70 | 5.38 | 54.00 | 31.74 | 20.88 | 16.63 | 86.69 | . |

Female – Femmes – Mujeres [4]

| 1975 | 24.76 | 1.16 | 3.07 | 2.57 | 0.19 | 0.71 | 2.11 | 1.03 | 2.06 | 11.86 | . |
| 1976 | 26.52 | 1.28 | 3.08 | 2.86 | 0.20 | 0.79 | 2.42 | 1.15 | 2.20 | 12.50 | . |

Zimbabwe [5] — Registered employees – Salariés inscrits – Asalariados registrados (Source – Fuente: III)

Total

1970	853.0	297.8	57.2	114.7	5.6	42.4	65.6	36.5	9.0	224.5	.
1971	891.0	310.9	58.0	121.6	5.8	46.8	67.5	38.9	9.4	232.1	.
1972	953.0	342.3	58.4	130.7	6.1	49.5	72.1	41.0	10.4	242.4	.
1973	997.0	356.6	58.1	139.4	6.6	56.8	76.7	42.3	11.1	249.9	.
1974	1 040.0	365.6	62.0	151.3	6.9	64.3	76.2	43.8	11.6	258.2	.
1975	1 052.0	363.8	63.6	156.0	6.9	60.8	77.3	45.3	12.1	267.6	.
1976	1 037.0	356.1	63.8	153.6	6.7	51.6	74.7	45.7	12.1	272.4	.
1977	1 015.0	348.2	61.6	145.1	6.6	46.5	72.5	45.5	12.2	277.0	.
1978	990.0	341.4	58.1	139.3	6.5	40.9	69.1	44.0	12.0	278.4	.
1979	989.6	335.2	59.5	144.7	6.6	40.6	67.6	43.4	12.1	278.9	.

Male – Hommes – Hombres

| 1979 | 819.1 | 249.5 | 58.4 | 133.6 | 6.4 | 40.1 | 55.7 | 40.3 | 7.1 | 228.0 | . |

Female – Femmes – Mujeres

| 1979 | 169.5 | 85.7 | 1.1 | 11.1 | 0.2 | 0.5 | 11.9 | 3.1 | 5.0 | 50.9 | . |

AMERICA – AMERIQUE – AMERICA

Bahamas — Insured persons – Personnes assurées – Personas aseguradas (Source – Fuente: II)

Total [6]

1976	60.410	1.916	0.642	3.376	1.116	3.271	19.024	3.843	6.224	20.757	0.236
1977	70.771	2.368	0.717	3.866	1.198	3.825	22.308	4.007	7.031	21.895	3.556
1978	69.876	2.350	0.713	3.792	1.176	3.884	22.094	3.952	7.069	21.279	3.567
1979	72.713	2.377	0.721	3.934	1.190	4.034	22.030	4.027	7.335	21.685	4.380

Barbados — Civilian employment – Emploi civil – Empleo civil (Source – Fuente: I)

Total [7]

1976	90.1	8.9	–	13.8	0.7	7.9	17.3	5.5	3.5	33.4	.
1977	90.2	8.7	–	14.8	0.3	7.7	17.4	5.5	4.0	31.8	.
1978 [8]	91.6	8.7	–	12.7	1.0	5.7	21.0	6.2	4.6	31.7	.

(a) Les libellés en français des branches d'activité économique sont indiqués à la page suivante. – La designación en español de las grandes divisiones de actividad económica figura en la página precedente.

[1] Dec. of each year. [2] Excl. domestic services. [3] June. [4] Dec. of each year. [5] Excl. employment in rural areas (except for large enterprises). [6] Jan. of each year. [7] Fourth quarter of each year. [8] First quarter.

[1] Déc. de chaque année. [2] Non compris les services domestiques. [3] Juin. [4] Déc. de chaque année. [5] Non compris l'emploi dans les zones rurales (à l'exception des grandes entreprises). [6] Janv. de chaque année. [7] Quatrième trimestre de chaque année. [8] Premier trimestre.

[1] Dic. de cada año. [2] Excl. los servicios domésticos. [3] Junio. [4] Dic. de cada año. [5] Excl. el empleo en las zonas rurales (con excepción de las grandes empresas). [6] Enero de cada año. [7] Cuarto trimestre de cada año. [8] Primer trimestre.

3 Structure of employment
Structure de l'emploi
Estructura del empleo

(Thousands – Milliers – Millares)

Pays Portée	Total	Branches d'activité économique [a]									
		1 Agriculture, chasse, sylviculture et pêche	2 Industries extractives	3 Industries manu-facturières	4 Electricité, gaz, eau	5 Construction	6 Commerce, restaurants et hôtels	7 Transports, entrepôts, communi-cations	8 Banques, assurances, aff. imm., serv. aux entreprises	9 Services à collectivité, services soc. et pers.	0 Activités mal désignées
Barbados				*Civilian employment – Emploi civil – Empleo civil (Source – Fuente: I)*							
Male – Hommes – Hombres [1]											
1976	53.4	5.4	–	6.6	0.6	7.7	8.2	4.8	1.6	18.5	.
1977	54.3	4.8	–	7.3	0.3	7.6	9.3	4.8	2.2	18.0	.
1978 [2]	51.9	4.4	–	6.6	0.5	5.5	11.2	5.0	2.6	16.1	.
Female – Femmes – Mujeres [2]											
1976	37.6	3.5	–	7.2	0.1	0.2	9.1	0.7	1.9	14.9	
1977	35.9	3.9	–	7.5	.	0.1	8.1	0.7	1.8	13.8	
1978 [2]	39.7	4.3	–	6.1	0.5	0.2	9.8	1.2	2.0	15.6	
Bolivia				*Civilian employment – Emploi civil – Empleo civil (Source – Fuente: IV)*							
Total											
1970	1 197.7	581.0	68.4	103.9	4.8	46.0	88.5	69.8	2.5	232.7	.
1971	1 236.1	592.9	71.1	108.2	5.1	48.2	91.9	72.3	2.8	243.6	.
1972	1 275.8	604.7	73.0	112.5	5.3	54.1	95.4	74.3	2.9	253.4	.
1973	1 316.7	616.9	75.4	117.1	5.4	60.8	98.9	78.2	3.1	260.9	.
1974	1 358.8	629.1	80.6	121.8	5.7	68.4	102.5	79.2	3.5	268.0	.
1975	1 402.3	641.7	82.4	126.6	5.7	76.9	106.3	82.1	3.9	276.7	.
1976	1 447.2	654.6	82.7	131.7	5.8	86.5	110.1	86.0	4.7	285.2	.
1977	1 485.3	667.7	82.7	137.2	6.1	88.6	113.1	90.8	4.9	299.2	.
1978	1 525.6	679.7	85.5	141.5	6.5	92.4	117.7	96.4	6.1	299.7	.
1979	1 565.7	687.6	86.3	146.9	7.6	93.7	121.4	111.5	6.2	304.5	.
Male – Hommes – Hombres											
1971	855.2	343.8	63.1	77.8	4.8	44.8	68.4	69.4	2.1	181.0	.
1972	884.1	350.7	64.7	81.0	5.0	50.3	71.0	70.6	2.2	188.6	.
1973	915.5	357.8	66.8	84.3	5.1	56.6	73.6	74.3	2.3	194.7	.
1974	947.1	364.9	71.3	87.7	5.3	63.6	76.3	74.5	2.6	200.9	.
1975	975.7	372.2	72.9	91.3	5.3	71.5	79.1	77.1	2.9	203.4	.
1976	1 006.9	379.7	73.7	14.8	4.7	90.4	81.9	80.8	3.6	207.4	.
1977	948.7	387.3	73.7	98.8	4.9	82.4	50.8	85.3	3.7	161.8	.
1978	976.4	394.2	76.2	101.9	5.3	86.0	52.8	90.6	4.6	164.9	.
1979	1 006.2	398.8	76.9	105.7	6.2	87.2	54.5	104.8	4.6	167.4	.
Female – Femmes – Mujeres											
1971	380.9	249.1	8.0	30.4	0.3	3.4	23.5	2.9	0.7	62.6	
1972	391.7	254.0	8.3	31.5	0.3	3.8	24.4	3.7	0.7	64.8	
1973	401.2	259.1	8.6	32.8	0.3	4.2	25.3	3.9	0.8	66.2	
1974	411.7	264.2	9.3	34.1	0.4	4.8	26.2	4.7	0.9	67.1	
1975	426.6	269.5	9.5	35.3	0.4	5.4	27.2	5.0	1.0	73.3	
1976	404.3	274.9	9.0	36.9	1.1	6.1	28.2	5.2	1.2	77.8	
1977	536.6	280.4	9.0	38.4	1.2	6.2	62.3	5.4	1.2	132.4	
1978	549.2	285.5	9.3	39.6	1.2	6.5	64.9	5.8	1.5	134.9	
1979	559.5	288.8	9.4	41.1	1.5	6.6	66.9	6.7	1.5	137.0	
Brasil				*Registered employees – Salariés inscrits – Asalariados registrados (Source – Fuente: III)*							
Total			[3]	[4]		[5]		[6]			
1970	5 730	23	81	2 499	31	647	844	435	277	817	76
1971	6 069	29	82	2 599	28	653	908	438	283	948	101
1972	6 876	24	80	2 830	17	819	1 029	499	331	1 121	126
1973	7 614	41	83	3 230	50	889	1 037	582	343	1 205	154
1974	8 803	40	97	3 720	71	1 059	1 260	638	377	1 353	188
1975	9 477	41	93	3 953	71	1 121	1 334	717	404	1 535	208

[a] La designación en español de las grandes divisiones de actividad económica figura en la página siguiente. – The English designation of major divisions of economic activity is shown on the preceding page.

[1] Fourth quarter of each year. [2] First quarter. [3] Growing and processing of agricultural products for basic industrial chemicals. [4] Mineral mining and quarrying. [5] Electricity only. [6] Excl. hotels.

[1] Quatrième trimestre de chaque année. [2] Premier trimestre. [3] Culture et traitement de plantes pour fabriquer des produits chimiques de base. [4] Industries extractives minérales. [5] Electricité seulement. [6] Non compris les hôtels.

[1] Cuarto trimestre de cada año. [2] Primer trimestre. [3] Cultivos y elaboración de plantas para fabricar substancias químicas básicas. [4] Minas y canteras minerales. [4] Electricidad solamente. [6] Excl. hoteles.

EMPLOYMENT

3 Structure of employment
Structure de l'emploi
Estructura del empleo

(Thousands – Milliers – Millares)

País / Alcance	Total	Grandes divisiones de actividad económica [a]									
		1 Agricultura, caza, silvicultura y pesca	2 Minas, canteras	3 Industrias manu-factureras	4 Electricidad, gas, agua	5 Construcción	6 Comercio, restaurantes y hoteles	7 Transportes, almacenaje, comuni-caciones	8 Bancos, seguros, bienes inm., serv. para empresas	9 Servicios comunales, sociales y personales	0 Activi-dades no bien especifi-cadas
Brasil		Registered employees – Salariés inscrits – Asalariados registrados (Source – Fuente: III)									
Male – Hommes – Hombres [1]											
1970	4 727	21	79	2 045	30	639	668	410	239	546	50
1971	4 945	27	80	2 106	27	645	713	415	234	631	67
1972	5 520	22	78	2 260	16	805	803	468	266	718	84
1973	6 033	37	81	2 555	47	872	779	525	270	764	103
1974	6 879	33	94	2 911	65	1 035	932	569	288	828	124
1975	7 326	35	89	3 093	65	1 085	974	629	301	921	134
Female – Femmes – Mujeres [1]											
1970	1 003	2	2	454	1	8	176	25	38	271	26
1971	1 124	2	2	493	1	8	195	23	49	317	34
1972	1 356	2	2	570	1	14	226	31	65	403	42
1973	1 581	4	2	675	3	17	258	57	73	441	51
1974	1 924	7	3	809	6	24	328	69	89	525	64
1975	2 151	6	4	860	6	36	360	88	103	614	74
Canada		Civilian employment – Emploi civil – Empleo civil (Source – Fuente: I)									
ISIC – CITI – CIIU 1958				[2]	[3]		[4]			[5]	
Total											
1970	7 778	582	125	1 768	88	467	1 667	599	.	2 483	–
1971	7 961	585	128	1 767	86	489	1 694	610	.	2 603	–
1972	8 210	555	123	1 828	92	495	1 775	631	.	2 710	–
1973	8 638	553	122	1 937	98	542	1 887	668	.	2 829	–
1974	9 011	560	126	1 994	95	591	1 998	688	.	2 959	–
1975	9 284	564	139	1 871	107	603	2 111	705	.	3 184	–
1976	9 479	562	145	1 921	111	635	2 141	714	.	3 252	–
1977	9 648	553	152	1 888	108	633	2 209	712	.	3 393	–
1978	9 972	573	158	1 956	119	632	2 283	738	.	3 512	–
1979	10 369	589	167	2 070	118	640	1 806	782	.	4 198	–
Male – Hommes – Hombres											
1970	5 233	514	118	1 376	76	446	1 033	505	.	1 166	–
1971	5 305	514	122	1 355	75	466	1 028	514	.	1 230	–
1972	5 447	480	116	1 394	82	471	1 069	530	.	1 304	–
1973	5 679	483	115	1 473	88	517	1 110	551	.	1 344	–
1974	5 885	484	118	1 507	82	559	1 171	566	.	1 398	–
1975	5 903	452	127	1 411	94	564	1 195	569	.	1 491	–
1976	5 965	443	133	1 426	97	592	1 196	567	.	1 511	–
1977	6 031	432	138	1 416	92	587	1 233	570	.	1 563	–
1978	6 148	448	143	1 456	103	584	1 262	585	.	1 567	–
1979	6 347	462	150	1 521	98	589	1 045	615	.	1 867	–

[a] The English designation of major divisions of economic activity is shown on the following page. – Les libellés en français des branches d'activité économique sont indiqués à la page précédente.

[1] See notes of line "Total", preceding page. [2] Incl. repair and installation services. [3] Incl. sanitary services. [4] Incl. financing, insurance and real estate; excl. restaurants and hotels. [5] Incl. restaurants and hotels; excl. repair and installation services and sanitary services.

[1] Voir notes de la ligne «Total» à la page précédente. [2] Y compris les services de réparation et d'installation. [3] Y compris les services sanitaires. [4] Y compris les banques, les assurances et affaires immobilières; non compris les restaurants et hôtels. [5] Y compris les restaurants et hôtels; non compris les services de réparation et d'installation, et les services sanitaires.

[1] Véanse notas de la línea «Total» en la página precedente. [2] Incl. los servicios de reparación y de instalación. [3] Incl. los servicios de saneamiento. [4] Incl. establecimientos financieros, seguros y bienes inmuebles; excl. restaurantes y hoteles. [5] Incl. restaurantes y hoteles; excl. los servicios de reparación y de instalación y los servicios de saneamiento.

3 Structure of employment
Structure de l'emploi
Estructura del empleo

(Thousands – Milliers – Millares)

Country Scope	Total	Major divisions of economic activity (a)									
		1 Agriculture, hunting, forestry and fishing	2 Mining, quarrying	3 Manu-facturing	4 Electricity, gas, water	5 Construction	6 Trade, restaurants and hotels	7 Transport, storage, communi-cation	8 Financing, insurance, real estate business services	9 Community, social and personal services	0 Activities not adequately defined
Canada		*Civilian employment – Emploi civil – Empleo civil (Source – Fuente: I)*									
Female – Femmes – Mujeres [1]											
1970	2 545	68	7	392	13	21	634	94	.	1 317	–
1971	2 657	71	7	412	11	24	665	96	.	1 372	–
1972	2 763	74	7	434	10	24	706	101	.	1 406	–
1973	2 958	70	7	464	11	26	777	117	.	1 485	–
1974	3 126	76	8	487	13	32	828	121	.	1 561	–
1975	3 381	112	11	460	13	40	916	136	.	1 693	–
1976	3 515	119	12	495	14	43	945	146	.	1 741	–
1977	3 617	120	14	472	16	47	976	142	.	1 830	–
1978	3 824	125	15	500	16	48	1 021	154	.	1 945	–
1979	4 022	127	17	549	20	51	761	166	.	2 331	–
Colombia [2]		*Civilian employment – Emploi civil – Empleo civil (Source – Fuente: I)*									
Total [3]											
1975	2 146.9	34.9	6.6	514.3	17.6	139.6	458.6	140.1	121.9	709.4	4.0
1976	2 239.3	34.8	8.4	577.8	17.2	132.6	462.7	146.2	127.2	731.9	0.5
1977	2 529.9	33.8	6.6	647.1	18.3	150.6	564.3	157.5	165.8	783.3	2.5
1978	2 751.3	38.7	8.3	713.6	18.7	184.3	616.2	168.3	178.6	824.1	0.6
1979	2 996.6	41.0	13.7	768.6	21.0	182.3	696.0	197.5	188.8	886.0	1.7
Male – Hommes – Hombres [3]											
1975	1 361.2	33.5	5.5	355.3	15.3	133.5	305.1	127.3	88.0	294.4	3.2
1976	1 449.2	31.7	7.9	401.2	15.7	131.0	318.4	136.5	93.2	313.4	0.4
1977	1 574.8	30.0	5.8	430.9	16.6	145.7	361.1	143.6	113.8	325.3	2.0
1978	1 716.1	35.1	7.2	465.6	16.3	175.8	390.1	150.1	113.8	354.8	0.2
1979	1 854.8	35.2	11.5	495.6	17.7	175.6	433.5	173.8	131.6	378.7	1.7
Female – Femmes – Mujeres [3]											
1975	785.7	1.4	1.1	158.9	2.2	6.1	153.5	12.8	34.0	414.9	0.8
1976	868.4	4.4	0.7	198.0	2.4	5.9	162.2	15.1	37.0	442.5	0.2
1977	955.1	3.8	0.8	216.2	1.7	4.9	203.3	13.8	52.0	458.0	0.6
1978	1 035.2	3.6	1.2	247.9	2.4	8.5	226.1	18.2	57.7	469.3	0.4
1979	1 141.9	5.9	2.2	273.0	3.4	6.7	262.5	23.7	57.2	507.3	–
Costa Rica		*Civilian employment – Emploi civil – Empleo civil (Source – Fuente: I)*									
Total [4]											
1973	542.332	207.175	1.518	68.297	5.445	37.414	66.243	24.316	13.491	117.252	1.181
1974	...	...	...	...	...	...	...	...	...	...	...
1975	...	...	...	...	...	...	...	...	...	...	...
1976	616.788	214.539	1.476	88.818	9.933	40.242	87.090	24.427	13.714	133.312	3.248
1977	653.265	215.555	0.662	102.517	9.616	41.849	97.161	26.034	16.935	141.547	1.389
1978	687.044	208.903	0.660	103.601	7.810	50.864	104.359	33.932	17.779	157.004	11.531
1979	707.135	202.649	1.436	113.941	9.025	54.765	105.695	31.241	19.181	167.472	1.730

(a) Les libellés en français des branches d'activité économique sont indiqués à la page suivante. – La designación en español de las grandes divisiones de actividad económica figura en la página precedente.

[1] See notes of line "Total", preceding page. [2] Seven main cities of the country. [3] Sep. of each year. [4] July of each year.

[1] Voir notes de la ligne «Total» à la page précédente. [2] Sept villes principales du pays. [3] Sept. de chaque année. [4] Juillet de chaque année.

[1] Véanse notas de la línea «Total» en la página precedente. [2] Siete ciudades principales del país. [3] Sept. de cada año. [4] Julio de cada año.

3 Structure of employment
Structure de l'emploi
Estructura del empleo

(Thousands – Milliers – Millares)

		Branches d'activité économique [a]									
		1	2	3	4	5	6	7	8	9	0
Pays Portée	Total	Agriculture, chasse, sylviculture et pêche	Industries extractives	Industries manu-facturières	Electricité, gaz, eau	Construction	Commerce, restaurants et hôtels	Transports, entrepôts, communi-cations	Banques, assurances, aff. imm., serv. aux entreprises	Services à collectivité, services soc. et pers.	Activités mal désignées
Cuba		*Employees – Salariés – Asalariados (Source – Fuente: IV)*									
Total				[1]						[2]	
1971	2 081.9	603.6	.	440.5	.	132.7	167.7	175.5	.	561.9	.
1972	2 125.9	636.9	.	438.5	.	153.7	165.9	177.3	.	553.6	.
1973	2 245.7	670.3	.	453.2	.	176.5	176.7	181.9	.	587.1	.
1974	2 313.3	674.5	.	466.7	.	183.5	184.2	186.3	.	618.1	.
1975	2 393.8	685.1	.	472.2	.	208.0	179.3	187.8	.	661.4	.
1976	2 469.2	684.9	.	477.4	.	243.2	179.1	198.6	.	686.0	.
1977	2 607.8	628.1	.	563.7	.	295.8	281.2	176.4	.	662.6	.
Chile		*Civilian employment – Emploi civil – Empleo civil (Source – Fuente: I)*									
Total											
1975	2 715.9	585.9	83.3	456.7	21.2	121.4	397.4	175.4	71.2	784.1	19.3
1976	2 741.9	543.1	134.7	383.8	24.0	101.9	416.8	173.3	50.6	906.0	7.7
1977	2 817.3	566.6	123.7	374.2	28.2	100.6	452.2	188.5	59.2	1 014.8	9.3
República Dominicana [3]		*Civilian employment – Emploi civil – Empleo civil (Source – Fuente: I)*									
Total											
1976	216.715	0.890	0.445	37.914	3.293	15.130	51.442	18.512	6.230	81.257	1.602
1977	...	...	...	...	...	...	...	...	...	...	...
1978	274.566	0.804	0.803	48.642	5.025	20.703	70.953	16.080	6.231	105.123	0.402
Guatemala		*Civilian employment – Emploi civil – Empleo civil (Source – Fuente: I)*									
Total											
1976	545.6	398.1	2.0	70.7	1.5	8.0	28.0	9.0	15.6	12.8	–
1977	592.7	408.2	3.6	80.9	1.5	12.9	38.8	10.7	16.2	19.9	–
Guyane française		*Employees – Salariés – Asalariados (Source – Fuente: IV)*									
Total [4]											
1970	10.812	0.348	0.053	1.378	0.355	2.039	0.816	0.206	0.844	4.773	–
1971	9.738	0.335	0.090	0.967	0.353	1.395	0.798	0.245	0.778	4.777	–
1972	9.986	0.349	0.100	0.879	0.349	1.298	1.018	0.252	0.866	4.875	–
1973	9.784	0.351	0.068	0.886	0.336	0.961	1.009	0.260	0.781	5.132	–
1974	10.795	0.383	0.066	0.753	0.317	0.948	0.920	0.294	0.750	6.364	–
1975	11.012	0.421	0.085	0.790	0.326	0.965	0.951	0.278	0.681	6.515	–
1976	12.580	0.348	0.118	0.681	0.350	1.220	0.981	0.269	0.726	7.887	–
1977	12.791	0.337	0.079	1.040	0.304	1.203	1.235	0.522	0.555	7.516	–
1978	13.475	0.503	0.089	0.427	0.334	1.345	1.073	0.564	0.995	8.145	–
1979	13.879	0.621	0.123	0.576	0.317	1.440	1.164	0.640	0.897	8.101	–
Male – Hommes – Hombres [4]											
1977	7.976	0.323	0.070	0.850	0.251	1.161	0.704	0.443	0.350	3.824	–
1978	8.274	0.485	0.073	0.303	0.276	1.291	0.513	0.475	0.658	4.200	–
1979	8.507	0.578	0.118	0.457	0.261	1.360	0.557	0.541	0.555	4.080	–
Female – Femmes – Mujeres [4]											
1977	4.815	0.014	0.009	0.190	0.053	0.042	0.531	0.079	0.205	0.205	–
1978	5.201	0.018	0.016	0.124	0.058	0.054	0.560	0.089	0.337	3.945	–
1979	5.372	0.043	0.005	0.119	0.056	0.080	0.607	0.099	0.342	4.021	–

[a] La designación en español de las grandes divisiones de actividad económica figura en la página siguiente. – The English designation of major divisions of economic activity is shown on the preceding page.

[1] Incl. mining, quarrying, electricity, gas and water (col. 2 and 4). [2] Incl. financing, insurance, real estate and activities not adequately defined (col. 9 and 0). [3] Santo Domingo only. [4] Dec. of each year.

[1] Y compris les industries extractives, l'électricité, le gaz et l'eau (col. 2 et 4). [2] Y compris les banques, les assurances, les affaires immobilières et les activités mal désignées (col. 9 et 0). [3] Santo Domingo seulement. [4] Déc. de chaque année.

[1] Incl. minas y canteras, electricidad, gas y agua (cols 2 y 4). [2] Incl. establecimientos financieros, seguros, bienes inmuebles y actividades no bien especificadas (cols. 10 y 0). [3] Santo Domingo solamente. [4] Dic. de cada año.

3 Structure of employment
Structure de l'emploi
Estructura del empleo

(Thousands – Milliers – Millares)

País Alcance	Total	Grandes divisiones de actividad económica (a)									
		1 Agricultura, caza, silvicultura y pesca	2 Minas, canteras	3 Industrias manu-factureras	4 Electricidad, gas, agua	5 Construcción	6 Comercio, restaurantes y hoteles	7 Transportes, almacenaje, comuni-caciones	8 Bancos, seguros, bienes inm., serv. para empresas	9 Servicios comunales, sociales y personales	0 Activi-dades no bien especifi-cadas

Haïti — Civilian employment – Emploi civil – Empleo civil (Source – Fuente: IV)

País Alcance	Total	1	2	3	4	5	6	7	8	9	0
Total [1]											
1970	1 928.62	1 428.62	0.97	118.70	1.35	17.59	185.15	11.79	0.64	157.47	7.20
1971	1 940.22	1 437.19	0.97	119.41	1.36	17.70	186.43	11.86	0.63	157.47	7.20
1972	1 951.89	1 445.82	0.98	120.13	1.37	17.80	187.68	11.93	0.66	158.28	7.24
1973	1 963.63	1 454.49	0.98	120.85	1.38	17.91	188.89	12.01	0.66	159.18	7.28
1974	1 975.44	1 463.22	0.99	121.51	1.38	18.02	190.11	12.08	0.70	160.04	7.33
1975	1 987.32	1 472.00	1.00	122.30	1.39	18.13	191.44	12.15	0.72	160.82	7.37
1976	1 883.52	1 395.28	0.94	115.93	1.32	17.18	181.49	11.52	0.84	152.03	6.99
1977	1 894.45	1 403.36	0.95	116.60	1.33	17.28	182.58	11.58	0.83	152.91	7.03
1978	1 904.16	1 410.37	0.95	117.18	1.34	17.37	183.50	11.64	1.07	153.68	7.06
Male – Hommes – Hombres [1]											
1970	1 053.76	889.87	0.87	52.02	1.26	17.41	11.17	11.26	0.48	64.47	4.96
1971	1 063.18	889.09	0.88	52.57	1.26	17.51	11.98	11.33	0.47	65.08	4.99
1972	1 072.65	904.37	0.88	53.12	1.27	17.62	12.75	11.40	0.50	65.71	5.03
1973	1 082.19	911.69	0.89	53.67	1.28	17.73	13.49	11.47	0.50	66.41	5.07
1974	1 091.80	919.06	0.89	54.23	1.29	17.83	14.25	11.54	0.52	67.08	5.11
1975	1 101.47	926.48	0.90	54.79	1.30	17.94	15.07	11.61	0.54	67.69	5.15
1976	995.46	848.40	0.85	48.25	1.22	16.99	4.68	10.97	0.63	58.71	4.76
1977	1 004.16	855.10	0.85	48.75	1.23	17.09	5.31	11.04	0.62	59.37	4.79
1978	1 009.43	859.38	0.86	48.99	1.24	17.18	5.34	11.10	0.87	59.66	4.81
Female – Femmes – Mujeres [1]											
1970	874.86	538.75	0.10	66.67	0.10	0.18	173.98	0.53	0.16	92.19	2.20
1971	877.05	540.10	0.10	66.84	0.10	0.18	174.15	0.53	0.16	92.38	2.20
1972	879.34	541.45	0.10	67.01	0.10	0.18	174.93	0.54	0.17	92.56	2.21
1973	881.44	542.80	0.10	67.17	0.10	0.18	175.39	0.54	0.17	92.77	2.21
1974	883.64	544.16	0.10	67.34	0.10	0.19	175.87	0.54	0.17	92.96	2.22
1975	885.85	545.52	0.10	67.51	0.10	0.19	175.37	0.54	0.18	93.13	2.22
1976	888.06	546.88	0.10	67.68	0.10	0.19	176.81	0.54	0.21	93.32	2.23
1977	890.29	548.25	0.10	67.85	0.10	0.19	177.27	0.54	0.21	93.55	2.23
1978	894.74	550.99	0.10	68.19	0.10	0.19	178.16	0.55	0.21	94.02	2.25

Jamaica — Civilian employment – Emploi civil – Empleo civil (Source – Fuente: I)

País Alcance	Total	1	2	3 [2]	4	5 [3]	6 [4]	7	8	9 [5]	0
Total											
1974	646.3	223.3	7.8	81.3	.	40.8	77.3	26.9	.	185.7	3.4
1975	682.3	226.8	7.5	74.0	.	44.6	81.7	31.6	.	213.0	3.2
1976	685.9	243.9	7.9	75.6	.	38.0	80.7	31.5	.	204.9	3.5
1977	689.8	243.9	7.4	76.2	.	32.9	88.4	29.6	.	207.3	4.1
1978	708.5	256.9	6.0	78.9	.	32.9	93.3	29.3	.	206.8	4.4
Male – Hommes – Hombres											
1978	429.7	189.7	5.2	59.4	.	31.8	33.7	21.9	.	85.0	3.0
Female – Femmes – Mujeres											
1978	278.8	67.2	0.8	19.5	.	1.1	59.6	7.4	.	121.8	1.4

México — Civilian employment – Emploi civil – Empleo civil (Source – Fuente: IV)

ISIC – CITI – CIIU 1958

País Alcance	Total	1	2	3 [2]	4 [7]	5	6 [4]	7	8	9 [5]	0
Total [6]											
1974	15 946	6 666	236	2 834	70	746	1 563	482	.	3 350	–
1975	16 597	6 783	241	2 961	71	756	1 654	490	.	3 641	–
1976	17 301	7 000	253	3 138	76	801	1 725	511	.	3 797	–
1977	18 043	7 271	265	3 277	79	835	1 806	534	.	3 975	–
1978	18 826	7 555	277	3 424	79	872	1 892	557	.	4 170	–
1979	19 651	7 886	289	3 574	83	910	1 975	582	.	4 353	–

(a) The English designation of major divisions of economic activity is shown on the following page. – Les libellés en français des branches d'activité économique sont indiqués à la page précédente.

[1] Year beginning in July of year indicated. [2] Incl. repair and installation services. [3] Incl. electricity. [4] Incl. financing, insurance and real estate; excl. restaurants and hotels. [5] Incl. restaurants and hotels; excl. repair and installation services and sanitary services. [6] June of each year. [7] Incl. sanitary services.

[1] Année commençant en juillet de l'année indiquée. [2] Y compris les services de réparation et d'installation. [3] Y compris l'électricité. [4] Y compris les banques, les assurances et affaires immobilières; non compris les restaurants et hôtels. [5] Y compris les restaurants et hôtels; non compris les services de réparation et d'installation, et les services sanitaires. [6] Juin de chaque année. [7] Y compris les services sanitaires.

[1] Año que comienza en julio del año indicado. [2] Incl. los servicios de reparación y de instalación. [3] Incl. electricidad. [4] Incl. establecimientos financieros, seguros y bienes inmuebles; excl. restaurantes y hoteles. [5] Incl. restaurantes y hoteles; excl. los servicios de reparación y de instalación y los servicios de saneamiento. [6] Junio de cada año. [7] Incl. los servicios de saneamiento.

EMPLOYMENT

3 Structure of employment
Structure de l'emploi
Estructura del empleo

(Thousands – Milliers – Millares)

Country Scope	Total	Major divisions of economic activity [a]									
		1	2	3	4	5	6	7	8	9	0
		Agriculture, hunting, forestry and fishing	Mining, quarrying	Manufacturing	Electricity, gas, water	Construction	Trade, restaurants and hotels	Transport, storage, communication	Financing, insurance, real estate business services	Community, social and personal services	Activities not adequately defined

México — Civilian employment – Emploi civil – Empleo civil (Source – Fuente: IV)

Male – Hommes – Hombres [1]

1975	13 016	6 355	219	2 242	64	728	1 117	462	.	1 830	–
1976	13 449	6 539	231	2 364	68	771	1 147	481	.	1 849	–
1977	13 897	6 752	235	2 399	68	788	1 198	495	.	1 962	–
1978	14 489	7 016	245	2 507	68	822	1 255	516	.	2 059	–
1979	14 843	7 189	251	2 568	70	843	1 285	528	.	2 109	–

Female – Femmes – Mujeres [1]

1975	3 581	429	22	719	8	29	537	28	.	1 811	–
1976	3 852	461	23	773	8	30	578	30	.	1 948	–
1977	4 145	519	30	878	11	47	608	39	.	2 012	–
1978	4 337	539	32	917	11	49	637	41	.	2 111	–
1979	4 808	697	38	1 007	13	67	689	53	.	2 243	–

Netherlands Antilles — Civilian employment – Emploi civil – Empleo civil (Source – Fuente: I)

Total

1977	78.354	0.833	0.407	11.071	1.296	6.015	22.796	5.012	3.692	24.561	2.671
1978	76.805	0.680	0.389	11.455	1.370	6.430	22.420	5.995	4.610	23.456	.

Male – Hommes – Hombres

1977	51.343	0.779	0.391	8.746	1.208	5.790	12.629	4.424	2.088	14.186	1.102
1978	50.036	0.637	0.376	9.096	1.279	6.047	11.591	4.697	2.708	13.605	.

Female – Femmes – Mujeres

1977	27.011	0.054	0.016	2.325	0.088	0.225	10.167	0.588	1.604	10.375	1.569
1978	26.769	0.043	0.013	2.359	0.091	0.383	10.829	1.298	1.902	9.851	.

Nicaragua [2] — Insured persons – Personnes assurées – Personas aseguradas (Source – Fuente: II)

Total

1970	86.665	0.999	1.991	22.237	0.960	5.230	16.227	4.141	3.700	31.180	.
1971	83.454	1.106	1.788	22.196	0.990	3.803	15.914	4.097	3.559	29.992	0.009
1972	89.858	1.388	1.309	23.581	1.321	3.276	14.802	4.533	4.186	35.273	0.189
1973	91.824	1.465	1.185	22.402	1.279	8.208	11.873	4.354	4.394	36.547	0.117
1974	98.399	1.546	2.789	25.011	1.830	10.382	14.335	4.907	4.734	32.681	0.184
1975	115.804	1.603	3.318	26.107	1.886	13.567	17.007	5.165	6.194	40.654	0.303
1976	129.170	2.133	1.783	30.461	2.095	11.361	19.383	5.952	6.280	48.897	0.825
1977	138.232	2.636	3.105	32.100	2.179	12.140	21.284	6.500	6.843	51.379	0.066
1978	132.294	2.928	1.543	29.166	2.349	7.313	20.866	6.076	7.040	54.221	0.792
1979	129.517	...	...	...	...	...	...	...	...	...	...

[a] Les libellés en français des branches d'activité économique sont indiqués à la page suivante. – La designación en español de las grandes divisiones de actividad económica figura en la página precedente.

[1] June of each year. See notes of line "Total", preceding page. [2] Eight main cities of the country.

[1] Juin de chaque année. Voir notes de la ligne «Total» à la page précédente. [2] Huit villes principales du pays.

[1] Junio de cada año. Véanse notas de la línea «Total» en la página precedente. [2] Ocho ciudades principales del país.

172

3 Structure of employment
Structure de l'emploi
Estructura del empleo

(Thousands – Milliers – Millares)

Pays Portée	Total	Branches d'activité économique [a]									
		1 Agriculture, chasse, sylviculture et pêche	2 Industries extractives	3 Industries manufacturières	4 Electricité, gaz, eau	5 Construction	6 Commerce, restaurants et hôtels	7 Transports, entrepôts, communications	8 Banques, assurances, aff. imm., serv. aux entreprises	9 Services à collectivité, services soc. et pers.	0 Activités mal désignées
Panamá		*Civilian employment – Emploi civil – Empleo civil (Source – Fuente: I)*									
Total											[1]
1970	434.3	158.2	0.5	42.6	3.8	23.6	61.5	16.4	9.2	95.9	22.6
1971	441.3	151.8	0.6	42.7	4.7	26.4	60.2	18.3	9.8	102.7	24.1
1972	455.4	152.9	0.4	43.8	5.3	31.1	64.6	18.1	10.9	105.2	23.1
1973	464.1	...	...	...	...	...	...	...	...	...	...
1974	487.4	150.0	0.3	51.2	4.7	30.8	66.0	25.3	15.9	122.4	20.8
1975	461.2	147.3	0.4	42.9	4.6	30.5	60.1	22.7	13.8	119.6	19.3
1976	471.5	148.7	0.2	47.9	5.6	29.2	64.7	24.1	15.5	118.0	17.6
1977	470.4	148.0	0.4	48.0	5.6	24.0	64.2	25.5	15.4	120.9	18.4
1978	499.2	144.3	0.9	48.6	7.0	25.7	65.9	27.5	19.4	141.6	18.3
Male – Hommes – Hombres											
1974	358.5	146.5	0.3	35.5	3.9	30.1	41.7	20.3	9.9	53.2	17.1
1975	336.3	142.8	0.4	29.3	4.1	29.4	36.6	19.0	8.7	49.3	16.7
1976	344.8	144.8	0.2	32.9	4.9	28.4	39.7	19.9	9.4	50.4	14.2
1977	344.3	143.0	0.4	33.8	4.7	23.5	39.7	19.9	9.4	50.4	14.2
1978	355.0	140.1	0.9	34.9	5.9	24.9	40.4	22.7	12.3	58.4	14.5
Female – Femmes – Mujeres											
1974	128.9	3.5	–	15.7	0.8	0.7	24.3	5.0	6.0	69.2	3.7
1975	124.1	4.5	–	13.6	0.5	1.1	23.5	3.7	5.1	70.3	2.6
1976	126.7	3.9	–	15.0	0.7	0.8	25.0	4.2	6.1	67.6	3.4
1977	126.1	5.0	–	14.2	0.9	0.5	23.8	4.3	5.7	68.4	3.3
1978	144.2	4.2	–	13.7	1.1	0.8	25.5	4.8	7.1	83.1	3.9
Paraguay		*Civilian employment – Emploi civil – Empleo civil (Source – Fuente: IV)*									
ISIC – CITI – CIIU 1958											
Total				[2]	[3]		[4]			[5]	
1972	730.6	372.2	1.0	102.4	2.0	28.3	60.0	20.4	.	129.2	15.0
1973	737.9	399.6	1.4	122.9	2.1	30.5	64.0	21.6	.	126.1	13.0
1974	786.8	424.2	1.4	130.6	2.4	32.4	69.4	23.7	.	132.1	15.0
1975	807.6	397.6	1.4	112.8	2.7	38.0	80.1	24.5	.	150.5	–
1976	854.4	420.4	1.5	119.5	3.0	40.2	84.7	25.9	.	159.2	–
1977	882.6	421.4	1.7	124.0	3.3	45.1	91.1	27.6	.	168.4	–
1978	911.8	428.3	1.8	128.9	3.6	48.6	95.9	28.5	.	175.8	–
1979	0.9	0.4	–	132.3	3.9	52.4	101.2	30.3	.	183.9	–
Puerto Rico [6]		*Civilian employment – Emploi civil – Empleo civil (Source – Fuente: I)*									
Total							[4]		[7]	[8]	
1970	694	66	–	132	12	78	126	34	16	224	.
1971	719	59	–	137	12	83	131	35	17	240	.
1972	747	54	–	140	14	77	135	36	18	269	.
1973	768	50	–	146	14	81	140	37	20	271	.
1974	764	52	–	147	15	77	148	38	19	272	.
1975	715	47	–	132	14	60	144	33	19	270	.
1976	734	47	–	137	13	47	140	35	19	294	.
1977	750	42	–	149	13	43	147	37	20	299	.
1978	796	39	1	160	13	48	152	37	22	324	.
1979	345	41	1	158	15	47	154	36	22	.	.

[a] La designación en español de las grandes divisiones de actividad económica figura en la página siguiente. – The English designation of major divisions of economic activity is shown on the preceding page.

[1] Canal Zone. [2] Incl. repair and installation services. [3] Incl. sanitary services. [4] Incl. financing, insurance and real estate; excl. restaurants and hotels. [5] Incl. restaurants and hotels; excl. repair and installation services and sanitary services. [6] Persons aged 14 years and over; beginning 1977: 16 years and over. [7] Excl. business services. [8] Incl. restaurants, hotels and business services; excl. repair and installation services and sanitary services.

[1] Zone du canal. [2] Y compris les services de réparation et d'installation. [3] Y compris les services sanitaires. [4] Y compris les banques, les assurances et affaires immobilières; non compris les restaurants et hôtels. [5] Y compris les restaurants et hôtels; non compris les services de réparation et d'installation, et les services sanitaires. [6] Personnes âgées de 14 ans et plus; à partir de 1977: 16 ans et plus. [7] Non compris les services aux entreprises. [8] Y compris les restaurants, les hôtels et les services aux entreprises; non compris les services de réparation et d'installation, et les services sanitaires.

[1] Zona del Canal. [2] Incl. los servicios de reparación y de instalación. [3] Incl. los servicios de saneamiento. [4] Incl. establecimientos financieros, seguros y bienes inmuebles; excl. restaurantes y hoteles. [5] Incl. restaurantes y hoteles; excl. los servicios de reparación y de instalación y los servicios de saneamiento. [6] Personas de 14 años y más; a partir de 1977: 16 años y más. [7] Excl. servicios para empresas. [8] Incl. restaurantes, hoteles y los servicios para empresas; excl. los servicios de reparación y de instalación, y los servicios de saneamiento.

EMPLOYMENT

3 Structure of employment
Structure de l'emploi
Estructura del empleo

(Thousands – Milliers – Millares)

País Alcance	Total	Grandes divisiones de actividad económica [a]									
		1 Agricultura, caza, silvicultura y pesca	2 Minas, canteras	3 Industrias manufactureras	4 Electricidad, gas, agua	5 Construcción	6 Comercio, restaurantes y hoteles	7 Transportes, almacenaje, comunicaciones	8 Bancos, seguros, bienes inm., serv. para empresas	9 Servicios comunales, sociales y personales	0 Actividades no bien especificadas
Puerto Rico [1]		*Civilian employment – Emploi civil – Empleo civil (Source – Fuente: I)*									
Male – Hommes – Hombres [2]											
1978	520	38	1	87	12	48	112	33	13	176	.
1979	188	40	1	85	14	46	112	32	13	.	.
Female – Femmes – Mujeres [2]											
1978	276	1	–	73	1	–	40	4	9	148	.
1979	288	1	–	73	1	1	42	4	9	157	.
Trinidad and Tobago [3]		*Civilian employment – Emploi civil – Empleo civil (Source – Fuente: I)*									
ISIC – CITI – CIIU 1958				4		5	6			7	
Total											
1970	317.2	77.8	.	65.7	.	41.8	44.8	20.6	.	66.5	–
1971 [8]	321.4	71.8	.	64.0	.	47.8	44.3	21.1	.	72.5	–
1972	...	...	...	...	...	...	...	...	...	...	...
1973	323.6	53.0	.	61.8	.	46.4	58.1	27.2	.	75.6	1.5
1974	333.9	54.6	.	65.0	.	45.8	61.1	29.3	.	77.5	0.6
1975	332.4	48.0	.	67.1	.	45.5	63.0	27.4	.	80.8	0.6
1976	...	...	...	...	...	...	...	...	...	...	...
1977 [8]	370.6	54.4	.	72.6	.	58.9	68.4	31.1	.	84.4	0.8
1978 [8]	385.4	50.4	.	75.4	.	69.1	65.7	29.9	.	94.6	0.4
United States		*Registered employees – Salariés inscrits – Asalariados registrados (Source – Fuente: III)*									
Total											
1970	70 880	.	623	19 367	691	3 588	15 757	3 824	6 049	20 981	–
1971	71 214	.	609	18 623	697	3 704	16 090	3 779	6 207	21 505	–
1972	73 675	.	628	19 151	712	3 889	16 724	3 830	6 512	22 231	–
1973	76 790	.	642	20 154	729	4 097	17 415	3 927	6 862	22 965	–
1974	78 265	.	697	20 077	743	4 020	17 811	3 982	7 121	23 814	–
1975	76 945	.	752	18 323	731	3 525	17 910	3 811	7 163	24 730	–
1976	79 382	.	779	18 997	733	3 576	18 640	3 849	7 433	25 375	–
1977	82 423	.	813	19 682	746	3 851	19 429	3 967	7 894	26 042	–
1978	86 446	.	851	20 476	777	4 271	20 427	4 150	8 514	26 981	–
1979	89 482	.	951	20 972	...	4 644	...	...	...	...	–
Male – Hommes – Hombres											
1970	44 748	.	586	13 919	587	3 402	9 396	2 971	3 246	10 642	–
1971	44 748	.	572	13 394	593	3 505	9 585	2 928	3 319	10 851	–
1972	46 134	.	588	13 681	607	3 670	9 977	2 981	3 481	11 150	–
1973	47 802	.	599	14 289	620	3 856	10 315	3 049	3 619	11 455	–
1974	48 141	.	648	14 228	628	3 758	10 402	3 079	3 698	11 700	–
1975	46 767	.	697	13 066	615	3 269	10 412	2 931	3 678	12 099	–
1976	47 812	.	719	13 390	614	3 295	10 776	2 958	3 774	12 286	–
1977	49 184	.	748	13 802	621	3 547	11 186	3 041	3 950	12 290	–
1978	51 193	.	775	14 245	645	3 936	11 671	3 150	4 188	12 584	–
1979	52 530	.	866	14 508	...	4 272	...	...	...	...	–
Female – Femmes – Mujeres											
1970	26 132	.	37	5 448	104	186	6 362	853	2 802	10 339	–
1971	26 466	.	37	5 229	103	199	6 504	852	2 888	10 654	–
1972	27 541	.	40	5 470	104	219	6 747	849	3 031	11 081	–
1973	28 988	.	43	5 865	109	241	7 100	878	3 243	11 510	–
1974	30 124	.	49	5 849	114	262	7 409	904	3 423	12 115	–
1975	30 178	.	55	5 257	116	256	7 497	880	3 485	12 632	–
1976	31 570	.	60	5 607	119	281	7 865	891	3 659	13 089	–
1977	33 239	.	65	5 880	124	304	8 243	927	3 944	13 752	–
1978	35 253	.	76	6 231	132	335	8 756	1 000	3 944	13 752	–
1979	36 952	.	91	6 464	...	372	...	...	...	...	–

[a] The English designation of major divisions of economic activity is shown on the following page. – Les libellés en français des branches d'activité économique sont indiqués à la page précédente.

[1] Persons aged 16 years and over. [2] See notes of line "Total", preceding page. [3] Persons aged 15 years and over. [4] Incl. mining, quarrying, repair and installation services. [5] Incl. electricity, gas, water and sanitary services. [6] Incl. financing, insurance and real estate; excl. restaurants and hotels. [7] Incl. restaurants and hotels; excl. repair and installation services and sanitary services. [8] First semester.

[1] Personnes âgées de 16 ans et plus. [2] Voir notes de la ligne «Total» à la page précédente. [3] Personnes âgées de 15 ans et plus. [4] Y compris les industries extractives, les services de réparation et d'installation. [5] Y compris l'électricité, le gaz, l'eau et les services sanitaires. [6] Y compris les banques, les assurances et affaires immobilières; non compris les restaurants et hôtels. [7] Y compris les restaurants et hôtels; non compris les services de réparation et d'installation, et les services sanitaires. [8] Premier semestre.

[1] Personas de 16 años y más. [2] Véanse notas de la línea «Total» en la página precedente. [3] Personas de 15 años y más. [4] Incl. minas, canteras y los servicios de reparación y de instalación. [5] Incl. electricidad, gas, agua y los servicios de saneamiento. [6] Incl. establecimientos financieros, seguros y bienes inmuebles; excl. restaurantes y hoteles. [7] Incl. restaurantes y hoteles; excl. los servicios de reparación y de instalación y los servicios de saneamiento. [8] Primer semestre.

3 Structure of employment
Structure de l'emploi
Estructura del empleo

(Thousands – Milliers – Millares)

Country Scope	Total	1 Agriculture, hunting, forestry and fishing	2 Mining, quarrying	3 Manufacturing	4 Electricity, gas, water	5 Construction	6 Trade, restaurants and hotels	7 Transport, storage, communication	8 Financing, insurance, real estate business services	9 Community, social and personal services	0 Activities not adequately defined
Uruguay [1]				*Civilian employment – Emploi civil – Empleo civil (Source – Fuente: I)*							
Total [2]											
1976	467.2	7.6	.	129.6	8.2	16.7	73.7	38.0	23.0	170.3	0.1
1977	478.5	7.3	.	139.5	7.4	14.8	78.5	36.4	23.2	171.2	0.2
1978	471.3	6.5	.	142.6	7.5	17.2	80.3	33.6	24.6	158.6	0.4
1979	484.3	6.7	.	141.8	8.0	19.3	77.6	35.5	25.2	169.8	0.4
Venezuela				*Civilian employment – Emploi civil – Empleo civil (Source – Fuente: I)*							
Total [2]											
1975	3 504.31	698.57	46.91	538.46	43.27	249.09	655.65	199.03	123.19	945.48	4.66
1976	3 703.21	696.39	43.62	587.58	39.76	295.48	687.30	219.75	139.27	991.66	2.40
1977	3 870.39	679.48	54.53	628.64	43.10	325.47	678.49	262.54	159.33	1 036.20	2.61
1978	3 994.52	640.04	48.69	677.86	46.71	369.20	696.68	281.86	170.54	1 059.90	3.02
Male – Hommes – Hombres [2]											
1975	2 546.73	650.02	44.16	370.29	38.46	243.50	460.17	183.57	85.60	467.80	3.16
1976	2 668.03	647.79	40.69	411.09	35.07	287.13	470.10	201.31	92.94	480.80	1.77
1977	2 806.73	636.01	51.15	444.49	37.57	317.56	465.25	242.55	103.08	507.32	1.75
1978	2 903.37	609.53	44.79	689.95	40.51	360.42	673.41	259.43	110.23	512.81	2.27
Female – Femmes – Mujeres [2]											
1975	957.79	48.55	2.76	168.17	4.82	5.59	195.48	15.46	37.59	477.67	1.50
1976	1 035.18	48.60	2.93	176.49	4.69	8.35	217.20	18.44	46.33	511.52	0.63
1977	1 063.66	43.48	3.38	184.14	5.53	7.92	213.24	19.99	56.24	528.88	0.86
1978	1 091.15	30.51	3.90	187.91	6.20	8.78	223.27	22.43	60.31	547.09	0.75

ASIA – ASIE – ASIA

Country Scope	Total	1	2	3	4	5	6	7	8	9	0
Bangladesh				*Registered employees – Salariés inscrits – Asalariados registrados (Source – Fuente: III)*							
ISIC – CITI – CIIU 1958											
Total [3]				[4]	[5]		[6]			[7]	
1975	885.8	114.5	0.1	298.8	20.9	44.9	26.4	31.3	.	348.9	.
1977	1 096.6	146.9	–	368.4	20.6	41.7	51.7	58.7	.	408.6	.
1979	1 172.9	136.0	0.5	398.1	22.4	33.7	65.4	68.8	.	447.7	.
Burma				*Civilian employment – Emploi civil – Empleo civil (Source – Fuente: IV)*							
Total										[8]	
1978	12 640	8 531	67	929	15	184	1 206	420	729	559	
1979	12 935	8 697	68	968	15	189	1 239	430	760	569	
Cyprus				*Civilian employment – Emploi civil – Empleo civil (Source – Fuente: III)*							
Total											
1976	159.3	45.2	2.3	27.8	1.3	10.8	24.3	7.7	4.7	35.2	–
1977	168.0	45.4	2.1	30.7	1.2	15.6	25.2	7.7	4.8	35.3	–
1978	174.0	44.4	2.1	34.5	1.3	16.9	25.6	8.0	5.0	36.2	–
1979	177.8	44.0	1.9	35.6	1.4	17.4	27.1	8.1	5.1	37.2	–

(a) Les libellés en français des branches d'activité économique sont indiqués à la page suivante. – La designación en español de las grandes divisiones de actividad económica figura en la página precedente.

[1] Montevideo only. [2] Second semester of each year. [3] Biennial survey. [4] Incl. repair and installation services. [5] Incl. sanitary services. [6] Incl. financing, insurance and real estate; excl. restaurants and hotels. [7] Incl. restaurants and hotels; excl. repair and installation services and sanitary services. [8] Incl. activities not adequately defined.

[1] Montevideo seulement. [2] Second semestre de chaque année. [3] Enquête biennale. [4] Y compris les services de réparation et d'installation. [5] Y compris les services sanitaires. [6] Y compris les banques, les assurances et affaires immobilières; non compris les restaurants et hôtels. [7] Y compris les restaurants et hôtels; non compris les services de réparation et d'installation, et les services sanitaires. [8] Y compris les activités mal désignées.

[1] Montevideo solamente. [2] Segundo semestre de cada año. [3] Encuesta bienal. [4] Incl. los servicios de reparación y de instalación. [5] Incl. los servicios de saneamiento. [6] Incl. establecimientos financieros, seguros y bienes inmuebles; excl. restaurantes y hoteles. [7] Incl. restaurantes y hoteles; excl. los servicios de reparación y de instalación y los servicios de saneamiento. [8] Incl. actividades no bien especificadas.

EMPLOYMENT

3 Structure of employment
Structure de l'emploi
Estructura del empleo

(Thousands – Milliers – Millares)

Pays Portée	Total	Branches d'activité économique (a)									
		1 Agriculture, chasse, sylviculture et pêche	2 Industries extractives	3 Industries manufacturières	4 Electricité, gaz, eau	5 Construction	6 Commerce, restaurants et hôtels	7 Transports, entrepôts, communications	8 Banques, assurances, aff. imm., serv. aux entreprises	9 Services à collectivité, services soc. et pers.	0 Activités mal désignées
Cyprus		*Civilian employment – Emploi civil – Empleo civil (Source – Fuente: III)*									
Male – Hommes – Hombres											
1976	100.6	20.5	2.2	16.3	1.2	10.1	16.0	6.7	3.1	24.5	–
1977	105.3	20.1	2.0	16.1	1.1	14.6	16.8	6.7	3.1	24.8	–
1978	111.0	22.0	2.0	17.9	1.2	15.7	16.8	6.9	3.2	25.3	–
1979	112.6	21.8	0.8	18.4	1.3	15.9	17.5	6.9	3.3	25.7	–
Female – Femmes – Mujeres											
1976	58.7	24.7	0.1	11.5	0.1	0.7	8.3	1.0	1.6	10.7	–
1977	62.7	25.3	0.1	14.6	0.1	1.0	8.4	1.0	1.7	10.5	–
1978	63.0	22.4	0.1	16.6	0.1	1.2	8.8	1.1	1.8	10.9	–
1979	65.2	22.2	0.1	17.2	0.1	1.5	9.6	1.2	1.8	11.5	–
Hong Kong [1]		*Registered employed – Effectif occupé – Efectivo ocupado (Source – Fuente: III)*									
Total						[2]		[2]		[2]	[3]
1970	690.2	.	1.1	549.2	6.7	.	.	45.8	19.8	67.6	.
1971	704.2	.	1.3	564.4	6.4	.	.	39.8	21.8	70.6	.
1972	724.9	.	1.1	578.9	6.0	.	.	41.2	23.8	74.4	.
1973	745.1	.	1.1	582.7	6.6	.	.	43.9	34.2	76.6	.
1974	768.7	.	0.8	600.1	6.3	.	.	45.3	37.1	79.0	.
1975	▮1 340.8	.	0.6	678.9	6.4	.	353.8	44.0	66.0	85.7	105.5
1976	▮1 555.7	.	0.5	773.7	6.5	48.8	371.1	51.5	72.5	124.0	107.2
1977	1 606.3	.	0.7	755.1	6.7	63.0	386.3	57.6	83.1	140.7	113.1
1978	1 742.6	.	0.6	816.7	7.2	73.7	411.4	61.5	98.2	152.5	120.8
1979	1 847.7	.	0.8	870.9	7.9	81.9	418.6	68.0	113.4	158.8	127.3
India [4]		*Registered employed – Effectif occupé – Efectivo ocupado (Source – Fuente: III)*									
Total [5]		[4]									
1975	19 671	1 158	816	5 127	547	1 083	362	2 442	660	7 477	–
1976	20 207	1 228	851	5 271	571	1 086	343	2 491	673	7 694	–
1977	20 744	1 314	887	5 391	598	1 092	350	2 538	720	7 855	–
1978	21 484	1 482	885	5 677	633	1 080	357	2 581	761	8 028	–
1979	22 186	1 621	896	5 839	670	1 114	379	2 661	846	8 159	–
Male – Hommes – Hombres [5]											
1975	17 440	752	733	4 674	537	1 016	343	2 390	617	6 379	–
1976	17 810	779	761	4 757	560	1 026	328	2 434	631	6 534	–
1977	18 250	830	795	4 864	587	1 034	333	2 478	672	6 657	–
1978	18 828	947	793	5 105	621	1 022	338	2 517	707	6 777	–
1979	19 426	1 036	810	5 266	656	1 055	358	2 594	780	780	–
Female – Femmes – Mujeres [5]											
1975	2 231	406	83	453	10	67	19	52	43	1 098	–
1976	2 397	449	90	514	11	60	15	57	42	1 160	–
1977	2 494	484	92	526	11	58	17	60	48	1 198	–
1978	2 656	535	92	572	12	58	18	64	54	1 251	–
1979	2 760	585	86	573	14	59	21	68	69	1 289	–
Israel [6]		*Civilian employment – Emploi civil – Empleo civil (Source – Fuente: I)*									
Total			[7]								
1970	963.2	84.8	.	233.3	11.3	80.1	125.0	72.2	49.7	303.8	3.0
1971	997.1	84.5	.	239.6	11.0	88.3	126.4	74.0	56.7	314.1	2.5
1972	1 047.0	83.4	.	248.3	8.8	99.3	137.0	76.9	60.2	328.7	4.4
1973	1 094.4	82.1	.	273.2	10.3	95.9	138.4	79.0	66.7	344.8	4.0
1974	1 096.5	71.5	.	278.4	10.3	88.6	131.2	83.2	68.4	358.1	6.8
1975	1 112.5	71.6	.	274.5	11.1	90.1	136.0	80.4	73.7	369.5	5.6
1976	1 126.8	72.2	.	274.1	11.7	86.3	139.6	78.7	76.2	381.4	7.0
1977	1 159.2	72.6	.	277.6	13.5	85.0	140.9	80.1	82.9	397.9	8.8
1978	1 212.6	73.9	.	285.0	13.3	80.3	143.4	82.7	91.4	429.4	13.2
1979	1 241.0	72.1	.	298.3	11.4	82.2	144.7	84.5	96.5	438.6	12.7

(a) La designación en español de las grandes divisiones de actividad económica figura en la página siguiente. – The English designation of major divisions of economic activity is shown on the preceding page.

[1] Fourth quarter of each year. [2] Major industry division not fully covered. [3] Public administration. [4] Excl. agricultural establishments in the private sector. [5] March of each year. [6] Persons aged 14 years and over. Data cover also certain territories under occupation by Israeli military forces since June 1967. [7] Incl. mining and quarrying.

[1] Quatrième trimestre de chaque année. [2] Branche d'activité économique non complètement couverte. [3] Administration publique. [4] Non compris les établissements agricoles du secteur privé. [5] Mars de chaque année. [6] Personnes âgées de 14 ans et plus. Les données couvrent aussi certains territoires occupés par les forces armées israéliennes depuis juin 1967. [7] Y compris les industries extractives.

[1] Cuarto trimestre de cada año. [2] Gran división de actividad económica no completamente cubierta. [3] Administración pública. [4] Excl. los establecimientos agrícolas del sector privado. [5] Marzo de cada año. [6] Personas de 14 años y más. Los datos cubren también ciertos territorios ocupados por las fuerzas armadas israelíes desde junio de 1967. [7] Incl. minas y canteras.

3 Structure of employment
Structure de l'emploi
Estructura del empleo

(Thousands – Milliers – Millares)

País Alcance	Total	1 Agricultura, caza, silvicultura y pesca	2 Minas, canteras	3 Industrias manufactureras	4 Electricidad, gas, agua	5 Construcción	6 Comercio, restaurantes y hoteles	7 Transportes, almacenaje, comunicaciones	8 Bancos, seguros, bienes inm., serv. para empresas	9 Servicios comunales, sociales y personales	0 Actividades no bien especificadas
Israel [1]				*Civilian employment – Emploi civil – Empleo civil (Source – Fuente: I)*							
Male – Hommes – Hombres [2]											
1973	746.8	62.4	.	207.4	9.6	92.7	91.9	68.0	36.5	176.7	2.1
1974	744.1	56.0	.	217.0	9.0	85.1	86.2	70.9	36.6	178.6	4.6
1975	748.2	54.5	.	215.4	9.6	86.7	88.5	69.3	39.8	180.7	3.8
1976	753.1	55.5	.	215.2	9.9	82.6	91.5	65.7	41.1	187.2	4.4
1977	769.7	56.2	.	217.1	11.8	81.2	93.3	67.1	44.1	193.2	6.0
1978	789.6	56.8	.	221.4	12.0	76.2	94.9	68.7	48.2	203.0	8.4
1979	799.7	55.1	.	227.6	9.7	77.4	95.9	70.1	50.9	205.0	8.0
Female – Femmes – Mujeres [2]											
1973	347.5	19.9	.	66.0	0.7	3.2	46.5	11.2	30.4	168.2	1.1
1974	352.7	15.5	.	61.5	1.2	3.2	45.0	12.4	31.9	179.2	2.5
1975	364.1	16.5	.	59.1	1.6	3.4	47.9	11.0	34.0	188.6	2.2
1976	374.1	16.7	.	59.0	1.6	3.8	47.9	12.9	35.1	194.3	2.8
1977	389.8	16.3	.	60.4	1.9	3.8	47.5	12.9	38.9	205.1	3.0
1978	423.2	17.1	.	63.5	1.4	4.1	48.6	14.1	43.1	226.6	4.7
1979	441.3	17.1	.	70.7	1.7	4.7	48.9	14.3	45.6	233.7	4.6
Japan [3]				*Civilian employment – Emploi civil – Empleo civil (Source – Fuente: I)*							
Total							[4]		[5]	[6]	
1970	50 940	8 860	200	13 770	280	3 940	10 120	3 240	1 320	9 120	70
1971	51 210	8 150	190	13 830	290	4 140	10 350	3 330	1 450	9 420	70
1972	51 260	7 550	160	13 830	290	4 330	10 500	3 270	1 490	9 420	70
1973	52 590	7 050	130	14 430	340	4 670	10 850	3 370	1 570	9 750	80
1974	52 370	6 750	140	14 270	330	4 640	10 970	3 310	1 630	10 060	100
1975	52 230	6 610	160	13 460	320	4 790	11 270	3 320	1 700	10 220	100
1976	52 710	6 430	180	13 450	330	4 920	11 510	3 410	2 760	10 510	100
1977	53 420	6 340	190	13 400	310	4 990	11 930	3 410	2 860	9 630	100
1978	54 080	6 330	150	13 260	320	5 200	12 100	3 420	2 960	9 880	120
1979	54 790	6 130	120	13 330	330	5 360	12 280	3 490	3 110	10 240	100
Male – Hommes – Hombres											
1970	30 910	4 360	170	8 590	250	3 410	5 470	2 820	710	5 080	50
1971	31 410	4 020	170	8 690	260	3 600	5 690	2 910	800	5 230	50
1972	31 680	3 780	140	8 780	250	3 770	5 730	2 870	810	5 500	50
1973	32 350	3 490	120	9 020	300	4 040	5 870	2 960	880	5 600	50
1974	32 650	3 400	120	9 100	290	4 020	6 030	2 920	920	5 770	70
1975	32 700	3 300	150	8 710	280	4 200	6 190	2 910	940	5 950	70
1976	32 940	3 270	170	8 550	280	4 270	6 360	2 990	1 660	5 390	70
1977	33 090	3 240	170	8 400	270	4 330	6 520	3 000	1 640	5 390	60
1978	33 250	3 230	140	8 180	280	4 510	6 540	3 040	1 720	5 430	80
1979	33 630	3 110	110	8 240	280	4 620	6 630	3 080	1 790	5 700	70
Female – Femmes – Mujeres											
1970	20 030	4 510	30	5 180	30	530	4 650	420	610	4 040	20
1971	19 820	4 120	30	5 140	30	550	4 650	420	650	4 190	20
1972	19 570	3 770	20	5 040	40	560	4 780	400	680	4 250	30
1973	20 230	3 560	10	5 430	40	630	4 990	410	690	4 450	30
1974	19 730	3 370	10	5 180	40	600	4 950	390	700	4 450	40
1975	19 530	3 310	10	4 750	40	590	5 080	400	760	4 560	30
1976	19 760	3 160	20	4 910	40	650	5 150	420	1 180	4 230	30
1977	20 330	3 090	10	5 000	40	660	5 410	400	1 230	4 440	40
1978	20 830	3 100	20	5 070	40	690	5 560	390	1 230	4 700	30
1979	21 170	3 020	20	5 080	50	740	5 650	400	1 330	4 850	40

(a) The English designation of major divisions of economic activity is shown on the following page. – Les libellés en français des branches d'activité économique sont indiqués à la page précédente.

[1] Persons aged 14 years and over. Data cover also certain territories under occupation by Israeli military forces since June 1967. [2] See notes of line "Total", preceding page. [3] Persons aged 15 years and over. [4] Excl. hotels. [5] Excl. business services. [6] Incl. hotels and business services.

[1] Personnes âgées de 14 ans et plus. Les données couvrent aussi certains territoires occupés par les forces armées israéliennes depuis juin 1967. [2] Voir notes de la ligne «Total» à la page précédente. [3] Personnes âgées de 15 ans et plus. [4] Non compris les hôtels. [5] Non compris les services aux entreprises. [6] Y compris les restaurants et les services aux entreprises.

[1] Personas de 14 años y más. Los datos cubren también ciertos territorios ocupados por las fuerzas armadas israelíes desde junio de 1967. [2] Véanse notas de la línea «Total» en la página precedente. [3] Personas de 15 años y más. [4] Excl. hoteles. [5] Excl. servicios para empresas. [6] Incl. restaurantes y los servicios para empresas.

3 Structure of employment
Structure de l'emploi
Estructura del empleo

(Thousands – Milliers – Millares)

Country Scope	Total	Major divisions of economic activity [a]									
		1 Agriculture, hunting, forestry and fishing	2 Mining, quarrying	3 Manu-facturing	4 Electricity, gas, water	5 Construction	6 Trade, restaurants and hotels	7 Transport, storage, communi-cation	8 Financing, insurance, real estate business services	9 Community, social and personal services	0 Activities not adequately defined

Jordan — Registered employees – Salariés inscrits – Asalariados registrados (Source – Fuente: III)

Total [1]

Year	Total	1	2	3	4	5	6	7	8	9	0
1972	61.67	–	1.13	8.89	1.13	0.28	3.45	2.79	3.04	40.94	–
1973	71.73	–	1.52	9.22	1.34	0.74	4.43	2.85	1.88	49.75	–
1974	84.22	–	3.00	11.84	1.41	3.16	5.02	2.96	2.46	54.37	–
1975	87.42	–	3.16	11.81	1.53	3.61	4.54	3.93	2.70	56.13	–
1976	92.88	–	3.82	11.97	1.72	4.82	0.50	4.37	3.17	58.10	–
1977	91.47	–	3.59	12.53	1.50	4.41	5.03	4.58	3.60	56.22	–

Korea, Republic of — Civilian employment – Emploi civil – Empleo civil (Source – Fuente: I)

Total [2]

Year	Total	1	2	3	4	5	6	7	8	9	0
1971	10 066	4 876	92	1 336	25	348	1 575	369	132	1 313	–
1972	10 559	5 346	54	1 445	45	392	1 588	355	103	1 231	–
1973	11 139	5 569	47	1 774	35	371	1 633	360	128	1 222	–
1974	11 586	5 584	50	2 012	35	450	1 760	359	147	1 189	–
1975	11 830	5 425	60	2 205	35	511	1 876	361	151	1 206	–
1976	12 556	5 601	65	2 678	38	529	1 878	390	156	1 221	–
1977	12 929	5 405	103	2 798	33	625	1 967	479	203	1 316	–
1978	13 490	5 181	107	3 016	30	821	2 130	531	246	1 428	–
1979	13 664	4 887	111	3 126	46	836	2 304	610	259	1 485	–

Male – Hommes – Hombres [2]

Year	Total	1	2	3	4	5	6	7	8	9	0
1971	6 371	2 837	81	870	24	339	881	344	108	887	–
1972	6 665	3 050	48	955	44	383	905	329	89	862	–
1973	6 923	3 223	43	1 090	33	360	895	330	105	844	–
1974	7 275	3 266	45	1 289	34	427	961	327	115	811	–
1975	7 489	3 172	55	1 450	34	486	1 038	327	112	815	–
1976	7 736	3 213	55	1 657	37	503	974	351	119	827	–
1977	8 126	3 157	97	1 702	30	576	1 053	439	151	921	–
1978	8 347	2 896	100	1 824	28	758	1 107	485	179	970	–
1979	8 409	2 709	102	1 888	40	772	1 176	554	182	986	–

Female – Femmes – Mujeres [2]

Year	Total	1	2	3	4	5	6	7	8	9	0
1971	3 695	2 039	11	466	1	9	694	25	24	426	–
1972	3 894	2 296	6	490	1	9	683	26	14	369	–
1973	4 216	2 346	4	684	2	11	738	30	23	378	–
1974	4 311	2 318	5	723	1	23	799	32	32	378	–
1975	4 341	2 253	5	755	1	25	838	34	39	391	–
1976	4 820	2 388	10	1 021	1	26	904	39	37	394	–
1977	4 803	2 248	6	1 096	3	49	914	40	52	395	–
1978	5 143	2 285	7	1 192	2	63	1 023	46	65	458	–
1979	5 255	2 178	9	1 238	6	64	1 128	56	77	499	–

Malaysia: Sabah — Registered employees – Salariés inscrits – Asalariados registrados (Source – Fuente: III)

ISIC – CITI – CIIU 1958
Total [3]

Year	Total	1	2	3	4	5	6	7	8	9	0
1973	47.189	26.976	0.218	1.658	0.785	8.934	0.838	3.000	.	2.245	2.535
1974	51.534	28.187	0.322	3.410	0.884	9.778	0.993	3.120	.	2.531	2.308
1975	54.988	31.936	0.848	2.525	0.975	8.446	0.945	3.088	.	1.632	3.121
1976	58.076	32.966	1.434	2.281	1.076	7.875	0.998	3.173	.	1.723	4.563
1977	58.299	36.719	1.706	2.139	1.165	7.352	1.274	3.366	.	1.916	2.662
1978	69.010	47.509	1.927	2.316	1.009	8.383	1.381	2.701	.	3.058	0.726
1979	80.312	50.389	1.878	3.826	1.367	9.966	2.406	2.971	.	4.901	2.608

[a] Les libellés en français des branches d'activité économique sont indiqués à la page suivante. – La designación en español de las grandes divisiones de actividad económica figura en la página precedente.

[1] Aug. of each year. [2] Persons aged 14 years and over. [3] Dec. of each year. [4] Incl. repair and installation services. [5] Incl. sanitary services. [6] Incl. financing, insurance and real estate; excl. restaurants and hotels. [7] Incl. restaurants and hotels; excl. repair and installation services and sanitary services.

[1] Août de chaque année. [2] Personnes âgées de 14 ans et plus. [3] Déc. de chaque année. [4] Y compris les services de réparation et d'installation. [5] Y compris les services sanitaires. [6] Y compris les banques, les assurances et affaires immobilières; non compris les restaurants et hôtels. [7] Y compris les restaurants et hôtels; non compris les services de réparation et d'installation, et les services sanitaires.

[1] Agosto de cada año. [2] Personas de 14 años y más. [3] Dic. de cada año. [4] Incl. los servicios de reparación y de instalación. [5] Incl. los servicios de saneamiento. [6] Incl. establecimientos financieros, seguros y bienes inmuebles; excl. restaurantes y hoteles. [7] Incl. restaurantes y hoteles; excl. los servicios de reparación y de instalación y los servicios de saneamiento.

3 Structure of employment
Structure de l'emploi
Estructura del empleo

(Thousands – Milliers – Millares)

Pays / Portée	Total	Branches d'activité économique (a)									
		1 Agriculture, chasse, sylviculture et pêche	2 Industries extractives	3 Industries manufacturières	4 Electricité, gaz, eau	5 Construction	6 Commerce, restaurants et hôtels	7 Transports, entrepôts, communications	8 Banques, assurances, aff. imm., serv. aux entreprises	9 Services à collectivité, services soc. et pers.	0 Activités mal désignées
Malaysia: Sabah — Registered employees – Salariés inscrits – Asalariados registrados (Source – Fuente: III)											
Male – Hommes – Hombres [1]											
1979	66.266	40.709	1.823	2.417	1.250	8.731	1.916	2.813	.	4.097	2.510
Female – Femmes – Mujeres [1]											
1979	14.046	9.680	0.055	1.409	0.117	1.235	0.490	0.158	.	0.804	0.098
Pakistan — Civilian employment – Emploi civil – Empleo civil (Source – Fuente: IV)											
Total											
1974	20 093	11 517	9	2 506	74	685	1 987	973	173	1 461	627
1975	20 424	11 192	31	2 783	1	858	2 265	994	137	1 997	67
1976	20 679	11 332	31	2 819	102	866	2 293	1 007	138	2 023	68
1977	21 295	11 670	32	2 903	105	891	2 362	1 037	142	2 083	70
1978	21 930	12 018	33	2 989	107	919	2 432	1 068	147	2 145	72
1979	22 596	12 383	34	3 080	111	946	2 506	1 100	151	2 210	75
Philippines [2] — Civilian employment – Emploi civil – Empleo civil (Source – Fuente: I)											
ISIC – CITI – CIIU 1958				[3]	[4]		[5]			[6]	
Total											
1970	11 358	6 100	52	1 354	33	438	839	498	.	1 861	183
1971	12 246	6 091	58	1 443	55	438	1 517	521	.	2 095	28
1972	12 834	6 907	52	1 396	42	429	1 558	486	.	1 954	10
1973	13 450	7 352	62	1 406	38	395	1 566	509	.	2 095	27
1974	13 885	7 727	47	1 442	38	394	1 559	510	.	2 143	25
1975	14 143	7 633	49	1 546	44	437	1 599	510	.	2 290	35
1976	14 238	7 659	81	1 598	51	428	1 398	600	.	2 374	49
1977	14 547	7 276	72	1 638	56	522	1 530	680	.	2 658	115
Male – Hommes – Hombres											
1970	7 893	4 930	49	621	32	435	380	487	.	823	136
1971	8 317	4 905	54	785	53	434	662	504	.	903	17
1972	8 725	5 492	44	765	39	425	652	468	.	835	5
1973	9 067	5 796	57	791	34	388	661	490	.	834	16
1974	9 437	6 088	42	806	35	388	706	494	.	863	15
1975	9 489	6 038	47	839	40	431	695	488	.	892	19
1976	9 630	5 949	78	919	47	424	583	570	.	1 024	36
1977	9 946	5 846	68	885	50	516	601	648	.	1 252	80

(a) La designación en español de las grandes divisiones de actividad económica figura en la página siguiente. – The English designation of major divisions of economic activity is shown on the preceding page.

[1] See notes of line "Total", preceding page. [2] Persons aged 10 years and over; beginning 1976: 15 years and over. [3] Incl. repair and installation services. [4] Incl. sanitary services. [5] Incl. financing, insurance and real estate; excl. restaurants and hotels. [6] Incl. restaurants and hotels; excl. repair and installation services and sanitary services.

[1] Voir notes de la ligne «Total» à la page précédente. [2] Personnes âgées de 10 ans et plus; à partir de 1976: 15 ans et plus. [3] Y compris les services de réparation et d'installation. [4] Y compris les services sanitaires. [5] Y compris les banques, les assurances et affaires immobilières; non compris les restaurants et hôtels. [6] Y compris les restaurants et hôtels; non compris les services de réparation et d'installation, et les services sanitaires.

[1] Véanse notas de la línea «Total» en la página precedente. [2] Personas de 10 años y más; a partir de 1976: 15 años y más. [3] Incl. los servicios de reparación y de instalación. [4] Incl. los servicios de saneamiento. [5] Incl. establecimientos financieros, seguros y bienes inmuebles; excl. restaurantes y hoteles. [6] Incl. restaurantes y hoteles; excl. los servicios de reparación y de instalación y los servicios de saneamiento.

3 Structure of employment
Structure de l'emploi
Estructura del empleo

(Thousands – Milliers – Millares)

País Alcance	Total	Grandes divisiones de actividad económica [a]									
		1 Agricultura, caza, silvicultura y pesca	2 Minas, canteras	3 Industrias manu-factureras	4 Electricidad, gas, agua	5 Construcción	6 Comercio, restaurantes y hoteles	7 Transportes, almacenaje, comuni-caciones	8 Bancos, seguros, bienes inm., serv. para empresas	9 Servicios comunales, sociales y personales	0 Activi-dades no bien especifi-cadas
Philippines [1]		*Civilian employment – Emploi civil – Empleo civil (Source – Fuente: I)*									
Female – Femmes – Mujeres [2]											
1970	3 465	1 170	3	733	1	3	459	11	.	1 038	47
1971	3 929	1 186	4	658	2	4	855	17	.	1 192	11
1972	4 109	1 415	8	631	3	4	906	18	.	1 119	5
1973	4 383	1 556	5	615	4	7	905	19	.	1 261	11
1974	4 448	1 639	5	636	3	6	853	16	.	1 280	10
1975	4 654	1 595	2	707	4	6	904	22	.	1 398	16
1976	4 608	1 710	3	679	4	4	815	30	.	1 350	13
1977	4 601	1 430	4	752	6	6	929	32	.	1 406	36
Singapore [3]		*Civilian employment – Emploi civil – Empleo civil (Source – Fuente: I)*									
Total [4]											
1973	799.6	21.4	1.1	189.9	11.2	51.5	196.1	93.7	28.7	205.8	0.2
1974	824.4	21.7	1.8	234.2	10.3	42.5	172.7	97.5	46.6	195.1	1.9
1975	833.5	17.4	3.1	218.1	8.9	39.2	191.7	97.9	50.7	204.0	2.5
1976	870.4	19.7	1.9	234.0	11.3	42.0	201.0	101.6	56.5	200.6	1.9
1977	903.9	19.8	1.6	245.5	11.4	42.0	212.7	105.6	59.7	204.3	1.3
1978	958.9	17.8	1.1	270.6	9.7	51.5	225.0	109.2	64.3	207.8	1.8
1979	1 021.0	15.2	1.5	294.7	9.8	54.3	237.3	118.9	72.0	216.4	1.0
Male – Hommes – Hombres [4]											
1974	562.2	15.4	1.5	129.3	9.2	38.5	122.5	86.3	30.6	127.6	1.3
1975	586.5	12.3	2.9	131.9	8.2	36.1	135.7	86.6	33.2	137.5	2.2
1976	600.4	15.0	1.4	139.3	10.5	38.2	140.0	86.5	36.0	132.0	1.5
1977	616.3	14.8	1.5	136.9	10.5	38.9	142.7	90.9	39.0	140.0	1.2
1978	640.9	13.0	1.0	146.7	8.5	46.3	150.3	93.1	39.0	141.1	1.6
1979	677.1	10.8	1.2	162.3	8.7	49.7	153.9	101.7	42.7	145.2	1.0
Female – Femmes – Mujeres [4]											
1974	262.2	6.3	0.3	105.0	1.1	4.0	50.2	11.2	16.0	67.5	0.7
1975	247.0	5.0	0.3	86.2	0.8	3.1	56.0	11.3	17.5	66.5	0.4
1976	270.0	4.7	0.5	94.6	0.7	3.9	61.0	15.1	20.6	68.6	0.3
1977	287.6	5.0	0.1	108.6	0.9	3.1	70.0	14.7	20.7	64.4	0.1
1978	318.0	4.7	0.1	123.8	1.2	5.1	74.6	16.1	25.4	66.6	0.1
1979	343.9	4.3	0.3	132.4	1.0	4.7	83.4	17.2	29.3	71.2	–
Sri Lanka		*Registered employees – Salariés inscrits – Asalariados registrados (Source – Fuente: III)*									
Total											
1971	978.9	551.5	2.8	202.0	5.8	27.8	72.3	72.8	14.6	29.3	–
1972	1 026.8	574.2	1.1	211.5	8.8	35.7	72.1	77.6	18.9	26.8	–
1973	1 058.5	568.5	4.3	206.5	7.1	86.5	74.4	75.8	21.2	14.2	–
1974	1 003.6	515.9	3.0	208.8	7.2	72.8	87.1	67.6	23.3	17.9	–
1975	999.0	508.6	4.6	189.0	6.9	94.4	97.9	61.3	18.8	17.5	–
1976	1 055.6	517.1	4.4	191.4	7.0	126.8	100.1	68.5	23.0	17.2	–
1977	1 039.7	516.3	4.0	194.7	7.8	113.0	97.6	61.3	26.7	18.2	–
1978	1 130.3	566.4	4.7	202.7	9.0	89.4	116.6	84.0	33.9	23.6	.

[a] The English designation of major divisions of economic activity is shown on the following page. – Les libellés en français des branches d'activité économique sont indiqués à la page précédente.

[1] Persons aged 10 years and over; beginning 1976: 15 years and over. [2] See notes of line "Total", preceding page. [3] Persons aged 10 years and over. [4] June of each year.

[1] Personnes âgées de 10 ans et plus; à partir de 1976: 15 ans et plus. [2] Voir notes de la ligne «Total» à la page précédente. [3] Personnes âgées de 10 ans et plus. [4] Juin de chaque année.

[1] Personas de 10 años y más; a partir de 1976: 15 años y más. [2] Véanse notas de la línea «Total» en la página precedente. [3] Personas de 10 años y más. [4] Junio de cada año.

3 Structure of employment
Structure de l'emploi
Estructura del empleo

(Thousands – Milliers – Millares)

Country Scope	Total	1 Agriculture, hunting, forestry and fishing	2 Mining, quarrying	3 Manu-facturing	4 Electricity, gas, water	5 Construction	6 Trade, restaurants and hotels	7 Transport, storage, communication	8 Financing, insurance, real estate business services	9 Community, social and personal services	0 Activities not adequately defined
Sri Lanka	*Registered employees – Salariés inscrits – Asalariados registrados (Source – Fuente: III)*										
Male – Hommes – Hombres											
1971	617.9	269.8	2.5	136.4	5.8	27.7	63.7	71.2	13.5	27.5	–
1972	649.9	285.9	0.9	136.2	8.7	35.3	64.6	76.4	16.8	25.0	–
1973	677.4	275.3	3.9	135.2	6.9	83.4	66.3	75.0	18.8	12.6	–
1974	649.9	249.8	2.5	141.2	6.9	70.5	76.5	66.6	20.2	15.7	–
1975	651.7	249.2	3.8	127.8	6.7	89.8	83.5	60.4	15.4	15.0	–
1976	696.3	249.7	3.7	131.2	6.8	120.1	83.6	67.3	19.1	14.7	–
1977	680.1	253.2	3.7	132.1	7.5	106.7	79.9	60.0	21.9	15.1	–
1978	750.0	290.1	4.4	140.4	8.7	84.0	93.6	81.6	27.7	19.5	.
Female – Femmes – Mujeres											
1971	361.1	281.7	0.3	65.7	0.1	0.1	8.5	1.6	1.2	1.8	–
1972	376.9	288.4	0.1	75.3	0.1	0.3	7.5	1.2	2.1	1.8	–
1973	376.6	293.3	0.3	66.8	0.2	3.0	8.1	0.8	2.5	1.6	–
1974	353.7	266.1	0.5	67.6	0.3	2.3	10.7	0.9	3.0	2.3	–
1975	347.3	259.4	0.8	61.1	0.2	4.6	14.3	1.0	3.4	2.4	–
1976	359.4	267.4	0.7	60.2	0.2	6.7	16.5	1.2	3.9	2.5	–
1977	359.6	263.0	0.4	62.6	0.3	6.3	17.7	1.4	4.9	3.1	–
1978	...	...	...	...	...	...	...	...	...	...	...
1979	380.3	276.4	0.3	62.3	0.3	5.4	23.0	2.4	6.2	4.1	.
République arabe syrienne	*Civilian employment – Emploi civil – Empleo civil (Source – Fuente: I)*										
Total [1]											
1971	1 522.3	891.8	1.6	172.3	7.0	70.6	140.8	45.9	9.9	182.0	0.5
1972	1 634.2	907.7	3.2	181.2	19.1	99.7	136.9	63.4	8.7	214.3	–
1973	1 612.1	850.2	14.4	161.2	7.3	88.3	153.6	64.5	10.1	262.5	–
1974	1 631.4	863.6	14.1	183.9	7.2	103.6	160.4	65.5	11.1	222.0	–
1975	1 750.5	894.9	11.5	205.8	9.5	121.9	185.7	75.9	9.9	235.4	–
1976	1 760.4	577.7	13.0	275.8	17.1	203.7	186.6	113.9	14.8	355.0	3.0
1977	1 894.4	740.2	7.9	256.3	16.6	170.1	196.5	117.2	12.9	375.6	1.0
1978	1 934.1	671.0	13.7	264.1	13.9	233.2	205.7	101.9	26.7	403.8	0.1
1979	2 092.0	686.8	0.5	333.6	31.9	287.4	216.6	95.4	21.4	418.5	.
Male – Hommes – Hombres [1]											
1977	1 562.9	523.6	7.6	214.2	16.1	169.7	190.5	114.7	11.3	314.1	0.9
1978	1 668.6	531.2	13.7	221.9	13.2	231.6	202.2	99.2	23.3	332.4	–
1979	1 762.2	487.3	–	293.6	30.2	283.2	211.4	93.5	18.6	344.4	.
Female – Femmes – Mujeres [1]											
1977	331.6	216.5	0.3	42.1	0.5	0.4	6.0	2.5	1.6	61.5	0.2
1978	265.5	139.8	–	42.2	0.8	1.6	3.5	2.7	3.4	71.4	0.1
1979	329.9	199.5	0.5	40.0	1.8	4.2	5.2	1.9	2.8	74.1	–
Thailand	*Civilian employment – Emploi civil – Empleo civil (Source – Fuente: I)*										
ISIC – CITI – CIIU 1958				[3]	[4]		[5]				[6]
Total [2]											
1971	16 618.6	13 157.6	19.0	659.0	18.5	188.9	1 180.8	213.3	.	1 171.9	9.2
1972	16 129.5	11 642.1	118.4	1 239.5	24.0	256.7	1 230.4	313.6	.	1 302.7	2.1
1973	17 042.7	12 270.5	110.9	1 201.1	48.4	258.0	1 392.3	383.9	.	1 375.6	2.0
1974	17 159.1	11 226.3	49.6	1 693.6	61.5	276.8	1 628.6	465.1	.	1 756.7	0.9
1975	18 181.6	13 269.9	28.4	1 355.7	41.4	205.7	1 377.2	381.3	.	1 521.6	–
1976	18 408.0	13 948.5	28.5	1 145.3	44.6	235.9	1 298.2	326.6	.	1 381.9	1.2
1977	20 307.8	14 921.5	50.2	1 329.2	48.3	331.7	1 674.5	382.8	.	1 567.1	0.7
1978	21 738.1	16 018.1	30.2	1 477.5	58.2	313.4	1 639.5	387.9	.	1 812.9	–

(a) Les libellés en français des branches d'activité économique sont indiqués à la page suivante. – La designación en español de las grandes divisiones de actividad económica figura en la página precedente.

[1] Sep. of each year. [2] Third quarter of each year. [3] Incl. repair and installation services. [4] Incl. sanitary services. [5] Incl. financing, insurance and real estate; excl. restaurants and hotels. [6] Incl. restaurants and hotels; excl. repair and installation services and sanitary services.

[1] Sept. de chaque année. [2] Troisième trimestre de chaque année. [3] Y compris les services de réparation et d'installation. [4] Y compris les services sanitaires. [5] Y compris les banques, les assurances et affaires immobilières; non compris les restaurants et hôtels. [6] Y compris les restaurants et hôtels; non compris les services de réparation et d'installation, et les services sanitaires.

[1] Sept. de cada año. [2] Tercer trimestre de cada año. [3] Incl. los servicios de reparación y de instalación. [4] Incl. los servicios de saneamiento. [5] Incl. establecimientos financieros, seguros y bienes inmuebles; excl. restaurantes y hoteles. [6] Incl. restaurantes y hoteles; excl. los servicios de reparación y de instalación y los servicios de saneamiento.

3 Structure of employment
Structure de l'emploi
Estructura del empleo

(Thousands – Milliers – Millares)

Pays Portée	Total	Branches d'activité économique [a]									
		1 Agriculture, chasse, sylviculture et pêche	2 Industries extractives	3 Industries manu-facturières	4 Electricité, gaz, eau	5 Construction	6 Commerce, restaurants et hôtels	7 Transports, entrepôts, communications	8 Banques, assurances, aff. imm., serv. aux entreprises	9 Services à collectivité, services soc. et pers.	0 Activités mal désignées
Thailand		Civilian employment – Emploi civil – Empleo civil (Source – Fuente: I)									
Male – Hommes – Hombres [1]											
1971	8 933.2	6 854.9	15.8	354.1	16.3	169.5	581.8	205.8	.	729.7	4.9
1972	8 925.9	6 307.2	98.8	692.2	21.2	242.7	542.1	298.0	.	742.6	2.0
1973	9 440.2	6 569.3	96.9	735.0	44.9	231.2	648.9	370.5	.	743.0	0.2
1974	9 492.3	6 015.3	41.5	931.4	49.1	243.5	748.2	437.7	.	1 016.5	–
1975	9 863.9	6 977.5	15.6	775.6	35.5	188.7	655.7	365.8	.	849.2	–
1976	10 103.3	7 489.2	25.2	603.0	40.8	211.7	629.4	311.9	.	791.7	–
1977	10 998.7	7 879.3	40.4	759.7	43.0	282.1	764.0	358.2	.	870.5	0.7
1978	11 510.5	8 184.4	23.5	858.8	50.2	271.2	772.5	363.5	.	985.7	–
Female – Femmes – Mujeres [1]											
1971	7 685.3	6 302.7	3.1	304.9	2.2	19.3	599.0	7.5	.	442.2	4.2
1972	7 206.5	5 334.8	19.5	547.2	2.7	35.1	688.2	15.6	.	560.0	–
1973	7 602.3	5 699.1	13.9	466.0	3.5	26.7	743.3	13.3	.	632.5	1.7
1974	7 666.8	5 210.9	7.9	754.2	12.3	33.2	880.3	27.4	.	330.6	0.1
1975	8 317.6	6 292.5	12.8	580.1	5.9	16.9	721.5	15.4	.	672.4	–
1976	8 307.5	6 459.2	3.2	542.3	3.7	24.1	668.7	14.6	.	590.1	1.2
1977	9 309.1	7 042.6	9.8	569.5	5.3	49.6	910.5	24.6	.	696.6	–
1978	10 227.5	7 833.6	6.5	625.1	7.9	42.1	9 867.0	24.1	.	827.0	–

EUROPE – EUROPE – EUROPA

	Total										
Austria		Insured persons – Personnes assurées – Personas aseguradas (Source – Fuente: II)									
Total [2]											
1972	2 537.5	56.5	31.9	914.5	30.3	269.8	388.4	148.2	106.5	591.4	.
1973	2 650.7	53.6	30.6	946.7	30.6	284.4	421.5	151.9	119.6	611.8	.
1974	2 687.4	50.1	30.4	944.5	31.4	278.0	433.9	158.5	127.6	633.0	.
1975	2 685.8	47.6	29.7	910.8	31.8	268.8	446.4	158.3	129.3	663.1	.
1976	2 704.4	46.7	28.4	905.5	31.9	266.2	459.1	156.6	132.8	677.2	.
1977	2 763.3	46.6	27.9	922.3	32.2	274.0	473.2	157.8	138.4	690.9	.
1978	2 784.3	45.2	27.2	913.1	31.5	274.1	478.5	159.5	144.7	710.5	.
1979	2 804.2	42.5	26.7	912.1	31.8	271.1	488.1	159.4	151.5	717.9	.

[a] La designación en español de las grandes divisiones de actividad económica figura en la página siguiente. – The English designation of major divisions of economic activity is shown on the preceding page.

[1] See notes of line "Total", preceding page. [2] July of each year.

[1] Voir notes de la ligne «Total» à la page précédente. [2] Juillet de chaque année.

[1] Véanse notas de la línea «Total» en la página precedente. [2] Julio de cada año.

3

Structure of employment
Structure de l'emploi
Estructura del empleo

(Thousands – Milliers – Millares)

País Alcance	Total	Grandes divisiones de actividad económica (a)									
		1 Agricultura, caza, silvicultura y pesca	2 Minas, canteras	3 Industrias manu-factureras	4 Electricidad, gas, agua	5 Construcción	6 Comercio, restaurantes y hoteles	7 Transportes, almacenaje, comuni-caciones	8 Bancos, seguros, bienes inm., serv. para empresas	9 Servicios comunales, sociales y personales	0 Activi-dades no bien especifi-cadas
Austria		Insured persons – Personnes assurées – Personas aseguradas (Source – Fuente: II)									
Male – Hommes – Hombres [1]											
1975	1 645.2	31.6	26.9	594.0	27.0	243.6	192.4	130.7	63.7	335.3	.
1976	1 650.8	31.3	25.7	592.5	27.1	240.9	198.2	129.0	65.6	340.5	.
1977	1 681.9	31.5	25.3	604.2	27.3	247.8	203.1	129.2	66.8	344.7	.
1978	1 687.0	30.7	24.6	601.5	26.6	247.2	203.9	129.9	66.8	344.7	.
1979	1 687.6	29.2	24.1	600.9	26.8	243.2	207.3	130.5	71.9	350.7	.
Female – Femmes – Mujeres [1]											
1975	1 040.6	16.0	2.8	316.8	4.8	25.2	254.0	27.6	65.6	327.8	.
1976	1 053.6	15.4	2.7	313.0	4.8	25.3	260.9	27.6	67.2	336.7	.
1977	1 081.4	15.1	2.6	318.1	4.9	26.2	270.1	28.6	71.6	346.2	.
1978	1 097.3	14.5	2.6	311.6	4.9	26.9	274.6	29.6	72.8	359.8	.
1979	1 116.6	13.3	2.6	311.3	4.9	28.0	280.8	28.9	76.3	370.4	.
Belgique [2]		Civilian employment – Emploi civil – Empleo civil (Source – Fuente: II)									
Total [3]											
1970	3 665.0	173.8	51.9	1 199.0	31.4	302.2	678.4	237.6	185.1	805.6	–
1971	3 701.5	161.7	49.0	1 197.4	32.7	302.3	683.8	246.1	198.9	829.9	–
1972	3 695.5	151.0	46.8	1 179.8	32.7	290.4	685.6	252.3	202.6	854.6	–
1973	3 744.5	144.2	42.1	1 190.3	32.9	288.3	693.8	260.8	209.6	882.5	–
1974	3 798.7	139.6	38.3	1 199.3	32.9	295.0	698.2	266.3	221.6	907.5	–
1975	3 743.6	135.9	37.2	1 128.3	33.2	295.2	697.0	268.9	222.0	925.9	–
1976	3 714.6	127.9	34.6	1 082.6	33.3	298.6	697.9	265.1	226.9	947.8	–
1977	3 707.2	122.6	32.2	1 041.7	33.4	300.2	704.3	265.8	230.0	977.0	–
1978	3 707.4	118.5	30.3	1 001.0	33.4	296.3	700.0	268.7	237.9	1 021.3	–
1979	3 749.3	118.5	29.2	973.2	33.2	298.7	702.5	273.0	247.8	1 073.1	.
Male – Hommes – Hombres [3]											
1970	2 467.2	136.2	51.0	888.1	29.6	294.4	380.1	214.1	119.1	354.6	
1971	2 476.9	129.2	48.2	883.5	30.8	293.9	382.5	220.0	125.3	363.5	
1972	2 455.2	120.1	45.9	867.3	30.8	281.8	382.8	225.7	127.7	373.1	
1973	2 471.2	114.2	41.3	873.8	31.0	279.3	387.7	230.6	130.6	382.7	
1974	2 495.4	110.2	37.6	878.8	31.0	285.3	389.7	234.4	138.0	390.4	
1975	2 457.0	106.2	36.6	834.8	31.2	285.4	388.0	236.7	137.8	400.3	
1976	2 436.5	100.8	34.0	807.7	31.2	288.6	388.2	233.0	141.3	411.7	
1977	2 422.0	97.8	31.6	784.2	31.3	289.8	391.2	232.9	141.5	421.6	
1978	2 406.6	93.1	29.8	756.7	31.1	285.6	386.8	234.7	145.3	443.5	
1979	2 420.3	90.7	28.7	739.3	30.8	288.1	388.1	238.0	150.8	465.8	.
Female – Femmes – Mujeres [3]											
1970	1 197.8	37.6	0.9	310.9	1.8	7.8	298.3	23.5	66.0	451.0	
1971	1 224.6	32.5	0.8	313.9	1.9	8.4	301.3	26.1	73.0	466.1	
1972	1 240.3	30.9	0.9	312.5	1.9	8.6	302.8	26.6	74.9	481.2	
1973	1 273.3	30.0	0.8	316.5	1.9	9.0	306.1	30.2	79.0	499.8	.
1974	1 303.3	29.4	0.7	320.5	1.9	9.7	308.5	31.9	83.6	517.1	.
1975	1 286.6	29.7	0.6	293.5	2.0	9.8	309.0	32.2	84.2	525.5	.
1976	1 278.1	27.1	0.6	274.9	2.1	10.0	309.7	32.0	85.6	536.1	.
1977	1 285.2	24.8	0.6	257.5	2.1	10.4	313.1	32.9	88.5	555.4	.
1978	1 300.7	25.4	0.5	244.3	2.2	10.7	313.2	34.0	92.6	577.8	.
1979	1 329.0	27.8	0.5	233.9	2.4	10.6	314.4	35.0	97.0	607.3	.

(a) The English designation of major divisions of economic activity is shown on the following page. – Les libellés en français des branches d'activité économique sont indiqués à la page précédente.

[1] July of each year. [2] Incl. persons working abroad (39,531 in 1979). [3] June of each year.

[1] Juillet de chaque année. [2] Y compris les personnes travaillant à l'étranger(39 531 en 1979). [3] Juin de chaque année.

[1] Julio de cada año. [2] Incl. las personas que trabajan en el extranjero (39 531 en 1979). [3] Junio de cada año.

3 Structure of employment
Structure de l'emploi
Estructura del empleo

(Thousands – Milliers – Millares)

Country Scope	Total	Major divisions of economic activity [a]									
		1 Agriculture, hunting, forestry and fishing	2 Mining, quarrying	3 Manu- facturing	4 Electricity, gas, water	5 Construction	6 Trade, restaurants and hotels	7 Transport, storage, communi- cation	8 Financing, insurance, real estate business services	9 Community, social and personal services	0 Activities not adequately defined
Bulgarie [1]		*Registered employees – Salariés inscrits – Asalariados registrados (Source – Fuente: III)*									
Total		[2]		[3]			[4]			[5]	
1970	2 748.7	292.9	.	1 156.0	.	303.8	232.1	226.6	.	512.5	24.8
1971	2 864.7	311.1	.	1 183.6	.	311.1	267.9	234.7	.	529.9	26.4
1972	2 993.4	358.2	.	1 210.3	.	315.3	283.1	240.3	.	558.2	28.0
1973	3 273.1	569.6	.	1 242.8	.	315.1	285.7	248.9	.	580.8	30.2
1974	3 424.8	642.9	.	1 277.1	.	315.5	290.2	259.1	.	608.6	31.4
1975	3 676.6	809.2	.	1 297.4	.	316.8	308.5	270.9	.	636.5	37.3
1976	3 886.8	964.8	.	1 310.1	.	312.7	319.9	281.6	.	660.7	37.0
1977	3 870.1	925.3	.	1 319.1	.	330.1	325.3	289.5	.	641.2	39.6
1978	3 895.6	917.3	.	1 336.4	.	338.8	329.8	293.6	.	639.1	40.6
1979	3 952.3*	934.3*	.	1 355.6*	.	339.6*	331.6*	297.4*	.	651.7*	42.0*
Czechoslovakia [6]		*Registered employed – Effectif occupé – Efectivo ocupado (Source – Fuente: III)*									
Total [7]				[8]	[9]						
1970	7 033	1 287	175	2 443	52	605	637	478	35	1 272	49
1971	7 115	1 270	176	2 465	53	624	668	479	36	1 295	49
1972	7 179	1 196	177	2 525	56	639	700	479	36	1 315	56
1973	7 254	1 165	177	2 566	56	659	724	483	37	1 334	56
1974	7 357	1 156	177	2 594	57	675	744	486	36	1 367	53
1975	7 435	1 129	174	2 627	58	689	766	486	37	1 403	66
1976	7 476	1 125	173	2 654	60	714	786	494	34	1 369	67
1977	7 538	1 102	175	2 667	61	723	807	497	34	1 402	70
1978	7 604	1 083	175	2 687	63	732	825	498	34	1 434	73
1979	7 674	1 075	177	2 697	64	741	838	502	35	1 474	71
Male – Hommes – Hombres [7]											
1970	3 748	665	150	1 315	39	511	189	326	12	518	23
1971	3 776	656	151	1 322	40	529	199	326	11	521	21
1972	3 774	607	151	1 351	42	536	211	327	11	513	25
1973	3 819	623	151	1 369	42	549	213	329	11	509	23
1974	3 849	615	151	1 381	43	563	217	325	11	517	26
1975	3 867	601	148	1 397	44	570	219	326	10	526	26
1976	3 879	601	147	1 407	45	592	225	331	11	494	26
1977	3 908	592	148	1 424	46	592	229	334	9	506	28
1978	3 950	593	148	1 437	47	599	232	334	9	521	30
1979	3 992	597	150	1 450	48	602	235	337	9	534	30
Female – Femmes – Mujeres [7]											
1970	3 286	615	25	1 137	13	92	448	148	23	758	27
1971	3 346	581	25	1 165	13	96	476	153	25	785	27
1972	3 400	542	26	1 196	14	102	496	151	25	817	21
1973	3 463	531	26	1 217	14	109	516	154	26	839	31
1974	3 527	517	26	1 231	14	112	536	159	26	866	40
1975	3 565	499	26	1 242	14	116	550	159	27	891	41
1976	3 596	498	26	1 252	15	122	567	162	24	889	41
1977	3 626	476	27	1 253	15	127	581	163	26	916	42
1978	3 662	467	27	1 255	16	131	599	163	26	935	43
1979	3 694	459	27	1 257	16	134	609	165	26	960	41

[a] Les libellés en français des branches d'activité économique sont indiqués à la page suivante. – La designación en español de las grandes divisiones de actividad económica figura en la página precedente.

[1] Socialised sector. [2] State agricultural undertakings. [3] Incl. mining, quarrying, electricity, gas and water (col. 2 and 4). [4] Incl. financing, insurance and real estate; excl. restaurants and hotels. [5] Incl. restaurants and hotels; excl. repair and installation services and water supply. [6] Excl. family workers and apprentices. [7] Dec. of each year. [8] Incl. water supply. [9] Excl. water supply.

[1] Secteur socialisé. [2] Entreprises agricoles d'Etat. [3] Y compris les industries extractives, l'électricité, le gaz et l'eau (col. 2 et 4). [4] Y compris les banques, les assurances et affaires immobilières; non compris les restaurants et hôtels. [5] Y compris les restaurants et hôtels; non compris les services de réparation et d'installation, et la distribution de l'eau. [6] Non compris les travailleurs familiaux et les apprentis. [7] Déc. de chaque année. [8] Y compris la distribution de l'eau. [9] Non compris la distribution de l'eau.

[1] Sector socializado. [2] Empresas agrícolas de Estado. [3] Incl. minas y canteras, electricidad, gas y agua (cols 2 y 4). [4] Incl. establecimientos financieros, seguros y bienes inmuebles; excl. restaurantes y hoteles. [5] Incl. restaurantes y hoteles; excl. los servicios de reparación y de instalación, y abastecimiento de agua. [6] Excl. los trabajadores familiares y los aprendices. [7] Dic. de cada año. [8] Incl. abastecimiento de agua. [9] Excl. abastecimiento de agua.

3 Structure of employment
Structure de l'emploi
Estructura del empleo

(Thousands – Milliers – Millares)

Pays Portée	Total	Branches d'activité économique [a]									
		1 Agriculture, chasse, sylviculture et pêche	2 Industries extractives	3 Industries manu-facturières	4 Electricité, gaz, eau	5 Construction	6 Commerce, restaurants et hôtels	7 Transports, entrepôts, communi-cations	8 Banques, assurances, aff. imm., serv. aux entreprises	9 Services à collectivité, services soc. et pers.	0 Activités mal désignées
Denmark [1]		*Civilian employment – Emploi civil – Empleo civil (Source – Fuente: I)*									
Total [2]											
1972	2 355.4	229.7	2.6	586.9	14.3	202.6	352.2	159.0	138.7	658.1	11.3
1973	2 385.2	227.3	2.4	588.7	13.4	201.3	360.8	165.7	140.4	673.2	12.0
1974	2 354.6	226.8	2.5	555.7	14.2	188.0	344.4	166.9	144.3	698.1	13.7
1975	2 332.2	227.6	2.1	528.6	13.6	189.6	343.6	157.7	145.7	711.4	12.3
1976	2 391.6	223.0	1.9	537.1	14.7	195.4	353.5	165.8	148.9	734.8	16.5
1977	2 413.9	218.5	2.1	521.6	14.3	196.5	351.0	166.7	154.9	768.7	19.6
1978	2 473.0	214.8	2.3	531.2	15.1	201.7	345.4	165.4	165.2	810.8	21.1
1979	2 501.2	208.3	1.7	534.1	17.5	201.7	333.7	175.4	177.0	826.1	25.7
Male – Hommes – Hombres [2]											
1972	1 390.5	167.2	2.3	406.1	13.1	187.8	182.5	124.6	72.8	228.8	5.3
1973	1 404.3	162.8	2.2	413.1	12.1	185.3	186.0	129.4	73.9	232.8	6.7
1974	1 377.7	165.0	2.3	396.1	12.7	172.8	178.9	130.5	74.9	238.3	6.2
1975	1 361.7	164.3	1.8	379.3	12.4	174.6	181.2	123.6	77.8	241.5	5.2
1976	1 391.3	162.4	1.7	383.8	13.3	180.5	187.3	130.1	78.6	247.7	5.9
1977	1 392.3	159.1	2.0	376.0	12.9	180.0	186.5	130.1	83.2	255.6	6.9
1978	1 408.6	152.3	2.1	381.0	13.3	183.8	179.5	128.2	88.2	273.0	7.2
1979	1 410.0	148.4	1.4	380.6	16.0	180.9	173.2	132.7	94.2	274.7	7.9
Female – Femmes – Mujeres [2]											
1972	964.9	62.5	0.3	180.8	1.2	14.8	169.7	34.4	65.9	429.3	6.0
1973	980.9	64.5	0.2	175.6	1.3	16.0	174.8	36.3	66.5	440.4	5.3
1974	976.9	61.8	0.2	159.6	1.5	15.2	165.5	36.4	69.4	459.8	7.5
1975	970.5	63.3	0.3	149.3	1.2	15.0	162.4	34.1	67.9	469.9	7.1
1976	1 000.3	60.6	0.2	153.3	1.4	14.9	166.2	35.7	70.3	487.1	10.6
1977	1 021.6	59.4	0.1	145.6	1.4	16.5	164.5	36.6	71.7	513.1	12.7
1978	1 064.4	62.5	0.2	150.2	1.8	17.9	165.9	37.2	77.0	537.8	13.9
1979	1 091.2	59.9	0.3	153.5	1.5	20.8	160.5	42.7	82.8	551.4	17.8
España [3]		*Civilian employment – Emploi civil – Empleo civil (Source – Fuente: I)*									
Total [4]											
1970	12 432.9	3 662.3	117.3	3 374.9	90.9	1 042.0	1 206.5	642.3	175.3	2 121.4	.
1971	12 499.2	3 552.9	112.9	3 433.8	91.6	1 026.1	1 252.8	658.2	187.9	2 183.0	.
1972	12 535.4	3 216.2	102.6	3 146.9	93.9	1 207.8	1 988.4	687.2	317.9	1 774.5	.
1973	12 850.7	3 128.0	101.4	3 285.4	83.3	1 244.5	2 119.3	673.1	338.2	1 877.3	.
1974	12 924.1	2 994.2	99.2	3 336.9	80.3	1 279.6	2 188.9	688.1	377.4	1 879.5	.
1975	12 691.9	2 798.6	102.9	3 393.7	86.6	1 274.2	2 130.1	668.0	400.2	1 837.6	.
1976	12 543.3	2 710.3	353.4	3 015.9	79.5	1 218.7	2 343.2	679.2	400.8	1 742.3	.
1977	12 434.8	2 568.1	358.2	2 993.2	87.1	1 240.7	2 341.5	652.5	411.4	1 782.1	.
1978	12 090.7	2 438.8	356.1	2 912.7	81.4	1 159.5	2 317.1	638.1	396.2	1 791.1	.
1979	11 837.3	2 314.3	339.8	2 801.9	74.2	1 087.2	2 316.0	680.5	406.1	1 817.3	.
Male – Hommes – Hombres [4]											
1970	9 329.1	2 857.3	115.8	2 567.8	87.9	1 024.4	793.5	594.1	148.6	1 139.7	.
1971	9 308.1	2 726.5	110.2	2 638.8	86.6	1 010.5	784.8	602.2	162.0	1 186.5	.
1972	9 228.5	2 464.6	100.8	2 306.8	88.6	1 187.2	1 228.4	632.6	257.7	961.8	.
1973	9 250.5	2 338.5	99.3	2 357.6	79.0	1 218.2	1 273.4	617.5	269.6	997.4	.
1974	9 254.1	2 230.4	97.6	2 401.8	75.4	1 254.7	1 285.5	635.9	298.6	974.2	.
1975	9 196.1	2 083.3	100.6	2 492.6	79.6	1 247.3	1 289.7	616.4	320.9	965.7	.
1976	8 871.3	1 953.1	324.0	2 173.4	74.8	1 191.6	1 453.9	618.1	315.3	767.1	.
1977	8 794.6	1 855.7	326.5	2 191.7	82.1	1 209.3	1 438.7	598.9	332.5	759.1	.
1978	8 564.5	1 767.7	326.8	2 140.3	77.8	1 133.2	1 446.5	582.2	308.2	781.9	.
1979	8 371.7	1 667.2	306.9	2 090.4	70.0	1 066.7	1 444.5	629.4	319.4	777.2	.

[a] La designación en español de las grandes divisiones de actividad económica figura en la página siguiente. – The English designation of major divisions of economic activity is shown on the preceding page.

[1] Persons aged 15 to 74 years. [2] Oct. of each year; prior to 1974: Nov. [3] Persons aged 14 years and over. [4] Fourth quarter of each year.

[1] Personnes âgées de 15 à 74 ans. [2] Oct. de chaque année; avant 1974: nov. [3] Personnes âgées de 14 ans et plus. [4] Quatrième trimestre de chaque année.

[1] Personas de 15 a 74 años. [2] Oct. de cada año; antes de 1974: nov. [3] Personas de 14 años y más. [4] Cuarto trimestre de cada año.

3 Structure of employment
Structure de l'emploi
Estructura del empleo

(Thousands – Milliers – Millares)

Grandes divisiones de actividad económica [a]

País Alcance	Total	1 Agricultura, caza, silvicultura y pesca	2 Minas, canteras	3 Industrias manufactureras	4 Electricidad, gas, agua	5 Construcción	6 Comercio, restaurantes y hoteles	7 Transportes, almacenaje, comunicaciones	8 Bancos, seguros, bienes inm., serv. para empresas	9 Servicios comunales, sociales y personales	0 Actividades no bien especificadas
España [1]				Civilian employment – Emploi civil – Empleo civil (Source – Fuente: I)							
Female – Femmes – Mujeres [2]											
1970	3 103.8	805.0	1.5	807.1	3.0	17.6	413.0	48.2	26.7	981.7	.
1971	3 191.1	826.4	2.7	795.0	5.0	15.6	468.0	56.0	25.9	996.5	.
1972	3 306.9	751.6	1.8	840.1	5.3	20.6	760.0	54.6	60.2	812.7	.
1973	3 600.2	789.5	2.1	927.8	4.3	26.5	845.9	55.6	68.6	879.9	.
1974	3 670.0	763.8	1.6	935.1	4.9	24.9	903.4	52.2	78.8	905.3	.
1975	3 495.8	715.3	2.3	901.1	7.0	26.9	840.4	51.6	79.3	871.9	.
1976	3 672.0	757.2	29.4	842.5	4.7	27.2	889.3	61.1	85.5	875.2	.
1977	3 640.3	712.4	31.7	801.5	5.0	31.4	902.8	53.6	78.9	1 023.0	.
1978	3 526.3	671.1	29.3	772.4	3.6	26.3	870.6	55.9	88.0	1 009.2	.
1979	3 465.6	647.1	32.9	711.5	4.2	20.5	871.5	51.1	86.7	1 040.1	.
Finland [3]				Civilian employment – Emploi civil – Empleo civil (Source – Fuente: I)							
Total											
1971	2 123	448	...	560	...	184	314	144	74	399	–
1972	2 118	399	...	570	...	180	320	150	79	419	–
1973	2 164	369	.	584	...	185	341	151	88	446	–
1974	2 229	362	.	613	...	187	350	154	99	464	–
1975	2 221	329	.	609	...	189	345	161	108	480	–
1976 [4]	▮2 163	▮298	9	▮550	28	▮161	▮321	▮161	▮116	▮492	27
1977	2 111	272	9	542	27	154	308	158	116	509	16
1978	2 084	256	9	527	25	151	301	162	118	518	17
1979	2 134	250	9	547	25	150	305	166	120	544	18
Male – Hommes – Hombres											
1971	1 166	251	...	358	...	175	119	106	26	131	–
1972	1 153	221	...	367	...	168	115	111	28	142	–
1973	1 171	209	...	376	...	170	123	110	30	153	–
1974	1 199	204	...	395	...	170	126	111	35	158	–
1975	1 187	181	...	391	...	174	127	121	38	155	–
1976 [4]	▮1 155	▮174	8	▮340	22	▮143	▮130	▮118	▮44	▮162	14
1977	1 116	160	8	340	22	135	119	117	42	165	8
1978	1 102	152	7	332	21	136	116	116	45	169	8
1979	1 128	148	8	347	21	136	123	118	46	172	9
Female – Femmes – Mujeres											
1971	957	197	...	202	...	9	195	38	48	268	–
1972	965	178	...	203	...	12	205	39	51	277	–
1973	993	160	...	208	...	15	218	41	58	293	–
1974	1 030	158	...	218	...	17	224	43	64	306	–
1975	1 034	148	...	218	...	15	218	40	70	325	–
1976 [4]	▮1 008	▮124	1	▮210	6	▮18	▮191	▮43	▮72	▮330	13
1977	995	112	1	202	5	19	189	41	74	344	8
1978	982	104	2	195	4	15	185	46	73	349	9
1979	1 006	102	1	200	4	14	182	48	74	372	9
France				Civilian employment – Emploi civil – Empleo civil (Source – Fuente: IV)							
Total											
1970	20 344	2 835	229	5 677	164	2 003	3 212	1 207	969	4 050	–
1971	20 438	2 683	216	5 742	162	1 981	3 251	1 204	1 025	4 174	–
1972	20 552	2 529	205	5 794	164	1 974	3 301	1 205	1 087	4 293	–
1973	20 815	2 379	192	5 907	166	1 989	3 398	1 221	1 154	4 410	–
1974	20 958	2 236	181	5 957	172	1 977	3 422	1 260	1 208	4 545	–
1975	20 714	2 104	177	5 780	172	1 896	3 215	1 259	1 299	4 812	–
1976	20 855	2 037	172	5 721	173	1 882	3 269	1 269	1 333	4 999	–
1977	21 034	1 978	165	5 695	176	1 877	3 309	1 296	1 385	5 154	–
1978	21 099	1 922	157	5 601	179	1 842	3 342	1 319	1 440	5 298	–
1979	21 100	1 867	150	5 496	183	1 820	3 374	1 334	1 492	5 385	.

[a] The English designation of major divisions of economic activity is shown on the following page. – Les libellés en français des branches d'activité économique sont indiqués à la page précédente.

[1] Persons aged 14 years and over. [2] Fourth quarter of each year. [3] Persons aged 15 to 74 years. [4] Sampling design revised; including 10,000 professional soldiers.

[1] Personnes âgées de 14 ans et plus. [2] Quatrième trimestre de chaque année. [3] Personnes âgées de 15 à 74 ans. [4] Plan d'échantillonnage révisé; y compris 10 000 militaires professionels.

[1] Personas de 14 años y más. [2] Cuarto trimestre de cada año. [3] Personas de 15 a 74 años. [4] Diseño de la muestra revisado; incl. 10 000 militares profesionales.

3 Structure of employment
Structure de l'emploi
Estructura del empleo

(Thousands – Milliers – Millares)

Country Scope	Total	Major divisions of economic activity (a)									
		1 Agriculture, hunting, forestry and fishing	2 Mining, quarrying	3 Manu-facturing	4 Electricity, gas, water	5 Construction	6 Trade, restaurants and hotels	7 Transport, storage, communi-cation	8 Financing, insurance, real estate business services	9 Community, social and personal services	0 Activities not adequately defined
German Democratic Rep. *Registered employees – Salariés inscrits – Asalariados registrados (Source – Fuente: III)*											
Total				[1]			[2]			[3]	
1970	6 874.4	281.0	.	3 170.7	.	505.8	824.9	592.8	.	1 499.3	.
1971	6 963.1	277.0	.	3 212.2	.	513.5	806.0	599.7	.	1 554.5	.
1972	7 136.6	266.9	.	3 343.1	.	524.1	812.1	602.2	.	1 588.3	.
1973	7 238.7	276.1	.	3 373.5	.	528.9	813.7	606.6	.	1 640.0	.
1974	7 336.0	293.5	.	3 378.5	.	536.9	829.3	615.3	.	1 682.5	.
1975	7 407.1	299.0	.	3 386.7	.	549.7	839.2	618.1	.	1 714.5	.
1976	7 496.7	305.9	.	3 417.1	.	560.9	845.9	626.3	.	1 740.4	.
1977	7 576.9	318.8	.	3 448.1	.	570.3	844.5	632.8	.	1 762.4	.
1978	7 651.9	333.1	.	3 468.4	.	574.6	843.3	633.2	.	1 799.2	.
1979	7 722.0*	334.1*	.	3 492.5*	.	576.9*	848.7*	633.5	.	1 836.5*	.
Germany, Fed. Rep. of *Civilian employment – Emploi civil – Empleo civil (Source – Fuente: I)*											
Total											
1972	26 125	2 038	434	9 550	219	2 230	3 799	1 530	1 298	5 027	–
1973	26 201	1 954	417	9 541	223	2 267	3 846	1 547	1 312	5 094	–
1974	25 688	1 882	387	9 410	226	2 135	3 708	1 508	1 326	5 106	–
1975	24 798	1 823	358	8 890	239	1 921	3 593	1 484	1 314	5 176	–
1976	24 556	1 743	355	8 784	215	1 836	3 525	1 521	1 272	5 305	–
1977	24 511	1 655	328	8 757	226	1 792	3 532	1 493	1 266	5 462	–
1978	24 700	1 608	337	8 744	216	1 815	3 566	1 488	1 309	5 617	–
1979	25 017	1 544	327	8 806	220	1 880	3 619	1 502	1 376	5 743	.
Male – Hommes – Hombres											
1972	16 512	961	411	6 640	190	2 074	1 720	1 247	708	2 561	–
1973	16 467	912	394	6 608	193	2 101	1 720	1 253	707	2 579	–
1974	16 061	879	365	6 563	193	1 969	1 653	1 222	702	2 515	–
1975	15 432	854	338	6 243	206	1 761	1 601	1 193	698	2 538	–
1976	15 280	828	336	6 099	187	1 688	1 571	1 253	709	2 609	–
1977	15 217	787	309	6 082	199	1 650	1 570	1 222	696	2 702	–
1978	15 323	773	318	6 060	189	1 668	1 612	1 225	715	2 763	–
1979	15 943	746	307	6 109	193	1 724	1 618	1 222	752	2 822	.
Female – Femmes – Mujeres											
1972	9 613	1 077	23	2 910	29	156	2 079	283	590	2 466	–
1973	9 734	1 042	23	2 933	30	166	2 126	294	605	2 515	–
1974	9 627	1 003	22	2 847	33	166	2 055	286	624	2 591	–
1975	9 366	969	20	2 647	33	160	1 992	291	616	2 638	–
1976	9 276	915	19	2 685	28	148	1 954	268	563	2 696	–
1977	9 294	868	19	2 675	27	142	1 962	271	570	2 760	–
1978	9 377	835	19	2 684	27	147	1 954	263	594	2 854	–
1979	9 524	798	20	2 697	27	156	2 001	280	624	2 921	.
Gibraltar *Registered employees – Salariés inscrits – Asalariados registrados (Source – Fuente: III)*											
Total											
1972	10.425	–	–	3.200	0.201	2.281	2.276	0.700	0.219	1.406	0.481
1973	11.339	–	–	3.176	0.214	2.750	2.434	0.633	0.240	1.416	0.476
1974	11.677	–	–	3.331	0.196	2.849	2.337	0.562	0.297	1.619	0.486
1975	11.954	–	–	3.313	0.195	2.850	2.375	0.695	0.316	1.714	0.496
1976	11.910	–	–	3.172	0.187	3.047	2.082	0.786	0.299	1.871	0.466
1977	11.229	–	–	3.223	0.189	2.560	1.931	0.662	0.266	1.960	0.438
1978	11.383	–	–	3.108	0.194	2.433	2.162	0.621	0.344	2.042	0.479
1979	11.423	.	.	3.002	0.179	2.597	1.977	0.688	0.388	2.096	0.496

(a) Les libellés en français des branches d'activité économique sont indiqués à la page suivante. – La designación en español de las grandes divisiones de actividad económica figura en la página precedente.

[1] Incl. mining, quarrying, electricity, gas and water (col. 2 and 4). [2] Incl. financing, insurance and real estate; excl. restaurants and hotels. [3] Incl. restaurants, hotels and activities not adequately defined; excl. repair and installation services and sanitary services.

[1] Y compris les industries extractives, l'électricité, le gaz et l'eau (col. 2 et 4). [2] Y compris les banques, les assurances et affaires immobilières; non compris les restaurants et hôtels. [3] Y compris les restaurants, les hôtels et les activités mal désignées; non compris les services de réparation et d'installation, et les services sanitaires.

[1] Incl. minas y canteras, electricidad, gas y agua (cols 2 y 4). [2] Incl. establecimientos financieros, seguros y bienes inmuebles; excl. restaurantes y hoteles. [3] Incl. restaurantes, hoteles y actividades no bien especificadas; excl. los servicios de reparación y de instalación, y los servicios de saneamiento.

3 Structure of employment
Structure de l'emploi
Estructura del empleo

(Thousands – Milliers – Millares)

Pays Portée	Total	Branches d'activité économique [a]									
		1 Agriculture, chasse, sylviculture et pêche	2 Industries extractives	3 Industries manufacturières	4 Electricité, gaz, eau	5 Construction	6 Commerce, restaurants et hôtels	7 Transports, entrepôts, communications	8 Banques, assurances, aff. imm., serv. aux entreprises	9 Services à collectivité, services soc. et pers.	0 Activités mal désignées

Hongrie [1] — Civilian employment – Emploi civil – Empleo civil (Source – Fuente: IV)

Pays Portée	Total	1	2	3[2]	4	5	6[3]	7	8	9[4]	0
Total											
1970	4 995.3	1 300.7	.	1 782.4	.	373.3	410.4	364.1	.	764.4	
1971	5 024.4	1 275.0	.	1 776.1	.	394.7	423.9	372.8	.	781.9	
1972	5 049.9	1 247.4	.	1 786.8	.	406.2	429.1	379.5	.	800.9	
1973	5 067.4	1 207.8	.	1 806.5	.	411.1	436.5	382.9	.	822.6	
1974	5 079.6	1 166.4	.	1 813.4	.	415.0	450.9	386.3	.	847.6	
1975	5 089.4	1 139.8	.	1 799.8	.	418.0	463.8	395.8	.	872.4	
1976	5 087.2	1 120.3	.	1 776.7	.	418.5	472.0	402.8	.	896.9	
1977	5 075.0	1 105.5	.	1 758.4	.	415.3	478.0	405.0	.	912.8	
1978	5 074.9	1 102.4	.	1 743.0	.	413.7	482.5	407.7	.	925.7	
1979	5 082.0*	1 110.4*	.	1 721.5*	.	410.6*	487.6*	409.3*	.	942.6*	
Male – Hommes – Hombres											
1970	2 906.2	804.5	.	1 009.2	.	320.4	157.1	283.3	.	331.7	.
1971	2 912.7	791.2	.	997.7	.	335.9	162.4	288.7	.	336.8	.
1972	2 902.2	769.7	.	998.8	.	342.2	162.1	291.9	.	337.5	.
1973	2 876.5	738.3	.	1 002.3	.	344.5	161.8	295.1	.	334.5	.
1974	2 856.1	709.7	.	1 000.1	.	345.8	164.3	296.6	.	339.6	.
1975	2 858.4	694.0	.	993.1	.	346.6	167.5	301.8	.	355.4	.
1976	2 855.5	682.6	.	983.6	.	346.3	171.5	306.2	.	365.3	.
1977	2 836.7	673.7	.	974.9	.	343.5	173.8	307.6	.	363.2	.
1978	2 824.5	670.4	.	964.5	.	341.8	174.5	309.3	.	364.0	.
1979	2 812.9*	671.4*	.	949.1*	.	338.4*	176.1*	310.3*	.	367.6*	.
Female – Femmes – Mujeres											
1970	2 089.1	496.2	.	773.2	.	52.9	253.3	80.8	.	432.7	.
1971	2 111.7	483.8	.	778.4	.	58.8	261.5	84.1	.	445.1	.
1972	2 147.7	477.7	.	788.0	.	64.0	267.0	87.6	.	463.4	.
1973	2 190.9	469.5	.	804.2	.	66.6	274.7	87.8	.	488.1	.
1974	2 223.5	456.7	.	813.3	.	69.2	286.6	89.7	.	508.0	.
1975	2 231.0	445.8	.	806.7	.	71.4	296.1	94.0	.	517.0	.
1976	2 231.7	437.7	.	793.1	.	72.2	300.5	96.6	.	531.6	.
1977	2 238.3	431.8	.	783.5	.	71.8	304.2	97.4	.	549.6	.
1978	2 250.4	432.0	.	778.5	.	71.9	308.0	98.3	.	561.7	.
1979	2 269.1*	439.0*	.	772.4*	.	72.2*	311.5*	99.0*	.	575.0*	.

Iceland — Insured persons – Personnes assurées – Personas aseguradas (Source – Fuente: II)

Pays Portée	Total	1	2	3[5]	4	5	6	7	8	9	0
Total											
1970	84.1	18.0	.	20.7	0.4	8.7	11.0	6.9	2.4	15.3	0.7
1971	87.9	17.4	.	22.0	0.5	9.6	11.8	7.3	2.5	16.1	0.7
1972	90.2	17.0	.	22.6	0.5	9.7	12.2	7.7	2.7	17.1	0.7
1973	92.6	16.9	.	22.6	0.7	10.8	12.7	7.7	2.8	17.7	0.7
1974	95.6	17.3	.	22.9	0.7	11.1	11.4	7.7	3.0	20.8	0.7
1975	97.1	16.7	.	23.6	0.7	11.5	13.1	7.7	3.2	19.8	0.8
1976	99.6	16.7	.	24.3	0.8	11.3	13.3	7.8	3.3	21.2	0.9

[a] La designación en español de las grandes divisiones de actividad económica figura en la página siguiente. – The English designation of major divisions of economic activity is shown on the preceding page.

[1] Socialised sector. [2] Incl. mining, quarrying, electricity and water. [3] Incl. financing, insurance and real estate; excl. restaurants and hotels. [4] Incl. gas, restaurants, hotels and activities not adequately defined; excl. repair and installation services and sanitary services. [5] Incl. mining and quarrying.

[1] Secteur socialisé. [2] Y compris les industries extractives, l'électricité et l'eau. [3] Y compris les banques, les assurances et affaires immobilières; non compris les restaurants et hôtels. [4] Y compris le gaz, les restaurants, les hôtels et les activités mal désignées; non compris les services de réparation et et d'installation, et les services sanitaires. [5] Y compris les industries extractives.

[1] Sector socializado. [2] Incl. minas y canteras, electricidad y agua. [3] Incl. establecimientos financieros, seguros y bienes inmuebles; excl. restaurantes y hoteles. [4] Incl. gas, restaurantes, hoteles y actividades no bien especificadas; excl. los servicios de reparación y de instalación, y los servicios de saneamiento. [5] Incl. minas y canteras.

3 Structure of employment
Structure de l'emploi
Estructura del empleo

(Thousands – Milliers – Millares)

País Alcance	Total	Grandes divisiones de actividad económica [a]									
		1 Agricultura, caza, silvicultura y pesca	2 Minas, canteras	3 Industrias manufactureras	4 Electricidad, gas, agua	5 Construcción	6 Comercio, restaurantes y hoteles	7 Transportes, almacenaje, comunicaciones	8 Bancos, seguros, bienes inm., serv. para empresas	9 Servicios comunales, sociales y personales	0 Actividades no bien especificadas
Ireland		*Civilian employment – Emploi civil – Empleo civil (Source – Fuente: IV)*									
Total [1]											
1970	1 045	283	10	213	13	76	171	60	23	193	3
1971	1 047	273	10	214	14	85	171	60	24	193	3
1972	1 040	267	10	212	14	81	171	61	25	196	3
1973	1 047	260	10	217	14	83	172	61	26	201	3
1974	1 058	254	10	224	14	85	172	63	27	206	3
1975	1 041	250	10	214	14	81	170	64	27	208	3
1976	1 023	242	10	207	14	76	170	63	28	210	3
1977	1 024	235	10	215	13	77	172	62	29	211	3
1978	1 036	230	10	219	13	82	173	63	30	214	3
Italie		*Civilian employment – Emploi civil – Empleo civil (Source – Fuente: I)*									
Total			[2]	[3]							
1977	19 948	3 149	208	5 477	.	1 982	3 605	1 127	427	3 975	–
1978	20 044	3 090	197	5 425	.	2 011	3 640	1 129	467	4 086	–
Male – Hommes – Hombres											
1977	13 759	2 030	191	3 780	.	1 933	2 441	1 018	322	2 044	–
1978	13 812	1 992	183	3 757	.	1 956	2 472	1 015	348	2 090	–
Female – Femmes – Mujeres											
1977	6 189	1 119	17	1 697	.	49	1 163	109	105	1 931	.
1978	6 232	1 098	14	1 668	.	55	1 168	114	119	1 996	–
Malta		*Employees – Salariés – Asalariados (Source – Fuente: IV)*									
ISIC – CITI – CIIU 1958											
Total [4]				[5]	[6]		[7]			[8]	
1970	99.5	5.9	0.6	24.8	0.9	12.6	13.5	4.5	.	37.5	–
1971	101.3	6.2	0.5	25.5	1.0	10.5	14.2	4.6	.	38.9	–
1972	98.9	6.4	0.5	27.0	0.9	6.6	13.7	4.5	.	37.9	–
1973	101.6	6.8	0.5	30.8	1.1	3.9	13.3	4.4	.	40.8	–
1974	102.3	6.9	0.5	31.8	0.8	4.6	13.4	4.6	.	39.7	–
1975	107.8	7.1	0.5	32.5	0.8	4.5	13.5	5.9	.	43.0	–
1976	110.5	7.3	0.6	33.2	0.8	4.1	13.8	5.7	.	45.0	–
1977	114.4	7.3	0.6	36.5	0.8	2.7	13.2	7.0	.	46.3	–
1978	116.2	7.4	0.6	32.9	0.9	4.5	13.9	7.2	.	48.8	–
Male – Hommes – Hombres [4]											
1970	79.4	5.2	0.6	17.8	0.8	12.6	8.3	4.2	.	29.9	–
1971	80.2	5.5	0.5	18.7	0.9	10.5	8.7	4.3	.	31.1	–
1972	76.2	5.6	0.5	18.7	0.8	6.6	8.4	4.1	.	31.5	–
1973	76.2	5.8	0.5	19.7	0.9	3.9	8.5	4.1	.	32.8	–
1974	75.7	5.9	0.5	20.0	0.7	4.6	8.1	4.3	.	31.6	–
1975	80.7	6.0	0.5	20.1	0.7	4.5	8.3	5.3	.	35.3	–
1976	81.7	6.0	0.6	20.4	0.7	4.1	8.3	5.2	.	36.4	–
1977	84.6	6.3	0.6	22.7	0.7	2.7	9.1	6.3	.	36.2	–
1978	85.6	6.6	0.6	18.5	0.8	4.5	9.5	6.5	.	38.6	–

[a] The English designation of major divisions of economic activity is shown on the following page. – Les libellés en français des branches d'activité économique sont indiqués à la page précédente.

[1] April of each year. [2] Energy and water. [3] Industrial transformations. [4] Nov. of each year; prior to 1972: Dec. [5] Incl. repair and installation services. [6] Incl. sanitary services. [7] Incl. financing, insurance and real estate; excl. restaurants and hotels. [8] Incl. restaurants and hotels; excl. repair and installation services and sanitary services.

[1] Avril de chaque année. [2] Energie et eau. [3] Transformations industrielles. [4] Nov. de chaque année; avant 1972: déc. [5] Y compris les services de réparation et d'installation. [6] Y compris les services sanitaires. [7] Y compris les banques, les assurances et affaires immobilières; non compris les restaurants et hôtels. [8] Y compris les restaurants et hôtels; non compris les services de réparation et d'installation, et les services sanitaires.

[1] Abril de cada año. [2] Energía y agua. [3] Transformaciones industriales. [4] Nov. de cada año; antes de 1972: dic. [5] Incl. los servicios de reparación y de instalación. [6] Incl. los servicios de saneamiento. [7] Incl. establecimientos financieros, seguros y bienes inmuebles; excl. restaurantes y hoteles. [8] Incl. restaurantes y hoteles; excl. los servicios de reparación y de instalación y los servicios de saneamiento.

3 Structure of employment
Structure de l'emploi
Estructura del empleo

(Thousands – Milliers – Millares)

Country Scope	Total	Major divisions of economic activity (a)									
		1 Agriculture, hunting, forestry and fishing	2 Mining, quarrying	3 Manu-facturing	4 Electricity, gas, water	5 Construction	6 Trade, restaurants and hotels	7 Transport, storage, communi-cation	8 Financing, insurance, real estate business services	9 Community, social and personal services	0 Activities not adequately defined
Malta					Employees – Salariés – Asalariados (Source – Fuente: IV)					
Female – Femmes – Mujeres [1]										
1970	20.1	0.7	–	7.0	0.1	–	5.2	0.3	.	6.8	–
1971	21.1	0.7	–	6.8	0.1	–	5.5	0.3	.	7.7	–
1972	22.7	0.8	–	8.3	0.1	–	5.3	0.4	.	7.8	–
1973	25.4	1.0	–	11.1	0.2	–	4.8	0.3	.	8.0	–
1974	26.6	1.0	–	11.8	0.1	–	5.3	0.3	.	8.1	–
1975	27.1	1.1	–	12.4	0.1	–	5.2	0.6	.	7.7	–
1976	28.8	1.3	–	12.8	0.1	–	5.5	0.5	.	8.6	–
1977	29.8	1.0	–	13.8	0.1	–	4.1	0.7	.	10.1	–
1978	30.6	0.8	–	14.4	0.1	–	4.4	0.7	.	10.2	–
Netherlands [2]					Civilian employment [3] – Emploi civil [3] – Empleo civil [3] (Source – Fuente: IV)					
Total										
1970	4 554	329	21	1 203	43	505	827	305	258	1 063	–
1971	4 581	320	19	1 186	43	495	834	309	270	1 105	–
1972	4 538	315	16	1 146	44	473	827	305	276	1 136	–
1973	4 546	309	10	1 131	45	472	826	305	283	1 165	–
1974	4 549	304	4	1 128	45	452	824	309	291	1 192	–
1975	4 523	299	4	1 088	45	436	819	310	296	1 226	–
1976	4 518	295	4	1 043	45	438	817	309	303	1 264	–
1977	4 528	289	4	1 015	45	442	821	308	312	1 292	–
Norway [4]					Civilian employment – Emploi civil – Empleo civil (Source – Fuente: I)					
Total										
1972	1 649	201	10	392	17	145	264	162	65	392	1
1973	1 654	189	12	389	17	142	270	163	66	405	1
1974	1 659	175	10	392	18	147	275	163	72	406	1
1975	1 707	159	12	411	17	147	271	158	79	452	1
1976	1 789	168	11	415	19	148	296	161	82	487	2
1977	1 824	165	10	409	15	156	309	171	85	501	3
1978	1 854	161	13	395	15	163	317	170	97	519	4
Portugal					Civilian employment – Emploi civil – Empleo civil (Source – Fuente: I)					
Total [5]										
1974	3 767	1 312	16	962	16	306	409	153	56	527	3
1975	3 734	1 265	16	939	16	297	429	158	61	547	–
1976	3 820	1 286	17	961	18	284	436	150	72	591	–
1977	3 781	1 228	16	905	19	313	454	163	70	607	–
1978	3 808	1 170	21	982	20	321	445	157	73	613	1
1979	3 906	1 179	22	1 000	13	329	461	161	76	660	–

(a) Les libellés en français des branches d'activité économique sont indiqués à la page suivante. – La designación en español de las grandes divisiones de actividad económica figura en la página precedente.

[1] See notes of line "Total", preceding page. [2] Excl. civil personnel employed by the Ministry of Defense. [3] Number of man-years. [4] Persons aged 16 to 74 years. [5] Second semester of each year.

[1] Voir notes de la ligne «Total» à la page précédente. [2] Non compris le personnel civil employé par le ministère de la Défense. [3] Nombre d'années-homme. [4] Personnes âgées de 16 à 74 ans. [5] Second semestre de chaque année.

[1] Véanse notas de la línea «Total» en la página precedente. [2] Excl. el personal civil empleado por el Ministerio de la Defensa. [3] Número de años–hombre. [4] Personas de 16 a 74 años. [5] Segundo semestre de cada año.

3 Structure of employment
Structure de l'emploi
Estructura del empleo

(Thousands – Milliers – Millares)

| Pays Portée | Total | Branches d'activité économique (a) | | | | | | | | | |
		1 Agriculture, chasse, sylviculture et pêche	2 Industries extractives	3 Industries manu-facturières	4 Electricité, gaz, eau	5 Construction	6 Commerce, restaurants et hôtels	7 Transports, entrepôts, communi-cations	8 Banques, assurances, aff. imm., serv. aux entreprises	9 Services à collectivité, services soc. et pers.	0 Activités mal désignées
Portugal		*Civilian employment – Emploi civil – Empleo civil (Source – Fuente: I)*									
Male – Hommes – Hombres [1]											
1974	2 260	690	15	567	16	301	254	127	37	245	1
1975	2 285	675	16	570	16	291	272	133	40	238	–
1976	2 339	681	16	597	17	279	281	125	45	293	–
1977	2 325	648	15	572	18	304	284	138	47	294	–
1978	2 349	601	20	632	18	316	279	130	51	295	–
1979	2 371	587	21	631	13	323	286	134	51	320	1
Female – Femmes – Mujeres [1]											
1974	1 507	622	1	395	–	5	155	26	19	282	2
1975	1 449	590	–	369	–	6	157	25	21	279	–
1976	1 481	605	1	364	1	5	155	25	27	298	–
1977	1 456	580	1	333	1	9	170	25	23	313	–
1978	1 459	569	1	350	2	5	166	27	22	318	–
1979	1 535	592	1	369	–	6	175	27	25	340	–
Roumanie		*Civilian employment – Emploi civil – Empleo civil (Source – Fuente: IV)*									
Total			[2]				[3]			[4]	
1970	9 875	4 868	.	2 277	.	768	427	414	.	1 012	109
1971	9 939	4 623	.	2 457	.	801	469	429	.	1 046	114
1972	9 971	4 403	.	2 601	.	840	509	440	.	1 066	112
1973	10 021	4 229	.	2 798	.	826	516	455	.	1 080	117
1974	10 070	4 036	.	2 983	.	813	542	459	.	1 107	130
1975	10 151	3 864	.	3 110	.	825	559	500	.	1 170	123
1976	10 227	3 670	.	3 268	.	848	592	506	.	1 211	132
1977	10 264	3 559	.	3 362	.	896	604	512	.	1 201	130
1978	10 290	3 375	.	3 447	.	922	618	538	.	1 254	136
1979	10 320	3 208	.	3 582	.	936	624	564	.	1 271	135
Sweden [5]		*Civilian employment* [6] *– Emploi civil* [6] *– Empleo civil* [6] *(Source – Fuente: I)*									
Total											
1970	3 854	314	21	1 064	24	371	557	266	192	1 046	–
1971	3 860	300	18	1 054	27	352	558	268	201	1 082	–
1972	3 862	287	19	1 046	26	331	546	268	206	1 134	–
1973	3 879	276	18	1 066	27	316	545	269	207	1 153	–
1974	3 962	264	20	1 121	31	294	560	271	212	1 191	–
1975	4 062	261	21	1 138	32	290	585	272	214	1 249	–
1976	4 088	254	21	1 100	33	294	592	275	241	1 276	–
1977	4 099	248	18	1 060	32	297	592	279	244	1 327	–
1978	4 115	250	15	1 023	32	290	594	277	253	1 382	–
1979	4 180	242	15	1 026	34	284	576	290	267	1 444	–
Male – Hommes – Hombres											
1970	2 335	242	19	792	20	352	246	206	101	358	–
1971	2 314	232	16	786	22	334	248	205	107	364	–
1972	2 295	220	17	787	22	316	245	203	107	378	–
1973	2 295	212	17	804	23	299	252	202	109	377	–
1974	2 316	200	18	830	27	275	268	203	113	380	–
1975	2 342	193	18	836	27	272	283	202	112	397	–
1976	2 338	190	18	812	29	274	286	203	128	397	–
1977	2 314	183	16	785	27	276	282	204	131	410	–
1978	2 297	186	13	753	27	266	287	201	137	426	–
1979	2 315	181	14	758	30	258	280	211	149	442	–

(a) La designación en español de las grandes divisiones de actividad económica figura en la página siguiente. – The English designation of major divisions of economic activity is shown on the preceding page.

[1] Second semester of each year. [2] Incl. mining, quarrying, electricity, gas and water (col. 2 and 4). [3] Incl. financing, insurance and real estate; excl. restaurants and hotels. [4] Incl. restaurants and hotels; excl. repair and installation services and sanitary services. [5] Persons aged 16 to 74 years. [6] Incl. certain categories of military personnel.

[1] Second semestre de chaque année. [2] Y compris les industries extractives, l'électricité, le gaz et l'eau (col. 2 et 4). [3] Y compris les banques, les assurances et affaires immobilières; non compris les restaurants et hôtels. [4] Y compris les restaurants et hôtels; non compris les services de réparation et d'installation, et les services sanitaires. [5] Personnes âgées de 16 à 74 ans. [6] Y compris certaines catégories de personnel militaire.

[1] Segundo semestre de cada año. [2] Incl. minas y canteras, electricidad, gas y agua (cols 2 y 4). [3] Incl. establecimientos financieros, seguros y bienes inmuebles; excl. restaurantes y hoteles. [4] Incl. restaurantes y hoteles; excl. los servicios de reparación y de instalación y los servicios de saneamiento. [5] Personas de 16 a 74 años. [6] Incl. ciertas categorías de personal militar.

3 Structure of employment
Structure de l'emploi
Estructura del empleo

(Thousands – Milliers – Millares)

País Alcance	Total	Grandes divisiones de actividad económica (a)									
		1 Agricultura, caza, silvicultura y pesca	2 Minas, canteras	3 Industrias manufactureras	4 Electricidad, gas, agua	5 Construcción	6 Comercio, restaurantes y hoteles	7 Transportes, almacenaje, comunicaciones	8 Bancos, seguros, bienes inm., serv. para empresas	9 Servicios comunales, sociales y personales	0 Actividades no bien especificadas
Sweden [1]		*Civilian employment [2] – Emploi civil [2] – Empleo civil [2] (Source – Fuente: I)*									
Female – Femmes – Mujeres											
1970	1 519	72	2	272	5	18	311	60	91	688	–
1971	1 546	69	2	267	5	18	310	63	94	718	–
1972	1 567	66	2	260	4	15	301	65	99	755	–
1973	1 584	64	1	262	4	17	293	67	99	776	–
1974	1 647	64	2	290	4	19	291	68	99	810	–
1975	1 720	68	2	302	4	18	302	70	102	852	–
1976	1 751	64	3	288	5	21	306	72	113	879	–
1977	1 785	65	2	275	5	21	310	75	114	917	–
1978	1 818	64	2	270	5	23	307	76	116	956	–
1979	1 865	61	2	276	5	26	296	79	118	1 082	–
Turquie		*Insured persons – Personnes assurées – Personas aseguradas (Source – Fuente: II)*									
Total											
1970	1 313.5	0.2	70.0	622.9	47.0	282.8	57.1	53.1	10.4	152.2	18.0
1971	1 404.8	0.1	84.9	671.1	51.2	275.9	80.9	59.5	10.5	149.9	20.7
1972	1 525.0	0.1	70.6	746.5	53.3	305.3	91.3	68.3	10.7	157.8	21.2
1973	1 649.1	0.1	72.8	815.2	60.5	329.1	98.1	68.0	11.4	173.0	20.8
1974	1 800.0	0.2	82.7	776.5	80.2	367.4	188.5	78.8	12.0	190.1	23.6
1975	1 823.3	0.2	78.9	850.4	75.8	397.8	107.8	79.1	12.5	197.7	23.1
1976	2 017.9	0.1	83.9	959.7	77.0	447.8	111.1	87.1	14.8	210.8	25.5
1977	2 191.3	0.1	124.2	1 010.0	82.0	487.1	116.1	94.8	15.4	235.8	25.7
1978	2 206.1	32.5	88.8	998.1	92.1	499.5	117.3	98.3	17.3	235.5	26.7
1979	2 152.4	38.5	84.3	1 004.3	87.2	453.6	121.1	97.6	17.8	223.0	24.9
United Kingdom [3]		*Civilian employment – Emploi civil – Empleo civil (Source – Fuente: IV)*									
Total [4]											
1970	24 381	782	411	8 465	391	1 653	4 005	1 640	1 214	5 820	–
1971	24 030	734	397	8 181	377	1 594	3 916	1 639	1 245	5 949	–
1972	24 020	709	380	7 907	356	1 674	3 958	1 614	1 270	6 149	1
1973	24 610	713	364	7 955	344	1 823	4 115	1 596	1 340	6 362	1
1974	24 714	680	350	7 995	347	1 767	4 130	1 583	1 401	6 461	1
1975	24 596	664	353	7 611	353	1 700	4 153	1 596	1 397	6 766	3
1976	24 429	660	349	7 367	353	1 695	4 137	1 553	1 405	6 903	9
1977	24 505	655	351	7 413	347	1 656	4 180	1 546	1 444	6 912	–
1978	24 552*	650*	346*	7 354*	348*	1 651*	4 213*	1 544*	1 470*	6 976*	–
1979	24 711*	632*	338*	7 276*	354*	1 679*	4 293*	1 560*	1 504*	7 076*	–
Male – Hommes – Hombres [4]											
1970	15 538	636	396	5 916	332	1 567	1 893	1 381	616	2 802	–
1971	15 248	598	382	5 755	316	1 508	1 846	1 375	628	2 840	–
1972	15 134	575	366	5 572	295	1 584	1 855	1 354	635	2 897	1
1973	15 345	564	350	5 571	283	1 726	1 895	1 332	665	1 958	–
1974	15 211	541	336	5 560	282	1 669	1 877	1 318	693	2 935	–
1975	15 050	531	339	5 366	285	1 599	1 884	1 325	699	3 021	2
1976	14 906	528	334	5 233	285	1 589	1 878	1 293	706	3 056	5
1977	14 877	531	336	5 244	282	1 549	1 895	1 283	715	3 044	–
1978	14 846*	526*	330*	5 207*	281*	1 544*	1 899*	1 275*	722*	3 061*	–
1979	14 838*	512*	323*	5 143*	284*	1 571*	1 923*	1 279*	731*	3 073*	–

(a) The English designation of major divisions of economic activity is shown on the following page. – Les libellés en français des branches d'activité économique sont indiqués à la page précédente.

[1] Persons aged 16 to 74 years. [2] Incl. certain categories of military personnel. [3] Excl. unpaid family workers as well as employees in private domestic services. [4] June of each year.

[1] Personnes âgées de 16 à 74 ans. [2] Y compris certaines catégories de personnel militaire. [3] Non compris les travailleurs familiaux non rémunérés et les personnes occupées à des services domestiques privés. [4] Juin de chaque année.

[1] Personas de 16 a 74 años. [2] Incl. ciertas categorías de personal militar. [3] Excl. los trabajadores familiares no remunerados y las personas ocupadas en los servicios domésticos privados. [4] Junio de cada año.

3 Structure of employment
Structure de l'emploi
Estructura del empleo

(Thousands – Milliers – Millares)

Country Scope	Total	Major divisions of economic activity (a)								
		1 Agriculture, hunting, forestry and fishing	2 Mining, quarrying	3 Manu-facturing	4 Electricity, gas, water	5 Construction	6 Trade, restaurants and hotels	7 Transport, storage, communi-cation	8 Financing, insurance, real estate business services	9 Community, social and personal services	0 Activities not adequately defined

United Kingdom [1]
Female – Femmes – Mujeres [2] — Civilian employment – Emploi civil – Empleo civil (Source – Fuente: IV)

Year	Total	1	2	3	4	5	6	7	8	9	0
1970	8 843	146	16	2 549	59	87	2 114	259	598	3 017	–
1971	8 782	138	15	2 426	61	85	2 068	264	615	3 111	–
1972	8 887	135	15	2 336	60	89	2 105	260	635	3 251	–
1973	9 266	149	14	2 383	61	98	2 219	263	675	3 404	–
1974	9 503	140	14	2 435	64	98	2 256	265	707	3 524	–
1975	9 546	133	14	2 245	68	101	2 268	271	696	3 748	–
1976	9 524	132	15	2 134	68	106	2 259	260	697	3 850	1
1977	9 627	125	15	2 169	66	107	2 285	263	728	3 869	4
1978	9 706*	124*	15*	2 147*	68*	107*	2 314*	269*	747*	3 915*	–
1979	9 873*	121*	16*	2 133*	70*	107*	2 371*	281*	7 723*	4 003*	–

Yugoslavia [3]
Total [4] — Registered employed – Effectif occupé – Efectivo ocupado (Source – Fuente: IV)

Year	Total	1	2	3	4	5	6	7	8	9	0
1970	3 765	235	101	1 294	98	412	470	291	93	771	–
1971	3 944	236	104	1 361	103	424	508	303	99	806	–
1972	4 115	238	107	1 437	107	430	542	315	101	838	–
1973	4 213	239	105	1 485	109	420	567	320	108	860	–
1974	4 423	247	111	1 566	114	444	600	329	116	896	–
1975	4 667	257	117	1 649	121	479	632	346	124	942	–
1976	4 833	256	121	1 697	125	500	658	357	134	985	–
1977	5 052	258	123	1 780	131	531	687	374	146	1 022	–
1978	5 280	263	123	1 838	138	567	714	381	163	1 093	–
1979	5 506	267	125	1 913	144	602	752	387	184	1 132	–

OCEANIA – OCEANIE – OCEANIA

Australia
Total [5] — Civilian employment – Emploi civil – Empleo civil (Source – Fuente: I)

Year	Total	1	2	3	4	5	6[6]	7	8[7]	9[8]	0
1970	5 395.6	433.9	81.7	1 423.8	.	456.5	1 087.4	416.5	383.5	908.9	.
1971	5 515.7	412.5	89.1	1 467.3	.	471.0	1 112.5	412.2	395.1	947.6	–
1972	5 609.9	442.3	81.1	1 428.4	.	466.0	1 162.8	408.9	398.9	1 013.4	–
1973	5 783.0	426.2	69.5	1 481.3	.	503.2	1 187.1	438.6	401.3	1 048.0	–
1974	5 855.2	404.8	73.8	1 478.4	.	506.3	1 165.7	444.1	429.4	1 102.2	–
1975	5 841.3	397.7	79.1	1 368.5	.	511.1	1 156.9	455.4	430.5	1 164.7	–
1976	5 897.8	384.6	79.7	1 384.3	.	493.8	1 156.9	442.3	456.3	1 222.1	–
1977	5 995.4	400.3	79.8	1 382.9	.	481.8	1 184.9	452.1	467.2	1 268.4	–
1978	5 969.6	1 238.5	79.5	1 299.9	.	485.0	1 238.6	455.6	465.8	1 283.9	–
1979	6 041.5	399.3	82.3	1 338.9	.	465.9	1 224.2	470.7	483.1	1 306.9	–

Male – Hommes – Hombres [5]

Year	Total	1	2	3	4	5	6	7	8	9	0
1970	3 647.7	357.2	77.2	1 073.0	.	435.2	646.7	352.9	216.5	349.5	.
1971	3 712.7	339.8	80.6	1 093.4	.	445.9	669.5	342.8	225.1	372.6	.
1972	3 757.7	366.5	75.5	1 080.9	.	443.8	690.1	343.0	217.7	391.1	–
1973	3 839.6	344.5	65.2	1 110.5	.	477.7	703.4	364.8	212.9	403.7	–
1974	3 847.1	332.9	69.8	1 100.5	.	479.3	670.5	367.2	232.9	422.8	–
1975	3 820.6	320.9	73.0	1 028.0	.	482.5	673.5	378.3	234.3	447.8	–
1976	3 836.3	301.4	74.4	1 046.3	.	458.9	687.2	372.7	247.6	465.6	–
1977	3 866.8	310.0	73.6	1 051.2	.	446.7	697.2	372.7	252.1	479.5	–
1978	3 832.3	296.1	74.2	980.1	.	440.9	729.1	379.0	247.0	491.8	–
1979	3 904.5	317.0	77.5	1 023.0	.	421.5	706.5	393.1	267.8	510.7	.

(a) Les libellés en français des branches d'activité économique sont indiqués à la page suivante. – La designación en español de las grandes divisiones de actividad económica figura en la página precedente.

[1] Excl. unpaid family workers as well as employees in private domestic services. [2] June of each year. [3] Socialised sector. [4] March and Sep. of each year. [5] Aug. of each year. [6] Incl. electricity, gas and water. [7] Incl. financing, insurance and real estate; excl. restaurants and hotels. [8] Incl. restaurants and hotels; excl. repair and installation services and sanitary services.

[1] Non compris les travailleurs familiaux non rémunérés et les personnes occupées à des services domestiques privés. [2] Juin de chaque année. [3] Secteur socialisé. [4] Mars et sept. de chaque année. [5] Août de chaque année. [6] Y compris l'électricité, le gaz et l'eau. [7] Y compris les banques, les assurances et affaires immobilières; non compris les restaurants et hôtels. [8] Y compris les restaurants et hôtels; non compris les services de réparation et d'installation, et les services sanitaires.

[1] Excl. los trabajadores familiares no remunerados y las personas ocupadas en los servicios domésticos privados. [2] Junio de cada año. [3] Sector socializado. [4] Marzo y sept. de cada año. [5] Agosto de cada año. [6] Incl. electricidad, gas y agua. [7] Incl. establecimientos financieros, seguros y bienes inmuebles; excl. restaurantes y hoteles. [8] Incl. restaurantes y hoteles; excl. los servicios de reparación y de instalación y los servicios de saneamiento.

3 Structure of employment
Structure de l'emploi
Estructura del empleo

(Thousands – Milliers – Millares)

Pays Portée	Total	1 Agriculture, chasse, sylviculture et pêche	2 Industries extractives	3 Industries manu-facturières	4 Electricité, gaz, eau	5 Construction	6 Commerce, restaurants et hôtels	7 Transports, entrepôts, communi-cations	8 Banques, assurances, aff. imm., serv. aux entreprises	9 Services à collectivité, services soc. et pers.	0 Activités mal désignées
Australia				Civilian employment – Emploi civil – Empleo civil (Source – Fuente: I)							
Female – Femmes – Mujeres [1]											
1970	1 747.8	76.7	4.5	350.8	.	21.3	440.7	63.7	167.0	559.3	.
1971	1 803.0	70.8	8.5	373.9	.	25.0	443.0	69.5	170.0	575.0	–
1972	1 852.1	75.0	5.7	347.6	.	22.2	472.7	65.9	181.2	622.4	–
1973	1 943.3	80.7	–	370.8	.	25.4	483.6	73.8	188.3	644.2	–
1974	2 008.1	70.9	–	377.9	.	27.1	495.2	77.0	196.5	679.4	–
1975	2 020.7	76.5	6.1	340.5	.	28.7	483.4	77.0	196.2	717.0	.
1976	2 061.5	82.9	5.3	338.0	.	34.9	469.7	69.6	208.7	756.4	–
1977	2 128.6	89.1	6.2	331.7	.	35.1	487.7	79.4	215.1	788.8	.
1978	2 137.2	78.1	5.4	319.8	.	44.0	509.5	76.7	218.8	792.0	.
1979	2 136.9	82.4	4.8	315.9	.	44.4	517.7	77.6	215.3	796.2	.
Fiji				Registered employed – Effectif occupé – Efectivo ocupado (Source – Fuente: III)							
Total [2]											
1970	51.60	3.80	2.10	9.10	1.10	7.40	8.70	3.90	1.50	14.00	.
1971	56.21	3.82	1.85	10.04	1.23	8.22	9.15	4.63	1.69	15.57	.
1972	58.40	2.78	1.74	9.83	1.44	8.24	9.89	5.22	2.03	17.23	.
1973	61.48	3.44	1.75	10.12	1.73	9.45	9.67	4.91	2.60	17.81	.
1974	67.00	3.90	2.00	11.80	1.70	8.30	10.00	6.20	3.30	19.80	.
1975	70.00	4.30	1.90	12.80	1.50	8.50	10.30	6.40	3.50	20.80	.
1976	70.00	3.80	1.50	11.40	1.80	7.70	11.70	6.80	3.70	21.60	.
1977	73.50	3.90	1.70	13.10	2.00	8.10	12.00	7.40	3.90	21.30	.
1978	74.90	4.20	0.40	13.50	2.20	8.20	12.40	7.90	4.30	21.80	.
1979	79.06	2.59	0.73	14.10	2.30	9.83	13.18	7.92	4.34	24.07	.
New Zealand [3]				Civilian employment – Emploi civil – Empleo civil (Source – Fuente: IV)							
Total											
1971	1 094	138	5	269	14	86	187	103	66	226	–
1972	1 103	139	4	269	14	87	187	103	67	233	–
1973	1 141	141	4	283	14	90	191	104	72	242	–
1974	1 178	142	4	295	15	93	195	107	75	252	–
1975	1 189	143	4	288	15	94	193	111	76	263	–
1976	1 198	143	4	294	15	92	191	111	78	269	–
1977	1 215	141	5	308	16	91	193	111	79	271	–
Male – Hommes – Hombres											
1977	830	117	4	225	14	88	110	89	44	138	–
Female – Femmes – Mujeres											
1977	385	24	–	84	2	4	83	22	35	133	–
Papua New Guinea				Employees – Salariés – Asalariados (Source – Fuente: IV)							
ISIC – CITI – CIIU 1958 *Total* [4]				[5]	[6]		[7]			[8]	
1973	142.18	36.58	4.47	10.25	1.56	7.74	12.31	5.34	.	63.93	–
1974	151.07	39.00	4.96	11.45	1.42	7.33	13.37	6.76	.	66.75	0.02
1975	131.20	31.38	5.10	10.56	1.59	6.84	12.10	6.37	.	57.06	0.19
1976	138.38	33.67	4.72	12.19	1.57	6.59	14.28	6.31	.	59.03	0.02
1977	137.56	33.69	4.50	12.19	1.96	7.19	14.09	6.41	.	57.50	0.03

(a) La designación en español de las grandes divisiones de actividad económica figura en la página siguiente. – The English designation of major divisions of economic activity is shown on the preceding page.

[1] See notes of line "Total", preceding page. [2] June of each year; beginning 1977: Sep. [3] Excl. unpaid family workers and members of producers' co-operatives. [4] June of each year. [5] Incl. repair and installation services. [6] Incl. sanitary services. [7] Incl. financing, insurance and real estate; excl. restaurants and hotels. [8] Incl. restaurants and hotels; excl. repair and installation services and sanitary services.

[1] Voir notes de la ligne «Total» à la page précédente. [2] Juin de chaque année; à partir de 1977: sept. [3] Non compris les travailleurs familiaux non rémunérés et les membres de coopératives de producteurs. [4] Juin de chaque année. [5] Y compris les services de réparation et d'installation. [6] Y compris les services sanitaires. [7] Y compris les banques, les assurances et affaires immobilières; non compris les restaurants et hôtels. [8] Y compris les restaurants et hôtels; non compris les services de réparation et d'installation, et les services sanitaires.

[1] Véanse notas de la línea «Total» en la página precedente. [2] Junio de cada año; a partir de 1977: sept. [3] Excl. los trabajadores familiares no remunerados y los miembros de cooperativas de producción. [4] Junio de cada año. [5] Incl. los servicios de reparación y de instalación. [6] Incl. los servicios de saneamiento. [7] Incl. establecimientos financieros, seguros y bienes inmuebles; excl. restaurantes y hoteles. [8] Incl. restaurantes y hoteles; excl. los servicios de reparación y de instalación y los servicios de saneamiento.

3 Structure of employment
Structure de l'emploi
Estructura del empleo

(Thousands – Milliers – Millares)

País Alcance	Total	Grandes divisiones de actividad económica (a)									
		1 Agricultura, caza, silvicultura y pesca	2 Minas, canteras [2]	3 Industrias manufactureras [3]	4 Electricidad, gas, agua [4]	5 Construcción [5]	6 Comercio, restaurantes y hoteles	7 Transportes, almacenaje, comunicaciones	8 Bancos, seguros, bienes inm., serv. para empresas	9 Servicios comunales, sociales y personales [6]	0 Actividades no bien especificadas [7]

USSR – URSS – URSS

URSS [1]   Registered employees – Salariés inscrits – Asalariados registrados (Source – Fuente: III)

Total											
1970	106 773	26 438	2 141	28 816	636	9 052	7 537	9 315	388	21 452	998
1971	108 874	26 256	2 119	29 443	648	9 549	7 816	9 597	411	22 193	1 022
1972	111 092	26 196	2 076	29 728	657	9 986	8 100	9 881	439	22 968	1 061
1973	113 152	26 282	2 051	30 163	661	10 091	8 392	10 170	465	22 968	1 061
1974	115 254	26 286	2 017	30 742	674	10 339	8 640	10 421	493	23 746	1 131
1975	117 132	25 944	2 027	31 338	689	10 574	8 857	10 743	519	24 455	1 187
1976 [8]	118 898	25 879	...	34 815	...	10 716	9 010	10 933	546	25 445	1 250
1977	120 588	25 646	...	35 417	...	10 880	9 204	11 184	574	25 926	1 290
1978	122 546	25 646	...	36 014	...	11 034	9 361	11 462	604	26 642	1 345
1979	124 123	25 370	...	36 456	...	11 156	9 526	11 723	632	27 642	1 391
										27 807	1 413

(a) Les libellés en français des branches d'activité économique sont indiqués à la page précédente.

[1] Socialised sector. [2] Excl. logging and industrial sea-fishing. [3] Excl. extraction of sand, stones and other minerals. [4] Excl. printing and publishing; incl. logging, industrial sea-fishing and water supply. [5] Excl. gas distribution and water supply. [6] Incl. gas distribution. [7] Incl. printing and publishing. [8] Beginning 1976: column 3 includes columns 2 and 4.

[1] Secteur socialisé. [2] Non compris les exploitations forestières et la pêche maritime industrielle. [3] Non compris l'extraction du sable, de la pierre et d'autres minéraux. [4] Non compris l'imprimerie et l'édition; y compris les exploitations forestières, la pêche industrielle et la distribution publique de l'eau. [5] Non compris la distribution du gaz. [6] Y compris la distribution du gaz. [7] Y compris l'imprimerie et l'édition. [8] A partir de 1976: la colonne 3 comprend les colonnes 2 et 4.

[1] Sector socializado. [2] Excl. la extracción de madera y la pesca marítima industrial. [3] Excl. la extracción de piedra, arena y otros minerales. [4] Excl. imprentas y editoriales; incl. la extracción de madera, la pesca marítima industrial y el abastecimiento de agua. [5] Excl. la distribución de gas. [6] Incl. la distribución de gas. [7] Incl. imprentas y editoriales. [8] A partir de 1977: la columna 3 incluye las columnas 2 y 4.

4 General level of employment
Niveau général de l'emploi
Nivel general del empleo

(Thousands – Milliers – Millares)

Country – Source Pays – Source País – Fuente	1970	1971	1972	1973	1974	1975	1976	1977	1978	1979
AFRICA – AFRIQUE – AFRICA										
Bénin (II)										
Total	.	.	.	35.528	37.197	33.127	.	39.262	42.681	43.553
Males – Hom.	.	.	.	33.127	34.706	30.791	.	36.462	39.826	40.608
Fem. – Muj.	.	.	.	2.401	2.491	2.336	.	2.800	2.855	2.945
Botswana (III)										
Total [1]	.	.	41.300	46.950	51.600	57.325	59.375	62.700	69.400	...
Males – Hom. [1]	.	.	.	.	.	.	48.276	49.030	54.405	...
Fem. – Muj. [1]	.	.	.	.	.	.	11.099	13.680	14.995	...
Burundi (IV)										
Total [2]	.	.	28.891	25.731	25.805	28.508	27.265	34.199	38.132	40.117
Rép.-Unie du Cameroun (III)										
Total	145.11	124.17	122.19	180.48	187.83	191.48	203.82	212.81	224.67	267.48
Egypt (I) [3]										
Total [4]	8 044.2	8 252.5	8 682.0	8 567.3	8 867.3	9 030.7	...	9 198.2	9 448.0	...
Males – Hom. [4]	7 259.5	7 714.5	8 106.5	8 100.8	8 362.2	8 482.7	...	8 572.3	8 704.7	...
Fem. – Muj. [4]	514.7	538.0	575.5	466.5	505.1	548.0	...	625.9	743.3	...
Gabon (II) [5]										
Total	63.03	65.04	68.51	...	...	113.20	128.90	138.60	...	...
Gambia (III)										
Total [6]	.	.	.	17.004	18.114	18.801	19.148	...	...	...
Males – Hom. [6]	.	.	.	.	16.137	16.871	17.336	...	...	...
Fem. – Muj. [6]	.	.	.	.	1.977	1.930	1.812	...	...	...
Kenya (III)										
Total [7]	.	.	719.8	761.7	826.3	819.1	857.5	902.9	911.6	972.3
Males – Hom. [7]	.	.	.	.	.	.	.	748.2	752.8	807.1
Fem. – Muj. [7]	.	.	.	.	.	.	.	154.7	158.7	165.2
Liberia (III)										
Total	45.948	46.116	46.503	43.464	38.205	46.882	46.182	40.304	93.101	126.46
Males – Hom.	40.250	40.378	40.728	38.063	33.464	39.136	40.447	34.149	79.370	86.922
Fem. – Muj.	5.698	5.738	5.775	5.401	4.741	7.746	5.735	6.155	13.731	39.542
Libyan Arab Jamahiriya (IV) [3]										
Total	.	459.0	488.0	538.1	607.2	677.1	732.7	765.0	773.2	...
Malawi [8] (III) [9]										
Total [5]	159.7	172.6	189.6	215.3	226.9	244.7	264.1	∎308.9[10]	353.7*	...
Males – Hom. [5]	146.5	158.7	173.8	193.5	203.1	221.3	239.4	∎276.4[10]	312.7*	...
Fem. – Muj. [5]	13.0	14.3	15.3	21.6	23.4	24.8	27.0	∎32.5[10]	41.0*	...

Explanatory notes and source: see p. 151 – Notes explicatives et source: voir p. 154 – Notas explicativas y fuente: véase p. 157

[1] Aug. of each year. [2] Dec. of each year. [3] Civilian labour force employed. [4] May of each year. [5] Excl. domestic services. [6] Third quarter of each year. [7] June of each year. [8] Establishments with 20 or more persons employed. [9] Incl. working proprietors and unpaid family workers. [10] Beginning 1977: sample of establishments and revised allocation of establishments in the industrial classification.

[1] Août de chaque année. [2] Déc. de chaque année. [3] Main-d'œuvre civile occupée. [4] Mai de chaque année. [5] Non compris les services domestiques. [6] Troisième trimestre de chaque année. [7] Juin de chaque année. [8] Etablissements occupant 20 personnes et plus. [9] Y compris les propriétaires–exploitants et les travailleurs familiaux non rémunérés. [10] A partir de 1977: échantillon d'établissements et changements dans leur répartition industrielle.

[1] Agosto de cada año. [2] Dic. de cada año. [3] Fuerza trabajadora civil ocupada. [4] Mayo de cada año. [5] Excl. los servicios domésticos. [6] Tercer trimestre de cada año. [7] Junio de cada año. [8] Establecimientos con 20 y más trabajadores. [9] Incl. los empresarios propietarios y los trabajadores familiares no remunerados. [10] A partir de 1977: muestra de establecimientos y cambios en la distribución industrial de los establecimientos.

4 General level of employment
Niveau général de l'emploi
Nivel general del empleo

(Thousands – Milliers – Millares)

Country – Source Pays – Source País – Fuente	1970	1971	1972	1973	1974	1975	1976	1977	1978	1979
Mauritius (III) [1]										
Total [2]	126.44	137.03	144.69	154.01	161.79	168.64	180.64	194.40	196.80	198.36
Males – Hom. [2]	101.91	110.33	116.89	123.04	126.86	131.54	138.18	147.04	148.60	147.49
Fem. – Muj. [2]	24.53	26.70	27.80	30.97	34.93	37.10	42.46	47.36	48.20	50.86
Seychelles (II)										
Total [3]	.	.	.	13.709	12.973	13.758	14.920	16.009	15.351	...
Sierra Leone (III)										
Total [4]	.	.	.	.	63.959	61.297	61.889	61.328	60.052	67.932
Swaziland (III)										
Total [5]	42.426	47.051	53.856	57.032	62.061	64.405	66.215[6]	66.225	71.256	...
Males – Hom. [5]	35.068	35.953	42.609	44.769	48.746	50.011	47.559[6]	47.266	54.017	...
Fem. – Muj. [5]	7.358	11.098	11.247	12.263	13.585	14.394	18.656[6]	17.572	17.239	...
Tunisie (IV)										
Total	1 276.4	1 312.0	1 386.7	1 417.3	1 455.8	1 366.5	1 440.1	1 480.0	1 524.0	1 567.9
Males – Hom.	.	.	.	.	.	1 105.9	1 163.5	...	...	...
Fem. – Muj.						260.6	276.6	...	...	...
Zambia (III)										
Total [4]	342.97	365.55	360.67	365.59	384.89	393.49	368.47	372.50*[7]	...	...
Zimbabwe [8] (III)										
Total	853.0	891.0	953.0	997.0	1 040.0	1 052.0	1 037.0	1 015.0	990.0	989.0

AMERICA – AMERIQUE – AMERICA

	1970	1971	1972	1973	1974	1975	1976	1977	1978	1979
Bahamas (II) [9]										
Total [10]	.	.	.	.	.	.	60.410	70.771	69.876	72.713
Barbados (III)										
Total	.	.	.	.	59.601	60.097	62.924	65.110	...	...
Bolivia (IV) [11]										
Total	1 197.7	1 236.1	1 275.8	1 316.7	1 358.8	1 402.3	1 447.2	1 485.3	1 525.6	1 565.7
Males – Hom.	.	855.2	884.1	915.5	947.1	975.7	1 006.9	948.7	976.4	1 006.2
Fem. – Muj.	.	380.9	391.7	401.2	411.7	426.6	404.3	536.6	549.2	559.5
Brasil (III) [12]										
Total [4]	5 730	6 069	6 876	7 614	8 803	9 477	▮11 289[13]	...	...	...
Males – Hom. [4]	4 727	4 945	5 520	6 033	6 879	7 326	▮8 568[13]	...	...	...
Fem. – Muj. [4]	1 003	1 124	1 356	1 581	1 924	2 151	▮2 721[13]	...	...	...
Canada (I) [14]										
Total	7 778	7 961	8 210	8 638	9 011	9 284	9 479	9 648	9 972	10 369
Males – Hom.	5 233	5 305	5 447	5 679	5 885	5 903	5 965	6 031	6 148	6 347
Fem. – Muj.	2 545	2 657	2 763	2 958	3 126	3 381	3 515	3 617	3 824	4 022

Explanatory notes and source: see p. 151 – Notes explicatives et source: voir p. 154 – Notas explicativas y fuente: véase p. 157

[1] Incl. development workers. [2] March and Sep. of each year. [3] Nov. of each year. [4] Dec. of each year. [5] June of each year. [6] Prior to 1976: Sep. of each year. [7] June. [8] Excl. small establishments in rural areas. [9] Insured persons. [10] Jan. of each year. [11] Civilian labour force employed. [12] Registered establishments on 31st Dec. of each year. [13] Beginning 1978: revised questionnaire. [14] Persons aged 15 years and over. Prior to 1975: 14 years and over.

[1] Y compris les personnes occupées à des travaux publics de développement. [2] Mars et sept. de chaque année. [3] Nov. de chaque année. [4] Déc. de chaque année. [5] Juin de chaque année. [6] Avant 1976: sept. de chaque année. [7] Juin. [8] Non compris les petites entreprises des zones rurales. [9] Personnes assurées. [10] Janv. de chaque année. [11] Main-d'œuvre civile occupée. [12] Etablissements enregistrés le 31 déc. de chaque année. [13] A partir de 1978: questionnaire révisé. [14] Personnes âgées de 15 ans et plus. Avant 1975: 14 ans et plus.

[1] Incl. las personas ocupadas en planes de desarrollo. [2] Marzo y sept. de cada año. [3] Nov. de cada año. [4] Dic. de cada año. [5] Junio de cada año. [6] Antes de 1976: sept. de cada año. [7] Junio. [8] Excl. las pequeñas empresas de las zonas rurales. [9] Personas aseguradas. [10] Enero de cada año. [11] Fuerza trabajadora civil ocupada. [12] Establecimientos registrados el 31 dic. de cada año. [13] A partir de 1978: cuestionario revisado. [14] Personas de 15 años y más. Antes de 1975: 14 años y más.

4 General level of employment
Niveau général de l'emploi
Nivel general del empleo

(Thousands – Milliers – Millares)

Country – Source Pays – Source País – Fuente	1970	1971	1972	1973	1974	1975	1976	1977	1978	1979
Colombia [1] (I)										
Total [2]	.	.	.	.	.	2 146.9	2 239.3	2 529.9	2 751.3	2 996.6
Males – Hom. [2]	.	.	.	.	.	1 361.2	1 449.2	1 574.8	1 716.1	1 854.8
Fem. – Muj. [2]	.	.	.	.	.	785.7	868.4	955.1	1 035.2	1 141.9
Costa Rica (I) [3]										
Total [4]	.	.	.	542.33	.	.	616.79	653.26	687.04	707.13
Males – Hom. [4]	.	.	.	.	.	.	484.06	503.17	519.42	530.11
Fem. – Muj. [4]	.	.	.	.	.	.	132.72	150.09	167.62	177.02
Cuba (IV) [5]										
Total	.	2 081.9	2 125.9	2 245.7	2 313.3	2 393.8	2 469.2	2 607.8*	...	...
Chile [6] (I) [3]										
Total	902.4	917.9	912.7	941.3	929.8	916.6	936.9	983.4	1 063.3	1 097.1
Guadeloupe (IV) [3]										
Total	.	.	.	.	83.4	84.1	80.9	83.9	83.9	...
Guyane française (IV)										
Total	10.812	9.738	9.986	9.784	10.795	11.012	12.580	12.791	13.475	13.879
Haïti (IV) [3]										
Total [7]	1 928.6	1 940.2	1 951.9	1 963.6	1 975.4	1 987.3	1 883.5	1 894.4	1 904.2	...
Males – Hom. [7]	1 053.8	1 063.2	1 072.7	1 082.2	1 091.8	1 101.5	995.5	1 004.2	1 009.4	...
Fem. – Muj. [7]	874.9	877.0	879.3	881.4	883.6	885.9	888.1	890.3	894.7	...
Jamaica (I) [3]										
Total	.	.	611.3	629.5	646.3	682.3	685.8	689.8	708.5	...
México (IV) [3]										
Total [8]	.	.	.	.	15 946	16 597	17 301	18 043	18 826	19 651
Males – Hom. [8]	.	.	.	.	.	13 016	13 449	13 897	14 489	14 843
Fem. – Muj. [8]	.	.	.	.	.	3 581	3 852	4 145	4 337	4 808
Nicaragua [9] (II) [10]										
Total	86.7	83.5	89.9	91.8	98.4	115.8	120.9	138.2	132.3	129.5
Panamá (I) [3]										
Total [11]	434.3	441.3	455.4	464.1	487.4[12]	461.2[13]	471.5	470.4[13]	499.2*	...
Males – Hom. [11]	.	.	.	.	358.5[12]	336.3[13]	344.8	344.3[13]	355.0*	...
Fem. – Muj. [11]	.	.	.	.	128.9[12]	124.1[13]	126.7	126.1[13]	144.2*	...
Paraguay (IV) [3]										
Total	.	.	730.6	737.9	786.8	807.6	854.4	882.6*	911.8*	0.9*
Perú (IV) [3]										
Total	3 960.0	4 086.9	4 214.8	4 338.9	4 482.5	4 582.2	4 708.9	4 826.5	4 910.1	5 054.3
Puerto Rico (I)										
Total	689	715	743	764	760	712	731	750	796	819

Explanatory notes and source: see p. 151 – Notes explicatives et source: voir p. 154 – Notas explicativas y fuente: véase p. 157

[1] Seven main cities of the country. [2] Sep. of each year. [3] Civilian labour force employed. [4] July of each year. [5] State sector. [6] Gran Santiago only. [7] Year beginning in July of year indicated. [8] June of each year. [9] Eight main cities of the country. [10] Insured persons. [11] Aug. of each year. [12] November. [13] October.

[1] Sept villes principales du pays. [2] Sept. de chaque année. [3] Main-d'œuvre civile occupée. [4] Juillet de chaque année. [5] Secteur d'Etat. [6] Seulement Gran Santiago. [7] Année commençant en juillet de l'année indiquée. [8] Juin de chaque année. [9] Huit villes principales du pays. [10] Personnes assurées. [11] Août de chaque année. [12] Novembre. [13] Octobre.

[1] Siete ciudades principales del país. [2] Sept. de cada año. [3] Fuerza trabajadora civil ocupada. [4] Julio de cada año. [5] Sector de Estado. [6] Gran Santiago solamente. [7] Año que comienza en julio del año indicado. [8] Junio de cada año. [9] Ocho ciudades principales del país. [10] Personas aseguradas. [11] Agosto de cada año. [12] Noviembre. [13] Octubre.

4 General level of employment
Niveau général de l'emploi
Nivel general del empleo

(Thousands – Milliers – Millares)

Country – Source Pays – Source País – Fuente	1970	1971	1972	1973	1974	1975	1976	1977	1978	1979
St. Kitts-Nevis-Anguilla (III)										
Total	.	.	.	19.67	19.89	19.98	21.10	22.17	22.89	22.90
Trinidad and Tobago (I) [1]										
Total	317.2	321.4[2]	.	323.6	333.9	332.3	.	370.8	385.4[2]	...
United States (I) [3]										
Total	78 627	79 120	81 702	84 409	85 936	84 783	87 485	90 546	94 373	96 945
Males – Hom.	48 960	49 245	50 630	51 963	52 519	51 230	52 390	53 861	55 491	56 499
Fem. – Muj.	29 667	29 875	31 072	32 446	33 417	33 553	35 095	36 685	38 882	40 446
Venezuela (I) [4]										
Total [5]	.	.	.	.	.	3 504.3	3 703.2	3 870.4	3 994.5	4 106.2
Males – Hom. [5]	.	.	.	.	.	2 546.7	2 668.0	2 806.7	2 903.4	...
Fem. – Muj. [5]	.	.	.	.	.	957.8	1 035.2	1 063.7	1 091.1	...
ASIA – ASIE – ASIA										
Brunei (III) [6]										
Total [7]	.	.	17.613	17.576	17.037	18.066	19.660	21.891	23.193	24.763
Cyprus (III) [4]										
Total	.	.	.	.	.	.	159.3	168.0	174.0	177.8*
Males – Hom.							100.6	105.3	111.0	112.6*
Fem. – Muj.							58.7	62.7	63.0	65.2*
India (III) [8]										
Total [9]	.	.	.	.	.	19 671	20 207	20 744	21 484	22 186*
Males – Hom. [9]	.	.	.	.	.	17 440	17 810	18 250	18 828	19 426*
Fem. – Muj. [9]	.	.	.	.	.	2 231	2 397	2 494	2 656	2 760*
Israel (I) [4]										
Total [4]	963.2	997.1	1 047.0	1 094.4	1 096.5	1 112.5	1 126.8	1 159.2	1 212.6	1 241.0
Males – Hom. [4]	...	...	...	746.8	744.1	748.2	753.1	769.7	789.6	799.7
Fem. – Muj. [4]	...	...	...	347.5	352.7	364.1	374.1	389.8	423.3	441.3
" " " " (II) [10]										
Total	828.7	875.3	911.8	930.1	940.1	976.9	1 004.3	1 034.0	1 065.6	∎ 1 153.4[11]
Japan (I) [4]										
Total	50 940	51 210	51 260	∎ 52 590[12]	52 370	52 230	52 710	53 420	54 080	54 790
Males – Hom.	30 910	31 410	31 680	∎ 32 350[12]	32 650	32 700	32 940	33 090	33 250	33 630
Fem. – Muj.	20 030	19 820	19 570	∎ 20 230[12]	19 730	19 530	19 760	20 330	20 830	21 170
Korea, Republic of (I) [4]										
Total	9 745	10 066	10 559	11 139	11 586	11 830	12 556	12 929	13 490	13 664
Males – Hom.	6 167	6 371	6 665	6 923	7 275	7 489	7 736	8 126	8 347	8 409
Fem. – Muj.	3 578	3 695	3 894	4 216	4 311	4 341	4 820	4 803	5 143	5 255

Explanatory notes and source: see p. 151 – Notes explicatives et source: voir p. 154 – Notas explicativas y fuente: véase p. 157

[1] First semester of each year. [2] First semester. [3] Persons aged 16 years and over. [4] Civilian labour force employed. [5] Second semester of each year. [6] Excl. government and personal services. [7] June of each year. [8] Employees and working proprietors. [9] March of each year. [10] Insured persons. [11] Beginning 1979: sample revised. [12] Prior to 1973: excl. Okinawa Prefecure.

[1] Premier semestre de chaque année. [2] Premier semestre. [3] Personnes âgées de 16 ans et plus. [4] Main-d'œuvre civile occupée. [5] Second semestre de chaque année. [6] Non compris les services gouvernementaux et personnels. [7] Juin de chaque année. [8] Salariés et propriétaires–exploitants. [9] Mars de chaque année. [10] Personnes assurées. [11] A partir de 1979: échantillon révisé. [12] Avant 1973: non compris la préfecture d'Okinawa.

[1] Primer semestre de cada año. [2] Primer semestre. [3] Personas de 16 años y más. [4] Fuerza trabajadora civil ocupada. [5] Segundo semestre de cada año. [6] Excl. los servicios gubernamentales y personales. [7] Junio de cada año. [8] Asalariados y empresarios propietarios. [9] Marzo de cada año. [10] Personas aseguradas. [11] A partir de 1979: muestra revisada. [12] Antes de 1973: excl. la Prefectura de Okinawa.

4 General level of employment
Niveau général de l'emploi
Nivel general del empleo

(Thousands – Milliers – Millares)

Country – Source Pays – Source País – Fuente	1970	1971	1972	1973	1974	1975	1976	1977	1978	1979
Malaysia: Sabah (III) [1]										
Total	38.965	40.763	43.032	45.450	51.213	53.666	56.457	59.960	68.522	75.370
Pakistan (IV) [2]										
Total	17 470	18 026	18 107	19 507	20 093	20 424	20 679	21 295	21 930	22 596
Philippines (I) [2]										
Total [3]	11 358	12 246	12 834	13 450	13 885	14 143	∎14 238[4]	14 334	16 087	16 544
Males – Hom. [3]	7 893	8 317	8 725	9 097	9 437	9 489	∎9 630[4]	9 890	...	...
Fem. – Muj. [3]	3 465	3 929	4 109	4 383	4 448	4 654	∎4 608[4]	4 444	...	...
Singapore (I) [5]										
Total [6]	650.9	.	.	799.6	824.3	833.5	870.4	903.9	958.9	1 021.0
Males – Hom. [6]	.	.	.	.	562.2	586.5	600.4	616.3	640.9	677.1
Fem. – Muj. [6]	.	.	.	.	262.3	247.0	270.0	287.6	318.0	343.9
Sri Lanka (III) [7]										
Total	.	978.9	1 026.8	1 058.5	1 003.6	999.0	1 055.6	1 039.7	1 130.3	...
Males – Hom.	.	617.9	649.9	677.4	649.9	651.7	696.3	680.1	750.0	...
Fem. – Muj.	.	361.1	376.9	376.6	353.7	347.3	359.4	359.6	380.3	...
République arabe syrienne (I) [2]										
Total [8]	.	1 522.3	1 634.2	1 612.1	1 631.4	1 750.5	1 760.4	1 894.4	1 934.1	2 092.1
Males – Hom. [8]	.	...	...	...	...	...	...	1 762.2	1 668.6	...
Fem. – Muj. [8]	.	...	...	...	...	...	...	331.6	265.5	329.9
Thailand (I) [2]										
Total [9]	.	16 619	16 129	17 043	17 159	18 182	18 411	20 308	21 738	...
Males – Hom. [9]	...	8 933.2	8 925.9	9 440.2	9 492.3	9 863.9	10 103	10 999	11 511	...
Fem. – Muj. [9]	...	7 685.3	7 206.5	7 602.3	7 666.8	8 317.6	8 307.5	9 309.1	10 228	...
EUROPE – EUROPE – EUROPA										
Austria (I) [2]										
Total	2 974	2 974	2 984	3 015	3 023	2 969	2 977	3 015	3 055	3 094
" " " " (II) [10]										
Total	2 389.2	2 454.9	2 512.7	2 608.3	2 656.9	2 656.4	2 685.9	2 737.1	2 757.7	2 773.7
Belgique (II) [2]										
Total [6]	3 665.0	3 701.5	3 695.5	3 744.5	3 798.7	3 743.6	3 714.6	3 707.2	3 707.4	3 749.3
Males – Hom. [6]	2 467.2	2 476.9	2 455.2	2 471.2	2 495.4	2 457.0	2 436.5	2 422.0	2 406.6	2 420.3
Fem. – Muj. [6]	1 197.8	1 224.6	1 240.3	1 273.3	1 303.3	1 286.6	1 278.1	1 285.2	1 300.7	1 329.0
Bulgarie (III) [7]										
Total	2 748.7	2 864.7	2 993.4	3 273.1	3 424.8	3 676.6	3 886.8	3 870.1	3 895.6	3 952.2*
Czechoslovakia [12] (III) [13]										
Total	5 901.6	5 950.0	6 029.2	6 106.0	6 182.2	6 253.2	6 310.5	6 392.3	6 473.5	6 545.7

Explanatory notes and source: see p. 151 – Notes explicatives et source: voir p. 154 – Notas explicativas y fuente: véase p. 157

[1] Establishments with 20 or more persons employed. [2] Civilian labour force employed. [3] Third quarter of each year. [4] Prior to 1976: annual averages. [5] Persons aged 10 years and over. [6] June of each year. [7] Registered employees. [8] Sep. of each year. [9] Second semester of each year. [10] Insured persons. [12] Socialised sector. [13] Employees; excl. women on maternity leave.

[1] Etablissements occupant 20 personnes et plus. [2] Main-d'œuvre civile occupée. [3] Troisième trimestre de chaque année. [4] Avant 1976: moyennes annuelles. [5] Personnes âgées de 10 ans et plus. [6] Juin de chaque année. [7] Salariés inscrits. [8] Sept. de chaque année. [9] Second semestre de chaque année. [10] Personnes assurées. [12] Secteur socialisé. [13] Salariés; non compris les femmes en congé de maternité.

[1] Establecimientos con 20 y más trabajadores. [2] Fuerza trabajadora civil ocupada. [3] Tercer trimestre de cada año. [4] Antes de 1976: medias anuales. [5] Personas de 10 años y más. [6] Junio de cada año. [7] Asalariados registrados. [8] Sept. de cada año. [9] Segundo semestre de cada año. [10] Personas aseguradas. [12] Sector socializado. [13] Asalariados; excl. las mujeres con permiso por maternidad.

4 General level of employment
Niveau général de l'emploi
Nivel general del empleo

(Thousands – Milliers – Millares)

Country – Source Pays – Source País – Fuente	1970	1971	1972	1973	1974	1975	1976	1977	1978	1979
Denmark (I) [1]										
Total	.	.	2 355.4	2 385.2	2 354.6	2 332.2	2 391.6	2 413.9	2 473.0	2 501.2
Males – Hom.	.	.	1 390.5	1 404.3	1 377.7	1 361.7	1 391.3	1 392.3	1 408.6	1 410.0
Fem. – Muj.	.	.	964.9	980.9	976.9	970.5	1 000.3	1 021.6	1 064.4	1 091.2
España (I) [1]										
Total [2]	12 433	12 499	12 535	12 851	12 924	12 692	12 543	12 435	12 091	11 837
Males – Hom. [2]	9 329	9 308	9 229	9 251	9 254	9 196	8 871	8 795	8 565	8 372
Fem. – Muj. [2]	3 104	3 191	3 307	3 600	3 670	3 496	3 672	3 640	3 526	3 466
Finland (I) [1]										
Total	2 126	2 123	2 118	2 164	2 229	2 221	2 163	2 111	2 084	2 134
Males – Hom.	1 177	1 166	1 153	1 171	1 199	1 187	1 155	1 116	1 102	1 128
Fem. – Muj.	949	957	965	993	1 030	1 034	1 008	995	982	1 006
France [3] (IV) [4]										
Total	20 589	20 696	20 805	21 068	21 235	21 014	21 161	21 339	21 404	21 404*
German Democratic Rep. (III) [5]										
Total	6 874.0	6 963.1	7 136.6	7 238.7	7 336.0	7 407.1	7 496.7	7 576.9	7 651.9	7 722.0
Germany, Fed. Rep. of (IV) [1]										
Total	26 169	26 225	26 125	26 201	256 888	24 798	24 556	24 511	24 700	25 017*
Males – Hom.	.	.	16 512	16 467	16 061	15 432	15 280	15 217	15 323	15 493
Fem. – Muj.	.	.	9 613	9 734	9 627	9 366	9 276	9 294	9 356	9 524
Hongrie [6] (III) [5]										
Total [7]	3 921	3 926	3 876	3 867	3 881	3 879	3 840	3 839	3 853	3 830
Ireland (IV) [1]										
Total [8]	1 045	1 047	1 040	1 047	1 058	1 041	1 023	1 024	1 036	1 049
Italie [1] (I)										
Total	19 512	19 541	19 241	19 429	19 844	19 958	20 100	20 302	20 398	20 615
Males – Hom.	14 130	14 086	13 926	13 965	14 165	14 212	14 198	14 113	14 166	14 203
Fem. – Muj.	5 442	5 455	5 315	5 464	5 679	5 746	5 902	6 189	6 232	6 412
Luxembourg (IV) [1]										
Total	144	148	151	...	150	150	151	150	150	...
Malta (IV) [5]										
Total	99.48	101.30	98.90	101.60	102.31	107.81	110.52	114.41	116.17	118.50
Netherlands (IV) [9]										
Total	4 554	4 581	4 538	4 546	4 549	4 523	4 518	4 528	4 548	4 588
Norway (I) [1]										
Total	.	.	1 649	1 654	1 659	1 707	1 789	1 824	1 854	1 872
Males – Hom.	.	.	1 048	1 049	1 056	1 066	1 092	1 108	1 114	1 110
Fem. – Muj.	.	.	601	605	603	641	697	716	740	762

Explanatory notes and source: see p. 151 – Notes explicatives et source: voir p. 154 – Notas explicativas y fuente: véase p. 157

[1] Civilian labour force employed. [2] Fourth quarter of each year. [3] Incl. professional army; excl. compulsory military service. [4] Registered employed. [5] Registered employees. [6] Excl. major divisions 8 and 9. [7] Socialised sector. [8] April of each year. [9] Civilian employment (man–years).

[1] Main–d'œuvre civile occupée. [2] Quatrième trimestre de chaque année. [3] Y compris les militaires de carrière; non compris les militaires du contingent. [4] Ensemble de l'effectif occupé. [5] Salariés inscrits. [6] Non compris les branches 8 et 9. [7] Secteur socialisé. [8] Avril de chaque année. [9] Emploi civil (années–homme).

[1] Fuerza trabajadora civil ocupada. [2] Cuarto trimestre de cada año. [3] Incl. los militares profesionales; excl. los militares en servicio obligatorio. [4] Todo el efectivo ocupado. [5] Asalariados registrados. [6] Excl. las grandes divisiones 8 y 9. [7] Sector socializado. [8] Abril de cada año. [9] Empleo civil (años–hombre).

4 General level of employment
Niveau général de l'emploi
Nivel general del empleo

(Thousands – Milliers – Millares)

Country – Source Pays – Source País – Fuente	1970	1971	1972	1973	1974	1975	1976	1977	1978	1979
Pologne [1] (III) [2]										
Total	9 817	10 124	10 568	10 979	11 368	11 632	11 744	11 910	11 981	11 993
Portugal (I) [3]										
Total	.	.	.	.	3 693.5	3 723.5	3 788.5	3 783.5	3 772.0	3 852.0
Males – Hom.					2 224.0	2 279.0	2 332.0	2 330.0	2 338.5	2 356.0
Fem. – Muj.					1 446.5	1 444.5	1 456.5	1 453.5	1 433.5	1 446.0
Roumanie [1] (III) [4]										
Total	5 108.7	5 374.5	5 629.6	5 829.6	6 024.6	6 300.8	6 558.8	6 740.2	6 956.3	7 183.0
Suisse (IV) [3]										
Total	3 124.1	3 166.9	3 189.2	3 202.9	3 187.1	3 017.0	2 918.2	2 922.7	2 939.9	2 961.8
Males – Hom.	2 060.9	2 093.1	2 111.2	2 112.6	2 099.3	1 985.5	1 919.0	1 915.8	1 922.5	1 931.7
Fem. – Muj.	1 063.2	1 073.8	1 078.0	1 090.3	1 087.8	1 031.5	999.2	1 006.9	1 017.4	1 030.1
Sweden (I) [3]										
Total	3 854	3 860	3 862	3 879	3 962	4 062	4 088	4 099	4 115	4 179
Males – Hom.	2 335	2 314	2 295	2 295	2 316	2 342	2 338	2 314	2 297	2 314
Fem. – Muj.	1 519	1 546	1 567	1 584	1 647	1 720	1 751	1 785	1 818	1 865
Turquie (II) [5]										
Total	1 313.5	1 404.8	1 525.0	1 649.1	1 800.0	1 823.3	2 017.9	2 191.3	2 206.1	2 152.4
United Kingdom (IV) [3]										
Total [6]	24 381	24 030	24 020	24 610	24 714	24 596	24 429	24 505	24 552*	24 711*
Males – Hom. [6]	15 538	15 248	15 134	15 345	15 211	15 050	14 906	14 877	14 846*	14 838*
Fem. – Muj. [6]	8 843	8 782	8 887	9 266	9 503	9 546	9 524	9 627	9 706*	9 873*
Yugoslavia (III) [4]										
Total [7]	3 765	3 944	4 115	4 213	4 423	4 667	4 833	5 052	5 280*	5 506*
" " " " (IV) [2]										
Total [7]	3 850	4 034	4 210	4 306	4 514	4 758	4 925	5 148	5 383*	5 615*

OCEANIA – OCEANIE – OCEANIA

	1970	1971	1972	1973	1974	1975	1976	1977	1978	1979
American Samoa (IV) [3]										
Total	7.000	7.400	7.800	8.200	7.994	7.878	7.297	7.815	9.302	8.812
Australia (I) [3]										
Total [8]	5 395.6	5 515.7	5 609.9	5 783.0	5 855.2	5 841.3	5 897.8	5 995.4	5 969.6	6 041.5
Males – Hom. [8]	3 647.7	3 712.7	3 757.7	3 839.6	3 847.1	3 820.6	3 836.3	3 866.8	3 832.3	3 904.5
Fem. – Muj. [8]	1 747.8	1 803.0	1 852.1	1 943.3	2 008.1	2 020.8	2 061.5	2 128.6	2 137.2	2 136.9
Fiji (III) [2]										
Total [9]	51.590	56.210	58.399	61.476	66.998	69.976	69.994	72.383	73.819	...
New Zealand (IV) [10]										
Total	1 076.5	1 093.5	1 103.4	1 140.8	1 178.1	1 188.5	1 198.5	...	...	...

Explanatory notes and source: see p. 151 – Notes explicatives et source: voir p. 154 – Notas explicativas y fuente: véase p. 157

[1] Socialised sector. [2] Registered employed. [3] Civilian labour force employed. [4] Registered employees. [5] Insured persons. [6] June of each year. [7] March and Sep. of each year. [8] Aug. of each year. [9] Sep. of each year. [10] Employers, workers on own account and employees.

[1] Secteur socialisé. [2] Ensemble de l'effectif occupé. [3] Main-d'œuvre civile occupée. [4] Salariés inscrits. [5] Personnes assurées. [6] Juin de chaque année. [7] Mars et sept. de chaque année. [8] Août de chaque année. [9] Sept. de chaque année. [10] Employeurs, personnes travaillant à leur propre compte et salariés.

[1] Sector socializado. [2] Todo el efectivo ocupado. [3] Fuerza trabajadora civil ocupada. [4] Asalariados registrados. [5] Personas aseguradas. [6] Junio de cada año. [7] Marzo y sept. de cada año. [8] Agosto de cada año. [9] Sept. de cada año. [10] Empleadores, trabajadores por cuenta propia y asalariados.

4 General level of employment
Niveau général de l'emploi
Nivel general del empleo

(Thousands – Milliers – Millares)

Country – Source Pays – Source País – Fuente	1970	1971	1972	1973	1974	1975	1976	1977	1978	1979
USSR – URSS – URSS										
URSS [1] (III) [2]										
Total	106 773	108 874	111 092	113 152	115 254	117 132	118 898	120 588	122 546	124 123
RSS de Biélorussie [1] (III) [2]										
Total	...	3 190	3 293	3 391	3 490	3 577	3 658	3 756	3 859	3 950
RSS d'Ukraine [1] (III) [2]										
Total	21 524	21 944	22 362	22 650	22 988	23 304	23 546	23 773	...	...

Explanatory notes and source: see p. 151 – Notes explicatives et source: voir p. 154 – Notas explicativas y fuente: véase p. 157

[1] Socialised sector. [2] Registered employees.   [1] Secteur socialisé. [2] Salariés inscrits.   [1] Sector socializado. [2] Asalariados registrados.

5 Employment in non-agricultural sectors
Emploi dans les secteurs non agricoles
Empleo en los sectores no agrícolas

(Thousands – Milliers – Millares)

Country – Source Pays – Source País – Fuente	1970	1971	1972	1973	1974	1975	1976	1977	1978	1979
AFRICA – AFRIQUE – AFRICA										
Botswana (III)										
Total [1]	.	.	36.475	42.325	47.150	53.075	55.350	58.450	64.200	...
Males – Hom. [1]	.	.	.	.	.	.	44.622	45.120	49.750	...
Fem. – Muj. [1]	.	.	.	.	.	.	10.728	13.340	14.450	...
Rép.-Unie du Cameroun (III)										
Total	105.93	100.98	89.32	145.42	150.73	141.02	146.99	155.70	163.45	200.67
Egypt (I) [2]										
Total [3]	3 935.7	3 783.0	4 028.6	4 168.0	4 669.4	4 607.1	...	5 008.3	5 472.2	...
Males – Hom. [3]	3 278.2	3 392.3	3 627.3	3 811.7	4 265.5	4 160.8	...	4 509.7	4 820.3	...
Fem. – Muj. [3]	387.5	390.7	401.3	356.3	403.9	446.3	...	498.6	651.9	...
Gabon (II) [4]										
Total	51.50	53.88	56.03	...	...	97.30	111.80	119.80	...	...
Gambia (III)										
Total [5]	.	.	.	15.738	17.148	17.629	18.101	...	...	
Males – Hom. [5]	.	.	.	.	15.283	15.828	16.396	...	...	
Fem. – Muj. [5]	.	.	.	.	1.865	1.800	1.705	...	...	
Kenya (III)										
Total [6]	.	.	472.9	496.3	565.2	578.5	614.5	642.6	668.6	717.8
Males – Hom. [6]	.	.	.	.	.	.	.	540.5	558.7	598.2
Fem. – Muj. [6]	.	.	.	.	.	.	.	102.1	109.8	119.6
Liberia (III)										
Total	37.307	37.443	37.759	35.291	31.022	36.319	37.487	22.166	54.664	93.024
Males – Hom.	33.233	33.335	33.627	31.426	27.631	29.782	33.386	19.420	48.159	60.170
Fem. – Muj.	4.074	4.108	4.132	3.865	3.391	6.537	4.101	2.746	6.505	32.854
Libyan Arab Jamahiriya (IV) [2]										
Total	.	332.0	360.3	408.6	475.8	544.0	591.5	620.1	625.3	...
Malawi [7] (III) [8]										
Total [4]	105.7	115.1	126.0	139.1	146.5	151.7	160.3	▌154.2[9]	182.9*	...
Males – Hom. [4]	99.1	108.1	117.6	129.8	136.6	141.1	148.5	▌142.0[9]	165.1*	...
Fem. – Muj. [4]	6.7	7.6	7.7	8.9	9.4	10.2	11.4	▌12.2[9]	17.8*	...
Mauritius (III) [10]										
Total [11]	69.26	79.42	84.64	93.52	101.85	107.33	118.82	131.05	137.21	140.97
Males – Hom. [11]	60.31	68.68	72.63	78.55	82.45	86.04	92.46	100.31	104.77	105.27
Fem. – Muj. [11]	8.95	10.74	12.01	14.97	19.42	21.29	26.36	30.74	32.44	35.70
Seychelles (II)										
Total [12]	.	.	.	12.012	10.975	11.666	12.734	13.850	13.791	...

Explanatory notes and source: see p. 151 – Notes explicatives et source: voir p. 154 – Notas explicativas y fuente: véase p. 157

[1] Aug. of each year. [2] Civilian labour force employed. [3] May of each year. [4] Excl. domestic services. [5] Third quarter of each year. [6] June of each year. [7] Establishments with 20 or more persons employed. [8] Incl. working proprietors and unpaid family workers. [9] Beginning 1977: sample of establishments and revised allocation of establishments in the industrial classification. [10] Incl. development workers. [11] March and Sep. of each year. [12] Nov. of each year.

[1] Août de chaque année. [2] Main-d'œuvre civile occupée. [3] Mai de chaque année. [4] Non compris les services domestiques. [5] Troisième trimestre de chaque année. [6] Juin de chaque année. [7] Etablissements occupant 20 personnes et plus. [8] Y compris les propriétaires–exploitants et les travailleurs familiaux non rémunérés. [9] A partir de 1977: échantillon d'établissements et changements dans leur répartition industrielle. [10] Y compris les personnes occupées à des travaux publics de développement. [11] Mars et sept. de chaque année. [12] Nov. de chaque année.

[1] Agosto de cada año. [2] Fuerza trabajadora civil ocupada. [3] Mayo de cada año. [4] Excl. los servicios domésticos. [5] Tercer trimestre de cada año. [6] Junio de cada año. [7] Establecimientos con 20 y más trabajadores. [8] Incl. los empresarios propietarios y los trabajadores familiares no remunerados. [9] A partir de 1977: muestra de establecimientos y cambios en la distribución industrial de los establecimientos. [10] Incl. las personas ocupadas en planes de desarrollo. [11] Marzo y sept. de cada año. [12] Nov. de cada año.

5 Employment in non-agricultural sectors
Emploi dans les secteurs non agricoles
Empleo en los sectores no agrícolas

(Thousands – Milliers – Millares)

Country – Source Pays – Source País – Fuente	1970	1971	1972	1973	1974	1975	1976	1977	1978	1979
Sierra Leone (III)										
Total [1]	.	.	.	.	59.044	56.366	57.015	56.183	54.925	62.237
Swaziland (III)										
Total [2]	24.107	26.211	29.524	33.377	33.992	35.998	37.695[3]	39.848	44.104	...
Males – Hom. [2]	19.799	21.383	23.949	26.666	27.578	28.826	28.873[3]	28.252	33.024	...
Fem. – Muj. [2]	4.308	4.828	5.575	6.711	6.724	7.802	8.822[3]	10.209	11.080	...
Tunisie (IV)										
Total	509.2	542.0	586.7	617.3	655.8	857.6	909.1	947.0	990.0	1 033.7
Males – Hom.	.	.	.	.	.	666.0	702.5	...	...	...
Fem. – Muj.	.	.	.	.	.	191.6	206.6	...	...	...
Zambia (III)										
Total [1]	308.36	326.23	330.88	335.15	351.28	357.39	335.97	340.00*[4]	...	...
Zimbabwe (III)										
Total	555.5	580.1	610.6	640.9	674.3	688.6	680.6	667.0	648.3	653.4
AMERICA – AMERIQUE – AMERICA										
Bahamas (II) [5]										
Total [6]	.	.	.	.	.	.	58.494	68.403	67.526	70.336
Barbados (III)										
Total	.	.	.	.	51.330	51.047	53.646	55.494	...	...
Bolivia (IV) [7]										
Total	616.7	643.2	671.1	699.8	729.7	760.6	792.6	817.6	845.9	878.1
Males – Hom.	.	511.4	533.4	557.7	582.2	603.5	627.3	561.4	582.2	607.4
Fem. – Muj.	.	131.8	137.7	142.1	147.5	157.1	129.3	256.2	263.7	270.7
Brasil (III) [8]										
Total [1]	5 707	6 040	6 852	7 573	8 763	9 436	∎ 11 190[9]	...	...	...
Males – Hom. [1]	4 706	4 918	5 498	5 996	6 846	7 291	∎ 8 485[9]	...	...	...
Fem. – Muj. [1]	1 001	1 122	1 354	1 577	1 917	2 145	∎ 2 705[9]	...	...	...
Canada (I) [10]										
Total	7 196	7 376	7 655	8 085	8 451	8 720	8 917	9 095	9 399	9 780
Males – Hom.	4 719	4 791	4 967	5 196	5 401	5 451	5 522	5 599	5 700	5 885
Fem. – Muj.	2 477	2 586	2 689	2 888	3 050	3 269	3 396	3 497	3 699	3 895
Colombia [11] (I)										
Total [12]	.	.	.	.	.	2 112.0	2 204.4	2 496.1	2 712.7	2 955.6
Males – Hom. [12]	.	.	.	.	.	1 327.7	1 417.5	1 544.7	1 681.1	1 819.6
Fem. – Muj. [12]	.	.	.	.	.	784.3	864.0	951.3	1 031.6	1 136.0
Costa Rica (I) [7]										
Total [13]	.	.	.	335.16	.	.	402.25	437.71	478.14	504.49

Explanatory notes and source: see p. 151 – Notes explicatives et source: voir p. 154 – Notas explicativas y fuente: véase p. 157

[1] Dec. of each year. [2] June of each year. [3] Prior to 1976: Sep. of each year. [4] June. [5] Insured persons. [6] Jan. of each year. [7] Civilian labour force employed. [8] Registered establishments on 31st Dec. of each year. [9] Beginning 1978: revised questionnaire. [10] Persons aged 15 years and over. Prior to 1975: 14 years and over. [11] Seven main cities of the country. [12] Sep. of each year. [13] July of each year.

[1] Déc. de chaque année. [2] Juin de chaque année. [3] Avant 1976: sept. de chaque année. [4] Juin. [5] Personnes assurées. [6] Janv. de chaque année. [7] Main-d'œuvre civile occupée. [8] Etablissements enregistrés le 31 déc. de chaque année. [9] A partir de 1978: questionnaire révisé. [10] Personnes âgées de 15 ans et plus. Avant 1975: 14 ans et plus. [11] Sept villes principales du pays. [12] Sept. de chaque année. [13] Juillet de chaque année.

[1] Dic. de cada año. [2] Junio de cada año. [3] Antes de 1976: sept. de cada año. [4] Junio. [5] Personas aseguradas. [6] Enero de cada año. [7] Fuerza trabajadora civil ocupada. [8] Establecimientos registrados el 31 dic. de cada año. [9] A partir de 1978: cuestionario revisado. [10] Personas de 15 años y más. Antes de 1975: 14 años y más. [11] Siete ciudades principales del país. [12] Sept. de cada año. [13] Julio de cada año.

5 Employment in non-agricultural sectors
Emploi dans les secteurs non agricoles
Empleo en los sectores no agrícolas

(Thousands – Milliers – Millares)

Country – Source Pays – Source País – Fuente	1970	1971	1972	1973	1974	1975	1976	1977	1978	1979
Cuba (IV) [1]										
Total	.	1 478.3	1 489.0	1 575.4	1 638.8	1 708.7	1 784.3	1 979.7*	...	...
El Salvador [2] (III)										
Total	.	.	.	.	.	121.32	145.50	143.71	147.13	162.79
Guadeloupe (IV) [3]										
Total	.	.	.	.	61.3	61.9	59.2	65.3	65.3	...
Guyane française (IV)										
Total	10.464	9.403	9.637	9.433	10.412	10.591	12.232	12.454	12.972	13.258
Haïti (IV) [3]										
Total [4]	500.0	503.0	506.1	509.1	512.2	515.3	488.2	491.1	493.8	...
Males – Hom. [4]	163.9	174.1	168.3	170.5	172.7	175.0	147.1	149.1	150.0	...
Fem. – Muj. [4]	336.1	336.9	337.9	338.6	339.5	340.3	341.2	342.0	343.7	...
Jamaica (I) [3]										
Total			406.9	420.8	423.0[5]	455.5	441.9	445.8	451.6	...
México (IV) [3]										
Total [6]				.	9 281	9 814	10 301	10 772	11 271	11 765
Males – Hom. [6]					.	6 661	6 910	7 145	7 472	7 655
Fem. – Muj. [6]					.	3 153	3 391	3 627	3 799	4 110
Nicaragua [7] (II) [8]										
Total	85.7	82.3	88.5	90.4	96.9	114.2	118.9	135.6	129.4	...
Panamá (I) [3]										
Total [9]	276.1	289.5	302.5	.	337.4[10]	313.9[11]	322.8	322.4[11]	354.9*	...
Males – Hom. [9]	.	.	.	.	212.0[10]	193.5[11]	200.0	201.3[11]	214.9*	...
Fem. – Muj. [9]	.	.	.	.	125.4[10]	119.6[11]	122.8	121.1[11]	140.0*	...
Paraguay (IV) [3]										
Total	.	.	358.3	338.3	362.6	410.0	434.0	461.2*	483.5*	0.5*
Perú (IV) [3]										
Total	2 093.0	2 193.2	2 302.7	2 410.1	2 542.5	2 631.5	2 735.9	2 821.6	2 894.0	3 018.4
Puerto Rico (I)										
Total	625	657	690	715	709	665	685	708	757	778
St. Kitts-Nevis-Anguilla (III)										
Total	.	.	.	9.22	9.29	9.28	9.84	10.62	11.24	11.30
Trinidad and Tobago (I) [12]										
Total	239.4	249.6[13]	.	270.6	279.3	284.3	.	321.8	335.0[13]	...
United States (I) [14]										
Total	75 165	75 733	78 230	80 957	82 444	81 403	84 188	87 302	91 031	93 648
Males – Hom.	46 099	46 456	47 791	49 130	49 619	48 429	49 675	51 222	52 810	53 854
Fem. – Muj.	29 066	29 277	30 439	31 827	32 825	32 974	34 513	36 080	38 221	39 794

Explanatory notes and source: see p. 151 – Notes explicatives et source: voir p. 154 – Notas explicativas y fuente: véase p. 157

[1] State sector. [2] Excl. the public administration. [3] Civilian labour force employed. [4] Year beginning in July of year indicated. [5] Prior to 1974: 45 industrial groups. [6] June of each year. [7] Eight main cities of the country. [8] Insured persons. [9] Aug. of each year. [10] November. [11] October. [12] Persons aged 15 years and over. [13] First semester. [14] Persons aged 16 years and over.

[1] Secteur d'Etat. [2] Non compris l'administration publique. [3] Main–d'œuvre civile occupée. [4] Année commençant en juillet de l'année indiquée. [5] Avant 1974: 45 classes industrielles. [6] Juin de chaque année. [7] Huit villes principales du pays. [8] Personnes assurées. [9] Août de chaque année. [10] Novembre. [11] Octobre. [12] Personnes âgées de 15 ans et plus. [13] Premier semestre. [14] Personnes âgées de 16 ans et plus.

[1] Sector de Estado. [2] Excl. la administración pública. [3] Fuerza trabajadora civil ocupada. [4] Año que comienza en julio del año indicado. [5] Antes de 1974: 45 clases industriales. [6] Junio de cada año. [7] Ocho ciudades principales del país. [8] Personas aseguradas. [9] Agosto de cada año. [10] Noviembre. [11] Octubre. [12] Personas de 15 años y más. [13] Primer semestre. [14] Personas de 16 años y más.

5 Employment in non-agricultural sectors
Emploi dans les secteurs non agricoles
Empleo en los sectores no agrícolas

(Thousands – Milliers – Millares)

Country – Source Pays – Source País – Fuente	1970	1971	1972	1973	1974	1975	1976	1977	1978	1979
United States (III)[1]										
Total	70 880	71 214	73 675	76 790	78 265	76 945	79 382	82 423	86 446	89 482
Males – Hom.	44 748	44 748	46 134	47 802	48 141	46 767	47 812	49 184	51 193	56 499
Fem. – Muj.	26 132	26 466	27 541	28 988	30 124	30 178	31 570	33 239	35 253	36 952
Uruguay (I)										
Total[2]	.	.	.	496.1[3]	427.8	...	459.6	471.2	464.8	477.6
Venezuela (I)[4]										
Total[2]	.	.	.	.	.	2 805.7	3 006.8	3 190.9	3 354.5	3 473.7
Males – Hom.[2]	.	.	.	.	.	1 896.7	2 020.2	2 170.7	2 293.8	...
Fem. – Muj.[2]	.	.	.	.	.	909.2	986.6	1 020.2	1 060.6	...
" " " " (III)[1]										
Males – Hom.	44 748	44 748	46 134	47 802	48 141	46 767	47 812	49 184	51 193	53
Virgin Islands(US) (III)										
Total	.	.	.	.	.	33.07	31.34	32.22	34.29	...
ASIA – ASIE – ASIA										
Bangladesh (III)[5]										
Total[6]	.	.	.	.	.	771.3	.	949.7	.	1 036.9
Brunei (III)[7]										
Total[8]	.	.	16.700	17.274	16.717	17.763	19.978	21.517	22.785	24.241
Cyprus (III)										
Total	.	.	.	.	.	.	114.1	122.6	129.6	133.8*
Males – Hom.	.	.	.	.	.	.	80.1	85.2	89.0	90.8*
Fem. – Muj.	.	.	.	.	.	.	34.0	37.4	40.6	43.0*
Hong Kong [9] (III)[10]										
Total[11]	690.2	704.2	724.9	745.1	768.7	▌1 340.8[12]	▌1 555.7[13]	1 606.3	1 742.6	1 847.7
India (III)[14]										
Total	16 259	16 435	17 171	17 761	18 194	18 541	19 002	19 487	20 067	20 565*[15]
Israel (I)										
Total[4]	878.4	912.6	963.6	1 012.3	1 025.0	1 040.9	1 055.0	1 086.8	1 138.6	1 168.9
Males – Hom.[4]	...	...	...	684.4	688.1	693.7	697.6	713.5	732.8	744.6
Fem. – Muj.[4]	...	...	...	327.9	336.9	347.2	357.4	373.3	405.8	424.2
" " " " (II)[16]										
Total	787.2	834.4	873.7	898.7	910.6	948.9	974.4	1 003.1	1 033.0	▌1 111.1[17]
Japan (I)[4]										
Total	42 070	43 080	43 710	▌45 540[18]	45 620	45 620	46 280	47 070	47 750	48 670
Males – Hom.	26 550	27 380	27 900	▌28 860[18]	29 250	29 400	29 680	29 850	30 030	30 520
Fem. – Muj.	15 520	15 690	15 800	▌16 690[18]	16 360	16 220	16 600	17 230	17 720	18 150

Explanatory notes and source: see p. 151 – Notes explicatives et source: voir p. 154 – Notas explicativas y fuente: véase p. 157

[1] Registered employees. [2] Second semester of each year. [3] First semester. [4] Civilian labour force employed. [5] Establishments with 20 or more persons employed. [6] Biennial survey. [7] Excl. government and personal services. [8] June of each year. [9] Excl. small establishments in rural areas. [10] Registered employed. [11] Fourth quarter of each year. [12] Incl. development workers. [13] Metal mining. [14] Employees and working proprietors. [15] March. [16] Insured persons. [17] Beginning 1979: sample revised. [18] Prior to 1973: excl. Okinawa Prefecure.

[1] Salariés inscrits. [2] Second semestre de chaque année. [3] Premier semestre. [4] Main–d'œuvre civile occupée. [5] Etablissements occupant 20 personnes et plus. [6] Enquête biennale. [7] Non compris les services gouvernementaux et personnels. [8] Juin de chaque année. [9] Non compris les petites entreprises des zones rurales. [10] Ensemble de l'effectif occupé. [11] Quatrième trimestre de chaque année. [12] Y compris les personnes occupées à des travaux publics de développement. [13] Extraction de minerais métalliques. [14] Salariés et propriétaires–exploitants. [15] Mars. [16] Personnes assurées. [17] A partir de 1979: échantillon révisé. [18] Avant 1973: non compris la préfecture d'Okinawa.

[1] Asalariados registrados. [2] Segundo semestre de cada año. [3] Primer semestre. [4] Fuerza trabajadora civil ocupada. [5] Establecimientos con 20 y más trabajadores. [6] Encuesta bienal. [7] Excl. los servicios gubernamentales y personales. [8] Junio de cada año. [9] Excl. las pequeñas empresas de las zonas rurales. [10] Todo el efectivo ocupado. [11] Cuarto trimestre de cada año. [12] Incl. las personas ocupadas en planes de desarrollo. [13] Extracción de minerales metálicos. [14] Asalariados y empresarios propietarios. [15] Marzo. [16] Personas aseguradas. [17] A partir de 1979: muestra revisada. [18] Antes de 1973: excl. la Prefectura de Okinawa.

5 **Employment in non-agricultural sectors**
Emploi dans les secteurs non agricoles
Empleo en los sectores no agrícolas

(Thousands – Milliers – Millares)

Country – Source Pays – Source País – Fuente	1970	1971	1972	1973	1974	1975	1976	1977	1978	1979
Jordan (III) [1]										
Total [2]	...	...	61.67	71.73	84.22	87.42	92.88	91.47	...	...
Males – Hom. [2]	...	...	...	54.03	70.42	75.07	78.03	74.67	...	...
Fem. – Muj. [2]	...	...	...	9.21	11.92	12.35	14.85	16.80	...	...
Korea, Republic of (I) [3]										
Total	4 829	5 190	5 213	5 570	6 002	6 405	6 955	7 524	8 309	8 777
Males – Hom.	3 297	3 534	3 615	3 700	4 009	4 317	4 523	4 969	5 451	5 700
Fem. – Muj.	1 532	1 656	1 598	1 870	1 993	2 088	2 432	2 555	2 858	3 077
Malaysia: Sabah (III) [4]										
Total	23.444	25.377	27.697	30.547	32.347	34.735	37.868	40.023	45.376	46.340
Pakistan (IV) [3]										
Total	7 195	7 384	7 582	8 326	8 576	9 232	9 347	9 625	9 911	10 213
Philippines (I) [3]										
Total [5]	5 258	6 155	5 927	6 098	6 158	6 510	▌6 579[6]	7 939	6 860	...
Males – Hom. [5]	2 963	3 412	3 233	3 271	3 349	3 451	▌3 681[6]	3 912	...	...
Fem. – Muj. [5]	2 295	2 743	2 694	2 827	2 809	3 059	▌2 898[6]	2 949	...	...
Singapore (I) [7]										
Total [8]	628.4	.	.	778.3	802.6	816.2	850.8	884.2	941.2	1 005.8
Males – Hom. [8]	.	.	.	.	546.8	574.2	585.4	601.5	627.9	666.3
Fem. – Muj. [8]	.	.	.	.	255.9	242.0	265.3	282.6	313.3	339.5
Sri Lanka (III) [9]										
Total	.	427.5	452.5	490.0	487.7	490.4	538.5	523.4	563.8	...
Males – Hom.	.	348.1	364.0	402.1	400.1	402.6	446.5	426.8	459.9	...
Fem. – Muj.	.	79.3	88.5	83.4	87.6	87.8	92.0	96.6	103.9	...
République arabe syrienne (I) [3]										
Total [10]	.	630.5	726.5	761.8	767.7	855.5	1 182.7	1 154.2	1 263.1	1 405.4
Males – Hom. [10]	.	...	...	...	...	...	...	1 039.2	1 137.4	1 274.9
Fem. – Muj. [10]	.	...	...	...	...	...	...	115.0	125.7	130.4
Thailand (I) [3]										
Total [11]	.	3 460.9	4 487.4	4 772.1	5 932.9	4 911.5	4 462.4	5 385.9	5 720.0	...
Males – Hom. [11]	...	2 078.3	2 618.7	2 870.9	3 477.0	2 886.4	2 614.1	3 119.4	3 326.1	...
Fem. – Muj. [11]	...	1 382.6	1 871.7	1 903.2	2 455.9	2 025.1	1 848.3	2 266.5	2 393.9	...
EUROPE – EUROPE – EUROPA										
Austria (I) [3]										
Total	2 418	2 452	2 490	2 527	2 632	2 598	2 612	2 661	2 724	2 767
Males – Hom.	1 552	1 564	1 586	1 616	1 654	1 638	1 643	1 673	1 701	1 729
Fem. – Muj.	866	888	904	911	978	960	969	988	1 023	1 038
Belgique [12] (II) [3]										
Males – Hom. [8]	2 331.0	2 347.7	2 335.1	2 357.0	2 385.2	2 350.8	2 335.7	2 324.2	2 313.5	2 329.6
Fem. – Muj. [8]	1 160.2	1 192.1	1 209.4	1 243.3	1 273.9	1 256.9	1 251.0	1 260.4	1 275.3	1 301.2

Explanatory notes and source: see p. 151 – Notes explicatives et source: voir p. 154 – Notas explicativas y fuente: véase p. 157

[1] Establishments with 5 or more persons employed. [2] Aug. of each year. [3] Civilian labour force employed. [4] Establishments with 20 or more persons employed. [5] Third quarter of each year. [6] Prior to 1976: annual averages. [7] Persons aged 10 years and over. [8] June of each year. [9] Registered employees. [10] Sep. of each year. [11] Second semester of each year. [12] [13] Incl. persons working abroad.

[1] Etablissements occupant 5 personnes et plus. [2] Août de chaque année. [3] Main-d'œuvre civile occupée. [4] Etablissements occupant 20 personnes et plus. [5] Troisième trimestre de chaque année. [6] Avant 1976: moyennes annuelles. [7] Personnes âgées de 10 ans et plus. [8] Juin de chaque année. [9] Salariés inscrits. [10] Sept. de chaque année. [11] Second semestre de chaque année. [12] [13] Y compris les travailleurs à l'étranger.

[1] Establecimientos con 5 y más trabajadores. [2] Agosto de cada año. [3] Fuerza trabajadora civil ocupada. [4] Establecimientos con 20 y más trabajadores. [5] Tercer trimestre de cada año. [6] Antes de 1976: medias anuales. [7] Personas de 10 años y más. [8] Junio de cada año. [9] Asalariados registrados. [10] Sept. de cada año. [11] Segundo semestre de cada año. [12] [13] Incl. las personas que trabajan en el extranjero.

5 Employment in non-agricultural sectors
Emploi dans les secteurs non agricoles
Empleo en los sectores no agrícolas

(Thousands – Milliers – Millares)

Country – Source Pays – Source País – Fuente	1970	1971	1972	1973	1974	1975	1976	1977	1978	1979
Belgique [1] (II) [2]										
Total [3]	3 491.9	3 539.8	3 544.5	3 600.3	3 659.1	3 607.7	3 586.7	3 584.6	3 588.9	3 630.8
Bulgarie (III) [4]										
Total	2 455.8	2 553.6	2 635.2	2 703.5	2 781.9	2 867.5	2 922.1	2 944.9	2 978.3	3 017.9*
Czechoslovakia [5] (III) [6]										
Total	5 483.4	5 532.0	5 635.0	5 711.0	5 787.8	5 863.8	5 918.5	5 995.6	6 151.0	6 284.0
Denmark (I) [2]										
Total	.	.	2 125.7	2 157.9	2 127.8	2 104.6	2 168.6	2 195.4	2 258.2	2 292.9
Males – Hom.	.	.	1 223.3	1 241.5	1 212.7	1 197.4	1 228.9	1 233.2	1 256.3	1 261.6
Fem. – Muj.	.	.	902.4	916.4	915.1	907.2	939.7	962.2	1 001.9	1 031.3
España (I) [2]										
Total [7]	8 771	8 946	9 319	9 723	9 930	9 893	9 833	9 867	9 652	9 523
Males – Hom. [7]	6 472	6 582	6 764	6 912	7 024	7 113	6 918	6 939	6 797	6 705
Fem. – Muj. [7]	2 299	2 365	2 555	2 811	2 906	2 781	2 915	2 928	2 855	2 819
Finland (I) [2]										
Total	1 645	1 675	1 719	1 795	1 867	1 892	1 865	1 839	1 828	1 884
Males – Hom.	.	915	932	962	995	1 006	981	956	950	980.
Fem. – Muj.	.	760	787	833	872	886	884	883	878	904
France [8] (IV) [4]										
Total	15 635	15 924	16 214	16 622	16 913	16 808	17 031	17 264	17 379	17 426
German Democratic Rep. (III) [4]										
Total	6 593.0	6 686.1	6 869.1	6 962.6	7 042.5	7 108.1	7 190.8	7 258.1	7 318.8	7 387.9
Germany, Fed. Rep. of (IV) [2]										
Total	23 907	24 081	24 087	24 247	23 806	22 975	22 813	22 856	23 092	23 473
Males – Hom.	.	.	15 551	15 555	15 182	14 578	14 452	14 430	14 550	14 747
Fem. – Muj.	.	.	8 536	8 692	8 624	8 397	8 361	8 426	8 521	8 726
Hongrie [9] (III) [4]										
Total [5]	2 854	2 894	2 885	2 923	2 970	2 996	3 004	3 016	2 991	2 991
Ireland (IV) [2]										
Total [10]	762	774	773	787	804	791	781	789	806	829
Italie (I) [2]										
Total	15 694	15 666	15 648	15 940	16 432	16 684	16 856	17 153	17 308	17 603
Males – Hom.	11 486	11 479	11 493	11 631	11 899	12 047	12 073	12 083	12 174	12 295
Fem. – Muj.	4 208	4 187	4 155	4 309	4 533	4 637	4 783	5 070	5 134	5 309
Luxembourg (IV) [2]										
Total	...	...	...	...	139.9	140.6	141.9	141.7	141.2	...
Malta (IV) [4]										
Total	93.57	95.14	92.50	94.80	95.44	100.78	103.20	107.06	108.83	118.50

Explanatory notes and source: see p. 151 – Notes explicatives et source: voir p. 154 – Notas explicativas y fuente: véase p. 157

[1] Incl. persons working abroad. [2] Civilian labour force employed. [3] June of each year. [4] Registered employees. [5] Socialised sector. [6] Employees; excl. women on maternity leave. [7] Fourth quarter of each year. [8] Incl. professional army; excl. compulsory military service. [9] Excl. major divisions 8 and 9. [10] April of each year.

[1] Y compris les travailleurs à l'étranger. [2] Main-d'œuvre civile occupée. [3] Juin de chaque année. [4] Salariés inscrits. [5] Secteur socialisé. [6] Salariés; non compris les femmes en congé de maternité. [7] Quatrième trimestre de chaque année. [8] Y compris les militaires de carrière; non compris les militaires du contingent. [9] Non compris les branches 8 et 9. [10] Avril de chaque année.

[1] Incl. las personas que trabajan en el extranjero. [2] Fuerza trabajadora civil ocupada. [3] Junio de cada año. [4] Asalariados registrados. [5] Sector socializado. [6] Asalariados; excl. las mujeres con permiso por maternidad. [7] Cuarto trimestre de cada año. [8] Incl. los militares profesionales; excl. los militares en servicio obligatorio. [9] Excl. las grandes divisiones 8 y 9. [10] Abril de cada año.

5 Employment in non-agricultural sectors
Emploi dans les secteurs non agricoles
Empleo en los sectores no agrícolas

(Thousands – Milliers – Millares)

Country – Source Pays – Source País – Fuente	1970	1971	1972	1973	1974	1975	1976	1977	1978	1979
Netherlands (IV) [1]										
Total	4 225	4 261	4 223	4 237	4 245	4 224	4 223	4 239	4 264	4 309
Norway (I) [2]										
Total	.	.	1 448	1 465	1 484	1 548	1 621	1 659	1 693	1 711
Males – Hom.	.	.	914	918	932	949	978	993	1 001	999
Fem. – Muj.	.	.	534	547	552	599	643	666	692	713
Pologne [3] **(III)** [4]										
Total	8 919	9 211	9 646	10 042	10 400	10 620	10 696	10 816	10 888	10 905
Portugal (I) [2]										
Total	.	.	.	.	2 405.5	2 461.0	2 504.5	2 538.0	2 593.5	2 675.5
Males – Hom.	.	.	.	.	1 544.5	1 601.5	1 641.0	1 671.0	1 719.0	1 760.5
Fem. – Muj.	.	.	.	.	861.0	859.5	863.5	867.0	874.5	915.0
Roumanie [3] **(III)** [5]										
Total	4 636.6	4 878.1	5 112.6	5 292.5	5 509.7	5 765.4	5 990.0	6 165.9	6 368.2	6 590.8
Suisse [6] **(III)** [4]										
Indices [7]	107.9	109.3	109.5	109.6	108.8	100.0	96.8	97.1	98.1	98.9
″ ″ ″ ″ **(IV)** [2]										
Total	2 855.6	2 904.6	2 934.6	2 955.6	2 943.6	2 779.6	2 683.1	2 693.4	2 716.8	2 741.4
Sweden (I) [2]										
Total	3 540	3 560	3 576	3 603	3 698	3 801	3 834	3 851	3 866	3 937
Males – Hom.	2 093	2 082	2 075	2 083	2 116	2 149	2 148	2 131	2 111	2 134
Fem. – Muj.	1 447	1 477	1 501	1 520	1 583	1 652	1 687	1 720	1 754	1 804
Turquie (II) [8]										
Total	1 313.3	1 404.7	1 524.9	1 648.9	1 799.8	1 823.2	2 017.7	2 191.1	2 173.5	2 113.9
United Kingdom (III) [5]										
Total [9]	22 013	21 690	21 694	22 232	22 374	22 312	22 150	22 231	22 283*	22 460*
″ ″ ″ ″ [10] **(IV)** [2]										
Total [9]	23 599	23 296	23 311	23 897	24 034	23 932	23 769	23 850	23 902*	24 079*
Males – Hom. [9]	14 902	14 650	14 559	14 781	14 670	14 519	14 378	14 836	14 320*	14 326*
Fem. – Muj. [9]	8 697	8 644	8 752	9 117	9 363	9 413	9 392	9 502	9 582*	9 752*
Yugoslavia (III) [5]										
Total [11]	3 539	3 717	3 886	3 983	4 185	4 419	4 586	4 792	5 018*	5 240*

OCEANIA – OCEANIE – OCEANIA

	1970	1971	1972	1973	1974	1975	1976	1977	1978	1979
Australia (I) [2]										
Total [12]	4 961.7	5 103.2	5 167.6	5 356.8	5 450.4	5 443.6	5 513.2	5 595.1	5 592.2	5 642.2
Males – Hom. [12]	3 290.5	3 372.9	3 391.2	3 495.1	3 514.2	3 499.7	3 534.9	3 556.8	3 536.3	3 587.5
Fem. – Muj. [12]	1 671.1	1 730.3	1 776.3	1 861.7	1 936.2	1 943.9	1 978.2	2 038.3	2 055.9	2 054.6

Explanatory notes and source: see p. 151 – Notes explicatives et source: voir p. 154 – Notas explicativas y fuente: véase p. 157

[1] Civilian employment (man–years). [2] Civilian labour force employed. [3] Socialised sector. [4] Registered employed. [5] Registered employees. [6] Third quarter of each year. [7] Index base: 1975 = 100. [8] Insured persons. [9] June of each year. [10] Persons aged 16 years and over. [11] March and Sep. of each year. [12] Aug. of each year.

[1] Emploi civil (années–homme). [2] Main–d'œuvre civile occupée. [3] Secteur socialisé. [4] Ensemble de l'effectif occupé. [5] Salariés inscrits. [6] Troisième trimestre de chaque année. [7] Indices base: 1975 = 100. [8] Personnes assurées. [9] Juin de chaque année. [10] Personnes âgées de 16 ans et plus. [11] Mars et sept. de chaque année. [12] Août de chaque année.

[1] Empleo civil (años–hombre). [2] Fuerza trabajadora civil ocupada. [3] Sector socializado. [4] Todo el efectivo ocupado. [5] Asalariados registrados. [6] Tercer trimestre de cada año. [7] Indices base 1975 = 100. [8] Personas aseguradas. [9] Junio de cada año. [10] Personas de 16 años y más. [11] Marzo y sept. de cada año. [12] Agosto de cada año.

5 Employment in non-agricultural sectors
Emploi dans les secteurs non agricoles
Empleo en los sectores no agrícolas

(Thousands – Milliers – Millares)

Country – Source Pays – Source País – Fuente	1970	1971	1972	1973	1974	1975	1976	1977	1978	1979
Fiji (III) [1]										
Total [2]	47.821	52.390	55.617	58.033	63.097	65.656	66.208	68.431	70.062	...
Guam (III) [3]										
Total	25.300	26.800	30.400	37.700	38.400	34.827	30.400	32.300	34.500	...
New Zealand [4] **(III)** [3]										
Total	764.05	779.04	788.07	810.80	839.72	851.73	860.73	864.92	859.62	878.87*[5]
Males – Hom.	...	...	...	...	...	...	581.27	580.46	576.43	582.76*[5]
Fem. – Muj.	...	...	...	...	...	...	279.46	284.46	283.19	296.12*[5]
Papua New Guinea (IV) [3]										
Total [6]	.	.	.	105.60	112.07	99.82	104.71	103.87	...	...
USSR – URSS – URSS										
URSS [7] **(III)** [3]										
Total	80 335	82 618	84 896	86 870	88 968	91 188	93 019	94 942	96 900	98 753

Explanatory notes and source: see p. 151 – Notes explicatives et source: voir p. 154 – Notas explicativas y fuente: véase p. 157

[1] Registered employed. [2] Sep. of each year. [3] Registered employees. [4] Incl. forestry. [5] April. [6] June of each year. [7] Socialised sector.

[1] Ensemble de l'effectif occupé. [2] Sept. de chaque année. [3] Salariés inscrits. [4] Y compris la sylviculture. [5] Avril. [6] Juin de chaque année. [7] Secteur socialisé.

[1] Todo el efectivo ocupado. [2] Sept. de cada año. [3] Asalariados registrados. [4] Incl. silvicultura. [5] Abril. [6] Junio de cada año. [7] Sector socializado.

EMPLOYMENT

6 Employment in manufacturing / Emploi dans les industries manufacturières / Empleo en las industrias manufactureras

 A All industries / Ensemble des industries / Todas las industrias

(Thousands – Milliers – Millares)

Country – Source Pays – Source País – Fuente	1970	1971	1972	1973	1974	1975	1976	1977	1978	1979
AFRICA – AFRIQUE – AFRICA										
Algérie (III)										
Total [1]	124.1	132.9	140.4	158.1	191.4	208.6	...	...	...	...
Botswana (III)										
Total [2]	.	.	2.650	2.850	3.300	3.850	4.275	4.150	4.400	...
Males – Hom. [2]	.	.	.	.	.	.	3.534	3.500	3.800	...
Fem. – Muj. [2]	.	.	.	.	.	.	0.741	0.660	0.600	...
Burundi (IV)										
Total [3]	.	.	2.245	2.453	2.543	2.673	2.539	2.783	2.771	2.830
Rép.-Unie du Cameroun (III)										
Total	18.14	20.43	20.85	30.89	33.49	41.33	47.37	49.85	50.12	70.22
Egypt (I) [4]										
Total [5]	1 211.7	1 030.2	1 108.6	1 208.4	1 354.5	1 295.8	...	1 353.4	1 427.8	...
Males – Hom. [5]	1 126.3	963.2	1 048.1	1 146.5	1 285.3	1 229.9	...	1 284.2	1 348.1	...
Fem. – Muj. [5]	85.4	67.0	60.5	61.9	69.2	65.9	...	69.2	79.7	...
Ethiopia (III)										
Total [6]	49.413	51.500	53.462	54.965	57.456	60.131	60.733	...	...	...
Gabon (II)										
Total	9.30	9.16	9.10	...	...	11.90	15.60	17.10	...	...
Gambia (III)										
Total [7]	.	.	.	2.741	2.594	2.302	1.694	...	...	...
Males – Hom. [7]	.	.	.	.	2.035	1.846	1.625	...	...	...
Fem. – Muj. [7]	.	.	.	.	0.559	0.456	0.069	...	...	...
Kenya (III)										
Total [8]	.	.	84.8	94.5	101.3	100.7	108.8	117.9	130.1	138.4
Males – Hom. [8]	.	.	.	.	.	.	.	106.1	116.2	126.9
Fem. – Muj. [8]	.	.	.	.	.	.	.	11.8	13.8	11.6
Liberia (III)										
Total	2.940	2.955	2.976	2.782	2.445	2.030	2.955	1.471	6.101	13.214
Males – Hom.	2.752	2.766	2.786	2.609	2.289	1.998	2.766	1.377	5.711	11.434
Fem. – Muj.	0.180	0.189	0.190	0.183	0.156	0.032	0.189	0.094	0.390	1.780
Libyan Arab Jamahiriya (IV) [4]										
Total	.	21.4	22.9	25.9	29.3	32.9	37.4	41.7	47.4	...
Malawi [9] (III) [10]										
Total	19.5	21.8	23.2	25.6	26.8	31.4	36.0	▌33.5[11]	36.0	...
Males – Hom.	18.1	21.3	22.3	24.5	25.8	29.8	34.4	▌31.7[11]	34.2	...
Fem. – Muj.	0.6	0.5	0.8	1.1	0.9	1.5	1.6	▌1.8[11]	1.8	...

Explanatory notes and source: see p. 151 – Notes explicatives et source: voir p. 154 – Notas explicativas y fuente: véase p. 157

[1] April of each year. [2] Aug. of each year. [3] Dec. of each year. [4] Civilian labour force employed. [5] May of each year. [6] Year ending in Sep. of the year indicated. [7] Third quarter of each year. [8] June of each year. [9] Establishments with 20 or more persons employed. [10] Incl. working proprietors and unpaid family workers. [11] Beginning 1977: sample of establishments and revised allocation of establishments in the industrial classification.

[1] Avril de chaque année. [2] Août de chaque année. [3] Déc. de chaque année. [4] Main–d'œuvre civile occupée. [5] Mai de chaque année. [6] Année se terminant en sept. de l'année indiquée. [7] Troisième trimestre de chaque année. [8] Juin de chaque année. [9] Etablissements occupant 20 personnes et plus. [10] Y compris les propriétaires–exploitants et les travailleurs familiaux non rémunérés. [11] A partir de 1977: échantillon d'établissements et changements dans leur répartition industrielle.

[1] Abril de cada año. [2] Agosto de cada año. [3] Dic. de cada año. [4] Fuerza trabajadora civil ocupada. [5] Mayo de cada año. [6] Año que termina en sept. del año indicado. [7] Tercer trimestre de cada año. [8] Junio de cada año. [9] Establecimientos con 20 y más trabajadores. [10] Incl. los empresarios propietarios y los trabajadores familiares no remunerados. [11] A partir de 1977: muestra de establecimientos y cambios en la distribución industrial de los establecimientos.

6 Employment in manufacturing
Emploi dans les industries manufacturières
Empleo en las industrias manufactureras

A All industries
Ensemble des industries
Todas las industrias

(Thousands – Milliers – Millares)

Country – Source Pays – Source País – Fuente	1970	1971	1972	1973	1974	1975	1976	1977	1978	1979
Mauritius (III)										
Total [1]	7.73	9.26	10.94	14.60	19.65	21.82	27.88	32.09	32.52	34.99
Males – Hom. [1]	6.20	6.92	7.72	9.08	10.27	11.25	13.21	14.39	14.58	15.31
Fem. – Muj. [1]	1.53	2.34	3.22	5.52	9.38	10.57	14.67	17.70	17.94	19.68
Nigeria (III) [2]										
Total	127.06	145.44	167.48	166.82	175.29	...	...	...	...	...
Sénégal (IV)										
Total	.	15.027	17.413	20.253	40.450	22.762	25.402	30.479	...	...
Seychelles (II)										
Total [3]	.	.	.	0.432	0.490	0.581	0.650	0.657	0.674	...
Sierra Leone (III)										
Total [4]	.	.	.	.	5.885	5.840	6.288	6.018	6.033	7.680
Swaziland (III)										
Total [5]	5.383	5.837	6.512	7.360	7.547	8.998	8.216[6]	8.411	8.743	...
Males – Hom. [5]	5.017	5.427	5.788	6.035	6.348	7.560	6.831[6]	6.553	6.543	...
Fem. – Muj. [5]	0.366	0.410	0.724	1.325	1.199	1.438	1.385[6]	1.858	2.200	...
Tunisie (III)										
Total	76.25	75.51	82.91	94.77	108.48	121.42	140.89	...	...	...
Males – Hom.	69.02	68.52	74.65	84.50	96.35	106.09	...	...	...	...
Fem. – Muj.	7.24	6.99	8.26	10.27	12.13	15.33	...	...	...	...
Zambia (III)										
Total [4]	38.16	42.02	43.30	43.60	44.07	44.37	41.66	40.88*[7]	...	...
Zimbabwe (III)										
Total	114.7	121.6	130.7	139.4	151.3	156.0	153.6	145.1	139.3	144.7
AMERICA – AMERIQUE – AMERICA										
Bahamas (II) [8]										
Total [9]	.	.	.	.	.	.	3.376	3.866	3.792	3.934
Barbados (III)										
Total	.	.	.	10.180	8.746	9.889	10.037	...	...	
Bolivia (IV) [10]										
Total	103.9	108.2	112.6	117.1	121.8	126.6	131.7	137.2	141.5	146.9
Males – Hom.	.	77.9	81.0	84.3	87.7	91.2	14.8	98.8	101.9	105.7
Fem. – Muj.	.	30.3	31.5	32.8	34.1	35.5	36.9	38.4	39.6	41.1
Brasil (III) [11]										
Total [4]	2 499	2 599	2 830	3 230	3 720	3 953	▌4 053[12]	...	...	...
Males – Hom. [4]	2 045	2 106	2 260	2 555	2 911	3 093	▌3 094[12]	...	...	...
Fem. – Muj. [4]	454	493	570	675	809	860	▌959[12]	...	...	...

Explanatory notes and source: see p. 151 – Notes explicatives et source: voir p. 154 – Notas explicativas y fuente: véase p. 157

[1] March and Sep. of each year. [2] Establishments with 10 or more persons employed. [3] Nov. of each year. [4] Dec. of each year. [5] June of each year. [6] Prior to 1976: Sep. of each year. [7] June. [8] Insured persons. [9] Jan. of each year. [10] Civilian labour force employed. [11] Registered establishments on 31st Dec. of each year. [12] Beginning 1978: revised questionnaire.

[1] Mars et sept. de chaque année. [2] Etablissements occupant 10 personnes et plus. [3] Nov. de chaque année. [4] Déc. de chaque année. [5] Juin de chaque année. [6] Avant 1976: sept. de chaque année. [7] Juin. [8] Personnes assurées. [9] Janv. de chaque année. [10] Main-d'œuvre civile occupée. [11] Etablissements enregistrés le 31 déc. de chaque année. [12] A partir de 1978: questionnaire révisé.

[1] Marzo y sept. de cada año. [2] Establecimientos con 10 y más trabajadores. [3] Nov. de cada año. [4] Dic. de cada año. [5] Junio de cada año. [6] Antes de 1976: sept. de cada año. [7] Junio. [8] Personas aseguradas. [9] Enero de cada año. [10] Fuerza trabajadora civil ocupada. [11] Establecimientos registrados el 31 dic. de cada año. [12] A partir de 1978: cuestionario revisado.

6 Employment in manufacturing / Emploi dans les industries manufacturières / Empleo en las industrias manufactureras

A All industries / Ensemble des industries / Todas las industrias

(Thousands – Milliers – Millares)

Country – Source / Pays – Source / País – Fuente	1970	1971	1972	1973	1974	1975	1976	1977	1978	1979
Canada (III) [1]										
Total	1 507.2	1 495.6	1 519.4	1 594.3	1 642.9	1 549.1	1 567.3	1 544.8	1 594.2	1 642.7
Colombia (III)										
Indices [2]	100.0	102.3	106.2	111.7	116.4	117.9	120.6	122.3	124.3	127.2
Costa Rica (I) [3]										
Total [4]						.	72.94	83.14	82.55	89.47
Cuba [5] (IV) [6]										
Total	.	440.5	438.5	453.2	466.7	472.2	477.4	563.7*	...	...
República Dominicana (III)										
Total	110.65	113.98	124.21	137.74	139.43	122.31	110.78	112.56	113.33	
Ecuador (III)										
El Salvador (III)[7]										
Total		.		.	.	49.49	54.16	56.37	57.70	58.84
Guatemala (III)										
Total	.	37.68	40.93	41.56	37.35	32.83	32.38	36.81	38.55	
Guyane française (IV)										
Total	1.378	0.967	0.879	0.886	0.753	0.790	0.681	1.040	0.427	0.576
Haïti (IV) [8]										
Total [9]	118.70	119.41	120.13	120.85	121.51	122.30	115.93	116.60	117.18	...
Males – Hom. [9]	52.02	52.57	53.12	53.67	54.23	54.79	48.25	48.75	48.99	...
Fem. – Muj. [9]	66.67	66.84	67.01	67.17	67.34	67.51	67.68	67.85	68.19	...
Jamaica (I) [8]										
Total	.	.	.	.	81.25	73.95	75.55	76.25	78.95	...
Males – Hom.					58.45	53.80	56.40	56.80	59.45	...
Fem. – Muj.					22.85	20.15	19.15	19.45	19.50	...
México [10] (III)										
Total	...	...	345.72	362.23	▌403.21[11]	413.51	▌468.74[12]	464.88	487.49	522.77*
″ ″ ″ ″ (IV) [8]										
Total [13]	.	.	.	.	2 833.7	2 961.2	3 137.6	3 276.6	3 424.5	3 574.5
Males – Hom. [13]	.	.	.	.	.	2 241.9	2 364.1	2 398.7	2 507.1	2 567.9
Fem. – Muj. [13]	.	.	.	.	.	719.3	773.5	877.9	917.4	1 006.6
Nicaragua [14] (II) [15]										
Total	22.237	22.196	23.581	22.402	25.011	26.107	30.461	32.100	29.166	26.594*
Panamá (I) [3]										
Total [16]	.	.	.	.	37.40[17]	33.71[18]	34.16	37.89[17]	39.55*	...
Males – Hom. [16]	.	.	.	.	29.80[17]	25.25[18]	27.01	29.42[17]	30.09*	...
Fem. – Muj. [16]	.	.	.	.	7.60[17]	8.46[18]	7.15	8.47[17]	9.46*	...

Explanatory notes and source: see p. 151 – Notes explicatives et source: voir p. 154 – Notas explicativas y fuente: véase p. 157

[1] Establishments with 20 or more persons employed. [2] Index base: July 1970–June 1971 = 100. [3] Wage earners and salaried employees. [4] July of each year. [5] Incl. mining and quarrying, electricity, gas and water. [6] State sector. [7] Index base: 1965 = 100. [8] Civilian labour force employed. [9] Year beginning in July of year indicated. [10] Figures include 57 industrial groups of the national classification. [11] Prior to 1974: 45 industrial groups. [12] Prior to 1976: 54 industrial groups. [13] June of each year. [14] Eight main cities of the country. [15] Insured persons. [16] Aug. of each year. [17] October. [18] November.

[1] Etablissements occupant 20 personnes et plus. [2] Indices base 100 en juillet 1970–juin 1971. [3] Population salariée ayant un emploi. [4] Juillet de chaque année. [5] Y compris les industries extractives, l'electricité, le gaz et l'eau. [6] Secteur d'Etat. [7] Indices base: 1965 = 100. [8] Main–d'œuvre civile occupée. [9] Année commençant en juillet de l'année indiquée. [10] Les chiffres comprennent 57 classes industrielles de la classification nationale. [11] Avant 1974: 45 classes industrielles. [12] Avant 1976: 54 classes industrielles. [13] Juin de chaque année. [14] Huit villes principales du pays. [15] Personnes assurées. [16] Août de chaque année. [17] Octobre. [18] Novembre.

[1] Establecimientos con 20 y más trabajadores. [2] Indices base: julio 1970–junio 1971 = 100. [3] Población ocupada asalariada. [4] Julio de cada año. [5] Incl. minas y canteras, electricidad, gas y agua. [6] Sector de Estado. [7] Indices base: 1965 = 100. [8] Fuerza trabajadora civil ocupada. [9] Año que comienza en julio del año indicado. [10] Las cifras comprenden 57 clases industriales de la clasificación nacional. [11] Antes de 1974: 45 clases industriales. [12] Antes de 1976: 54 clases industriales. [13] Junio de cada año. [14] Ocho ciudades principales del país. [15] Personas aseguradas. [16] Agosto de cada año. [17] Octubre. [18] Noviembre.

6 Employment in manufacturing
Emploi dans les industries manufacturières
Empleo en las industrias manufactureras

All industries
Ensemble des industries
Todas las industrias

(Thousands – Milliers – Millares)

Country – Source Pays – Source País – Fuente	1970	1971	1972	1973	1974	1975	1976	1977	1978	1979
Paraguay (IV) [1]										
Total	.	.	102.4	122.9	130.6	112.8	119.5	124.0*	128.9*	132.3*
Perú [2] (III) [3]										
Total			.	.	66.445	70.702	74.134	75.675	74.146	74.308
" " " " (IV) [1]										
Total	574.0	601.3	627.4	658.4	694.7	727.9	744.0	741.2	772.3	803.9
St. Kitts-Nevis-Anguilla (III)										
Total	.	.	.	1.01	1.07	1.25	1.25	1.50	1.90	2.00
Trinidad and Tobago [4] (III) [5]										
Total	23.6	28.1	25.4	29.3	26.3	26.9	28.0*	...	...	...
United States (III) [6]										
Total	19 367	18 263	19 151	20 154	20 077	18 323	18 997	19 682	20 476	20 972*
Males – Hom.	13 919	13 034	13 681	14 289	14 228	13 066	13 390	13 802	14 245	14 508*
Venezuela (III) [6]										
Total [7]	61.406	62.104	62.905	65.447	70.099	75.003	82.230	85.854	89.914*	...
Virgin Islands(US) (III)										
Total	.	.	.	.	.	3.06	3.16	3.14	2.95	...
ASIA – ASIE – ASIA										
Afghanistan (III) [6]										
Total [8]	.	.	.	22.7	28.2	33.5	34.5	39.9	43.0	...
Males – Hom. [8]	.	.	.	21.8	27.3	32.3	33.7	37.1	40.7	...
Fem. – Muj. [8]	.	.	.	0.9	0.9	1.2	0.8	2.8	2.3	...
Bangladesh (III) [9]										
Total [10]	.	.	.	.	.	298.75	.	368.42	.	398.11
Brunei (III)										
Total [11]	.	.	1.592	1.970	1.893	2.168	2.193	2.456	2.189	2.312
Cyprus (III) [12]										
Total	.	.	.	.	.	22.353	23.626	27.232	28.100[13]	
Males – Hom.	.	.	.	.	.	11.419	11.767	13.349	13.706[13]	
Fem. – Muj.	.	.	.	.	.	10.934	11.859	13.883	14.394[13]	
Hong Kong (III) [14]										
Total [15]	549.2	564.4	578.9	582.7	600.1	678.9	773.7	755.1	816.7	870.9
Males – Hom. [15]	268.1	275.7	282.9	280.8	294.4	328.2	374.8	368.9	402.7	428.7
Fem. – Muj. [15]	281.1	288.7	295.9	301.9	305.8	350.6	399.0	386.3	413.9	442.2
India (III) [16]										
Total	4 594	4 697	4 895	5 014	5 138	5 087	5 210	5 391	5 610	5 839*[17]
Males – Hom. [18]	.	.	.	.	.	.	4 732	4 875	5 074	5 266*[17]
Fem. – Muj. [18]	.	.	.	.	.	.	478	516	536	573*[17]

Explanatory notes and source: see p. 151 – Notes explicatives et source: voir p. 154 – Notas explicativas y fuente: véase p. 157

[1] Civilian labour force employed. [2] Lima metropolis only. [3] Establishments with 50 or more persons employed. [4] Excl. sugar distilleries and petroleum refineries. [5] Establishments with 10 or more persons employed. [6] Registered employees. [7] Second semester of each year. [8] Year beginning in July of year indicated. [9] Establishments with 20 or more persons employed. [10] Biennial survey. [11] June of each year. [12] Employees and unpaid family workers. [13] [14] Registered employed. [15] Dec. of each year. [16] Employees and working proprietors. [17] March. [18] March of each year.

[1] Main-d'œuvre civile occupée. [2] Métropole de Lima seulement. [3] Etablissements occupant 50 personnes et plus. [4] Non compris les raffineries de sucre et de pétrole. [5] Etablissements occupant 10 personnes et plus. [6] Salariés inscrits. [7] Second semestre de chaque année. [8] Année commençant en juillet de l'année indiquée. [9] Etablissements occupant 20 personnes et plus. [10] Enquête biennale. [11] Juin de chaque année. [12] Salariés et travailleurs familiaux non rémunérés. [13] [14] Ensemble de l'effectif occupé. [15] Déc. de chaque année. [16] Salariés et propriétaires–exploitants. [17] Mars. [18] Mars de chaque année.

[1] Fuerza trabajadora civil ocupada. [2] Lima metropolitana solamente. [3] Establecimientos con 50 y más trabajadores. [4] Excl. las refinerías de azúcar y de petróleo. [5] Establecimientos con 10 y más trabajadores. [6] Asalariados registrados. [7] Segundo semestre de cada año. [8] Año que comienza en julio del año indicado. [9] Establecimientos con 20 y más trabajadores. [10] Encuesta bienal. [11] Junio de cada año. [12] Asalariados y trabajadores familiares no remunerados. [13] [14] Todo el efectivo ocupado. [15] Dic. de cada año. [16] Asalariados y empresarios propietarios. [17] Marzo. [18] Marzo de cada año.

6 Employment in manufacturing
Emploi dans les industries manufacturières
Empleo en las industrias manufactureras

A All industries
Ensemble des industries
Todas las industrias

(Thousands – Milliers – Millares)

Country – Source Pays – Source País – Fuente	1970	1971	1972	1973	1974	1975	1976	1977	1978	1979
Israel [1] (I) [2]										
Total	192.5	200.8	208.4	226.0	231.8	231.0	228.7	232.3	238.3	252.0
Males – Hom.	147.9	155.0	157.8	170.8	179.5	180.8	178.8	180.0	184.1	190.2
Fem. – Muj.	44.6	45.8	50.6	55.2	52.3	50.2	49.9	52.3	54.2	61.8
Japan (I) [3]										
Total	11 440	11 560	11 550	12 030[4]	12 010	11 380	11 330	11 260	11 090	11 070
Males – Hom.	7 540	7 680	7 790	7 990[4]	8 110	7 760	7 620	7 470	7 270	7 340
Fem. – Muj.	3 900	3 880	3 770	4 040[4]	3 900	3 610	3 700	3 790	3 820	3 730
Jordan (III) [5]										
Total [6]	...	...	...	8.77	11.12	11.61	11.98	12.53	...	...
Males – Hom. [6]	...	...	...	...	9.91	10.23	10.73	11.15	...	...
Fem. – Muj. [6]	...	...	...	...	1.21	1.38	1.34	1.38	...	...
Korea, Republic of (I) [3]										
Total	887	855	1 027	1 289	1 535	1 722	2 071	2 197	2 409	2 524
Males – Hom.	618	615	733	865	1 059	1 216	1 389	1 420	1 519	1 555
Fem. – Muj.	269	240	294	424	476	506	682	777	890	969
Peninsular Malaysia (III) [7]										
Total	...	...	...	...	...	...	232.43	253.95	277.42	...
Malaysia: Sabah (III) [8]										
Total [9]	.	.	.	1.658	3.410	2.525	2.281	2.139	2.316	3.826
Pakistan (III) [7]										
Total	.	.	494.92	343.40	535.13	551.31	558.16	572.45	550.47	...
Singapore (I) [3]										
Total [10]	.	.	.	.	213.8	194.0	213.7	224.7	251.2	273.6
Males – Hom. [10]	.	.	.	.	116.8	115.0	124.4	122.6	134.2	148.5
Fem. – Muj. [10]	.	.	.	.	97.0	79.0	89.3	102.1	116.9	125.1
" " " " [11] (III) [12]										
Total	120.51	140.55	170.35	198.57	206.07	191.53	207.23	219.11	243.72	267.45*
Sri Lanka (III) [7]										
Total	.	202.01	211.52	206.47	208.77	188.95	191.42	194.71	202.74	...
Males – Hom.	.	136.36	136.19	135.18	141.20	127.84	131.25	132.13	140.42	...
Fem. – Muj.	.	65.66	75.34	66.77	67.57	61.11	60.18	62.58	62.32	...
Thailand (I) [2]										
Total [13]	.	659.0	1 239.5	1 201.1	1 693.6	1 355.7	1 145.3	1 329.2	1 477.5	...
Males – Hom. [13]	.	354.1	692.2	735.0	931.4	775.6	603.0	759.7	858.8	...
Fem. – Muj. [13]	.	304.9	547.2	466.0	754.2	580.1	542.3	569.5	625.1	...

Explanatory notes and source: see p. 151 – Notes explicatives et source: voir p. 154 – Notas explicativas y fuente: véase p. 157

[1] Incl. mining and quarrying. [2] Civilian labour force employed. [3] Wage earners and salaried employees. [4] Prior to 1973: excl. Okinawa Prefecure. [5] Establishments with 5 or more persons employed. [6] Aug. of each year. [7] Registered employees. [8] Establishments with 20 or more persons employed. [9] Dec. of each year. [10] June of each year. [11] Excl. rubber processing. [12] Establishments with 10 or more persons employed. [13] Second semester of each year.

[1] Y compris les industries extractives. [2] Main-d'œuvre civile occupée. [3] Population salariée ayant un emploi. [4] Avant 1973: non compris la préfecture d'Okinawa. [5] Etablissements occupant 5 personnes et plus. [6] Août de chaque année. [7] Salariés inscrits. [8] Etablissements occupant 20 personnes et plus. [9] Déc. de chaque année. [10] Juin de chaque année. [11] Non compris le travail du caoutchouc naturel. [12] Etablissements occupant 10 personnes et plus. [13] Second semestre de chaque année.

[1] Incl. las minas y canteras. [2] Fuerza trabajadora civil ocupada. [3] Población ocupada asalariada. [4] Antes de 1973: excl. la Prefectura de Okinawa. [5] Establecimientos con 5 y más trabajadores. [6] Agosto de cada año. [7] Asalariados registrados. [8] Establecimientos con 20 y más trabajadores. [9] Dic. de cada año. [10] Junio de cada año. [11] Excl. la elaboración de caucho natural. [12] Establecimientos con 10 y más trabajadores. [13] Segundo semestre de cada año.

6 Employment in manufacturing
Emploi dans les industries manufacturières
Empleo en las industrias manufactureras

A All industries
Ensemble des industries
Todas las industrias

(Thousands – Milliers – Millares)

Country – Source / Pays – Source / País – Fuente	1970	1971	1972	1973	1974	1975	1976	1977	1978	1979
EUROPE – EUROPE – EUROPA										
Austria (II) [1]										
Total [2]	.	.	914.5	946.7	944.5	910.8	905.5	922.3	913.1	912.1
Males – Hom. [2]	.	.	...	...	...	594.0	592.5	604.3	601.5	600.9
Fem. – Muj. [2]	.	.	...	...	...	316.8	313.0	318.1	311.6	311.3
" " " " (III) [3]										
Total	629.3	648.0	662.3	676.3	673.9	640.1	629.3	634.4	623.2	622.7
Belgique (II) [3]										
Total [4]	1 087.2	1 088.5	1 074.4	1 088.3	1 102.1	1 033.1	990.9	952.1	912.6	887.9
Males – Hom. [4]	803.7	801.3	788.2	797.1	804.2	762.4	737.4	715.0	688.1	673.1
Fem. – Muj. [4]	283.5	287.2	286.2	291.2	298.0	270.7	253.6	237.1	224.5	214.8
Bulgarie (III) [3]										
Total	1 008.7	1 173.0	1 198.2	1 227.4	1 135.4	1 155.6	1 169.3	1 179.6	1 190.5	...
Czechoslovakia (III) [5]										
Total	2 205	2 220	2 236	2 256	2 271	2 290	2 302	2 323	2 337	2 358
" " " " (IV) [6]										
Total [7]	2 452	2 487	2 547	2 586	2 612	2 639	2 659	2 677	2 692	2 707
Males – Hom. [7]	1 315	1 322	1 351	1 369	1 381	1 397	1 407	1 424	1 437	1 450
Fem. – Muj. [7]	1 137	1 165	1 196	1 217	1 231	1 242	1 252	1 253	1 255	1 257
Denmark (I) [8]										
Total	.	.	586.9	588.7	555.7	528.6	537.1	521.6	531.2	534.1
Males – Hom.	.	.	406.1	413.1	396.1	379.3	383.8	376.0	381.0	380.6
Fem. – Muj.	.	.	180.8	175.6	159.6	149.3	153.3	145.6	150.2	153.5
" " " " (III) [3]										
Total	419.3	405.6	412.8	425.0	412.5	374.7	375.5	377.1	375.9	378.9
España (I) [9]										
Total [10]	2 825.8	2 883.2	2 786.7	2 911.3	2 957.6	3 018.4	2 676.6	2 660.1	2 600.1	2 497.0
Males – Hom. [10]	2 179.9	2 241.7	2 072.2	2 129.3	2 178.1	2 248.2	1 963.7	1 973.2	1 935.5	1 879.1
Fem. – Muj. [10]	645.9	641.5	714.5	782.0	779.5	770.2	712.9	686.9	664.6	617.9
Finland [11] (I) [9]										
Total	541	540	550	563	598	593	572	563	554	571
Males – Hom.	.	346	354	366	385	381	362	364	355	368
Fem. – Muj.	.	194	196	197	213	212	213	204	199	203
France (III) [3]										
Total	5 328	5 411	5 477	5 601	5 660	▌5 502[12]	5 449	5 426	5 335	5 233*
German Democratic Rep. [11] (III) [3]										
Total	3 170.7	3 212.2	3 343.1	3 373.5	3 378.5	3 386.7	3 417.1	3 448.1	3 468.4	3 492.5

Explanatory notes and source: see p. 151 – Notes explicatives et source: voir p. 154 – Notas explicativas y fuente: véase p. 157

[1] Insured persons. [2] July of each year. [3] Registered employees. [4] June of each year. [5] Employees; excl. women on maternity leave. [6] Registered employed. [7] Dec. of each year. [8] Civilian labour force employed. [9] Wage earners and salaried employees. [10] Fourth quarter of each year. [11] Incl. mining and quarrying, electricity, gas and water. [12] Change of industrial classification.

[1] Personnes assurées. [2] Juillet de chaque année. [3] Salariés inscrits. [4] Juin de chaque année. [5] Salariés; non compris les femmes en congé de maternité. [6] Ensemble de l'effectif occupé. [7] Déc. de chaque année. [8] Main-d'œuvre civile occupée. [9] Population salariée ayant un emploi. [10] Quatrième trimestre de chaque année. [11] Y compris les industries extractives, l'électricité, le gaz et l'eau. [12] Changement de classification industrielle.

[1] Personas aseguradas. [2] Julio de cada año. [3] Asalariados registrados. [4] Junio de cada año. [5] Asalariados; excl. las mujeres con permiso por maternidad. [6] Todo el efectivo ocupado. [7] Dic. de cada año. [8] Fuerza trabajadora civil ocupada. [9] Población ocupada asalariada. [10] Cuarto trimestre de cada año. [11] Incl. minas y canteras, electricidad, gas y agua. [12] Cambio de clasificación industrial.

6 Employment in manufacturing
Emploi dans les industries manufacturières
Empleo en las industrias manufactureras

A All industries
Ensemble des industries
Todas las industrias

(Thousands – Milliers – Millares)

Country – Source Pays – Source País – Fuente	1970	1971	1972	1973	1974	1975	1976	1977	1978	1979
Germany, Fed. Rep. of (IV) [1]										
Total	.	.	8 995	8 995	8 858	8 347	8 313	8 274	8 282	8 342
Males – Hom.	.	.	6 260	6 228	6 183	5 865	5 749	5 733	5 721	5 767
Fem. – Muj.	.	.	2 735	2 767	2 675	2 482	2 564	2 541	2 561	2 575
Grèce (III) [2]										
Indices [3]	112.3	119.2	124.1	131.4	132.8	133.9	142.1	148.6	153.3	157.5
Hongrie [4] (III) [2]										
Total	1 448	1 454	1 451	1 479	1 496	1 456	1 447	1 444	1 446	1 422
Ireland (III) [2]										
Total [5]	.	.	.	207.6	210.2	195.1	199.1	205.0	210.8	...
" " " " (IV) [6]										
Total [7]	213	214	212	217	224	214	207	215	219	227
Italie (I) [2]										
Total	4 851	4 947	4 903	4 989	5 189	5 201	5 215	▮4 800[8]	4 732	4 754
Males – Hom.	...	...	...	...	...	...	...	3 297	3 254	3 251
Fem. – Muj.	...	...	...	...	...	...	...	1 503	1 477	1 503
Luxembourg (III) [9]										
Total	41.225	42.303	43.278	44.785	46.381	44.371	43.357	...	...	...
Malta (IV) [2]										
Total	21.330	22.520	23.630	27.430	28.011	28.891	33.196	36.483	32.827	39.454
Males – Hom.	15.280	15.910	16.090	17.280	17.668	18.028	17.672	20.196	18.459	24.276
Fem. – Muj.	6.050	6.610	7.540	10.150	10.343	10.953	12.612	13.608	14.368	15.178
Netherlands (III) [2]										
Indices [10]	...	...	...	105	104	100	96	94	91	90
" " " " (IV) [11]										
Total	1 203	1 186	1 146	1 131	1 128	1 088	1 043	1 015	988	973
Norway (I) [1]										
Total	.	.	367	389	392	395	398	393	380	370
Pologne [4] (III) [12]										
Total	4 072.3	4 200.1	4 366.4	4 490.2	4 600.0	4 729.9	4 745.3	4 792.3	4 785.5	4 774.3
" " " " [4] (III) [2]										
Total	3 483.9	3 607.9	3 757.8	3 880.2	3 986.3	4 271.4	4 084.9	4 128.6	4 110.6	4 077.2
Portugal (I) [1]										
Total	.	.	.	.	816.0	821.5	854.5	810.0	845.0	865.0
Males – Hom.	.	.	.	.	488.5	511.5	540.5	522.5	557.5	563.5
Fem. – Muj.	.	.	.	.	327.5	310.5	314.0	287.5	287.5	301.5
Roumanie [4] (III) [2]										
Total [13]	2 066.0	2 201.7	2 324.2	2 484.6	2 660.4	2 802.1	2 909.2	3 027.4	3 107.5	3 227.4

Explanatory notes and source: see p. 151 – Notes explicatives et source: voir p. 154 – Notas explicativas y fuente: véase p. 157

[1] Wage earners and salaried employees. [2] Registered employees. [3] Index base: 1964 = 100. [4] Socialised sector. [5] Sep. of each year. [6] Civilian labour force employed. [7] April of each year. [8] Change of industrial classification. [9] Establishments with 20 or more persons employed. [10] Index base: 1975 = 100. [11] Civilian employment (man-years). [12] Registered employed. [13] Incl. mining and quarrying, electricity, gas and water.

[1] Population salariée ayant un emploi. [2] Salariés inscrits. [3] Indices base: 1964 = 100. [4] Secteur socialisé. [5] Sept. de chaque année. [6] Main-d'œuvre civile occupée. [7] Avril de chaque année. [8] Changement de classification industrielle. [9] Etablissements occupant 20 personnes et plus. [10] Indices base: 1975 = 100. [11] Emploi civil (années-homme). [12] Ensemble de l'effectif occupé. [13] Y compris les industries extractives, l'électricité, le gaz et l'eau.

[1] Población ocupada asalariada. [2] Asalariados registrados. [3] Indices base 1964 = 100. [4] Sector socializado. [5] Sept. de cada año. [6] Fuerza trabajadora civil ocupada. [7] Abril de cada año. [8] Cambio de clasificación industrial. [9] Establecimientos con 20 y más trabajadores. [10] Indices base 1975 = 100. [11] Empleo civil (años-hombre). [12] Todo el efectivo ocupado. [13] Incl. minas y canteras, electricidad, gas y agua.

6 Employment in manufacturing
Emploi dans les industries manufacturières
Empleo en las industrias manufactureras

A All industries
Ensemble des industries
Todas las industrias

(Thousands – Milliers – Millares)

Country – Source Pays – Source País – Fuente	1970	1971	1972	1973	1974	1975	1976	1977	1978	1979
Suisse (III) [1]										
Total [2]	879.89	873.18	848.42	814.27	805.24	714.90	683.20	681.82	683.69	678.18
" " " " (III) [3]										
Indices [4]	144.2	142.2	138.6	136.5	136.1	123.8	115.1	114.8	114.9	113.6
Sweden (III) [3]										
Total	664.01	646.39	635.30	650.03	667.39	669.17	664.17	634.24	608.47	...
Males – Hom.	523.20	510.07	503.05	513.28	521.17	519.62	515.05	491.83	472.58	...
Fem. – Muj.	140.81	136.32	132.25	136.75	146.22	149.55	149.13	142.41	135.89	...
" " " " (III) [5]										
Total	664.01	646.39	635.30	650.03	667.39	669.17	658.23 *	636.74	607.70	610.20
Turquie (III) [3]										
Total	504.1	519.3	576.9	637.6	657.8	699.6	724.4	...	...	...
United Kingdom (III) [3]										
Total [6]	8 342	8 058	7 780	7 829	7 873	7 490	7 246	7 292	7 233*	7 155*
Males – Hom. [6]	5 817	5 653	5 465	5 467	5 458	5 264	5 131	5 142	5 105*	5 041*
Fem. – Muj. [6]	2 525	2 405	2 315	2 362	2 415	2 226	2 115	2 150	2 128*	2 114*
Yugoslavia (III) [3]										
Total [7]	1 294	1 361	1 437	1 485	1 565	1 649	1 697	1 780	1 838*	1 913*

OCEANIA – OCEANIE – OCEANIA

	1970	1971	1972	1973	1974	1975	1976	1977	1978	1979
Fiji (III) [1]										
Total [2]	9.135	10.040	9.828	10.116	11.840	12.760	11.444	11.253	...	13.096
Guam (III) [3]										
Total	0.900	1.100	1.000	1.100	1.700	1.200	0.933	0.992	1.233	...
New Zealand (III) [3]										
Total	.	246.77	246.54	257.25	266.47	261.37	266.74	268.78	257.80	269.55*[8]
Males – Hom.	.	.	.	.	196.78	194.35	197.39	197.28	192.55	199.34*[8]
Fem. – Muj.	.	.	.	.	70.41	66.93	69.36	71.51	65.25	70.21*[8]
Papua New Guinea (IV) [3]										
Total [6]	9.179	9.568	10.121	10.252	11.450	10.565	12.188	12.192	...	...

USSR – URSS – URSS

	1970	1971	1972	1973	1974	1975	1976	1977	1978	1979
URSS [9] (III) [3]										
Total [10]	31 593	32 030	32 461	32 875	33 433	34 054	34 815	35 417	36 014	36 456

Explanatory notes and source: see p. 151 – Notes explicatives et source: voir p. 154 – Notas explicativas y fuente: véase p. 157

[1] Registered employed. [2] Sep. of each year. [3] Registered employees. [4] Index base: 1949 = 100. [5] Wage earners only. [6] June of each year. [7] March and Sep. of each year. [8] April. [9] Socialised sector. [10] Incl. mining and quarrying, electricity, gas and water.

[1] Ensemble de l'effectif occupé. [2] Sept. de chaque année. [3] Salariés inscrits. [4] Indices base: 1949 = 100. [5] Ouvriers seulement. [6] Juin de chaque année. [7] Mars et sept. de chaque année. [8] Avril. [9] Secteur socialisé. [10] Y compris les industries extractives, l'electricité, le gaz et l'eau.

[1] Todo el efectivo ocupado. [2] Sept. de cada año. [3] Asalariados registrados. [4] Indices base 1949 = 100. [5] Obreros solamente. [6] Junio de cada año. [7] Marzo y sept. de cada año. [8] Abril. [9] Sector socializado. [10] Incl. minas y canteras, electricidad, gas y agua.

6 B

Employment in manufacturing
Emploi dans les industries manufacturières
Empleo en las industrias manufactureras

By major groups of industry
Par classe d'industrie
Por agrupaciones de industria

(Thousands – Milliers – Millares)

Country – ISIC code (a) Pays – Code CITI (a) País – Clave CIIU (a)	1970	1971	1972	1973	1974	1975	1976	1977	1978	1979
AFRICA – AFRIQUE – AFRICA										
Burundi [1] (III)										
311–12	0.187	0.198	0.192	0.215	0.222	0.218	0.232	0.458	0.401	0.370
313	0.312	0.339	0.457	0.563	0.548	0.593	0.554	0.572	0.636	0.676
321	0.224	0.144	0.144	0.142	0.153	0.158	0.152	0.152	0.153	0.171
322	0.203	0.220	0.218	0.222	0.251	0.265	0.228	0.233	0.234	0.231
323	0.074	0.070	0.019	0.089	0.046	0.046	0.058	0.060	0.049	0.058
324	0.077	0.092	0.075	0.066	0.066	0.030	0.030	0.033	0.033	0.041
33	0.104	0.134	0.135	0.152	0.164	0.131	0.143	0.141	0.161	0.169
34	0.100	0.104	0.101	0.119	0.127	0.133	0.131	0.130	0.124	0.124
35	0.116	0.164	0.116	0.135	0.147	0.152	0.191	0.280	0.296	0.222
36	0.121	0.125	0.105	0.157	0.150	0.365	0.253	0.154	0.172	0.178
381	0.572	0.556	0.514	0.520	0.529	0.449	0.469	0.485	0.495	0.573
383	0.014	0.008	0.007	0.029	0.029	0.030	0.020	0.018	0.017	0.017
390	0.015	0.192	0.162	0.144	0.104	0.203	0.078	0.069	–	–
Total	**2.119**	**2.346**	**2.245**	**2.553**	**2.536**	**2.773**	**2.539**	**2.785**	**2.771**	**2.830**
Rép.-Unie du Cameroun (III)										
311–12	.	.	.	3.717	4.975	5.341	5.430	4.837	5.375	6.847
313	.	.	.	3.983	5.331	6.195	6.324	7.431	7.843	8.013
314	.	.	.	0.405	0.537	0.742	0.812	0.918	1.184	1.354
323–24	.	.	.	0.308	0.410	0.497	0.513	0.937	1.317	1.611
321	.	.	.	3.353	4.483	4.837	4.987	5.138	4.955	5.219
322	.	.	.	5.403	7.232	6.963	7.011	6.844	7.084	7.395
331	.	.	.	3.048	4.072	4.841	4.941	5.393	5.836	6.772
332	.	.	.	0.999	1.327	1.705	1.835	1.741	1.694	2.395
341	.	.	.	–	–	–	–	0.452	2.193	2.916
342	.	.	.	0.675	0.896	0.749	0.836	0.871	1.164	1.749
351	.	.	.	–	–	–	0.023	0.059	0.057	0.103
353	.	.	.	–	–	–	–	–	0.896	1.131
356	.	.	.	–	–	–	–	–	0.375	0.437
361	.	.	.	–	–	–	–	–	0.178	0.298
362	.	.	.	–	–	–	–	–	0.271	0.298
381	.	.	.	–	–	–	–	–	0.840	1.012
Total	.	.	.	**21.891**	**29.263**	**31.870**	**32.712**	**34.621**	**41.262**	**47.550**

(a) ISIC – CITI – CIIU 1968: See Annex. – Voir annexe – Véase anexo.

[1] Dec. of each year.   [1] Déc. de chaque année.   [1] Dic. de cada año.

6

Employment in manufacturing
Emploi dans les industries manufacturières
Empleo en las industrias manufactureras

B

By major groups of industry
Par classe d'industrie
Por agrupaciones de industria

(Thousands – Milliers – Millares)

Country – ISIC code (a) Pays – Code CITI (a) País – Clave CIIU (a)	1970	1971	1972	1973	1974	1975	1976	1977	1978	1979
Egypt [1] (III) [2]										
311–12	88.0	95.0	94.0	91.0	104.0	105.0	100.0	...	...	...
313	6.0	6.0	6.0	5.0	6.0	6.0	6.0			
314	9.0	6.0	12.0	11.0	12.0	12.0	12.0			
321	249.0	223.0	259.0	269.0	274.0	293.0	279.0			
322	4.0	8.0	3.0	3.0	3.0	3.0	3.0	...	...	...
323	3.0	4.0	4.0	3.0	4.0	4.0	4.0			
324	5.0	5.0	6.0	6.0	6.0	5.0	5.0			
331	5.0	4.0	5.0	5.0	6.0	4.0	6.0			
332	3.0	4.0	3.0	3.0	5.0	3.0	3.0			
341	10.0	9.0	11.0	13.0	11.0	13.0	11.0	...	...	...
342	16.0	13.0	16.0	14.0	14.0	15.0	16.0			
351	11.0	11.0	13.0	20.0	16.0	20.0	19.0			
352	24.0	23.0	24.0	27.0	21.0	28.0	26.0			
353	5.0	5.0	8.0	5.0	10.0	11.0	4.0			
354	3.0	4.0	4.0	3.0	4.0	4.0	6.0	...	...	...
355	5.0	4.0	5.0	5.0	3.0	5.0	5.0			
356	4.0	4.0	6.0	6.0	8.0	7.0	4.0			
361	1.0	1.0	1.0	1.0	4.0	3.0	3.0			
362	10.0	6.0	9.0	10.0	9.0	8.0	10.0			
369	20.0	20.0	20.0	19.0	19.0	22.0	23.0	...	...	...
371	23.0	12.0	17.0	32.0	11.0	38.0	33.0			
372	4.0	4.0	5.0	8.0	7.0	4.0	4.0			
381	30.0	43.0	37.0	24.0	32.0	33.0	33.0			
382	14.0	12.0	18.0	27.0	30.0	29.0	33.0			
384	27.0	19.0	21.0	24.0	25.0	25.0	28.0	...	...	...
385	1.0	2.0	1.0	1.0	1.0	1.0	6.0			
390	1.0	1.0	1.0	2.0	2.0	2.0	1.0			
Total	**581.0**	**548.0**	**609.0**	**637.0**	**647.0**	**703.0**	**683.0**	...	...	...
Ethiopia [3] (III)										
311–12	8.350	8.643	9.066	9.732	11.639	13.471	10.782	...	...	...
313	3.040	2.924	2.971	2.898	2.915	3.077	3.629	...	...	...
314	0.432	0.542	0.581	0.603	0.477	0.689	0.662	...	...	...
321	21.105	21.409	22.563	22.827	22.296	22.599	26.083	...	...	...
322	0.549	0.967	1.011	1.125	1.214	1.216	1.207			
323	0.918	0.895	0.978	1.199	1.206	1.215	1.143			
324	1.272	1.293	1.186	1.421	1.548	1.688	1.569	...	...	...
331	2.840	3.551	3.521	3.376	3.628	3.816	4.275			
332	0.497	0.480	0.577	0.629	0.655	0.651	0.689			
341	0.366	0.687	0.680	0.713	0.685	0.566	0.640	...	...	...
342	1.602	1.566	1.558	1.537	1.508	1.507	1.642			
351	0.160	0.109	0.081	0.087	0.051	0.047	0.187			
352	0.752	0.687	0.750	0.766	0.835	0.824	0.941	...	...	
353	0.656	0.673	0.745	0.757	0.736	0.740	0.799			
354	–	–	–	–	–	–	–			
355	0.312	0.339	0.347	0.499	1.477	1.792	1.025	...	...	...
356	0.608	0.643	0.686	0.748	0.522	0.449	0.928			
361	–	–	–	–	–	–	–	...		
362	0.380	0.375	0.368	0.407	0.506	0.514	0.565			
369	3.764	3.510	3.657	3.674	3.576	3.452	2.788			
371	0.514	0.635	0.658	0.672	0.601	0.572	0.561			
372	–	–	–	–	–	–	–			
381	1.244	1.509	1.411	1.219	1.324	1.188	0.561	...	...	...
382	–	–	–	–	–	–	–			
383	0.052	0.063	0.067	0.076	0.057	0.058	0.057			
384	–	–	–	–	–	–	–			
385	–	–	–	–	–	–	–	...	...	
390	–	–	–	–	–	–	–			
Total	**49.413**	**51.500**	**53.462**	**54.965**	**57.456**	**60.131**	**60.733**	...	...	...

(a) ISIC – CITI – CIIU 1968: See Annex. – Voir annexe – Véase anexo.

[1] Oct. of each year. [2] Public sector and establishments with 10 or more persons employed. [3] Year ending in Sep. of the year indicated.

[1] Oct. de chaque année. [2] Secteur publique et établissements occupant 10 personnes et plus. [3] Année se terminant en sept. de l'année indiquée.

[1] Oct. de cada año. [2] Sector póblico y establecimientos con 10 y más trabajadores. [3] Año que termina en sept. del año indicado.

6 Employment in manufacturing
Emploi dans les industries manufacturières
Empleo en las industrias manufactureras

B By major groups of industry
Par classe d'industrie
Por agrupaciones de industria

(Thousands – Milliers – Millares)

Country – ISIC code [a] Pays – Code CITI [a] País – Clave CIIU [a]	1970	1971	1972	1973	1974	1975	1976	1977	1978	1979
Kenya [1] (III)										
311–12	13.98	16.23	15.41	17.29	19.33	19.87	22.83	25.67	31.33	33.58
313–14	3.81	4.12	4.19	4.23	4.66	4.55	5.52	5.72	5.50	6.21
321	7.39	8.81	9.65	11.56	12.35	12.72	13.64	14.82	18.22	20.08
322	2.96	3.89	3.84	3.85	4.37	4.28	4.78	4.91	5.01	5.31
323	0.56	0.93	0.89	1.02	1.30	1.13	1.23	1.42	1.42	1.66
324	1.54	1.62	▌1.23[2]	1.71	1.66	1.67	1.66	1.78	2.15	2.12
331	5.43	6.09	6.20	6.41	7.53	7.70	7.87	7.20	8.42	8.52
332	2.25	2.64	2.36	2.91	3.16	2.52	2.67	2.90	3.11	3.09
341	1.17	1.73	1.94	2.54	2.48	3.17	3.38	3.38	3.61	3.76
342	3.99	4.39	3.92	4.06	4.39	4.35	4.51	4.03	3.93	4.21
35	4.31	4.84	6.18	7.13	.	.	.	.	.	.
351	.	.	.	.	1.84	1.91	1.91	2.08	2.26	2.22
352	.	.	.	.	3.33	3.17	3.92	4.88	5.23	5.27
353	.	.	.	.	0.28	0.29	0.29	0.29	0.30	0.33
355	0.70	0.81	0.99	1.10	1.25	1.34	1.36	1.60	1.64	1.87
356	.	.	.	.	1.02	1.15	1.31	1.63	1.83	2.36
361+369	1.92	1.94	2.41	2.78	.	.	.	.	.	.
361	.	.	.	.	0.08	0.07	0.08	0.08	0.13	...
362	0.59	0.55	0.59	0.34	0.63	0.66	0.69	0.76	0.84	1.03
369	.	.	.	.	3.35	3.61	3.43	4.00	4.02	5.56
37	.	.	.	.	1.09	0.94	1.12	1.34	1.77	...
381	3.96	5.90	5.86	6.60	6.06	5.99	6.93	7.56	8.30	9.16
382	1.83	1.56	1.65	1.42	1.28	1.28	1.30	1.27	1.29	1.26
383	6.93	6.45	0.69	0.86	0.77	1.04	1.11	1.30	1.37	1.41
384	18.11	18.70	15.84	18.39	17.47	16.04	15.84	17.75	17.04	17.41
385	.	.	.	.	0.05	0.04	0.02	0.17	0.18	...
390	1.48	1.94	1.55	1.11	1.59	1.22	1.36	1.38	1.13	1.03
Total	**82.93**	**93.15**	**85.42**	**95.31**	**101.34**	**100.73**	**108.78**	**117.95**	**130.06**	**137.46**
Malawi [3] (III)										
311–12	2.278	2.378	2.504	2.843	3.404	4.069	8.304	▌8.528[4]	9.526	...
313	4.043	4.091	4.360	4.821	5.029	5.575	5.876	▌1.205[4]	1.330	...
314	4.823	5.878	6.520	7.092	6.093	8.334	9.771	▌8.702[4]	8.587	...
321	2.343	2.509	2.654	2.958	3.134	3.152	3.208	▌3.597[4]	4.079	...
322	1.238	1.488	1.276	1.601	1.898	2.032	1.948	▌1.807[4]	1.993	...
323	0.036	0.053	0.056	0.061	0.055	0.061	0.056	▌0.058[4]	0.064	...
324	0.135	0.135	0.134	0.119	0.132	0.135	0.214	▌0.235[4]	0.283	...
331	0.709	0.764	1.020	1.334	1.222	1.109	1.598	▌1.555[4]	1.352	...
332	0.384	0.400	0.261	0.255	0.285	0.353	0.449	▌0.641[4]	0.714	...
341	0.040	0.057	0.137	0.165	0.171	0.237	0.245	▌0.226[4]	0.220	...
342	0.676	0.790	0.589	0.760	0.824	0.974	0.526	▌1.002[4]	1.036	...
351	0.035	0.064	0.050	0.195	0.120	0.166	0.166	▌0.150[4]	0.198	...
352	0.603	0.613	0.776	0.453	0.947	1.047	1.062	▌1.077[4]	1.112	...
355	0.077	0.080	0.119	0.195	0.166	0.206	0.178	▌0.206[4]	0.181	...
356	0.026	0.030	0.039	0.046	0.067	0.107	0.121	▌0.201[4]	0.313	...
369	1.181	1.342	1.432	1.419	1.629	1.690	2.717	▌2.070[4]	2.436	...
371	–	–	–	–	–	0.004	–	▌–[4]	0.015	...
372	–	–	–	–	0.034	0.038	0.035	▌–[4]	–	...
381	0.417	0.604	0.855	0.965	1.104	1.399	1.597	▌1.301[4]	1.553	...
382	0.173	0.187	0.169	0.167	0.236	0.251	0.255	▌0.366[4]	0.439	...
383	0.085	0.099	0.120	0.117	0.093	0.105	0.101	▌0.118[4]	0.135	...
384	0.039	0.049	0.074	0.074	0.077	0.088	0.102	▌0.207[4]	0.179	...
390	0.124	0.149	0.073	–	0.110	0.229	0.242	▌0.227[4]	0.210	...
Total	**19.465**	**21.760**	**23.218**	**25.640**	**26.830**	**31.361**	**38.771**	**▌33.479[4]**	**35.955**	**...**

[a] ISIC – CITI – CIIU 1968: See Annex. – Voir annexe – Véase anexo.

[1] June of each year. [2] Prior to 1972: incl. repair services. [3] Establishments with 20 or more persons employed. [4] Beginning 1977: sample of establishments and revised allocation of establishments in the industrial classification.

[1] Juin de chaque année. [2] Avant 1972: y compris les services de réparation. [3] Etablissements occupant 20 personnes et plus. [4] A partir de 1977: échantillon d'établissements et changements dans leur répartition industrielle.

[1] Junio de cada año. [2] Antes de 1972: incl. los servicios de reparación. ñ[3] Establecimientos con 20 y más trabajadores. [4] A partir de 1977: muestra de establecimientos y cambios en la distribución industrial de los establecimientos.

6 Employment in manufacturing
Emploi dans les industries manufacturières
Empleo en las industrias manufactureras

B By major groups of industry
Par classe d'industrie
Por agrupaciones de industria

(Thousands – Milliers – Millares)

Country – ISIC code (a) Pays – Code CITI (a) País – Clave CIIU (a)	1970	1971	1972	1973	1974	1975	1976	1977	1978	1979
Mauritius [1] (III) [2]										
323+355	0.141	0.174	0.205	0.409	0.385	0.341	0.590	0.556	0.681	0.563
311–12 [3]	0.767	0.821	1.254	1.571	1.881	1.955	1.969	2.438	2.417	2.446
313–14	1.258	1.354	1.499	1.557	1.787	1.995	2.279	2.432	2.639	2.535
321	0.737	0.860	0.698	0.646	0.778	0.992	2.208	2.868	1.994	2.248
322	0.374	1.044	2.222	4.007	6.625	7.574	11.484	13.675	14.280	15.670
324	0.274	0.369	0.412	0.465	0.454	0.430	0.399	0.491	0.479	0.449
33	0.299	0.389	0.571	0.835	0.913	0.904	0.866	1.000	0.969	1.047
341	–	–	–	–	–	–	–	–	0.364	0.302
342	0.702	0.784	0.784	0.962	1.064	0.986	1.049	1.077	1.266	1.141
351–54	0.347	0.384	0.482	0.487	0.604	0.790	0.861	0.963	0.963	0.974
356	–	–	–	–	–	–	–	–	0.123	0.127
36 [4]	0.571	0.588	0.638	0.846	0.910	0.980	1.108	1.355	1.474	1.477
371	–	–	–	–	–	–	–	–	0.365	0.489
381	0.358	0.451	0.588	0.827	0.785	0.795	0.798	0.734	0.576	0.615
382	0.566	0.552	0.599	0.517	0.600	0.681	0.786	0.849	0.768	0.772
383	0.149	0.151	0.161	0.837	2.023	1.731	2.560	2.175	1.726	2.097
384	0.792	0.626	0.752	0.938	0.964	0.977	0.862	0.745	0.749	0.715
385	–	–	–	–	–	–	–	–	0.153	0.213
390	0.486	1.228	0.711	0.818	1 040	1.386	1.529	1.883	1.091	1.172
Total	**7.821**	**9.775**	**11.576**	**15.722**	**1 059.8**	**22.517**	**29.348**	**33.241**	**33.077**	**35.052**
Sierra Leone [5] (III)										
311–12	1.209	1.106	1.175	1.150	1.223	1.242	1.076	1.248	1.248	1.283
313	0.669	0.628	0.749	0.656	0.594	0.613	0.582	0.993	0.993	2.176
314	0.315	0.307	0.352	0.354	0.381	0.323	0.373	0.435	0.435	0.424
32	0.153	0.158	0.143	0.154	0.138	0.134	0.049	0.131	0.131	0.058
331	1.225	1.212	1.231	1.229	1.377	1.398	1.383	1.371	1.370	1.371
332	0.091	0.091	0.029	0.030	0.027	0.027	0.028	0.031	0.031	0.106
34	0.518	0.527	0.526	0.536	0.547	0.547	0.550	0.540	0.550	0.558
351	0.034	0.030	0.033	0.043	0.046	0.044	0.034	0.045	0.045	0.199
352	0.135	0.143	0.134	0.150	0.090	0.093	0.097	0.091	0.091	0.114
353	0.120	0.111	0.109	0.131	0.123	0.135	0.138	0.136	0.130	0.159
356	0.047	0.052	0.127	0.127	0.064	0.004	0.035	0.037	0.037	0.123
369	0.044	0.044	0.044	0.022	0.024	0.024	–	0.024	0.036	0.061
381	0.035	0.035	0.027	0.027	0.036	0.037	0.034	0.034	0.036	0.158
384	1.084	0.848	1.208	1.214	1.215	1.219	1.249	0.902	0.904	0.890
Total	**5.679**	**5.292**	**5.887**	**5.823**	**5.885**	**5.840**	**5.628**	**6.018**	**6.037**	**7.680**

(a) ISIC – CITI – CIIU 1968: See Annex. – Voir annexe – Véase anexo.

[1] Sep. of each year. [2] Excl. developments workers. [3] Excl. sugar and tea factories. [4] Excl. pottery, china, earthenware and glass. [5] Dec. of each year.

[1] Sept. de chaque année. [2] Non compris les personnes occupées à des travaux publics de développement. [3] Non compris les fabriques de sucre et de thé. [4] Non compris le grès, les porcelaines, les faïences et le verre. [5] Déc. de chaque année.

[1] Sept. de cada año. [2] Excl. las personas ocupadas en planes de desarrollo. [3] Excl. las industrias del azúcar y del tó. [4] Excl. el barro, la loza, la porcelana y el vidrio. [5] Dic. de cada año.

6 Employment in manufacturing
Emploi dans les industries manufacturières
Empleo en las industrias manufactureras

B By major groups of industry
Par classe d'industrie
Por agrupaciones de industria

(Thousands – Milliers – Millares)

Country – ISIC code (a) Pays – Code CITI (a) País – Clave CIIU (a)	1970	1971	1972	1973	1974	1975	1976	1977	1978	1979
South Africa, Rep. of ¹ (III)										
311–12	131.3	134.6	135.5	141.8	148.4	156.7	159.8	161.4	161.6	...
313	21.1	24.0	24.3	25.1	26.5	26.0	26.5	25.5	25.3	...
314	4.1	3.8	3.8	3.7	3.7	3.7	3.7	4.1	4.3	...
321	97.8	100.0	101.9	106.3	110.3	110.0	112.4	109.5	108.4	...
322	85.4	88.8	91.5	94.3	96.2	97.4	97.4	94.1	93.4	...
323	7.9	8.2	8.4	8.3	8.9	9.5	9.5	9.2	9.3	...
324	24.4	24.1	24.5	24.0	22.4	21.0	20.4	17.0	17.6	...
331	43.4	45.9	46.4	48.8	50.9	52.8	53.5	52.0	51.2	...
332	25.3	25.7	25.0	25.2	27.6	25.6	25.3	24.5	24.2	...
341	29.9	31.3	32.2	33.6	34.6	34.3	35.2	34.8	34.2	...
342	30.9	32.3	33.4	33.8	34.7	35.2	35.2	34.6	35.0	...
351–54	67.5	69.4	70.8	73.6	74.4	74.5	76.8	78.7	80.4	...
355	15.6	16.1	16.2	16.8	16.7	16.6	17.1	17.2	17.2	...
356	15.7	15.6	15.9	17.5	19.9	19.5	20.1	19.2	21.0	...
36	76.2	79.0	80.5	82.7	86.4	88.0	86.8	85.3	85.3	...
37	83.3	85.9	86.7	92.0	97.3	104.5	106.9	105.5	108.0	...
381	108.1	109.9	112.5	115.1	120.1	123.4	123.8	118.7	115.7	...
382	65.1	66.1	66.5	68.1	71.3	76.7	78.1	76.5	76.0	...
383	43.0	48.2	50.0	53.0	57.9	60.1	62.9	59.6	59.8	...
385	3.1	3.2	4.0	5.6	6.7	6.1	6.8	5.9	5.6	...
390	14.7	15.1	16.4	18.2	21.0	21.2	22.5	22.1	23.3	...
Total	**993.9**	**1 027.2**	**1 046.4**	**1 087.5**	**1 135.9**	**1 162.8**	**1 180.7**	**1 155.4**	**1 156.8**	**...**
Zimbabwe (III)										
311–12	.	.	.	.	.	20.5	21.6	21.6	22.0	22.4
313	.	.	.	.	.	6.7	7.0	7.0	6.8	6.3
314	.	.	.	.	.	5.2	5.6	4.9	5.2	5.4
321	.	.	.	.	.	15.3	15.7	15.3	14.8	15.2
322	.	.	.	.	.	14.7	14.3	13.2	12.0	13.4
323	.	.	.	.	.	0.4	0.5	0.6	0.6	0.7
324	.	.	.	.	.	4.1	4.1	4.0	3.8	3.9
331	.	.	.	.	.	6.1	5.5	4.9	4.4	4.4
332	.	.	.	.	.	5.7	5.2	4.5	4.1	4.4
341	.	.	.	.	.	2.4	2.4	2.4	2.4	2.4
342	.	.	.	.	.	4.2	4.4	4.3	4.3	4.5
351–54	.	.	.	.	.	0.4	0.4	0.4	0.3	0.3
351	.	.	.	.	.	2.5	2.5	2.6	2.7	2.9
352	.	.	.	.	.	4.0	3.8	3.7	3.6	3.5
355	.	.	.	.	.	2.0	2.1	2.0	2.0	2.0
356	.	.	.	.	.	2.0	1.9	2.0	2.1	2.2
361	.	.	.	.	.	0.2	0.3	0.3	0.3	0.3
362	.	.	.	.	.	0.6	0.5	0.5	0.5	0.5
369	.	.	.	.	.	8.0	7.1	6.1	5.4	5.8
371	.	.	.	.	.	13.7	14.7	13.3	12.2	12.9
372	.	.	.	.	.	0.8	0.8	0.7	0.7	0.8
381–82	.	.	.	.	.	21.9	19.9	18.3	17.3	17.9
383	.	.	.	.	.	5.7	5.1	4.8	4.5	4.8
384	.	.	.	.	.	5.4	5.4	5.0	4.6	5.1
385	.	.	.	.	.	0.2	0.2	0.2	0.2	0.2
390	.	.	.	.	.	2.7	2.6	2.5	2.5	2.5
Total	**.**	**.**	**.**	**.**	**.**	**155.4**	**153.6**	**145.1**	**139.3**	**144.7**

(a) ISIC – CITI – CIIU 1968: See Annex. – Voir annexe – Véase anexo.

¹ June of each year.   ¹ Juin de chaque année.   ¹ Junio de cada año.

6 Employment in manufacturing
Emploi dans les industries manufacturières
Empleo en las industrias manufactureras

B By major groups of industry
Par classe d'industrie
Por agrupaciones de industria

(Thousands – Milliers – Millares)

Country – ISIC code (a) Pays – Code CITI (a) País – Clave CIIU (a)	1970	1971	1972	1973	1974	1975	1976	1977	1978	1979
AMERICA – AMERIQUE – AMERICA										
Argentina (III)										
311–12	26.49	27.26	27.12	31.33	33.29	34.80	35.26	36.60	34.23	...
313	5.72	4.80	4.49	4.25	4.97	5.07	4.56	3.77	2.21	...
314	5.67	5.96	5.88	6.01	6.43	6.53	6.76	6.26	5.88	...
321	.	1.12	1.10	1.04	1.06	1.11	1.21	1.15	1.10	...
341	11.83	12.81	13.19	13.84	14.31	15.24	16.01	15.73	15.31	...
351	18.87	19.10	19.34	20.01	20.53	20.99	20.80	20.04	19.09	...
352	12.61	12.61	12.83	12.93	13.90	13.90	14.02	14.02	13.32	...
355	5.33	5.62	6.11	6.60	7.07	7.39	7.48	7.67	7.28	...
356	0.77	0.69	0.74	0.92	0.86	0.93	0.80	0.89	0.59	...
369	8.68	9.08	9.20	9.02	9.22	10.01	10.70	10.73	10.94	...
371	13.16	14.17	14.32	14.81	16.01	18.01	18.99	19.39	18.29	...
381	5.43	5.66	5.87	5.71	6.27	6.58	6.22	5.58	4.70	...
382	6.46	5.85	5.45	5.56	6.43	6.91	6.26	5.99	4.64	...
383	4.56	4.46	4.25	4.24	4.62	5.38	4.94	4.88	4.62	...
384	52.13	53.70	55.82	60.55	67.80	73.98	69.09	64.88	34.32	...
Total	**177.71**	**182.89**	**185.74**	**196.83**	**212.78**	**226.83**	**223.10**	**217.58**	**176.52**	...
Barbados (III)										
31	.	.	.	.	3.216	2.983	3.035	3.195	...	...
32	.	.	.	.	2.256	2.009	2.422	2.325	...	...
33	.	.	.	.	0.347	0.302	0.539	0.538	...	...
34	.	.	.	.	0.659	0.596	0.529	0.748	...	...
35	.	.	.	.	0.351	0.379	0.398	0.434	...	...
36	.	.	.	.	0.413	0.295	0.287	0.258	...	...
38	.	.	.	.	2.309	1.658	2.011	1.900	...	...
390	.	.	.	.	0.628	0.526	0.668	0.639	...	...
Total	.	.	.	.	**10.179**	**8.748**	**9.889**	**10.037**	...	...
Bolivia (III)										
31	6.74	6.46	6.68	6.74	8.89	11.09	17.57	27.22	27.68	28.69
32	7.92	7.79	7.65	7.83	8.40	8.26	16.64	26.31	26.46	27.43
33	1.41	1.29	1.31	1.23	1.48	3.41	6.32	9.98	10.38	10.76
34	0.98	1.07	1.02	1.09	1.16	1.59	2.72	4.54	4.58	4.75
35	1.11	1.27	1.30	0.29	0.47	0.54	4.35	6.80	7.11	7.37
36	1.23	1.22	0.76	1.11	1.54	1.59	3.25	4.99	5.24	5.43
37	0.11	0.11	0.07	0.09	0.63	0.76	1.10	1.63	2.55	2.52
38	0.79	0.70	0.95	1.06	1.58	1.94	5.12	7.98	8.32	8.63
390	0.69	0.56	1.65	0.06	0.11	0.23	0.87	1.27	1.31	1.36
Total	**20.98**	**20.46**	**21.39**	**19.49**	**24.27**	**29.41**	**57.94**	**90.74**	**93.62**	**96.92**

(a) ISIC – CITI – CIIU 1968: See Annex. – Voir annexe – Véase anexo.

6 Employment in manufacturing
Emploi dans les industries manufacturières
Empleo en las industrias manufactureras

B By major groups of industry
Par classe d'industrie
Por agrupaciones de industria

(Thousands – Milliers – Millares)

Country – ISIC code (a) / Pays – Code CITI (a) / País – Clave CIIU (a)	1970	1971	1972	1973	1974	1975	1976	1977	1978	1979
Canada (III) [1]										
311–12	172.4	171.8	170.7	173.7	174.8	167.7	171.7	173.4	178.3	181.1
313	28.0	28.1	27.8	29.1	29.7	30.1	31.3	31.5	31.1	32.2
314	9.6	9.5	9.3	9.2	9.4	8.8	8.9	9.9	8.3	8.3
321	68.1	68.7	72.8	76.1	75.2	66.7	65.8	63.2	65.1	66.4
322	86.6	86.2	87.3	90.5	89.6	87.4	88.1	84.8	87.9	88.8
323	9.4	9.4	9.7	10.4	10.3	9.9	9.1	8.1	8.4	8.4
324	17.4	17.5	16.6	16.6	16.6	15.8	16.1	13.8	14.9	15.5
331	77.1	82.2	85.9	94.3	94.0	82.9	92.0	92.4	98.2	100.4
332	34.0	34.2	36.7	39.7	41.4	36.4	37.2	33.1	35.0	36.7
341	117.8	116.2	115.8	117.6	127.9	113.0	124.1	124.7	125.5	126.8
342	69.6	67.8	67.0	69.6	73.1	72.7	73.2	73.0	76.5	78.7
351	19.9	18.7	17.6	17.4	18.4	19.3	20.6	21.3	22.4	23.0
352	52.0	50.6	50.7	52.9	55.6	55.3	55.5	56.0	56.2	57.3
353	10.1	10.0	9.7	9.7	10.8	10.8	10.3	10.7	11.3	11.6
354	6.7	6.8	6.9	6.9	7.0	7.2	7.9	8.5	9.9	10.5
355	24.3	24.2	24.3	27.2	26.3	26.2	26.8	27.1	26.7	28.0
356	18.2	18.5	19.9	22.4	21.9	19.6	20.7	20.6	22.7	23.4
361	5.2	4.8	4.5	4.8	4.9	4.6	4.6	4.7	4.4	4.5
362	11.9	11.2	11.9	12.9	13.0	12.1	12.3	12.1	12.2	12.2
369	28.7	29.2	30.9	33.1	35.2	34.0	32.9	31.3	32.2	33.3
371	102.7	101.8	100.2	104.4	109.8	108.1	101.6	103.7	105.2	106.0
372	13.2	12.9	13.4	13.5	13.4	12.1	12.5	12.8	13.6	14.6
381	119.6	116.8	119.0	126.8	132.9	124.1	124.4	119.9	125.5	132.1
382	73.6	70.9	68.8	75.7	82.1	81.0	75.0	73.2	75.3	81.2
383	124.2	118.4	119.3	125.7	135.7	121.5	120.5	111.9	111.9	116.0
384	139.0	141.7	149.7	161.3	159.0	149.1	154.0	156.7	168.6	176.4
385	17.2	16.9	17.3	17.6	18.7	18.0	10.2	17.6	16.9	18.5
390	50.6	50.6	55.7	55.0	56.2	54.7	60.0	48.8	50.0	51.2
Total	**1 507.1**	**1 495.6**	**1 519.4**	**1 594.1**	**1 642.9**	**1 549.1**	**1 567.3**	**1 544.8**	**1 594.2**	**1 642.7**
Colombia (III)										
311–12	.	47.59	53.25	56.89	60.68	63.92	62.60	64.05*	...	...
313	.	16.54	18.38	19.74	19.67	20.76	22.24	23.08*	...	...
314	.	3.50	3.54	3.56	3.73	4.59	3.78	3.76*	...	...
321	.	63.16	68.00	73.05	74.91	75.73	75.49	78.50*	...	...
322	.	28.62	32.37	38.85	39.42	38.71	45.50	44.10*	...	...
323	.	5.19	4.78	5.85	6.40	7.66	8.13	8.23*	...	...
324	.	7.62	6.70	7.72	7.29	8.86	9.00	9.15*	...	...
331	.	7.38	7.77	8.42	8.64	8.43	8.59	6.77*	...	...
332	.	6.63	6.64	6.98	7.45	7.36	7.44	6.96*	...	...
341	.	8.14	8.79	9.59	11.89	11.12	11.44	11.62*	...	...
342	.	13.09	14.47	15.46	16.88	17.79	17.77	18.79*	...	...
351	.	8.73	9.53	10.14	10.38	11.41	11.59	10.93*	...	...
352	.	18.28	19.48	21.43	23.75	23.28	23.55	24.64*	...	...
353	.	2.25	2.40	2.87	3.92	4.05	3.99	4.32*	...	...
354	.	0.26	0.32	0.37	0.48	0.41	0.45	0.56*	...	...
355	.	5.51	7.39	7.98	9.20	8.01	7.71	8.62*	...	...
356	.	6.79	8.47	9.87	10.64	10.44	12.26	13.80*	...	...
361	.	3.93	4.49	4.77	5.08	5.17	5.67	5.56*	...	...
362	.	4.99	5.04	5.77	6.33	6.73	7.02	7.81*	...	...
369	.	17.37	17.99	19.34	19.34	19.02	19.43	19.28*	...	...
371	.	10.96	11.35	12.38	12.17	13.73	13.78	14.56*	...	...
372	.	2.07	2.23	2.51	2.48	2.41	2.76	2.72*	...	...
381	.	24.67	26.66	28.35	30.36	29.50	29.13	31.71*	...	...
382	.	13.11	13.68	14.84	15.45	14.64	15.59	16.81*	...	...
383	.	9.29	10.06	11.78	12.78	13.11	14.73	14.92*	...	...
384	.	10.34	10.99	14.19	17.59	18.63	19.60	21.32*	...	...
385	.	1.30	1.67	1.93	2.21	2.80	2.50	2.68*	...	...
390	.	6.95	7.52	8.35	8.31	8.54	8.31	8.65*	...	...
Total	**.**	**354.25**	**383.98**	**423.01**	**447.45**	**456.82**	**470.05**	**483.93***	**...**	**...**

(a) ISIC – CITI – CIIU 1968: See Annex. – Voir annexe – Véase anexo.

[1] Establishments with 20 or more persons employed.　　[1] Etablissements occupant 20 personnes et plus.　　[1] Establecimientos con 20 y más trabajadores.

6 Employment in manufacturing
Emploi dans les industries manufacturières
Empleo en las industrias manufactureras

B By major groups of industry
Par classe d'industrie
Por agrupaciones de industria

(Thousands – Milliers – Millares)

Country – ISIC code (a) Pays – Code CITI (a) País – Clave CIIU (a)	1970	1971	1972	1973	1974	1975	1976	1977	1978	1979
Chile [1] (III)										
311–12	29.24	29.70	33.43	35.29	33.72	34.93	37.28	37.87	...	...
313	5.46	5.31	6.15	6.74	6.59	5.84	5.14	5.75	...	...
314	1.39	1.42	1.87	2.12	2.20	2.11	1.48	1.35	...	...
322+324	24.57	23.81	24.10	23.35	21.89	19.67	19.00	19.49	...	...
321	37.25	37.44	45.71	46.77	43.60	36.84	30.79	30.68	...	...
323	2.24	2.12	2.13	2.29	2.28	2.12	2.14	2.29	...	...
331	6.33	6.31	6.10	5.80	5.57	4.85	4.31	4.79	...	...
332	8.31	6.80	6.71	6.44	7.94	7.53	6.82	6.41	...	...
341	2.51	2.52	2.72	2.56	2.64	2.79	2.45	3.35	...	...
342	8.24	7.98	9.31	9.77	9.42	8.14	7.25	7.43	...	...
351–52	17.08	17.15	20.08	20.30	20.21	19.96	17.80	18.54	...	...
353–54	0.92	0.91	0.90	0.95	0.96	0.93	0.77	0.73	...	...
355	3.41	3.23	3.93	4.16	3.84	3.66	3.39	3.34	...	...
36	9.11	8.62	9.54	10.41	10.78	10.18	7.99	7.40	...	...
37	12.14	12.16	13.20	14.05	13.78	13.39	11.75	11.11	...	...
381	13.19	12.19	13.67	14.35	13.85	13.21	12.24	11.79	...	...
382	4.35	3.68	3.91	5.72	4.83	4.40	3.01	3.09	...	...
383	6.25	5.85	5.85	6.12	6.02	5.51	4.51	4.27	...	...
384	7.65	6.63	6.22	6.03	5.58	5.11	4.71	1.90	...	...
390	3.63	3.24	3.04	3.29	2.88	3.04	2.58	2.11	...	...
Total	**203.31**	**197.10**	**218.59**	**226.54**	**218.57**	**204.20**	**185.41**	**183.72**	...	...
República Dominicana (III)										
311–12	95.13	97.88	103.89	113.88	114.97	95.42	82.16	81.75	81.32	...
313	1.63	1.65	1.81	1.80	1.91	2.20	2.47	3.19	3.36	...
314	0.85	0.80	1.58	1.08	1.15	1.43	0.82	0.83	0.86	...
321	2.26	2.20	2.49	4.33	2.49	2.61	3.01	3.56	3.48	...
322	0.99	1.08	1.28	1.60	1.75	2.18	2.74	2.57	2.64	...
323	0.38	0.38	0.57	0.52	0.71	0.72	0.80	0.93	1.00	...
324	0.52	0.50	0.60	0.62	0.73	0.99	1.06	1.12	1.29	...
331	0.09	0.11	0.10	0.11	0.11	0.10	0.14	0.11	0.12	...
332	0.56	0.60	0.78	0.88	0.99	1.00	1.02	1.10	1.05	...
341	0.88	0.83	1.01	1.21	1.37	1.38	1.45	1.69	1.83	...
342	0.80	0.82	0.99	1.24	1.16	1.11	1.23	1.20	1.27	...
351	0.70	0.75	0.81	0.91	1.02	1.11	1.19	1.24	1.38	...
352	1.18	1.30	1.66	1.44	1.70	1.84	2.15	2.30	2.43	...
353	–	–	–	0.18	0.16	0.13	0.10	0.10	0.10	...
354	–	–	–	–	–	–	–	0.02	–	...
355	0.45	0.47	0.69	0.78	0.87	0.93	0.92	0.99	0.92	...
356	0.44	0.49	0.57	0.71	0.68	0.88	1.08	1.24	1.24	...
362	0.27	0.28	0.30	0.36	0.36	0.36	0.35	0.41	0.51	...
369	1.61	1.65	2.42	2.97	3.64	3.90	3.94	3.98	4.07	...
371	0.80	0.83	0.86	0.93	1.15	1.09	1.05	0.94	0.98	...
372	0.04	0.04	0.05	0.05	0.05	0.05	0.08	0.08	0.08	...
381	0.84	0.98	1.42	1.67	1.91	2.05	2.12	2.23	2.32	...
382	0.06	0.08	0.08	0.14	0.17	0.26	0.32	0.35	0.39	...
383	0.15	0.23	0.20	0.23	0.28	0.46	0.44	0.47	0.55	...
384	–	–	–	0.04	0.02	0.02	0.02	0.01	0.01	...
385	0.01	0.03	0.03	0.03	0.04	0.03	0.04	0.04	0.04	...
390	0.01	0.01	0.02	0.02	0.05	0.05	0.07	0.09	0.08	...
Total	**110.65**	**114.00**	**124.21**	**137.74**	**139.46**	**122.31**	**110.78**	**112.56**	**113.34**	...

(a) ISIC – CITI – CIIU 1968: See Annex. – Voir annexe – Véase anexo.

[1] April of each year. [1] Avril de chaque année. [1] Abril de cada año.

6 Employment in manufacturing
Emploi dans les industries manufacturières
Empleo en las industrias manufactureras

B By major groups of industry
Par classe d'industrie
Por agrupaciones de industria

(Thousands – Milliers – Millareş)

Country – ISIC code [a] Pays – Code CITI [a] País – Clave CIIU [a]	1970	1971	1972	1973	1974	1975	1976	1977	1978	1979
Guatemala (III)										
311–12	.	5.776	8.213	6.544	9.482	9.241	8.852	10.185	11.977	...
313	.	1.054	1.228	1.196	1.884	1.409	1.515	1.795	1.938	...
314	.	0.946	0.653	0.570	0.842	0.744	0.476	0.467	0.520	...
321	.	7.937	7.837	7.222	5.791	5.010	4.655	5.964	5.524	...
322	.	1.549	1.229	2.557	2.354	2.242	2.346	1.667	1.568	...
323	.	0.562	0.562	0.520	0.533	0.599	0.613	0.622	0.649	...
324	.	1.665	1.713	1.840	0.899	1.203	1.160	1.177	1.221	...
331	.	2.864	2.517	2.636	1.496	1.261	1.139	1.245	1.234	...
332	.	0.806	1.070	0.751	0.286	0.272	0.285	0.220	0.197	...
341	.	1.058	0.867	1.068	1.176	1.047	1.092	0.858	0.804	...
342	.	1.734	2.414	2.461	1.572	1.255	1.178	0.563	0.709	...
351	.	0.165	0.302	0.379	0.513	0.262	0.313	0.487	0.435	...
352	.	2.177	1.803	2.265	2.008	1.689	1.746	1.613	1.617	...
353	.	0.111	0.118	0.054	0.077	0.056	0.056	0.057	0.060	...
354	.	0.023	0.018	0.022	0.014	0.027	0.029	0.050	0.058	...
355	.	0.805	0.758	1.032	0.517	0.315	0.353	0.589	0.690	...
356	.	0.040	0.930	0.845	0.556	0.512	0.550	1.218	1.001	...
361	.	0.025	0.033	0.060	–	–	–	0.067	0.062	...
362	.	0.533	0.582	0.989	0.922	0.836	0.791	0.978	0.992	...
369	.	2.299	2.651	3.137	2.051	1.632	1.776	2.065	2.215	...
371	.	0.779	0.829	0.688	0.825	0.295	0.338	0.421	0.430	...
372	.	0.015	0.062	0.033	–	0.011	0.010	0.062	0.062	...
381	.	2.004	2.452	2.473	1.996	1.707	1.895	2.333	2.319	...
382	.	0.185	0.297	0.379	0.219	0.173	0.205	0.326	0.263	...
383	.	1.172	0.919	0.898	0.760	0.655	0.646	0.843	1.000	...
384	.	0.337	0.458	0.494	0.339	0.326	0.305	0.564	0.634	...
385	.	0.080	0.132	0.056	0.034	0.025	0.028	0.065	0.054	...
390	.	0.977	0.287	0.387	0.204	0.026	0.022	0.309	0.319	...
Total	.	**37.678**	**40.934**	**41.556**	**37.350**	**32.830**	**32.374**	**36.810**	**38.552**	...
Jamaica (III)										
311–12	14.373	14.760	14.391	14.540	15.595	15.577	14.755	13.642	13.271	...
313	1.545	1.637	1.788	1.994	2.460	2.044	2.586	2.513	1.831	...
314	1.053	1.079	1.215	1.215	1.801	1.882	1.770	1.776	1.804	...
321	1.442	1.695	1.702	1.799	1.821	1.823	1.408	1.225	1.382	...
323	0.280	0.341	0.432	0.417	0.355	0.410	0.420	0.371	0.346	...
324	1.808	1.744	1.636	1.725	1.544	1.272	1.324	1.441	0.952	...
331	0.692	0.698	0.702	0.716	0.702	0.683	0.560	0.950	0.464	...
332	1.854	1.866	1.931	2.069	2.790	2.753	2.889	2.434	2.125	...
341	0.569	0.671	0.738	0.742	0.917	0.947	1.023	0.922	0.982	...
342	2.038	2.424	2.143	2.183	1.703	2.409	2.622	0.278	2.088	...
351	1.750	1.745	2.054	2.087	2.316	2.319	2.171	2.332	2.379	...
353	0.084	0.084	0.105	0.105	0.099	0.089	0.091	0.105	–	...
354	0.125	0.078	0.091	0.010	0.117	0.055	0.040	0.268	0.124	...
355	0.429	0.458	0.452	0.452	0.501	0.525	0.523	0.581	0.569	...
36	1.989	1.993	2.075	2.135	1.790	2.076	1.961	1.941	1.587	...
37	0.302	0.269	0.580	0.681	0.927	1.005	0.900	0.956	0.784	...
381–82	2.174	2.232	2.226	2.350	2.756	2.641	2.720	2.685	2.453	...
383	0.792	1.021	1.280	1.279	1.954	1.141	1.121	1.132	1.343	...
384	3.922	4.063	4.104	4.228	4.415	3.951	3.758	3.343	3.431	...
390	1.365	1.484	1.332	1.220	1.839	1.485	1.511	1.577	1.634	...
Total	**38.586**	**40.342**	**40.977**	**41.947**	**46.402**	**45.087**	**44.153**	**40.472**	**39.549**	...

[a] ISIC – CITI – CIIU 1968: See Annex. – Voir annexe – Véase anexo.

6 Employment in manufacturing
Emploi dans les industries manufacturières
Empleo en las industrias manufactureras

B By major groups of industry
Par classe d'industrie
Por agrupaciones de industria

(Thousands – Milliers – Millares)

Country – ISIC code (a) Pays – Code CITI (a) País – Clave CIIU (a)	1970	1971	1972	1973	1974	1975	1976	1977	1978	1979
México ¹ (III)										
311–12	.	.	...	...	59.00	58.94	62.97	62.92	64.17	67.12
313	.	.	...	...	18.22	18.74	50.57	52.09	55.34	61.29
314	.	.	...	...	5.19	4.71	4.65	4.90	4.95	5.17
321	.	.	...	...	55.84	56.36	57.55	55.45	55.11	56.91
331	.	.	...	...	4.53	4.88	5.41	5.46	5.34	5.37
341	.	.	...	...	24.88	25.07	26.71	27.18	28.13	29.24
351	.	.	...	...	22.42	24.62	25.81	25.08	26.36	28.18
352	.	.	...	...	15.55	13.82	14.00	14.77	16.02	17.05
353	.	.	...	...	0.70	0.73	0.76	0.77	0.78	0.83
354	.	.	...	...	2.42	2.47	3.22	3.81	3.99	3.88
355	.	.	...	...	7.38	8.23	9.29	8.93	9.38	9.44
362	.	.	...	...	19.15	19.90	19.39	20.01	21.15	22.43
369	.	.	...	...	15.11	15.93	16.99	16.96	17.74	19.14
371	.	.	...	...	44.55	46.98	48.35	52.82	57.80	61.75
372	.	.	...	...	13.76	13.98	14.31	13.89	14.03	17.26
381	.	.	...	...	22.27	22.86	23.95	23.00	23.84	25.43
382	.	.	...	...	2.03	2.74	2.66	2.23	2.74	2.90
383	.	.	...	...	30.82	30.59	37.15	36.17	36.93	40.00
384	.	.	...	...	41.40	41.93	44.98	38.44	43.67	50.52
Total	.	.	...	...	**405.21**	**413.51**	**468.74**	**464.88**	**487.49**	**523.93**
Nicaragua (II)										
311–12	2.752	2.935	3.079	2.719	2.880	7.867	8.564	8.451	8.322	...
313	1.414	1.503	1.356	0.979	1.337	1.627	1.690	2.653	2.537	...
314	0.252	0.278	0.296	0.256	0.254	0.244	0.230	0.259	0.276	...
321	2.488	2.446	2.332	1.492	1.659	2.736	3.289	3.091	2.722	...
322	2.610	2.713	2.467	1.734	2.103	2.232	2.465	3.057	2.974	...
323	0.060	0.053	0.052	0.064	0.064	0.129	0.149	0.196	0.204	...
331	0.375	0.432	0.588	0.574	0.599	1.130	1.149	1.254	1.166	...
332	0.616	0.634	0.283	0.167	0.175	0.263	0.299	0.404	0.402	...
341	0.245	0.250	0.401	0.663	0.789	0.921	0.766	0.495	0.478	...
342	0.710	0.780	1.056	0.945	0.816	0.801	0.823	0.893	0.891	...
351	1.935	2.263	2.379	2.186	2.474	2.725	2.944	3.168	3.106	...
354	0.139	0.162	0.076	0.040	0.039	0.042	0.044	0.048	0.048	...
355	0.319	0.323	0.372	0.361	0.421	0.439	0.532	0.702	0.548	...
36	0.691	0.736	0.808	0.827	0.828	0.396	0.371	0.393	1.293	...
37	0.099	0.144	0.390	0.481	0.686	1.155	0.987	1.110	1.026	...
381	–	–	–	–	0.330	0.411	0.440	0.566	0.555	...
382	0.365	0.350	0.804	0.971	1.070	1.269	1.244	1.341	...	...
383	0.379	0.243	0.406	0.304	0.359	1.705	0.481	0.626	...	...
384	0.026	0.038	0.147	0.182	0.185	0.181	0.158	0.139	...	...
385	–	–	0.011	0.010	0.002	0.134	0.141	0.145	...	...
390	0.413	0.413	0.308	0.236	0.281	0.354	0.406	0.516	...	...
Total	**15.888**	**16.696**	**17.611**	**15.191**	**17.351**	**26.761**	**27.172**	**29.507**	**26.548**	...

(a) ISIC – CITI – CIIU 1968: See Annex. – Voir annexe – Véase anexo.

¹ Oct. of each year.   ¹ Oct. de chaque année.   ¹ Oct. de cada año.

229

6 Employment in manufacturing / Emploi dans les industries manufacturières / Empleo en las industrias manufactureras

B By major groups of industry / Par classe d'industrie / Por agrupaciones de industria

(Thousands – Milliers – Millares)

Country – ISIC code (a) / Pays – Code CITI (a) / País – Clave CIIU (a)	1970	1971	1972	1973	1974	1975	1976	1977	1978	1979
Puerto Rico ¹ (III) ²										
311–12	13.42	14.49	16.24	15.73	16.60	16.65	16.74	16.16	17.10	16.66
314	5.02	5.36	5.31	5.27	5.00	4.65	4.24	3.00	2.66	2.07
321	8.27	6.19	7.13	7.04	6.59	4.56	3.97	4.52	4.65	3.86
322	34.85	34.31	37.13	38.44	35.53	33.83	34.74	34.98	33.96	31.99
323	3.61	3.45	2.47	2.64	2.15	2.06	1.57	1.77	1.97	1.86
324	4.22	2.71	3.25	3.64	3.65	2.76	3.10	3.57	3.83	3.63
33	3.79	3.88	3.91	3.79	3.17	2.95	2.91	2.77	3.05	3.32
341	1.02	1.13	0.93	1.03	0.83	0.89	1.09	1.17	1.03	1.19
342	1.51	1.48	1.60	1.61	1.75	1.57	1.68	1.72	1.88	1.81
353–56	5.01	5.07	5.02	4.88	4.75	3.72	4.53	4.26	4.82	5.44
351	3.17	4.77	6.42	7.65	8.17	6.96	8.36	10.40	10.67	11.47
361	1.33	1.23	1.31	1.30	1.33	1.13	0.88	0.57	0.58	0.62
362	0.63	0.68	0.74	0.83	0.91	0.89	0.95	1.03	1.21	1.22
369	3.35	3.64	3.76	3.50	3.25	2.65	2.25	2.20	2.45	2.24
381	4.68	4.87	5.38	5.22	5.18	4.30	4.44	4.28	4.73	4.59
382	1.06	1.15	1.08	0.95	2.64	2.34	3.33	3.69	4.40	5.51
383	9.25	10.88	10.56	12.62	10.25	8.55	11.62	12.21	14.37	15.25
384	0.42	0.42	0.33	0.48	0.35	0.32	0.26	0.37	0.38	0.36
385	4.73	5.64	6.89	8.17	8.27	9.49	9.23	10.04	10.84	11.73
390	3.91	3.33	3.04	2.88	2.30	2.61	2.74	2.47	3.39	3.73
Total	**113.26**	**114.71**	**122.50**	**127.67**	**122.68**	**112.89**	**118.62**	**121.19**	**128.00**	**128.57**
United States (III)										
311–12	1 530	1 534	1 518	1 487	1 482	1 436	1 468	1 483	1 490	1 486
313	236	231	228	228	225	221	221	228	232	230
314	83	77	75	78	77	76	77	71	70	66
321	975	955	986	1 010	965	868	919	910	900	892
322	1 364	1 343	1 383	1 438	1 363	1 243	1 318	1 316	1 333	1 313
323	107	101	103	101	99	91	99	98	98	95
324	222	198	193	183	172	158	164	157	158	149
331	646	669	726	759	712	615	680	722	752	758
332	440	444	483	507	489	417	444	464	491	487
341	706	682	689	705	706	642	676	692	701	714
342	1 104	1 081	1 094	1 111	1 111	1 083	1 099	1 141	1 193	1 243
351–52	1 049	1 011	.	.	.	.	.	.	.	.
351	.	.	569	591	603	582	596	610	615	623
352	.	.	440	447	457	433	447	464	481	489
353	154	153	151	149	153	153	157	160	165	169
354	38	41	44	44	44	42	42	43	44	45
355	277	273	288	304	311	272	258	291	290	285
356	313	308	343	385	384	336	381	423	462	482
361	44	42	44	46	49	43	45	46	46	46
362	156	151	156	163	156	144	152	155	156	152
369	444	452	478	499	504	442	448	468	496	513
371	627	574	568	605	610	548	549	554	560	567
372	633	597	605	655	679	591	606	627	653	677
381	1 560	1 480	1 547	1 651	1 639	1 458	1 511	1 583	1 673	1 727
382	1 986	1 815	1 889	2 089	2 208	2 057	2 065	2 175	2 319	2 463
383	1 871	1 744	1 813	1 970	1 968	1 702	1 774	1 878	2 000	2 109
384	1 853	1 761	1 790	1 929	1 868	1 715	1 799	1 872	1 992	2 048
385	527	495	516	557	592	550	575	615	654	690
390	426	412	433	454	452	407	429	438	454	452
Total	**19 367**	**18 623**	**19 151**	**20 142**	**20 077**	**18 323**	**18 997**	**19 682**	**20 476**	**20 972**

(a) ISIC – CITI – CIIU 1968: See Annex. – Voir annexe – Véase anexo.

¹ Oct. of each year. ² Wage earners only.　　　¹ Oct. de chaque année. ² Ouvriers seulement.　　　¹ Oct. de cada año. ² Obreros solamente.

6 B

Employment in manufacturing
Emploi dans les industries manufacturières
Empleo en las industrias manufactureras

By major groups of industry
Par classe d'industrie
Por agrupaciones de industria

(Thousands – Milliers – Millares)

Country – ISIC code [a] Pays – Code CITI [a] País – Clave CIIU [a]	1970	1971	1972	1973	1974	1975	1976	1977	1978	1979
ASIA – ASIE – ASIA										
Afghanistan [1] (III)										
31	.	.	.	4.321	4.845	5.103	5.147	11.541	13.220	...
321	.	.	.	11.961	13.579	15.611	16.592	16.656	18.485	...
323	.	.	.	0.229	0.205	0.326	0.287	0.303	0.365	...
324	.	.	.	0.496	0.515	0.548	0.553	0.617	0.627	
332	.	.	.	0.551	0.602	0.799	0.825	0.701	0.974	
342	.	.	.	1.287	1.326	1.447	1.465	1.747	1.713	
351	.	.	.	–	3.026	3.705	4.108	2.622	1.135	...
352	.	.	.	0.259	0.255	0.341	0.369	0.377	0.341	
354	.	.	.	0.109	0.091	0.091	0.092	0.137	0.088	...
356	.	.	.	0.360	0.427	0.829	0.583	0.623	0.690	...
369	.	.	.	1.186	1.144	1.555	1.243	1.325	1.858	...
381	.	.	.	1.390	1.442	1.522	1.492	1.539	1.609	
390	.	.	.	0.594	0.664	1.591	1.755	1.728	1.914	
Total	.	.	.	**22.743**	**28.121**	**33.468**	**34.511**	**39.916**	**43.019**	...
Brunei [2] (III)										
31	.	.	.	.	0.143	0.190	0.164	0.204	0.187	...
32	.	.	.	.	0.278	0.355	0.350	0.370	0.342	...
331	.	.	.	.	0.521	0.553	0.544	0.670	0.578	...
332	.	.	.	.	0.175	0.199	0.259	0.318	0.314	...
342	.	.	.	.	0.199	0.201	0.204	0.205	0.197	...
353	.	.	.	.	0.173	0.164	0.149	0.175	0.193	...
369	.	.	.	.	0.121	0.172	0.193	0.145	0.092	...
38	.	.	.	.	0.111	0.102	0.111	0.125	0.136	...
390	.	.	.	.	0.172	0.232	0.219	0.244	0.150	...
Total	.	.	.	.	**1.893**	**2.168**	**2.193**	**2.456**	**2.189**	...
Cyprus (IV)										
311–12	5.071	5.412	5.110	5.077	4.256	3.224	3.765	3.934	3.975	3.986*
313	1.865	1.892	1.959	1.956	1.821	1.526	1.468	1.398	1.658	1.630*
314	0.524	0.449	0.417	0.411	0.372	0.327	0.416	0.565	0.510	0.523*
321	1.376	1.467	2.084	2.090	1.542	1.538	1.882	1.704	1.953	1.812*
322	5.448	5.590	5.501	5.640	4.470	4.234	5.474	6.985	8.155	8.750*
323	0.336	0.329	0.435	0.448	0.380	0.390	0.462	0.536	0.620	0.651*
324	2.158	2.423	2.067	2.068	1.680	1.585	1.771	2.047	2.220	2.264*
33	3.268	3.338	3.281	2.602	2.479	2.884	3.106	3.253	3.616	3.711*
341	0.192	0.273	0.273	0.292	0.253	0.161	0.227	0.178	0.426	0.567*
342	1.174	1.210	1.339	1.300	1.128	1.078	1.239	1.276	1.388	1.312*
351	0.040	0.041	0.038	0.129	0.023	0.027	0.042	0.031	0.142	0.281*
352	0.587	0.627	0.683	0.629	0.585	0.514	0.611	0.738	0.804	0.794*
353	–	–	0.155	0.154	0.149	0.128	0.134	0.145	0.146	0.296*
355	0.223	0.225	0.237	0.240	0.170	0.077	0.163	0.153	0.217	0.221*
356	0.322	0.371	0.447	0.561	0.316	0.210	0.419	0.484	0.569	0.696*
361	0.082	0.084	0.041	0.040	0.028	0.014	0.039	0.041	0.037	0.035*
362	0.013	0.013	0.005	0.005	0.004	0.005	0.004	0.005	0.005	0.005*
369	2.309	2.295	2.480	2.512	1.858	1.373	1.529	1.864	2.271	2.300*
381	2.666	2.751	2.750	2.128	2.071	1.474	1.642	1.602	1.784	1.847*
382	0.843	0.830	1.038	1.036	0.798	0.566	0.717	0.963	1.034	1.051*
383	0.343	0.334	0.519	0.182	0.419	0.106	0.153	0.212	0.234	0.236*
384	0.418	0.436	0.412	0.345	0.368	0.193	0.409	0.485	0.586	0.550*
385	0.016	0.017	0.021	–	0.018	0.014	–	–	0.002	0.002*
390	0.691	0.725	0.825	0.729	0.611	0.531	0.630	▌2.084[4]	2.175	2.097*
Total	**29.965**	**31.132**	**32.117**	**30.574**	**25.799**	**22.179**	**26.302**	**30.683**	**34.527**	**35.617***

[a] ISIC – CITI – CIIU 1968: See Annex. – Voir annexe – Véase anexo.

[1] Year beginning in July of year indicated. [2] June of each year. [3] Registered employed. [4] Beginning 1978: incl. cottage industry.

[1] Année commençant en juillet de l'année indiquée. [2] Juin de chaque année. [3] Ensemble de l'effectif occupé. [4] A partir de 1978: y compris les industries fermières.

[1] Año que comienza en julio del año indicado. [2] Junio de cada año. [3] Todo el efectivo ocupado. [4] A partir de 1978: incl. industrias granjeras.

6 Employment in manufacturing
Emploi dans les industries manufacturières
Empleo en las industrias manufactureras

B By major groups of industry
Par classe d'industrie
Por agrupaciones de industria

(Thousands – Milliers – Millares)

Country – ISIC code (a) Pays – Code CITI (a) País – Clave CIIU (a)	1970	1971	1972	1973	1974	1975	1976	1977	1978	1979
Hong Kong [1] (III) [2]										
311–12	11.11	11.12	11.82	12.58	14.22	14.35	15.21	15.27	16.45	16.57
313	2.63	2.88	2.96	3.09	2.89	2.68	2.96	3.26	3.54	3.44
314	1.02	1.03	0.95	0.82	0.82	0.79	0.78	0.77	0.77	0.81
321	127.47	126.50	120.90	120.31	117.12	134.55	137.31	123.98	122.96	126.75
322	110.97	131.43	143.19	148.61	169.56	217.33	244.51	229.76	246.96	251.34
323	0.79	1.36	1.29	1.35	2.08	2.46	2.36	2.07	2.18	2.60
324	3.89	4.82	4.49	3.90	4.22	4.33	4.98	5.00	5.11	6.11
331	6.06	6.14	6.36	5.41	7.00	7.59	7.69	7.87	8.13	8.31
332	3.63	4.17	4.72	5.89	7.44	7.53	8.49	8.73	9.39	9.41
341	6.27	6.19	6.79	7.17	7.24	7.44	9.00	9.62	10.05	11.18
342	18.48	19.11	18.99	18.71	19.30	19.81	22.35	22.09	23.94	25.13
351	0.69	0.61	0.68	0.72	0.76	0.59	0.85	1.02	1.29	1.46
352	3.68	3.37	4.40	4.41	4.97	4.61	4.68	4.80	5.07	5.41
353	0.01	0.01	0.01	0.01	0.01	0.01	–	0.01	0.01	0.01
354	–	–	–	–	–	0.00	0.01	0.02	0.07	0.11
355	12.04	10.91	8.40	7.12	6.90	6.10	6.31	5.39	6.20	5.30
356	70.96	68.95	72.12	68.12	59.07	63.71	76.99	78.45	86.51	87.85
361	0.23	0.29	0.31	0.37	0.52	0.50	0.51	0.61	0.70	0.72
362	2.05	2.04	2.13	2.26	1.73	1.83	2.18	1.98	2.19	2.21
369	0.94	0.86	0.89	0.79	0.99	1.01	1.25	1.46	1.68	1.88
371	2.01	1.78	1.69	1.71	2.07	2.02	2.33	2.56	2.75	2.74
372	0.87	1.03	1.16	0.85	1.03	1.08	1.48	1.54	1.69	1.46
381	46.67	45.85	49.69	50.91	52.45	57.32	69.78	70.93	80.11	84.80
382	7.45	8.41	9.33	10.02	10.90	11.93	11.97	11.97	12.91	13.58
383	48.83	52.54	62.40	69.13	64.67	66.35	88.06	89.52	97.96	117.71
384	13.49	15.72	14.48	13.10	14.06	11.13	11.81	12.20	13.48	14.13
385	7.15	7.58	7.90	9.48	11.22	13.18	18.45	20.63	26.79	39.34
390	39.78	29.68	20.80	15.84	16.90	18.59	21.41	23.57	27.80	30.51
Total	**549.18**	**564.37**	**578.85**	**582.70**	**600.13**	**678.86**	**773.75**	**755.11**	**816.68**	**870.90**
India [3] (III)										
311–12	675	682	711	744	793	513	543	556	630	...
313	18	19	24	22	23	48	54	55	56	...
314	121	127	161	175	131	184	205	231	237	...
321	1 250	1 396	1 479	1 480	1 509	1 667	1 671	1 643	1 750	...
322	29	30	32	35	38	24	27	31	33	...
323	24	24	25	24	25	23	16	17	17	...
324	7	20	21	18	19	21	21	21	28	...
331	87	84	84	87	92	44	47	43	44	...
332	18	14	14	15	17	6	6	6	6	...
341	70	72	75	79	84	80	96	100	104	...
342	135	136	145	142	143	145	149	154	100	...
351–52	246	269	283	292	312	323	337	350	367	...
353	11	7	7	7	7	14	14	14	14	...
354	12	12	14	15	19	10	5	9	10	...
355	70	62	63	67	70	64	68	71	71	...
356	17	27	30	31	32	6	7	9	9	...
361	27	24	25	26	27	29	30	30	31	...
362	55	53	56	58	61	45	44	45	48	...
369	178	195	198	209	213	175	175	179	181	...
371	249	280	302	309	325	345	363	374	378	...
372	38	45	49	46	51	30	34	35	39	...
381	211	185	193	196	204	295	284	286	289	...
382	360	370	379	388	415	308	323	336	361	...
383	204	215	229	243	251	274	283	297	308	...
384	494	430	435	472	488	347	363	375	398	...
385	19	21	21	22	22	17	17	17	18	...
390	137	131	131	136	139	23	29	31	32	...
Total	**4 762**	**4 930**	**5 186**	**5 338**	**5 510**	**5 060**	**5 211**	**5 315**	**5 559**	**...**

(a) ISIC – CITI – CIIU 1968: See Annex. – Voir annexe – Véase anexo.

[1] Dec. of each year. [2] Registered employed. [3] Employees and working proprietors.

[1] Déc. de chaque année. [2] Ensemble de l'effectif occupé. [3] Salariés et propriétaires–exploitants.

[1] Dic. de cada año. [2] Todo el efectivo ocupado. [3] Asalariados y empresarios propietarios.

6 B

6 Employment in manufacturing
Emploi dans les industries manufacturières
Empleo en las industrias manufactureras

B By major groups of industry
Par classe d'industrie
Por agrupaciones de industria

(Thousands – Milliers – Millares)

Country – ISIC code [a] Pays – Code CITI [a] País – Clave CIIU [a]	1970	1971	1972	1973	1974	1975	1976	1977	1978	1979
Indonesia [1] (III) [2]										
311–12	...	...	...	188.7	190.8	219.3	221.4	224.2	...	...
313	...	...	...	4.9	4.7	6.4	6.0	5.9	...	...
314	...	...	...	116.0	128.0	133.5	169.5	162.6	...	...
323–24	...	...	...	6.5	6.6	8.7	9.0	9.0	...	...
321	...	...	...	178.3	165.0	232.0	215.0	198.7	...	...
322	...	...	...	2.4	2.6	4.1	4.1	4.9	...	...
33	...	...	...	20.6	22.4	38.5	41.6	45.2	...	...
341	...	...	...	7.0	7.3	8.1	9.2	8.8	...	...
342	...	...	...	14.8	14.7	17.9	18.4	17.7	...	...
351,2,6	...	...	...	36.5	38.1	53.8	58.2	58.3	...	...
355	...	...	...	44.6	45.7	46.8	48.2	49.3	...	...
36	...	...	...	23.9	24.6	33.5	34.3	35.5	...	...
371	...	...	...	1.6	2.1	2.9	4.7	5.0	...	...
381	...	...	...	18.6	21.3	22.4	31.2	29.5	...	...
382	...	...	...	6.7	7.3	8.8	7.2	10.6	...	...
383	...	...	...	8.7	12.2	10.5	17.9	20.6	...	...
384	...	...	...	13.7	14.6	22.1	25.9	25.0	...	...
390	...	...	...	8.9	8.9	5.1	4.6	5.1	...	...
Total	...	...	...	**702.4**	**716.9**	**874.4**	**926.4**	**915.9**	...	...
Jordan [3] (III) [2]										
311–12	...	...	...	1.699	2.091	1.368	2.106	1.240	...	...
313	...	...	...	–	–	0.145	0.302	0.593	...	...
314	...	...	...	–	–	0.480	0.312	0.501	...	...
321	...	...	...	2.033	2.725	2.820	2.500	2.362	...	...
322	...	...	...	–	–	2.134	1.820	1.823	...	...
323	...	...	...	–	–	0.232	0.203	0.166	...	...
324	...	...	...	–	–	0.371	0.366	0.584	...	...
331	...	...	...	0.250	0.385	0.367	0.397	0.295	...	...
341	...	...	...	0.724	0.822	0.691	0.792	0.818	...	...
342	...	...	...	–	0.418	0.404	0.432	0.465	...	...
351	...	...	...	1.498	2.093	0.960	1.402	1.252	...	...
353	...	...	...	–	–	1.569	1.713	1.959	...	...
356	...	...	...	–	0.444	0.387	0.296	0.328	...	...
362	...	...	...	1.285	1.472	2.411	1.863	2.036	...	...
371	...	...	...	–	0.230	0.310	0.281	0.334	...	...
372	...	...	...	–	1.715	2.120	2.096	2.149	...	...
383	...	...	...	–	0.422	0.388	0.427	0.430	...	...
384	...	...	...	–	0.143	0.077	0.077	0.088	...	...
390	...	...	...	–	0.157	0.172	0.190	0.210	...	...
Total	...	...	...	**7.489**	**13.117**	**17.406**	**17.575**	**17.633**	...	...

[a] ISIC – CITI – CIIU 1968: See Annex. – Voir annexe – Véase anexo.

[1] Establishments with 20 or more persons employed. [2] Registered employed. [3] Aug. of each year; establishments with 5 or more persons employed.

[1] Etablissements occupant 20 personnes et plus. [2] Ensemble de l'effectif occupé. [3] Août de chaque année; établissements occupant 5 personnes et plus.

[1] Establecimientos con 20 y más trabajadores. [2] Todo el efectivo ocupado. [3] Agosto de cada año; establecimientos con 5 y más trabajadores.

6 B

Employment in manufacturing
Emploi dans les industries manufacturières
Empleo en las industrias manufactureras

By major groups of industry
Par classe d'industrie
Por agrupaciones de industria

(Thousands – Milliers – Millares)

Country – ISIC code (a) Pays – Code CITI (a) País – Clave CIIU (a)	1970	1971	1972	1973	1974	1975	1976	1977	1978	1979
Pakistan (III)										
311–12	...	...	...	45.35	42.68	44.52	45.22	29.90	50.93	...
313	...	...	...	1.94	10.82	10.73	10.89	11.51	8.33	...
314	...	...	...	7.48	11.87	10.31	10.74	11.61	17.24	...
321	...	...	...	227.90	249.77	230.63	233.03	216.63	194.18	...
322	...	...	...	0.25	1.94	1.51	1.53	1.46	1.43	...
323	...	...	...	1.93	3.76	1.51	2.48	2.82	3.66	...
324	...	...	...	4.02	4.93	5.17	5.13	5.12	4.79	...
331	...	...	...	2.21	1.02	1.13	1.53	1.56	1.88	...
332	...	...	...	0.81	1.63	1.61	1.71	1.72	1.51	...
341	...	...	...	13.55	13.06	12.99	13.39	13.82	13.29	...
342	...	...	...	6.18	7.89	7.67	8.31	8.84	7.85	...
353–54	...	...	...	4.43	7.11	7.86	7.11	6.78	5.46	...
351	...	...	...	22.80	4.99	4.81	6.92	6.44	8.30	...
352	...	...	...	3.08	9.34	8.86	2.59	2.67	3.41	...
353	...	...	...	1.59	9.38	2.20	2.39	2.37	2.52	...
356	...	...	...	0.23	–	–	–	–	–	...
361	...	...	...	7.82	1.01	1.02	1.32	1.25	1.33	...
362	...	...	...	1.44	1.49	1.47	1.43	1.23	1.11	...
369	...	...	...	3.66	4.26	4.59	4.64	4.70	4.63	...
371	...	...	...	6.72	3.33	3.74	4.02	5.00	4.63	...
372	...	...	...	0.24	0.54	–	–	0.08	0.05	...
381	...	...	...	29.69	5.62	10.16	11.03	5.85	6.88	...
382	...	...	...	12.54	18.14	15.12	13.05	18.35	18.13	...
383	...	...	...	8.00	17.78	17.26	14.46	13.94	13.00	...
384	...	...	...	5.41	49.06	38.02	40.02	39.02	40.30	...
385	...	...	...	3.63	3.08	3.81	3.24	2.60	2.45	...
390	...	...	...	25.90	22.41	19.10	15.66	11.72	16.66	...
Total	...	...	...	**448.82**	**506.91**	**465.81**	**461.85**	**427.01**	**433.95**	...
Singapore [1] (III) [2]										
311–12	9.06	9.70	9.90	9.42	9.28	8.72	8.57	9.20	9.64	9.82
313	2.35	2.35	2.55	2.71	2.66	2.64	2.64	2.51	2.60	2.62
314	1.05	1.01	1.10	1.19	1.14	1.30	1.18	1.22	1.26	1.23
321	7.05	8.85	12.41	14.10	12.18	11.38	11.62	10.54	9.81	8.72
322	9.99	13.39	18.12	20.91	18.56	17.97	20.69	23.28	28.99	27.38
323	0.71	0.75	0.76	0.71	0.70	0.86	0.97	1.22	1.35	1.21
324	2.00	2.19	2.39	1.96	1.85	1.90	1.74	1.47	1.59	1.59
331	9.20	10.79	12.25	13.11	11.97	9.42	8.77	8.83	10.01	9.35
332	1.79	2.07	2.09	2.36	2.64	2.64	2.95	3.43	4.70	5.18
341	2.56	2.70	3.06	3.41	3.33	3.37	3.62	3.60	3.80	3.89
342	7.01	7.33	7.59	7.73	8.28	8.51	9.08	9.81	11.06	11.42
353–54	2.20	2.53	2.66	3.06	3.10	3.33	3.17	3.09	3.08	3.15
351	0.81	1.03	1.21	1.30	1.31	1.45	1.41	1.37	1.50	1.56
352	3.06	3.03	2.99	3.47	3.41	3.57	3.48	3.76	3.81	3.91
355	1.88	1.92	1.94	1.86	1.73	1.67	1.64	1.61	1.70	1.72
356	2.19	2.99	3.95	4.77	4.66	4.97	5.47	6.49	7.89	7.03
361–62	1.79	0.98	1.02	0.99	1.02	0.68	0.72	0.76	0.77	0.86
369	3.04	3.20	3.34	3.65	3.91	4.28	4.37	4.00	3.79	4.37
371	1.08	1.25	1.31	1.38	1.52	1.41	1.36	1.37	1.43	1.49
372	0.41	0.55	0.39	0.53	0.56	0.44	0.14	0.52	0.62	0.63
381	8.69	9.11	9.70	10.23	10.75	10.97	11.53	12.25	14.37	14.90
382	3.81	4.45	5.35	7.79	11.78	13.68	15.45	15.28	18.94	23.68
383	13.59	18.75	31.48	44.43	48.91	34.56	47.06	52.18	59.47	73.75
384	16.21	20.44	22.55	25.46	28.44	30.42	27.70	28.22	28.37	32.91
385	0.89	1.29	3.18	6.50	8.09	6.94	7.38	7.89	8.13	9.42
390	8.07	7.89	7.06	5.52	4.25	4.43	4.53	5.21	5.03	5.65
Total	**120.51**	**140.55**	**170.35**	**198.57**	**206.07**	**191.53**	**207.23**	**219.11**	**243.72**	**267.45**

(a) ISIC – CITI – CIIU 1968: See Annex. – Voir annexe – Véase anexo.

[1] June of each year; establishments with 10 or more persons employed.

[1] Juin de chaque année; établissements occupant 10 personnes et plus. [2] Ensemble de l'effectif occupé.

[1] Junio de cada año; establecimientos con 10 y más trabajadores. [2] Todo el efectivo ocupado.

6 B Employment in manufacturing
Emploi dans les industries manufacturières
Empleo en las industrias manufactureras

By major groups of industry
Par classe d'industrie
Por agrupaciones de industria

(Thousands – Milliers – Millares)

Country – ISIC code (a) Pays – Code CITI (a) País – Clave CIIU (a)	1970	1971	1972	1973	1974	1975	1976	1977	1978	1979
Sri Lanka (III)										
311–12	.	57.40	57.59	59.80	57.38	35.90	40.97	35.26	37.72	...
313	.	3.26	3.70	2.93	2.72	3.22	4.17	4.55	5.84	...
314	.	8.23	4.90	3.81	6.69	5.56	4.63	3.04	3.42	...
321	.	52.54	65.42	61.89	61.46	66.09	61.17	66.38	65.73	...
322	.	5.03	4.42	4.78	6.25	4.91	6.17	8.81	7.55	...
323	.	0.73	1.47	1.08	0.88	0.83	0.93	1.38	1.13	...
324	.	2.68	1.79	2.01	1.57	2.13	2.41	2.64	3.01	...
331	.	6.51	6.61	5.27	5.66	5.68	5.20	5.34	5.65	...
332	.	3.10	0.53	1.38	0.92	1.12	0.90	1.26	1.43	...
341	.	2.77	3.09	3.50	3.71	4.20	3.80	3.94	5.61	...
342	.	8.85	6.39	8.13	8.51	8.37	8.33	9.12	6.67	...
352–54	.	9.76	10.03	7.27	7.07	6.61	6.75	6.56	6.47	...
351	.	3.74	2.25	1.77	1.97	1.71	1.54	2.15	2.25	...
355	.	13.42	10.90	11.15	11.82	8.39	8.76	7.52	8.49	...
356	.	0.28	0.41	0.56	0.38	0.67	0.55	0.31	0.57	...
361	.	1.16	1.70	1.67	2.21	2.47	1.95	3.48	5.05	...
362	.	1.31	1.23	0.90	0.70	1.34	1.23	1.07	1.05	...
369	.	8.23	8.87	8.00	8.23	8.02	9.05	8.36	9.88	...
371	.	2.34	3.23	0.30	0.14	0.29	0.37	0.46	0.41	...
372	.	0.51	0.47	0.39	0.18	0.14	0.13	0.13	0.33	...
381	.	4.09	6.46	7.25	7.58	6.54	7.65	7.94	8.49	...
382	.	1.63	4.09	2.59	1.65	7.61	3.38	3.51	4.22	...
383	.	1.85	2.74	2.38	3.28	2.77	2.89	2.58	3.00	...
384	.	1.41	1.79	5.82	6.10	1.94	6.50	6.46	6.31	...
385	.	0.82	0.60	0.43	0.39	0.38	0.38	0.41	0.40	...
390	.	1.34	1.33	1.43	1.34	2.05	2.04	1.72	2.27	...
Total	.	**203.01**	**212.02**	**206.47**	**208.77**	**188.95**	**191.86**	**194.38**	**202.96**	**...**

EUROPE – EUROPE – EUROPA

	1970	1971	1972	1973	1974	1975	1976	1977	1978	1979
Austria [1] (II) [2]										
31	...	...	...	110.96	109.34	109.58	109.81	112.78	111.22	109.54
323–24	...	...	...	6.66	6.11	5.69	5.86	5.89	5.48	5.40
321	...	...	...	73.83	69.91	61.98	60.57	59.36	55.53	56.39
322	...	...	...	70.05	75.22	71.82	69.90	70.62	66.49	65.04
33	...	...	...	80.75	82.45	80.56	83.24	86.86	88.18	88.36
341	...	...	...	29.26	29.01	27.75	27.45	27.08	25.98	25.44
342	...	...	...	36.24	36.74	36.75	36.10	35.94	35.67	35.95
35	...	...	...	79.35	79.89	77.08	76.09	77.82	77.07	76.97
36	...	...	...	44.70	44.71	42.13	40.61	40.49	39.96	39.64
37	...	...	...	63.00	67.20	68.30	66.10	66.20	65.10	66.29
38	...	...	...	342.90	344.90	329.10	329.80	339.30	342.50	343.12
390	...	...	...	5.70	6.00	5.90	6.40	7.70	7.60	–
Total	**...**	**...**	**...**	**943.40**	**951.49**	**916.65**	**911.93**	**930.03**	**920.80**	**912.14**

(a) ISIC – CITI – CIIU 1968: See Annex. – Voir annexe – Véase anexo.

[1] July of each year. [2] Insured persons.　　　　　[1] Juillet de chaque année. [2] Personnes assurées.　　　　　[1] Julio de cada año. [2] Personas aseguradas.

6 Employment in manufacturing
Emploi dans les industries manufacturières
Empleo en las industrias manufactureras

B By major groups of industry
Par classe d'industrie
Por agrupaciones de industria

(Thousands – Milliers – Millares)

Country – ISIC code (a) Pays – Code CITI (a) País – Clave CIIU (a)	1970	1971	1972	1973	1974	1975	1976	1977	1978	1979
Belgique ¹ (II) ²										
311–12	.	.	.	81.6	82.0	78.7	77.1	75.3	75.5	...
313	.	.	.	23.5	21.7	20.6	17.9	19.4	18.9	...
314	.	.	.	8.7	8.8	8.1	7.6	7.3	7.6	...
321	.	.	.	107.8	104.5	94.7	90.0	81.6	73.3	...
322	.	.	.	86.6	84.0	75.9	69.9	61.7	56.1	...
323	.	.	.	6.2	5.8	5.4	5.0	4.6	4.0	...
324	.	.	.	7.2	6.8	5.6	4.5	3.8	3.3	...
33	.	.	.	53.4	54.3	49.3	48.5	46.6	43.8	...
341	.	.	.	26.7	27.1	24.8	23.1	21.2	20.4	...
342	.	.	.	40.8	41.1	38.2	34.8	34.1	34.0	...
351–52	.	.	.	74.6	77.3	76.9	75.8	75.5	75.0	...
353	.	.	.	6.1	5.7	5.4	5.2	5.5	5.9	...
354	.	.	.	1.6	1.5	1.6	1.5	1.6	1.4	...
355	.	.	.	9.1	9.2	8.6	7.8	7.6	7.6	...
356	.	.	.	15.3	16.0	14.4	15.2	14.8	14.3	...
362	.	.	.	25.5	25.8	22.1	20.9	20.2	18.8	...
369	.	.	.	42.8	43.2	41.2	39.1	38.5	36.9	...
371	.	.	.	103.4	109.7	105.1	99.7	95.6	86.8	...
381	.	.	.	109.2	106.7	100.7	94.1	91.2	87.0	...
382	.	.	.	62.7	69.1	66.8	62.1	60.4	58.0	...
383	.	.	.	100.9	102.5	96.2	92.1	87.6	85.5	...
384	.	.	.	71.6	74.0	71.3	76.7	77.2	77.0	...
385	.	.	.	4.9	5.2	5.3	5.1	5.1	5.2	...
390	.	.	.	18.3	18.2	16.2	15.4	15.6	16.5	...
Total	.	.	.	**1 088.4**	**1 100.1**	**1 033.2**	**988.9**	**952.0**	**912.6**	...
Bulgarie ³ (III)										
31	168.5	152.8	154.5	156.3	171.9	170.6	174.4	171.6	165.5*	...
323–24	24.2	26.8	27.2	27.7	27.0	26.6	27.3	27.6	27.4*	...
321	111.1	119.7	121.8	123.9	125.8	128.9	130.1	129.4	128.8*	...
322	39.1	42.0	42.3	43.9	45.1	44.9	44.3	44.9	46.4*	...
33	73.5	78.2	77.6	78.6	76.2	75.2	73.1	70.9	69.3*	...
341	10.3	11.2	11.6	12.5	13.7	14.0	13.6	13.7	13.9*	...
342	8.7	8.4	8.3	9.5	9.4	9.7	10.3	11.3	11.4*	...
353–54	57.1	58.3	55.5	59.1	52.6	51.6	50.8	50.5	50.8*	...
351–56	59.0	65.0	68.8	72.1	74.9	76.3	76.5	78.7	80.9*	...
361–62	19.6	20.2	20.3	20.8	22.4	23.3	23.7	23.8	24.7*	...
369 ⁴	48.7	50.7	54.4	53.9	56.8	58.7	57.9	57.4	59.0*	...
371	29.1	29.2	29.5	30.2	30.0	31.0	31.7	32.2	33.2*	...
372	38.6	37.9	...	...	...	...	...	...	...	...
38	245.2	270.1	283.1	296.7	310.8	321.0	328.7	338.0	350.1*	...
410	17.0	16.5	16.8	17.2	18.1	19.5	20.3	21.3	22.5*	...
390	69.4	73.4	78.3	...	...	...	...	...	...	...
Total	**1 019.1**	**1 060.5**	**1 050.1**	**1 002.2**	**1 034.8**	**1 051.3**	**1 062.7**	**1 071.3**	**1 083.9***	...

(a) ISIC – CITI – CIIU 1968: See Annex. – Voir annexe – Véase anexo.

¹ June of each year. ² Insured employees. ³ State sector.
⁴ Products for construction.

¹ Juin de chaque année. ² Salariés assurés. ³ Secteur d'état. ⁴ Matériaux de construction.

¹ Junio de cada año. ² Asalariados asegurados. ³ Sector del estado. ⁴ Productos para la construcción.

6 B

Employment in manufacturing
Emploi dans les industries manufacturières
Empleo en las industrias manufactureras

By major groups of industry
Par classe d'industrie
Por agrupaciones de industria

(Thousands – Milliers – Millares)

Country – ISIC code (a) Pays – Code CITI (a) País – Clave CIIU (a)	1970	1971	1972	1973	1974	1975	1976	1977	1978	1979
Czechoslovakia (III) [1]										
311–12	119.0	120.6	120.4	120.9	121.3	122.6	126.0	127.4	128.9	128.9
313	24.4	24.8	25.0	25.0	24.9	24.3	24.3	24.3	24.2	24.2
314	3.2	3.3	3.3	3.3	3.4	3.5	3.4	3.4	3.4	3.3
321	185.7	186.6	186.4	185.4	184.7	183.8	180.1	178.2	176.3	176.3
322	99.4	98.9	97.1	96.2	93.8	92.1	91.0	89.0	87.5	86.7
323	21.9	22.0	22.1	21.9	21.7	21.7	21.6	21.5	21.3	21.3
324	58.1	59.4	60.3	60.4	59.4	59.4	59.1	58.5	57.5	57.0
331	52.4	52.5	52.7	53.5	53.8	54.4	51.6	51.7	51.7	51.7
332	48.1	48.0	47.7	47.7	48.1	48.8	48.9	49.0	49.2	49.9
341	33.2	33.7	33.6	33.6	34.2	34.4	34.3	34.7	34.8	34.5
342	21.5	21.8	21.5	22.0	21.6	21.3	22.5	23.0	23.1	23.3
351	58.9	60.7	61.2	62.6	63.4	64.1	63.8	63.2	63.0	63.3
352	18.0	20.1	20.5	20.3	20.5	20.6	15.7	16.1	15.6	15.7
353	13.8	13.9	13.8	13.4	13.6	14.2	14.4	14.5	14.7	14.9
354	3.2	3.1	3.1	3.1	3.1	3.1	4.2	4.3	4.4	4.4
355	19.6	18.2	18.8	19.3	19.6	19.9	20.0	20.2	20.2	20.3
356	.	.	.	.	.	.	5.8	5.8	5.7	5.6
361	8.5	8.5	8.4	8.4	8.3	8.0	7.8	7.7	7.7	7.6
362	55.7	56.5	56.1	56.6	57.0	57.0	57.4	56.8	56.3	56.3
369	66.0	66.9	64.5	63.2	62.9	64.9	65.7	65.2	64.6	64.5
371	135.7	135.9	135.5	135.7	135.7	135.7	116.5	116.8	117.5	118.2
372	29.4	29.7	31.5	31.4	27.9	28.1	20.4	20.6	20.8	21.0
381	95.7	98.5	98.0	97.9	96.0	95.2	125.4	129.6	130.1	130.7
382	290.2	290.2	291.8	294.1	296.9	276.9	314.0	320.1	324.6	328.3
383	96.4	96.8	97.2	96.8	97.2	97.8	103.8	101.1	101.9	102.7
384	139.8	139.8	141.0	140.7	140.8	164.1	165.1	165.7	167.2	168.6
385	60.1	60.6	61.9	62.5	62.2	62.3	12.8	13.0	13.1	13.2
390	29.4	29.7	31.5	31.4	31.0	30.4	32.5	31.9	32.2	32.3
Total	**1 787.3**	**1 800.7**	**1 804.9**	**1 807.3**	**1 803.0**	**1 808.6**	**1 808.1**	**1 813.3**	**1 817.5**	**1 824.7**
Denmark (III) [1]										
311–12	53.60	55.04	55.27	55.96	55.18	51.20	51.19	51.59	52.22	...
313	11.89	11.96	12.34	12.94	12.41	11.85	11.75	11.55	11.62	...
314	5.84	5.36	5.07	4.24	4.39	3.53	3.68	3.53	3.29	...
321	22.46	20.98	21.59	21.16	18.57	16.44	17.09	16.09	14.78	...
322	20.09	17.93	18.17	17.46	14.87	14.08	14.59	13.89	12.97	...
323	2.24	2.13	2.07	1.85	1.69	1.75	1.64	1.61	1.51	...
324	3.94	3.62	3.81	3.58	3.10	2.69	2.98	2.99	2.70	...
331	11.40	10.76	11.13	11.51	10.50	9.04	9.37	9.36	9.47	...
332	13.28	12.27	13.34	14.18	12.71	11.35	12.68	12.75	12.56	...
341	10.61	10.11	9.99	10.57	10.35	9.22	8.97	8.81	8.77	...
342	29.31	29.49	28.84	29.22	28.17	26.03	25.65	25.56	25.94	...
351	10.52	10.15	10.02	11.06	10.76	10.57	11.01	10.99	10.87	...
352	11.99	11.80	12.14	12.13	12.18	11.52	11.22	11.46	11.58	...
353	0.62	0.61	0.60	0.58	0.59	0.58	0.56	0.56	0.58	...
354	1.57	1.55	1.55	1.33	1.55	1.40	1.29	1.30	1.31	...
355	3.98	3.56	3.67	3.55	3.45	3.12	3.11	3.00	3.06	...
356	7.38	7.59	8.20	8.89	8.43	7.21	7.98	8.11	8.34	...
361	3.15	3.26	3.46	3.56	3.65	3.24	3.23	3.48	3.78	...
362	2.90	2.85	3.12	3.37	3.38	3.46	3.66	3.57	3.32	...
369	20.10	19.75	20.32	21.11	18.75	15.99	16.71	16.98	17.02	...
371	6.60	6.56	5.87	5.91	6.25	5.85	6.01	5.80	5.38	...
372	2.48	2.28	2.23	2.48	2.51	2.23	2.33	2.45	2.46	...
381	31.84	30.57	31.88	33.22	30.99	27.02	28.02	28.82	30.45	...
382	53.26	51.71	51.99	56.85	58.35	52.40	52.19	54.55	54.19	...
383	31.53	27.80	27.52	30.23	29.38	24.80	24.91	24.81	24.95	...
384	32.85	33.00	34.05	34.70	35.72	34.39	31.74	29.97	28.69	...
385	6.83	6.59	6.57	7.18	7.99	7.53	7.32	8.14	8.37	...
390	7.06	6.38	6.65	6.98	6.73	6.20	5.98	5.91	5.70	...
Total	**419.33**	**405.69**	**411.48**	**425.82**	**412.61**	**374.73**	**376.86**	**377.65**	**375.89**	**...**

(a) ISIC – CITI – CIIU 1968: See Annex. – Voir annexe – Véase anexo.

[1] Wage earners only.　　　　　　　　　　[1] Ouvriers seulement.　　　　　　　　　　[1] Obreros solamente.

6 Employment in manufacturing
Emploi dans les industries manufacturières
Empleo en las industrias manufactureras

B By major groups of industry
Par classe d'industrie
Por agrupaciones de industria

(Thousands – Milliers – Millares)

Country – ISIC code (a) Pays – Code CITI (a) País – Clave CIIU (a)	1970	1971	1972	1973	1974	1975	1976	1977	1978	1979
España (I) [1]										
31	347.5	...	...	374.3	383.2	394.8	381.3	372.2	379.3	353.2
32	514.9	...	...	615.2	617.5	603.2	567.8	554.1	535.3	522.3
33	240.8	...	...	226.5	228.2	238.9	235.2	233.8	232.0	202.3
34	150.9	...	...	161.7	150.0	167.9	159.5	158.4	159.6	149.8
35	200.1	...	...	305.1	287.5	300.8	402.6	403.7	413.2	391.6
36	184.1	...	...	191.5	190.9	201.4	...	...	...	...
371,72,81	535.2	...	...	377.2	363.1	390.4	297.5	305.7	291.4	287.4
382–83	264.5	...	...	315.2	371.9	355.5	341.8	349.8	321.3	306.3
384	302.8	...	...	254.1	270.6	288.5	272.3	268.4	265.6	270.7
385	...	...	...	...	...	...	18.6	14.0	12.4	13.4
390	85.0	...	...	90.5	94.7	77.0	–	–	–	–
Total	**2 825.8**	...	...	**2 911.3**	**2 957.6**	**3 018.4**	**2 676.6**	**2 660.1**	**2 610.1**	**2 497.0**
Finland (III) [2]										
311–12	51.07	51.08	52.78	54.11	53.90	54.06	54.65	52.89	52.00	...
313	6.24	6.18	6.28	6.46	6.41	6.12	6.28	6.06	5.69	...
314	1.45	1.45	1.45	1.52	1.52	1.52	1.45	1.40	1.37	...
321	31.12	29.05	29.02	29.71	30.21	28.00	25.93	24.38	22.69	...
322	25.35	31.83	32.80	34.64	35.19	35.37	34.46	32.87	32.14	...
323	3.37	3.35	3.40	3.42	3.26	3.39	3.11	2.98	2.69	...
324	7.43	7.30	7.17	6.49	6.09	6.24	6.45	6.52	6.50	...
331	37.89	44.29	44.13	45.43	44.94	38.71	39.43	40.07	40.55	...
332	15.23	10.38	11.85	12.03	12.42	10.46	11.96	11.84	11.27	...
341	47.54	49.17	48.76	50.26	52.45	51.67	51.39	50.68	48.46	...
342	27.73	28.04	28.08	29.80	30.57	30.87	30.87	30.60	30.99	...
351	8.36	11.78	12.61	13.07	13.19	14.32	14.11	13.45	13.09	...
352	7.69	8.57	8.77	9.25	9.62	9.26	9.57	9.42	9.40	...
353	1.60	1.77	1.97	2.15	2.22	2.36	2.68	2.67	2.71	...
354	0.61	0.59	0.69	0.65	0.74	0.74	0.74	0.80	0.72	...
355	6.17	4.86	4.93	5.32	5.50	5.38	5.05	4.79	4.53	...
356	7.53	5.75	6.24	6.80	6.56	5.72	6.05	6.03	6.53	...
361	2.44	2.43	2.46	2.43	2.31	1.95	1.76	1.52	1.41	...
362	3.92	3.94	3.91	3.98	4.21	4.14	3.92	3.58	3.27	...
369	13.59	13.93	15.20	15.71	16.95	16.41	15.73	15.45	14.50	...
371	9.23	11.82	12.58	11.82	12.46	15.02	15.61	14.83	14.13	...
372	4.70	4.19	4.47	5.14	5.38	5.44	5.22	5.19	5.06	...
381	29.11	24.76	25.87	28.10	30.39	29.65	30.07	28.49	27.67	...
382	44.58	57.46	58.90	60.14	62.73	63.73	61.79	60.78	57.44	...
383	21.90	22.76	24.68	26.62	30.95	31.74	31.03	29.88	28.94	...
384	30.20	31.61	36.20	35.42	35.52	37.94	39.07	36.72	35.74	...
385	1.74	1.82	1.91	3.15	3.56	4.15	3.81	3.85	4.15	...
390	3.55	4.67	4.91	5.40	4.97	4.97	4.85	5.00	4.80	...
Total	**451.35**	**474.83**	**492.06**	**509.03**	**524.26**	**519.31**	**517.05**	**502.75**	**488.46**	...

(a) ISIC – CITI – CIIU 1968: See Annex. – Voir annexe – Véase anexo.

[1] Wage earners and salaried employees. [2] Establishments with 5 or more persons employed.

[1] Population salariée ayant un emploi. [2] Etablissements occupant 5 personnes et plus.

[1] Población ocupada asalariada. [2] Establecimientos con 5 y más trabajadores.

6 Employment in manufacturing
Emploi dans les industries manufacturières
Empleo en las industrias manufactureras

B By major groups of industry
Par classe d'industrie
Por agrupaciones de industria

(Thousands – Milliers – Millares)

Country – ISIC code (a) Pays – Code CITI (a) País – Clave CIIU (a)	1970	1971	1972	1973	1974	1975	1976	1977	1978	1979
France [1] (III)										
31	.	490	487	492	513	509	507	516	514	...
32	.	864	876	862	785	739	728	702	669	...
33	.	226	230	240	239	228	230	229	226	...
34	.	377	380	384	350	335	336	333	329	...
35	.	577	590	604	616	601	606	608	603	...
36	.	247	250	255	243	235	234	230	225	...
37	.	304	301	307	277	269	269	256	240	...
38	.	2 221	2 250	2 337	2 470	2 403	2 438	2 407	2 360	...
390	.	96	99	104	99	97	99	101	97	...
Total	.	**5 402**	**5 463**	**5 585**	**5 592**	**5 416**	**5 447**	**5 382**	**5 263**	**...**
Germany, Fed. Rep. of (IV) [2]										
31	.	.	749	728	706	685	703	727	732	...
32	.	.	1 084	1 035	937	861	847	823	818	...
33	.	.	496	500	482	477	462	475	477	...
34	.	.	538	541	523	485	452	445	475	...
35	.	.	968	976	987	987	972	927	916	...
36	.	.	343	338	316	272	288	293	285	...
37	.	.	606	597	599	564	485	618	518	...
38	.	.	4 132	4 198	4 233	3 948	4 037	3 902	3 996	...
390	.	.	79	82	75	68	67	64	65	...
Total	.	.	**8 995**	**8 995**	**8 858**	**8 347**	**8 313**	**8 274**	**8 282**	**...**
Hongrie (III) [3]										
311–12	151.8	152.6	155.1	158.1	161.6	163.7	163.7	166.5	168.9	...
313	22.1	22.1	22.8	23.6	24.1	24.9	25.1	25.1	26.1	...
314	6.2	6.2	6.3	6.1	6.0	6.1	6.0	6.0	6.0	...
321	144.8	141.6	139.9	139.9	138.1	132.6	130.2	128.0	126.7	...
322	78.5	80.0	80.2	82.5	84.9	81.7	81.4	79.3	79.0	...
323	15.2	14.6	14.6	14.6	14.9	14.3	13.8	15.0	14.2	...
324	44.0	43.3	41.7	42.2	43.2	40.9	40.1	38.7	38.4	...
331	20.7	19.6	19.1	18.9	22.5	22.3	21.8	20.2	19.6	...
332	33.1	32.9	32.3	32.8	32.8	32.6	32.4	32.2	32.1	...
341	16.1	16.0	16.0	16.3	16.1	15.8	16.2	16.3	16.0	...
342	20.6	21.1	21.0	20.5	20.5	19.8	20.2	20.2	20.1	...
351	37.4	38.1	39.5	42.0	42.7	42.1	42.4	42.7	42.6	...
352	26.2	26.7	27.0	27.6	27.9	27.7	27.8	27.4	27.4	...
353	6.7	6.9	7.0	7.3	7.4	7.4	7.3	7.2	7.1	...
354	–	–	–	–	–	–	–	–	–	
355	12.0	11.8	11.8	12.1	11.9	11.8	11.3	11.2	11.1	...
356	14.6	14.8	14.6	14.7	14.7	14.2	14.6	13.2	12.8	...
361	13.3	13.4	13.5	14.2	15.0	15.1	14.6	14.9	15.2	...
362	14.1	14.4	14.7	15.6	16.3	16.9	16.6	16.6	17.0	...
369	46.2	46.7	47.0	46.8	45.4	43.0	42.0	41.5	42.1	...
371	80.9	82.1	80.9	82.4	82.2	80.8	79.1	78.3	78.0	...
372	20.3	21.0	21.4	21.6	21.6	21.2	20.4	21.3	21.0	...
381	82.6	81.7	75.3	77.6	76.8	74.4	72.6	63.3	62.8	...
382	151.8	150.6	147.1	147.9	149.1	142.9	137.6	138.4	133.4	...
383	138.7	139.1	144.3	151.9	155.6	155.5	160.3	169.6	171.4	...
384	108.9	107.5	109.5	110.6	109.8	105.3	106.6	106.8	110.4	...
385	51.9	52.8	53.3	56.2	57.7	56.9	58.0	60.0	61.2	...
390	89.1	96.2	95.6	95.3	97.1	85.7	84.6	84.6	85.2	...
Total	**1 447.5**	**1 453.8**	**1 451.3**	**1 479.5**	**1 495.8**	**1 455.7**	**1 446.6**	**1 444.3**	**1 445.8**	**...**

(a) ISIC – CITI – CIIU 1968: See Annex. – Voir annexe – Véase anexo.

[1] Dec. of each year. [2] Wage earners and salaried employees. [3] State sector.

[1] Déc. de chaque année. [2] Population salariée ayant un emploi. [3] Secteur d'état.

[1] Dic. de cada año. [2] Población ocupada asalariada. [3] Sector del estado.

6 Employment in manufacturing
Emploi dans les industries manufacturières
Empleo en las industrias manufactureras

B By major groups of industry
Par classe d'industrie
Por agrupaciones de industria

(Thousands – Milliers – Millares)

Country – ISIC code (a) Pays – Code CITI (a) País – Clave CIIU (a)	1970	1971	1972	1973	1974	1975	1976	1977	1978	1979
Ireland [1] (III) [2]										
311–12	.	.	.	46.2	47.4	45.9	45.6	45.8	46.8	...
313	.	.	.	7.9	8.0	7.8	7.6	7.6	7.9	...
314	.	.	.	2.3	2.4	2.4	2.4	2.5	2.5	...
321	.	.	.	21.2	20.3	16.6	17.6	18.2	17.9	...
322	.	.	.	17.5	16.9	16.3	15.3	15.2	15.3	...
323	.	.	.	2.1	2.2	2.1	1.9	1.9	1.8	...
324	.	.	.	4.9	4.6	3.4	3.6	3.8	3.8	...
331	.	.	.	5.2	5.1	4.6	4.7	4.4	4.5	...
332	.	.	.	3.5	3.4	3.4	3.3	3.2	3.4	...
341	.	.	.	5.8	5.8	5.5	5.3	5.4	5.4	...
342	.	.	.	10.5	10.8	10.7	10.1	10.0	10.6	...
351–52	.	.	.	9.7	10.2	9.1	10.0	10.2	11.1	...
353–54	.	.	.	0.3	0.3	0.3	0.3	0.3	0.3	...
355	.	.	.	3.1	3.1	2.8	2.8	3.0	3.1	...
356	.	.	.	3.5	3.5	3.5	4.1	4.3	4.6	...
36	.	.	.	13.0	13.6	13.1	13.2	13.9	14.9	...
37	.	.	.	4.1	4.1	3.5	3.5	3.5	2.2	...
381	.	.	.	11.4	11.8	11.2	12.1	12.7	13.6	...
382	.	.	.	5.5	5.7	5.4	6.1	6.8	7.2	...
383	.	.	.	12.1	12.3	10.9	12.2	13.7	14.6	...
384	.	.	.	13.4	13.8	12.5	12.0	12.3	12.2	...
385	.	.	.	2.4	2.7	2.9	3.7	4.6	5.4	...
390	.	.	.	2.0	2.2	1.2	1.7	1.7	1.7	...
Total	.	.	.	**207.6**	**210.2**	**195.1**	**199.1**	**205.0**	**210.8**	**...**
Italie (III)										
311–12	139.8	136.8	139.3	141.7	143.5	139.5	137.0	282.4	...	...
313	24.4	23.8	23.9	23.3	22.8	21.7	20.4	19.1	...	...
314	19.0	18.5	17.6	17.0	17.3	16.5	15.6	16.3	...	...
322+324	269.9	268.4	266.1	271.6	270.9	261.2	253.9	246.5	...	...
321	371.1	351.5	331.1	328.0	318.0	299.7	286.8	276.6	...	...
323	27.5	26.8	26.8	26.1	25.6	24.8	24.5	24.5	...	...
331	63.1	63.9	61.8	62.4	61.6	57.5	55.9	55.7	...	...
332	68.3	69.2	70.3	71.6	71.8	68.0	68.5	66.7	...	...
341	64.1	62.9	62.7	63.4	64.1	60.8	60.0	56.8	...	...
342	59.1	58.9	59.2	61.2	61.6	60.5	59.4	57.9	...	...
351–53	165.3	167.8	165.0	166.7	171.5	167.9	163.5	161.2	...	...
354	13.3	13.0	13.1	13.3	13.6	14.1	14.1	14.1	...	...
355	51.5	54.4	54.4	55.3	56.2	55.1	53.0	52.9	...	...
36	210.8	203.4	194.5	196.3	200.6	196.7	189.5	185.2	...	...
37	213.3	218.9	221.8	229.9	240.4	241.1	240.7	199.5	...	...
382	537.9	533.2	530.7	546.1	562.1	547.0	532.3	442.6	...	...
383	177.8	182.3	187.3	201.0	210.6	207.4	203.8	199.0	...	...
384	234.2	242.3	250.8	271.5	276.4	267.5	263.8	265.5	...	...
390	95.1	97.2	96.9	103.0	107.0	103.9	101.5	149.6	...	...
Total	**2 805.4**	**2 793.2**	**2 773.2**	**2 849.5**	**2 895.6**	**2 810.8**	**2 744.4**	**2 772.3**	**...**	**...**

(a) ISIC – CITI – CIIU 1968: See Annex. – Voir annexe – Véase anexo.

[1] Establishments with 3 or more persons employed. [2] Registered employed.

[1] Etablissements occupant 3 personnes et plus. [2] Ensemble de l'effectif occupé.

[1] Establecimientos con 3 y más trabajadores. [2] Todo el efectivo ocupado.

6 Employment in manufacturing
Emploi dans les industries manufacturières
Empleo en las industrias manufactureras

B By major groups of industry
Par classe d'industrie
Por agrupaciones de industria

(Thousands – Milliers – Millares)

Country – ISIC code (a) Pays – Code CITI (a) País – Clave CIIU (a)	1970	1971	1972	1973	1974	1975	1976	1977	1978	1979
Luxembourg [1] (III)										
311–12	1.041	1.086	1.116	1.157	1.341	1.347	1.285	...	...	...
313–14	1.519	1.516	1.460	1.515	1.527	1.452	1.428	...	...	...
321–22	0.642	0.661	0.746	0.768	0.729	0.652	0.597	...	...	...
33	0.169	0.177	0.209	0.261	0.280	0.233	0.268	...	...	...
34	0.785	0.917	0.791	0.702	0.888	0.776	0.816	...	...	...
35	4.826	5.190	5.648	5.718	5.921	5.815	5.927	...	...	...
36	2.022	2.167	2.164	2.190	2.237	2.244	2.220	...	...	...
371	23.646	23.547	23.595	24.349	25.274	25.020	23.899	...	...	...
372	0.801	0.717	0.783	0.858	0.998	0.812	0.791	...	...	...
38	4.540	5.092	5.536	6.018	6.227	6.052	6.024	...	...	...
Total	**39.991**	**41.070**	**42.048**	**43.536**	**45.422**	**44.403**	**43.255**	...	...	...
Malta [2] (III)										
311–12	1.300	1.280	1.210	1.430	1.563	1.659	1.668	1.773	2.112	...
313	1.470	1.310	1.510	1.250	1.173	1.216	1.149	1.182	1.264	...
314	0.170	0.130	0.200	0.340	0.395	0.460	0.486	0.502	0.706	...
322+324	1.420	1.700	1.650	2.790	4.318	5.147	6.221	6.838	9.233	...
321	2.780	2.970	3.410	3.770	2.634	3.267	3.301	3.538	3.259	...
323	0.190	0.210	0.210	0.990	0.882	0.838	0.805	1.125	1.145	...
331	0.060	0.060	0.040	0.050	0.011	0.077	0.081	0.017	0.059	...
332	1.030	1.390	1.490	1.630	1.435	1.495	1.231	1.711	2.648	...
341	0.160	0.170	0.190	0.190	0.177	0.208	0.203	0.287	0.286	...
342	0.880	1.190	1.130	1.160	0.970	1.017	1.175	1.359	1.449	...
351–53	0.290	0.240	0.310	0.650	0.657	0.615	0.758	0.967	1.307	...
354	0.010	0.010	0.020	0.020	–	–	–	–	–	...
355	1.080	1.290	1.360	1.350	1.481	0.970	0.994	1.058	1.036	...
36	0.930	0.800	0.800	1.020	1.079	1.163	1.080	0.784	0.935	...
381	0.610	0.710	0.640	0.510	0.378	0.491	0.466	0.808	1.314	...
383	0.990	1.140	1.510	2.250	2.213	1.846	2.107	2.261	2.998	...
384	6.480	6.090	6.150	6.110	6.386	6.351	6.340	6.753	7.613	...
390	0.940	1.150	1.090	1.150	1.383	1.313	1.414	1.822	2.090	...
Total	**20.790**	**21.840**	**22.920**	**26.660**	**27.135**	**28.133**	**29.479**	**32.785**	**39.454**	...
Netherlands (IV) [3]										
311–12	147	146	144	142	140	136	132	129	126	...
313–14	28	28	27	26	26	25	24	24	23	...
323–24	14	13	11	10	10	9	8	8	7	...
321	79	74	67	61	58	53	48	44	40	...
322	62	57	53	47	40	33	29	26	24	...
33	58	57	56	55	54	51	49	48	47	...
341	34	32	31	31	32	31	30	29	28	...
342	80	80	78	78	77	75	74	74	74	...
353–54	11	11	11	14	14	14	14	14	14	...
351–56	121	120	117	117	124	121	116	115	113	...
36	51	50	48	48	46	43	41	40	40	...
37,38,390	460	460	447	447	453	446	431	417	405	...
Total	**1 145**	**1 128**	**1 090**	**1 076**	**1 074**	**1 037**	**996**	**968**	**941**	...

(a) ISIC – CITI – CIIU 1968: See Annex. – Voir annexe – Véase anexo.

[1] Establishments with 20 or more persons employed. [2] Nov. of each year; prior to 1972: Dec. [3] Employees (man–years).

[1] Etablissements occupant 20 personnes et plus. [2] Nov. de chaque année avant 1972: déc. [3] Salariés (années–homme).

[1] Establecimientos con 20 y más trabajadores. [2] Nov. de cada año; antes de 1972: dic. [3] Asalariados (años–hombre).

6 Employment in manufacturing / Emploi dans les industries manufacturières / Empleo en las industrias manufactureras

B By major groups of industry / Par classe d'industrie / Por agrupaciones de industria

(Thousands – Milliers – Millares)

Country – ISIC code (a) Pays – Code CITI (a) País – Clave CIIU (a)	1970	1971	1972	1973	1974	1975	1976	1977	1978	1979
Norway (I) [1]										
311–12	.	.	51	50	50	49	45	48	50	...
313	.	.	5	5	4	5	5	5	6	...
314	.	.	1	1	2	2	2	2	2	...
321	.	.	18	14	16	19	15	16	17	...
322	.	.	16	16	14	12	17	14	9	...
323	.	.	3	2	1	2	2	1	1	...
324	.	.	2	2	1	2	2	1	2	...
331	.	.	30	29	32	33	32	33	28	...
332	.	.	7	9	13	11	12	12	11	...
341	.	.	16	17	17	20	23	23	19	...
342	.	.	26	26	27	28	32	29	32	...
35	.	.	37	37	28	32	35	35	35	...
36	.	.	19	17	15	16	16	15	16	...
371	.	.	27	26	15	16	12	11	10	...
372	.	.	6	5	13	14	14	10	9	...
381	.	.	33	29	27	29	28	29	26	...
382	.	.	14	14	25	27	27	32	35	...
383	.	.	27	27	25	26	27	26	24	...
384	.	.	44	57	61	63	63	60	57	...
385	.	.	2	2	1	1	1	1	1	...
390	.	.	8	4	5	4	5	6	5	...
Total	.	.	**392**	**389**	**392**	**411**	**415**	**409**	**395**	**...**
Pologne [2] (III) [3]										
311–12	387.3	408.6	420.2	436.7	455.3	463.9	460.7	462.3	465.3	461.1
313	54.3	54.9	56.1	59.6	60.4	54.8	53.8	53.0	50.9	49.4
314	10.6	11.2	11.2	10.1	10.0	9.7	10.0	10.4	9.6	9.4
321	437.3	444.2	459.6	471.3	481.6	482.9	480.8	472.9	462.9	452.0
322	167.3	174.0	187.7	194.1	195.4	200.8	202.5	208.5	207.7	202.1
323	34.2	34.7	36.5	39.6	40.6	40.7	41.7	40.7	40.6	40.7
324	90.7	93.7	99.8	102.4	105.3	103.1	100.9	101.4	101.5	99.3
331	102.7	105.9	109.3	111.3	112.9	113.6	112.9	113.0	110.1	106.3
332	93.3	93.9	97.3	100.8	103.1	104.0	107.6	112.6	113.7	109.0
341	53.6	55.3	57.8	58.4	58.6	59.9	57.9	57.1	56.6	55.0
342	46.6	48.3	50.0	51.4	53.5	53.3	53.1	52.1	49.7	49.0
351	126.9	127.1	129.0	131.0	135.8	133.8	131.7	133.5	130.2	127.0
352	61.2	66.5	78.3	76.5	77.6	85.8	74.4	71.6	69.9	68.5
353	9.8	10.1	10.9	12.6	13.8	14.4	15.0	15.1	14.7	15.0
354	21.8	21.7	21.8	22.1	22.3	26.6	26.7	22.4	22.6	22.3
355	41.1	41.5	44.2	45.9	46.7	46.1	47.1	47.8	47.8	47.9
356	26.1	32.3	32.2	36.1	38.3	38.8	51.5	51.0	50.7	50.5
361	22.4	23.7	24.3	24.5	25.5	26.8	27.2	27.8	28.7	29.0
362	51.8	54.2	57.1	59.5	61.0	62.1	62.6	63.2	63.0	63.1
369	158.4	157.2	160.6	159.9	160.5	161.9	154.5	155.4	151.3	145.2
371	159.1	163.0	167.3	169.3	173.4	177.4	183.4	186.4	187.6	185.8
372	30.9	33.1	35.0	35.9	38.3	42.5	42.4	43.0	43.8	43.2
381	216.1	224.7	232.1	251.6	250.7	252.8	252.0	261.9	254.7	252.1
382	430.1	445.4	462.8	479.4	492.6	503.4	512.4	541.3	552.9	561.6
383	211.2	230.3	241.5	255.8	280.1	309.8	314.4	316.7	317.9	321.1
384	327.0	336.5	347.8	356.4	359.5	368.4	374.1	373.7	372.3	369.2
385	48.1	49.5	56.5	56.5	60.2	53.9	55.4	55.3	55.8	54.7
390	38.4	41.7	46.6	48.1	50.5	50.2	55.6	57.3	57.8	67.5
Total	**3 458.4**	**3 583.2**	**3 733.5**	**3 856.8**	**3 963.5**	**4 041.4**	**4 062.3**	**4 107.4**	**4 090.3**	**4 057.0**

(a) ISIC – CITI – CIIU 1968: See Annex. – Voir annexe. – Véase anexo.

[1] Civilian labour force employed. [2] Socialised sector. [3] Excl. apprentices; figures include full–time eqivalent of part–time workers.

[1] Main–d'œuvre civile occupée. [2] Secteur socialisé. [3] Non compris les apprentis; les personnes employées à temps partiel sont converties en unité de travail à temps complet.

[1] Fuerza trabajadora civil ocupada. [2] Sector socializado. [3] Excl. los aprendices; las personas empleadas a tiempo parcial son convertidas en unidad de trabajo a pleno tiempo.

6 Employment in manufacturing
Emploi dans les industries manufacturières
Empleo en las industrias manufactureras

B By major groups of industry
Par classe d'industrie
Por agrupaciones de industria

(Thousands – Milliers – Millares)

Country – ISIC code (a) Pays – Code CITI (a) País – Clave CIIU (a)	1970	1971	1972	1973	1974	1975	1976	1977	1978	1979
Portugal (III)										
311–12	...	65.39	70.53	68.56	68.83	71.57	73.68	78.66	76.81	...
313	...	6.88	7.18	7.85	8.09	8.22	8.98	9.47	9.76	...
314	...	1.34	1.21	1.38	1.44	1.61	1.58	1.74	1.63	...
322+324	...	29.25	32.95	38.31	42.94	43.82	.	.	.	.
321	...	121.16	129.11	134.68	141.15	135.47	137.64	136.93	135.46	...
322	...	.	.	.	.	.	30.52	30.28	35.14	...
323	...	4.63	5.08	4.80	4.36	4.33	4.39	4.48	4.67	...
324	...	.	.	.	.	.	14.96	14.86	15.01	...
331	...	38.92	45.20	45.20	46.06	44.64	42.54	45.10	42.84	
332	...	12.00	15.32	16.48	16.85	18.24	16.60	17.52	16.28	
341	...	12.76	13.72	13.97	15.55	15.54	16.23	17.08	16.73	
342	...	15.54	24.99	25.39	25.08	24.63	22.81	22.63	22.85	
351	...	11.76	12.14	12.97	12.31	12.33	12.19	13.04	13.86	...
352	...	14.53	16.76	17.09	16.93	17.95	19.49	20.16	21.06	
353	...	1.59	1.42	1.77	2.06	2.11	2.38	1.88	2.18	
354	...	0.04	0.03	0.03	0.01	0.01	0.00	0.00	0.00	
355	...	7.47	7.47	7.35	7.00	7.30	7.41	7.78	7.88	
356	...	9.21	9.40	11.89	13.01	12.52	13.25	14.26	14.96	...
361	...	10.52	10.55	10.80	10.18	10.23	10.50	11.25	11.25	...
362	...	10.72	9.19	10.77	10.85	10.25	10.34	10.51	10.50	...
369	...	26.49	28.90	28.81	29.96	30.61	31.21	33.15	34.07	...
371	...	4.93	10.84	12.32	13.11	13.04	12.89	13.23	15.09	...
372	...	1.23	4.70	4.28	4.17	3.76	3.78	3.76	3.70	...
381	...	20.17	23.82	26.97	27.20	29.17	34.14	34.22	35.97	...
382	...	7.69	9.43	10.49	13.88	12.69	15.59	17.10	17.84	...
383	...	18.11	22.59	25.34	26.73	23.17	25.23	25.47	28.48	...
384	...	28.42	32.80	31.72	34.71	35.68	41.37	45.47	47.18	...
385	...	0.50	0.92	1.11	1.62	1.92	2.18	2.33	2.25	...
390	...	3.40	3.14	3.25	3.25	2.88	3.01	3.00	2.87	...
Total	...	**484.67**	**549.40**	**573.60**	**597.34**	**593.70**	**614.90**	**635.36**	**646.33**	...
Roumanie ¹ (III)										
31	175.8	186.9	196.5	202.3	211.8	215.0	220.9	232.5	226.2	229.9
323–24	84.6	91.5	96.2	98.3	102.9	102.7	106.5	110.3	112.0	114.7
321	222.7	249.3	275.0	298.8	318.2	317.1	335.8	352.3	359.6	371.0
322	118.9	131.0	144.1	158.9	170.9	179.6	187.2	190.6	191.2	195.8
33	293.3	298.4	300.5	303.7	311.0	313.5	312.7	314.6	314.3	314.0
341	28.9	29.7	30.8	32.6	34.4	35.1	36.6	37.3	37.3	37.3
342	20.9	21.4	21.6	22.0	20.9	19.8	19.8	19.6	19.6	19.7
35 ²	134.8	144.3	149.9	161.4	177.8	191.8	198.9	207.0	218.5	224.7
361–62	28.6	31.9	34.3	36.8	39.5	42.7	44.2	46.2	45.8	53.5
369	109.7	113.7	115.3	117.6	120.5	121.5	121.9	131.4	133.5	133.2
371	71.8	72.5	74.0	76.3	78.7	88.3	94.4	100.2	104.5	110.5
372 ³	61.1	64.0	65.2	67.6	72.6	73.7	74.2	74.9	77.1	77.5
38	546.4	599.2	651.6	736.4	824.6	912.2	963.9	1 012.5	1 068.8	1 138.3
Total	**1 897.5**	**2 033.8**	**2 155.0**	**2 312.7**	**2 483.8**	**2 613.0**	**2 717.0**	**2 829.4**	**2 908.4**	**3 020.1**

(a) ISIC – CITI – CIIU 1968: See Annex. – Voir annexe – Véase anexo.

¹ Socialised sector. ² Excl. petroleum refineries (353).
³ Incl. ore mining.

¹ Secteur socialisé. ² Non compris les raffineries de pétrole (353). ³ Y compris l'extraction des minerais.

¹ Sector socializado. ² Excl. las refinerías de petróleo (353). ³ Incl. la extracción de minerales.

EMPLOYMENT

<table>
<tr><td>6</td><td>Employment in manufacturing
Emploi dans les industries manufacturières
Empleo en las industrias manufactureras</td><td>B</td><td>By major groups of industry
Par classe d'industrie
Por agrupaciones de industria</td></tr>
</table>

(Thousands – Milliers – Millaręs)

Country – ISIC code [a] Pays – Code CITI [a] País – Clave CIIU [a]	1970	1971	1972	1973	1974	1975	1976	1977	1978	1979
Suisse [1] (III) [2]										
311–12	45.97	45.57	45.43	44.39	43.83	40.92	40.27	41.06	41.32	41.23
313	9.32	9.47	9.40	9.03	8.62	8.04	7.55	7.32	7.22	7.26
314	7.04	6.63	6.53	6.13	5.69	5.03	4.68	4.54	4.45	4.17
323–24	3.99	3.78	3.59	3.36	3.13	2.71	2.51	2.50	2.49	2.37
321	59.99	57.43	54.21	50.80	48.08	41.22	41.18	40.07	38.26	36.68
322	62.81	60.02	57.58	53.24	48.67	41.81	41.05	40.24	38.80	36.50
33	42.53	42.37	42.40	39.92	37.14	30.94	28.48	28.30	28.48	28.35
341	20.59	20.33	19.83	19.41	19.33	17.39	16.77	16.54	16.43	16.26
342	52.35	52.03	51.27	50.18	48.84	43.85	41.96	41.88	42.56	43.19
351–52	64.70	66.69	67.78	65.37	66.41	63.53	61.51	61.08	61.50	62.26
353–54	0.51	0.53	0.54	0.50	0.50	0.53	0.51	0.49	0.47	0.45
355–56	15.25	15.71	15.82	16.54	17.14	14.53	14.67	15.06	14.67	15.05
36	27.81	27.73	27.75	27.32	25.83	20.77	18.64	18.55	18.87	19.03
37	35.10	35.36	33.90	32.45	30.52	26.61	25.56	25.36	25.44	24.98
382–83	227.95	231.80	222.95	220.83	231.06	213.23	202.73	202.23	207.33	210.96
381	85.77	85.37	83.77	81.76	80.19	69.47	66.41	67.29	67.43	66.75
384	39.49	37.14	35.84	23.84	20.60	17.67	16.78	16.71	16.47	16.25
385	72.81	69.43	64.50	64.04	64.59	52.26	47.63	48.02	46.78	41.87
390	5.89	5.78	5.31	5.15	5.06	4.37	4.30	4.59	4.70	4.54
Total	**879.89**	**873.18**	**848.42**	**814.27**	**805.24**	**714.90**	**683.20**	**681.82**	**683.69**	**678.18**
Sweden (III)										
311–12	49.41	48.43	47.38	47.63	47.79	48.86	49.89	48.89	49.49	...
313	5.62	5.49	4.72	4.48	4.16	4.20	4.32	3.99	3.68	...
314	0.94	0.99	0.98	0.99	0.99	1.02	1.11	1.12	1.09	...
321	27.07	24.47	22.90	23.08	22.23	20.39	20.32	18.64	16.71	...
322	28.14	24.42	23.05	22.49	21.48	20.38	18.43	15.72	13.52	...
323	3.35	2.95	2.75	2.48	2.46	2.36	2.23	2.12	1.94	...
324	4.31	3.52	3.38	3.40	3.46	3.25	3.06	2.99	2.63	...
331	53.58	51.65	51.27	53.23	53.02	49.26	47.74	46.36	45.74	...
332	12.71	11.64	12.19	12.76	13.58	13.71	13.60	13.68	13.20	...
341	47.34	45.64	46.23	47.03	47.90	47.65	49.31	48.21	46.71	...
342	28.18	27.22	26.43	26.11	25.77	25.98	25.56	24.98	24.70	...
351	11.15	11.03	11.23	11.68	11.97	13.18	13.47	12.97	12.59	...
352	11.31	11.16	11.32	11.52	11.68	10.31	10.56	10.05	10.00	...
353	0.56	0.58	0.63	0.62	0.69	0.85	0.92	0.94	0.94	...
354	0.96	0.99	0.84	0.79	0.77	0.84	0.96	0.91	0.94	...
355	11.22	11.34	10.68	10.81	10.91	10.16	9.17	8.50	8.15	...
356	7.86	7.78	8.31	9.39	9.43	9.43	9.86	9.26	9.06	...
361	3.63	3.31	3.48	3.63	3.88	3.91	3.51	3.27	2.99	...
362	5.33	4.82	4.62	4.70	4.73	4.74	4.72	4.47	4.22	...
369	21.52	19.46	18.01	17.40	16.88	16.29	15.75	15.03	14.31	...
371	42.52	41.39	40.34	41.07	42.91	43.60	42.97	40.14	37.07	...
372	7.57	7.79	7.92	8.48	9.49	9.31	9.52	9.30	9.12	...
381	65.08	63.88	62.80	65.03	67.00	67.42	66.26	63.15	58.18	...
382	87.41	85.23	83.12	85.34	89.35	90.21	88.82	84.81	80.34	...
383	45.50	47.33	45.65	46.46	50.99	51.93	51.86	50.37	48.44	...
384	71.94	74.46	76.24	79.55	83.63	88.56	88.97	84.03	82.71	...
385	5.28	5.02	4.44	5.01	5.30	6.45	6.35	5.87	5.53	...
390	4.50	4.39	4.35	4.85	4.91	4.91	4.91	4.45	4.46	...
Total	**664.01**	**646.39**	**635.30**	**650.03**	**667.39**	**669.17**	**664.17**	**634.24**	**608.47**	...

[a] ISIC – CITI – CIIU 1968: See Annex. – Voir annexe – Véase anexo.

[1] Sep. of each year. [2] Incl. working proprietors.

[1] Sept. de chaque année. [2] Y compris les propriétaires–exploitants.

[1] Sept. de cada año. [2] Incl. los empresarios propietarios.

6 Employment in manufacturing
Emploi dans les industries manufacturières
Empleo en las industrias manufactureras

B By major groups of industry
Par classe d'industrie
Por agrupaciones de industria

(Thousands – Milliers – Millares)

Country – ISIC code (a) Pays – Code CITI (a) País – Clave CIIU (a)	1970	1971	1972	1973	1974	1975	1976	1977	1978	1979
Turquie [1] (III)										
311–12	76.05	81.27	87.94	93.26	96.26	97.35	102.12	...	...	...
313	9.93	9.83	10.12	10.97	11.26	11.88	11.79	...	...	...
314	34.73	32.26	41.85	40.90	37.03	38.45	38.53	...	...	...
322+324	5.41	6.74						...	...	...
321	129.22	126.28	129.45	142.46	147.29	151.07	162.70	...	...	...
322	.	.	8.46	6.34	7.37	9.60	9.37	...	...	...
323	2.58	3.58	2.82	2.98	3.50	5.08	4.00	...	...	...
324	.	.	9.88	2.90	3.25	3.64	3.84	...	...	...
331	8.82	9.28	10.59	12.66	12.28	12.67	12.49	...	...	...
332	2.59	2.64	3.96	1.56	1.86	3.90	3.06	...	...	...
341	12.14	15.10	19.68	14.64	15.44	15.78	16.32	...	...	...
342	9.56	9.73	10.03	10.35	10.42	9.75	10.28	...	...	...
351–52	30.41	28.54	32.02	.	.	.	.	...	...	...
353–54	2.16	5.43	4.19	.	.	.	.	...	...	...
351	.	.	.	13.76	15.18	17.30	19.12	...	...	...
352	.	.	.	21.63	21.63	23.07	23.34	...	...	...
353	.	.	.	2.02	2.15	2.42	2.54	...	...	...
354	.	.	.	2.72	2.72	2.69	2.77	...	...	...
355	8.62	8.65	10 060	11.47	10.44	10.95	10.57	...	...	...
356	.	.	.	10.33	9.65	9.93	11.25	...	...	...
36	36.45	37.25	35.99	.	.	.	.	...	...	...
361	.	.	.	5.67	6.42	6.94	7.67	...	...	...
362	.	.	.	8.25	9.50	9.43	5.61	...	...	...
369	.	.	.	29.75	32.44	33.96	37.75	...	...	...
37	30.90	34.10	36.53	.	.	.	.	...	...	...
371	.	.	.	31.76	35.85	44.78	48.73	...	...	...
372	.	.	.	15.37	17.76	19.65	20.51	...	...	...
381	33.26	29.55	33.59	33.63	32.80	34.53	28.81	...	...	...
382	20.94	21.56	27.32	37.96	37.35	41.36	40.53	...	...	...
383	9.80	13.98	17.04	20.06	23.00	25.75	27.01	...	...	...
384	32.91	33.79	42.87	49.05	49.87	52.00	54.33	...	...	...
385	.	.	.	1.32	1.38	1.26	1.33	...	...	...
390	8.15	9.70	2.53	3.93	3.63	4.43	4.03	...	...	...
Total	**504.63**	**519.27**	**10 627**	**637.72**	**657.76**	**699.61**	**720.41**	...	...	...
United Kingdom [2] (III)										
311–12	620	▮597[3]	586	584	590	555	546	544	538*	533*
313	132	▮131[3]	128	129	135	130	129	129	130*	129*
314	41	▮42[3]	41	40	41	41	39	38	38*	36*
321	678	▮622[3]	597	594	585	529	513	512	492*	480*
322	360	▮361[3]	360	353	340	326	307	313	305*	306*
323	49	▮47[3]	46	45	43	42	40	41	40*	39*
324	95	▮93[3]	90	88	86	77	74	74	74*	74*
331	137	▮132[3]	132	138	136	124	126	123	124*	124*
332	134	▮137[3]	143	154	147	140	138	135	134*	136*
341	246	▮225[3]	224	220	229	220	205	200	198*	201*
342	380	▮371[3]	355	354	359	345	336	336	338*	342*
351	205	▮205[3]	199	194	196	197	197	202	203*	205*
352	238	▮233[3]	227	233	238	234	226	233	235*	235*
353	26	▮23[3]	22	21	20	20	19	19	19*	18*
354	22	▮22[3]	20	20	19	19	18	17	17*	17*
355	123	▮122[3]	121	123	125	119	115	107	106*	99*
356	108	▮111[3]	114	124	128	114	115	124	124*	125*
361	56	▮54[3]	54	57	60	59	58	59	61*	58*
362	78	▮76[3]	73	74	73	69	65	69	69*	69*
369	184	▮177[3]	174	175	168	147	140	135	133*	130*
371	449	▮422[3]	390	389	382	384	359	366	348*	335*
372	145	▮135[3]	126	129	125	117	111	117	116*	115*
381	577	▮556[3]	537	548	559	524	501	512	511*	503*
382	1 106	▮1 051[3]	975	967	977	960	929	925	924*	904*
383	828	▮812[3]	792	808	843	781	739	753	756*	750*
384	1 033	▮1 011[3]	972	986	979	943	929	933	935*	923*
385	163	▮166[3]	157	161	161	156	150	150	147*	148*
390	129	▮124[3]	125	121	129	118	122	126	118*	121*
Total	**8 342**	**▮8 058[3]**	**7 780**	**7 829**	**7 873**	**7 490**	**7 246**	**7 292**	**7 233***	**7 155***

(a) ISIC – CITI – CIIU 1968: See Annex. – Voir annexe – Véase anexo.

[1] Sep. of each year. [2] June of each year. [3] Prior to 1971: National insurance statistics.

[1] Sept. de chaque année. [2] Juin de chaque année. [3] Avant 1971: statistiques de l'assurance nationale.

[1] Sept. de cada año. [2] Junio de cada año. [3] Antes de 1971: estadísticas del Seguro Nacional.

6 Employment in manufacturing
Emploi dans les industries manufacturières
Empleo en las industrias manufactureras

B By major groups of industry
Par classe d'industrie
Por agrupaciones de industria

(Thousands – Milliers – Millares)

Country – ISIC code (a) Pays – Code CITI (a) País – Clave CIIU (a)	1970	1971	1972	1973	1974	1975	1976	1977	1978	1979
Yugoslavia [1] (III) [2]										
311–12	110	116	127	132	141	147	151	157	165	172
313	23	24	26	27	28	30	31	32	32	33
314	15	15	15	15	16	16	16	17	18	18
321	153	160	172	182	190	199	204	207	211	218
322	87	90	96	102	105	109	113	114	117	121
323	20	22	23	25	26	27	29	29	28	29
324	36	39	42	45	47	50	53	55	58	60
331	79	75	77	79	83	88	90	92	90	89
332	57	61	64	66	70	72	73	78	81	85
341	29	30	31	31	34	37	37	39	40	39
342	46	47	48	50	52	55	56	58	59	61
351	28	30	32	33	35	37	39	46	45	44
352	26	28	29	31	33	35	36	39	42	43
353	6	7	7	8	8	8	9	10	9	10
354	2	2	2	2	2	2	3	3	3	3
355	19	20	22	23	24	25	25	27	28	29
356	17	18	19	20	21	22	23	23	24	24
361	10	11	11	11	12	12	13	13	14	14
362	13	14	14	14	15	16	16	17	18	19
369	47	49	51	51	53	55	54	55	55	56
371	35	37	38	40	42	45	48	48	48	53
372	21	21	22	22	24	25	26	27	29	29
381	143	156	162	164	175	184	192	198	213	225
382	59	63	65	66	70	73	76	83	87	99
383	90	96	102	106	112	121	125	132	138	143
384	104	110	115	118	126	133	137	140	149	147
385	9	10	10	10	11	11	12	13	13	13
390	10	10	15	12	10	15	10	28	24	37
Total	**1 294**	**1 361**	**1 437**	**1 485**	**1 565**	**1 649**	**1 697**	**1 780**	**1 838**	**1 913**

OCEANIA – OCEANIE – OCEANIA

	1970	1971	1972	1973	1974	1975	1976	1977	1978	1979
Australia [3] (III)										
31	...	197.4	201.5	197.6	200.0	194.6	196.7	197.2	187.4	185.2
322–23	...	95.9	93.9	91.2	90.4	74.1	77.2	69.9	69.8	70.3
321	...	56.1	53.9	53.7	51.9	42.8	43.3	37.9	37.5	36.6
324	...	19.5	18.7	17.7	16.3	14.3	13.3	12.4	12.5	12.9
331	...	53.9	53.0	54.2	54.8	51.4	51.6	50.6	48.2	47.0
332	...	23.7	23.3	25.3	26.4	25.1	25.7	25.3	24.6	24.5
34	...	107.8	105.1	105.5	108.6	99.9	99.4	99.3	98.6	99.2
351,2,5,6	...	60.6	59.6	60.2	62.6	58.3	57.7	57.3	57.3	57.8
353–54	...	5.7	5.7	5.5	5.8	5.6	5.7	5.9	6.2	6.2
36	...	52.1	51.3	52.0	54.2	49.3	49.3	48.8	46.5	45.9
371	...	72.6	69.2	70.2	72.1	69.6	67.4	66.3	66.1	68.2
372	...	24.7	23.8	24.9	26.2	24.2	24.4	25.0	25.1	25.8
381–82	...	118.4	114.6	117.6	124.3	112.0	110.7	108.3	106.8	107.3
383	...	106.9	100.3	106.0	111.1	92.7	88.5	82.2	79.1	82.0
384	...	161.3	161.1	160.2	170.8	152.4	153.6	149.3	143.7	150.2
385	...	90.2	85.8	87.0	92.2	87.1	84.3	82.8	78.6	79.7
390	...	70.1	69.5	72.4	76.1	66.6	68.3	65.7	64.4	65.7
Total	**...**	**1 316.9**	**1 290.3**	**1 301.2**	**1 343.8**	**1 220.0**	**1 217.1**	**1 184.2**	**1 152.4**	**1 164.5**

(a) ISIC – CITI – CIIU 1968: See Annex. – Voir annexe – Véase anexo.

[1] March and Sep. of each year. [2] Socialised sector. [3] June of each year.   [1] Mars et sept. de chaque année. [2] Secteur socialisé. [3] Juin de chaque année.   [1] Marzo y sept. de cada año. [2] Sector socializado. [3] Junio de cada año.

6 Employment in manufacturing
Emploi dans les industries manufacturières
Empleo en las industrias manufactureras

B By major groups of industry
Par classe d'industrie
Por agrupaciones de industria

(Thousands – Milliers – Millares)

Country – ISIC code (a) Pays – Code CITI (a) País – Clave CIIU (a)	1970	1971	1972	1973	1974	1975	1976	1977	1978	1979
Fiji ¹ (III)										
311–12	3.949	4.181	4.083	4.344	4.521	4.301	4.666	5.028	5.252	...
313–14	0.422	0.397	0.445	0.483	0.488	0.404	0.439	0.541	0.524	...
322	0.397	0.443	0.457	0.420	0.460	0.509	0.706	0.609	0.484	...
324	0.030	0.036	0.036	0.032	0.022	0.024	0.045	0.039	0.030	
331	0.782	0.975	1.036	0.938	1.111	0.293	0.879	0.951	0.927	...
332	0.681	0.743	0.763	0.789	0.608	0.414	0.908	0.734	1.160	...
341	0.057	0.063	0.073	0.087	0.089	0.107	0.114	0.126	0.072	
342	0.570	0.572	0.605	0.667	0.642	0.433	0.669	0.699	0.711	
351–54	0.234	0.261	0.211	0.213	0.217	0.168	0.212	0.196	0.305	...
355	0.074	0.071	0.053	0.076	0.045	0.044	0.053	0.071	0.077	
356	0.010	0.037	0.054	0.073	0.070	0.090	0.046	0.169	0.176	
36	0.351	0.428	0.414	0.346	0.482	0.262	0.294	0.356	0.359	
381	0.536	0.745	0.749	0.690	0.709	0.994	0.573	0.997	0.959	
382	0.254	0.162	0.150	0.148	0.173	0.185	0.775	0.048	0.232	
383	0.067	0.088	0.046	0.122	0.073	0.136	0.143	0.060	0.135	
384	0.709	0.803	0.607	0.644	0.589	0.162	0.693	0.140	0.745	
390	0.012	0.035	0.046	0.044	0.054	0.029	0.032	0.037	0.080	...
Total	**9.135**	**10.040**	**9.828**	**10.116**	**10.353**	**8.555**	**11.247**	**10.801**	**12.228**	**...**
New Zealand ² (III)										
311–12	42.97	44.35	45.35	46.01	62.60	66.24	66.98	...	...	...
313	2.99	3.15	3.31	3.26	4.55	4.36	4.71	...	...	...
314	1.17	1.20	1.19	1.24	1.18	1.35	1.33	...	...	...
321	15.64	15.53	15.09	15.47	18.68	19.12	19.57	...	...	...
322	23.53	23.28	22.59	22.85	21.55	20.77	21.99	...	...	...
323	2.38	2.47	2.51	2.58	3.01	3.28	3.42	...	...	...
324	5.37	5.29	4.98	5.04	5.20	4.79	5.12	...	...	...
331	14.69	14.29	14.55	15.53	16.24	16.45	16.96	...	...	...
332	5.45	5.64	6.08	6.51	6.70	7.23	7.30	...	...	...
341	9.22	9.17	9.50	9.86	9.67	9.89	10.44	...	...	...
342	15.74	15.60	15.78	15.51	18.07	17.98	18.08	...	...	...
351	7.04	7.34	7.35	7.55	5.25	5.70	5.96	...	...	...
352	.	.	.	.	7.18	6.95	6.88	...	...	...
353					0.32	0.35	0.37	...	...	...
354	0.69	0.68	0.66	0.66	0.37	0.40	0.37	...	...	...
355	3.96	3.87	3.83	3.86	4.87	4.61	4.60	...	...	...
356	5.19	5.96	6.09	6.76	5.01	4.99	6.22	...	...	...
361	0.97	0.97	0.94	1.01	0.90	1.10	1.29	...	...	...
362	2.09	2.27	2.09	2.34	2.23	2.48	2.67	...	...	...
369	5.65	5.41	5.29	5.66	7.67	7.56	7.31	...	...	...
37	3.32	3.88	4.23	4.58				.	.	...
371	.	.	.	.	3.13	3.11	3.40	...	...	...
372	.	.	.	.	3.05	3.15	3.30	...	...	...
381	17.77	18.35	19.30	20.50	22.98	22.97	24.33	...	...	...
382	16.43	15.89	16.75	17.14	14.21	13.50	14.38	...	...	...
383	10.02	10.00	10.34	11.39	17.98	18.47	17.50	...	...	...
384	12.39	13.25	13.47	14.59	19.51	20.57	20.06	...	...	...
385	0.36	0.34	0.38	0.40	0.84	1.04	1.11	...	...	...
390	4.08	4.24	4.00	4.33	4.22	4.47	4.43	...	...	...
Total	**229.10**	**232.42**	**235.65**	**244.64**	**287.19**	**292.88**	**300.06**	**...**	**...**	**...**

(a) ISIC – CITI – CIIU 1968: See Annex. – Voir annexe – Véase anexo.

¹ June of each year. ² Year finishing in March of the following year.

¹ Juin de chaque année. ² Année finissant en mars de l'année suivante.

¹ Junio de cada año. ² Año que termina en marzo del año siguiente.

6 Employment in manufacturing
Emploi dans les industries manufacturières
Empleo en las industrias manufactureras

B By major groups of industry
Par classe d'industrie
Por agrupaciones de industria

(Thousands – Milliers – Millares)

Country – ISIC code (a) Pays – Code CITI (a) País – Clave CIIU (a)	1970	1971	1972	1973	1974	1975	1976	1977	1978	1979
Papua New Guinea [1] (III)										
311–12	0.967	1.595	1.766	1.817	1.616	1.335	1.517	2.006	...	...
313	0.631	0.847	0.765	0.783	0.487	0.496	1.070	1.271	...	...
314	0.690	0.453	0.672	0.687	0.817	0.776	0.684	0.539	...	...
321	0.011	0.021	0.042	0.089	0.056	0.056	0.070	0.061	...	...
322	0.009	0.117	0.235	0.193	0.020	0.020	0.327	0.145	...	...
323	–	–	–	–	–	–	–	–	...	...
324	0.053	0.006	0.010	0.002	0.002	–	–	–	...	...
331	3.666	3.272	3.033	2.003	3.168	3.416	3.782	3.546	...	...
332	0.084	0.128	0.201	0.064	0.074	0.121	0.153	0.120	...	...
341	0.029	0.058	0.045	0.071	0.110	0.125	0.137	0.114	...	...
342	0.308	0.461	0.387	0.399	0.636	0.580	0.589	0.596	...	...
351	0.003	0.051	0.024	0.058	0.038	0.048	0.039	0.040	...	...
352	0.239	0.094	0.093	0.097	0.127	0.174	0.262	0.195	...	...
353	–	–	–	–	–	–	–	–	...	...
354	–	–	–	0.011	0.022	–	–	–	...	...
355	0.022	0.022	0.036	0.172	0.004	0.006	0.004	0.006	...	...
356	0.018	0.005	0.010	0.022	0.016	0.024	0.029	0.024	...	...
361	0.004	–	–	0.002	–	–	–	–	...	...
362	0.240	0.199	0.161	0.169	0.160	0.163	0.149	0.178	...	...
369	0.250	0.102	0.163	0.173	0.148	0.206	0.204	0.198	...	...
371	0.222	0.051	0.042	0.086	0.071	0.128	0.277	0.466	...	...
372	–	–	–	–	–	–	–	–	...	...
381	0.407	0.764	0.614	0.586	0.752	0.818	0.672	0.687	...	...
382	0.122	0.169	0.193	0.154	0.180	0.289	0.341	0.270	...	...
383	0.107	0.113	0.127	0.142	0.163	0.143	0.092	0.161	...	...
384	0.693	0.738	0.717	0.637	0.766	0.749	0.872	0.846	...	...
385	–	–	–	–	–	–	–	–	...	...
390	0.404	0.302	0.785	0.884	1.061	0.608	0.918	0.991	...	...
Total	**9.179**	**9.568**	**10.121**	**9.301**	**10.494**	**10.281**	**12.188**	**12.460**	...	...

(a) ISIC – CITI – CIIU 1968: See Annex. – Voir annexe – Véase anexo.

[1] June of each year.   [1] Juin de chaque année.   [1] Junio de cada año.

7 Employment in mining and quarrying
Emploi dans les industries extractives
Empleo en las minas y canteras

(Thousands – Milliers – Millares)

Country – Source Pays – Source País – Fuente	1970	1971	1972	1973	1974	1975	1976	1977	1978	1979
AFRICA – AFRIQUE – AFRICA										
Algérie (III)										
Total [1]	31.0	36.2	37.6	47.1	59.3	65.4	...	...	...	...
Botswana (III)										
Total [2]	.	.	1.675	3.525	4.100	4.525	5.450	5.500	4.700	...
Males – Hom. [2]	.	.	.	.	.	.	5.149	5.280	4.470	...
Fem. – Muj. [2]	.	.	.	.	.	.	0.301	0.230	0.230	...
Burundi (IV)										
Total [3]	.	.	0.260	0.502	0.697	0.746	0.511	0.785	1.270	1.480
Egypt (I) [4]										
Total [5]	29.8	7.2	19.8	15.4	20.2	13.1	...	19.9	35.7	...
Males – Hom. [5]	28.6	7.1	19.6	15.2	19.8	12.1	...	19.7	32.6	...
Fem. – Muj. [5]	1.2	0.1	0.2	0.2	0.4	1.0	...	0.2	3.1	...
Kenya (III)										
Total [6]	.	.	3.2	3.1	3.9	3.5	3.9	3.4	2.5	2.6
Males – Hom. [6]	.	.	.	.	.	.	.	3.3	2.5	2.6
Fem. – Muj. [6]	.	.	.	.	.	.	.	0.1	–	0.1
Liberia (III)										
Total	7.535	7.566	7.628	7.128	6.265	7.928	7.573	6.611	10.491	10.376
Males – Hom.	6.300	6.316	6.378	5.960	5.238	6.328	6.332	5.527	8.771	9.116
Fem. – Muj.	1.235	1.240	1.250	1.168	1.027	1.600	1.241	1.084	1.720	1.260
Libyan Arab Jamahiriya (IV) [4]										
Total	.	14.2	14.4	15.3	16.3	17.6	18.5	19.2	20.4	...
Malawi [7] (III) [8]										
Total	0.7	0.6	0.8	0.8	0.9	0.9	1.1	∎0.6[9]	0.6*	...
Mauritius (III)										
Total [10]	0.16	0.16	0.15	0.14	0.15	0.16	0.15	0.12	0.20	0.15
Males – Hom. [10]	0.12	0.12	0.10	0.10	0.10	0.11	0.09	0.06	0.12	0.07
Fem. – Muj. [10]	0.04	0.05	0.04	0.05	0.05	0.06	0.06	0.06	0.07	0.08
Nigeria (III) [11]										
Total	52.56	56.72	56.32	59.84	57.99	45.85	48.13	...	...	...
Sénégal (IV)										
Total	.	1.861	1.744	3.513	4.039	4.536	5.062	6.010	...	...
Sierra Leone (III)										
Total [3]	.	.	.	.	9.603	4.686	5.349	5.258	5.258	5.248

Explanatory notes and source: see p. 151 – Notes explicatives et source: voir p. 154 – Notas explicativas y fuente: véase p. 157

[1] April of each year. [2] Aug. of each year. [3] Dec. of each year. [4] Civilian labour force employed. [5] May of each year. [6] June of each year. [7] Establishments with 20 or more persons employed. [8] Incl. working proprietors and unpaid family workers. [9] Beginning 1977: sample of establishments and revised allocation of establishments in the industrial classification. [10] Sep. of each year. [11] Metal mining.

[1] Avril de chaque année. [2] Août de chaque année. [3] Déc. de chaque année. [4] Main-d'œuvre civile occupée. [5] Mai de chaque année. [6] Juin de chaque année. [7] Etablissements occupant 20 personnes et plus. [8] Y compris les propriétaires–exploitants et les travailleurs familiaux non rémunérés. [9] A partir de 1977: échantillon d'établissements et changements dans leur répartition industrielle. [10] Sept. de chaque année. [11] Extraction de minerais métalliques.

[1] Abril de cada año. [2] Agosto de cada año. [3] Dic. de cada año. [4] Fuerza trabajadora civil ocupada. [5] Mayo de cada año. [6] Junio de cada año. [7] Establecimientos con 20 y más trabajadores. [8] Incl. los empresarios propietarios y los trabajadores familiares no remunerados. [9] A partir de 1977: muestra de establecimientos y cambios en la distribución industrial de los establecimientos. [10] Sept. de cada año. [11] Extracción de minerales metálicos.

7 Employment in mining and quarrying
Emploi dans les industries extractives
Empleo en las minas y canteras

(Thousands – Milliers – Millares)

Country – Source Pays – Source País – Fuente	1970	1971	1972	1973	1974	1975	1976	1977	1978	1979
Swaziland (III)										
Total [1]	2.907	2.926	2.950	2.924	3.020	3.079	3.076[2]	3.086	2.607	...
Males – Hom. [1]	2.827	2.855	2.877	2.854	2.953	3.008	3.013[2]	3.007	2.567	...
Fem. – Muj. [1]	0.080	0.071	0.073	0.070	0.067	0.071	0.063[2]	0.079	0.040	...
Tunisie (III)										
Total	18.53	19.08	19.59	18.84	18.71	18.37	18.98	...	...	...
Zambia (III)										
Total [3]	57.60	58.16	60.65	61.74	65.11	64.75	64.58	68.10*[4]	...	...
Zimbabwe (III)										
Total	57.2	58.0	58.4	58.1	62.0	63.6	63.8	61.6	58.1	59.5
AMERICA – AMERIQUE – AMERICA										
Bahamas (II) [5]										
Total [6]	.	.	.	.	.	.	0.642	0.717	0.713	0.721
Bolivia (IV) [7]										
Total	68.4	71.1	73.0	75.4	80.6	82.4	82.7	82.7	85.5	86.3
Males – Hom.	.	63.1	64.7	66.8	71.3	72.9	73.7	73.7	76.2	76.9
Fem. – Muj.	.	8.0	8.3	8.6	9.3	9.5	9.0	9.0	9.3	9.4
Brasil (III) [8]										
Total [3]	81	82	80	83	97	93	▌83[9]	...	...	...
Males – Hom. [3]	79	80	78	81	94	89	▌80[9]	...	...	...
Fem. – Muj. [3]	2	2	2	2	3	4	▌3[9]	...	...	...
Canada (III) [10]										
Total	.	119.7	115.3	116.6	121.1	119.2	123.3	128.0	125.1	...
Colombia [11] (I) [7]										
Total [12]	.	.	.	.	.	6.611	8.392	6.567	8.310	13.715
Males – Hom. [12]	.	.	.	.	.	5.519	7.903	5.810	7.153	11.468
Fem. – Muj. [12]	.	.	.	.	.	1.092	0.659	0.757	1.157	2.247
República Dominicana (III)										
Total	0.927	0.899	2.933	3.074	3.205	3.627	3.816	3.901	3.241	...
Guyane française (IV)										
Total	0.053	0.090	0.100	0.068	0.066	0.085	0.118	0.079	0.089	0.123
Haïti (IV) [7]										
Total [13]	0.967	0.972	0.978	0.984	0.990	0.997	0.944	0.949	0.954	...
Males – Hom. [13]	0.871	0.876	0.881	0.887	0.893	0.900	0.846	0.851	0.856	...
Fem. – Muj. [13]	0.096	0.096	0.097	0.097	0.097	0.097	0.098	0.098	0.098	...

Explanatory notes and source: see p. 151 – Notes explicatives et source: voir p. 154 – Notas explicativas y fuente: véase p. 157

[1] June of each year. [2] Prior to 1976: Sep. of each year. [3] Dec. of each year. [4] June. [5] Insured persons. [6] Jan. of each year. [7] Civilian labour force employed. [8] Registered establishments on 31st Dec. of each year. [9] Beginning 1978: revised questionnaire. [10] Establishments with 20 or more persons employed. [11] Seven main cities of the country. [12] Sep. of each year. [13] Year beginning in July of year indicated.

[1] Juin de chaque année. [2] Avant 1976: sept. de chaque année. [3] Déc. de chaque année. [4] Juin. [5] Personnes assurées. [6] Janv. de chaque année. [7] Main-d'œuvre civile occupée. [8] Etablissements enregistrés le 31 déc. de chaque année. [9] A partir de 1978: questionnaire révisé. [10] Etablissements occupant 20 personnes et plus. [11] Sept villes principales du pays. [12] Sept. de chaque année. [13] Année commençant en juillet de l'année indiquée.

[1] Junio de cada año. [2] Antes de 1976: sept. de cada año. [3] Dic. de cada año. [4] Junio. [5] Personas aseguradas. [6] Enero de cada año. [7] Fuerza trabajadora civil ocupada. [8] Establecimientos registrados el 31 dic. de cada año. [9] A partir de 1978: cuestionario revisado. [10] Establecimientos con 20 y más trabajadores. [11] Siete ciudades principales del país. [12] Sept. de cada año. [13] Año que comienza en julio del año indicado.

7 Employment in mining and quarrying
Emploi dans les industries extractives
Empleo en las minas y canteras

(Thousands – Milliers – Millares)

Country – Source / Pays – Source / País – Fuente	1970	1971	1972	1973	1974	1975	1976	1977	1978	1979
Jamaica (I) [1]										
Total	.	.	.	.	7.80	7.50	7.85	7.35	5.95	...
México (IV) [1]										
Total [2]	.	.	.	.	236.0	240.5	253.3	265.2	276.7	288.9
Males – Hom. [2]	.	.	.	.	.	218.8	230.5	234.9	245.1	250.8
Fem. – Muj. [2]	.	.	.	.	.	21.7	22.7	30.4	31.7	38.0
Nicaragua [3] **(II)** [4]										
Total	1.991	1.788	1.309	1.185	2.789	3.318	1.783	3.105	1.543	...
Panamá (I) [5]										
Total [6]	.	.	.	.	0.20[7]	0.31[8]	0.24	0.25[7]	0.87*	...
Paraguay (IV) [1]										
Total	.	.	1.0	1.4	1.4	1.4	1.5	1.7*	1.8*	0.0*
Perú (IV) [1]										
Total	78.5	79.8	82.2	83.4	85.1	85.1	90.0	95.5	99.8	103.9
Trinidad and Tobago [9] **(III)** [10]										
Total	14.5	15.7	17.8	17.7	18.2	18.3	16.3*	...	...	...
United States (III) [11]										
Total	623	609	628	642	697	752	779	813	851	951
Males – Hom.	586	572	588	599	648	697	719	748	775	866
Fem. – Muj.	37	37	40	43	49	55	60	65	76	91
Venezuela [12] **(III)** [11]										
Total [13]	25.346	24.837	24.289	23.873	23.883	24.159	24.699	26.089	...	...
ASIA – ASIE – ASIA										
Afghanistan (III) [11]										
Total [14]	.	.	.	2.2	2.8	3.2	3.1	3.4	...	...
Bangladesh (III) [15]										
Total [16]	.	.	.	.	.	0.121	.	–	.	0.482
Brunei (III)										
Total [2]	.	.	2.913	3.108	3.286	3.460	3.472	4.028	4.517	4.531
Cyprus (III) [17]										
Total	.	.	.	.	.	.	2.098	1.974	1.954	1.772*
Hong Kong (III) [18]										
Total [19]	1.140	1.275	1.104	1.062	0.762	0.637	0.459	0.657	0.617	0.814

Explanatory notes and source: see p. 151 – Notes explicatives et source: voir p. 154 – Notas explicativas y fuente: véase p. 157

[1] Civilian labour force employed. [2] June of each year. [3] Eight main cities of the country. [4] Insured persons. [5] Wage earners and salaried employees. [6] Aug. of each year. [7] October. [8] November. [9] Incl. refining of oil and asphalt. [10] Establishments with 10 or more persons employed. [11] Registered employees. [12] Iron ore and prospecting, extraction and refining of crude oil. [13] Second semester of each year. [14] Year beginning in July of year indicated. [15] Establishments with 20 or more persons employed. [16] Biennial survey. [17] Employees and unpaid family workers. [18] Registered employed. [19] Dec. of each year.

[1] Main-d'œuvre civile occupée. [2] Juin de chaque année. [3] Huit villes principales du pays. [4] Personnes assurées. [5] Population salariée ayant un emploi. [6] Août de chaque année. [7] Octobre. [8] Novembre. [9] Y compris le raffinage du pétrole et d'asphalte. [10] Etablissements occupant 10 personnes et plus. [11] Salariés inscrits. [12] Minerai de fer et prospection, exploitation et raffinage du pétrole brut. [13] Second semestre de chaque année. [14] Année commençant en juillet de l'année indiquée. [15] Etablissements occupant 20 personnes et plus. [16] Enquête biennale. [17] Salariés et travailleurs familiaux non rémunérés. [18] Ensemble de l'effectif occupé. [19] Déc. de chaque année.

[1] Fuerza trabajadora civil ocupada. [2] Junio de cada año. [3] Ocho ciudades principales del país. [4] Personas aseguradas. [5] Población ocupada asalariada. [6] Agosto de cada año. [7] Octubre. [8] Noviembre. [9] Incl. refinación de petróleo y asfalto. [10] Establecimientos con 10 y más trabajadores. [11] Asalariados registrados. [12] Mineral de hierro y exploración, explotación y refinación del petróleo crudo. [13] Segundo semestre de cada año. [14] Año que comienza en julio del año indicado. [15] Establecimientos con 20 y más trabajadores. [16] Encuesta bienal. [17] Asalariados y trabajadores familiares no remunerados. [18] Todo el efectivo ocupado. [19] Dic. de cada año.

7 Employment in mining and quarrying
Emploi dans les industries extractives
Empleo en las minas y canteras

(Thousands – Milliers – Millares)

Country – Source Pays – Source País – Fuente	1970	1971	1972	1973	1974	1975	1976	1977	1978	1979
India (III) [1]										
Total	638	631	658	719	772	821	853	864	886	896*[2]
Japan (I) [3]										
Total	180	180	150	▮130[4]	130	150	180	180	150	120
Jordan (III) [5]										
Total [6]	...	...	1.13	1.52	3.00	3.16	3.82	3.59	...	...
Korea, Republic of (I) [3]										
Total	107	82	51	45	47	59	62	99	103	106
Peninsular Malaysia (III) [7]										
Total	50.03	46.64	45.31	42.03	43.49	41.07	35.81	36.58	...	...
Malaysia: Sabah (III) [8]										
Total [9]	.	.	.	0.218	0.322	0.848	1.434	1.706	1.927	1.878
Pakistan (III) [7]										
Total	.	.	11.155	8.556	10.203	9.828	11.817	27.389	32.712	...
Philippines (III) [7]										
Indices [10]	.	.	100.0	103.9	106.8	103.2	108.2	116.3	118.5	...
Singapore (I) [3]										
Total [11]	.	.	.	.	1.408	3.139	1.751	1.573	1.000	1.393
Sri Lanka (III) [7]										
Total	.	2.783	1.081	4.285	2.981	4.595	4.429	4.044	4.696	...
Males – Hom.	.	2.459	0.940	3.935	2.520	3.831	3.746	3.674	4.365	...
Fem. – Muj.	.	0.324	0.141	0.350	0.461	0.764	0.683	0.370	0.331	...
Thailand (I) [12]										
Total [13]	.	19.0	118.4	110.9	49.6	28.4	28.5	50.2	30.2	...

EUROPE – EUROPE – EUROPA

	1970	1971	1972	1973	1974	1975	1976	1977	1978	1979
Austria (III) [7]										
Total	...	...	31.908	30.581	30.355	29.676	28.394	27.930	27.185	26.736
Belgique (II) [7]										
Total [11]	51.4	48.4	46.3	41.6	37.8	36.7	34.2	31.8	29.9	28.9
Bulgarie (III) [7]										
Total	121.94	120.84	116.48	113.71	111.42	109.79	106.90	103.49	104.68	...
Czechoslovakia (III) [14]										
Total [9]	175	176	177	177	177	174	173	175	175	177

Explanatory notes and source: see p. 151 – Notes explicatives et source: voir p. 154 – Notas explicativas y fuente: véase p. 157

[1] Employees and working proprietors. [2] March. [3] Wage earners and salaried employees. [4] Prior to 1973: excl. Okinawa Prefecure. [5] Establishments with 5 or more persons employed. [6] Aug. of each year. [7] Registered employees. [8] Establishments with 20 or more persons employed. [9] Dec. of each year. [10] Index base: 1972 = 100. [11] June of each year. [12] Civilian labour force employed. [13] Second semester of each year. [14] Registered employed.

[1] Salariés et propriétaires–exploitants. [2] Mars. [3] Population salariée ayant un emploi. [4] Avant 1973: non compris la préfecture d'Okinawa. [5] Etablissements occupant 5 personnes et plus. [6] Août de chaque année. [7] Salariés inscrits. [8] Etablissements occupant 20 personnes et plus. [9] Déc. de chaque année. [10] Indices base: 1972 = 100. [11] Juin de chaque année. [12] Main-d'œuvre civile occupée. [13] Second semestre de chaque année. [14] Ensemble de l'effectif occupé.

[1] Asalariados y empresarios propietarios. [2] Marzo. [3] Población ocupada asalariada. [4] Antes de 1973: excl. la Prefectura de Okinawa. [5] Establecimientos con 5 y más trabajadores. [6] Agosto de cada año. [7] Asalariados registrados. [8] Establecimientos con 20 y más trabajadores. [9] Dic. de cada año. [10] Indices base: 1972 = 100. [11] Junio de cada año. [12] Fuerza trabajadora civil ocupada. [13] Segundo semestre de cada año. [14] Todo el efectivo ocupado.

7 Employment in mining and quarrying
Emploi dans les industries extractives
Empleo en las minas y canteras

(Thousands – Milliers – Millares)

Country – Source Pays – Source País – Fuente	1970	1971	1972	1973	1974	1975	1976	1977	1978	1979
Denmark (I) [1]										
Total	.	.	2.6	2.4	2.5	2.1	1.9	2.1	2.3	1.7
Males – Hom.	.	.	2.3	2.2	2.3	1.8	1.7	2.0	2.1	1.4
Fem. – Muj.	.	.	0.3	0.2	0.2	0.3	0.2	0.1	0.2	0.3
España (I) [2]										
Total [3]	111.6	...	...	...	...	98.2	328.8	334.8	342.2	325.4
France (III) [4]										
Total	226	213	202	189	178	▌173[5]	168	161	153	145*
Germany, Fed. Rep. of (IV) [2]										
Total	.	.	426	408	380	351	350	323	331	321
Grèce (III) [4]										
Total	22.083	22.168	22.452	22.292	23.252	23.922	24.351	23.410	21.518	...
Hongrie [6] (III) [4]										
Total	151.59	148.28	141.63	139.75	139.05	129.27	127.70	125.67	123.51	122.02
Iceland (III)										
Total	11	11	11	11	11	10	11	11	11	...
Ireland (IV) [1]										
Total [7]	10	10	10	10	10	10	10	10	10	11
Italie [8] (I) [4]										
Total	282	281	302	310	305	326	318	▌193[5]	181	195
Luxembourg (III) [9]										
Total	1.592	1.547	1.476	1.212	1.221	1.218	1.060	...	...	...
Malta (IV) [4]										
Total	0.470	0.410	0.530	0.400	0.344	0.459	0.654	0.609	0.683	0.868
Netherlands (IV) [10]										
Total	21	19	16	10	4	4	4	4	4	4
Norway (I) [1]										
Total	.	.	10	12	10	12	11	10	13	13
Pologne [6] (III) [11]										
Total	450.8	456.0	464.1	460.2	460.7	460.9	462.8	465.1	473.9	490.9
Portugal (I) [12]										
Total [13]	.	.	.	.	14	15	16	15	20	20
Sweden (III) [4]										
Total	10.908	10.829	10.564	10.886	11.240	11.845	12.019	11.280	10.266	...

Explanatory notes and source: see p. 151 – Notes explicatives et source: voir p. 154 – Notas explicativas y fuente: véase p. 157

[1] Civilian labour force employed. [2] Wage earners and salaried employees. [3] Fourth quarter of each year. [4] Registered employees. [5] Change of industrial classification. [6] Socialised sector. [7] April of each year. [8] Incl. electricity, gas and water. [9] Establishments with 20 or more persons employed. [10] Civilian employment (man–years). [11] Registered employed. [12] Insured persons. [13] Second semester of each year.

[1] Main-d'œuvre civile occupée. [2] Population salariée ayant un emploi. [3] Quatrième trimestre de chaque année. [4] Salariés inscrits. [5] Changement de classification industrielle. [6] Secteur socialisé. [7] Avril de chaque année. [8] Y compris l'électricité, le gaz et l'eau. [9] Etablissements occupant 20 personnes et plus. [10] Emploi civil (années-homme). [11] Ensemble de l'effectif occupé. [12] Personnes assurées. [13] Second semestre de chaque année.

[1] Fuerza trabajadora civil ocupada. [2] Población ocupada asalariada. [3] Cuarto trimestre de cada año. [4] Asalariados registrados. [5] Cambio de clasificación industrial. [6] Sector socializado. [7] Abril de cada año. [8] Incl. electricidad, gas y agua. [9] Establecimientos con 20 y más trabajadores. [10] Empleo civil (años-hombre). [11] Todo el efectivo ocupado. [12] Personas aseguradas. [13] Segundo semestre de cada año.

7 Employment in mining and quarrying
Emploi dans les industries extractives
Empleo en las minas y canteras

(Thousands – Milliers – Millares)

Country – Source Pays – Source País – Fuente	1970	1971	1972	1973	1974	1975	1976	1977	1978	1979
Turquie (III) [1]										
Total	76.22	80.90	80.41	83.77	90.10	92.48	95.44	100.38	94.88	...
United Kingdom (IV) [1]										
Total [2]	.	346	330	315	300	303	298	299	294*	286*
Yugoslavia (III) [1]										
Total [3]	97	108	109	108	112	118	123	123	123*	...

OCEANIA – OCEANIE – OCEANIA

Country – Source Pays – Source País – Fuente	1970	1971	1972	1973	1974	1975	1976	1977	1978	1979
Australia (III) [1]										
Total [4]	70.5	75.5	75.2	75.1	76.6	80.7	78.3	78.9	74.7	76.7
Fiji (III) [5]										
Total [6]	2.135	1.853	1.745	1.748	1.963	1.897	1.550	1.841	0.809	...
New Zealand (III) [1]										
Total [7]	4.274	3.930	3.647	3.622	3.692	3.778	3.752	3.826	3.896	...

Explanatory notes and source: see p. 151 – Notes explicatives et source: voir p. 154 – Notas explicativas y fuente: véase p. 157

[1] Registered employees. [2] June of each year. [3] March and Sep. of each year. [4] Aug. of each year. [5] Registered employed. [6] Sep. of each year. [7] April and Oct. of each year.

[1] Salariés inscrits. [2] Juin de chaque année. [3] Mars et sept. de chaque année. [4] Août de chaque année. [5] Ensemble de l'effectif occupé. [6] Sept. de chaque année. [7] Avril et oct. de chaque année.

[1] Asalariados registrados. [2] Junio de cada año. [3] Marzo y sept. de cada año. [4] Agosto de cada año. [5] Todo el efectivo ocupado. [6] Sept. de cada año. [7] Abril y oct. de cada año.

8 Employment in construction
Emploi dans la construction
Empleo en la construcción

(Thousands – Milliers – Millares)

Country – Source Pays – Source País – Fuente	1970	1971	1972	1973	1974	1975	1976	1977	1978	1979
AFRICA – AFRIQUE – AFRICA										
Algérie (III)										
Total [1]	106.9	116.6	124.5	140.0	152.0	161.0	...	...	...	...
Botswana (III)										
Total [2]	.	.	6.475	7.225	8.075	9.000	6.125	6.900	9.200	...
Males – Hom. [2]							5.929	6.750	8.970	...
Fem. – Muj. [2]							0.196	0.140	0.230	...
Burundi (IV)										
Total [3]	.	.	1.945	2.211	2.087	2.286	1.920	3.875	4.207	4.052
Rép.-Unie du Cameroun (III)										
Total	11.13	11.19	10.75	16.92	18.18	22.65	21.26	23.19	25.74	31.21
Egypt (I) [4]										
Total [5]	192.2	193.2	205.8	242.3	232.8	247.3	...	334.3	384.9	...
Males – Hom. [5]	189.8	190.0	201.4	239.2	229.4	243.3	...	329.0	379.9	...
Fem. – Muj. [5]	2.4	3.2	4.4	3.1	3.4	4.0	...	5.3	5.0	...
Gambia (III)										
Total [6]	.	.	.	3.529	4.182	5.180	3.873	...	...	...
Males – Hom. [6]				.	4.035	5.040	3.855	...	...	...
Fem. – Muj. [6]				.	0.147	0.140	0.018	...	...	...
Kenya (III)										
Total [7]	.	.	37.6	41.2	44.5	40.5	47.1	48.9	55.3	61.3
Males – Hom. [7]	.	.	.	.	.	.	.	46.7	53.8	59.1
Fem. – Muj. [7]	.	.	.	.	.	.	.	2.2	1.5	2.2
Liberia (III)										
Total	4.502	4.522	4.557	4.259	3.744	4.128	4.525	1.694	4.205	2.188
Males – Hom.	4.061	4.079	4.110	3.842	3.378	3.263	4.082	1.528	3.793	1.602
Fem. – Muj.	0.441	0.443	0.447	0.417	0.366	0.865	0.443	0.166	0.412	0.586
Libyan Arab Jamahiriya (IV) [4]										
Total	.	56.7	66.6	87.4	118.1	148.5	167.8	171.4	164.3	...
Malawi [8] (III) [9]										
Total	18.6	17.8	18.2	21.1	22.9	21.1	21.1	23.3[10]	31.5*	...
Mauritius (III)										
Total [11]	2.33	2.52	3.31	4.86	5.43	6.03	7.25	7.75	9.76	8.98
Males – Hom. [11]	2.30	2.49	3.28	4.83	5.39	5.99	7.19	7.66	9.63	8.85
Fem. – Muj. [11]	0.03	0.03	0.03	0.03	0.04	0.04	0.06	0.09	0.14	0.13

Explanatory notes and source: see p. 151 – Notes explicatives et source: voir p. 154 – Notas explicativas y fuente: véase p. 157

[1] April of each year. [2] Aug. of each year. [3] Dec. of each year. [4] Civilian labour force employed. [5] May of each year. [6] Third quarter of each year. [7] June of each year. [8] Establishments with 20 or more persons employed. [9] Incl. working proprietors and unpaid family workers. [10] Beginning 1977: sample of establishments and revised allocation of establishments in the industrial classification. [11] Sep. of each year.

[1] Avril de chaque année. [2] Août de chaque année. [3] Déc. de chaque année. [4] Main–d'œuvre civile occupée. [5] Mai de chaque année. [6] Troisième trimestre de chaque année. [7] Juin de chaque année. [8] Etablissements occupant 20 personnes et plus. [9] Y compris les propriétaires-exploitants et les travailleurs familiaux non rémunérés. [10] A partir de 1977: échantillon d'établissements et changements dans leur répartition industrielle. [11] Sept. de chaque année.

[1] Abril de cada año. [2] Agosto de cada año. [3] Dic. de cada año. [4] Fuerza trabajadora civil ocupada. [5] Mayo de cada año. [6] Tercer trimestre de cada año. [7] Junio de cada año. [8] Establecimientos con 20 y más trabajadores. [9] Incl. los empresarios propietarios y los trabajadores familiares no remunerados. [10] A partir de 1977: muestra de establecimientos y cambios en la distribución industrial de los establecimientos. [11] Sept. de cada año.

8 Employment in construction
Emploi dans la construction
Empleo en la construcción

(Thousands – Milliers – Millares)

Country – Source Pays – Source País – Fuente	1970	1971	1972	1973	1974	1975	1976	1977	1978	1979
Sénégal (IV)										
Total	.	2.900	3.355	3.231	3.453	3.888	4.339	5.151	...	...
Seychelles (II)										
Total [1]	.	.	.	3.353	1.760	1.364	1.783	2.086	1.454	...
Sierra Leone (III)										
Total [2]	.	.	.	.	6.959	7.549	7.850	7.803	7.807	8.470
Swaziland (III)										
Total [3]	2.328	2.537	3.629	3.950	4.421	3.341	3.075[4]	4.081	7.909	...
Males – Hom. [3]	2.293	2.522	3.614	3.922	4.388	3.302	3.027[4]	3.978	7.762	...
Fem. – Muj. [3]	0.035	0.015	0.015	0.028	0.033	0.039	0.048[4]	0.103	0.147	...
Tunisie (IV)										
Total	.	.	.	.	.	128.4	139.6	147.0	155.0	162.0
Zambia (III)										
Total [2]	68.80	65.88	72.32	70.49	70.58	71.75	50.27	45.40*[5]	...	...
Zimbabwe (III)										
Total	42.4	46.8	49.5	56.8	64.3	60.8	51.6	46.5	40.9	40.6
AMERICA – AMERIQUE – AMERICA										
Bahamas (II) [6]										
Total [7]	.	.	.	.	.	.	3.271	3.825	3.884	4.034
Barbados (III)										
Total	.	.	.	.	2.556	2.774	2.837	2.030	...	...
Bolivia (IV) [8]										
Total	46.0	48.2	54.1	60.8	68.4	76.9	86.5	88.6	92.4	93.7
Males – Hom.	.	44.8	50.3	56.6	63.6	71.5	90.4	82.4	86.0	87.2
Fem. – Muj.	.	3.4	3.8	4.2	4.8	5.4	6.1	6.2	6.5	6.6
Brasil (III) [9]										
Total [2]	647	653	819	889	1 059	1 121	▮882[10]	...	...	...
Males – Hom. [2]	639	645	805	872	1 035	1 085	▮855[10]	...	...	...
Fem. – Muj. [2]	8	8	14	17	24	36	▮27[10]	...	...	...
Canada (III) [11]										
Total	.	220.8	209.4	210.1	223.6	223.3	220.0	214.6	208.6	...
Colombia [12] (I) [8]										
Total [13]	.	.	.	.	.	139.58	132.61	150.61	184.27	182.32
Males – Hom. [13]	.	.	.	.	.	133.52	130.98	145.67	175.80	175.62
Fem. – Muj. [13]	.	.	.	.	.	6.07	5.90	4.94	8.47	6.70

Explanatory notes and source: see p. 151 – Notes explicatives et source: voir p. 154 – Notas explicativas y fuente: véase p. 157

[1] Nov. of each year. [2] Dec. of each year. [3] June of each year. [4] Prior to 1976: Sep. of each year. [5] June. [6] Insured persons. [7] Jan. of each year. [8] Civilian labour force employed. [9] Registered establishments on 31st Dec. of each year. [10] Beginning 1978: revised questionnaire. [11] Establishments with 20 or more persons employed. [12] Seven main cities of the country. [13] Sep. of each year.

[1] Nov. de chaque année. [2] Déc. de chaque année. [3] Juin de chaque année. [4] Avant 1976: sept. de chaque année. [5] Juin. [6] Personnes assurées. [7] Janv. de chaque année. [8] Main-d'œuvre civile occupée. [9] Etablissements enregistrés le 31 déc. de chaque année. [10] A partir de 1978: questionnaire révisé. [11] Etablissements occupant 20 personnes et plus. [12] Sept villes principales du pays. [13] Sept. de chaque année.

[1] Nov. de cada año. [2] Dic. de cada año. [3] Junio de cada año. [4] Antes de 1976: sept. de cada año. [5] Junio. [6] Personas aseguradas. [7] Enero de cada año. [8] Fuerza trabajadora civil ocupada. [9] Establecimientos registrados el 31 dic. de cada año. [10] A partir de 1978: cuestionario revisado. [11] Establecimientos con 20 y más trabajadores. [12] Siete ciudades principales del país. [13] Sept. de cada año.

8 Employment in construction
Emploi dans la construction
Empleo en la construcción

(Thousands – Milliers – Millares)

Country – Source Pays – Source País – Fuente	1970	1971	1972	1973	1974	1975	1976	1977	1978	1979
Costa Rica (I) [1]										
Total [2]	.	.	.	.	.	.	...	36.72	41.24	45.64
Males – Hom. [2]	.	.	.	.	.	.	...	35.21	40.65	45.17
Fem. – Muj. [2]	.	.	.	.	.	.	...	1.50	0.59	0.47
Cuba (IV) [3]										
Total	.	132.7	153.7	176.5	183.5	208.0	243.2	295.8*	...	...
Guadeloupe (IV) [4]										
Total	.	.	.	.	11.5	11.6	10.9	10.2	10.2	...
Guyane française (IV)										
Total	2.039	1.395	1.298	0.961	0.948	0.965	1.220	1.203	1.345	1.440
Haïti (IV) [4]										
Total [5]	17.592	17.698	17.804	17.911	18.018	18.126	17.181	17.281	17.367	...
Males – Hom. [5]	17.408	17.514	17.619	17.726	17.832	17.940	16.995	17.094	17.179	...
Fem. – Muj. [5]	0.184	0.184	0.185	0.185	0.186	0.186	0.186	0.187	0.188	...
Jamaica (I) [4]										
Total	.	.	.	.	40.75	44.60	37.95	32.95	32.90	...
México (IV) [4]										.
Total [6]	.	.	.	.	746.3	756.1	801.1	835.4	871.7	909.8
Males – Hom. [6]	.	.	.	.	.	727.6	771.0	788.3	822.5	843.1
Fem. – Muj. [6]	.	.	.	.	.	28.5	30.0	47.1	49.2	66.7
Nicaragua [7] (II) [8]										
Total	5.230	3.803	3.276	8.208	10.382	13.567	11.361	12.140	7.313	...
Panamá (I) [1]										
Total [9]	.	.	.	.	24.40[10]	23.57[11]	22.41	17.86[10]	18.52*	...
Paraguay (IV) [4]										
Total	.	.	28.3	30.5	32.4	38.0	40.2	45.1*	48.6*	52.4*
Perú (IV) [4]										
Total	121.8	134.2	145.7	159.7	178.5	190.7	194.9	158.8	160.4	161.6
Trinidad and Tobago (III) [12]										
Total	5.6	5.9	6.7	7.0	7.4	9.6	10.4*	...	...	...
United States (III) [13]										
Total	3 588	3 704	3 889	4 097	4 020	3 525	3 576	3 851	4 271	4 644
Males – Hom.	3 402	3 505	3 670	3 856	3 758	3 269	3 295	3 547	3 936	4 272
Fem. – Muj.	186	199	219	241	262	256	281	304	335	372
Virgin Islands (US) [14] (III)										
Total	.	.	.	.	.	4.48	2.76	2.51	2.41	...

Explanatory notes and source: see p. 151 – Notes explicatives et source: voir p. 154 – Notas explicativas y fuente: véase p. 157

[1] Wage earners and salaried employees. [2] July of each year. [3] State sector. [4] Civilian labour force employed. [5] Year beginning in July of year indicated. [6] June of each year. [7] Eight main cities of the country. [8] Insured persons. [9] Aug. of each year. [10] October. [11] November. [12] Establishments with 10 or more persons employed. [13] Registered employees. [14] Incl. mining and quarrying.

[1] Population salariée ayant un emploi. [2] Juillet de chaque année. [3] Secteur d'Etat. [4] Main-d'œuvre civile occupée. [5] Année commençant en juillet de l'année indiquée. [6] Juin de chaque année. [7] Huit villes principales du pays. [8] Personnes assurées. [9] Août de chaque année. [10] Octobre. [11] Novembre. [12] Etablissements occupant 10 personnes et plus. [13] Salariés inscrits. [14] Y compris les industries extractives.

[1] Población ocupada asalariada. [2] Julio de cada año. [3] Sector de Estado. [4] Fuerza trabajadora civil ocupada. [5] Año que comienza en julio del año indicado. [6] Junio de cada año. [7] Ocho ciudades principales del país. [8] Personas aseguradas. [9] Agosto de cada año. [10] Octubre. [11] Noviembre. [12] Establecimientos con 10 y más trabajadores. [13] Asalariados registrados. [14] Incl. las minas y canteras.

8 Employment in construction
Emploi dans la construction
Empleo en la construcción

(Thousands – Milliers – Millares)

Country – Source Pays – Source País – Fuente	1970	1971	1972	1973	1974	1975	1976	1977	1978	1979
ASIA – ASIE – ASIA										
Bangladesh (III) [1]										
Total [2]	.	.	.	.	.	44.89	.	41.71	.	33.67
Brunei (III)										
Total	.	.	7.296	6.304	5.600	5.487	6.836	7.124	7.717	8.761
Cyprus (III) [3]										
Total	.	.	.	.	.	9.954	11.671	13.179	16.001*	
Hong Kong (III) [4]										
Total [5]	.	.	.	.	.	.	49	63	74	82
India (III) [6]										
Total	...	...	...	...	1 094	1 067	1 078	1 069	1 084	1 114*[7]
Israel (II) [8]										
Total	74.0	81.9	88.8	87.3	84.5	85.0	77.7	70.4	67.6	▮71.6[9]
Japan (I) [10]										
Total	3 050	3 240	3 430	▮3 670[11]	3 620	3 770	3 850	3 900	4 030	4 170
Jordan (III) [12]										
Total [13]	...	...	0.28	0.74	3.16	3.61	4.82	1.41	...	...
Korea, Republic of (I) [10]										
Total	246	317	363	348	421	485	501	588	769	784
Malaysia: Sabah (III) [1]										
Total [5]	.	.	.	8.934	9.778	8.446	7.875	7.352	8.383	9.966
Pakistan (III) [14]										
Total	.	.	49.261	31.845	43.075	42.819	43.701	48.355	45.048	...
Philippines (III) [14]										
Indices [15]	.	.	100.0	93.6	113.2	125.3	211.9	202.9	167.7	...
Singapore (I) [10]										
Total [16]	.	.	.	.	36.473	35.068	36.666	36.732	44.500	47.981
Sri Lanka (III) [14]										
Total	.	27.83	35.65	86.45	72.84	94.40	126.85	112.96	89.37	▮0[17]
Males – Hom.	.	27.72	35.32	83.43	70.49	89.81	120.11	106.69	83.99	▮0[17]
Fem. – Muj.	.	0.10	0.33	3.02	2.35	4.59	6.74	6.27	5.38	▮0[17]
Thailand (I) [18]										
Total [19]	.	188.9	256.7	258.0	276.8	205.7	235.9	331.7	313.4	...

Explanatory notes and source: see p. 151 – Notes explicatives et source: voir p. 154 – Notas explicativas y fuente: véase p. 157

[1] Establishments with 20 or more persons employed. [2] Biennial survey. [3] Employees and unpaid family workers. [4] Registered employed. [5] Dec. of each year. [6] Employees and working proprietors. [7] March. [8] Insured persons. [9] Beginning 1979: sample revised. [10] Wage earners and salaried employees. [11] Prior to 1973: excl. Okinawa Prefecure. [12] Establishments with 5 or more persons employed. [13] Aug. of each year. [14] Registered employees. [15] Index base: 1972 = 100. [16] June of each year. [17] Drop due to an abnormal response rate. [18] Civilian labour force employed. [19] Second semester of each year.

[1] Etablissements occupant 20 personnes et plus. [2] Enquête biennale. [3] Salariés et travailleurs familiaux non rémunérés. [4] Ensemble de l'effectif occupé. [5] Déc. de chaque année. [6] Salariés et propriétaires–exploitants. [7] Mars. [8] Personnes assurées. [9] A partir de 1979: échantillon révisé. [10] Population salariée ayant un emploi. [11] Avant 1973: non compris la préfecture d'Okinawa. [12] Etablissements occupant 5 personnes et plus. [13] Août de chaque année. [14] Salariés inscrits. [15] Indices base: 1972 = 100. [16] Juin de chaque année. [17] Baisse due à un taux anormal de réponse. [18] Main-d'œuvre civile occupée. [19] Second semestre de chaque année.

[1] Establecimientos con 20 y más trabajadores. [2] Encuesta bienal. [3] Asalariados y trabajadores familiares no remunerados. [4] Todo el efectivo ocupado. [5] Dic. de cada año. [6] Asalariados y empresarios propietarios. [7] Marzo. [8] Personas aseguradas. [9] A partir de 1979: muestra revisada. [10] Población ocupada asalariada. [11] Antes de 1973: excl. la Prefectura de Okinawa. [12] Establecimientos con 5 y más trabajadores. [13] Agosto de cada año. [14] Asalariados registrados. [15] Indices base: 1972 = 100. [16] Junio de cada año. [17] Baja debida a una tasa anormal de respuestas. [18] Fuerza trabajadora civil ocupada. [19] Segundo semestre de cada año.

8 Employment in construction
Emploi dans la construction
Empleo en la construcción

(Thousands – Milliers – Millares)

Country – Source Pays – Source País – Fuente	1970	1971	1972	1973	1974	1975	1976	1977	1978	1979
EUROPE – EUROPE – EUROPA										
Austria (III) [1]										
Total	...	...	269.80	284.38	278.04	268.75	266.15	273.97	274.08	271.15
Belgique (II) [1]										
Total [2]	249.3	251.9	240.8	238.3	245.9	246.6	250.3	251.5	247.7	249.1
Bulgarie (III) [1]										
Total	303.76	311.05	315.27	315.07	315.53	316.82	312.61	330.13	338.83	293.57*
Czechoslovakia (III) [3]										
Total [4]	605	624	639	659	675	689	714	723	732	741
Denmark (I) [5]										
Total	.	.	202.6	201.3	188.0	189.6	195.4	196.5	201.7	201.7
Males – Hom.	.	.	187.8	185.3	172.8	174.6	180.5	180.0	183.8	180.9
Fem. – Muj.	.	.	14.8	16.0	15.2	15.0	14.9	16.5	17.9	20.8
España (I) [6]										
Total [7]	930.8	...	...	...	...	1 111.4	1 044.9	1 057.2	977.6	878.6
Finland (I) [6]										
Total	174	170	167	167	174	178	153	147	143	142
France (III) [1]										
Total	1 710	1 690	1 683	1 695	1 681	∎1 608[8]	1 592	1 580	1 536	1 505*
German Democratic Rep. (III) [1]										
Total	505.8	513.5	524.1	528.9	536.9	549.7	560.9	570.3	574.6	576.9
Germany, Fed. Rep. of (IV) [6]										
Total	.	.	2 014	2 042	1 917	1 709	1 643	1 607	1 623	1 682*
Hongrie [9] (III) [1]										
Total	345.60	363.68	368.75	374.22	379.14	385.58	384.53	382.70	383.65	377.33
Iceland (IV)										
Total	76	85	81	83	85	81	76	77	82	...
Ireland (IV) [5]										
Total [10]	76	85	81	83	85	81	76	77	82	83
Italie (I) [1]										
Total	1 704	1 712	1 650	1 581	1 583	1 565	1 475	∎1 609[8]	1 624	1 607
Luxembourg (III) [11]										
Total	9.805	12.487	12.700	13.297	15.481	110.83	9.721	...	...	...

Explanatory notes and source: see p. 151 – Notes explicatives et source: voir p. 154 – Notas explicativas y fuente: véase p. 157

[1] Registered employees. [2] June of each year. [3] Registered employed. [4] Dec. of each year. [5] Civilian labour force employed. [6] Wage earners and salaried employees. [7] Fourth quarter of each year. [8] Change of industrial classification. [9] Socialised sector. [10] April of each year. [11] Establishments with 20 or more persons employed.

[1] Salariés inscrits. [2] Juin de chaque année. [3] Ensemble de l'effectif occupé. [4] Déc. de chaque année. [5] Main-d'œuvre civile occupée. [6] Population salariée ayant un emploi. [7] Quatrième trimestre de chaque année. [8] Changement de classification industrielle. [9] Secteur socialisé. [10] Avril de chaque année. [11] Etablissements occupant 20 personnes et plus.

[1] Asalariados registrados. [2] Junio de cada año. [3] Todo el efectivo ocupado. [4] Dic. de cada año. [5] Fuerza trabajadora civil ocupada. [6] Población ocupada asalariada. [7] Cuarto trimestre de cada año. [8] Cambio de clasificación industrial. [9] Sector socializado. [10] Abril de cada año. [11] Establecimientos con 20 y más trabajadores.

EMPLOYMENT

8 Employment in construction
Emploi dans la construction
Empleo en la construcción

(Thousands – Milliers – Millares)

Country – Source Pays – Source País – Fuente	1970	1971	1972	1973	1974	1975	1976	1977	1978	1979
Malta (IV) [1]										
Total	12.010	10.020	6.410	3.900	4.302	4.320	4.051	2.745	4.559	4.867
Netherlands (IV) [2]										
Total	505	495	473	472	452	436	438	442	450	459
Norway (I) [3]										
Total	.	.	145	142	147	147	148	156	163	151
Pologne [4] (III) [5]										
Total	1 004.8	1 055.2	1 123.1	1 236.5	1 320.2	1 320.0	1 297.5	1 289.6	1 298.4	1 273.6
Portugal (I) [6]										
Total [7]	.	.	.	.	288	277	261	287	297	299
Roumanie [4] (III) [1]										
Total	682.5	714.2	746.2	739.5	715.1	736.4	749.2	777.3	827.6	839.6
Suisse (IV) [3]										
Total	249.6	260.9	269.5	264.1	246.9	200.0	184.0	183.5	181.1	182.9
Turquie (II) [6]										
Total	282.8	275.9	305.3	329.1	367.4	397.8	447.8	487.1	499.5	453.6
United Kingdom (IV) [1]										
Total [8]	.	1 261.8	1 299.7	1 379.5	1 328.3	1 313.7	1 309.1	1 270.0	1 264.9*	1 292.8*
Yugoslavia (III) [1]										
Total [9]	423	433	436	424	448	485	497	531	567*	...

OCEANIA – OCEANIE – OCEANIA

Australia (III) [1]										
Total [10]	381.1	393.7	397.3	395.2	400.1	411.6	376.4	367.5	357.2	346.1
Fiji (III) [5]										
Total [11]	7.404	8.225	8.239	9.454	8.291	8.449	7.672	8.129	7.974	...
Guam (III) [1]										
Total	4.400	5.500	7.100	7.700	8.300	5.388	3.300	4.014	4.900	...
New Zealand (III) [1]										
Total [12]	61.215	61.602	62.438	64.510	66.792	67.499	65.337	63.308	60.803	...
Papua New Guinea (IV) [1]										
Total [8]	.	.	.	7.741	7.335	6.841	6.593	7.194	...	...

Explanatory notes and source: see p. 151 – Notes explicatives et source: voir p. 154 – Notas explicativas y fuente: véase p. 157

[1] Registered employees. [2] Civilian employment (man-years). [3] Civilian labour force employed. [4] Socialised sector. [5] Registered employed. [6] Insured persons. [7] Second semester of each year. [8] June of each year. [9] March and Sep. of each year. [10] Aug. of each year. [11] Sep. of each year. [12] April and Oct. of each year.

[1] Salariés inscrits. [2] Emploi civil (années–homme). [3] Main-d'œuvre civile occupée. [4] Secteur socialisé. [5] Ensemble de l'effectif occupé. [6] Personnes assurées. [7] Second semestre de chaque année. [8] Juin de chaque année. [9] Mars et sept. de chaque année. [10] Août de chaque année. [11] Sept. de chaque année. [12] Avril et oct. de chaque année.

[1] Asalariados registrados. [2] Empleo civil (años-hombre). [3] Fuerza trabajadora civil ocupada. [4] Sector socializado. [5] Todo el efectivo ocupado. [6] Personas aseguradas. [7] Segundo semestre de cada año. [8] Junio de cada año. [9] Marzo y sept. de cada año. [10] Agosto de cada año. [11] Sept. de cada año. [12] Abril y oct. de cada año.

8 Employment in construction
Emploi dans la construction
Empleo en la construcción

Country – Source Pays – Source País – Fuente	1970	1971	1972	1973	1974	1975	1976	1977	1978	1979
USSR – URSS – URSS										
URSS [1] (III) [2]										
Total	9 052	9 549	9 986	10 091	10 339	10 574	10 716	10 880	11 034	11 156

Explanatory notes and source: see p. 151 – Notes explicatives et source: voir p. 154 – Notas explicativas y fuente: véase p. 157

[1] Socialised sector. [2] Registered employees.   [1] Secteur socialisé. [2] Salariés inscrits.   [1] Sector socializado. [2] Asalariados registrados.

9 Employment in transport, storage and communication
Emploi dans les transports, entrepôts et communications
Empleo en los transportes, almacenaje y comunicaciones

(Thousands – Milliers – Millares)

Country – Source Pays – Source País – Fuente	1970	1971	1972	1973	1974	1975	1976	1977	1978	1979
AFRICA – AFRIQUE – AFRICA										
Algérie (III)										
Total [1]	32.7	36.0	37.3	40.0	43.2	45.2	...	...	...	...
Botswana (III)										
Total [2]	.	.	1.125	1.350	1.650	1.975	2.025	1.850	2.000	...
Males – Hom. [2]	.	.					1.959	1.780	1.910	...
Fem. – Muj. [2]	.	.					0.066	0.060	0.090	...
Burundi (IV)										
Total [3]	.	.	0.924	0.880	0.906	0.821	0.731	0.669	0.973	1.058
Rép.-Unie du Cameroun (III)										
Total	13.12	8.75	8.47	13.22	16.34	18.68	18.84	19.35	20.81	8.83
Egypt (I) [4]										
Total [5]	366.9	323.1	339.1	353.1	396.4	419.5	...	428.0	467.3	...
Males – Hom. [5]	357.7	314.2	331.5	341.2	384.9	405.6	...	412.5	448.6	...
Fem. – Muj. [5]	9.2	8.9	7.6	11.9	11.5	13.9	...	15.5	18.7	...
Gambia (III)										
Total [6]	.	.	.	2.398	2.800	2.909	3.381	...	...	...
Males – Hom. [6]	.	.	.		2.732	2.844	3.272	...	...	...
Fem. – Muj. [6]	.	.	.		0.068	0.065	0.109	...	...	...
Kenya (III)										
Total [7]	.	.	45.3	44.4	46.3	45.5	47.7	48.1	50.9	54.8
Males – Hom. [7]	.	.						45.0	47.4	51.0
Fem. – Muj. [7]	.	.						3.1	3.6	3.7
Liberia (III)										
Total	2.710	2.723	2.743	2.564	2.254	6.380	2.724	1.013	4.038	5.529
Males – Hom.	2.559	2.563	2.581	2.413	2.122	6.066	2.564	0.954	3.800	4.561
Fem. – Muj.	0.159	0.160	0.162	0.151	0.132	0.314	0.160	0.059	0.238	0.968
Libyan Arab Jamahiriya (IV) [4]										
Total	.	38.4	41.7	45.0	48.8	53.5	57.9	63.1	67.5	...
Malawi [8] (III) [9]										
Total	8.5	9.0	9.8	10.5	11.4	12.0	12.9	❚16.6[10]	17.6*	...
Mauritius (III)										
Total [11]	5.24	6.57	6.89	7.91	9.07	9.41	9.93	11.15	10.49	8.28
Males – Hom. [11]	5.15	6.45	6.75	7.70	8.86	9.15	9.63	10.82	10.10	7.86
Fem. – Muj. [11]	0.09	0.11	0.14	0.21	0.21	0.26	0.30	0.33	0.38	0.41

Explanatory notes and source: see p. 151 – Notes explicatives et source: voir p. 154 – Notas explicativas y fuente: véase p. 157

[1] April of each year. [2] Aug. of each year. [3] Dec. of each year. [4] Civilian labour force employed. [5] May of each year. [6] Third quarter of each year. [7] June of each year. [8] Establishments with 20 or more persons employed. [9] Incl. working proprietors and unpaid family workers. [10] Beginning 1977: sample of establishments and revised allocation of establishments in the industrial classification. [11] Sep. of each year.

[1] Avril de chaque année. [2] Août de chaque année. [3] Déc. de chaque année. [4] Main-d'œuvre civile occupée. [5] Mai de chaque année. [6] Troisième trimestre de chaque année. [7] Juin de chaque année. [8] Etablissements occupant 20 personnes et plus. [9] Y compris les propriétaires-exploitants et les travailleurs familiaux non rémunérés. [10] A partir de 1977: échantillon d'établissements et changements dans leur répartition industrielle. [11] Sept. de chaque année.

[1] Abril de cada año. [2] Agosto de cada año. [3] Dic. de cada año. [4] Fuerza trabajadora civil ocupada. [5] Mayo de cada año. [6] Tercer trimestre de cada año. [7] Junio de cada año. [8] Establecimientos con 20 y más trabajadores. [9] Incl. los empresarios propietarios y los trabajadores familiares no remunerados. [10] A partir de 1977: muestra de establecimientos y cambios en la distribución industrial de los establecimientos. [11] Sept. de cada año.

9 Employment in transport, storage and communication
Emploi dans les transports, entrepôts et communications
Empleo en los transportes, almacenaje y comunicaciones

(Thousands – Milliers – Millares)

Country – Source Pays – Source País – Fuente	1970	1971	1972	1973	1974	1975	1976	1977	1978	1979
Sénégal (IV)										
Total	.	10.409	11.987	11.616	12.128	13.528	15.097	17.922	...	...
Seychelles (II)										
Total [1]	.	.	.	0.851	0.947	0.979	0.995	1.230	1.608	...
Sierra Leone (III)										
Total [2]	.	.	.	.	8.027	8.823	6.359	5.854	5.919	7.397
Swaziland (III)										
Total [3]	1.877	2.050	2.280	2.688	2.483	2.540	2.566[4]	2.768	2.934	...
Males – Hom. [3]	1.756	1.915	2.128	2.527	2.318	2.321	2.376[4]	2.508	2.631	...
Fem. – Muj. [3]	0.121	0.135	0.152	0.161	0.165	0.219	0.190[4]	0.260	0.303	...
Tunisie (III)										
Total	23.98	24.20	24.45	25.89	26.79	31.64	35.76	...	...	...
Zambia (III)										
Total [2]	22.30	22.58	25.04	24.21	22.15	22.05	21.08	21.30*[5]	...	...
Zimbabwe (III)										
Total	36.5	38.9	41.0	42.3	43.8	45.3	45.7	45.5	44.0	43.4
AMERICA – AMERIQUE – AMERICA										
Bahamas (II) [6]										
Total [7]	.	.	.	.	.	3.843	4.007	3.952	4.027	
Barbados (III)										
Total	.	.	.	.	4.801	4.891	4.736	3.596	...	...
Bolivia (IV) [8]										
Total	69.8	72.2	74.3	78.3	79.3	82.1	86.0	90.8	96.4	111.5
Males – Hom.	.	69.4	70.6	74.3	74.5	77.1	80.8	85.3	90.6	104.8
Fem. – Muj.	.	2.9	3.7	3.9	4.7	5.0	5.2	5.4	5.8	6.7
Brasil (III) [9]										
Total [2]	435	438	499	582	638	717	▌1 182[10]	...	...	...
Males – Hom. [2]	410	415	468	525	569	629	▌1 017[10]	...	...	...
Fem. – Muj. [2]	25	23	31	57	69	88	▌165[10]	...	...	...
Canada (III) [11]										
Total	.	607.3	613.3	628.8	661.7	665.0	681.0	688.0	704.5	...
Colombia [12] (I) [8]										
Total [13]	.	.	.	.	.	140.13	146.16	157.46	168.27	197.54
Males – Hom. [13]	.	.	.	.	.	127.30	136.45	143.64	150.11	173.81
Fem. – Muj. [13]	.	.	.	.	.	12.82	15.07	13.82	18.16	23.74

Explanatory notes and source: see p. 151 – Notes explicatives et source: voir p. 154 – Notas explicativas y fuente: véase p. 157

[1] Nov. of each year. [2] Dec. of each year. [3] June of each year. [4] Prior to 1976: Sep. of each year. [5] June. [6] Insured persons. [7] Jan. of each year. [8] Civilian labour force employed. [9] Registered establishments on 31st Dec. of each year. [10] Beginning 1978: revised questionnaire; incl. persons employed in auxiliary services. [11] Establishments with 20 or more persons employed. [12] Seven main cities of the country. [13] Sep. of each year.

[1] Nov. de chaque année. [2] Déc. de chaque année. [3] Juin de chaque année. [4] Avant 1976: sept. de chaque année. [5] Juin. [6] Personnes assurées. [7] Janv. de chaque année. [8] Main-d'œuvre civile occupée. [9] Établissements enregistrés le 31 déc. de chaque année. [10] A partir de 1978: questionnaire révisé; y compris les personnes employées dans les services auxiliaires. [11] Établissements occupant 20 personnes et plus. [12] Sept villes principales du pays. [13] Sept. de chaque année.

[1] Nov. de cada año. [2] Dic. de cada año. [3] Junio de cada año. [4] Antes de 1976: sept. de cada año. [5] Junio. [6] Personas aseguradas. [7] Enero de cada año. [8] Fuerza trabajadora civil ocupada. [9] Establecimientos registrados el 31 dic. de cada año. [10] A partir de 1978: cuestionario revisado; incl. las personas ocupadas en los servicios auxiliares. [11] Establecimientos con 20 y más trabajadores. [12] Siete ciudades principales del país. [13] Sept. de cada año.

9 Employment in transport, storage and communication
Emploi dans les transports, entrepôts et communications
Empleo en los transportes, almacenaje y comunicaciones

(Thousands – Milliers – Millares)

Country – Source Pays – Source País – Fuente	1970	1971	1972	1973	1974	1975	1976	1977	1978	1979
Cuba (IV) [1]										
Total	.	175.5	177.3	181.9	186.3	187.8	198.6	176.4*	...	...
Guadeloupe (IV) [2]										
Total		.	.	.	6.5	6.5	6.1	4.0	4.0	
Guyane française (IV)										
Total	0.206	0.245	0.252	0.260	0.294	0.278	0.269	0.522	0.564	0.640
Haïti (IV) [2]										
Total [3]	11.792	11.863	11.934	12.006	12.078	12.150	11.517	11.584	11.642	...
Males – Hom. [3]	11.259	11.328	11.398	11.468	11.539	11.610	10.975	11.041	11.096	
Fem. – Muj. [3]	0.533	0.535	0.536	0.538	0.539	0.540	0.542	0.543	0.546	
Jamaica [4] (I) [2]										
Total	.			.	26.90	31.55	31.50	29.55	29.30	...
México (IV) [2]										
Total [5]				.	481.6	489.7	511.0	534.1	557.3	581.7
Males – Hom. [5]					.	461.8	480.6	494.7	516.2	528.4
Fem. – Muj. [5]					.	28.0	30.4	39.3	41.0	53.2
Nicaragua [6] (II) [7]										
Total	4.141	4.097	4.533	4.354	4.907	5.165	5.952	6.500	6.076	...
Panamá (I) [8]										
Total [9]			.		15.50[10]	13.83[11]	14.71	15.51[10]	16.31*	...
Paraguay (IV) [2]										
Total	.	.	20.4	21.6	23.7	24.5	25.9	27.6*	28.5*	30.3*
Trinidad and Tobago (III) [12]										
Total	7.5	9.8	10.0	11.3	11.6	11.3	6.3*	...	...	...
United States (III) [13]										
Total	3 824	3 779	3 830	3 927	3 982	3 811	3 849	3 967	4 150	...
Males – Hom.	2 971	2 928	2 981	3 049	3 079	2 931	2 958	3 041	3 150	...
Fem. – Muj.	853	852	849	878	904	880	891	927	1 000	...
Virgin Islands(US) (III)										
Total	.	.		.		1.74	1.66	1.66	1.76	...

ASIA – ASIE – ASIA

Bangladesh (III) [14]										
Total [15]	.	.	.	.	.	31.35	.	58.75	.	68.82

Explanatory notes and source: see p. 151 – Notes explicatives et source: voir p. 154 – Notas explicativas y fuente: véase p. 157

[1] State sector. [2] Civilian labour force employed. [3] Year beginning in July of year indicated. [4] Incl. electricity. [5] June of each year. [6] Eight main cities of the country. [7] Insured persons. [8] Wage earners and salaried employees. [9] Aug. of each year. [10] October. [11] November. [12] Establishments with 10 or more persons employed. [13] Registered employees. [14] Establishments with 20 or more persons employed. [15] Biennial survey.

[1] Secteur d'Etat. [2] Main-d'œuvre civile occupée. [3] Année commençant en juillet de l'année indiquée. [4] Y compris l'électricité. [5] Juin de chaque année. [6] Huit villes principales du pays. [7] Personnes assurées. [8] Population salariée ayant un emploi. [9] Août de chaque année. [10] Octobre. [11] Novembre. [12] Etablissements occupant 10 personnes et plus. [13] Salariés inscrits. [14] Etablissements occupant 20 personnes et plus. [15] Enquête biennale.

[1] Sector de Estado. [2] Fuerza trabajadora civil ocupada. [3] Año que comienza en julio del año indicado. [4] Incl. electricidad. [5] Junio de cada año. [6] Ocho ciudades principales del país. [7] Personas aseguradas. [8] Población ocupada asalariada. [9] Agosto de cada año. [10] Octubre. [11] Noviembre. [12] Establecimientos con 10 y más trabajadores. [13] Asalariados registrados. [14] Establecimientos con 20 y más trabajadores. [15] Encuesta bienal.

9 Employment in transport, storage and communication
Emploi dans les transports, entrepôts et communications
Empleo en los transportes, almacenaje y comunicaciones

(Thousands – Milliers – Millares)

Country – Source Pays – Source País – Fuente	1970	1971	1972	1973	1974	1975	1976	1977	1978	1979
Brunei (III)										
Total [1]	.	.	1.063	1.600	1.710	1.004	1.051	1.338	1.511	1.516
Cyprus (III) [2]										
Total	.	.	.	.	.	.	5.814	5.350	5.458	5.519*
Hong Kong (III) [3]										
Total [4]	45.80	39.76	41.15	43.85	45.28	43.96	51.46	57.57	61.46	68.00
India (III) [5]										
Total	1 923	1 969	2 000	2 023	2 426	2 460	2 486	2 536	2 592	2 661*[6]
Israel (II) [7]										
Total	55.1	58.6	60.1	60.9	62.0	64.5	66.0	67.6	69.8	▌71.0[8]
Japan (I) [9]										
Total	3 110	3 200	3 110	▌3 200[10]	3 120	3 140	3 250	3 230	3 240	3 310
Jordan (III) [11]										
Total [12]	...	...	2.79	2.85	2.96	3.93	4.37	4.58	...	...
Korea, Republic of (I) [9]										
Total	317	342	306	317	310	316	349	428	463	525
Peninsular Malaysia (III) [13]										
Total	24.160	32.340	32.550	33.591	34.406	34.917	34.776	34.295	...	...
Malaysia: Sabah (III) [14]										
Total [15]	.	.	3.000	3.120	3.088	3.173	3.366	2.701	2.971	
Pakistan (III) [13]										
Total	.	.	103.63	58.60	108.62	102.41	89.19	89.51	89.39	...
Philippines (III) [13]										
Indices [16]	.	.	100.0	105.0	108.4	111.0	100.9	102.2	110.0	...
Singapore (I) [9]										
Total [1]	.	.	.	.	82.22	84.69	85.11	88.76	91.60	99.79
Sri Lanka (III) [13]										
Total	.	72.79	77.58	75.77	67.55	61.32	68.53	61.35	83.95	...
Males – Hom.	.	71.18	76.40	74.97	66.62	60.37	67.34	59.99	81.59	...
Fem. – Muj.	.	1.61	1.18	0.81	0.93	0.95	1.20	1.36	2.36	...
Thailand (I) [17]										
Total [18]	.	213.3	313.6	383.9	465.1	381.3	326.6	382.8	387.9	...

Explanatory notes and source: see p. 151 – Notes explicatives et source: voir p. 154 – Notas explicativas y fuente: véase p. 157

[1] June of each year. [2] Employees and unpaid family workers. [3] Registered employed. [4] Nov. of each year. [5] Employees and working proprietors. [6] March. [7] Insured persons. [8] Beginning 1979: sample revised. [9] Wage earners and salaried employees. [10] Prior to 1973: excl. Okinawa Prefecure. [11] Establishments with 5 or more persons employed. [12] Aug. of each year. [13] Registered employees. [14] Establishments with 20 or more persons employed. [15] Dec. of each year. [16] Index base: 1972 = 100. [17] Civilian labour force employed. [18] Second semester of each year.

[1] Juin de chaque année. [2] Salariés et travailleurs familiaux non rémunérés. [3] Ensemble de l'effectif occupé. [4] Nov. de chaque année. [5] Salariés et propriétaires-exploitants. [6] Mars. [7] Personnes assurées. [8] A partir de 1979: échantillon révisé. [9] Population salariée ayant un emploi. [10] Avant 1973: non compris la préfecture d'Okinawa. [11] Etablissements occupant 5 personnes et plus. [12] Août de chaque année. [13] Salariés inscrits. [14] Etablissements occupant 20 personnes et plus. [15] Déc. de chaque année. [16] Indices base: 1972 = 100. [17] Main-d'œuvre civile occupée. [18] Second semestre de chaque année.

[1] Junio de cada año. [2] Asalariados y trabajadores familiares no remunerados. [3] Todo el efectivo ocupado. [4] Nov. de cada año. [5] Asalariados y empresarios propietarios. [6] Marzo. [7] Personas aseguradas. [8] A partir de 1979: muestra revisada. [9] Población ocupada asalariada. [10] Antes de 1973: excl. la Prefectura de Okinawa. [11] Establecimientos con 5 y más trabajadores. [12] Agosto de cada año. [13] Asalariados registrados. [14] Establecimientos con 20 y más trabajadores. [15] Dic. de cada año. [16] Indices base: 1972 = 100. [17] Fuerza trabajadora civil ocupada. [18] Segundo semestre de cada año.

9 Employment in transport, storage and communication
Emploi dans les transports, entrepôts et communications
Empleo en los transportes, almacenaje y comunicaciones

(Thousands – Milliers – Millares)

Country – Source Pays – Source País – Fuente	1970	1971	1972	1973	1974	1975	1976	1977	1978	1979
EUROPE – EUROPE – EUROPA										
Austria (III) [1]										
Total	...	...	148.17	151.89	158.47	158.27	156.63	157.79	159.49	159.45
Belgique (II) [1]										
Total [2]	218.4	227.4	233.9	242.0	247.8	250.5	247.4	248.0	251.6	255.3
·Bulgarie (III) [1]										
Total	226.64	234.63	240.30	248.89	259.14	270.95	281.62	289.49	293.57	297.40*
Czechoslovakia (III) [3]										
Total [4]	478	479	479	483	486	486	494	497	498	502
Denmark (I) [5]										
Total	.	.	159.0	165.7	166.9	157.7	165.8	166.7	165.4	175.4
Males – Hom.	.	.	124.6	129.4	130.5	123.6	130.1	130.1	128.2	132.7
Fem. – Muj.	.	.	34.4	36.3	36.4	34.1	35.7	36.6	37.2	42.7
España (I) [6]										
Total [7]	509.4	...	...	...	...	529.0	523.2	511.3	500.1	519.6
Finland (I) [6]										
Total	130	124	131	130	134	141	144	144	148	152
France (III) [1]										
Total	1 140	1 139	1 142	1 157	1 198	∎ 1 201[8]	1 214	1 238	1 262	1 279*
German Democratic Rep. (III) [1]										
Total	592.8	599.7	602.2	606.6	615.3	618.1	626.3	632.8	633.2	633.5
Germany, Fed. Rep. of (IV) [6]										
Total	.	.	1 422	1 439	1 406	1 388	1 424	1 394	1 389	1 401
Hongrie [9] (III) [1]										
Total	353	359	361	363	369	381	385	389	392	392
Iceland (IV)										
Total	60	60	61	61	63	64	63	62	63	...
Ireland (IV) [5]										
Total [10]	60	60	61	61	63	64	63	62	63	65
Italie (I) [1]										
Total	823	829	855	867	902	901	944	∎ 972[8]	958	961
Malta (IV) [1]										
Total	4.110	4.010	3.770	3.600	3.700	4.867	5.740	7.001	7.230	7.739

Explanatory notes and source: see p. 151 – Notes explicatives et source: voir p. 154 – Notas explicativas y fuente: véase p. 157

[1] Registered employees. [2] June of each year. [3] Registered employed. [4] Dec. of each year. [5] Civilian labour force employed. [6] Wage earners and salaried employees. [7] Fourth quarter of each year. [8] Change of industrial classification. [9] Socialised sector. [10] April of each year.

[1] Salariés inscrits. [2] Juin de chaque année. [3] Ensemble de l'effectif occupé. [4] Déc. de chaque année. [5] Main-d'œuvre civile occupée. [6] Population salariée ayant un emploi. [7] Quatrième trimestre de chaque année. [8] Changement de classification industrielle. [9] Secteur socialisé. [10] Avril de chaque année.

[1] Asalariados registrados. [2] Junio de cada año. [3] Todo el efectivo ocupado. [4] Dic. de cada año. [5] Fuerza trabajadora civil ocupada. [6] Población ocupada asalariada. [7] Cuarto trimestre de cada año. [8] Cambio de clasificación industrial. [9] Sector socializado. [10] Abril de cada año.

9 Employment in transport, storage and communication
Emploi dans les transports, entrepôts et communications
Empleo en los transportes, almacenaje y comunicaciones

(Thousands – Milliers – Millares)

Country – Source Pays – Source País – Fuente	1970	1971	1972	1973	1974	1975	1976	1977	1978	1979
Netherlands (IV) [1]										
Total	305	309	305	305	309	310	309	308	310	315
Norway (I) [2]										
Total	.	.	127	129	130	121	124	138	133	130
Pologne [3] (III) [4]										
Total	932.5	959.8	991.5	1 000.8	1 029.7	1 049.1	1 066.1	1 078.5	1 092.5	1 098.6
Portugal (I) [5]										
Total [6]	.	.	.	.	143	146	137	148	143	147
Roumanie [3] (III) [7]										
Total	397.0	406.7	418.9	434.6	434.5	470.1	479.3	483.5	505.7	529.2
Suisse (IV) [2]										
Total	171.6	175.5	180.0	182.7	184.2	182.8	178.7	177.4	177.8	179.1
Turquie (II) [5]										
Total	53.1	59.5	68.3	68.0	78.8	79.1	87.1	94.8	98.3	97.6
United Kingdom (IV) [7]										
Total [8]	.	1 568.0	1 543.2	1 524.5	1 506.0	1 518.0	1 474.6	1 467.9	1 466.4*	1 482.3*
Yugoslavia (III) [7]										
Total [9]	308	319	331	336	344	360	361	372	381*	...

OCEANIA – OCEANIE – OCEANIA

Australia (III) [7]										
Total [10]	363.9	373.4	371.6	379.2	398.3	404.6	399.3	397.0	396.4	399.6
Fiji (III) [4]										
Total [11]	3.883	4.629	5.225	4.909	6.180	6.423	6.774	7.196	6.967	...
New Zealand (III) [7]										
Total [12]	77.593	81.652	81.906	83.678	86.667	90.472	91.532	90.786	91.347	...
Papua New Guinea (IV) [7]										
Total [8]	.	.	.	5.342	6.760	6.371	6.309	6.409	...	...

USSR – URSS – URSS

URSS [3] (III) [7]										
Total	9 315	9 597	9 881	10 170	10 421	10 743	10 933	11 184	11 462	11 723

Explanatory notes and source: see p. 151 – Notes explicatives et source: voir p. 154 – Notas explicativas y fuente: véase p. 157

[1] Civilian employment (man–years). [2] Civilian labour force employed. [3] Socialised sector. [4] Registered employed. [5] Insured persons. [6] Second semester of each year. [7] Registered employees. [8] June of each year. [9] Dec. of each year. [10] Aug. of each year. [11] Sep. of each year. [12] April and Oct. of each year.

[1] Emploi civil (années–homme). [2] Main–d'œuvre civile occupée. [3] Secteur socialisé. [4] Ensemble de l'effectif occupé. [5] Personnes assurées. [6] Second semestre de chaque année. [7] Salariés inscrits. [8] Juin de chaque année. [9] Déc. de chaque année. [10] Août de chaque année. [11] Sept. de chaque année. [12] Avril et oct. de chaque année.

[1] Empleo civil (años–hombre). [2] Fuerza trabajadora civil ocupada. [3] Sector socializado. [4] Todo el efectivo ocupado. [5] Personas aseguradas. [6] Segundo semestre de cada año. [7] Asalariados registrados. [8] Junio de cada año. [9] Dic. de cada año. [10] Agosto de cada año. [11] Sept. de cada año. [12] Abril y oct. de cada año.

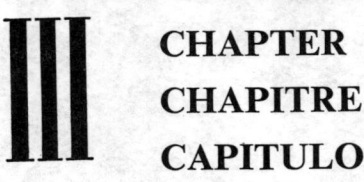

Unemployment

Chômage

Desempleo

Unemployment

Unemployment is defined as follows in the Resolution concerning statistics of the labour force, employment and unemployment, adopted by the Eighth International Conference of Labour Statisticians (Geneva, 1954):[1]

"(1) Persons in unemployment consist of all persons above a specified age who, on the specified day or for a specified week, were in the following categories:

(a) workers available for employment whose contract of employment had been terminated or temporarily suspended and who were without a job and seeking work for pay or profit;

(b) persons who were available for work (except for minor illness) during the specified period and were seeking work for pay or profit, who were never previously employed or whose most recent status was other than that of employee (i.e. former employers, etc.), or who had been in retirement;

(c) persons without a job and currently available for work who had made arrangements to start a new job at a date subsequent to the specified period;

(d) persons on temporary or indefinite lay-off without pay.

(2) The following categories of persons are not considered to be unemployed:

(a) persons intending to establish their own business or farm, but who had not yet arranged to do so, who were not seeking work for pay or profit;

(b) former unpaid family workers not at work and not seeking work for pay or profit."

For various reasons, national definitions of unemployment often differ from the recommended international standard definition. The national definitions used vary from one country to another as regards *inter alia* age limits, reference periods, criteria for seeking work, treatment of persons temporarily laid off, and treatment of first-time job seekers.

Intercountry comparisons are further hampered by the variety of types of systems used to obtain information on unemployment and the differences in the scope and coverage of such systems.[2]

In most cases, the series on unemployment presented in this chapter relate to the entire geographical area of a country but rural areas are often less well covered than other areas in most unemployment statistics.

In some cases, the statistics cover all members of the civilian labour force or all employees; however, usually the data refer only to wage earners and lower-paid salaried employees. Persons employed in mining and quarrying and in manufacturing are more fully covered than persons employed in other economic activities.

In general, two main sources of unemployment statistics may be distinguished. These sources, described below are identified in the tables by the codes I and II.

Source I. *Labour force sample surveys.* Labour force sample surveys generally yield the best over-all statistics on unemployment since, in particular, they include groups of persons who are often not covered in unemployment statistics obtained by other methods, particularly persons seeking work for the first time. Generally the definition of unemployment used for this type of statistics follows more closely the international recommendations and such statistics are more comparable internationally than those obtained from other sources. Likewise the percentages of unemployment are generally more reliable since they are calculated by relating the estimated numbers of persons unemployed to the estimate of the civilian labour force (employed plus unemployed) derived from the same surveys.

Source II. *Administrative records.* There are three types of administrative records which serve as sources of information on unemployment. The most common of these sources is *Type a*: *Employment office statistics.* The

---

[1] See ILO: *International Recommendations on Labour Statistics* (Geneva, 1976).

[2] For the descriptions of the various national series, sources, scopes, definitions and methods of compilation used, etc., see ILO: *Technical Guide 1980* (description of general series published in the *Bulletin* and the *Year Book of Labour Statistics*), Vol. II, "Employment—Unemployment—Hours of work—Wages" (Geneva, 1980).

statistics from these series usually refer to the numbers of applicants for work on the registers at the end of each month. They may include, in addition to persons without a job, persons on strike, or temporarily ill and unable to work and persons engaged on unemployment relief projects. In principle, these statistics do not include persons who, although in employment, wish to change their job and are therefore registered at employment offices. This series is identified by the Code IIa, however, if the series also includes persons in employment but seeking a change of job, the series is then identified by the Code II A.

The value of these statistics varies widely. In cases where the employment offices function in close connection with unemployment insurance, registration being a qualifying condition for the receipt of unemployment benefits, they are comparable in reliability to compulsory unemployment insurance statistics (see *type b* below). Employment offices operating in close connection with large unemployment relief schemes may also provide reasonably satisfactory figures during the currency of such schemes. However, where registration is entirely voluntary, and especially where the employment offices function only in the more populous regions of a country or are not widely patronised by employees seeking work or by employers seeking workers, the data are generally very incomplete and do not give a reliable indication of the extent of unemployment. The scope of the figures is determined partly by the manner in which the system of exchanges is organised and the advantages which registration brings, and partly by the extent to which workers are accustomed to register. In many cases persons engaged in agriculture and living in less populous areas are scarcely represented in the statistics, if at all. The scope of employment exchange statistics is therefore most difficult to ascertain, and in very few cases can satisfactory percentages of unemployment be calculated. In general, these statistics are not comparable from country to country. However, if there are no changes in legislation, administrative regulations and the like, fluctuations within a country may reflect changes in the prevalence of unemployment.

In certain cases, unemployment statistics are derived from other *administrative records* such as *Compulsory unemployment insurance schemes (Type b)* which, as a rule, have a broad industrial coverage and generally relate to wage earners and salaried employees or to wage earners only; and *Statistics of trade union benefit funds (Type c)*, the scope of which is determined by the degree of development of trade unions, the rules for admission of members to the unions or to the union benefit fund, the number of unions reporting, etc. These series are identified by the Codes IIb and IIc respectively. For both of the latter schemes, unemployment rates are computed by comparing the number of recipients of insurance benefits to the total number of insured persons covered by the schemes. However, the extent to which the numbers and percentages of unemployed reported are representative of the actual general level of unemployment in a given country is difficult if not impossible to ascertain.

Lastly, a few countries issue *official national estimates* of unemployment. Such estimates are primarily based on data obtained from *type b* or *type c* sources but supplemented by data from *type a* sources for persons not covered by such schemes. These estimates are identified in the tables by the Codes II a/b or IIa/c.

Table 10

General level of unemployment

As far as possible, the statistics in this table are presented both in absolute numbers (in thousands), and in percentages. The *numbers* indicate the size of the problem of unemployment within the fields covered by the respective series. Fluctuations in numbers unemployed reflect not only seasonal and other variations in economic activity but also, over a period, the effects of changes in the size of the population of working age; depending on the source and type of series used, they may also be influenced by changes in legislation or administrative organisation.

The *percentages* illustrate the severity of unemployment within the fields covered by the respective series. They are calculated by relating the number of workers in the given group who are unemployed during the reference period (usually a particular day or a given week) to the total of employed and unemployed persons in the group at the same date (Source I). The percentages for the Source II series should be interpreted with due regard to their representativeness.

Table 11

Structure of unemployment

This table provides data on the previous job experiences of the unemployed. Data are arranged, so far as possible, according to the major divisions of economic activity of the *International Standard Industrial Classification of All Economic Activities (ISIC-1968)* or the major groups of the *International Standard Classification of Occupations (ISCO-1968)*, as the case may be. Unemployed persons with previous experience are classified according to the industry or occupation in which they are usually or were most frequently engaged. Unemployed persons seeking work for the first time are classified under *activities not adequately defined (ISIC-1968)* or *workers not classifiable by occupation (ISCO-1968)*. Abridged versions of the ISIC and ISCO classifications are shown in the Appendix.

The remarks made on the general series in table 10 apply here also.

Chômage

La résolution concernant les statistiques de la main-d'œuvre, de l'emploi et du Chômage, adoptée par la huitième Conférence internationale des statisticiens du travail (Genève, 1954) [1], donne du chômage la définition suivante:

« 1) Les personnes en chômage sont toutes les personnes qui ont dépassé un âge spécifié, et qui, un jour spécifié ou une semaine spécifiée, rentrent dans les catégories suivantes:

a) travailleurs à même de prendre un emploi et dont le contrat d'emploi a pris fin ou a été temporairement interrompu, et qui se trouvent sans emploi et en quête de travail rémunéré;

b) personnes à même de travailler (sauf maladies bénignes) durant la période spécifiée et en quête de travail rémunéré, qui n'ont jamais eu d'emploi auparavant, ou dont la dernière position dans la profession n'était pas celle de salarié (c'est-à-dire les anciens employeurs, etc.) ou qui avaient cessé de travailler;

c) personnes sans emploi qui sont normalement à même de travailler immédiatement et ont pris leurs dispositions en vue de commencer à travailler dans un nouvel emploi à une date postérieure à la période spécifiée;

d) personnes mises à pied temporairement ou pour une durée indéfinie, sans rémunération;

2) Ne sont pas considérées comme personnes en chômage:

a) les personnes qui ont l'intention d'ouvrir une entreprise ou une exploitation agricole à leur propre compte, mais qui n'ont pas encore pris leurs dispositions pour ce faire et qui ne sont pas en quête de travail rémunéré;

b) les travailleurs familiaux non rémunérés qui ont cessé leur activité et ne sont pas en quête de travail rémunéré. »

Pour diverses raisons, les définitions nationales du mot « chômage » s'écartent souvent de la définition normalisée internationale qui est recommandée. Les définitions nationales varient d'un pays à un autre en ce qui concerne entre autres les limites d'âge, les périodes de référence, les critères retenus en matière de recherche d'emploi, le traitement des données concernant les personnes mises à pied temporairement et celles qui cherchent du travail pour la première fois.

Les comparaisons de pays à pays sont, de plus, affectées par la variété des méthodes utilisées pour rassembler les informations sur le chômage ainsi que par les différences dans le champ d'application et la portée propres à ces méthodes [2].

Les séries sur le chômage présentées dans ce chapitre se rapportent, le plus souvent, à l'ensemble du territoire national d'un pays donné, mais, dans la plupart des statistiques sur le chômage, les données relatives aux zones rurales sont fréquemment moins complètes que celles qui concernent d'autres régions.

Les statistiques ne couvrent l'ensemble de la main-d'œuvre civile ou tous les salariés que dans quelques cas; cependant, elles sont habituellement limitées aux ouvriers et aux employés dont la rémunération est peu élevée. Elles sont plus complètes pour les travailleurs des industries extractives et des industries manufacturières que pour ceux qui sont occupés dans d'autres activités économiques.

On distingue, en général, deux principaux types de statistiques (indiqués dans les en-têtes du tableau par les codes I et II).

Source 1. *Enquêtes par sondage sur la main-d'œuvre.* Les enquêtes par sondage sur la main-d'œuvre fournissent généralement les meilleures statistiques d'ensemble sur le chômage, car elles permettent en particulier de couvrir des groupes (tels que les personnes en quête d'emploi pour la première fois) qui, souvent, ne sont pas compris dans les statistiques du chômage obtenues par d'autres méthodes. En général, la définition du chômage adoptée pour ce type de statistiques suit plus fidèlement les recommandations internationales et de telles statistiques sont plus comparables sur le plan international que celles obtenues d'autres sources. De même, les pourcentages de chômage sont généralement plus fiables du fait qu'ils sont calculés en rapportant

---

[1] Voir BIT: *Recommandations internationales sur les statistiques du travail* (Genève, 1975).

[2] Pour les descriptions des diverses séries nationales, sources, portées, définitions et méthodes de calcul utilisées, etc., voir BIT: *Guide technique 1980* (descriptions des séries générales publiées dans le *Bulletin* et l'*Annuaire des statistiques du travail*), vol. II, « Emploi — Chômage — Durée du travail — Salaires » (Genève, 1980).

le nombre évalué des personnes en chômage à l'effectif évalué de la main-d'œuvre civile (personnes occupées, plus chômeurs) dérivé des mêmes enquêtes.

Source II. *Registres administratifs*. Trois types de registres administratifs qui servent de sources d'informations sur le chômage. La plus commune de ces sources est du *type a : Statistiques des bureaux de placement*. Ces statistiques donnent généralement le nombre de demandeurs d'emploi figurant sur les registres à la fin de chaque mois. Elles peuvent comprendre, outre les personnes sans travail, des personnes en grève ou dans l'incapacité temporaire de travailler par suite de maladie et des personnes occupées à des travaux entrepris pour secourir les chômeurs. En principe, ces statistiques ne comprennent pas les personnes qui, bien que pourvues d'un emploi, sont désireuses d'en changer et sont, en conséquence, inscrites dans des bureaux de placement; cette série est identifiée par le Code IIa; cependant, si la série comprend également les personnes déjà pourvues d'emploi mais désireuses d'en changer, elle est alors identifiée par le Code IIA.

La valeur de ces statistiques est très variable. Lorsque les bureaux de placement fonctionnent en rapport étroit avec une assurance-chômage, l'inscription étant une des conditions mises à l'octroi des indemnités, les données sont aussi fiables que celles des statistiques d'assurance-chômage obligatoire (voir *Type b* ci-dessous). Quand les bureaux sont en étroite relation avec des régimes d'assistance publique d'une large portée, les chiffres relevés peuvent également fournir des données satisfaisantes durant l'existence de tels régimes. Toutefois, lorsque les inscriptions sont purement volontaires et surtout lorsque les bureaux de placement ne fonctionnent que dans les régions à forte densité de population ou ne sont pas utilisés largement par les salariés en quête de travail ou par les employeurs qui cherchent des travailleurs, les statistiques sont en général très incomplètes et ne fournissent pas une indication sûre du niveau du chômage. La portée des données dépend

donc, d'une part, de l'organisation du réseau des bureaux et, d'autre part, de l'habitude qu'ont les travailleurs de s'y inscrire et de l'intérêt qu'ils ont à le faire. Dans bien des cas, les personnes occupées dans l'agriculture et habitant des régions à population moins dense sont parfois à peine couvertes par les statistiques, quand elles le sont. La portée des statistiques des bureaux de placement est de ce fait très difficile à préciser et il est très rare que les données permettent de calculer des pourcentages de chômage satisfaisants. En général, ces statistiques ne seront donc pas comparables d'un pays à un autre. Cependant, s'il n'y a pas de changements dans la législation ou dans les réglementations administratives et similaires, leurs fluctuations au sein d'un même pays peuvent indiquer les variations dans l'étendue du chômage.

Dans certains cas, les statistiques de chômage sont dérivées d'autres *registres administratifs*, tels que: *Régimes d'assurance-chômage obligatoire (Type b)* qui ont ordinairement une vaste portée industrielle et qui portent, en général, sur les ouvriers et les employés ou sur les ouvriers seulement; et *Statistiques des caisses syndicales (Type c)*, dont la portée dépend du degré de développement des syndicats, des conditions réglant l'affiliation aux syndicats ou à la caisse syndicale, du nombre des syndicats fournissant des données, etc. Ces séries sont identifiées, respectivement, par les Codes IIb et IIc.

Pour les deux derniers régimes, les pourcentages de chômage sont calculés en comparant le nombre de bénéficiaires d'allocations de chômage et le nombre total des travailleurs assurés couverts par les régimes. Toutefois il est difficile, sinon impossible, de déterminer jusqu'à quel point de telles statistiques peuvent être considérées comme fournissant une indication exacte du niveau général du chômage dans un pays donné.

Enfin, quelques pays publient des *évaluations officielles nationales* du chômage. De telles estimations sont principalement basées sur des données obtenues à partir des sources du *type b* ou du *type c* et complétées, en ce qui concerne les personnes non couvertes par ces régimes, par des données tirées des sources du *type a*. Dans les tableaux, ces estimations sont identifiées par les Codes IIa/b ou IIa/c.

Tableau 10

Niveau général du chômage

Dans la mesure du possible, les statistiques sont présentées en chiffres absolus (en milliers) et en pourcentages. Les *nombres* indiquent l'étendue du problème du chômage dans les limites couvertes par les diverses séries. Les fluctuations du nombre des chômeurs reflètent non seulement les variations saisonnières et autres de l'activité économique, mais aussi l'effet des changements dans une période donnée de l'importance numérique de la population en âge de travailler; elles peuvent aussi être influencées par des changements intervenus dans la législation ou dans l'organisation administrative, selon la source et le type de série utilisé.

Les *pourcentages* font ressortir la gravité du chômage, dans les limites couvertes par les diverses séries. Ils sont calculés en rapportant le nombre de travailleurs d'un certain groupe qui se trouvaient en chômage pendant la période de référence (en général, un jour donné ou une semaine donnée) au nombre total des personnes occupées et des chômeurs dans ce groupe à la même date (source I). Les pourcentages de chômage des séries de la source II doivent être interprétés avec une attention particulière quant à leur degré de représentativité.

Tableau 11

Structure du chômage

Ce tableau fournit des données sur les chômeurs ayant déjà occupé un emploi. Les données sont disposées, dans toute la mesure possible, par industrie selon la *Classification internationale type, par industrie, de toutes les branches d'activité économique (CITI-1968)* ou les classes de la *Classification internationale type des professions (CITP-1968)*, selon les cas. Les personnes en chômage ayant déjà occupé un emploi sont classées selon la branche d'activité économique ou le groupe de professions dans lequel elles ont habituellement ou le plus fréquemment travaillé. Les personnes en quête d'emploi pour la première fois sont classées sous *activités mal désignées (CITI-1968)* ou sous *travailleurs ne pouvant être classés selon la profession (CITP-1968)*. Des versions abrégées de ces classifications sont présentées dans l'Annexe.

Les observations concernant les séries générales du tableau 10 s'appliquent également au tableau 11.

Desempleo

El desempleo se halla definido en la forma siguiente en la resolución sobre estadísticas de la fuerza del trabajo, del empleo y del desempleo, adoptada por la octava Conferencia Internacional de Estadígrafos del Trabajo (Ginebra, 1954) [1]:

« 1) Las personas comprendidas en el desempleo serán todas aquellas que tengan más de cierta edad especificada y que, en un día especificado o en una semana especificada, se hallen en las siguientes categorías:

a) los trabajadores disponibles para el empleo cuyo contrato de trabajo haya expirado o esté suspendido temporalmente, que estén sin empleo y busquen trabajo remunerado durante un breve período especificado, con preferencia una semana;

b) las personas que no hayan estado empleadas nunca y aquellas cuya categoría de ocupación más reciente sea distinta de la de asalariado (es decir, antiguos empleadores, etc.) en unión de las que estén jubiladas, cuyas personas se hallen disponibles para trabajar (salvo los casos de enfermedad benigna) en el curso del período especificado y estén buscando trabajo remunerado;

c) las personas sin empleo que en el momento de que se trate se hallen disponibles para trabajar y hayan logrado un nuevo empleo que deba empezar en una fecha subsiguiente al período especificado;

d) las personas que hayan sido suspendidas temporal o indefinidamente, sin goce de remuneración.

2) No se considerará desempleadas a las personas comprendidas en las categorías siguientes:

a) las que tengan el propósito de establecer por su cuenta un negocio cualquiera o explotación agrícola, pero que no hayan tomado medidas en esa dirección y que no estén buscando trabajo remunerado;

b) los antiguos trabajadores familiares no remunerados que no estén trabajando ni buscando trabajo remunerado. »

Por varias razones, las definiciones nacionales del « desempleo » difieren a menudo de la definición recomendada por la Clasificación internacional uniforme. Las definiciones nacionales varían de un país a otro respecto de los límites de edad, los períodos de referencia, los criterios para determinar que una persona está buscando trabajo, los criterios para determinar que una persona se halla temporalmente suspendida, y aquellos que buscan un empleo por primera vez.

Las comparaciones entre los países están igualmente afectadas por la variedad de métodos utilizados para recoger la información de desempleo, y además por las diferencias inherentes a dichos métodos en cuanto al alcance de la investigación [2].

En la mayoría de los casos, las estadísticas de desempleo que figuran en este capítulo se refieren a toda un área geográfica de un país determinado, pero con frecuencia las regiones rurales no se hallan comprendidas en el mismo grado que otras regiones en la mayoría de las estadísticas de desempleo.

En algunos casos, las estadísticas comprenden todos los sectores de la fuerza de trabajo civil o todos los asalariados; sin embargo, las cifras se refieren generalmente sólo a los obreros y a los empleados de baja remuneración. Las personas empleadas en las minas y canteras y en las industrias manufactureras están incluidas en mayor grado que las personas ocupadas en otras actividades económicas.

Pueden distinguirse, en general, dos fuentes principales de estadísticas de desempleo, las cuales se indican en los encabezamientos de los cuadros por las claves I y II.

Fuente I. *Encuestas por muestra sobre la fuerza de trabajo.* Estas encuestas proporcionan generalmente las mejores cifras de conjunto sobre el desempleo, porque comprenden grupos de individuos no incluidos por lo regular en las estadísticas de desempleo obtenidas por otros métodos, en particular las personas en busca de ocupación por primera vez. En general, la

---

[1] Véase OIT: *Recomendaciones internacionales sobre estadísticas del trabajo* (Ginebra, 1975).

[2] Para las descripciones de las diversas series nacionales, fuentes, su alcance, definiciones y métodos de compilación utilizados, etc., véase OIT: *Guía Técnica 1980* (descripciones de las series generales publicadas en el *Boletín* y el *Anuario de Estadísticas del Trabajo*), vol. II, « Empleo — Desempleo — Horas de trabajo — Salarios » (Ginebra, 1980).

definición del desempleo utilizada en este tipo de estadísticas se ajusta bastante a las recomendaciones internacionales, por lo que dichas estadísticas son más comparables internacionalmente que las obtenidas de otras fuentes. De igual manera, los porcentajes de desempleo son por lo regular más confiables, puesto que se calculan relacionando el número estimado de personas desempleadas con el conjunto estimado de la fuerza de trabajo civil (personas empleadas más personas desempleadas), derivados de las mismas encuestas.

Fuente II. *Registros administrativos.* Existen tres tipos de registros administrativos que sirven de fuentes de información sobre el desempleo. El más común es el *Tipo a: Estadísticas de las oficinas de coloración.* Estas estadísticas generalmente se refieren al número de solicitantes de empleo que figuran en los registros al fin de cada mes. Las mismas pueden comprender, además de las personas sin trabajo, a las personas en huelga o en incapacidad temporal de trabajar por causa de enfermedad y a las ocupadas en trabajos creados como medio de auxilio a los desempleados. En principio, dichas estadísticas no abarcan a las personas que, aunque ya poseen un empleo, desean cambiarlo y, en consecuencia, se hallan inscritas en las oficinas de colocación. Esta serie se identifica por la clave IIa; sin embargo, si se incluyen las personas que ya poseen un empleo pero que desean cambiarlo, la serie será identificada por la clave IIA.

El valor de dichas estadísticas es muy variable. Cuando las oficinas de colocación funcionan en íntima relación con un seguro de desempleo, siendo la inscripción una de las condiciones exigidas para la concesión de indemnizaciones de desempleo, los datos son tan fiables como los de las estadísticas del seguro obligatorio de desempleo (ver *Tipo b* más adelante). Cuando las oficinas de colocación están en relación íntima con sistemas amplios de asistencia pública, las cifras recogidas pueden proporcionar también datos satisfactorios durante la vigencia de tales sistemas. Sin embargo, cuando las inscripciones son totalmente voluntarias y, sobre todo, cuando las oficinas de colocación no funcionan sino en las regiones de gran densidad de población de un país, o no son utilizadas ampliamente por los obreros en busca de trabajo o por los empleadores en demanda de mano de obra, las estadísticas son generalmente muy incompletas y no proporcionan una indicación fidedigna de la extensión del desempleo. El alcance de los datos depende, pues, por una parte, de la organización de la red de oficinas y, por otra, de las ventajas que proporciona el registro y de la costumbre que tengan los trabajadores de inscribirse en ellas. Con frecuencia sucede que las personas que trabajan en la agricultura y que viven en territorios de población poco densa apenas si están englobadas en las estadísticas, si es que no están excluidas del todo. El alcance de las estadísticas de las oficinas de colocación es, por esto, muy difícil de precisar, y sólo raramente sus datos permiten calcular porcentajes satisfactorios de desempleo. En general, dichas estadísticas no son comparables de un país a otro; sin embargo, si no han habido cambios en la legislación, reglamentos administrativos y similares, sus fluctuaciones dentro de un mismo país pueden indicar las variaciones en la extensión del desempleo.

En ciertos casos, las estadísticas del desempleo son derivadas de otros *registros administrativos,* como: *a) Sistemas de seguro obligatorio de desempleo (Tipo b),* que tienen ordinariamente un vasto alcance industrial y que comprenden, en general, los obreros y los empleados o los obreros solamente, y *Estadísticas de las cajas de los sindicatos (Tipo c),* cuyo alcance depende del grado de desarrollo de los sindicatos, de las reglas que rigen la afiliación a los sindicatos o a las cajas sindicales, del número de sindicatos que facilitan informaciones, etc. Estas series se identifican por las claves IIb y IIc respectivamente. Para los dos últimos sistemas, los porcentajes de desempleo se calculan comparando el número de quienes reciben pagos por desempleo, con el total de asegurados que abarca el sistema. Sin embargo, es difícil, si no imposible, definir hasta qué punto puede considerarse que estas estadísticas procuran una indicación exacta del nivel general del desempleo en un país dado.

Finalmente, algunos países publican *estimaciones nacionales oficiales* del desempleo. Estas se basan principalmente en datos provenientes de fuentes de *tipo b* o *tipo c* y completadas, para las personas fuera de esos sistemas, con datos provenientes de fuentes de *tipo a*. Estas estimaciones se identifican en los cuadros por las claves IIa/b o IIa/c.

Cuadro 10

Nivel general del desempleo

En la medida de lo posible, las estadísticas de este cuadro presentan cifras absolutas (millares) y porcentajes. Las *cifras* indican la extensión del problema del desempleo en las actividades comprendidas en las respectivas series. Las fluctuaciones de las personas desempleadas reflejan no sólo variaciones estacionales y otros cambios de la actividad económica, sino también los efectos en las modificaciones del volumen de la población en edad de trabajar, dentro de un período determinado, todo lo cual depende de la fuente y del tipo utilizados; pueden hallarse influidas también por cambios de la legislación y la organización administrativa.

Los *porcentajes* hacen resaltar la gravedad del desempleo dentro de los límites que abarcan las diversas series. Se calculan relacionando el número de trabajadores de cierto grupo, que se

encuentran desempleados en un período determinado (generalmente un día o una semana), con el conjunto de las personas empleadas y desempleadas de ese grupo en la misma fecha (fuente I). Los porcentajes de desempleo de las series de la fuente II deben interpretarse teniendo muy en cuenta su representatividad.

Cuadro 11

Estructura del desempleo

Este cuadro entrega información sobre los trabajos anteriores de los desempleados. Los datos se clasifican, en la medida de lo posible y según el caso, por industria de acuerdo con la *Clasificación industrial internacional uniforme de todas las actividades económicas (CIIU-1968)* o las agrupaciones de la *Clasificación internacional uniforme de ocupaciones (CIUO-1968)*. Las personas desempleadas que trabajaban previamente se clasifican según la industria u ocupación en las que normalmente, o con mayor frecuencia, han trabajado. Las personas desempleadas que buscan trabajo por primera vez se clasifican en *actividades no bien especificadas (CIIU-1968)* o en *trabajadores que no pueden ser clasificados según la ocupación (CIUO-1968)*. Las clasificaciones, abreviadas, figuran en el apéndice.

Las observaciones formuladas respecto a las series generales del cuadro 10 se aplican también en este caso.

UNEMPLOYMENT

10 General level of unemployment
Niveau général du chômage
Nivel general del desempleo

(Thousands — *Milliers* — Millares)

Country — *Pays* — País	Code *Code* Clave	1970	1971	1972	1973	1974	1975	1976	1977	1978	1979
AFRICA — AFRIQUE **AFRICA**											
Burundi (Bjumbura)	II A	.	.	.	.	.	.	.	.	5.40	5.80
Rép.-Unie du Cameroun[1]	II a	2.17	2.38	2.94	4.04	4.23	4.28	4.20	3.84	4.62	3.41
République centrafricaine (Bangui)	II A	.	0.32	0.16	0.36	0.49	0.42[2]	...	...	...	...
Egypt	I[3]	198.0	153.1	134.6	145.1	208.6	233.4	.	296.1	354.5	...
» . . . . (%)		*(2.4)*	*(1.8)*	*(1.5)*	*(1.6)*	*(2.3)*	*(2.5)*	.	*(3.1)*	*(3.6)*	...
Ghana	II a	16.5	18.4	31.2	26.3	28.3	30.5	32.7	31.9	34.8	31.3
Haute-Volta[4]	II A	0.99	0.74	0.66	3.62	2.49	3.20	3.31	4.99	1.98	...
Liberia	II A	.	.	0.11	0.14	0.11	0.48	...	...	...	...
Libyan Arab Jamahiriya	II a	2.58	1.34	5.31	7.28	4.85	4.99	4.97	3.23	1.91	...
Madagascar	II a	8.6	11.1	12.8	17.6	13.4	13.0	29.2	46.5	35.6	39.9
Maroc	II a	31.6	26.3	29.8	29.1	26.3	23.0	17.4	22.4	17.0	18.8
Mauritius	II a	21.0	30.7	34.5	27.2	21.2	20.5	20.8	17.1	16.8	22.0
Niger (Niamey)	II a	0.13	0.22	0.29	0.66	0.38	0.39	0.35	0.39	0.70	...
Nigeria	II a	13.5	14.4	15.4	19.1	20.5	20.0	19.0	15.8	16.7	
Réunion	II a	1.74	3.82	8.10	9.38	14.9	15.7[5]	16.5	17.3	17.6	...
Sénégal (Dakar)	II A[6]	2.03	3.29	2.35	3.50	2.90	4.69	2.92	4.63	...	...
Sierra Leone	II A[7]	9.51	8.03	6.80	5.75	5.56	6.64	7.67	7.34	7.78	5.26
» » .	II A[8]	5.76	5.75	5.92	5.90	6.31	6.73	8.02	8.65	8.79	8.90
South Africa, Rep. of[9]	II a	8.5	8.6	12.2	10.8	8.3	10.3	14.5	28.5	30.9	28.2
Sudan	II a	4.79	4.95	4.08	4.06	4.42	5.49	6.68	6.45	3.56	6.62
Togo (Lomé)	II a	0.43	0.52	0.41	0.39	0.41	0.34	0.40[10]	.	0.29	0.25
Tunisie	II a	63.7	52.5	31.9	37.0	32.4	29.4	32.6	64.5	59.4	58.14
Zambia	II a	10.3	10.2	12.6	9.3	10.6	12.4	...	...		8.90
AMERICA — AMÉRIQUE **AMÉRICA**											
Argentina (Gran Buenos Aires) . .	I	158.0	196.5[11]	221.5	173.0	121.2	97.0	159.1	103.3	101.6	68.9[12]
» » » » (%)		*(4.8)*	*(6.0)*	*(6.6)*	*(5.6)*	*(3.4)*	*(2.3)*	*(4.5)*	*(2.8)*	*(2.8)*	*(2.0)*
Barbados	I	.	.	.	.	.	.	16.8	16.3	14.0	14.0
» . . . . (%)		.	.	.	.	.	.	*(15.6)*	*(16.3)*	*(13.8)*	*(13.1)*
Bolivia	II.[13]	.	122.7	112.1	100.9	89.1	76.6	63.4	62.1	54.1	...
» . . . . (%)			*(9.0)*	*(8.1)*	*(7.1)*	*(6.1)*	*(5.2)*	*(4.2)*	*(4.0)*	*(3.4)*	...
Brasil[14]	I[15]	.	.	1 033.9	968.0	.	.	721.7	...	...	...

EXPLANATORY NOTES: See p. 271.

Codes: See p. 284.

[1] Douala, Yaoundé, Nkongsamba and Garoua. [2] Jan.-Feb. and April-Dec. [3] May. [4] Ouagadougou and Bobo-Dioulasso. [5] Prior to 1975: data relate to December. [6] Excl. persons seeking work for the first time. [7] Excl. applicants for work registered at the Maritime Pool. [8] Applicants for work registered at the Maritime Pool. [9] Non-indigenous population. [10] Jan.-June. [11] April and July. [12] April. [13] Official estimates. [14] Excl. rural areas of Rondonía, Acre, Amazonas, Roraima, Pará, Amapá, Mato Grosso and Goiás. [15] Fourth quarter.

NOTES EXPLICATIVES: Voir p. 274.

Codes: Voir p. 284.

[1] Douala, Yaoundé, Nkongsamba et Garoua. [2] Janv.-fév. et avril-déc. [3] Mai. [4] Ouagadougou et Bobo-Dioulasso. [5] Avant 1975 : les données se réfèrent à décembre. [6] Non compris les personnes en quête d'emploi pour la première fois. [7] Non compris les demandeurs d'emploi enregistrés au bureau de placement maritime. [8] Demandeurs d'emploi enregistrés au bureau de placement maritime. [9] Population non indigène. [10] Janv.-juin. [11] Avril et juillet. [12] Avril. [13] Evaluations officielles. [14] Non compris les zones rurales de Rondonia, Acre, Amazonas, Roraima, Pará, Amapá, Mato Grosso et Goiás. [15] Quatrième trimestre.

NOTAS EXPLICATIVAS: Véase pág. 277.

Claves: Véase pág. 284.

[1] Duala, Yaundé, Nkongsamba y Garoua. [2] Enero-febr. y abril-dic. [3] Mayo. [4] Uagadugú y Bobo-Diulasso. [5] Antes de 1975: los datos se refieren a diciembre. [6] Excl. las personas en busca de trabajo por primera vez. [7] Excl. los solicitantes de trabajo registrados en la oficina de colocación marítima. [8] Solicitantes de trabajo registrados en la oficina de colocación marítima. [9] Población no indígena. [10] Enero-junio. [11] Abril y julio. [12] Abril. [13] Estimaciones oficiales. [14] Excl. las áreas urbanas de Rondonia, Acre, Amazonas, Roraima, Pará, Amapá, Mato Grosso y Goiás. [15] Cuarto trimestre.

10 General level of unemployment
Niveau général du chômage
Nivel general del desempleo

(Thousands — *Milliers* — Millares)

Country — *Pays* — País	Code *Code* Clave	1970	1971	1972	1973	1974	1975	1976	1977	1978	1979
Canada	I	487.0	543.0	553.0	512.0	515.0	690.0	727.0	850.0	911.0	838.0
» . . . . (%)		(5.9)	(6.4)	(6.3)	(5.6)	(5.4)	(6.9)	(7.1)	(8.1)	(8.4)	(7.5)
Colombia[1]	I	.	.	.	.	.	253.1[2]	276.0	266.7	261.7	...
» . . . . (%)							(10.5)	(10.8)	(9.8)	(8.9)	...
Costa Rica	I	.	.	.	.	.	.	30.3[3]	32.8[4]	33.8[4]	34.2[5]
» » (%)		.	.	.	.	.	.	(4.4)	(4.7)	(4.6)	(4.7)
Chile	I[6]	.	.	.	.	.	467.6	409.6	361.7	472.2	460.8
» . . . . (%)		(3.4)	(3.8)	(3.1)	.	.	(14.7)	(13.0)	(11.6)	(13.9)	(13.6)
» (Gran Santiago)	I	42.8	43.7	34.0	47.6	83.9	157.7	192.9	158.2	169.4	169.4
» » » . . . . (%)		(4.1)	(4.2)	(3.3)	(4.8)	(8.3)	(15.0)	(17.1)	(13.9)	(13.7)	(13.4)
Guadeloupe	II a	0.65	0.59	0.74	0.78	1.01	1.04	0.92	1.38	6.41	...
Guatemala[7]	II a	0.66	0.66	0.62	0.57	0.44	0.93	0.36	0.22	0.24	0.22
Guyana[8]	II a	5.18	4.45	3.39	2.90	2.27	3.16	2.97	2.46	...	...
Guyane française[9]	II a	0.22	0.29	0.71	0.53	0.68	0.85	0.80	0.84	0.84	0.86
Honduras	II.[10]	49.4	51.1	51.7	53.1	52.3	78.6	80.8	86.6	91.8	
Jamaica	I	.	.	184.5	176.4	173.8	175.4	197.8	220.2	230.5	
» (%)		.	.	(23.2)	(21.9)	(21.2)	(20.5)	(22.4)	(24.2)	(24.5)	
Nicaragua	II.[10]	20.3	20.5	35.4	54.5	45.9	...	...	...	...	...
» . . . . (%)		(3.7)	(3.6)	(6.0)	(9.1)	(7.3)	...	...	...	...	...
Panamá	I	33.3	36.3	33.2	34.9	30.0[11]	31.6[12]	33.7[13]	44.8[11]	43.8[13]	...
» . . . . (%)		(7.1)	(7.6)	(6.8)	(7.0)	(5.8)	(6.4)	(6.7)	(8.7)	(8.1)	...
Perú	I	201.2	195.7	194.0	191.5	186.9	236.9	258.3	298.2	341.5	387.6
»		(4.7)	(4.4)	(4.2)	(4.2)	(4.0)	(4.9)	(5.2)	(5.8)	(6.5)	(7.1)
Puerto Rico	I[14]	83.0	94.0	100.0	101.0	116.0	157.0	177.0	187.0	175.0	168.0
» » . . . . (%)		(10.7)	(11.6)	(11.9)	(11.6)	(13.2)	(18.1)	(19.5)	(19.9)	(18.1)	(17.0)
Saint-Pierre-et-Miquelon	II a	.	.	.	.	.	.	.	0.08	0.06	0.04
Suriname	II a	2.25	0.96	0.86	1.97	2.20	2.36	1.94	1.66	1.60[15]	...
Trinidad and Tobago	I	46.4	46.4[16]	.	58.9	60.1	58.6	.	57.5	53.5[16]	...
» » » . . . (%)		(12.5)	(12.6)	.	(15.4)	(15.3)	(15.0)	.	(13.4)	(12.2)	...
United States	I	4 088.0	4 993.0	4 840.0	4 304.0	5 076.0	7 830.0	7 288.0	6 855.0	6 047.0	5 963.0
» » . . . . . . (%)		(4.9)	(5.9)	(5.6)	(4.9)	(5.6)	(8.5)	(7.7)	(7.0)	(6.0)	(5.8)
Uruguay (Montevideo)	I	39.3	41.2	41.7[16]	49.4[16]	38.2[17]	.	68.2	64.1	53.0	43.2
» . . . . (%)		(7.5)	(7.6)	(7.7)	(8.9)	(8.1)	.	(12.8)	(11.8)	(10.2)	(8.4)
Venezuela	I	198.8	195.2	.	.	219.5	268.7	221.6[18]	192.6	180.4[18]	244.6[18]
» . . . . (%)		(6.3)	(6.0)	.	.	...	...	...	(4.8)	(4.3)	(5.6)
Virgin Is. (US)	II a	.	.	.	.	.	2.58	2.78	...	...	...

EXPLANATORY NOTES: See p. 271.

Codes: See p. 284.

[1] Bogotá, Barranquilla, Bucaramanga, Cali, Manizales, Medellín and Pasto. [2] Sep. [3] July and Nov. [4] March, July and Nov. [5] March and July. [6] Fourth quarter. [7] Guatemala City, Quezaltenango, Escuintla and Puerto Barrios; prior to 1973: Guatemala City only. [8] Georgetown, New Amsterdam and Anna Regina districts. [9] Cayenne and Kourou. [10] Official estimates. [11] Oct. [12] Nov. [13] Aug. [14] Excl. persons temporarily laid off. [15] Jan.-Sep. [16] First semester. [17] Aug. 1974-Feb. 1975. [18] Second semester.

NOTES EXPLICATIVES: Voir p. 274.

Codes: Voir p. 284.

[1] Bogotá, Barranquilla, Bucaramanga, Cali, Manizales, Medellín et Pasto. [2] Sept. [3] Juillet et nov. [4] Mars, juillet et nov. [5] Mars et juillet. [6] Quatrième trimestre. [7] Ville de Guatemala, Quezaltenango, Escuintla et Puerto Barrios ; avant 1973 : ville de Guatemala seulement. [8] Districts de Georgetown, de New Amsterdam et d'Anna Regina. [9] Cayenne et Kourou. [10] Evaluations officielles. [11] Oct. [12] Nov. [13] Août. [14] Non compris les personnes temporairement mises à pied. [15] Janv.-sept. [16] Premier semestre. [17] Août 1974-fév. 1975. [18] Deuxième semestre.

NOTAS EXPLICATIVAS: Véase pág. 277.

Claves: Véase pág. 284.

[1] Bogotá, Barranquilla, Bucaramanga, Cali, Manizales, Medellín y Pasto. [2] Sept. [3] Julio y nov. [4] Marzo, julio y nov. [5] Marzo y julio. [6] Cuarto trimestre. [7] Ciudad de Guatemala, Quezaltenango, Escuintla y Puerto Barrios; antes de 1973: Ciudad de Guatemala solamente. [8] Distritos de Georgetown, de Nueva Amsterdam y de Anna Regina. [9] Cayena y Kourou. [10] Estimaciones oficiales. [11] Oct. [12] Nov. [13] Agosto. [14] Excl. las personas temporalmente despedidas. [15] Enero-sept. [16] Primer semestre. [17] Agosto 1974-febr. 1975. [18] Segundo semestre.

UNEMPLOYMENT

10 General level of unemployment
Niveau général du chômage
Nivel general del desempleo

(Thousands — *Milliers* — Millares)

Country — *Pays* — País	Code *Code* Clave	1970	1971	1972	1973	1974	1975	1976	1977	1978	1979
ASIA — ASIE ASIA											
Brunei	II	.	.	.	.	1.28 [1]	1.63	1.68	1.92	2.21	2.76
» . . . . (%)		.	.	.	.	.	(8.2)	(7.9)	(8.1)	(8.7)	(10.0)
Burma	II	76.4	90.0	108.2	194.1 [2]	193.9	197.3	227.7	296.8	415.0	445.0
Cyprus	II a	2.81	2.85	2.52	3.31	11.2 [3]	22.5	14.5	6.14	4.02	3.69
» . . . . (%)		(1.1)	(1.1)	(0.9)	(1.2)	(4.3)	(10.9)	(7.1)	(3.1)	(2.0)	(1.8)
Hong Kong	I	.	.	.	.	.	180.0 [4]	98.5	83.0	57.8	61.4
» » . . . . . (%)							(9.1)	(5.1)	(4.3)	(2.9)	(2.9)
India	II A	3 725.7	4 602.3	5 927.6	7 713.8	8 378.3	8 917.6	9 563.2	10 512.7	11 837.3	13 794.0
Indonesia	II A	30.7	37.1	90.5	84.3 [5]	89.1	115.1	157.0	153.5	157.2 [6]	160.5
Iraq	II	5.18	5.03	8.02	9.99	9.03	8.62	9.58	9.58	10.5	8.10
Israel [7]	I	38.3	35.7	29.1	29.7	34.3	35.1	42.5	47.4	44.7	37.0
» . . . . (%)		(3.8)	(3.5)	(2.7)	(2.6)	(3.0)	(3.1)	(3.6)	(3.9)	(3.6)	(2.9)
Japan	I	590.0	640.0	730.0	680.0	730.0	1 000.0	1 080.0	1 100.0	1 240.0	1 170.0
» . . . . (%)		(1.1)	(1.2)	(1.4)	(1.3)	(1.4)	(1.9)	(2.0)	(2.0)	(2.2)	(2.1)
Korea, Rep. of	I	454.0	476.0	499.0	461.0	494.0	510.0	505.0	511.0	442.0	542.0
» » » . . . . . (%)		(4.5)	(4.5)	(4.5)	(4.0)	(4.1)	(4.1)	(3.9)	(3.8)	(3.2)	(3.8)
Malaysia :											
Peninsular Malaysia	II A	169.3	157.1	160.7	154.7	134.5	125.1	110.6	112.8	107.2	94.4
Sabah	II A	...	...	0.86	0.81	0.82	0.93	1.12	1.02	0.79	0.63
Sarawak	II A	...	...	2.48	5.47	9.53	6.60	6.75	8.83	9.34	10.5
Pakistan	II A	.	188.4	157.4	167.6	189.6	205.2	198.5	155.3	146.4	146.4
Philippines	I	.	666.0	867.0	690.0	584.0	581.0 [8]	780.0	781.1 [9]	873.0	761.0 [10]
» . . . . (%)		.	(5.2)	(6.3)	(4.8)	(4.0)	(3.9)	(5.2)	(5.1)	(5.2)	(4.4)
Singapore	I [11]	42.0	35.0	36.0	37.8	34.0	39.5	40.5	36.9	35.7	35.3
» . . . . (%)		(6.0)	(4.8)	(4.7)	(4.5)	(4.0)	(4.5)	(4.5)	(3.9)	(3.6)	(3.3)
»	II a	50.5	37.8	36.2	35.7	32.5	41.6	34.9	31.7 [12]	19.4 [13]	10.9
Sri Lanka	II A	381.0	419.7	440.3	457.7	489.3	521.7	547.2	572.6	...	...
République arabe syrienne	I [14]	.	123.4	80.9	76.5	87.2	88.5	113.4	100.3	90.3	82.1
» » » . . (%)		(6.4)	(7.5)	(4.7)	(4.5)	(5.1)	(4.8)	(6.2)	(5.0)	(4.5)	(3.8)
Thailand	I	.	31.9	83.1	71.8	92.1	66.7	142.2	190.4	173.4	...
» . . . . (%)		.	(0.2)	(0.5)	(0.4)	(0.6)	(0.4)	(0.9)	(1.0)	(0.9)	...
EUROPE — EUROPE EUROPA											
Austria	II a	59.4	52.9	50.0	41.3	41.3	55.5	55.3	51.2	58.6	56.7
» . . . . (%)		(2.4)	(2.1)	(1.9)	(1.6)	(1.5)	(2.0)	(2.0)	(1.8)	(2.1)	(2.0)
Belgique	II a/b [15]	82.0	84.5	105.2	111.2	124.1	207.8	266.6	307.6	333.4	351.8
» . . . . (%)		(2.9)	(2.9)	(3.4)	(3.6)	(4.0)	(6.7)	(8.5)	(9.8)	(10.5)	(10.9)
» . . . . (%)	II [16]	33.7	39.6	36.6	34.3	42.0	82.5	58.5	69.0	69.4	69.6
»		(1.3)	(1.5)	(1.4)	(1.3)	(1.5)	(3.1)	(2.2)	(2.6)	(2.6)	(2.6)

EXPLANATORY NOTES: See p. 271.

Codes: See p. 284.

[1] May-Dec. [2] Prior to 1973: Greater Rangoon (Rangoon, Insein, Kamayut, Okkalapa) and Mandalay only. [3] Beginning July 1974: due to a change in the geographical scope of the series, data are not comparable with those for preceding period. [4] Sep. [5] Prior to 1973: code II a. [6] April-Dec. [7] Incl. persons who did not work in the country during the previous 12 months. [8] Feb. and Aug. [9] First, third and fourth quarters. [10] First, second and third quarters. [11] June. [12] Jan.-Nov. [13] Prior to 1977: code II A. [14] Sep. [15] Wholly unemployed. Unemployment rates refer only to wholly unemployed receiving insurance benefits. [16] Daily average of partially unemployed (prior to 1975: controlled partially unemployed only).

NOTES EXPLICATIVES: Voir p. 274.

Codes: Voir p. 284.

[1] Mai-déc. [2] Avant 1973 : Grand Rangoon (Rangoon, Insein, Kamayut, Okkalapa) et Mandalay seulement. [3] A partir de juillet 1974 : en raison d'un changement de la portée géographique de la série, les données ne sont pas comparables avec celles de la période précédente. [4] Sept. [5] Avant 1973 : code II a. [6] Avril-déc. [7] Y compris les personnes qui n'ont pas travaillé dans le pays pendant les 12 mois précédents. [8] Fév. et août. [9] Premier, troisième et quatrième trimestres. [10] Premier, second et troisième trimestres. [11] Juin. [12] Janv.-nov. [13] Avant 1977 : code II A. [14] Sept. [15] Chômeurs complets. Les taux de chômage se réfèrent uniquement aux chômeurs complets indemnisés. [16] Moyenne journalière du nombre de chômeurs partiels (avant 1975 : chômeurs partiels contrôlés seulement).

NOTAS EXPLICATIVAS: Véase pág. 277.

Claves: Véase pág. 284.

[1] Mayo-dic. [2] Antes de 1973: Gran Rangún (Rangún, Insein, Kamayut, Okkalapa) y Mandalay únicamente. [3] A partir de julio de 1974: en razón de un cambio del alcance geográfico de la serie, los datos no son comparables a los del período precedente. [4] Sept. [5] Antes de 1973: clave IIa. [6] Abril-dic. [7] Incl. las personas que no trabajaron en el país en los 12 meses precedentes. [8] Febr. y agosto. [9] Primero, tercero y cuarto trimestres. [10] Primero, segundo y tercer trimestres. [11] Junio. [12] Enero-nov. [13] Antes de 1977: clave IIA. [14] Sept. [15] Desempleados completos. Las tasas de desempleo se refieren solamente a los desempleados completos que reciben prestaciones. [16] Promedio diario de desempleados parciales (antes de 1975: desempleados parciales controlados únicamente).

10 General level of unemployment
Niveau général du chômage
Nivel general del desempleo

(Thousands — *Milliers* — Millares)

Country — *Pays* — País	Code / *Code* / Clave	1970	1971	1972	1973	1974	1975	1976	1977	1978	1979
Denmark	II a/c	24.6	32.2	32.9	21.4	50.1	123.6	133.2 [1]	163.6	190.7	161.8
» (%)		.	.	.	(1.1)	(2.5)	(6.0)	(5.3)	(6.4)	(7.3)	(6.1)
España	I	.	.	.	321.9	381.1	536.4	680.9	756.7	1 001.6	1 218.2
» (%)		.	.	.	(2.5)	(2.9)	(4.0)	(5.1)	(5.7)	(7.6)	(9.2)
»	II a	145.6	190.3	190.9	149.6	150.3	256.6	376.4	539.6	818.5	1 037.2
» (%)		(1.1)	(1.5)	(1.5)	(1.1)	(1.1)	(1.9)	(2.8)	(4.1)	(6.2)	(7.9)
Finland	I	41.0	49.0	55.0	51.0	39.0	51.0	90.0 [2]	137.0	169.0	139.0
» (%)		(1.9)	(2.3)	(2.5)	(2.3)	(1.7)	(2.2)	(4.0)	(6.1)	(7.5)	(6.1)
France [3]	II a	262.1	338.2	383.5	393.9	497.7	839.7	933.5	1 071.7	1 166.9	1 349.8
Germany, Fed. Rep. of	II a	148.8	185.1	246.4	273.5	582.5	1 074.2	1 060.3	1 030.0	992.9	876.1
» » » (%)		(0.7)	(0.8)	(1.1)	(1.2)	(2.6)	(4.7)	(4.6)	(4.5)	(4.3)	(3.8)
Gibraltar	II a	0.04	0.04	0.05	0.04	0.06	0.11	0.15	0.17	0.17	0.15
Grèce	II a [4]	48.7	30.3	23.8	21.4	27.1	35.0	28.5	27.7	30.9	31.6
Iceland	II a	1.10	0.57	0.46	0.37	0.37	0.64	0.51	0.37	0.45	0.50
» (%)		(1.3)	(0.7)	(0.5)	(0.4)	(0.4)	(0.7)	(0.5)	(0.4)	(0.4)	(0.5)
Ireland	II b [5]	41.6	42.4	48.2	44.0	48.1	75.4	83.5	81.9	74.7	66.4
» (%)		(7.2)	(7.2)	(8.1)	(7.2)	(7.9)	(12.2)	(12.3)	(11.8)	(10.7)	(9.3)
»	II a	58.8	57.2	66.6	52.0	67.1	96.2	107.8	106.4	99.2	89.6
Isle of Man	II a	.	.	0.50	0.38	0.35	0.52	0.70	0.76	0.63	0.47
» » » (%)		.	.	.	(2.6)	(2.4)	(3.1)	(3.5)	(3.7)	(3.1)	(2.3)
Italie	I	1 111.0	1 109.0	1 297.0	1 305.0	1 113.0	1 230.0	1 426.0	1 545.0	1 571.0	1 698.0
» (%)		(5.4)	(5.4)	(6.4)	(6.4)	(5.4)	(5.9)	(6.7)	(7.2)	(7.2)	(7.7)
Luxembourg	II a	0.04	0.02	0.04	0.05	0.06	0.26	0.46	0.82	1.17	1.06
Malta	II a	3.93	5.34	6.88	6.64	5.85	5.13	4.52	4.62	4.27	3.39
» (%)		(4.9)	(5.6)	(5.8)	(4.5)	(6.1)	(4.3)	(4.2)	(4.3)	(3.5)	(2.7)
Netherlands	II a	46.4	62.0	107.9	109.9	134.9	195.3	210.9	203.5	205.6 [6]	210.0
» (%)		(1.1)	(1.6)	(2.8)	(2.8)	(3.5)	(5.0)	(5.3)	(5.1)	(5.0)	(5.1)
Norway	I	.	.	28.0	26.0	25.0	40.0	32.0	27.0	35.0	38.0
» (%)		.	.	(1.7)	(1.5)	(1.5)	(2.3)	(1.8)	(1.5)	(1.7)	(2.0)
»	II a	12.5	12.2	14.8	12.8	10.7	19.6	19.9	16.1	20.0	24.1
» (%)		(0.8)	(0.8)	(1.0)	(0.8)	(0.7)	(1.3)	(1.3)	(1.1)	(1.3)	(1.5)
Portugal	I	.	.	.	.	66.5	177.5	260.0	308.5	333.5	343.5
» (%)		.	.	.	.	(1.8)	(4.5)	(6.4)	(7.5)	(8.1)	(8.2)
Suisse	II a	0.10	0.10	0.11	0.08	0.22	10.2	20.7	12.0	10.2	10.3
» (%)		(—)	(—)	(—)	(—)	(—)	(0.3)	(0.7)	(0.4)	(0.4)	(0.3)
Sweden	I	59.0	101.0	107.0	98.0	80.0	67.0	66.0	75.0	94.0	88.0
» (%)		(1.5)	(2.5)	(2.7)	(2.5)	(2.0)	(1.6)	(1.6)	(1.8)	(2.2)	(2.1)
»	II a/b [7]	29.5	45.3	48.2	46.0	39.0	36.7	32.7	34.2	45.7	45.1
» (%)		(1.4)	(2.0)	(2.0)	(1.9)	(1.5)	(1.4)	(1.2)	(1.2)	(1.6)	(1.5)
Turquie	II a	43.8	44.9	43.9	44.8	81.7	116.8	141.3	142.7	166.8	170.7

EXPLANATORY NOTES: See p. 271.

Codes: See p. 284.

1 Prior to 1976: excl. part-time insured unemployed. Unemployment rates are computed in relation to the labour force (prior to 1976: employees). 2 Beginning 1976: sampling design revised. 3 Beginning June 1972: excl. certain unemployed over 60 years of age (recipients of " income maintenance benefits "). 4 Excl. persons who do not re-register after one month (prior to April 1976: six months). 5 Excl. agriculture, fishing and private domestic service. 6 Persons seeking work for 25 hours or more a week (prior to 1978: 30 hours or more). 7 Unemployment among members of unemployment insurance funds.

NOTES EXPLICATIVES: Voir p. 274.

Codes: Voir p. 284.

1 *Avant 1976 : non compris les chômeurs assurés partiellement. Les taux de chômage sont calculés par rapport à la population active (avant 1976 : salariés).* 2 *A partir de 1976 : plan d'échantillonnage révisé.* 3 *A partir de juin 1972 : non compris certains chômeurs de plus de 60 ans (bénéficiaires de la « garantie de ressources »).* 4 *Non compris les personnes qui ne renouvellent pas leur inscription après un mois (avant avril 1976 : six mois).* 5 *Non compris l'agriculture, la pêche et les services domestiques privés.* 6 *Personnes en quête d'un emploi de 25 heures ou plus par semaine (avant 1978 : 30 heures ou plus).* 7 *Chômage parmi les membres des caisses d'assurance-chômage.*

NOTAS EXPLICATIVAS: Véase pág. 277.

Claves: Véase pág. 284.

1 Antes de 1976: excl. los desempleados parcialmente asegurados. Las tasas de desempleo se calculan con respecto a la población activa (antes de 1976: asalariados). 2 A partir de 1976: diseño de la muestra revisado. 3 A partir de junio de 1972: excl. ciertos desempleados de más de 60 años (beneficiarios de la « garantía de recursos »). 4 Excl. las personas que no renuevan su inscripción después de un mes (antes de abril de 1976: seis meses). 5 Excl. la agricultura, la pesca y el servicio doméstico particular. 6 Personas que buscan trabajo de 25 horas o más por semana (antes de 1978: 30 horas o más). 7 Desempleo entre los afiliados a las cajas de seguro de desempleo.

UNEMPLOYMENT

10 General level of unemployment
Niveau général du chômage
Nivel general del desempleo

(Thousands — *Milliers* — Millares)

Country — *Pays* — País	Code *Code* Clave	1970	1971	1972	1973	1974	1975	1976	1977	1978	1979
United Kingdom	II a[1]	612.2	792.1	875.6	618.8	614.9[2]	977.6	1 358.8[3]	1 483.6	1 475.0	1 390.5
» » . . . . (%)		(2.6)	(3.5)	(3.8)	(2.7)	(2.6)	(4.1)	(5.7)	(6.2)	(6.1)	(5.7)
» »	II a[4]	21.9	49.4	79.2	11.6	207.4[5]	62.6[6]	25.0[7]	20.6	11.2	13.0
» » . . . . . . (%)		(0.1)	(0.2)	(0.3)	(0.1)	(0.9)	(0.3)	(0.1)	(0.1)	(—)	(0.1)
Yugoslavia	II a	319.6	291.3	315.3	381.6	448.6	540.1	635.3	700.4	734.8	762.0
» . . . . (%)		(7.7)	(6.7)	(7.0)	(8.1)	(9.0)	(10.2)	(11.4)	(11.9)	(12.0)	(11.9)
OCEANIA — OCÉANIE OCEANÍA											
American Samoa	I	.	.	.	1.23	1.11	1.64	1.72	1.36	1.36	1.32
» » . . . . . (%)		.	.	.	...	...	...	(19.4)	(15.0)	(14.0)	(13.0)
Australia	I	90.6	107.3	150.1	136.3	161.6	302.5	298.1	358.1	402.1	404.7
» . . . . (%)		(1.6)	(1.9)	(2.6)	(2.3)	(2.7)	(4.9)	(4.8)	(5.7)	(6.3)	(6.2)
Fiji	II a	0.22	0.13	0.13	0.20	0.91	0.14	0.19	0.29	0.16	0.17
Guam	I	.	.	.	.	2.90[8]	2.70[8]	2.64	2.04	2.62	2.80
» . . . . (%)		.	.	.	.	(9.6)	(9.6)	(9.7)	(7.3)	(8.3)	(8.0)
New Zealand	II a	1.60	3.11	5.68	2.32	0.95	4.17	5.36	7.38	22.3	25.2
Nouvelle Calédonie	II a	.	.	.	0.69	0.50	0.58	0.74	0.78	0.83	0.86
Polynésie française	II a	.	.	.	.	.	.	0.05	0.06	0.19	0.25

EXPLANATORY NOTES: See p. 271.   NOTES EXPLICATIVES: Voir p. 274.   NOTAS EXPLICATIVAS: Véase pág. 277.

I: Labour force sample surveys.

II: Administrative records.
II a: Registered unemployed.
II A: Registered applicants for work (incl. persons in employment). } Employment office statistics.
II b: Compulsory unemployment insurance schemes.
II c: Statistics of trade union benefit funds.

I: *Enquêtes par sondage sur la main-d'œuvre.*

II: *Registres administratifs.*
II a: *Chômeurs enregistrés.*
II A: *Demandeurs d'emploi enregistrés (y compris les personnes ayant un emploi).* } *Statistiques des bureaux de placement.*
II b: *Régimes d'assurance-chômage obligatoire.*
II c: *Statistiques des caisses syndicales.*

I: Encuestas por muestra sobre la fuerza trabajadora.

II: Registros administrativos.
II a: Desempleados registrados.
II A: Solicitantes de trabajo registrados (incl. las personas que tienen trabajo). } Estadísticas de las oficinas de colocación.
II b: Regímenes del seguro obligatorio de desempleo.
II c: Estadísticas de las cajas de los sindicatos.

[1] Excl. persons temporarily laid off. [2] Jan-Nov. [3] Jan-Oct. and Dec. [4] Persons temporarily laid off. [5] Jan-Sep. [6] Feb.-Dec. [7] Jan.-Oct. [8] Sep.

[1] *Non compris les personnes temporairement mises à pied.* [2] *Janv.-nov.* [3] *Janv.-oct. et déc.* [4] *Personnes temporairement mises à pied.* [5] *Janv.-sept.* [6] *Fév.-déc.* [7] *Janv.-oct.* [8] *Sept.*

[1] Excl. las personas temporalmente despedidas. [2] Enero-nov. [3] Enero-oct. y dic. [4] Personas temporalmente despedidas. [5] Enero-sept. [6] Febr.-dic. [7] Enero-oct. [8] Sept.

11 Structure of unemployment
Structure du chômage
Estructura del desempleo

AFRICA — AFRIQUE — AFRICA

Rép.-Unie du Cameroun [1]

A Industrial groups *(Employment office statistics)*
Groupes d'activité économique *(Statistiques des bureaux de placement)*
Grupos de actividad económica *(Estadísticas de las oficinas de colocación)*

		1	2	3	4	5	6	7	8	9	0
Date / Date / Fecha	Total	Agriculture, forestry, fishing / Agriculture, sylviculture, pêche / Agricultura, silvicultura, pesca	Mining, quarrying / Industries extractives / Minas, canteras	Manufacturing / Industries manufacturières / Industrias manufactureras	Electricity, gas, water / Electricité, gaz, eau / Electricidad, gas, agua	Construction / Construction / Construcción	Trade, restaurants and hotels / Commerce, restaurants et hôtels / Comercio, restaurantes y hoteles	Transport, storage, communication / Transports, entrepôts, communications / Transportes, almacenaje, comunicaciones	Financing, insur., real est., business serv. / Banques, assur., aff. imm., serv. aux entreprises / Bancos, seguros, bienes inm., serv. para empresas	Community, social, and pers. services / Services à collectivité, services sociaux et pers. / Servicios comunales, sociales y personales	Activities not adequately described [2] / Activités mal désignées [2] / Actividades no bien especificadas [2]
1970	2 167	37	9	56	14	323	174	99	12	152	1 291
1971	2 383	75	12	44	17	408	252	147	15	71	1 342
1972	2 938	74	8	48	41	541	267	292	14	183	1 470
1973	4 040	84	11	53	19	896	378	417	18	295	1 869
1974	4 233	98	16	64	18	916	441	425	21	325	1 909
1975	4 284	101	18	76	21	1 001	398	348	19	421	1 881
1976	4 202	119	21	84	23	1 251	397	318	22	443	1 524
1977	3 840	225	23	101	32	1 349	546	345	21	524	674
1978	4 625	276	26	129	44	1 397	563	431	31	474	1 254
1979	3 407	2 111	21	145	38	1 157	486	229	27	367	696

B Occupational groups *(Employment office statistics)*
Groupes de professions *(Statistiques des bureaux de placement)*
Grupos de ocupaciones *(Estadísticas de las oficinas de colocación)*

		0/1	2	3	4	5	6	7/8/9	X
Date / Date / Fecha	Total	Professional, technical and related workers / Personnel des professions scientifiques, techniques, libérales et assimilées / Profesionales, técnicos y trabajadores asimilados	Administrative and managerial workers / Directeurs et cadres administratifs supérieurs / Directores y funcionarios públicos superiores	Clerical and related workers / Personnel administratif et travailleurs assimilés / Personal administrativo y trabajadores asimilados	Sales workers / Personnel commercial et vendeurs / Comerciantes y vendedores	Service workers / Travailleurs spécialisés dans les services / Trabajadores de los servicios	Agricultural, animal husbandry and forestry workers, fishermen and hunters / Agriculteurs, éleveurs, forestiers, pêcheurs et chasseurs / Obreros agrícolas y forestales, pescadores y cazadores	Production and related workers, transport equipment operators and labourers / Ouvriers et manœuvres non agricoles et conducteurs d'engins de transport / Trabajadores no agrícolas, conductores de máquinas y vehículos de transporte y trabajadores asimilados	Workers not classifiable by occupation [2] / Travailleurs ne pouvant être classés selon la profession [2] / Trabajadores que no pueden ser clasificados según la ocupación [2]
1974	4 233	98	16	64	18	916	441	771	1 909
1975	4 284	101	18	76	21	1 001	398	788	1 881
1976	4 202	119	21	84	23	1 251	397	783	1 524
1977	3 840	117	12	93	21	1 377	270	691	1 259
1978	4 625	341	11	173	26	1 431	319	934	1 390

[1] Douala, Yaoundé, Nkongsamba and Garoua.
[2] Incl. persons seeking work for the first time.

[1] *Douala, Yaoundé, Nkongsamba et Garoua.* [2] *Y compris les personnes en quête d'emploi pour la première fois.*

[1] Duala, Yaundé, Nkongsamba y Garoua. [2] Incl. las personas en busca de trabajo por primera vez.

11 Structure of unemployment
Structure du chômage
Estructura del desempleo

Egypt

A Industrial groups *(Labour force sample surveys)*
Groupes d'activité économique *(Enquêtes par sondage sur la main-d'œuvre)*
Grupos de actividad económica *(Encuestas por muestra sobre la fuerza trabajadora)*

Date [1] / Date [1] / Fecha [1]	Total	1 Agriculture, forestry, fishing / Agriculture, sylviculture, pêche / Agricultura, silvicultura, pesca	2 Mining, quarrying / Industries extractives / Minas, canteras	3 Manufacturing / Industries manufacturières / Industrias manufactureras	4 Electricity, gas, water / Electricité, gaz, eau / Electricidad, gas, agua	5 Construction / Construction / Construcción	6 Trade, restaurants and hotels / Commerce, restaurants et hôtels / Comercio, restaurantes y hoteles	7 Transport, storage, communication / Transports, entrepôts, communications / Transportes, almacenaje, comunicaciones	8 Financing, insur., real est., business serv. / Banques, assur., aff. imm., serv. aux entreprises / Bancos, seguros, bienes inm., serv. para empresas	9 Community, social, and pers. services / Services à collectivité, serv. sociaux et pers. / Servicios comunales, sociales y personales	0 Activities not adequately described [2] / Activités mal désignées [2] / Actividades no bien especificadas [2]
1971	153 100	2 000	—	7 800	—	1 700	6 000	800	300	4 500	130 000
1972	134 600	2 300	—	5 000	—	1 100	2 700	1 600	300	2 100	119 500
1973	145 100	1 000	—	2 000	100	100	1 700	1 100	100	1 200	137 800
1974	208 600	400	—	1 200	—	100	100	200	—	100	206 500
1975	233 400	1 200	—	300	—	200	700	900	—	100	230 000
1977	296 100	27 500	—	1 300	—	800	400	400	100	1 400	264 200
1978	354 500	900	—	2 500	200	900	300	200	—	600	348 900

B Occupational groups *(Labour force sample surveys)*
Groupes de professions *(Enquêtes par sondage sur la main-d'œuvre)*
Grupos de ocupaciones *(Encuestas por muestra sobre la fuerza trabajadora)*

Date [1] / Date [1] / Fecha [1]	Total	0/1 Professional, technical and related workers / Personnel des professions scientifiques, techniques, libérales et assimilées / Profesionales, técnicos y trabajadores asimilados	2 Administrative and managerial workers / Directeurs et cadres administratifs supérieurs / Directores y funcionarios públicos superiores	3 Clerical and related workers / Personnel administratif et travailleurs assimilés / Personal administrativo y trabajadores asimilados	4 Sales workers / Personnel commercial et vendeurs / Comerciantes y vendedores	5 Service workers / Travailleurs spécialisés dans les services / Trabajadores de los servicios	6 Agricultural, animal husbandry and forestry workers, fishermen and hunters / Agriculteurs, éleveurs, forestiers, pêcheurs et chasseurs / Trabajadores agrícolas y forestales, pescadores y cazadores	7/8/9 Production and related workers, transport equipment operators and labourers / Ouvriers et manœuvres non agricoles et conducteurs d'engins de transport / Obreros no agrícolas, conductores de máquinas y vehículos de transp. y trabaj. asimilados	X Workers not classifiable by occupation [2] / Travailleurs ne pouvant être classés selon la profession [2] / Trabajadores que no pueden ser clasificados según la ocupación [2]
1970	198 000	2 600	600	3 300	4 200	6 500	10 000	42 100	128 700
1971	153 100	3 300	1 200	1 200	1 800	1 300	2 800	11 300	130 200
1972	134 600	3 100	300	1 000	1 400	1 300	2 500	9 500	115 500
1973	145 100	1 400	—	2 800	600	1 800	600	5 200	132 700
1974	208 600	1 200	—	1 000	1 300	1 900	1 200	12 800	189 200
1975	233 400	1 600	100	1 500	300	100	400	1 000	228 400
1977	296 100	2 800	—	100	300	1 200	1 800	5 500	284 400
1978	354 500	4 500	700	1 800	600	1 000	2 300	7 600	336 000

[1] May of each year. [2] Incl. persons seeking work for the first time.

[1] *Mai de chaque année.* [2] *Y compris les personnes en quête d'emploi pour la première fois.*

[1] Mayo de cada año. [2] Incl. las personas en busca de trabajo por primera vez.

11 Structure of unemployment
Structure du chômage
Estructura del desempleo

Ghana

A Industrial groups *(Employment office statistics)*
Groupes d'activité économique *(Statistiques des bureaux de placement)*
Grupos de actividad económica *(Estadísticas de las oficinas de colocación)*

Date [1] / Date [1] / Fecha [1]	Total	1 Agriculture, forestry, fishing / Agriculture, sylviculture, pêche / Agricultura, silvicultura, pesca	2 Mining, quarrying / Industries extractives / Minas, canteras	3 Manufacturing [2] / Industries manufacturières [2] / Industrias manufactureras [2]	4 Electricity, gas, water / Electricité, gaz, eau / Electricidad, gas, agua	5 Construction / Construction / Construcción	6× Trade [3] / Commerce [3] / Comercio [3]	7 Transport, storage, communication / Transports, entrepôts, communications / Transportes, almacenaje, comunicaciones	8 Financing, insur., real est., business serv. / Banques, assur., aff. imm., serv. aux entreprises / Bancos, seguros, bienes inm., serv. para empresas	6×;9× Community, social, and pers. services [4] / Services à collectivité, serv. sociaux et pers. [4] / Servicios comunales, sociales y personales [4]	Activities not adequately described [5] / Activités mal désignées [5] / Actividades no bien especificadas [5]
1970	15 763	731	227	1 044	256	2 802	296	415	197	1 232	8 563
1971	18 866	2 263	281	1 097	357	3 096	382	417	256	152	10 565
1972	31 961	2 885	587	1 374	412	5 615	62	709	42	2 434	17 841
1973	25 173	2 523	639	1 719	30	4 014	412	635	275	2 044	12 882
1974	28 752	1 959	749	1 656	1 336	2 355	1 072	780	768	1 769	16 308
1975	30 723	978	475	1 827	611	4 073	434	561	1 284	1 610	18 870
1976	32 924	3 783	369	2 076	578	4 735	1 116	619	806	3 305	15 537
1977	32 154	3 232	379	3 175	380	4 929	711	403	775	1 691	16 478
1978	33 824	4 043	307	2 404	290	4 185	599	380	513	2 165	19 038
1979	30 927	4 266	530	2 366	678	2 745	569	496	674	2 453	16 150

B Occupational groups *(Employment office statistics)*
Groupes de professions *(Statistiques des bureaux de placement)*
Grupos de ocupaciones *(Estadísticas de las oficinas de colocación)*

Date [1] / Date [1] / Fecha [1]	Total	0/1 Professional, technical and related workers / Personnel des professions scientifiques, techniques, libérales et assimilées / Profesionales, técnicos y trabajadores asimilados	2 Administrative and managerial workers / Directeurs et cadres administratifs supérieurs / Directores y funcionarios públicos superiores	3 Clerical and related workers / Personnel administratif et travailleurs assimilés / Personal administrativo y trabajadores asimilados	4 Sales workers / Personnel commercial et vendeurs / Comerciantes y vendedores	5 Service workers / Travailleurs spécialisés dans les services / Trabajadores de los servicios	6 Agricultural, animal husbandry and forestry workers, fishermen and hunters / Agriculteurs, éleveurs, forestiers, pêcheurs et chasseurs / Trabajadores agrícolas y forestales, pescadores y cazadores	7/8/9 Production and related workers, transport equipment operators and labourers / Ouvriers et manœuvres non agricoles et conducteurs d'engins de transport / Obreros no agrícolas, conductores de máquinas y vehículos de transporte y trabajadores asimilados	X Workers not classifiable by occupation [5] / Travailleurs ne pouvant être classés selon la profession [5] / Trabajadores que no pueden ser clasificados según la ocupación [5]
1970	15 763	76	2	1 136	29	690	80	7 507	6 243
1971	18 866	125	2	986	31	691	58	8 585	8 388
1972	31 961	67	2	1 602	37	1 225	69	13 265	15 694
1973	25 173	64	2	1 425	89	934	83	9 846	12 730
1974	28 752	110	12	1 191	124	1 046	56	10 198	15 589
1975	30 723	140	3	1 091	120	1 075	82	12 158	16 054
1976	32 924	125	29	1 466	67	1 266	82	14 255	15 634
1977	32 154	108	—	1 208	150	1 269	94	12 836	16 489
1978	33 824	100	3	1 085	86	1 084	81	12 347	19 038
1979	30 927	93	1	1 063	36	1 068	74	12 442	16 150

[1] March, June, Sep. and Dec. [2] Incl. repair services. [3] Excl. restaurants and hotels. [4] Excl. repair services. Incl. restaurants and hotels. [5] Incl. persons seeking work for the first time.

[1] Mars, juin, sept. et déc. [2] Y compris les services de réparation. [3] Non compris les restaurants et les hôtels. [4] Non compris les services de réparation. Y compris les restaurants et les hôtels. [5] Y compris les personnes en quête d'emploi pour la première fois.

[1] Marzo, junio, sept. y dic. [2] Incl. los servicios de reparación. [3] Excl. los restaurantes y los hoteles. [4] Excl. los servicios de reparación. Incl. los restaurantes y los hoteles. [5] Incl. las personas en busca de trabajo por primera vez.

11 Structure of unemployment
Structure du chômage
Estructura del desempleo

Liberia

Occupational groups *(Employment office statistics)*
Groupes de professions *(Statistiques des bureaux de placement)*
Grupos de ocupaciones *(Estadísticas de las oficinas de colocación)*

		0/1	2	3	4	5	6	7/8/9	X
Date / *Date* / Fecha	Total	Professional, technical and related workers / *Personnel des professions scientifiques, techniques, libérales et assimilées* / Profesionales, técnicos y trabajadores asimilados	Administrative and managerial workers / *Directeurs et cadres administratifs supérieurs* / Directores y funcionarios públicos superiores	Clerical and related workers / *Personnel administratif et travailleurs assimilés* / Personal administrativo y trabajadores asimilados	Sales workers / *Personnel commercial et vendeurs* / Comerciantes y vendedores	Service workers / *Travailleurs spécialisés dans les services* / Trabajadores de los servicios	Agricultural, animal husbandry and forestry workers, fishermen and hunters / *Agriculteurs, éleveurs, forestiers, pêcheurs et chasseurs* / Trabajadores agrícolas y forestales, pescadores y cazadores	Production and related workers, transport equipment operators and labourers / *Ouvriers et manœuvres non agricoles et conducteurs d'engins de transport* / Obreros no agrícolas, conductores de máquinas y vehiculos de transp. y trabaj. asimilados	Workers not classifiable by occupation / *Travailleurs ne pouvant être classés selon la profession* / Trabajadores que no pueden ser clasificados según la ocupación
1972	107	3	1	22	5	1	52	7	16
1973	140	69	1	7	10	11	34	—	9
1974	108	71	1	6	16	4	7	1	2
1975	476	23	1	53	18	24	82	200	75

Mauritius

(ISCO — CITP — CIUO 1958)

Occupational groups *(Employment office statistics)*
Groupes de professions *(Statistiques des bureaux de placement)*
Grupos de ocupaciones *(Estadísticas de las oficinas de colocación)*

Date / *Date* / Fecha	Total	Professional, technical and related workers / *Professions libérales, techniciens et assimilés* / Profesiones liberales, técnicos y asimilados	Administrative, executive, managerial workers / *Directeurs, cadres administratifs supérieurs* / Administradores, gerentes, directores	Clerical workers / *Employés de bureau* / Empleados de oficina	Sales workers / *Vendeurs* / Vendedores	Farmers, fishermen and related workers / *Agriculteurs, pêcheurs et assimilés* / Agricultores, pescadores y asimilados	Miners, quarrymen and related workers / *Mineurs, carriers et assimilés* / Mineros, canteros y asimilados	Workers in transport and communication occupations / *Travailleurs dans les professions des transports et des communications* / Trabajadores de los transportes y comunicaciones	Craftsmen, prod. process workers, labourers not elsewhere classified / *Artisans, ouvriers de métier et à la production, manœuvres non classés ailleurs* / Artesanos, trabaj. ocupados en los div. procesos de prod., peones no clasif. bajo otros epígrafes	Service workers / *Travailleurs spécialisés dans les services* / Trabajadores de los servicios	Workers not classifiable by occupation / *Personnes ne pouvant être classées selon la profession* / Trabajadores que no pueden ser clasificados según la ocupación
1970	20 992	149	1	172	656	5 787	18	598	6 023	1 070	6 518
1971	30 659	196	—	211	974	8 567	29	727	7 547	1 198	11 210
1972	34 463	198	2	196	975	9 577	38	716	7 640	1 116	14 005
1973	27 217	148	1	212	731	6 576	20	475	5 478	911	12 665
1974	21 157	126	—	209	589	5 613	10	325	4 359	681	9 245
1975	20 513	120	—	182	582	6 062	11	309	4 445	809	7 992
1976	20 841	142	1	210	608	5 586	14	385	5 039	1 025	7 831
1977	17 071	145	2	209	479	3 141	9	343	4 780	956	7 007
1978	16 804	156	—	223	412	3 282	12	329	2 975	993	8 422
1979	22 039	168	—	255	490	4 307	13	625	4 530	1 198	10 453

11 Structure of unemployment
Structure du chômage
Estructura del desempleo

Nigeria

Occupational groups *(Employment office statistics)*
Groupes de professions *(Statistiques des bureaux de placement)*
Grupos de ocupaciones *(Estadísticas de las oficinas de colocación)*

Date / Date / Fecha	Total	0/1 Professional, technical and related workers — Personnel des professions scientifiques, techniques, libérales et assimilées — Profesionales, técnicos y trabajadores asimilados	2 Administrative and managerial workers — Directeurs et cadres administratifs supérieurs — Directores y funcionarios públicos superiores	3 Clerical and related workers — Personnel administratif et travailleurs assimilés — Personal administrativo y trabajadores asimilados	4 Sales workers — Personnel commercial et vendeurs — Comerciantes y vendedores	5 Service workers — Travailleurs spécialisés dans les services — Trabajadores de los servicios	6 Agricultural, animal husbandry and forestry workers, fishermen and hunters — Agriculteurs, éleveurs, forestiers, pêcheurs et chasseurs — Trabajadores agrícolas y forestales, pescadores y cazadores	7/8/9 Production and related workers, transport equipment operators and labourers — Ouvriers et manœuvres non agricoles et conducteurs d'engins de transport — Obreros no agrícolas, conductores de máquinas y vehículos de transporte y trabajadores asimilados	X Workers not classifiable by occupation [1] — Travailleurs ne pouvant être classés selon la profession [1] — Trabajadores que no pueden ser clasificados según la ocupación [1]
1970	13 507	104	1	857	107	587	61	7 362	4 428
1971	14 410	104	1	844	163	589	73	7 818	4 818
1972	15 371	96	—	823	177	1 189	50	8 113	4 923
1973	19 096	93	—	1 078	188	1 451	87	10 046	6 153
1974	20 471	58	2	821	173	862	44	11 944	6 567
1975	19 969	35	2	744	150	475	55	12 442	6 066
1976	18 970	53	8	736	166	440	147	13 382	4 038
1977	15 849	38	4	721	224	310	78	10 706	3 768

[1] Incl. persons seeking work for the first time.

[1] *Y compris les personnes en quête d'emploi pour la première fois.*

[1] Incl. las personas en busca de trabajo por primera vez.

Sierra Leone

Occupational groups *(Employment office statistics)* [1]
Groupes de professions *(Statistiques des bureaux de placement)* [1]
Grupos de ocupaciones *(Estadísticas de las oficinas de colocación)* [1]

Date / Date / Fecha	Total	0/1 Professional, technical and related workers — Personnel des professions scientifiques, techniques, libérales et assimilées — Profesionales, técnicos y trabajadores asimilados	2 Administrative and managerial workers — Directeurs et cadres administratifs supérieurs — Directores y funcionarios públicos superiores	3 Clerical and related workers — Personnel administratif et travailleurs assimilés — Personal administrativo y trabajadores asimilados	4 Sales workers — Personnel commercial et vendeurs — Comerciantes y vendedores	5 Service workers — Travailleurs spécialisés dans les services — Trabajadores de los servicios	6 Agricultural, animal husbandry and forestry workers, fishermen and hunters — Agriculteurs, éleveurs, forestiers, pêcheurs et chasseurs — Trabajadores agrícolas y forestales, pescadores y cazadores	7/8/9 Production and related workers, transport equipment operators and labourers — Ouvriers et manœuvres non agricoles et conducteurs d'engins de transport — Obreros no agrícolas, conductores de máquinas y vehículos de transp. y trabaj. asimilados	X Workers not classifiable by occupation — Travailleurs ne pouvant être classés selon la profession — Trabajadores que no pueden ser clasificados según la ocupación
1973	5 746	5	—	1 040	378	509	8	1 121	2 685
1974	5 559	5	—	1 015	390	322	14	746	3 067
1975	6 638	5	—	1 000	242	122	15	822	4 432
1976	7 670	6	—	1 039	380	194	11	1 132	4 908
1977	7 342	7	—	1 693	416	344	7	1 543	3 332

[1] Excl. applicants for work registered at the Maritime Pool (8,654 in 1977).

[1] *Non compris les demandeurs d'emploi enregistrés au bureau de placement maritime (8 654 en 1977).*

[1] Excl. los solicitantes de trabajo registrados en la oficina de colocación marítima (8 654 en 1977).

11 Structure of unemployment
Structure du chômage
Estructura del desempleo

South Africa, Rep. of [1]

Occupational groups *(Employment office statistics)*
Groupes de professions *(Statistiques des bureaux de placement)*
Grupos de ocupaciones *(Estadísticas de las oficinas de colocación)*

Date / Date / Fecha	Total	Civil and clerical workers / *Fonctionnaires et employés de bureau* / Funcionarios y oficinistas	Commercial employees / *Employés de commerce* / Empleados de comercio	Professional and semi-professional workers / *Professions libérales et semi-libérales* / Profesiones liberales y semiliberales	Transport, storage, communication, personnel services / *Transports, entrepôts, communications, services personnels* / Transportes, almacenaje, comunicaciones, servicios personales	Skilled workers / *Ouvriers qualifiés* / Obreros calificados	Semi-skilled and unskilled workers / *Ouvriers semi-qualifiés et non qualifiés* / Obreros semicalificados y no calificados
1970	8 489	1 943	751	101	997	437	4 259
1971	8 577	2 105	753	78	936	538	4 167
1972	12 200	3 047	997	100	1 319	1 184	5 553
1973	10 785	2 636	930	124	1 048	929	5 118
1974	8 350	2 126	772	110	836	631	3 875
1975	10 305	2 572	891	128	1 011	1 082	4 621
1976	14 515	3 610	1 190	172	1 296	1 897	6 350
1977	28 495	6 023	2 173	303	2 299	4 965	12 732
1978	30 925	6 918	2 474	364	2 851	5 528	12 792
1979	28 240	6 857	2 340	420	2 900	4 096	11 627

[1] Non-indigenous population.   [1] *Population non indigène.*   [1] Población no indígena.

Tunisie

Occupational groups *(Employment office statistics)*
Groupes de professions *(Statistiques des bureaux de placement)*
Grupos de ocupaciones *(Estadísticas de las oficinas de colocación)*

(ISCO — CITP — CIUO 1958)

Date / Date / Fecha	Total	Professional, technical and related workers / *Professions libérales, techniciens et assimilés* / Profesiones liberales, técnicos y asimilados	Administrative, executive, managerial workers / *Directeurs, cadres administratifs supérieurs* / Administradores, gerentes, directores	Clerical workers / *Employés de bureau* / Empleados de oficina	Sal workers / *Vendeurs* / Vendedores	Farmers, fishermen and related workers / *Agriculteurs, pêcheurs et assimilés* / Agricultores, pescadores y asimilados	Miners, quarrymen and related workers / *Mineurs, carriers et assimilés* / Mineros, canteros y asimilados	Workers in transport and communication occupations / *Travailleurs dans les professions des transports et des communications* / Trabajadores de los transportes y comunicaciones	Craftsmen, prod. process workers, labourers not elsewhere classified / *Artisans, ouvriers de métier et à la prod., manœuvres non classés ailleurs* / Artesanos, trabaj. ocupados en los div. procesos de prod., peones no clasif. bajo otros epígrafes	Service workers / *Travailleurs spécialisés dans les services* / Trabajadores de los servicios	Persons seeking work for the first time [1] / *Personnes en quête d'emploi pour la première fois* [1] / Personas en busca de trabajo por primera vez [1]
1970	63 683	33	5	646	39	10 440	28	630	41 652	1 746	8 464
1971	52 476	42	2	597	37	9 456	31	778	31 597	1 870	8 066
1972	31 929	49	2	481	38	4 892	35	458	17 529	1 306	7 139
1973	36 971	58	3	432	41	6 132	26	439	21 029	835	7 976
1975 [2]	28 819	80	24	434	23	196	10	577	18 382	843	8 250
1976 [2]	36 058	99	32	1 182	51	266	.	1 079	26 186	998	6 165
1977 [2]	79 184	95	17	830	60	715	.	1 313	61 849	1 579	12 726
1978 [2]	55 582	49	6	765	50	365	.	1 075	40 479	1 094	11 699
1979 [2]	63 448	143	13	568	63	325	.	45 446		1 099	15 791

[1] Incl. workers not classifiable by occupation.   [2] Dec.

[1] *Y compris les personnes ne pouvant être classées selon la profession.*   [2] *Déc.*

[1] Incl. los trabajadores que no pueden ser clasificados según la ocupación.   [2] Dic.

11 Structure of unemployment
Structure du chômage
Estructura del desempleo

AMERICA — AMÉRIQUE — AMERICA

Canada

(ISIC — CITI — CIIU 1958)

A Industrial groups *(Labour force sample surveys)*
Groupes d'activité économique *(Enquêtes par sondage sur la main-d'œuvre)*
Grupos de actividad económica *(Encuestas por muestra sobre la fuerza trabajadora)*

Date / Date / Fecha	Total	Agriculture, forestry, fishing / Agriculture, sylviculture, pêche / Agricultura, silvicultura, pesca	Mining, quarrying / Industries extractives / Minas, canteras	Manufacturing / Industries manufacturières / Industrias manufactureras	Construction / Construction / Construcción	Commerce / Commerce / Comercio	Electricity, gas, water, sanitary services, transport, storage, communication / Electricité, gaz, eau, services sanitaires, transports, entrepôts, communications / Electricidad, gas, agua, servicios sanitarios, transportes, almacenaje, comunicaciones	Services [1] / Services [1] / Servicios [1]	Persons seeking work for the first time / Personnes en quête d'emploi pour la première fois / Personas en busca de trabajo por primera vez
1970	487 000	43 000		112 000	84 000	57 000	35 000	95 000	61 000
1971	543 000	45 000		123 000	84 000	66 000	37 000	116 000	73 000
1972	553 000	39 000		122 000	87 000	69 000	38 000	137 000	62 000
1973	512 000	35 000		107 000	79 000	66 000	36 000	136 000	53 000
1974	515 000	42 000		114 000	80 000	62 000	36 000	136 000	47 000
1975	690 000	40 000		149 000	80 000	96 000	42 000	188 000	94 000
1976	727 000	42 000		150 000	88 000	110 000	47 000	236 000	53 000
1977	850 000	48 000		168 000	109 000	134 000	49 000	280 000	62 000
1978	911 000	53 000		169 000	120 000	138 000	53 000	305 000	72 000
1979	838 000	48 000		152 000	99 000	125 000	48 000	293 000	73 000

[1] Incl. finance, insurance and real estate.

[1] *Y compris les établissements financiers, les assurances et les affaires immobilières.*

[1] Incl. los establecimientos financieros, los seguros y los bienes inmuebles.

(ISCO — CITP — CIUO 1958)

B Occupational groups *(Labour force sample surveys)*
Groupes de professions *(Enquêtes par sondage sur la main-d'œuvre)*
Grupos de ocupaciones *(Encuestas por muestra sobre la fuerza trabajadora)*

Date / Date / Fecha	Total	Professional, technical and related workers / Professions libérales, techniciens et assimilés / Profesiones liberales, técnicos y asimilados	Administrative, executive, managerial workers / Directeurs, cadres administratifs supérieurs / Administradores, gerentes, directores	Clerical workers / Employés de bureau / Empleados de oficina	Sales workers / Vendeurs / Vendedores	Farmers, fishermen and related workers / Agriculteurs, pêcheurs et assimilés / Agricultores, pescadores y asimilados	Miners, quarrymen and related workers / Mineurs, carriers et assimilés / Mineros, canteros y asimilados	Workers in transport occupations / Travailleurs dans les professions des transports / Trabajadores de los transportes	Craftsmen, prod. process workers, labourers not elsewhere classified / Artisans, ouvriers de métier et à la production, manœuvres non classés ailleurs / Artesanos, trabaj. ocupados en los div. procesos de prod., peones no clasif. bajo otros epígrafes	Service workers / Travailleurs spécialisés dans les services / Trabajadores de los servicios	Persons seeking work for the first time / Personnes en quête d'emploi pour la première fois / Personas en busca de trabajo por primera vez
1973	512 000	131 000				37 000	33 000		194 000	65 000	53 000
1974	515 000	131 000				43 000	33 000		200 000	65 000	47 000
1975	690 000	202 000				41 000	27 000		236 000	90 000	94 000
1976	727 000	244 000				45 000	30 000		248 000	107 000	53 000
1977	850 000	280 000				51 000	34 000		288 000	135 000	62 000
1978	911 000	305 000				54 000	35 000		295 000	149 000	72 000
1979	838 000	269 000				52 000	33 000		266 000	145 000	73 000

[1] Incl. workers in communication occupations.

[1] *Y compris les travailleurs des communications.*

[1] Incl. los trabajadores de las comunicaciones.

11 Structure of unemployment
Structure du chômage
Estructura del desempleo

Colombia [1]

A Industrial groups (Labour force sample surveys)
Groupes d'activité économique (Enquêtes par sondage sur la main-d'œuvre)
Grupos de actividad económica (Encuestas por muestra sobre la fuerza trabajadora)

Date / Date / Fecha	Total	1 Agriculture, forestry, fishing / Agriculture, sylviculture, pêche / Agricultura, silvicultura, pesca	2 Mining, quarrying / Industries extractives / Minas, canteras	3 Manufacturing / Industries manufacturières / Industrias manufactureras	4 Electricity, gas, water / Electricité, gaz, eau / Electricidad, gas, agua	5 Construction / Construction / Construcción	6 Trade, restaurants and hotels / Commerce, restaurants et hôtels / Comercio, restaurantes y hoteles	7 Transport, storage, communication / Transports, entrepôts, communications / Transportes, almacenaje, comunicaciones	8 Financing, insur., real est., business serv. / Banques, assur., aff. imm., serv. aux entreprises / Bancos, seguros, bienes inm., serv. para empresas	9 Community, social, and pers. services / Services à collectivité, serv. sociaux et pers. / Servicios comunales, sociales y personales	0 Activities not adequately described / Activités mal désignées / Actividades no bien especificadas
1976	276 009	1 683	615	74 647	2 913	26 632	88 869	12 889	12 898	44 667	10 196
1977	266 663	1 842	484	76 553	2 196	23 513	83 873	10 856	13 390	47 320	6 636
1978	261 719	2 226	412	64 494	2 154	19 978	91 294	9 991	17 404	50 988	2 778

B Occupational groups (Labour force sample surveys)
Groupes de professions (Enquêtes par sondage sur la main-d'œuvre)
Grupos de ocupaciones (Encuestas por muestra sobre la fuerza trabajadora)

Date / Date / Fecha	Total	0/1 Professional, technical and related workers / Personnel des professions scientifiques, techniques, libérales et assimilées / Profesionales, técnicos y trabajadores asimilados	2 Administrative and managerial workers / Directeurs et cadres administratifs supérieurs / Directores y funcionarios públicos superiores	3 Clerical and related workers / Personnel administratif et travailleurs assimilés / Personal administrativo y trabajadores asimilados	4 Sales workers / Personnel commercial et vendeurs / Comerciantes y vendedores	5 Service workers / Travailleurs spécialisés dans les services / Trabajadores de los servicios	6 Agricultural, animal husbandry and forestry workers, fishermen and hunters / Agriculteurs, éleveurs, forestiers, pêcheurs et chasseurs / Trabajadores agrícolas y forestales, pescadores y cazadores	7/8/9 Production and related workers, transport equipment operators and labourers / Ouvriers et manœuvres non agricoles et conducteurs d'engins de transport / Obreros no agrícolas, conductores de máquinas y vehículos de transporte y trabajadores asimilados	X Workers not classifiable by occupation / Travailleurs ne pouvant être classés selon la profession / Trabajadores que no pueden ser clasificados según la ocupación
1976	276 009	18 109	1 109	72 031	40 712	34 464	1 756	107 419	409
1977	266 663	17 389	1 389	71 877	37 644	35 303	1 866	100 115	1 080
1978	261 719	20 445	1 085	74 689	41 399	29 825	1 125	91 916	1 235

[1] Bogotá, Barranquilla, Bucaramanga, Cali, Manizales, Medellín and Pasto.

[1] Bogotá, Barranquilla, Bucaramanga, Cali, Manizales, Medellín et Pasto.

[1] Bogotá, Barranquilla, Bucaramanga, Cali, Manizales, Medellín y Pasto.

11 Structure of unemployment
Structure du chômage
Estructura del desempleo

Costa Rica

(ISIC — CITI — CIIU 1958)

A   Industrial groups *(Labour force sample surveys)*
Groupes d'activité économique *(Enquêtes par sondage sur la main-d'œuvre)*
Grupos de actividad económica *(Encuestas por muestra sobre la fuerza trabajadora)*

Date [1] / Date [1] / Fecha [1]	Total	Agriculture, forestry, fishing / Agriculture, sylviculture, pêche / Agricultura, silvicultura, pesca	Mining, quarrying / Industries extractives / Minas, canteras	Manufacturing / Industries manufacturières / Industrias manufactureras	Construction / Construction / Construcción	Trade, financing, insurance [2] / Commerce, banques, assurances [2] / Comercio, bancos, seguros [2]	Electricity, gas, water / Electricité, gaz, eau / Electricidad, gas, agua	Transport, storage, communication / Transports, entrepôts, communications / Transportes, almacenaje, comunicaciones	Services [3] / Services [3] / Servicios [3]	Activities not adequately described / Activités mal désignées / Actividades no bien especificadas	Persons seeking work for the first time / Personnes en quête d'emploi pour la première fois / Personas en busca de trabajo por primera vez
1976	40 921	4 741	4 292		4 382	4 172	248	791	4 412	144	17 739
1977	31 433	4 663	5 330		2 814	4 262	216	1 432	3 111	500	9 105
1978	32 666	4 393		5 643	2 169	4 648	1 199		5 215	.	9 399
1979	36 251	3 932		6 185	3 118	5 931	117	1 373	4 273 *	241	11 081

B   Occupational groups *(Labour force sample surveys)*
Groupes de professions *(Enquêtes par sondage sur la main-d'œuvre)*
Grupos de ocupaciones *(Encuestas por muestra sobre la fuerza trabajadora)*

(ISCO — CITP — CIUO 1958)

Date [1] / Date [1] / Fecha [1]	Total	Professional, technical and related workers / Professions libérales, techniciens et assimilés / Profesiones liberales, técnicos y asimilados	Administrative, executive, managerial workers / Directeurs, cadres administratifs supérieurs / Administradores, gerentes, directores	Clerical workers / Employés de bureau / Empleados de oficina	Sales workers / Vendeurs / Vendedores	Farmers, fishermen and related workers / Agriculteurs, pêcheurs et assimilés / Agricultores, pescadores y asimilados	Workers in transport occupations / Travailleurs dans les professions des transports / Trabajadores de los transportes	Craftsmen, prod. process workers, labourers not elsewhere classified / Artisans, ouvriers de métier et à la production, manœuvres non classés ailleurs / Artesanos, trabaj. ocupados en los div. procesos de prod., peones no clasif. bajo otros epígrafes	Service workers / Travailleurs spécialisés dans les services / Trabajadores de los servicios	Workers not classifiable by occupation / Travailleurs ne pouvant être classés selon la profession / Trabajadores que no pueden ser clasificados según la ocupación	Persons seeking work for the first time / Personnes en quête d'emploi pour la première fois / Personas en busca de trabajo por primera vez
1976	40 921	778	439	4 454		13 476			3 809	226	17 739
1977	31 433	486	891	4 147		12 955			3 433	416	9 105
1978	32 666	798	507	5 025		12 345			4 556	36	9 399
1979	36 251	427	533	5 371		14 326			4 396	117	11 081

[1] July. [2] Incl. restaurants and hotels. [3] Excl. restaurants and hotels.

[1] *Juillet.* [2] *Y compris les restaurants et les hôtels.* [3] *Non compris les restaurants et les hôtels.*

[1] Julio. [2] Incl. los restaurantes y los hoteles. [3] Excl. los restaurantes y los hoteles.

11 Structure of unemployment
Structure du chômage
Estructura del desempleo

Chile

Industrial groups *(Labour force sample surveys)*
Groupes d'activité économique *(Enquêtes par sondage sur la main-d'œuvre)*
Grupos de actividad económica *(Encuestas por muestra sobre la fuerza trabajadora)*

Date / Date / Fecha	Total	1 Agriculture, forestry, fishing / Agriculture, sylviculture, pêche / Agricultura, silvicultura, pesca	2 Mining, quarrying / Industries extractives / Minas, canteras	3 Manufacturing / Industries manufacturières / Industrias manufactureras	4 Electricity, gas, water / Electricité, gaz, eau / Electricidad, gas, agua	5 Construction / Construction / Construcción	6 Trade, restaurants and hotels / Commerce, restaurants et hôtels / Comercio, restaurantes y hoteles	7 Transport, storage, communication / Transports, entrepôts, communications / Transportes, almacenaje, comunicaciones	8 Financing, insur., real est., business serv. / Banques, assur., aff. imm., serv. aux entreprises / Bancos, seguros, bienes inm., serv. para empresas	9 Community, social, and pers. services / Services à collectivité, services sociaux et pers. / Servicios comunales, sociales y personales	0 Activities not adequately described / Activités mal désignées / Actividades no bien especificadas	Persons seeking work for the first time / Personnes en quête d'emploi pour la première fois / Personas en busca de trabajo por primera vez
1975	467 600	24 400	6 400	71 800	4 800	48 900	38 600	24 000	8 500	75 800	5 000	159 400
1976	409 600	27 200	8 800	43 200	3 500	38 200	34 000	19 700	4 000	65 500	6 300	159 200
1977	399 500	33 200	10 300	41 400	2 500	36 900	31 600	16 000	4 700	71 300	9 900	141 700

Honduras

Industrial groups *(Official estimates)*
Groupes d'activité économique *(Evaluations officielles)*
Grupos de actividad económica *(Estimaciones oficiales)*

Date / Date / Fecha	Total	1 Agriculture, forestry, fishing / Agriculture, sylviculture, pêche / Agricultura, silvicultura, pesca	2 Mining, quarrying / Industries extractives / Minas, canteras	3 Manufacturing / Industries manufacturières / Industrias manufactureras	4 Electricity, gas, water / Electricité, gaz, eau / Electricidad, gas, agua	5 Construction / Construction / Construcción	6 Trade, restaurants and hotels / Commerce, restaurants et hôtels / Comercio, restaurantes y hoteles	7 Transport, storage, communication / Transports, entrepôts, communications / Transportes, almacenaje, comunicaciones	8 Financing, insur., real est., business serv. / Banques, assur., aff. imm., serv. aux entreprises / Bancos, seguros, bienes inm., serv. para empresas	9 Community, social, and pers. services / Services à collectivité, services sociaux et pers. / Servicios comunales, sociales y personales
1970	49 436	29 800	133	5 119	137	1 301	3 441	1 195	7 009	1 301
1971	51 053	30 035	139	6 003	127	1 384	3 538	1 296	7 263	1 268
1972	51 739	30 368	160	5 666	143	1 470	3 786	1 347	7 577	1 222
1973	53 099	30 713	163	5 971	150	1 548	4 019	1 488	7 875	1 172
1974	52 320	30 892	167	6 292	159	1 617	4 292	1 604	6 167	1 130

11 Structure of unemployment
Structure du chômage
Estructura del desempleo

Jamaica

(ISIC — CITI — CIIU 1958)

A Industrial groups *(Labour force sample surveys)*
Groupes d'activité économique *(Enquêtes par sondage sur la main-d'œuvre)*
Grupos de actividad económica *(Encuestas por muestra sobre la fuerza trabajadora)*

Date / Date / Fecha	Total	Agriculture, forestry, fishing and mining / Agriculture, sylviculture, pêche et mines / Agricultura, silvicultura, pesca y minas	Manufacturing / Industries manufacturières / Industrias manufactureras	Construction / Construction / Construcción	Electricity, gas, water, sanitary services, transport and communication / Electricité, gaz, eau, services sanitaires, transports et communications / Electricidad, gas, agua, servicios sanitarios, transportes y comunicaciones	Commerce / Commerce / Comercio	Services / Services / Servicios	Activities not adequately described / Activités mal désignées / Actividades no bien especificadas	Persons seeking work for the first time / Personnes en quête d'emploi pour la première fois / Personas en busca de trabajo por primera vez
1972	184 500	13 600	13 650	12 000	3 050	10 000	49 400	3 950	78 850
1973	176 400	12 250	15 600	13 250	3 200	10 900	62 100	2 750	56 350
1974	173 750	13 650	17 150	11 650	3 800	10 950	55 150	2 350	59 050
1975	175 400	12 600	15 350	12 650	3 850	12 400	62 450	1 300	54 800
1976	197 750	15 800	20 300	15 450	3 900	13 950	70 850	1 350	56 150
1977	220 200	17 100	22 800	16 900	4 400	15 500	81 400	1 900	60 200
1978	230 500	17 400	20 000	15 200	4 200	15 600	81 700	1 500	74 900

B Occupational groups *(Labour force sample surveys)*
Groupes de professions *(Enquêtes par sondage sur la main-d'œuvre)*
Grupos de ocupaciones *(Encuestas por muestra sobre la fuerza trabajadora)*

Date / Date / Fecha	Total	Professional, technical and related workers / Professions libérales, techniciens et assimilés / Profesiones liberales, técnicos y trabajadores asimilados	Administrative, executive and managerial workers / Directeurs et cadres administratifs supérieurs / Administradores, gerentes y directores	Clerical workers / Employés de bureau / Empleados de oficina	Sales workers / Vendeurs * / Vendedores	Workers on own account / Personnes travaillant à leur propre compte / Trabajadores por cuenta propia	Craftsmen, prod. process workers, labourers not elsewhere classified / Artisans, ouvriers de métier et à la production, manœuvres non classés ailleurs / Artesanos, trab. ocupados en los div. procesos de prod., peones no clasif. bajo otros epígrafes	Service workers / Travailleurs spécialisés dans les services / Trabajadores de los servicios	Workers not classifiable by occupation / Personnes ne pouvant être classées selon la profession / Trabajadores que no pueden ser clasificados según la ocupación	Persons seeking work for the first time / Personnes en quête d'emploi pour la première fois / Personas en busca de trabajo por primera vez
1972	184 500	1 650			11 800		8 100	44 050	37 500	2 550	78 850
1973	176 400	2 450			14 600		11 800	48 150	42 350	700	56 350
1974	173 750	2 100			14 300		10 650	47 150	39 500	1 000	59 050
1975	175 400	3 350			16 100		12 300	47 400	40 850	600	54 800
1976	197 750	4 400			18 900		16 150	56 150	45 600	400	56 150
1977	220 200	6 950			23 200		16 050	67 600	46 050	200	60 200

UNEMPLOYMENT

11 Structure of unemployment
Structure du chômage
Estructura del desempleo

Panamá

A Industrial groups *(Labour force sample surveys)*
Groupes d'activité économique *(Enquêtes par sondage sur la main-d'œuvre)*
Grupos de actividad económica *(Encuestas por muestra sobre la fuerza trabajadora)*

Date / Date / Fecha	Total	1 Agriculture, forestry, fishing / Agriculture, sylviculture, pêche / Agricultura, silvicultura, pesca	2 Mining, quarrying / Industries extractives / Minas, canteras	3 Manufacturing / Industries manufacturières / Industrias manufactureras	4 Electricity, gas, water / Electricité, gaz, eau / Electricidad, gas, agua	5 Construction / Construction / Construcción	6 Trade, restaurants and hotels / Commerce, restaurants et hôtels / Comercio, restaurantes y hoteles	7 Transport, storage, communication / Transports, entrepôts, communications / Transportes, almacenaje, comunicaciones	8 Financing, insur., real est., business serv. / Banques, assur., aff. imm., serv. aux entreprises / Bancos, seguros, bienes inm., serv. para empresas	9 Community, social, and pers. services / Services à collectivité, serv. sociaux et pers. / Servicios comunales, sociales y personales	Canal zone / Zone du canal / Zona del Canal	Persons seeking work for the first time / Personnes en quête d'emploi pour la première fois / Personas en busca de trabajo por primera vez
1971	36 300	1 500	—	2 900	—	4 000	4 200	1 900	500	10 600	2 100	8 600
1972	33 200	1 500	—	2 200	200	2 900	3 700	900	300	5 800	500	15 200
1974 [1]	30 000	2 700	100	2 200	100	4 100	3 500	1 700	500	5 800	800	8 500
1975 [2]	31 600	2 160	20	2 720	350	4 270	3 840	1 550	880	7 770	810	7 230
1976 [3]	33 700	1 850	40	3 090	100	4 610	4 670	1 400	690	7 220	930	9 100
1977 [1]	44 820 [4]	2 050	—	3 720	40	3 890	4 820	1 520	1 130	5 870	750	20 330
1978 [3] *	43 800	1 250	40	2 850	110	3 120	4 090	940	1 030	7 130	660	22 580

B Occupational groups *(Labour force sample surveys)*
Groupe de professions *(Enquêtes par sondage sur la main-d'œuvre)*
Grupos de ocupaciones *(Encuestas por muestra sobre la fuerza trabajadora)*

Date / Date / Fecha	Total	0/1 Professional, technical and related workers / Personnel des professions scientifiques, techniques, libérales et assimilées / Profesionales, técnicos y trabajadores asimilados	2 Administrative and managerial workers / Directeurs et cadres administratifs supérieurs / Directores y funcionarios públicos superiores	3 Clerical and related workers / Personnel administratif et travailleurs assimilés / Personal administrativo y trabajadores asimilados	4 Sales workers / Personnel commercial et vendeurs / Comerciantes y vendedores	5 Service workers / Travailleurs spécialisés dans les services / Trabajadores de los servicios	6 Agricultural, animal husbandry and forestry workers, fishermen and hunters / Agriculteurs, éleveurs, forestiers, pêcheurs et chasseurs / Trabajadores agrícolas y forestales, pescadores y cazadores	7/8/9 Production and related workers, transport equipment, operators and labourers / Ouvriers et manœuvres non agricoles et conducteurs d'engins de transport / Obreros no agrícolas, conductores de máquinas y vehículos de transporte y trabajadores asimilados	Persons seeking work for the first time / Personnes en quête d'emploi pour la première fois / Personas en busca de trabajo por primera vez
1975 [2]	31 600	2 400	600	3 200	2 200	6 200	1 600	8 100	7 200
1976 [3]	33 700	1 100	500	3 100	2 000	6 100	1 800	10 000	9 100

[1] Oct. [2] Nov. [3] Aug. [4] Incl. 700 persons whose activity is not adequately described.

[1] Oct. [2] Nov. [3] Août. [4] Y compris 700 personnes dont l'activité est mal désignée.

[1] Oct. [2] Nov. [3] Agosto. [4] Incl. 700 personas con actividades no bien especificadas.

11 Structure of unemployment
Structure du chômage
Estructura del desempleo

Perú

(ISIC — CITI — CIIU 1958)

Industrial groups *(Labour force sample surveys)*
Groupes d'activité économique *(Enquêtes par sondage sur la main-d'œuvre)*
Grupos de actividad económica *(Encuestas por muestra sobre la fuerza trabajadora)*

Date *Date* Fecha	Total	Agriculture, forestry, fishing *Agriculture, sylviculture, pêche* Agricultura, silvicultura, pesca	Mining, quarrying *Industries extractives* Minas, canteras	Manufacturing *Industries manufacturières* Industrias manufactureras	Construction *Construction* Construcción	Commerce *Commerce* Comercio	Electricity, gas, water and sanitary services *Electricité, gaz, eau et services sanitaires* Electricidad, gas, agua y servicios sanitarios	Transport, storage, communication *Transports, entrepôts, communications* Transportes, almacenaje, comunicaciones	Services *Services* Servicios	Activities not adequately described *Activités mal désignées* Actividades no bien especificadas	Persons seeking work for the first time *Personnes en quête d'emploi pour la première fois* Personas en busca de trabajo por primera vez
1970	201 200	6 100	300	30 400	2 200	10 200		20 000		84 900	47 100
1971	195 700	6 200	600	27 200	2 100	9 800		19 000		84 600	46 200
1972	194 000	6 300	600	26 400	2 200	6 200		10 600		92 200	49 500
1973	191 500	6 300	600	24 400	2 000	8 400		11 800		86 000	52 000
1974	186 900	6 100	400	24 500	1 900	7 400		11 100		80 900	54 600
1975	236 900	5 900	1 600	33 500	2 100	12 400		17 500		163 900	
1976	258 300	5 900	1 700	32 600	3 800	18 500		19 600		176 200	
1977	298 200	6 000	1 700	52 500	26 400	17 000		14 600		180 000	
1978	341 500	6 000	700	50 200	30 600	22 800		36 600		194 600	
1979	387 600	6 100	700	45 500	28 900	36 900		59 400		210 100	

UNEMPLOYMENT

11 Structure of unemployment
Structure du chômage
Estructura del desempleo

Puerto Rico

A
Industrial groups *(Labour force sample surveys)* [1]
Groupes d'activité économique *(Enquêtes par sondage sur la main-d'œuvre)* [1]
Grupos de actividad económica *(Encuestas por muestra sobre la fuerza trabajadora)* [1]

Date / Date / Fecha	Total	1 — Agriculture, forestry, fishing / Agriculture, sylviculture, pêche / Agricultura, silvicultura, pesca	3 — Manufacturing / Industries manufacturières / Industrias manufactureras	4 — Electricity, gas, water / Électricité, gaz, eau / Electricidad, gas, agua	5 — Construction / Construction / Construcción	6 × — Trade [2] / Commerce [2] / Comercio [2]	7 — Transport, storage, communication / Transports, entrepôts, communications / Transportes, almacenaje, comunicaciones	8 — Financing, insur., real est., business serv. / Banques, assur., aff. imm., serv. aux entreprises / Bancos, seguros, bienes inm., serv. para empresas	6 × ; 9 — Community, social, and pers. services [3] / Services à collectivité, serv. sociaux et pers. [3] / Servicios comunales, sociales y personales [3]	0 — Activities not adequately described [4] / Activités mal désignées [4] / Actividades no bien especificadas [4]
1970	84 000	11 000	24 000	—	16 000	9 000	3 000	—	13 000	8 000
1971	95 000	10 000	27 000	—	19 000	11 000	3 000	—	16 000	9 000
1972	101 000	8 000	27 000	—	22 000	13 000	3 000	—	17 000	10 000
1973	102 000	7 000	26 000	—	22 000	12 000	4 000	—	20 000	9 000
1974	117 000	9 000	27 000	—	26 000	13 000	4 000	1 000	23 000	12 000
1975	159 000	12 000	39 000	2 000	36 000	18 000	5 000	2 000	34 000	13 000
1976	179 000	15 000	40 000	2 000	39 000	21 000	6 000	1 000	40 000	14 000
1977	187 000	16 000	41 000	—	37 000	22 000	5 000	2 000	47 000	15 000
1978	175 000	13 000	37 000	1 000	33 000	22 000	4 000	2 000	46 000	16 000
1979	168 000	14 000	33 000	1 000	33 000	21 000	4 000	2 000	45 000	14 000

B
Occupational groups *(Labour force sample surveys)* [1]
Groupes de professions *(Enquêtes par sondage sur la main-d'œuvre)* [1]
Grupos de ocupaciones *(Encuestas por muestra sobre la fuerza trabajadora)* [1]

Date / Date / Fecha	Total	0/1 — Professional, technical and related workers / Personnel des professions scientifiques, techniques, libérales et assimilées / Profesionales, técnicos y trabajadores asimilados	2 — Administrative and managerial workers / Directeurs et cadres administratifs supérieurs / Directores y funcionarios públicos superiores	3 — Clerical and related workers / Personnel administratif et travailleurs assimilés / Personal administrativo y trabajadores asimilados	4 — Sales workers / Personnel commercial et vendeurs / Comerciantes y vendedores	5 — Service workers / Travailleurs spécialisés dans les services / Trabajadores de los servicios	6 — Agricultural, animal husbandry and forestry workers, fishermen and hunters / Agriculteurs, éleveurs, forestiers, pêcheurs et chasseurs / Trabajadores agrícolas y forestales, pescadores y cazadores	7/8/9 — Production and related workers, transport equipment operators and labourers / Ouvriers et manœuvres non agricoles et conducteurs d'engins de transport / Obreros no agrícolas, conductores de máquinas y vehículos de transporte y trabajadores asimilados	X — Workers not classifiable by occupation [4] / Travailleurs ne pouvant être classés selon la profession [4] / Trabajadores que no pueden ser clasificados según la ocupación [4]
1970	84 000	—	—	4 000	3 000	7 000	10 000	48 000	8 000
1971	95 000	—	—	5 000	4 000	8 000	9 000	56 000	9 000
1972	101 000	2 000	—	7 000	5 000	8 000	7 000	61 000	10 000
1973	102 000	3 000	2 000	7 000	5 000	9 000	7 000	61 000	9 000
1974	117 000	3 000	2 000	9 000	5 000	11 000	8 000	67 000	12 000
1975	159 000	5 000	3 000	12 000	7 000	14 000	11 000	94 000	13 000
1976	179 000	5 000	4 000	13 000	8 000	17 000	14 000	104 000	14 000
1977	187 000	6 000	5 000	15 000	8 000	19 000	15 000	104 000	15 000
1978	175 000	5 000	4 000	14 000	8 000	19 000	12 000	96 000	16 000
1979	168 000	5 000	5 000	13 000	7 000	17 000	13 000	94 000	14 000

[1] Persons aged 15 years and over (beginning 1977: 16 years and over). Excl. persons temporarily laid off. Figures of less than 1,000 persons are indicated by a dash. [2] Excl. restaurants and hotels. [3] Incl. restaurants and hotels. [4] Incl. persons seeking work for the first time.

[1] *Personnes âgées de 14 ans et plus (à partir de 1977: 16 ans et plus). Non compris les personnes temporairement mises à pied. Les chiffres inférieurs à 1 000 personnes sont désignés par un tiret.* [2] *Non compris les restaurants et les hôtels.* [3] *Y compris les restaurants et les hôtels.* [4] *Y compris les personnes en quête d'emploi pour la première fois.*

[1] Personas de 14 años y más (a partir de 1977: 16 años y más). Excl. las personas temporalmente despedidas. Las cifras inferiores a 1 000 personas están indicadas con un guión. [2] Excl. los restaurantes y los hoteles. [3] Incl. los restaurantes y los hoteles. [4] Incl. las personas en busca de trabajo por primera vez.

11 Structure of unemployment
Structure du chômage
Estructura del desempleo

Trinidad and Tobago

(ISIC — CITI — CIIU 1958)

A Industrial groups *(Labour force sample surveys)*
Groupes d'activité économique *(Enquêtes par sondage sur la main-d'œuvre)*
Grupos de actividad económica *(Encuestas por muestra sobre la fuerza trabajadora)*

Date / Date / Fecha	Total	Agriculture, forestry, fishing / Agriculture, sylviculture, pêche / Agricultura, silvicultura, pesca	Mining, quarrying, manufacturing / Industries extractives, industries manufacturières / Minas, canteras, industrias manufactureras	Construction [1] / Construction [1] / Construcción [1]	Commerce / Commerce / Comercio	Transport, storage, communication / Transports, entrepôts, communications / Transportes, almacenaje, comunicaciones	Services / Services / Servicios	Activities not adequately described / Activités mal désignées / Actividades no bien especificadas	Persons seeking work for the first time / Personnes en quête d'emploi pour la première fois / Personas en busca de trabajo por primera vez
1970	46 400	4 600	8 000	11 200	3 900	1 900	6 400	—	10 400
1971 [2]	46 400	3 500	7 500	12 800	3 400	2 400	6 600	—	10 200
1972	.	.	.	.	.	.	.	.	.
1973	58 900	2 400	9 100	14 500	6 800	2 000	8 600	2 600	13 000
1974	60 100	3 300	9 700	15 600	6 700	2 400	9 500	700	12 200
1975	58 600	3 900	8 000	15 500	5 000	1 800	7 500	1 800	15 000
1976	.	.	.	.	.	.	.	.	.
1977	57 500	2 800	7 200	19 300	5 100	2 100	7 500	1 800	11 800
1978 [2]	53 500	3 100	5 500	21 000	5 100	2 000	8 900	1 100	6 800

[1] Incl. electricity, gas, water and sanitary services.
[2] First semester.

[1] Y compris l'électricité, le gaz, l'eau et les services sanitaires. [2] Premier semestre.

[1] Incl. la electricidad, el gas, el agua y los servicios sanitarios. [2] Primer semestre.

(ISCO — CITP — CIUO 1958)

B Occupational groups *(Labour force sample surveys)*
Groupes de professions *(Enquêtes par sondage sur la main-d'œuvre)*
Grupos de ocupaciones *(Encuestas por muestra sobre la fuerza trabajadora)*

Date / Date / Fecha	Total	Professional, technical and related workers / Professions libérales, techniciens et assimilés / Profesiones liberales, técnicos y asimilados	Administrative, executive, managerial, clerical and related workers / Directeurs, cadres adm. sup., employés de bureau et assimilés / Administradores, gerentes, directores, empleados de oficina y asimilados	Sales workers / Vendeurs / Vendedores	Farmers, fishermen and related workers / Agriculteurs, pêcheurs et assimilés / Agricultores, pescadores y asimilados	Craftsmen, prod. process workers, labourers not elsewhere classified [1] / Artisans, ouvriers de métier et à la production, manœuvres non classés ailleurs [1] / Artesanos, trabaj. ocupados en los div. procesos de prod., peones no clasif. bajo otros epígr. [1]	Workers in transport and communication occupations / Travailleurs des transports et des communications / Trabajadores de los transportes y comunicaciones	Service workers / Travailleurs spécialisés dans les services / Trabajadores de los servicios	Workers not classifiable by occupation / Personnes ne pouvant être classées selon la profession / Trabajadores que no pueden ser clasificados según la ocupación	Persons seeking work for the first time / Personnes en quête d'emploi pour la première fois / Personas en busca de trabajo por primera vez
1970	46 400	200	2 400	2 400	4 400	19 900	2 100	4 700	—	10 400
1971 [2]	46 400	300	2 100	1 600	3 400	21 900	1 700	5 300	—	10 200
1972	.	.	.	.	.	.	.	.	.	.
1973	58 900	1 500	3 300	4 000	2 000	24 200	1 200	6 900	2 700	13 000
1974	60 100	1 000	2 900	3 600	3 100	26 700	1 400	8 800	400	12 200
1975	58 600	1 200	2 700	2 700	3 200	25 100	1 500	5 600	1 500	15 000
1976	.	.	.	.	.	.	.	.	.	.
1977	57 500	600	3 600	2 300	3 000	28 300	1 300	5 000	1 800	11 800
1978 [2]	53 500	700	3 700	2 600	3 000	28 500	1 700	5 400	1 000	6 800

[1] Incl. miners, quarrymen and related workers.
[2] First semester.

[1] Y compris les mineurs, carriers et travailleurs assimilés. [2] Premier semestre.

[1] Incl. los mineros, canteros y trabajadores asimilados. [2] Primer semestre.

11

Structure of unemployment
Structure du chômage
Estructura del desempleo

United States

(ISIC — CITI — CIIU 1958)

A

Industrial groups *(Labour force sample surveys)* [1]
Groupes d'activité économique *(Enquêtes par sondage sur la main-d'œuvre)* [1]
Grupos de actividad económica *(Encuestas por muestra sobre la fuerza trabajadora)* [1]

Date / *Date* / Fecha	Total [2]	Wage earners and salaried employees — *Ouvriers et employés* — Obreros y empleados						
		Agriculture, forestry, fishing / *Agriculture, sylviculture, pêche* / Agricultura, silvicultura, pesca	Mining, quarrying / *Industries extractives* / Minas, canteras	Manufacturing / *Industries manufacturières* / Industrias manufactureras	Construction / *Construction* / Construcción	Commerce / *Commerce* / Comercio	Transport, storage, communication [3] / *Transports, entrepôts, communications* [3] / Transportes, almacenaje, comunicaciones [3]	Services / *Services* / Servicios
1970	4 088 000	100 000	16 000	1 197 000	394 000	842 000	163 000	811 000
1971	4 993 000	108 000	23 000	1 404 000	447 000	1 081 000	191 000	1 026 000
1972	4 840 000	108 000	19 000	1 155 000	466 000	1 134 000	183 000	1 021 000
1973	4 304 000	99 000	18 000	932 000	417 000	1 011 000	152 000	963 000
1974	5 076 000	115 000	19 000	1 247 000	499 000	1 197 000	174 000	942 000
1975	7 830 000	157 000	30 000	2 320 000	831 000	1 708 000	303 000	1 339 000
1976	7 288 000	189 000	36 000	1 683 000	718 000	1 718 000	270 000	1 450 000
1977	6 855 000	186 000	32 000	1 452 000	607 000	1 644 000	271 000	1 394 000
1978	6 047 000	151 000	35 000	1 219 000	541 000	1 439 000	221 000	1 286 000
1979	5 963 000	157 000	44 600	1 273 000	548 000	1 390 000	229 000	1 236 000

[1] Persons aged 16 years and over. [2] Incl. casual workers. Incl. industrial groups not specified in the table. [3] Incl. electricity, gas, water and sanitary services.

[1] *Personnes âgées de 16 ans et plus.* [2] *Y compris les travailleurs occasionnels. Y compris des groupes d'activité économique non spécifiés dans le tableau.* [3] *Y compris l'électricité, le gaz, l'eau et les services sanitaires.*

[1] Personas de 16 años y más. [2] Incl. los trabajadores ocasionales. Incl. grupos de actividad económica no especificados en el cuadro. [3] Incl. la electricidad, el gas, el agua y los servicios sanitarios.

B

Occupational groups *(Labour force sample surveys)* [1]
Groupes de professions *(Enquêtes par sondage sur la main-d'œuvre)* [1]
Grupos de ocupaciones *(Encuestas por muestra sobre la fuerza trabajadora)* [1]

(ISCO — CITP — CIUO 1958)

Date / *Date* / Fecha	Total [2]	Professional, technical and related workers / *Professions libérales, techniciens et assimilés* / Profesiones liberales, técnicos y trabajadores asimilados	Farmers, farm managers / *Agriculteurs, directeurs d'exploitations agric.* / Agricultores, directores de empresas agrícolas	Executive and managerial workers [3] / *Directeurs et cadres adm. supérieurs* [3] / Administradores, gerentes y directores [3]	Clerical and related workers / *Employés de bureau et assimilés* / Empleados de oficina y asimilados	Sales workers / *Vendeurs* / Vendedores	Craftsmen, foremen and related workers [4] / *Artisans, contre-maîtres et assimilés* [4] / Artesanos, contramaestres y asimilados [4]	Operative and related workers / *Ouvriers spécialisés et assimilés* / Operarios especializados y asimilados	Housekeeping service workers / *Personnel domestique* / Trabajadores del servicio doméstico	Service workers [5] / *Travailleurs dans les services* [5] / Trabajadores de los servicios [5]	Farm labourers and foremen / *Ouvriers et contre-maîtres agricoles* / Obreros y contramaestres agrícolas	Labourers not elsewhere classified / *Ouvriers non classés ailleurs* / Obreros no clasificados en otras partes
1970	4 088 000	227 000	4 000	112 000	579 000	195 000	398 000	1 057 000	69 000	472 000	79 000	391 000
1971	4 993 000	333 000	5 000	145 000	683 000	225 000	507 000	1 182 000	69 000	650 000	76 000	488 000
1972	4 840 000	282 000	3 000	145 000	704 000	238 000	482 000	1 009 000	60 000	677 000	80 000	483 000
1973	4 304 000	260 000	2 000	123 000	630 000	205 000	434 000	857 000	62 000	612 000	76 000	397 000
1974	5 076 000	285 000	4 000	168 000	725 000	240 000	523 000	1 123 000	56 000	708 000	75 000	492 000
1975	7 830 000	425 000	3 000	276 000	1 063 000	336 000	994 000	1 955 000	67 000	1 024 000	106 000	756 000
1976	7 288 000	440 000	4 000	296 000	1 062 000	312 000	831 000	1 493 000	68 000	1 084 000	128 000	685 000
1977	6 855 000	426 000	4 000	276 000	1 004 000	318 000	708 000	1 333 000	60 000	1 042 000	129 000	616 000
1978	6 047 000	381 000	3 000	214 000	866 000	256 000	603 000	1 155 000	63 000	966 000	107 000	566 000
1979	5 963 000	373 000	3 000	225 000	853 000	252 000	604 000	1 206 000	54 000	925 000	103 000	566 000

[1] Persons aged 16 years and over. [2] Incl. casual workers. [3] Excl. farm managers. [4] Excl. farm foremen. [5] Excl. house-keeping service workers.

[1] *Personnes âgées de 16 ans et plus.* [2] *Y compris les travailleurs occasionnels.* [3] *Non compris les directeurs d'exploitations agricoles.* [4] *Non compris les contre-maîtres agricoles.* [5] *Non compris le personnel domestique.*

[1] Personas de 16 años y más. [2] Incl. los trabajadores ocasionales. [3] Excl. los directores de empresas agrícolas. [4] Excl. los contramaestres agrícolas. [5] Excl. los trabajadores del servicio doméstico.

11 Structure of unemployment
Structure du chômage
Estructura del desempleo

Uruguay (Montevideo)

(ISIC — CITI — CIIU 1958)

A Industrial groups *(Labour force sample surveys)*
Groupes d'activité économique *(Enquêtes par sondage sur la main-d'œuvre)*
Grupos de actividad económica *(Encuestas por muestra sobre la fuerza trabajadora)*

Date / Date / Fecha	Total	Agriculture, forestry, fishing / Agriculture, sylviculture, pêche / Agricultura, silvicultura, pesca	Manufacturing / Industries manufacturières / Industrias manufactureras	Construction / Construction / Construcción	Electricity, gas, water and sanitary services / Électricité, gaz, eau et services sanitaires / Electricidad, gas, agua y servicios sanitarios	Commerce / Commerce / Comercio	Transport, storage, communication / Transports, entrepôts, communications / Transportes, almacenaje comunicaciones	Services / Services / Servicios	Activities not adequately described / Activités mal désignées / Actividades no bien especificadas	Persons seeking work for the first time / Personnes en quête d'emploi pour la première fois / Personas en busca de trabajo por primera vez
1970	39 250	350	11 650	2 350	100	4 300	850	5 200	1 050	13 400
1971	41 200	250	13 900	2 300	200	4 450	1 400	6 500	500	11 700
1972 [1]	41 700	400	13 500	2 200	100	6 100	2 200	5 900	—	11 300
1973 [1]	49 400	300	14 700	3 600	300	6 000	1 500	8 600	500	13 900
1974 [2]	38 200	300	9 800	3 100	—	4 100	400	4 600	300	15 600
1976	68 200	500	18 600	3 200	100	8 800	2 200	11 800	900	22 100
1977	64 100	700	16 400	3 000	300	8 600	1 500	11 800	21 800	
1978	53 000	300	13 900	2 300	300	7 200	1 200	9 800	18 000	
1979	43 200	400	12 100	1 400	—	6 300	1 400	8 100	13 500	

(ISCO — CITP — CIUO 1958)

B Occupational groups *(Labour force sample surveys)*
Groupes de professions *(Enquêtes par sondage sur la main-d'œuvre)*
Grupos de ocupaciones *(Encuestas por muestra sobre la fuerza trabajadora)*

Date / Date / Fecha	Total	Professional, technical and related workers / Professions libérales, techniciens et assimilés / Profesiones liberales, técnicos y asimilados	Administrative, executive, managerial workers / Directeurs, cadres administratifs supérieurs / Administradores, gerentes, directores	Clerical workers / Employés de bureau / Empleados de oficina	Sales workers / Vendeurs / Vendedores	Farmers, fishermen and related workers / Agriculteurs, pêcheurs et assimilés / Agricultores, pescadores y asimilados	Workers in transport occupations / Travailleurs dans les professions des transports / Trabajadores de los transportes	Craftsmen, prod. process workers, labourers not elsewhere classified / Artisans, ouvriers de métier et à la production, manœuvres non classés ailleurs / Artesanos, trabaj. ocupados en los div. procesos de prod., peones no clasif. bajo otros epígrafes	Service workers / Travailleurs spécialisés dans les services / Trabajadores de los servicios	Workers not classifiable by occupation [3] / Travailleurs ne pouvant être classés selon la profession [3] / Trabajadores que no pueden ser clasificados según la ocupación [3]
1970	39 250	550	50	2 700	3 050	1 200	400	13 450	3 600	14 250
1971	41 200	1 200	200	3 550	3 000	300	1 250	14 950	3 700	13 050
1972 [1]	41 700	1 500	200	3 100	3 300	500	1 000	12 600	4 000	15 500
1973 [1]	49 400	1 800	300	4 500	3 500	500	1 100	18 300	4 400	15 000
1974 [2]	38 200	500	300	1 900	2 000	300	400	13 000	3 700	16 100
1976	68 200	2 300	300	4 800	5 200	600	1 400	22 800	7 400	23 400
1977	64 100	2 350	100	4 500	4 750	700	21 100		8 450	22 150
1978	53 000	1 400	—	4 700	3 500	400	17 700		6 500	18 800
1979	43 200	1 600	—	4 100	3 000	400	14 400		5 300	14 400

[1] First semester. [2] Aug. 1974–Feb. 1975. [3] Incl. persons seeking work for the first time.

[1] *Premier semestre.* [2] *Août 1974–fév. 1975.* [3] *Y compris les personnes en quête d'emploi pour la première fois.*

[1] Primer semestre. [2] Agosto 1974–febr. 1975. [3] Incl. las personas en busca de trabajo por primera vez.

301

11 Structure of unemployment
Structure du chômage
Estructura del desempleo

Venezuela

(ISIC — CITI — CIIU 1958)

A Industrial groups *(Labour force sample surveys)*
Groupes d'activité économique *(Enquêtes par sondage sur la main-d'œuvre)*
Grupos de actividad económica *(Encuestas por muestra sobre la fuerza trabajadora)*

Date [1] Date [1] Fecha [1]	Total [2]	Agriculture, forestry, fishing *Agriculture, sylviculture, pêche* Agricultura, silvicultura, pesca	Mining, quarrying *Industries extractives* Minas, canteras	Manufacturing *Industries manufacturières* Industrias manufactureras	Construction *Construction* Construcción	Electricity, gas, water and sanitary services *Électricité, gaz, eau et services sanitaires* Electricidad, gas, agua y servicios sanitarios	Commerce *Commerce* Comercio	Transport, storage, communication *Transports, entrepôts, communications* Transportes, almacenaje, comunicaciones	Services *Services* Servicios	Activities not adequately described *Activités mal désignées* Actividades no bien especificadas
1970	198 847	17 329	4 842	33 213	30 089	3 419	24 020	12 454	36 089	407
1971	195 161	15 538	3 566	39 674	29 817	2 832	25 207	14 271	32 663	209
1974	219 474	15 436	3 263	38 345	34 021	1 718	36 152	13 060	41 026	658
1975 [3]	241 752	16 595	2 200	25 015	34 127	2 620	35 769	11 751	42 524	37 245
1976 [3]	221 585	15 837	1 336	39 224	36 442	784	31 596	9 874	43 193	13 747
1977 [3]	185 409	9 266	2 447	30 109	29 967	1 943	27 203	7 959	36 352	11 960
1978	180 360	8 817	2 580	32 300	32 924	1 239	22 841	9 316	30 793	10 755
1979	244 646	12 340	1 907	42 686	44 024	3 019	28 212	15 566	45 683	14 415

(ISCO — CITP — CIUO 1958)

B Occupational groups *(Labour force sample surveys)*
Groupes de professions *(Enquêtes par sondage sur la main-d'œuvre)*
Grupos de ocupaciones *(Encuestas por muestra sobre la fuerza trabajadora)*

Date [1] Date [1] Fecha [1]	Total [2]	Professional, technical and related workers *Professions libérales, techniciens et assimilés* Profesiones liberales, técnicos y asimilados	Administrative, executive, managerial workers *Directeurs, cadres administratifs supérieurs* Administradores, gerentes, directores	Clerical workers *Employés de bureau* Empleados de oficina	Sales workers *Vendeurs* Vendedores	Farmers, fishermen and related workers *Agriculteurs, pêcheurs et assimilés* Agricultores, pescadores y asimilados	Miners, quarrymen and related workers *Mineurs, carriers et assimilés* Mineros, canteros y asimilados	Workers in transport and communication occupations *Travailleurs dans les professions des transports et des communications* Trabajadores de los transportes y comunicaciones	Craftsmen, prod. process workers, labourers not elsewhere classified *Artisans, ouvriers de métier et à la production, manœuvres non classés ailleurs* Artesanos, trabaj. ocupados en los div. procesos de prod., peones no clasif. bajo otros epígrafes	Service workers *Travailleurs spécialisés dans les services* Trabajadores de los servicios	Workers not classifiable by occupation *Personnes ne pouvant être classées selon la profession* Trabajadores que no pueden ser clasificados según la ocupación
1970	198 847	10 869	3 316	19 075	16 139	14 185	2 017	14 296	64 725	17 140	100
1971	195 161	8 296	1 788	18 688	16 493	11 972	2 201	15 837	71 908	16 385	209
1974	219 474	9 947	2 517	18 925	23 673	11 497	2 268	17 951	71 348	23 786	1 767
1975 [3]	241 752	10 271	3 299	14 265	18 428	17 526	854	15 454	66 918	26 156	34 675
1976 [3]	221 585	10 516	2 707	17 421	16 236	16 889	907	15 774	74 939	22 672	13 972
1977 [3]	185 409	8 808	4 260	17 275	13 663	9 837	1 071	14 271	57 069	19 594	11 358
1978	180 360	7 415	3 215	16 227	12 949	9 244	1 766	14 454	58 912	16 548	10 835
1979	244 646	10 635	2 810	26 601	15 689	12 276	1 291	22 495	81 176	20 375	14 504

[1] Second semester. Prior to 1975, average of the two semesters. [2] Incl. persons seeking work for the first time.

[1] *Deuxième semestre. Avant 1975, moyenne de deux semestres.* [2] *Y compris les personnes en quête d'emploi pour la première fois.*

[1] Segundo semestre. Antes de 1975, promedio de los dos semestres. [2] Incl. las personas en busca de trabajo por primera vez.

11 Structure of unemployment
Structure du chômage
Estructura del desempleo

ASIA — ASIE — ASIA

Brunei

Industrial groups *(Employment office statistics)*
Groupes d'activité économique *(Statistiques des bureaux de placement)*
Grupos de actividad económica *(Estadísticas de las oficinas de colocación)*

Date [1] / Date [1] / Fecha [1]	Total	0/1	2	3	4	5	6	7/8/9	X
		Professional, technical and related workers / Personnel des professions scientifiques, techniques, libérales et assimilées / Profesionales, técnicos y trabajadores asimilados	Administrative and managerial workers / Directeurs et cadres administratifs supérieurs / Directores y funcionarios públicos superiores	Clerical and related workers / Personnel administratif et travailleurs assimilés / Personal administrativo y trabajadores asimilados	Sales workers / Personnel commercial et vendeurs / Comerciantes y vendedores	Service workers / Travailleurs spécialisés dans les services / Trabajadores de los servicios	Agricultural, animal husbandry and forestry workers, fishermen and hunters / Agriculteurs, éleveurs, forestiers, pêcheurs et chasseurs / Trabajadores agrícolas y forestales, pescadores y cazadores	Production and related workers, transport equipment operators and labourers / Ouvriers et manœuvres non agricoles et conducteurs d'engins de transport / Obreros no agrícolas, conductores de máquinas y vehículos de transporte y trabajadores asimilados	Workers not classifiable by occupation / Travailleurs ne pouvant être classés selon la profession / Trabajadores que no pueden ser clasificados según la ocupación
1974	1 417	.	.	443	48	466	7	453	.
1975	1 531	.	.	448	25	473	2	583	.
1976	1 872	.	.	557	23	690	15	587	.
1977	1 965	.	.	623	20	726	51	545	.
1978	2 649	.	.	873	15	940	51	717	.
1979	2 229	.	.	888	24	817	65	435	.

[1] December.

[1] *Décembre.*

[1] Diciembre.

UNEMPLOYMENT

11 Structure of unemployment
Structure du chômage
Estructura del desempleo

Cyprus

A Industrial groups (Employment office statistics)
Groupes d'activité économique (Statistiques des bureaux de placement)
Grupos de actividad económica (Estadísticas de las oficinas de colocación)

Date / Date / Fecha	Total	1 — Agriculture, forestry, fishing / Agriculture, sylviculture, pêche / Agricultura, silvicultura, pesca	2 — Mining, quarrying / Industries extractives / Minas, canteras	3 — Manufacturing / Industries manufacturières / Industrias manufactureras	4 — Electricity, gas, water / Electricité, gaz, eau / Electricidad, gas, agua	5 — Construction / Construction / Construcción	6 — Trade, restaurants and hotels / Commerce, restaurants et hôtels / Comercio, restaurantes y hoteles	7 — Transport, storage, communication / Transports, entrepôts, communications / Transportes, almacenaje, comunicaciones	8 — Financing, insur., real est., business serv. / Banques, assur., aff. imm., serv. aux entreprises / Bancos, seguros, bienes inm., serv. para empresas	9 — Community, social, and pers. services / Services à collectivité, serv. sociaux et pers. / Servicios comunales, sociales y personales	0 — Activities not adequately described [2] / Activités mal désignées [2] / Actividades no bien especificadas [2]
1970	2 810	144	67	237	18	489	284	81	32	348	1 110
1971	2 846	104	108	254	11	437	260	101	40	316	1 215
1972	2 524	119	43	208	14	310	169	112	31	299	1 219
1973	3 314	379	66	255	17	417	208	103	53	401	1 415
1974 [1]	11 206	1 206	239	2 339	33	2 493	1 591	503	218	1 266	1 318
1975	22 543	2 832	478	4 731	61	6 356	3 075	1 222	364	2 062	1 362
1976	14 518	1 763	271	1 753	133	3 637	2 108	888	151	1 663	2 151
1977	6 144	469	89	531	44	714	901	334	98	798	2 166
1978	4 017	205	42	309	33	320	508	169	72	569	1 790
1979	3 691	173	70	277	22	287	419	122	73	504	1 744

B Occupational groups (Employment office statistics)
Groupes de professions (Statistiques des bureaux de placement)
Grupos de ocupaciones (Estadísticas de las oficinas de colocación)

Date / Date / Fecha	Total	0/1 — Professional, technical and related workers / Personnel des professions scientifiques, techniques, libérales et assimilées / Profesionales, técnicos y trabajadores asimilados	2 — Administrative and managerial workers / Directeurs et cadres administratifs supérieurs / Directores y funcionarios públicos superiores	3 — Clerical and related workers / Personnel administratif et travailleurs assimilés / Personal administrativo y trabajadores asimilados	4 — Sales workers / Personnel commercial et vendeurs / Comerciantes y vendedores	5 — Service workers / Travailleurs spécialisés dans les services / Trabajadores de los servicios	6 — Agricultural, animal husbandry and forestry workers, fishermen and hunters / Agriculteurs, éleveurs, forestiers, pêcheurs et chasseurs / Trabajadores agrícolas y forestales, pescadores y cazadores	7/8/9 — Production and related workers, transport equipment operators and labourers / Ouvriers et manœuvres non agricoles et conducteurs d'engins de transport / Obreros no agrícolas, conductores de máquinas y vehículos de transporte y trabajadores asimilados	X — Workers not classifiable by occupation [3] / Travailleurs ne pouvant être classés selon la profession [3] / Trabajadores que no pueden ser clasificados según la ocupación [3]
1972	2 524	296	16	318	42	226	18	841	767
1973	3 314	453	20	435	48	248	30	1 285	795
1974 [1]	11 206	571	51	1 239	491	1 257	184	6 723	690
1975	22 543	509	87	2 030	1 128	2 354	911	14 812	712
1976	14 518	629	38	1 271	715	1 300	790	8 736	1 039
1977	6 144	661	37	981	303	563	181	2 256	1 162
1978	4 017	694	34	715	159	359	81	1 135	840
1979	3 691	753	55	593	123	277	59	1 015	816

[1] Beginning July 1974: due to a change in the geographical scope of the series, data are not comparable with those for preceding period. [2] Incl. persons seeking work for the first time. [3] Incl. certain persons seeking work for the first time.

[1] A partir de juillet 1974 : en raison d'un changement de la portée géographique de la série, les données ne sont pas comparables avec celles de la période précédente. [2] Y compris les personnes en quête d'emploi pour la première fois. [3] Y compris certaines personnes en quête d'emploi pour la première fois.

[1] A partir de julio de 1974: en razón de un cambio del alcance geográfico de la serie, los datos no son comparables a los del período precedente. [2] Incl. las personas en busca de trabajo por primera vez. [3] Incl. ciertas personas en busca de trabajo por primera vez.

11 Structure of unemployment
Structure du chômage
Estructura del desempleo

Hong Kong

Occupational groups *(Labour force sample surveys)* [1]
Groupes de professions *(Enquêtes par sondage sur la main-d'œuvre)* [1]
Grupos de ocupaciones *(Encuestas por muestra sobre la fuerza trabajadora)* [1]

Date [1] Date [1] Fecha [1]	Total	0/1 Professional, technical and related workers *Personnel des professions scientifiques, techniques, libérales et assimilées* Profesionales, técnicos y trabajadores asimilados	2 Administrative and managerial workers *Directeurs et cadres administratifs supérieurs* Directores y funcionarios públicos superiores	3 Clerical and related workers *Personnel administratif et travailleurs assimilés* Personal administrativo y trabajadores asimilados	4 Sales workers *Personnel commercial et vendeurs* Comerciantes y vendedores	5 Service workers *Travailleurs spécialisés dans les services* Trabajadores de los servicios	6 Agricultural, animal husbandry and forestry workers, fishermen and hunters *Agriculteurs, éleveurs, forestiers, pêcheurs et chasseurs* Trabajadores agrícolas y forestales, pescadores y cazadores	7/8/9 Production and related workers, transport equipment operators and labourers *Ouvriers et manœuvres non agricoles et conducteurs d'engins de transport* Obreros no agrícolas, conductores de máquinas y vehículos de transporte y trabajadores asimilados	X Workers not classifiable by occupation *Travailleurs ne pouvant être classés selon la profession* Trabajadores que no pueden ser clasificados según la ocupación	Persons seeking work for the first time *Personnes en quête d'emploi pour la première fois* Personas en busca de trabajo por primera vez
1977	80 000	2 800	200	4 200	3 600	8 400	1 100	41 600	100	18 000
1978	55 600	1 200	300	3 600	2 900	6 700	6 700	25 200	300	15 100
1979	74 600	1 600	300	4 000	2 800	7 500	600	32 200	300	25 400

[1] September.   [1] *Septembre.*   [1] Septiembre.

India

Occupational groups *(Employment office statistics)* [1]
Groupes de professions *(Statistiques des bureaux de placement)* [1]
Grupos de ocupaciones *(Estadísticas de las oficinas de colocación)* [1]

Date [2] Date [2] Fecha [2]	Total	0/1 Professional, technical and related workers *Personnel des professions scientifiques, techniques, libérales et assimilées* Profesionales, técnicos y trabajadores asimilados	2 Administrative and managerial workers *Directeurs et cadres administratifs supérieurs* Directores y funcionarios públicos superiores	3 Clerical and related workers *Personnel administratif et travailleurs assimilés* Personal administrativo y trabajadores asimilados	4 Sales workers *Personnel commercial et vendeurs* Comerciantes y vendedores	5 Service workers *Travailleurs spécialisés dans les services* Trabajadores de los servicios	6 Agricultural, animal husbandry and forestry workers, fishermen and hunters *Agriculteurs, éleveurs, forestiers, pêcheurs et chasseurs* Trabajadores agrícolas y forestales, pescadores y cazadores	7/8/9 Production and related workers, transport equipment operators and labourers *Ouvriers et manœuvres non agricoles et conducteurs d'engins de transport* Obreros no agrícolas, conductores de máquinas y vehículos de transp. y trabaj. asimilados	X Workers not classifiable by occupation [3] *Travailleurs ne pouvant être classés selon la profession* [3] Trabajadores que no pueden ser clasificados según la ocupación [3]
1974	8 393 355	433 668	7 757	462 387	2 173	235 778	24 436	932 594	6 294 562
1975	9 059 367	491 088	7 125	523 989	2 406	261 218	29 840	1 020 083	6 723 618
1976	9 696 639	544 672	7 738	547 039	2 009	273 210	29 953	998 807	7 293 211
1977	10 665 225	625 515	9 323	595 174	2 335	299 107	34 792	1 063 998	8 034 981
1978 [4]	12 677 821	705 779	9 979	683 046	2 406	343 970	41 500	1 175 437	9 715 704

[1] Applicants for work on the "live" register. [2] June and Dec. [3] Incl. persons seeking work for the first time. [4] Dec.

[1] *Demandeurs d'emploi restant inscrits.* [2] *Juin et déc.* [3] *Y compris les personnes en quête d'emploi pour la première fois.* [4] *Déc.*

[1] Solicitantes de trabajo que continúan inscritos. [2] Junio y dic. [3] Incl. las personas en busca de trabajo por primera vez. [4] Dic.

UNEMPLOYMENT

11 Structure of unemployment
Structure du chômage
Estructura del desempleo

Israel

A

Industrial groups *(Labour force sample surveys)* [1]
Groupes d'activité économique *(Enquêtes par sondage sur la main-d'œuvre)* [1]
Grupos de actividad económica *(Encuestas por muestra sobre la fuerza trabajadora)* [1]

Date / Date / Fecha	Total	1 Agriculture, forestry, fishing / *Agriculture, sylviculture, pêche* / Agricultura, silvicultura, pesca	2-3 Mining, quarrying, manufacturing / *Industries extractives, industries manufacturières* / Minas, canteras, industrias manufactureras	4 Electricity, gas, water / *Electricité, gaz, eau* / Electricidad, gas, agua	5 Construction / *Construction* / Construcción	6 Trade, restaurants and hotels / *Commerce, restaurants et hôtels* / Comercio, restaurantes y hoteles	7 Transport, storage, communication / *Transports, entrepôts, communications* / Transportes, almacenaje, comunicaciones	8 Financing, insur., real est., business serv. / *Banques, assur., aff. imm., serv. aux entreprises* / Bancos, seguros, bienes inm., serv. para empresas	9 Community, social, and pers. services / *Services à collectivité, serv. sociaux et pers.* / Servicios comunales, sociales y personales	0 Activities not adequately described / *Activités mal désignées* / Actividades no bien especificadas
1970	18 600	1 600	5 500	100	2 700	2 300	1 200	1 000	4 200	—
1971	18 900	1 200	5 100	200	2 500	2 900	1 600	800	4 600	—
1972	15 300	800	4 700	100	2 300	2 100	1 100	500	3 700	—
1973	16 000	300	4 600	100	3 100	2 300	1 000	800	3 800	100
1974	16 500	400	4 100	100	2 500	2 200	1 200	1 000	4 500	400
1975	16 500	300	4 000	100	2 800	2 300	1 200	1 200	4 500	200
1976	22 400	600	4 900	100	4 100	3 100	1 800	1 200	5 900	600
1977	22 200	500	4 800	100	4 100	2 500	1 800	1 200	6 300	800
1978	21 400	500	5 600	100	2 800	2 800	1 500	1 600	5 800	700
1979	19 000	500	4 700	200	2 200	2 400	1 300	1 700	5 200	800

B

Occupational groups *(Labour force sample surveys)* [1]
Groupes de professions *(Enquêtes par sondage sur la main-d'œuvre)* [1]
Grupos de ocupaciones *(Encuestas por muestra sobre la fuerza trabajadora)* [1]

Date / Date / Fecha	Total	0/1 Professional, technical and related workers / *Personnel des professions scientifiques, techniques, libérales et assimilées* / Profesionales, técnicos y trabajadores asimilados	2 Administrative and managerial workers / *Directeurs et cadres administratifs supérieurs* / Directores y funcionarios públicos superiores	3 Clerical and related workers / *Personnel administratif et travailleurs assimilés* / Personal administrativo y trabajadores asimilados	4 Sales workers / *Personnel commercial et vendeurs* / Comerciantes y vendedores	5 Service workers / *Travailleurs spécialisés dans les services* / Trabajadores de los servicios	6 Agricultural, animal husbandry and forestry workers, fishermen and hunters / *Agriculteurs, éleveurs, forestiers, pêcheurs et chasseurs* / Trabajadores agrícolas y forestales, pescadores y cazadores	7/8/9 Production and related workers, transport equipment operators and labourers / *Ouvriers et manœuvres non agricoles et conducteurs d'engins de transport* / Obreros no agrícolas, conductores de máquinas y vehículos de transporte y trabajadores asimilados	X Workers not classifiable by occupation / *Travailleurs ne pouvant être classés selon la profession* / Trabajadores que no pueden ser clasificados según la ocupación
1972	15 300	1 400	100	2 000	600	2 400	700	7 700	400
1973	16 000	1 900	—	2 900	800	2 100	400	8 100	100
1974	16 500	1 800	200	2 600	700	2 700	400	7 500	200
1975	16 500	2 000	300	2 800	1 200	2 100	400	7 900	200
1976	22 400	2 400	400	3 300	1 200	3 300	600	10 600	600
1977	22 200	2 300	400	3 700	1 100	3 000	500	10 600	600
1978	21 400	2 200	300	4 300	1 400	2 800	400	9 400	600
1979	19 000	1 900	200	3 400	1 300	2 600	600	8 300	700

[1] Excl. persons who did not work in the country during the previous 12 months.

[1] *Non compris les personnes qui n'ont pas travaillé dans le pays pendant les 12 mois précédents.*

[1] Excl. las personas que no trabajaron en el país en los 12 meses precedentes.

11 Structure of unemployment
Structure du chômage
Estructura del desempleo

Korea, Rep. of

A — Industrial groups (*Labour force sample surveys*)
Groupes d'activité économique (*Enquêtes par sondage sur la main-d'œuvre*)
Grupos de actividad económica (*Encuestas por muestra sobre la fuerza trabajadora*)

Date / Date / Fecha	Total	1 — Agriculture, forestry, fishing / Agriculture, sylviculture, pêche / Agricultura, silvicultura, pesca	2 — Mining, quarrying / Industries extractives / Minas, canteras	3 — Manufacturing / Industries manufacturières / Industrias manufactureras	4 — Electricity, gas, water / Electricité, gaz, eau / Electricidad, gas, agua	5 — Construction / Construction / Construcción	6 — Trade, restaurants and hotels / Commerce, restaurants et hôtels / Comercio, restaurantes y hoteles	7 — Transport, storage, communication / Transports, entrepôts, communications / Transportes, almacenaje, comunicaciones	8 — Financing, insur., real est., business serv. / Banques, assur., aff. imm., serv. aux entreprises / Bancos, seguros, bienes inm., serv. para empresas	9 — Community, social, and pers. services / Services à collectivité, serv. sociaux et pers. / Servicios comunales, sociales y personales	0 — Activities not adequately described [1] / Activités mal désignées [1] / Actividades no bien especificadas [1]
1971	476 000	31 000	4 000	54 000	3 000	17 000	35 000	19 000	4 000	39 000	270 000
1972	499 000	23 000	2 000	82 000	3 000	44 000	53 000	24 000	5 000	51 000	212 000
1973	461 000	19 000	4 000	91 000	3 000	35 000	62 000	20 000	6 000	49 000	172 000
1974	494 000	35 000	1 000	106 000	1 000	34 000	62 000	23 000	8 000	48 000	176 000
1975	510 000	19 000	1 000	128 000	1 000	36 000	60 000	21 000	4 000	38 000	202 000
1976	505 000	20 000	2 000	117 000	1 000	54 000	62 000	20 000	4 000	44 000	181 000
1977	511 000	22 000	4 000	104 000	1 000	34 000	58 000	20 000	6 000	32 000	230 000
1978	442 000	15 000	2 000	103 000	1 000	40 000	51 000	20 000	11 000	27 000	172 000
1979	542 000	18 000	3 000	155 000	1 000	73 000	69 000	28 000	13 000	32 000	150 000

B — Occupational groups (*Labour force sample surveys*)
Groupes de professions (*Enquêtes par sondage sur la main-d'œuvre*)
Grupos de ocupaciones (*Encuestas por muestra sobre la fuerza trabajadora*)

Date / Date / Fecha	Total	0/1 — Professional, technical and related workers / Personnel des professions scientifiques, techniques, libérales et assimilées / Profesionales, técnicos y trabajadores asimilados	2 — Administrative and managerial workers / Directeurs et cadres administratifs supérieurs / Directores y funcionarios públicos superiores	3 — Clerical and related workers / Personnel administratif et travailleurs assimilés / Personal administrativo y trabajadores asimilados	4 — Sales workers / Personnel commercial et vendeurs / Comerciantes y vendedores	5 — Service workers / Travailleurs spécialisés dans les services / Trabajadores de los servicios	6 — Agricultural, animal husbandry and forestry workers, fishermen and hunters / Agriculteurs, éleveurs, forestiers, pêcheurs et chasseurs / Trabajadores agrícolas y forestales, pescadores y cazadores	7/8/9 — Production and related workers, transport equipment operators and labourers / Ouvriers et manœuvres non agricoles et conducteurs d'engins de transport / Obreros no agrícolas, conductores de máquinas y vehículos de transp. y trabaj. asimilados	X — Workers not classifiable by occupation [1] / Travailleurs ne pouvant être classés selon la profession [1] / Trabajadores que no pueden ser clasificados según la ocupación [1]
1970	454 000	5 000	1 000	27 000	24 000	21 000	31 000	67 000	278 000
1971	476 000	7 000	3 000	30 000	35 000	17 000	27 000	88 000	269 000
1972	499 000	7 000	2 000	32 000	46 000	18 000	23 000	156 000	215 000
1973	461 000	7 000	3 000	40 000	52 000	18 000	19 000	150 000	172 000
1974	494 000	10 000	3 000	40 000	54 000	25 000	34 000	152 000	176 000
1975	510 000	7 000	3 000	41 000	55 000	21 000	23 000	166 000	194 000
1976	505 000	6 000	4 000	34 000	54 000	23 000	20 000	183 000	181 000
1977	511 000	7 000	4 000	37 000	49 000	19 000	21 000	144 000	230 000
1978	442 000	8 000	5 000	39 000	44 000	18 000	14 000	142 000	172 000
1979	542 000	13 000	7 000	51 000	58 000	23 000	18 000	222 000	150 000

[1] Incl. persons seeking work for the first time.

[1] Y compris les personnes en quête d'emploi pour la première fois.

[1] Incl. las personas en busca de trabajo por primera vez.

11 Structure of unemployment
Structure du chômage
Estructura del desempleo

Malaysia:

Occupational groups *(Employment office statistics)* [1]
Groupes de professions *(Statistiques des bureaux de placement)* [1]
Grupos de ocupaciones *(Estadísticas de las oficinas de colocación)* [1]

Date [2] / Date [2] / Fecha [2]	Total	0/1 Professional, technical and related workers / *Personnel des professions scientifiques, techniques, libérales et assimilées* / Profesionales, técnicos y trabajadores asimilados	2 Administrative and managerial workers / *Directeurs et cadres administratifs supérieurs* / Directores y funcionarios públicos superiores	3 Clerical and related workers / *Personnel administratif et travailleurs assimilés* / Personal administrativo y trabajadores asimilados	4 Sales workers / *Personnel commercial et vendeurs* / Comerciantes y vendedores	5 Service workers / *Travailleurs spécialisés dans les services* / Trabajadores de los servicios	6 Agricultural, animal husbandry and forestry workers, fishermen and hunters / *Agriculteurs, éleveurs, forestiers, pêcheurs et chasseurs* / Trabajadores agrícolas y forestales, pescadores y cazadores	7/8/9 Production and related workers, transport equipment operators and labourers / *Ouvriers et manœuvres non agricoles et conducteurs d'engins de transport* / Obreros no agrícolas, conductores de máquinas y vehículos de transp. y trabaj. asimilados
Peninsular Malaysia								
1970	157 705	9 405	43	37 721	866	17 932	6 470	85 268
1971	155 902	9 976	9	34 225	633	14 810	6 862	89 387
1972	162 420	9 316	69	32 656	683	16 718	7 728	95 250
1973	140 157	6 030	73	27 947	481	12 438	7 436	85 752
1974	128 637	4 979	122	25 350	521	9 784	6 550	81 331
1975	108 242	4 758	212	25 307	446	7 978	5 061	64 480
1976	104 617	4 950	339	26 913	336	7 355	4 772	59 952
1977	104 201	5 762	548	30 529	446	6 532	4 204	56 180
1978	96 657	4 289	458	31 741	288	6 486	3 502	49 893
1979	76 628	2 797	387	28 919	205	5 420	2 366	36 534
Sabah								
1972	863	4	.	253	5	105	101	395
1973	806	14	.	338	4	84	76	290
1974	824	13	.	374	9	89	44	295
1975	1 013	6	.	372	9	115	53	458
1976	916	24	1	373	8	104	81	325
1977	932	15	.	446	3	83	92	293
1978	622	6	.	301	4	42	56	213
1979	552	6	.	241	29	41	34	201
Sarawak								
1972	4 049	69	.	1 578	34	336	60	1 972
1973	7 267	90	.	2 934	38	555	62	3 588
1974	9 095	131	.	3 422	63	652	60	4 767
1975	4 865	58	1	1 776	43	364	59	2 564
1976	7 866	113	8	2 651	65	780	107	4 143
1977	9 084	240	10	3 243	67	830	102	4 592
1978	9 486	375	15	3 577	68	800	106	4 545
1979	11 484	524	24	4 684	81	829	122	5 220

[1] Applicants for work on the " live " register. [2] Dec.

[1] *Demandeurs d'emploi restant inscrits.* [2] *Déc.*

[1] Solicitantes de trabajo que continúan inscritos. [2] Dic.

11 Structure of unemployment
Structure du chômage
Estructura del desempleo

Pakistan

Occupational groups *(Employment office statistics)* [1]
Groupes de professions *(Statistiques des bureaux de placement)* [1]
Grupos de ocupaciones *(Estadísticas de las oficinas de colocación)* [1]

Date [2] / Date [2] / Fecha [2]	Total	0/1	2	3	4	5	6	7/8/9
		Professional, technical and related workers / *Personnel des professions scientifiques, techniques, libérales et assimilées* / Profesionales, técnicos y trabajadores asimilados	Administrative and managerial workers / *Directeurs et cadres administratifs supérieurs* / Directores y funcionarios públicos superiores	Clerical and related workers / *Personnel administratif et travailleurs assimilés* / Personal administrativo y trabajadores asimilados	Sales workers / *Personnel commercial et vendeurs* / Comerciantes y vendedores	Service workers / *Travailleurs spécialisés dans les services* / Trabajadores de los servicios	Agricultural, animal husbandry and forestry workers, fishermen and hunters / *Agriculteurs, éleveurs, forestiers, pêcheurs et chasseurs* / Trabajadores agrícolas y forestales, pescadores y cazadores	Production and related workers, transport equipment operators and labourers / *Ouvriers et manœuvres non agricoles et conducteurs d'engins de transport* / Obreros no agrícolas, conductores de máquinas y vehículos de transp. y trabaj. asimilados
1974	191 217 [3]	20 464	712	64 408	209	46 381	3 004	56 141
1975	199 249 [3]	31 109	834	64 958	175	47 185	4 590	48 782

[1] Applicants for work on the " live " register. [2] Dec.
[3] Data for occupational groups are provisional.

[1] *Demandeurs d'emploi restant inscrits.* [2] *Déc.*
[3] *Les données par groupes de professions sont provisoires.*

[1] Solicitantes de trabajo que continúan inscritos.
[2] Dic. [3] Los datos por grupos de ocupaciones son provisionales.

11 Structure of unemployment
Structure du chômage
Estructura del desempleo

Philippines

(ISIC — CITI — CIIU 1958)

A Industrial groups *(Labour force sample surveys)*
Groupes d'activité économique *(Enquêtes par sondage sur la main-d'œuvre)*
Grupos de actividad económica *(Encuestas por muestra sobre la fuerza trabajadora)*

Date / Date / Fecha	Total	Agriculture, forestry, fishing / Agriculture, sylviculture, pêche / Agricultura, silvicultura, pesca	Mining, quarrying / Industries extractives / Minas, canteras	Manufacturing / Industries manufacturières / Industrias manufactureras	Construction / Construction / Construcción	Electricity, gas, water and sanitary services / Electricité, gaz, eau et services sanitaires / Electricidad, gas, agua y servicios sanitarios	Commerce / Commerce / Comercio	Transport, storage, communication / Transports, entrepôts, communications / Transportes, almacenaje, comunicaciones	Services / Services / Servicios	Activities not adequately described / Activités mal désignées / Actividades no bien especificadas	Persons seeking work for the first time / Personnes en quête d'emploi pour la première fois / Personas en busca de trabajo por primera vez
1971	666 000	91 000	4 000	46 000	38 000	2 000	42 000	20 000	71 000	10 000	342 000
1972	867 000	122 000	2 000	59 000	47 000	2 000	51 000	27 000	84 000	7 000	468 000
1973	690 000	90 000	3 000	61 000	53 000	3 000	48 000	29 000	78 000	3 000	323 000
1974	584 000	101 000	1 000	55 000	45 000	1 000	39 000	29 000	60 000	1 000	249 000
1975	581 000	90 000	2 000	61 000	47 000	2 000	34 000	19 000	67 000	2 000	257 000

B Occupational groups *(Labour force sample surveys)*
Groupes de professions *(Enquêtes par sondage sur la main-d'œuvre)*
Grupos de ocupaciones *(Encuestas por muestra sobre la fuerza trabajadora)*

Date / Date / Fecha	Total	0/1 Professional, technical and related workers / Personnel des professions scientifiques, techniques, libérales et assimilées / Profesionales, técnicos y trabajadores asimilados	2 Administrative and managerial workers / Directeurs et cadres administratifs supérieurs / Directores y funcionarios públicos superiores	3 Clerical and related workers / Personnel administratif et travailleurs assimilés / Personal administrativo y trabajadores asimilados	4 Sales workers / Personnel commercial et vendeurs / Comerciantes y vendedores	5 Service workers / Travailleurs spécialisés dans les services / Trabajadores de los servicios	6 Agricultural, animal husbandry and forestry workers, fishermen and hunters / Agriculteurs, éleveurs, forestiers, pêcheurs et chasseurs / Trabajadores agrícolas y forestales, pescadores y cazadores	7/8/9 Production and related workers, transport equipment operators and labourers / Ouvriers et manœuvres non agricoles et conducteurs d'engins de transport / Obreros no agrícolas, conductores de máquinas y vehículos de transp. y trabaj. asimilados	X Workers not classifiable by occupation / Travailleurs ne pouvant être classés selon la profession / Trabajadores que no pueden ser clasificados según la ocupación	Persons seeking work for the first time / Personnes en quête d'emploi pour la première fois / Personas en busca de trabajo por primera vez
1971	666 000	13 000	1 000	17 000	40 000	41 000	92 000	109 000	9 000	342 000
1972	867 000	16 000	2 000	24 000	46 000	48 000	120 000	136 000	6 000	468 000
1973	690 000	14 000	1 000	29 000	41 000	42 000	89 000	147 000	2 000	323 000
1974	584 000	9 000	2 000	20 000	35 000	40 000	100 000	130 000	1 000	249 000
1975	581 000	10 000	2 000	27 000	28 000	38 000	89 000	132 000	1 000	257 000

11 Structure of unemployment
Structure du chômage
Estructura del desempleo

Singapore

Occupational groups *(Labour force sample surveys)*
Groupes de professions *(Enquêtes par sondage sur la main-d'œuvre)*
Grupos de ocupaciones *(Encuestas por muestra sobre la fuerza trabajadora)*

Date [1] *Date* [1] Fecha [1]	Total	0/1 Professional, technical and related workers *Personnel des professions scientifiques, techniques, libérales et assimilées* Profesionales, técnicos y trabajadores asimilados	2 Administrative and managerial workers *Directeurs et cadres administratifs supérieurs* Directores y funcionarios públicos superiores	3 Clerical and related workers *Personnel administratif et travailleurs assimilés* Personal administrativo y trabajadores asimilados	4 Sales workers *Personnel commercial et vendeurs* Comerciantes y vendedores	5 Service workers *Travailleurs spécialisés dans les services* Trabajadores de los servicios	6 Agricultural, animal husbandry and forestry workers, fishermen and hunters *Agriculteurs, éleveurs, forestiers, pêcheurs et chasseurs* Trabajadores agrícolas y forestales, pescadores y cazadores	7/8/9 Production and related workers, transport equipment operators and labourers *Ouvriers et manœuvres non agricoles et conducteurs d'engins de transport* Obreros no agrícolas, conductores de máquinas y vehículos de transporte y trabajadores asimilados	X Workers not classifiable by occupation *Travailleurs ne pouvant être classés selon la profession* Trabajadores que no pueden ser clasificados según la ocupación
1974	34 044	2 623	340	9 373	2 477	2 817	340	9 665	6 409
1975	39 452	3 355	162	8 713	4 871	4 005	162	14 233	3 951
1976	40 487	2 600	318	10 135	3 502	3 290	371	16 025	4 246
1977	36 861	3 145	259	10 621	2 930	3 124	151	15 447	1 184
1978	35 703	2 608	276	8 714	3 413	3 074	21	14 544	3 053
1979	35 294	2 745	333	9 692	3 265	3 161	166	13 706	2 226

[1] June.　　　　　[1] *Juin.*　　　　　[1] Junio.

Sri Lanka

Occupational groups *(Employment office statistics)* [1]
Groupes de professions *(Statistiques des bureaux de placement)* [1]
Grupos de ocupaciones *(Estadísticas de las oficinas de colocación)* [1]

Date *Date* Fecha	Total	Professional, technical and clerical workers *Professions libérales, techniciens et employés de bureau* Profesiones liberales, técnicos y empleados de oficina	Skilled workers *Ouvriers qualifiés* Obreros calificados	Semi-skilled workers *Ouvriers semi-qualifiés* Obreros semicalificados	Unskilled workers *Ouvriers non qualifiés* Obreros no calificados
1970	380 962	93 228	34 636	94 509	158 589
1971	419 679	96 156	39 764	96 730	187 029
1972	440 342	91 429	43 087	100 576	205 250
1973	457 671	86 425	43 402	105 188	222 657
1974	489 348	89 087	44 818	112 574	242 869
1975	521 714	96 450	47 323	120 379	257 562
1976	547 244	103 993	49 836	127 728	265 687
1977	572 583	110 644	52 564	134 787	274 588

[1] Applicants for work.　　　　　[1] *Demandeurs d'emploi.*　　　　　[1] Solicitantes de trabajo.

11 Structure of unemployment
Structure du chômage
Estructura del desempleo

République arabe syrienne

A Industrial groups *(Labour force sample surveys)*
Groupes d'activité économique *(Enquêtes par sondage sur la main-d'œuvre)*
Grupos de actividad económica *(Encuestas por muestra sobre la fuerza trabajadora)*

Date [1] / Date [1] / Fecha [1]	Total	1 Agriculture, forestry, fishing / Agriculture, sylviculture, pêche / Agricultura, silvicultura, pesca	2 Mining, quarrying / Industries extractives / Minas, canteras	3 Manufacturing / Industries manufacturières / Industrias manufactureras	4 Electricity, gas, water / Electricité, gaz, eau / Electricidad, gas, agua	5 Construction / Construction / Construcción	6 Trade, restaurants and hotels / Commerce, restaurants et hôtels / Comercio, restaurantes y hoteles	7 Transport, storage, communication / Transports, entrepôts, communications / Transportes, almacenaje, comunicaciones	8 Financing, insur., real est., business serv. / Banques, assur., aff. imm., serv. aux entreprises / Bancos, seguros, bienes inm., serv. para empresas	9 Community, social, and pers. services / Services à collectivité, serv. sociaux et pers. / Servicios comunales, sociales y personales	Persons seeking work for the first time / Personnes en quête d'emploi pour la première fois / Personas en busca de trabajo por primera vez
1971	123 387	34 364	556	9 605	205	7 102	7 619	2 060	207	8 045	53 624
1972	80 907	17 641	93	4 182	281	5 986	3 532	1 986	379	4 663	42 164
1973	76 489	7 410	563	4 916	278	7 500	5 642	2 082	283	6 988	40 827
1974	87 190	10 188	—	5 666	—	6 149	3 980	2 588	—	6 021	52 598
1975	88 482	21 500	283	4 852	91	7 724	3 399	2 359	91	3 228	44 955
1976	113 439										
1977	100 328	14 286	126	8 580	—	8 384	6 116	1 451	262	5 621	55 502
1978	90 314	10 021	—	6 186	—	10 283	3 225	3 345	530	4 864	51 879
1979	82 094	5 775	—	5 225	—	10 468	4 455	2 427	363	3 650	49 731

B Occupational groups *(Labour force sample surveys)*
Groupes de professions *(Enquêtes par sondage sur la main-d'œuvre)*
Grupos de ocupaciones *(Encuestas por muestra sobre la fuerza trabajadora)*

Date [1] / Date [1] / Fecha [1]	Total	0/1 Professional, technical and related workers / Personnel des professions scientifiques, techniques, libérales et assimilées / Profesionales, técnicos y trabajadores asimilados	2 Administrative and managerial workers / Directeurs et cadres administratifs supérieurs / Directores y funcionarios públicos superiores	3 Clerical and related workers / Personnel administratif et travailleurs assimilés / Personal administrativo y trabajadores asimilados	4 Sales workers / Personnel commercial et vendeurs / Comerciantes y vendedores	5 Service workers / Travailleurs spécialisés dans les services / Trabajadores de los servicios	6 Agricultural, animal husbandry and forestry workers, fishermen and hunters / Agriculteurs, éleveurs, forestiers, pêcheurs et chasseurs / Trabajadores agrícolas y forestales, pescadores y cazadores	7/8/9 Production and related workers, transport equipment, operators and labourers / Ouvriers et manœuvres non agricoles et conducteurs d'engins de transport / Obreros no agrícolas, conductores de máquinas y vehículos de transporte y trabajadores asimilados	Persons seeking work for the first time / Personnes en quête d'emploi pour la première fois / Personas en busca de trabajo por primera vez
1971	123 387	2 637	104	1 398	5 490	2 348	34 646	23 140	53 624
1972	80 907	1 388	—	650	3 540	930	17 926	14 309	42 164
1973	76 489	1 134	—	2 170	4 888	1 609	7 599	18 262	40 827
1974	87 190	567	94	1 046	2 374	1 230	10 284	18 997	52 598
1975	88 482	1 088	—	1 294	2 496	541	21 591	16 517	44 955
1976	113 439	2 532	45	1 288	4 772	1 114	13 808	20 985	68 895
1977	100 328	1 782	181	1 955	5 865	302	14 125	20 616	55 502
1978	90 314	1 423	192	2 566	2 617	1 429	9 245	20 966	51 879
1979	82 094	1 682	—	1 037	4 378	649	5 275	19 342	49 731

[1] September.　　　[1] *Septembre.*　　　[1] Septiembre.

11 Structure of unemployment
Structure du chômage
Estructura del desempleo

Thailand

(ISCO — CITP — CIUO 1958)

Occupational groups *(Labour force sample surveys)* [1]
Groupes de professions *(Enquêtes par sondage sur la main-d'œuvre)* [1]
Grupos de ocupaciones *(Encuestas por muestra sobre la fuerza trabajadora)* [1]

Date / Date / Fecha	Total	Professional, technical and related workers	Administrative, executive, managerial workers	Clerical workers	Sales workers	Farmers, fishermen and related workers	Workers in transport occupations	Craftsmen, prod. process workers, labourers not elsewhere classified	Service workers	Workers not classifiable by occupation	Persons seeking work for the first time
1972	83 100	1 500	380	3 050	3 240	10 320	3 740	16 330	2 340	860	41 340
1973	71 820	1 490	1 260	3 610	3 670	4 410	3 870	14 550	1 030	1 040	36 890
1974	92 110	1 140	460	2 550	1 180	6 160	1 520	12 780	2 240	30	64 050
1975	66 670	360	120	1 210	1 310	2 970	1 430	4 040	560	110	54 560
1976 [2]	129 770	3 070	60	1 840	2 920	22 650	1 790	12 430	1 720	—	83 290
1977 [2]	212 500	4 100	800	7 100	5 900	46 100	4 300	31 400	6 000	—	106 500

[1] Persons aged 11 years and over. [2] Jan.-March.   [1] *Personnes âgées de 11 ans et plus.* [2] *Janv.-mars.*   [1] Personas de 11 años y más. [2] Enero-marzo.

313

11 Structure of unemployment
Structure du chômage
Estructura del desempleo

EUROPE — EUROPE — EUROPA

Austria (1)

A Industrial or occupational groups *(Employment office statistics)*
Groupes d'activité économique ou de professions *(Statistiques des bureaux de placement)*
Grupos de actividad económica o de ocupaciones *(Estadísticas de las oficinas de colocación)*

Date / *Date* / Fecha	Total [1]	Agriculture, forestry / *Agriculture, sylviculture* / Agricultura, silvicultura	Mining / *Mines* / Minas	Stone, glass, ceramics / *Pierre, verre, céramique* / Piedra, vidrio, cerámica	Food, beverages, tobacco / *Aliments, boissons, tabac* / Alimentos, bebidas, tabaco	Textiles	Clothing [2] / *Habillement* [2] / Vestido [2]	Leather / *Cuir* / Cuero	Paper / *Papier* / Papel
1970	58 444	5 683	514	1 371	802	1 399	3 880	175	358
1971	52 020	4 724	450	973	756	1 424	3 843	163	374
1972	49 135	4 102	394	750	698	1 262	3 780	154	361
1973	41 327	3 472	159	569	521	1 014	3 619	153	252
1974	41 306	3 100	115	649	540	977	3 180	135	225
1975	55 464	3 426	142	1 169	763	1 282	3 081	237	312
1976	55 257	3 390	182	1 098	854	716	2 552	117	254
1977	51 165	3 249	207	966	719	695	2 281	111	219
1978	58 570	3 261	232	1 061	894	827	2 610	147	303
1979	56 719	3 042	97	882	853	606	2 019	123	260

Date / *Date* / Fecha	Printing / *Imprimerie* / Imprentas	Chemicals, rubber / *Produits chimiques, caoutchouc* / Productos químicos, caucho	Wood / *Bois* / Madera	Metal and electrical workers / *Electriciens, ouvriers sur métaux* / Electricistas, obreros metalúrgicos	Construction / *Construction* / Construcción	Hotels, restaurants / *Hôtels, restaurants* / Hoteles, restaurantes	Transport, communication / *Transports, communications* / Transportes, comunicaciones	Unskilled workers [3] / *Ouvriers non qualifiés* [3] / Obreros no calificados [3]	Commercial employees and clerical workers / *Employés de commerce et de bureau* / Empleados de comercio y de oficina
1970	227	518	1 040	2 882	10 862	6 185	1 194	4 372	9 718
1971	233	546	843	2 779	6 869	6 167	950	4 419	10 354
1972	256	551	795	2 810	5 095	6 377	898	4 217	9 575
1973	193	452	460	1 997	3 980	6 038	629	2 791	9 037
1974	198	490	589	2 397	4 487	6 425	752	2 907	8 456
1975	284	866	1 152	6 035	8 053	6 967	1 493	4 552	9 224
1976	313	655	956	4 796	8 724	7 320	1 601	4 242	10 401
1977	291	515	824	3 831	7 581	7 792	1 360	3 633	10 235
1978	329	570	1 130	4 592	9 542	8 102	1 681	4 039	11 731
1979	331	541	1 195	4 478	9 228	8 195	1 737	3 750	11 774

[1] Incl. occupational groups not specified in the table. [2] Incl. shoemakers. [3] Incl. semi-skilled workers of certain occupations.

[1] *Y compris des groupes de professions non spécifiés dans le tableau.* [2] *Y compris les cordonniers.* [3] *Y compris les ouvriers semi-qualifiés de certains métiers.*

[1] Incl. grupos de ocupaciones no especificados en el cuadro. [2] Incl. los zapateros. [3] Incl. obreros semicalificados de ciertas ocupaciones.

11 Structure of unemployment
Structure du chômage
Estructura del desempleo

Austria (2)

B Occupational groups *(Employment office statistics)* [1]
Groupes de professions *(Statistiques des bureaux de placement)* [1]
Grupos de ocupaciones *(Estadísticas de las oficinas de colocación)* [1]

Date / *Date* / Fecha	Total	0/1	2	3	4	5	6	7/8/9
		Professional, technical and related workers / *Personnel des professions scientifiques, techniques, libérales et assimilées* / Profesionales, técnicos y trabajadores asimilados	Administrative and managerial workers / *Directeurs et cadres administratifs supérieurs* / Directores y funcionarios públicos superiores	Clerical and related workers / *Personnel administratif et travailleurs assimilés* / Personal administrativo y trabajadores asimilados	Sales workers / *Personnel commercial et vendeurs* / Comerciantes y vendedores	Service workers / *Travailleurs spécialisés dans les services* / Trabajadores de los servicios	Agricultural, animal husbandry and forestry workers, fishermen and hunters / *Agriculteurs, éleveurs, forestiers, pêcheurs et chasseurs* / Trabajadores agrícolas y forestales, pescadores y cazadores	Production and related workers, transport equipment operators and labourers / *Ouvriers et manœuvres non agricoles et conducteurs d'engins de transport* / Obreros no agrícolas, conductores de máquinas y vehículos de transp. y trabaj. asimilados
1972	49 135	1 946	198	7 004	3 994	10 329	4 122	18 647
1973	41 327	1 816	170	6 330	3 759	9 119	3 807	15 868
1974	41 306	1 775	206	5 634	3 386	8 892	3 332	16 439
1975	55 464	2 210	252	6 650	3 711	9 341	3 614	29 686
1976	55 257	2 698	316	6 876	3 963	9 684	3 727	25 371
1977	51 165	2 695	308	6 532	3 973	9 537	3 335	22 029
1978	58 570	3 117	395	7 214	4 710	9 774	3 381	26 965
1979	56 719	3 176	427	6 918	4 674	9 820	3 116	23 425

[1] Totals represent the average of monthly figures; data for occupational groups are calculated on the basis of quarterly figures.

[1] *Les totaux représentent la moyenne des chiffres mensuels ; les données par groupes de professions sont calculées sur la base de chiffres trimestriels.*

[1] Los totales representan el promedio de las cifras mensuales; los datos por grupos de ocupaciones son calculados en base a cifras trimestrales.

11 Structure of unemployment
Structure du chômage
Estructura del desempleo

Belgique

Industrial groups *(Employment office statistics)* [1]
Groupes d'activité économique *(Statistiques des bureaux de placement)* [1]
Grupos de actividad económica *(Estadísticas de las oficinas de colocación)* [1]

Date / Date / Fecha	Total	Agriculture, forestry, fishing / Agriculture, sylviculture, pêche / Agricultura, silvicultura, pesca	Mining, quarrying / Industries extractives / Minas, canteras	Manufacturing / Industries manufacturières / Industrias manufactureras	Electricity, gas, water / Electricité, gaz, eau / Electricidad, gas, agua	Construction / Construction / Construcción	Trade, financing, insurance / Commerce, banques, assurances / Comercio, bancos, seguros	Transport, storage, communication / Transports, entrepôts, communications / Transportes, almacenaje, comunicaciones	Restaurants and hotels / Restaurants et hôtels / Restaurantes y hoteles	Services / Services / Servicios	Activities not adequately described / Activités mal désignées / Actividades no bien especificadas
1970	71 261	1 277	4 128	35 026	99	8 880	6 705	2 090	2 628	8 478	1 950
1971	80 876	1 185	3 610	34 020	90	10 098	6 625	1 954	2 572	8 579	2 143
1972	86 822	1 177	3 734	41 148	98	13 106	8 511	2 276	2 817	10 735	3 220
1973	91 702	1 085	3 569	43 167	119	10 373	10 284	2 321	3 044	13 245	4 495
1974	104 720	1 057	3 636	48 588	125	9 708	12 477	2 568	3 389	16 418	6 754
1975	177 367	1 351	3 613	85 431	210	18 079	20 085	4 267	4 853	24 531	14 947
1976	228 537	1 461	3 646	107 657	238	21 897	27 915	5 507	6 504	32 915	20 797
1977	264 284	1 563	3 642	122 788	275	25 963	33 498	5 938	7 625	39 964	23 028
1978	282 164	1 564	3 768	127 914	343	29 019	36 558	6 325	8 517	43 939	24 217
1979	294 416	1 578	3 432	129 565	379	28 104	39 585	6 481	9 493	50 097	25 702

[1] Wholly unemployed receiving insurance benefits only.

[1] *Chômeurs complets indemnisés seulement.*

[1] Desempleados completos que reciben prestaciones solamente.

Denmark

Industrial groups *(Trade union fund statistics)* [1]
Groupes d'activité économique *(Statistiques des caisses syndicales)* [1]
Grupos de actividad económica *(Estadísticas de las cajas sindicales)* [1]

Date / Date / Fecha	Total	Agriculture, forestry, fishing / Agriculture, sylviculture, pêche / Agricultura, silvicultura, pesca	Mining, quarrying / Industries extractives / Minas, canteras	Manufacturing / Industries manufacturières / Industrias manufactureras	Electricity, gas, water / Electricité, gaz, eau / Electricidad, gas, agua	Construction / Construction / Construcción	Trade, restaurants and hotels [2] / Commerce, restaurants et hôtels [2] / Comercio, restaurantes y hoteles [2]	Transport, storage, communication / Transports, entrepôts, communications / Transportes, almacenaje, comunicaciones	Services / Services / Servicios
1970	28 981	2 095	141	8 257	115	11 992	3 325	2 229	827
1971	33 910	1 863	121	11 536	109	12 746	3 922	2 638	975
1972	31 801	1 662	93	10 576	112	11 346	4 323	2 608	1 081
1973	23 784	1 366	63	7 577	83	8 109	3 310	2 042	1 234
1974	46 976	1 726	79	19 467	115	14 808	5 475	3 204	2 102
1975	106 275	3 272	126	51 031	271	26 656	12 795	5 714	6 410
1976	101 600	3 358	104	44 859	321	19 301	15 892	5 160	12 605
1977	130 762	4 735	110	56 022	410	24 112	21 610	5 872	17 891

[1] Average of counts taken on one Wednesday of each month. Data relate to unemployed members of trade union funds only. [2] Incl. financing, insurance and real estate.

[1] *Moyenne des relevés effectués un mercredi de chaque mois. Les données se réfèrent uniquement aux chômeurs membres des caisses syndicales.* [2] *Y compris les banques, assurances et affaires immobilières.*

[1] Promedio de los informes obtenidos un miércoles de cada mes. Los datos se refieren únicamente a los desempleados miembros de las cajas sindicales. [2] Incl. los bancos, seguros y bienes inmuebles.

11 Structure of unemployment
Structure du chômage
Estructura del desempleo

España

A
Industrial groups *(Labour force sample surveys)*
Groupes d'activité économique *(Enquêtes par sondage sur la main-d'œuvre)*
Grupos de actividad económica *(Encuestas por muestra sobre la fuerza trabajadora)*

Date [1] / Date [1] / Fecha [1]	Total	1 Agriculture, forestry, fishing / Agriculture, sylviculture, pêche / Agricultura, silvicultura, pesca	2 Mining, quarrying / Industries extractives / Minas, canteras	3 Manufacturing / Industries manufacturières / Industrias manufactureras	4 Electricity, gas, water / Electricité, gaz, eau / Electricidad, gas, agua	5 Construction / Construction / Construcción	6 Trade, restaurants and hotels / Commerce, restaurants et hôtels / Comercio, restaurantes y hoteles	7 Transport, storage, communication / Transports, entrepôts, communications / Transportes, almacenaje, comunicaciones	8 Financing, insur., real est., business serv. / Banques, assur., aff. imm., serv. aux entreprises / Bancos, seguros, bienes inm., serv. para empresas	9 Community, social, and pers. services / Services à collectivité, services sociaux et pers. / Servicios comunales, sociales y personales	0 Activities not adequately described / Activités mal désignées / Actividades no bien especificadas
1971	256 000	57 100		80 500		80 600		378 000			
1972	391 500	60 000		52 100		44 300		57 500			177 600
1973	362 700	48 400		52 000		47 700		78 800			135 800
1974	434 100	65 700		57 300		63 400		100 000			147 700
1975 [2]	624 500	103 000		95 900		150 200		125 200			150 100
1976	704 200	73 300	12 900	84 500	2 100	147 000	81 100	11 100	5 000	30 300	256 900
1977	841 100	90 800	9 500	101 500	3 000	161 600	92 900	11 500	6 500	36 900	326 900
1978	1 094 900	101 700	15 400	150 400	2 200	203 300	110 800	18 500	10 400	58 800	423 300
1979	1 348 600	91 800	12 700	199 700	2 700	264 300	133 500	17 700	13 000	76 800	536 400

B
Occupational groups *(Labour force sample surveys)*
Groupes de professions *(Enquêtes par sondage sur la main-d'œuvre)*
Grupos de ocupaciones *(Encuestas por muestra sobre la fuerza trabajadora)*

Date [1] / Date [1] / Fecha [1]	Total	0/1 Professional, technical and related workers / Personnel des professions scientifiques, techniques, libérales et assimilées / Profesionales, técnicos y trabajadores asimilados	2 Administrative and managerial workers / Directeurs et cadres administratifs supérieurs / Directores y funcionarios públicos superiores	3 Clerical and related workers / Personnel administratif et travailleurs assimilés / Personal administrativo y trabajadores asimilados	4 Sales workers / Personnel commercial et vendeurs / Comerciantes y vendedores	5 Service workers / Travailleurs spécialisés dans les services / Trabajadores de los servicios	6 Agricultural, animal husbandry and forestry workers, fishermen and hunters / Agriculteurs, éleveurs, forestiers, pêcheurs et chasseurs / Trabajadores agrícolas y forestales, pescadores y cazadores	7/8/9 Production and related workers, transport equipment operators and labourers / Ouvriers et manœuvres non agricoles et conducteurs d'engins de transport / Obreros no agrícolas, conductores de máquinas y vehículos de transporte y trabajadores asimilados	X Workers not classifiable by occupation / Travailleurs ne pouvant être classés selon la profession / Trabajadores que no pueden ser clasificados según la ocupación
1976	704 200	10 500	600	31 400	24 600	48 700	68 500	263 000	256 900
1977	841 100	11 600	700	34 800	30 400	57 700	83 500	295 500	326 900
1978	1 094 900	16 200	4 100	50 500	36 900	79 700	93 200	391 000	423 300
1979	1 348 600	19 100	3 200	59 600	43 200	90 600	76 900	485 200	570 800

[1] Fourth quarter. [2] Prior to 1976: distribution according to the 1958 ISIC.

[1] Quatrième trimestre. [2] Avant 1976; répartition selon la CITI 1958.

[1] Cuarto trimestre. [2] Antes de 1976: repartición según la CIIU 1958.

11 Structure of unemployment
Structure du chômage
Estructura del desempleo

Finland

A Industrial groups *(Labour force sample surveys)* [1]
Groupes d'activité économique *(Enquêtes par sondage sur la main-d'œuvre)* [1]
Grupos de actividad económica *(Encuestas por muestra sobre la fuerza trabajadora)* [1]

Date / Date / Fecha	Total	1	2	3	4	5	6	7	8	9	0
		Agriculture, forestry, fishing / *Agriculture, sylviculture, pêche* / Agricultura, silvicultura, pesca	Mining, quarrying / *Industries extractives* / Minas, canteras	Manufacturing / *Industries manufacturières* / Industrias manufactureras	Electricity, gas, water / *Electricité, gaz, eau* / Electricidad, gas, agua	Construction / *Construction* / Construcción	Trade, restaurants and hotels / *Commerce, restaurants et hôtels* / Comercio, restaurantes y hoteles	Transport, storage, communication / *Transports, entrepôts, communications* / Transportes, almacenaje, comunicaciones	Financing, insur., real est., business serv. / *Banques, assur., aff. imm., serv. aux entreprises* / Bancos, seguros, bienes inm., serv. para empresas	Community, social, and pers. services / *Services à collectivité, services sociaux et pers.* / Servicios comunales, sociales y personales	Activities not adequately described / *Activités mal désignées* / Actividades no bien especificadas
1971	49 000	8 000		6 000		12 000	4 000	2 000	—	5 000	12 000
1972	55 000	8 000		8 000		12 000	4 000	2 000	—	6 000	15 000
1973	51 000	7 000		8 000		9 000	5 000	2 000	1 000	5 000	14 000
1974	39 000	4 000		7 000		6 000	6 000	2 000	.	5 000	9 000
1975	51 000	5 000		8 000		9 000	5 000	3 000	1 000	5 000	15 000
1976 [2]	90 000	6 000		14 000		16 000	7 000	3 000	1 000	8 000	35 000
1977	137 000	12 000		28 000		24 000	12 000	6 000	2 000	14 000	39 000
1978	169 000	14 000		35 000		29 000	18 000	7 000	3 000	18 000	45 000
1979	139 000	11 000		23 000		22 000	16 000	5 000	3 000	19 000	40 000

B Occupational groups *(Labour force sample surveys)* [1]
Groupes de professions *(Enquêtes par sondage sur la main-d'œuvre)* [1]
Grupos de ocupaciones *(Encuestas por muestra sobre la fuerza trabajadora)* [1]

Date / Date / Fecha	Total	0/1	2	3	4	5	6	7/8/9	X
		Professional, technical and related workers / *Personnel des professions scientifiques, techniques, libérales et assimilées* / Profesionales, técnicos y trabajadores asimilados	Administrative and managerial workers / *Directeurs et cadres administratifs supérieurs* / Directores y funcionarios públicos superiores	Clerical and related workers / *Personnel administratif et travailleurs assimilés* / Personal administrativo y trabajadores asimilados	Sales workers / *Personnel commercial et vendeurs* / Comerciantes y vendedores	Service workers / *Travailleurs spécialisés dans les services* / Trabajadores de los servicios	Agricultural, animal husbandry and forestry workers, fishermen and hunters / *Agriculteurs, éleveurs, forestiers, pêcheurs et chasseurs* / Trabajadores agrícolas y forestales, pescadores y cazadores	Production and related workers, transport equipment operators and labourers / *Ouvriers et manœuvres non agricoles et conducteurs d'engins de transport* / Obreros no agrícolas, conductores de máquinas y vehículos de transporte y trabajadores asimilados	Workers not classifiable by occupation / *Travailleurs ne pouvant être classés selon la profession* / Trabajadores que no pueden ser clasificados según la ocupación
1971	49 000	3 000	—	1 000	2 000	4 000	8 000	19 000	12 000
1972	55 000	3 000	—	1 000	2 000	4 000	9 000	21 000	15 000
1973	51 000	2 000	—	2 000	2 000	5 000	8 000	19 000	13 000
1974	39 000	2 000	—	2 000	2 000	6 000	5 000	13 000	9 000
1975	51 000	3 000	—	2 000	2 000	5 000	7 000	22 000	10 000

[1] Persons aged 15 to 74 years. [2] Beginning 1976: sampling design revised.

[1] *Personnes âgées de 15 à 74 ans.* [2] *A partir de 1976: plan d'échantillonnage révisé.*

[1] Personas de 15 a 74 años. [2] A partir de 1976: diseño de la muestra revisado.

11 Structure of unemployment
Structure du chômage
Estructura del desempleo

France

Occupational groups *(Employment office statistics)* [1]
Groupes de professions *(Statistiques des bureaux de placement)* [1]
Grupos de ocupaciones *(Estadísticas de las oficinas de colocación)* [1]

Date / Date / Fecha	Total	Materials handling and warehousing / *Manutention et stockage* / Transporte de materiales y almacenaje	Fishing and water transport / *Pêche et navigation* / Pesca y transporte por agua	Agriculture, forestry / *Agriculture, sylviculture* / Agricultura, silvicultura	Earthworks and mining / *Terrassement et extraction* / Terraplenes y minas	Metal workers / *Ouvriers sur métaux* / Obreros metalúrgicos	Electricity / *Electricité* / Electricidad	Building, construction / *Bâtiment, construction* / Edificación y construcción	Food, beverages / *Aliments, boissons* / Alimentos, bebidas	Textiles
1970	262 085	54 262	851	5 406	1 403	16 856	3 957	17 108	4 891	15 636
1971	338 159	67 215	881	5 892	1 726	23 097	5 441	23 144	5 698	15 966
1972	383 465	70 518	812	5 891	1 679	26 891	6 104	21 832	6 392	14 598
1973	393 900	66 334	783	5 431	1 227	24 279	5 773	17 125	6 496	14 759
1974	497 711	78 583	943	5 898	1 371	32 666	8 435	21 537	8 104	18 413
1975	839 715	115 921	1 430	10 346	3 258	76 707	23 205	55 158	12 157	27 813
1976	933 461	99 859	1 540	12 706	3 812	87 912	32 275	53 799	13 834	29 394
1977	1 071 748	106 617	1 689	14 786	4 890	111 661	29 856	60 114	15 620	35 195
1978 [2]	1 328 308	121 227	2 268	18 647	6 864	157 300	28 407	79 046	21 238	43 521

Date / Date / Fecha	Skins, leather / *Peaux, cuir* / Pieles, cuero	Wood / *Bois* / Madera	Printing / *Imprimerie* / Imprentas	Drivers / *Conducteurs d'automobiles* / Conductores de automóviles	Commercial employees / *Employés de commerce* / Empleados de comercio	Domestic personnel / *Personnel domestique* / Personal doméstico	Clerical workers / *Employés de bureau* / Empleados de oficina	Professional, executive and managerial workers / *Professions libérales, directeurs et cadres adm. sup.* / Profesiones liberales, administradores, gerentes y directores	Entertainment / *Emplois artistiques et du spectacle* / Diversiones	Others / *Autres* / Otros
1970	2 412	2 665	1 988	5 306	21 410	27 966	44 739	16 650	2 497	16 082
1971	2 576	3 143	2 767	7 250	27 540	34 748	62 298	25 399	3 314	20 064
1972	2 217	2 857	3 361	8 088	32 919	39 180	78 225	33 718	4 775	23 408
1973	2 281	2 417	3 113	7 405	38 671	42 161	88 165	36 617	5 394	25 469
1974	2 201	3 317	4 070	10 015	50 656	50 513	115 098	44 347	6 745	34 799
1975	3 252	7 648	7 097	20 604	76 703	74 602	185 522	75 332	8 697	54 263
1976	4 804	7 550	8 140	21 400	90 277	85 718	220 311	84 755	9 827	65 548
1977	4 753	8 688	7 797	25 960	107 238	97 574	252 828	94 285	10 929	81 268
1978 [2]	5 268	12 988	9 256	35 958	133 834	90 241	306 337	114 412	12 614	128 882

[1] Beginning June 1972: excl. certain unemployed over 60 years of age (recipients of " income maintenance benefits "). [2] December.

[1] *A partir de juin 1972 : non compris certains chômeurs de plus de 60 ans (bénéficiaires de la « garantie de ressources »).* [2] *Décembre.*

[1] A partir de junio de 1972: excl. ciertos desempleados de más de 60 años (beneficiarios de la « garantía de recursos »). [2] Diciembre.

11 Structure of unemployment
Structure du chômage
Estructura del desempleo

Germany, Fed. Rep. of

A Industrial groups *(Employment office statistics)*
Groupes d'activité économique *(Statistiques des bureaux de placement)*
Grupos de actividad económica *(Estadísticas de las oficinas de colocación)*

Date / Date / Fecha	Total	1 Agriculture, forestry, fishing / *Agriculture, sylviculture, pêche* / Agricultura, silvicultura, pesca	2 Mining, quarrying / *Industries extractives* / Minas, canteras	3 Manufacturing / *Industries manufacturières* / Industrias manufactureras	4 Electricity, gas, water / *Electricité, gaz, eau* / Electricidad, gas, agua	5 Construction / *Construction* / Construcción	6 Trade, restaurants and hotels / *Commerce, restaurants et hôtels* / Comercio, restaurantes y hoteles	7 Transport, storage, communication / *Transports, entrepôts, communications* / Transportes, almacenaje, comunicaciones	8 Financing, insur., real est., business serv. / *Banques, assur., aff. imm., serv. aux entreprises* / Bancos, seguros, bienes inm., serv. para empresas	9 Community, social, and pers. services / *Services à collectivité, services sociaux et pers.* / Servicios comunales, sociales y personales	0 Activities not adequately described / *Activités mal désignées* / Actividades no bien especificadas
1975	1 074 217	10 352	7 924	412 164	1 697	151 052	182 768	27 211	35 326	115 229	130 494
1976	1 060 336	10 894	7 292	362 141	1 627	105 907	215 767	27 875	45 507	157 116	126 210
1977	1 029 995	10 325	8 283	304 879	1 548	93 682	201 536	25 817	40 115	160 386	183 424
1978	992 948	11 824	8 325	287 909	1 986	74 470	187 454	24 152	33 409	159 544	203 875
1979	876 137	9 426	9 215	250 653	1 293	50 873	163 237	21 397	28 834	148 966	192 243

B Occupational groups *(Employment office statistics)*
Groupes de professions *(Statistiques des bureaux de placement)*
Grupos de ocupaciones *(Estadísticas de las oficinas de colocación)*

Date / Date / Fecha	Total	0/1 Professional, technical and related workers / *Personnel des professions scientifiques, techniques, libérales et assimilées* / Profesionales, técnicos y trabajadores asimilados	2 Administrative and managerial workers / *Directeurs et cadres administratifs supérieurs* / Directores y funcionarios públicos superiores	3 Clerical and related workers / *Personnel administratif et travailleurs assimilés* / Personal administrativo y trabajadores asimilados	4 Sales workers / *Personnel commercial et vendeurs* / Comerciantes y vendedores	5 Service workers / *Travailleurs spécialisés dans les services* / Trabajadores de los servicios	6 Agricultural, animal husbandry and forestry workers, fishermen and hunters / *Agriculteurs, éleveurs, forestiers, pêcheurs et chasseurs* / Trabajadores agrícolas y forestales, pescadores y cazadores	7/8/9 Production and related workers, transport equipment operators and labourers / *Ouvriers et manœuvres non agricoles et conducteurs d'engins de transport* / Obreros no agrícolas, conductores de máquinas y vehículos de transp. y trabaj. asimilados	X Workers not classifiable by occupation / *Travailleurs ne pouvant être classés selon la profession* / Trabajadores que no pueden ser clasificados según la ocupación
1970	148 846	10 897	14 676		9 502	12 823	10 048	88 049	2 851
1971	185 072	13 752	18 975		11 869	16 325	6 922	113 574	3 655
1972	246 433	20 072	27 872		16 622	22 326	7 851	146 601	5 089
1973	273 498	26 541	36 306		23 086	25 745	8 114	147 769	5 937
1974	582 481	48 070	69 206		51 042	45 199	8 439	347 595	12 930
1975	1 074 217	88 066	134 699		91 363	73 608	13 259	650 934	22 288
1976	1 060 336	115 539	168 212		106 011	86 282	14 881	545 743	23 668
1977	1 029 995	125 065	164 639		109 311	89 710	14 739	496 054	30 477
1978	992 948	114 288	147 167		102 562	92 185	16 318	490 335	30 093
1979	876 137	102 475	127 299		90 747	87 812	17 727	422 837	27 240

11 Structure of unemployment
Structure du chômage
Estructura del desempleo

Grèce

(ISCO — CITP — CIUO 1958)

Occupational groups *(Employment office statistics)* [1]
Groupes de professions *(Statistiques des bureaux de placement)* [1]
Grupos de ocupaciones *(Estadísticas de las oficinas de colocación)* [1]

Date / Date / Fecha	Total	Professional, technical and related workers / *Professions libérales, techniciens et assimilés* / Profesiones liberales, técnicos y trabajadores asimilados	Administrative, executive and managerial workers / *Directeurs et cadres administratifs supérieurs* / Administradores, gerentes y directores	Clerical workers / *Employés de bureau* / Empleados de oficina	Sales workers / *Vendeurs* / Vendedores	Farmers, fishermen and related workers / *Agriculteurs, pêcheurs et assimilés* / Agricultores, pescadores y asimilados	Miners, quarrymen and related workers / *Mineurs, carriers et assimilés* / Mineros, canteros y asimilados	Workers in transport and communication occupations / *Travailleurs des transports et des communications* / Trabajadores de los transportes y comunicaciones	Craftsmen, prod. process workers, labourers not elsewhere classified / *Artisans, ouvriers de métier et à la prod., manœuvres non classés ailleurs* / Artesanos, trabaj. ocupados en los div. procesos de prod., peones no clasif. bajo otros epígr.	Service workers and workers not classifiable by occupation / *Travailleurs des services et personnes ne pouvant être classées selon la prof.* / Trabajadores de los servicios y trab. que no pueden ser clasif. según la ocupación
1970	48 687	1 240	43	4 508	1 957	996	552	1 380	32 643	5 368
1971	30 317	912	31	2 746	1 144	658	401	929	20 064	3 432
1972	23 833	747	36	1 938	849	615	365	640	15 692	2 951
1973	21 445	712	49	1 847	649	478	301	503	13 983	2 923
1974	27 101	950	80	2 132	749	503	385	810	17 654	3 838
1975	34 969	1 156	105	2 493	982	644	522	1 132	23 728	4 207
1976	28 474	973	83	2 195	866	601	393	945	18 343	4 075
1977	27 668	1 056	79	2 236	922	559	415	819	17 512	4 070.
1978	30 918	1 226	90	2 665	1 064	585	472	956	19 380	4 480

[1] Excl. persons who do not re-register after one month (prior to April 1976: six months).

[1] *Non compris les personnes qui ne renouvellent pas leur inscription après un mois (avant avril 1976 : six mois).*

[1] Excl. las personas que no renueven su inscripción después de un mes (antes de abril de 1976: seis meses).

11 Structure of unemployment
Structure du chômage
Estructura del desempleo

Ireland

Industrial groups *(Employment office statistics)* [1]
Groupes d'activité économique *(Statistiques des bureaux de placement)* [1]
Grupos de actividad económica *(Estadísticas de las oficinas de colocación)* [1]

(ISIC — CITI — CIIU 1958)

Date / Date / Fecha	Total	Agriculture, forestry, fishing / Agriculture, sylviculture, pêche / Agricultura, silvicultura, pesca	Mining, quarrying / Industries extractives / Minas, canteras	Manufacturing / Industries manufacturières / Industrias manufactureras	Construction / Construction / Construcción	Electricity, gas, water and sanitary services / Electricité, gaz, eau et services sanitaires / Electricidad, gas, agua y servicios sanitarios	Commerce / Commerce / Comercio	Transport, storage, communication / Transports, entrepôts, communications / Transportes, almacenaje, comunicaciones	Services / Services / Servicios	Activities not adequately described / Activités mal désignées / Actividades no bien especificadas
1970	64 865	20 826	492	12 150	12 799	443	5 832	3 562	6 900	1 861
1971	61 988	17 369	434	13 723	11 816	383	5 839	3 405	7 186	1 833
1972 [2]	71 527	20 722	435	15 296	13 968	447	6 550	3 609	8 075	2 425
1973	66 785	20 004	409	13 464	12 465	394	6 177	3 457	7 839	2 576
1974	71 392	19 923	453	16 002	13 484	434	6 523	3 487	8 325	2 761
1975	103 234	22 751	690	29 937	20 768	607	9 420	4 439	10 917	3 705
1976	112 834	23 936	847	30 089	24 533	762	10 514	5 058	12 976	4 119
1977	111 036	23 295	700	28 227	24 605	741	10 209	4 902	13 888	4 469
1978	102 908	21 732	613	25 287	22 285	672	9 472	4 460	13 462	4 925
1979	92 864	19 440	415	21 843	19 903	606	8 320	3 863	12 922	5 552

[1] Applicants for work on the "live" register. Incl. persons on systematic short-time working and persons aged 65 years and over. [2] Jan.-March and May-Dec.

[1] *Demandeurs d'emploi restant inscrits. Y compris les personnes qui travaillent systématiquement à mi-temps et les personnes âgées de 65 ans et plus.* [2] *Janv.-mars et mai-déc.*

[1] Solicitantes de trabajo que continúan inscritos. Incl. las personas que trabajan sistemáticamente medio tiempo y las personas de 65 años y más de edad. [2] Enero-marzo y mayo-dic.

Italie

Industrial groups *(Labour force sample surveys)*
Groupes d'activité économique *(Enquêtes par sondage sur la main-d'œuvre)*
Grupos de actividad económica *(Encuestas por muestra sobre la fuerza trabajadora)*

Date / Date / Fecha	Total	1 Agriculture, forestry, fishing / Agriculture, sylviculture, pêche / Agricultura, silvicultura, pesca	2 Mining, quarrying / Industries extractives / Minas, canteras	4 Electricity, gas, water / Electricité, gaz, eau / Electricidad, gas, agua	3 Manufacturing / Industries manufacturières / Industrias manufactureras	5 Construction / Construction / Construcción	6 Trade, restaurants and hotels / Commerce, restaurants et hôtels / Comercio, restaurantes y hoteles	7 Transport, storage, communication / Transports, entrepôts, communications / Transportes, almacenaje, comunicaciones	8 Financing, insur., real est., business serv. / Banques, assur., aff. imm., serv. aux entreprises / Bancos, seguros, bienes inm., serv. para empresas	9 Community, social, and pers. services / Services à collectivité, services sociaux et pers. / Servicios comunales, sociales y personales	Persons seeking work for the first time / Personnes en quête d'emploi pour la première fois / Personas en busca de trabajo por primera vez
1972	697 000	29 000	3 000		93 000	56 000	36 000	13 000	32 000		435 000
1973	668 000	35 000	3 000		82 000	50 000	33 000	13 000	32 000		420 000
1974	560 000	23 000	1 000		67 000	37 000	27 000	10 000	29 000		366 000
1975	654 000	31 000	2 000		93 000	47 000	29 000	13 000	31 000		408 000
1976	732 000	28 000	2 000		107 000	42 000	31 000	12 000	33 000		477 000

11 Structure of unemployment
Structure du chômage
Estructura del desempleo

Netherlands

Occupational groups *(Employment office statistics)*
Groupes de professions *(Statistiques des bureaux de placement)*
Grupos de ocupaciones *(Estadísticas de las oficinas de colocación)*

Date / Date / Fecha	Total [1]	Agriculture, hunting, fishing / Agriculture, chasse, pêche / Agricultura, caza, pesca	Mining, quarrying / Industries extractives / Minas, canteras	Pottery, glass, stone / Poterie, verre, pierre / Alfarería, vidrio, piedra	Diamonds / Diamants / Diamantes	Printing / Imprimerie / Imprentas	Textiles	Clothing, cleaning / Habillement, nettoyage / Vestido, limpieza	Wood / Bois / Madera
1970	46 414	1 608	115	63	18	279	307	930	188
1971	61 999	1 984	105	66	14	494	301	1 085	314
1972	107 930	2 616	139	115	11	932	548	1 407	593
1973	109 891	2 372	127	109	9	957	517	1 642	451
1974	134 905	2 651	136	138	3	1 037	438	2 456	633
1975	195 302	3 838	142	319	24	1 541	712	3 794	1 341
1976	210 873	4 575	178	361	39	1 819	651	3 707	1 240
1977	203 528	4 146	158	276	38	1 784	586	3 564	874
1978 [2]	205 608	3 959	160	218	28	1 515	551	3 385	703
1979	209 988	3 854	158	159	20	1 345	510	3 293	696

Date / Date / Fecha	Leather, rubber / Cuir, caoutchouc / Cuero, caucho	Food, beverages, tobacco / Aliments, boissons, tabac / Alimentos, bebidas, tabaco	Metal workers / Ouvriers sur métaux / Obreros metalúrgicos	Building / Bâtiment / Edificación	Commerce / Commerce / Comercio	Transport / Transports / Transportes	Hotels / Hôtels / Hoteles	Clerical workers / Employés de bureau / Empleados de oficina	Unskilled workers / Ouvriers non qualifiés / Obreros no calificados
1970	255	377	3 005	6 382	3 562	2 123	2 933	5 761	5 882
1971	194	420	5 149	11 259	4 501	3 061	2 998	7 660	8 315
1972	322	704	12 681	22 356	5 718	5 352	4 119	13 477	14 591
1973	308	783	11 588	20 295	7 532	4 761	4 801	15 605	13 004
1974	283	806	12 761	31 089	9 310	5 073	5 331	18 099	15 691
1975	481	1 193	21 597	38 445	12 677	7 189	6 726	26 272	27 045
1976	433	1 328	24 283	28 070	14 200	7 831	8 021	30 124	...
1977	355	1 191	20 394	20 702	15 804	7 295	8 195	33 859	...
1978 [2]	311	1 036	17 332	16 458	17 652	6 919	8 456	38 163	...
1979	248	892	14 008	16 718	19 392	6 502	8 790	41 564	...

[1] Incl. occupational groups not specified in the table.
[2] Persons seeking work for 25 hours or more a week (prior to 1978: 30 hours or more).

[1] *Y compris des groupes de professions non spécifiés dans le tableau.* [2] *Personnes en quête d'un emploi de 25 heures ou plus par semaine (avant 1978 : 30 heures ou plus).*

[1] Incl. grupos de ocupaciones no especificados en el cuadro. [2] Personas que buscan trabajo de 25 horas o más por semana (antes de 1978: 30 horas o más).

UNEMPLOYMENT

11 Structure of unemployment
Structure du chômage
Estructura del desempleo

Norway

Occupational groups *(Employment office statistics)*
Groupes de professions *(Statistiques des bureaux de placement)*
Grupos de ocupaciones *(Estadísticas de las oficinas de colocación)*

Date / Date / Fecha	Total	0/1 Professional, technical and related workers / *Personnel des professions scientifiques, techniques, libérales et assimilées* / Profesionales, técnicos y trabajadores asimilados	2 Administrative and managerial workers / *Directeurs et cadres administratifs supérieurs* / Directores y funcionarios públicos superiores	3 Clerical and related workers / *Personnel administratif et travailleurs assimilés* / Personal administrativo y trabajadores asimilados	4 Sales workers / *Personnel commercial et vendeurs* / Comerciantes y vendedores	5 Service workers / *Travailleurs spécialisés dans les services* / Trabajadores de los servicios	6 Agricultural, animal husbandry and forestry workers, fishermen and hunters / *Agriculteurs, éleveurs, forestiers, pêcheurs et chasseurs* / Trabajadores agrícolas y forestales, pescadores y cazadores	7/8/9 Production and related workers, transport equipment operators and labourers / *Ouvriers et manœuvres non agricoles et conducteurs d'engins de transport* / Obreros no agrícolas, conductores de máquinas y vehículos de transporte y trabajadores asimilados	X Workers not classifiable by occupation / *Travailleurs ne pouvant être classés selon la profession* / Trabajadores que no pueden ser clasificados según la ocupación
1970	12 458	398	15	483	475	915	1 042	8 161	969
1971	12 193	338	14	486	469	959	1 041	7 895	991
1972	14 812	580	29	658	602	1 278	1 282	9 153	1 230
1973	12 811	594	35	637	627	1 300	975	7 508	1 135
1974	10 662	533	33	664	626	1 238	707	5 761	1 100
1975	19 558	987	46	1 114	935	1 953	1 071	11 413	2 039
1976	19 859	1 201	77	1 268	1 155	2 274	1 279	10 425	2 180
1977	16 127	894	62	1 057	969	2 072	981	7 986	2 106
1978	20 003	1 278	94	1 284	1 137	2 544	970	10 055	2 641
1979	24 106	1 760	114	1 659	1 431	2 870	1 233	11 790	3 249

11 Structure of unemployment
Structure du chômage
Estructura del desempleo

Portugal

A — Industrial groups (Labour force sample surveys)
Groupes d'activité économique (Enquêtes par sondage sur la main-d'œuvre)
Grupos de actividad económica (Encuestas por muestra sobre la fuerza trabajadora)

Date / Date / Fecha	Total [1]	1 Agriculture, forestry, fishing / Agriculture, sylviculture, pêche / Agricultura, silvicultura, pesca	2 Mining, quarrying / Industries extractives / Minas, canteras	3 Manufacturing / Industries manufacturières / Industrias manufactureras	4 Electricity, gas, water / Electricité, gaz, eau / Electricidad, gas, agua	5 Construction / Construction / Construcción	6 Trade, restaurants and hotels / Commerce, restaurants et hôtels / Comercio, restaurantes y hoteles	7 Transport, storage, communication / Transports, entrepôts, communications / Transportes, almacenaje, comunicaciones	8 Financing, insur., real est., business serv. / Banques, assur., aff. imm., serv. aux entreprises / Bancos, seguros, bienes inm., serv. para empresas	9 Community, social, and pers. services / Services à collectivité, serv. sociaux et pers. / Servicios comunales, sociales y personales	Persons seeking work for the first time / Personnes en quête d'emploi pour la première fois / Personas en busca de trabajo por primera vez
1974	66 500	1 000		11 000	—	3 500	5 500	1 000	1 000	5 500	32 500
1975	177 500	4 000	-	35 000	—	17 500	20 500	3 500	3 500	19 500	69 000
1976	260 000	5 000	—	48 500	.	23 500	30 500	6 000	7 000	25 000	108 500
1977	308 500	6 000	500	52 000	.	23 000	29 000	5 500	5 000	28 000	154 000
1978	333 500	5 500	500	56 000	—	15 000	27 500	6 000	4 000	24 500	188 500
1979	343 500	8 000	—	60 000	—	13 500	27 500	4 500	2 500	27 500	195 000

B — Occupational groups (Labour force sample surveys)
Groupes de professions (Enquêtes par sondage sur la main-d'œuvre)
Grupos de ocupaciones (Encuestas por muestra sobre la fuerza trabajadora)

Date / Date / Fecha	Total [1]	0/1 Professional, technical and related workers / Personnel des professions scientifiques, techniques, libérales et assimilées / Profesionales, técnicos y trabajadores asimilados	2 Administrative and managerial workers / Directeurs et cadres administratifs supérieurs / Directores y funcionarios públicos superiores	3 Clerical and related workers / Personnel administratif et travailleurs assimilés / Personal administrativo y trabajadores asimilados	4 Sales workers / Personnel commercial et vendeurs / Comerciantes y vendedores	5 Service workers / Travailleurs spécialisés dans les services / Trabajadores de los servicios	6 Agricultural, animal husbandry and forestry workers, fishermen and hunters / Agriculteurs, éleveurs, forestiers, pêcheurs et chasseurs / Obreros agrícolas y forestales, pescadores y cazadores	7/8/9 Production and related workers, transport equipment operators and labourers / Ouvriers et manœuvres non agricoles et conducteurs d'engins de transport / Trabajadores no agrícolas, conductores de máquinas y vehículos de transporte y trabajadores asimilados	Persons seeking work for the first time / Personnes en quête d'emploi pour la première fois / Personas en busca de trabajo por primera vez
1974	66 500	2 000	—	5 500	2 500	3 500	1 000	15 500	32 500
1975	177 500	6 000	1 000	18 000	9 000	12 500	4 000	54 500	69 000
1976	260 000	9 000	2 500	26 000	16 500	16 500	5 000	73 500	108 500
1977	308 500	10 500	500	22 000	16 000	19 000	6 000	76 500	154 000
1978	333 500	7 000	500	21 000	13 500	22 500	5 500	71 000	188 500
1979	343 500	7 000	500	20 000	12 500	25 000	8 000	72 000	195 000

[1] Figures are rounded off independently; consequently the total differs from the sum of the groups.

[1] Les chiffres sont arrondis indépendamment ; en conséquence le total diffère de la somme des groupes.

[1] Las cifras están redondeadas independientemente; en consecuencia, el total difiere de la suma de los grupos.

11 Structure of unemployment
Structure du chômage
Estructura del desempleo

Suisse

Occupational groups *(Employment office statistics)*
Groupes de professions *(Statistiques des bureaux de placement)*
Grupos de ocupaciones *(Estadísticas de las oficinas de colocación)*

Date / Date / Fecha	Total	Agriculture / Agriculture / Agricultura	Food, beverages, tobacco / Aliments, boissons, tabac / Alimentos, bebidas, tabaco	Clothing / Habillement / Vestido	Leather, rubber / Cuir, caoutchouc / Cuero, caucho	Building / Bâtiment / Edificación	Wood, cork / Bois, liège / Madera, corcho	Textiles	Printing, publishing / Imprimerie, édition / Imprentas, editoriales
1970	104	1	1	1	—	26	1	—	—
1971	100	—	—	1	—	14	1	1	2
1972	106	—	1	4	—	4	1	1	1
1973	81	1	—	2	—	6	1	1	1
1974	221	1	2	3	—	26	3	1	20
1975	10 170	37	88	135	28	791	291	109	427
1976	20 703	77	190	246	49	1 560	495	119	673
1977	12 020	83	87	149	24	758	164	59	306
1978	10 483	92	86	168	21	642	99	50	159
1979	10 333	79	92	173	20	455	77	46	134

Date / Date / Fecha	Metal industries, machinery / Industrie métallurgique, machines / Industria metalúrgica, maquinaria	Watchmaking, jewellery / Horlogerie, bijouterie / Relojería, joyería	Commerce, administration / Commerce, administration / Comercio, administración	Hotels, restaurants / Hôtels, restaurants / Hoteles, restaurantes	Transport, communication / Transports, communications / Transportes, comunicaciones	Professional workers / Professions libérales / Profesiones liberales	Domestic workers / Personnel domestique / Personal doméstico	Labourers / Manœuvres / Peones	Others / Autres / Otros
1970	2	1	15	7	2	11	2	18	16
1971	4	16	18	5	1	9	2	10	16
1972	4	21	23	6	1	7	3	15	14
1973	4	3	20	5	2	6	2	15	12
1974	22	4	43	9	7	34	1	28	17
1975	2 675	794	1 619	228	327	1 162	27	824	608
1976	4 750	1 336	4 122	588	614	3 160	80	1 537	1 107
1977	1 672	341	2 788	535	381	2 912	—	—	1 761
1978	970	340	2 568	649	327	2 621	—	—	1 691
1979	834	704	2 573	718	301	2 419	—	—	1 708

11 Structure of unemployment
Structure du chômage
Estructura del desempleo

Sweden

A Industrial groups *(Labour force sample surveys)* [1]
Groupes d'activité économique *(Enquêtes par sondage sur la main-d'œuvre)* [1]
Grupos de actividad económica *(Encuestas por muestra sobre la fuerza trabajadora)* [1]

Date / Date / Fecha	Total	1 Agriculture, forestry, fishing / Agriculture, sylviculture, pêche / Agricultura, silvicultura, pesca	2 Mining, quarrying / Industries extractives / Minas, canteras	3 Manufacturing / Industries manufacturières / Industrias manufactureras	4 Electricity, gas, water / Electricité, gaz, eau / Electricidad, gas, agua	5 Construction / Construction / Construcción	6 Trade, restaurants and hotels / Commerce, restaurants et hôtels / Comercio, restaurantes y hoteles	7 Transport, storage, communication / Transports, entrepôts, communications / Transportes, almacenaje, comunicaciones	8 Financing, insur., real est., business serv. / Banques, assur., aff. imm., serv. aux entreprises / Bancos, seguros, bienes inm., serv. para empresas	9 Community, social, and pers. services / Services à collectivité, services sociaux et pers. / Servicios comunales, sociales y personales	0 Activities not adequately described / Activités mal désignées / Actividades no bien especificadas
1970	59 000	4 000		14 000		11 000	9 000	3 000	2 000	12 000	4 000
1971	101 000	5 000	—	25 000	—	21 000	15 000	4 000	2 000	20 000	7 000
1972	107 000	7 000	—	28 000	1 000	20 000	17 000	6 000	4 000	25 000	—
1973	98 000	6 000	—	26 000	—	17 000	17 000	5 000	3 000	24 000	—
1974	80 000	4 000	—	22 000	—	11 000	14 000	4 000	2 000	22 000	—
1975	67 000	4 000	—	19 000	—	8 000	12 000	3 000	3 000	18 000	—
1976	66 000	4 000	—	15 000	—	8 000	11 000	3 000	2 000	17 000	7 000
1977	75 000	4 000	—	17 000	—	7 000	12 000	4 000	3 000	20 000	7 000
1978	94 000	6 000	1 000	23 000	—	11 000	13 000	4 000	3 000	24 000	9 000
1979	88 000	5 000	—	20 000	—	8 000	13 000	4 000	3 000	26 000	—

B Occupational groups *(Labour force sample surveys)* [1]
Groupes de professions *(Enquêtes par sondage sur la main-d'œuvre)* [1]
Grupos de ocupaciones *(Encuestas por muestra sobre la fuerza trabajadora)* [1]

(ISCO — CITP — CIUO 1958)

Date / Date / Fecha	Total	Professional, technical and related workers [2] / Professions libérales, techniciens et assimilés [2] / Profesiones liberales, técnicos y asimilados [2]	Clerical workers / Employés de bureau / Empleados de oficina	Sales workers / Vendeurs / Vendedores	Farmers, fishermen and related workers / Agriculteurs, pêcheurs et assimilés / Agricultores, pescadores y asimilados	Workers in transport and communication occupations / Travailleurs dans les professions des transports et des communications / Trabajadores de los transportes y comunicaciones	Craftsmen, prod. process workers, labourers not elsewhere classified [3] / Artisans, ouvriers de métier et à la production, manœuvres non classés ailleurs [3] / Artesanos, trabaj. ocupados en los div. procesos de prod., peones no clasif. bajo otros epígrafes [3]	Service workers / Travailleurs spécialisés dans les services / Trabajadores de los servicios	Workers not classifiable by occupation / Personnes ne pouvant être classées selon la profession / Trabajadores que no pueden ser clasificados según la ocupación
1970	59 000	7 000	4 000	5 000	4 000	3 000	24 000	8 000	4 000
1971	101 000	10 000	8 000	7 000	6 000	4 000	45 000	14 000	7 000
1972	107 000	12 000	9 000	8 000	8 000	6 000	47 000	17 000	—
1973	98 000	13 000	9 000	8 000	6 000	5 000	42 000	15 000	—
1974	80 000	10 000	8 000	6 000	5 000	4 000	32 000	15 000	—
1975	67 000	9 000	7 000	6 000	5 000	3 000	26 000	11 000	—
1976	66 000	7 000	6 000	5 000	4 000	3 000	23 000	11 000	7 000
1977	75 000	9 000	6 000	6 000	5 000	4 000	24 000	14 000	7 000
1978	94 000	11 000	8 000	6 000	6 000	5 000	34 000	15 000	9 000
1979	88 000	10 000	8 000	6 000	6 000	4 000	30 000	15 000	9 000

[1] Persons aged 16 to 74 years. [2] Incl. administrative, executive and managerial workers. [3] Incl. miners, quarrymen and related workers.

[1] *Personnes âgées de 16 à 74 ans.* [2] *Y compris les directeurs et les cadres administratifs supérieurs.* [3] *Y compris les mineurs, carriers et travailleurs assimilés.*

[1] Personas de 16 a 74 años. [2] Incl. los administradores, gerentes y directores. [3] Incl. los mineros, canteros y trabajadores asimilados.

11 Structure of unemployment
Structure du chômage
Estructura del desempleo

Turquie

(ISCO — CITP — CIUO 1958)

Occupational groups *(Employment office statistics)* [1]
Groupes de professions *(Statistiques des bureaux de placement)* [1]
Grupos de ocupaciones *(Estadísticas de las oficinas de colocación)* [1]

Date / *Date* / Fecha	Total	Profesional, technical and related workers / *Professions libérales, techniciens et assimilés* / Profesiones liberales, técnicos y asimilados	Administrative, executive, managerial workers / *Directeurs, cadres administratifs supérieurs* / Administradores, gerentes, directores	Clerical workers / *Employés de bureau* / Empleados de oficina	Sales workers / *Vendeurs* / Vendedores	Farmers, fishermen and related workers / *Agriculteurs, pêcheurs et assimilés* / Agricultores, pescadores y asimilados	Miners, quarrymen and related workers / *Mineurs, carriers et assimilés* / Mineros, canteros y asimilados	Workers in transport and communication occupations / *Travailleurs dans les professions des transports et des communications* / Trabajadores de los transportes y comunicaciones	Craftsmen, prod. process workers, labourers not elsewhere classified / *Artisans, ouvriers de métier et à la production, manœuvres non classés ailleurs* / Artesanos, trabaj. ocupados en los div. procesos de prod., peones no clasif. bajo otros epígrafes	Service workers / *Travailleurs spécialisés dans les services* / Trabajadores de los servicios
1976	141 276	2 149	121	21 651	121	2 870	437	8 230	87 041	18 656
1977	142 654	2 089	101	23 763	82	2 957	390	9 088	87 117	17 067
1978	152 954	3 210	263	28 000	93	2 725	286	7 605	97 205	13 567
1979	189 467	4 120	281	40 094	154	1 936	371	13 135	113 069	16 307

[1] Registered unemployed.   [1] *Chômeurs enregistrés.*   [1] Desempleados registrados.

11 Structure of unemployment
Structure du chômage
Estructura del desempleo

United Kingdom

Industrial groups *(Employment office statistics)* [1]
Groupes d'activité économique *(Statistiques des bureaux de placement)* [1]
Grupos de actividad económica *(Estadísticas de las oficinas de colocación)* [1]

Date / Date / Fecha	Total [2]	1 Agriculture, forestry, fishing / *Agriculture, sylviculture, pêche* / Agricultura, silvicultura, pesca	2 Mining, quarrying / *Industries extractives* / Minas, canteras	3 Manufacturing / *Industries manufacturières* / Industrias manufactureras	4 Electricity, gas, water / *Electricité, gaz, eau* / Electricidad, gas, agua	5 Construction / *Construction* / Construcción	6 Trade, restaurants and hotels / *Commerce, restaurants et hôtels* / Comercio, restaurantes y hoteles	7 Transport, storage, communication / *Transports, entrepôts, communications* / Transportes, almacenaje, comunicaciones	8 Financing, insur., real est., business serv. / *Banques, assur., aff. imm., serv. aux entreprises* / Bancos, seguros, bienes inm., serv. para empresas	9 Community, social, and pers. services / *Services à collectivité, services sociaux et pers.* / Servicios comunales, sociales y personales	0 Activities not adequately described / *Activités mal désignées* / Actividades no bien especificadas
1973	625 846	12 758	18 198	174 757	7 046	97 297	84 421	40 007	18 937	85 510	86 915
1974	623 296	12 504	16 404	161 987	5 971	112 432	81 556	35 411	19 735	86 598	90 695
1975	1 005 678	19 396	16 272	285 120	6 905	172 641	138 866	50 330	29 237	126 456	160 455
1976	1 329 407	24 994	17 436	366 979	9 044	220 017	196 397	63 210	37 023	168 879	255 428
1977	1 474 611	26 963	19 422	351 066	9 511	222 040	215 796	62 790	40 250	200 352	326 421
1978	1 473 954	26 558	23 578	346 615	8 799	200 331	211 429	60 307	38 584	210 290	347 463
1979	1 390 467	24 225	24 394	331 146	8 037	178 464	200 806	57 051	38 514	204 499	323 331

[1] Excl. persons temporarily laid off. [2] For 1973-75, average of 12 monthly figures; for 1976, average of 3 monthly figures (Feb., May and Aug.); for 1977-78, average of 4 monthly figures (Feb., May, Aug. and Nov.).

[1] *Non compris les personnes temporairement mises à pied.* [2] *Pour 1973-75, moyenne de 12 données mensuelles; pour 1976, moyenne de 3 données mensuelles (fév., mai et août); pour 1977-78, moyenne de 4 données mensuelles (fév., mai, août et nov.).*

[1] Excl. las personas temporalmente despedidas. [2] Para 1973-1975, promedio de 12 cifras mensuales; para 1976, promedio de 3 cifras mensuales (febr., mayo y agosto); para 1977-78, promedio de 4 cifras mensuales (febr., mayo, agosto y nov.).

Industrial groups *(Employment office statistics)* [1]
Groupes d'activité économique *(Statistiques des bureaux de placement)* [1]
Grupos de actividad económica *(Estadísticas de las oficinas de colocación)* [1]

Date / Date / Fecha	Total [2]	1 Agriculture, forestry, fishing / *Agriculture, sylviculture, pêche* / Agricultura, silvicultura, pesca	2 Mining, quarrying / *Industries extractives* / Minas, canteras	3 Manufacturing / *Industries manufacturières* / Industrias manufactureras	4 Electricity, gas, water / *Electricité, gaz, eau* / Electricidad, gas, agua	5 Construction / *Construction* / Construcción	6 Trade, restaurants and hotels / *Commerce, restaurants et hôtels* / Comercio, restaurantes y hoteles	7 Transport, storage, communication / *Transports, entrepôts, communications* / Transportes, almacenaje, comunicaciones	8 Financing, insur., real est., business serv. / *Banques, assur., aff. imm., serv. aux entreprises* / Bancos, seguros, bienes inm., serv. para empresas	9 Community, social, and pers. services / *Services à collectivité, services sociaux et pers.* / Servicios comunales, sociales y personales	0 Activities not adequately described / *Activités mal désignées* / Actividades no bien especificadas
1973	10 952	1 819	4	8 276	65	425	127	115	7	114	—
1974	210 990	2 237	304	194 921	15	1 285	1 484	541	570	1 290	8 343
1975	61 431	2 190	45	57 296	15	698	459	384	27	314	3
1976	25 530	2 629	26	20 642	7	1 014	711	205	27	269	
1977	16 530	2 781	23	12 147	2	902	316	136	16	207	—
1978	9 046	2 603	5	5 268	11	553	255	174	15	162	—

[1] Persons temporarily laid off. [2] For 1973, average of 12 monthly figures; for 1974 average of 9 monthly figures (Jan.-Sep.); for 1975, average of 11 monthly figures (Feb.-Dec.); for 1976, average of 3 monthly figures (Feb., May and Aug.); for 1977 and 1978, average of 4 monthly figures (Feb., May, Aug. and Nov.).

[1] *Personnes temporairement mises à pied.* [2] *Pour 1973, moyenne de 12 données mensuelles; pour 1974, moyenne de 9 données mensuelles (janv.-sep.); pour 1975, moyenne de 11 données mensuelles (fév.-déc.); pour 1976, moyenne de 3 données mensuelles (fév., mai et août); pour 1977 et 1978, moyenne de 4 données mensuelles (fév., mai, août et nov.).*

[1] Personas temporalmente despedidas. [2] Para 1973, promedio de 12 cifras mensuales; para 1974, promedio de 9 cifras mensuales (enero-sept.); para 1975, promedio de 11 cifras mensuales (febr.-dic.); para 1976, promedio de 3 cifras mensuales (febr., mayo y agosto); para 1977 y 1978, promedio de 4 cifras mensuales (febr., mayo, agosto y nov.).

11 Structure of unemployment
Structure du chômage
Estructura del desempleo

Yugoslavia

A Industrial groups *(Employment office statistics)* [1]
Groupes d'activité économique *(Statistiques des bureaux de placement)* [1]
Grupos de actividad económica *(Estadísticas de las oficinas de colocación)* [1]

Date [2] Date [2] Fecha [2]	Total	1 Agriculture, forestry, fishing *Agriculture, sylviculture, pêche* Agricultura, silvicultura, pesca	2-3 Mining, quarrying, manufacturing *Industries extractives, industries manufacturières* Minas, canteras, industrias manufactureras	4 Electricity, gas, water *Electricité, gaz, eau* Electricidad, gas, agua	5 Construction *Construction* Construcción	6 Trade, restaurants and hotels *Commerce, restaurants et hôtels* Comercio, restaurantes y hoteles	7 Transport, storage, communication *Transports, entrepôts, communications* Transportes, almacenaje, comunicaciones	8 Financing, insur., real est., business serv. *Banques, assur., aff. imm., serv. aux entreprises* Bancos, seguros, bienes inm., serv. para empresas	9 Community, social, and pers. services *Services à collectivité, services sociaux et pers.* Servicios comunales, sociales y personales	0 Activities not adequately described *Activités mal désignées* Actividades no bien especificadas
1970	141 451	30 143	40 724	6 606	31 657	10 793	4 356	15 956		1 216
1971	143 867	30 658	41 420	6 719	32 197	10 977	4 431	16 228		1 237
1972	153 764	32 767	44 269	7 181	34 412	11 732	4 736	17 345		1 322
1973	178 320	38 000	51 338	8 328	39 908	13 606	5 492	20 114		1 534
1974	194 082	41 359	55 876	9 064	43 436	14 808	5 978	21 892		1 669
1975	234 698	50 014	67 570	10 960	52 525	17 908	7 229	26 474		2 018
1976	263 496	56 151	75 861	12 305	58 970	20 105	8 116	29 722		2 266
1977	267 156	56 931	76 914	12 476	59 790	20 384	8 228	30 135		2 298
1978	250 988	53 486	72 260	11 721	56 171	19 150	7 730	28 312		2 158
1979	246 465	52 522	70 957	11 510	55 159	18 805	7 591	27 801		2 120

[1] Excl. persons seeking work for the first time. [2] Dec.

[1] *Non compris les personnes en quête d'emploi pour la première fois.* [2] *Déc.*

[1] Excl. las personas en busca de trabajo por primera vez. [2] Dic.

(ISCO — CITP — CIUO 1958)

B Occupational groups *(Employment office statistics)*
Groupes de professions *(Statistiques des bureaux de placement)*
Grupos de ocupaciones *(Estadísticas de las oficinas de colocación)*

Date [1] Date [1] Fecha [1]	Total	Professional, technical and related workers *Professions libérales, techniciens et assimilés* Profesiones liberales, técnicos y asimilados	Administrative, executive, managerial workers *Directeurs, cadres administratifs supérieurs* Administradores, gerentes, directores	Clerical workers *Employés de bureau* Empleados de oficina	Sales workers *Vendeurs* Vendedores	Farmers, fishermen and related workers *Agriculteurs, pêcheurs et assimilés* Agricultores, pescadores y asimilados	Miners, quarrymen and related workers *Mineurs, carriers et assimilés* Mineros, canteros y asimilados	Workers in transport and communication occupations *Travailleurs dans les professions des transports et des communications* Trabajadores de los transportes y comunicaciones	Craftsmen, prod. process workers, labourers not elsewhere classified *Artisans, ouvriers de métier et à la production, manœuvres non classés ailleurs* Artesanos, trabaj. ocupados en los div. procesos de prod., peones no clasif. bajo otros epígrafes	Service workers *Travailleurs spécialisés dans les services* Trabajadores de los servicios	Workers not classifiable by occupation [2] *Personnes ne pouvant être classées selon la profession [2]* Trabajadores que no pueden ser clasificados según la ocupación [2]
1970	294 096	21 060	1	23 344	4 782	2 428	900	4 204	30 422	3 888	203 067
1971	264 050	11 388	—	14 955	5 813	3 289	453	2 379	27 374	1 950	196 449
1972	288 878	13 577	—	14 267	7 706	3 122	463	2 395	32 702	2 569	212 077
1973	353 881	17 796	—	16 484	11 746	3 856	558	3 705	46 066	3 250	250 420
1974	417 765	20 333	—	20 986	17 013	4 492	547	5 349	59 839	4 245	284 961
1975	501 607	21 000	—	25 245	22 507	5 043	647	7 586	70 530	5 126	343 923
1976	604 317	23 513	—	28 386	29 827	5 775	622	9 830	90 423	6 046	409 895
1977	660 268	27 640	—	33 539	35 872	6 398	703	10 282	103 727	7 663	434 444
1978	708 374	32 822	—	40 236	40 078	6 815	844	10 597	110 490	7 631	458 861
1979	720 064	33 339	—	40 900	40 756	6 913	864	10 801	112 330	7 777	466 384

[1] June. [2] Incl. persons seeking work for the first time.

[1] *Juin.* [2] *Y compris les personnes en quête d'emploi pour la première fois.*

[1] Junio. [2] Incl. las personas en busca de trabajo por primera vez.

11 — Structure of unemployment / Structure du chômage / Estructura del desempleo

OCEANIA — OCÉANIE — OCEANIA

Australia

A — Industrial groups *(Labour force sample surveys)*
Groupes d'activité économique *(Enquêtes par sondage sur la main-d'œuvre)*
Grupos de actividad económica *(Encuestas por muestra sobre la fuerza trabajadora)*

		1	2	3	4	5	6 ×	7	8	6 × ; 9	
Date [1] / Date [1] / Fecha [1]	Total [2]	Agriculture, forestry, fishing / *Agriculture, sylviculture, pêche* / Agricultura, silvicultura, pesca	Mining, quarrying / *Industries extractives* / Minas, canteras	Manufacturing / *Industries manufacturières* / Industrias manufactureras	Electricity, gas, water / *Electricité, gaz, eau* / Electricidad, gas, agua	Construction / *Construction* / Construcción	Trade [3] / *Commerce* [3] / Comercio [3]	Transport, storage, communication / *Transports, entrepôts, communications* / Transportes, almacenaje, comunicaciones	Financing, insur., real est., business serv. / *Banques, assur., aff. imm., serv. aux entreprises* / Bancos, seguros, bienes inm., serv. para empresas	Community, social and pers. services [4] / *Services à collectivité, services sociaux et pers.* [4] / Servicios comunales, sociales y personales [4]	Persons seeking work for the first time / *Personnes en quête d'emploi pour la première fois* / Personas en busca de trabajo por primera vez
1970	78 200	4 600	—	17 200		7 000	15 800	—	5 000	15 300	7 800
1971	92 700	—	—	22 000		10 000	16 900	—	5 000	18 800	7 600
1972	144 000	7 100	—	35 900		13 200	29 900	6 300	6 300	24 900	14 300
1973	105 800	—	—	21 300		10 100	27 400	5 300	—	19 100	13 400
1974	140 900	8 100	—	38 400		13 700	27 400	5 700	8 100	22 400	12 900
1975	278 400	9 200	—	68 800		28 500	55 100	13 200	13 700	46 700	34 100
1976	292 700	13 300	—	71 200		32 300	60 300	11 600	12 400	44 200	37 500
1977	359 300	19 600	—	83 100		34 600	83 400	14 400	12 200	52 400	49 800
1978	395 700	18 000	—	66 200		42 600	63 500	13 400	12 300	43 300	125 900 [5]
1979	373 800	12 400	—	61 100		27 800	58 500	9 400	10 200	46 000	134 200

B — Occupational groups *(Labour force sample surveys)*
Groupes de professions *(Enquêtes par sondage sur la main-d'œuvre)*
Grupos de ocupaciones *(Encuestas por muestra sobre la fuerza trabajadora)*

(ISCO — CITP — CIUO 1958)

Date [1] / Date [1] / Fecha [1]	Total [2]	Professional, technical and related workers / *Professions libérales, techniciens et assimilés* / Profesiones liberales, técnicos y asimilados	Administrative, executive, managerial workers / *Directeurs, cadres administratifs supérieurs* / Administradores, gerentes, directores	Clerical workers / *Employés de bureau* / Empleados de oficina	Sales workers / *Vendeurs* / Vendedores	Farmers, fishermen and related workers / *Agriculteurs, pêcheurs et assimilés* / Agricultores, pescadores y asimilados	Workers in transport and communication occupations / *Travailleurs dans les professions des transports et des communications* / Trabajadores de los transportes y comunicaciones	Miners, quarrymen and related workers / *Mineurs, carriers et assimilés* / Mineros, canteros y asimilados	Craftsmen, prod. process workers, labourers not elsewhere classified / *Artisans, ouvriers de métier et à la production, manœuvres non classés ailleurs* / Artesanos, trabaj. ocupados en los div. procesos de prod., peones no clasif. bajo otros epígrafes	Service workers / *Travailleurs spécialisés dans les services* / Trabajadores de los servicios	Persons seeking work for the first time / *Personnes en quête d'emploi pour la première fois* / Personas en busca de trabajo por primera vez
1971	92 700	5 700	—	15 400	8 200	—	—		33 500	12 300	7 600
1972	144 000	8 400	—	15 600	17 700	7 600	5 600		53 900	18 800	14 300
1973	105 800	4 700	—	13 700	14 300	—	5 400		33 600	15 000	13 400
1974	140 900	8 300	—	16 600	12 400	8 500	7 300		54 000	18 300	12 900
1975	278 400	13 100	—	35 400	23 600	11 100	13 400		107 900	34 600	34 100
1976	292 700	18 000	—	29 400	31 200	13 200	14 900		113 000	30 400	37 500
1977	359 300	16 500	4 800	39 600	39 600	22 000	10 300		133 200	42 200	49 800
1978	395 700	12 100	—	30 600	28 500	20 000	15 100		129 000	29 300	125 900 [5]
1979	373 800	12 400	5 100	30 900	23 300	17 500	11 000		107 500	32 000	134 200

[1] Aug. [2] Figures of less than 4,000 persons are indicated by a dash. Total may differ from the sum of the groups. [3] Excl. restaurants and hotels. [4] Incl. restaurants and hotels. [5] Incl. unemployed persons who had never worked for two weeks or more in a full time job. Prior to 1978 these persons were classified according to the industry or occupation of their last employment.

[1] Août. [2] Les chiffres inférieurs à 4 000 personnes sont indiqués par un tiret. Le total peut différer de la somme des groupes. [3] Non compris les restaurants et les hôtels. [4] Y compris les restaurants et les hôtels. [5] Y compris les chômeurs qui n'ont jamais travaillé pour deux semaines ou plus dans un emploi à plein temps. Avant 1978 ces personnes étaient réparties selon l'activité économique ou la profession de leur dernier emploi.

[1] Agosto. [2] Las cifras inferiores a 4 000 personas están indicadas por un guión. El total puede diferir de la suma de grupos. [3] Excl. los restaurantes y los hoteles. [4] Incl. los restaurantes y los hoteles. [5] Incl. los desempleados que nunca han trabajado dos o más semanas en un empleo a tiempo completo. Antes de 1978 estas personas se clasificaban según su actividad económica u ocupación en el último empleo.

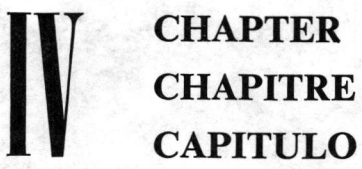

CHAPTER
CHAPITRE
CAPITULO

Hours of work

Durée du travail

Horas de trabajo

Hours of work

Tables 12 to 16 generally show the *average number of hours of work per week per wage earner*. In a few cases hours per day or per month have been shown in the absence of hours per week. Some of the series refer to average hours per week for all employees or even for all categories of workers, as indicated in footnotes. Unless otherwise stated, the series relate to workers of both sexes, irrespective of age.

Where possible, the data presented are statistics of average *hours actually worked*; where such data are lacking, statistics of average *hours paid for* are given. In a few cases where absolute data are not available, index numbers of hours of work have been provided.[1] Statistics of hours actually worked generally comprise all hours worked during normal periods of work, overtime, time spent at the place of work waiting or standing by, as well as time corresponding to short rest periods at the workplace, including tea and coffee breaks. In addition to hours actually worked, statistics of hours paid for include hours paid for but not worked, such as paid annual vacation, paid public holidays, paid sick leave and other paid leave.

Statistics of average hours of work are mostly obtained from payrolls data supplied by a sample of establishments often furnishing at the same time data on wages and on employment. Average hours worked or paid for per week or per month are usually compiled by dividing the total number of man-hours actually worked or paid for during a week or a month by the average number of workers on the payrolls during the same period. Average hours actually worked or paid for per day are generally compiled by dividing the total number of man-hours actually worked or paid for during a week, fortnight or month by the total number of man-days actually worked or paid for during the same period.

In a few cases, statistics on hours worked are obtained from household *sample surveys*. The information is collected from individuals and the data obtained are therefore not fully comparable with the data obtained from establishments.

In making comparisons of data on hours of work, it should be borne in mind that the data are influenced by the number of days normally worked per week, regulations and customs regarding Saturday and overtime work, the extent of absenteeism, labour turnover, etc. Differences in national definitions of hours worked, the coverage of the series and the methods of compilation must also be taken into account.[2]

Table 12

Hours of work in non-agricultural sectors

Unless otherwise indicated in footnotes, the data shown in this table cover the following divisions of economic activity: Mining and quarrying; Manufacturing; Electricity, gas and water; Construction; Wholesale and retail trade, restaurants and hotels; Transport, storage and communication; Financing, insurance, real estate and business services; Community, social and personal services. In some cases, however, these divisions are only represented by certain of the groups composing them.

---

[1] For the descriptions of the various national series, their scope, methods of compilation and definitions used, etc., see ILO: *Technical Guide 1980* (description of general series published in the *Bulletin* and the *Year Book of Labour Statistics*), Vol. II, " Employment—Unemployment—Hours of Work—Wages " (Geneva, 1980).

[2] For a review of the problems concerning definitions, methods of collection and tabulation of data on hours of work, see ILO: *Statistics of Hours of Work*, Tenth International Conference of Labour Statisticians, Report III, as well as the resolution concerning statistics of hours of work adopted by the Tenth International Conference of Labour Statisticians. See ILO: *International Recommendations on Labour Statistics* (Geneva, 1976).

Table 13

Hours of work in manufacturing

Part A of table 13 generally shows hours of work per worker in manufacturing industries as a whole; where in a few cases other industries are also included in the series, this is indicated in footnotes.

Part B of table 13 shows hours of work in specified manufacturing industries for most of the countries represented in Part A. So far as possible, the different manufacturing industries have been arranged according to the International Standard Classification of All Economic Activities (see Appendix) with the corresponding code number of the different industrial major groups.

Tables 14 to 16

Hours of work in mining and quarrying; construction; transport, storage and communication

Tables 14 to 16 show statistics of average hours of work per week in three major divisions of economic activity as follows: Table 14. Mining and quarrying; table 15. Construction; and table 16. Transport, storage and communication (excl. sea transport).

The statistics of hours of work in mining often exclude coal mining owing to the particular conditions regulating work in that industry in the different countries (especially the widespread application of systems of payment by results and of payment for travelling time). The statistics of hours of work in construction refer in many cases to building or to certain categories of building workers.

Durée du travail

Les tableaux 12 à 16 donnent généralement la *durée moyenne du travail par semaine, par ouvrier*. Dans quelques cas, c'est la durée du travail par jour ou par mois qui est indiquée, en l'absence de la durée hebdomadaire. Certaines des séries se rapportent à la durée hebdomadaire moyenne pour tous les travailleurs salariés ou même pour toutes les catégories de travailleurs, selon ce qu'indiquent les notes de bas de page. Sauf indication contraire, les séries couvrent les travailleurs des deux sexes, sans considération d'âge.

Dans la mesure du possible, les données présentées sont des statistiques du nombre moyen d'*heures réellement effectuées*; lorsque ces données manquent, elles sont remplacées par des statistiques du nombre moyen d'*heures rémunérées*. Dans quelques cas où l'on ne dispose pas de données en chiffres absolus, ce sont les nombres-indices de la durée du travail qui ont été reproduits [1]. Les statistiques du nombre d'heures de travail réellement effectuées englobent généralement toutes les heures de travail effectuées au cours des périodes normales de travail, les heures supplémentaires, les heures passées sur le lieu de travail à attendre ou à rester à la disposition, ainsi que le temps correspondant à de courtes périodes de repos passées sur le lieu de travail, y compris les pauses pour le thé et le café. Outre les heures de travail réellement effectuées, les statistiques des heures rémunérées comprennent les heures de travail payées mais non effectuées, telles que congés annuels, jours fériés, congés de maladie et autres congés payés.

Les statistiques de la durée moyenne du travail sont tirées le plus souvent des bordereaux de salaires remis par un échantillon d'établissements, qui fournissent fréquemment en même temps des données sur les salaires et sur l'emploi. Le nombre moyen d'heures de travail réellement effectuées ou rémunérées par semaine ou par mois est généralement obtenu en divisant le nombre total des heures-homme réellement effectuées ou rémunérées pendant une semaine ou un mois par le nombre moyen des travailleurs figurant sur les bordereaux de salaires pendant la même période. La durée moyenne de la journée de travail effectuée ou rémunérée est généralement obtenue en divisant le nombre total d'heures-homme réellement effectuées ou rémunérées pendant une semaine, une quinzaine ou un mois par le nombre total des journées-homme réellement effectuées ou rémunérées pendant la même période.

Dans quelques cas peu nombreux, les statistiques de la durée du travail ont été obtenues à partir d'*enquêtes par sondage* dans les ménages. Les renseignements sont recueillis auprès des particuliers; les données obtenues ne sont donc pas entièrement comparables avec celles que fournissent les établissements.

En comparant les données relatives à la durée du travail, il ne faut pas perdre de vue que ces données sont influencées par le nombre de journées normalement effectuées par semaine, par les règlements et les usages concernant le travail du samedi et les heures supplémentaires, par le degré d'absentéisme, le mouvement de la main-d'œuvre, etc. Il faut également tenir compte des différences dans les définitions nationales du travail effectif, la portée des séries et les méthodes d'établissement de ces séries [2].

---

[1] Pour les descriptions des diverses séries nationales, de leur portée, des méthodes de calcul et des définitions utilisées, etc., voir BIT: *Guide technique 1980* (descriptions des séries générales publiées dans le *Bulletin* et l'*Annuaire des statistiques du travail*), vol. II, « Emploi — Chômage — Durée du travail — Salaires » (Genève, 1980).

[2] Pour une étude des problèmes relatifs aux définitions, aux méthodes d'établissement des séries et à la tabulation des données concernant la durée du travail, voir BIT, dixième Conférence internationale des statisticiens du travail, rapport III: *Statistiques de la durée du travail*, ainsi que la résolution concernant les statistiques des heures de travail, adoptée par la dixième Conférence internationale des statisticiens du travail. Voir BIT: *Recommandations internationales sur les statistiques du travail* (Genève, 1975).

Tableau 12

Durée du travail dans les secteurs non agricoles

Sauf indication contraire figurant en notes de bas de page, les données présentées dans ce tableau couvrent les branches d'activité économique ci-après: industries extractives; industries manufacturières; électricité, gaz et eau; construction; commerce de gros et de détail, restaurants et hôtels; transports, entrepôts et communications; banque, assurances, affaires immobilières et services fournis aux entreprises; services fournis à la collectivité, services sociaux et services personnels. Dans certains cas, toutefois, ces branches d'activité ne sont représentées que par une partie seulement des classes qui les composent.

Tableau 13

Durée du travail dans les industries manufacturières

La partie A du tableau 13 indique généralement la durée du travail par travailleur dans l'ensemble des industries manufacturières; dans les quelques cas où d'autres branches d'activité sont également comprises dans la série, une indication est donnée à ce sujet en notes de bas de page.

La partie B du tableau 13 indique la durée du travail dans des industries manufacturières spécifiées, pour la plupart des pays représentés dans la partie A. Dans la mesure du possible, les différentes industries manufacturières ont été ordonnées conformément à la Classification internationale type, par industrie, de toutes les branches d'activité économique (voir annexe), avec indication du numéro de code correspondant aux différentes classes d'industries.

Tableaux 14 à 16

Durée du travail dans les industries extractives; la construction; les transports, entrepôts et communications

Les tableaux 14 à 16 contiennent des statistiques de la durée moyenne du travail par semaine dans trois branches d'activité économique particulièrement importantes, à savoir: tableau 14, industries extractives; tableau 15, construction; tableau 16, transports, entrepôts et communications (non compris les transports par mer).

Les statistiques de la durée du travail dans les industries extractives font fréquemment exclusion des mines de charbon, en raison des conditions particulières régissant le travail dans cette branche d'activité dans les différents pays (notamment l'application très étendue de systèmes de rémunération au rendement et de rémunération du temps nécessaire aux trajets). Les statistiques de la durée du travail dans la construction concernent très souvent l'industrie du bâtiment ou certaines catégories de travailleurs du bâtiment.

Horas de trabajo

Los cuadros 12 a 16 representan generalmente el *promedio de horas de trabajo por semana y por obrero*. En ciertos casos, cuando no existen horas de trabajo por semana, se presentan las horas de trabajo por día o por mes. Tal como se indica en las notas de pie de página, algunas de las series se refieren al promedio de las horas semanales para todas las personas empleadas e inclusive para todas las categorías de trabajadores. Salvo indicación contraria, las series abarcan los trabajadores de ambos sexos, sin distinción de edad.

Cada vez que es posible, los datos que se presentan son estadísticas de promedios de *horas efectivamente trabajadas*; cuando faltan dichos datos, se dan estadísticas de promedios de *horas pagadas*. En ciertos casos, cuando no se dispone de cifras absolutas, se presentan índices de horas de trabajo [1]. Las estadísticas de las horas efectivamente trabajadas comprenden generalmente todas las horas trabajadas durante el tiempo normal de trabajo, las horas extraordinarias, el tiempo empleado en el lugar de trabajo esperando o permaneciendo disponible, así como los cortos períodos de descanso en el lugar de trabajo, incluidas las pausas para tomar el café o el té. Las estadísticas de horas pagadas incluyen, además de las horas efectivamente trabajadas, las horas remuneradas pero no trabajadas, tales como las vacaciones anuales, días feriados, ausencias por motivo de enfermedad y otros permisos pagados.

Las estadísticas de promedios de horas de trabajo se obtienen generalmente de los datos de las nóminas de salarios proporcionados por una muestra de establecimientos que presentan también datos sobre los salarios y el empleo. El promedio de las horas efectivamente trabajadas o pagadas por semana o por mes se obtiene generalmente dividiendo el número total de horas-hombre efectivamente trabajadas o pagadas durante una semana o un mes por el promedio de trabajadores que figuren en las nóminas de salarios durante el mismo período. El promedio de las horas efectivamente trabajadas o pagadas por día se obtiene generalmente dividiendo el número total de horas-hombre efectivamente trabajadas o pagadas durante una semana, una quincena o un mes por el número total de días-hombre efectivamente trabajados o pagados durante el mismo período.

En ciertos casos, las estadísticas de horas efectivamente trabajadas se obtienen mediante *encuestas por muestras* sobre las familias. La información se obtiene de los individuos y, por lo tanto, los datos pueden no ser enteramente comparables con aquellos que se obtienen de los establecimientos.

Al hacer comparaciones sobre los datos de horas de trabajo debe tenerse presente que los mismos están influidos por el número normal de días de trabajo por semana, por las disposiciones reglamentarias y costumbres respecto al trabajo durante el sábado y a las horas extraordinarias, la frecuencia del absentismo, la rotación de la mano de obra, etc. Deben tenerse presentes también las diferencias en las definiciones de cada país sobre las horas efectivamente trabajadas, el alcance de las series y los métodos de compilación [2].

---

[1] Para las descripciones de las diversas series nacionales, su alcance, métodos de compilación y definiciones utilizados, etc., véase OIT: *Guía Técnica 1980* (descripciones generales de las series publicadas en el *Boletín* y el *Anuario de Estadísticas del Trabajo*), vol. II, « Empleo — Desempleo — Horas de trabajo — Salarios» (Ginebra, 1980).

[2] Como revisión de los problemas relativos a las definiciones, métodos de obtención y tabulación de los datos sobre las horas de trabajo, véase OIT: *Estadísticas de la duración del trabajo*, décima Conferencia Internacional de Estadígrafos del Trabajo, Informe III, así como la resolución sobre las estadísticas de las horas de trabajo, adoptada por la décima Conferencia Internacional de Estadígrafos del Trabajo. Véase OIT: *Recomendaciones internacionales sobre estadísticas del trabajo* (Ginebra, 1975).

Cuadro 12

Horas de trabajo en los sectores no agrícolas

Salvo indicación contraria en notas de pie de página, los datos que se presentan en este cuadro incluyen las siguientes divisiones de la actividad económica: minas y canteras; industrias manufactureras; electricidad, gas y agua; construcción; comercio al por mayor y al por menor y restaurantes y hoteles; transportes, almacenaje y comunicaciones; establecimientos financieros, seguros, bienes inmuebles y servicios prestados a las empresas; servicios comunales, sociales y personales. En algunos casos, estas divisiones sólo están representadas por una parte de los grupos que las componen.

Cuadro 13

Horas de trabajo en las industrias manufactureras

La parte A del cuadro 13 indica generalmente las horas de trabajo por obrero en todas las industrias manufactureras; cuando en ciertos casos se incluyen otras industrias, así se indica en notas de pie de página.

La parte B del cuadro 13 presenta las horas de trabajo en industrias manufactureras especificadas para la mayoría de los países que figuran en la parte A. En la medida de lo posible, las diferentes industrias manufactureras han sido ordenadas según la Clasificación industrial internacional uniforme de todas las actividades económicas (véase apéndice) con indicación del correspondiente número de código de los diferentes grupos de industrias.

Cuadros 14 a 16

Horas de trabajo en minas y canteras; construcción; transportes, almacenaje y comunicaciones

Los cuadros 14 a 16 presentan las estadísticas del promedio de horas de trabajo por semana en tres divisiones principales de actividad económica, a saber: cuadro 14: minas y canteras; cuadro 15: construcción; cuadro 16: transportes, almacenaje y comunicaciones (excl. el transporte marítimo).

Las estadísticas sobre horas de trabajo en las minas excluyen frecuentemente las minas de carbón, a causa de las condiciones particulares que regulan el trabajo en esa industria en los distintos países (especialmente debido a la extensa aplicación de los sistemas de pago por rendimiento y al pago por el tiempo empleado en ir al trabajo). Las estadísticas de horas de trabajo en la construcción se refieren, en muchos casos, solamente a la edificación o a ciertas categorías de trabajadores de esta rama.

12 Hours of work in non-agricultural sectors
Durée du travail dans les secteurs non agricoles
Horas de trabajo en los sectores no agrícolas

Hours of work per week — Durée du travail par semaine — Horas de trabajo por semana

Country — Pays — País	Code Code Clave	1970	1971	1972	1973	1974	1975	1976	1977	1978	1979	1980 (VI)
AFRICA — AFRIQUE ÁFRICA												
Algérie [1]	(a)	43.2	42.5	42.8	42.8	43.0	43.0	44.2	44.5	...	...	.
Egypt [2]	(b)	56	56	55	56	60	58 *	56 *	...	...	...	.
Mali [3]	(a)	.	42.3	43.0	42.4	43.1	...	...	...	...	...	.
Sierra Leone [4,5]	(a)	48.3	48.0	49.4	54.3	47.9	41.8	40.6	40.3	40.1	44.0	.
AMERICA — AMÉRIQUE AMÉRICA												
Guyana [6,7]	(b)	45.3	46.5	44.8	43.9	46.2	45.9	47.4	45.4	45.8	...	.
Perú (Lima-Callao) [8,9]	(a)	.	.	.	48.5	48.6	47.9	49.4	46.9	46.8	46.0	.
Puerto Rico [10]	(a)	37.8	37.8	37.7	37.9	36.8	36.6	35.7	I 36.9 [11]	37.1	37.2	37.1 [22]
United States	(b)	37.1	36.9	37.0	36.9	36.5	36.1	36.1	36.0	35.8	35.6	35.3
Venezuela [12]	(a)	42.9	42.6	42.7	42.8	42.7	42.3	42.4	42.9	44.2	...	...
ASIA — ASIE ASIA												
Brunei [2,13]	(a)	.	.	48.8	49.4	48.5	49.1	48.9	49.5	49.8	50.0	.
Cyprus [2,5]	(b)	45	45	45	44	I 42 [14]	44	45	44	44	43	.
Israel [13,15]	(a)	39.6	39.6	40.1	37.3	37.6	37.9	37.6	36.5	35.8	36.6	37.1 [23]
Japan [13]	(a)	43.1	42.7	42.4	I 42.0 [16]	40.5	39.7	I 40.3 [16]	40.3	40.5	I 40.7 [16]	41.6
Korea, Rep. of [13]	(a)	51.6	50.6	50.9	50.7	49.6	50.0	51.1	51.4	51.3	50.5	...
Philippines [10,17]	(a)	.	.	44.7	45.8	47.0	48.2	47.6	...	...	...	.
Singapore [17,18]	(a) [19]	47.8	48.4	48.6	48.4	47.5	47.8	47.8	48.3	48.7	48.4	.
Sri Lanka [6,20]	(b) [21]	9.1	9.1	9.1	9.1	9.3	9.3	8.8	9.1	10.0	9.5	.

EXPLANATORY NOTES: See p. 335.   NOTES EXPLICATIVES: Voir p. 337.   NOTAS EXPLICATIVAS: Véase pág. 339.

(a): Hours actually worked — *Heures réellement effectuées* — Horas efectivamente trabajadas.
(b): Hours paid for — *Heures rémunérées* — Horas pagadas.

[1] April of each year. [2] Oct. of each year. [3] Dec. of each year. [4] Excl. electricity, gas and water, commerce, financing, etc., and services. May and Nov. of each year. [5] Adults. [6] Excl. electricity, gas and water, financing, etc., and services. [7] Prior to 1973: excl. commerce. [8] Excl. mining, quarrying, electricity, gas and water. [9] June of each year. [10] Civilian labour force employed. [11] Beginning July 1977: persons aged 16 years and over. [12] Excl. construction and transport. [13] Incl. salaried employees. [14] Beginning July 1974: due to a change in the geographical scope of the series, data are not comparable with those for the preceding period. [15] Incl. agriculture, forestry and fishing. [16] Sampling design revised. [17] Aug. of each year. [18] Incl. agriculture, fishing and sea transport. [19] Prior to 1975: July. [20] March and Sep. of each year. [21] Per day. [22] April. [23] First quarter.

[1] *Avril de chaque année.* [2] *Oct. de chaque année.* [3] *Déc. de chaque année.* [4] *Non compris l'électricité, le gaz et l'eau, le commerce, les banques, etc., et les services. Mai et nov. de chaque année.* [5] *Adultes.* [6] *Non compris l'électricité, le gaz et l'eau, les banques, etc., et les services.* [7] *Avant 1973 : non compris le commerce.* [8] *Non compris les industries extractives, l'électricité, le gaz et l'eau.* [9] *Juin de chaque année.* [10] *Main-d'œuvre civile occupée.* [11] *A partir de juillet 1977 : personnes âgées de 16 ans et plus.* [12] *Non compris la construction et les transports.* [13] *Y compris les employés.* [14] *A partir de juillet 1974 : en raison d'un changement de la portée géographique de la série, les données ne sont pas comparables avec celles de la période précédente.* [15] *Y compris l'agriculture, la sylviculture et la pêche.* [16] *Plan d'échantillonnage révisé.* [17] *Août de chaque année.* [18] *Y compris l'agriculture, la pêche et les transports par mer.* [19] *Avant 1975 : juillet.* [20] *Mars et sept. de chaque année.* [21] *Par jour.* [22] *Avril.* [23] *Premier trimestre.*

[1] Abril de cada año. [2] Oct. de cada año. [3] Dic. de cada año. [4] Excl. la electricidad, el gas y el agua, el comercio, los establecimientos financieros, etc., y los servicios. Mayo y nov. de cada año. [5] Adultos. [6] Excl. la electricidad, el gas y el agua, los establecimientos financieros, etc., y los servicios. [7] Antes de 1973: excl. el comercio. [8] Excl. las minas y canteras, la electricidad, el gas y el agua. [9] Junio de cada año. [10] Fuerza trabajadora civil ocupada. [11] A partir de julio de 1977: personas de 16 años y más. [12] Excl. la construcción y los transportes. [13] Incl. los empleados. [14] A partir de julio de 1974: en razón de un cambio del alcance geográfico de la serie, los datos no son comparables a los del período precedente. [15] Incl. la agricultura, la silvicultura y la pesca. [16] Diseño de la muestra revisado. [17] Agosto de cada año. [18] Incl. la agricultura, la pesca y el transporte marítimo. [19] Antes de 1975: julio. [20] Marzo y sept. de cada año. [21] Por día. [22] Abril. [23] Primer trimestre.

12 Hours of work in non-agricultural sectors
Durée du travail dans les secteurs non agricoles
Horas de trabajo en los sectores no agrícolas

Hours of work per week — Durée du travail par semaine — Horas de trabajo por semana

Country — Pays — País	Code Code Clave	1970	1971	1972	1973	1974	1975	1976	1977	1978	1979	1980 (VI)
EUROPE — EUROPE EUROPA												
Belgique [1,2]	(a)[3]	40.2	40.0	|39.2[4]	38.0	36.7	35.4	36.1	35.4	35.5	35.8	.
España [5,6]	(a)	43.9	43.6	44.6	44.0	43.7	42.8	41.7	|43.9[7]	43.5	42.9	...
France [8]	(a)	.	.	44.6	44.4	43.7	42.7	|42.4[9]	41.8	41.4	41.2	41.1
Germany, Fed. Rep. of [2]	(b)	44.0	43.2	42.8	|42.8[9]	41.9	40.5	41.6	41.7	41.6	41.9	41.8[33]
Gibraltar [10,11]	(b)	48.1	47.6	47.7	49.4	47.4	47.3	46.4	47.5	47.1	45.9	.
Iceland (Reykjavik) [12,13]	(b)	.	.	.	.	52.6	51.7	52.0	50.3	50.5	50.1	.
Ireland [14,15]	(a)[16]	42.8	42.4	42.5	42.4	39.9	41.6	...	...	...	...	.
Italie [2]	(a)[17]	7.80	7.83	7.80	7.70	7.70	7.72	7.72	7.73	|7.75[18]	...	.
Luxembourg [1,19]	(a)	45.0	44.7	|43.9[4]	43.7	43.6	40.9	40.3	39.5	40.2	40.8	.
Malta [20,21]	(b)	43.2	43.1	42.5	42.0	41.2	44.8	41.0	40.0	40.0	40.0	.
Netherlands [1,22]	(b)	.		.	.	42.3	41.4	41.4	41.4	41.3	...	.
Portugal [2]	(a)	.	40.8	42.2	42.7	42.6	40.7	39.0	38.5	38.7	...	.
Suisse [23,24]	(b)	.	.	.	45.4	45.4	44.9	44.8	44.8	44.7	44.5	44.5[34]
Sweden [25]	(a)	.	38.2	37.0	36.8	36.8	36.6	36.3	35.9	35.7	35.7	36.1
United Kingdom [1,26]												
Males [21] — Hommes [21] — Hombres [21]	(a)[27]	45.7	44.7	45.0	45.6	45.1	43.6	44.0	44.2	44.2	44.0	
Females [21] — Femmes [21] — Mujeres [21]	(a)[27]	37.9	37.7	37.9	37.7	37.4	37.0	37.4	37.4	37.4	37.4	
Yugoslavia [20,28]	(b)[29]	183	182	182	182	181	183	185	185	185 *	185 *	
OCEANIA — OCÉANIE OCEANÍA												
Australia [1,30]												
Males [21] — Hommes [21] — Hombres [21]	(b)[20]	43.5	43.2	|42.0[31]	42.3	41.3	40.6	40.7	40.7	40.6	40.9	.
Females [21] — Femmes [21] — Mujeres [21]	(b)[20]	39.4	39.3	|38.9[31]	39.0	38.5	38.4	38.4	38.4	38.2	38.6	.
New Zealand [20,32]	(b)[16]	38.3	37.7	37.6	37.7	37.6	37.2	36.9	36.7	36.4	37.6	...

EXPLANATORY NOTES: See p. 335.   NOTES EXPLICATIVES: Voir p. 337.   NOTAS EXPLICATIVAS: Véase pág. 339.

(a): Hours actually worked — Heures réellement effectuées — Horas efectivamente trabajadas.
(b): Hours paid for — Heures rémunérées — Horas pagadas.

[1] Oct. of each year. [2] Excl. commerce, transport, financing, etc., and services. [3] Beginning Oct. 1976: excl. electricity, gas and water. [4] New industrial classification. [5] Civilian labour force employed. Prior to 1977: wage earners and salaried employees. [6] Prior to 1977: excl. transport and services. [7] Series replacing former series. [8] Excl. water, communication, public administrations and private domestic services. [9] Sampling design revised. [10] Excl. mining and quarrying. [11] Oct. of each year, except for 1970-72: April and Oct. and 1974-75: April. [12] Excl. mining, quarrying, electricity, gas, water, financing, etc., and services. [13] Skilled males. [14] Sep. of each year. [15] Excl. commerce, transport and financing, etc. [16] Incl. juveniles. [17] Per day. [18] Scope of series revised. [19] Excl. electricity, gas and water, commerce, transport, financing, etc., and services. [20] Incl. salaried employees. [21] Adults. [22] Incl. juveniles. Prior to 1977: excl. services. [23] Accident insurance statistics; excl. overtime. [24] Incl. horticulture and forestry but excl. mining, quarrying, financing, etc., and services. [25] Civilian labor force employed. [26] Excl. coal mines, commerce, railways, financing, etc. [27] Full-time wage earners. [28] Socialised sector. [29] Per month. [30] Incl. forestry, trapping and sea transport. [31] Scope of series enlarged. [32] Incl. forestry and logging. April and Oct. of each year. [33] April. [34] Second quarter.

[1] Oct. de chaque année. [2] Non compris le commerce, les transports, les banques, etc., et les services. [3] A partir d'oct. 1976 : non compris l'électricité, le gaz et l'eau. [4] Nouvelle classification industrielle. [5] Main-d'œuvre civile occupée. Avant 1977 : ouvriers et employés. [6] Avant 1977 : non compris les transports et les services. [7] Série remplaçant la précédente. [8] Non compris l'eau, les communications, les administrations publiques et les services domestiques privés. [9] Plan d'échantillonnage révisé. [10] Non compris les industries extractives. [11] Oct. de chaque année, sauf pour 1970-1972 : avril et oct., et 1974-1976 : avril. [12] Non compris les industries extractives, l'électricité, le gaz, l'eau, les banques, etc., et les services. [13] Hommes qualifiés. [14] Sept. de chaque année. [15] Non compris le commerce, les transports et les banques, etc. [16] Y compris les jeunes gens. [17] Par jour. [18] Portée de la série révisée. [19] Non compris l'électricité, le gaz et l'eau, le commerce, les transports, les banques, etc., et les services. [20] Y compris les employés. [21] Adultes. [22] Y compris les jeunes gens. Avant 1977 : non compris les services. [23] Statistiques d'assurance-accidents ; non compris les heures supplémentaires. [24] Y compris l'horticulture et la sylviculture, mais non compris les industries extractives, les banques, etc., et les services. [25] Main-d'œuvre civile occupée. [26] Non compris les mines de charbon, le commerce, les chemins de fer, les banques, etc. [27] Ouvriers à temps complet. [28] Secteur socialisé. [29] Par mois. [30] Y compris la sylviculture, la pêche, le piégeage et les transports par mer. [31] Portée de la série élargie. [32] Y compris la sylviculture et l'exploitation forestière. Avril et oct. de chaque année. [33] Avril. [34] Deuxième trimestre.

[1] Oct. de cada año. [2] Excl. el comercio, los transportes, los establecimientos financieros, etc., y los servicios. [3] A partir de oct. de 1976: excl. la electricidad, el gas y el agua. [4] Nueva clasificación industrial. [5] Fuerza trabajadora civil ocupada. Antes de 1977: obreros y empleados. [6] Antes de 1977: excl. los transportes y los servicios. [7] Serie que substituye a la anterior. [8] Excl. el agua, las comunicaciones, las administraciones públicas y los servicios domésticos privados. [9] Diseño de la muestra revisado. [10] Excl. las minas y canteras. [11] Oct. de cada año, salvo para 1970-1972: abril y oct., y 1974-1976: abril. [12] Excl. las minas y canteras, la electricidad, el gas, el agua, los establecimientos financieros, etc., y los servicios. [13] Hombres calificados. [14] Sept. de cada año. [15] Excl. el comercio, los transportes y los establecimientos financieros, etc. [16] Incl. los jóvenes. [17] Por día. [18] El alcance de la serie es revisado. [19] Excl. la electricidad, el gas y el agua, el comercio, los transportes, los establecimientos financieros, etc., y los servicios. [20] Incl. los empleados. [21] Adultos. [22] Incl. los jóvenes. Antes de 1977: excl. los servicios. [23] Estadísticas del seguro de accidentes; excl. las horas extraordinarias. [24] Incl. la horticultura y la silvicultura, pero excl. las minas, las canteras, los establecimientos financieros, etc., y los servicios. [25] Fuerza trabajadora civil ocupada. [26] Excl. las minas de carbón, el comercio, los ferrocarriles, los establecimientos financieros, etc. [27] Obreros a tiempo completo. [28] Sector socializado. [29] Por mes. [30] Incl. la silvicultura, la pesca, la caza con trampas y los transportes por mar. [31] El alcance de la serie es mayor. [32] Incl. la silvicultura y la explotación de la madera. Abril y oct. de cada año. [33] Abril. [34] Segundo trimestre.

13 Hours of work in manufacturing
Durée du travail dans les industries manufacturières
Horas de trabajo en las industrias manufactureras

A All industries
Ensemble des industries
Todas las industrias

Hours of work per week Durée du travail par semaine Horas de trabajo por semana

Country — Pays — País	Code Code Clave	1970	1971	1972	1973	1974	1975	1976	1977	1978	1979	1980 (VI)
AFRICA — AFRIQUE AFRICA												
Algérie [1]	(a)	42.4	41.1	40.7	40.8	41.6	41.6	43.8	44.4	...	...	.
Egypt [2]	(b)	55	55	54	55	59	59 *	56 *	...	...	...	.
Mali [3]	(a)	.	42.3	43.3	44.2	44.6	...	...	...	...	...	.
Sierra Leone [4,5]	(a)	45.1	41.5	42.8	49.6	46.6	43.8	41.5	40.5	40.2	40.2	.
South Africa, Rep. of [6]	(a)	47.1	47.1	46.5	47.5	48.4	48.2	47.3	47.5	47.6	48.0	...
« « « « . . . . . Total	(a)	47.0	46.3	45.9	46.8	46.9	46.6	46.1	46.5	47.0	47.7	...
AMERICA — AMÉRIQUE AMÉRICA												
Canada	(b)	39.7	39.7	40.0	39.6	38.9	38.6	38.7	38.7	38.8	38.8	38.3
Ecuador	(a)	48	48	48	49	51	51	50	51	...	...	.
El Salvador (San Salvador) [7]												
Males — Hommes — Hombres	(a)	48.0	47.5	46.4	47.0	48.2	44.3	44.3	44.3	44.6	44.6	...
Females — Femmes — Mujeres . . .	(a)	45.2	46.0	45.3	46.2	47.5	43.9	44.1	44.3	44.6	44.6	...
Guatemala [8]	(a)	45.9	46.3	46.6	47.6	|48.2 [9]	47.2	47.3	48.5	47.5	...	.
Guyana	(b)	46.3	47.0	46.3	46.4	47.8	48.2	48.8	46.9	45.6	...	.
México [2]	(a)	44.9	44.8	45.9	45.6	45.5	45.6	45.6	45.5	...	...	.
Panamá	(a)	42.3	44.7	43.8	43.1	45.7	45.5	45.9	45.9	...	...	.
Perú (Lima-Callao) [10]	(a)	.	.	.	.	47.2	46.1	48.1	45.4	45.8	45.7	.
Puerto Rico	(b)	36.7	37.2	37.2	37.1	36.9	37.0	37.5	37.6	37.9	37.6	...
United States	(b)	39.8	39.9	40.5	40.7	40.0	39.5	40.1	40.3	40.4	40.2	39.4
Venezuela	(a)	44.4	43.3	43.6	43.8	43.7	42.3	43.1	43.7	43.9	...	...
Virgin Is. (US) [11, 12]	(b)	.	.	.	.	40.3	38.8	41.1	37.4	...	...	...
ASIA — ASIE ASIA												
Brunei [2, 11]	(a) [13]	.	.	50.2	50.2	49.6	49.3	50.7	50.3	49.8	50.0	.
Burma [14]	(a) [15]	7.7	7.6	7.5 [16]	7.7	7.6	7.6	7.7	7.7	7.4	...	.
Cyprus [2, 4]	(b)	46	45	44	43	|43 [17]	43	45	44	44	43	.

EXPLANATORY NOTES: See p. 335.   NOTES EXPLICATIVES: Voir p. 337.   NOTAS EXPLICATIVAS: Véase pág. 339.

(a): Hours actually worked — *Heures réellement effectuées* — Horas efectivamente trabajadas.
(b): Hours paid for — *Heures rémunérées* — Horas pagadas.

[1] April of each year. [2] Oct. of each year. [3] Dec. of each year. [4] Adults. [5] May and Nov. of each year. [6] White manual workers. [7] Department of San Salvador. Prior to 1975: metropolitan area. [8] Prior to 1974: Guatemala City only. [9] Series replacing former series. [10] June of each year. [11] Incl. salaried employees. [12] First quarter of each year. [13] Incl. mining, quarrying and construction. [14] Workers engaged for less than 30 days (excl. casual workers). [15] Per day. Beginning 1973: March and Sep. of each year. [16] April and Sep. [17] Beginning July 1974: due to a change in the geographical scope of the series, data are not comparable with those for the preceding period.

[1] Avril de chaque année. [2] Oct. de chaque année. [3] Déc. de chaque année. [4] Adultes. [5] Mai et nov. de chaque année. [6] Travailleurs manuels (population blanche). [7] Département de San Salvador. Avant 1975 : région métropolitaine. [8] Avant 1974 : ville de Guatemala seulement. [9] Série remplaçant la précédente. [10] Juin de chaque année. [11] Y compris les employés. [12] Premier trimestre de chaque année. [13] Y compris les industries extractives et la construction. [14] Travailleurs engagés pour moins de 30 jours (non compris les travailleurs occasionnels). [15] Par jour. A partir de 1973 : mars et sept. de chaque année. [16] Avril et sept. [17] A partir de juillet 1974 : en raison d'un changement de la portée géographique de la série, les données ne sont pas comparables avec celles de la période précédente.

[1] Abril de cada año. [2] Oct. de cada año. [3] Dic. de cada año. [4] Adultos. [5] Mayo y nov. de cada año. [6] Trabajadores manuales (población blanca). [7] Departamento de San Salvador. Antes de 1975: área metropolitana. [8] Antes de 1974: ciudad de Guatemala solamente. [9] Serie que substituye a la anterior. [10] Junio de cada año. [11] Incl. los empleados. [12] Primer trimestre de cada año. [13] Incl. las minas y canteras y la construcción. [14] Trabajadores ocupados durante menos de 30 días (excl. los trabajadores ocasionales). [15] Por día. A partir de 1973: marzo y sept. de cada año. [16] Abril y sept. [17] A partir de julio de 1974: en razón de un cambio del alcance geográfico de la serie, los datos no son comparables a los del período precedente.

343

13 Hours of work in manufacturing — Durée du travail dans les industries manufacturières — Horas de trabajo en las industrias manufactureras

A All industries — Ensemble des industries — Todas las industrias

Hours of work per week · Durée du travail par semaine · Horas de trabajo por semana

Country — Pays — País	Code Code Clave	1970	1971	1972	1973	1974	1975	1976	1977	1978	1979	1980 (VI)
Israel [1,2]	(a)	42.1	41.7	42.8	39.2	39.7	40.3	40.3	38.8	38.0	39.3	39.2 [26]
Japan [2]	(a)	43.3	42.6	42.3	|42.0 [3]	40.0	38.8	|40.2 [4]	40.3	40.6	|40.6 [3]	42.6
Korea, Rep. of [2]	(a)	52.3	51.9	51.6	51.2	49.9	50.5	52.5	52.9	52.9	52.0	...
Philippines [4,5]	(a)	.	.	44.2	43.6	44.8	45.3	43.7	...	...	...	.
Singapore [4,6]	(a)	48.7	49.4	49.5	48.8	47.9	48.4	48.4	48.8	49.0	48.5	.
Sri Lanka [7]	(b) [8]	9.2	9.1	9.3	9.3	9.8	9.2	8.8	9.0	10.0	9.6	.
République arabe syrienne [9,10]	(a)	48.0	44.9	47.1	46.3	44.7	43.2	47.1	46.7	...	...	
EUROPE — EUROPE EUROPA												
Austria [1]	(a)	37.4	|37.1 [11]	36.4	36.0	36.0	33.9	34.4	33.9	33.4	33.6	33.4 [27]
Belgique [12,13]	(a)	39.9	39.7	|38.7 [14]	37.6	36.6	34.8	35.8	35.1	35.2	35.4	.
Czechoslovakia [15]	(a)	43.8	43.8	43.7	43.6	43.6	43.6	43.6	43.7	43.5	43.5	43.4 [27]
Denmark [1]	(a)	36.2	35.8	35.4	33.5	34.2	33.1	33.3	32.7	32.6	33.1	.
España [16]	(a)	44.1	43.9	44.9	44.2	43.8	42.7	41.6	43.4 [17]	43.1	42.1	...
Finland [1]	(a)	38.3	38.5	38.2	38.0	38.4	38.4	38.2	38.4	38.5	41.0	...
France	(a)	44.8	44.5	|44.0 [18]	43.6	42.9	41.7	|41.6 [3]	41.3	41.0	40.8	40.7
Germany, Fed. Rep. of	(b)	43.8	43.0	42.7	|42.8 [3]	41.9	40.4	41.4	41.7	41.6	41.8	41.8 [26]
Gibraltar [19]	(b)	49.5	53.5	52.4	51.2	48.0	46.4	45.6	44.9	49.3	48.5	.
Grèce	(b)	44.6	44.1	44.6	43.4	43.8	|42.7 [3]	41.9	41.0	41.2	41.2	42.0 [29]
Hongrie [20]	(a) [21]	165.5	165.8	164.2	162.6	161.5	161.8	164.3	163.5	161.9	160.9	156.3
Ireland [22,23]	(a)	42.7	42.3	42.3	|42.4 [14]	41.8	41.5	42.3	42.6	42.3	42.4	...
Italie	(a) [8]	7.80	7.73	7.78	7.67	7.67	7.68	7.67	7.70	|7.72 [24]	...	...
Luxembourg [12]	(a)	44.0	43.6	|42.4 [15]	42.3	42.4	40.8	40.6	38.9	39.8	40.5	.
Malta [2,9]	(b)	44.2	43.4	42.4	42.5	41.5	44.7	41.0	41.0	41.0	41.0	.
Netherlands [12,23]	(b) [25]	44.2	43.8	43.4	43.0	|41.9	41.2	41.3	41.2	41.1	...	.
Norway [23]												
Males — Hommes — Hombres	(a)	35.3	34.8	34.4	34.0	33.5	33.5	32.6	31.7	31.3	31.0	32.8 [26]
Females — Femmes — Mujeres	(a)	30.9	30.0	29.9	29.3	28.8	28.1	27.8	27.0	26.4	25.9	27.4 [26]

EXPLANATORY NOTES: See p. 335.   NOTES EXPLICATIVES: Voir p. 337.   NOTAS EXPLICATIVAS: Véase pág. 339.

(a) : Hours actually worked — Heures réellement effectuées — Horas efectivamente trabajadas.
(b) : Hours paid for — Heures rémunérées — Horas pagadas.

[1] Incl. mining and quarrying. [2] Incl. salaried employees. [3] Sampling design revised. [4] Aug. of each year. [5] Civilian labour force employed. [6] Prior to 1975: July. [7] March and Sep. of each year. [8] Per day. [9] Adults. [10] May of each year. Prior to 1973: Nov. [11] Scope of series enlarged. [12] Oct. of each year. [13] Excl. primary iron and steel. [14] New industrial classification. [15] State industry. [16] Civilian labour force employed. Prior to 1977: wage earners and salaried employees. [17] Series replacing former series. [18] Beginning Dec. 1972: revised series. [19] Oct. of each year except for 1970-72: April and Oct. and 1974-76: April. [20] Socialised sector. [21] Per month. [22] Sep. of each year. [23] Incl. juveniles. [24] Scope of series revised. [25] Prior to 1974: hours actually worked. [26] First quarter. [27] Second quarter. [28] April. [29] May.

[1] Y compris les industries extractives. [2] Y compris les employés. [3] Plan d'échantillonnage révisé. [4] Août de chaque année. [5] Main-d'œuvre civile occupée. [6] Avant 1975 : juillet. [7] Mars et sept. de chaque année. [8] Par jour. [9] Adultes. [10] Mai de chaque année. Avant 1973 : nov. [11] Portée de la série élargie. [12] Oct. de chaque année. [13] Non compris la sidérurgie. [14] Nouvelle classification industrielle. [15] Industrie d'Etat. [16] Main-d'œuvre civile occupée. Avant 1977 : ouvriers et employés. [17] Série remplaçant la précédente. [18] A partir de déc. 1972 : série révisée. [19] Oct. de chaque année, sauf pour 1970-1972 : avril et oct., et 1974-1976 : avril. [20] Secteur socialisé. [21] Par mois. [22] Sept. de chaque année. [23] Y compris les jeunes gens. [24] Portée de la série révisée. [25] Avant 1974 : heures réellement effectuées. [26] Premier trimestre. [27] Deuxième trimestre. [28] Avril. [29] Mai.

[1] Incl. las minas y canteras. [2] Incl. los empleados. [3] Diseño de la muestra revisado. [4] Agosto de cada año. [5] Fuerza trabajadora civil ocupada. [6] Antes de 1975: julio. [7] Marzo y sept. de cada año. [8] Por día. [9] Adultos. [10] Mayo de cada año. Antes de 1973: nov. [11] El alcance de la serie es mayor. [12] Oct. de cada año. [13] Excl. la siderurgia. [14] Nueva clasificación industrial. [15] Industria de Estado. [16] Fuerza trabajadora civil ocupada. Antes de 1977: obreros y empleados. [17] Serie que substituye a la anterior. [18] A partir de dic. de 1972: serie revisada. [19] Oct. de cada año, salvo para 1970-1972: abril y oct., y 1974-1976: abril. [20] Sector socializado. [21] Por mes. [22] Sept. de cada año. [23] Incl. los jóvenes. [24] El alcance de la serie es revisado. [25] Antes de 1974: horas efectivamente trabajadas. [26] Primer trimestre. [27] Segundo trimestre. [28] Abril. [29] Mayo.

13 Hours of work in manufacturing
Durée du travail dans les industries manufacturières
Horas de trabajo en las industrias manufactureras

A All industries
Ensemble des industries
Todas las industrias

Hours of work per week   Durée du travail par semaine   Horas de trabajo por semana

Country — *Pays* — País	Code *Code* Clave	1970	1971	1972	1973	1974	1975	1976	1977	1978	1979	1980 (VI)
Pologne [1]	*(a)* [2]	*172*	*165*	*169*	*168*	*166*	*164*	*166*	*165*	*163*	*163*	.
Portugal	*(a)*	44.8	❘ 43.6 [3]	44.7	44.7	42.8	41.9	40.1	39.8	39.2	...	.
Suisse [4]	*(b)*	44.7	44.6	44.4	❘ 44.9 [3]	44.8	44.5	44.4	44.6	44.4	44.2	43.9 [16]
Sweden	*(a)* [2]	*151*	*148*	*143*	*140*	*137*	*136*	*133*	*132*	...	...	.
United Kingdom [5, 6]												
Males [7] — *Hommes* [7] — *Hombres* [7]	*(a)*	44.9	43.6	44.1	44.7	44.0	42.7	43.5	43.6	43.5	43.2	.
Females [7] — *Femmes* [7] — *Mujeres* [7]	*(a)*	37.7	37.5	37.7	37.5	37.2	36.8	37.2	37.2	37.2	37.2	.
Yugoslavia [8, 9]	*(b)* [2]	*184*	*182*	*181*	*181*	*181*	*182*	*185*	*185*	*185*	*185* *	.
OCEANIA — OCÉANIE												
OCEANÍA												
Australia [5, 9]												
Males [6] — *Hommes* [6] — *Hombres* [6]	*(b)*	44.0	43.5	❘ 43.1 [10]	43.6	42.2	41.3	41.3	41.3	41.7	42.1	.
Females [6] — *Femmes* [6] — *Mujeres* [6] . . .	*(b)*	39.7	39.6	❘ 39.6 [10]	39.8	38.9	38.7	38.8	39.0	39.1	39.5	.
New Zealand [9, 11]	*(b)* [12]	40.4	❘ 39.8 [13]	39.8	40.1	39.8	39.3	39.0	38.9	38.6	39.3	...
URSS [8, 14]	*(a)*	40.6	40.5	40.7	40.9	40.6	40.7	❘ 40.7 [15]	40.6	40.4	40.6	.
RSS de Biélorussie [8]	*(a)*	39.2	39.1	40.4	40.3	40.4	40.4	❘ 40.3 [15]	40.4	40.4	40.4	.

EXPLANATORY NOTES: See p. 335.   NOTES EXPLICATIVES: Voir p. 337.   NOTAS EXPLICATIVAS: Véase pág. 339.

(a) :   Hours actually worked — *Heures réellement effectuées* —   Horas efectivamente trabajadas.
(b) :   Hours paid for   — *Heures rémunérées*   —   Horas pagadas.

[1] Socialised sector. Incl. fishing, mining and quarrying, electricity and gas. [2] Per month. [3] Series replacing former series. [4] Beginning 1973: accident insurance statistics; excl. overtime. [5] Oct. of each year. [6] Adults. [7] Full-time wage earners. [8] Socialised sector. [9] Incl. salaried employees. [10] Scope of series enlarged. [11] April and Oct. of each year. [12] Incl. juveniles. [13] New industrial classification. [14] Incl. Byelorussian SSR, shown separately in this table. [15] Beginning 1976: incl. mining and quarrying. [16] Second quarter.

[1] *Secteur socialisé. Y compris la pêche, les industries extractives, l'électricité et le gaz.* [2] *Par mois.* [3] *Série remplaçant la précédente.* [4] *A partir de 1973 : statistiques d'assurance-accidents ; non compris les heures supplémentaires.* [5] *Oct. de chaque année.* [6] *Adultes.* [7] *Ouvriers à temps complet.* [8] *Secteur socialisé.* [9] *Y compris les employés.* [10] *Portée de la série élargie.* [11] *Avril et oct. de chaque année.* [12] *Y compris les jeunes gens.* [13] *Nouvelle classification industrielle.* [14] *Y compris la RSS de Biélorussie, figurant séparément dans ce tableau.* [15] *A partir de 1976 : y compris les industries extractives.* [16] *Deuxième trimestre.*

[1] Sector socializado. Incl. la pesca, las minas y canteras, la electricidad y el gas. [2] Por mes. [3] Serie que substituye a la anterior. [4] A partir de 1973: estadísticas del seguro de accidentes; excluidas las horas extraordinarias. [5] Oct. de cada año. [6] Adultos. [7] Obreros a tiempo completo. [8] Sector socializado. [9] Incl. los empleados. [10] El alcance de la serie es mayor. [11] Abril y oct. de cada año. [12] Incl. los jóvenes. [13] Nueva clasificación industrial. [14] Incl. la RSS de Bielorrusia, que figura separadamente en este cuadro. [15] A partir de 1976: incl. las minas y canteras. [16] Segundo trimestre.

13 Hours of work in manufacturing
Durée du travail dans les industries manufacturières
Horas de trabajo en las industrias manufactureras

B By industry
Par industrie
Por industria

AFRICA — AFRIQUE — AFRICA

Algérie

Hours actually worked per week
Heures réellement effectuées par semaine
Horas efectivamente trabajadas por semana

Date [1] Date [1] Fecha [1]	311-313 Food, beverages *Aliments, boissons* Alimentos, bebidas	321-322 Textiles, clothing *Textiles, habillement* Textiles, vestidos	323-324 Leather, leather products, footwear *Cuir, articles en cuir, chaussures* Cuero, artículos de cuero, calzado	33 Wood, furniture *Bois, ameublement* Madera, mobiliario	34 Paper, printing, publishing *Papier, imprimerie, édition* Papel, imprentas, editoriales
1970	43.0	41.5	41.5	41.2	43.0
1971	40.5	38.8	41.8	41.0	42.8
1972	41.2	38.2	41.2	41.2	42.2
1973	41.2	39.2	41.5	40.8	41.0
1974	41.5	40.5	41.0	40.0	42.5
1975	41.0	40.2	40.5	40.0	42.5
1976	44.2	43.5	41.5	44.0	44.2
1977	44.2	44.2	43.2	44.2	

Date [1] Date [1] Fecha [1]	351-352; 355 Chemicals, rubber products *Industrie chimique, caoutchouc* Productos químicos, caucho	369 × Building material *Matériaux de construction* Materiales de construcción	37 Basic metal industries *Industrie métallurgique de base* Industrias metalúrgicas básicas	381-383 Metal products, machinery, etc. *Produits métalliques, machines, etc.* Productos metálicos, maquinaria, etc.	390 Other manufacturing industries *Autres industries manufacturières* Otras industrias manufactureras
1970	41.8	44.8	41.5	43.2	43.0
1971	42.0	44.2	41.2	42.8	41.2
1972	41.8	42.8	41.5	41.2	39.8
1973	43.0	41.8	40.0	41.0	44.2
1974	43.2	44.8	40.8	42.2	44.8
1975	40.8	45.8	44.6	41.5	40.0
1976	42.8	44.0	43.8	44.2	43.2
1977	44.2	45.5	44.8		43.5

[1] April of each year.   [1] *Avril de chaque année.*   [1] Abril de cada año.

13 Hours of work in manufacturing
Durée du travail dans les industries manufacturières
Horas de trabajo en las industrias manufactureras

B By industry
Par industrie
Por industria

Egypt (1)

Hours paid for per week
Heures rémunérées par semaine
Horas pagadas por semana

Date [1] Date [1] Fecha [1]	311-312 Food Aliments Alimentos	313 Beverages Boissons Bebidas	314 Tobacco Tabac Tabaco	321 Textiles	322 Clothing Habillement Vestido	323 Leather, leather products Cuir, articles en cuir Cuero, artículos de cuero	324 Footwear Chaussures Calzado	331 Wood Bois Madera	332 Furniture Ameublement Mobiliario
1970	56	52	54	54	52	54	50	54	55
1971	58	59	56	55	49	60	47	55	54
1972	56	51	52	53	52	51	46	56	57
1973	59	55	53	54	58	62	47	55	53
1974	63	57	52	60	54	56	57	55	53
1975 *	64	67	51	53	53	53	57	58	55
1976 *	60	60	55	56	53	52	50	50	50

Date [1] Date [1] Fecha [1]	341 Paper, paper products Papier, articles en papier Papel, artículos de papel	342 Printing, publishing Imprimerie, édition Imprentas, editoriales	351 Industrial chemicals Chimie industrielle Química industrial	352 Other chemical products Autres produits chimiques Otros productos químicos	353 Petroleum refineries Raffineries de pétrole Refinerías de petróleo	354 Products of petroleum and coal Dérivés du pétrole et du charbon Derivados del petróleo y del carbón	355 Rubber products Produits en caoutchouc Productos de caucho	356 Plastic products Articles en matière plastique Productos plásticos	361 Pottery, china, earthenware Grès, porcelaines, faïences Barro, loza, porcelana
1970	51	50	53	53	46	46	48	51	51
1971	52	52	56	56	48	46	50	54	49
1972	54	50	52	56	47	47	55	52	47
1973	55	53	53	54	73	48	54	53	48
1974	58	50	52	55	54	66	56	51	46
1975 *	52	51	54	56	58	64	56	50	46
1976 *	59	50	55	51	65	61	59	53	45

[1] Oct. of each year.

[1] Oct. de chaque année.

[1] Oct. de cada año.

13 Hours of work in manufacturing
Durée du travail dans les industries manufacturières
Horas de trabajo en las industrias manufactureras

B By industry
Par industrie
Por industria

Egypt (2)

Hours paid for per week
Heures rémunérées par semaine
Horas pagadas por semana

Date [1] / Date [1] / Fecha [1]	362 Glass, and glass products / Verre / Vidrio	369 Other non-metallic mineral products / Autres produits minéraux non métalliques / Otros productos minerales no metálicos	371 Basic metal industries / Industrie métallurgique de base / Industrias metalúrgicas básicas — Iron and steel / Sidérurgie / Hierro y acero	372 Non-ferrous metal / Métaux non ferreux / Metales no ferrosos	381 Metal products / Produits métalliques / Productos metálicos	382 Machinery (non-electrical) / Machines (non électriques) / Maquinaria (no eléctrica)	383 Electrical machinery and apparatus / Machines et appareils électriques / Maquinaria y aparatos eléctricos	384 Transport equipment / Matériel de transport / Material de transporte	385 Scientific, measuring, optical, etc., equipment / Matériel scientifique, de précision, d'optique, etc. / Equipo científico, de medida, de óptica, etc.	390 Other manufacturing industries / Autres industries manufacturières / Otras industrias manufactureras
1970	58	55	48	62	54	50	48	61	57	51
1971	55	54	55	62	52	52	49	58	54	52
1972	56	55	50	50	51	50	51	58	55	54
1973	53	56	57	46	53	50	51	59	55	52
1974	55	63	53	57	54	56	53	63	50	52
1975 *	52	58	51	54	50	49	52	61	56	50
1976 *	56	66	49	54	42	52	51	58	51	54

[1] Oct. of each year. [1] Oct. de chaque année. [1] Oct. de cada año.

13

Hours of work in manufacturing
Durée du travail dans les industries manufacturières
Horas de trabajo en las industrias manufactureras

B

By industry
Par industrie
Por industria

South Africa, Rep. of

Hours actually worked per week [1]
Heures réellement effectuées par semaine [1]
Horas efectivamente trabajadas por semana [1]

Date / Date / Fecha	311-312 Food / Aliments / Alimentos	313 Beverages / Boissons / Bebidas	314 Tobacco / Tabac / Tabaco	321 Textiles	322 Clothing / Habillement / Vestido	323 Leather, leather products / Cuir, articles en cuir / Cuero, artículos de cuero	324 Footwear / Chaussures / Calzado	331 Wood / Bois / Madera	332 Furniture / Ameublement / Mobiliario	341 Paper, paper products / Papier, articles en papier / Papel, artículos de papel
1970	48.0	48.2	43.3	47.1	40.8	41.6	41.5	45.9	44.0	46.8
1971	48.2	47.6	43.7	46.8	41.4	42.8	41.3	47.1	45.1	48.1
1972	47.9	47.6	43.0	47.2	41.2	42.8	41.1	45.7	42.9	47.8
1973	48.3	48.0	43.0	47.2	42.5	42.5	42.4	46.0	44.1	48.0
1974	48.2	47.8	42.4	46.1	42.3	45.0	41.5	45.7	44.4	48.6
1975	48.2	48.6	45.5	46.9	42.1	43.3	42.6	45.7	44.2	48.3

Date / Date / Fecha	342 Printing, publishing / Imprimerie, édition / Imprentas, editoriales	351 Industrial chemicals / Chimie industrielle / Química industrial	355 Rubber products / Produits en caoutchouc / Productos de caucho	36 Non-metallic mineral products / Produits minéraux non métalliques / Productos minerales no metálicos	37 Basic metal industries / Industrie métallurgique de base / Industrias metalúrgicas básicas	381 Metal products / Produits métalliques / Productos metálicos	382 Machinery (non-electrical) / Machines (non électriques) / Maquinaria (no eléctrica)	383 Electrical machinery and apparatus / Machines et appareils électriques / Maquinaria y aparatos eléctricos	384 Transport equipment / Matériel de transport / Material de transporte	390 Other manufacturing industries / Autres industries manufacturières / Otras industrias manufactureras
1970	42.0	45.1	48.3	48.3	48.9	49.4	48.1	46.3	46.5	44.8
1971	41.5	45.2	48.6	48.9	49.9	49.1	47.9	46.7	46.0	44.8
1972	40.7	44.7	46.7	47.6	49.6	48.0	46.9	46.3	45.8	43.8
1973	41.6	44.7	47.6	48.1	48.4	49.4	47.1	47.2	47.5	46.0
1974	43.2	47.0	48.3	49.1	52.9	49.5	47.5	47.2	47.5	44.2
1975	42.4	47.6	47.4	48.3	52.4	49.8	48.0	46.1	47.4	43.3

[1] White manual workers.   [1] *Travailleurs manuels (population blanche).*   [1] Trabajadores manuales (población blanca).

HOURS

13 Hours of work in manufacturing
Durée du travail dans les industries manufacturières
Horas de trabajo en las industrias manufactureras

B By industry
Par industrie
Por industria

AMERICA — AMÉRIQUE — AMERICA

Canada (1)

Hours paid for per week
Heures rémunérées par semaine
Horas pagadas por semana

Date / Date / Fecha	311-312	313	314	321 ×	322	323; 324	324	331
	Food	Beverages	Tobacco		Clothing	Leather, leather products, footwear	Footwear	Wood
	Aliments	*Boissons*	*Tabac*	Textiles [1]	*Habillement*	*Cuir, articles en cuir, chaussures*	*Chaussures*	*Bois*
	Alimentos	Bebidas	Tabaco		Vestido	Cuero, artículos de cuero, calzado	Calzado	Madera
1970	39.3	40.1	37.5	40.4	36.0	38.2	38.1	38.7
1971	38.8	40.2	36.8	40.5	36.3	38.5	38.5	39.1
1972	38.9	40.0	36.6	40.7	36.4	38.5	38.3	39.6
1973	38.5	39.8	36.6	40.4	36.0	37.9	38.0	39.2
1974	37.8	39.2	36.8	39.3	35.7	37.3	37.4	37.9
1975	37.8	39.4	36.6	38.9	35.4	36.7	36.8	38.0
1976	37.6	38.7	36.0	39.1	35.0	36.7	36.7	38.1
1977	37.3	38.8	36.0	39.0	34.8	36.3	36.3	37.9
1978	37.6	38.7	35.9	39.3	35.0	37.0	37.1	38.6
1979	37.7	38.9	36.0	39.2	35.2	36.8	37.1	37.7

Date / Date / Fecha	332	341	342	351-352	353	354	355	356
	Furniture	Paper, paper products	Printing, publishing	Chemicals	Petroleum refineries	Products of petroleum and coal	Rubber products	Plastic products
	Ameublement	*Papier, articles en papier*	*Imprimerie, édition*	*Industrie chimique*	*Raffineries de pétrole*	*Dérivés du pétrole et du charbon*	*Produits en caoutchouc*	*Articles en matière plastique*
	Mobiliario	Papel, artículos de papel	Imprentas, editoriales	Productos químicos	Refinerías de petróleo	Derivados del petróleo y del carbón	Productos de caucho	Productos plásticos
1970	40.5	40.9	37.2	40.6	42.3	42.2	40.7	40.0
1971	41.3	40.4	37.2	40.2	42.0	41.9	40.6	40.6
1972	41.7	40.8	37.7	40.8	42.6	42.5	40.9	40.1
1973	40.6	40.4	37.2	40.8	43.4	43.2	41.0	39.0
1974	39.8	40.0	36.1	40.0	42.0	41.6	39.9	38.1
1975	39.0	39.6	35.5	39.8	41.8	41.6	39.3	38.3
1976	39.2	39.7	35.7	39.5	40.9	40.8	39.7	38.5
1977	39.1	39.2	35.3	39.8	40.9	41.0	39.6	38.8
1978	39.2	39.5	35.2	39.8	40.7	41.0	39.7	38.9
1979	39.2	39.6	34.9	40.1	41.4	41.8	40.1	39.1

[1] Excl. knitting mills. [1] *Non compris les fabriques de bonneterie et de tricot.* [1] Excl. las fábricas de tejidos de punto.

13 Hours of work in manufacturing
Durée du travail dans les industries manufacturières
Horas de trabajo en las industrias manufactureras

B By industry
Par industrie
Por industria

Canada (2)

Hours paid for per week
Heures rémunérées par semaine
Horas pagadas por semana

Date / Date / Fecha	36 — Non-metallic mineral products / Produits minéraux non métalliques / Productos minerales no metálicos	371 — Iron and steel / Sidérurgie / Hierro y acero	372 — Non-ferrous metal / Métaux non ferreux / Metales no ferrosos	381 — Metal products / Produits métalliques / Productos metálicos	382 — Machinery (non-electrical) / Machines (non électriques) / Maquinaria (no eléctrica)	383 — Electrical machinery and apparatus / Machines et appareils électriques / Maquinaria y aparatos eléctricos	384 — Transport equipment / Matériel de transport / Material de transporte	385 — Scientific, measuring, optical, etc., equipment / Matériel scientifique, de précision, d'optique, etc. / Equipo científico, de medida, de óptica, etc.	390 — Other manufacturing industries / Autres industries manufacturières / Otras industrias manufactureras
1970	41.7	40.2	40.8	40.5	40.7	39.3	40.3	39.1	39.8
1971	42.0	39.9	41.7	40.4	40.4	39.3	39.9	41.5	41.0
1972	42.2	40.2	41.7	40.8	40.5	39.7	40.8	40.6	40.5
1973	41.6	39.8	41.3	40.4	40.7	39.5	40.6	40.5	39.4
1974	40.7	40.0	40.5	39.4	39.7	39.0	39.8	39.3	38.3
1975	40.4	39.7	39.6	38.9	39.3	38.8	39.3	38.9	38.4
1976	40.4	39.7	40.6	39.5	39.6	38.8	40.2	39.0	38.5
1977	40.2	39.4	40.3	39.4	39.4	38.9	40.6	39.5	38.8
1978	40.6	39.9	40.6	39.5	39.1	39.1	40.5	39.2	38.8
1979	40.5	40.1	41.0	39.6	40.0	39.0	39.9	38.9	38.9

13 Hours of work in manufacturing
Durée du travail dans les industries manufacturières
Horas de trabajo en las industrias manufactureras

B By industry
Par industrie
Por industria

Ecuador

Hours actually worked per week
Heures réellement effectuées par semaine
Horas efectivamente trabajadas por semana

Date / Date / Fecha	311-312 Food / Aliments / Alimentos	313 Beverages / Boissons / Bebidas	314 Tobacco / Tabac / Tabaco	321 Textiles	322; 324 Clothing, footwear / Habillement, chaussures / Vestido, calzado	323 Leather, leather products / Cuir, articles en cuir / Cuero, artículos de cuero	331 Wood / Bois / Madera	341 Paper, paper products / Papier, articles en papier / Papel, artículos de papel
1970	49	56	45	45	43	45	51	49
1971	51	55	46	45	43	46	51	48
1972	52	53	44	45	41	42	54	48
1973	54	52	45	45	42	44	56	49
1974	58	51	44	46	45	45	53	45
1975	58	52	38	44	43	44	55	44
1976	53	55	43	46	41	47	52	46
1977	56	57	43	45	41	50	55	48 *

Date / Date / Fecha	342 Printing, publishing / Imprimerie, édition / Imprentas, editoriales	351 Industrial chemicals / Chimie industrielle / Química industrial	355 Rubber products / Produits en caoutchouc / Productos de caucho	36 Non-metallic mineral products / Produits minéraux non métalliques / Productos minerales no metálicos	381 Metal products / Produits métalliques / Productos metálicos	382 Machinery (non-electrical) / Machines (non électriques) / Maquinaria (no eléctrica)	383 Electrical machinery and apparatus / Machines et appareils électriques / Maquinaria y aparatos eléctricos	384 Transport equipment / Matériel de transport / Material de transporte	390 Other manufacturing industries / Autres industries manufacturières / Otras industrias manufactureras
1970	50	46	48	49	46	41	41	52	47
1971	47	48	44	46	45	42	40	50	47
1972	47	46	41	52	47	43	37	45	49
1973	47	46	44	53	46	46	35	46	48
1974	50	49	39	49	47	50	37	48	47
1975	49	52	38	49	45	51	39	51	49
1976	50	52	37	52	47	55	37	52	49
1977	50	51	38	48	47	46	40	57	52

13 B

Hours of work in manufacturing
Durée du travail dans les industries manufacturières
Horas de trabajo en las industrias manufactureras

By industry
Par industrie
Por industria

El Salvador (San Salvador) [1]

Hours actually worked per week
Heures réellement effectuées par semaine
Horas efectivamente trabajadas por semana

Date / Date / Fecha	311-312 Food / Aliments / Alimentos	313 Beverages / Boissons / Bebidas	321 Textiles	322; 324 Clothing, footwear / Habillement, chaussures / Vestido, calzado	332 Furniture / Ameublement / Mobiliario	34 Paper, printing, publishing / Papier, imprimerie, édition / Papel, imprentas, editoriales	36 Non-metallic mineral products / Produits minéraux non métalliques / Productos minerales no metálicos	371 Iron and steel basic industries / Sidérurgie / Industrias básicas de hierro y acero	384 Transport equipment / Matériel de transport / Material de transporte	390 Other manufacturing industries / Autres industries manufacturières / Otras industrias manufactureras
				Males — *Hommes* — Hombres						
1970	51.6	57.9	44.3	44.1	46.1	46.3	53.7	45.8	50.7	48.0
1971	52.9	56.7	42.6	45.5	47.7	47.7	51.1	46.1	43.7	48.8
1972	48.5	57.8	41.5	44.4	45.1	49.6	47.4	46.0	42.7	48.4
1973	48.1	59.3	45.0	44.2	43.9	46.8	49.7	45.8	45.2	47.8
1974	53.3	57.7	43.3	43.5	44.9	50.8	50.0	48.0	43.9	49.5
1975	...	47.1	...	43.8	42.2	44.1	41.9	31.2	43.9	54.6
1976	...	44.2	...	44.2	44.1	44.1	44.1	44.3	44.2	43.5
1977	...	44.6	...	44.2	44.4	44.1	44.0	44.8	44.3	44.5

Date / Date / Fecha	311-312 Food / Aliments / Alimentos	313 Beverages / Boissons / Bebidas	321 Textiles	322; 324 Clothing, footwear / Habillement, chaussures / Vestido, calzado	34 Paper, printing, publishing / Papier, imprimerie, édition / Papel, imprentas, editoriales	390 Other manufacturing industries / Autres industries manufacturières / Otras industrias manufactureras
			Females — *Femmes* — Mujeres			
1970	47.2	51.4	44.1	43.8	45.4	46.4
1971	50.8	51.4	43.1	45.0	48.8	46.6
1972	50.6	53.2	40.5	46.2	53.6	46.7
1973	50.9	47.5	44.4	44.1	45.8	47.5
1974	51.6	47.4	43.9	47.5	46.6	54.4
1975	...	42.1	...	45.4	42.9	...
1976	...	43.7	...	44.3	43.1	43.8
1977	...	45.0	...	44.1	44.6	44.4

[1] Department of San Salvador. Prior to 1975: metropolitan area.

[1] *Département de San Salvador. Avant 1975: région métropolitaine.*

[1] Departamento de San Salvador. Antes de 1975: área metropolitana.

13 Hours of work in manufacturing
Durée du travail dans les industries manufacturières
Horas de trabajo en las industrias manufactureras

B By industry
Par industrie
Por industria

Guatemala [1]

Hours actually worked per week
Heures réellement effectuées par semaine
Horas efectivamente trabajadas por semana

Date / Date / Fecha	311-312 Food / Aliments / Alimentos	313 Beverages / Boissons / Bebidas	314 Tobacco / Tabac / Tabaco	321 Textiles	322; 324 Clothing, footwear / Habillement, chaussures / Vestido, calzado	323 Leather, leather products / Cuir, articles en cuir / Cuero, artículos de cuero	331 Wood / Bois / Madera
1970	45.5	48.9	45.0	44.5	44.9	46.9	46.2
1971	45.0	47.9	45.2	44.4	45.5	46.9	46.1
1972	46.8	49.3	45.5	45.0	45.4	48.8	46.7
1973	46.5	50.7	44.9	46.4	45.4	47.8	48.0
1974 [2]	56.8	48.2	47.9	46.1	46.4	45.5	45.6
1975	49.0	46.3	43.5	45.6	43.9	45.9	44.2
1976	50.0	46.4	47.1	45.1	43.7	45.9	44.1
1977	50.6	51.9	48.7	45.5	44.4	44.1	44.1
1978	47.9	51.8	48.2	46.0	45.1	44.8	43.9

Date / Date / Fecha	332 Furniture / Ameublement / Mobiliario	34 Paper, printing, publishing / Papier, imprimerie, édition / Papel, imprentas, editoriales	351-352; 355 Chemicals, rubber products / Industrie chimique, produits en caoutchouc / Productos químicos y de caucho	36 Non-metallic mineral products / Produits minéraux non métalliques / Productos minerales no metálicos	37 Basic metal industries / Industrie métallurgique de base / Industrias metalúrgicas basicas	383 Electrical machinery and apparatus / Machines et appareils électriques / Maquinaria y aparatos eléctricos	384 Transport equipment / Matériel de transport / Material de transporte
1970	45.4	48.6	46.2	47.3	45.6	44.6	45.1
1971	46.5	46.8	48.2	46.7	46.0	44.5	45.6
1972	46.4	48.0	48.2	46.7	46.6	44.9	46.0
1973	45.5	47.9	50.3	48.2	48.4	45.0	48.0
1974 [2]	45.5	50.4	46.9	52.3	45.4	50.6	47.2
1975	43.2	49.6	46.8	50.4	45.4	49.9	45.5
1976	42.3	49.8	45.9	48.9	47.8	50.8	44.2
1977	44.3	52.8	47.2	48.9	47.6	49.4	46.3
1978	42.0	51.1	47.4	49.0	50.8	44.3	43.5

[1] Prior to 1974: Guatemala City only. [2] Series replacing former series.

[1] *Avant 1974: ville de Guatemala seulement.* [2] *Série remplaçant la précédente.*

[1] Antes de 1974: ciudad de Guatemala solamente. [2] Serie que substituye a la anterior.

13 Hours of work in manufacturing
Durée du travail dans les industries manufacturières
Horas de trabajo en las industrias manufactureras

B By industry
Par industrie
Por industria

México (1)

Hours actually worked per week
Heures réellement effectuées par semaine
Horas efectivamente trabajadas por semana

Date [1] Date [1] Fecha [1]	311-312 Food Aliments Alimentos	313 Beverages Boissons Bebidas	314 Tobacco Tabac Tabaco	321 Textiles	322 Clothing Habillement Vestido	323 Leather, leather products Cuir, articles en cuir Cuero, artículos de cuero	324 Footwear Chaussures Calzado
1970	44.5	41.9	40.5	42.5	45.6	47.4	46.5
1971	45.5	39.6	42.4	45.1	46.0	45.5	46.8
1972	47.8	38.6	40.6	46.0	45.8	45.6	47.2
1973	51.2	39.2	39.1	45.4	45.3	44.7	47.6
1974	46.4	39.5	40.0	45.7	45.6	46.1	47.3
1975	46.2	36.6	46.3	45.4	45.2	47.1	40.4
1976	47.0	46.4	46.6	45.3	45.3	45.2	47.6
1977	46.7	42.0	46.4	45.9	45.6	45.2	41.1

Date [1] Date [1] Fecha [1]	331 Wood Bois Madera	332 Furniture Ameublement Mobiliario	341 Paper, paper products Papier, articles en papier Papel, artículos de papel	342 Printing, publishing Imprimerie, édition Imprentas, editoriales	351 Industrial chemicals Chimie industrielle Química industrial	352 Other chemical products Autres produits chimiques Otros productos químicos	353 Petroleum refineries Raffineries de pétrole Refinerías de petróleo
1970	48.0	45.0	46.6	45.9	45.1	45.8	38.0
1971	46.9	44.5	46.6	45.6	45.4	45.3	37.8
1972	46.0	45.8	47.7	46.5	45.7	45.3	45.0
1973	45.0	45.5	48.2	46.5	46.3	44.1	44.4
1974	45.0	44.9	47.0	46.4	44.9	46.6	44.0
1975	44.8	44.6	47.2	45.9	45.1	45.9	43.1
1976	44.9	45.8	47.8	45.5	44.3	45.7	44.0
1977	46.7	46.2	46.8	...	44.9	45.6	38.1

[1] Oct. of each year.

[1] *Oct. de chaque année.*

[1] Oct. de cada año.

13 Hours of work in manufacturing
Durée du travail dans les industries manufacturières
Horas de trabajo en las industrias manufactureras

B By industry
Par industrie
Por industria

México (2)

Hours actually worked per week
Heures réellement effectuées par semaine
Horas efectivamente trabajadas por semana

Date [1] / Date [1] / Fecha [1]	355 Rubber products / Produits en caoutchouc / Productos de caucho	361 Pottery, china, earthenware / Grès, porcelaines, faïences / Barro, loza, porcelana	362 Glass / Verre / Vidrio	369 Other non-metallic mineral products / Autres produits minéraux non métalliques / Otros productos minerales no metálicos	371 Basic metal industries — Iron and steel / Sidérurgie / Hierro y acero	372 Basic metal industries — Non-ferrous metal / Métaux non ferreux / Metales no ferrosos	384 Transport equipment / Matériel de transport / Material de transporte	390 Other manufacturing industries / Autres industries manufacturières / Otras industrias manufactureras
1970	46.8	47.3	46.8	46.2	44.8	48.3	45.1	31.3
1971	44.8	46.0	45.2	48.0	46.7	44.6	44.8	30.0
1972	46.1	47.9	46.8	47.5	43.0	45.7	46.7	32.6
1973	45.6	47.7	47.4	48.3	43.9	47.0	46.5	27.6
1974	46.2	47.3	47.6	46.4	43.9	47.7	46.6	27.3
1975	43.6	46.6	47.3	47.8	43.1	50.2	45.8	48.6
1976	42.7	47.1	47.1	47.1	44.7	47.7	44.5	...
1977	42.5	47.1	46.9	47.3	45.1	46.3	44.3	48.2

[1] Oct. of each year.

[1] *Oct. de chaque année.*

[1] *Oct. de cada año.*

13

Hours of work in manufacturing
Durée du travail dans les industries manufacturières
Horas de trabajo en las industrias manufactureras

B

By industry
Par industrie
Por industria

Panamá (1)

Hours actually worked per week
Heures réellement effectuées par semaine
Horas efectivamente trabajadas por semana

Date / Date / Fecha	311-312 Food / Aliments / Alimentos	313 Beverages / Boissons / Bebidas	314 Tobacco / Tabac / Tabaco	321 Textiles	322 Clothing / Habillement / Vestido	323 Leather, leather products / Cuir, articles en cuir / Cuero, artículos de cuero	324 Footwear / Chaussures / Calzado	331 Wood / Bois / Madera	332 Furniture / Ameublement / Mobiliario
1970	43.5	46.3	35.6	41.9	37.1	44.0	40.8	42.6	42.5
1971	46.9	45.2	38.3	45.9	38.6	46.7	41.8	46.4	45.4
1972	45.6	47.4	40.6	42.5	40.0	44.7	44.8	45.0	46.4
1973	45.3	48.2	40.7	47.2	40.8	45.2	45.3	46.6	44.6
1974	46.7	47.8	39.6	42.7	41.2	44.5	43.5	47.7	45.6
1975	46.1	47.5	36.6	45.0	41.3	42.7	45.0	47.9	44.7
1976	46.4	48.9	44.4	46.3	40.8	46.6	44.7	43.5	42.6
1977	48.2	48.5	38.9	44.5	41.0	47.6	43.9	45.4	44.2

Date / Date / Fecha	341 Paper, paper products / Papier, articles en papier / Papel, artículos de papel	342 Printing, publishing / Imprimerie, édition / Imprentas, editoriales	351 Industrial chemicals / Chimie industrielle / Química industrial	352 Other chemical products / Autres produits chimiques / Otros productos químicos	355 Rubber products / Produits en caoutchouc / Productos de caucho	356 Plastic products / Articles en matière plastique / Productos plásticos	362 Glass / Verre / Vidrio	369 Other non-metallic mineral products / Autres produits minéraux non métalliques / Otros productos minerales no metálicos
1970	42.6	44.8	45.2	46.5	41.7	42.9	43.3	43.8
1971	43.5	47.3	49.4	46.1	43.6	43.9	45.4	47.3
1972	46.1	50.8	45.1	46.6	46.3	44.3	46.8	49.4
1973	43.4	49.8	46.8	44.6	45.7	44.6	44.0	47.2
1974	45.9	47.4	47.1	44.1	44.8	49.3	46.0	46.8
1975	46.9	48.4	45.8	44.7	47.3	44.0	46.6	48.4
1976	47.0	49.0	48.0	44.5	45.2	47.0	47.4	51.1
1977	46.3	46.4	52.3	46.2	45.5	53.7	40.4	49.9

13 Hours of work in manufacturing
Durée du travail dans les industries manufacturières
Horas de trabajo en las industrias manufactureras

B By industry
Par industrie
Por industria

Panamá (2)

Hours actually worked per week
Heures réellement effectuées par semaine
Horas efectivamente trabajadas por semana

Date / Date / Fecha	371 Iron and steel basic industries / Sidérurgie / Industrias básicas de hierro y acero	381 Metal products / Produits métalliques / Productos metálicos	382 Machinery (non-electrical) / Machines (non électriques) / Maquinaria (no eléctrica)	383 Electrical machinery and apparatus / Machines et appareils électriques / Maquinaria y aparatos eléctricos	384 Transport equipment / Matériel de transport / Material de transporte	385 Scientific, measuring, optical, etc., equipment / Matériel scientifique, de précision, d'optique, etc. / Equipo científico, de medida, de óptica, etc.	353-354; 372; 390 Miscellaneous manufacturing / Industries manufacturières diverses / Industrias manufactureras diversas
1970	43.3	41.9	42.0	39.8	40.9	42.5	35.6
1971	48.8	43.5	47.2	42.8	43.1	46.0	43.8
1972	47.9	42.8	47.4	43.8	46.7	43.2	45.6
1973	43.3	39.3	46.6	43.3	42.3	42.8	52.9
1974	47.5	44.8	46.5	42.4	44.2	43.8	48.6
1975	46.5	45.7	44.8	44.5	46.6	39.9	48.3
1976	44.9	45.5	49.5	41.8	51.1	43.8	49.8
1977	44.4	44.9	44.3	41.3	41.6	46.0	39.5

Puerto Rico (1)

Hours paid for per week
Heures rémunérées par semaine
Horas pagadas por semana

Date [1] / Date [1] / Fecha [1]	311-313 Food, beverages / Aliments, boissons / Alimentos, bebidas	314 Tobacco / Tabac / Tabaco	321 Textiles	322 Clothing / Habillement / Vestido	323 Leather, leather products / Cuir, articles en cuir / Cuero, artículos de cuero	324 Footwear / Chaussures / Calzado	33 Wood, furniture / Bois, ameublement / Madera, mobiliario
1970	39.0	37.6	38.1	34.8	38.1	36.5	39.2
1971	36.4	37.4	37.7	35.2	37.3	34.0	35.2
1972	37.3	38.2	37.8	35.1	38.9	36.1	37.0
1973	39.1	37.7	37.0	34.6	37.5	37.2	37.0
1974	37.6	38.5	36.7	34.5	36.8	36.2	37.3
1975	35.3	39.9	38.2	35.8	38.2	37.3	35.5
1976	37.4	39.8	33.3	35.1	36.8	37.0	35.5
1977	37.6	38.3	36.5	35.4	36.6	36.5	36.3
1978	39.1	37.6	36.8	33.5	37.0	34.8	35.1
1979	37.8	37.4	38.3	35.8	37.4	37.6	36.0

[1] Oct. of each year.   [1] Oct. de chaque année.   [1] Oct. de cada año.

13 Hours of work in manufacturing
Durée du travail dans les industries manufacturières
Horas de trabajo en las industrias manufactureras

B By industry
Par industrie
Por industria

Puerto Rico (2)

Hours paid for per week
Heures rémunérées par semaine
Horas pagadas por semana

	341	342	351-352	353-354	355-356	361	362
Date [1]	Paper, paper products	Printing, publishing	Chemicals	Refineries and products of petroleum and coal	Rubber and plastic products	Pottery, china, earthenware	Glass
Date [1]	*Papier, articles en papier*	*Imprimerie, édition*	*Industrie chimique*	*Raffineries et dérivés du pétrole et du charbon*	*Produits en caoutchouc et en plastique*	*Grès, porcelaines, faïences*	*Verre*
Fecha [1]	Papel, artículos de papel	Imprentas, editoriales	Productos químicos	Refinerías y derivados del petróleo y del carbón	Productos de caucho, de plástico	Barro, loza, porcelana	Vidrio
1970	37.1	39.2	40.1	40.9	36.6	41.6	37.6
1971	38.7	39.0	40.5	38.5	36.8	42.6	38.2
1972	39.5	40.1	40.8	42.5	36.4	43.4	38.7
1973	39.4	40.3	40.1	41.1	37.1	42.1	40.9
1974	40.4	38.8	40.8	38.8	38.2	46.1	40.9
1975	38.5	40.6	41.6	40.9	35.5	41.6	38.7
1976	39.4	39.0	41.4	38.9	37.8	42.0	39.3
1977	39.7	40.1	42.4	41.1	38.1	45.3	39.8
1978	40.7	40.1	42.1	40.1	38.6	46.4	40.9
1979	39.5	39.8	42.0	40.4	38.5	46.3	38.4

	369	381	382	383	384	385	390
Date [1]	Other non-metallic mineral products	Metal products	Machinery (non-electrical)	Electrical machinery and apparatus	Transport equipment	Scientific, measuring, optical, etc., equipment	Other manufacturing industries
Date [1]	*Autres produits minéraux non métalliques*	*Produits métalliques*	*Machines (non électriques)*	*Machines et appareils électriques*	*Matériel de transport*	*Matériel scientifique, de précision, d'optique, etc.*	*Autres industries manufacturières*
Fecha [1]	Otros productos minerales no metálicos	Productos metálicos	Maquinaria (no eléctrica)	Maquinaria y aparatos eléctricos	Material de transporte	Equipo científico, de medida, de óptica, etc.	Otras industrias manufactureras
1970	38.6	39.5	41.9	39.3	38.4	40.3	34.7
1971	37.7	38.6	39.4	39.1	33.9	39.0	36.9
1972	38.5	38.8	42.0	40.2	36.8	39.0	36.3
1973	37.9	39.2	38.1	40.0	40.5	38.5	38.2
1974	38.7	38.3	39.5	38.5	38.6	38.7	36.5
1975	38.1	38.1	40.3	38.2	36.9	39.5	39.7
1976	36.5	38.2	42.2	39.0	35.9	39.4	38.2
1977	39.1	38.1	39.1	39.1	36.3	40.0	38.4
1978	38.6	39.0	40.4	40.2	33.1	38.9	40.0
1979	37.7	38.7	42.0	39.9	36.4	40.2	40.2

[1] Oct. of each year.   [1] *Oct. de chaque année.*   [1] Oct. de cada año.

HOURS

13 Hours of work in manufacturing
Durée du travail dans les industries manufacturières
Horas de trabajo en las industrias manufactureras

B By industry
Par industrie
Por industria

United States (1)

Hours paid for per week
Heures rémunérées par semaine
Horas pagadas por semana

Date / Date / Fecha	311-313 Food, beverages / Aliments, boissons / Alimentos, bebidas	314 Tobacco / Tabac / Tabaco	321 Textiles	322 Clothing / Habillement / Vestido	323-324 Leather, leather products, footwear / Cuir, articles en cuir, chaussures / Cuero, artículos de cuero, calzado	331 Wood / Bois / Madera	332 Furniture / Ameublement / Mobiliario
1970	40.5	37.8	39.9	35.3	37.2	39.5	39.2
1971	40.3	37.8	40.6	35.6	37.7	39.8	39.8
1972	40.5	37.6	41.3	36.0	38.3	40.4	40.2
1973	40.4	38.6	40.9	35.9	37.8	39.9	40.0
1974	40.4	38.3	39.5	35.2	36.9	39.2	39.1
1975	40.3	38.2	39.3	35.2	37.1	38.7	38.0
1976	40.5	37.5	40.1	35.8	37.4	39.9	38.8
1977	40.0	37.8	40.4	35.6	36.9	39.8	39.0
1978	39.7	38.1	40.4	35.6	37.1	39.8	39.3
1979	39.9	38.0	40.3	35.2	36.5	39.5	38.6

Date / Date / Fecha	341 Paper, paper products / Papier, articles en papier / Papel, artículos de papel	342 Printing, publishing / Imprimerie, édition / Imprentas, editoriales	351-352 Chemicals / Industrie chimique / Productos químicos	353-354 Refineries and products of petroleum and coal / Raffineries et dérivés du pétrole et du charbon / Refinerías y derivados del petróleo y del carbón	355-356 Rubber and plastic products / Produits en caoutchouc et en plastique / Productos de caucho, de plástico	36 Non-metallic mineral products / Produits minéraux non métalliques / Productos minerales no metálicos
1970	41.9	37.7	41.6	42.8	40.2	41.2
1971	42.1	37.5	41.6	42.8	40.3	41.6
1972	42.8	37.7	41.7	42.7	41.1	42.1
1973	42.9	37.7	41.8	42.4	41.1	41.9
1974	42.2	37.5	41.5	42.1	40.5	41.3
1975	41.6	36.9	41.0	41.2	39.9	40.4
1976	42.5	37.5	41.6	42.1	40.7	41.1
1977	42.9	37.7	41.7	42.7	41.0	41.3
1978	42.9	37.6	41.9	43.6	40.9	41.6
1979	42.6	37.5	41.8	43.8	40.5	41.5

13 Hours of work in manufacturing
Durée du travail dans les industries manufacturières
Horas de trabajo en las industrias manufactureras

B By industry
Par industrie
Por industria

United States (2)

Hours paid for per week
Heures rémunérées par semaine
Horas pagadas por semana

	37	381	382	383	384	385	390
Date *Date* Fecha	Basic metal industries *Industrie métallurgique de base* Industrias metalúrgicas básicas	Metal products *Produits métalliques* Productos metálicos	Machinery (non-electrical) *Machines (non électriques)* Maquinaria (no eléctrica)	Electrical machinery and apparatus *Machines et appareils électriques* Maquinaria y aparatos eléctricos	Transport equipment *Matériel de transport* Material de transporte	Scientific, measuring, optical, etc., equipment *Matériel scientifique, de précision, d'optique, etc.* Equipo científico, de medida, de óptica, etc.	Other manufacturing industries *Autres industries manufacturières* Otras industrias manufactureras
1970	40.4	40.7	41.1	39.8	40.3	40.2	38.7
1971	40.1	40.4	40.6	39.9	40.7	39.8	38.9
1972	41.4	41.2	42.1	40.4	41.7	40.6	39.5
1973	42.3	41.6	42.8	40.4	42.1	40.9	39.0
1974	41.6	40.8	42.1	39.7	40.5	40.4	38.7
1975	40.0	40.1	40.8	39.5	40.4	39.5	38.5
1976	40.8	40.8	41.2	40.0	41.7	40.3	38.8
1977	41.3	41.0	41.5	40.4	42.5	40.6	38.8
1978	41.8	41.0	42.0	40.3	42.2	40.9	38.8
1979	41.4	40.8	41.8	40.3	41.2	40.8	38.9

Venezuela (1)

Hours actually worked per week
Heures réellement effectuées par semaine
Horas efectivamente trabajadas por semana

	311-312	313	314	321-322	324	331	341
Date *Date* Fecha	Food *Aliments* Alimentos	Beverages *Boissons* Bebidas	Tobacco *Tabac* Tabaco	Textiles, clothing *Textiles, habillement* Textiles, vestido	Footwear *Chaussures* Calzado	Wood *Bois* Madera	Paper, paper products *Papier, articles en papier* Papel, artículos de papel
1970	44.3	44.4	44.8	46.4	43.3	45.8	44.5
1971	43.0	43.2	42.6	45.7	43.1	43.7	43.9
1972	41.3	42.8	42.3	42.5	41.9	43.6	45.9
1973	41.2	44.2	41.4	43.6	44.9	44.3	46.4
1974	43.6	44.7	44.5	44.9	43.8	45.7	47.1
1975	40.7	44.9	39.4	44.7	42.9	46.3	44.2
1976	42.2	44.7	40.5	44.6	42.9	43.7	44.4
1977 *	41.3	43.9	41.2	43.3	43.3	44.1	45.1

13 Hours of work in manufacturing
Durée du travail dans les industries manufacturières
Horas de trabajo en las industrias manufactureras

B By industry
Par industrie
Por industria

Venezuela (2)

Hours actually worked per week
Heures réellement effectuées par semaine
Horas efectivamente trabajadas por semana

Date / Date / Fecha	342 Printing, publishing / Imprimerie, édition / Imprentas, editoriales	351-352 Chemicals / Industrie chimique / Productos químicos	355 Rubber products / Produits en caoutchouc / Productos de caucho	371 Iron and steel basic industries / Sidérurgie / Industrias básicas de hierro y acero	381 Metal products / Produits métalliques / Productos metálicos	384 Transport equipment / Matériel de transport / Material de transporte
1970	42.9	42.1	43.3	45.7	45.4	40.3
1971	42.0	40.8	42.1	44.5	44.5	40.3
1972	43.6	42.8	44.4	45.3	44.7	40.8
1973	43.6	44.1	44.3	43.7	44.0	41.0
1974	44.3	45.9	45.5	44.4	45.3	41.5
1975	42.3	41.7	41.7	42.0	43.0	41.9
1976	41.2	38.4	42.4	40.8	40.3	37.7
1977 *	42.5	44.1	42.8	42.6	42.1	38.3

Virgin Is. (US)

Hours paid for per week [1]
Heures rémunérées par semaine [1]
Horas pagadas por semana [1]

Date [2] / Date [2] / Fecha [2]	311-312 Food / Aliments / Alimentos	321 Textiles	332 Furniture / Ameublement / Mobiliario	342 Printing, publishing / Imprimerie, édition / Imprentas, editoriales	353 Petroleum refineries / Raffineries de pétrole / Refinerías de petróleo	361 Pottery, china, earthenware / Grès, porcelaines, faïences / Barro, loza, porcelana	381 Metal products / Produits métalliques / Productos metálicos	385 Scientific, measuring, optical, etc., equipment / Matériel scientifique, de précision, d'optique, etc. / Equipo científico, de medida, de óptica, etc.	390 Other manufacturing industries / Autres industries manufacturières / Otras industrias manufactureras
1973	40.9	39.3	35.3	37.2	44.5	44.1	39.6	35.0	39.0
1974	41.4	38.5	39.9	39.0	39.9	28.8	35.9	38.1	32.4
1975	39.5	35.8	35.2	39.3	44.2	37.2	36.8	37.5	35.8

[1] Incl. salaried employees. [2] First quarter of each year.

[1] Y compris les employés. [2] Premier trimestre de chaque année.

[1] Incl. los empleados. [2] Primer trimestre de cada año.

13 Hours of work in manufacturing
Durée du travail dans les industries manufacturières
Horas de trabajo en las industrias manufactureras

B By industry
Par industrie
Por industria

ASIA — ASIE — ASIA

Burma

Hours actually worked per day [1]
Heures réellement effectuées par jour [1]
Horas efectivamente trabajadas por día [1]

Date [2] Date [2] Fecha [2]	311-312 Food Aliments Alimentos	313 Beverages Boissons Bebidas	314 Tobacco Tabac Tabaco	321 Textiles 	322; 324 Clothing, footwear Habillement, chaussures Vestido, calzado	323 Leather, leather products Cuir, articles en cuir Cuero, artículos de cuero	331 Wood Bois Madera
1970	7.7	7.3	7.7	7.5	7.6	7.0	7.5
1971	7.8	7.1	7.6	7.5	7.4	7.3	7.5
1972 [3]	7.6	7.7	7.4	7.2	7.3	7.4	7.5
1973	7.8	7.7	7.6	7.6	7.9	7.0	7.5
1974	7.8	7.7	7.6	7.7	7.0	7.7	7.5
1975	7.8	7.7	7.6	7.6	7.0	8.0	7.5
1976	7.9	8.0	7.4	7.5	7.0	8.0	7.6
1977	7.7	7.4	7.6	7.3	8.0	8.0	7.5
1978	7.5	7.8	7.7	7.6	8.0	8.0	7.6

Date [2] Date [2] Fecha [2]	342 Printing, publishing Imprimerie édition Imprentas, editoriales	352 Chemical products Produits chimiques Productos químicos	355 Rubber products Produits en caoutchouc Productos de caucho	362 Glass Verre Vidrio	369 Other non-metallic mineral products Autres produits minéraux non métalliques Otros productos minerales no metálicos	381 Metal products Produits métalliques Productos metálicos	384 Transport equipment Matériel de transport Material de transporte
1970	7.4	7.4	7.4	.		7.7	7.9
1971	7.4	7.5	7.4	.		7.7	7.9
1972 [3]	7.8	7.7	7.7	7.8	8.0	7.1	7.9
1973	7.7	6.6	7.4	7.5	8.0	7.1	7.5
1974	7.6	7.9	7.3	7.5	8.0	7.8	7.9
1975	7.3	7.9	7.2	7.2	...	7.3	8.0
1976	7.4	8.0	7.0	7.6	8.0	7.0	8.0
1977	7.3	8.0	7.2	7.7	8.0	7.2	8.0
1978	7.5	8.0	7.4	7.3	8.0	7.4	8.0

[1] Workers engaged for less than 30 days (excl. casual workers). [2] Beginning 1973: March and Sep. of each year. [3] April and Sep.

[1] *Travailleurs engagés pour moins de 30 jours (non compris les travailleurs occasionnels).* [2] *A partir de 1973 : mars et sept. de chaque année.* [3] *Avril et sept.*

[1] Trabajadores ocupados durante menos de 30 días (excl. los trabajadores ocasionales). [2] A partir de 1973: marzo y sept. de cada año. [3] Abril y sept.

13 Hours of work in manufacturing
Durée du travail dans les industries manufacturières
Horas de trabajo en las industrias manufactureras

B By industry
Par industrie
Por industria

Cyprus

Hours paid for per week [1]
Heures rémunérées par semaine [1]
Horas pagadas por semana [1]

	311-312	313	314	321	322	323	324	331	332
Date [2]	Food	Beverages	Tobacco		Clothing	Leather, leather products	Footwear	Wood	Furniture
Date [2] Fecha [2]	Aliments	Boissons	Tabac	Textiles	Habillement	Cuir, articles en cuir	Chaussures	Bois	Ameublement
	Alimentos	Bebidas	Tabaco		Vestido	Cuero, artículos de cuero	Calzado	Madera	Mobiliario
1970	44	46	44	44	43	44	44	46	44
1971	48	49	42	45	43	44	42	43	44
1972	43	48	42	44	42	44	41	43	44
1973	43	46	35	43	43	43	41	41	44
1974 [3]	44	45	41	42	41	41	40	46	40
1975	43	49	39	43	43	42	41	41	42
1976	45	49	44	44	43	44	43	45	43
1977	45	47	43	44	43	41	42	42	44
1978	42	50	44	42	42	40	42	42	43
1979	43	47	44	42	40	40	42	42	42

	341	342	351	355	369	381	382	383	384	390
Date [2]	Paper, paper products	Printing, publishing	Industrial chemicals	Rubber products	Non-metallic mineral products [4]	Metal products	Machinery (non-electrical)	Electrical machinery and apparatus	Transport equipment	Other manufacturing industries
Date [2] Fecha [2]	Papier, articles en papier	Imprimerie, édition	Chimie industrielle	Produits en caoutchouc	Produits minéraux non métalliques [4]	Produits métalliques	Machines (non électriques)	Machines et appareils électriques	Matériel de transport	Autres industries manufacturières
	Papel, artículos de papel	Imprentas, editoriales	Química industrial	Productos de caucho	Productos minerales no metálicos [4]	Productos metálicos	Maquinaria (no eléctrica)	Maquinaria y aparatos eléctricos	Material de transporte	Otras industrias manufactureras
1970	44	47	44	44	47	45	44	44	45	44
1971	44	48	48	46	46	44	43	50	44	45
1972	47	46	44	43	45	44	47	50	45	46
1973	47	45	44	45	49	43	43	43	44	45
1974 [3]	32	42	45	41	43	41	40	43	46	44
1975	42	38	43	41	45	44	41	43	44	43
1976	43	44	44	41	45	44	43	44	41	43
1977	48	45	44	41	46	45	45	55	44	42
1978	47	46	44	41	46	45	45	42	44	42
1979	43	47	43	39	45	44	41	42	40	42

[1] Adults only. [2] Oct. of each year. [3] Beginning July 1974: due to a change in the geographical scope of the series, data are not comparable with those for the preceding period. [4] Excl. pottery, china, earthenware and glass.

[1] Adultes seulement. [2] Oct. de chaque année. [3] A partir de juillet 1974 : en raison d'un changement de la portée géographique de la série, les données ne sont pas comparables avec celles de la période précédente. [4] Non compris le grès, les porcelaines, les faïences et le verre.

[1] Adultos solamente. [2] Oct. de cada año. [3] A partir de julio de 1974: en razón de un cambio del alcance geográfico de la serie, los datos no son comparables a los del periodo precedente. [4] Excl. el barro, la loza, la porcelana y el vidrio.

13 Hours of work in manufacturing
Durée du travail dans les industries manufacturières
Horas de trabajo en las industrias manufactureras

B By industry
Par industrie
Por industria

Israel (1)

Hours actually worked per week [1]
Heures réellement effectuées par semaine [1]
Horas efectivamente trabajadas por semana [1]

Date / Date / Fecha	31 Food, beverages, tobacco *Aliments, boissons, tabac* Alimentos, bebidas, tabaco	321 Textiles	322 Clothing *Habillement* Vestido	323-324 Leather, leather products, footwear *Cuir, articles en cuir, chaussures* Cuero, artículos de cuero, calzado	33 Wood, furniture *Bois, ameublement* Madera, mobiliario	341 Paper, paper products *Papier, articles en papier* Papel, artículos de papel
1972	42.2	43.6	41.9	42.7	43.1	43.9
1973	39.0	40.1	40.0	36.3	38.2	41.5
1974	39.7	40.2	39.2	38.0	39.1	41.3
1975	40.8	41.3	40.0	38.6	40.4	40.3
1976	40.0	39.8	38.6	40.3	41.1	42.2
1977	39.0	39.5	37.4	37.7	38.0	40.3
1978	38.7	40.1	36.6	40.0	38.2	34.1
1979	39.9	39.5	37.4	36.8	39.9	42.1

Date / Date / Fecha	342 Printing, publishing *Imprimerie, édition* Imprentas, editoriales	351-354 Chemicals, petroleum, refineries [2] *Industrie chimique, raffineries de pétrole* [2] Productos químicos, refinerías de petróleo [2]	355-356 Rubber and plastic products *Produits en caoutchouc et en plastique* Productos de caucho, de plástico	36 Non-metallic mineral products *Produits minéraux non métalliques* Productos minerales no metálicos	37 Basic metal industries *Industrie métallurgique de base* Industrias metalúrgicas básicas	381 Metal products *Produits métalliques* Productos metálicos
1972	39.6	43.2	41.7	44.0	44.8	42.7
1973	38.4	38.6	38.3	40.4	39.4	39.4
1974	40.1	39.4	38.2	39.6	39.0	39.8
1975	38.2	40.0	40.5	39.1	38.9	39.7
1976	38.5	39.7	41.5	41.2	39.8	40.8
1977	37.4	38.2	38.9	39.8	39.1	38.8
1978	37.9	36.9	38.6	38.8	36.6	37.8
1979	36.9	38.9	39.5	38.8	41.9	39.7

[1] Incl. salaried employees. [2] Incl. products of petroleum and coal. [1] *Y compris les employés.* [2] *Y compris les dérivés du pétrole et du charbon.* [1] Incl. los empleados. [2] Incl. los derivados del petróleo y del carbón.

13 Hours of work in manufacturing
Durée du travail dans les industries manufacturières
Horas de trabajo en las industrias manufactureras

B By industry
Par industrie
Por industria

Israel (2)

Hours actually worked per week [1]
Heures réellement effectuées par semaine [1]
Horas efectivamente trabajadas por semana [1]

Date / Date / Fecha	382 Machinery (non-electrical) / Machines (non électriques) / Maquinaria (no eléctrica)	383 Electrical machinery and apparatus / Machines et appareils électriques / Maquinaria y aparatos eléctricos	384 Transport equipment / Matériel de transport / Material de transporte	390 Diamonds / Diamants / Diamantes	Other manufacturing industries / Autres industries manufacturières / Otras industrias manufactureras
1972	44.3	43.2	43.6	43.0	40.9
1973	39.9	38.8	40.7	38.4	37.8
1974	40.2	39.9	41.8	38.9	39.4
1975	39.7	40.6	40.8	39.7	37.2
1976	39.4	40.4	41.3	39.7	39.9
1977	41.7	39.9	39.0	39.2	36.1
1978	38.0	38.7	37.1	38.2	35.1
1979	39.3	40.5	39.3	38.5	36.9

[1] Incl. salaried employees.　　　　[1] Y compris les employés.　　　　[1] Incl. los empleados.

Japan (1)

Hours actually worked per week [1]
Heures réellement effectuées par semaine [1]
Horas efectivamente trabajadas por semana [1]

Date / Date / Fecha	31 Food, beverages, tobacco / Aliments, boissons, tabac / Alimentos, bebidas, tabaco	321 Textiles	322 Clothing / Habillement / Vestido	323-324 Leather, leather products, footwear / Cuir, articles en cuir, chaussures / Cuero, artículos de cuero, calzado	331 Wood / Bois / Madera	332 Furniture / Ameublement / Mobiliario
1970	42.4	43.5	42.3	43.3	44.1	44.2
1971	42.2	43.4	42.2	42.5	43.8	43.9
1972	41.9	43.2	41.8	42.4	44.2	44.0
1973 [2]	41.4	42.4	41.2	42.8	43.9	43.1
1974	40.4	40.1	39.7	41.9	41.9	40.9
1975	40.5	39.8	40.0	40.3	40.2	41.3
1976 [2]	40.8	40.6	40.6	40.9	42.4	42.1
1977	40.8	40.1	40.6	40.9	42.5	42.2
1978	41.0	40.8	41.2	41.4	43.4	42.7
1979 [2]	41.0	41.4	41.1	41.1	43.7	43.3

[1] Incl. salaried employees. [2] Sampling design revised.　　[1] Y compris les employés. [2] Plan d'échantillonnage révisé.　　[1] Incl. los empleados. [2] Diseño de la muestra revisado.

13 Hours of work in manufacturing / Durée du travail dans les industries manufacturières / Horas de trabajo en las industrias manufactureras

B By industry / Par industrie / Por industria

Japan (2)

Hours actually worked per week [1]
Heures réellement effectuées par semaine [1]
Horas efectivamente trabajadas por semana [1]

Date / Date / Fecha	341 Paper, paper products / Papier, articles en papier / Papel, artículos de papel	342 Printing, publishing / Imprimerie, édition / Imprentas, editoriales	351-352 Chemicals / Industrie chimique / Productos químicos	353-354 Refineries and products of petroleum and coal / Raffineries et dérivés du pétrole et du charbon / Refinerías y derivados del petróleo y del carbón	355 Rubber products / Produits en caoutchouc / Productos de caucho	36 Non-metallic mineral products / Produits minéraux non métalliques / Productos minerales no metálicos	371 Iron and steel basic industries / Sidérurgie / Industrias básicas de hierro y acero
1970	43.5	45.0	40.9	42.6	41.7	43.8	44.4
1971	42.7	44.8	40.4	42.5	41.1	43.1	42.7
1972	42.1	44.4	39.7	41.4	40.8	43.0	42.2
1973 [2]	41.8	43.6	39.1	41.2	40.8	43.1	42.6
1974	39.5	41.7	37.9	40.6	38.5	41.1	41.0
1975	38.4	41.6	36.9	39.5	37.4	39.2	37.7
1976 [2]	40.1	42.0	37.5	39.4	38.5	40.3	38.7
1977	40.0	42.2	37.6	39.5	38.8	40.6	38.9
1978	40.4	42.4	37.8	39.5	39.2	41.3	38.9
1979 [2]	41.2	42.7	38.0	39.6	40.0	41.4	39.9

Date / Date / Fecha	372 Non-ferrous metal basic industries / Métaux non ferreux (industrie de base) / Industrias básicas de metales no ferrosos	381 Metal products / Produits métalliques / Productos metálicos	382 Machinery (non-electrical) / Machines (non électriques) / Maquinaria (no eléctrica)	383 Electrical machinery and apparatus / Machines et appareils électriques / Maquinaria y aparatos eléctricos	384 Transport equipment / Matériel de transport / Material de transporte	385 Scientific, measuring, optical, etc., equipment / Matériel scientifique, de précision, d'optique, etc. / Equipo científico, de medida, de óptica, etc.	390 Other manufacturing industries / Autres industries manufacturières / Otras industrias manufactureras
1970	44.4	44.6	44.9	41.6	44.5	41.6	43.2
1971	43.3	44.1	43.2	40.6	43.6	41.0	42.9
1972	43.0	43.7	42.8	41.0	43.3	40.5	42.7
1973 [2]	42.8	43.2	43.0	40.8	43.5	40.1	41.8
1974	39.7	40.5	40.7	38.3	40.9	38.7	39.6
1975	37.2	39.0	38.1	37.6	39.1	37.5	39.4
1976 [2]	39.8	41.2	40.3	39.9	40.6	39.1	40.3
1977	39.6	41.4	40.9	39.7	41.2	39.2	40.2
1978	40.4	41.6	40.9	40.3	40.9	39.1	40.6
1979 [2]	41.0	42.5	41.5	40.9	41.7	39.8	40.8

[1] Incl. salaried employees. [2] Sampling design revised.   [1] Y compris les employés. [2] Plan d'échantillonnage révisé.   [1] Incl. los empleados. [2] Diseño de la muestra revisado.

13 Hours of work in manufacturing
Durée du travail dans les industries manufacturières
Horas de trabajo en las industrias manufactureras

B By industry
Par industrie
Por industria

Korea, Rep. of (1)

Hours actually worked per week [1]
Heures réellement effectuées par semaine [1]
Horas efectivamente trabajadas por semana [1]

Date / Date / Fecha	311-312 Food / Aliments / Alimentos	313 Beverages / Boissons / Bebidas	321 Textiles	322; 324 Clothing, footwear / Habillement, chaussure / Vestido, calzado	323 Leather, leather products / Cuir, articles en cuir / Cuero, artículos de cuero	331 Wood / Bois / Madera	332 Furniture / Ameublement / Mobiliario	341 Paper, paper products / Papier, articles en papier / Papel, artículos de papel	342 Printing, publishing / Imprimerie, édition / Imprentas, editoriales
1970	53.4	52.0	53.1	53.9	49.5	58.1	51.0	52.8	52.2
1971	52.3	51.5	52.0	54.3	50.2	58.8	51.6	51.2	52.6
1972	51.3	50.1	51.7	55.3	52.7	55.0	51.0	52.6	49.9
1973	51.6	51.1	53.0	54.6	49.9	59.3	50.1	51.8	48.4
1974	48.2	50.5	49.8	49.8	49.1	53.6	50.0	48.7	49.0
1975	47.3	49.7	51.1	52.9	48.8	56.2	48.0	49.5	47.9
1976	51.0	48.9	53.1	54.9	50.0	55.1	48.3	51.9	50.7
1977	53.2	52.5	52.9	55.4	52.6	58.6	51.2	53.9	51.2
1978	53.3	52.7	52.7	55.0	51.8	59.0	53.0	53.6	50.2
1979	52.6	52.9	52.3	54.1	50.6	55.9	53.2	53.3	50.4

Date / Date / Fecha	351 Industrial chemicals / Chimie industrielle / Química industrial	352 Other chemical products / Autres produits chimiques / Otros productos químicos	353 Petroleum refineries / Raffineries de pétrole / Refinerías de petróleo	354 Products of petroleum and coal / Dérivés du pétrole et du charbon / Derivados del petróleo y del carbón	355 Rubber products / Produits en caoutchouc / Productos de caucho	356 Plastic products / Articles en matière plastique / Productos plásticos	361 Pottery, china, earthenware / Grès, porcelaines, faïences / Barro, loza, porcelana	362 Glass, and glass products / Verre / Vidrio	369 Other non-metallic mineral products / Autres produits minéraux / Otros productos minerales
1970	53.9	52.9	52.9	50.8	53.0	52.9	44.9		
1971	50.8	52.7	52.7	52.1	53.9	52.7	52.0		
1972	50.5	49.4	49.5	53.6	52.7	56.3	52.0		
1973	50.0	48.8	46.7	46.9	52.8	53.0			
1974	49.5	48.6	45.6	49.0	51.6	50.7	50.3	51.3	50.9
1975	50.4	47.7	45.5	49.3	55.8	53.6	47.8	50.6	49.6
1976	50.3	49.0	46.9	53.3	58.6	53.7	48.1	48.8	49.9
1977	51.2	49.2	46.4	54.6	55.6	53.3	50.5	51.6	51.5
1978	51.6	49.8	47.0	43.5	57.8	52.7	51.6	50.1	53.9
1979	52.4	48.4	46.4	42.7	56.2	52.1	50.4	48.9	54.1

[1] Incl. salaried employees.　　　[1] Y compris les employés.　　　[1] Incl. los empleados.

13 Hours of work in manufacturing
Durée du travail dans les industries manufacturières
Horas de trabajo en las industrias manufactureras

B By industry
Par industrie
Por industria

Korea, Rep. of (2)

Hours actually worked per week [1]
Heures réellement effectuées par semaine [1]
Horas efectivamente trabajadas por semana [1]

	371	372	381	382	383	384	385	390
Date *Date* Fecha	Basic metal industries *Industrie métallurgique de base* Industrias metalúrgicas básicas		Metal products *Produits métalliques* Productos metálicos	Machinery (non-electrical) *Machines (non électriques)* Maquinaria (no eléctrica)	Electrical machinery and apparatus *Machines et appareils électriques* Maquinaria y aparatos eléctricos	Transport equipment *Matériel de transport* Material de transporte	Scientific, measuring, optical, etc., equipment *Matériel scientifique, de précision, d'optique, etc.* Equipo científico, de medida, de óptica, etc.	Other manufacturing industries *Autres industries manufacturières* Otras industrias manufactureras
	Iron and steel *Sidérurgie* Hierro y acero	Non-ferrous metal *Métaux non ferreux* Metales no ferrosos						
1970	55.3		53.8	53.3	49.7	50.5	.	48.9
1971	52.9		52.7	51.9	51.0	51.4	.	49.1
1972	52.0		50.8	49.8	49.4	52.5	.	48.7
1973	54.4	53.4	52.2	51.7	49.4	49.2	48.9	49.9
1974	51.8	48.0	51.7	50.7	47.6	50.3	47.7	49.5
1975	50.7	48.6	51.4	50.2	46.9	49.1	47.5	50.2
1976	52.9	50.9	54.1	53.2	48.9	52.3	52.0	52.2
1977	53.4	55.4	53.6	53.9	48.1	53.0	50.1	52.4
1978	54.0	53.3	52.9	54.2	49.2	54.0	49.5	51.0
1979	53.4	54.4	51.3	50.7	48.9	52.9	47.4	50.4

[1] Incl. salaried employees.   [1] *Y compris les employés.*   [1] Incl. los empleados.

Singapore (1)

Hours actually worked per week
Heures réellement effectuées par semaine
Horas efectivamente trabajadas por semana

	311-312	313	314	321	322	323	324	331	332
Date [1] *Date* [1] Fecha [1]	Food *Aliments* Alimentos	Beverages *Boissons* Bebidas	Tobacco *Tabac* Tabaco	Textiles	Clothing *Habillement* Vestido	Leather, leather products *Cuir, articles en cuir* Cuero, artículos de cuero	Footwear *Chaussures* Calzado	Wood *Bois* Madera	Furniture *Ameublement* Mobiliario
1971	47.4	47.4	43.9	49.7	47.6	46.6	46.6	50.4	46.7
1972	46.8	48.0	43.0	49.0	45.6	42.7	46.1	51.0	47.3
1973	47.1	48.0	44.4	47.9	47.5	45.6	44.7	51.0	47.7
1974	46.5			46.0		46.7			46.2
1975	47.0			46.3		47.2			49.5
1976	46.5			47.2		46.7			48.0
1977	46.7			47.8		48.5			49.7
1978	48.0			47.8		48.0			49.8
1979	48.8			47.1		47.7			50.6

[1] Aug. of each year. Prior to 1975: July.   [1] *Août de chaque année. Avant 1975 : juillet.*   [1] Agosto de cada año. Antes de 1975: julio.

13 Hours of work in manufacturing
Durée du travail dans les industries manufacturières
Horas de trabajo en las industrias manufactureras

B By industry
Par industrie
Por industria

Singapore (2)

Hours actually worked per week
Heures réellement effectuées par semaine
Horas efectivamente trabajadas por semana

Date [1] / Date [1] / Fecha [1]	341 Paper, paper products / Papier, articles en papier / Papel, artículos de papel	342 Printing, publishing / Imprimerie, édition / Imprentas, editoriales	351 Industrial chemicals / Chimie industrielle / Química industrial	352 Other chemical products / Autres produits chimiques / Otros productos químicos	353 Petroleum refineries / Raffineries de pétrole / Refinerías de petróleo	355 Rubber products / Produits en caoutchouc / Productos de caucho	356 Plastic products / Articles en matière plastique / Productos plásticos	361-362 Pottery, china, earthenware and glass / Grès, porcelaines, faïences et verre / Barro, loza, porcelana y vidrio	369 Other non-metallic mineral products / Autres produits minéraux non métalliques / Otros productos minerales no metálicos
1971	49.6	47.7	49.8	46.6	45.6	45.5	47.7	47.6	48.7
1972	51.1	48.9	53.5	46.4	46.6	45.4	48.6	48.3	49.6
1973	49.7	51.2	53.6	46.7	48.8	46.0	48.1	45.7	50.0
1974	49.1				45.9				50.4
1975	51.7				45.5				48.6
1976	49.8				46.6				48.4
1977	50.0				46.9				49.4
1978	51.2				47.3				51.9
1979	50.5				46.3				50.0

Date [1] / Date [1] / Fecha [1]	371 Basic metal industries / Industrie métallurgique de base / Industrias metalúrgicas básicas — Iron and steel / Sidérurgie / Hierro y acero	372 Non-ferrous metal / Métaux non ferreux / Metales no ferrosos	381 Metal products / Produits métalliques / Productos metálicos	382 Machinery (non-electrical) / Machines (non électriques) / Maquinaria (no eléctrica)	383 Electrical machinery and apparatus / Machines et appareils électriques / Maquinaria y aparatos eléctricos	384 Transport equipment / Matériel de transport / Material de transporte	385 Scientific, measuring, optical, etc., equipment / Matériel scientifique, de précision, d'optique, etc. / Equipo científico, de medida, de óptica, etc.	390 Other manufacturing industries / Autres industries manufacturières / Otras industrias manufactureras
1971	52.1	49.0	49.5	51.2	46.2	57.6	47.2	49.9
1972	49.1	48.1	49.3	50.5	48.5	57.7	46.5	46.3
1973	48.8	42.6	49.4	50.4	45.9	57.3	46.2	45.1
1974	48.9		47.8	50.5	44.9	57.0	47.4	46.1
1975	50.6		48.0	50.4	45.0	55.8	45.3	46.4
1976	50.1		47.4	49.5	46.9	56.2	46.0	45.7
1977	50.4		47.5	50.4	46.8	56.5	46.0	45.7
1978	51.8		48.2	49.7	47.2	56.7	46.1	45.6
1979	53.2		46.7	49.5	46.4	56.7	48.1	46.1
							48.6	47.9

[1] Aug. of each year. Prior to 1975: July. [1] Août de chaque année. Avant 1975 : juillet. [1] Agosto de cada año. Antes de 1975: julio.

13 Hours of work in manufacturing
Durée du travail dans les industries manufacturières
Horas de trabajo en las industrias manufactureras

B By industry
Par industrie
Por industria

République arabe syrienne (1)

Hours actually worked per week [1]
Heures réellement effectuées par semaine [1]
Horas efectivamente trabajadas por semana [1]

Date [2] / Date [2] / Fecha [2]	311-312 Food / Aliments / Alimentos	313 Beverages / Boissons / Bebidas	314 Tobacco / Tabac / Tabaco	321 Textiles	322 Clothing / Habillement / Vestido	323 Leather, leather products / Cuir, articles en cuir / Cuero, artículos de cuero	331 Wood / Bois / Madera
1970	50.6	55.8	36.7	.	50.3	45.9	50.3
1971	49.4	48.8	36.8	43.2	49.0	41.2	43.5
1972	52.5	53.1	39.1	46.7	44.2	42.7	41.0
1973	49.2	73.5	39.9	48.7	45.2	42.2	42.0
1974	45.1	59.3	41.6	44.0	50.3	41.9	54.0
1975	44.1	55.2	40.2	43.1	48.9	45.2	46.5
1976	47.1	56.9	39.6	47.5	47.7	45.9	49.2
1977	49.1	55.3	43.8	46.1	48.6	42.3	46.9

Date [2] / Date [2] / Fecha [2]	341 Paper, paper products / Papier, articles en papier / Papel, artículos de papel	342 Printing, publishing / Imprimerie, édition / Imprentas, editoriales	351 Industrial chemicals / Chimie industrielle / Química industrial	352 Other chemical products / Autres produits chimiques / Otros productos químicos	353 Petroleum refineries / Raffineries de pétrole / Refinerías de petróleo	354 Products of petroleum and coal / Dérivés du pétrole et du charbon / Derivados del petróleo y del carbón	355 Rubber products / Produits en caoutchouc / Productos de caucho
1970	49.0	35.2	42.7		.	.	48.2
1971	47.4	40.2	49.6		41.1	37.5	45.8
1972	45.6	46.7	49.1		40.1	40.1	45.7
1973	44.4	41.2	48.9	51.0	39.1	43.9	53.7
1974	47.7	50.2	47.8	48.2	44.6	44.0	50.8
1975	48.1	...	49.7	45.0	43.9	40.4	46.0
1976	46.7	52.9	48.5	45.4	43.6	43.7	49.7
1977	51.2	53.2	54.5	44.5	41.6	46.5	46.9

[1] Adults only. [2] May of each year. Prior to 1973: Nov.

[1] Adultes seulement. [2] Mai de chaque année. Avant 1973 : nov.

[1] Adultos solamente. [2] Mayo de cada año. Antes de 1973: nov.

13 Hours of work in manufacturing
Durée du travail dans les industries manufacturières
Horas de trabajo en las industrias manufactureras

B By industry
Par industrie
Por industria

République arabe syrienne (2)

Hours actually worked per week [1]
Heures réellement effectuées par semaine [1]
Horas efectivamente trabajadas por semana [1]

Date [2] / Fecha [2]	356 Plastic products / Articles en matière plastique / Productos plásticos	361 Pottery, china, earthenware / Grès, porcelaines, faïences / Barro, loza, porcelana	362 Glass / Verre / Vidrio	369 × Cement / Ciment / Cemento	371 Iron and steel basic industries / Sidérurgie / Industrias básicas de hierro y acero	381 Metal products / Produits métalliques / Productos metálicos	382 Machinery (non-electrical) / Machines (non électriques) / Maquinaria (no eléctrica)	383 Electrical machinery and apparatus / Machines et appareils électriques / Maquinaria y aparatos eléctricos
1970	.	.	.	.	45.7	.	.	43.9
1971	42.2	46.7	42.5	47.4	43.0	44.2	38.7	36.5
1972	47.5	44.4	42.5	49.2	46.3	48.7	43.6	40.6
1973	48.8	42.3	38.7	47.1	46.5	44.1	45.0	40.5
1974	44.1	42.0	39.8	48.0	48.0	43.9	45.0	45.3
1975	42.2	41.3	36.7	44.2	45.6	45.7	...	44.1
1976	43.5	43.4	40.6	49.0	45.9	47.1	55.4	48.4
1977	45.8	45.0	40.6	53.2	46.6	47.1	55.4	48.4

[1] Adults only. [2] May of each year. Prior to 1973: Nov.

[1] Adultes seulement. [2] Mai de chaque année. Avant 1973 : nov.

[1] Adultos solamente. [2] Mayo de cada año. Antes de 1973: nov.

13 Hours of work in manufacturing
Durée du travail dans les industries manufacturières
Horas de trabajo en las industrias manufactureras

B By industry
Par industrie
Por industria

EUROPE — EUROPE — EUROPA

Austria (1)

Hours actually worked per week
Heures réellement effectuées par semaine
Horas efectivamente trabajadas por semana

Date / Date / Fecha	31 Food, beverages, tobacco *Aliments, boissons, tabac* Alimentos, bebidas, tabaco	321 Textiles	322 Clothing *Habillement* Vestido	323 × Leather *Cuir* Cuero	323 × -324 Leather products, footwear *Articles en cuir, chaussures* Artículos de cuero, calzado	33 Wood, furniture *Bois, ameublement* Madera, mobiliario
1970	38.5	36.6	35.7	38.3	36.7	38.4
1971 [1]	38.2	36.2	35.9	39.0	39.1	38.7
1972	38.0	35.6	34.4	38.1	35.8	38.0
1973	37.9	35.1	33.9	37.3	34.9	37.5
1974	38.0	35.2	34.3	37.4	34.1	37.3
1975	36.4	33.5	32.9	34.3	32.3	35.6
1976	36.3	34.0	33.7	34.5	33.0	36.0
1977	35.8	33.8	32.6	34.8	33.1	35.4
1978	37.1	34.5	33.5	34.5	33.9	36.2
1979	36.6	34.9	33.5	36.4	34.9	36.7

Date / Date / Fecha	341 Paper *Papier* Papel	Paper products *Articles en papier* Artículos de papel	35 × Chemicals, products of petroleum and coal, rubber, plastics [2] *Industrie chimique, dérivés du pétrole et du charbon, caoutchouc, plastique [2]* Productos químicos, derivados del petróleo y del carbón, caucho, plástico [2]	353 Petroleum refineries [3] *Raffineries de pétrole [3]* Refinerías de petróleo [3]	36 × Non-metallic mineral products [4] *Produits minéraux non métalliques [4]* Productos minerales no metálicos [4]	362 Glass *Verre* Vidrio
1970	37.9	37.9	35.6	36.7	39.8	36.9
1971 [1]	37.5	38.0	36.2	36.8	40.0	37.3
1972	37.8	36.8	35.5	35.7	39.3	36.5
1973	38.1	36.2	35.2	35.3	38.8	35.9
1974	37.3	36.6	35.2	35.0	38.9	36.3
1975	34.0	34.4	33.5	34.3	36.2	33.3
1976	35.0	35.7	34.0	34.3	36.2	35.1
1977	34.4	35.1	34.0	33.4	36.0	35.0
1978	35.4	35.9	34.5	35.0	37.1	36.1
1979	35.8	36.1	34.8	35.1	36.8	36.2

[1] Scope of series enlarged.   [2] Excl. petroleum refineries.   [3] Incl. crude petroleum and natural gas production.   [4] Excl. glass.

[1] *Portée de la série élargie.*   [2] *Non compris les raffineries de pétrole.*   [3] *Y compris la production de pétrole brut et de gaz naturel.*   [4] *Non compris le verre.*

[1] El alcance de la serie es mayor.   [2] Excl. las refinerías de petróleo.   [3] Incl. la producción de petróleo crudo y gas natural.   [4] Excl. el vidrio.

13 Hours of work in manufacturing
Durée du travail dans les industries manufacturières
Horas de trabajo en las industrias manufactureras

B By industry
Par industrie
Por industria

Austria (2)

Hours actually worked per week
Heures réellement effectuées par semaine
Horas efectivamente trabajadas por semana

	371			381; 385	382; 384 ×	383	384 ×
	Basic metal industries *Industrie métallurgique de base* Industrias metalúrgicas básicas			Metal products [2]	Machinery (non-electrical), transport equipment [3]	Electrical machinery and apparatus	Motor vehicles
Date *Date* Fecha	Iron and steel *Sidérurgie* Hierro y acero	Foundries *Fonderie* Fundición	Non-ferrous metal *Métaux non ferreux* Metales no ferrosos	*Produits métalliques* [2] Productos metálicos [2]	*Machines (non électriques), matériel de transport* [3] Maquinaria (no eléctrica), material de transporte [3]	*Machines et appareils électriques* Maquinaria y aparatos eléctricos	*Véhicules automobiles* Vehículos automóviles
1970	38.9	38.3	37.8	37.3	38.5	36.1	36.7
1971 [1]	36.6	37.9	37.1	36.8	38.1	36.0	35.6
1972	36.0	36.5	36.6	36.1	37.1	35.2	34.8
1973	36.2	36.3	36.8	35.9	36.7	34.8	34.7
1974	36.3	36.4	36.6	35.7	36.4	34.8	34.5
1975	32.8	33.9	33.4	33.4	34.4	32.8	32.9
1976	33.7	33.8	34.4	34.0	34.4	33.7	33.4
1977	32.8	33.6	33.3	33.7	33.9	33.3	33.1
1978	35.9	34.8	35.0	34.8	35.4	34.9	33.8
1979	35.3	35.4	35.0	34.9	35.7	34.5	34.5

[1] Scope of series enlarged. [2] Incl. scientific, measuring, optical, etc. equipment. [3] Excl. motor vehicles.

[1] *Portée de la série élargie.* [2] *Y compris le matériel scientifique, de précision, d'optique, etc.* [3] *Non compris les véhicules automobiles.*

[1] El alcance de la serie es mayor. [2] Incl. el equipo científico, de medida, de óptica, etc. [3] Excl. los vehículos automóviles.

Belgique (1)

Hours actually worked per week
Heures réellement effectuées par semaine
Horas efectivamente trabajadas por semana

	311 ×-312	313	314	321	322 ×	323	324	331	332
Date [1] *Date* [1] Fecha [1]	Food *Aliments* Alimentos	Beverages *Boissons* Bebidas	Tobacco *Tabac* Tabaco	Textiles	Clothing *Habillement* Vestido	Leather, leather products *Cuir, articles en cuir* Cuero, artículos de cuero	Footwear *Chaussures* Calzado	Wood *Bois* Madera	Furniture *Ameublement* Mobiliario
1970	40.9	40.0	39.9	39.5	38.7	40.6	38.7	41.4	40.9
1971	40.3	40.5	38.7	39.3	39.6	39.8	38.5	42.1	40.5
1972 [2]	39.2	38.9	37.5	38.0	38.3	38.6	36.2	40.7	40.4
1973	38.7	39.1	37.0	36.2	36.1	37.4	35.8	39.9	39.8
1974	36.8	36.9	37.3	34.3	35.6	36.5	32.4	36.9	38.4
1975	36.5	37.1	35.7	32.7	33.9	35.4	28.9	36.4	35.8
1976	36.4	36.0	35.7	34.2	34.2	36.7	25.3	36.9	37.1
1977	35.7	35.4	34.7	32.7	33.8	35.9	31.3	36.7	35.8
1978	35.9	35.3	35.8	32.7	34.2	34.1	33.2	36.1	35.1
1979	36.0	36.4	35.9	34.0	34.3	34.0	32.2	36.5	34.3

[1] Oct. of each year. [2] New industrial classification.

[1] *Oct. de chaque année.* [2] *Nouvelle classification industrielle.*

[1] Oct. de cada año. [2] Nueva clasificación industrial.

13 Hours of work in manufacturing
Durée du travail dans les industries manufacturières
Horas de trabajo en las industrias manufactureras

B By industry
Par industrie
Por industria

Belgique (2)

Hours actually worked per week
Heures réellement effectuées par semaine
Horas efectivamente trabajadas por semana

	341	342	351			353	355	361	362
Date [1]	Paper, paper products	Printing, publishing	Basic industrial chemicals	Fertilizers and pesticides [2]	Synthetic and man-made fibres	Petroleum refineries	Rubber products	Pottery, china, earthenware	Glass
Date [1]	Papier, articles en papier	Imprimerie, édition	Industrie chimique de base	Engrais et pesticides [2]	Fibres synthétiques et artificielles	Raffineries de pétrole	Produits en caoutchouc	Grès, porcelaines, faïences	Verre
Fecha [1]	Papel, artículos de papel	Imprentas, editoriales	Química industrial básica	Abonos y plaguicidas [2]	Fibras sintéticas y artificiales	Refinerías de petróleo	Productos de caucho	Barro, loza, porcelana	Vidrio
1970	41.2	39.7	39.0	40.4	37.4	37.6	39.7	35.0	39.1
1971	40.2	39.7	38.9	39.0	38.5	38.9	40.9	40.5	38.3
1972 [3]	38.9	38.7	37.9	37.6	37.2	36.4	39.3	39.4	39.6
1973	38.3	38.0	36.7	37.5	36.3	38.7	38.4	38.3	38.7
1974	37.1	37.5	35.5	36.3	33.7	38.8	37.7	37.7	36.3
1975	34.0	35.7	34.6	34.8	27.7	34.5	35.2	32.9	33.8
1976	36.6	37.4	36.1	35.7	35.6	35.5	37.4	31.4	36.4
1977	36.0	36.8	35.6	36.1	33.4	35.1	36.4	35.2	34.8
1978	36.7	36.8	35.6	35.9	35.4	35.2	35.8	36.1	35.4
1979	36.0	35.8	34.9	35.1	35.7	33.8	36.7	35.5	36.1

	369 ×	372	381	382	383	384	385	390
Date [1]	Cement	Non-ferrous metal basic industries	Metal products	Machinery (non-electrical)	Electrical machinery and apparatus	Transport equipment	Scientific, measuring optical, etc., equipment	Other manufacturing industries
Date [1]	Ciment	Métaux non ferreux (industrie de base)	Produits métalliques	Machines (non électriques)	Machines et appareils électriques	Matériel de transport	Matériel scientifique, de précision, d'optique, etc.	Autres industries manufacturières
Fecha [1]	Cemento	Industrias básicas de metales no ferrosos	Productos metálicos	Maquinaria (no eléctrica)	Maquinaria y aparatos eléctricos	Material de transporte	Equipo científico, de medida, de óptica, etc.	Otras industrias manufactureras
1970	40.1	40.2	38.9	40.4	40.1	40.4	.	.
1971	39.9	40.4	39.6	40.2	38.8	39.4	.	.
1972 [3]	37.6	38.9	38.3	38.6	38.9	38.6	38.6	39.3
1973	36.3	38.4	36.7	38.1	36.6	38.3	37.2	38.4
1974	35.8	37.4	37.3	37.5	36.3	37.5	38.0	37.4
1975	35.4	34.2	35.1	34.7	34.8	35.7	35.3	35.8
1976	36.8	37.0	35.6	35.8	35.1	37.6	36.1	36.8
1977	37.0	36.0	34.7	35.3	34.1	34.9	36.8	35.3
1978	36.2	35.9	34.7	34.6	34.6	36.3	36.7	36.1
1979	35.1	36.0	35.6	35.6	34.7	36.4	35.9	35.2

[1] Oct. of each year. [2] Incl. drugs and medicines. [3] New industrial classification.

[1] Oct. de chaque année. [2] Y compris les produits pharmaceutiques. [3] Nouvelle classification industrielle.

[1] Oct. de cada año. [2] Incl. los productos farmacéuticos y medicamentos. [3] Nueva clasificación industrial.

13 Hours of work in manufacturing
Durée du travail dans les industries manufacturières
Horas de trabajo en las industrias manufactureras

B By industry
Par industrie
Por industria

Czechoslovakia (1)[1]

Hours actually worked per week
Heures réellement effectuées par semaine
Horas efectivamente trabajadas por semana

Date / Date / Fecha	311-312 Food / Aliments / Alimentos	313 Beverages / Boissons / Bebidas	314 Tobacco / Tabac / Tabaco	321 Textiles	322 Clothing / Habillement / Vestido	323 Leather, leather products / Cuir, articles en cuir / Cuero, artículos de cuero	324 Footwear / Chaussures / Calzado	331 Wood / Bois / Madera	332 Furniture / Ameublement / Mobiliario
1970	46.1	.	.	41.9	40.9	41.9	41.6	43.8	43.2
1971	46.1	45.6	43.2	41.9	40.8	42.2	41.5	43.8	43.2
1972	46.3	45.6	42.8	41.7	40.7	42.0	41.5	43.8	43.4
1973	46.1	45.4	43.0	41.7	40.6	42.0	41.5	43.6	43.0
1974	46.5	45.2	43.2	41.6	40.9	41.9	41.9	43.6	43.0
1975	46.2	45.1	42.8	41.4	40.8	41.7	42.2	43.5	42.9
1976	45.5	45.1	42.8	41.3	40.7	41.7	42.2	43.8	43.0
1977	46.0	45.2	42.9	41.3	40.7	41.6	41.8	43.9	43.1
1978	45.8	45.1	42.8	41.1	40.5	41.3	41.6	43.8	43.1
1979	45.8	45.2	42.5	41.3	40.5	41.4	41.7	43.9	43.3

Date / Date / Fecha	341 Paper, paper products / Papier, articles en papier / Papel, artículos de papel	342 Printing, publishing / Imprimerie, édition / Imprentas, editoriales	351 Industrial chemicals / Chimie industrielle / Química industrial	352 Other chemical products / Autres produits chimiques / Otros productos químicos	353 Petroleum refineries / Raffineries de pétrole / Refinerías de petróleo	354 Products of petroleum and coal / Dérivés du pétrole et du charbon / Derivados del petróleo y del carbón	355 Rubber products / Produits en caoutchouc / Productos de caucho	356 Plastic products / Article en matière plastique / Productos plásticos	361 Pottery, china, earthenware / Grès, porcelaines, faïences / Barro, loza, porcelana
1970	44.2	43.3	43.3	42.9	42.7	43.3	42.6	.	.
1971	44.2	43.2	43.3	42.9	43.1	43.7	42.7	.	43.1
1972	44.2	43.1	43.2	43.0	42.8	43.8	42.8	.	42.7
1973	43.9	43.4	43.0	42.7	42.8	43.5	42.6	.	42.2
1974	43.9	43.2	42.9	42.7	42.7	43.6	42.5	.	42.1
1975	43.9	43.0	42.9	42.8	42.7	43.4	42.8	.	41.7
1976	43.9	43.0	42.9	42.1	42.7	43.6	42.8	43.0	41.7
1977	43.8	42.9	43.0	42.2	42.8	43.7	42.7	42.4	41.6
1978	44.0	42.8	42.6	42.2	42.9	43.7	42.8	42.4	41.4
1979	44.1	42.8	43.1	42.2	43.0	44.0	42.7	42.5	41.8

[1] State industry.   [1] Industrie d'Etat.   [1] Industria de Estado.

13 Hours of work in manufacturing
Durée du travail dans les industries manufacturières
Horas de trabajo en las industrias manufactureras

B By industry
Par industrie
Por industria

Czechoslovakia (2) [1]

Hours actually worked per week
Heures réellement effectuées par semaine
Horas efectivamente trabajadas por semana

Date / Date / Fecha	362 Glass / Verre / Vidrio	369 Other non-metallic mineral products / Autres produits minéraux non métalliques / Otros productos minerales no metálicos	371 Iron and steel / Sidérurgie / Hierro y acero	372 Non-ferrous metal / Métaux non ferreux / Metales no ferrosos	381 Metal products / Produits métalliques / Productos metálicos	382 Machinery (non-electrical) / Machines (non électriques) / Maquinaria (no eléctrica)	383 Electrical machinery and apparatus / Machines et appareils électriques / Maquinaria y aparatos eléctricos	384 Transport equipment / Matériel de transport / Material de transporte	385 Scientific, measuring, optical, etc., equipment / Matériel scientifique, de précision, d'optique, etc. / Equipo científico, de medida, de óptica, etc.	390 Other manufacturing industries / Autres industries manufacturières / Otras industrias manufactureras
			Basic metal industries / Industrie métallurgique de base / Industrias metalúrgicas básicas							
1970	.	.	43.3	43.6	.	.	.	.	.	43.2
1971	42.7	45.2	43.4	43.7	43.3	45.4	42.8	44.1	43.8	43.3
1972	42.7	45.3	43.3	44.0	43.5	45.3	42.9	44.0	43.9	43.3
1973	42.5	45.0	43.0	43.7	43.2	45.2	42.9	43.9	43.8	43.2
1974	42.3	44.7	42.8	43.7	43.2	45.2	42.8	44.0	43.8	43.2
1975	42.4	44.6	42.8	43.9	43.2	45.2	42.8	43.9	43.8	43.0
1976	42.3	44.7	42.8	43.8	43.4	45.2	42.8	44.1	43.9	42.4
1977	42.3	44.9	42.7	42.4	43.8	45.1	43.0	44.4	43.2	42.5
1978	42.1	44.9	42.6	42.2	43.7	44.9	42.7	44.1	43.1	42.3
1979	42.3	45.0	42.7	42.3	43.9	44.9	42.7	44.2	43.2	42.2

[1] State industry.   [1] Industrie d'Etat.   [1] Industria de Estado.

Denmark (1)

Hours actually worked per week
Heures réellement effectuées par semaine
Horas efectivamente trabajadas por semana

Date / Date / Fecha	311-312 Food / Aliments / Alimentos	313 Beverages / Boissons / Bebidas	314 Tobacco / Tabac / Tabaco	321 Textiles	322 Clothing / Habillement / Vestido	323 Leather, leather products / Cuir, articles en cuir / Cuero, artículos de cuero	324 Footwear / Chaussures / Calzado	331 Wood / Bois / Madera	332 Furniture / Ameublement / Mobiliario
1971	36.3	35.1	34.2	34.4	32.2	35.4	34.0	36.9	36.0
1972	35.8	34.8	34.2	33.8	32.0	35.0	34.7	37.2	36.3
1973	34.6	33.2	30.6	31.9	30.9	33.4	32.7	35.2	34.5
1974	34.4	33.0	31.7	31.9	30.1	34.1	33.6	34.9	34.9
1975	34.0	32.6	30.4	31.6	29.7	32.6	32.2	32.8	33.5
1976	33.6	33.1	30.4	31.7	29.8	32.4	32.1	34.4	34.3
1977	32.9	32.7	30.3	30.7	28.1	30.9	30.4	33.6	33.2
1978	...	32.4	29.6	30.6	28.2	31.1	29.6	33.2	32.7
1979	...	32.0	29.7	31.6	28.2	31.4	30.7	34.1	33.7

13 Hours of work in manufacturing
Durée du travail dans les industries manufacturières
Horas de trabajo en las industrias manufactureras

B By industry
Par industrie
Por industria

Denmark (2)

Hours actually worked per week
Heures réellement effectuées par semaine
Horas efectivamente trabajadas por semana

Date / Date / Fecha	341 Paper, paper products / Papier, articles en papier / Papel, artículos de papel	342 Printing, publishing / Imprimerie, édition / Imprentas, editoriales	351 Industrial chemicals / Chimie industrielle / Química industrial	352 Other chemical products / Autres produits chimiques / Otros productos químicos	353 Petroleum refineries / Raffineries de pétrole / Refinerías de petróleo	354 Products of petroleum and coal / Dérivés du pétrole et du charbon / Derivados del petróleo y del carbón	355 Rubber products / Produits en caoutchouc / Productos de caucho	356 Plastic products / Articles en matière plastique / Productos plásticos	361 Pottery, china, earthenware / Grès, porcelaines, faïences / Barro, loza, porcelana
1971	36.4	36.5	37.1	34.7	39.4	41.9	36.6	35.6	33.9
1972	36.2	36.2	37.1	34.4	36.4	40.3	35.6	35.0	32.5
1973	33.6	34.9	35.4	33.1	34.6	38.7	33.1	33.8	29.6
1974	34.5	34.9	35.7	33.2	35.8	40.0	35.2	34.7	31.2
1975	31.2	34.5	33.6	32.7	36.3		32.6	33.8	29.5
1976	32.2	34.4	33.1	32.9	36.3		34.0	33.4	26.9
1977	31.7	32.5	33.8	31.6	39.3		33.9	32.8	29.7
1978	32.5	...	33.5	31.9	38.4		33.2	32.4	...
1979	33.5	...	34.9	31.8	35.2		33.2	33.1	...

Date / Date / Fecha	362 Glass / Verre / Vidrio	369 Other non-metallic mineral products / Autres produits minéraux non métalliques / Otros productos minerales no metálicos	371 Basic metal industries — Iron and steel / Sidérurgie / Hierro y acero	372 Basic metal industries — Non-ferrous metal / Métaux non ferreux / Metales no ferrosos	381 Metal products / Produits métalliques / Productos metálicos	382 Machinery (non-electrical) / Machines (non électriques) / Maquinaria (no eléctrica)	383 Electrical machinery and apparatus / Machines et appareils électriques / Maquinaria y aparatos eléctricos	384 × Transport equipment / Matériel de transport / Material de transporte	385 Scientific, measuring, optical, etc., equipment / Matériel scientifique, de précision, d'optique, etc. / Equipo científico, de medida, de óptica, etc.	390 Other manufacturing industries / Autres industries manufacturières / Otras industrias manufactureras
1971	36.5	38.4	36.7	35:5	35.6	36.9	34.6	35.9	34.5	35.3
1972	35.6	38.2	36.3	35.1	35.4	36.3	34.5	35.5	34.7	34.5
1973	34.4	35.6	33.9	32.1	33.9	33.9	32.0	33.3	32.4	32.3
1974	36.2	36.9	35.9	34.0	34.5	35.1	33.2	34.9	33.2	32.8
1975	33.1	34.7	33.8		33.3	34.3	31.8	33.4	32.9	31.8
1976	34.3	35.3	33.3		33.6	34.1	32.9	34.0	32.3	32.2
1977	33.0	34.7	32.9		33.2	33.6	32.7	33.2	32.0	31.5
1978	...	34.7	33.0		32.9	33.6	32.1	...	32.3	31.4
1979	...	34.4	33.1		34.0	34.3	32.2	...	33.0	31.5

13 B

Hours of work in manufacturing
Durée du travail dans les industries manufacturières
Horas de trabajo en las industrias manufactureras

By industry
Par industrie
Por industria

España

Hours actually worked per week [1]
Heures réellement effectuées par semaine [1]
Horas efectivamente trabajadas por semana [1]

Date / Date / Fecha	31 — Food, beverages, tobacco / Aliments, boissons, tabac / Alimentos, bebidas, tabaco	321 — Textiles	322-324 — Clothing, leather, leather products, footwear / Habillement, cuir, articles en cuir, chaussures / Vestido, cuero, artículos de cuero, calzado	33 — Wood, furniture / Bois, ameublement / Madera, mobiliario	341 — Paper, paper products / Papier, articles en papier / Papel, artículos de papel
1970	42.2	42.2	44.7	44.3	45.2
1971	42.8	41.9	44.5	44.3	45.6
1972	44.0	42.8	45.9	46.1	47.0
1973	44.1	41.8	45.0	44.6	44.0
1974	44.5	41.9	44.2	45.4	47.0
1975	44.7	41.2	44.0	43.7	44.7
1976	43.6	40.6	43.4	43.4	44.0

Date / Date / Fecha	342 — Printing, publishing / Imprimerie, édition / Imprentas, editoriales	351-352 — Chemicals / Industrie chimique / Productos químicos	353-354 — Refineries and products of petroleum and coal / Raffineries et dérivés du pétrole et du charbon / Refinerías y derivados del petróleo y del carbón	355 — Rubber products / Produits en caoutchouc / Productos de caucho	37-38 × — Metal industries, machinery, etc. [2] / Industrie métallurgique, machines, etc. [2] / Industrias metalúrgicas, maquinaria, etc. [2]
1970	41.2	45.8	45.4	43.5	45.0
1971	41.5	45.6	45.1	41.9	44.7
1972	42.1	46.3	46.6	43.3	45.5
1973	43.2	44.1	45.6	49.6	44.7
1974	41.8	44.7	44.8	41.6	44.0
1975	41.1	43.2	43.9	41.5	42.5
1976	41.2	42.5	42.5	40.5	41.1

[1] Incl. salaried employees. [2] Excl. scientific, measuring, optical, etc., equipment.

[1] Y compris les employés. [2] Non compris le matériel scientifique, de précision, d'optique, etc.

[1] Incl. los empleados. [2] Excl. el equipo científico, de medida, de óptica, etc.

HOURS

13 Hours of work in manufacturing
Durée du travail dans les industries manufacturières
Horas de trabajo en las industrias manufactureras

B By industry
Par industrie
Por industria

Finland

Hours actually worked per week
Heures réellement effectuées par semaine
Horas efectivamente trabajadas por semana

Date / Date / Fecha	311-312 Food / Aliments / Alimentos	321 Textiles	323 Leather, leather products / Cuir, articles en cuir / Cuero, artículos de cuero	331 × Sawmills / Scieries / Aserraderos	341 Paper, paper products / Papier, articles en papier / Papel, artículos de papel	351-352 Chemicals / Industrie chimique / Productos químicos	36 Non-metallic mineral products / Produits minéraux non métalliques / Productos minerales no metálicos	371; 381-382 Metal industries, machinery (non-electrical) / Industrie métallurgique, machines (non électriques) / Industrias metalúrgicas, maquinaria (no eléctrica)
1970	40.5	38.8	38.3	40.1	40.9	40.3	39.6	40.3
1971	38.8	37.6	37.5	38.3	39.0	38.8	38.3	38.8
1972	39.1	37.9	37.3	38.2	38.4	39.0	38.5	38.3
1973	40.4	37.2	37.4	38.4	38.7	39.4	38.4	38.4
1974	39.1	37.6	34.4	37.4	37.8	38.5	39.8	38.5	38.1
1975	39.0	37.6	37.2	38.0	39.4	39.6	39.0	38.5
1976	39.1	38.0	36.0	38.4	39.5	40.0	38.9	37.8
1977	39.0	37.5	36.4	37.7	39.6	39.3	39.0	37.6
1978	38.7	37.4	37.7	38.6	39.4	39.7	39.0	38.8
1979	41.1	40.8	40.4	41.1	41.3	41.0	41.1	41.0

France (1)

Hours actually worked per week
Heures réellement effectuées par semaine
Horas efectivamente trabajadas por semana

Date [1] / Date [1] / Fecha [1]	31 Food, beverages, tobacco / Aliments, boissons, tabac / Alimentos, bebidas, tabaco	321 Textiles	322 Clothing / Habillement / Vestido	323 Leather, leather products / Cuir, articles en cuir / Cuero, artículos de cuero	324 Footwear / Chaussures / Calzado	33 Wood, furniture / Bois, ameublement / Madera, mobiliario	341 Paper, paper products / Papier, articles en papier / Papel, artículos de papel
1972	46.1	43.2	41.5	44.1	42.8	46.4	44.2
1973	45.6	42.5	41.1	43.0	42.7	46.1	43.7
1974	44.7	41.7	40.7	43.2	42.4	44.8	42.3
1975	43.6	39.9	40.4	42.2	41.1	42.8	40.1
1976 [2]	42.8	40.9	40.5	41.7	41.6	42.9	40.6
1977	42.5	40.3	40.3	40.9	41.0	42.4	40.3
1978	42.0	40.3	40.4	40.5	40.8	41.8	40.3
1979	41.6	40.3	40.3	40.6	40.9	41.5	40.3

[1] Oct. of each year. [2] Sampling design revised.   [1] *Oct. de chaque année.* [2] *Plan d'échantillonnage révisé.*   [1] Oct. de cada año. [2] Diseño de la muestra revisado.

13 B

Hours of work in manufacturing — By industry
Durée du travail dans les industries manufacturières — Par industrie
Horas de trabajo en las industrias manufactureras — Por industria

France (2)

Hours actually worked per week
Heures réellement effectuées par semaine
Horas efectivamente trabajadas por semana

	342	351 ×	351-352 ×	353-354	355	356	36	
Date [1] Date [1] Fecha [1]	Printing, publishing Imprimerie, édition Imprentas, editoriales	Synthetic and man-made fibres Fibres synthétiques et artificielles Fibras sintéticas y artificiales	Chemicals Industrie chimique Productos químicos	Refineries and products of petroleum and coal Raffineries et dérivés du pétrole et du charbon Refinerías y derivados del petróleo y del carbón	Rubber products Produits en caoutchouc Productos de caucho	Plastic products Articles en matière plastique Productos plásticos	Non-metallic mineral products *Produits minéraux non métalliques* Productos minerales no metálicos	
							Total	Glass *Verre* Vidrio
1972	43.7	42.1	42.0	40.6	44.1	44.9	44.2	41.2
1973	43.5	41.6	41.0	40.6	43.5	44.0	43.9	41.2
1974	43.2	40.8	40.4	40.3	42.7	42.8	43.3	40.9
1975	42.0	39.1	39.7	40.3	41.7	41.5	42.0	39.9
1976 [2]	41.8	39.8	40.2	40.4	41.9	42.0	42.0	40.8
1977	41.6	39.7	40.2	40.3	41.3	41.3	41.3	40.4
1978	41.2	39.9	40.2	40.3	41.0	40.7	41.1	40.4
1979	40.9	39.5	40.1	40.3	41.0	40.4	41.0	40.3

	37	381	382	383	384 ×		385	390
Date [1] Date [1] Fecha [1]	Basic metal industries Industrie métallurgique de base Industrias metalúrgicas básicas	Metal products Produits métalliques Productos metálicos	Machinery (non-electrical) Machines (non électriques) Maquinaria (no eléctrica)	Electrical machinery and apparatus Machines et appareils électriques Maquinaria y aparatos eléctricos	Manufacture of motor vehicles Construction de véhicules automobiles Fabricación de vehículos automóviles	Other Autres Otras	Scientific, measuring, optical, etc., equipment Matériel scientifique, de précision, d'optique, etc. Equipo científico, de medida, de óptica, etc.	Other manufacturing industries Autres industries manufacturières Otras industrias manufactureras
1972	44.0	45.3	44.5	43.6	43.7	44.1	44.0	43.9
1973	43.4	44.7	44.1	42.9	43.1	43.3	43.6	43.2
1974	42.7	44.0	43.3	42.3	42.3	43.0	42.8	42.4
1975	40.9	42.3	41.4	41.1	41.6	42.0	41.5	41.3
1976 [2]	41.6	42.5	41.8	41.3	41.4	41.8	42.0	41.3
1977	40.2	42.0	41.3	41.0	41.1	41.2	41.6	40.8
1978	40.4	41.5	40.9	40.6	41.2	40.6	40.9	40.5
1979	41.0	41.4	40.8	40.2	40.9	40.6	40.7	40.4

[1] Oct. of each year. [2] Sampling design revised.

[1] *Oct. de chaque année.* [2] *Plan d'échantillonnage révisé.*

[1] Oct. de cada año. [2] Diseño de la muestra revisado.

13 Hours of work in manufacturing
Durée du travail dans les industries manufacturières
Horas de trabajo en las industrias manufactureras

B By industry
Par industrie
Por industria

Germany, Fed. Rep. of (1)

Hours paid for per week
Heures rémunérées par semaine
Horas pagadas por semana

Date / Date / Fecha	31 Food, beverages, tobacco / Aliments, boissons, tabac / Alimentos, bebidas, tabaco — Total	31 — Tobacco / Tabac / Tabaco	321 Textiles	322 Clothing / Habillement / Vestido	323 × Leather, leather products [2] / Cuir, articles en cuir [2] / Cuero, artículos de cuero [2]	324 Footwear / Chaussures / Calzado	331 Wood / Bois / Madera	332 Furniture / Ameublement / Mobiliario	341 Paper, paper products / Papier, articles en papier / Papel, artículos de papel	342 Printing, publishing / Imprimerie, édition / Imprentas, editoriales
1970	45.1	40.7	42.6	40.7	41.5	40.7	45.6	43.0	46.2	43.3
1971	44.8	40.9	42.3	40.4	41.3	40.5	45.1	43.0	45.7	43.0
1972	44.4	40.7	42.2	40.2	41.0	39.8	44.7	42.9	45.7	43.0
1973 [1]	44.5	40.5	41.9	39.6	41.1	39.3	44.5	42.5	45.3	42.7
1974	43.8	40.1	40.9	39.2	40.3	39.3	43.7	41.3	44.5	41.8
1975	43.5	40.1	39.7	38.8	39.4	39.7	42.1	40.6	40.7	41.5
1976	43.8	40.2	40.9	39.0	40.4	40.3	43.5	41.7	43.9	42.0
1977	43.8	40.4	40.9	39.5	40.0	40.1	43.4	42.3	44.2	42.5
1978	43.5	40.3	41.0	39.3	40.2	40.3	43.3	42.0	44.1	42.3
1979	43.4	40.2	41.2	39.5	40.7	40.4	43.0	41.5	43.9	42.3

Date / Date / Fecha	351 Industrial chemicals [3] / Chimie industrielle [3] / Química industrial [3]	352 Synthetic fibres / Fibres synthétiques / Fibras sintéticas	353 Other chemical products / Autres produits chimiques / Otros productos químicos	355 Petroleum refineries / Raffineries de pétrole / Refinerías de petróleo	355 Rubber products / Produits en caoutchouc / Productos de caucho	356 Plastic products / Articles en matière plastique / Productos plásticos	361 Pottery, china, earthenware / Grès, porcelaines, faïences / Barro, loza, porcelana	362 Glass, and glass products / Verre / Vidrio	369 Other non-metallic mineral products / Autres produits minéraux non métalliques / Otros productos minerales no metálicos
1970	43.2	42.0	42.2	42.7	...	43.4	...	43.3	48.7
1971	42.6	42.0	41.9	42.0	...	43.0	...	43.1	48.3
1972	42.3	41.6	42.1	41.3	...	42.7	...	43.1	47.8
1973 [1]	43.1	41.5	42.3	41.7	42.1	42.7	42.1	42.8	46.7
1974	42.6	41.0	41.8	41.4	40.5	41.5	41.4	41.4	45.2
1975	40.6	36.5	40.9	40.9	38.9	39.6	38.6	39.9	43.7
1976	41.7	39.8	41.5	41.1	41.0	41.9	41.0	41.6	44.5
1977	42.1	40.7	41.5	41.5	41.2	41.8	41.7	42.3	44.5
1978	41.6	41.1	41.4	41.4	41.0	41.7	41.1	41.7	44.9
1979	41.6	41.1	41.2	41.5	41.5	41.7	41.0	41.6	44.9

[1] Sampling design revised. [2] Excl. tanneries and leather finishing, fur dressing and dyeing industries. [3] Excl. synthetic fibres.

[1] Plan d'échantillonnage révisé. [2] Non compris la tannerie-mégisserie, la préparation et teinture des fourrures. [3] Non compris les fibres synthétiques.

[1] Diseño de la muestra revisado. [2] Excl. la curtiduría y talleres de acabado y la industria de la preparación y teñido de pieles. [3] Excl. las fibras sintéticas.

13 Hours of work in manufacturing
Durée du travail dans les industries manufacturières
Horas de trabajo en las industrias manufactureras

B By industry
Par industrie
Por industria

Germany, Fed. Rep. of (2)

Hours paid for per week
Heures rémunérées par semaine
Horas pagadas por semana

Date / Date / Fecha	371	372	381	382	383	384 ×			385	390
	Basic metal industries *Industrie métallurgique de base* Industrias metalúrgicas básicas		Metal products *Produits métalliques* Productos metálicos	Machinery (non-electrical) *Machines (non électriques)* Maquinaria (no eléctrica)	Electrical machinery and apparatus *Machines et appareils électriques* Maquinaria y aparatos eléctricos	Motor vehicles [2] *Véhicules à moteur* [2] Vehículos de motor [2]	Ship building *Construction navale* Construcciones navales	Manufacture of aircraft *Construction aéronautique* Fabricación de aeronaves	Scientific, measuring, optical, etc., equipment *Matériel scientifique, de précision, d'optique, etc.* Equipo científico, de medida, de óptica, etc.	Other manufacturing industries *Autres industries manufacturières* Otras industrias manufactureras
	Iron and steel *Sidérurgie* Hierro y acero	Non-ferrous metal *Métaux non ferreux* Metales no ferrosos								
1970	44.8	44.4	44.6	45.3	42.5	44.0	48.3	43.1	41.8	42.2
1971	43.1	43.4	43.6	43.9	41.5	42.8	47.7	42.8	40.8	41.3
1972	42.9	43.6	43.3	43.3	41.7	41.6	46.9	42.1	40.9	41.3
1973 [1]	43.6	44.0	43.5	43.6	41.5	42.1	46.9	42.4	41.3	41.5
1974	43.1	43.0	42.4	43.2	40.8	39.2	46.9	42.6	40.6	40.8
1975	40.2	40.3	40.7	41.1	38.7	39.3	46.3	41.4	38.8	39.0
1976	40.9	42.5	42.1	41.4	40.4	41.7	44.6	40.9	40.1	40.2
1977	40.5	42.7	42.2	42.2	40.6	41.8	44.3	40.4	40.4	40.8
1978	41.2	42.3	41.9	42.1	40.6	41.3	42.1	41.2	40.3	40.5
1979	42.3	42.7	42.1	42.4	40.8	41.5	42.7	41.4	40.8	40.7

[1] Sampling design revised. [2] Incl. bicycles and miscellaneous transport equipment.

[1] *Plan d'échantillonnage révisé.* [2] *Y compris les cycles et matériel de transport divers.*

[1] Diseño de la muestra revisado. [2] Incl. las bicicletas y material de transporte diverso.

13 Hours of work in manufacturing
Durée du travail dans les industries manufacturières
Horas de trabajo en las industrias manufactureras

B By industry
Par industrie
Por industria

Grèce

Hours paid for per week
Heures rémunérées par semaine
Horas pagadas por semana

	311-312	313	314	321	322; 324	323	331	332	341	342
Date [1]	Food	Beverages	Tobacco		Clothing, footwear	Leather, leather products	Wood	Furniture	Paper, paper products	Printing, publishing
Date [1]	Aliments	Boissons	Tabac	Textiles	Habillement, chaussures	Cuir, articles en cuir	Bois	Ameublement	Papier, articles en papier	Imprimerie, édition
Fecha [1]	Alimentos	Bebidas	Tabaco		Vestido, calzado	Cuero, artículos de cuero	Madera	Mobiliario	Papel, artículos de papel	Imprentas, editoriales
1970	42.3	45.0	39.2	45.8	42.1	44.5	42.1	42.1	44.6	45.8
1971	41.4	45.5	44.7	44.5	43.3	46.3	41.8	41.2	47.2	45.4
1972	41.8	44.5	45.6	44.5	42.9	45.3	40.7	40.8	46.6	46.0
1973	42.6	41.8	42.7	43.7	41.5	45.0	41.9	42.6	44.8	45.3
1974	40.9	43.4	43.2	44.2	44.3	46.1	42.8	43.8	45.3	46.5
1975 [2]	37.7	41.9	42.2	43.6	41.6	44.4	45.7	42.6	44.9	45.2
1976	39.7	40.6	34.3	42.5	40.8	43.3	43.0	40.3	42.9	43.3
1977	38.9	42.1	40.7	41.4	38.7	43.2	43.1	40.7	42.4	43.8
1978	40.5	43.9	40.2	43.3	41.3	43.6	44.0	42.9	43.2	43.1
1979	38.9	42.3	38.7	40.6	37.7	43.3	41.7	39.4	39.8	40.1

	351	354	355	36	37	381	382	383	384	390
Date [1]	Industrial chemicals	Products of petroleum and coal	Rubber products	Non-metallic mineral products	Basic metal industries	Metal products	Machinery (non-electrical)	Electrical machinery and apparatus	Transport equipment	Other manufacturing industries
Date [1]	Chimie industrielle	Dérivés du pétrole et du charbon	Produits en caoutchouc	Produits minéraux non métalliques	Industrie métallurgique de base	Produits métalliques	Machines (non électriques)	Machines et appareils électriques	Matériel de transport	Autres industries manufacturières
Fecha [1]	Química industrial	Derivados del petróleo y del carbón	Productos de caucho	Productos minerales no metálicos	Industrias metalúrgicas básicas	Productos metálicos	Maquinaria (no eléctrica)	Maquinaria y aparatos eléctricos	Material de transporte	Otras industrias manufactureras
1970	45.4	46.2	44.7	46.4	50.6	44.5	44.4	44.4	47.7	43.7
1971	46.3	46.3	43.4	45.4	50.6	44.3	46.0	44.2	44.8	42.6
1972	46.1	45.5	45.4	45.5	57.1	44.3	46.6	43.4	46.3	43.8
1973	44.7	46.9	42.2	42.9	51.8	44.8	45.3	40.9	42.6	43.5
1974	44.7	47.7	43.3	43.6	50.4	43.9	43.4	43.6	43.6	41.1
1975 [2]	44.8	45.6	42.6	43.7	50.2	44.8	43.5	42.8	44.8	41.8
1976	44.0	45.0	41.4	42.8	44.8	43.0	42.8	41.9	43.9	40.9
1977	43.3	46.5	40.9	41.7	45.2	43.3	43.1	40.0	42.2	40.5
1978	44.4	46.4	39.2	43.4	46.5	43.4	39.6	41.2	42.4	43.1
1979	41.9	43.3	40.7	41.2	44.7	41.5	39.2	41.0	43.7	39.2

[1] Nov. of each year.　[2] Sampling design revised.　　[1] Nov. de chaque année.　[2] Plan d'échantillonnage révisé.　　[1] Nov. de cada año.　[2] Diseño de la muestra revisado.

13 Hours of work in manufacturing
Durée du travail dans les industries manufacturières
Horas de trabajo en las industrias manufactureras

B By industry
Par industrie
Por industria

Hongrie (1) [1]

Hours actually worked per month
Heures réellement effectuées par mois
Horas efectivamente trabajadas por mes

Date / Date / Fecha	311-312 Food / Aliments / Alimentos	313 Beverages / Boissons / Bebidas	314 Tobacco / Tabac / Tabaco	321 Textiles	322 Clothing / Habillement / Vestido	323 Leather, leather products / Cuir, articles en cuir / Cuero, artículos de cuero	324 Footwear / Chaussures / Calzado	331 Wood / Bois / Madera	332 Furniture / Ameublement / Mobiliario
1970	171	171	164	164	165	162	167	168	167
1971	172	171	166	164	165	161	166	169	167
1972	170	169	164	163	164	162	166	167	166
1973	168	170	161	161	162	157	163	165	165
1974	168	169	159	159	162	148	162	163	163
1975	170	176	160	158	160	156	161	162	164
1976	172	177	162	162	162	161	164	165	165
1977	172	176	161	161	162	149	162	163	165
1978	169	173	160	159	158	155	160	160	163
1979	168	173	159	157	157	156	159	160	163

Date / Date / Fecha	341 Paper, paper products / Papier, articles en papier / Papel, artículos de papel	342 Printing, publishing / Imprimerie, édition / Imprentas, editoriales	351 Industrial chemicals / Chimie industrielle / Química industrial	352 Other chemical products / Autres produits chimiques / Otros productos químicos	353 Petroleum refineries / Raffineries de pétrole / Refinerías de petróleo	355 Rubber products / Produits en caoutchouc / Productos de caucho	356 Plastic products / Articles en matière plastique / Productos plásticos	361 Pottery, china, earthenware / Grès, porcelaines, faïences / Barro, loza, porcelana	362 Glass / Verre / Vidrio
1970	162	157	161	158	162	163	164	159	159
1971	161	158	161	158	163	164	165	161	160
1972	161	157	160	157	161	162	165	160	160
1973	159	156	158	155	160	161	164	159	159
1974	158	154	157	154	158	161	162	157	157
1975	158	153	158	155	157	160	161	158	156
1976	159	155	159	157	161	162	163	161	159
1977	159	154	158	156	159	163	160	160	159
1978	158	153	158	155	160	160	160	158	159
1979	157	152	157	155	162	160	158	157	157

[1] Socialised sector.   [1] *Secteur socialisé.*   [1] Sector socializado.

13 Hours of work in manufacturing
Durée du travail dans les industries manufacturières
Horas de trabajo en las industrias manufactureras

B By industry
Par industrie
Por industria

Hongrie (2) [1]

Hours actually worked per month
Heures réellement effectuées par mois
Horas efectivamente trabajadas por mes

Date / Date / Fecha	369 Other non-metallic mineral products *Autres produits minéraux non métalliques* Otros productos minerales no metálicos	371 Basic metal industries / *Industrie métallurgique de base* / Industrias metalúrgicas básicas Iron and steel *Sidérurgie* Hierro y acero	372 Non-ferrous metal *Métaux non ferreux* Metales no ferrosos	381 Metal products *Produits métalliques* Productos metálicos	382 Machinery (non-electrical) *Machines (non électriques)* Maquinaria (no eléctrica)	383 Electrical machinery and apparatus *Machines et appareils électriques* Maquinaria y aparatos eléctricos	384 Transport equipment *Matériel de transport* Material de transporte	385 Scientific, measuring, optical, etc., equipment *Matériel scientifique, de précision, d'optique, etc.* Equipo científico, de medida, de óptica, etc.	390 Other manufacturing industries *Autres industries manufacturières* Otras industrias manufactureras
1970	171	162	163	164	167	166	166	163	168
1971	168	162	161	165	168	167	167	166	168
1972	163	160	162	163	165	166	164	165	166
1973	162	161	161	162	164	164	162	163	163
1974	160	159	159	160	163	164	162	162	161
1975	162	159	159	160	163	164	161	159	161
1976	165	162	161	163	166	166	164	164	163
1977	164	161	161	163	165	165	164	163	162
1978	164	160	159	161	164	163	163	162	159
1979	164	160	158	160	162	162	162	161	159

[1] Socialised sector.

[1] *Secteur socialisé.*

[1] Sector socializado.

13 Hours of work in manufacturing
Durée du travail dans les industries manufacturières
Horas de trabajo en las industrias manufactureras

B By industry
Par industrie
Por industria

Ireland

Hours actually worked per week
Heures réellement effectuées par semaine
Horas efectivamente trabajadas por semana

Date [1] / Date [1] / Fecha [1]	311-312	313	314	321	322; 324	323; 355	33	34	35 ×	36	381-383
	Food / *Aliments* / Alimentos	Beverages / *Boissons* / Bebidas	Tobacco / *Tabac* / Tabaco	Textiles	Clothing, footwear / *Habillement, chaussures* / Vestido, calzado	Leather, leather products, rubber / *Cuir, articles en cuir, caoutchouc* / Cuero, artículos de cuero, caucho	Wood, furniture / *Bois, ameublement* / Madera, mobiliario	Paper, printing, publishing / *Papier, imprimerie, édition* / Papel, imprentas, editoriales	Chemicals, refineries and products of petroleum and coal, plastics [3] / *Industrie chimique, raffineries et dérivés du pétrole et du charbon, plastique* [3] / Productos químicos, refinerías y derivados del petróleo y del carbón, plástico [3]	Non-metallic mineral products / *Produits minéraux non métalliques* / Productos minerales no metálicos	Metal products, machinery, etc. / *Produits métalliques, machines, etc.* / Productos metálicos, maquinaria, etc.
Males [2] — *Hommes* [2] — Hombres [2]											
1970	47.8	45.6	46.4	43.8	41.8	44.9	42.8	45.0	44.3	46.2	44.1
1971	47.7	45.4	44.9	42.5	41.7	44.1	42.2	43.3	45.6	44.7	43.6
1972	47.6	47.6	44.8	43.7	40.9	42.9	43.0	44.2	46.1	43.8	43.5
1973 [4]	47.3	47.1	46.5	42.9	41.6	40.3	42.2	44.6	45.2	45.0	43.7
1974	47.4	47.1	45.5	42.4	39.9	41.9	41.7	43.6	45.3	42.9	42.0
1975	46.4	49.0	47.2	40.9	40.3	42.2	41.8	42.5	41.8	42.9	41.1
1976	47.2	50.9	46.1	40.8	40.3	43.3	43.3	43.7	43.6	43.8	42.7
1977	47.5	52.7	45.2	40.7	40.9	43.6	41.8	43.2	43.8	44.7	43.0
1978	46.0	49.2	45.6	41.4	40.3	41.0	41.9	43.7	45.5	44.2	42.6
1979	46.7	49.0	45.9	42.0	41.4	42.0	41.1	44.0	44.8	43.5	43.1
Females [2] — *Femmes* [2] — Mujeres [2]											
1970	37.5	29.3	41.5	39.3	38.8	39.4	38.4	40.1	38.4	39.6	38.7
1971	37.4	29.3	40.7	38.4	38.1	39.2	40.0	40.2	38.6	40.2	38.5
1972	36.3	30.6	40.8	39.3	38.1	38.9	36.7	38.6	38.3	37.0	39.5
1973 [4]	36.8	32.2	42.5	37.4	38.2	36.1	38.1	39.7	38.0	37.4	37.9
1974	35.7	31.0	41.0	38.2	37.4	38.1	37.1	37.9	37.1	38.0	37.7
1975	37.7	31.5	42.1	38.0	37.6	38.0	37.5	37.7	37.7	36.9	37.7
1976	37.2	32.2	41.4	38.5	37.9	37.3	38.9	38.9	38.5	37.4	38.2
1977	38.9	31.0	40.6	38.1	38.0	37.8	38.5	38.4	38.4	36.0	39.6
1978	38.5	31.4	41.5	38.3	38.3	36.4	38.9	37.9	38.9	36.2	38.5
1979	38.5	32.2	39.4	38.5	38.1	38.8	38.4	37.8	40.0	36.4	38.3

[1] Sep. of each year. [2] Workers on adult rates of pay. [3] Excl. rubber products. [4] New industrial classification.

[1] *Sept. de chaque année.* [2] *Travailleurs rémunérés sur la base de taux de salaire pour adultes.* [3] *Non compris les produits en caoutchouc.* [4] *Nouvelle classification industrielle.*

[1] Sept. de cada año. [2] Trabajadores pagados sobre la base de tarifas de salarios para adultos. [3] Excl. los productos de caucho. [4] Nueva clasificación industrial.

HOURS

13 Hours of work in manufacturing
Durée du travail dans les industries manufacturières
Horas de trabajo en las industrias manufactureras

B By industry
Par industrie
Por industria

Italie (1)

Hours actually worked per month
Heures réellement effectuées par mois
Horas efectivamente trabajadas por mes

Date / Date / Fecha	311-312 Food / Aliments / Alimentos	313 Beverages / Boissons / Bebidas	314 Tobacco / Tabac / Tabaco	321 Textiles	322 Clothing / Habillement / Vestido	323 Leather, leather products / Cuir, articles en cuir / Cuero, artículos de cuero	324 Footwear / Chaussures / Calzado	331 Wood / Bois / Madera	332 Furniture / Ameublement / Mobiliario
1970	155	160	122	137	138	145	131	150	152
1971	151	157	112	133	134	142	132	146	149
1972	147	150	120	134	130	139	129	143	147
1973	144	150	122	130	126	135	124	140	143
1974	138	146	114	127	124	131	128	138	141
1975	136	142	116	122	116	130	125	129	132
1976	138	143	124	128	120	134	128	136	138
1977	137	143	128	126	123	135	128	138	138

Date / Date / Fecha	341 Paper, paper products / Papier, articles en papier / Papel, artículos de papel	342 Printing, publishing / Imprimerie, édition / Imprentas, editoriales	351 Industrial chemicals / Chimie industrielle / Química industrial	353 Petroleum refineries / Raffineries de pétrole / Refinerías de petróleo	354 Products of petroleum and coal / Dérivés du pétrole et du charbon / Derivados del petróleo y del carbón	355 Rubber products / Produits en caoutchouc / Productos de caucho	356 Plastic products / Articles en matière plastique / Productos plásticos	361 Pottery, china, earthenware / Grès, porcelaines, faïences / Barro, loza, porcelana	362 Glass, and glass products / Verre / Vidrio
1970	156	156	156	165	164	149	151	153	158
1971	148	149	149	158	157	144	147	146	150
1972	149	148	140	151	151	142	144	142	145
1973	145	141	140	152	151	132	137	137	140
1974	139	139	134	145	145	130	130	137	136
1975	126	135	132	110	141	124	123	124	123
1976	137	139	132	118	144	133	132	130	129
1977	134	127	133	146	145	133	132	131	132

13 B

Hours of work in manufacturing
Durée du travail dans les industries manufacturières
Horas de trabajo en las industrias manufactureras

By industry
Par industrie
Por industria

Italie (2)

Hours actually worked per month
Heures réellement effectuées par mois
Horas efectivamente trabajadas por mes

Date *Date* Fecha	369 × Cement *Ciment* Cemento	371 / 372 Basic metal industries *Industrie métallurgique de base* Industrias metalúrgicas básicas		381 Metal products *Produits métalliques* Productos metálicos	382 Machinery (non-electrical) *Machines (non électriques)* Maquinaria (no eléctrica)	383 Electrical machinery and apparatus *Machines et appareils électriques* Maquinaria y aparatos eléctricos	384 Transport equipment *Matériel de transport* Material de transporte	385 Scientific, measuring, optical, etc., equipment *Matériel scientifique, de précision, d'optique, etc.* Equipo científico, de medida, de óptica, etc.	390 Other manufacturing industries *Autres industries manufacturières* Otras industrias manufactureras
		Iron and steel *Sidérurgie* Hierro y acero	Non-ferrous metal *Métaux non ferreux* Metales no ferrosos						
1970	166	153	158	155	155	150	152	...	150
1971	158	146	148	146	149	139	146	...	145
1972	153	142	142	140	142	133	138	...	142
1973	151	137	136	136	136	126	131	...	137
1974	147	137	137	137	138	125	128	120 [1]	131
1975	145	130	127	124	131	114	122	128	123
1976	146	134	133	131	132	119	126	129	131
1977	147	134	134	129	138	124	128	132	132

[1] Third quarter.　　　　　　　　　　　　[1] *Troisième trimestre.*　　　　　　　　　　　　[1] Tercer trimestre.

13 Hours of work in manufacturing
Durée du travail dans les industries manufacturières
Horas de trabajo en las industrias manufactureras

B By industry
Par industrie
Por industria

Luxembourg

Hours actually worked per week
Heures réellement effectuées par semaine
Horas efectivamente trabajadas por semana

	311-312	313	314	322; 324	331	332	34		351
Date [1]	Food	Beverages	Tobacco	Clothing, footwear	Wood	Furniture	Paper, printing, publishing		Synthetic and man-made fibres
Date [1] Fecha [1]	Aliments	Boissons	Tabac	Habillement, chaussures	Bois	Ameublement	Papier, imprimerie, édition	Total	Fibres synthétiques et artificielles
	Alimentos	Bebidas	Tabaco	Vestido, calzado	Madera	Mobiliario	Papel, imprentas, editoriales		Fibras sintéticas y artificiales
1970	47.0	50.3	44.7	43.9	47.1	48.6	44.1	46.1	.
1971	45.9	46.1	44.5	42.7	44.8	47.4	44.1	46.0	.
1972 [2]	46.5	46.9	44.6	41.4	44.5	46.9	42.9	42.3	39.8
1973	45.2	48.0	42.3	41.1	44.3	46.1	43.6	43.6	39.6
1974	46.0	46.7	41.2	41.3	43.8	46.7	42.0	43.0	41.4
1975	41.9	42.8	40.4	40.5	40.9	42.8	41.9	37.4	38.3
1976	43.7	41.3	40.5	40.4	40.8	41.9	43.7	40.3	40.2
1977	42.9	42.1	40.3	40.1	41.1	40.3	43.7	39.4	40.1
1978	41.4	41.1	40.3	40.1	40.4		44.3	39.6	37.8
1979	40.3	40.7	40.2	38.6	40.0		41.3	40.7	...

	355	346	36	371	381	382	383	384
Date [1]	Rubber products	Plastic products	Non-metallic mineral products	Iron and steel basic industries	Metal products	Machinery (non-electrical)	Electrical machinery and apparatus	Transport equipment
Date [1] Fecha [1]	Produits en caoutchouc	Articles en matière plastique	Produits minéraux non métalliques	Sidérurgie	Produits métalliques	Machines (non électriques)	Machines et appareils électriques	Matériel de transport
	Productos de caucho	Productos plásticos	Productos minerales no metálicos	Industrias básicas de hierro y acero	Productos metálicos	Maquinaria (no eléctrica)	Maquinaria y aparatos eléctricos	Material de transporte
1970	.	45.6	47.8	.	50.8	47.3	46.4	45.4
1971	.	44.0	47.0	.	48.7	48.2	44.7	43.8
1972 [2]	44.9	44.8	45.2	40.8	46.0	46.6	45.8	42.4
1973	45.0	42.5	44.8	40.9	46.1	43.4	46.5	46.7
1974	42.0	42.5	43.9	41.2	44.9	44.9	44.0	43.4
1975	37.9	39.2	39.8	40.9	40.8	42.5	42.2	40.3
1976	40.2	41.5	42.3	38.7 [3]	41.3	41.9	42.4	41.7
1977	39.9	39.2	38.9	37.1	40.9	41.9	41.2	41.9
1978	41.1	39.8	38.6	39.1	40.9	41.2	37.9	44.3
1979	42.2	39.8	40.4	40.0	40.8	41.7	39.6	38.8

[1] Oct. of each year. [2] New industrial classification [3] April.

[1] Oct. de chaque année. [2] Nouvelle classification industrielle. [3] Avril.

[1] Oct. de cada año. [2] Nueva clasificación industrial. [3] Abril.

13 Hours of work in manufacturing
Durée du travail dans les industries manufacturières
Horas de trabajo en las industrias manufactureras

B By industry
Par industrie
Por industria

Malta

Hours paid for per week [1]
Heures rémunérées par semaine [1]
Horas pagadas por semana [1]

Date / Date / Fecha	Food / Aliments / Alimentos	Beverages / Boissons / Bebidas	Tobacco / Tabac / Tabaco	Textiles	Clothing / Habillement / Vestido	Wood, cork / Bois, liège / Madera, corcho	Furniture / Ameublement / Mobiliario	Printing, publishing / Imprimerie, édition / Imprentas, editoriales
1970	46.4	43.6	41.8	42.6	46.0	46.7	45.9	43.9
1971	44.8	43.1	42.1	42.2	43.4	46.5	44.7	41.5
1972	44.8	43.6	40.5	41.1	41.7	46.5	43.1	41.3
1973	43.8	43.0	39.8	41.0	41.2	45.0	42.5	41.0
1974	41.8	41.0	40.5	39.8	40.8	43.5	42.0	41.0
1975	44.5	41.5	40.2	40.0	40.0	39.2	40.8	39.8
1976	44.0	41.0	40.0	39.5	40.0	39.5	41.0	40.0

Date / Date / Fecha	Chemicals / Industrie chimique / Productos químicos	Products of petroleum and coal / Dérivés du pétrole et du charbon / Derivados del petróleo y del carbón	Non-metallic mineral products / Produits minéraux non métalliques / Productos minerales no metálicos	Metal products / Produits métalliques / Productos metálicos	Machinery (non-electrical) / Machines (non électriques) / Maquinaria (no eléctrica)	Electrical machinery / Machines électriques / Maquinaria eléctrica	Transport equipment / Matériel de transport / Material de transporte	Miscellaneous manufacturing / Industries manufacturières diverses / Industrias manufactureras diversas
1970	42.3	48.2	45.4	44.7	44.2	43.9	38.5	43.7
1971	44.2	48.1	45.5	43.0	42.6	42.3	38.5	42.2
1972	43.3	45.1	44.7	40.4	40.8	41.0	38.6	41.3
1973	43.5	…	44.8	40.8	40.5	41.2	40.2	40.8
1974	41.8	…	44.0	40.5	40.5	40.2	40.0	40.5
1975	42.5	…	43.8	40.0	40.8	41.5	41.0	39.8
1976	40.0	…	44.0	40.0	40.0	40.0	40.5	40.8

[1] Incl. salaried employees; adults only.

[1] Y compris les employés ; adultes seulement.

[1] Incl. los empleados; adultos solamente.

13 B
Hours of work in manufacturing — By industry
Durée du travail dans les industries manufacturières — Par industrie
Horas de trabajo en las industrias manufactureras — Por industria

Netherlands (1)

Hours paid for per week [1]
Heures rémunérées par semaine [1]
Horas pagadas por semana [1]

Date [2] / Date [2] / Fecha [2]	311-312 Food / Aliments / Alimentos	313 Beverages / Boissons / Bebidas	314 Tobacco / Tabac / Tabaco	321 Textiles	322 Clothing / Habillement / Vestido	323 Leather, leather products / Cuir, articles en cuir / Cuero, artículos de cuero	324 Footwear / Chaussures / Calzado
1974	42.4	41.8	40.9	41.7	42.3	41.3	41.0
1975	41.9	41.7	40.6	41.0	40.5	40.6	40.4
1976	41.9	41.5	40.6	41.2	40.5	41.0	41.0
1977	41.9	41.3	40.6	41.1	40.2	41.0	41.1
1978	41.9	41.2	40.4	41.0	40.2	41.0	40.8

Date [2] / Date [2] / Fecha [2]	331 Wood / Bois / Madera	332 Furniture / Ameublement / Mobiliario	341 Paper, paper products / Papier, articles en papier / Papel, artículos de papel	342 Printing, publishing / Imprimerie, édition / Imprentas, editoriales	351 Industrial chemicals / Chimie industrielle / Química industrial	352 Other chemical products / Autres produits chimiques / Otros productos químicos	353-354 Refineries and products of petroleum and coal / Raffineries et dérivés du pétrole et du charbon / Refinerías y derivados del petróleo y del carbón
1974	42.3	42.3	41.5	41.3	40.9	41.2	41.6
1975	41.3	40.8	41.0	41.0	40.6	41.0	41.4
1976	41.5	40.7	41.1	41.2	40.8	40.8	41.1
1977	41.3	41.3	41.2	41.2	40.7	40.9	40.9
1978	41.2	40.9	41.3	40.9	40.7	41.1	40.9

[1] Incl. juveniles. [2] Oct. of each year.   [1] Y compris les jeunes gens. [2] Oct. de chaque année.   [1] Incl. los jóvenes. [2] Oct. de cada año.

| | 13 | Hours of work in manufacturing
Durée du travail dans les industries manufacturières
Horas de trabajo en las industrias manufactureras | B | By industry
Par industrie
Por industria |

Netherlands (2)

Date [2] Date [2] Fecha [2]	355-356 Rubber and plastic products *Produits en caoutchouc et en plastique* Productos de caucho, de plástico	36 Non-metallic mineral products *Produits minéraux non métalliques* Productos minerales no metálicos	37 Basic metal industries *Industrie métallurgique de base* Industrias metalúrgicas básicas	381 Metal products *Produits métalliques* Productos metálicos	382 Machinery (non-electrical) *Machines (non électriques)* Maquinaria (no eléctrica)	383 Electrical machinery and apparatus *Machines et appareils électriques* Maquinaria y aparatos eléctricos	384 Transport equipment *Matériel de transport* Material de transporte	385; 390 Other manufac- turing industries [3] *Autres industries manufac- turières [3]* Otras industrias manufac- tureras [3]
1974	41.9	43.4	41.1	42.2	41.9	40.6	42.0	41.3
1975	41.1	42.6	40.5	40.9	41.1	40.3	41.2	40.6
1976	41.6	42.7	40.7	41.4	41.3	40.3	41.2	40.5
1977	41.6	42.2	40.5	41.3	41.3	40.3	41.2	40.4
1978	41.4	42.4	40.5	41.1	41.0	40.4	41.0	40.4

[1] Incl. juveniles. [2] Oct. of each year. [3] Incl. scientific, measuring, optical, etc., equipment.

[1] *Y compris les jeunes gens.* [2] *Oct. de chaque année.* [3] *Y compris le matériel scientifique, de précision, d'optique, etc.*

[1] Incl. los jóvenes. [2] Oct. de cada año. [3] Incl. el equipo científico, de medida, de óptica, etc.

13 — B

Hours of work in manufacturing — **By industry**
Durée du travail dans les industries manufacturières — **Par industrie**
Horas de trabajo en las industrias manufactureras — **Por industria**

Norway (1)

Hours actually worked per week [1]
Heures réellement effectuées par semaine [1]
Horas efectivamente trabajadas por semana [1]

Date / Date / Fecha	311-312 Food / Aliments / Alimentos	313 Beverages / Boissons / Bebidas	314 Tobacco / Tabac / Tabaco	321 Textiles	322 Clothing / Habillement / Vestido	323 Leather, leather products / Cuir, articles en cuir / Cuero, artículos de cuero	324 Footwear / Chaussures / Calzado	331 Wood / Bois / Madera	332 Furniture / Ameublement / Mobiliario	341 Paper, paper products / Papier, articles en papier / Papel, artículos de papel
Males — Hommes — Hombres										
1971	36.6	36.9	36.7	34.4	35.0	34.3	34.9	35.0	35.8	34.5
1972	36.2	36.7	36.0	34.5	35.1	34.6	34.8	35.0	35.5	34.4
1973	35.3	35.4	35.3	34.5	34.5	34.6	34.1	34.6	35.0	34.3
1974	34.4	35.7	31.3	33.9	34.2	34.3	34.6	33.9	35.0	34.3
1975	34.4	36.5	31.8	33.3	34.4	34.0	33.8	34.0	33.8	34.0
1976	33.3	35.4	31.5	33.0	32.9	30.9	32.8	33.0	34.2	32.5
1977	32.6	35.9	29.4	31.8	32.4	31.6	30.8	32.1	33.3	32.1
1978	31.9	33.6	30.1	31.3	31.1	31.8	30.8	32.1	32.2	30.3
1979	31.3	32.3	31.6	30.5	30.6	32.0	29.9	30.9	31.7	30.5
Females — Femmes — Mujeres										
1971	29.5	31.9	30.0	29.5	30.6	28.4	31.7	.	31.8	29.1
1972	29.2	31.9	30.9	30.3	30.7	29.7	31.5	.	31.5	29.0
1973	28.7	32.0	30.6	29.5	30.2	31.0	31.0	.	30.9	28.9
1974	28.2	30.2	27.7	28.7	29.7	29.2	31.0	.	30.9	28.2
1975	26.5	31.0	28.2	27.7	29.4	28.4	30.5	.	30.1	27.2
1976	26.5	28.3	27.2	27.6	28.6	28.5	29.2	.	28.1	27.7
1977	25.8	29.1	27.8	26.8	26.9	27.8	29.6	.	27.5	26.9
1978	25.9	29.2	26.7	26.1	26.2	28.5	26.8	.	27.2	27.1
1979	25.2	28.0	24.6	26.0	26.5	27.1	27.9	.	25.6	27.0

[1] Incl. juveniles.

[1] Y compris les jeunes gens.

[1] Incl. los jóvenes.

13 Hours of work in manufacturing
Durée du travail dans les industries manufacturières
Horas de trabajo en las industrias manufactureras

B By industry
Par industrie
Por industria

Norway (2)

Hours actually worked per week [1]
Heures réellement effectuées par semaine [1]
Horas efectivamente trabajadas por semana [1]

Date / Date / Fecha	342 Printing, publishing / Imprimerie, édition / Imprentas, editoriales	351-354 Chemicals, petroleum refineries [2] / Industrie chimique, raffineries de pétrole [2] / Productos químicos, refinerías de petróleo [2]	355 Rubber products / Produits en caoutchouc / Productos de caucho	356 Plastic products / Articles en matière plastique / Productos plásticos	361 Pottery, china, earthenware / Grès, porcelaines, faïences / Barro, loza, porcelana	362 Glass, and glass products / Verre / Vidrio	369 Other non-metallic mineral products / Autres produits minéraux / Otros productos minerales	37-38 Metal industries, machinery, etc. / Industrie métallurgique, machines, etc. / Industrias metalúrgicas, maquinaria, etc.	390 Other manufacturing industries / Autres industries manufacturières / Otras industrias manufactureras
Males *(concl.)* — *Hommes* (fin) — Hombres *(fin)*									
1971	37.6	34.8	33.3	34.2	35.3	33.5	35.6	34.3	35.6
1972	37.4	34.4	33.3	34.4	34.5	33.7	35.1	33.6	35.4
1973	36.8	34.4	33.5	33.8	34.6	33.1	34.5	32.9	34.7
1974	36.2	33.9	32.9	33.1	33.8	33.6	34.3	32.7	34.4
1975	36.4	32.8	32.4	32.8	33.8	32.1	34.4	33.4	34.9
1976	35.1	31.8	31.2	32.5	33.3	32.1	33.3	32.4	33.7
1977	34.3	31.2	31.8	31.7	32.2	32.0	32.3	31.5	32.9
1978	33.7	30.5	30.7	30.9	31.0	29.7	31.8	31.2	32.3
1979	33.4	31.0	30.0	30.9	28.6	29.5	31.0	30.9	32.4
Females *(concl.)* — *Femmes* (fin) — Mujeres *(fin)*									
1971	33.1	30.7	25.6	30.3	31.1	31.8	.	30.3	28.3
1972	32.9	29.6	26.1	30.7	31.2	31.3	.	29.3	30.3
1973	32.4	29.9	26.2	29.4	30.0	31.0	.	28.2	30.2
1974	32.0	29.8	27.1	29.1	29.1	28.4	.	27.7	30.6
1975	32.3	29.8	27.0	28.3	30.8	28.7	.	27.8	30.3
1976	31.4	29.5	25.2	26.9	30.2	28.6	.	27.9	28.9
1977	30.2	28.3	26.4	25.9	28.3	27.8	.	27.4	28.3
1978	29.5	27.0	26.5	25.8	26.4	26.1	.	25.9	27.9
1979	29.0	26.9	25.7	25.6	23.4	24.9	.	25.5	27.2

[1] Incl. juveniles. [2] Incl. products of petroleum and coal.

[1] *Y compris les jeunes gens.* [2] *Y compris les dérivés du pétrole et du charbon.*

[1] Incl. los jóvenes. [2] Incl. los derivados del petróleo y del carbón.

13 Hours of work in manufacturing
Durée du travail dans les industries manufacturières
Horas de trabajo en las industrias manufactureras

B By industry
Par industrie
Por industria

Pologne (1) [1]

Hours actually worked per month
Heures réellement effectuées par mois
Horas efectivamente trabajadas por mes

Date / Date / Fecha	311-312 Food / Aliments / Alimentos	313 Beverages / Boissons / Bebidas	314 Tobacco / Tabac / Tabaco	321 Textiles	322 Clothing / Habillement / Vestido	323 Leather, leather products / Cuir, articles en cuir / Cuero, artículos de cuero	324 Footwear / Chaussures / Calzado	331 Wood / Bois / Madera	332 Furniture / Ameublement / Mobiliario
1970	178	180	171	166	169	169	172	173	173
1971	178	180	171	161	168	168	169	172	172
1972	177	179	166	159	166	166	167	172	170
1973	177	179	167	158	165	166	166	171	170
1974	175	176	166	156	163	160	163	169	168
1975	172	172	164	154	160	158	159	167	164
1976	172	172	172	156	161	159	160	168	166
1977	170	170	171	153	160	158	160	167	165
1978	168	168	169	153	158	156	158	165	163
1979	168	168	169	153	156	155	157	165	160

Date / Date / Fecha	341 Paper, paper products / Papier, articles en papier / Papel, artículos de papel	342 Printing, publishing / Imprimerie, édition / Imprentas, editoriales	351 Industrial chemicals / Chimie industrielle / Química industrial	352 Other chemical products / Autres produits chimiques / Otros productos químicos	353 Petroleum refineries / Raffineries de pétrole / Refinerías de petróleo	354 Products of petroleum and coal / Dérivés du pétrole et du charbon / Derivados del petróleo y del carbón	355 Rubber products / Produits en caoutchouc / Productos de caucho	356 Plastic products / Articles en matière plastique / Productos plásticos	361 Pottery, china, earthenware / Grès, porcelaines, faïences / Barro, loza, porcelana
1970	173	157	167	170	180	168	166	169	172
1971	167	152	163	168	175	166	167	169	169
1972	166	150	160	165	172	165	165	168	167
1973	165	150	158	164	169	164	166	167	166
1974	162	148	157	159	162	162	163	163	165
1975	161	147	155	157	159	159	160	161	160
1976	162	148	156	159	161	160	160	160	161
1977	163	148	155	158	160	160	160	159	159
1978	161	147	154	156	159	159	158	156	158
1979	161	147	154	157	161	159	157	155	159

[1] Socialised sector.   [1] *Secteur socialisé.*   [1] Sector socializado.

13 Hours of work in manufacturing
Durée du travail dans les industries manufacturières
Horas de trabajo en las industrias manufactureras

B By industry
Par industrie
Por industria

Pologne (2) [1]

Hours actually worked per month
Heures réellement effectuées par mois
Horas efectivamente trabajadas por mes

Date / Date / Fecha	362 Glass, and glass products / Verre / Vidrio	369 Other non-metallic mineral products / Autres produits minéraux non métalliques / Otros productos minerales no metálicos	371 Basic metal industries / Industrie métallurgique de base / Industrias metalúrgicas básicas — Iron and steel / Sidérurgie / Hierro y acero	372 Non-ferrous metal / Métaux non ferreux / Metales no ferrosos	381 Metal products / Produits métalliques / Productos metálicos	382 Machinery (non-electrical) / Machines (non électriques) / Maquinaria (no eléctrica)	383 Electrical machinery and apparatus / Machines et appareils électriques / Maquinaria y aparatos eléctricos	384 Transport equipment / Matériel de transport / Material de transporte	385 Scientific, measuring, optical, etc., equipment / Matériel scientifique, de précision, d'optique, etc. / Equipo científico, de medida, de óptica, etc.	390 Other manufacturing industries / Autres industries manufacturières / Otras industrias manufactureras
1970	169	176	175	172	176	174	167	173	161	169
1971	164	174	174	172	172	172	170	173	171	170
1972	161	173	172	170	170	173	169	172	170	168
1973	158	173	171	169	170	173	169	173	170	167
1974	156	172	169	165	167	170	166	170	167	164
1975	153	168	167	160	164	167	163	168	164	162
1976	155	170	168	163	166	167	164	168	165	163
1977	154	169	169	164	165	166	162	166	163	162
1978	153	167	168	163	162	164	160	165	161	160
1979	153	167	168	162	163	165	160	165	162	160

[1] Socialised sector. [1] *Secteur socialisé.* [1] Sector socializado.

Portugal (1)

Hours actually worked per week
Heures réellement effectuées par semaine
Horas efectivamente trabajadas por semana

Date / Date / Fecha	311-312 Food / Aliments / Alimentos	313 Beverages / Boissons / Bebidas	314 Tobacco / Tabac / Tabaco	321 Textiles	322 Clothing [1] / Habillement [1] / Vestido [1]	323 Leather, leather products / Cuir, articles en cuir / Cuero, artículos de cuero	324 Footwear / Chaussures / Calzado	331 Wood / Bois / Madera	332 Furniture / Ameublement / Mobiliario	341 Paper, paper products / Papier, articles en papier / Papel, artículos de papel
1971	41.7	45.4	45.1	45.0	43.8	45.2	.	42.1	44.6	47.3
1972	45.4	46.4	47.1	46.3	43.7	41.4	.	41.8	44.6	45.7
1973	43.9	45.4	48.5	44.3	44.7	44.7	.	43.5	42.3	44.9
1974	42.1	44.6	45.9	42.7	42.5	46.3	.	42.6	41.7	40.8
1975	41.6	43.5	45.2	40.2	44.6	43.1	.	40.2	40.9	46.1
1976	41.0	43.1	48.1	38.0	37.9	44.1	41.2	41.1	41.7	44.8
1977	41.1	43.5	46.7	37.1	40.4	41.8	40.5	41.4	43.3	44.3
1978	40.5	41.9	49.1	38.6	37.5	40.2	37.9	39.0	40.5	43.6

[1] Prior to 1976: incl. footwear. [1] *Avant 1976 : y compris les chaussures.* [1] Antes de 1976: incl. el calzado.

13 Hours of work in manufacturing
Durée du travail dans les industries manufacturières
Horas de trabajo en las industrias manufactureras

B · By industry
Par industrie
Por industria

Portugal (2)

Hours actually worked per week
Heures réellement effectuées par semaine
Horas efectivamente trabajadas por semana

Date / Date / Fecha	342 Printing, publishing / Imprimerie, édition / Imprentas, editoriales	351 Industrial chemicals / Chimie industrielle / Química industrial	352 Other chemical products / Autres produits chimiques / Otros productos químicos	353 Petroleum refineries / Raffineries de pétrole / Refinerías de petróleo	354 × Briquettes and packaged fuel / Briquettes et agglomérés / Briquetas y combustible aglomerado	355 Rubber products / Produits en caoutchouc / Productos de caucho	356 Plastic products / Articles en matière plastique / Productos plásticos	361 Pottery, china, earthenware / Grès, porcelaines, faïences / Barro, loza, porcelana	362 Glass and glass products / Verre / Vidrio
1971	46.2	45.4	42.4	43.6	49.2	44.6	45.2	44.8	41.2
1972	46.0	45.1	39.8	45.4	48.5	44.5	47.7	42.4	47.2
1973	48.0	40.6	45.8	43.8	42.0	45.7	47.7	46.5	44.0
1974	45.5	47.7	42.5	41.1	48.1	43.9	43.5	47.3	46.2
1975	44.3	44.5	39.9	37.6	43.3	51.2	39.3	48.6	43.3
1976	42.5	40.8	40.0	37.3	38.5	37.3	40.3	44.7	43.5
1977	41.0	40.3	41.7	36.3	52.9	37.1	37.8	41.9	39.9
1978	41.5	40.2	38.8	40.2	43.3	38.3	37.0	43.0	42.6

Date / Date / Fecha	369 Other non-metallic mineral products / Autres produits minéraux non métalliques / Otros productos minerales no metálicos	371 Iron and steel / Sidérurgie / Hierro y acero	372 Non-ferrous metal / Métaux non ferreux / Metales no ferrosos	381 Metal products / Produits métalliques / Productos metálicos	382 Machinery (non-electrical) / Machines (non électriques) / Maquinaria (no eléctrica)	383 Electrical machinery and apparatus / Machines et appareils électriques / Maquinaria y aparatos eléctricos	384 Transport equipment / Matériel de transport / Material de transporte	385 Scientific, measuring, optical, etc., equipment / Matériel scientifique, de précision, d'optique, etc. / Equipo científico, de medida, de óptica, etc.	390 Other manufacturing industries / Autres industries manufacturières / Otras industrias manufactureras
1971	43.5	43.4	46.3	45.3	44.3	36.9	40.9	36.4	43.6
1972	44.9	46.8	44.9	45.8	46.5	38.6	43.8	44.7	42.9
1973	44.7	47.6	43.7	43.6	53.2	40.6	48.8	35.9	44.8
1974	43.3	43.9	43.7	43.5	43.4	37.5	44.2	42.6	42.6
1975	42.9	41.4	43.6	42.0	42.7	38.7	41.6	44.3	39.6
1976	42.6	41.1	42.5	38.2	42.3	39.3	39.0	38.1	41.3
1977	42.0	41.3	42.8	40.3	42.0	39.4	35.9	40.1	41.6
1978	41.4	36.3	42.3	39.2	41.9	36.7	35.8	39.8	41.6

Note for 371/372 spanning header: Basic metal industries / Industrie métallurgique de base / Industrias metalúrgicas básicas

13 Hours of work in manufacturing
Durée du travail dans les industries manufacturières
Horas de trabajo en las industrias manufactureras

B By industry
Par industrie
Por industria

Suisse

Hours paid for per week [1]
Heures rémunérées par semaine [1]
Horas pagadas por semana [1]

Date / Date / Fecha	311-312 Food / Aliments / Alimentos	313 Beverages / Boissons / Bebidas	314 Tobacco / Tabac / Tabaco	321 Textiles	322; 324 Clothing, footwear / Habillement, chaussures / Vestido, calzado	323 Leather, leather products / Cuir, articles en cuir / Cuero, artículos de cuero	33 Wood, furniture / Bois, ameublement / Madera, mobiliario	341 Paper, paper products / Papier, articles en papier / Papel, artículos de papel
1973	44.8	45.4	44.0	44.6	44.7	44.6	46.5	44.8
1974	44.7	45.4	43.9	44.5	44.6	44.7	46.3	44.6
1975	44.7	45.2	43.6	44.0	44.2	44.4	45.9	44.4
1976	44.5	45.0	43.1	44.3	44.5	44.3	45.7	44.6
1977	44.3	45.1	43.1	44.4	44.4	44.4	45.7	44.5
1978	44.3	45.1	43.0	44.2	44.3	44.2	45.8	43.7
1979	44.0	44.8	43.0	44.2	44.1	44.2	45.7	43.5

Date / Date / Fecha	342 Printing, publishing / Imprimerie, édition / Imprentas, editoriales	351-352 Chemicals / Industrie chimique / Productos químicos	355-356 Rubber and plastic products / Produits en caoutchouc et en plastique / Productos de caucho y de plástico	36 Non-metallic mineral products / Produits minéraux non métalliques / Productos minerales no metálicos	37 Basic metal industry / Industrie métallurgique de base / Industrias metalúrgicas basicas	382-383 Machinery / Machines / Maquinaria	385 × Watchmaking / Horlogerie / Relojería
1973	43.2	43.9	44.6	46.0	45.5	44.9	43.8
1974	43.4	43.7	44.6	45.8	45.5	44.8	43.7
1975	43.2	43.6	44.1	45.1	44.9	44.5	43.2
1976	43.1	43.5	44.2	44.9	44.8	44.5	43.4
1977	42.9	43.6	44.1	44.7	45.0	44.6	43.5
1978	42.4	43.5	44.1	44.7	45.0	44.6	43.1
1979	41.6	43.3	44.0	44.7	44.6	44.2	42.9

[1] Accident insurance statistics. Excl. overtime.

[1] *Statistiques d'assurance-accidents. Non compris les heures supplémentaires.*

[1] Estadísticas del seguro de accidentes. Excl. las horas extraordinarias.

HOURS

13 Hours of work in manufacturing
Durée du travail dans les industries manufacturières
Horas de trabajo en las industrias manufactureras

B By industry
Par industrie
Por industria

Sweden (1)

Hours actually worked per month
Heures réellement effectuées par mois
Horas efectivamente trabajadas por mes

Date / Date / Fecha	311-312 Food / Aliments / Alimentos	313 Beverages / Boissons / Bebidas	314 Tobacco / Tabac / Tabaco	321 Textiles	322 Clothing / Habillement / Vestido	323 Leather, leather products / Cuir, articles en cuir / Cuero, artículos de cuero	324 Footwear / Chaussures / Calzado	331 Wood / Bois / Madera	332 Furniture / Ameublement / Mobiliario
1970	150	158	142	149	139	144	145	153	149
1971	148	159	132	145	140	144	138	151	146
1972	143	157	137	144	138	141	140	147	143
1973	138	155	126	138	134	136	135	146	142
1974	139	152	128	128	136	131	134	142	139
1975	136	152	126	136	133	130	129	139	136
1976	131	146	129	135	130	129	127	139	137
1977	133	152	123	130	131	128	128	139	135

Date / Date / Fecha	341 Paper, paper products / Papier, articles en papier / Papel, artículos de papel	342 Printing, publishing / Imprimerie, édition / Imprentas, editoriales	351 Industrial chemicals / Chimie industrielle / Química industrial	352 Other chemical products / Autres produits chimiques / Otros productos químicos	353 Petroleum refineries / Raffineries de pétrole / Refinerías de petróleo	354 Products of petroleum and coal / Dérivés du pétrole et du charbon / Derivados del petróleo y del carbón	355 Rubber products / Produits en caoutchouc / Productos de caucho	356 Plastic products / Articles en matière plastique / Productos plásticos	361 Pottery, china, earthenware / Grès, porcelaines, faïences / Barro, loza, porcelana
1970	154	152	155	147	167	155	147	147	145
1971	153	150	153	143	162	153	145	147	148
1972	145	145	145	138	144	148	138	138	132
1973	144	143	145	131	147	141	138	136	124
1974	142	144	142	129	127	143	136	134	124
1975	137	140	136	131	118	134	133	131	122
1976	132	139	131	128	140	143	131	130	119
1977	129	139	130	129	136	138	132	130	120

13 Hours of work in manufacturing
Durée du travail dans les industries manufacturières
Horas de trabajo en las industrias manufactureras

B By industry
Par industrie
Por industria

Sweden (2)

Hours actually worked per month
Heures réellement effectuées par mois
Horas efectivamente trabajadas por mes

Date / Date / Fecha	362 Glass, and glass products / Verre / Vidrio	369 Other non-metallic mineral products / Autres produits minéraux non métalliques / Otros productos minerales no metálicos	371 Iron and steel / Sidérurgie / Hierro y acero	372 Non-ferrous metal / Métaux non ferreux / Metales no ferrosos	381 Metal products / Produits métalliques / Productos metálicos	382 Machinery (non-electrical) / Machines (non électriques) / Maquinaria (no eléctrica)	383 Electrical machinery and apparatus / Machines et appareils électriques / Maquinaria y aparatos eléctricos	384 Transport equipment / Matériel de transport / Material de transporte	385 Scientific, measuring, optical, etc., equipment / Matériel scientifique, de précision, d'optique, etc. / Equipo científico, de medida, de óptica, etc.	390 Other manufacturing industries / Autres industries manufacturières / Otras industrias manufactureras
1970	149	151	157	152	151	152	146	152	145	144
1971	147	149	153	151	148	148	143	147	147	141
1972	142	144	146	145	144	145	140	142	143	137
1973	138	145	144	141	140	140	136	140	136	132
1974	135	142	142	141	139	139	133	138	138	133
1975	131	140	139	135	137	137	130	134	134	134
1976	129	137	134	135	134	133	130	134	131	128
1977	128	136	131	132	133	133	124	129	130	130

Note: Columns 371 and 372 fall under the heading *Basic metal industries / Industrie métallurgique de base / Industrias metalúrgicas básicas*.

HOURS

13 Hours of work in manufacturing
Durée du travail dans les industries manufacturières
Horas de trabajo en las industrias manufactureras

B By industry
Par industrie
Por industria

United Kingdom (1)

Hours actually worked per week [1]
Heures réellement effectuées par semaine [1]
Horas efectivamente trabajadas por semana [1]

Date [2] / Fecha [2]	31 Food, beverages, tobacco / Aliments, boissons, tabac / Alimentos, bebidas, tabaco	321 Textiles	322 Clothing / Habillement / Vestido	323 Leather, leather products / Cuir, articles en cuir / Cuero, artículos de cuero	324 Footwear / Chaussures / Calzado	33 Wood, furniture / Bois, ameublement / Madera, mobiliario	34 Paper, printing, publishing / Papier, imprimerie, édition / Papel, imprentas, editoriales	351-352 Chemicals / Industrie chimique / Productos químicos
Adult males — *Hommes adultes* — Hombres adultos								
1970	46.8	44.7	41.9	44.8	40.7	45.6	45.3	44.9
1971	46.4	44.1	41.6	44.5	40.6	44.7	44.4	44.0
1972	46.4	44.7	42.1	44.1	40.5	45.0	44.7	44.2
1973	47.1	44.9	42.4	44.3	41.5	45.1	45.1	44.6
1974	46.6	44.0	42.2	43.9	39.4	43.8	43.9	43.7
1975	46.2	42.6	41.6	43.7	38.9	43.1	42.4	42.4
1976	45.9	43.6	41.3	43.1	40.3	42.8	43.6	43.9
1977	46.4	43.4	41.9	43.4	40.5	43.0	44.5	44.0
1978	46.2	43.7	41.7	42.9	40.7	43.0	44.6	44.4
1979	46.3	43.2	41.5	42.8	40.3	43.2	43.8	44.2
Adult females — *Femmes adultes* — Mujeres adultas								
1970	38.5	37.3	37.3	37.1	36.9	37.4	38.9	38.7
1971	38.2	37.3	36.8	37.0	36.9	37.7	38.7	38.4
1972	38.2	37.6	36.8	37.3	36.6	38.1	38.9	38.7
1973	38.6	37.3	36.4	36.7	36.6	37.5	38.6	38.5
1974	38.0	37.2	36.2	36.0	35.3	37.7	38.7	38.3
1975	37.7	36.1	35.6	36.2	35.2	37.0	37.9	37.8
1976	37.9	36.7	36.0	36.2	35.7	37.3	38.4	38.3
1977	38.1	36.4	36.1	36.1	36.3	37.2	38.5	38.1
1978	37.9	36.6	36.0	36.5	36.2	37.5	38.1	38.2
1979	38.1	36.3	36.0	36.6	36.3	36.7	38.3	38.5

[1] Full-time wage earners. [2] Oct. of each year.　　[1] *Ouvriers à temps complet.* [2] *Oct. de chaque année.*　　[1] Obreros a tiempo completo. [2] Oct. de cada año.

402

13 Hours of work in manufacturing
Durée du travail dans les industries manufacturières
Horas de trabajo en las industrias manufactureras

B By industry
Par industrie
Por industria

United Kingdom (2)

Hours actually worked per week [1]
Heures réellement effectuées par semaine [1]
Horas efectivamente trabajadas por semana [1]

Date [2] Date [2] Fecha [2]	353-354 Refineries and products of petroleum and coal Raffineries et dérivés du pétrole et du charbon Refinerías y derivados del petróleo y del carbón	355 Rubber products Produits en caoutchouc Productos de caucho	356 Plastic products Articles en matière plastique Productos plásticos	361 Pottery, china, earthenware Grès, porcelaines, faïences Barro, loza, porcelana	362 Glass Verre Vidrio	369 Other non-metallic mineral products Autres produits minéraux non métalliques Otros productos minerales no metálicos	371 Iron and steel basic industries Sidérurgie Industrias básicas de hierro y acero
	Adult males (cont.) — Hommes adultes (suite) — Hombres adultos (cont.)						
1970	44.0	44.7	45.9	45.0	45.7	47.6	45.3
1971	43.6	42.7	44.9	43.8	44.3	50.4	43.2
1972	42.9	43.2	45.3	44.1	45.2	47.4	44.7
1973	42.3	43.9	46.0	44.7	44.8	48.3	45.2
1974	43.8	43.0	44.6	44.5	43.8	47.2	45.0
1975	42.6	41.7	43.1	42.6	42.9	45.5	41.7
1976	42.9	42.2	44.6	44.0	43.9	46.1	43.9
1977	43.0	42.6	44.4	44.7	43.7	46.7	43.9
1978	43.0	42.2	44.6	44.7	42.8	46.6	43.8
1979	44.4	42.6	44.0	43.8	43.0	46.0	42.9
	Adult females (cont.) — Femmes adultes (suite) — Mujeres adultas (cont.)						
1970	39.2	38.3	38.1	35.8	38.8	38.1	37.3
1971	39.3	37.9	37.5	35.9	37.9	36.5	37.5
1972	38.6	38.0	38.0	36.0	39.2	36.3	38.4
1973	38.6	37.4	38.0	35.5	37.7	37.7	37.3
1974	38.8	38.1	37.3	35.6	37.5	36.7	37.1
1975	38.6	38.1	37.4	35.3	37.7	35.1	36.7
1976	36.5	38.3	38.2	36.1	37.9	36.6	37.8
1977	37.7	38.1	37.9	36.3	37.7	37.3	37.8
1978	38.7	37.6	38.1	36.5	37.4	36.7	38.1
1979	38.7	38.3	37.8	36.4	37.8	37.2	38.1

[1] Full-time wage earners. [2] Oct. of each year.   [1] Ouvriers à temps complet. [2] Oct. de chaque année.   [1] Obreros a tiempo completo. [2] Oct. de cada año.

13 Hours of work in manufacturing
Durée du travail dans les industries manufacturières
Horas de trabajo en las industrias manufactureras

B By industry
Par industrie
Por industria

United Kingdom (3)

Hours actually worked per week [1]
Heures réellement effectuées par semaine [1]
Horas efectivamente trabajadas por semana [1]

	372	381	382	383	384	385	390
Date [2] Date [2] Fecha [2]	Non-ferrous metal basic industries *Métaux non ferreux (industrie de base)* Industrias básicas de metales no ferrosos	Metal products *Produits métalliques* Productos metálicos	Machinery (non-electrical) *Machines (non électriques)* Maquinaria (no eléctrica)	Electrical machinery and apparatus *Machines et appareils électriques* Maquinaria y aparatos eléctricos	Transport equipment *Matériel de transport* Material de transporte	Scientific, measuring, optical, etc., equipment *Matériel scientifique, de précision, d'optique, etc.* Equipo científico, de medida, de óptica, etc.	Other manufacturing industries *Autres industries manufacturières* Otras industrias manufactureras
Adult males *(concl.)* — *Hommes adultes* (fin) — Hombres adultos *(fin)*							
1970	44.2	45.2	44.9	44.4	43.1	44.1	46.7
1971	43.4	43.2	43.0	43.4	41.8	42.8	46.0
1972	44.4	43.9	43.5	43.4	42.6	43.4	45.1
1973	44.6	44.7	44.6	44.0	43.2	43.9	45.1
1974	44.3	43.7	44.2	43.4	42.5	43.7	44.6
1975	42.6	42.1	42.6	42.2	41.9	42.0	43.0
1976	44.4	43.2	42.9	42.3	42.8	42.7	43.3
1977	43.6	43.1	43.3	42.6	42.5	43.0	43.4
1978	43.2	43.1	43.0	42.9	41.9	42.5	43.4
1979	43.7	42.7	42.5	42.3	41.9	42.3	44.0
Adult females *(concl.)* — *Femmes adultes* (fin) — Mujeres adultas *(fin)*							
1970	37.5	37.4	38.1	37.7	37.9	38.2	37.4
1971	37.0	37.1	37.9	37.7	37.7	38.2	37.5
1972	38.2	37.7	38.4	37.8	38.2	38.2	37.7
1973	37.9	37.3	38.1	37.4	37.9	38.2	37.5
1974	37.9	37.1	38.0	37.2	37.8	37.9	37.3
1975	36.6	36.8	36.5	37.1	37.5	37.4	36.8
1976	37.7	37.5	38.0	37.6	37.7	37.6	36.3
1977	36.6	37.0	37.8	37.8	38.0	37.7	36.9
1978	37.4	37.2	37.9	37.9	37.4	38.3	36.0
1979	37.9	37.2	37.6	37.6	37.7	38.7	36.8

[1] Full-time wage earners. [2] Oct. of each year.   [1] *Ouvriers à temps complet.* [2] *Oct. de chaque année.*   [1] Obreros a tiempo completo. [2] Oct. de cada año.

13

**Hours of work in manufacturing
Durée du travail dans les industries manufacturières
Horas de trabajo en las industrias manufactureras**

B

**By industry
Par industrie
Por industria**

Yugoslavia (1) [1]

Hours paid for per month
Heures rémunérées par mois
Horas pagadas por mes

	311-312	313	314	321	322	323	324	331	332
Date / Date / Fecha	Food / Aliments / Alimentos	Beverages / Boissons / Bebidas	Tobacco / Tabac / Tabaco	Textiles	Clothing / Habillement / Vestido	Leather, leather products / Cuir, articles en cuir / Cuero, artículos de cuero	Footwear / Chaussures / Calzado	Wood / Bois / Madera	Furniture / Ameublement / Mobiliario
1970	184	181	177	176	179	186	180	185	183
1971	183	181	177	176	179	183	178	180	177
1972	181	182	177	175	178	180	174	179	176
1973	181	182	177	175	178	180	174	179	176
1974	181	182	177	175	178	180	174	179	176
1975	181	182	180	179	180	181	178	180	176
1976	181	182	180	179	180	181	178	180	176

	341	342	351; 356	352	353	354	355	361	362
Date / Date / Fecha	Paper, paper products / Papier, articles en papier / Papel, artículos de papel	Printing, publishing / Imprimerie, édition / Imprentas, editoriales	Industrial chemicals [2] / Chimie industrielle [2] / Química industrial [2]	Other chemical products / Autres produits chimiques / Otros productos químicos	Petroleum refineries / Raffineries de pétrole / Refinerías de petróleo	Products of petroleum and coal / Dérivés du pétrole et du charbon / Derivados del petróleo y del carbón	Rubber products / Produits en caoutchouc / Productos de caucho	Pottery, china, earthenware / Grès, porcelaines, faïences / Barro, loza, porcelana	Glass, and glass products / Verre / Vidrio
1970	187	182	187	181	183	178	180	181	182
1971	184	182	186	180	183	178	178	180	181
1972	182	182	184	178	182	177	175	180	181
1973	182	182	184	178	182	177	175	180	181
1974	182	182	184	178	182	177	175	180	181
1975	183	184	184	180	183	179	179	181	181
1976	183	184	184	180	183	179	179	181	181

[1] Socialised sector; incl. salaried employees. [2] Incl. plastic products.

[1] *Secteur socialisé; y compris les employés.* [2] *Y compris les articles en matière plastique.*

[1] Sector socializado; incl. los empleados. [2] Incl. productos plásticos.

13

Hours of work in manufacturing
Durée du travail dans les industries manufacturières
Horas de trabajo en las industrias manufactureras

B

By industry
Par industrie
Por industria

Yugoslavia (2) [1]

Hours paid for per month
Heures rémunérées par mois
Horas pagadas por mes

Date *Date* Fecha	369 Other non-metallic mineral products *Autres produits minéraux non métalliques* Otros productos minerales no metálicos	371 Basic metal industries [2] *Industrie métallurgique de base* [2] Industrias metalúrgicas básicas [2] Iron and steel *Sidérurgie* Hierro y acero	372 Non-ferrous metal *Métaux non ferreux* Metales no ferrosos	381 Metal products *Produits métalliques* Productos metálicos	382 Machinery (non-electrical) *Machines (non électriques)* Maquinaria (no eléctrica)	383 Electrical machinery and apparatus *Machines et appareils électriques* Maquinaria y aparatos eléctricos	384 Transport equipment *Matériel de transport* Material de transporte	385 Scientific, measuring, optical, etc., equipment *Matériel scientifique, de précision, d'optique, etc.* Equipo científico, de medida, de óptica, etc.	390 Other manufacturing industries *Autres industries manufacturières* Otras industrias manufactureras
1970	185	188	181	187	188	174	183	182	181
1971	186	186	180	185	186	176	182	180	180
1972	184	184	178	182	183	180	180	177	176
1973	184	184	178	182	183	180	180	177	176
1974	184	184	178	182	183	180	180	177	176
1975	184	184	180	184	183	181	180	180	179
1976	184	184	180	184	183	181	180	180	179

[1] Socialized sector; incl. salaried employees. [2] Incl. ores extraction.

[1] *Secteur socialisé ; y compris les employés.* [2] *Y compris l'extraction des minerais.*

[1] Sector socializado; incl. los empleados. [2] Incl. la extracción de minerales.

13 Hours of work in manufacturing
Durée du travail dans les industries manufacturières
Horas de trabajo en las industrias manufactureras

B By industry
Par industrie
Por industria

OCEANIA — OCÉANIE — OCEANIA

Australia

Hours paid for per week [1]
Heures payées par semaine [1]
Horas pagadas por semana [1]

	31	321-322; 324	34	351-353	37	381-383	384	.
Date [2] Date [2] Fecha [2]	Food, beverages, tobacco *Aliments, boissons, tabac* Alimentos, bebidas, tabaco	Textiles, clothing, footwear *Textiles, habillement, chaussures* Textiles, vestido, calzado	Paper, printing, publishing *Papier, imprimerie, édition* Papel, imprentas, editoriales	Chemicals, petroleum refineries *Industrie chimique, raffineries de pétrole* Productos químicos, refinerías de petróleo	Basic metal industries *Industrie métallurgique de base* Industrias metalúrgicas básicas	Metal products, machinery, etc. *Produits métalliques, machines, etc.* Productos metálicos, maquinaria, etc.	Transport equipment *Matériel de transport* Material de transporte	Other manufacturing industries *Autres industries manufacturières* Otras industrias manufactureras
			Adult males — *Hommes adultes* — Hombres adultos					
1970	43.6	43.6	42.7	42.9	45.0	44.8	43.0	44.2
1971	43.6	43.7	42.3	42.5	43.8	44.1	42.6	43.8
1972 [3]	43.4	43.4	42.5	42.5	44.0	43.2	41.9	43.9
1973	43.6	44.1	42.8	42.1	44.8	43.9	42.7	44.2
1974	42.7	41.4	41.4	41.5	44.0	42.4	40.7	42.4
1975	42.2	42.4	41.2	40.8	40.9	41.0	39.9	41.9
1976	41.9	41.8	41.1	40.5	41.2	41.4	40.8	41.5
1977	42.2	42.3	41.5	40.8	41.3	40.9	40.6	41.4
1978	42.3	42.0	42.2	41.8	41.8	41.4	41.3	41.3
1979	41.5	42.5	42.2	40.9	42.8	42.5	41.1	43.0
			Adult females — *Femmes adultes* — Mujeres adultas					
1970	39.1	39.5	39.5	39.6	40.5	40.5	39.5	39.8
1971	39.3	39.2	39.6	39.2	39.7	40.2	39.9	39.8
1972 [3]	39.8	39.3	39.7	38.6	40.0	39.9	39.9	39.7
1973	40.4	39.3	40.2	39.5	40.1	40.0	40.3	39.9
1974	39.4	38.3	39.0	38.6	39.2	39.3	38.6	39.1
1975	38.7	38.6	38.8	38.5	38.9	39.0	38.9	38.7
1976	39.1	38.3	39.4	38.7	39.3	38.9	39.4	38.8
1977	39.2	38.7	39.4	39.0	39.2	38.8	39.0	39.4
1978	39.2	38.8	39.1	38.6	39.7	40.2	40.2	38.9
1979	39.5	39.6	39.6	39.1	39.5	39.9	39.1	39.2

[1] Incl. salaried employees. [2] Oct. of each year. [3] Scope of the series enlarged.

[1] *Y compris les employés.* [2] *Oct. de chaque année.* [3] *Portée de la série élargie.*

[1] Incl. los empleados. [2] Oct. de cada año. [3] El alcance de la serie es mayor.

13 Hours of work in manufacturing
Durée du travail dans les industries manufacturières
Horas de trabajo en las industrias manufactureras

B By industry
Par industrie
Por industria

New Zealand (1)

Hours paid for per week [1]
Heures payées par semaine [1]
Horas pagadas por semana [1]

Date [2] / Date [2] / Fecha [2]	311-312 Food / Aliments / Alimentos	313 Beverages / Boissons / Bebidas	314 Tobacco / Tabac / Tabaco	321 Textiles	322 Clothing / Habillement / Vestido	323 Leather, leather products / Cuir, articles en cuir / Cuero, artículos de cuero	324 Footwear / Chaussures / Calzado	331 Wood / Bois / Madera	332 Furniture / Ameublement / Mobiliario
1971	40.5	42.4	39.7	38.4	34.6	37.9	36.6	41.0	39.4
1972	40.2	42.4	41.8	38.6	34.3	37.3	37.1	40.9	39.5
1973	40.2	42.0	41.2	39.0	34.1	36.8	36.9	41.5	40.1
1974	40.0	41.0	39.8	38.3	33.8	36.7	36.4	41.5	39.3
1975	39.7	40.9	39.7	37.8	34.3	36.5	35.9	40.4	38.5
1976	39.7	40.3	39.0	38.5	34.6	36.7	35.9	40.8	38.3
1977	38.6	40.0	39.3	38.1	34.9	36.0	36.2	39.8	37.9
1978	37.5	39.8	38.7	38.2	34.7	37.1	37.1	39.4	37.8

Date [2] / Date [2] / Fecha [2]	341 Paper, paper products / Papier, articles en papier / Papel, artículos de papel	342 Printing, publishing / Imprimerie, édition / Imprentas, editoriales	351 Industrial chemicals / Chimie industrielle / Química industrial	352 Other chemical products / Autres produits chimiques / Otros productos químicos	353 Petroleum refineries / Raffineries de pétrole / Refinerías de petróleo	354 Products of petroleum and coal / Dérivés du pétrole et du charbon / Derivados del petróleo y del carbón	355 Rubber products / Produits en caoutchouc / Productos de caucho	356 Plastic products / Articles en matière plastique / Productos plásticos	361 Pottery, china, earthenware / Grès, porcelaines, faïences / Barro, loza, porcelana	362 Glass / Verre / Vidrio
1971	41.6	38.4	42.3	38.2	40.2	41.8	40.5	41.2	37.8	43.0
1972	41.5	38.3	43.1	38.1	40.3	42.7	40.7	41.2	41.3	43.5
1973	42.4	38.4	43.3	38.0	40.6	44.1	41.1	41.9	35.7	42.4
1974	47.7	38.3	43.2	38.0	40.3	44.1	39.8	41.0	33.5	39.2
1975	41.3	37.9	41.8	34.2	41.7	42.7	40.0	40.4	36.6	41.0
1976	41.4	37.6	42.9	37.8	41.4	41.7	39.3	39.8	39.9	42.7
1977	41.6	37.9	43.3	37.8	41.7	43.6	39.0	40.3	38.3	41.6
1978	39.6	37.3	43.3	38.5	43.1	42.7	39.5	39.7	39.1	40.4

[1] Incl. salaried employees and juveniles. [2] April and Oct. of each year.

[1] Y compris les employés et les jeunes gens. [2] Avril et oct. de chaque année.

[1] Incl. los empleados y los jóvenes. [2] Abril y oct. de cada año.

13 Hours of work in manufacturing
Durée du travail dans les industries manufacturières
Horas de trabajo en las industrias manufactureras

B By industry
Par industrie
Por industria

New Zealand (2)

Hours paid for per week [1]
Heures payées par semaine [1]
Horas pagadas por semana [1]

Date [2] / Date [2] / Fecha [2]	369 — Other non-metallic mineral products / Autres produits minéraux non métalliques / Otros productos minerales no metálicos	371 — Iron and steel / Sidérurgie / Hierro y acero	372 — Non-ferrous metal / Métaux non ferreux / Metales no ferrosos	381 — Metal products / Produits métalliques / Productos metálicos	382 — Machinery (non-electrical) / Machines (non électriques) / Maquinaria (no eléctrica)	383 — Electrical machinery and apparatus / Machines et appareils électriques / Maquinaria y aparatos eléctricos	384 — Transport equipment / Matériel de transport / Material de transporte	385 — Scientific, measuring, optical, etc., equipment / Matériel scientifique, de précision, d'optique, etc. / Equipo científico, de medida, de óptica, etc.	390 — Other manufacturing industries / Autres industries manufacturières / Otras industrias manufactureras
		Basic metal industries / Industrie métallurgique de base / Industrias metalúrgicas básicas							
1971	42.8	44.0	42.8	41.4	41.6	39.0	41.1	37.6	36.4
1972	43.3	43.5	43.3	41.5	41.6	39.2	40.8	37.6	36.9
1973	44.2	45.8	43.8	41.9	42.0	39.5	41.5	38.1	36.8
1974	42.9	45.1	43.2	41.4	41.6	38.8	42.3	37.7	36.0
1975	43.3	40.9	39.6	40.5	39.9	38.8	41.2	37.9	35.9
1976	42.1	41.7	41.8	39.8	40.0	38.3	39.2	37.8	36.0
1977	42.4	41.6	41.9	40.1	39.8	38.5	39.9	37.3	36.4
1978	41.6	41.4	41.7	39.7	39.5	38.6	40.1	37.2	36.8

[1] Incl. salaried employees and juveniles. [2] April and Oct. of each year.

[1] Y compris les employés et les jeunes gens. [2] Avril et oct. de chaque année.

[1] Incl. los empleados y los jóvenes. [2] Abril y oct. de cada año.

HOURS

13 Hours of work in manufacturing
Durée du travail dans les industries manufacturières
Horas de trabajo en las industrias manufactureras

B By industry
Par industrie
Por industria

URSS [1]

Hours actually worked per week
Heures réellement effectuées par semaine
Horas efectivamente trabajadas por semana

Date / Date / Fecha	31 Food, beverages, tobacco / Aliments, boissons, tabac / Alimentos, bebidas, tabaco		321 Textiles	322 Clothing / Habillement / Vestido	323-324 Leather, leather products, footwear / Cuir, articles en cuir, chaussures / Cuero, artículos de cuero, calzado	33 Wood, furniture / Bois, ameublement / Madera, mobiliario	
	Total	Tobacco / Tabac / Tabaco				Total	Furniture / Ameublement / Mobiliario
1970	41.0	40.8	40.4	40.4	40.4	40.8	40.5
1971	41.0	40 8	40.6	40.2	40.2	40.7	40.6
1972	41.0	40.8	40.7	40.3	40.5	40.8	40.7
1973	41.0	40.8	40.6	40.3	40.4	40.9	40.7
1974	41.0	41.0	40.7	40.3	40.3	40.7	40.8
1975	41.0	41.0	40.4	40.3	40.5	40.8	40.8

Date / Date / Fecha	341 Paper, paper products / Papier, articles en papier / Papel, artículos de papel	35 Chemicals / Industrie chimique / Productos químicos			371 Iron and steel basic industries / Sidérurgie / Industrias básicas de hierro y acero	38 Metal products, machinery, etc. / Produits métalliques, machines, etc. / Productos metálicos, maquinaria, etc.	
		Total	Petroleum refineries / Raffineries de pétrole / Refinerías de petróleo	Rubber products / Produits en caoutchouc / Productos de caucho		Total	Electrical machinery / Machines électriques / Maquinaria eléctrica
1970	41.0	39.9	40.3	40.4	40.6	40.5	40.1
1971	40.9	39.7	40.0	40.6	40.6	40.4	40.0
1972	41.0	39.8	40.2	40.5	40.9	40.6	40.0
1973	41.0	39.7	40.1	40.2	40.8	40.6	40.1
1974	41.0	39.8	40.3	40.3	40.9	40.6	40.4
1975	41.0	39.9	40.3	40.3	40.9	40.8	40.4

[1] Socialised sector. Incl. Byelorussian SSR, shown separately in this table.

[1] Secteur socialisé. Y compris la RSS de Biélorussie, figurant séparément dans ce tableau.

[1] Sector socializado. Incl. la RSS de Bielorrusia, que figura separadamente en este cuadro.

13 Hours of work in manufacturing
Durée du travail dans les industries manufacturières
Horas de trabajo en las industrias manufactureras

B By industry
Par industrie
Por industria

RSS de Biélorussie [1]

Hours actually worked per week
Heures réellement effectuées par semaine
Horas efectivamente trabajadas por semana

Date / Date / Fecha	31 — Food. beverages, tobacco / Aliments, boissons, tabac / Alimentos, bebidas, tabaco		321 Textiles	322 Clothing / Habillement / Vestido	323-324 Leather and fur products footwear / Articles en cuir et en fourrure, chaussure / Productos de cuero y piel, calzado
	Total	Tobacco / Tabac / Tabaco			
1970	39.4	39.9	39.3	39.7	39.6
1971	39.3	40.2	39.2	39.8	39.7
1972	41.0	40.2	40.3	40.2	40.6
1973	40.9	...	40.1	40.0	39.4
1974	40.9	...	40.3	40.1	40.4
1975	41.0	...	40.1	40.0	40.2

Date / Date / Fecha	33 — Wood, furniture / Bois, ameublement / Madera, mobiliario		341 Paper, paper products / Papier, articles en papier / Papel, artículos de papel	38 — Metal products, machinery, etc. / Produits métalliques, machines, etc. / Productos metálicos, maquinaria, etc.	
	Total	Furniture / Ameublement / Mobiliario		Total	Electrical machinery / Machines électriques / Maquinaria eléctrica
1970	39.2	39.7	39.2	39.1	39.0
1971	39.4	39.5	39.2	39.1	39.1
1972	40.8	39.1	40.9	40.2	39.3
1973	40.7	...	41.0	40.3	...
1974	40.7	...	40.9	40.4	...
1975	40.7	...	41.0	40.4	...

[1] Socialised sector.   [1] *Secteur socialisé.*   [1] Sector socializado.

14 Hours of work in mining and quarrying
Durée du travail dans les industries extractives
Horas de trabajo en las minas y canteras

Hours of work per week — Durée du travail par semaine — Horas de trabajo por semana

Date / Date / Fecha	AFRICA — AFRIQUE — AFRICA			AMERICA — AMÉRIQUE — AMÉRICA				
				Canada			Colombia [4]	
	Algérie [1]	Egypt [2]	Sierra Leone [3]	Coal mining / Mines de charbon / Minas de carbón	Metal mining / Mines métallifères / Minas metalíferas	All mining and quarrying / Ensemble des industries extractives / Todas las minas y canteras	Petroleum / Pétrole / Petróleo	Ecuador
	(a)	(b)	(a)	(b)	(b)	(b)	(a) [5]	(a)
1970	41.4	49	47.5	42.1	40.3	41.0	210	57
1971	42.6	52	47.1	41.1	39.3	40.4	224	55
1972	40.5	54	49.8	40.4	39.0	40.3	239	53
1973	40.5	53	55.8	40.7	39.6	40.9	241	51
1974	43.0	55	48.3	39.8	39.4	40.4	263	47
1975	41.5	64 *	41.6	38.2	39.4	40.0	238	49
1976	44.0	60 *	41.6	39.5	39.6	40.3	246 [6]	53
1977	44.0	...	41.6	40.6	39.8	40.6	237	47
1978	...	...	40.5	40.1	39.4	40.5	...	...
1979	...	...	40.5	40.4	40.4	41.1	...	...

Date / Date / Fecha	AMERICA — AMÉRIQUE — AMÉRICA						ASIA — ASIE — ASIA	
					Venezuela		Burma [7]	
	Guyana	México [2]	Puerto Rico	United States	Petroleum extraction / Extraction du pétrole / Extracción de petróleo	Iron ore mining / Extraction du minerai de fer / Extracción de mineral de hierro	Metal mining / Mines métallifères / Minas metalíferas	Cyprus [10]
	(b)	(a)	(b)	(b)	(a)	(a)	(a) [8]	(b) [2]
1970	43.1	48.0	37.5	42.7	36.1	40.2	7.9	42
1971	45.7	48.0	39.8	42.4	36.4	39.9	8.0	44
1972	40.1	44.0	39.3	42.6	37.3	36.9	7.7 [9]	46
1973	40.1	44.0	39.1	42.4	36.8	37.3	7.6	45
1974	43.6	...	37.6	41.9	38.3	40.2	7.9	44 [11]
1975	43.3	...	38.3	41.9	38.7	38.5	7.9	43
1976	48.0	...	39.1	42.4	36.6	37.3	7.9	43
1977	43.4	...	37.5	43.4	37.2	38.0	8.0	44
1978	46.6	...	38.5	43.3	45.7	47.4	8.0	45
1979	...	...	...	43.0	45.5	49.2	...	46

EXPLANATORY NOTES: See p. 335. — NOTES EXPLICATIVES: Voir p. 337. — NOTAS EXPLICATIVAS: Véase pág. 339.

(a) : Hours actually worked — *Heures réellement effectuées* — Horas efectivamente trabajadas.
(b) : Hours paid for — *Heures rémunérées* — Horas pagadas.

[1] April of each year. [2] Oct. of each year. [3] Adults. May and Nov. of each year. [4] Males. [5] Per month. [6] Jan.-Nov. [7] Workers engaged for less than 30 days (excl. casual workers). [8] Per day. Beginning 1973: March and Sep. of each year. [9] April and Sep. [10] Adults. [11] Beginning July 1974: due to a change in the geographical scope of the series, data are not comparable with those for the preceding period.

[1] *Avril de chaque année.* [2] *Oct. de chaque année.* [3] *Adultes. Mai et nov. de chaque année.* [4] *Hommes.* [5] *Par mois.* [6] *Janv.-nov.* [7] *Travailleurs engagés pour moins de 30 jours (non compris les travailleurs occasionnels).* [8] *Par jour. A partir de 1973 : mars et sept. de chaque année.* [9] *Avril et sept.* [10] *Adultes.* [11] *A partir de juillet 1974 : en raison d'un changement de la portée géographique de la série, les données ne sont pas comparables avec celles de la période précédente.*

[1] Abril de cada año. [2] Oct. de cada año. [3] Adultos. Mayo y nov. de cada año. [4] Hombres. [5] Por mes. [6] Enero-nov. [7] Trabajadores ocupados durante menos de 30 días (excl. los trabajadores ocasionales). [8] Por día. A partir de 1973: marzo y sept. de cada año. [9] Abril y sept. [10] Adultos. [11] A partir de julio de 1974: en razón de un cambio del alcance geográfico de la serie, los datos no son comparables a los del período precedente.

14 Hours of work in mining and quarrying
Durée du travail dans les industries extractives
Horas de trabajo en las minas y canteras

Hours of work per week   Durée du travail par semaine   Horas de trabajo por semana

Date / Date / Fecha	India Coal mining / Mines de charbon / Minas de carbón (a)	India Metal mining / Mines métallifères / Minas metalíferas (a)	Japan (a)[1]	Korea, Rep. of (a)[1]	Philippines[3] (a)[4]	Singapore[3,5] (a)	Sri Lanka[6] Plumbago mining / Mines de plombagine / Minas de plombagina (b)[7]	Rép. arabe syrienne[8] Phosphate mining / Mines de phosphate / Minas de fosfato (a)[9]
	ASIA — ASIE — ASIA							
1970	47.74	47.3	44.6	45.1	.	47.3	8.8	35.2
1971	47.87	47.2	43.9	45.4		48.2	9.1	47.8
1972	47.92	47.5	43.8	42.7	50.6	50.4	8.4	49.0
1973	47.83	47.4	44.3[2]	43.7	45.8	51.3	8.7	51.0
1974	47.85	47.7	44.1	43.0	49.8	47.8	8.2	42.1
1975	47.81	47.4	42.7	43.1	50.2	51.1	7.6	39.9
1976	47.50	46.9	42.8[2]	41.5	46.9	50.0	8.0	38.9
1977	47.82	47.1 *	43.0	41.7	...	51.3	9.0	43.7
1978	...	...	43.4	41.1	...	52.5	8.2	...
1979	...	...	43.6[2]	40.2	...	49.8	8.5	...

Date / Date / Fecha	Belgique[10,11] (a)	Czechoslovakia[13] (a)	Denmark (a)	España (a)[1]	Finland (a)	France (a)	Germany, Fed. Rep. of[15] All mining / Ensemble des mines / Todas las minas (b)	Germany, Fed. Rep. of[15] Coal mining / Mines de charbon / Minas de carbón (b)
	EUROPE — EUROPE — EUROPA							
1970	42.5	43.3	41.1	37.3	30.5	43.4	42.7	42.0
1971	42.9	43.5	40.7	36.9	39.6	42.6	41.7	41.0
1972	40.5[12]	43.0	41.5	38.2	40.8	42.1[14]	40.6	39.9
1973	39.1	43.0	39.6	34.9	40.8	41.6	41.8[2]	41.3[2]
1974	38.9	43.0	39.8	36.4	40.4	41.2	41.7	41.3
1975	36.8	43.0	37.0	37.6	39.6	40.9	41.5	41.3
1976	37.6	43.3	37.2	34.4	39.3	40.8[2]	40.6	40.3
1977	36.7	43.5	36.6	...	39.4	40.4	40.8	40.4
1978	36.3	43.8	36.3	...	39.6	40.1	40.8	40.4
1979	37.3	43.9	38.3	...	41.0	40.1	41.3	40.9

EXPLANATORY NOTES: See p. 335.   NOTES EXPLICATIVES: Voir p. 337.   NOTAS EXPLICATIVAS: Véase pág. 339.

(a) : Hours actually worked — Heures réellement effectuées — Horas efectivamente trabajadas.
(b) : Hours paid for — Heures rémunérées — Horas pagadas.

14 Hours of work in mining and quarrying
Durée du travail dans les industries extractives
Horas de trabajo en las minas y canteras

Hours of work per week   Durée du travail par semaine   Horas de trabajo por semana

Date / Date / Fecha	Hongrie [1]	Ireland [3]	Italie	Luxembourg [8] Mining and quarrying / Industries extractives / Minas y canteras	Luxembourg [8] Iron ore mining / Extraction du minerai de fer / Extracción de mineral de hierro	Malta Stone quarrying and clay pits / Carrières de pierre et argile / Canteras de piedra y arcilla	Netherlands [8]	Norway
	(a) [2]	(a) [4,5]	(a) [6]	(a) [4]		(b) [10,11]	(b) [12]	(a) [13]
1970	165.7	47.4	7.87	43.1	41.1	43.8	.	34.5
1971	164.4	48.4	7.92	41.9	39.8	44.3	.	34.2
1972	160.9	48.3	7.92	42.2 [9]	40.4 [9]	44.7	.	33.8
1973	160.2	48.3	7.93	43.1	40.8	44.2	.	33.5
1974	159.8	44.9	7.98	44.6	42.6	40.8	45.1	33.5
1975	160.0	43.9	7.97	40.0	39.5	43.2	43.9	32.5
1976	161.8	45.2	7.88	40.3	39.1	43.0	43.2	31.4
1977	161.8	45.7	7.92	39.7	37.6	42.0	43.1	30.7
1978	160.9	45.3	8.03 [7]	40.8	40.2	42.0	43.0	30.3
1979	161.0	...	...	41.7	41.3	...	...	29.6

Date / Date / Fecha	Portugal	Sweden	United Kingdom [8] Miscellaneous minerals, excl. coal / Minerais divers, non compris le charbon / Minerales varios, excl. el carbón	Yugoslavia [1]	Australia [8]	New Zealand [16] Coal mining / Mines de charbon / Minas de carbón	New Zealand [16] Other mining and quarrying / Autres industries extractives / Otras minas y canteras	URSS [1]
	(a)	(a) [2]	(a) [13,14]	(b) [2,11]	(b) [11,13]	(b) [11,12]		(a)
1970	.	143	51.8	187	44.8	34.8	47.4	38.6
1971	37.7	146	49.3	185	44.0	35.5	45.1	38.8
1972	40.3	140	49.0	184	43.6 [15]	36.9	45.5	38.5
1973	40.6	138	48.8	185	43.9	37.5	47.4	38.5
1974	40.2	135	48.0	184	42.4	38.0	47.0	38.7
1975	38.6	128	47.2	185	41.1	37.8	46.3	38.7
1976	36.3	127	46.4	185	41.5	39.5	45.0	...
1977	34.2	132	47.2	185	41.2	38.8	45.5	...
1978	37.2	...	47.2	185	40.0	39.5	45.5	...
1979	...	...	46.8	185 *	41.7	...	44.9	...

EXPLANATORY NOTES: See p. 335.   NOTES EXPLICATIVES: Voir p. 337.   NOTAS EXPLICATIVAS: Véase pág. 339.

(a) : Hours actually worked — *Heures réellement effectuées* — Horas efectivamente trabajadas.
(b) : Hours paid for — *Heures rémunérées* — Horas pagadas.

[1] Socialised sector. [2] Per month. [3] Sep. of each year. [4] Males. [5] Workers on adult rates of pay. [6] Per day. [7] Scope of series revised. [8] Oct. of each year. [9] New industrial classification. [10] Adults. [11] Incl. salaried employees. [12] Incl. juveniles. [13] Adult males. [14] Full-time wage earners. [15] Scope of series enlarged. [16] April and Oct. of each year.

[1] *Secteur socialisé.* [2] *Par mois.* [3] *Sept. de chaque année.* [4] *Hommes.* [5] *Travailleurs rémunérés sur la base de taux de salaire pour adultes.* [6] *Par jour.* [7] *Portée de la série révisée.* [8] *Oct. de chaque année.* [9] *Nouvelle classification industrielle.* [10] *Adultes.* [11] *Y compris les employés.* [12] *Y compris les jeunes gens.* [13] *Hommes adultes.* [14] *Ouvriers à temps complet.* [15] *Portée de la série élargie.* [16] *Avril et oct. de chaque année.*

[1] Sector socializado. [2] Por mes. [3] Sept. de cada año. [4] Hombres. [5] Trabajadores pagados sobre la base de tarifas de salarios para adultos. [6] Por día. [7] El alcance de la serie es revisado. [8] Oct. de cada año. [9] Nueva clasificación industrial. [10] Adultos. [11] Incl. los empleados. [12] Incl. los jóvenes. [13] Hombres adultos. [14] Obreros a tiempo completo. [15] El alcance de la serie es mayor. [16] Abril y oct. de cada año.

15 Hours of work in construction
Durée du travail dans la construction
Horas de trabajo en la construcción

Hours of work per week | Durée du travail par semaine | Horas de trabajo por semana

Date / Date / Fecha	AFRICA — AFRIQUE — AFRICA						AMERICA AMÉRIQUE AMÉRICA
	Algerie [1]	Egypt [2]	Mali	Sierra Leone [4]	South Africa, Rep. of		Canada
					Total	[5]	
	(a)	(b)	(a) [3]	(a)	(a)		(b)
1970	45.0	57	.	55.3	45.4	47.6	39.2
1971	46.2	59	42.0	47.1	45.0	46.1	39.2
1972	47.2	56	42.9	50.3	44.8	45.5	40.1
1973	45.8	56	44.4	42.2	45.6	46.7	39.5
1974	44.5	57	45.3	48.6	46.1	47.3	39.1
1975	44.5	58 *	...	46.8	45.9	47.2	39.0
1976	45.2	53 *	...	45.6	45.2	45.5	38.9
1977	45.0	...	...	45.5	46.0	47.3	38.7
1978	...	...	...	45.5	46.2	46.8	39.0
1979	...	...	...	45.5	45.0	46.3	39.4

Date / Date / Fecha	AMERICA — AMÉRIQUE — AMÉRICA					ASIA — ASIE — ASIA	
	El Salvador (San Salvador) [6]	Guyana	México [2]	Perú [7] (Lima-Callao)	United States	Cyprus [2,8]	Israel
	(a)	(b)	(a)	(a)	(b)	(b)	(a) [10]
1970	44.7	49.4	49.7	.	37.3	44	42.2
1971	44.8	52.6	45.5	.	37.2	44	41.9
1972	44.5	50.5	46.2	. .	36.5	43	42.9
1973	43.2	45.7	47.1	.	36.8	44	39.2
1974	42.9	46.3	47.4	46.0	36.6	42 [9]	39.2
1975	...	47.7	47.3	49.1	36.4	41	39.9
1976	...	46.4	47.8	50.0	36.8	42	39.4
1977	...	47.5	44.9	49.0	36.5	43	38.6
1978	...	43.1	...	49.0	36.8	43	37.8
1979	...	...	...	48.4	36.9	41	39.9

EXPLANATORY NOTES: See p. 335.   NOTES EXPLICATIVES: Voir p. 337.   NOTAS EXPLICATIVAS: Véase pág. 339.

(a) : Hours actually worked — *Heures réellement effectuées* — Horas efectivamente trabajadas.
(b) : Hours paid for — *Heures rémunérées* — Horas pagadas.

[1] April of each year. [2] Oct. of each year. [3] Dec. of each year. [4] Adults. May and Nov. of each year. [5] White manual workers. [6] Metropolitan area. Males. [7] June of each year. [8] Adults. [9] Beginning July 1974: due to a change in the geographical scope of the series, data are not comparable with those for the preceding period. [10] Incl. salaried employees.

[1] *Avril de chaque année.* [2] *Oct. de chaque année.* [3] *Déc. de chaque année.* [4] *Adultes. Mai et nov. de chaque année.* [5] *Travailleurs manuels (population blanche).* [6] *Région métropolitaine. Hommes.* [7] *Juin de chaque année.* [8] *Adultes.* [9] *A partir de juillet 1974 : en raison d'un changement de la portée géographique de la série, les données ne sont pas comparables avec celles de la période précédente.* [10] *Y compris les employés.*

[1] Abril de cada año. [2] Oct. de cada año. [3] Dic. de cada año. [4] Adultos. Mayo y nov. de cada año. [5] Trabajadores manuales (población blanca). [6] Area metropolitana. Hombres. [7] Junio de cada año. [8] Adultos. [9] A partir de julio de 1974: en razón de un cambio del alcance geográfico de la serie, los datos no son comparables a los del período precedente. [10] Incl. los empleados.

15 Hours of work in construction
Durée du travail dans la construction
Horas de trabajo en la construcción

Hours of work per week — Durée du travail par semaine — Horas de trabajo por semana

Date / Date / Fecha	ASIA — ASIE — ASIA				
	Japan	Korea, Rep. of	Philippines [3]	Singapore [3, 5]	Sri Lanka [6]
	(a) [1]	(a) [1]	(a) [4]	(a)	(b) [7, 8]
1970	46.0	47.3	.	48.5	8.0
1971	46.1	51.2	.	50.6	8.0
1972	46.1	48.8	46.1	49.9	8.0
1973	45.5 [2]	47.8	43.6	53.2	7.5
1974	44.3	48.1	44.8	48.7	8.5
1975	43.0	48.9	47.3	49.4	8.6
1976	42.9 [2]	46.9	45.8	48.8	8.6
1977	43.1	49.0	...	48.5	9.0
1978	43.6	48.5	...	48.9	8.3
1979	43.6 [2]	49.4	...	48.5	7.9

Date / Date / Fecha	EUROPE — EUROPE — EUROPA					
	Austria	Belgique [9]	España	France	Germany, Fed. Rep. of [6]	Gibraltar [13]
	(b)	(a)	(a) [1]	(a)	(b) [12]	(b)
1970	38.6	41.3	45.7	49.0	44.7	53.8
1971	38.1	41.3	45.0	48.6	44.1	54.4
1972	37.9	41.3 [10]	45.9	48.1 [11]	43.6	52.0
1973	37.4	39.8	46.1	47.9	43.1 [2]	54.4
1974	37.1	37.3	46.0	47.2	42.0	52.2
1975	37.8	38.3	44.9	45.8	41.4	49.7
1976	39.1	37.2	43.3	44.6 [2]	41.6	49.0
1977	39.5	37.1	...	43.3	41.1	51.8
1978	39.5	37.1	...	42.5	41.6	52.8
1979	...	37.3	...	42.2	42.4	46.0

EXPLANATORY NOTES: See p. 335.   NOTES EXPLICATIVES: Voir p. 337.   NOTAS EXPLICATIVAS: Véase pág. 339.

(a) : Hours actually worked — *Heures réellement effectuées* — Horas efectivamente trabajadas.
(b) : Hours paid for — *Heures rémunérées* — Horas pagadas.

[1] Incl. salaried employees. [2] Sampling design revised. [3] Aug. of each year. [4] Civilian labour force employed. [5] Prior to 1975: July. [6] Building. [7] March and Sep. of each year. [8] Per day. [9] Oct. of each year. [10] New industrial classification. [11] Beginning Dec. 1972: revised series. [12] Males. [13] Oct. of each year, except for 1970-72: April and Oct. and 1974-76: April.

[1] *Y compris les employés.* [2] *Plan d'échantillonnage révisé.* [3] *Août de chaque année.* [4] *Main-d'œuvre civile occupée.* [5] *Avant 1975 : juillet.* [6] *Bâtiment.* [7] *Mars et sept. de chaque année.* [8] *Par jour.* [9] *Oct. de chaque année.* [10] *Nouvelle classification industrielle.* [11] *A partir de déc. 1972 : série révisée.* [12] *Hommes.* [13] *Oct. de chaque année, sauf pour 1970-1972 : avril et oct., et 1974-1976 : avril.*

[1] Incl. los empleados. [2] Diseño de la muestra revisado. [3] Agosto de cada año. [4] Fuerza trabajadora civil ocupada. [5] Antes de 1975: julio. [6] Edificación. [7] Marzo y sept. de cada año. [8] Por día. [9] Oct. de cada año. [10] Nueva clasificación industrial. [11] A partir de dic. de 1972: serie revisada. [12] Hombres. [13] Oct. de cada año, salvo 1970-1972: abril y oct., y 1974-1976: abril.

15 Hours of work in construction
Durée du travail dans la construction
Horas de trabajo en la construcción

Hours of work per week　　　　　　Durée du travail par semaine　　　　　　Horas de trabajo por semana

Date / Date / Fecha	EUROPE — EUROPE — EUROPA						
	Hongrie [1]	Ireland [3]		Italie	Luxembourg [8]	Malta	Netherlands [8]
	(a) [2]	(a) [4]	(a) [5]	(a) [6]	(a) [9]	(b) [11, 12]	(b) [13]
1970	170.3	46.6	46.6	7.68	50.4	45.9	.
1971	168.9	47.6	47.7	7.78	50.6	45.8	.
1972	166.0	46.7	46.3	7.83	50.7 [10]	44.5	.
1973	164.7	47.1	46.5	7.87	51.4	44.2	.
1974	164.4	45.7	45.5	7.88	48.4	44.8	42.2
1975	164.5	44.4	44.3	7.90	41.6	44.0	41.0
1976	168.8	45.1	45.4	7.88	41.5	43.0	40.9
1977	168.1	45.4	45.2	7.85	42.0	40.0	40.8
1978	167.8	46.7	46.7	7.82 [7]	41.8	40.0	40.7
1979	166.0	46.5	47.1	...	42.0	...	...

Date / Date / Fecha	EUROPE — EUROPE — EUROPA				OCEANIA — OCÉANIE — OCEANÍA		URSS [1]
	Portugal	Suisse	United Kingdom [8]	Yugoslavia [1]	Australia [8]	New Zealand [19]	
	(a)	(b) [14]	(a) [16, 17]	(b) [2, 11]	(b) [11, 16]	(b) [11, 13]	(a)
1970	.	46.3	47.5	187	44.8	44.1	40.9
1971	34.9	46.4	47.2	182	45.6	43.6	40.8
1972	36.7	46.7	47.0	184	42.9 [18]	43.4	40.9
1973	38.3	47.3 [15]	47.2	184	42.4	44.3	40.9
1974	42.3	47.0	46.8	184	41.9	44.1	40.7
1975	37.8	46.1	45.2	184	40.8	43.8	41.0
1976	36.2	45.8	44.3	187	40.6	43.0	40.7
1977	35.4	45.9	44.7	187	41.8	43.2	40.6
1978	37.3	45.8	44.9	187	41.3	43.2	41.0
1979	...	45.8	44.9	187 *	41.3	...	41.0

EXPLANATORY NOTES: See p. 335.　　　　　NOTES EXPLICATIVES: Voir p. 337.　　　　　NOTAS EXPLICATIVAS: Véase pág. 339.

(a): Hours actually worked — *Heures réellement effectuées* — Horas efectivamente trabajadas.
(b): Hours paid for — *Heures rémunérées* — Horas pagadas.

[1] Socialised sector. [2] Per month. [3] Sep. of each year. Private sector only. [4] Skilled workers. [5] Semi-skilled and unskilled workers. [6] Per day. [7] Scope of series revised. [8] Oct. of each year. [9] Males. [10] New industrial classification. [11] Incl. salaried employees. [12] Adults. [13] Incl. juveniles. [14] Beginning 1973: accident insurance statistics; excl. overtime. [15] Series replacing former series. [16] Adult males. [17] Full-time wage earners. [18] Scope of series enlarged. [19] April and Oct. of each year.

[1] *Secteur socialisé.* [2] *Par mois.* [3] *Sept. de chaque année. Secteur privé seulement.* [4] *Ouvriers qualifiés.* [5] *Ouvriers semi-qualifiés et non qualifiés.* [6] *Par jour.* [7] *Portée de la série révisée.* [8] *Oct. de chaque année.* [9] *Hommes.* [10] *Nouvelle classification industrielle.* [11] *Y compris les employés.* [12] *Adultes.* [13] *Y compris les jeunes gens.* [14] *A partir de 1973: statistiques d'assurance-accidents: non compris les heures supplémentaires.* [15] *Série remplaçant la précédente.* [16] *Hommes adultes.* [17] *Ouvriers à temps complet.* [18] *Portée de la série élargie.* [19] *Avril et oct. de chaque année.*

[1] Sector socializado. [2] Por mes. [3] Sept. de cada año. Sector privado solamente. [4] Obreros calificados. [5] Obreros semicalificados y no calificados. [6] Por día. [7] El alcance de la serie es revisado. [8] Oct. de cada año. [9] Hombres. [10] Nueva clasificación industrial. [11] Incl. los empleados. [12] Adultos. [13] Incl. los jóvenes. [14] A partir de 1973: estadísticas del seguro de accidentes; excl. las horas extraordinarias. [15] Serie que substituye a la anterior. [16] Hombres adultos. [17] Obreros a tiempo completo. [18] El alcance de la serie es mayor. [19] Abril y oct. de cada año.

16 Hours of work in transport, storage and communication (Excl. sea transport)
Durée du travail dans les transports, entrepôts et communications (Non compris les transports par mer)
Horas de trabajo en los transportes, almacenaje y comunicaciones (Excl. el transporte marítimo)

Hours of work per week — Durée du travail par semaine — Horas de trabajo por semana

Date / Date / Fecha	AFRICA — AFRIQUE — AFRICA			AMERICA — AMÉRIQUE — AMÉRICA			
	Algérie [1]	Egypt [2]	Sierra Leone [3]	Canada — Local transport — Transports locaux — Transportes locales	Guyana — Transport and communication — Transports et communications — Transportes y comunicaciones	Perú [4],[5] (Lima-Callao) — Transport — Transports — Transportes	United States — Principal railways — Grandes lignes de chemin de fer — Líneas principales de ferrocarriles
	(a)	(b)	(a)	(b)	(b)	(a)	(b)
1970	44.8	59	46.6	42.0	43.4	.	44.2
1971	45.0	58	58.6	41.9	42.4	.	43.2
1972	47.5	56	49.5	42.1	44.8	.	43.9
1973	43.8	70	55.9	41.9	42.2	.	44.5
1974	43.8	66	45.3	41.6	48.9	47.0	44.0
1975	43.8	65 *	44.2	40.5	45.6	56.4	43.3
1976	44.0	61 *	43.8	40.7	46.0	66.4	43.7
1977	44.0	...	43.2	40.9	46.8	55.8	43.5
1978	...	...	43.0	40.9	54.2	54.9	43.7
1979	...	...	44.0	40.3	...	53.3	43.9

Date / Date / Fecha	AMERICA AMÉRIQUE AMÉRICA	ASIA — ASIE — ASIA					
	United States [6] — Local railways — Chemins de fer et autobus locaux — Ferrocarriles y autobuses locales	Burma [7] — Transport — Transports — Transportes	Cyprus [2]	Israel	Japan	Korea, Rep. of	Malaysia [14] — Peninsular Malaysia — Road haulage — Camionnage — Camionaje
	(b)	(a) [8]	(b) [10]	(a) [12]	(a) [12]	(a) [12]	(a) [12],[15]
1970	42.1	7.6	50	42.8	44.2	53.7	.
1971	41.8	7.7	50	42.7	43.7	55.5	215
1972	41.5	7.9 [9]	47	42.8	43.6	50.8	213
1973	41.4	7.9	51	39.0	43.9 [13]	51.3	213
1974	40.7	7.9	48 [11]	39.8	42.7	51.9	213
1975	40.1	7.9	48	41.0	42.2	51.0	225
1976	41.2	8.0	49	40.9	42.1 [13]	50.5	225
1977	41.5	8.0	52	39.5	41.9	49.5	196
1978	41.3	7.5	53	38.7	41.7	49.4	212
1979	41.1	...	50	40.5	42.2 [13]	49.5	...

EXPLANATORY NOTES: See p. 335.   NOTES EXPLICATIVES: Voir p. 337.   NOTAS EXPLICATIVAS: Véase pág. 339.

(a): Hours actually worked — *Heures réellement effectuées* — Horas efectivamente trabajadas.
(b): Hours paid for — *Heures rémunérées* — Horas pagadas.

[1] April of each year. [2] Oct. of each year. [3] Incl. sea transport. Adults. May and Nov. of each year. [4] June of each year. [5] Incl. sea transport, except for 1974. [6] Excl. government-operated transport. [7] Incl. sea transport. Workers engaged for less than 30 days (excl. casual workers). [8] Per day. Beginning 1973: March and Sep. of each year. [9] April and Sep. [10] Adults. [11] Beginning July 1974: due to a change in the geographical scope of the series, data are not comparable with those for the preceding period. [12] Incl. salaried employees. [13] Sampling design revised. [14] July of each year. [15] Per month.

[1] *Avril de chaque année.* [2] *Oct. de chaque année.* [3] *Y compris les transports par mer. Adultes. Mai et nov. de chaque année.* [4] *Juin de chaque année.* [5] *Y compris les transports par mer, sauf pour 1974.* [6] *Non compris les transports gérés par le gouvernement.* [7] *Y compris les transports par mer. Travailleurs engagés pour moins de 30 jours (non compris les travailleurs occasionnels).* [8] *Par jour. A partir de 1973: mars et sept. de chaque année.* [9] *Avril et sept.* [10] *Adultes.* [11] *A partir de juillet 1974: en raison d'un changement de la portée géographique de la série, les données ne sont pas comparables avec celles de la période précédente.* [12] *Y compris les employés.* [13] *Plan d'échantillonnage révisé.* [14] *Juillet de chaque année.* [15] *Par mois.*

[1] Abril de cada año. [2] Oct. de cada año. [3] Incl. el transporte marítimo. Adultos. Mayo y nov. de cada año. [4] Junio de cada año. [5] Incl. el transporte marítimo, salvo para 1974. [6] Excl. los transportes administrados por el Gobierno. [7] Incl. el transporte marítimo. Trabajadores ocupados durante menos de 30 días (excl. los trabajadores ocasionales). [8] Por día. A partir de 1973: marzo y sept. de cada año. [9] Abril y sept. [10] Adultos. [11] A partir de julio de 1974: en razón de un cambio del alcance geográfico de la serie, los datos no son comparables a los del período precedente. [12] Incl. los empleados. [13] Diseño de la muestra revisado. [14] Julio de cada año. [15] Por mes.

16 Hours of work in transport, storage and communication (Excl. sea transport)
Durée du travail dans les transports, entrepôts et communications (Non compris les transports par mer)
Horas de trabajo en los transportes, almacenaje y comunicaciones (Excl. el transporte marítimo)

Hours of work per week — Durée du travail par semaine — Horas de trabajo por semana

Date / Date / Fecha	ASIA — ASIE — ASIA		Sri Lanka [5] Transport / Transports / Transportes	EUROPE — EUROPE — EUROPA		Malta [11,12] Transport / Transports / Transportes	Storage and warehousing / Entrepôts et magasins / Depósito y almacenamiento
	Philippines [1]	Singapore [1,3]		France [7]	Gibraltar [10]		
	(a) [2]	(a) [4]	(b) [6]	(a)	(b)	(b)	(b)
1970	.	47.7	9.0	45.8	48.6	45.5	44.8
1971	.	48.4	9.5	45.2 [8]	49.2	46.0	44.5
1972	50.4	43.2	9.2	44.1	48.8	47.8	42.5
1973	49.9	45.8	9.0	43.5	50.0	44.0	42.3
1974	49.8	47.5	8.9	42.8	46.8	46.5	41.5
1975	51.7	49.1	9.8	42.2	45.6	40.8	40.0
1976	50.7	47.5	8.5	42.6 [9]	45.1	41.0	40.0
1977	...	49.0	9.0	42.2	45.3	41.0	...
1978	...	50.2	9.8	42.1	...	...	...
1979	...	50.1	7.7	41.9	48.1	...	...

Date / Date / Fecha	EUROPE — EUROPE — EUROPA				OCEANIA — OCÉANIE — OCEANÍA	
	Netherlands [13] Transport / Transports / Transportes	Suisse	United Kingdom [13,16]	Yugoslavia [4,18]	Australia [4,13]	New Zealand [22]
	(b) [14]	(b) [15]	(a) [17]	(b) [11,19]	(b) [11,20]	(a) [11,14]
1970	.	.	49.2	189	46.1	41.5
1971	.	.	48.0	187	44.9	41.0
1972	.	.	48.5	188	42.5 [21]	40.9
1973	.	46.6	49.6	188	43.3	41.7
1974	45.3	46.3	49.5	188	42.1	42.1
1975	44.0	46.2	47.3	188	40.8	41.3
1976	43.9	46.0	47.5	189	41.4	41.0
1977	43.4	45.8	48.0	189	41.1	41.3
1978	43.6	45.7	48.8	189	40.8	40.9
1979	...	45.6	48.6	189 *	41.1	...

EXPLANATORY NOTES: See p. 335.   NOTES EXPLICATIVES: Voir p. 337.   NOTAS EXPLICATIVAS: Véase pág. 339.

(a) : Hours actually worked — *Heures réellement effectuées* — Horas efectivamente trabajadas.
(b) : Hours paid for — *Heures rémunérées* — Horas pagadas.

[1] August of each year. [2] Civilian labour force employed. [3] Prior to 1975: July. [4] Incl. sea transport. [5] March and Sep. of each year. [6] Per day. [7] Excl. communication. [8] Beginning 1972: revised series. [9] Sampling design revised. [10] April of each year, except for 1970-72: April and Oct.; 1973 and 1977: Oct. [11] Incl. salaried employees. [12] Adults. [13] Oct. of each year. [14] Incl. juveniles. [15] Accident insurance statistics; excl. overtime. [16] Excl. railways and London Transport. [17] Full-time adult males. [18] Socialised sector. [19] Per month. [20] Adult males. [21] Scope of series enlarged. Prior to 1972: excl. communication. [22] April and Oct. of each year.

[1] Août de chaque année. [2] Main-d'œuvre civile occupée. [3] Avant 1975: juillet. [4] Y compris les transports par mer. [5] Mars et sept. de chaque année. [6] Par jour. [7] Non compris les communications. [8] A partir de déc. 1972: série révisée. [9] Plan d'échantillonnage révisé. [10] Avril de chaque année, sauf pour 1970-1972: avril et oct.; 1973 et 1977: oct. [11] Y compris les employés. [12] Adultes. [13] Oct. de chaque année. [14] Y compris les jeunes gens. [15] Statistiques d'assurance-accidents: non compris les heures supplémentaires. [16] Non compris les chemins de fer et les services de transports londoniens. [17] Hommes adultes à temps complet. [18] Secteur socialisé. [19] Par mois. [20] Hommes adultes. [21] Portée de la série élargie. Avant 1972: non compris les communications. [22] Avril et oct. de chaque année.

[1] Agosto de cada año. [2] Fuerza trabajadora civil ocupada. [3] Antes de 1975: julio. [4] Incl. el transporte marítimo. [5] Marzo y sept. de cada año. [6] Por día. [7] Excl. las comunicaciones. [8] A partir de dic. de 1972: serie revisada. [9] Diseño de la muestra revisado. [10] Abril de cada año, salvo 1970-1972: abril y oct.; 1973 y 1977: oct. [11] Incl. los empleados. [12] Adultos. [13] Oct. de cada año. [14] Incl. los jóvenes. [15] Estadísticas del seguro de accidentes; excl. las horas extraordinarias. [16] Excl. los ferrocarriles y los transportes londinenses. [17] Hombres adultos a tiempo completo. [18] Sector socializado. [19] Por mes. [20] Hombres adultos. [21] El alcance de la serie es mayor. Antes de 1972: excl. las comunicaciones. [22] Abril y oct. de cada año.

V CHAPTER
CHAPITRE
CAPITULO

Wages
Salaires
Salarios

Wages

Tables 17 to 22 generally present *average gross money wages* per wage earner (i.e. wages before deduction of income taxes and social security contributions payable by the worker). Where in some cases the series also cover salaried employees, this is indicated in a footnote.

The statistics shown are, in general, *average earnings*; only where such data are lacking are *wage rates* given. Occasionally wage indices are given in the absence of absolute wage data. Wages per hour and per week are shown for each country whenever available; in the absence of such data, wages per day or per month have been given, especially in table 22 on wages in agriculture. Data are shown, as far as possible, for both sexes combined and for each sex separately. Where not otherwise stated, the series relate to workers of both sexes, irrespective of age.

Statistics of average earnings are usually derived from payroll data supplied by a sample of establishments often furnishing at the same time data on hours of work and on employment.[1] Average earnings per hour (or day) are normally compiled by dividing the total wages paid in a given period by total man-hours (or man-days) actually worked or paid for in that period, and earnings per week (or month) by dividing the total wages paid in a given week (or month) by the average number of workers employed in the same period. The data usually cover cash payments received from employers, i.e. remuneration for normal working hours, overtime pay, incentive pay, earnings of piece workers; remuneration for time not worked (annual vacation, public holidays, sick leave and other paid leave); bonuses and gratuities, cost-of-living allowances and special premiums (such as end-of-year bonuses). They frequently also include the value of payments in kind, while family allowances are mostly excluded from statistics of earnings. In a few cases average earnings are compiled on the basis of

social insurance records. Social insurance statistics usually yield lower averages than payroll data because overtime pay, incentive pay and the like may be excluded as well as wages exceeding a certain upper limit. Moreover, the insurance scheme may be restricted to lower-paid workers only, or higher-paid workers may be under-represented in the compilation of average earnings.

Statistics of wage rates are in most cases based on collective agreements, arbitration awards or other wage-setting decisions, which generally specify minimum rates for particular occupations or groups of workers. In some countries rates actually paid correspond closely to these minima. In countries where the fixing of wage rates is widespread, series of average wage rates in particular industries or groups of industries are calculated, using as weights the numerical importance in a given year of the different occupations for which rates are available in the industries covered. Data on wage rates usually refer only to rates for adults working normal hours, and therefore payments for overtime premiums and other supplementary wage elements are not taken into account; cost-of-living allowances, however, are often included, and other allowances fixed in the wage-setting process, such as housing allowances, are sometimes included. Some countries obtain average *rates actually paid* (straight-time earnings) from establishment payrolls in a similar way as average earnings are obtained. Rates actually paid usually cover the remuneration on the basis of normal time worked, both for normal and overtime hours, but exclude incentive pay and other bonuses as well as the premium part of overtime pay. Rates actually paid are sometimes also gathered by labour inspectors.

In making comparisons between wage series account must be taken of differences in concepts, scope, methods of compilation and of presentation of the data.[2] Earnings data show fluctua-

---

[1] For a detailed discussion of wage statistical methods, see ILO: *Wages and Payrolls Statistics*, Studies and Reports, New Series, No. 16 (Geneva, 1949) and *International Recommendations on Labour Statistics* (Geneva, 1976).

[2] For the descriptions of the various national series, their scope, methods of compilation and definitions used, etc., see ILO: *Technical Guide 1980* (descriptions of general series published in the *Bulletin* and the *Year Book of Labour Statistics*), Vol. II. "Employment—Unemployment—Hours of Work—Wages" (Geneva, 1980).

tions which reflect the influence both of changes in wage rates and supplementary wage payments. Weekly, daily and monthly earnings are in addition much dependent on variations in average hours of work. Statistics of wage rates do not reflect the influence of changes in wage supplements nor the influence of variations in hours of work. The fluctuations of average earnings obtained from global payrolls are also influenced by changes in the employment structure, i.e. the relative importance of males, females, unskilled and skilled labour, etc., while average wage rates are normally compiled using the employment structure of a given year as weights. Average hourly earnings are generally higher than hourly rates because the former include overtime payments, premiums, bonuses and allowances which do not enter into statistics of wage rates. Average weekly or monthly earnings should also be higher than the corresponding rates, but may sometimes fall short of wage rates because of loss of working time through sickness, absenteeism or part-time work.

Time comparisons are less affected by differences in concepts, definitions and methods of compilation of the data than comparisons of wage levels at a given date.

The assessment of international differences in the *real wage income* of workers involves a conversion of the data into a common reference currency by means of particular conversion factors reflecting the relative purchasing power (with regard to consumer goods and services) of the currencies concerned. Satisfactory comparisons of this kind can only be made for countries with similar characteristics and are preferably based on special uniform inquiries which normally use the concept of net earnings and include family allowances. [1] Crude indicators of trends of real wages are usually obtained in an easier way by dividing average gross earnings (or indices of gross earnings) by an index of consumer prices.

Comparisons of *total labour cost* between different industries of one country or between different countries cannot be based on wage statistics alone. Although gross earnings obviously represent the most important component of labour cost, wage supplements such as family allowances, certain bonuses and gratuities or contributions paid by the employer to social security funds or in respect of welfare services furnished by the establishment to its workers, form an important element of total labour cost in certain industries and countries which are not usually included in statistics of earnings. Statistics of total labour cost are therefore mostly the subject of special studies. [2]

Table 17

Wages in non-agricultural sectors

Unless otherwise indicated in footnotes, the wage series shown in this table cover the following divisions of economic activity: Mining and quarrying; Manufacturing; Electricity, gas and water; Construction; Wholesale and retail trade, restaurants and hotels; Transports, storage and communication; Financing, insurance, real estate and business services; Community, social and personal services. In some cases, however, these divisions are only represented by certain of the groups composing them.

Table 18

Wages in manufacturing

Part A of table 18 shows wages in manufacturing industries as a whole; where in a few cases other industries are also included in the series, this is indicated in a footnote.

Part B of table 18 shows wages in specified manufacturing industries. The data are presented separately for each country.

So far as possible, the different manufacturing industries have been arranged according to the International Standard Industrial Classification

---

[1] See, e.g. Statistical Office of the European Communities: *Salaires CEE, 1964*, Statistiques sociales, 1966, No. 5 (in French only).

[2] See, e.g. ILO: *Labour Costs in European Industry*, Studies and Reports, New Series, No. 52 (Geneva, 1959).

of All Economic Activities (see Appendix) with the corresponding code number of the different industrial major groups.

Tables 19 to 21

Wages in mining and quarrying; construction; and transport, storage and communication

Tables 19 to 21 show statistics of wages in three major divisions of economic activity as follows: table 19, Mining and quarrying; table 20, Construction; and table 21, Transport, storage and communication (excl. sea transport).

Table 22

Wages in agriculture

The statistics of agricultural wages presented in table 22 refer in most cases to general farm labourers. A distinction is made between *permanent* workers, *seasonal* workers and *day* workers; in the last-mentioned group, *regular* day labourers and *casual* day labourers are distinguished.

The methods of payment and the types of labour contracts and arrangements in agriculture are often quite different from those in other activities. To indicate the nature of the wage statistics given in each column a special notation has been adopted: the sign I at the top of the column indicates that the statistics refer to total wages which are paid entirely in cash; the sign II standing alone indicates that the figures refer to the money part of the wages only, although the workers receive payments in kind in addition; where the sign *a* is added, it indicates that the value of meals furnished is included in the amounts of wages shown and, similarly, *b* indicates that the value of lodging furnished is included. Although the figures are identified in some cases as representing rates of pay or earnings, it should be noted that in most countries there is little or no difference between the nominal rates of remuneration and the actual earnings of agricultural workers.

International comparisons of wages are subject to greater reservations with respect to agriculture than for other activities. The nature of the work carried out by the different categories of farm workers and the length of the working day and week also show considerable variation from one country to another. Seasonal fluctuations in agricultural wages are more important in some countries than in others.

In general, series marked I, representing the complete wage of workers who are remunerated entirely in cash, are more comparable internationally than series marked either II + *a* + *b* or II alone. Comparisons between series marked II alone, in which the figures do not include the value of board and lodging provided by the employer, are subject to special reservations owing to differences in each case in the relative importance of these payments in kind.

A major drawback for international comparisons of series marked II + *a* + *b* lies in the lack of uniformity in the methods followed in the different countries for estimating the money value of the payments in kind included. Where the data relate to similar occupations and units of time (day, week or month), these series may nevertheless be considered to be roughly comparable with one another and with series marked I, which also refer to the complete wage of the workers covered.

Salaires

Les tableaux 17 à 22 indiquent généralement les *salaires nominaux bruts moyens* par ouvrier (autrement dit, les salaires avant déduction de l'impôt sur le revenu et des cotisations de sécurité sociale à la charge du travailleur). Quand les employés sont également compris dans une série, ce fait est indiqué en note de bas de page.

Les statistiques fournies sont en général celles des *gains moyens*; les *taux de salaire* ne sont donnés que lorsque les gains moyens ne sont pas disponibles. Exceptionnellement, ce sont les indices des salaires qui sont reproduits, à défaut de données absolues sur les salaires. Les salaires horaires et hebdomadaires ont été fournis pour chaque pays lorsqu'ils étaient disponibles; en l'absence de ces données, ce sont les salaires journaliers ou mensuels qui ont été indiqués, notamment au tableau 22, qui concerne les salaires payés dans l'agriculture. Les données sont présentées, dans la mesure du possible, pour l'ensemble des deux sexes et aussi pour chaque sexe séparément. Sauf indication contraire, les séries couvrent les travailleurs des deux sexes, sans considération d'âge.

Les *statistiques des gains moyens* sont généralement tirées des bordereaux de salaires remis par un échantillon d'établissements, qui fournissent fréquemment en même temps des données sur la durée du travail et sur l'emploi [1]. Les gains moyens horaires (ou journaliers) sont généralement obtenus en divisant le total des salaires payés au cours d'une période déterminée par le nombre total d'heures-homme (ou de journées-homme) réellement effectuées ou rémunérées pendant cette période, et les gains hebdomadaires (ou mensuels) en divisant le total des salaires payés au cours d'une semaine donnée (ou d'un mois donné) par le nombre moyen de travailleurs employés pendant la même période. Les données comprennent généralement les paiements en espèces reçus de l'employeur, c'est-à-dire la rémunération pour les heures normales de travail, le paiement des heures supplémentaires, les primes de stimulation, les gains des travailleurs aux pièces; la rémunération pour les heures de travail payées, mais non effectuées (congés annuels, jours fériés, congés de maladie et autres congés payés); les primes et gratifications, les allocations de cherté de vie et les versements spéciaux (par exemple, les gratifications de fin d'année). Elles englobent souvent la valeur des paiements en nature; par contre les allocations familiales sont généralement exclues des statistiques des gains. Dans quelques cas, les gains moyens sont calculés à partir de *registres d'assurances sociales*. Les données sur les gains tirées des statistiques d'assurances sociales fournissent généralement des moyennes inférieures à celles qui sont obtenues à partir des bordereaux de salaires, les heures supplémentaires, les primes de stimulation, etc., pouvant en être exclues, de même que les salaires qui dépassent un certain niveau. De plus, le régime d'assurance peut ne couvrir que les travailleurs à salaires modestes ou, si les travailleurs à salaires élevés sont inclus, ils peuvent ne pas être représentés entièrement pour le calcul des gains moyens.

Les *statistiques des taux de salaire* se fondent le plus souvent sur les conventions collectives, les décisions d'arbitrage ou les décisions d'autorités réglementant les salaires, qui spécifient généralement des taux minima pour des professions particulières ou des catégories de travailleurs déterminées. Dans quelques pays, les taux effectivement payés sont très proches de ces minima. Dans d'autres, où il est d'usage de fixer des taux de salaire, on calcule les séries des taux de salaire moyens dans des branches d'activité économique particulières ou dans des groupes de branches d'activité, en pondérant ces taux suivant l'importance numérique que revêtent, au cours d'une année donnée, les différentes professions pour lesquelles on connaît les taux appliqués dans les branches d'activité couvertes par ces statistiques. Les données relatives aux taux de salaire ne concernent généralement que les taux de rémunération des adultes travaillant pendant l'horaire normal. Par conséquent, il n'est pas tenu compte de la rémunéra-

---

[1] On trouvera une étude plus détaillée des méthodes statistiques d'enregistrement des salaires dans BIT: *Statistiques des bordereaux de salaires et des gains*, Etudes et documents, nouvelle série, n° 16 (Genève, 1949); voir également: *Recommandations internationales sur les statistiques du travail* (Genève, 1975).

tion des heures supplémentaires et des autres éléments qui s'ajoutent au salaire; cependant, les allocations de cherté de vie sont souvent comprises dans les calculs, de même que d'autres allocations déterminées par la procédure de fixation des salaires, par exemple l'indemnité de logement. Dans quelques pays, on obtient les *taux* moyens *effectivement payés* (rémunération au temps exclusivement) en utilisant les bordereaux de salaires des établissements, de la même façon que pour les gains moyens. En général, les taux effectivement payés comprennent la rémunération calculée sur la base de la durée normale du travail, aussi bien pour les heures supplémentaires que pour la durée normale du travail, mais ils ne tiennent pas compte des primes de stimulation et d'autres versements spéciaux, pas plus que de la part de la rémunération des heures supplémentaires correspondant aux primes. Parfois, ce sont les inspecteurs du travail qui prennent note des taux effectivement payés.

Lorsqu'on fait une comparaison entre des séries concernant les salaires, il y a lieu de tenir compte des différences que peuvent présenter les notions, la portée économique, les méthodes d'établissement des séries et la présentation des données[1]. Les données concernant les gains sont sujettes à des fluctuations qui traduisent des changements survenus aussi bien dans les taux de salaire que dans les paiements supplémentaires. En outre, les gains hebdomadaires, journaliers et mensuels dépendent très fortement des variations de la durée moyenne du travail. Par contre, les statistiques des taux de salaire ne subissent pas l'influence des changements affectant les suppléments de salaire, ni celle des variations de la durée du travail. Les fluctuations des gains moyens obtenus à partir de l'ensemble des bordereaux de salaires sont également influencées par les changements survenus dans la structure de l'emploi, c'est-à-dire par l'importance relative des travailleurs, des travailleuses, de la main-d'œuvre non qualifiée et de la main-d'œuvre qualifiée, etc., tandis que les taux de salaire moyens sont calculés le plus souvent en prenant la structure de l'emploi d'une année donnée comme coefficient de pondération. Les gains horaires moyens sont généralement plus élevés que les taux de salaire horaires, les premiers comprenant la rémunération des heures supplémentaires, les gratifications, les primes et les allocations, qui n'entrent pas dans les statistiques des taux de salaire. Les gains hebdomadaires ou mensuels moyens devraient aussi être plus élevés que les taux de salaire correspondants, mais il arrive qu'ils leur soient inférieurs en raison des heures de travail perdues du fait de la maladie, de l'absentéisme ou du travail à temps partiel.

Les comparaisons dans le temps se ressentent moins des différences de notions, de définitions et de méthodes de calcul que les comparaisons des niveaux de salaire à une date donnée.

Pour évaluer les différences internationales du *revenu réel provenant des salaires* il faut convertir les données en prenant une devise commune de référence, au moyen de facteurs de conversion particuliers traduisant le pouvoir d'achat relatif (en ce qui concerne les biens de consommation et les services) des devises entrant en considération. On ne peut faire des comparaisons de ce genre avec des résultats satisfaisants que pour des pays ayant des caractéristiques analogues; ces comparaisons se fonderont de préférence sur des enquêtes spéciales uniformes, utilisant habituellement la notion de gain net et englobant les allocations familiales[2]. On obtient généralement avec plus de facilité des indicateurs approximatifs des tendances des salaires réels en divisant les gains bruts moyens (ou les indices des gains bruts) par un indice des prix à la consommation.

Une comparaison du *coût total de la main-d'œuvre* entre différentes branches d'activité d'un même pays ou entre différents pays ne peut pas se fonder sur les seules statistiques des salaires. Bien que les gains bruts représentent

[1] Pour les descriptions des diverses séries nationales, de leur portée, des méthodes de calcul et des définitions utilisées, etc., voir BIT: *Guide technique 1980* (description des séries générales publiées dans le *Bulletin* et l'*Annuaire des statistiques du travail*), vol. II, « Emploi — Chômage — Durée du travail — Salaires » (Genève, 1980).

[2] Voir notamment Office statistique des Communautés européennes: *Salaires CEE, 1964*, Statistiques sociales, 1966, n° 5.

incontestablement l'élément le plus important du coût de la main-d'œuvre, les suppléments de rémunération tels que les allocations familiales, certaines primes et gratifications, les cotisations payées par l'employeur à des caisses de sécurité sociale ou les versements qu'il fait au titre de services sociaux fournis par l'établissement à son personnel, constituent un élément important du coût total de la main-d'œuvre dans certaines branches d'activité et dans certains pays; toutefois, ces prestations ne sont généralement pas comprises dans les statistiques des gains. C'est pourquoi les statistiques concernant le coût total de la main-d'œuvre font le plus souvent l'objet d'études spéciales [1].

Tableau 17

Salaires dans les secteurs non agricoles

Sauf indication contraire figurant en notes de bas de page, les séries présentées dans ce tableau couvrent les branches d'activité économique ci-après: industries extractives; industries manufacturières; électricité, gaz et eau; construction; commerce de gros et de détail, restaurants et hôtels; transports, entrepôts et communications; banque, assurances, affaires immobilières et services fournis aux entreprises; services fournis à la collectivité, services sociaux et services personnels. Dans quelques cas, toutefois, ces branches d'activité ne sont représentées que par une partie seulement des classes qui les composent.

Tableau 18

Salaires dans les industries manufacturières

La partie A du tableau 18 indique les salaires dans l'ensemble des industries manufacturières; dans les quelques cas où d'autres branches d'activité sont également comprises dans la série,

une indication est donnée à ce sujet en note de bas de page.

La partie B du tableau 18 concerne les salaires dans les industries manufacturières spécifiées. Les données sont présentées séparément pour chaque pays.

Dans toute la mesure possible, les différentes industries manufacturières ont été ordonnées conformément à la Classification internationale type, par industrie, de toutes les branches d'activité économique (voir annexe), avec indication du numéro de code correspondant aux différentes classes d'industries.

Tableaux 19 à 21

Salaires dans les industries extractives, dans la construction, ainsi que dans les transports, entrepôts et communications

Les tableaux 19 à 21 contiennent les statistiques des salaires dans trois branches d'activité économique principales, à savoir: tableau 19, industries extractives; tableau 20, construction; tableau 21, transports, entrepôts et communications (non compris les transports par mer).

Tableau 22

Salaires dans l'agriculture

Les statistiques des salaires dans l'agriculture présentées au tableau 22 se rapportent, dans la plupart des cas, aux travailleurs agricoles non spécialisés. Une distinction est faite entre les travailleurs *permanents*, les travailleurs *saisonniers* et les travailleurs *journaliers*; dans ce dernier groupe, on distingue les travailleurs journaliers *réguliers* et les travailleurs journaliers *occasionnels*.

Les modes de rémunération, les types de contrats de travail et les dispositions prises dans l'agriculture sont souvent très différents de ceux

---

[1] Voir notamment BIT: *Coût de la main-d'œuvre dans l'industrie européenne*, Etudes et documents, nouvelle série, n° 52 (Genève, 1959).

qui prévalent dans les autres branches d'activité. Pour indiquer le genre de statistiques des salaires présentées dans chaque colonne, on a adopté une notation spéciale: le symbole I placé en haut de la colonne indique que les statistiques se rapportent aux salaires totaux payés entièrement en espèces; le symbole II représenté seul indique que les chiffres se rapportent seulement à la partie du salaire payée en espèces, bien que les travailleurs reçoivent en outre des prestations en nature; l'adjonction du symbole a indique que la valeur des repas fournis est comprise dans le montant des salaires, tandis que le symbole b indique que le montant des salaires englobe la valeur du logement fourni. Bien qu'il soit précisé dans certains cas que les chiffres représentent des taux de salaire ou des gains, il y a lieu de relever que, dans la plupart des pays, on ne note que peu ou pas de différence entre les taux nominaux de rémunération et les gains effectifs des travailleurs agricoles.

Les comparaisons internationales des salaires sont sujettes à de plus grandes réserves pour l'agriculture que pour les autres branches d'activité. La nature du travail effectué par les différentes catégories de travailleurs agricoles et la durée de la journée de travail ou de la semaine de travail présentent également des différences considérables d'un pays à un autre. Les fluctuations saisonnières des salaires agricoles sont plus accusées dans certains pays que dans d'autres.

En général, les séries marquées I, qui représentent le salaire complet des travailleurs rémunérés entièrement en espèces, se prêtent mieux à une comparaison internationale que les séries marquées $II + a + b$ ou simplement II. Les comparaisons entre les séries marquées II, dans lesquelles les chiffres ne comprennent pas la valeur des repas et du logement fournis par l'employeur, doivent faire l'objet de réserves spéciales car l'importance relative de ces paiements en nature diffère dans chaque cas.

Une réserve importante concernant les comparaisons internationales des séries marquées $II + a + b$ réside dans le manque d'uniformité des méthodes suivies dans les différents pays pour estimer la valeur nominale des paiements en nature. Quand les données se rapportent aux mêmes professions et unités de temps (journée, semaine ou mois), ces séries peuvent néanmoins être considérées comme approximativement comparables entre elles ainsi qu'avec les séries marquées I, qui se rapportent également aux salaires complets des travailleurs couverts par ces séries.

Salarios

Los cuadros 17 a 22 presentan generalmente el *promedio de los salarios nominales brutos* por obrero (es decir, antes de la deducción de los impuestos a la renta y las cotizaciones del seguro social a cargo del trabajador). Cuando en ciertos casos los empleados han sido incluidos, así se indica en una nota de pie de página.

Las estadísticas presentadas se refieren generalmente a las *ganancias medias*; sólo cuando faltan datos de éstas se las reemplaza por estadísticas de *tarifas de salarios*. Cuando faltan cifras absolutas, se ofrecen índices de salarios. Los salarios por hora y por semana se presentan por países; a falta de tales datos, se dan los salarios por día o por mes, especialmente en el cuadro 22, relativo a los salarios en la agricultura. Los datos se refieren, en la medida de lo posible, a uno y otro sexo o bien a cada sexo por separado. Salvo indicación contraria, las series abarcan a los trabajadores de uno y otro sexo, sin distinción de edades.

Las *estadísticas de ganancias medias* se obtienen por lo general de los datos de las nóminas de salarios proporcionados por una muestra de establecimientos, los que suelen dar al mismo tiempo indicaciones concernientes a las horas de trabajo y al empleo [1]. Por regla general, las ganancias medias por hora (o por día) se obtienen dividiendo el total de los salarios pagados en un período dado por el número de horas-hombre (o días-hombre) efectivamente trabajadas o pagadas durante ese mismo período; las ganancias por semana (o por mes) se calculan dividiendo el total de los salarios pagados en una semana dada (o mes) por el promedio de trabajadores empleados durante el período. Generalmente, los datos comprenden los pagos en dinero recibidos de los empleadores, es decir, la remuneración por las horas normales de trabajo, pagos por horas extraordinarias, las primas de estímulo, las ganancias de los trabajadores a destajo; la remuneración por horas de trabajo pagadas pero no efectuadas (vacaciones anuales, días feriados, ausencias por motivo de enfermedad y otros permisos pagados); las primas y gratificaciones, las asignaciones por carestía de vida y primas especiales (tales como la bonificación de fin de año). Con frecuencia incluyen también el valor de los pagos en especie; las asignaciones familiares se excluyen en la mayoría de los casos de las estadísticas de ganancias. En ciertos casos, las ganancias medias se obtienen de los *registros del seguro social*. Las estadísticas del seguro social arrojan, generalmente, promedios más bajos que los que se obtienen de las planillas de pago, pues aquéllos pueden excluir los pagos por horas extraordinarias, las primas de estímulo, etc., y además pueden no comprender los salarios de un valor superior a cierto límite. Más aún: el sistema de seguro puede limitarse solamente a los trabajadores de salarios bajos, o, si incluye a los de salarios altos, éstos pueden estar representados de manera incompleta en la compilación de las ganancias medias.

Las *estadísticas de tarifas de salarios* se basan de ordinario en los contratos colectivos, en las decisiones arbitrales o en otros procedimientos de fijación de salarios, donde generalmente se especifican las tarifas mínimas en determinadas ocupaciones o para grupos particulares de trabajadores. En algunos países las tarifas realmente pagadas se aproximan mucho a esos mínimos. En países donde está muy generalizada la práctica de fijar las tarifas de salarios, se calculan las series de las tarifas medias de salarios en determinadas industrias o grupos de industrias utilizando como ponderaciones las cifras correspondientes a la importancia numérica en un año dado de las diferentes ocupaciones sobre las cuales se dispone de tarifas en las industrias comprendidas en las estadísticas. Las estadísticas de tarifas de salarios se refieren generalmente sólo a las tarifas para los adultos que trabajan las horas normales, y por lo mismo no se incluyen los pagos por horas extraordinarias y por suplementos de salarios. En cambio, con frecuencia se incluyen en las estadísticas tanto las asignaciones por carestía de vida como otras asignaciones determinadas por el sistema de fijación de salarios (por ejemplo, los subsidios de vivienda). Algunos países establecen promedios de *tarifas efectiva-*

---

[1] Para un estudio detallado de los métodos estadísticos de salarios, véase *Estadísticas de nóminas de salarios y de ganancias,* Estudios y documentos, nueva serie, núm. 16 (Ginebra, 1949), y *Recomendaciones internacionales sobre estadísticas del trabajo* (Ginebra, 1975).

mente pagadas (ganancias de tiempo seguido) sirviéndose de las nóminas de pagos de establecimientos y utilizando el mismo método que para las ganancias medias. Las tarifas efectivamente pagadas comprenden en general la remuneración del tiempo normalmente trabajado, es decir, las horas ordinarias y las extraordinarias, pero excluyen las primas de estímulo y otras gratificaciones, como también la porción correspondiente a las primas en la remuneración por horas extraordinarias. Las tarifas efectivamente pagadas son compiladas a veces por los inspectores del trabajo.

Al hacer comparaciones entre las series de salarios se deben tener presentes las diferencias de conceptos, alcance, métodos de compilación y de presentación de las estadísticas [1]. Los datos sobre las ganancias presentan fluctuaciones que reflejan la influencia tanto de los cambios en las tarifas de salarios como en los demás suplementos de los salarios. Además, las ganancias diarias, semanales o mensuales dependen en gran parte de las variaciones en el promedio de horas de trabajo. Las estadísticas de las tarifas de salarios no revelan la influencia de las modificaciones de los suplementos de los salarios ni la influencia de las variaciones de las horas de trabajo. Las fluctuaciones de las ganancias medias que se obtienen de las nóminas de salarios globales dependen también de los cambios en la estructura del empleo, es decir, la mayor o menor importancia relativa que tengan los hombres, las mujeres, los trabajadores no calificados y los trabajadores calificados, etc.; las tarifas medias de salarios se calculan ordinariamente utilizando como ponderación la estructura del empleo en un año determinado. Las ganancias medias por hora son ordinariamente mayores que las tarifas por hora, ya que las primeras incluyen el pago de las horas extraordinarias, las primas, las bonificaciones y otras gratificaciones que no se incluyen en las estadísticas de tarifas de salarios.

Las ganancias medias por semana o por mes son más elevadas que sus correspondientes tarifas, pero a veces pueden no existir dichas tarifas de salarios por razón de la pérdida de tiempo laborable a causa de enfermedad, absentismo o trabajo a media jornada.

Las comparaciones en el tiempo se ven menos afectadas por las diferencias de conceptos, definiciones y métodos de compilación de los datos que las comparaciones de los niveles de salarios en una fecha determinada.

La determinación de las diferencias internacionales en el *ingreso real en salario* de los trabajadores requiere la conversión de los datos a una moneda común de referencia mediante el empleo de factores particulares que indiquen el poder de compra de las monedas en cuestión respecto de los bienes de consumo y los servicios. Sólo pueden hacerse comparaciones satisfactorias de este género entre países de características similares, y ellas deben basarse de preferencia en encuestas uniformes especiales que utilicen ordinariamente el concepto de ganancias netas e incluyan las asignaciones familiares [2]. En general, pueden obtenerse más fácilmente indicaciones aproximadas de las tendencias de los salarios reales dividiendo las ganancias brutas medias (o los índices de ganancias brutas) por el índice de precios del consumo.

Las comparaciones del *costo total de la mano de obra* entre diferentes industrias de un país o entre diversos países no pueden efectuarse utilizando sólo las estadísticas de salarios. Aunque las ganancias brutas constituyen evidentemente la parte más importante del costo de la mano de obra, los suplementos de los salarios tales como las asignaciones familiares, ciertas bonificaciones y gratificaciones o las contribuciones pagadas por el empleador a las cajas del seguro social o los servicios de bienestar proporcionados a los trabajadores por los establecimientos constituyen una porción considerable del costo total de la mano de obra en determinadas industrias y en ciertos países que no figuran normalmente en las estadísticas de ganancias. Las estadísticas

[1] Para las descripciones de las diversas series nacionales, su alcance, métodos de compilación y definiciones utilizados, etc., véase OIT: *Guía Técnica 1980* (descripciones de las series generales publicadas en el *Boletín* y el *Anuario de Estadísticas del Trabajo*), vol. II, « Empleo — Desempleo — Horas de trabajo — Salarios » (Ginebra, 1980).

[2] Véase, por ejemplo, Office statistique des Communautés européennes: *Salaires CEE, 1964*, Statistiques sociales, 1966, nº 5 (en francés solamente).

del costo total de la mano de obra son, por lo tanto, en la mayoría de los casos, objeto de estudios especiales [1].

Cuadro 17

Salarios en los sectores no agrícolas

Salvo indicación contraria en notas de pie de página, las series de salarios de este cuadro incluyen las siguientes divisiones de la actividad económica: minas y canteras; industrias manufactureras; electricidad, gas y agua; construcción; comercio al por mayor y al por menor y restaurantes y hoteles; transportes, almacenaje y comunicaciones; establecimientos financieros, seguros, bienes inmuebles y servicios prestados a las empresas; servicios comunales, sociales y personales. En algunos casos, estas divisiones sólo están representadas por una parte de los grupos que las componen.

Cuadro 18

Salarios en las industrias manufactureras

La parte A del cuadro 18 indica las estadísticas de salarios en todas las industrias manufactureras; cuando en ciertos casos se incluyen otras industrias, así se indica en notas de pie de página.

La parte B del cuadro 18 presenta las estadísticas de salarios en industrias manufactureras especificadas. Se presentan los datos de cada país por separado.

En la medida de lo posible, las diferentes industrias manufactureras han sido ordenadas según la Clasificación industrial internacional uniforme de todas las actividades económicas (véase apéndice), con indicación del correspondiente número de código de los diferentes grupos de industrias.

---

[1] Véase, por ejemplo, OIT: *Coût de la main-d'œuvre dans l'industrie européenne*, Etudes et documents, nouvelle série, nº 52 (Ginebra, 1959; en inglés y francés solamente).

Cuadros 19 a 21

Salarios en minas y canteras; construcción; transportes, almacenaje y comunicaciones

Los cuadros 19 a 21 presentan las estadísticas de salarios en tres divisiones principales de actividad económica, a saber: cuadro 19: minas y canteras; cuadro 20: construcción; cuadro 21: transportes, almacenaje y comunicaciones (excl. el transporte marítimo).

Cuadro 22

Salarios en la agricultura

Las estadísticas de los salarios en la agricultura presentadas en el cuadro 22 se refieren ordinariamente a los trabajadores agrícolas en general. Se distingue entre trabajadores *permanentes*, trabajadores *de temporada* y *jornaleros*; este último grupo se subdivide en jornaleros *regulares* y jornaleros *ocasionales*.

Los sistemas de remuneración y los tipos de contratos y de acuerdos en la agricultura son a menudo muy diferentes de los que rigen en otras actividades. Para indicar el género de las estadísticas de salarios presentadas en cada columna se ha adoptado una notación especial: el símbolo I en la parte superior de la columna indica que las cifras se refieren a salarios totales pagados por entero en dinero. El símbolo II, a solas, indica que las cifras se refieren únicamente a la porción en dinero de los salarios, aun cuando los trabajadores reciban pagos en especie; cuando se ha agregado el símbolo *a*, las cifras incluyen, como parte del salario, las comidas suministradas, y, del mismo modo, el símbolo *b* indica que se incluye el valor del alojamiento proporcionado. Aunque se indica en ciertos casos que las cifras representan tarifas de salarios o ganancias, es característico de la agricultura que en la mayoría de los países haya poca o ninguna diferencia entre las tarifas nominales de salarios y las ganancias efectivas de los agricultores.

Las comparaciones internacionales de salarios en la agricultura se hallan sujetas a reservas aún mayores que las de otras actividades. La naturaleza del trabajo que efectúan las diferentes categorías de trabajadores agrícolas y la duración de la jornada o de la semana de trabajo varían considerablemente de un país a otro. En ciertos países, los salarios agrícolas sufren variaciones estacionales más importantes que en otros.

En general, las series marcadas con el símbolo I, que representan el salario total de aquellos trabajadores cuya remuneración se paga enteramente en efectivo, se prestan mejor a la comparación internacional que las series marcadas ya sea con II + a + b o simplemente con II. Las comparaciones entre las series marcadas solamente II, en las que las cifras no incluyen el valor de la alimentación ni el del alojamiento proporcionados por el empleador, deben ser objeto de especiales reservas, dadas las diferencias en la importancia relativa de estos pagos en especie.

Un inconveniente importante en las comparaciones internacionales de las series marcadas II + a + b es la falta de uniformidad de los métodos utilizados en los diferentes países para estimar el valor en dinero de los pagos en especie incluidos en los datos. Cuando las informaciones se refieren a las mismas ocupaciones y unidades de tiempo (día, semana o mes), estas series pueden considerarse como aproximadamente comparables, tanto entre sí como con las series marcadas I, que corresponden también a los salarios totales de los trabajadores comprendidos.

17 Wages in non-agricultural sectors
Salaires dans les secteurs non agricoles
Salarios en los sectores no agrícolas

Earnings (E.G.) or rates (R.T.) per hour, day, week or month

Gains (E.G.) ou taux (R.T.) par heure, jour, semaine ou mois

Ganancias (E.G.) o tarifas (R.T.) por hora, día, semana o mes

Date / Date / Fecha	Algérie	Burundi (Bujumbura)	Egypt			Kenya	Malawi
	Hour / Heure / Hora	Month / Mois / Mes	Week[4] — Semaine[4] — Semana[4]			Month[5] / Mois[5] / Mes[5]	Month / Mois / Mes
			Males / Hommes / Hombres	Females / Femmes / Mujeres	M. + F. / H. + F. / H. + M.		
	(E.G.)[1]	(E.G.)[2,3]	(E.G.)			(E.G.)[2,6]	(E.G.)[2]
	Dinars	Francs	Piastres	Piastres	Piastres	Shillings	Kwacha
1970	2.80	.	410	252	401	578.20	37.13
1971	2.63	.	406	274	399	591.60	37.06
1972	2.88	.	458	321	450	634.70	36.84
1973	2.94	3 726	476	311	467	679.80	37.71
1974	3.27	5 109	540	370	531	719.10	40.99
1975	3.56	5 028	569	385	558	802.10	42.64
1976	3.79	...	662 *	497 *	652 *	905.90	44.94
1977	4.12	6 193	...	...	...	986.50	48.76[7]
1978	...	7 693	...	...	...	1 066.70	55.87
1979	...	8 344	...	...	...	1 162.50	...
1980: VI	.	.	.		.	.	...

AFRICA — AFRIQUE — AFRICA

Date / Date / Fecha	Mauritius	Nigeria	Sierra Leone[9]	Swaziland[11]		Tanzania (Tanganyika)[14]	Zambia	
	Day / Jour / Día	Day / Jour / Día	Week[10] / Semaine[10] / Semana[10]	Month — Mois — Mes		Month[5] / Mois[5] / Mes[5]	Month[16] — Mois[16] — Mes[16]	
				Skilled / Qualifiés / Calificados	Unskilled / Non qualifiés / No calificados		Zambians / Zambiens / Zambianos	Others / Autres / Otros
	(E.G.)[8]	(R.T.)	(E.G.)	(E.G.)[12,13]		(E.G.)[15]	(E.G.)[2]	
	Rupees	Naira	Leones	Emalangeni	Emalangeni	Shillings	Kwacha	Kwacha
1970	6.95	.	8.36	.	.	340	...	...
1971	6.70		8.48	.	.	354	...	...
1972	7.70	0.88	8.89	208	23	369	...	...
1973	8.21	0.92	8.77	204	25	419	89	384
1974	9.46	1.36	9.35	187	38	617	100	421
1975	11.44	1.97	10.33	283	49	...	99	460
1976	15.98	1.99	11.35	315	51	...	101	475
1977	18.96	2.21	11.55	284	78	...	131	585
1978	22.26	2.36	12.05	404	71	...	138	606
1979	24.38	2.60	13.50	...	...	...	...	...
1980: VI	.	.	.	...	...	...	...	...

EXPLANATORY NOTES: See p. 423.

[1] April of each year. [2] Incl. salaried employees. [3] Incl. family allowances. [4] Oct. of each year. [5] June of each year. [6] Incl. the value of payments in kind. [7] Scope of series enlarged. [8] Sep. of each year. [9] Excl. electricity, gas, water, commerce, financing, etc., and services. Adults. [10] May and Nov. of each year. [11] Incl. agriculture and forestry. [12] June of each year. Prior to 1976: Sep. [13] Males. [14] Incl. agriculture. [15] Adult males. [16] Fourth quarter of each year.

NOTES EXPLICATIVES: Voir p. 426.

[1] Avril de chaque année. [2] Y compris les employés. [3] Y compris les allocations familiales. [4] Oct. de chaque année. [5] Juin de chaque année. [6] Y compris la valeur des paiements en nature. [7] Portée de la série élargie. [8] Sept. de chaque année. [9] Non compris l'électricité, le gaz, l'eau, le commerce, les banques, etc., et les services. Adultes. [10] Mai et nov. de chaque année. [11] Y compris l'agriculture et la sylviculture. [12] Juin de chaque année. Avant 1976 : sept. [13] Hommes. [14] Y compris l'agriculture. [15] Hommes adultes. [16] Quatrième trimestre de chaque année.

NOTAS EXPLICATIVAS: Véase pág. 430.

[1] Abril de cada año. [2] Incl. los empleados. [3] Incl. las asignaciones familiares. [4] Oct. de cada año. [5] Junio de cada año. [6] Incl. el valor de los pagos en especie. [7] El alcance de la serie es mayor. [8] Sept. de cada año. [9] Excl. la electricidad, el gas, el agua, los establecimientos financieros, etc., y los servicios. Adultos. [10] Mayo y nov. de cada año. [11] Incl. la agricultura y la silvicultura. [12] Junio de cada año. Antes de 1976: sept. [13] Hombres. [14] Incl. la agricultura. [15] Hombres adultos. [16] Cuarto trimestre de cada año.

17 Wages in non-agricultural sectors
Salaires dans les secteurs non agricoles
Salarios en los sectores no agrícolas

Earnings *(E.G.)* or rates *(R.T.)* per hour, day, week or month

Gains *(E.G.)* ou taux *(R.T.)* par heure, jour, semaine ou mois

Ganancias *(E.G.)* o tarifas *(R.T.)* por hora, día, semana o mes

Date / *Date* / Fecha	AMERICA — AMÉRIQUE — AMÉRICA							
	Bahamas [1]	Barbados [1]	Bolivia	Canada [6]	Costa Rica	Cuba	Guyana [7]	Honduras
	Hour / *Heure* / Hora	Week / *Semaine* / Semana	Month / *Mois* / Mes	Week / *Semaine* / Semana	Month / *Mois* / Mes	Month / *Mois* / Mes	Week / *Semaine* / Semana	Week / *Semaine* / Semana
	(R.T.)	*(E.G.)* [2]	*(R.T.)* [5]	*(E.G.)* [5]	*(E.G.)*	*(E.G.)* [5]	*(E.G.)*	*(E.G.)*
	Dollars	Dollars	Pesos	Dollars	Colones	Pesos	Dollars	Lempiras
1970	.	44.23	1 015	126.82	.	.	47.99	.
1971	.	52.14	1 095	137.64	.	120.08	49.78	.
1972	2.08	48.40 [3]	1 129	149.22	.	127.25	51.88	.
1973	2.51	58.58	1 260	160.46	956	129.92	53.13	48.72
1974	2.75	76.03 [4]	1 750	178.09	1 109	134.00	58.74	40.53
1975	2.88	81.47	1 750	203.34	1 338	140.00	61.70	43.21
1976	2.79	95.82	1 750	228.03	1 487	143.00	70.58	58.54
1977	...	113.22	2 518	249.95	1 639	145.00	73.83	53.09
1978	...	...	2 716	265.37	1 854	...	...	68.47
1979	...	...	...	288.25	2 104	...	...	77.54
1980: VI	.	...	.	315.47	.	.	...	.

Date / *Date* / Fecha	AMERICA — AMÉRIQUE — AMÉRICA							
	Netherlands Antilles	Nicaragua	Perú [8] (Lima-Callao)	Trinidad and Tobago	United States		Uruguay [1, 13]	Venezuela [15]
	Month / *Mois* / Mes	Hour / *Heure* / Hora	Day / *Jour* / Día	Day [10] / *Jour* [10] / Día [10]	Hour / *Heure* / Hora	Week / *Semaine* / Semana	Month / *Mois* / Mes	Month / *Mois* / Mes
	(E.G.) [5]	*(E.G.)*	*(E.G.)* [9]	*(R.T.)* [11]	*(E.G.)*		*(R.T.)* [5, 14]	*(E.G.)*
	Córdobas		Soles	(1970 = 100)			(1970 = 100)	Bolívares
1970	.	3.55	115.12	**100.0**	3.23	119.83	**100.0**	1 201
1971	.	3.72	123.52	106.5	3.45	127.31	127.9	1 254
1972	.	3.87	154.32	120.3	3.70	136.90	187.6	1 316
1973	449	...	189.17	132.8	3.94	145.39	362.0	1 356
1974	520	4.72	218.22	148.6	4.24	154.76	629.8	1 667
1975	601	5.23	259.79	193.1	4.53	163.53	1 056.9	1 862
1976	652	5.62	314.20	231.3 [12]	4.86	175.45	1 476.8	1 816
1977	902	5.58	379.06	265.8	5.25	189.00	2 035.7	1 915
1978	896	...	515.95	299.8	5.69	203.70	2 814.9	2 646
1979	...	...	753.08	...	6.16	219.30	4 233.1	...
1980: VI	.	.	...	.	6.61	233.33	...	...

EXPLANATORY NOTES: See p. 423.

NOTES EXPLICATIVES: Voir p. 426.

NOTAS EXPLICATIVAS: Véase pág. 430.

[1] Excl. mining and quarrying. [2] Adult males. [3] March and Sep. [4] Series replacing former series. [5] Incl. salaried employees. [6] Incl. forestry and logging. [7] Excl. electricity, gas, water, financing, etc., and services. [8] Excl. mining, quarrying, electricity, gas, water. [9] June of each year. [10] May and Nov. of each year. [11] Minimum rates. Adults. [12] Beginning Nov. 1976: series linked to former series. [13] Montevideo; private sector only. [14] Average rates. [15] Excl. construction and transport.

[1] *Non compris les industries extractives.* [2] *Hommes adultes.* [3] *Mars et sept.* [4] *Série remplaçant la précédente.* [5] *Y compris les employés.* [6] *Y compris la sylviculture et l'exploitation forestière.* [7] *Non compris l'électricité, le gaz, l'eau, les banques, etc., et les services.* [8] *Non compris les industries extractives, l'électricité, le gaz et l'eau.* [9] *Juin de chaque année.* [10] *Mai et nov. de chaque année.* [11] *Taux minima. Adultes.* [12] *A partir de nov. 1976 : série enchaînée à la précédente.* [13] *Montevideo ; secteur privé seulement.* [14] *Taux moyens.* [15] *Non compris la construction et les transports.*

[1] Excl. las minas y canteras. [2] Hombres adultos. [3] Marzo y sept. [4] Serie que substituye a la anterior. [5] Incl. los empleados. [6] Incl. la silvicultura y la explotación de la madera. [7] Excl. la electricidad, el gas, el agua, los establecimientos financieros, etc., y los servicios. [8] Excl. las minas y canteras, la electricidad, el gas y el agua. [9] Junio de cada año. [10] Mayo y nov. de cada año. [11] Tarifas mínimas. Adultos. [12] A partir de nov. de 1976: serie enlazada con la anterior. [13] Montevideo; sector privado solamente. [14] Tarifas medias. [15] Excl. la construcción y los transportes.

WAGES

17 Wages in non-agricultural sectors
Salaires dans les secteurs non agricoles
Salarios en los sectores no agrícolas

Earnings *(E.G.)* or rates *(R.T.)* per hour, day, week or month

Gains *(E.G.)* ou taux *(R.T.)* par heure, jour, semaine ou mois

Ganancias *(E.G.)* o tarifas *(R.T.)* por hora, día, semana o mes

Date / *Date* / Fecha	Brunei Hour *Heure* Hora *(E.G.)* [1,2]	Cyprus Week [2] *Semaine* [2] Semana [2] *(E.G.)* [3,4]	Israel Month *Mois* Mes *(E.G.)* [1,6]	Japan Males *Hommes* Hombres *(E.G.)* [1,9]	Japan Females *Femmes* Mujeres	Japan M. + F. H. + F. H. + M.	Jordan [1] Day *Jour* Día *(E.G.)* [3,10]
	Dollars	Pounds	Pounds	Yen	Yen	Yen	Fils
1970	.	9.38	692	89 934	45 801	75 670	.
1971	.	10.15	797	102 486	53 577	86 834	.
1972	1.64	11.87	904	117 816	62 882	100 586	.
1973	1.87	13.90	1 147	143 619 [8]	76 324 [8]	122 545 [8]	1 290
1974	2.05	15.12 [5]	1 561	180 686	97 392	154 967	1 384
1975	1.86	15.09	2 162 [7]	204 295	114 067	177 213	1 503
1976	1.86	15.75	2 875	230 999 [8]	129 675 [8]	200 242 [8]	1 884
1977	2.17	19.57	4 252	253 698	141 644	219 620	2 085
1978	2.87	24.22	6 565	271 121	152 420	235 378	...
1979	2.98	29.62	12 600 [8]	289 052 [8]	158 825 [8]	247 933 [8]	...
1980: VI	.	.	21 954 [18]	416 769	227 568	355 551	

ASIA — ASIE — ASIA

Date / *Date* / Fecha	Korea, Rep. of [1] Month *Mois* Mes *(E.G.)* [4]	Philippines Month *Mois* Mes *(E.G.)* [11]	Philippines (Manila) Day — *Jour* — Día Skilled workers *Ouvriers qualifiés* Obreros calificados *(R.T.)* [12]	Philippines (Manila) Unskilled workers *Ouvriers non qualifiés* Obreros no calificados	Singapore [13] Hour *Heure* Hora *(E.G.)* [14]	Sri Lanka Hour *Heure* Hora *(E.G.)* [15,16]	Sri Lanka Day *Jour* Día	Sri Lanka Day [12,16] *Jour* [12,16] Día [12,16] *(R.T.)* [3,17]
	Won	Pesos	Pesos	Pesos	Cents	Cents	Rupees	Rupees
1970	17 831	252	11.30	9.21	96	98.97	8.94	4.85
1971	20 581	272	11.89	9.84	99	104.25	9.29	5.15
1972	24 179	301	12.48	10.42	104	114.80	10.35	5.30
1973	26 954	337	13.14	10.69	119	109.18	9.97	5.83
1974	35 542	381	14.35	11.54	136	134.10	12.48	6.88
1975	46 019	413	14.93	12.51	154	148.88	13.72	8.04
1976	62 362	...	15.48	13.14	163	158.00	14.40	8.77
1977	82 355	...	17.15	13.84	170	186.00	19.19	8.81
1978	111 201	...	19.27	14.42	181	279.00	26.95	10.83
1979	142 665	...	20.57	15.19	200	266.00	25.41	12.65
1980: VI	165 644 [19]	.	.	.				15.17

EXPLANATORY NOTES: See p. 423.

[1] Incl. salaried employees. [2] Oct. of each year. [3] Adults. [4] Incl. family allowances and the value of payments in kind. [5] Beginning July 1974: due to a change in the geographical scope of the series, data are not comparable with those for the preceding period. [6] Prior to July 1975: incl. family allowances. Beginning July 1975: incl. payments subject to income tax and the value of payments in kind. [7] Scope of series enlarged. [8] Sampling design revised. [9] Incl. family allowances, mid- and end-of-year bonuses. [10] April of each year. [11] Excl. construction. [12] Excl. mining, quarrying and services. [13] Incl. agriculture, fishing and sea transport. [14] Aug. of each year. Prior to 1975: July. [15] March and Sep. of each year. [16] Excl. electricity, gas, water, financing, etc., and services. [17] Minimum rates. [18] April. [19] March.

NOTES EXPLICATIVES: Voir p. 426.

[1] *Y compris les employés.* [2] *Oct. de chaque année.* [3] *Adultes.* [4] *Y compris les allocations familiales et la valeur des paiements en nature.* [5] *A partir de juillet 1974: en raison d'un changement de la portée géographique de la série, les données ne sont pas comparables avec celles de la période précédente.* [6] *Avant juillet 1975: y compris les allocations familiales. A partir de juillet 1975: y compris les versements soumis à l'impôt sur le revenu et la valeur des paiements en nature.* [7] *Portée de la série élargie.* [8] *Plan d'échantillonnage révisé.* [9] *Y compris les allocations familiales et les primes de mi et de fin d'année.* [10] *Avril de chaque année.* [11] *Non compris la construction.* [12] *Non compris les industries extractives et les services.* [13] *Y compris l'agriculture, la pêche et les transports par mer.* [14] *Août de chaque année. Avant 1975: juillet.* [15] *Mars et sept. de chaque année.* [16] *Non compris l'électricité, le gaz, l'eau, les banques, etc., et les services.* [17] *Taux minima.* [18] *Avril.* [19] *Mars.*

NOTAS EXPLICATIVAS: Véase pág. 430.

[1] Incl. los empleados. [2] Oct. de cada año. [3] Adultos. [4] Incl. las asignaciones familiares y el valor de los pagos en especie. [5] A partir de julio de 1974: en razón de un cambio del alcance geográfico de la serie, los datos no son comparables a los del período precedente. [6] Antes de julio de 1975: incl. las asignaciones familiares. A partir de julio de 1975: incl. los pagos sometidos al impuesto sobre la renta y el valor de los pagos en especie. [7] El alcance de la serie es mayor. [8] Diseño de la muestra revisado. [9] Incl. las asignaciones familiares y las primas de mitad y de fin de año. [10] Abril de cada año. [11] Excl. la construcción. [12] Excl. las minas, las canteras y los servicios. [13] Incl. la agricultura, la pesca y el transporte marítimo. [14] Agosto de cada año. Antes de 1975: julio. [15] Marzo y sept. de cada año. [16] Excl. la electricidad, el gas, el agua, los establecimientos financieros, etc., y los servicios. [17] Tarifas mínimas. [18] Abril. [19] Marzo.

17 Wages in non-agricultural sectors
Salaires dans les secteurs non agricoles
Salarios en los sectores no agrícolas

Earnings (E.G.) or rates (R.T.) per hour, day, week or month

Gains (E.G.) ou taux (R.T.) par heure, jour, semaine ou mois

Ganancias (E.G.) o tarifas (R.T.) por hora, día, semana o mes

Date / Date / Fecha	Austria [1]	Belgique [2]				Bulgarie [6]	Czechoslovakia [6]
	Month / Mois / Mes	Hour / Heure / Hora	Hour — Heure — Hora			Month / Mois / Mes	Month / Mois / Mes
			Males / Hommes / Hombres	Females / Femmes / Mujeres	M. + F. / H. + F. / H. + M.		
	(E.G.)	(E.G.)	(E.G.) [3, 4]			(E.G.) [7, 8]	(E.G.) [7]
	Schilling	(1970 = 100)	Francs	Francs	Francs	Leva	Korunas
1970	4 590	100	73.04	48.70	68.39	123.8	1 945
1971	5 270	112	82.04	55.41	76.96	126.5	2 018
1972	5 820	128	94.81 [5]	64.95 [5]	88.71 [5]	130.9	2 099
1973	6 590	149	108.18	74.48	101.33	139.2	2 165
1974	7 530	180	135.47	94.20	127.01	142.0	2 236
1975	8 440	216	156.07	111.06	146.85	146.4	2 308
1976	9 170	240	173.94	121.84	163.28	148.1	2 373
1977	10 010	262	190.51	133.39	178.88	151.4	2 447
1978	10 660	280	201.59	140.92	189.23	157.3	2 521
1979	11 236	302	217.77	151.68	204.27	164.3 *	2 583
1980: VI	.	325	.	.	.	.	2 629 [16]

EUROPE — EUROPE — EUROPA

Date / Date / Fecha	Denmark [9]			España [11]	France			
	Hour — Heure — Hora			Hour / Heure / Hora	Hour [3] / Heure [3] / Hora [3]	Hour — Heure — Hora		
	Males [10] / Hommes [10] / Hombres [10]	Females [10] / Femmes [10] / Mujeres [10]	M. + F. [10] / H. + F. [10] / H. + M. [10]			Males [10] / Hommes [10] / Hombres [10]	Females [10] / Femmes [10] / Mujeres [10]	M. + F. [10] / H. + F. [10] / H. + M. [10]
	(E.G.)			(E.G.) [7]	(E.G.) [12]	(R.T.) [12]		
	Öre	Öre	Öre	Pesetas	Francs	Francs	Francs	Francs
1970	1 790	1 296	1 712	40.09	5.84	4.82	4.19	4.66
1971	2 046	1 510	1 965	45.73	6.55	5.34	4.66	5.17
1972	2 278	1 721	2 193	53.55	7.46 [13]	5.97 [15]	5.24 [15]	5.80 [15]
1973	2 616	2 073	2 532	64.10	8.57	7.16	6.12	6.93
1974	3 105	2 540	3 020	81.30	10.29	8.50	7.33	8.24
1975	3 682	3 062	3 594	107.28	11.88	9.95	8.63	9.66
1976	4 103	3 455	4 008	138.40	13.74 [14]	11.48 [14]	9.92 [14]	11.11 [14]
1977	4 500	3 832	4 397	...	15.51	13.00	11.20	12.57
1978	4 967	4 212	4 849	...	17.37	14.59	12.68	14.13
1979	5 540	4 694	5 400	...	19.46	16.44	14.37	15.95
1980: VI	5 958 [17]	5 046 [17]	5 797 [17]	...	.	19.02	16.60	18.44

EXPLANATORY NOTES: See p. 423.

[1] Excl. commerce. [2] Excl. commerce, transport, financing, etc., and services. [3] Oct. of each year. [4] Beginning Oct. 1976: excl. electricity, gas and water. [5] New industrial classification. [6] Socialised sector. [7] Incl. salaried employees. [8] Incl. agriculture and sea transport. [9] Excl. mining and quarrying, commerce, transport, financing, etc., and services. [10] Adults. [11] Excl. transport and services. [12] Excl. mining and quarrying, electricity, gas, water, state-operated transport (SNCF and RATP), communication, public administrations and private domestic services. [13] Series replacing former series. [14] Sampling design revised. [15] Beginning Dec. 1972: revised series. [16] Second quarter. [17] First quarter.

NOTES EXPLICATIVES: Voir p. 426.

[1] Non compris le commerce. [2] Non compris le commerce, les transports, les banques, etc., et les services. [3] Oct. de chaque année. [4] A partir d'oct. 1976: non compris l'électricité, le gaz et l'eau. [5] Nouvelle classification industrielle. [6] Secteur socialisé. [7] Y compris les employés. [8] Y compris l'agriculture et les transports par mer. [9] Non compris les industries extractives, le commerce, les transports, les banques, etc., et les services. [10] Adultes. [11] Non compris les transports et les services. [12] Non compris les industries extractives, l'électricité, le gaz, l'eau, les transports gérés par l'Etat (SNCF et RATP), les communications, les administrations publiques et les services domestiques privés. [13] Série remplaçant la précédente. [14] Plan d'échantillonnage révisé. [15] A partir de déc. 1972: série révisée. [16] Deuxième trimestre. [17] Premier trimestre.

NOTAS EXPLICATIVAS: Véase pág. 430.

[1] Excl. el comercio. [2] Excl. el comercio, los transportes, los establecimientos financieros, etc., y los servicios. [3] Oct. de cada año. [4] A partir de oct. de 1976: excl. la electricidad, el gas y el agua. [5] Nueva clasificación industrial. [6] Sector socializado. [7] Incl. los empleados. [8] Incl. la agricultura y los transportes por mar. [9] Excl. las minas y las canteras, el comercio, los transportes, los establecimientos financieros, etc., y los servicios. [10] Adultos. [11] Excl. los transportes y los servicios. [12] Excl. las minas y las canteras, la electricidad, el gas, el agua, los transportes administrados por el Estado (SNCF y RATP), las comunicaciones, las administraciones públicas y los servicios domésticos privados. [13] Serie que substituye a la anterior. [14] Diseño de la muestra revisado. [15] A partir de dic. de 1972: serie revisada. [16] Segundo trimestre. [17] Primer trimestre.

WAGES

17 Wages in non-agricultural sectors
Salaires dans les secteurs non agricoles
Salarios en los sectores no agrícolas

Earnings *(E.G.)* or rates *(R.T.)* per hour, day, week or month

Gains *(E.G.)* ou taux *(R.T.)* par heure, jour, semaine ou mois

Ganancias *(E.G.)* o tarifas *(R.T.)* por hora, día, semana o mes

Date / *Date* / Fecha	German Democratic Republic [1], [2] Month *Mois* Mes (E.G.) [3], [4]	Germany, Fed. Rep. of [5] Hour — *Heure* — Hora Males *Hommes* Hombres (E.G.) [6]	Germany, Fed. Rep. of [5] Hour — *Heure* — Hora Females *Femmes* Mujeres (E.G.) [6]	Germany, Fed. Rep. of [5] Hour — *Heure* — Hora M. + F. *H. + F.* H. + M. (E.G.) [6]	Germany, Fed. Rep. of [5] Week *Semaine* Semana M. + F. *H. + F.* H. + M. (E.G.) [6]	Gibraltar [8] Week [9] *Semaine* [9] Semana [9] (E.G.)	Hongrie [10], [11] Month *Mois* Mes (E.G.) [12]
	Mark	Mark	Mark	Mark	Mark	£	Forints
1970	762	6.49	4.49	6.09	268	13.72	2 139
1971	792	7.25	5.05	6.82	295	16.06	2 239
1972	818	7.89	5.53	7.42	319	17.60	2 342
1973	843	8.76 [7]	6.16 [7]	8.23 [7]	353 [7]	23.40	2 512
1974	867	9.68	6.90	9.13	382	24.44	2 682
1975	897	10.40	7.52	9.85	402	30.46	2 846
1976	927	11.08	8.02	10.49	438	33.89	3 009
1977	954	11.89	8.64	11.27	471	41.09	3 248
1978	985	12.52	9.13	11.88	496	60.78	3 515
1979	1 014 *	13.25	9.62	12.55	527	68.98	3 719
1980: VI		14.03 [18]	10.17 [18]	13.30 [18]	556 [18]		3 802 [19]

EUROPE — EUROPE — EUROPA

Date / *Date* / Fecha	Iceland [13] (Reykjavik) Hour — *Heure* — Hora Males — *Hommes* — Hombres Skilled *Qualifiés* Calificados (E.G.)	Iceland [13] (Reykjavik) Hour — *Heure* — Hora Males — *Hommes* — Hombres Unskilled *Non qualifiés* No calificados (E.G.)	Iceland [13] (Reykjavik) Hour — *Heure* — Hora Females *Femmes* Mujeres (E.G.)	Iceland [13] (Reykjavik) Hour — *Heure* — Hora Total (E.G.)	Ireland (1) [14] Hour [15] — *Heure* [15] — Hora [15] Males [16] *Hommes* [16] Hombres [16] (E.G.)	Ireland (1) [14] Hour [15] — *Heure* [15] — Hora [15] Females [16] *Femmes* [16] Mujeres [16] (E.G.)	Ireland (1) [14] Hour [15] — *Heure* [15] — Hora [15] M. + F. [17] *H. + F.* [17] H. + M. [17] (E.G.)
	Kronur	Kronur	Kronur	Kronur	Pence	Pence	Pence
1970	146.82	116.41	90.89	123.23	51.8	29.8	43.4
1971	174.77	133.16	105.14	143.52	59.2	34.3	50.2
1972	225.20	177.12	139.64	188.25	67.8	39.5	57.4
1973	289.89	224.44	169.76	239.15	80.9	49.3	69.8
1974	469.70	346.90	258.37	376.60	97.0	59.1	88.1
1975	596.13	445.15	337.45	481.84	127.0	78.4	111.2
1976	771.22	582.12	454.53	629.17	...	...	...
1977	1 056.98	800.61	641.55	861.20	...	...	...
1978	1 565.21	1 223.70	1 021.76	1 305.42	...	...	...
1979	2 254.00	1 731.00	1 457.00	1 863.00	...	...	...
1980: VI	.	.	.	.			

EXPLANATORY NOTES: See p. 423.

[1] State sector. [2] Incl. agriculture. [3] Incl. salaried employees. [4] Incl. family allowances. [5] Excl. commerce, transport, financing, etc., and services. [6] Incl. family allowances paid directly by the employers. [7] Sampling design revised. [8] Excl. mining and quarrying. [9] Oct. of each year, except for 1970-72: April and Oct., and 1974-76: April. [10] Socialised sector. [11] Prior to 1975: incl. agriculture and forestry. [12] Incl. the value of payments in kind. Incl. loyalty money. [13] Excl. mining and quarrying, electricity, gas, water, financing, etc., and services. [14] Excl. commerce, transport and financing, etc. [15] Sep. of each year. [16] Workers on adult rates of pay. [17] Incl. juveniles. [18] April. [19] Second quarter.

NOTES EXPLICATIVES: Voir p. 426.

[1] *Secteur d'Etat.* [2] *Y compris l'agriculture.* [3] *Y compris les employés.* [4] *Y compris les allocations familiales.* [5] *Non compris le commerce, les transports, les banques, etc., et les services.* [6] *Y compris les allocations familiales payées directement par les employeurs.* [7] *Plan d'échantillonnage révisé.* [8] *Non compris les industries extractives.* [9] *Oct. de chaque année, sauf pour 1970-1972: avril et oct., et 1974-1976: avril.* [10] *Secteur socialisé.* [11] *Avant 1975: y compris l'agriculture et la sylviculture.* [12] *Y compris la valeur des paiements en nature. Y compris les primes d'assiduité.* [13] *Non compris les industries extractives, l'électricité, le gaz, l'eau, les banques, etc., et les services.* [14] *Non compris le commerce, les transports et les banques, etc.* [15] *Sept. de chaque année.* [16] *Travailleurs rémunérés sur la base de taux de salaire pour adultes.* [17] *Y compris les jeunes gens.* [18] *Avril.* [19] *Deuxième trimestre.*

NOTAS EXPLICATIVAS: Véase pág. 430.

[1] Sector de Estado. [2] Incl. la agricultura. [3] Incl. los empleados. [4] Incl. las asignaciones familiares. [5] Excl. el comercio, los transportes, los establecimientos financieros, etc., y los servicios. [6] Incl. las asignaciones familiares pagadas directamente por los empleadores. [7] Diseño de la muestra revisado. [8] Excl. las minas y canteras. [9] Oct. de cada año, salvo para 1970-1972: abril y oct., y 1974-1976: abril. [10] Sector socializado. [11] Antes de 1975: incl. la agricultura y la silvicultura. [12] Incl. el valor de los pagos en especie. Incl. las primas de asiduidad. [13] Excl. las minas y canteras, la electricidad, el gas, el agua, los establecimientos financieros, etc., y los servicios. [14] Excl. el comercio, los transportes y los establecimientos financieros, etc. [15] Sept. de cada año. [16] Trabajadores pagados sobre la base de tarifas de salarios para adultos. [17] Incl. los jóvenes. [18] Abril. [19] Segundo trimestre.

17 Wages in non-agricultural sectors
Salaires dans les secteurs non agricoles
Salarios en los sectores no agrícolas

Earnings *(E.G.)* or rates *(R.T.)* per hour, day, week or month

Gains *(E.G.)* ou taux *(R.T.)* par heure, jour, semaine ou mois

Ganancias *(E.G.)* o tarifas *(R.T.)* por hora, día, semana o mes

Date *Date* Fecha	EUROPE — EUROPE — EUROPA					
	Ireland (2) [1]			Italie [5]		Luxembourg
	Week [2] — *Semaine* [2] — Semana [2]			Hour *Heure* Hora		Hour — *Heure* — Hora
	Males [3] *Hommes* [3] Hombres [3]	Females [3] *Femmes* [3] Mujeres [3]	M. + F. [4] *H. + F.* [4] H. + M. [4]			Males *Hommes* Hombres
	(E.G.)			*(E.G.)* [6]	*(R.T.)*	*(E.G.)* [9],[10]
	Pounds	Pounds	Pounds	Lire	(1970 = 100)	Francs
1970	23.14	11.47	18.58	617	**100.0**	88.18
1971	26.17	13.07	21.26	712	111.9	94.50
1972	30.05	15.01	24.38	797	122.2	103.53 [11]
1973	35.86	18.58	29.63	974	150.4	118.87
1974	42.21	21.94	35.12	1 212	180.6	148.10
1975	54.41	29.40	42.26	1 787 [7]	231.2	162.69
1976	...	...	...	2 130	279.2	187.97
1977	...	...	...	2 670	355.8	202.85
1978	...	...	...	3 266 [8]	414.5	212.89
1979	...	...	...	...	494.5	223.11
1980: VI	.	.	.	...	604.3	.

Date *Date* Fecha	EUROPE — EUROPE — EUROPA					
	Luxembourg		Netherlands			
	Hour — *Heure* — Hora		Hour — *Heure* — Hora			
	Females *Femmes* Mujeres	M. + F. *H. + F.* H. + M.	Males [12] *Hommes* [12] Hombres [12]	Females [12] *Femmes* [12] Mujeres [12]	M. + F. [4] *H. + F.* [4] H. + M. [4]	M. + F. [12] *H. + F.* [12] H. + M. [12]
	(E.G.) [9],[10]		*(E.G.)* [9],[13]			*(R.T.)* [14]
	Francs	Francs	Guilders	Guilders	Guilders	(1970 = 100)
1970	50.27	86.48	5.47	4.03	5.06	**100**
1971	56.25	92.61	6.33	4.66	5.85	112
1972	65.13 [11]	101.86 [11]	7.05	5.24	6.52	126
1973	69.02	116.34	8.08	6.15	7.54	142
1974	89.67	144.85	9.36	7.40	8.78	165
1975	103.06	159.36	10.67	8.48	10.09	189
1976	125.33	184.16	11.50	9.36	10.92	207
1977	131.88	198.52	12.74	10.11	12.03	222
1978	135.63	208.21	13.61	10.64	12.81	236
1979	137.61	218.38	...	...	...	248
1980: VI	.	.	.	.	.	256

EXPLANATORY NOTES: See p. 423.

[1] Excl. commerce, transport and financing, etc. [2] Sep. of each year. [3] Workers on adult rates of pay. [4] Incl. juveniles. [5] Excl. commerce, transport, financing, etc., and services. [6] Incl. the value of payments in kind. Prior to 1975: excl. payments for annual vacation and public holidays. [7] Series replacing former series. [8] Scope of series revised. [9] Oct. of each year. [10] Excl. electricity, gas and water, commerce, transport, financing, etc., and services. [11] New industrial classification. [12] Adults. [13] Prior to 1977: excl. services. [14] Incl. salaried employees.

NOTES EXPLICATIVES: Voir p. 426.

[1] *Non compris le commerce, les transports et les banques, etc.* [2] *Sept. de chaque année.* [3] *Travailleurs rémunérés sur la base de taux de salaire pour adultes.* [4] *Y compris les jeunes gens.* [5] *Non compris le commerce, les transports, les banques, etc., et les services.* [6] *Y compris la valeur des paiements en nature. Avant 1975: non compris la rémunération pour congés annuels et jours fériés.* [7] *Série remplaçant la précédente.* [8] *Portée de la série révisée.* [9] *Oct. de chaque année.* [10] *Non compris l'électricité, le gaz et l'eau, le commerce, les transports, les banques, etc., et les services.* [11] *Nouvelle classification industrielle.* [12] *Adultes.* [13] *Avant 1977: non compris les services.* [14] *Y compris les employés.*

NOTAS EXPLICATIVAS: Véase pág. 430.

[1] Excl. el comercio, los transportes y los establecimientos financieros, etc. [2] Sept. de cada año. [3] Trabajadores pagados sobre la base de tarifas de salarios para adultos. [4] Incl. los jóvenes. [5] Excl. el comercio, los transportes, los establecimientos financieros, etc., y los servicios. [6] Incl. el valor de los pagos en especie. Antes de 1975: excl. los pagos por vacaciones anuales y días feriados. [7] Serie que substituye a la anterior. [8] El alcance de la serie es revisado. [9] Oct. de cada año. [10] Excl. la electricidad, el gas y el agua, el comercio, los transportes, los establecimientos financieros, etc., y los servicios. [11] Nueva clasificación industrial. [12] Adultos. [13] Antes de 1977: excl. los servicios. [14] Incl. los empleados.

17 Wages in non-agricultural sectors
Salaires dans les secteurs non agricoles
Salarios en los sectores no agrícolas

Earnings *(E.G.)* or rates *(R.T.)* per hour, day, week or month

Gains *(E.G.)* ou taux *(R.T.)* par heure, jour, semaine ou mois

Ganancias *(E.G.)* o tarifas *(R.T.)* por hora, día, semana o mes

Date / Date / Fecha	Pologne [1,2] Month / Mois / Mes (E.G.) [3,4] Zlotys	Portugal [5] Hour / Heure / Hora (E.G.) Escudos	Roumanie [1,6] Month / Mois / Mes (E.G.) [3] Lei	Suisse [8] Hour — Heure — Hora Males / Hommes / Hombres (E.G.) [9] Francs	Suisse [8] Females / Femmes / Mujeres (E.G.) [9] Francs	Suisse [8] M. + F. / H. + F. / H. + M. (E.G.) [9] Francs
1970	2 277	.	1 434	6.99	4.39	.
1971	2 399	10.90	1 471	7.85	5.01	.
1972	2 542	12.60	1 498	8.75	5.54	.
1973	2 830	14.90	1 563	9.29 [10]	6.18 [10]	8.79
1974	3 221	22.20	1 663	10.57	7.06	10.01
1975	3 601	32.20	1 813	11.37	7.58	10.76
1976	4 128	39.50	1 964	11.55	7.73	10.93
1977	4 416	46.80	1 818 [7]	11.81	7.75	11.16
1978	4 670	53.01	2 011	12.14	8.03	11.48
1979	5 093 *	...	2 108	12.50	8.32	11.83
1980: VI	.	.	.	13.15 [18]	8.66 [18]	12.43 [18]

Date / Date / Fecha	Suisse [11] Hour — Heure — Hora Males [12] / Hommes [12] / Hombres [12] Skilled / Qualifiés / Calificados (E.G.) [13] Francs	Suisse [11] Semi-skilled and unskilled / Semi-qualifiés et non qualifiés / Semicalificados y no calificados (E.G.) [13] Francs	Suisse [11] Total (E.G.) [13] Francs	Suisse [11] Females [12] / Femmes [12] / Mujeres [12] (E.G.) [13] Francs	Turquie Day [14] / Jour [14] / Día [14] (E.G.) [3,15] Liras	United Kingdom (1) Week [16] / Semaine [16] / Semana [16] M. + F. [17] / H. + F. [17] / H. + M. [17] (R.T.) (1970 = 100)
1970	7.96	6.70	7.22	4.77	35.32	**100.0**
1971	8.97	7.60	8.16	5.42	39.32	112.9
1972	10.04	8.49	9.13	6.05	43.88	128.5
1973	11.25	9.52	10.23	6.83	54.41	146.1
1974	12.61	10.72	11.50	7.76	68.26	175.0
1975	13.44	11.54	12.33	8.32	85.55	226.7
1976	13.60	11.73	12.50	8.57	115.30	270.4
1977	14.17	12.23	13.10	8.72	132.25	288.2
1978	14.57	12.54	13.45	9.03	220.42	328.9
1979	15.09	12.97	13.92	9.35	292.49	377.8
1980: VI	.	.	.	.	.	450.6

EXPLANATORY NOTES: See p. 423.

[1] Socialised sector. [2] Incl. sea fishing. [3] Incl. salaried employees. [4] Incl. the value of payments in kind. [5] Excl. commerce, transport, financing, etc., and services. [6] Incl. agriculture and forestry. [7] Beginning 1977: net earnings after deduction of income taxes. [8] Incl. forestry and horticulture but excl. mining, quarrying, financing, etc. and services. Prior to 1975: incl. family allowances. [9] Accident insurance statistics. [10] Series replacing former series. [11] Statistics of establishments. Incl. horticulture. Incl. family allowances. [12] Adults. [13] Oct. of each year. [14] Sep. of each year. [15] Incl. fishing. [16] Incl. agriculture, forestry and fishing, but excl. financing, etc. [17] Incl. juveniles. [18] Second quarter.

NOTES EXPLICATIVES: Voir p. 426.

[1] *Secteur socialisé.* [2] *Y compris la pêche maritime.* [3] *Y compris les employés.* [4] *Y compris la valeur des paiements en nature.* [5] *Non compris le commerce, les transports, les banques, etc., et les services.* [6] *Y compris l'agriculture et la sylviculture.* [7] *A partir de 1977: gains nets après déduction de l'impôt sur le revenu.* [8] *Y compris la sylviculture et l'horticulture, mais non compris les industries extractives, les banques, etc. et les services. Avant 1975: y compris les allocations familiales.* [9] *Statistiques d'assurance-accidents.* [10] *Série remplaçant la précédente.* [11] *Statistiques d'établissements. Y compris l'horticulture. Y compris les allocations familiales.* [12] *Adultes.* [13] *Oct. de chaque année.* [14] *Sept. de chaque année.* [15] *Y compris la pêche.* [16] *Y compris l'agriculture, la sylviculture et la pêche, mais non compris les banques, etc.* [17] *Y compris les jeunes gens.* [18] *Deuxième trimestre.*

NOTAS EXPLICATIVAS: Véase pág. 430.

[1] Sector socializado. [2] Incl. la pesca marítima. [3] Incl. los empleados. [4] Incl. el valor de los pagos en especie. [5] Excl. el comercio, los transportes, los establecimientos financieros, etc., y los servicios. [6] Incl. la agricultura y la silvicultura. [7] A partir de 1977: ganancias netas después de deducir los impuestos sobre la renta. [8] Incl. la silvicultura y la horticultura, pero excl. las minas, las canteras, los establecimientos financieros, etc., y los servicios. Antes de 1975: incl. las asignaciones familiares. [9] Estadísticas del seguro de accidentes. [10] Serie que substituye a la anterior. [11] Estadísticas de establecimientos. Incl. la horticultura. Incl. las asignaciones familiares. [12] Adultos. [13] Oct. de cada año. [14] Sept. de cada año. [15] Incl. la pesca. [16] Incl. la agricultura, la silvicultura y la pesca, pero excl. los establecimientos financieros, etc. [17] Incl. los jóvenes. [18] Segundo trimestre.

17 Wages in non-agricultural sectors
Salaires dans les secteurs non agricoles
Salarios en los sectores no agrícolas

Earnings *(E.G.)* or rates *(R.T.)* per hour, day, week or month

Gains *(E.G.)* ou taux *(R.T.)* par heure, jour, semaine ou mois

Ganancias *(E.G.)* o tarifas *(R.T.)* por hora, día, semana o mes

Date / Date / Fecha	EUROPE — EUROPE — EUROPA					OCEANIA — OCÉANIE — OCEANÍA			
	United Kingdom (2)[1]				Yugoslavia[4]	Australia			
	Hour — *Heure* — Hora		Week — *Semaine* — Semana		Month / *Mois* / Mes	Hour — *Heure* — Hora		Hour[2] — *Heure*[2] — Hora[2]	
	Males / *Hommes* / Hombres	Females / *Femmes* / Mujeres	Males / *Hommes* / Hombres	Females / *Femmes* / Mujeres		Males[6] / *Hommes*[6] / Hombres[6]	Females[6,8] / *Femmes*[6,8] / Mujeres[6,8]	Males[6] / *Hommes*[6] / Hombres[6]	Females[6] / *Femmes*[6] / Mujeres[6]
	(E.G.)[2,3]				*(E.G.)*[5]	*(R.T.)*[7]		*(E.G.)*[5,9]	
	Pence	Pence	£	£	Dinars	Cents	Cents	Dollars	Dollars
1970	61.4	36.9	28.05	13.99	1 177	131.6	97.3	1.84	1.20
1971	69.2	41.9	30.93	15.80	1 431	148.2	111.7	2.08	1.39
1972	79.6	48.3	35.82	18.30	1 613	161.4	125.9	2.35[10]	1.73[10]
1973	89.7	56.1	40.92	21.16	1 919	182.8	147.0	2.72	2.08
1974	107.8	72.2	48.63	27.01	2 468	233.6	201.3	3.58	2.86
1975	136.7	92.4	59.58	34.19	3 045	280.6	260.0	4.05	3.39
1976	152.2	108.6	66.97	40.61	3 543	322.8	302.0	4.61	3.95
1977	164.9	118.5	72.89	44.31	4 213	358.3	336.9	5.10	4.41
1978	188.9	138.8	83.50	50.03	5 099	383.2	359.4	5.46	4.70
1979	220.3	155.7	96.94	58.24	6 168	412.2	382.6	5.93	5.07
1980: VI	.	.	.	.	...	443.0	407.8	.	.

Date / Date / Fecha	OCEANIA — OCÉANIE — OCEANÍA					URSS[4,16]	RSS de Biélorussie[4]	RSS d'Ukraine[4]
	Fiji[11]	New Zealand[13]				Month / *Mois* / Mes	Month / *Mois* / Mes	Month / *Mois* / Mes
	Day[12] / *Jour*[12] / Día[12]	Hour — *Heure* — Hora			Week *Semaine* Semana			
		Males[15] / *Hommes*[15] / Hombres[15]	Females[15] / *Femmes*[15] / Mujeres[15]	M. + F.[15] / H. + F.[15] / H. + M.[15]	Males[6] / *Hommes*[6] / Hombres[6]			
	(R.T.)	*(E.G.)*[5,14]			*(R.T.)*[7]	*(E.G.)*[5]	*(E.G.)*[5]	*(E.G.)*[5]
	Dollars	Dollars	Dollars	Dollars	Dollars	Roubles	Roubles	Roubles
1970	2.47	.	.	1.29	43.84	124.6	112.0	116.8
1971	2.72	.	.	1.54	55.01	128.4	115.8	120.1
1972	3.08	.	.	1.72	59.74	132.5	119.6	123.4
1973	3.98	.	.	1.94	66.46	137.1	123.7	126.5
1974	4.90	2.48	1.78	2.26	75.63	143.2	126.9	129.6
1975	5.97	2.82	2.08	2.58	86.33	148.2	130.2	134.9
1976	6.68	3.17	2.43	2.92	96.91	153.4	138.2	141.1
1977	7.11	3.61	2.78	3.33	109.58	157.2	141.0	144.2
1978	7.89	4.08	3.14	3.76	...	162.0	144.5	147.5
1979	8.44 *	4.78	3.73	4.41	...	162.5	147.8	151.1
1980: VI	.	.	.	.	.	.	.	.

EXPLANATORY NOTES: See p. 423.

[1] Excl. coal mining, commerce, railways, financing, etc. [2] Oct. of each year. [3] Full-time adults. [4] Socialised sector. [5] Incl. salaried employees. [6] Adults. [7] Minimum rates. [8] Excl. mining, quarrying and construction. [9] Incl. forestry, fishing and trapping. [10] Scope of series enlarged. [11] Incl. agriculture. [12] June of each year. [13] Incl. forestry and logging. [14] April and Oct. of each year. [15] Incl. juveniles. [16] Incl. Byelorussian SSR and Ukrainian SSR, shown separately in this table.

NOTES EXPLICATIVES: Voir p. 426.

[1] *Non compris les mines de charbon, le commerce, les chemins de fer, les banques, etc.* [2] *Oct. de chaque année.* [3] *Adultes à temps complet.* [4] *Secteur socialisé.* [5] *Y compris les employés.* [6] *Adultes.* [7] *Taux minima.* [8] *Non compris les industries extractives et la construction.* [9] *Y compris la sylviculture, la pêche et le piégeage.* [10] *Portée de la série élargie.* [11] *Y compris l'agriculture.* [12] *Juin de chaque année.* [13] *Y compris la sylviculture et l'exploitation forestière.* [14] *Avril et oct. de chaque année.* [15] *Y compris les jeunes gens.* [16] *Y compris les RSS de Biélorussie et d'Ukraine, figurant séparément dans ce tableau.*

NOTAS EXPLICATIVAS: Véase pág. 430.

[1] Excl. las minas de carbón, el comercio, los ferrocarriles, los establecimientos financieros, etc. [2] Oct. de cada año. [3] Adultos a tiempo completo. [4] Sector socializado. [5] Incl. los empleados. [6] Adultos. [7] Tarifas mínimas. [8] Excl. las minas, las canteras y la construcción. [9] Incl. la silvicultura, la pesca y la caza mediante trampas. [10] El alcance de la serie es mayor. [11] Incl. la agricultura. [12] Junio de cada año. [13] Incl. la silvicultura y la explotación de la madera. [14] Abril y oct. de cada año. [15] Incl. los jóvenes. [16] Incl. las RSS de Bielorrusia y de Ucrania, que figuran separadamente en este cuadro.

WAGES

18 Wages in manufacturing
Salaires dans les industries manufacturières
Salarios en las industrias manufactureras

A All industries
Ensemble des industries
Todas las industrias

Earnings *(E.G.)* or rates *(R.T.)* per hour, day, week or month

Gains *(E.G.)* ou taux *(R.T.)* par heure, jour, semaine ou mois

Ganancias *(E.G.)* o tarifas *(R.T.)* por hora, día, semana o mes

	AFRICA — AFRIQUE — AFRICA					
Date	Algérie	Burundi (Bujumbura)	Egypt			Kenya
			Week [4] — *Semaine* [4] — Semana [4]			
Date	Hour	Month	Males	Females	M. + F.	Month
	Heure	*Mois*	*Hommes*	*Femmes*	*H. + F.*	*Mois*
Fecha	Hora	Mes	Hombres	Mujeres	H. + M.	Mes
	(E.G.) [1]	*(E.G.)* [2,3]	*(E.G.)*			*(E.G.)* [3,5]
	Dinars	Francs	Piastres	Piastres	Piastres	Shillings
1970	2.56	.	407	283	397	607.20
1971	2.63	.	401	269	392	620.70
1972	2.85	.	468	320	458	634.80
1973	3.38	5 205	476	308	466	682.50
1974	3.01	5 100	534	336	524	728.00
1975	3.13	5 469	553	375	541	830.50
1976	...	...	663 *	498 *	651 *	884.00
1977	...	5 915	...	...	...	978.30
1978	...	5 740	...	...	...	1 027.70
1979	...	7 048	...	...	...	1 084.70
1980: VI	.				.	.

	AFRICA — AFRIQUE — AFRICA						
Date	Malawi	Maroc (Casablanca)	Mauritius	Nigeria	Sierra Leone	South Africa, Rep. of	
Date	Month	Hour	Day [8]	Day	Week [9]	Month — *Mois* — Mes	
	Mois	*Heure*	*Jour* [8]	*Jour*	*Semaine* [9]		
Fecha	Mes	Hora	Día [8]	Día	Semana [9]	Total	11
	(E.G.) [3]	*(R.T.)* [7]	*(E.G.)*	*(R.T.)*	*(E.G.)* [10]	*(E.G.)*	
	Kwacha	Dirhams	Rupees	Naira	Leones	Rand	Rand
1970	28.16	0.85	6.04	.	8.28	115.20	299.50
1971	29.56	0.96	6.21	.	8.35	126.20	334.40
1972	32.59	0.96	6.48	1.30	8.15	135.50	357.40
1973	32.26	1.15	6.03	1.42	12.23	150.50	390.70
1974	37.82	2.21	7.19	1.56	10.13	172.80	447.60
1975	38.84	...	8.60	1.77	11.31	200.80	510.50
1976	39.77	...	11.55	1.96	12.13	230.90	571.40
1977	43.31 [6]	...	14.13	2.16	12.65	257.40	625.40
1978	46.99	...	16.56	2.30	13.25	292.60	698.20
1979	...	...	17.37	3.30	13.80	335.40	805.40
1980: VI	...	.	.	.	.	...	...

EXPLANATORY NOTES: See p. 423.

NOTES EXPLICATIVES: Voir p. 426.

NOTAS EXPLICATIVAS: Véase pág. 430.

[1] April of each year. [2] Incl. family allowances. [3] Incl. salaried employees. [4] Oct. of each year. [5] June of each year Incl. the value of payments in kind. [6] Scope of series enlarged. [7] Minimum rates. Adult males. Dec. of each year. [8] Sep. of each year. [9] May and Nov. of each year. [10] Adults. [11] White population.

[1] *Avril de chaque année.* [2] *Y compris les allocations familiales.* [3] *Y compris les employés.* [4] *Oct. de chaque année.* [5] *Juin de chaque année. Y compris la valeur des paiements en nature.* [6] *Portée de la série élargie.* [7] *Taux minima. Hommes adultes. Déc. de chaque année.* [8] *Sept. de chaque année.* [9] *Mai et nov. de chaque année.* [10] *Adultes.* [11] *Population blanche.*

[1] Abril de cada año. [2] Incl. las asignaciones familiares. [3] Incl. los empleados. [4] Oct. de cada año. [5] Junio de cada año. Incl. el valor de los pagos en especie. [6] El alcance de la serie es mayor. [7] Tarifas mínimas. Hombres adultos. Dic. de cada año. [8] Sept. de cada año. [9] Mayo y nov. de cada año. [10] Adultos. [11] Población blanca.

18 Wages in manufacturing
Salaires dans les industries manufacturières
Salarios en las industrias manufactureras

A All industries
Ensemble des industries
Todas las industrias

Earnings (E.G.) or rates (R.T.) per hour, day, week or month

Gains (E.G.) ou taux (R.T.) par heure, jour, semaine ou mois

Ganancias (E.G.) o tarifas (R.T.) por hora, día, semana o mes

	AFRICA — AFRIQUE — AFRICA					AMERICA — AMÉRIQUE — AMÉRICA		
Date / Date / Fecha	Swaziland		Tanzania (Tanganyka)	Zambia		Argentina	Bahamas	Barbados
	Month — Mois — Mes		Month [2]	Month — Mois — Mes		Hour	Hour	Week
	Skilled / Qualifiés / Calificados	Unskilled / Non qualifiés / No calificados	Mois [2] / Mes [2]	Zambians / Zambiens / Zambianos	Others / Autres / Otros	Heure / Hora	Heure / Hora	Semaine / Semana
	(E.G.) [1]		(E.G.) [3]	(E.G.) [4,5]		(E.G.) [6]	(R.T.)	(E.G.) [3]
	Emalangeni	Emalangeni	Shillings	Kwacha	Kwacha	Pesos	Dollars	Dollars
1970	·	·	368	...	...	1.65	·	44.21
1971	·	·	385	...	...	2.27	1.80	47.84
1972	241	34	397	85	437	3.31	2.25	49.57 [7]
1973	205	34	443	89	510	5.82	2.85	60.63
1974	410	41	616	89	489	7.49	2.57	76.13 [8]
1975	383	43	...	98	471	20.33	2.50	88.23
1976	370	67	...	141	721	62.31	2.49	98.52
1977	477	68	...	127	647	133.98	...	116.64
1978	521	90	...	...	...	...	...	...
1979	...	...	...	...	...	...	...	...
1980: VI . . .	...	...	...	...	·	...	...	...

	AMERICA — AMÉRIQUE — AMÉRICA							
Date / Date / Fecha	Bolivia	Brésil	Canada		Colombia	Costa Rica	Cuba	Chile
	Month / Mois / Mes	Month / Mois / Mes	Hour / Heure / Hora	Week / Semaine / Semana	Hour / Heure / Hora	Month / Mois / Mes	Month / Mois / Mes	Month [10] / Mois [10] / Mes [10]
	(R.T.) [4]	(E.G.) [4]	(E.G.)		(E.G.)	(E.G.)	(E.G.) [4,9]	(E.G.)
	Pesos	Cruzeiros	Dollars	Dollars	Pesos	Colones	Pesos	Pesos
1970	902	535	3.01	119.69	·	·	·	1 041.63
1971	1 054	670	3.28	130.16	7.26	·	121.92	1 480.69
1972	1 088	849	3.54	141.47	7.91	·	130.42	2 408.20
1973	1 219	1 049	3.85	152.46	9.00	795	133.58	7 265.56
1974	1 709	1 370	4.37	170.01	10.70	945	135.50	45 776.21
1975	1 709	1 938	5.06	195.01	13.18	1 123	141.08	205.50 [11]
1976	1 709	2 844	5.76	222.79	16.34	1 290	140.67	805.30
1977	2 339	...	6.38	246.73	20.54	1 445	150.00	2 258.29
1978	1 898	...	6.84	265.03	26.56	1 642	...	3 885.93
1979	...	...	7.44	288.39	35.69	1 889	...	5 720.81
1980: VI . . .	·	·	8.10	312.06 *	43.58 [12]	·	·	...

EXPLANATORY NOTES: See p. 423.

[1] June of each year. Prior to 1976: Sep. Males. [2] June of each year. [3] Adult males. [4] Incl. salaried employees. [5] Fourth quarter of each year. [6] Unskilled workers. [7] March and Sep. [8] Series replacing former series. [9] Incl. mining and quarrying, elect., gas and water. [10] April of each year. Incl. the value of payments in kind. [11] New currency introduced in Sep. 1975: 1 peso = 1,000 old escudos. [12] March.

NOTES EXPLICATIVES: Voir p. 426.

[1] Juin de chaque année. Avant 1976: sept. Hommes. [2] Juin de chaque année. [3] Hommes adultes. [4] Y compris les employés. [5] Quatrième trimestre de chaque année. [6] Ouvriers non qualifiés. [7] Mars et sept. [8] Série remplaçant la précédente. [9] Y compris les industries extractives, l'électricité, le gaz et l'eau. [10] Avril de chaque année. Y compris la valeur des paiements en nature. [11] Nouvelle monnaie introduite en sept. 1975: 1 peso = 1 000 anciens escudos. [12] Mars.

NOTAS EXPLICATIVAS: Véase pág. 430.

[1] Junio de cada año. Antes de 1976: sept. Hombres. [2] Junio de cada año. [3] Hombres adultos. [4] Incl. los empleados. [5] Cuarto trimestre de cada año. [6] Obreros no calificados. [7] Marzo y sept. [8] Serie que substituye a la anterior. [9] Incl. las minas y las canteras, la electricidad, el gas y el agua. [10] Abril de cada año. Incl. el valor de los pagos en especie. [11] Nueva moneda adoptada en sept. de 1975: 1 peso = 1 000 antiguos escudos. [12] Marzo.

WAGES

18 Wages in manufacturing
Salaires dans les industries manufacturières
Salarios en las industrias manufactureras

A All industries
Ensemble des industries
Todas las industrias

Earnings *(E.G.)* or rates *(R.T.)* per hour, day, week or month

Gains *(E.G.)* ou taux *(R.T.)* par heure, jour, semaine ou mois

Ganancias *(E.G.)* o tarifas *(R.T.)* por hora, día, semana o mes

Date / *Date* / Fecha	República Dominicana	Ecuador		El Salvador (San Salvador) [2]			
	Month / *Mois* / Mes	Hour / *Heure* / Hora	Week / *Semaine* / Semana	Hour — *Heure* — Hora		Week — *Semaine* — Semana	
				Males / *Hommes* / Hombres	Females / *Femmes* / Mujeres	Males / *Hommes* / Hombres	Females / *Femmes* / Mujeres
	(E.G.) [1]	*(E.G.)*		*(E.G.)*			
	Pesos	Sucres	Sucres	Colones	Colones	Colones	Colones
1970	72.06	6.10	293	0.94	0.77	45.08	34.80
1971	73.14	6.80	331	0.96	0.75	45.73	34.33
1972	78.15	8.10	391	0.99	0.78	45.70	35.19
1973	74.42	8.90	440	1.03	0.85	48.63	39.06
1974	85.28	10.80	545	1.13	0.94	54.63	44.75
1975	120.25	13.20	672	1.14	1.03	50.41	45.11
1976	136.28	16.30	812	1.45	1.25	64.36	55.06
1977	138.84	18.20	921	1.56	1.26	69.24	55.72
1978	143.48	...	...	1.69	1.39	75.31	62.03
1979	...	...	...	1.90	1.50	84.80	...
1980: VI	.	...	...	...	...	...	...

Date / *Date* / Fecha	Guatemala [3]	Guyana	Honduras	México		Netherlands Antilles	Nicaragua	Panamá	Perú (Lima-Callao)
	Hour / *Heure* / Hora	Week / *Semaine* / Semana	Week / *Semaine* / Semana	Hour / *Heure* / Hora	Month / *Mois* / Mes	Month / *Mois* / Mes	Hour / *Heure* / Hora	Hour / *Heure* / Hora	Day / *Jour* / Día
	(E.G.)	*(E.G.)*	*(E.G.)*	*(E.G.)* [5]	*(E.G.)*	*(E.G.)* [1]	*(E.G.)*	*(E.G.)*	*(E.G.)* [6]
	Centavos	Dollars	Lempiras	Pesos	Pesos	Guilders	Córdobas	Balboas	Soles
1970	43.3	36.13	.	7.32	1 703	.	3.24	0.80	120.50
1971	43.5	37.19	.	7.94	1 851	.	3.27	0.81	128.65
1972	43.6	38.27	.	8.68	1 956	.	3.42	0.78	159.39
1973	43.6	40.87	44.78	10.64	2 202	414	3.68	0.87	195.50
1974	44.2 [4]	46.72	34.47	13.80	2 804	597	4.25	1.02	242.06
1975	46.0	52.41	41.30	15.44	3 412	635	4.73	1.14	255.41
1976	49.4	58.57	50.13	22.16	4 285	767	5.03	1.12	324.87
1977	53.0	59.94	48.54	25.56	5 619	1 096	5.09	1.19	394.40
1978	60.2	...	55.71	...	6 465	1 286	6.69	...	539.11
1979	...	...	87.24	...	7 509	...	...	...	785.91
1980: VI	...	.	.	.	...	.	.	.	...

EXPLANATORY NOTES: See p. 423.

NOTES EXPLICATIVES: Voir p. 426.

NOTAS EXPLICATIVAS: Véase pág. 430.

[1] Incl. salaried employees. [2] Department of San Salvador. Prior to 1975: metropolitan area. [3] Prior to 1974: Guatemala city only. [4] Series replacing former series. [5] Oct. of each year. [6] June of each year.

[1] Y compris les employés. [2] Département de San Salvador. Avant 1975 : région métropolitaine. [3] Avant 1974 : ville de Guatemala seulement. [4] Série remplaçant la précédente. [5] Oct. de chaque année. [6] Juin de chaque année.

[1] Incl. los empleados. [2] Departamento de San Salvador. Antes de 1975: área metropolitana. [3] Antes de 1974: ciudad de Guatemala solamente. [4] Serie que substituye a la anterior. [5] Oct. de cada año. [6] Junio de cada año.

18 Wages in manufacturing / Salaires dans les industries manufacturières / Salarios en las industrias manufactureras

A All industries / Ensemble des industries / Todas las industrias

Earnings *(E.G.)* or rates *(R.T.)* per hour, day, week or month

Gains *(E.G.)* ou taux *(R.T.)* par heure, jour, semaine ou mois

Ganancias *(E.G.)* o tarifas *(R.T.)* por hora, día, semana o mes

Date / *Date* / Fecha	AMERICA — AMÉRIQUE — AMÉRICA							
	Puerto Rico		Suriname	United States		Uruguay [1]	Venezuela	Virgin Is. (US)
	Hour / *Heure* / Hora	Week / *Semaine* / Semana	Month / *Mois* / Mes	Hour / *Heure* / Hora	Week / *Semaine* / Semana	Month / *Mois* / Mes	Month / *Mois* / Mes	Hour [4] / *Heure* [4] / Hora [4]
	(E.G.)		(E.G.)	(E.G.)		(R.T.) [2, 3]	(E.G.)	(E.G.) [2]
	$	$	Guilders	$	$	(1970 = 100)	Bolívares	Dollars
1970	1.76	64.59	.	3.35	133.33	100.0	960	.
1971	1.87	69.56	126	3.57	142.44	128.3	1 021	.
1972	2.00	74.40	132	3.82	154.71	190.4	1 094	.
1973	2.11	78.28	138	4.09	164.46	362.4	1 093	3.28
1974	2.32	85.61	144	4.42	176.80	637.3	1 289	3.79
1975	2.56	94.72	...	4.83	190.79	1 049.3	1 473	4.43
1976	2.78	104.25	...	5.22	209.32	1 428.0	1 514	4.78
1977	3.02	113.55	...	5.68	228.90	1 940.1	1 653	...
1978	3.36	127.34	...	6.17	249.27	2 664.1	1 870	...
1979	3.69	138.74	...	6.69	268.94	3 998.8	...	...
1980: VI	3.97 [15]	...		7.20	283.68	...	...	...

Date / *Date* / Fecha	ASIA — ASIE — ASIA							
	Bangladesh (Dacca)		Brunei [5]	Burma		Cyprus	Hong Kong	India [13]
	Day — *Jour* — Día		Hour / *Heure* / Hora	Month — *Mois* — Mes		Week [8] / *Semaine* [8] / Semana [8]	Day [12] / *Jour* [12] / Día [12]	Month / *Mois* / Mes
	Skilled / *Qualifiés* / Calificados	Unskilled / *Non qualifiés* / No calificados		Males [2] / *Hommes* [2] / Hombres [2]	Females [2] / *Femmes* [2] / Mujeres [2]			
	(R.T.)		(E.G.) [2]	(E.G.) [6]		(E.G.) [9, 10]	(R.T.)	(E.G.) [14]
	Taka	Taka	Dollars	Kyats	Kyats	Pounds	Dollars	Rupees
1970	6.91	4.90	.	162.57	136.25	8.12	14.79	227.2
1971	7.49	5.41	.	163.28	136.57	8.78	17.31	235.2
1972	7.95	5.58	1.68	139.90 [7]	132.12 [7]	10.16	19.14	250.7
1973	9.62	6.87	1.92	172.49	152.91	11.66	21.37	261.3
1974	9.50	7.42	2.18	179.42	152.22	13.71 [11]	22.49	260.9
1975	12.81	9.72	2.12	182.71	161.62	13.71	23.35	262.2
1976	15.38	10.62	2.25	216.32	178.20	14.64	27.06	433.6
1977	15.56	10.53	2.27	223.67	230.80	17.62	29.96	467.8 *
1978	...	...	2.89	212.34	184.52	21.39	33.79	...
1979	...	...	3.03	...	...	27.17	39.73	...
1980: VI	.	.	.	...	...	...	43.78 [15]	.

EXPLANATORY NOTES: See p. 423.

[1] Montevideo; private sector. [2] Incl. salaried employees. [3] Average rates. [4] First quarter of each year. [5] Incl. mining, quarrying and construction. Oct. of each year. [6] Beginning 1973: March and Sep. of each year. [7] April and Sep. [8] Oct. of each year. [9] Adults. [10] Incl. family allowances and the value of payments in kind. [11] Beginning July 1974: due to a change in the geographical scope of the series, data are not comparable with those for the preceding period. [12] March and Sep. of each year. [13] The number of states covered by the series varies according to the years. [14] Incl. electricity, gas, water and services. [15] March.

NOTES EXPLICATIVES: Voir p. 426.

[1] *Montevideo ; secteur privé.* [2] *Y compris les employés.* [3] *Taux moyens.* [4] *Premier trimestre de chaque année.* [5] *Y compris les industries extractives et la construction. Oct. de chaque année.* [6] *A partir de 1973 : mars et sept. de chaque année.* [7] *Avril et sept.* [8] *Oct. de chaque année.* [9] *Adultes.* [10] *Y compris les allocations familiales et la valeur des paiements en nature.* [11] *A partir de juillet 1974 : en raison d'un changement de la portée géographique de la série, les données ne sont pas comparables avec celles de la période précédente.* [12] *Mars et sept. de chaque année.* [13] *Le nombre d'Etats couverts par la série varie selon les années.* [14] *Y compris l'électricité, le gaz, l'eau et les services.* [15] *Mars.*

NOTAS EXPLICATIVAS: Véase pág. 430.

[1] Montevideo; sector privado. [2] Incl. los empleados. [3] Tarifas medias. [4] Primer trimestre de cada año. [5] Incl. las minas, las canteras y la construcción. Oct. de cada año. [6] A partir de 1973: marzo y sept. de cada año. [7] Abril y sept. [8] Oct. de cada año. [9] Adultos. [10] Incl. las asignaciones familiares y el valor de los pagos en especie. [11] A partir de julio de 1974: en razón de un cambio del alcance geográfico de la serie, los datos no son comparables a los del período precedente. [12] Marzo y sept. de cada año. [13] El número de Estados cubiertos por la serie varía según los años. [14] Incl. la electricidad, el gas, el agua y los servicios. [15] Marzo.

18 Wages in manufacturing
Salaires dans les industries manufacturières
Salarios en las industrias manufactureras

A All industries
Ensemble des industries
Todas las industrias

Earnings *(E.G.)* or rates *(R.T.)* per hour, day, week or month

Gains *(E.G.)* ou taux *(R.T.)* par heure, jour, semaine ou mois

Ganancias *(E.G.)* o tarifas *(R.T.)* por hora, día, semana o mes

	ASIA — ASIE — ASIA							
	Israel [1, 2]		Japan			Jordan [1]	Korea, Rep. of	Pakistan
Date	Day	Month	Month — *Mois* — Mes			Day	Month	Month
Date	*Jour*	*Mois*	Males	Females	M. + F.	*Jour*	*Mois*	*Mois*
			Hommes	*Femmes*	H. + F.			
Fecha	Día	Mes	Hombres	Mujeres	H. + M.	Día	Mes	Mes
	(E.G.) [3]	*(E.G.)* [3, 5]	*(E.G.)* [1, 7]			*(E.G.)* [8, 9]	*(E.G.)* [1, 10]	*(E.G.)*
	Pounds	Pounds	Yen	Yen	Yen	Fils	Won	Rupees
1970	26.2	664	88 212	39 272	71 447	.	14 301	152.7
1971	29.0	756	99 011	45 387	81 010	.	16 611	150.6
1972	33.0	863	113 243	53 043	93 627	.	18 923	160.3
1973	40.8	1 071	140 672 [4]	65 455 [4]	116 271 [4]	1 149	22 330	283.1
1974	56.0	1 479	176 441	82 132	146 464	1 229	30 209	302.5
1975	80.4	2 182 [6]	193 940	92 938	163 729	1 169	38 378	353.6
1976	106.5	3 039	217 893 [4]	102 257 [4]	183 557 [4]	1 884	51 685	388.4
1977	157.4	4 327	238 434	109 694	200 754	1 919	69 168	...
1978	278.4	6 756	253 419	117 246	214 575	...	92 907	...
1979	525.0 [4]	13 001 [4]	273 248 [4]	122 743 [4]	227 753 [4]	...	119 515	...
1980: VI	1 053.0 [15]	23 370 [16]	351 593	147 360	288 381		137 482 [15]	.

	ASIA — ASIE — ASIA							
	Philippines	Singapore	Sri Lanka		République arabe syrienne [8]			
Date	Month	Hour [11]	Hour [12]	Day [12]	Week — *Semaine* — Semana			Month
Date	*Mois*	*Heure* [11]	*Heure* [12]	*Jour* [12]	Males	Females	M. + F.	*Mois*
					Hommes	*Femmes*	H. + F.	
Fecha	Mes	Hora [11]	Hora [12]	Día [12]	Hombres	Mujeres	H. + M.	Mes
	(E.G.)	*(E.G.)*	*(E.G.)*		*(E.G.)* [13]			*(R.T.)* [1, 14]
	Pesos	Cents	Cents	Rupees	Pounds	Pounds	Pounds	Pounds
1970	215	90	90.52	8.28	54.90	32.90	51.10	148
1971	245	92	93.39	8.24	58.40	31.70	54.10	148
1972	275	98	109.27	9.89	65.90	36.30	61.60	148
1973	301	108	104.67	9.75	80.10	47.45	75.35	148
1974	317	126	127.21	12.30	76.70	49.75	72.75	...
1975	334	146	141.36	12.83	85.68	59.82	82.22	253
1976	...	153	145.60	12.99	111.35	72.05	105.85	...
1977	...	160	206.00	19.05	115.40	79.35	110.00	...
1978	...	171	295.00	28.75	...	...	...	...
1979	...	189	253.00	24.85	...	...	...	...
1980: VI			...	...	.	.	.	...

EXPLANATORY NOTES: See p. 423.

[1] Incl. salaried employees. [2] Incl. mining and quarrying. [3] Beginning July 1975: incl. payments subject to income tax and the value of payments in kind. [4] Sampling design revised. [5] Prior to July 1975: incl. family allowances. [6] Scope of series enlarged. [7] Incl. family allowances, mid- and end-of-year bonuses. [8] Adults. [9] April of each year. [10] Incl. family allowances and the value of payments in kind. [11] Aug. of each year. Prior to 1975: July. [12] March and Sep. of each year. [13] May of each year. [14] Minimum rates. [15] May. [16] April.

NOTES EXPLICATIVES: Voir p. 426.

[1] *Y compris les employés.* [2] *Y compris les industries extractives.* [3] *A partir de juillet 1975 : y compris les versements soumis à l'impôt sur le revenu et la valeur des paiements en nature.* [4] *Plan d'échantillonnage révisé.* [5] *Avant juillet 1975 : y compris les allocations familiales.* [6] *Portée de la série élargie.* [7] *Y compris les allocations familiales et les primes de mi- et de fin d'année.* [8] *Adultes.* [9] *Avril de chaque année.* [10] *Y compris les allocations familiales et la valeur des paiements en nature.* [11] *Août de chaque année. Avant 1975 : juillet.* [12] *Mars et sept. de chaque année.* [13] *Mai de chaque année.* [14] *Taux minima.* [15] *Mai.* [16] *Avril.*

NOTAS EXPLICATIVAS: Véase pág. 430.

[1] Incl. los empleados. [2] Incl. las minas y canteras. [3] A partir de julio de 1975: incl. los pagos sometidos al impuesto sobre la renta y el valor de los pagos en especie. [4] Diseño de la muestra revisado. [5] Antes de julio de 1975: incl. las asignaciones familiares. [6] El alcance de la serie es mayor. [7] Incl. las asignaciones familiares y las primas de mitad y de fin de año. [8] Adultos. [9] Abril de cada año. [10] Incl. las asignaciones familiares y el valor de los pagos en especie. [11] Agosto de cada año. Antes de 1975: julio. [12] Marzo y sept. de cada año. [13] Mayo de cada año. [14] Tarifas mínimas. [15] Mayo. [16] Abril.

18 A

Wages in manufacturing
Salaires dans les industries manufacturières
Salarios en las industrias manufactureras

All industries
Ensemble des industries
Todas las industrias

Earnings *(E.G.)* or rates *(R.T.)* per hour, day, week or month

Gains *(E.G.)* ou taux *(R.T.)* par heure, jour, semaine ou mois

Ganancias *(E.G.)* o tarifas *(R.T.)* por hora, día, semana o mes

	EUROPE — EUROPE — EUROPA								
	Austria	Belgique			Bulgarie [4,5]	Czechoslovakia [7]	Denmark		
Date	Month	Hour — *Heure* — Hora			Month	Month	Hour [8] — *Heure* [8] — Hora [8]		
Date	*Mois*	Males	Females	M. + F.	*Mois*	*Mois*	Males [9]	Females [9]	M. + F. [9]
Fecha	Mes	*Hommes*	*Femmes*	*H. + F.*	Mes	Mes	*Hommes* [9]	*Femmes* [9]	*H. + F.* [9]
		Hombres	Mujeres	H. + M.			Hombres [9]	Mujeres [9]	H. + M. [9]
	(E.G.) [1]	*(E.G.)* [2]			*(E.G.)* [6]	*(E.G.)*	*(E.G.)* [10]		
	Schilling	Francs	Francs	Francs	Leva	Korunas	Ore	Ore	Ore
1970	.	71.98	48.70	66.16	124	1 841	1 654	1 231	1 569
1971	5 297	81 72	55.41	75.14	127	1 904	1 871	1 434	1 789
1972	5 912	95.35 [3]	64.91 [3]	87.58 [3]	132	1 979	2 080	1 621	1 993
1973	6 665	108.51	74.5	99.83	141	2 038	2 421	1 992	2 337
1974	7 710	136.00	94.20	125.28	144	2 115	2 899	2 430	2 813
1975	8 730	155.79	111.06	144.32	150	2 200	3 441	2 901	3 350
1976	9 553	172.73	121.85	159.68	151	2 267	3 838	3 253	3 734
1977	10 355	188.69	133.39	174.59	155	2 355	4 173	3 609	4 071
1978	10 942	199.46	140.92	184.44	161	2 434	4 574	3 941	4 459
1979	11 586	217.77	151.68	199.61	170	2 505	5 059	4 370	4 922
1980: VI	14 125	.	.	.	177 [16]	2 594 [17]	.	.	.

	EUROPE — EUROPE — EUROPA								
	España	Finland [5]			France				German Dem. Rep. [1,14]
Date	Hour	Hour — *Heure* — Hora			Hour — *Heure* — Hora			Hour	Month
Date	*Heure*	Males	Females	M. + F.	Males	Females	M. + F.	*Heure*	*Mois*
Fecha	Hora	*Hommes*	*Femmes*	*H. + F.*	*Hommes*	*Femmes*	*H. + F.*	Hora	Mes
		Hombres	Mujeres	H. + M.	Hombres	Mujeres	H. + M.		
	(E.G.) [6]	*(E.G.)* [11]			*(E.G.)* [2]			*(R.T.)* [9]	*(E.G.)* [15]
	Pesetas	Markkaa	Markkaa	Markkaa	Francs	Francs	Francs	Francs	Mark
1970	39.47	5.64	3.97	5.06	.	.	5.92	4.66	748
1971	44.81	6.51	4.61	5.85	.	.	6.66	5.18	777
1972	52.20	7.43	5.30	6.69	7.98	6.12	7.47	5.82 [13]	799
1973	62.48	8.68	6.22	7.78	9.19	7.06	8.57	7.05	828
1974	78.82	10.60	7.67	9.54	11.18	8.50	10.40	8.39	838
1975	104.73	12.87	9.34	11.59	12.88	9.84	11.99	9.82	869
1976	135.97	14.78	10.85	13.42	14.99 [12]	11.33 [12]	13.87 [12]	11.11 [12]	910
1977	...	16.00	11.88	14.60	16.88	12.80	15.61	12.58	939
1978	...	17.15	12.82	15.69	18.91	14.50	17.49	14.20	973
1979	...	19.08	14.37	17.49	21.16	16.26	19.56	16.04	1 002 *
1980: VI	...	20.25 [16]	15.11 [16]	18.52 [16]	.	.	.	18.50	

EXPLANATORY NOTES: See p. 423.

[1] Incl. mining and quarrying. [2] Oct. of each year. [3] New industrial classification. [4] Socialised sector. [5] Incl. mining, quarrying and electricity. [6] Incl. salaried employees. [7] State industry. [8] July-Sep. of each year. [9] Adults. [10] Excl. vacation pay. [11] Incl. the value of payments in kind. [12] Sampling design revised. [13] Beginning Dec. 1972: revised series. [14] State sector. [15] Incl. family allowances. [16] First quarter. [17] Second quarter.

NOTES EXPLICATIVES: Voir p. 426.

[1] *Y compris les industries extractives.* [2] *Oct. de chaque année.* [3] *Nouvelle classification industrielle.* [4] *Secteur socialisé.* [5] *Y compris les industries extractives et l'électricité.* [6] *Y compris les employés.* [7] *Industrie d'Etat.* [8] *Juillet-sept. de chaque année.* [9] *Adultes.* [10] *Non compris les versements pour congés payés.* [11] *Y compris la valeur des paiements en nature.* [12] *Plan d'échantillonnage révisé.* [13] *A partir de déc. 1972: série révisée.* [14] *Secteur d'Etat.* [15] *Y compris les allocations familiales.* [16] *Premier trimestre.* [17] *Deuxième trimestre.*

NOTAS EXPLICATIVAS: Véase pág. 430.

[1] Incl. las minas y canteras. [2] Oct. de cada año. [3] Nueva clasificación industrial. [4] Sector socializado. [5] Incl. las minas, las canteras y la electricidad. [6] Incl. los empleados. [7] Industria de Estado. [8] Julio-sept. de cada año. [9] Adultos. [10] Excl. los pagos por vacaciones. [11] Incl. el valor de los pagos en especie. [12] Diseño de la muestra revisado. [13] A partir de dic. de 1972: serie revisada. [14] Sector de Estado. [15] Incl. las asignaciones familiares. [16] Primer trimestre. [17] Segundo trimestre.

18 Wages in manufacturing / Salaires dans les industries manufacturières / Salarios en las industrias manufactureras

A All industries / Ensemble des industries / Todas las industrias

Earnings (E.G.) or rates (R.T.) per hour, day, week or month

Gains (E.G.) ou taux (R.T.) par heure, jour, semaine ou mois

Ganancias (E.G.) o tarifas (R.T.) por hora, día, semana o mes

EUROPE — EUROPE — EUROPA

Date / Date / Fecha	Germany, Fed. Rep. of				Gibraltar	Grèce		
	Hour — Heure — Hora			Week Semaine Semana	Week Semaine Semana	Hour — Heure — Hora		
	Males Hommes Hombres	Females Femmes Mujeres	M. + F. H. + F. H. + M.	M. + F. H. + F. H. + M.		Males Hommes Hombres	Females Femmes Mujeres	M. + F. H. + F. H. + M.
	(E.G.) [1]				(E.G.) [3]	(E.G.)		
	Mark	Mark	Mark	Mark	£	Drachmas	Drachmas	Drachmas
1970	6.45	4.49	5.96	261	13.10	17.93	12.19	15.95
1971	7.20	5.05	6.66	287	15.35	19.70	13.04	17.35
1972	7.82	5.53	7.24	309	16.42	21.42	14.39	18.94
1973	8.69 [2]	6.16 [2]	8.03 [2]	343 [2]	23.71	25.12	16.46	22.04
1974	9.64	6.90	8.94	373	26.04	31.84	21.30	27.87
1975	10.41	7.51	9.69	392	32.84	39.26 [1]	27.29 [2]	34.74 [2]
1976	11.10	8.01	10.35	431	35.61	50.46	35.45	44.66
1977	11.92	8.62	11.14	465	41.27	61.67	42.42	53.99
1978	12.54	9.13	11.73	488	67.08	76.45	52.78	66.74
1979	13.21	9.62	12.36	518	78.96	93.20	63.30	80.50
1980: VI	14.10 [13]	10.17 [13]	13.17 [13]	550 [13]	.	116.70 [14]	78.60 [14]	101.00 [14]

EUROPE — EUROPE — EUROPA

Date / Date / Fecha	Hongrie [4]	Ireland					Italie	
	Month Mois Mes	Hour [6] — Heure [6] — Hora [6]			Week [6] — Semaine [6] Semana [6]		Hour Heure Hora	
		Males [7] Hommes [7] Hombres [7]	Females [7] Femmes [7] Mujeres [7]	M. + F. [8] H. + F. [8] H. + M. [8]	M. + F. [8] H. + F. [8] H. + M. [8]			
	(E.G.) [5]	(E.G.)					(E.G.) [10]	(R.T.)
	Forints	Pence	Pence	Pence	Pounds		Lire	(1970 = 100)
1970	2 016	53.0	29.8	42.4	18.10		606	100.0
1971	2 088	60.7	34.3	49.1	20.74		703	113.5
1972	2 181	69.2	39.6	55.9	23.64		788	125.4
1973	2 402	81.8 [9]	49.0 [9]	68.8 [9]	29.16 [9]		966	155.7
1974	2 573	98.0	58.6	83.0	34.69		1 209	190.7
1975	2 733	128.0	77.9	109.9	45.57		1 794 [11]	241.6
1976	2 895	145.8	88.9	126.2	53.40		2 133	292.1
1977	3 145	170.1	104.4	147.3	62.79		2 673	373.5
1978	3 417	195.7	124.6	170.0	71.92		3 244 [12]	516.3
1979	3 601	227.8	151.8	200.7	85.10		...	516.3
1980: VI	3 577	...	...	...	...		...	624.8

EXPLANATORY NOTES: See p. 423.

[1] Incl. family allowances paid directly by the employers. [2] Sampling design revised. [3] Oct. of each year, except for 1970-72: April and Oct., and 1974-76: April. [4] Socialised sector. Incl. mining, quarrying and electricity. [5] Incl. the value of payments in kind. Incl. loyalty money. [6] Sep. of each year. [7] Workers on adult rates of pay. [8] Incl. juveniles. [9] New industrial classification. [10] Incl. the value of payments in kind. Prior to 1975: excl. payments for annual vacation and public holidays. [11] Series replacing former series. [12] Scope of series revised. [13] April. [14] May.

NOTES EXPLICATIVES: Voir p. 426.

[1] Y compris les allocations familiales payées directement par les employeurs. [2] Plan d'échantillonnage révisé. [3] Oct. de chaque année, sauf pour 1970-1972: avril et oct., et 1974-1976: avril. [4] Secteur socialisé. Y compris les industries extractives et l'électricité. [5] Y compris la valeur des paiements en nature. Y compris les primes d'assiduité. [6] Sept. de chaque année. [7] Travailleurs rémunérés sur la base de taux de salaire pour adultes. [8] Y compris les jeunes gens. [9] Nouvelle classification industrielle. [10] Y compris la valeur des paiements en nature. Avant 1975: non compris les paiements pour congés annuels et jours fériés. [11] Série remplaçant la précédente. [12] Portée de la série révisée. [13] Avril. [14] Mai.

NOTAS EXPLICATIVAS: Véase pág. 430.

[1] Incl. las asignaciones familiares pagadas directamente por los empleadores. [2] Diseño de la muestra revisado. [3] Oct. de cada año, salvo para 1970-1972: abril y oct., y 1974-1976: abril. [4] Sector socialista. Incl. las minas y las canteras y la electricidad. [5] Incl. el valor de los pagos en especie. Incl. las primas de asiduidad. [6] Sept. de cada año. [7] Trabajadores pagados sobre la base de tarifas de salarios para adultos. [8] Incl. los jóvenes. [9] Nueva clasificación industrial. [10] Incl. el valor de los pagos en especie. Antes de 1975: excl. los pagos por vacaciones anuales y días feriados. [11] Serie que substituye a la anterior. [12] El alcance de la serie es revisado. [13] Abril. [14] Mayo.

18 Wages in manufacturing
Salaires dans les industries manufacturières
Salarios en las industrias manufactureras

A All industries
Ensemble des industries
Todas las industrias

Earnings *(E.G.)* or rates *(R.T.)* per hour, day, week or month

Gains *(E.G.)* ou taux *(R.T.)* par heure, jour, semaine ou mois

Ganancias *(E.G.)* o tarifas *(R.T.)* por hora, día, semana o mes

	EUROPE — EUROPE — EUROPA						
	Luxembourg			Netherlands			
Date *Date* Fecha	Hour — *Heure* — Hora			Hour — *Heure* — Hora			
	Males *Hommes* Hombres	Females *Femmes* Mujeres	M. + F. *H. + F.* H. + M.	Males [3] *Hommes* [3] Hombres [3]	Females [3] *Femmes* [3] Mujeres [3]	M. + F. [4] *H. + F.* [4] H. + M. [4]	M. + F. [3] *H. + F.* [3] H. + M. [3]
	(E.G.) [1]			*(E.G.)* [1]			*(R.T.)* [5]
	Francs	Francs	Francs	Guilders	Guilders	Guilders	(1970 = 100)
1970	90.78	50.27	88.51	5.49	3.94	4.82	**100**
1971	97.74	56.25	95.18	6.29	4.56	5.53	112
1972	111.66 [2]	65.13 [2]	108.91 [2]	6.98	5.06	6.38	127
1973	124.84	69.02	131.18	7.96	6.01	7.36	144
1974	156.78	89.67	151.94	9.36	7.26	8.70	168
1975	169.25	103.06	164.45	10.60	8.39	9.95	191
1976	195.50	125.33	190.10	11.41	9.11	10.77	208
1977	211.13	131.88	205.00	12.52	10.02	11.83	223
1978	224.52	135.63	217.57	13.22	10.63	12.49	236
1979	234.60	137.61	227.77	...	...	...	246
1980: VI	.	.	.	.	.	.	255

	EUROPE — EUROPE — EUROPA							
	Norway		Pologne [7]	Portugal	Roumanie [8]	Suisse (1)		
Date *Date* Fecha	Hour — *Heure* — Hora		Month *Mois* Mes	Hour *Heure* Hora	Month *Mois* Mes	Hour — *Heure* — Hora		
	Males [3] *Hommes* [3] Hombres [3]	Females [3] *Femmes* [3] Mujeres [3]				Males *Hommes* Hombres	Females *Femmes* Mujeres	M. + F. *H. + F.* H. + M.
	(E.G.) [6]		*(E.G.)* [5, 6]	*(E.G.)*	*(E.G.)* [5]	*(E.G.)* [10]		
	Kroner	Kroner	Zlotys	Escudos	Lei	Francs	Francs	Francs
1970	13.75	10.32	2 224	.	1 324	6.96	4.39	.
1971	15.45	11.65	2 344	10.50	1 461	7.82	5.01	.
1972	16.82	12.82	2 459	12.20	1 482	8.72	5.54	.
1973	18.61	14.18	2 689	14.30	1 549	9.07 [11]	6.14 [11]	8.43
1974	21.83	16.75	3 050	22.60	1 660	10.23	7.02	9.53
1975	26.15	20.41	3 667	32.60	1 823	11.11	7.55	10.34
1976	30.44	24.16	4 049	40.70	1 942	11.33	7.70	10.54
1977	33.77	26.96	4 354	47.70	1 815 [9]	11.55	7.70	10.71
1978	36.44	29.24	4 598	55.40	2 019	11.92	7.98	11.06
1979	37.47	30.15	5 400 *	...	2 118	12.30	8.26	11.42
1980: VI	38.06 [12]	31.00 [12]			.	12.97 [13]	8.61 [13]	12.02 [13]

EXPLANATORY NOTES: See p. 423.

[1] Oct. of each year. [2] New industrial classification. [3] Adults. [4] Incl. juveniles. [5] Incl. salaried employees. [6] Incl. the value of payments in kind. [7] Socialised sector. [8] Socialised sector. Incl. mining quarrying, electricity, gas and water. [9] Beginning 1977: net earnings after deduction of income taxes. [10] Accident insurance statistics. Prior to 1975: incl. family allowances. [11] Series replacing former series. [12] First quarter. [13] Second quarter.

NOTES EXPLICATIVES: Voir p. 426.

[1] *Oct. de chaque année.* [2] *Nouvelle classification industrielle.* [3] *Adultes.* [4] *Y compris les jeunes gens.* [5] *Y compris les employés.* [6] *Y compris la valeur des paiements en nature.* [7] *Secteur socialisé.* [8] *Secteur socialisé. Y compris les industries extractives, l'électricité, le gaz et l'eau.* [9] *A partir de 1977: gains nets après déduction de l'impôt sur le revenu.* [10] *Statistiques d'assurance-accidents. Avant 1975: y compris les allocations familiales.* [11] *Série remplaçant la précédente.* [12] *Premier trimestre.* [13] *Deuxième trimestre.*

NOTAS EXPLICATIVAS: Véase pág. 430.

[1] Oct. de cada año. [2] Nueva clasificación industrial. [3] Adultos. [4] Incl. los jóvenes. [5] Incl. los empleados. [6] Incl. el valor de los pagos en especie. [7] Sector socializado. [8] Sector socializado. Incl. las minas, las canteras, la electricidad, el gas y el agua. [9] A partir de 1977: ganancias netas después de deducir los impuestos sobre la renta. [10] Estadísticas del seguro de accidentes. Antes de 1975: incl. las asignaciones familiares. [11] Serie que substituye a la anterior. [12] Primer trimestre. [13] Segundo trimestre.

18 Wages in manufacturing / Salaires dans les industries manufacturières / Salarios en las industrias manufactureras — A — All industries / Ensemble des industries / Todas las industrias

Earnings *(E.G.)* or rates *(R.T.)* per hour, day, week or month

Gains *(E.G.)* ou taux *(R.T.)* par heure, jour, semaine ou mois

Ganancias *(E.G.)* o tarifas *(R.T.)* por hora, día, semana o mes

	EUROPE — EUROPE — EUROPA						
	Suisse (2)				Sweden		
	Hour [1] — *Heure* [1] — Hora [1]				Hour — *Heure* — Hora		
Date / *Date* / Fecha	Males [2] — *Hommes* [2] — Hombres [2]			Females [2] / *Femmes* [2] / Mujeres [2]	Males [2] / *Hommes* [2] / Hombres [2]	Females [2] / *Femmes* [2] / Mujeres [2]	M. + F. [4] / H. + F. [4] / H. + M. [4]
	Skilled / *Qualifiés* / Calificados	Semi-skilled and unskilled / *Semi-qualifiés et non qualifiés* / Semicalificados y no calificados	Total				
	(E.G.) [3]				(E.G.) [5, 6]		
	Francs	Francs	Francs	Francs	Kronor	Kronor	Kronor
1970	8.01	6.85	7.33	4.74	.	.	.
1971	8.97	7.78	8.27	5.37	15.64	12.88	14.91
1972	10.07	8.66	9.24	5.98	17.49	14.65	16.76
1973	11.31	9.75	10.40	6.80	19.00	15.97	18.19
1974	12.71	11.03	11.73	7.71	21.26 [7]	17.85 [7]	20.30 [7]
1975	13.53	11.89	12.57	8.29	24.84	21.16	23.79
1976	13.73	12.13	12.80	8.51	28.04	24.38	27.01
1977	14.24	12.59	13.37	8.74	30.27	26.47	29.22
1978	14.74	13.00	13.82	9.13	33.04 [7]	29.32 [7]	32.31 [7]
1979	15.29	13.43	14.30	9.43	36.77	32.83	35.75
1980: VI	.	.	.	.	.	.	.

	EUROPE — EUROPE — EUROPA						
	Turquie	United Kingdom					Yugoslavia [11]
	Day [8] / *Jour* [8] / Día [8]	Hour — *Heure* — Hora		Week — *Semaine* — Semana		Week — *Semaine* — Semana	Month / *Mois* / Mes
Date / *Date* / Fecha		Males / *Hommes* / Hombres	Females / *Femmes* / Mujeres	Males / *Hommes* / Hombres	Females / *Femmes* / Mujeres	M. + F. [4] / H. + F. [4] / H. + M. [4]	
	(E.G.) [9]	(E.G.) [1, 10]				(R.T.)	(E.G.) [9]
	Liras	Pence	Pence	£	£	1970 = 100	Dinars
1970	35.72	64.4	37.1	28.91	13.98	100.0	1 097
1971	40.74	72.0	42.1	31.37	15.80	112.5	1 335
1972	45.21	82.1	48.7	36.20	18.34	127.9	1 559
1973	57.28	92.9	56.4	41.52	21.15	144.4	1 854
1974	70.92	111.6	72.7	49.12	27.05	168.9	2 369
1975	89.75	139.9	93.0	59.74	34.23	219.8	2 901
1976	126.29	155.9	109.4	67.83	40.71	263.5	3 313
1977	127.52	168.7	119.5	73.56	44.45	275.9	3 907
1978	224.13	194.9	134.6	84.77	50.08	326.2	4 651
1979	304.20	227.5	157.1	98.28	58.44	375.0	5 617
1980: VI	.	.	.	.	.	439.4	...

EXPLANATORY NOTES: See p. 423.

NOTES EXPLICATIVES: Voir p. 426.

NOTAS EXPLICATIVAS: Véase pág. 430.

[1] Oct. of each year. [2] Adults. [3] Statistics of establishments. Incl. family allowances. [4] Incl. juveniles. [5] Beginning 1976: second quarter of each year. [6] Incl. holiday and sick-leave payments and the value of payments in kind. [7] Sampling design revised. [8] Sep. of each year. [9] Incl. salaried employees. [10] Full-time adult wage earners. [11] Socialised sector.

[1] *Oct. de chaque année.* [2] *Adultes.* [3] *Statistiques d'établissements. Y compris les allocations familiales.* [4] *Y compris les jeunes gens.* [5] *A partir de 1976 : deuxième trimestre de chaque année.* [6] *Y compris les versements au titre des vacances et congés de maladie et la valeur des paiements en nature.* [7] *Plan d'échantillonnage révisé.* [8] *Sept. de chaque année.* [9] *Y compris les employés.* [10] *Ouvriers adultes à temps complet.* [11] *Secteur socialisé.*

[1] Oct. de cada año. [2] Adultos. [3] Estadísticas de establecimientos. Incl. las asignaciones familiares. [4] Incl. los jóvenes. [5] A partir de 1976: segundo trimestre de cada año. [6] Incl. los pagos por vacaciones y licencias de enfermedad y el valor de los pagos en especie. [7] Diseño de la muestra revisado. [8] Sept. de cada año. [9] Incl. los empleados. [10] Obreros adultos a tiempo completo. [11] Sector socializado.

18 | Wages in manufacturing | A | All industries
Salaires dans les industries manufacturières | | Ensemble des industries
Salarios en las industrias manufactureras | | Todas las industrias

Earnings *(E.G.)* or rates *(R.T.)* per hour, day, week or month

Gains *(E.G.)* ou taux *(R.T.)* par heure, jour, semaine ou mois

Ganancias *(E.G.)* o tarifas *(R.T.)* por hora, día, semana o mes

		OCEANIA — OCÉANIE — OCEANÍA					Fiji	New Zealand
Date		Australia						
		Hour [2] — *Heure* [2] — Hora [2]		Hour — *Heure* — Hora			Day [6]	Week — *Semaine* Semana
Date	American Samoa						*Jour* [6]	
		Males [3]	Females [6]	Males [3]	Females [3]			Males [3]
Fecha		*Hommes* [3]	*Femmes* [3]	*Hommes* [3]	*Femmes* [3]		Día [6]	*Hommes* [3]
		Hombres [3]	Mujeres [6]	Hombres [3]	Mujeres [3]			Hombres [3]
	(R.T./h.) [1]	*(E.G.)* [4]		*(R.T.)* [1]			*(R.T.)*	*(R.T.)* [1]
	Dollars	Dollars	Dollars	Cents	Cents		Dollars	Dollars
1970	.	1.79	1.14	128.1	91.8		2.55	44.57
1971	.	2.04	1.34	143.6	105.0		2.69	56.96
1972		2.20 [5]	1.49 [5]	156.4	118.9		3.21	61.48
1973	.	2.58	1.79	176.3	135.1		3.78	68.20
1974	1.35	3.44	2.55	224.9	189.3		4.82	77.22
1975	1.42	3.82	3.00	268.1	245.5		6.19	88.39
1976	1.54	4.33	3.42	307.3	288.5		6.64	98.80
1977	1.66	4.79	3.83	341.5	322.4		6.87	111.79
1978	1.81	5.11	4.08	365.8	344.2		8.10	...
1979	1.96	5.66	4.38	393.7	367.2		8.67 *	...
1980: VI		.	.	426.4	391.3		.	

		OCEANIA — OCÉANIE — OCEANÍA		Nouvelle-Calédonie	Samoa	URSS [13, 14]	RSS de Biélorussie [13]	RSS d'Ukraine [13]
Date		New Zealand						
		Hour — *Heure* — Hora		Hour — *Heure* Hora				
Date					Week	Month	Month	Month
	Males [7]	Females [7]	M. + F. [7]	Labourers [10]	*Semaine*	*Mois*	*Mois*	*Mois*
Fecha	*Hommes* [7]	*Femmes* [7]	*H. + F.* [7]	*Manœuvres* [10]	Semana	Mes	Mes	Mes
	Hombres [7]	Mujeres [7]	H. + M. [7]	Obreros no calificados [10]				
		(E.G.) [8]		*(R.T.)* [11]	*(E.G.)* [4, 7]	*(E.G.)* [4]	*(E.G.)* [4]	*(E.G.)* [4]
	Dollars	Dollars	Dollars	Francs (CFP)	Sene	Roubles	Roubles	Roubles
1970	.	.	1.28	105.05	872	127.5	.	120.0
1971	.	.	1.54 [9]	113.70	1 077	131.7	.	123.9
1972	.	.	1.68	108.20 [12]	1 041	136.4	125.4	127.7
1973	.	.	1.92	112.73	992	141.3	129 6	131.5
1974	2.43	1.60	2.22	127.13	1 004	149.8	134.1	135.7
1975	2.76	1.90	2.54	142.81	1 324	155.8	138.8	143.1
1976	3.14	2.24	2.91	150.89	1 638	163.2 [15]	...	161.9 [15]
1977	3.60	2.64	3.34	159.81	1 939	166.3	...	165.6
1978	4.12	2.99	3.83	171.41	...	170.8	...	169.1
1979	4.78	3.46	4.42	181.97	...	174.3	...	172.4
1980: VI	...	...	...	.	.	.	.	.

EXPLANATORY NOTES: See p. 423.

[1] Minimum rates. [2] Oct. of each year. [3] Adults. [4] Incl. salaried employees. [5] Scope of series enlarged. [6] June of each year. [7] Incl. juveniles. [8] April and Oct. of each year. [9] New industrial classification. [10] First category. [11] Prior to Sep. 1972: incl. production bonuses. [12] Sep.-Dec. [13] Socialised sector. [14] Incl. Byelorussian SSR and Ukrainian SSR, shown separately in this table. [15] Beginning 1976: incl. mining and quarrying.

NOTES EXPLICATIVES: Voir p. 426.

[1] *Taux minima.* [2] *Oct. de chaque année.* [3] *Adultes.* [4] *Y compris les employés.* [5] *Portée de la série élargie.* [6] *Juin de chaque année.* [7] *Y compris les jeunes gens.* [8] *Avril et oct. de chaque année.* [9] *Nouvelle classification industrielle.* [10] *Première catégorie.* [11] *Avant sept. 1972: y compris les primes de productivité.* [12] *Sept.-déc.* [13] *Secteur socialisé.* [14] *Y compris les RSS de Biélorussie et d'Ukraine, figurant séparément dans ce tableau.* [15] *A partir de 1976: y compris les industries extractives.*

NOTAS EXPLÍCATIVAS: Véase pág. 430.

[1] Tarifas mínimas. [2] Oct. de cada año. [3] Adultos. [4] Incl. los empleados. [5] El alcance de la serie es mayor. [6] Junio de cada año. [7] Incl. los jóvenes. [8] Abril y oct. de cada año. [9] Nueva clasificación industrial. [10] Primera categoría. [11] Antes de sept. de 1972: incl. las primas de producción. [12] Sept.-dic. [13] Sector socializado. [14] Incl. las RSS de Bielorrusia y de Ucrania, que figuran separadamente en este cuadro. [15] A partir de 1976: incl. las minas y canteras.

WAGES

18 Wages in manufacturing
Salaires dans les industries manufacturières
Salarios en las industrias manufactureras

B By industry
Par industrie
Por industria

AFRICA — AFRIQUE — AFRICA

Algérie

Average hourly earnings *(dinars)*
Gains horaires moyens *(dinars)*
Promedio de ganancias por hora *(dinars)*

	311-313	321-322	323-324	33	34
Date [1]	Food, beverages	Textiles, clothing	Leather, leather products, footwear	Wood, furniture	Paper, printing, publishing
Date [1]	*Aliments, boissons*	*Textiles, habillement*	*Cuir, articles en cuir, chaussures*	*Bois, ameublement*	*Papier, imprimerie, édition*
Fecha [1]	Alimentos, bebidas	Textiles, vestidos	Cuero, artículos de cuero, calzado	Madera, mobiliario	Papel, imprentas, editoriales
1970	2.30	2.30	2.25	2.90	2.55
1971	2.59	2.38	2.64	2.42	2.81
1972	2.49	2.52	2.91	2.82	2.84
1973	2.94	3.42	3.03	2.99	3.18
1974	3.52	3.74	3.68	3.69	3.52
1975	3.11	3.85	4.35	4.17	3.51

	351-352; 355	369 ×	37	381-383	390
Date [1]	Chemicals, rubber products	Building material	Basic metal industries	Metal products, machinery, etc.	Other manufacturing industries
Date [1]	*Industrie chimique, caoutchouc*	*Matériaux de construction*	*Industrie métallurgique de base*	*Produits métalliques, machines, etc.*	*Autres industries manufacturières*
Fecha [1]	Productos químicos, caucho	Materiales de construcción	Industrias metalúrgicas básicas	Productos metálicos, maquinaria, etc.	Otras industrias manufactureras
1970	2.40	2.15	3.05	2.95	2.85
1971	3.28	1.84	3.44	3.18	2.14
1972	3.48	2.58	3.99	3.46	1.73
1973	3.59	3.44	3.94	3.61	3.48
1974	4.12	2.55	4.09	4.03	3.01
1975	4.69	3.80	4.91	3.82	3.13

[1] April of each year.   [1] *Avril de chaque année.*   [1] Abril de cada año.

18 B

Wages in manufacturing
Salaires dans les industries manufacturières
Salarios en las industrias manufactureras

By industry
Par industrie
Por industria

Egypt (1)

Average weekly earnings *(piastres)*
Gains hebdomadaires moyens *(piastres)*
Promedio de ganancias por semana *(piastres)*

Date [1] / Date [1] / Fecha [1]	311-312 Food / Aliments / Alimentos	313 Beverages / Boissons / Bebidas	314 Tobacco / Tabac / Tabaco	321 Textiles	322 Clothing / Habillement / Vestido	323 Leather, leather products / Cuir, articles en cuir / Cuero, artículos de cuero	324 Footwear / Chaussures / Calzado	331 Wood / Bois / Madera	332 Furniture / Ameublement / Mobiliario
1970	392	548	642	430	307	425	410	354	300
1971	408	522	519	422	446	490	408	364	303
1972	460	600	572	515	362	434	474	387	324
1973	482	618	724	517	296	447	418	441	367
1974	535	633	761	551	390	508	511	489	596
1975	561	649	855	570	417	608	494	499	562
1976 *	637	745	899	689	897	667	523	625	540

Date [1] / Date [1] / Fecha [1]	341 Paper, paper products / Papier, articles en papier / Papel, artículos de papel	342 Printing, publishing / Imprimerie, édition / Imprentas, editoriales	351 Industrial chemicals / Chimie industrielle / Química industrial	352 Other chemical products / Autres produits chimiques / Otros productos químicos	353 Petroleum refineries / Raffineries de pétrole / Refinerías de petróleo	354 Products of petroleum and coal / Dérivés du pétrole et du charbon / Derivados del petróleo y del carbón	355 Rubber products / Produits en caoutchouc / Productos de caucho	356 Plastic products / Articles en matière plastique / Productos plásticos	361 Pottery china, earthenware / Grès, porcelaines, faïences / Barro, loza, porcelana
1970	367	573	524	586	794	404	474	421	293
1971	388	743	534	512	803	429	474	436	355
1972	444	681	553	555	692	661	521	448	421
1973	541	721	443	554	821	705	751	505	342
1974	510	791	643	693	864	801	674	558	687
1975	531	857	601	612	875	877	730	572	733
1976 *	680	818	737	735	982	960	758	573	617

[1] Oct. of each year.   [1] *Oct. de chaque année.*   [1] *Oct. de cada año.*

18 Wages in manufacturing
Salaires dans les industries manufacturières
Salarios en las industrias manufactureras

B By industry
Par industrie
Por industria

Egypt (2)

Average weekly earnings *(piastres)*
Gains hebdomadaires moyens *(piastres)*
Promedio de ganancias por semana *(piastres)*

| Date [1] / Date [1] / Fecha [1] | 362 | 369 | 371 Basic metal industries / Industrie métallurgique de base / Industrias metalúrgicas básicas | | 381 | 382 | 383 | 384 | 385 | 390 |
| | | | 372 | | | | | | | |
	Glass, and glass products / Verre / Vidrio	Other non-metallic mineral products / Autres produits minéraux / Otros productos minerales	Iron and steel / Sidérurgie / Hierro y acero	Non-ferrous metal / Métaux non ferreux / Metales no ferrosos	Metal products / Produits métallurgiques / Productos metálicos	Machinery (non-electrical) / Machines (non électriques) / Maquinaria (no eléctrica)	Electrical machinery and apparatus / Machines et appareils électriques / Maquinaria y aparatos eléctricos	Transport equipment / Matériel de transport / Material de transporte	Scientific, measuring, optical, etc., equipment / Matériel scientifique, de précision, d'optique, etc. / Equipo científico, de medida, de óptica, etc.	Other manufacturing industries / Autres industries manufacturières / Otras industrias manufactureras
1970	385	465	717	647	448	639	428	667	441	388
1971	340	471	639	642	546	601	450	602	406	318
1972	468	560	636	552	580	576	490	595	439	452
1973	454	533	716	649	469	679	504	600	399	489
1974	487	558	767	629	589	765	564	665	449	668
1975	557	645	628	516	707	708	572	727	516	504
1976 *	760	717	932	641	795	825	799	762	951	631

[1] Oct. of each year.   [1] *Oct. de chaque année.*   [1] Oct. de cada año.

18 Wages in manufacturing
Salaires dans les industries manufacturières
Salarios en las industrias manufactureras

B By industry
Par industrie
Por industria

Malawi (1)

Average monthly earnings [1] *(kwacha)*
Gains mensuels moyens [1] *(kwacha)*
Promedio de ganancias por mes [1] *(kwacha)*

Date / Date / Fecha	311-312 Food / Aliments / Alimentos	313 Beverages / Boissons / Bebidas	314 Tobacco / Tabac / Tabaco	321 Textiles	322 Clothing / Habillement / Vestido	323 Leather, leather products / Cuir, articles en cuir / Cuero, artículos de cuero	324 Footwear / Chaussures / Calzado
1970	34.40	23.00	28.20	24.40	19.60 [3]	20.20	.
1971	.	.	.	.	.	.	.
1972	30.88	24.12	23.82	29.41	23.22	19.34	26.70
1973	34.20	28.00	25.14	29.94	26.26	16.74	39.24
1974	41.40	32.29	33.21	33.27	29.72	20.36	37.89
1975	43.70	35.44	30.44	41.68	35.31	20.88	38.15
1976	32.89	87.34	28.43	41.70	39.33	20.45	81.57
1977 [2]	28.37	84.14	34.80	47.06	33.11	35.11	101.73
1978	34.65	73.08	37.31	48.22	33.13	48.36	93.32

Date / Date / Fecha	331 Wood / Bois / Madera	332 Furniture / Ameublement / Mobiliario	341 Paper, paper products / Papier, articles en papier / Papel, artículos de papel	342 Printing, publishing / Imprimerie, édition / Imprentas, editoriales	351 Industrial chemicals / Chimie industrielle / Química industrial	352 Other chemical products / Autres produits chimiques / Otros productos químicos	355 Rubber products / Produits en caoutchouc / Productos de caucho
1970	.	24.40	52.80	.	56.00	.	55.00
1971	.	.	.	.	.	.	.
1972	23.96	23.22	65.38	41.74	78.58	73.13	58.80
1973	20.38	22.04	36.20	90.91	93.69	74.10	60.10
1974	20.54	34.83	35.78	46.35	92.71	90.10	65.01
1975	22.95	33.68	46.21	51.25	78.84	108.48	55.61
1976	31.92	23.87	48.67	80.00	94.28	90.26	61.39
1977 [2]	22.81	45.37	56.30	72.19	170.92	100.82	71.21
1978	24.39	53.39	67.54	85.38	175.69	114.64	61.14

[1] Incl. salaried employees. [2] Scope of series enlarged.
[3] Incl. footwear.

[1] *Y compris les employés.* [2] *Portée de la série élargie.*
[3] *Y compris la chaussure.*

[1] Incl. los empleados. [2] El alcance de la serie es mayor. [3] Incl. el calzado.

18 Wages in manufacturing
Salaires dans les industries manufacturières
Salarios en las industrias manufactureras

B By industry
Par industrie
Por industria

Malawi (2)

Average monthly earnings [1] *(kwacha)*
Gains mensuels moyens [1] *(kwacha)*
Promedio de ganancias por mes [1] *(kwacha)*

	356	369	381	382	383	384	390
Date *Date* Fecha	Plastic products *Articles en matière plastique* Productos plásticos	Non-metallic mineral products *Produits minéraux non métalliques* Productos minerales no metálicos	Metal products *Produits métalliques* Productos metálicos	Machinery (non-electrical) *Machines (non électriques)* Maquinaria (no eléctrica)	Electrical machinery and apparatus *Machines et appareils électriques* Maquinaria y aparatos eléctricos	Transport equipment *Matériel de transport* Material de transporte	Other manufacturing industries *Autres industries manufacturières* Otras industrias manufactureras
1970	.	38.20	47.40	.	.	104.00	48.40
1971	.	.	.	.	.	.	.
1972	24.71	38.05	41.49	48.37	47.35	97.26	51.55
1973	44.42	31.40	48.99	60.97	59.08	108.96	...
1974	67.68	41.30	46.57	54.87	57.24	117.87	56.50
1975	46.19	41.13	49.69	63.33	68.68	144.23	20.29
1976	52.56	33.47	57.32	74.47	87.66	121.09	26.24
1977 [2]	68.86	38.36	60.24	84.81	95.77	86.94	40.68
1978	70.90	36.49	50.66	70.29	83.79	77.76	40.85

[1] Incl. salaried employees. [2] Scope of series enlarged.   [1] *Y compris les employés.* [2] *Portée de la série élargie.*   [1] Incl. los empleados. [2] El alcance de la serie es mayor.

Mauritius (1)

Average daily earnings *(rupees)*
Gains journaliers moyens *(rupees)*
Promedio de ganancias por día *(rupees)*

	311-312	313	314	321	322	323; 355	324	33	341
Date [1] *Date [1]* Fecha [1]	Food *Aliments* Alimentos	Beverages *Boissons* Bebidas	Tobacco *Tabac* Tabaco	Textiles	Clothing *Habillement* Vestido	Leather, leather products, rubber *Cuir, articles en cuir, caoutchouc* Cuero, artículos de cuero, caucho	Footwear *Chaussures* Calzado	Wood, furniture *Bois, ameublement* Madera, mobiliario	Paper, paper products *Papier, articles en papier* Papel, artículos de papel
1970	6.11	5.08	6.72	5.23	3.85	4.47	5.95	7.47	.
1971	6.52	4.35	7.13	5.21	4.92	3.55	7.02	7.72	.
1972	6.40	5.31	6.57	5.32	3.35	4.23	6.56	7.20	.
1973	6.14	6.00	8.96	5.82	3.33	3.60	7.19	9.48	.
1974	8.65	7.40	7.81	6.51	4.44	5.77	8.79	9.87	.
1975	9.05	7.08	11.07	9.32	6.34	9.30	9.85	13.04	.
1976	12.46	10.33	12.83	11.22	8.99	10.45	14.00	19.34	.
1977	16.59	13.92	13.42	14.23	10.61	11.84	17.09	21.09	.
1978	21.30	15.60	15.13	16.35	12.98	13.56	19.05	30.98	13.49
1979	24.83	15.84	16.25	18.75	14.62	16.19	20.24	25.50	16.50

[1] Sep. of each year.   [1] *Sept. de chaque année.*   [1] Sept. de cada año.

18 Wages in manufacturing
Salaires dans les industries manufacturières
Salarios en las industrias manufactureras

B By industry
Par industrie
Por industria

Mauritius (2)

Average daily earnings *(rupees)*
Gains journaliers moyens *(rupees)*
Promedio de ganancias por día *(rupees)*

	342	351-352	356	381	382	383	384	390	
Date [1] *Date [1]* Fecha [1]	Printing, publishing *Imprimerie, édition* Imprentas, editoriales	Chemicals *Industrie chimique* Productos químicos	Plastic products *Articles en matière plastique* Productos plásticos	Metal products *Produits métalliques* Productos metálicos	Machinery (non-electrical) *Machines (non électriques)* Maquinaria (no eléctrica)	Electrical machinery and apparatus *Machines et appareils électriques* Maquinaria y aparatos eléctricos	Transport equipment *Matériel de transport* Material de transporte	Jewelry and related articles *Bijouterie, orfèvrerie et joaillerie* Joyas y artículos conexos	Other manufacturing industries *Autres industries manufacturières* Otras industrias manufactureras
1970	7.51	4.57	.	6.43	7.45	5.06	5.98	.	6.32
1971	7.35	4.53	.	6.03	7.15	6.26	11.49	.	3.64
1972	8.76	4.86	.	6.84	8.34	7.26	15.39	.	4.27
1973	8.55	5.29	.	7.08	8.06	5.27	10.16	.	4.24
1974	11.35	6.27	.	9.95	11.69	5.38	16.84	.	6.97
1975	13.87	6.82	.	13.17	14.79	6.00	13.43	.	8.23
1976	16.56	11.86	.	19.19	19.10	8.41	26.12	.	12.22
1977	22.66	16.71	.	20.28	43.65	10.86	33.56	.	13.23
1978	27.27	19.88	13.37	19.62	30.63	13.34	35.00	15.33	12.53
1979	29.87	17.39	14.76	21.46	31.19	13.25	35.02	13.06	15.59

[1] Sep. of each year.

[1] *Sept. de chaque année.*

[1] Sept. de cada año.

18 Wages in manufacturing
Salaires dans les industries manufacturières
Salarios en las industrias manufactureras

B By industry
Par industrie
Por industria

AMERICA — AMÉRIQUE — AMERICA

Argentina

Average hourly earnings [1] *(pesos)*
Gains horaires moyens [1] *(pesos)*
Promedio de ganancias por hora [1] *(pesos)*

Date / Date / Fecha	311-312 Food / Aliments / Alimentos	313 Beverages / Boissons / Bebidas	314 Tobacco / Tabac / Tabaco	321 × Textiles — Cotton / Coton / Algodón	321 × Textiles — Wool / Laine / Lana	322 Clothing / Habillement / Vestido	323 Leather, leather products / Cuir, articles en cuir / Cuero, artículos de cuero	324 Footwear / Chaussure / Calzado	331 Wood / Bois / Madera
1970	1.56	1.48	1.59	1.58	1.66	1.48	1.75	1.36	1.66
1971	2.16	2.14	2.17	2.21	2.29	2.02	2.38	1.94	2.30
1972	3.18	3.18	3.17	3.25	3.36	2.96	3.47	2.83	3.36
1973	5.60	5.73	5.43	5.75	5.85	5.19	5.97	5.22	5.65
1974	7.16	7.29	7.00	7.32	7.42	6.76	7.53	7.00	7.35
1975	19.46	19.43	21.63	18.93	19.19	19.17	22.45	21.65	19.75
1976	70.81	71.20	59.52	61.01	61.64	67.49	64.38	59.48	56.24
1977	142.51	152.70	126.87	131.06	133.63	135.01	154.16	120.35	127.19

Date / Date / Fecha	341 Paper, paper products / Papier, articles en papier / Papel, artículos de papel	342 Printing, publishing / Imprimerie, édition / Imprentas, editoriales	351 Industrial chemicals / Chimie industrielle / Química industrial	355 Rubber products / Produits en caoutchouc / Productos de caucho	361 × Ceramics / Céramique / Cerámica	362 Glass / Verre / Vidrio	37 Basic metal industries / Industrie métallurgique de base / Industrias metalúrgicas básicas	384 Transport equipment / Matériel de transport / Material de transporte
1970	1.80	1.52	2.20	1.60	1.58	1.68	1.75	2.00
1971	2.46	2.08	2.94	2.20	2.16	2.21	2.43	2.68
1972	3.58	3.06	4.23	3.23	3.17	3.21	3.55	3.97
1973	6.20	5.41	6.54	5.76	5.71	5.65	6.40	7.00
1974	7.77	6.98	8.11	7.70	7.57	7.22	8.47	9.13
1975	20.05	18.34	19.84	21.06	22.55	15.12	21.15	24.87
1976	58.14	61.84	55.07	57.04	69.46	48.27	57.45	65.76
1977	137.28	123.19	125.70	137.25	145.88	107.59	129.44	146.62

[1] Unskilled workers.　　　[1] *Ouvriers non qualifiés.*　　　[1] Obreros no calificados.

18 Wages in manufacturing / Salaires dans les industries manufacturières / Salarios en las industrias manufactureras

B By industry / Par industrie / Por industria

Barbados

Average weekly earnings [1] *(dollars)*
Gains hebdomadaires moyens [1] *(dollars)*
Promedio de ganancias por semana [1] *(dollars)*

Date / Date / Fecha	31 Food, beverages, tobacco / Aliments, boissons, tabac / Alimentos, bebidas, tabaco	32 Textiles, clothing, leather, / Textiles, habillement, cuir / Textiles, vestido, cuero	33 Wood, furniture / Bois, ameublement / Madera, mobiliario	34 Paper, printing, publishing / Papier, imprimerie, édition / Papel, imprentas, editoriales	35 Chemicals, etc. / Industrie chimique, etc. / Productos químicos, etc.	36 Non-metallic mineral products / Produits minéraux non métalliques / Productos minerales no metálicos	38 Metal products, machinery, etc. / Produits métalliques, machines, etc. / Productos metálicos, maquinaria, etc.	39 Other manufacturing industries / Autres industries manufacturières / Otras industrias manufactureras
1974	80.88	38.79	56.82	63.12	70.02	75.41	47.78	43.93
1975	99.46	44.39	59.46	72.81	72.93	86.03	60.03	48.53
1976	112.26	46.89	68.57	92.06	90.98	91.05	66.52	50.92
1977	129.17	66.20	93.06	101.68	102.23	109.16	78.27	62.69

[1] Adults only.   [1] *Adultes seulement.*   [1] Adultos solamente.

Bolivia (1)

Monthly rates [1] *(pesos)*
Taux mensuels [1] *(pesos)*
Tarifas por mes [1] *(pesos)*

Date / Date / Fecha	311-312 Food / Aliments / Alimentos	313 Beverages / Boissons / Bebidas	314 Tobacco / Tabac / Tabaco	321 Textiles	322; 324 Clothing, footwear / Habillement, chaussures / Vestido, calzado	323 Leather, leather products / Cuir, articles en cuir / Cuero, artículos de cuero
1971	1 131	1 792	1 155	987	1 017	778
1972	1 266	1 927	1 290	1 122	1 152	913
1973	1 386	2 047	1 410	1 242	1 272	1 033
1974	1 786	2 447	1 810	1 642	1 672	1 433
1975	1 786	2 447	1 810	1 642	1 672	1 433
1976	1 786	2 447	1 810	1 642	1 672	1 433
1977	2 086	2 747	2 110	1 942	1 972	1 733

[1] Incl. salaried employees.   [1] *Y compris les employés.*   [1] Incl. los empleados.

WAGES

18 Wages in manufacturing
Salaires dans les industries manufacturières
Salarios en las industrias manufactureras

B By industry
Par industrie
Por industria

Bolivia (2)

Monthly rates [1] *(pesos)*
Taux mensuels [1] *(pesos)*
Tarifas por mes [1] *(pesos)*

Date / Date / Fecha	331 Wood / Bois / Madera	332 Furniture / Ameublement / Mobiliario	341 Paper, paper products / Papier, articles en papier / Papel, artículos de papel	342 Printing, publishing / Imprimerie, édition / Imprentas, editoriales	351-352 Chemicals / Industrie chimique / Productos químicos	355 Rubber products / Produits en caoutchouc / Productos de caucho
1971	607	676	905	1 050	1 125	899
1972	742	811	1 040	1 185	1 260	1 034
1973	862	931	1 160	1 305	1 380	1 154
1974	1 262	1 331	1 560	1 705	1 780	1 554
1975	1 262	1 331	1 560	1 705	1 780	1 554
1976	1 262	1 331	1 560	1 705	1 780	1 554
1977	1 562	1 631	1 860	2 005	2 080	1 854

Date / Date / Fecha	369 Other non-metallic mineral products / Autres produits minéraux non métalliques / Otros productos minerales no metálicos	37 Basic metal industries / Industrie métallurgique de base / Industrias metalúrgicas básicas	381 Metal products / Produits métalliques / Productos metálicos	382 Machinery (non-electrical) / Machines (non électriques) / Maquinaria (no eléctrica)	383 Electrical machinery and apparatus / Machines et appareils électriques / Maquinaria y aparatos eléctricos	384 Transport equipment / Matériel de transport / Material de transporte	390 Other manufacturing industries / Autres industries manufacturières / Otras industrias manufactureras
1971	1 121	1 452	692	898	634	796	780
1972	1 256	1 587	827	1 033	769	931	915
1973	1 376	1 707	947	1 153	889	1 051	1 035
1974	1 776	2 107	1 347	1 553	1 289	1 451	1 435
1975	1 776	2 107	1 347	1 553	1 289	1 451	1 435
1976	1 776	2 107	1 340	1 553	1 289	1 451	1 435
1977	2 076	2 407	1 647	1 853	1 589	1 741	1 735

[1] Incl. salaried employees.　　　[1] *Y compris les employés.*　　　[1] Incl. los empleados.

18 Wages in manufacturing / Salaires dans les industries manufacturières / Salarios en las industrias manufactureras

B By industry / Par industrie / Por industria

Brésil

Average monthly earnings [1] *(cruzeiros)*
Gains mensuels moyens [1] *(cruzeiros)*
Promedio de ganancias por mes [1] *(cruzeiros)*

Date / Date / Fecha	311-312 Food / Aliments / Alimentos	313 Beverages / Boissons / Bebidas	314 Tobacco / Tabac / Tabaco	321 Textiles	322; 324 Clothing, footwear / Habillement, chaussures / Vestido, calzado	341 Paper, paper products / Papier, articles en papier / Papel, artículos de papel	351 Industrial chemicals / Chimie industrielle / Química industrial
1971 [2]	559	748	631	483	368	743	978
1972 [2]	672	936	792	604	465	947	1 277
1973	750	1 024	886	651	532	1 072	1 380
1974	998	1 340	1 071	835	699	1 437	1 798
1975	1 378	1 847	1 486	1 145	982	2 041	2 728
1976	1 990	2 683	2 325	1 654	1 452	2 981	3 906

Date / Date / Fecha	352 × Soap, perfumes, candles / Savons, parfums, bougies / Jabones, perfumes, velas	355 Rubber products / Produits en caoutchouc / Productos de caucho	356 Plastic products / Articles en matière plastique / Productos plásticos	36 Non-metallic mineral products / Produits minéraux non métalliques / Productos minerales no metálicos	371 Iron and steel basic industries / Sidérurgie / Industrias básicas de hierro y acero	383 Metal products / Produits métalliques / Productos metálicos	383 Electrical machinery and apparatus / Machines et appareils électriques / Maquinaria y aparatos eléctricos	384 Transport equipment / Matériel de transport / Material de transporte
1971 [2]	810	880	677	638	813	910	841	1 089
1972 [2]	1 013	1 088	795	820	986	1 117	1 067	1 401
1973	1 136	1 157	889	898	1 104	1 217	1 131	1 601
1974	1 541	1 471	1 182	1 225	1 465	1 571	1 453	1 958
1975	1 855	2 065	1 687	1 666	2 127	2 245	2 155	2 677
1976	2 581	3 023	2 468	2 444	3 212	3 365	3 197	3 833

[1] Incl. salaried employees. [2] Dec.   [1] *Y compris les employés.* [2] *Déc.*   [1] Incl. los empleados. [2] Dic.

461

18 Wages in manufacturing / Salaires dans les industries manufacturières / Salarios en las industrias manufactureras

B By industry / Par industrie / Por industria

Canada (1)

Average hourly earnings *(dollars)*
Gains horaires moyens *(dollars)*
Promedio de ganancias por hora *(dollars)*

	311-312	313	314	321 ×	322	323-324	324	331
Date	Food	Beverages	Tobacco		Clothing	Leather, leather products	Footwear	Wood
Date	Aliments	Boissons	Tabac	Textiles 1	Habillement	Cuir, articles en cuir	Chaussures	Bois
Fecha	Alimentos	Bebidas	Tabaco		Vestido	Cuero, artículos de cuero	Calzado	Madera
1970	2.60	3.37	3.41	2.37	2.00	2.03	1.97	2.89
1971	2.85	3 66	3.84	2.57	2.18	2.21	2.12	3.22
1972	3.09	4.09	4.09	2.76	2.35	2.35	2.25	3.51
1973	3.38	4.38	4.52	2.97	2.54	2.57	2.47	3.92
1974	3.90	4.94	5.06	3.39	2.90	2.95	2.86	4.51
1975	4.62	5.76	5.94	3.95	3.40	3.46	3.32	5.17
1976	5.25	6.51	6.69	4.50	3.86	3.93	3.77	6.06
1977	5.75	7.08	7.56	5.00	4.23	4.27	4.13	6.74
1978	6.14	7.49	7.95	5.38	4.59	4.54	4.38	7.31
1979	6.71	8.54	8.84	5.90	4.95	4.91	4.78	7.95

	332	341	342	351-352	353	354	355	356
Date	Furniture	Paper, paper products	Printing, publishing	Chemicals	Petroleum refineries	Products of petroleum and coal	Rubber products	Plastic products
Date	Ameublement	Papier, articles en papier	Imprimerie, édition	Industrie chimique	Raffineries de pétrole	Dérivés du pétrole et du charbon	Produits en caoutchouc	Articles en matière plastique
Fecha	Mobiliario	Papel, artículos de papel	Imprentas, editoriales	Productos químicos	Refinerías de petróleo	Derivados del petróleo y del carbón	Productos de caucho	Productos plásticos
1970	2.40	3.49	3.56	3.22	4.25	4.21	3.13	2.39
1971	2.57	3.88	3.86	3.48	4.54	4.48	3.33	2.59
1972	2.74	4.18	4.20	3.74	4.96	4.92	3.67	2.76
1973	3.00	4.47	4.56	4.01	5.26	5.19	3.90	2.98
1974	3.41	5.17	5.00	4.49	6.01	5.95	4.25	3.35
1975	4.00	5.87	5.76	5.22	6.91	6.84	5.07	3.97
1976	4.55	6.89	6.41	5.89	7.73	7.63	5.64	4.44
1977	5.07	7.69	6.98	6.51	8.74	8.60	6.11	4.85
1978	5.36	8.24	7.46	6.97	9.48	9.26	6.61	5.16
1979	5.86	8.93	8.21	7.67	10.31	10.04	7.38	5.62

1 Excl. knitting mills.   1 Non compris les fabriques de bonneterie et de tricot.   1 Excl. las fábricas de tejidos de punto.

18 Wages in manufacturing
Salaires dans les industries manufacturières
Salarios en las industrias manufactureras

B By industry
Par industrie
Por industria

Canada (2)

Average hourly earnings *(dollars)*
Gains horaires moyens *(dollars)*
Promedio de ganancias por hora *(dollars)*

	36	371	372	381	382	383	384	385	390
Date *Date* Fecha	Non-metallic mineral products *Produits minéraux non métalliques* Productos minerales no metálicos	Basic metal industries / *Industrie métallurgique de base* / Industrias metalúrgicas básicas — Iron and steel / *Sidérurgie* / Hierro y acero	Non-ferrous metal / *Métaux non ferreux* / Metales no ferrosos	Metal products *Produits métalliques* Productos metálicos	Machinery (non-electrical) *Machines (non électriques)* Maquinaria (no eléctrica)	Electrical machinery and apparatus *Machines et appareils électriques* Maquinaria y aparatos eléctricos	Transport equipment *Matériel de transport* Material de transporte	Scientific, measuring, optical, etc., equipment *Matériel scientifique, de précision, d'optique, etc.* Equipo científico, de medida, de óptica, etc.	Other manufacturing industries *Autres industries manufacturières* Otras industrias manufactureras
1970	3.18	3.86	3.12	3.25	3.41	2.91	3.55	2.74	2.42
1971	3.53	4.18	3.38	3.52	3.74	3.12	3.93	3.00	2.62
1972	3.85	4.55	3.66	3.75	4.00	3.30	4.26	3.21	2.80
1973	4.24	4.98	4.02	4.08	4.36	3.53	4.64	3.49	3.03
1974	4.75	5.41	4.54	4.61	4.88	4.04	5.18	3.82	3.41
1975	5.56	6.06	5.25	5.38	5.63	4.70	5.81	4.38	3.98
1976	6.25	7.01	5.93	6.06	6.24	5.24	6.60	4.83	4.46
1977	6.89	7.75	6.50	6.69	6.84	5.76	7.34	5.50	4.93
1978	7.43	8.37	6.82	7.10	7.34	6.13	7.85	5.84	5.25
1979	8.17	9.11	7.35	7.72	8.01	6.57	8.45	6.34	5.72

Colombia (1)

Average hourly earnings *(pesos)*
Gains horaires moyens *(pesos)*
Promedio de ganancias por hora *(pesos)*

Date *Date* Fecha	Food *Aliments* Alimentos	Beverages *Boissons* Bebidas	Tobacco *Tabac* Tabaco	Textiles	Clothing *Habillement* Vestido	Wood *Bois* Madera	Furniture *Ameublement* Mobiliario	Paper, paper products *Papier, articles en papier* Papel, artículos de papel	Printing, publishing *Imprimerie, édition* Imprentas, editoriales	Leather, leather products *Cuir, articles en cuir* Cuero, artículos de cuero
1971	6.54	8.40	8.24	8.13	4.26	4.72	4.99	8.26	7.96	5.77
1972	7.28	9.15	8.91	8.72	4.74	5.08	5.45	9.78	8.35	5.96
1973	8.08	10.58	9.93	9.72	5.34	5.77	6.21	11.30	9.07	6.70
1974	9.74	12.98	10.71	11.45	6.66	6.90	7.49	13.77	11.01	8.07
1975	13.07	15.58	11.62	13.28	8.45	8.85	9.83	16.19	13.37	10.73
1976	15.69	19.24	14.08	16.56	10.89	10.73	11.63	21.46	15.38	13.36
1977	19.41	24.21	19.07	20.43	13.62	15.13	15.73	27.95	19.39	16.11
1978	23.81	32.30	25.08	27.80	17.53	18.66	19.66	37.12	24.88	21.11
1979	32.99	42.41	34.07	37.95	24.46	25.83	26.41	50.17	33.44	29.30

WAGES

18 Wages in manufacturing / Salaires dans les industries manufacturières / Salarios en las industrias manufactureras

B By industry / Par industrie / Por industria

Colombia (2)

Average hourly earnings *(pesos)*
Gains horaires moyens *(pesos)*
Promedio de ganancias por hora *(pesos)*

Date / Date / Fecha	Rubber products / Industrie du caoutchouc / Productos de caucho	Chemicals / Industrie chimique / Productos químicos	Products of petroleum and coal / Dérivés du pétrole et du charbon / Derivados del petróleo y del carbón	Non-metallic mineral products / Produits minéraux non métalliques / Productos minerales no metálicos	Basic metal industries / Industrie métallurgique de base / Industrias metalúrgicas básicas	Metal products / Produits métalliques / Productos metálicos	Machinery (non-electrical) / Machines (non électriques) / Maquinaria (no eléctrica)	Electrical machinery / Machines électriques / Maquinaria eléctrica	Transport equipment / Matériel de transport / Material de transporte	Miscellaneous manufacturing / Industries manufacturières diverses / Industrias manufactureras diversas
1971	9.23	7.96	14.70	7.51	8.85	5.86	6.75	6.65	7.11	5.56
1972	10.24	8.58	15.98	8.11	10.04	6.17	7.19	7.43	7.85	6.51
1973	12.01	10.42	16.90	9.36	11.87	7.01	8.31	8.61	9.26	7.10
1974	14.61	12.52	19.77	10.90	12.33	8.68	10.02	10.03	10.76	8.40
1975	17.35	15.36	22.08	13.48	15.23	10.94	12.23	12.76	14.19	10.96
1976	24.62	19.17	22.68	16.71	19.81	14.04	14.87	16.02	16.93	13.52
1977	28.40	24.61	30.35	20.92	22.88	18.35	18.09	20.37	22.01	16.74
1978	35.24	31.36	38.02	27.35	29.17	23.85	23.08	25.62	27.56	21.51
1979	46.39	39.41	50.53	37.04	36.51	31.65	31.15	34.18	37.20	29.70

Chile (1)

Average monthly earnings [1] *(pesos)*
Gains mensuels moyens [1] *(pesos)*
Promedio de ganancias por mes [1] *(pesos)*

Date [2] / Date [2] / Fecha [2]	311-312 Food / Aliments / Alimentos	313 Beverages / Boissons / Bebidas	314 Tobacco / Tabac / Tabaco	321 Textiles	322; 324 Clothing, footwear / Habillement, chaussures / Vestido, calzado	323 Leather, leather products / Cuir, articles en cuir / Cuero, artículos de cuero	331 Wood / Bois / Madera
1970	902.83	924.13	1 423.96	934.12	913.87	923.96	571.08
1971	1 228.79	1 779.74	1 737.38	1 323.84	1 516.36	1 288.37	963.53
1972	1 950.75	2 239.71	2 893.75	2 467.66	2 246.23	1 998.48	1 456.75
1973	6 373.86	6 942.34	9 295.41	6 708.75	6 123.40	9 238.09	4 486.12
1974	42 369.34	42 479.11	71 110.21	41 457.26	36 728.27	46 473.95	31 720.95
1975 [3]	202.76	196.71	324.59	175.08	172.73	188.07	171.99
1976	828.57	752.99	1 752.74	689.77	673.66	689.02	570.82
1977	2 245.31	2 003.04	4 659.33	1 900.87	1 873.64	1 692.16	1 729.83
1978	3 982.97	3 813.74	8 224.86	3 366.95	3 102.66	2 941.53	3 081.58

[1] Incl. the value of payments in kind. [2] April of each year. [3] New currency introduced in Sep. 1975: 1 peso = 1,000 old escudos.

[1] Y compris la valeur des paiements en nature. [2] Avril de chaque année. [3] Nouvelle monnaie introduite en sept. 1975 : 1 peso = 1 000 anciens escudos.

[1] Incl. el valor de los pagos en especie. [2] Abril de cada año. [3] Nueva moneda adoptada en sept. de 1975: 1 peso = 1 000 antiguos escudos.

18 B

Wages in manufacturing
Salaires dans les industries manufacturières
Salarios en las industrias manufactureras

By industry
Par industrie
Por industria

Chile (2)

Average monthly earnings [1] *(pesos)*
Gains mensuels moyens [1] *(pesos)*
Promedio de ganancias por mes [1] *(pesos)*

	332	341	342	351-352	353-354	355	36
Date [2]	Furniture	Paper, paper products	Printing, publishing	Chemicals	Refineries and products of petroleum and coal	Rubber products	Non-metallic mineral products
Date [2]	*Ameublement*	*Papier, articles en papier*	*Imprimerie, édition*	*Industrie chimique*	*Raffineries et dérivés du pétrole et du charbon*	*Produits en caoutchouc*	*Produits minéraux non métalliques*
Fecha [2]	Mobiliario	Papel, artículos de papel	Imprentas, editoriales	Productos químicos	Refinerías y derivados del petróleo y del carbón	Productos de caucho	Productos minerales no metálicos
1970	924.62	2 288.76	1 411.70	1 068.58	2 818.15	1 037.92	1 262.00
1971	1 267.90	2 531.22	2 200.33	1 460.69	3 990.02	1 620.68	1 921.04
1972	2 297.72	5 706.74	2 839.62	2 288.36	3 075.39	2 365.64	2 686.97
1973	6 090.13	16 018.01	8 720.17	5 832.57	16 854.86	8 469.94	8 446.25
1974	46 760.58	66 358.85	48 428.33	48 364.37	168 913.08	58 069.26	51 958.16
1975 [3]	208.08	268.72	194.91	259.62	627.52	231.87	253.88
1976	762.20	1 014.16	847.53	1 071.31	2 633.53	953.41	860.15
1977	2 093.51	2 691.83	2 487.09	2 915.80	5 780.70	2 907.12	2 390.04
1978	3 477.29	5 264.15	4 093.84	4 676.43	9 225.54	4 545.19	4 264.80

	37	381	382	383	384	390
Date [2]	Basic metal industries	Metal products	Machinery (non-electrical)	Electrical machinery and apparatus	Transport equipment	Other manufacturing industries
Date [2]	*Industrie métallurgique de base*	*Produits métallurgiques*	*Machines (non électriques)*	*Machines et appareils électriques*	*Matériel de transport*	*Autres industries manufacturières*
Fecha [2]	Industrias metalúrgicas básicas	Productos metálicos	Maquinaria (no eléctrica)	Maquinaria y aparatos eléctricos	Material de transporte	Otras industrias manufactureras
1970	1 741.95	1 052.61	990.90	668.45	974.84	963.69
1971	2 863.00	1 495.96	1 672.63	946.52	1 216.48	1 021.22
1972	4 126.07	2 404.14	2 431.59	1 689.94	1 995.77	1 821.19
1973	11 164.71	7 738.51	7 340.35	5 795.94	9 070.02	6 213.54
1974	68 612.71	59 680.79	47 318.38	36 902.67	37 509.78	38 578.00
1975 [3]	280.08	218.17	224.70	199.63	200.85	169.93
1976	1 053.97	940.73	870.90	719.17	726.54	656.64
1977	3 237.64	2 476.63	2 299.77	2 242.37	3 008.21	1 619.69
1978	5 077.66	3 870.25	4 169.79	3 932.98	5 757.66	3 275.64

[1] Incl. the value of payments in kind. [2] April of each year. [3] New currency introduced in Sep. 1975: 1 peso = 1,000 old escudos.

[1] *Y compris la valeur des paiements en nature.* [2] *Avril de chaque année.* [3] *Nouvelle monnaie introduite en sept. 1975 : 1 peso = 1 000 anciens escudos.*

[1] Incl. el valor de los pagos en especie. [2] Abril de cada año. [3] Nueva moneda adoptada en sept. de 1975: 1 peso = 1 000 antiguos escudos.

WAGES

18 Wages in manufacturing
Salaires dans les industries manufacturières
Salarios en las industrias manufactureras

B By industry
Par industrie
Por industria

República Dominicana (1)

Average monthly earnings [1] *(pesos)*
Gains mensuels moyens [1] *(pesos)*
Promedio de ganancias por mes [1] *(pesos)*

Date / Date / Fecha	311-312 Food / Aliments / Alimentos	313 Beverages / Boissons / Bebidas	314 Tobacco / Tabac / Tabaco	321 Textiles	322 Clothing / Habillement / Vestido	323 Leather, leather products / Cuir, articles en cuir / Cuero, artículos de cuero	324 Footwear / Chaussures / Calzado	331 Wood / Bois / Madera
1970	59.64	179.94	102.16	134.59	72.54	130.85	105.81	105.04
1971	59.54	187.45	116.75	135.61	70.56	137.57	89.91	94.52
1972	63.24	201.84	144.40	133.36	75.92	112.10	112.89	86.44
1973	57.17	225.66	183.79	93.92	77.61	124.37	127.28	80.93
1974	65.32	235.17	199.17	145.17	102.37	121.08	111.58	97.00
1975	101.83	245.16	193.75	168.32	104.08	122.49	122.72	105.87
1976	114.45	248.24	238.36	157.63	100.20	115.71	121.94	97.58
1977	113.49	229.88	253.76	166.88	111.37	130.87	133.84	93.35
1978	114.01	262.02	270.22	174.62	119.76	128.45	152.96	112.67

Date / Date / Fecha	332 Furniture / Ameublement / Mobiliario	341 Paper, paper products / Papier, articles en papier / Papel, artículos de papel	342 Printing, publishing / Imprimerie, édition / Imprentas, editoriales	351 Industrial chemicals / Chimie industrielle / Química industrial	352 Other chemical products / Autres produits chimiques / Otros productos químicos	355 Rubber products / Produits en caoutchouc / Productos de caucho	356 Plastic products / Articles en matière plastique / Productos plásticos	36 Non-metallic mineral products / Produits minéraux non métalliques / Productos minerales no metálicos
1970	94.30	179.48	159.22	205.42	155.12	139.62	113.54	176.81
1971	109.35	201.39	167.77	221.15	158.30	159.99	113.19	194.71
1972	108.58	196.37	156.31	148.91	148.91	148.73	127.02	169.42
1973	99.60	179.00	166.52	198.11	167.15	139.99	125.00	168.05
1974	120.16	207.83	187.91	234.41	174.83	136.66	159.50	182.66
1975	150.45	225.89	225.68	238.55	178.56	157.37	143.96	189.90
1976	159.58	291.54	210.91	262.23	215.56	182.99	146.86	210.00
1977	164.12	283.25	225.29	259.00	225.39	184.60	159.85	218.51
1978	176.15	269.86	238.40	262.37	245.85	219.31	178.87	225.73

[1] Incl. salaried employees.   [1] *Y compris les employés.*   [1] Incl. los empleados.

466

18 Wages in manufacturing
Salaires dans les industries manufacturières
Salarios en las industrias manufactureras

B By industry
Par industrie
Por industria

República Dominicana (2)

Average monthly earnings [1] *(pesos)*
Gains mensuels moyens [1] *(pesos)*
Promedio de ganancias por mes [1] *(pesos)*

Date *Date* Fecha	371	372	381	382	383	384	385	390
	Basic metal industries *Industrie métallurgique de base* Industrias metalúrgicas básicas		Metal products	Machinery (non-electrical)	Electrical machinery and apparatus	Transport equipment	Scientific, measuring, optical, etc. equipment	Other manufacturing industries
	Iron and steel *Sidérurgie* Hierro y acero	Non-ferrous metal *Métaux non ferreux* Metales no ferrosos	*Produits métallurgiques* Productos metálicos	*Machines (non électriques)* Maquinaria (no eléctrica)	*Machines et appareils électriques* Maquinaria y aparatos eléctricos	*Matériel de transport* Material de transporte	*Matériel scientifique, de précision, d'optique, etc.* Equipo científico, de medida, de óptica, etc.	*Autres industries manufacturières* Otras industrias manufactureras
1970	178.99	133.33	158.19	182.91	182.80	129.33	90.76	100.69
1971	195.32	146.67	160.65	192.93	156.33	141.56	136.02	104.98
1972	142.86	142.86	160.57	211.98	220.05	144.36	122.11	112.36
1973	278.35	143.74	160.04	200.49	241.33	145.39	137.36	87.53
1974	190.58	139.22	178.08	155.66	231.50	159.16	129.85	219.00
1975	175.67	208.91	204.69	149.12	178.83	129.43	137.35	220.84
1976	273.97	191.09	208.24	135.82	274.65	93.53	156.17	114.60
1977	320.26	205.63	220.67	193.72	283.02	62.67	163.30	102.60
1978	294.01	222.17	232.93	203.32	261.12	78.60	197.51	241.07

[1] Incl. salaried employees.

[1] *Y compris les employés.*

[1] Incl. los empleados.

18 Wages in manufacturing
Salaires dans les industries manufacturières
Salarios en las industrias manufactureras

B By industry
Par industrie
Por industria

Ecuador

Average hourly earnings *(sucres)*
Gains horaires moyens *(sucres)*
Promedio de ganancias por hora *(sucres)*

	311-312	313	314	321	322; 324	323	331	341	342
Date / Date / Fecha	Food / Aliments / Alimentos	Beverages / Boissons / Bebidas	Tobacco / Tabac / Tabaco	Textiles	Clothing, footwear / Habillement, chaussures / Vestido, calzado	Leather, leather products / Cuir, articles en cuir / Cuero, artículos de cuero	Wood / Bois / Madera	Paper, paper products / Papier, articles en papier / Papel, artículos de papel	Printing, publishing / Imprimerie, édition / Imprentas, editoriales
1970	5.40	8.60	9.20	5.60	4.20	5.60	5.10	8.60	7.20
1971	5.70	9.00	11.90	6.60	5.10	6.20	6.10	9.00	8.60
1972	6.80	10.40	11.60	7.60	5.50	7.20	7.80	13.40	9.60
1973	7.50	11.40	13.40	8.50	6.20	7.30	8.70	14.90	11.00
1974	9.00	13.20	16.60	10.30	8.50	9.00	11.00	18.20	12.60
1975	11.20	15.40	21.90	12.80	10.40	11.60	13.50	23.70	15.10
1976	15.40	17.10	21.80	14.50	12.80	12.50	17.60	26.70	17.80
1977	16.80	18.40	25.90	16.30	13.90	12.00	20.80	29.30	20.40

	351	355	369	381	382	383	384	390
Date / Date / Fecha	Industrial chemicals / Chimie industrielle / Química industrial	Rubber products / Produits en caoutchouc / Productos de caucho	Non-metallic mineral products / Produits minéraux non métalliques / Productos minerales no metálicos	Metal products / Produits métalliques / Productos metálicos	Machinery (non-electrical) / Machines (non électriques) / Maquinaria (no eléctrica)	Electrical machinery and apparatus / Machines et appareils électriques / Maquinaria y aparatos eléctricos	Transport equipment / Matériel de transport / Material de transporte	Other manufacturing industries / Autres industries manufacturières / Otras industrias manufactureras
1970	7.50	15.30	7.80	6.20	8.10	7.90	6.00	5.60
1971	8.40	19.30	9.80	6.60	8.80	9.40	7.00	6.40
1972	10.50	23.70	9.90	7.50	9.50	12.30	8.00	6.90
1973	12.30	23.70	11.00	9.00	9.20	14.50	8.90	7.70
1974	13.80	30.80	13.10	11.10	10.40	18.70	10.80	9.80
1975	14.50	39.90	17.70	14.10	13.90	18.60	13.90	11.80
1976	17.00	55.00	18.90	16.90	15.50	22.20	16.70	13.60
1977	20.80	57.10	20.90	19.30	19.50	24.20	17.20	14.20

18 **Wages in manufacturing**
Salaires dans les industries manufacturières
Salarios en las industrias manufactureras

B By industry
Par industrie
Por industria

El Salvador (San Salvador) [1]

Average hourly earnings *(colones)*
Gains horaires moyens *(colones)*
Promedio de ganancias por hora *(colones)*

	311-312	313	321	322; 324	332	34	36	371	384	390
Date Date Fecha	Food *Aliments* Alimentos	Beverages *Boissons* Bebidas	Textiles	Clothing, footwear *Habillement, chaussures* Vestido, calzado	Furniture *Ameublement* Mobiliario	Paper printing, publishing *Papier, imprimerie, édition* Papel, imprentas, editoriales	Non-metallic mineral products *Produits minéraux non métalliques* Productos minerales no metálicos	Iron and steel basic industries *Sidérurgie* Industrias básicas de hierro y acero	Transport equipment *Matériel de transport* Material de transporte	Other manufacturing industries *Autres industries manufacturières* Otras industrias manufactureras
Males — *Hommes* — Hombres										
1970	1.01	1.15	0.96	0.94	0.86	0.96	0.68	0.99	0.82	0.97
1971	1.08	1.15	0.97	0.99	0.85	0.96	0.72	0.99	0.79	0.93
1972	1.05	1.19	1.01	1.01	0.80	1.04	0.74	0.95	0.84	1.01
1973	1.12	1.23	1.07	1.06	0.80	1.05	0.81	0.98	0.93	1.08

	311-312	313	321	322; 324	34	390
Date Date Fecha	Food *Aliments* Alimentos	Beverages *Boissons* Bebidas	Textiles	Clothing, footwear *Habillement, chaussures* Vestido, calzado	Paper, printing, publishing *Papier, imprimerie, édition* Papel, imprentas, editoriales	Other manufacturing industries *Autres industries manufacturières* Otras industrias manufactureras
Females — *Femmes* — Mujeres						
1970	0.62	0.68	0.87	0.70	0.83	0.76
1971	0.59	0.64	0.85	0.76	0.88	0.72
1972	0.61	0.62	0.90	0.79	0.82	0.78
1973	0.68	0.68	0.98	0.84	0.78	0.83

[1] Metropolitan area.   [1] *Région métropolitaine.*   [1] Area metropolitana.

WAGES

18 Wages in manufacturing
Salaires dans les industries manufacturières
Salarios en las industrias manufactureras

B By industry
Par industrie
Por industria

Guatemala [1]

Average hourly earnings *(centavos)*
Gains horaires moyens *(centavos)*
Promedio de ganancias por hora *(centavos)*

	311-312	313	314	321	322; 324	323	331
Date *Date* Fecha	Food *Aliments* Alimentos	Beverages *Boissons* Bebidas	Tobacco *Tabac* Tabaco	Textiles	Clothing, footwear *Habillement, chaussures* Vestido, calzado	Leather, leather products *Cuir, articles en cuir* Cuero, artículos de cuero	Wood *Bois* Madera
1970	34.5	47.2	69.3	35.4	30.9	26.7	27.3
1971	35.3	46.1	72.9	37.5	30.9	23.8	28.8
1972	35.2	46.5	71.1	37.7	30.9	23.8	28.9
1973	35.9	46.8	73.6	39.7	29.8	25.9	29.5
1974 [2]	36.9	59.8	49.0	39.3	35.4	34.8	34.0
1975	42.3	59.2	54.0	40.7	36.6	30.6	37.0
1976	45.4	62.5	60.3	44.6	38.8	32.4	39.0
1977	47.6	60.9	66.5	46.3	44.4	37.1	43.7
1978	52.4	76.2	62.1	49.5	48.7	37.4	47.0

	332	34	351-352; 355	36	37	383	384
Date *Date* Fecha	Furniture *Ameublement* Mobiliario	Paper, printing, publishing *Papier, imprimerie, édition* Papel, imprentas, editoriales	Chemicals, rubber products *Industrie chimique, produits en caoutchouc* Productos químicos y de caucho	Non-metallic mineral products *Produits minéraux non métalliques* Productos minerales no metálicos	Basic metal industries *Industrie métallurgique de base* Industrias metalúrgicas básicas	Electrical machinery and apparatus *Machines et appareils électriques* Maquinaria y aparatos eléctricos	Transport equipment *Matériel de transport* Material de transporte
1970	33.1	50.4	39.3	56.1	33.6	37.9	48.3
1971	31.2	51.5	36.4	57.4	35.9	38.3	51.3
1972	31.8	52.6	36.7	57.7	35.9	38.1	53.0
1973	30.1	51.8	35.9	50.4	38.5	39.8	54.5
1974 [2]	37.6	55.3	40.0	55.6	45.3	55.4	40.8
1975	40.4	55.6	54.3	74.6	49.6	53.4	46.7
1976	39.8	59.6	55.5	65.2	50.5	58.3	48.9
1977	30.5	64.1	65.7	72.0	63.3	63.5	45.2
1978	36.9	80.9	85.3	78.5	59.7	76.2	54.4

[1] Prior to 1974: Guatemala City only. [2] Series replacing former series.

[1] *Avant 1974 : ville de Guatemala seulement.* [2] *Série remplaçant la précédente.*

[1] Antes de 1974: ciudad de Guatemala solamente. [2] Serie que substituye a la anterior.

18 Wages in manufacturing
Salaires dans les industries manufacturières
Salarios en las industrias manufactureras

B By industry
Par industrie
Por industria

México (1)

Average hourly earnings *(pesos)*
Gains horaires moyens *(pesos)*
Promedio de ganancias por hora *(pesos)*

Date [1] Date [1] Fecha [1]	311-312 Food *Aliments* Alimentos	313 Beverages *Boissons* Bebidas	314 Tobacco *Tabac* Tabaco	321 Textiles	322 Clothing *Habillement* Vestido	323 Leather, leather products *Cuir, articles en cuir* Cuero, artículos de cuero	324 Footwear *Chaussures* Calzado
1970	6.49	8.09	7.82	7.89	5.15	8.03	7.75
1971	6.99	8.42	9.05	8.33	5.29	7.62	8.00
1972	7.81	8.94	9.89	8.92	5.78	8.48	8.88
1973	9.64	10.74	12.27	11.02	7.55	9.87	11.05
1974	12.51	13.91	14.72	13.88	10.19	13.24	13.11
1975	13.28	15.00	16.07	15.93	11.03	15.01	13.85
1976	19.11	20.29	21.78	21.67	14.47	20.04	27.84
1977	22.78	23.52	23.66	24.10	25.97	22.68	25.97

Date [1] Date [1] Fecha [1]	331 Wood *Bois* Madera	332 Furniture *Ameublement* Mobiliario	341 Paper, paper products *Papier, articles en papier* Papel, artículos de papel	342 Printing, publishing *Imprimerie, édition* Imprentas, editoriales	351 Industrial chemicals *Chimie industrielle* Química industrial	352 Other chemical products *Autres produits chimiques* Otros productos químicos	353 Petroleum refineries *Raffineries de pétrole* Refinerías de petróleo
1970	5.50	6.11	7.24	8.21	7.37	6.70	7.90
1971	6.57	6.56	7.85	8.81	8.05	7.10	9.00
1972	8.09	7.19	8.42	9.52	8.72	8.09	9.16
1973	8.48	9.35	10.44	10.39	11.24	10.15	9.26
1974	11.15	12.34	13.89	15.21	14.79	13.44	12.36
1975	12.99	13.54	15.15	15.96	16.91	13.59	13.63
1976	24.22	19.91	21.73	23.21	25.01	21.60	19.17
1977	27.33	22.15	25.55	25.72	27.26	23.86	26.41

[1] Oct. of each year.　　　[1] *Oct. de chaque année.*　　　[1] Oct. de cada año.

471

18 Wages in manufacturing
Salaires dans les industries manufacturières
Salarios en las industrias manufactureras

B By industry
Par industrie
Por industria

México (2)

Average hourly earnings *(pesos)*
Gains horaires moyens *(pesos)*
Promedio de ganancias por hora *(pesos)*

	355	361	362	369	371	372	384	390
Date [1] *Date* [1] Fecha [1]	Rubber products *Produits en caoutchouc* Productos de caucho	Pottery, china, earthenware *Grès, porcelaines, faïences* Barro, loza, porcelana	Glass *Verre* Vidrio	Other non-metallic mineral products *Autres produits minéraux non métalliques* Otros productos minerales no metálicos	Basic metal industries / *Industrie métallurgique de base* / Industrias metalúrgicas básicas — Iron and steel / *Sidérurgie* / Hierro y acero	Non-ferrous metal / *Métaux non ferreux* / Metales no ferrosos	Transport equipment *Matériel de transport* Material de transporte	Other manufacturing industries *Autres industries manufacturières* Otras industrias manufactureras
1970	9.88	7.14	6.79	7.40	8.04	6.74	8.42	7.05
1971	11.23	8.40	6.90	8.06	7.41	8.35	9.48	7.25
1972	11.81	8.53	7.94	8.55	9.23	8.49	10.36	8.24
1973	16.47	11.66	10.18	10.24	10.54	10.98	11.35	10.28
1974	20.14	13.61	12.43	13.81	14.64	13.76	15.12	12.83
1975	24.30	16.44	14.89	15.59	17.08	15.69	17.61	17.86
1976	35.29	22.98	21.03	22.32	25.08	21.61	23.51	17.17
1977	39.63	24.76	23.87	25.89	28.44	23.59	30.06	20.81

[1] Oct. of each year.   [1] *Oct. de chaque année.*   [1] Oct. de cada año.

Nicaragua (1)

Average hourly earnings *(córdobas)*
Gains horaires moyens *(córdobas)*
Promedio de ganancias por hora *(córdobas)*

	311-312	313	314	321	322; 324	323
Date *Date* Fecha	Food *Aliments* Alimentos	Beverages *Boissons* Bebidas	Tobacco *Tabac* Tabaco	Textiles	Clothing, footwear *Habillement, chaussures* Vestido, calzado	Leather, leather products *Cuir, articles en cuir* Cuero, artículos de cuero
1970	3.45	3.93	5.64	2.98	2.31	1.96
1971	3.53	3.93	5.93	2.72	2.33	1.81
1972	3.55	4.36	6.11	2.78	2.22	1.85
1973	4.02	4.52	6.60	3.00	2.34	1.87
1974	3.35	4.98	7.21	3.38	2.82	2.18
1975	5.05	5.07	8.18	3.88	3.07	2.49

18 **Wages in manufacturing**
Salaires dans les industries manufacturières
Salarios en las industrias manufactureras

B **By industry**
Par industrie
Por industria

Nicaragua (2)

Average hourly earnings *(córdobas)*
Gains horaires moyens *(córdobas)*
Promedio de ganancias por hora *(córdobas)*

	331	332	341	342	351-352	353-354	355
Date	Wood	Furniture	Paper, paper products	Printing, publishing	Chemicals	Refineries and products of petroleum and coal	Rubber products
Date	*Bois*	*Ameublement*	*Papier, articles en papier*	*Imprimerie, édition*	*Industrie chimique*	*Raffineries et dérivés du pétrole et du charbon*	*Produits en caoutchouc*
Fecha	Madera	Mobiliario	Papel, artículos de papel	Imprentas, editoriales	Productos químicos	Refinerías y derivados del petróleo y del carbón	Productos de caucho
1970	3.04	2.51	2.69	3.31	3.87	9.89	3.84
1971	3.13	2.62	2.70	3.34	3.84	10.33	3.30
1972	3.33	2.58	3.03	3.30	3.98	10.79	3.50
1973	3.35	2.92	4.13	3.33	4.03	10.47	3.98
1974	3.87	3.76	4.63	3.80	4.54	12.22	4.41
1975	3.83	4.49	5.03	4.30	...	13.68	8.13

	36	37	381	382	383	384	385
Date	Non-metallic mineral products	Basic metal industries	Metal products	Machinery (non-electrical)	Electrical machinery and apparatus	Transport equipment	Scientific, measuring, optical, etc., equipment
Date	*Produits minéraux non métalliques*	*Industrie métallurgique de base*	*Produits métalliques*	*Machines (non électriques)*	*Machines et appareils électriques*	*Matériel de transport*	*Matériel scientifique, de précision, d'optique, etc.*
Fecha	Productos minerales no metálicos	Industrias metalúrgicas básicas	Productos metálicos	Maquinaria (no eléctrica)	Maquinaria y aparatos eléctricos	Material de transporte	Equipo científico, de medida, de óptica, etc.
1970	3.25	2.54	3.35	3.82	3.29	3.16	.
1971	3.39	2.50	3.28	4.06	3.39	3.60	.
1972	3.61	3.14	2.87	5.18	3.29	2.75	2.41
1973	3.81	3.28	2.80	5.53	3.58	2.91	2.78
1974	4.28	4.11	3.12	6.37	3.94	3.84	2.14
1975	4.58	4.91	3.73	6.56	...	4.75	4.55

WAGES

18 Wages in manufacturing
Salaires dans les industries manufacturières
Salarios en las industrias manufactureras

B By industry
Par industrie
Por industria

Panamá (1)

Average hourly earnings *(balboas)*
Gains horaires moyens *(balboas)*
Promedio de ganancias por hora *(balboas)*

Date / Date / Fecha	311-312 Food / Aliments / Alimentos	313 Beverages / Boissons / Bebidas	314 Tobacco / Tabac / Tabaco	321 Textiles	322 Clothing / Habillement / Vestido	323 Leather, leather products / Cuir, articles en cuir / Cuero, artículos de cuero	324 Footwear / Chaussures / Calzado	331 Wood / Bois / Madera	332 Furniture / Ameublement / Mobiliario
1970	0.67	0.70	0.76	0.57	0.67	0.71	0.72	0.65	0.73
1971	0.68	0.82	0.89	0.61	0.71	0.73	0.83	0.66	0.76
1972	0.67	0.79	0.88	0.83	0.71	0.69	0.79	0.66	0.85
1973	0.76	1.01	0.93	0.80	0.71	0.70	0.79	0.68	0.91
1974	0.79	0.89	1.34	0.93	0.82	0.89	0.88	0.85	1.01
1975	0.90	1.00	1.22	0.98	0.93	1.00	0.96	0.88	1.09
1976	0.96	1.01	1.25	1.06	0.89	0.91	1.03	0.95	1.17
1977	1.00	1.13	1.48	0.97	0.99	1.02	1.06	0.93	1.18

Date / Date / Fecha	341 Paper, paper products / Papier, articles en papier / Papel, artículos de papel	342 Printing, publishing / Imprimerie, édition / Imprentas, editoriales	351 Industrial chemicals / Chimie industrielle / Química industrial	352 Industrial chemical products / Autres produits chimiques / Otros productos químicos	355 Other products / Produits en caoutchouc / Productos de caucho	356 Rubber products / Articles en matière plastique / Productos plásticos	362 Glass / Verre / Vidrio	369 Other non-metallic mineral products / Autres produits minéraux non métalliques / Otros productos minerales no metálicos
1970	0.89	0.91	0.84	0.69	1.11	0.80	0.92	0.77
1971	0.96	0.95	1.06	0.80	0.95	0.81	0.76	0.78
1972	0.87	0.97	0.91	0.81	1.04	0.89	0.72	0.76
1973	1.02	1.03	1.00	0.82	1.10	0.91	0.73	0.94
1974	1.05	1.22	1.06	1.01	1.16	0.98	1.04	0.98
1975	1.26	1.36	1.18	1.20	1.23	1.15	0.97	1.14
1976	1.34	1.48	1.23	1.24	1.32	1.17	1.26	1.17
1977	1.41	1.52	1.37	1.28	1.25	1.04	1.45	1.23

18 Wages in manufacturing
Salaires dans les industries manufacturières
Salarios en las industrias manufactureras

B By industry
Par industrie
Por industria

Panamá (2)

Average hourly earnings *(balboas)*
Gains horaires moyens *(balboas)*
Promedio de ganancias por hora *(balboas)*

Date / Date / Fecha	371 Iron and steel basic industries / *Sidérurgie* / Industrias básicas de hierro y acero	381 Metal products / *Produits métalliques* / Productos metálicos	382 Machinery (non-electrical) / *Machines (non électriques)* / Maquinaria (no eléctrica)	383 Electrical machinery and apparatus / *Machines et appareils électriques* / Maquinaria y aparatos eléctricos	384 Transport equipment / *Matériel de transport* / Material de transporte	385 Scientific, measuring, optical, etc., equipment / *Matériel scientifique, de précision, d'optique, etc.* / Equipo científico, de medida, de óptica, etc.	353-354; 372; 390 Miscellaneous manufacturing / *Industries manufacturières diverses* / Industrias manufactureras diversas
1970	0.86	0.95	0.99	0.90	1.27	0.89	2.66
1971	0.78	0.86	0.89	0.89	1.04	1.03	1.93
1972	0.81	0.83	1.08	0.77	1.29	1.11	2.17
1973	0.79	0.90	1.11	0.87	0.97	0.92	1.83
1974	1.04	1.02	1.08	1.07	1.03	1.02	2.15
1975	1.22	1.10	1.39	1.02	1.30	1.26	2.25
1976	1.21	1.31	1.38	1.14	1.46	1.18	2.23
1977	1.15	1.48	1.66	1.02	1.97	1.15	3.16

Puerto Rico (1)

Average hourly earnings *(dollars)*
Gains horaires moyens *(dollars)*
Promedio de ganancias por hora *(dollars)*

Date [1] / Date [1] / Fecha [1]	311-313 Food, beverages / *Aliments, boissons* / Alimentos, bebidas	314 Tobacco / *Tabac* / Tabaco	321 Textiles	322 Clothing / *Habillement* / Vestido	323 Leather, leather products / *Cuir, articles en cuir* / Cuero, artículos de cuero	324 Footwear / *Chaussures* / Calzado	33 Wood, furniture / *Bois, ameublement* / Madera, mobiliario
1970	1.82	1.49	1.61	1.60	1.47	1.62	1.67
1971	1.94	1.56	1.73	1.70	1.56	1.65	1.73
1972	2.07	1.63	1.79	1.76	1.58	1.66	1.82
1973	2.23	1.81	1.94	1.83	1.66	1.71	1.95
1974	2.42	1.96	2.10	1.97	1.83	1.84	2.11
1975	2.60	2.21	2.15	2.14	2.01	2.02	2.25
1976	2.86	2.41	2.36	2.34	2.23	2.16	2.40
1977	3.07	2.59	2.57	2.52	2.41	2.32	2.64
1978	3.32	2.96	2.87	2.80	2.71	2.59	2.84
1979	3.69	3.36	3.22	3.11	3.09	2.91	3.15

[1] Oct. of each year.   [1] *Oct. de chaque année.*   [1] Oct. de cada año.

18 Wages in manufacturing / Salaires dans les industries manufacturières / Salarios en las industrias manufactureras

B By industry / Par industrie / Por industria

Puerto Rico (2)

Average hourly earnings *(dollars)*
Gains horaires moyens *(dollars)*
Promedio de ganancias por hora *(dollars)*

Date [1] / Date [1] / Fecha [1]	341 Paper, paper products / Papier, articles en papier / Papel, artículos de papel	342 Printing, publishing / Imprimerie, édition / Imprentas, editoriales	351-352 Chemicals / Industrie chimique / Productos químicos	353-354 Refineries and products of petroleum and coal / Raffineries et dérivés du pétrole et du charbon / Refinerías y derivados del petróleo y del carbón	355-356 Rubber and plastic products / Produits en caoutchouc et en plastique / Productos de caucho y de plástico	361 Pottery, china, earthenware, / Grès, porcelaines, faïences / Barro, loza, porcelana	362 Glass / Verre / Vidrio
1970	2.05	2.30	2.26	3.20	1.71	2.52	2.22
1971	2.21	2.38	2.36	3.55	1.78	2.84	2.47
1972	2.36	2.70	2.64	4.00	1.87	3.31	2.54
1973	2.49	2.99	2.87	4.32	2.02	3.47	2.52
1974	2.72	3.10	3.22	4.52	2.20	3.91	2.83
1975	2.85	3.07	3.64	5.28	2.55	3.55	2.83
1976	3.07	3.57	3.90	6.01	2.75	3.79	3.24
1977	3.25	3.76	4.22	6.51	3.00	4.42	3.48
1978	3.71	4.03	4.60	7.36	3.27	4.50	3.76
1979	3.80	4.16	4.90	7.93	3.46	4.58	3.98

Date [1] / Date [1] / Fecha [1]	369 Other non-metallic mineral products / Autres produits minéraux non métalliques / Otros productos minerales no metálicos	381 Metal products / Produits métalliques / Productos metálicos	382 Machinery (non-electrical) / Machines (non électriques) / Maquinaria (no eléctrica)	383 Electrical machinery and apparatus / Machines et appareils électriques / Maquinaria y aparatos eléctricos	384 Transport equipment / Matériel de transport / Material de transporte	385 Scientific, measuring, optical, etc., equipment / Matériel scientifique, de précision, d'optique, etc. / Equipo científico, de medida, de óptica, etc.	390 Other manufacturing industries / Autres industries manufacturières / Otras industrias manufactureras
1970	1.94	2.03	2.25	1.91	2.22	1.92	1.66
1971	2.00	2.17	2.62	2.00	2.21	2.06	1.78
1972	2.19	2.23	2.96	2.16	2.35	2.16	1.91
1973	2.32	2.53	2.97	2.24	2.63	2.32	2.07
1974	2.59	2.79	2.91	2.55	2.87	2.57	2.40
1975	2.67	2.95	3.24	2.82	2.87	2.81	2.59
1976	2.82	3.20	3.50	3.05	3.13	3.05	2.78
1977	3.16	3.46	3.52	3.31	3.37	3.31	3.09
1978	3.37	3.82	3.91	3.69	3.37	3.31	3.09
1979	3.77	4.17	4.08	3.95	3.62	3.81	3.75

[1] Oct. of each year.

[1] *Oct. de chaque année.*

[1] Oct. de cada año.

18 Wages in manufacturing / Salaires dans les industries manufacturières / Salarios en las industrias manufactureras

B By industry / Par industrie / Por industria

United States (1)

Average hourly earnings *(dollars)*
Gains horaires moyens *(dollars)*
Promedio de ganancias por hora *(dollars)*

Date / Date / Fecha	311-313 Food, beverages / Aliments, boissons / Alimentos, bebidas	314 Tobacco / Tabac / Tabaco	321 Textiles	322 Clothing / Habillement / Vestido	323-324 Leather, leather products, footwear / Cuir, articles en cuir, chaussures / Cuero, artículos de cuero, calzado	331 Wood / Bois / Madera	332 Furniture / Ameublement / Mobiliario
1970	3.16	2.91	2.45	2.39	2.49	2.96	2.77
1971	3.38	3.16	2.57	2.49	2.59	3.17	2.90
1972	3.60	3.47	2.75	2.60	2.68	3.33	3.08
1973	3.85	3.76	2.95	2.76	2.79	3.61	3.29
1974	4.19	4.12	3.20	2.97	2.99	3.89	3.53
1975	4.61	4.55	3.42	3.17	3.21	4.26	3.78
1976	4.98	4.98	3.69	3.40	3.40	4.72	3.99
1977	5.37	5.54	3.99	3.62	3.61	5.10	4.34
1978	5.80	6.13	4.30	3.94	3.89	5.60	4.68
1979	6.27	6.69	4.66	4.24	4.23	6.08	5.06

Date / Date / Fecha	341 Paper, paper products / Papier, articles en papier / Papel, artículos de papel	342 Printing, publishing / Imprimerie, édition / Imprentas, editoriales	351-352 Chemicals / Industrie chimique / Productos químicos	353-354 Refineries and products of petroleum and coal / Raffineries et dérivés du pétrole et du charbon / Refinerías y derivados del petróleo y del carbón	355-356 Rubber and plastic products / Produits en caoutchouc et en plastique / Productos de caucho y de plástico	36 Non-metallic mineral products / Produits minéraux non métalliques / Productos minerales no metálicos
1970	3.44	3.92	3.69	4.28	3.20	3.40
1971	3.67	4.20	3.97	4.57	3.39	3.67
1972	3.95	4.51	4.26	4.96	3.61	3.94
1973	4.20	4.75	4.51	5.28	3.81	4.22
1974	4.53	5.03	4.88	5.68	4.06	4.54
1975	5.01	5.38	5.39	6.48	4.39	4.92
1976	5.47	5.71	5.91	7.21	4.66	5.33
1977	5.96	6.12	6.43	7.83	5.17	5.81
1978	6.52	6.50	7.01	8.63	5.52	6.32
1979	7.12	6.91	7.59	9.37	5.96	6.84

WAGES

18 Wages in manufacturing
Salaires dans les industries manufacturières
Salarios en las industrias manufactureras

B By industry
Par industrie
Por industria

United States (2)

Average hourly earnings *(dollars)*
Gains horaires moyens *(dollars)*
Promedio de ganancias por hora *(dollars)*

	37	381	382	383	384	385	390
Date *Date* Fecha	Basic metal industries *Industrie métallurgique de base* Industrias metalúrgicas básicas	Metal products *Produits métalliques* Productos metálicos	Machinery (non-electrical) *Machines (non électriques)* Maquinaria (no eléctrica)	Electrical machinery and apparatus *Machines et appareils électriques* Maquinaria y aparatos eléctricos	Transport equipment *Matériel de transport* Material de transporte	Scientific, measuring, optical, etc., equipment *Matériel scientifique, de précision, d'optique, etc.* Equipo científico, de medida, de óptica, etc.	Other manufacturing industries *Autres industries manufacturières* Otras industrias manufactureras
1970	3.93	3.53	3.77	3.28	4.06	3.34	2.83
1971	4.23	3.77	4.02	3.49	4.45	3.50	2.97
1972	4.66	4.04	4.32	3.91	4.81	3.66	3.11
1973	5.04	4.29	4.60	3.91	5.15	3.83	3.29
1974	5.60	4.61	4.94	4.21	5.54	4.11	3.53
1975	6.18	5.05	5.37	4.64	6.07	4.53	3.81
1976	6.77	5.49	5.79	4.96	6.62	4.93	4.04
1977	7.40	5.91	6.26	5.39	7.28	5.29	4.36
1978	8.20	6.34	6.77	5.82	7.91	5.71	4.69
1979	8.97	6.82	7.33	6.31	8.53	6.17	5.04

Uruguay [1] (1)

Monthly rates [2] *(Indices)*
Taux mensuels [2] *(Indices)*
Tarifas por mes [2] *(Indices)*

(1970 = 100)

	311-312	313	314	321	322	341	342
Date *Date* Fecha	Food *Aliments* Alimentos	Beverages *Boissons* Bebidas	Tobacco *Tabac* Tabaco	Textiles	Clothing *Habillement* Vestido	Paper, paper products *Papier, articles en papier* Papel, artículos de papel	Printing, publishing *Imprimerie, édition* Imprentas, editoriales
1970	100.0	100.0	100.0	100.0	100.0	100.0	100.0
1971	125.1	127.0	121.8	127.4	128.4	129.7	109.7
1972	183.0	222.6	183.7	186.4	193.6	195.6	225.4
1973	343.5	451.4	341.5	361.0	380.3	348.8	439.6
1974	610.8	823.6	581.0	640.6	645.2	618.7	809.7
1975	1 023.0	1 323.3	940.4	1 037.8	1 062.6	1 076.0	1 280.8
1976	1 404.6	1 786.3	1 293.0	1 408.4	1 453.3	1 479.0	1 720.2
1977	1 904.3	2 421.5	1 753.5	1 908.2	1 969.9	2 005.8	2 367.0
1978	2 602.6	3 269.6	2 400.8	2 611.6	2 917.6	2 746.1	2 434.3

[1] Montevideo; private sector only. Incl. salaried employees. [2] Average rates.

[1] *Montevideo; secteur privé seulement. Y compris les employés.* [2] *Taux moyens.*

[1] Montevideo; sector privado solamente. Incl. los empleados. [2] Tarifas medias.

18 Wages in manufacturing
Salaires dans les industries manufacturières
Salarios en las industrias manufactureras

B By industry
Par industrie
Por industria

Uruguay [1] (2)

Monthly rates [2] *(Indices)*
Taux mensuels [2] *(Indices)*
Tarifas por mes [2] *(Indices)*

(1970 = 100)

Date / Date / Fecha	351-353 Chemicals, petroleum refineries / Industrie chimique, raffineries de pétrole / Productos químicos, refinerías de petróleo	354 Products of petroleum and coal / Dérivés du pétrole et du charbon / Derivados del petróleo y del carbón	355 Rubber products / Produits en caoutchouc / Productos de caucho	381 Metal products / Produits métalliques / Productos metálicos	382-383; 385 Machinery [3] / Machines [3] / Maquinaria [3]	384 Transport equipment / Matériel de transport / Material de transporte	390 Other manufacturing industries / Autres industries manufacturières / Otras industrias manufactureras
1970	100.0	100.0	100.0	100.0	100.0	100.0	100.0
1971	127.1	127.5	125.9	126.8	127.5	97.1	126.8
1972	182.6	201.5	183.8	187.7	183.7	181.7	181.7
1973	357.4	410.0	341.8	407.2	345.0	371.5	339.3
1974	647.6	644.6	582.2	577.1	581.0	577.2	577.2
1975	1 104.9	1 167.8	947.9	947.2	952.1	951.1	942.8
1976	1 515.6	1 582.7	1 284.4	1 291.2	1 290.2	1 297.2	1 286.7
1977	2 055.3	2 146.0	1 741.5	1 763.1	1 750.1	1 759.2	1 744.8
1978	2 813.9	2 938.1	2 384.3	2 408.9	2 395.7	2 408.6	2 388.7

[1] Montevideo; private sector only. Incl. salaried employees. [2] Average rates. [3] Incl. scientific, measuring, optical, etc., equipment.

[1] *Montevideo; secteur privé seulement. Y compris les employés.* [2] *Taux moyens.* [3] *Y compris le matériel scientifique, de précision, d'optique, etc.*

[1] Montevideo; sector privado solamente. Incl. los empleados. [2] Tarifas medias. [3] Incl. el equipo científico, de medida, de óptica, etc.

Venezuela (1)

Average monthly earnings *(bolívares)*
Gains mensuels moyens *(bolívares)*
Promedio de ganancias por mes *(bolívares)*

Date / Date / Fecha	311-312 Food / Aliments / Alimentos	313 Beverages / Boissons / Bebidas	314 Tobacco / Tabac / Tabaco	321-322 Textiles, clothing / Textiles, habillement / Textiles, vestido	324 Footwear / Chaussures / Calzado	33 Wood, furniture / Bois, ameublement / Madera, mobiliario	341 Paper, paper products / Papier, articles en papier / Papel, artículos de papel
1970	651	1 014	833	736	649	635	809
1971	756	1 096	919	860	763	655	886
1972	788	1 283	1 033	895	749	657	985
1973	886	1 319	1 215	918	829	777	1 079
1974	964	1 361	1 334	1 034	878	823	1 231
1975	1 009	1 438	1 451	1 141	921	892	1 273
1976	1 128	1 673	1 621	1 260	1 058	985	1 354
1977 *	1 341	1 631	1 876	1 281	1 207	803	1 100

WAGES

18 Wages in manufacturing
Salaires dans les industries manufacturières
Salarios en las industrias manufactureras

B By industry
Par industrie
Por industria

Venezuela (2)

Average monthly earnings *(bolívares)*
Gains mensuels moyens *(bolívares)*
Promedio de ganancias por mes *(bolívares)*

Date / Date / Fecha	342 Printing, publishing / *Imprimerie, édition* / Imprentas, editoriales	351-352 Chemicals / *Industrie chimique* / Productos químicos	355 Rubber products / *Produits en caoutchouc* / Productos de caucho	371 Basic metal industries / *Industrie métallurgique de base* / Industrias metalúrgicas básicas — Iron and steel / *Sidérurgie* / Hierro y acero	372 Non-ferrous metal / *Métaux non ferreux* / Metales no ferrosos	384 Transport equipment / *Matériel de transport* / Material de transporte
1970	1 348	899	1 136	1 096	925	1 329
1971	1 410	1 047	1 152	1 155	1 005	1 473
1972	1 506	1 098	1 310	1 236	1 230	1 675
1973	1 585	1 371	1 450	1 284	1 145	1 493
1974	1 758	1 523	1 648	1 367	1 300	1 721
1975	1 756	1 564	1 670	1 372	1 469	1 948
1976	1 859	1 814	1 902	1 584	1 501	2 466
1977 *	1 836	1 908	2 343	1 396	1 708	2 589

Virgin Is. (US)

Average hourly earnings [1] *(dollars)*
Gains horaires moyens [1] *(dollars)*
Promedio de ganancias por hora [1] *(dollars)*

Date [2] / Date [2] / Fecha [2]	311-312 Food / *Aliments* / Alimentos	321 Textiles	332 Furniture / *Ameublement* / Mobiliario	342 Printing, publishing / *Imprimerie, édition* / Imprentas, editoriales	353 Petroleum refineries / *Raffineries de pétrole* / Refinerías de petróleo	361 Pottery, china, earthenware / *Grès, porcelaines, faïences* / Barro, loza, porcelana	381 Metal products / *Produits métalliques* / Productos metálicos	385 Scientific, measuring, optical, etc., equipment / *Matériel scientifique, de précision, d'optique, etc.* / Equipo científico, de medida, de óptica, etc.	390 Other manufacturing industries / *Autres industries manufacturières* / Otras industrias manufactureras
1973	2.71	2.65	3.57	3.58	4.04	4.06	3.00	2.37	2.51
1974	3.13	3.16	3.83	3.97	4.46	4.75	2.61	2.79	2.37
1975	2.95	3.73	3.35	3.83	5.19	5.30	2.81	3.01	1.91
1976	3.78	4.67	3.14	4.00	5.95	5.16	2.53	2.87	2.22

[1] Incl. salaried employees. [2] First quarter of each year.   [1] *Y compris les employés.* [2] *Premier trimestre de chaque année.*   [1] Incl. los empleados. [2] Primer trimestre de cada año.

18 Wages in manufacturing
Salaires dans les industries manufacturières
Salarios en las industrias manufactureras

B By industry
Par industrie
Por industria

ASIA — ASIE — ASIA

Burma

Average hourly earnings [1] *(kyats)*
Gains horaires moyens [1] *(kyats)*
Promedio de ganancias por hora [1] *(kyats)*

	311-312	313	314	321	322; 324	323	331
Date [2]	Food	Beverages	Tobacco		Clothing, footwear	Leather, leather products	Wood
Date [2]	*Aliments*	*Boissons*	*Tabac*	Textiles	*Habillement, chaussures*	*Cuir, articles en cuir*	*Bois*
Fecha [2]	Alimentos	Bebidas	Tabaco		Vestido, calzado	Cuero, artículos de cuero	Madera
1970	0.51	0.60	0.32	0.62	0.69	0.54	0.49
1971	0.50	0.63	0.34	0.72	0.87	0.52	0.50
1972 [3]	0.47	0.53	0.33	0.63	0.96	0.67	0.51
1973	0.59	0.54	0.35	0.75	0.61	0.56	0.56
1974	0.53	0.55	0.36	0.74	0.83	0.55	0.50
1975	0.56	0.54	0.38	0.77	0.74	0.51	0.56
1976	0.60	0.54	0.48	0.67	0.73	0.51	0.51
1977	0.64	0.72	0.57	0.65	1.33	0.59	0.77
1978	0.66	0.67	0.58	1.17	1.20	0.51	0.77

	342	352	355	362	369	381	384
Date [2]	Printing, publishing	Chemical products	Rubber products	Glass	Other non-metallic mineral products	Metal products	Transport equipment
Date [2]	*Imprimerie, édition*	*Produits chimiques*	*Produits en caoutchouc*	*Verre*	*Autres produits minéraux non métalliques*	*Produits métalliques*	*Matériel de transport*
Fecha [2]	Imprentas, editoriales	Productos químicos	Productos de caucho	Vidrio	Otros productos minerales no metálicos	Productos metálicos	Material de transporte
1970	0.63	0.64	0.64	·	·	...	0.44
1971	0.60	0.63	0.60	·	·	0.63	0.85
1972 [3]	0.53	0.72	0.45	0.59	0.45	0.52	0.75
1973	0.66	0.75	0.70	0.88	0.39	0.61	0.88
1974	0.62	0.65	0.72	0.82	0.46	0.55	0.55
1975	0.68	0.53	0.81	1.06	...	0.63	0.53
1976	0.66	0.51	0.91	0.90	0.49	0.53	1.72
1977	0.76	0.63	0.80	0.90	0.69	0.47	0.76
1978	0.75	0.62	0.74	1.28	0.81	0.51	0.68

[1] Workers engaged for less than 30 days (excl. casual workers). [2] Beginning 1973: March and Sep. of each year. [3] April and Sept.

[1] *Travailleurs engagés pour moins de 30 jours (non compris les travailleurs occasionnels).* [2] *A partir de 1973 : mars et sept. de chaque année.* [3] *Avril et sept.*

[1] Trabajadores ocupados durante menos de 30 días (excl. los trabajadores ocasionales). [2] A partir de 1973: marzo y sept. de cada año. [3] Abril y sept.

18 — B

Wages in manufacturing
Salaires dans les industries manufacturières
Salarios en las industrias manufactureras

By industry
Par industrie
Por industria

Cyprus

Average weekly earnings[1] *(pounds)*
Gains hebdomadaires moyens[1] *(pounds)*
Promedio de ganancias por semana[1] *(pounds)*

	311-312	313	314	321	322	323	324	331	332	341
Date[2]	Food	Beverages	Tobacco		Clothing	Leather, leather products	Footwear	Wood	Furniture	Paper, paper products
Date[2]	Aliments	Boissons	Tabac	Textiles	Habillement	Cuir, articles en cuir	Chaussures	Bois	Ameublement	Papier, articles en papier
Fecha[2]	Alimentos	Bebidas	Tabaco		Vestido	Cuero, artículos de cuero	Calzado	Madera	Mobiliario	Papel, artículos de papel
1970	6.39	8.20	6.90	5.47	4.94	6.32	8.05	8.80	10.05	6.65
1971	7.77	9.98	7.48	5.67	6.08	6.87	9.33	8.90	11.10	7.07
1972	8.52	12.19	6.56	6.69	6.67	8.48	10.74	10.80	11.93	9.60
1973	9.45	13.18	5.87	8.21	7.81	8.68	12.15	11.41	13.96	11.50
1974 [3]	12.91	16.96	10.81	8.55	8.49	8.75	14.06	16.04	17.15	9.23
1975	11.31	17.56	11.19	9.59	8.41	10.69	14.92	13.82	16.02	12.78
1976	11.66	17.54	13.74	11.28	9.40	12.33	16.49	16.74	16.76	14.40
1977	13.78	20.62	15.62	13.86	11.71	13.84	19.17	18.05	20.09	17.11
1978	15.92	24.75	19.22	16.06	13.86	17.21	23.17	23.65	25.92	20.96
1978	20.38	32.37	22.54	21.20	17.58	21.08	28.85	32.31	32.15	20.33

	342	351	355	369	381	382	383	384	390
Date[2]	Printing, publishing	Industrial chemicals	Rubber products	Non-metallic mineral products [4]	Metal products	Machinery (non-electrical)	Electrical machinery and apparatus	Transport equipment	Other manufacturing industries
Date[2]	Imprimerie, édition	Chimie industrielle	Produits en caoutchouc	Produits minéraux non métalliques [4]	Produits métalliques	Machines (non électriques)	Machines et appareils électriques	Matériel de transport	Autres industries manufacturières
Fecha[2]	Imprentas, editoriales	Química industrial	Productos de caucho	Productos minerales no metálicos [4]	Productos metálicos	Maquinaria (no eléctrica)	Maquinaria y aparatos eléctricos	Material de transporte	Otras industrias manufactureras
1970	10.79	7.10	9.76	10.90	9.31	10.24	8.11	10.00	7.76
1971	11.49	8.45	9.96	11.74	10.50	11.05	10.02	11.35	8.72
1972	13.85	8.50	11.05	13.04	11.57	14.45	12.65	13.17	10.24
1973	16.83	10.03	13.29	16.92	13.76	15.82	13.35	14.57	11.96
1974 [3]	16.25	12.82	14.38	20.59	14.03	12.82	15.00	15.60	17.27
1975	16.70	12.31	16.51	23.00	14.87	15.05	16.35	15.59	11.20
1976	19.76	19.47	15.17	24.18	16.18	16.87	33.30	15.75	12.06
1977	23.78	15.53	18.68	28.06	19.64	21.88	32.00	21.48	14.07
1978	28.27	22.36	23.51	33.97	27.01	26.96	29.18	26.83	16.97
1979	36.96	30.50	28.28	39.91	34.50	32.71	35.72	32.43	20.69

[1] Adults only. Incl. family allowances and the value of payments in kind. [2] Oct. of each year, except 1969: Sep. [3] Beginning July 1974: due to a change in the geographical scope of the series, data are not comparable with those for the preceding period. [4] Excl. pottery, china, earthenware and glass.

[1] *Adultes seulement. Y compris les allocations familiales et la valeur des paiements en nature.* [2] *Oct. de chaque année, sauf pour 1969 : sept.* [3] *A partir de juillet 1974 : en raison d'un changement de la portée géographique de la série, les données ne sont pas comparables avec celles de la période précédente.* [4] *Non compris les grès, les porcelaines, les faïences et le verre.*

[1] Adultos solamente. Incl. las asignaciones familiares y el valor de los pagos en especie. [2] Oct. de cada año, salvo 1969: sept. [3] A partir de julio de 1974: en razón de un cambio del alcance geográfico de la serie, los datos no son comparables a los del período precedente. [4] Excl. el barro, la loza, la porcelana y el vidrio.

18 Wages in manufacturing
Salaires dans les industries manufacturières
Salarios en las industrias manufactureras

B By industry
Par industrie
Por industria

India [1]

Average monthly earnings *(rupees)*
Gains mensuels moyens *(rupees)*
Promedio de ganancias por mes *(rupees)*

Date / Date / Fecha	321 Textiles	322; 324 Clothing, footwear / Habillement, chaussures / Vestido, calzado	323 Leather, leather products / Cuir, articles en cuir / Cuero, artículos de cuero	331 Wood / Bois / Madera	332 Furniture / Ameublement / Mobiliario	341 Paper, paper products / Papier, articles en papier / Papel, artículos de papel	342 Printing, publishing / Imprimerie, édition / Imprentas, editoriales	351-352 Chemicals / Industrie chimique / Productos químicos	354 Products of petroleum and coal / Dérivés du pétrole et du charbon / Derivados del petróleo y del carbón
1970	230.3	201.6	171.2	131.7	188.3	223.8	226.3	232.2	314.8
1971	233.7	207.1	237.7	146.9	165.3	233.6	242.5	241.6	302.7
1972	257.0	232.7	239.3	172.3	169.8	209.8	277.6	249.7	293.4
1973	277.4	241.7	239.3	173.2	167.2	269.6	267.3	251.9	253.8
1974	284.4	257.9	231.5	176.1	223.4	284.3	259.3	267.0	252.5
1975	291.0	231.2	273.4	191.4	231.3	271.4	259.4	254.0	259.9
1976	412.2	356.1	370.0	215.5	254.4	464.1	412.0	356.5	458.5
1977 *	467.2	370.7	451.3	193.7	305.7	459.4	455.8	449.8	526.8

Date / Date / Fecha	355 Rubber products / Industrie du caoutchouc / Productos de caucho	36 Non-metallic mineral products / Produits minéraux non métalliques / Productos minerales no metálicos	37 Basic metal industries / Industrie métallurgique de base / Industrias metalúrgicas básicas	381 Metal products / Produits métalliques / Productos metálicos	382 Machinery (non-electrical) / Machines (non électriques) / Maquinaria (no eléctrica)	383 Electrical machinery / Machines électriques / Maquinaria eléctrica	384 Transport equipment / Matériel de transport / Material de transporte	390 Miscellaneous manufacturing / Industries manufacturières diverses / Industrias manufactureras diversas
1970	237.4	151.1	239.4	203.9	229.0	276.1	254.8	229.7
1971	199.4	156.7	263.8	214.7	232.9	256.3	292.5	250.6
1972	216.2	167.1	268.2	210.6	254.8	273.0	310.9	232.2
1973	222.5	184.8	262.3	233.7	252.9	272.5	301.7	215.2
1974	213.6	182.9	249.5	234.6	255.5	269.9	265.0	230.2
1975	238.2	182.8	255.0	246.1	267.1	255.7	242.4	252.9
1976	409.7	288.2	534.0	376.3	488.2	589.4	519.0	433.7
1977 *	398.0	302.0	542.1	447.4	515.8	649.6	534.0	444.2

[1] The number of states covered by the series varies according to the years.

[1] *Le nombre d'Etats couverts par la série varie selon les années.*

[1] El número de Estados cubiertos por la serie varía según los años.

Wages in manufacturing
Salaires dans les industries manufacturières
Salarios en las industrias manufactureras

B **By industry**
Par industrie
Por industria

Israel

Average daily earnings [1] *(pounds)*
Gains journaliers moyens [1] *(pounds)*
Promedio de ganancias por día [1] *(pounds)*

	31	321	322	323-324	33	341	342	351-354
Date *Date* Fecha	Food, beverages, tobacco *Aliments, boissons, tabac* Alimentos, bebidas, tabaco	Textiles	Clothing *Habillement* Vestido	Leather, leather products, footwear *Cuir, articles en cuir, chaussures* Cuero, artículos de cuero, calzado	Wood, furniture *Bois, ameublement* Madera, mobiliario	Paper, paper products *Papier, articles en papier* Papel, artículos de papel	Printing, publishing *Imprimerie, édition* Imprentas, editoriales	Chemicals, petroleum refineries [3] *Industrie chimique, raffineries de pétrole [3]* Productos químicos, refinerías de petróleo [3]
1970	23.6	21.9	17.9	22.8	25.8	24.5	31.5	31.3
1971	26.2	24.6	19.7	23.9	29.0	25.9	35.0	35.1
1972	29.3	29.3	23.4	27.0	31.4	30.0	38.8	40.9
1973	37.0	38.6	29.0	32.6	37.1	37.6	47.2	52.4
1974	50.0	51.8	37.9	43.8	51.1	51.3	62.6	71.2
1975	72.0	72.8	52.9	63.9	74.1	75.1	87.6	104.7
1976	95.6	99.3	71.8	88.0	98.1	104.3	119.1	140.6
1977	139.7	139.8	99.6	122.6	135.7	148.8	168.3	212.4
1978	240.4	236.9	169.6	194.8	220.4	264.6	275.4	345.7
1979 [2]	427.0	428.0	300.0	398.0	377.0	377.0	499.0	628.0

	355-356	36	37	381	382	383	384	390	
Date *Date* Fecha	Rubber and plastic products *Produits en caoutchouc et en plastique* Productos de caucho y de plástico	Non-metallic mineral products *Produits minéraux non métalliques* Productos minerales no metálicos	Basic metal industries *Industrie métallurgique de base* Industrias metalúrgicas básicas	Metal products *Produits métallurgiques* Productos metálicos	Machinery (non-electrical) *Machines (non électriques)* Maquinaria (no eléctrica)	Electrical machinery and apparatus *Machines et appareils électriques* Maquinaria y aparatos eléctricos	Transport equipment *Matériel de transport* Material de transporte	Diamonds *Diamants* Diamantes	Other manufacturing industries *Autres industries manufacturières* Otras industrias manufactureras
1970	25.1	30.4	32.8	26.5	29.7	26.9	32.4	26.9	21.8
1971	28.1	34.3	36.9	29.9	32.5	30.0	34.6	28.9	25.0
1972	30.8	37.8	41.3	33.7	36.6	33.8	38.8	33.2	29.2
1973	37.2	48.5	51.2	42.1	46.0	41.6	51.0	40.1	34.2
1974	51.8	66.8	68.2	57.7	61.8	58.4	72.4	53.5	46.8
1975	74.1	91.1	95.1	83.5	88.0	80.7	101.5	79.9	70.9
1976	101.1	116.4	126.9	109.5	119.8	114.1	126.3	107.3	96.5
1977	148.4	165.7	184.5	158.9	187.0	175.4	209.1	158.0	141.3
1978	268.6	283.3	328.7	284.2	315.5	350.0	367.3	230.9	261.8
1979 [2]	472.4	519.7	593.0	564.0	586.0	682.0	749.0	...	463.0

[1] Incl. salaried employees. Beginning July 1975: incl. payments subject to income tax and the value of payments in kind. [2] Sampling design revised. [3] Incl. products of petroleum and coal.

[1] *Y compris les employés. A partir de juillet 1975: y compris les versements soumis à l'impôt sur le revenu et la valeur des paiements en nature.* [2] *Plan d'échantillonnage révisé.* [3] *Y compris les dérivés du pétrole et du charbon.*

[1] Incl. los empleados. A partir de julio de 1975: incl. los pagos sometidos al impuesto sobre la renta y el valor de los pagos en especie. [2] Diseño de la muestra revisado. [3] Incl. los derivados del petróleo y del carbón.

18 Wages in manufacturing
Salaires dans les industries manufacturières
Salarios en las industrias manufactureras

B By industry
Par industrie
Por industria

Japan (1)

Average monthly earnings [1] *(yen)*
Gains mensuels moyens [1] *(yen)*
Promedio de ganancias por mes [1] *(yen)*

Date / Date / Fecha	31 Food, beverages, tobacco / Aliments, boissons, tabac / Alimentos, bebidas, tabaco	321 Textiles	322 Clothing / Habillement / Vestido	323-324 Leather, leather products, footwear / Cuir, articles en cuir, chaussures / Cuero, artículos de cuero, calzado	331 Wood / Bois / Madera	332 Furniture / Ameublement / Mobiliario
1970	62 801	52 657	40 041	59 400	54 777	55 250
1971	73 643	59 924	45 876	65 919	63 214	63 164
1972	85 366	70 069	53 416	75 398	75 702	73 863
1973 [2]	96 328	89 536	69 948	93 573	98 460	92 050
1974	123 998	103 992	85 686	118 303	118 780	117 021
1975	146 592	113 878	96 001	128 588	128 661	131 385
1976 [2]	161 666	129 883	107 948	142 722	141 442	144 060
1977	179 251	137 625	113 226	155 136	149 288	154 450
1978	193 323	150 864	122 015	165 914	159 234	163 232
1979 [2]	194 491	165 474	129 695	172 406	176 667	183 640

Date / Date / Fecha	341 Paper, paper products / Papier, articles en papier / Papel, artículos de papel	342 Printing, publishing / Imprimerie, édition / Imprentas, editoriales	351-352 Chemicals / Industrie chimique / Productos químicos	353-354 Refineries and products of petroleum and coal / Raffineries et dérivés du pétrole et du charbon / Refinerías y derivados del petróleo y del carbón	355 Rubber products / Produits en caoutchouc / Productos de caucho	36 Non-metallic mineral products / Produits minéraux non métalliques / Productos minerales no metálicos	371 Iron and steel basic industries / Sidérurgie / Industrias básicas de hierro y acero
1970	73 159	87 257	86 785	98 028	64 740	70 543	100 710
1971	85 171	100 810	98 657	114 112	75 270	79 395	109 798
1972	97 084	115 881	112 969	127 114	89 652	91 606	122 362
1973 [2]	118 919	140 006	140 429	153 822	113 173	110 784	155 080
1974	157 377	178 142	183 213	200 264	143 607	143 251	200 001
1975	165 698	207 045	198 811	224 261	161 240	157 476	217 512
1976 [2]	188 779	239 107	219 699	248 059	181 115	176 097	238 137
1977	203 774	259 006	239 795	269 441	197 448	194 219	261 602
1978	217 721	278 760	253 984	295 702	208 135	207 497	270 504
1979 [2]	229 988	288 914	282 613	322 938	223 644	217 485	291 121

[1] Incl. salaried employees. Incl. family allowances, mid- and end-of-year bonuses. [2] Sampling design revised.

[1] Y compris les employés. Y compris les allocations familiales et les primes de mi- et de fin d'année. [2] Plan d'échantillonnage révisé.

[1] Incl. los empleados. Incl. las asignaciones familiares y las primas de mitad y de fin de año. [2] Diseño de la muestra revisado.

WAGES

18 Wages in manufacturing
Salaires dans les industries manufacturières
Salarios en las industrias manufactureras

B By industry
Par industrie
Por industria

Japan (2)

Average monthly earnings [1] *(yen)*
Gains mensuels moyens [1] *(yen)*
Promedio de ganancias por mes [1] *(yen)*

Date / Date / Fecha	372	381	382	383	384	385	390
	Non-ferrous metal basic industries *Métaux non ferreux (industrie de base)* Industrias básicas de metales no ferrosos	Metal products *Produits métalliques* Productos metálicos	Machinery (non-electrical) *Machines (non électriques)* Maquinaria (no eléctrica)	Electrical machinery and apparatus *Machines et appareils électriques* Maquinaria y aparatos eléctricos	Transport equipment *Matériel de transport* Material de transporte	Scientific, measuring, optical, etc., equipment *Matériel scientifique, de précision, d'optique, etc.* Equipo científico, de medida, de óptica, etc.	Other manufacturing industries *Autres industries manufacturières* Otras industrias manufactureras
1970	85 419	71 353	81 222	63 830	82 769	69 153	60 398
1971	95 818	80 408	88 782	72 841	94 784	76 955	69 713
1972	110 617	92 436	102 513	87 086	106 169	90 637	82 286
1973 [2]	136 760	117 647	131 647	105 419	132 231	111 277	102 047
1974	170 487	148 247	165 863	129 570	163 382	137 227	130 443
1975	181 078	165 626	176 417	151 089	181 768	152 940	149 216
1976 [2]	204 979	176 330	199 694	173 641	208 825	174 437	166 698
1977	224 291	194 548	221 157	190 525	229 529	190 604	182 937
1978	241 919	209 708	232 126	209 515	239 834	204 957	193 583
1979 [2]	258 516	225 639	254 174	217 004	254 654	219 409	211 629

[1] Incl. salaried employees. Incl. family allowances, mid- and end-of-year bonuses. [2] Sampling design revised.

[1] *Y compris les employés. Y compris les allocations familiales et les primes de mi- et de fin d'année.* [2] *Plan d'échantillonnage révisé.*

[1] Incl. los empleados. Incl. las asignaciones familiares y las primas de mitad y de fin de año. [2] Diseño de la muestra revisado.

18 Wages in manufacturing
Salaires dans les industries manufacturières
Salarios en las industrias manufactureras

B By industry
Par industrie
Por industria

Korea, Rep. of (1)

Average monthly earnings [1] *(won)*
Gains mensuels moyens [1] *(won)*
Promedio de ganancias por mes [1] *(won)*

	311-312	313	321	322	323	331	332	341
Date *Date* Fecha	Food *Aliments* Alimentos	Beverages *Boissons* Bebidas	Textiles	Clothing *Habillement* Vestido	Leather, leather products *Cuir, articles en cuir* Cuero, artículos de cuero	Wood *Bois* Madera	Furniture *Ameublement* Mobiliario	Paper, paper products *Papier, articles en papier* Papel, artículos de papel
1970	15 661	16 389	11 505	9 974	11 864	15 250	11 166	18 174
1971	18 072	19 062	13 335	12 071	13 861	18 009	12 660	20 425
1972	19 877	22 760	15 508	14 633	16 226	19 392	14 399	22 962
1973	23 479	27 560	19 143	14 952	19 197	23 623	14 919	25 313
1974	30 313	39 519	37 571	19 931	24 469	30 548	20 398	34 074
1975	40 124	52 012	33 393	25 152	32 655	38 835	31 444	44 508
1976	53 332	71 079	45 681	35 789	44 688	51 921	34 555	57 594
1977	76 760	109 840	56 698	45 737	49 901	68 623	56 681	88 400
1978	102 094	127 269	74 480	60 878	68 600	94 716	91 366	121 854
1979	134 440	169 515	98 574	80 478	89 220	115 883	110 545	155 582

	342	351	352	353	354	355	356	361
Date *Date* Fecha	Printing, publishing *Imprimerie, édition* Imprentas, editoriales	Industrial chemicals *Chimie industrielle* Química industrial	Other chemical products *Autres produits chimiques* Otros productos químicos	Petroleum refineries *Raffineries de pétrole* Refinerías de petróleo	Products of petroleum and coal *Dérivés du pétrole et du charbon* Derivados del petróleo y del carbón	Rubber products *Produits en caoutchouc* Productos de caucho	Plastic products *Articles en matière plastique* Productos plásticos	Pottery, china, earthenware *Grès, porcelaines, faïences* Barro, loza, porcelana
1970	18 872	22 194	19 465	30 917	15 241	12 358	16 162	11 129
1971	22 227	26 654	21 983	36 624	20 688	13 841	19 065	12 640
1972	23 680	32 418	24 967	44 213	22 496	17 818	21 306	14 356
1973	29 844	49 143	29 776	61 487	28 473	17 549	24 999	15 571
1974	38 013	58 711	39 457	92 311	34 420	24 096	33 067	21 652
1975	49 000	79 132	50 659	124 145	46 699	34 748	46 420	29 874
1976	71 183	106 919	68 515	179 611	64 999	43 421	58 271	40 092
1977	95 436	132 339	96 465	225 091	92 778	55 752	73 551	51 139
1978	128 603	166 604	127 019	289 017	111 537	71 773	103 016	73 572
1979	182 842	210 447	161 222	345 565	144 875	91 721	138 445	92 758

[1] Incl. salaried employees. Incl. family allowances and the value of payments in kind.

[1] *Y compris les employés. Y compris les allocations familiales et la valeur des paiements en nature.*

[1] Incl. los empleados. Incl. las asignaciones familiares y el valor de los pagos en especie.

18 Wages in manufacturing / Salaires dans les industries manufacturières / Salarios en las industrias manufactureras — B By industry / Par industrie / Por industria

Korea, Rep. of (2) — Average monthly earnings [1] *(won)* / Gains mensuels moyens [1] *(won)* / Promedio de ganancias por mes [1] *(won)*

Date / Date / Fecha	362 Glass, and glass products / Verre / Vidrio	369 Other non-metallic mineral products / Autres produits minéraux / Otros productos minerales	371 Iron and steel / Sidérurgie / Hierro y acero	372 Non-ferrous metal / Métaux non ferreux / Metales no ferrosos	381 Metal products / Produits métallurgiques / Productos metálicos	382 Machinery (non-electrical) / Machines (non électriques) / Maquinaria (no eléctrica)	383 Electrical machinery and apparatus / Machines et appareils électriques / Maquinaria y aparatos eléctricos	384 Transport equipment / Matériel de transport / Material de transporte	385 Scientific, measuring, optical, etc., equipment / Matériel scientifique, de précision, d'optique, etc. / Equipo científico, de medida, de óptica, etc.	390 Other manufacturing industries / Autres industries manufacturières / Otras industrias manufactureras
			Basic metal industries / Industrie métallurgique de base / Industrias metalúrgicas básicas							
1970	15 141	16 067	20 857	18 770	15 319	15 105	15 213	18 535	14 652	10 546
1971	17 483	18 376	24 505	22 717	18 632	18 109	18 682	20 189	17 207	12 204
1972	20 351	22 724	29 638	29 202	18 980	21 272	18 980	22 391	21 042	14 165
1973	30 554	27 236	38 707	35 609	20 653	25 697	20 243	26 141	22 520	15 970
1974	36 991	37 050	49 014	48 056	29 352	33 449	27 848	41 141	26 660	22 291
1975	51 299	44 902	51 344	58 835	38 406	40 520	37 898	51 098	34 638	29 053
1976	72 957	57 714	71 894	76 901	51 518	57 658	49 833	71 920	47 548	38 051
1977	93 330	88 913	102 988	117 869	66 659	85 557	62 223	116 312	61 993	50 589
1978	123 054	123 499	138 225	161 366	93 148	116 031	79 240	154 636	81 610	70 829
1979	156 291	153 617	167 738	185 369	120 549	145 445	99 930	176 414	104 457	96 759

[1] Incl. salaried employees. Incl. family allowances and the value of payments in kind.

[1] *Y compris les employés. Y compris les allocations familiales et la valeur des paiements en nature.*

[1] Incl. los empleados. Incl. las asignaciones familiares y el valor de los pagos en especie.

Pakistan — Average monthly earnings *(rupees)* / Gains mensuels moyens *(rupees)* / Promedio de ganancias por mes *(rupees)*

Date / Date / Fecha	Food, beverages, tobacco / Aliments, boissons, tabac / Alimentos, bebidas, tabaco	Textiles	Wood, stone, glass / Bois, pierre, verre / Madera, piedra, vidrio	Paper, printing, publishing / Papier, imprimerie, édition / Papel, imprentas, editoriales	Skins, hides / Peaux, cuirs / Pieles, cuero	Chemicals / Industrie chimique / Productos químicos	Minerals, metals / Minéraux, métaux / Minerales, metales	Engineering / Mécanique / Mecánica	Miscellaneous manufacturing / Industries manufacturières diverses / Industrias manufactureras diversas
1970	.	143.1	127.1	168.9	161.2	168.5	142.6	154.9	140.1
1971	.	154.5	156.8	148.4	146.2	198.5	155.3	133.0	128.6
1972	165.8	164.0	171.6	169.3	169.1	168.2	174.3	155.9	172.3
1973	253.3	230.5	235.3	368.4	235.7	304.7	266.6	322.2	311.2
1974	255.6	288.1	282.7	562.7	...	376.8	...	...	259.8
1975	271.1	366.2	330.6	427.9	...	389.0	...	...	477.8
1976	320.5	360.4	437.5	510.1	...	472.4	...	...	510.4

18 Wages in manufacturing / Salaires dans les industries manufacturières / Salarios en las industrias manufactureras — B By industry / Par industrie / Por industria

Singapore (1)

Average hourly earnings *(cents)*
Gains horaires moyens *(cents)*
Promedio de ganancias por hora *(cents)*

Date [1] / Date [1] / Fecha [1]	311-312 Food / Aliments / Alimentos	313 Beverages / Boissons / Bebidas	314 Tobacco / Tabac / Tabaco	321 Textiles	322 Clothing / Habillement / Vestido	323 Leather, leather products / Cuir, articles en cuir / Cuero, artículos de cuero	324 Footwear / Chaussures / Calzado	331 Wood / Bois / Madera	332 Furniture / Ameublement / Mobiliario
1971	76	110	116	63	58	65	69	96	100
1972	81	118	119	68	60	61	74	99	103
1973	99	135	146	85	71	77	83	112	106
1974	125			98	83			125	
1975	140			109	102			134	
1976	152			114	106			146	
1977	163			127	110			150	
1978	176			145	120			161	
1979	197			166	142			182	

Date [1] / Date [1] / Fecha [1]	341 Paper, paper products / Papier, articles en papier / Papel, artículos de papel	342 Printing, publishing / Imprimerie, édition / Imprentas, editoriales	351 Industrial chemicals / Chimie industrielle / Química industrial	352 Other chemical products / Autres produits chimiques / Otros productos químicos	353 Petroleum refineries / Raffineries de pétrole / Refinerías de petróleo	355 Rubber products / Produits en caoutchouc / Productos de caucho	356 Plastic products / Articles en matière plastique / Productos plásticos	361-362 Pottery, china, earthenware and glass / Grès, porcelaines, faïences et verre / Barro, loza, porcelana y vidrio	369 Other non-metallic mineral products / Autres produits minéraux non métalliques / Otros productos minerales no metálicos
1971	65	107	118	76	230	81	68	107	111
1972	72	117	117	96	232	86	73	121	112
1973	79	128	126	107	264	97	91	139	115
1974	138				136			149	
1975	147				158			178	
1976	166				161			182	
1977	169				175			192	
1978	176				192			215	
1979	196				210			236	

[1] Aug. of each year. Prior to 1975: July.　　　[1] *Août de chaque année. Avant 1975 : juillet.*　　　[1] Agosto de cada año. Antes de 1975: julio.

WAGES

18 Wages in manufacturing
Salaires dans les industries manufacturières
Salarios en las industrias manufactureras

B By industry
Par industrie
Por industria

Singapore (2)

Average hourly earnings *(cents)*
Gains horaires moyens *(cents)*
Promedio de ganancias por hora *(cents)*

Date [1] Date [1] Fecha [1]	371 Basic metal industries *Industrie métallurgique de base* Industrias metalúrgicas básicas Iron and steel *Sidérurgie* Hierro y acero	372 Non-ferrous metal *Métaux non ferreux* Metales no ferrosos	381 Metal products *Produits métalliques* Productos metálicos	382 Machinery (non-electrical) *Machines (non électriques)* Maquinaria (no eléctrica)	383 Electrical machinery and apparatus *Machines et appareils électriques* Maquinaria y aparatos eléctricos	384 Transport equipment *Matériel de transport* Material de transporte	385 Scientific, measuring, optical, etc., equipment *Matériel scientifique, de précision, d'optique, etc.* Equipo científico, de medida, de óptica, etc.	390 Other manufacturing industries *Autres industries manufacturières* Otras industrias manufactureras
1971	110	108	93	109	75	135	68	65
1972	126	115	94	118	81	148	77	66
1973	132	148	108	134	93	157	96	86
1974	153		120	157	111	176	102	98
1975	166		135	174	127	208	120	109
1976	180		147	197	137	217	130	124
1977	195		158	200	146	217	140	138
1978	224		171	209	153	242	144	144
1979	263		198	225	173	252	159	172

[1] Aug. of each year. Prior to 1975: July.   [1] *Août de chaque année. Avant 1975 : juillet.*   [1] Agosto de cada año. Antes de 1975: julio.

République arabe syrienne (1)

Average weekly earnings [1] *(pounds)*
Gains hebdomadaires moyens [1] *(pounds)*
Promedio de ganancias por semana [1] *(pounds)*

Date [2] Date [2] Fecha [2]	311-312 Food *Aliments* Alimentos	313 Beverages *Boissons* Bebidas	314 Tobacco *Tabac* Tabaco	321 Textiles	322 Clothing *Habillement* Vestido	323 Leather, leather products *Cuir, articles en cuir* Cuero, artículos de cuero	331 Wood *Bois* Madera
1970	47.20	59.90	46.55	. .	39.65	51.35	45.10
1971	47.10	53.50	43.05	57.10	42.35	57.10	55.80
1972	55.65	68.15	48.50	65.55	48.55	77.10	54.20
1973	72.50	91.70	61.65	78.40	58.95	79.05	55.10
1974	64.20	82.40	59.50	74.50	61.10	73.10	64.80
1975	70.21	98.61	72.98	79.91	67.67	107.39	71.72
1976	97.25	130.50	87.95	104.85	81.90	122.70	105.10
1977	101.95	120.45	98.80	109.80	78.15	114.75	95.10

[1] Adults only.   [2] May of each year. Prior to 1973: Nov.   [1] *Adultes seulement.*   [2] *Mai de chaque année. Avant 1973 : nov.*   [1] Adultos solamente.   [2] Mayo de cada año. Antes de 1973: nov.

18 Wages in manufacturing
Salaires dans les industries manufacturières
Salarios en las industrias manufactureras

B By industry
Par industrie
Por industria

République arabe syrienne (2)

Average weekly earnings [1] *(pounds)*
Gains hebdomadaires moyens [1] *(pounds)*
Promedio de ganancias por semana [1] *(pounds)*

Date [2] *Date [2]* Fecha [2]	341 Paper, paper products *Papier, articles en papier* Papel, artículos de papel	342 Printing, publishing *Imprimerie, édition* Imprentas, editoriales	351 Industrial chemicals *Chimie industrielle* Química industrial	352 Other chemical products *Autres produits chimiques* Otros productos químicos	353 Petroleum refineries *Raffineries de pétrole* Refinerías de petróleo	354 Products of petroleum and coal *Dérivés du pétrole et du charbon* Derivados del petróleo y del carbón	355 Rubber products *Produits en caoutchouc* Productos de caucho
1970	50.80	56.25	.	46.40	.	.	47.75
1971	42.00	59.90	.	53.90	75.85	45.70	51.60
1972	50.35	66.00	.	69.35	80.70	45.75	63.45
1973	62.55	78.25	102.10	78.30	91.15	54.00	76.60
1974	64.10	84.70	101.25	78.95	94.40	53.25	80.40
1975	82.22	...	127.71	87.07	132.79	63.51	84.76
1976	94.70	96.65	147.35	106.70	158.60	88.75	108.15
1977	105.95	107.15	151.45	113.50	151.50	106.05	113.20

Date [2] *Date [2]* Fecha [2]	356 Plastic products *Articles en matière plastique* Productos plásticos	361 Pottery, china, earthenware *Grès, porcelaines, faïences* Barro, loza, porcelana	362 Glass *Verre* Vidrio	369 × Cement *Ciment* Cemento	371 Iron and steel basic industries *Sidérurgie* Industrias básicas de hierro y acero	381 Metal products *Produits métalliques* Productos metálicos	382 Machinery (non-electrical) *Machines (non électriques)* Maquinaria (no eléctrica)	383 Electrical machinery and apparatus *Machines et appareils électriques* Maquinaria y aparatos eléctricos
1970	.	.	.	.	53.55	...	...	49.30
1971	39.20	43.90	49.65	57.80	43.80	50.10	56.50	51.35
1972	55.30	47.55	67.30	81.15	54.45	63.50	56.60	64.05
1973	52.25	57.65	75.70	97.55	67.05	68.10	69.75	69.00
1974	51.45	64.10	84.15	89.90	68.05	66.55	73.60	74.50
1975	63.74	82.68	87.53	101.85	79.91	79.21	...	80.60
1976	91.95	106.55	112.50	137.55	108.55	103.80	115.85	97.15
1977	97.55	107.35	112.50	135.25	116.25	103.80	115.85	97.15

[1] Adults only. [2] May of each year. Prior to 1973: Nov.

[1] *Adultes seulement.* [2] *Mai de chaque année. Avant 1973 : nov.*

[1] Adultos solamente. [2] Mayo de cada año. Antes de 1973: nov.

WAGES

18 Wages in manufacturing
Salaires dans les industries manufacturières
Salarios en las industrias manufactureras

B By industry
Par industrie
Por industria

EUROPE — EUROPE — EUROPA

Austria

Average monthly earnings *(schilling)*
Gains mensuels moyens *(schilling)*
Promedio de ganancias por mes *(schilling)*

Date / Date / Fecha	311-312	321	322	323 ×	323 × ; 324	331-332	341	
	Food, beverages, tobacco / *Aliments, boissons, tabac* / Alimentos, bebidas, tabaco	Textiles	Clothing / *Habillement* / Vestido	Leather / *Cuir* / Cuero	Leather products, footwear / *Articles en cuir, chaussures* / Artículos de cuero, calzado	Wood [2], furniture / *Bois [2], ameublement* / Madera [2], mobiliario	Paper / *Papier* / Papel	Paper products / *Articles en papier* / Artículos de papel
1970	4 807	3 474	3 047	3 804	3 349	4 361	6 262	4 233
1971 [1]	5 372	3 925	3 344	4 206	3 861	4 950	6 820	4 588
1972	6 139	4 387	3 718	4 665	4 462	5 655	7 483	5 081
1973	6 855	4 964	4 104	5 061	4 853	6 322	8 400	5 614
1974	7 864	5 606	4 588	5 705	5 437	7 264	9 668	6 655
1975	8 987	6 160	5 193	6 513	6 072	7 980	10 706	7 380
1976	9 988	6 798	5 703	6 855	6 489	8 899	12 054	8 326
1977	10 845	7 298	6 214	7 414	6 994	9 671	13 046	9 012
1978	11 342	7 738	6 575	7 809	7 267	10 481	13 735	9 475
1979	11 996	8 156	6 802	8 357	7 830	11 404	14 674	10 139

Date / Date / Fecha	35	36		371	372	381; 385; 390	382	383	384
	Chemicals [3] / *Industrie chimique [3]* / Productos químicos [3]	Non-metallic mineral products / *Produits minéraux non métalliques* / Productos minerales no metálicos — Total	Glass / *Verre* / Vidrio	Basic metal industries / *Industrie métallurgique de base* / Industrias metalúrgicas básicas — Iron and steel / *Sidérurgie* / Hierro y acero	Non-ferrous metal / *Métaux non ferreux* / Metales no ferrosos	Metal products, miscellaneous manufacturing [4] / *Produits métalliques, industries manufacturières diverses [4]* / Productos metálicos, industrias manufactureras diversas [4]	Machinery (non-electrical) / *Machines (non électriques)* / Maquinaria (no eléctrica)	Electrical machinery / *Machines électriques* / Maquinaria eléctrica	Transport equipment / *Matériel de transport* / Material de transporte
1970	4 902	5 267	4 648	5 238	5 466	4 428	5 258	4 278	4 621
1971 [1]	5 614	5 916	5 442	6 271	6 030	5 101	6 099	4 839	5 541
1972	6 251	6 856	6 104	6 805	6 819	5 707	6 792	5 367	6 140
1973	6 997	7 540	6 947	7 678	7 749	6 453	7 698	6 049	6 908
1974	8 203	8 619	8 047	9 008	8 992	7 447	8 833	6 881	7 949
1975	9 317	9 566	8 727	10 102	9 909	8 443	9 905	8 068	8 954
1976	10 163	10 581	9 898	10 869	10 757	9 256	10 751	8 869	9 731
1977	11 051	11 600	11 019	11 685	11 305	9 992	11 632	9 690	10 594
1978	11 817	12 436	11 667	12 379	12 030	10 481	12 374	10 321	10 992
1979	12 391	13 119	11 940	12 869	12 840	10 930	13 072	10 900	11 927

[1] Scope of series enlarged. [2] Excl. sawmills. [3] Incl. refineries and products of petroleum and coal, rubber and plastic products. [4] Incl. scientific, measuring, optical, etc., equipment.

[1] *Portée de la série élargie.* [2] *Non compris les scieries.* [3] *Y compris les raffineries et dérivés du pétrole et du charbon, et les produits en caoutchouc et en plastique.* [4] *Y compris le matériel scientifique, de précision, d'optique, etc.*

[1] El alcance de la serie es mayor. [2] Excl. los aserraderos. [3] Incl. las refinerías y derivados del petróleo y del carbón y los productos de caucho y de plástico. [4] Incl. el equipo científico, de medida, de óptica, etc.

18 Wages in manufacturing
Salaires dans les industries manufacturières
Salarios en las industrias manufactureras

B By industry
Par industrie
Por industria

Belgique (1)

Average hourly earnings *(francs)*
Gains horaires moyens *(francs)*
Promedio de ganancias por hora *(francs)*

	311-312	313	314	321	322 ×	323	324	331	332
Date [1]	Food	Beverages	Tobacco		Clothing	Leather, leather products	Footwear	Wood	Furniture
Date [1]	*Aliments*	*Boissons*	*Tabac*	Textiles	*Habillement*	*Cuir, articles en cuir*	*Chaussures*	*Bois*	*Ameublement*
Fecha [1]	Alimentos	Bebidas	Tabaco		Vestido	Cuero, artículos de cuero	Calzado	Madera	Mobiliario
1970	58.40	63.90	57.40	56.05	46.13	55.01	57.50	62.88	65.14
1971	67.95	72.77	66.30	63.67	50.61	62.12	63.86	70.22	70.48
1972 [2]	77.44	83.71	81.67	74.68	58.46	72.66	72.76	81.03	80.00
1973	88.21	94.61	92.45	85.20	65.59	82.04	84.23	90.14	87.57
1974	111.34	119.51	113.33	107.06	82.09	98.11	102.70	116.03	114.54
1975	132.52	140.65	130.77	123.07	99.72	114.78	119.76	135.95	132.53
1976	149.74	157.82	155.57	135.63	108.95	130.70	132.10	149.90	146.22
1977	166.83	174.62	160.23	145.47	118.05	145.60	142.83	165.78	161.77
1978	177.04	186.81	168.29	150.91	129.11	149.80	151.30	177.15	178.16
1979	186.24	198.23	184.35	164.15	137.69	161.33	164.14	187.36	182.42

	341	342	351		353	355	361	362
Date [1]	Paper, paper products	Printing, publishing	Basic industrial chemicals	Fertilizers and pesticides [3]	Synthetic and man-made fibres	Petroleum refineries	Rubber products	Pottery, china, earthenware	Glass
Date [1]	*Papier, articles en papier*	*Imprimerie, édition*	*Industrie chimique de base*	*Engrais et pesticides [3]*	*Fibres synthétiques et artificielles*	*Raffineries de pétrole*	*Produits en caoutchouc*	*Grès, porcelaines, faïences*	*Verre*
Fecha [1]	Papel, artículos de papel	Imprentas, editoriales	Química industrial básica	Abonos y plaguicidas [3]	Fibras sintéticas y artificiales	Refinerías de petróleo	Productos de caucho	Barro, loza, porcelana	Vidrio
1970	65.91	72.40	81.38	70.40	73.08	105.03	69.11	59.78	66.28
1971	74.88	85.15	94.35	81.72	84.37	123.38	78.02	67.88	75.03
1972 [2]	85.41	93.32	115.23	95.96	100.27	143.02	93.00	79.14	88.51
1973	96.52	108.96	126.62	107.60	114.18	158.29	104.50	90.83	102.29
1974	119.92	142.21	157.25	137.19	141.15	190.20	132.76	112.61	128.39
1975	138.44	170.32	184.90	160.97	166.86	224.19	150.84	132.17	149.57
1976	153.55	185.02	205.97	176.92	182.82	255.77	164.30	146.84	167.74
1977	165.89	197.67	230.72	200.65	191.48	274.41	183 69	164.08	182.28
1978	179.50	204.66	248.32	210.61	198.72	288.33	194.83	173.30	194.92
1979	196.03	221.55	259.91	223.66	220.38	333.22	207.68	183.96	209.54

[1] Oct. of each year. [2] New industrial classification.
[3] Incl. drugs and medicines.

[1] *Oct. de chaque année.* [2] *Nouvelle classification industrielle.* [3] *Y compris les produits pharmaceutiques et les médicaments.*

[1] Oct. de cada año. [2] Nueva clasificación industrial.
[3] Incl. los productos farmacéuticos y medicamentos.

WAGES

18 Wages in manufacturing
Salaires dans les industries manufacturières
Salarios en las industrias manufactureras

B By industry
Par industrie
Por industria

Belgique (2)

Average hourly earnings *(francs)*
Gains horaires moyens *(francs)*
Promedio de ganancias por hora *(francs)*

Date [1] *Date* [1] Fecha [1]	369 × Cement *Ciment* Cemento	371	372	381 Metal products *Produits métalliques* Productos metálicos	382 Machinery (non- electrical) *Machines (non électriques)* Maquinaria (no eléctrica)	383 Electrical machinery and apparatus *Machines et appareils électriques* Maquinaria y aparatos eléctricos	384 Transport equipment *Matériel de transport* Material de transporte	385 Scientific, measuring, optical, etc., equipment *Matériel scientifique, de précision, d'optique, etc.* Equipo científico, de medida, de óptica, etc.	390 Other manufacturing industries *Autres industries manufacturières* Otras industrias manufactureras
		Basic metal industries *Industrie métallurgique de base* Industrias metalúrgicas básicas							
		Iron and steel *Sidérurgie* Hierro y acero	Non-ferrous metal *Métaux non ferreux* Metales no ferrosos						
1970	84.43	88.67	76.30	67.65	71.66	67.59	79.46	.	.
1971	93.34	103.50	88.37	75.62	81.42	76.89	88.52		
1972 [2]	111.31	119.49	104.41	88.99	94.23	86.96	102.11	79.03	65.03
1973	123.78	134.89	120.57	102.41	107.99	100.59	115.78	91.43	75.23
1974	151.93	171.89	151.86	128.28	133.94	126.83	144.76	117.18	90.01
1975	175.82	185.07	171.27	147.13	153.05	145.37	170.50	135.98	104.25
1976	199.82	209.83	188.12	160.02	167.56	160.52	180.13	147.94	120.05
1977	227.52	227.11	207.00	174.84	183.22	173.48	194.46	164.09	129.31
1978	243.82	237.80	221.18	186.12	193.37	183.15	200.05	173.86	142.53
1979	257.85	270.58	235.60	203.32	209.29	200.79	213.87	185.49	158.07

[1] Oct. of each year. [2] New industrial classification.

[1] *Oct. de chaque année.* [2] *Nouvelle classification industrielle.*

[1] Oct. de cada año. [2] Nueva clasificación industrial.

18 B

Wages in manufacturing
Salaires dans les industries manufacturières
Salarios en las industrias manufactureras

By industry
Par industrie
Por industria

Bulgarie [1]

Average monthly earnings [2] *(leva)*
Gains mensuels moyens [2] *(leva)*
Promedio de ganancias por mes [2] *(leva)*

	31	321	322	323-324	33	341	342
Date *Date* Fecha	Food, beverage, tobacco *Aliments, boissons, tabac* Alimentos, bebidas, tabaco	Textiles	Clothing *Habillement* Vestido	Leather, leather products, footwear *Cuir, articles en cuir, chaussures* Cuero, artículos de cuero, calzado	Wood, furniture [3] *Bois, ameublement [3]* Madera, mobiliario [3]	Paper, paper products *Papier, articles en papier* Papel, artículos de papel	Printing, publishing *Imprimerie, édition* Imprentas, editoriales
1970	115.2	106.2	99.5	109.0	127.3	118.2	122.2
1971	118.8	109.7	99.7	114.4	131.3	117.4	121.8
1972	123.1	114.6	104.2	119.7	136.4	119.3	128.3
1973	132.0	123.7	112.1	125.1	143.2	124.5	136.4
1974	134.4	124.3	113.8	128.9	149.3	128.2	129.8
1975	140.0	130.3	115.6	131.5	155.3	139.3	139.8
1976	141.3	131.4	115.9	132.8	156.0	138.4	141.2
1977	140.5	135.3	117.2	139.3	158.7	142.0	145.0
1978	147.1	140.8	119.4	142.1	162.2	159.5	158.2
1979 *	151.8	150.3	126.6	148.8	169.5	170.8	172.4

	351-352; 355	354	361 ×-362	369 ×	371	381-382	390
Date *Date* Fecha	Chemicals, rubber products [4] *Industrie chimique, caoutchouc [4]* Productos químicos, caucho [4]	Products of petroleum and coal *Dérivés du pétrole et du charbon* Derivados del petróleo y del carbón	China, earthenware, glass *Porcelaines, faïences, verre* Loza, porcelana, vidrio	Building material *Matériaux de construction* Materiales de construcción	Iron and steel basic industries [5] *Sidérurgie [5]* Industrias básicas de hierro y acero [5]	Metal products, machinery (non-electrical) *Produits métalliques, machines (non électriques)* Productos metálicos, maquinaria (no eléctrica)	Other manufacturing industries *Autres industries manufacturières* Otras industrias manufactureras
1970	127.8	165.8	117.7	132.5	148.2	129.8	108.9
1971	129.5	167.4	127.4	137.7	157.2	133.3	110.2
1972	133.7	174.0	132.7	141.2	171.8	138.5	114.5
1973	143.4	186.2	137.4	148.5	176.7	146.9	120.3
1974	146.7	193.6	138.5	155.1	182.6	149.3	124.5
1975	151.8	204.5	147.8	162.0	186.8	158.3	128.1
1976	154.3	205.0	148.8	161.6	191.3	159.3	130.1
1977	160.4	210.9	154.5	166.7	197.2	164.5	...
1978	171.8	219.8	160.6	172.3	200.3	172.2	...
1979 *	182.3	226.3	170.8	187.5	225.1	180.1	...

[1] Socialised sector. [2] Incl. salaried employees. [3] Incl. logging. [4] Incl. salt mining. [5] Incl. ore mining.

[1] *Secteur socialisé.* [2] *Y compris les employés.* [3] *Y compris l'exploitation forestière.* [4] *Y compris l'extraction du sel.* [5] *Y compris l'extraction des minerais.*

[1] Sector socializado. [2] Incl. los empleados. [3] Incl. la explotación de la madera. [4] Incl. la explotación de minas de sal. [5] Incl. la extracción de minerales.

18 Wages in manufacturing
Salaires dans les industries manufacturières
Salarios en las industrias manufactureras

B By industry
Par industrie
Por industria

Czechoslovakia [1] (1)

Average monthly earnings *(korunas)*
Gains mensuels moyens *(korunas)*
Promedio de ganancias por mes *(korunas)*

	311-312	313	314	321	322	323	324	331	332
Date *Date* Fecha	Food *Aliments* Alimentos	Beverages *Boissons* Bebidas	Tobacco *Tabac* Tabaco	Textiles	Clothing *Habillement* Vestido	Leather, leather products *Cuir, articles en cuir* Cuero, artículos de cuero	Footwear *Chaussures* Calzado	Wood *Bois* Madera	Furniture *Ameublement* Mobiliario
1970	1 832	1 791	1 502	1 485	1 431	1 585	1 739	1 775	1 717
1971	1 881	1 880	1 597	1 536	1 459	1 641	1 797	1 842	1 770
1972	1 959	1 962	1 661	1 592	1 523	1 734	1 853	1 907	1 858
1973	2 017	2 014	1 733	1 644	1 572	1 787	1 885	1 955	1 919
1974	2 087	2 086	1 825	1 713	1 645	1 852	1 978	2 027	1 976
1975	2 160	2 152	1 888	1 791	1 718	1 909	2 068	2 104	2 057
1976	2 189	2 199	1 941	1 860	1 770	1 965	2 106	2 178	2 109
1977	2 285	2 274	2 004	1 934	1 850	2 013	2 186	2 253	2 167
1978	2 342	2 327	2 071	2 010	1 914	2 082	2 270	2 329	2 234
1979	2 381	2 396	2 109	2 065	1 979	2 161	2 350	2 396	2 295

	341	342	351	352	353	354	355	356	361	362
Date *Date* Fecha	Paper, paper products *Papier, articles en papier* Papel, artículos de papel	Printing, publishing *Imprimerie, édition* Imprentas, editoriales	Industrial chemicals *Chimie industrielle* Química industrial	Other chemical products *Autres produits chimiques* Otros productos químicos	Petroleum refineries *Raffineries de pétrole* Refinerías de petróleo	Products of petroleum and coal *Dérivés du pétrole et du charbon* Derivados del petróleo y del carbón	Rubber products *Produits, en caoutchouc* Productos de caucho	Plastic products *Articles en matière plastique* Productos plásticos	Pottery, china, earthenware *Grès, porcelaines, faïences* Barro, loza, porcelana	Glass *Verre* Vidrio
1970	1 742	1 900	1 967	1 676	2 130	2 322	1 835	.	1 649	1 662
1971	1 808	1 929	2 045	1 716	2 208	2 388	1 978	.	1 681	1 710
1972	1 872	1 997	2 123	1 777	2 281	2 444	2 059	.	1 729	1 790
1973	1 938	2 025	2 172	1 834	2 341	2 479	2 111	.	1 769	1 841
1974	2 008	2 076	2 241	1 906	2 430	2 586	2 189	.	1 818	1 932
1975	2 083	2 134	2 329	1 980	2 499	2 711	2 291	.	1 913	2 018
1976	2 175	2 165	2 392	1 959	2 556	2 631	2 373	2 042	1 946	2 061
1977	2 238	2 227	2 472	2 040	2 659	2 728	2 466	2 128	2 006	2 143
1978	2 297	2 296	2 561	2 102	2 754	2 820	2 558	2 190	2 061	2 224
1979	2 383	2 358	2 648	2 163	2 924	2 926	2 670	2 263	2 133	2 286

[1] State industry.   [1] *Industrie d'Etat.*   [1] Industria de Estado.

18 Wages in manufacturing
Salaires dans les industries manufacturières
Salarios en las industrias manufactureras

B By industry
Par industrie
Por industria

Czechoslovakia [1] (2)

Average monthly earnings *(korunas)*
Gains mensuels moyens *(korunas)*
Promedio de ganancias por mes *(korunas)*

Date / Date / Fecha	369 Other non-metallic mineral products / Autres produits minéraux non métalliques / Otros productos minerales no metálicos	371 Iron and steel / Sidérurgie / Hierro y acero	372 Non-ferrous metal / Métaux non ferreux / Metales no ferrosos	381 Metal products / Produits métalliques / Productos metálicos	382 Machinery (non-electrical) / Machines (non électriques) / Maquinaria (no eléctrica)	383 Electrical machinery and apparatus / Machines et appareils électriques / Maquinaria y aparatos eléctricos	384 Transport equipment / Matériel de transport / Material de transporte	385 Scientific, measuring, optical, etc., equipment / Matériel scientifique, de précision, d'optique, etc. / Equipo científico, de medida, de óptica, etc.	390 Other manufacturing industries / Autres industries manufacturières / Otras industrias manufactureras
		Basic metal industries / Industrie métallurgique de base / Industrias metalúrgicas básicas							
1970	2 027	2 253	1 986	1 749	2 088	1 664	1 986	1 819	1 624
1971	2 102	2 345	2 053	1 817	2 168	1 711	2 071	1 879	1 682
1972	2 174	2 446	2 157	1 880	2 262	1 771	2 148	1 945	1 726
1973	2 230	2 534	2 204	1 940	2 324	1 835	2 205	2 005	1 781
1974	2 317	2 630	2 278	2 006	2 409	1 896	2 272	2 080	1 853
1975	2 402	2 709	2 385	2 084	2 491	1 980	2 411	2 171	1 922
1976	2 467	2 858	2 506	2 200	2 547	2 050	2 487	2 233	1 981
1977	2 543	2 947	2 589	2 278	2 651	2 128	2 585	2 331	2 046
1978	2 616	3 045	2 678	2 354	2 738	2 202	2 662	2 408	2 104
1979	2 676	3 130	2 757	2 426	2 818	2 260	2 736	2 478	2 158

[1] State industry.   [1] *Industrie d'Etat.*   [1] Industria de Estado.

Denmark [1] (1)

Average hourly earnings [2] *(öre)*
Gains horaires moyens [2] *(öre)*
Promedio de ganancias por hora [2] *(öre)*

Date [3] / Date [3] / Fecha [3]	311-312 Food / Aliments / Alimentos	313 Beverages / Boissons / Bebidas	314 Tobacco / Tabac / Tabaco	321 Textiles	322; 324 Clothing, footwear / Habillement, chaussures / Vestido, calzado	323 Leather, leather products / Cuir, articles en cuir / Cuero, artículos de cuero
1972	1 779	2 461	1 625	1 704	1 645	1 696
1973	2 092	3 053	1 936	2 050	1 917	1 991
1974	2 472	3 554	2 411	2 475	2 315	2 423
1975	2 965	4 310	2 901	2 877	2 771	2 893
1976	3 292	4 786	3 259	3 261	3 105	3 244
1977	3 684	5 177	3 582	3 631	3 500	3 677
1978	4 226	5 625	4 375	4 139	3 855	3 975
1979	4 607	6 164	4 835	4 590	4 305	4 484

[1] Adults only. [2] Excl. vacation pay. [3] July-Sep. of each year.   [1] *Adultes seulement.* [2] *Non compris les versements pour congés payés.* [3] *Juillet-sept. de chaque année.*   [1] Adultos solamente. [2] Excl. los pagos por vacaciones. [3] Julio-sept. de cada año.

18 Wages in manufacturing
Salaires dans les industries manufacturières
Salarios en las industrias manufactureras

B By industry
Par industrie
Por industria

Denmark[1] (2)

Average hourly earnings [2] *(öre)*
Gains horaires moyens [2] *(öre)*
Promedio de ganancias por hora [2] *(öre)*

	331	332; 381 ×	341	342	351-352	353-354
Date [3] Date [3] Fecha [3]	Wood Bois Madera	Furniture [4] Ameublement [4] Mobiliario [4]	Paper, paper products Papier, articles en papier Papel, artículos de papel	Printing, publishing Imprimerie, édition Imprentas, editoriales	Chemicals Industrie chimique Productos químicos	Refineries and products of petroleum and coal Raffineries et dérivés du pétrole et du charbon Refinerías y derivados del petróleo y del carbón
1972	1 933	1 867	2 005	2 346	1 844	2 020
1973	2 228	2 176	2 346	2 704	2 201	2 375
1974	2 578	2 560	2 874	3 273	2 668	2 746
1975	3 006	3 004	3 368	4 017	3 081	3 140
1976	3 260	3 362	3 798	4 634	3 434	3 592
1977	3 577	3 721	4 219	5 107	3 818	3 902
1978	4 117	4 116	4 747	5 890	4 244	4 305
1979	4 579	4 551	5 359	6 612	4 689	4 854

	355	36	381 ×	382-383	384	356; 385; 390
Date [3] Date [3] Fecha [3]	Rubber products Produits en caoutchouc Productos de caucho	Non-metallic mineral products Produits minéraux non métalliques Productos minerales no metálicos	Metal products Produits métalliques Productos metálicos	Machinery Machines Maquinaria	Transport equipment Matériel de transport Material de transporte	Miscellaneous manufacturing Industries manufacturières diverses Industrias manufactureras diversas
1972	1 786	1 967	1 986	1 956	2 174	1 761
1973	2 091	2 316	2 330	2 292	2 475	2 061
1974	2 489	2 655	2 805	2 792	2 988	2 471
1975	2 921	3 145	3 291	3 306	3 547	2 949
1976	3 279	3 544	3 667	3 645	3 895	3 255
1977	3 675	3 944	3 996	3 962	4 154	3 608
1978	4 029	4 325	4 427	4 453	4 154	3 608
1979	4 431	4 782	4 922	4 938	4 542	4 135

[1] Adults only. [2] Excl. vacation pay. [3] July-Sep. of each year. [4] Incl. metal furniture.

[1] *Adultes seulement.* [2] *Non compris les versements pour congés payés.* [3] *Juillet-sept. de chaque année.* [4] *Y compris les meubles en métal.*

[1] Adultos solamente. [2] Excl. los pagos por vacaciones. [3] Julio-sept. de cada año. [4] Incl. los muebles metálicos.

18 Wages in manufacturing
Salaires dans les industries manufacturières
Salarios en las industrias manufactureras

B By industry
Par industrie
Por industria

España

Average hourly earnings [1] *(pesetas)*
Gains horaires moyens [1] *(pesetas)*
Promedio de ganancias por hora [1] *(pesetas)*

Date / Date / Fecha	31 Food, beverages, tobacco / Aliments, boissons, tabac / Alimentos, bebidas, tabaco	321 Textiles	322-324 Clothing, leather, leather products, footwear / Habillement, cuir, articles en cuir, chaussures / Vestido, cuero, artículos de cuero, calzado	33 Wood, furniture / Bois, ameublement / Madera, mobiliario	341 Paper, paper products / Papier, articles en papier / Papel, artículos de papel
1970	35.26	33.77	26.70	27.00	39.75
1971	39.66	37.92	29.55	30.27	48.45
1972	44.88	43.68	33.86	34.50	57.35
1973	51.71	51.01	39.75	40.74	68.69
1974	61.86	62.99	49.67	49.58	87.27
1975	79.46	79.33	61.74	64.52	115.64
1976	114.01	110.14	88.87	86.63	151.01

Date / Date / Fecha	342 Printing, publishing / Imprimerie, édition / Imprentas, editoriales	351-352 Chemicals / Industrie chimique / Productos químicos	353-354 Refineries and products of petroleum and coal / Raffineries et dérivés du pétrole et du charbon / Refinerías y derivados del petróleo y del carbón	355 Rubber products / Produits en caoutchouc / Productos de caucho	37-38 × Metal industries, machinery, etc. [2] / Industrie métallurgique, machines, etc. [2] / Industrias metalúrgicas, maquinaria, etc. [2]
1970	43.10	43.05	35.38	57.19	45.04
1971	49.51	49.14	41.38	65.56	51.20
1972	57.59	56.11	47.36	71.41	60.82
1973	68.37	69.03	58.58	86.70	73.56
1974	83.22	87.63	87.40	114.69	93.45
1975	107.57	116.95	97.76	138.81	127.37
1976	139.23	149.96	126.15	175.05	159.35

[1] Incl. salaried employees. [2] Excl. scientific, measuring, optical, etc., equipment.

[1] *Y compris les employés.* [2] *Non compris le matériel scientifique, de précision, d'optique, etc.*

[1] Incl. los empleados. [2] Excl. el equipo científico, de medida, de óptica, etc.

WAGES

18 Wages in manufacturing
Salaires dans les industries manufacturières
Salarios en las industrias manufactureras

B By industry
Par industrie
Por industria

Finland

Average hourly earnings [1] *(markkaa)*
Gains horaires moyens [1] *(markkaa)*
Promedio de ganancias por hora [1] *(markkaa)*

	311-312	313	314	321	322	323	324	331
Date	Food	Beverages	Tobacco		Clothing	Leather, leather products	Footwear	Wood
Date	*Aliments*	*Boissons*	*Tabac*	Textiles	*Habillement*	*Cuir, articles en cuir*	*Chaussures*	*Bois*
Fecha	Alimentos	Bebidas	Tabaco		Vestido	Cuero, artículos de cuero	Calzado	Madera
1972	6.23	6.34	5.99	5.29	4.91	5.24	5.38	6.18
1973	7.21	7.55	7.02	6.22	5.74	6.02	6.08	7.25
1974	8.71	9.05	8.65	7.82	7.04	7.32	7.23	8.79
1975	10.66	11.21	10.61	9.37	8.50	8.95	8.86	10.28
1976	12.41	12.74	12.26	10.67	9.76	10.02	10.20	11.99
1977	14.31	14.33	13.84	11.40	10.51	10.93	11.32	13.27
1978	15.16	15.50	15.40	12.16	11.31	11.82	12.03	14.44
1979	17.06	17.10	16.87	13.59	12.68	12.97	13.43	16.33

	332	341	342	35 ×	355	36	37	38
Date	Furniture	Paper, paper products	Printing, publishing	Chemicals, refineries and products of petroleum and coal, plastics [2]	Rubber products	Non-metallic mineral products	Basic metal industries	Metal products, machinery, etc.
Date	*Ameublement*	*Papier, articles en papier*	*Imprimerie, édition*	*Industrie chimique, raffineries et dérivés du pétrole et du charbon, plastique* [2]	*Produits en caoutchouc*	*Produits minéraux non métalliques*	*Industrie métallurgique de base*	*Produits métalliques, machines, etc.*
Fecha	Mobiliario	Papel, artículos de papel	Imprentas, editoriales	Productos químicos, refinerías y derivados del petróleo y del carbón, plástico [2]	Productos de caucho	Productos minerales no metálicos	Industrias metalúrgicas básicas	Productos metálicos, maquinaria, etc.
1972	5.94	7.41	7.39	6.61	6.10	6.89	7.50	7.24
1973	7.06	8.75	8.61	7.81	7.24	8.14	8.75	8.42
1974	8.74	10.76	10.32	9.61	8.70	9.98	10.55	10.26
1975	10.45	12.94	12.38	11.65	10.80	11.92	12.78	12.56
1976	11.91	14.85	14.31	13.14	11.98	13.58	14.97	14.44
1977	12.94	15.90	16.26	14.22	12.81	14.81	16.52	15.54
1978	13.95	17.31	17.38	15.27	13.98	15.84	17.98	16.55
1979	15.39	19.59	19.58	17.13	15.63	17.55	20.27	18.34

[1] Incl. the value of payments in kind.   [2] Excl. rubber products.

[1] *Y compris la valeur des paiements en nature.*   [2] *Non compris les produits en caoutchouc.*

[1] Incl. el valor de los pagos en especie.   [2] Excl. los productos de caucho.

18 Wages in manufacturing
Salaires dans les industries manufacturières
Salarios en las industrias manufactureras

B By industry
Par industrie
Por industria

France (1)

Average hourly earnings *(francs)*
Gains horaires moyens *(francs)*
Promedio de ganancias por hora *(francs)*

	31	321	322	323	324	33	341	342
Date [1] *Date [1]* Fecha [1]	Food beverages, tobacco *Aliments, boissons, tabac* Alimentos, bebidas, tabaco	Textiles	Clothing *Habillement* Vestido	Leather, leather products *Cuir, articles en cuir* Cuero, artículos de cuero	Footwear *Chaussures* Calzado	Wood, furniture *Bois, ameublement* Madera, mobiliario	Paper, paper products *Papier, articles en papier* Papel, artículos de papel	Printing, publishing *Imprimerie, édition* Imprentas, editoriales
1972	7.04	6.39	5.80	5.97	5.97	6.27	7.66	9.65
1973	8.11	7.43	6.70	6.80	6.96	7.48	8.88	11.01
1974	9.91	8.94	7.88	8.23	8.74	8.92	11.46	12.87
1975	11.52	10.26	9.22	9.67	10.24	10.26	12.92	14.48
1976 [2]	13.25	11.78	10.60	11.08	11.52	12.36	14.73	16.45
1977	15.07	13.02	11.90	12.71	12.86	14.05	16.69	18.00
1978	17.02	14.74	13.57	14.20	14.44	15.60	18.67	20.80
1979	19.30	16.34	15.10	16.03	16.47	17.53	21.42	22.95

	351 ×	351-352 ×	355	356	36		371	372
					Non-metallic mineral products *Produits minéraux non métalliques* Productos minerales no metálicos		Basic metal industries *Industrie métallurgique de base* Industrias metalúrgicas básicas	
Date [1] *Date [1]* Fecha [1]	Synthetic and man-made fibres *Fibres synthétiques et artificielles* Fibras sintéticas y artificiales	Chemicals *Industrie chimique* Productos químicos	Rubber products *Produits en caoutchouc* Productos de caucho	Plastic products *Articles en matière plastique* Productos plásticos	Total	Glass *Verre* Vidrio	Iron and steel *Sidérurgie* Hierro y acero	Non-ferrous metal *Métaux non ferreux* Metales no ferrosos
1972	9.11	8.57	7.18	6.78	7.78	9.19	8.07	7.99
1973	10.19	9.86	8.68	7.89	9.09	10.54	9.20	9.55
1974	12.91	12.02	10.34	9.68	10.94	12.43	11.71	11.20
1975	14.21	13.65	12.27	11.24	12.60	14.06	14.25	12.96
1976 [2]	15.75	15.52	13.74	12.52	14.54	16.05	15.97	15.08
1977	17.69 [3]	17.42	15.27	14.37	16.43	17.91	17.79	17.34
1978	...	20.13	17.09	16.17	18.27	19.89	19.64	19.39
1979	...	22.70	19.17	18.47	20.73	22.62	21.11	21.44

[1] Oct. of each year. [2] Sampling design revised. [3] April.

[1] *Oct. de chaque année.* [2] *Plan d'échantillonnage révisé.* [3] *Avril.*

[1] Oct. de cada año. [2] Diseño de la muestra revisado. [3] Abril.

WAGES

18 B
Wages in manufacturing — By industry
Salaires dans les industries manufacturières — Par industrie
Salarios en las industrias manufactureras — Por industria

France (2)

Average hourly earnings *(francs)*
Gains horaires moyens *(francs)*
Promedio de ganancias por hora *(francs)*

Date [1] / Date [1] / Fecha [1]	381 Metal products / Produits métalliques / Productos metálicos	382 Machinery (non-electrical) / Machines (non électriques) / Maquinaria (no eléctrica)	383 Electrical machinery and apparatus / Machines et appareils électriques / Maquinaria y aparatos eléctricos	384 × Manufacture of motor vehicles / Construction de véhicules automobiles / Fabricación de vehículos automóviles	Other / Autres / Otras	385 Scientific, measuring, optical, etc., equipment / Matériel scientifique, de précision, d'optique, etc. / Equipo científico, de medida, de óptica, etc.	390 Other manufacturing industries / Autres industries manufacturières / Otras industrias manufactureras
1972	7.46	8.10	7.33	8.34	9.08	7.05	7.07
1973	8.59	9.13	8.22	9.15	10.25	8.11	8.00
1974	10.34	11.04	9.95	11.22	12.36	10.11	9.64
1975	11.95	12.75	11.68	12.43	14.22	11.49	11.52
1976 [2]	13.95	14.87	13.51	15.43	16.56	13.21	12.80
1977	15.68	16.86	15.25	17.28	19.33	15.43	14.97
1978	17.39	18.61	17.35	19.36	20.82	17.02	16.42
1979	19.57	20.84	19.52	21.08	23.46	18.96	18.41

[1] Oct. of each year. [2] Sampling design revised.

[1] *Oct. de chaque année.* [2] *Plan d'échantillonnage révisé.*

[1] Oct. de cada año. [2] Diseño de la muestra revisado.

Germany, Fed. Rep. of (1)

Average hourly earnings [1] *(mark)*
Gains horaires moyens [1] *(mark)*
Promedio de ganancias por hora [1] *(mark)*

Date / Date / Fecha	31 Food, beverages, tobacco / Aliments, boissons, tabac / Alimentos, bebidas, tabaco — Total	31 — Tobacco / Tabac / Tabaco	321 Textiles	322 Clothing / Habillement / Vestido	323 × Leather, leather products [3] / Cuir, articles en cuir [3] / Cuero, artículos de cuero [3]	324 Footwear / Chaussures / Calzado	331 Wood / Bois / Madera	332 Furniture / Ameublement / Mobiliario	341 Paper, paper products / Papier, articles en papier / Papel, artículos de papel	342 Printing, publishing / Imprimerie, édition / Imprentas, editoriales
1970	5.28	4.88	5.08	4.53	4.50	4.75	5.41	5.97	6.19	6.94
1971	5.95	5.53	5.56	5.06	4.95	5.31	6.11	6.68	6.94	7.71
1972	6.55	6.24	6.07	5.55	5.40	5.78	6.76	7.38	7.52	8.41
1973 [2]	7.29	6.73	6.83	6.19	6.02	6.40	7.50	8.17	8.31	9.34
1974	8.16	7.60	7.59	6.78	6.58	7.00	8.32	9.04	9.38	10.33
1975	8.87	8.34	8.21	7.38	7.16	7.46	8.86	9.71	9.91	11.00
1976	9.57	9.15	8.74	7.83	7.53	7.82	9.48	10.47	10.89	11.68
1977	10.23	9.82	9.30	8.40	8.08	8.37	10.18	11.21	11.56	12.61
1978	10.79	10.58	9.82	8.88	8.68	8.90	10.76	11.81	12.29	13.24
1979	11.35	11.17	10.29	9.28	9.22	9.45	11.42	12.55	12.95	13.87

[1] Incl. family allowances paid directly by the employers. [2] Sampling design revised. [3] Excl. tanneries and leather finishing, fur dressing and dyeing industries.

[1] *Y compris les allocations familiales payées directement par les employeurs.* [2] *Plan d'échantillonnage révisé.* [3] *Non compris la tannerie-mégisserie, la préparation et teinture des fourrures.*

[1] Incl. las asignaciones familiares pagadas directamente por los empleadores. [2] Diseño de la muestra revisado. [3] Excl. la curtiduría y talleres de acabado y la industria de la preparación y teñido de pieles.

18 Wages in manufacturing
Salaires dans les industries manufacturières
Salarios en las industrias manufactureras

B By industry
Par industrie
Por industria

Germany, Fed. Rep. of (2)

Average hourly earnings [1] *(mark)*
Gains horaires moyens [1] *(mark)*
Promedio de ganancias por hora [1] *(mark)*

Date / Date / Fecha	351 Industrial chemicals [3] / Chimie industrielle [3] / Química industrial [3]	351 Synthetic fibres / Fibres synthétiques / Fibras sintéticas	352 Other chemical products / Autres produits chimiques / Otros productos químicos	353 Petroleum refineries / Raffineries de pétrole / Refinerías de petróleo	355 Rubber products / Produits en caoutchouc / Productos de caucho	356 Plastic products / Articles en matière plastique / Productos plásticos	361 Pottery, china, earthenware / Grès, porcelaines, faïences / Barro, loza, porcelana	362 Glass, and glass products / Verre / Vidrio	369 Other non-metallic mineral products / Autres produits minéraux / Otros productos minerales
1970	7.06	6.65	5.76	7.34	...	5.34	...	6.01	6.36
1971	7.84	7.40	6.41	8.35	...	5.97	...	6.79	7.12
1972	8.49	8.07	6.97	9.27	...	6.54	...	7.41	7.82
1973 [2]	9.27	9.00	7.74	10.29	8.27	7.21	6.95	8.11	8.62
1974	10.55	10.18	8.71	11.73	9.20	8.01	7.79	8.98	9.52
1975	11.30	10.91	9.43	12.79	9.94	8.68	8.45	9.69	10.08·
1976	12.21	11.90	10.09	13.75	10.57	9.30	8.99	10.44	10.74
1977	13.20	12.94	10.84	14.77	11.22	9.97	9.59	11.21	11.38
1978	13.86	13.59	11.47	15.71	11.87	10.57	10.11	11.80	12.01
1979	14.49	14.18	11.97	16.62	12.49	11.13	10.65	12.40	12.79

Date / Date / Fecha	371 Basic metal industries / Industrie métallurgique de base / Industrias metalúrgicas básicas — Iron and steel / Sidérurgie / Hierro y acero	372 Non-ferrous metal / Métaux non ferreux / Metales no ferrosos	381 Metal products / Produits métallurgiques / Productos metálicos	382 Machinery (non-electrical) / Machines (non électriques) / Maquinaria (no eléctrica)	383 Electrical machinery and apparatus / Machines et appareils électriques / Maquinaria y aparatos eléctricos	384 × Motor vehicles [4] / Véhicules à moteur [4] / Vehículos de motor [4]	384 × Ship building / Construction navale / Construcciones navales	384 × Manufacture of aircraft / Construction aéronautique / Fabricación de aeronaves	385 Scientific, measuring, optical, etc. equipment / Matériel scientifique, de précision, d'optique, etc. / Equipo científico, de medida, de óptica, etc.	390 Other manufacturing industries / Autres industries manufacturières / Otras industrias manufactureras
1970	6.83	6.22	5.84	6.41	5.43	6.83	6.58	6.26	5.41	4.99
1971	7.38	6.93	6.50	7.19	6.17	7.74	7.34	7.06	6.09	5.62
1972	7.90	7.53	7.05	7.82	6.74	8.33	7.97	7.68	6.63	6.20
1973 [2]	8.83	8.38	7.79	8.68	7.44	9.21	8.88	8.64	7.32	6.85
1974	9.84	9.30	8.56	9.58	8.26	10.23	9.95	9.68	8.12	7.66
1975	10.47	10.05	9.21	10.39	9.06	11.28	10.61	10.57	8.92	8.36
1976	11.14	10.80	9.83	10.98	9.61	12.02	11.25	11.24	9.45	8.90
1977	11.92	11.64	10.59	11.83	10.38	12.96	12.14	12.19	10.21	9.56
1978	12.47	12.22	11.12	12.38	10.89	13.65	12.79	12.97	10.74	10.02
1979	13.23	12.89	11.72	13.07	11.50	14.29	13.54	13.67	11.27	10.57

[1] Incl. family allowances paid directly by the employers. [2] Sampling design revised. [3] Excl. synthetic fibres. [4] Incl. bicycles and miscellaneous transport equipment.

[1] *Y compris les allocations familiales payées directement par les employeurs.* [2] *Plan d'échantillonnage révisé.* [3] *Non compris les fibres synthétiques.* [4] *Y compris les cycles et matériel de transport divers.*

[1] Incl. las asignaciones familiares pagadas directamente por los empleadores. [2] Diseño de la muestra revisado. [3] Excl. las fibras sintéticas. [4] Incl. las bicicletas y material de transporte diverso.

WAGES

18 Wages in manufacturing
Salaires dans les industries manufacturières
Salarios en las industrias manufactureras

B By industry
Par industrie
Por industria

Grèce

Average hourly earnings *(drachmas)*
Gains horaires moyens *(drachmas)*
Promedio de ganancias por hora *(drachmas)*

	311-312	313	314	321	322; 324	323	331	332	341	342
Date [1] Date [1] Fecha [1]	Food *Aliments* Alimentos	Beverages *Boissons* Bebidas	Tobacco *Tabac* Tabaco	Textiles	Clothing, footwear *Habillement, chaussures* Vestido, calzado	Leather, leather products *Cuir, articles en cuir* Cuero, artículos de cuero	Wood *Bois* Madera	Furniture *Ameublement* Mobiliario	Paper, paper products *Papier, articles en papier* Papel, artículos de papel	Printing, publishing *Imprimerie, édition* Imprentas, editoriales
1970	16.02	15.12	14.29	15.12	14.89	17.46	14.60	16.45	16.38	20.92
1971	16.23	16.08	15.62	16.45	16.89	18.34	15.92	18.28	17.18	22.75
1972	17.02	17.14	15.72	17.83	17.73	19.34	16.75	19.62	18.69	23.61
1973	19.29	22.16	18.89	20.26	17.26	21.65	20.73	21.31	19.86	29.34
1974	26.69	29.36	24.57	28.59	23.96	29.71	27.25	27.47	29.37	37.48
1975 [2]	34.81	34.95	37.11	36.05	31.21	36.57	37.06	35.36	38.91	46.29
1976	43.01	43.05	43.42	45.21	38.53	47.34	44.96	41.57	50.41	58.58
1977	50.10	53.90	53.40	51.70	44.10	56.90	52.30	50.50	59.30	77.80
1978	62.48	67.63	70.17	65.39	54.08	69.23	65.96	65.11	71.65	96.97
1979	80.02	84.34	79.42	79.37	66.56	84.03	82.44	78.99	89.96	116.74

	351	354	355	36	37	381	382	383	384	390
Date [1] Date [1] Fecha [1]	Industrial chemicals *Chimie industrielle* Química industrial	Products of petroleum and coal *Dérivés du pétrole et du charbon* Derivados del petróleo y del carbón	Rubber products *Produits en caoutchouc* Productos de caucho	Non-metallic mineral products *Produits minéraux non métalliques* Productos minerales no metálicos	Basic metal industries *Industrie métallurgique de base* Industrias metalúrgicas básicas	Metal products *Produits métalliques* Productos metálicos	Machinery (non-electrical) *Machines (non électriques)* Maquinaria (no eléctrica)	Electrical machinery and apparatus *Machines et appareils électriques* Maquinaria y aparatos eléctricos	Transport equipment *Matériel de transport* Material de transporte	Other manufacturing industries *Autres industries manufacturières* Otras industrias manufactureras
1970	16.17	19.42	16.92	18.04	26.14	17.21	16.52	16.51	18.79	14.06
1971	16.86	21.42	17.67	19.05	29.23	18.59	18.13	17.37	20.21	15.19
1972	18.54	22.28	19.68	20.08	29.88	19.56	19.09	18.88	21.45	15.82
1973	23.58	27.38	23.83	22.35	34.64	23.16	23.83	21.18	28.92	19.51
1974	28.97	35.10	29.25	30.24	43.15	29.89	31.83	28.69	37.53	28.28
1975 [2]	39.67	46.92	35.18	42.28	59.33	39.96	37.18	38.52	49.98	33.13
1976	49.71	61.91	42.85	53.09	76.74	48.34	45.74	48.48	62.18	39.10
1977	59.40	79.40	52.40	64.20	93.70	59.60	54.50	57.20	73.00	45.30
1978	75.87	90.38	65.55	81.02	119.50	75.87	71.60	72.24	94.22	56.59
1979	89.66	114.35	79.00	99.18	143.25	92.03	85.15	87.78	109.39	71.58

[1] Nov. of each year. [2] Sampling design revised.

[1] *Nov. de chaque année.* [2] *Plan d'échantillonnage révisé.*

[1] Nov. de cada año. [2] Diseño de la muestra revisado.

18 Wages in manufacturing / Salaires dans les industries manufacturières / Salarios en las industrias manufactureras — B By industry / Par industrie / Por industria

Hongrie [1] (1)

Average monthly earnings [2] *(forints)*
Gains mensuels moyens [2] *(forints)*
Promedio de ganancias por mes [2] *(forints)*

Date / Date / Fecha	311-312 Food / Aliments / Alimentos	313 Beverages / Boissons / Bebidas	314 Tobacco / Tabac / Tabaco	321 Textiles	322 Clothing / Habillement / Vestido	323 Leather, leather products / Cuir, articles en cuir / Cuero, artículos de cuero	324 Footwear / Chaussures / Calzado	331 Wood / Bois / Madera	332 Furniture / Ameublement / Mobiliario
1970	1 858	1 753	1 688	1 762	1 610	1 954	1 774	1 876	1 893
1971	1 959	1 849	1 757	1 812	1 646	2 016	1 775	1 959	1 936
1972	2 082	1 940	1 872	1 907	1 737	2 132	1 862	2 041	2 008
1973	2 320	2 956	2 036	2 119	1 914	2 298	2 018	2 218	2 171
1974	2 499	2 293	2 183	2 267	2 021	2 398	2 144	2 389	2 315
1975	2 668	2 510	2 299	2 424	2 119	2 520	2 272	2 514	2 442
1976	2 803	2 652	2 457	2 566	2 250	2 692	2 416	2 636	2 559
1977	3 067	2 869	2 680	2 845	2 477	2 892	2 618	2 874	2 719
1978	3 300	3 102	2 934	3 125	2 706	3 180	2 851	3 107	2 917
1979	3 466	3 277	3 076	3 265	2 831	3 443	3 003	3 262	3 086

Date / Date / Fecha	341 Paper, paper products / Papier, articles en papier / Papel, artículos de papel	342 Printing, publishing / Imprimerie, édition / Imprentas, editoriales	351 Industrial chemicals / Chimie industrielle / Química industrial	352 Other chemical products / Autres produits chimiques / Otros productos químicos	353 Petroleum refineries / Raffineries de pétrole / Refinerías de petróleo	355 Rubber products / Produits en caoutchouc / Productos de caucho	356 Plastic products / Articles en matière plastique / Productos plásticos	361 Pottery, china, earthenware / Grès, porcelaines, faïences / Barro, loza, porcelana	362 Glass / Verre / Vidrio
1970	1 911	1 959	1 962	1 881	1 999	1 967	1 720	1 792	1 871
1971	2 003	2 091	2 038	1 984	2 142	2 114	1 809	1 922	1 948
1972	2 086	2 224	2 165	2 082	2 227	2 180	1 894	2 002	2 081
1973	2 329	2 450	2 421	2 308	2 517	2 363	2 084	2 255	2 308
1974	2 544	2 632	2 626	2 514	2 745	2 542	2 242	2 410	2 450
1975	2 685	2 757	2 771	2 713	2 195	2 729	2 385	2 593	2 560
1976	3 140	2 890	2 929	2 860	3 107	2 902	2 500	2 762	2 713
1977	3 348	3 091	3 202	3 126	3 452	3 180	2 816	2 993	3 036
1978	3 550	3 341	3 508	3 417	3 822	3 426	3 119	3 242	3 359
1979	3 715	3 531	3 742	3 585	4 129	3 603	3 335	3 455	3 533

[1] Socialised sector. [2] Incl. the value of payments in kind.

[1] *Secteur socialisé.* [2] *Y compris la valeur des paiements en nature.*

[1] Sector socializado. [2] Incl. el valor de los pagos en especie.

18 Wages in manufacturing
Salaires dans les industries manufacturières
Salarios en las industrias manufactureras

B By industry
Par industrie
Por industria

Hongrie [1] (2)

Average monthly earnings [2] *(forints)*
Gains mensuels moyens [2] *(forints)*
Promedio de ganancias por mes [2] *(forints)*

	369	371	372	381	382	383	384	385	390
		Basic metal industries							
	Other non-metallic mineral products	*Industrie métallurgique de base*		Metal products	Machinery (non-electrical)	Electrical machinery and apparatus	Transport equipment	Scientific, measuring, optical, etc., equipment	Other manufacturing industries
Date		Industrias metalúrgicas básicas							
Date	*Autres produits minéraux non métalliques*	Iron and steel	Non-ferrous metal	*Produits métalliques*	*Machines (non électriques)*	*Machines et appareils électriques*	*Matériel de transport*	*Matériel scientifique, de précision, d'optique, etc.*	*Autres industries manufacturières*
Fecha	Otros productos minerales no metálicos	*Sidérurgie* Hierro y acero	*Métaux non ferreux* Metales no ferrosos	Productos metálicos	Maquinaria (no eléctrica)	Maquinaria y aparatos eléctricos	Material de transporte	Equipo científico, de medida, de óptica, etc.	Otras industrias manufactureras
1970	2 111	2 195	2 144	1 894	2 068	1 878	2 096	1 973	1 736
1971	2 182	2 288	2 251	1 971	2 149	1 941	2 187	2 076	1 813
1972	2 239	2 400	2 351	2 061	2 234	2 047	2 295	2 165	1 894
1973	2 440	2 699	2 616	2 263	2 459	2 259	2 540	2 380	1 994
1974	2 599	2 935	2 953	2 394	2 623	2 440	2 736	2 526	2 130
1975	2 738	3 128	3 143	2 528	2 778	2 607	2 902	2 662	2 240
1976	2 902	3 310	3 356	2 686	2 943	2 773	3 085	2 815	2 353
1977	3 135	3 624	3 718	2 914	3 174	2 978	3 320	3 013	2 531
1978	3 442	3 942	4 055	3 135	3 459	3 202	3 598	3 223	2 726
1979	3 609	4 143	4 328	3 319	3 647	3 350	3 779	3 407	2 829

[1] Socialised sector. [2] Incl. the value of payments in kind.

[1] *Secteur socialisé.* [2] *Y compris la valeur des paiements en nature.*

[1] Sector socializado. [2] Incl. el valor de los pagos en especie.

18 Wages in manufacturing
Salaires dans les industries manufacturières
Salarios en las industrias manufactureras

B By industry
Par industrie
Por industria

Ireland

Average hourly earnings *(pence)*
Gains horaires moyens *(pence)*
Promedio de ganancias por hora *(pence)*

Date [1] Date [1] Fecha [1]	311-312 Food *Aliments* Alimentos	313 Beverages *Boissons* Bebidas	314 Tobacco *Tabac* Tabaco	321 Textiles	322; 324 Clothing, footwear *Habille- ment, chaussures* Vestido, calzado	323; 355 Leather, leather products, rubber *Cuir, articles en cuir, caoutchouc* Cuero, artículos de cuero, caucho	33 Wood, furniture *Bois, ameublement* Madera, mobiliario	34 Paper, printing, publishing *Papier, imprimerie, édition* Papel, imprentas, editoriales	35 × Chemicals, refineries and products of petroleum and coal, plastics [3] *Industrie chimique, raffineries et dérivés du pétrole et du charbon, plastique* [3] Productos químicos, refinerías y derivados del petróleo y del carbón, plástico [3]	36 Non- metallic mineral products *Produits minéraux non métalliques* Productos minerales no metálicos	381-383 Metal products, machinery, etc *Produits métalliques, machines, etc.* Productos metálicos, maquinaria, etc.
				Males [2] — *Hommes* [2] — Hombres [2]							
1970	49.4	63.4	65.6	47.2	51.7	56.3	45.5	62.6	57.2	53.5	53.9
1971	55.4	71.0	70.7	55.7	57.6	68.0	52.7	69.4	65.7	62.8	62.9
1972	62.1	79.5	84.0	63.0	62.5	75.3	60.7	80.5	74.9	74.4	71.3
1973 [4]	75.7	98.2	96.4	77.0	75.6	93.1	70.4	93.7	88.2	87.7	81.6
1974	91.2	115.3	114.4	91.5	87.1	109.0	85.2	113.1	105.7	103.8	98.2
1975	123.2	141.2	152.6	119.5	109.4	136.1	108.3	145.3	136.2	138.2	127.3
1976	135.2	159.1	166.5	136.7	124.6	154.3	123.5	169.5	150.9	169.5	147.7
1977	158.5	186.0	190.8	159.9	140.3	179.6	134.5	202.6	181.0	180.9	174.4
1978	185.5	224.3	228.2	176.7	161.6	204.5	151.9	233.1	209.3	211.0	197.3
1979	211.3	268.7	274.0	203.4	192.5	245.7	173.1	278.5	253.5	246.7	228.2
				Females [2] — *Femmes* [2] — Mujeres [2]							
1970	30.8	39.1	39.5	27.4	31.0	31.1	29.9	31.6	28.9	28.4	27.8
1971	34.7	44.5	44.9	32.7	34.8	35.3	36.3	36.2	33.0	32.8	32.4
1972	40.4	49.9	54.4	38.1	38.5	38.2	42.0	41.1	39.8	39.4	38.9
1973 [4]	51.1	57.5	61.4	48.5	47.5	47.1	48.3	50.2	46.6	50.8	48.7
1974	60.6	70.1	80.7	56.4	55.6	53.1	56.8	58.9	58.0	61.6	60.9
1975	83.3	96.7	118.1	72.7	71.3	75.9	75.9	84.1	76.4	85.3	78.6
1976	97.7	111.2	147.4	84.7	80.8	89.4	86.3	98.8	89.1	94.5	91.7
1977	111.3	128.0	166.9	99.4	92.5	102.0	102.5	118.3	103.1	110.9	106.7
1978	133.8	147.6	191.2	113.3	107.6	117.4	113.4	140.3	128.1	141.2	134.8
1979	164.1	183.4	229.7	136.0	133.0	133.2	127.8	174.9	150.8	177.6	161.8

[1] Sep. of each year. [2] Workers on adult rates of pay.
[3] Excl. rubber products. [4] New industrial clasification.

[1] *Sept. de chaque année.* [2] *Travailleurs rémunérés sur la base de taux de salaire pour adultes.* [3] *Non compris les produits en caoutchouc.* [4] *Nouvelle classification industrielle.*

[1] Sept. de cada año. [2] Trabajadores pagados sobre la base de tarifas de salarios para adultos. [3] Excl. los productos de caucho. [4] Nueva clasificación industrial.

18 Wages in manufacturing
Salaires dans les industries manufacturières
Salarios en las industrias manufactureras

B By industry
Par industrie
Por industria

Italie (1)

Average hourly earnings [1] *(lire)*
Gains horaires moyens [1] *(lire)*
Promedio de ganancias por hora [1] *(lire)*

	311-312	313	314	321	322	323	324	331	332
Date	Food	Beverages	Tobacco		Clothing	Leather, leather products	Footwear	Wood	Furniture
Date	Aliments	Boissons	Tabac	Textiles	Habillement	Cuir, articles en cuir	Chaussures	Bois	Ameublement
Fecha	Alimentos	Bebidas	Tabaco		Vestido	Cuero, artículos de cuero	Calzado	Madera	Mobiliario
1970	572	610	737	503	383	459	379	445	441
1971	651	688	831	593	517	571	495	555	554
1972	792	785	873	659	585	640	542	612	610
1973	930	973	913	762	715	789	666	769	782
1974	1 171	1 216	1 291	1 032	903	988	848	1 008	1 013
1975 [2]	1 882	2 130	1 723	1 719	1 528	1 608	1 412	1 562	1 590
1976	2 114	2 129	1 839	1 999	1 637	1 761	1 570	1 698	1 722
1977	2 673	2 697	2 309	2 345	2 111	2 286	2 088	2 202	2 238

	341	342	351	353	354	355	356	361	362
Date	Paper, paper products	Printing, publishing	Industrial chemicals	Petroleum refineries	Products of petroleum and coal	Rubber products	Plastic products	Pottery, china, earthenware	Glass
Date	Papier, articles en papier	Imprimerie, édition	Chimie industrielle	Raffineries de pétrole	Dérivés du pétrole et du charbon	Produits en caoutchouc	Articles en matière plastique	Grès, porcelaines, faïences	Verre
Fecha	Papel, artículos de papel	Imprentas, editoriales	Química industrial	Refinerías de petróleo	Derivados del petróleo y del carbón	Productos de caucho	Productos plásticos	Barro, loza, porcelana	Vidrio
1970	625	784	727	1 008	961	669	507	545	583
1971	731	943	840	1 187	1 128	851	652	697	724
1972	851	1 025	948	1 377	1 295	960	753	782	877
1973	1 033	1 269	1 180	1 553	1 487	1 083	873	963	985
1974	1 280	1 414	1 455	1 831	1 774	1 445	1 177	1 324	1 332
1975 [2]	2 294	2 482	2 315	2 456	2 929	2 500	1 957	2 056	2 216
1976	2 382	2 509	2 414	2 573	2 939	2 447	1 998	2 159	2 258
1977	2 970	3 115	3 013	3 685	3 579	2 106	2 595	2 707	2 799

[1] Incl. the value of payments in kind. [2] Series replacing former series. Prior to 1975: excl. the payments for annual vacation and public holidays.

[1] Y compris la valeur des paiements en nature. [2] Série remplaçant la précédente. Avant 1975 : non compris les paiements pour congés annuels et jours fériés.

[1] Incl. el valor de los pagos en especie. [2] Serie que substituye a la anterior. Antes de 1975: excl. los pagos por vacaciones anuales y días feriados.

18 Wages in manufacturing
Salaires dans les industries manufacturières
Salarios en las industrias manufactureras

B By industry
Par industrie
Por industria

Italie (2)

Average hourly earnings [1] *(lire)*
Gains horaires moyens [1] *(lire)*
Promedio de ganancias por hora [1] *(lire)*

	369 ×	371	372	381	382	383	384	385	390
Date *Date* Fecha	Cement *Ciment* Cemento	Basic metal industries *Industrie métallurgique de base* Industrias metalúrgicas básicas		Metal products *Produits métalliques* Productos metálicos	Machinery (non-electrical) *Machines (non électriques)* Maquinaria (no eléctrica)	Electrical machinery and apparatus *Machines et appareils électriques* Maquinaria y aparatos eléctricos	Transport equipment *Matériel de transport* Material de transporte	Scientific, measuring, optical, etc., equipment *Matériel scientifique, de précision, d'optique, etc.* Equipo científico, de medida, de óptica, etc.	Other manufacturing industries *Autres industries manufacturières* Otras industrias manufactureras
		Iron and steel *Sidérurgie* Hierro y acero	Non-ferrous metal *Métaux non ferreux* Metales no ferrosos						
1970	706	828	683	690	625	643	772	...	526
1971	814	933	765	759	694	714	854	...	656
1972	874	1 013	861	837	777	788	943	...	752
1973	1 153	1 248	1 082	1 043	973	984	1 117	...	891
1974	1 441	1 516	1 375	1 283	1 217	1 201	1 327	...	1 174
1975 [2]	2 040	2 497	2 275	2 169	2 100	2 142	2 248	2 057	1 972
1976	2 193	2 625	2 403	2 317	2 255	2 227	2 353	2 212	2 016
1977	2 707	3 192	2 952	2 704	2 287	2 759	2 873	2 716	2 603

[1] Incl. the value of payments in kind. [2] Series replacing former series. Prior to 1975: excl. the payments for annual vacation and public holidays.

[1] *Y compris la valeur des paiements en nature.* [2] *Série remplaçant la précédente. Avant 1975: non compris la rémunération pour congés annuels et jours fériés.*

[1] Incl. el valor de los pagos en especie. [2] Serie que substituye a la anterior. Antes de 1975: excl. la remuneración por vacaciones anuales y días feriados.

509

WAGES

18 Wages in manufacturing
Salaires dans les industries manufacturières
Salarios en las industrias manufactureras

B By industry
Par industrie
Por industria

Luxembourg

Average hourly earnings *(francs)*
Gains horaires moyens *(francs)*
Promedio de ganancias por hora *(francs)*

Date [1] / Date [1] / Fecha [1]	311-312 Food / Aliments / Alimentos	313 Beverages / Boissons / Bebidas	314 Tobacco / Tabac / Tabaco	322; 324 Clothing, footwear / Habillement, chaussure / Vestido, calzado	331 Wood / Bois / Madera	332 Furniture / Ameublement / Mobiliario	34 Paper, printing, publishing / Papier, imprimerie, édition / Papel, imprentas, editoriales	351 Industrial chemicals — Total	351 Synthetic and man-made fibres
1970	63.79	65.74	61.35	39.53	54.27	66.52	81.50	62.23	.
1971	72.87	75.51	65.19	46.77	60.64	81.80	94.35	70.64	
1972 [2]	78.54	84.64	72.48	54.87	72.55	89.69	99.94	69.18	122.78
1973	87.10	95.71	82.40	60.48	83.35	101.73	117.39	87.70	127.25
1974	100.62	114.84	97.16	68.64	103.43	122.18	135.02	110.44	154.90
1975	126.91	138.28	120.77	83.12	119.79	141.42	159.02	133.68	166.71
1976	139.93	158.06	138.16	92.60	127.87	160.31	184.99	150.68	206.17
1977	147.25	171.37	147.86	102.61	144.28	168.67	202.41	159.90	209.33
1978	159.13	176.49	156.02	106.78	152.84		208.08	161.98	221.41
1979	162.65	183.82	167.72	114.19	163.84		218.65	175.04	...

Date [1] / Date [1] / Fecha [1]	355 Rubber products / Produits en caoutchouc / Productos de caucho	356 Plastic products / Articles en matière plastique / Productos plásticos	36 Non-metallic mineral products / Produits minéraux non métalliques / Productos minerales no metálicos	371 Iron and steel / Sidérurgie / Hierro y acero	372 Non-ferrous metal / Métaux non ferreux / Metales no ferrosos	381 Metal products / Produits métalliques / Productos metálicos	382 Machinery (non-electrical) / Machines (non électriques) / Maquinaria (no eléctrica)	383 Electrical machinery and apparatus / Machines et appareils électriques / Maquinaria y aparatos eléctricos	384 Transport equipment / Matériel de transport / Material de transporte
1970	.	63.39	68.76	98.48	.	69.92	72.62	69.52	65.29
1971	.	82.57	81.31	104.68	.	77.33	82.05	83.60	69.55
1972 [2]	105.50	96.42	89.30	121.02	90.58	87.24	91.11	85.44	75.23
1973	119.86	109.92	100.75	136.75	97.95	98.25	100.67	98.12	88.47
1974	156.26	128.30	120.97	174.26	128.27	121.38	126.69	115.33	112.82
1975	183.01	159.78	138.91	172.23	143.81	143.31	151.32	143.94	130.80
1976	211.83	185.39	162.26	205.66	155.16	162.78	172.78	174.27	138.30
1977	227.41	200.89	169.08	224.49	179.07	175.33	182.86	179.30	150.16
1978	232.56	206.80	173.91	248.40	173.40	181.86	191.90	184.93	143.46
1979	243.27	217.78	183.38	256.51	200.04	190.97	210.15	197.90	154.99

[1] Oct. of each year. [2] New industrial classification.
[1] *Oct. de chaque année.* [2] *Nouvelle classification industrielle.*
[1] Oct. de cada año. [2] Nueva clasificación industrial.

18 Wages in manufacturing
Salaires dans les industries manufacturières
Salarios en las industrias manufactureras

B By industry
Par industrie
Por industria

Malta (1)

Average hourly earnings [1] *(cents)*
Gains horaires moyens [1] *(cents)*
Promedio de ganancias por hora [1] *(cents)*

Date / Date / Fecha	Food / Aliments / Alimentos	Beverages / Boissons / Bebidas	Tobacco / Tabac / Tabaco	Textiles	Clothing / Habillement / Vestido	Wood, cork / Bois, liège / Madera, corcho	Furniture / Ameublement / Mobiliario	Printing, publishing / Imprimerie, édition / Imprentas, editoriales
			Adult males — *Hommes adultes* — Hombres adultos					
1970	18.8	21.5	27.6	21.8	18.7	18.2	19.6	22.7
1971	20.1	21.5	28.8	22.4	20.7	19.5	21.6	25.9
1972	21.4	23.8	32.4	26.2	22.1	19.3	24.0	27.9
1973	...	...	...	...	...	...	...	...
1974	28.3	32.5	37.4	31.9	30.4	29.4	28.9	33.8
1975	32.6	36.8	46.8	38.0	40.9	36.1	33.2	39.0
1976	33.9	41.4	47.4	43.8	42.2	39.0	44.9	43.2

Date / Date / Fecha	Chemicals / Industrie chimique / Productos químicos	Products of petroleum and coal / Dérivés du pétrole et du charbon / Derivados del petróleo y del carbón	Non-metallic mineral products / Produits minéraux non métalliques / Productos minerales no metálicos	Metal products / Produits métalliques / Productos metálicos	Machinery (non-electrical) / Machines (non électriques) / Maquinaria (no eléctrica)	Electrical machinery / Machines électriques / Maquinaria eléctrica	Transport equipment / Matériel de transport / Material de transporte	Miscellaneous manufacturing / Industries manufacturières diverses / Industrias manufactureras diversas
			Adult males (concl.) — *Hommes adultes* (fin) — Hombres adultos *(fin)*					
1970	20.3	16.7	20.6	21.0	22.5	21.8	29.4	20.5
1971	22.0	16.7	21.9	23.6	24.2	25.6	30.6	23.5
1972	22.8	21.1	24.2	27.0	29.4	27.0	32.3	25.5
1973	...	...	...	...	...	...	...	...
1974	31.0	...	27.3	34.2	37.4	36.8	44.2	30.4
1975	37.2	...	33.8	37.7	39.9	43.6	46.9	32.9
1976	44.4	...	37.2	53.2	46.4	44.2	47.0	41.2

[1] Incl. salaried employees.   [1] *Y compris les employés.*   [1] Incl. los empleados.

18 Wages in manufacturing
Salaires dans les industries manufacturières
Salarios en las industrias manufactureras

B By industry
Par industrie
Por industria

Malta (2)

Average hourly earnings [1] *(cents)*
Gains horaires moyens [1] *(cents)*
Promedio de ganancias por hora [1] *(cents)*

Date / Date / Fecha	Food / Aliments / Alimentos	Beverages / Boissons / Bebidas	Tobacco / Tabac / Tabaco	Textiles	Clothing / Habillement / Vestido	Printing, publishing / Imprimerie, édition / Imprentas, editoriales	Chemicals / Industrie chimique / Productos químicos	Miscellaneous manufacturing / Industries manufacturières diverses / Industrias manufactureras diversas
Adult females — Femmes adultes — Mujeres adultas								
1970	11.1	12.9	14.4	13.0	11.7	13.2	13.0	13.2
1971	12.3	13.3	14.4	14.5	13.5	14.6	13.4	14.7
1972	13.5	14.5	16.3	16.3	15.3	15.4	15.5	15.8
1973	...	...	...	...	...	...	...	...
1974	19.4	23.0	21.5	20.1	21.2	20.0	17.4	21.4
1975	22.4	25.5	25.9	26.2	28.1	26.1	25.9	25.8
1976	30.5	39.0	34.5	34.0	33.6	33.9	32.0	33.2

[1] Incl. salaried employees.　　　　[1] *Y compris les employés.*　　　　[1] Incl. los empleados.

Netherlands (1)

Average hourly earnings [1] *(guilders)*
Gains horaires moyens [1] *(guilders)*
Promedio de ganancias por hora [1] *(guilders)*

Date [2] / Date [2] / Fecha [2]	311-312 Food / Aliments / Alimentos	313 Beverages / Boissons / Bebidas	314 Tobacco / Tabac / Tabaco	321 Textiles	322 Clothing / Habillement / Vestido	323 Leather, leather products / Cuir, articles en cuir / Cuero, artículos de cuero	324 Footwear / Chaussures / Calzado
1970	5.36	5.39	5.11	5.16	4.87	4.97	4.81
1971	6.19	6.18	6.04	5.92	5.43	5.75	5.60
1972	6.79	7.01	6.56	6.55	6.10	6.42	6.29
1973	7.85	8.22	7.64	7.58	7.39	7.26	7.19
1974	9.05	9.27	9.10	9.02	8.04	8.39	8.30
1975	10.38	10.43	10.25	10.08	9.29	9.36	9.25
1976	11.16	11.37	10.95	10.76	9.93	10.00	9.91
1977	12.31	12.59	12.18	11.93	.	.	.
1978	13.04	13.47	12.62	12.55	.	.	.

[1] Adult males.　[2] Oct. of each year.　　　　[1] *Hommes adultes.*　[2] *Oct. de chaque année.*　　　　[1] Hombres adultos.　[2] Oct. de cada año.

18 B

Wages in manufacturing
Salaires dans les industries manufacturières
Salarios en las industrias manufactureras

By industry
Par industrie
Por industria

Netherlands (2)

Average hourly earnings [1] *(guilders)*
Gains horaires moyens [1] *(guilders)*
Promedio de ganancias por hora [1] *(guilders)*

	331	332	341	342	352	351	353-354
Date [2]	Wood	Furniture	Paper, paper products	Printing, publishing	Industrial chemicals	Other chemical products	Refineries and products of petroleum and coal
Date [2]	*Bois*	*Ameublement*	*Papier, articles en papier*	*Imprimerie, édition*	*Chimie industrielle*	*Autres produits chimiques*	*Raffineries et dérivés du pétrole et du charbon*
Fecha [2]	Madera	Mobiliario	Papel, artículos de papel	Imprentas, editoriales	Química industrial	Otros productos químicos	Refinerías y derivados del petróleo y del carbón
1970	4.98	5.20	5.87	5.85	6.11	5.50	7.43
1971	5.76	6.05	6.73	6.86	6.99	6.28	8.48
1972	6.43	6.34	7.48	7.86	7.88	6.92	8.81
1973	7.38	7.42	8.49	8.86	9.17	8.07	9.93
1974	8.61	8.41	9.95	10.38	10.60	9.37	11.29
1975	9.79	9.59	11.00	11.49	12.18	10.36	12.93
1976	10.46	10.30	11.88	12.26	13.02	11.25	13.84
1977	11.75	11.38	13.07	13.32	14.35	12.46	15.50
1978	12.55	12.00	13.68	14.01	14.99	13.00	16.09

	355-356	36	37	381	382	383	384	385; 390
Date [2]	Rubber and plastic products	Non-metallic mineral products	Basic metal industries	Metal products	Machinery (non-electrical)	Electrical machinery and apparatus	Transport equipment	Other manufacturing industries [3]
Date [2]	*Produits en caoutchouc et en plastique*	*Produits minéraux non métalliques*	*Industrie métallurgique de base*	*Produits métalliques*	*Machines (non électriques)*	*Machines et appareils électriques*	*Matériel de transport*	*Autres industries manufacturières [3]*
Fecha [2]	Productos de caucho, de plástico	Productos minerales no metálicos	Industrias metalúrgicas básicas	Productos metálicos	Maquinaria (no eléctrica)	Maquinaria y aparatos eléctricos	Material de transporte	Otras industrias manufactureras [3]
1970	5.52	5.45	6.05	5.33	5.53	5.20	5.66	5.12
1971	6.50	6.29	6.80	6.07	6.32	5.91	6.47	5.76
1972	7.12	6.97	7.60	6.75	6.88	6.55	7.10	6.60
1973	8.01	7.93	8.73	7.62	7.85	7.44	8.10	7.63
1974	9.31	9.20	10.73	9.14	9.47	8.73	9.63	9.09
1975	10.51	10.28	11.91	10.33	10.63	10.08	10.94	10.30
1976	11.33	11.17	12.87	11.06	11.41	10.86	11.66	10.90
1977	12.43	12.40	14.05	12.20	12.44	11.94	12.57	11.78
1978	13.08	12.98	14.89	12.86	13.08	12.67	13.21	13.01

[1] Adult males. [2] Oct. of each year. [3] Incl. scientific measuring, optical, etc., equipment.

[1] *Hommes adultes.* [2] *Oct. de chaque année.* [3] *Y compris le matériel scientifique, de précision, d'optique, etc.*

[1] Hombres adultos. [2] Oct. de cada año. [3] Incl. el equipo científico, de medida, de óptica, etc.

18 Wages in manufacturing / Salaires dans les industries manufacturières / Salarios en las industrias manufactureras

B By industry / Par industrie / Por industria

Norway (1)

Average hourly earnings [1] *(kroner)*
Gains horaires moyens [1] *(kroner)*
Promedio de ganancias por hora [1] *(kroner)*

Date [2] / Date [2] / Fecha [2]	311-312	313	314	321	322	323	324	331	332
	Food / *Aliments* / Alimentos	Beverages / *Boissons* / Bebidas	Tobacco / *Tabac* / Tabaco	Textiles	Clothing / *Habillement* / Vestido	Leather, leather products / *Cuir, articles en cuir* / Cuero, artículos de cuero	Footwear / *Chaussures* / Calzado	Wood / *Bois* / Madera	Furniture / *Ameublement* / Mobiliario
Adult males — *Hommes adultes* — Hombres adultos									
1972	15.53	15.73	15.03	14.70	14.73	15.39	14.77	15.45	15.90
1973	17.08	18.32	16.51	16.02	16.05	16.64	16.64	16.94	17.16
1974	20.34	21.50	19.54	19.58	19.34	19.44	18.92	20.80	20.48
1975	23.49	24.54	23.11	22.36	21.81	22.09	21.38	23.21	22.91
1976	27.97	29.29	27.56	26.79	26.10	26.38	25.20	28.29	27.54
1977	30.74	32.64	30.99	29.59	28.25	28.89	28.30	30.46	30.27
1978	33.24	34.62	33.22	30.92	30.95	28.66	29.34	33.38	32.38
1979	33.59	34.79	33.84	31.67	30.43	31.12	29.94	33.78	33.13
Adult females — *Femmes adultes* — Mujeres adultas									
1972	12.46	13.40	13.23	12.20	12.34	12.00	12.00	13.56	14.12
1973	13.76	14.99	14.36	13.27	13.36	13.43	13.33	14.81	15.52
1974	16.57	18.25	17.51	16.49	15.77	15.59	15.65	17.74	18.52
1975	19.73	21.58	20.40	18.66	18.42	18.42	18.28	21.17	21.40
1976	23.85	25.05	24.42	22.93	22.16	22.18	22.35	26.15	25.79
1977	25.93	27.87	26.99	24.92	24.23	24.90	24.47	28.83	27.98
1978	28.31	29.59	29.77	26.72	26.47	25.85	26.24	31.31	30.18
1979	28.38	30.09	30.24	27.01	27.14	25.56	26.95	31.82	30.90

[1] Incl. the value of payments in kind. [2] Third quarter of each year.

[1] *Y compris la valeur des paiements en nature.* [2] *Troisième trimestre de chaque année.*

[1] Incl. el valor de los pagos en especie. [2] Tercer trimestre de cada año.

18 B

Wages in manufacturing
Salaires dans les industries manufacturières
Salarios en las industrias manufactureras

By industry
Par industrie
Por industria

Norway (2)

Average hourly earnings [1] *(kroner)*
Gains horaires moyens [1] *(kroner)*
Promedio de ganancias por hora [1] *(kroner)*

Date [2] / Date [2] / Fecha [2]	341	342	351	352	354	355	356	361	362
	Paper, paper products / *Papier, articles en papier* / Papel, artículos de papel	Printing, publishing / *Imprimerie, édition* / Imprentas, editoriales	Industrial chemicals / *Chimie industrielle* / Química industrial	Other chemical products / *Autres produits chimiques* / Otros productos químicos	Products of petroleum and coal / *Dérivés du pétrole et du charbon* / Derivados del petróleo y del carbón	Rubber products / *Produits en caoutchouc* / Productos de caucho	Plastic products / *Articles en matière plastique* / Productos plásticos	Pottery, china, earthenware / *Grès, porcelaines, faïences* / Barro, loza, porcelana	Glass / *Verre* / Vidrio
Adult males *(cont.)* — *Hommes adultes* (suite) — Hombres adultos *(cont.)*									
1972	16.61	19.76	17.13	16.58	17.10	16.05	16.29	16.04	16.25
1973	18.24	21.67	18.83	18.70	18.24	17.52	17.93	17.94	18.04
1974	22.53	24.99	24.55	21.59	22.87	20.44	21.54	21.85	21.10
1975	26.52	29.23	28.30	25.43	27.65	23.45	24.04	25.18	24.75
1976	31.03	35.89	33.32	30.10	33.09	27.91	28.31	29.20	29.55
1977	33.88	40.58	36.30	33.09	37.02	30.82	31.09	32.63	33.06
1978	36.08	44.74	37.93	35.84	37.03	32.22	33.96	34.78	35.92
1979	36.32	44.90	39.14	36.26	39.94	33.98	33.91	35.43	36.14
Adult females *(cont.)* — *Femmes adultes* (suite) — Mujeres adultas *(cont.)*									
1972	13.34	15.12	.	13.29	.	12.88	13.04	11.33	14.17
1973	14.73	16.74	.	15.12	.	14.79	14.42	12.84	15.84
1974	18.18	19.57	.	17.45	.	17.72	18.32	16.50	18.66
1975	21.31	22.93	.	20.10	.	20.55	20.56	19.22	21.45
1976	25.85	28.59	.	25.48	.	25.63	24.65	22.82	26.82
1977	28.37	31.52	.	28.22	.	28.54	26.70	27.09	29.78
1978	30.31	35.53	.	30.63	.	30.76	29.32	28.84	32.73
1979	31.04	35.25	.	30.33	.	31.37	29.79	29.83	32.57

[1] Incl. the value of payments in kind. [2] Third quarter of each year.

[1] *Y compris la valeur des paiements en nature.* [2] *Troisième trimestre de chaque année.*

[1] Incl. el valor de los pagos en especie. [2] Tercer trimestre de cada año.

18 Wages in manufacturing
Salaires dans les industries manufacturières
Salarios en las industrias manufactureras

B By industry
Par industrie
Por industria

Norway (3)

Average hourly earnings [1] *(kroner)*
Gains horaires moyens [1] *(kroner)*
Promedio de ganancias por hora [1] *(kroner)*

	369	371	372	381	382	383	384	385	390
		Basic metal industries		Metal products	Machinery (non-electrical)	Electrical machinery and apparatus	Transport equipment	Scientific, measuring, optical, etc., equipment	Other manufacturing industries
Date [2]	Other non-metallic mineral products	*Industrie métallurgique de base*							
Date [2]		Industrias metalúrgicas básicas		*Produits métalliques*	*Machines (non électriques)*	*Machines et appareils électriques*	*Matériel de transport*	*Matériel scientifique, de précision, d'optique, etc.*	*Autres industries manufacturières*
Fecha [2]	*Autres produits minéraux non métalliques*	Iron and steel	Non-ferrous metal						
	Otros productos minerales no metálicos	*Sidérurgie* Hierro y acero	*Métaux non ferreux* Metales no ferrosos	Productos metálicos	Maquinaria (no eléctrica)	Maquinaria y aparatos eléctricos	Material de transporte	Equipo científico, de medida, de óptica, etc.	Otras industrias manufactureras
Adult males (concl.) — Hommes adultes (fin) — Hombres adultos (fin)									
1972	17.38	17.93	17.38	16.78	18.08	17.81	18.04	15.44	16.63
1973	18.83	19.80	18.68	18.85	19.90	19.93	20.04	16.75	18.15
1974	23.14	23.80	23.25	22.97	23.25	22.98	23.81	21.54	21.58
1975	25.70	28.73	27.58	25.39	27.45	27.28	27.97	24.49	23.71
1976	31.56	33.81	31.68	31.12	32.65	32.16	32.93	30.03	28.53
1977	33.78	36.02	35.49	33.56	35.63	35.89	35.13	34.95	31.62
1978	36.67	38.78	37.07	36.49	39.95	38.20	38.48	35.93	33.93
1979	37.41	39.49	36.89	36.75	40.49	39.09	38.78	35.63	37.38
Adult females (concl.) — Femmes adultes (fin) — Mujeres adultas (fin)									
1972	.	.	13.92	14.00	15.73	15.05	.	.	13.43
1973	.	.	...	15.82	17.67	16.60	.	.	15.09
1974	.	.	...	18.69	19.84	19.71	.	.	18.13
1975	.	.	...	21.80	24.41	23.67	.	.	20.22
1976	.	.	...	26.74	28.84	27.32	.	.	24.78
1977	.	29.57	31.82	29.08	31.80	31.11	.	31.33	27.27
1978	.	.	.	31.85	34.19	33.68	.	.	29.40
1979	.	.	.	32.65	37.40	33.74	.	.	29.86

[1] Incl. the value of payments in kind. [2] Third quarter of each year.

[1] *Y compris la valeur des paiements en nature.* [2] *Troisième trimestre de chaque année.*

[1] Incl. el valor de los pagos en especie. [2] Tercer trimestre de cada año.

18 Wages in manufacturing
Salaires dans les industries manufacturières
Salarios en las industrias manufactureras

B By industry
Par industrie
Por industria

Pologne [1] (1)

Average monthly earnings [2] *(zlotys)*
Gains mensuels moyens [2] *(zlotys)*
Promedio de ganancias por mes [2] *(zlotys)*

	311-312	313	314	321	322	323	324	331	332
Date	Food	Beverages	Tobacco		Clothing	Leather, leather products	Footwear	Wood	Furniture
Date	*Aliments*	*Boissons*	*Tabac*	Textiles	*Habillement*	*Cuir, articles en cuir*	*Chaussures*	*Bois*	*Ameublement*
Fecha	Alimentos	Bebidas	Tabaco		Vestido	Cuero, artículos de cuero	Calzado	Madera	Mobiliario
1970	2 063	1 857	1 770	2 006	1 864	2 106	1 952	1 951	2 068
1971	2 191	1 982	1 881	2 113	1 963	2 206	2 049	2 053	2 171
1972	2 359	2 114	1 941	2 188	2 038	2 264	2 117	2 163	2 272
1973	2 566	2 356	2 154	2 429	2 185	2 414	2 302	2 346	2 474
1974	2 916	2 676	2 623	2 703	2 469	2 748	2 601	2 666	2 805
1975	3 293	3 174	2 989	3 195	2 929	2 223	3 017	3 433	3 470
1976	3 578	3 414	3 364	3 549	3 253	3 627	3 357	3 661	3 768
1977	4 025	3 736	3 665	3 893	3 571	4 056	3 700	3 959	4 056
1978	4 280	3 915	3 992	4 095	3 789	4 283	3 945	4 189	4 293
1979 *	4 681	4 199	4 470	4 500	4 116	4 653	4 334	4 541	4 532

	341	342	351	352	353	354	355	356	361
Date	Paper, paper products	Printing, publishing	Industrial chemicals	Other chemical products	Petroleum refineries	Products of petroleum and coal	Rubber products	Plastic products	Pottery, china, earthenware
Date	*Papier, articles en papier*	*Imprimerie, édition*	*Chimie industrielle*	*Autres produits chimiques*	*Raffineries de pétrole*	*Dérivés du pétrole et du charbon*	*Produits en caoutchouc*	*Articles en matière plastique*	*Grès, porcelaines, faïences*
Fecha	Papel, artículos de papel	Imprentas, editoriales	Química industrial	Otros productos químicos	Refinerías de petróleo	Derivados del petróleo y del carbón	Productos de caucho	Productos plásticos	Barro, loza, porcelana
1970	1 959	2 191	2 387	2 159	2 427	2 746	2 131	2 053	1 970
1971	2 065	2 306	2 522	3 248	2 504	2 951	2 219	2 143	2 101
1972	2 154	2 375	2 661	2 357	2 641	3 051	2 314	2 244	2 262
1973	2 285	2 593	2 951	2 652	2 954	3 244	2 579	2 386	2 558
1974	2 644	2 964	3 415	2 977	3 431	3 857	2 877	2 643	2 911
1975	3 249	3 240	3 789	3 496	3 790	4 311	3 333	3 112	3 329
1976	3 540	3 586	4 139	3 709	4 161	4 615	3 672	3 667	3 616
1977	3 810	3 983	4 518	4 016	4 544	5 222	3 978	4 003	3 967
1978	4 033	4 215	4 737	4 243	4 719	5 693	4 232	4 246	4 254
1979 *	4 531	4 728	5 282	4 660	5 391	6 476	4 811	4 629	4 575

[1] Socialised sector. Incl. salaried employees. [2] Incl. the value of payments in kind.

[1] *Secteur socialisé. Y compris les employés.* [2] *Y compris la valeur des paiements en nature.*

[1] Sector socializado. Incl. los empleados. [2] Incl. el valor de los pagos en especie.

WAGES

18 Wages in manufacturing / Salaires dans les industries manufacturières / Salarios en las industrias manufactureras

B By industry / Par industrie / Por industria

Pologne [1] (2)

Average monthly earnings [2] *(zlotys)*
Gains mensuels moyens [2] *(zlotys)*
Promedio de ganancias por mes [2] *(zlotys)*

	362	369	371	372	381	382	383	384	385	390
			Basic metal industries *Industrie métallurgique de base* Industrias metalúrgicas básicas							
Date / *Date* / Fecha	Glass, and glass products *Verre* Vidrio	Other non-metallic mineral products *Autres produits minéraux* Otros productos minerales	Iron and steel *Sidérurgie* Hierro y acero	Non-ferrous metal *Métaux non ferreux* Metales no ferrosos	Metal products *Produits métalliques* Productos metálicos	Machinery (non-electrical) *Machines (non électriques)* Maquinaria (no eléctrica)	Electrical machinery and apparatus *Machines et appareils électriques* Maquinaria y aparatos eléctricos	Transport equipment *Matériel de transport* Material de transporte	Scientific, measuring, optical, etc., equipment *Matériel scientifique, de précision, d'optique, etc.* Equipo científico, de medida, de óptica, etc.	Other manufacturing industries *Autres industries manufacturières* Otras industrias manufactureras
1970	2 062	2 189	2 939	2 814	2 226	2 463	2 243	2 489	2 371	2 040
1971	2 149	2 323	3 093	3 000	2 327	2 582	2 350	2 664	2 477	2 160
1972	2 347	2 476	3 234	3 101	2 432	2 704	2 442	2 787	2 590	2 236
1973	2 676	2 700	3 502	3 350	2 655	2 974	2 654	3 048	2 795	2 387
1974	3 002	3 159	4 101	3 967	2 966	3 341	2 979	3 428	3 117	2 671
1975	3 451	3 698	4 861	4 799	3 468	3 968	3 459	4 130	3 649	3 247
1976	3 685	3 909	5 340	5 164	3 953	4 414	3 873	4 518	4 117	3 564
1977	4 061	4 231	5 673	5 570	4 435	4 929	4 356	4 956	4 595	3 937
1978	4 413	4 513	6 089	5 877	4 649	5 141	4 596	5 184	4 806	4 169
1979 *	4 854	4 897	6 901	6 613	4 953	5 485	4 919	5 517	5 146	4 394

[1] Socialised sector. Incl. salaried employees. [2] Incl. the value of payments in kind.

[1] *Secteur socialisé. Y compris les employés.* [2] *Y compris la valeur des paiements en nature.*

[1] Sector socializado. Incl. los empleados. [2] Incl. el valor de los pagos en especie.

Portugal (1)

Average hourly earnings *(escudos)*
Gains horaires moyens *(escudos)*
Promedio de ganancias por hora *(escudos)*

	311-312	313	314	321	322	323	324	331	332	341
Date / *Date* / Fecha	Food *Aliments* Alimentos	Beverages *Boissons* Bebidas	Tobacco *Tabac* Tabaco	Textiles	Clothing [1] *Habillement* [1] Vestido [1]	Leather, leather products *Cuir, articles en cuir* Cuero, artículos de cuero	Footwear *Chaussures* Calzado	Wood *Bois* Madera	Furniture *Ameublement* Mobiliario	Paper, paper products *Papier, articles en papier* Papel, artículos de papel
1971	9.20	13.70	13.40	8.00	6.70	9.20	.	8.60	9.90	13.00
1972	9.80	15.90	24.50	9.10	7.20	10.90	.	9.60	11.30	15.70
1973	12.00	20.40	25.40	11.30	8.70	11.80	.	11.50	12.90	17.30
1974	18.40	31.90	45.90	17.30	14.30	16.70	.	16.90	18.60	27.80
1975	29.00	38.50	49.80	28.40	22.20	27.90		24.80	26.90	38.10
1976	36.20	45.70	47.40	33.60	30.10	36.60	28.90	30.50	28.70	46.20
1977	43.20	49.30	64.70	39.60	35.60	46.60	34.50	34.50	30.80	54.10
1978	51.00	60.20	110.80	45.00	39.50	54.40	39.10	41.30	38.50	66.00

[1] Prior to 1976: incl. footwear.

[1] *Avant 1976 : y compris la chaussure.*

[1] Antes de 1976: incl. el calzado.

18 B

Wages in manufacturing
Salaires dans les industries manufacturières
Salarios en las industrias manufactureras

By industry
Par industrie
Por industria

Portugal (2)

Average hourly earnings *(escudos)*
Gains horaires moyens *(escudos)*
Promedio de ganancias por hora *(escudos)*

Date / Date / Fecha	342 Printing, publishing *Imprimerie, édition* Imprentas, editoriales	351 Industrial chemicals *Chimie industrielle* Química industrial	352 Other chemical products *Autres produits chimiques* Otros productos químicos	353 Petroleum refineries *Raffineries de pétrole* Refinerías de petróleo	354 × Briquettes and packaged fuel *Briquettes et agglomérés* Briquetas y combustible aglomerado	355 Rubber products *Produits en caoutchouc* Productos de caucho	356 Plastic products *Articles en matière plastique* Productos plásticos	361 Pottery, china, earthenware *Grès, porcelaines, faïences* Barro, loza, porcelana	362 Glass *Verre* Vidrio
1971	22.30	15.30	13.10	30.60	10.50	11.60	9.90	10.30	13.40
1972	15.70	17.60	15.10	33.50	12.30	13.20	12.00	12.60	17.20
1973	17.70	20.70	17.50	37.10	13.80	17.30	13.20	12.30	18.60
1974	24.60	24.50	29.00	65.70	16.90	23.90	21.50	19.10	29.70
1975	32.80	44.90	41.40	79.50	13.30	33.80	33.10	26.80	38.50
1975	34.00	46.10	41.50	79.50	13.30	33.40	32.40	26.80	38.70
1976	40.30	57.90	46.50	88.30	17.50	50.10	42.40	36.10	45.20
1977	48.70	64.80	52.10	105.30	14.10	59.50	52.90	48.30	61.60
1978	55.60	76.00	65.10	111.00	13.90	67.10	58.50	56.00	63.70

Date / Date / Fecha	369 Other non-metallic mineral products *Autres produits minéraux non métalliques* Otros productos minerales no metálicos	371 Iron and steel *Sidérurgie* Hierro y acero	372 Non-ferrous metal *Métaux non ferreux* Metales no ferrosos	381 Metal products *Produits métalliques* Productos metálicos	382 Machinery (non-electrical) *Machines (non électriques)* Maquinaria (no eléctrica)	383 Electrical machinery and apparatus *Machines et appareils électriques* Maquinaria y aparatos eléctricos	384 Transport equipment *Matériel de transport* Material de transporte	385 Scientific, measuring, optical, etc., equipment *Matériel scientifique, de précision, d'optique, etc.* Equipo científico, de medida, de óptica, etc.	390 Other manufacturing industries *Autres industries manufacturières* Otras industrias manufactureras
1971	11.20	22.50	12.40	11.10	12.30	12.20	19.80	18.00	8.00
1972	12.30	19.80	13.90	14.40	15.50	14.00	22.10	11.80	9.90
1973	14.70	21.20	15.60	16.70	17.60	16.90	26.60	15.00	11.60
1974	21.80	23.90	26.00	26.90	29.20	36.50	36.60	22.00	16.70
1975	32.20	48.00	34.80	35.70	38.00	45.40	52.10	30.30	26.10
1976	37.40	61.40	44.20	44.50	37.90	53.00	69.20	43.90	31.60
1977	47.20	65.80	49.50	51.80	54.20	60.50	78.90	51.10	34.60
1978	56.30	81.90	58.00	59.10	62.40	65.80	88.30	57.70	43.90

Note: columns 371 and 372 are grouped under "Basic metal industries / *Industrie métallurgique de base* / Industrias metalúrgicas básicas".

WAGES

18 **Wages in manufacturing**
    Salaires dans les industries manufacturières
    Salarios en las industrias manufactureras

B   By industry
    Par industrie
    Por industria

Roumanie [1]

Average monthly earnings [2] *(lei)*
Gains mensuels moyens [2] *(lei)*
Promedio de ganancias por mes [2] *(lei)*

Date / *Date* / Fecha	Food / *Aliments* / Alimentos	Textiles	Clothing [3] / *Habillement* [3] / Vestido [3]	Leather, fur, footwear / *Cuir, fourrure, chaussures* / Cuero, piel, calzado	Wood [4] / *Bois* [4] / Madera [4]	Cellulose, paper / *Cellulose, papier* / Celulosa, papel
1970	1 287	1 202	1 170	1 267	1 362	1 409
1971	1 329	1 212	1 195	1 285	1 391	1 437
1972	1 352	1 224	1 232	1 292	1 424	1 460
1973	1 413	1 327	1 303	1 421	1 483	1 460
1974	1 444	1 453	1 366	1 536	1 582	1 558

Date / *Date* / Fecha	Printing, publishing / *Imprimerie, édition* / Imprentas, editoriales	Chemicals / *Industrie chimique* / Productos químicos	Non-ferrous mineral products [5] / *Produits minéraux non ferreux* [5] / Productos minerales no ferrosos [5]	Glass, china, earthenware / *Verre, porcelaines, faïences* / Vidrio, porcelana, loza	Building material / *Matériaux de construction* / Materiales de construcción	Primary iron and steel [5] / *Sidérurgie* [5] / Siderurgia [5]	Metal products, machinery, etc. / *Produits métalliques, machines, etc.* / Productos metálicos, maquinaria, etc.
1970	1 398	1 491	1 829	1 398	1 369	1 725	1 544
1971	1 431	1 512	1 885	1 425	1 407	1 775	1 577
1972	1 458	1 527	1 914	1 443	1 444	1 800	1 598
1973	1 473	1 571	1 967	1 557	1 525	1 800	1 598
1974	1 525	1 676	2 053	1 720	1 606	2 020	1 794

[1] Socialised sector. [2] Incl. salaried employees. [3] Excl. footwear. [4] Incl. exploitation. [5] Incl. ore mining.

[1] *Secteur socialisé.* [2] *Y compris les employés.* [3] *Non compris la chaussure.* [4] *Y compris l'exploitation.* [5] *Y compris l'extraction des minerais.*

[1] Sector socializado. [2] Incl. los empleados. [3] Excl. el calzado. [4] Incl. la explotación. [5] Incl. la extracción de minerales.

18 B Wages in manufacturing / Salaires dans les industries manufacturières / Salarios en las industrias manufactureras — By industry / Par industrie / Por industria

Suisse (1)

Average hourly earnings [1] *(francs)*
Gains horaires moyens [1] *(francs)*
Promedio de ganancias por hora [1] *(francs)*

Date [2] / Date [2] / Fecha [2]	311-312 Food / Aliments / Alimentos	313 Beverages / Boissons / Bebidas	314 Tobacco / Tabac / Tabaco	321 Textiles	322 Clothing / Habillement / Vestido	323 Leather, leather products / Cuir, articles en cuir / Cuero, artículos de cuero	324 Footwear / Chaussures / Calzado	331 Wood / Bois / Madera	332 Furniture / Ameublement / Mobiliario
Adult males — *Hommes adultes* — Hombres adultos									
1972	8.78	8.88	8.73	8.66	8.67	8.50	8.61	8.97	9.27
1973	9.93	9.65	9.50	9.78	9.74	9.61	9.61	9.44	10.40
1974	11.12	10.94	11.02	11.07	10.78	10.95	10.71	10.70	11.62
1975	12.01	11.97	12.16	11.68	11.29	11.62	10.91	11.44	12.29
1976	12.28	12.42	12.61	11.82	11.51	12.06	11.27	11.52	12.35
1977	12.76	12.70	13.66	12.39	11.62	12.55	11.68	11.98	12.77
1978	13.25	13.02	14.41	12.86	12.22	13.06	12.52	12.37	13.11
1979	13.85	13.38	14.81	13.35	12.85	13.61	12.91	12.87	13.52
Adult females — *Femmes adultes* — Mujeres adultas									
1972	5.74	5.74	5.61	5.82	5.90	5.73	6.05	6.06	6.56
1973	6.52	6.54	6.37	6.69	6.62	6.42	6.72	6.41	7.39
1974	7.29	7.36	7.13	7.56	7.36	7.11	7.45	7.00	8.30
1975	8.06	8.12	7.68	7.96	7.61	7.64	7.48	7.74	8.96
1976	8.31	8.51	8.08	8.47	7.74	7.91	7.75	7.61	8.93
1977	8.42	8.60	8.44	8.49	7.73	8.42	7.93	7.57	9.07
1978	8.91	9.09	9.03	8.74	8.06	8.75	8.53	7.78	9.36
1979	9.30	9.41	8.98	9.06	8.32	9.10	8.81	8.40	9.66

[1] Statistics of establishments. Incl. family allowances. [2] Oct. of each year.

[1] *Statistiques d'établissements. Y compris les allocations familiales.* [2] *Oct. de chaque année.*

[1] Estadísticas de establecimientos. Incl. las asignaciones familiares. [2] Oct. de cada año.

18 Wages in manufacturing
Salaires dans les industries manufacturières
Salarios en las industrias manufactureras

B By industry
Par industrie
Por industria

Suisse (2)

Average hourly earnings [1] *(francs)*
Gains horaires moyens [1] *(francs)*
Promedio de ganancias por hora [1] *(francs)*

Date [2] / Date [2] / Fecha [2]	341 — Paper, paper products / Papier, articles en papier / Papel, artículos de papel	342 — Printing, publishing / Imprimerie, édition / Imprentas, editoriales	351-352 — Chemicals / Industrie chimique / Productos químicos	355-356 — Rubber and plastic products / Produits en caoutchouc et en plastique / Productos de caucho y de plástico	36 — Non-metallic mineral products / Produits minéraux non métalliques / Productos minerales no metálicos — Total	36 — Glass / Verre / Vidrio	37; 38 × — Metal industries, machinery, etc.[3] / Industrie métallurgique, machines, etc.[3] / Industrias metalúrgicas, maquinaria, etc.[3]	385 × — Watchmaking / Horlogerie / Relojería	390 × — Jewellery / Bijouterie / Joyería
Adult males *(concl.)* — Hommes adultes (fin) — Hombres adultos *(fin)*									
1972	9.28	10.92	10.32	9.78	10.32	9.64	9.27	8.60	9.23
1973	10.49	12.21	11.69	10.98	10.24	10.84	10.44	9.67	10.38
1974	11.78	13.78	13.54	12.41	11.56	12.36	11.75	11.14	11.48
1975	12.68	14.95	14.52	12.87	12.45	13.27	12.60	12.10	12.28
1976	12.85	15.40	15.16	13.07	12.72	13.60	12.79	12.13	12.80
1977	13.32	15.96	15.50	13.38	13.27	...	13.29	12.31	13.01
1978	13.95	17.01	15.91	13.18	13.65	...	13.66	13.34	13.56
1979	14.55	18.20	16.35	13.67	14.04	...	14.07	13.72	14.13
Adult females *(concl.)* — Femmes adultes (fin) — Mujeres adultas *(fin)*									
1972	5.97	6.18	6.07	6.02	6.96	6.04	6.16	5.94	6.23
1973	6.71	7.24	7.98	6.80	7.08	6.88	7.00	6.64	6.88
1974	7.66	8.34	9.16	7.66	8.00	7.84	7.93	7.87	7.93
1975	8.17	9.37	10.04	8.08	8.64	8.18	8.71	8.48	8.34
1976	8.30	9.44	10.57	8.22	8.91	8.41	8.90	8.45	8.65
1977	8.79	9.97	10.81	8.35	9.13	...	9.07	8.69	8.57
1978	9.23	10.52	11.21	8.66	9.39	...	9.37	9.28	8.98
1979	9.42	11.29	11.59	9.00	9.64	...	9.66	9.46	9.44

[1] Statistics of establishments. Incl. family allowances. [2] Oct. of each year. [3] Excl. scientific, measuring, optical, etc., equipment.

[1] *Statistiques d'établissements. Y compris les allocations familiales.* [2] *Oct. de chaque année.* [3] *Non compris le matériel scientifique, de précision, d'optique, etc.*

[1] Estadísticas de establecimientos. Incl. las asignaciones familiares. [2] Oct. de cada año. [3] Excl. el equipo científico, de medida, de óptica, etc.

SALAIRES
SALARIOS

18 Wages in manufacturing
Salaires dans les industries manufacturières
Salarios en las industrias manufactureras

B By industry
Par industrie
Por industria

Sweden (1)

Average hourly earnings [1] *(kronor)*
Gains horaires moyens [1] *(kronor)*
Promedio de ganancias por hora [1] *(kronor)*

Date [2] / Date [2] / Fecha [2]	311-312 Food / Aliments / Alimentos	313 Beverages / Boissons / Bebidas	314 Tobacco / Tabac / Tabaco	321 Textiles	322 Clothing / Habillement / Vestido	323 Leather, leather products / Cuir, articles en cuir / Cuero, artículos de cuero	324 Footwear / Chaussures / Calzado	331 Wood / Bois / Madera	332 Furniture / Ameublement / Mobiliario
Adult males — *Hommes adultes* — Hombres adultos									
1971	15.18	14.88	16.37	13.98	13.27	14.54	14.20	14.30	14.32
1972	17.24	17.58	18.98	15.89	14.98	16.36	16.05	16.18	15.78
1973	18.53	18.88	20.25	17.24	16.41	17.58	17.21	17.61	17.32
1974 [3]	20.53	20.72	21.95	19.44	18.03	19.26	19.13	20.01	19.35
1975	24.22	24.57	25.40	22.58	20.77	23.00	22.14	23.15	22.41
1976	27.90	27.69	27.86	25.64	23.70	26.29	25.06	25.91	25.01
1977	29.82	29.05	30.46	27.16	25.93	28.70	27.51	27.96	27.30
1978	33.04	32.77	34.35	30.01	27.83	30.88	29.74	31.11	29.85
1979	36.62	36.85	37.89	33.64	31.25	34.02	32.49	34.01	33.22
Adult females — *Femmes adultes* — Mujeres adultas									
1971	12.66	13.45	13.49	11.94	11.57	12.19	11.81	12.90	12.85
1972	14.61	15.95	16.30	13.70	13.16	13.89	13.70	14.58	14.29
1973	15.70	17.16	17.49	14.88	14.49	14.95	14.79	15.99	15.70
1974 [3]	17.37	18.82	19.20	16.62	16.02	16.50	16.55	18.07	17.49
1975	20.54	22.41	22.83	19.57	19.00	19.19	19.62	20.94	20.60
1976	23.92	25.80	25.76	22.63	22.08	22.57	22.48	23.92	23.47
1977	25.82	26.54	27.97	24.48	24.35	24.50	24.97	26.02	25.40
1978	28.75	30.53	31.94	27.21	26.84	27.28	27.55	29.20	28.27
1979	32.07	34.30	35.18	30.46	29.89	30.52	30.52	32.39	31.61

[1] Incl. holiday and sick-leave payments and the value of payments in kind. [2] Beginning 1976: second quarter of each year. [3] Sampling design revised.

[1] *Y compris les versements au titre des vacances et congés de maladie et la valeur des paiements en nature.* [2] *A partir de 1976 : deuxième trimestre de chaque année.* [3] *Plan d'échantillonnage révisé.*

[1] Incl. los pagos por vacaciones y licencias de enfermedad y el valor de los pagos en especie. [2] A partir de 1976: segundo trimestre de cada año. [3] Diseño de la muestra revisado.

523

18 Wages in manufacturing
Salaires dans les industries manufacturières
Salarios en las industrias manufactureras

B By industry
Par industrie
Por industria

Sweden (2)

Average hourly earnings [1] *(kronor)*
Gains horaires moyens [1] *(kronor)*
Promedio de ganancias por hora [1] *(kronor)*

	341	342	351	352	353-354	355	356	361	362
Date [2]	Paper, paper products	Printing, publishing	Industrial chemicals	Other chemical products	Refineries and products of petroleum and coal	Rubber products	Plastic products	Pottery, china, earthenware	Glass
Date [2]	*Papier, articles en papier*	*Imprimerie, édition*	*Chimie industrielle*	*Autres produits chimiques*	*Raffineries et dérivés du pétrole et du charbon*	*Produits en caoutchouc*	*Articles en matière plastique*	*Grès, porcelaines, faïences*	*Verre*
Fecha [2]	Papel, artículos de papel	Imprentas, editoriales	Química industrial	Otros productos químicos	Refinerías y derivados del petróleo y del carbón	Productos de caucho	Productos plásticos	Barro, loza, porcelana	Vidrio
Adult males *(cont.)* — *Hommes adultes* (suite) — Hombres adultos *(cont.)*									
1971	15.55	18.35	14.96	14.98	15.74	15.02	14.57	14.63	15.37
1972	17.83	20.67	16.92	16.65	18.08	16.69	16.35	16.54	17.43
1973	19.30	22.29	18.28	18.00	19.54	17.83	17.49	17.80	19.01
1974 [3]	22.55	24.71	21.10	20.04	22.04	19.87	19.50	19.27	21.04
1975	27.03	28.43	25.09	23.45	26.13	22.93	22.92	22 95	24.75
1976	30.83	32.49	29.59	26.62	30.65	25.65	26.37	26.01	28.45
1977	32.77	35.88	31.17	28.56	33.24	28.27	28.75	28.08	30.86
1978	35.85	38.96	34.54	31.72	36.70	30.44	31.24	29.90	34.00
1979	41.01	43.24	38.23	35.63	40.06	33.96	34.83	33.34	37.03
Adult females *(cont.)* — *Femmes adultes* (suite) — Mujeres adultas *(cont.)*									
1971	12.70	13.67	12.67	12.74	.	12.82	12.44	12.40	12.65
1972	14.75	15.66	14.63	14.39	.	14.64	14.03	14.31	14.54
1973	15.93	17.21	15.93	15.66	.	15.90	15.25	15.63	15.94
1974 [3]	18.55	19.43	18.21	17.61	.	17.91	17.07	17.17	17.84
1975	22.51	22.78	22.33	20.89	.	20.98	20.26	20.76	21.24
1976	25.75	26.75	26.46	23.93	.	23.72	23.68	23.38	25.14
1977	27.58	29.50	27.96	25.53	.	25.97	25.91	25.20	26.84
1978	30.85	32.62	30.78	28.71	.	28.39	28.38	27.53	29.84
1979	34.20	36.53	33.89	32.09	.	31.86	31.99	30.44	32.96

[1] Incl. holiday and sick-leave payments and the value of payments in kind. [2] Beginning 1976: second quarter of each year. [3] Sampling design revised.

[1] *Y compris les versements au titre des vacances et congés de maladie et la valeur des paiements en nature.* [2] *A partir de 1976 : deuxième trimestre de chaque année.* [3] *Plan d'échantillonnage révisé.*

[1] Incl. los pagos por vacaciones y licencias de enfermedad y el valor de los pagos en especie. [2] A partir de 1976: segundo trimestre de cada año. [3] Diseño de la muestra revisado.

18 B

Wages in manufacturing
Salaires dans les industries manufacturières
Salarios en las industrias manufactureras

By industry
Par industrie
Por industria

Sweden (3)

Average hourly earnings [1] *(kronor)*
Gains horaires moyens [1] *(kronor)*
Promedio de ganancias por hora [1] *(kronor)*

Date [2] Date [2] Fecha [2]	369 Other non-metallic mineral products *Autres produits minéraux non métalliques* Otros productos minerales no metálicos	371	372	381 Metal products *Produits métalliques* Productos metálicos	382 Machinery (non-electrical) *Machines (non électriques)* Maquinaria (no eléctrica)	383 Electrical machinery and apparatus *Machines et appareils électriques* Maquinaria y aparatos eléctricos	384 Transport equipment *Matériel de transport* Material de transporte	385 Scientific, measuring, optical, etc., equipment *Matériel scientifique, de précision, d'optique, etc.* Equipo científico, de medida, de óptica, etc.	390 Other manufacturing industries *Autres industries manufacturières* Otras industrias manufactureras
		Basic metal industries *Industrie métallurgique de base* Industrias metalúrgicas básicas							
		Iron and steel *Sidérurgie* Hierro y acero	Non-ferrous metal *Métaux non ferreux* Metales no ferrosos						
Adult males *(concl.)* — *Hommes adultes* (fin) — Hombres adultos *(fin)*									
1971	15.16	16.44	15.64	15.78	15.88	15.57	16.43	15.60	14.72
1972	17.19	18.52	17.46	17.23	17.43	17.15	18.46	17.07	16.11
1973	18.40	20.28	18.96	18.77	18.84	18.64	20.22	18.49	17.38
1974 [3]	20.70	22.94	21.33	20.77	20.81	20.56	22.49	20.21	19.57
1975	24.11	27.15	25.22	24.27	24.32	24.11	25.93	23.74	22.48
1976	27.33	30.73	28.28	27.21	27.30	27.22	28.86	26.30	25.00
1977	29.60	32.33	30.85	29.70	29.59	29.52	31.19	29.13	26.96
1978	32.52	35.22	33.45	32.04	32.21	31.91	33.71	30.85	29.88
1979	36.19	40.11	37.29	35.53	35.50	35.22	37.20	35.17	32.64
Adult females *(concl.)* — *Femmes adultes* (fin) — Mujeres adultas *(fin)*									
1971	12.76	14.71	13.87	13.23	14.08	13.27	14.98	13.50	12.49
1972	14.77	17.08	15.43	14.71	15.78	14.89	16.84	15.11	13.79
1973	16.02	18.67	16.90	16.07	16.91	16.19	18.65	16.10	15.22
1974 [3]	18.26	21.09	18.91	17.81	18.68	17.86	20.74	17.76	17.02
1975	21.45	25.61	22.76	21.06	21.93	21.24	24.01	21.02	20.15
1976	24.82	29.00	25.67	24.15	24.74	24.55	27.12	24.30	23.25
1977	27.78	30.97	27.88	26.61	27.13	26.61	29.07	26.91	24.79
1978	31.12	34.12	30.75	29.17	30.14	29.13	31.97	28.87	28.01
1979	33.83	38.72	33.94	32.57	33.06	32.72	35.70	32.62	30.81

[1] Incl. holiday and sick-leave payments and the value of payments in kind. [2] Beginning 1976: second quarter of each year. [3] Sampling design revised.

[1] *Y compris les versements au titre des vacances et congés de maladie et la valeur des paiements en nature.* [2] *A partir de 1976 : deuxième trimestre de chaque année.* [3] *Plan d'échantillonnage révisé.*

[1] Incl. los pagos por vacaciones y licencias de enfermedad y el valor de los pagos en especie. [2] A partir de 1976: segundo trimestre de cada año. [3] Diseño de la muestra revisado.

18 Wages in manufacturing
Salaires dans les industries manufacturières
Salarios en las industrias manufactureras

B By industry
Par industrie
Por industria

Turquie

Average daily earnings [1] *(liras)*
Gains journaliers moyens [1] *(liras)*
Promedio de ganancias por día [1] *(liras)*

	311-312	313	314	321	322	323	331	332	341	342
Date [2]	Food	Beverages	Tobacco		Clothing	Leather, leather products	Wood	Furniture	Paper, paper products	Printing, publishing
Date [2]	*Aliments*	*Boissons*	*Tabac*	Textiles	*Habillement*	*Cuir, articles en cuir*	*Bois*	*Ameublement*	*Papier, articles en papier*	*Imprimerie, édition*
Fecha [2]	Alimentos	Bebidas	Tabaco		Vestido	Cuero, artículos de cuero	Madera	Mobiliario	Papel, artículos de papel	Imprentas, editoriales
1970	30.36	50.45	54.68	28.26	28.39	33.02	24.54	25.64	39.75	44.79
1971	33.88	45.76	37.33	34.81	29.27	33.49	29.17	27.29	40.07	43.76
1972	37.26	47.28	35.82	40.76	30.84	34.04	30.14	29.08	53.51	50.28
1973	45.86	58.96	64.34	66.02	38.40	41.88	35.16	35.35	76.92	55.91
1974	70.46	77.51	77.63	57.27	52.92	54.40	49.15	50.80	77.40	76.91
1975	82.62	92.51	95.36	65.81	61.78	67.68	63.27	64.50	123.88	87.09
1976	116.87	137.73	125.15	121.87	86.26	111.26	86.55	86.31	168.05	113.90
1977	159.72	182.95	185.14	130.00	111.14	147.13	115.19	112.12	226.63	137.60

	351	354	355	36	37	381	382	383	384	390
Date [2]	Industrial chemicals	Products of petroleum and coal	Rubber products	Non-metallic mineral products	Basic metal industries	Metal products	Machinery (non-electrical)	Electrical machinery and apparatus	Transport equipment	Miscellaneous manu-facturing
Date [2]	*Chimie industrielle*	*Dérivés du pétrole et du charbon*	*Produits en caoutchouc*	*Produits minéraux non métalliques*	*Industrie métallur-gique de base*	*Produits métalliques*	*Machines (non électriques)*	*Machines et appareils électriques*	*Matériel de transport*	*Industries manu-facturières diverses*
Fecha [2]	Química industrial	Derivados del petróleo y del carbón	Productos de caucho	Productos minerales no metálicos	Industrias metalúrgicas básicas	Productos metálicos	Maquinaria (no eléctrica)	Maquinaria y aparatos eléctricos	Material de transporte	Industrias manu-factureras diversas
1970	42.75	54.50	32.97	31.14	50.61	34.20	37.89	41.17	39.07	30.92
1971	47.68	67.97	41.30	38.19	56.70	40.15	45.33	48.43	61.52	31.49
1972	59.40	76.80	48.56	40.88	67.94	44.91	48.87	54.85	65.05	36.68
1973	63.59	96.58	56.88	54.44	68.14	52.06	55.48	60.22	70.65	40.84
1974	83.89	95.11	79.90	67.00	98.41	66.39	68.48	73.72	92.00	55.25
1975	103.83	150.92	129.67	86.23	136.50	87.38	103.35	95.23	125.80	71.87
1976	132.47	158.76	134.88	121.99	161.86	109.76	118.83	123.20	148.63	100.22
1977	183.49	228.48	171.57	160.87	203.49	...	117.36	168.35	179.41	127.12

[1] Incl. salaried employees. [2] Sep. of each year.   [1] *Y compris les employés.* [2] *Sept. de chaque année.*   [1] Incl. los empleados. [2] Sept. de cada año.

18   Wages in manufacturing
Salaires dans les industries manufacturières
Salarios en las industrias manufactureras

B   By industry
Par industrie
Por industria

United Kingdom (1)

Average hourly earnings [1] *(pence)*
Gains horaires moyens [1] *(pence)*
Promedio de ganancias por hora [1] *(pence)*

Date [2] Date [2] Fecha [2]	31 Food, beverages, tobacco / Aliments, boissons, tabac / Alimentos, bebidas, tabaco	321 Textiles	322 Clothing / Habillement / Vestido	323 Leather, leather products / Cuir, articles en cuir / Cuero, artículos de cuero	324 Footwear / Chaussures / Calzado	33 Wood, furniture / Bois, ameublement / Madera, mobiliario	34 Paper, printing, publishing / Papier, imprimerie, édition / Papel, imprentas, editoriales	351-352 Chemicals / Industrie chimique / Productos químicos
Adult males — Hommes adultes — Hombres adultos								
1970	59.8	56.6	55.5	53.5	62.9	57.2	74.4	65.1
1971	68.1	63.5	59.4	59.0	68.9	65.4	81.2	74.4
1972	77.1	71.7	67.9	67.5	76.9	75.7	92.2	83.2
1973	85.4	81.9	76.2	76.9	87.8	87.3	108.0	92.6
1974	102.9	97.4	92.0	93.1	108.9	104.1	125.2	117.0
1975	130.5	121.9	109.1	115.5	134.3	129.5	153.7	149.2
1976	145.6	136.4	122.4	128.0	142.8	143.6	169.4	163.5
1977	156.2	147.0	136.3	141.0	169.0	157.3	184.5	175.8
1978	181.6	168.2	152.8	162.3	179.7	181.0	217.0	204.8
1979	215.5	195.5	183.8	184.4	214.4	210.8	262.3	243.1
Adult females — Femmes adultes — Mujeres adultas								
1970	37.3	35.9	34.2	32.0	42.3	38.6	39.9	36.9
1971	43.6	40.5	38.2	36.6	46.6	45.3	44.2	42.7
1972	50.8	46.0	43.9	40.6	53.2	51.7	51.1	47.9
1973	58.8	53.3	50.7	48.3	61.5	61.2	59.0	55.8
1974	75.7	68.4	64.8	61.8	78.6	76.6	77.8	75.2
1975	98.9	87.5	77.8	77.1	99.8	99.4	101.6	99.6
1976	115.3	102.9	91.5	89.4	106.1	113.0	117.7	115.6
1977	124.7	111.9	102.3	101.6	126.0	124.2	126.9	128.2
1978	142.1	124.9	114.4	114.6	130.5	143.0	145.2	144.2
1979	165.0	143.5	137.5	135.1	156.8	168.5	175.3	167.9

[1] Full-time wage earners.   [2] Oct. of each year.

[1] *Ouvriers et ouvrières à temps complet.*   [2] *Oct. de chaque année.*

[1] Obreros y obreras de tiempo completo.   [2] Oct. de cada año.

18 Wages in manufacturing
Salaires dans les industries manufacturières
Salarios en las industrias manufactureras

B By industry
Par industrie
Por industria

United Kingdom (2)

Average hourly earnings [1] *(pence)*
Gains horaires moyens [1] *(pence)*
Promedio de ganancias por hora [1] *(pence)*

	353-354	355	356	361	362	369	371
Date [2]	Refineries and products of petroleum and coal	Rubber products	Plastic products	Pottery, china, earthenware	Glass	Other non-metallic mineral products	Iron and steel basic industries
Date [2] Fecha [2]	*Raffineries et dérivés du pétrole et du charbon*	*Produits en caoutchouc*	*Articles en matière plastique*	*Grès, porcelaines, faïences*	*Verre*	*Autres produits minéraux non métalliques*	*Sidérurgie*
	Refinerías y derivados del petróleo y del carbón	Productos de caucho	Productos plásticos	Barro, loza, porcelana	Vidrio	Otros productos minerales no metálicos	Industrias básicas de hierro y acero
Adult males *(cont.)* — *Hommes adultes* (suite) — Hombres adultos *(cont.)*							
1970	70.1	68.2	61.1	59.7	65.0	60.3	66.8
1971	78.3	76.4	68.1	67.5	74.6	63.4	73.5
1972	90.6	86.5	77.2	76.4	87.2	88.8	85.6
1973	100.3	95.4	88.2	84.8	97.9	89.0	97.8
1974	130.2	117.0	108.1	100.8	120.1	107.3	116.1
1975	163.7	148.8	133.5	127.5	147.5	135.5	151.4
1976	178.9	165.8	148.4	142.8	160.8	150.7	171.0
1977	191.5	172.8	161.1	154.0	169.7	164.7	183.7
1978	222.4	205.7	189.1	180.3	209.8	189.2	212.8
1979	262.6	232.7	225.9	208.7	243.3	225.9	243.0
Adult females *(cont.)* — *Femmes adultes* (suite) — Mujeres adultas *(cont.)*							
1970	39.0	37.7	35.3	36.9	39.6	37.1	35.8
1971	45.3	44.3	40.2	41.7	47.1	41.6	39.6
1972	53.0	51.5	46.1	47.1	57.2	47.6	48.1
1973	66.7	57.4	53.9	54.7	66.2	57.0	54.4
1974	81.0	74.9	71.4	71.2	87.7	73.0	71.5
1975	111.2	99.2	90.4	94.8	106.3	97.7	96.6
1976	132.8	119.4	106.1	112.3	122.4	113.7	115.9
1977	148.5	129.8	116.0	120.7	132.0	121.9	125.7
1978	153.9	148.2	134.9	135.6	159.0	137.9	142.5
1979	176.7	163.1	154.0	156.5	183.1	158.1	166.7

[1] Full-time wage earners.   [2] Oct. of each year.   [1] *Ouvriers et ouvrières à temps complet.*   [2] *Oct. de chaque année.*   [1] Obreros y obreras de tiempo completo.   [2] Oct. de cada año.

18 Wages in manufacturing
Salaires dans les industries manufacturières
Salarios en las industrias manufactureras

B By industry
Par industrie
Por industria

United Kingdom (3)

Average hourly earnings [1] *(pence)*
Gains horaires moyens [1] *(pence)*
Promedio de ganancias por hora [1] *(pence)*

	372	381	382	383	384	385	390
Date [2] *Date* [2] Fecha [2]	Non-ferrous metal basic industries *Métaux non ferreux (industrie de base)* Industrias básicas de metales no ferrosos	Metal products *Produits métalliques* Productos metálicos	Machinery (non-electrical) *Machines (non électriques)* Maquinaria (no eléctrica)	Electrical machinery and apparatus *Machines et appareils électriques* Maquinaria y aparatos eléctricos	Transport equipment *Matériel de transport* Material de transporte	Scientific, measuring, optical, etc., equipment *Matériel scientifique, de précision, d'optique, etc.* Equipo científico, de medida, de óptica, etc.	Other manufacturing industries *Autres industries manufacturières* Otras industrias manufactureras
	Adult males *(concl.)* — *Hommes adultes* (fin) — Hombres adultos *(fin)*							
1970	65.7	61.5	63.3	62.4	73.8	60.6	55.4
1971	72.2	67.2	69.4	69.4	83.2	66.5	61.9
1972	83.7	77.5	79.8	79.5	94.3	74.1	69.8
1973	95.5	88.3	90.8	89.0	103.8	84.3	80.2
1974	113.4	107.5	109.7	106.4	122.9	101.4	99.0
1975	141.1	133.3	138.2	134.6	151.6	127.0	118.4
1976	155.2	150.2	154.1	150.1	169.1	144.4	135.8
1977	171.6	163.9	169.5	162.3	178.3	158.0	149.7
1978	202.6	189.5	193.9	187.3	204.6	179.8	174.5
1979	231.0	220.0	226.8	218.3	232.3	213.6	201.3
	Adult females *(concl.)* — *Femmes adultes* (fin) — Mujeres adultas *(fin)*							
1970	37.2	35.8	40.2	38.6	44.7	38.1	33.9
1971	42.1	40.2	45.3	43.9	51.9	41.4	38.2
1972	50.2	47.6	53.2	51.1	61.5	47.1	42.9
1973	57.9	56.1	61.7	59.8	68.9	56.4	50.3
1974	74.9	72.2	79.0	75.8	87.7	70.9	66.3
1975	96.4	93.5	103.8	98.1	112.6	94.9	82.0
1976	114.9	112.6	123.1	115.8	133.1	112.6	98.5
1977	127.9	122.4	135.3	124.4	140.5	120.7	109.1
1978	145.4	139.9	149.8	142.4	161.0	135.9	124.0
1979	165.9	161.6	170.3	166.4	182.5	160.5	140.4

[1] Full-time wage earners. [2] Oct. of each year.

[1] *Ouvriers et ouvrières à temps complet.* [2] *Oct. de chaque année.*

[1] Obreros y obreras de tiempo completo. [2] Oct. de cada año.

18

Wages in manufacturing
Salaires dans les industries manufacturières
Salarios en las industrias manufactureras

B

By industry
Par industrie
Por industria

Yugoslavia [1] (1)

Average monthly earnings [2] *(dinars)*
Gains mensuels moyens [2] *(dinars)*
Promedio de ganancias por mes [2] *(dinars)*

	311-312	313	314	321	322	323	324	331	332
Date *Date* Fecha	Food *Aliments* Alimentos	Beverages *Boissons* Bebidas	Tobacco *Tabac* Tabaco	Textiles	Clothing *Habillement* Vestido	Leather, leather products *Cuir, articles en cuir* Cuero, artículos de cuero	Footwear *Chaussures* Calzado	Wood *Bois* Madera	Furniture *Ameublement* Mobiliario
1970	1 073	1 246	938	901	832	1 031	913	947	1 031
1971	1 318	1 537	1 225	1 145	1 043	1 257	1 185	1 187	1 253
1972	1 558	1 753	1 537	1 442	1 340	1 535	1 422	1 410	1 468
1973	1 857	1 933	1 822	1 676	1 520	1 835	1 679	1 661	1 705
1974	2 364	2 461	2 229	2 122	1 924	2 207	2 018	2 158	2 208
1975	2 864	2 982	2 866	2 509	2 275	2 681	2 452	2 496	2 554
1976	3 298	3 434	3 312	2 778	2 520	3 020	2 762	2 856	2 922
1977	3 903	4 011	3 781	3 136	3 001	3 397	3 214	3 264	3 591
1978	4 706	4 762	4 485	3 725	3 615	4 500	3 830	4 055	4 272
1979	5 495	5 772	5 333	4 528	4 378	5 662	4 638	5 002	5 269

	341	342	351; 356	352	353	354	355	361	362
Date *Date* Fecha	Paper, paper products *Papier, articles en papier* Papel, artículos de papel	Printing, publishing *Imprimerie, édition* Imprentas, editoriales	Industrial chemicals [3] *Chimie industrielle [3]* Química industrial [3]	Other chemical products *Autres produits chimiques* Otros productos químicos	Petroleum refineries *Raffineries de pétrole* Refinerías de petróleo	Products of petroleum and coal *Dérivés du pétrole et du charbon* Derivados del petróleo y del carbón	ubber products *Produits en caoutchouc* Productos de caucho	Pottery, china, earthenware *Grès, porcelaines, faïences* Barro, loza, porcelana	Glass *Verre* Vidrio
1970	1 171	1 288	1 206	1 258	1 793	1 672	1 050	1 008	1 111
1971	1 363	1 503	1 494	1 465	2 213	2 019	1 268	1 220	1 497
1972	1 587	1 695	1 720	1 734	2 423	2 168	1 522	1 468	1 542
1973	1 878	1 915	2 052	2 032	2 954	2 410	1 775	1 718	1 787
1974	2 637	2 468	2 764	2 736	3 796	3 282	2 273	2 097	2 270
1975	3 126	3 017	3 352	3 319	4 779	4 060	2 886	2 534	2 756
1976	3 447	3 517	3 779	3 742	5 269	4 572	3 245	3 023	2 553
1977	3 966	4 445	4 355	4 364	5 804	4 619	3 888	3 721	3 527
1978	4 761	5 381	5 278	5 058	6 843	5 797	4 451	4 272	4 126
1979	5 765	6 488	6 376	6 025	8 147	6 916	5 627	5 173	4 827

[1] Socialised sector. [2] Incl. salaried employees. [3] Incl. plastic products.

[1] *Secteur socialisé.* [2] *Y compris les employés.* [3] *Y compris les articles en matière plastique.*

[1] Sector socializado. [2] Incl. los empleados. [3] Incl. productos plásticos.

18 B

Wages in manufacturing
Salaires dans les industries manufacturières
Salarios en las industrias manufactureras

By industry
Par industrie
Por industria

Yugoslavia [1] (2)

Average monthly earnings [2] *(dinars)*
Gains mensuels moyens [2] *(dinars)*
Promedio de ganancias por mes [2] *(dinars)*

Date / Date / Fecha	369 Other non-metallic mineral products [3] / Autres produits minéraux non métalliques [3] / Otros productos minerales no metálicos [3]	371-372 Basic metal industries [3] / Industrie métallurgique de base [3] / Industrias metalúrgicas básicas [3]		381 Metal products / Produits métalliques / Productos metálicos	382 Machinery (non-electrical) / Machines (non électriques) / Maquinaria (no eléctrica)	383 Electrical machinery and apparatus / Machines et appareils électriques / Maquinaria y aparatos eléctricos	384 Transport equipment / Matériel de transport / Material de transporte	385 Scientific, measuring, optical, etc., equipment / Matériel scientifique, de précision, d'optique, etc. / Equipo científico, de medida, de óptica, etc.	390 Other manufacturing industries / Autres industries manufacturières / Otras industrias manufactureras
		371 Iron and steel / Sidérurgie / Hierro y acero	372 Non-ferrous metal / Métaux non ferreux / Metales no ferrosos						
1970	1 101	1 256	1 261	1 143	1 181	1 143	1 257	1 261	1 095
1971	1 199	1 560	1 500	1 376	1 446	1 335	1 501	1 473	1 353
1972	1 583	1 846	1 700	1 622	1 680	1 520	1 723	1 649	1 556
1973	1 827	2 143	2 017	1 826	1 954	1 801	1 968	1 930	1 877
1974	2 312	2 796	2 776	2 358	2 502	2 318	2 499	2 440	2 347
1975	2 813	3 383	3 257	2 969	3 134	2 913	3 137	3 119	2 841
1976	3 040	3 746	3 711	3 453	3 688	3 404	3 607	3 662	3 305
1977	3 850	4 221	4 468	4 083	4 396	4 139	4 250	4 508	4 295
1978	4 775	5 093	5 343	4 978	5 417	4 968	5 206	5 522	5 063
1979	5 682	6 250	6 516	5 928	6 717	5 847	6 207	6 405	5 873

[1] Socialised sector. [2] Incl. salaried employees. [3] Incl. ores extraction.

[1] *Secteur socialisé.* [2] *Y compris les employés.* [3] *Y compris l'extraction des minerais.*

[1] Sector socializado. [2] Incl. los empleados. [3] Incl. la extracción de minerales.

18 Wages in manufacturing / Salaires dans les industries manufacturières / Salarios en las industrias manufactureras — B By industry / Par industrie / Por industria

OCEANIA — OCÉANIE — OCEANIA

Australia

Average hourly earnings [1] *(dollars)*
Gains horaires moyens [1] *(dollars)*
Promedio de ganancias por hora [1] *(dollars)*

	31	321-322; 324	34	351-353	37	381-383	384	.
Date [2]	Food, beverages, tobacco	Textiles, clothing, footwear	Paper, printing, publishing	Chemicals, petroleum refineries	Basic metal industries	Metal products, machinery, etc.	Transport equipment	Other manufacturing industries
Date [2]	*Aliments, boissons, tabac*	*Textiles, habillement, chaussures*	*Papier, imprimerie, édition*	*Industrie chimique, raffineries de pétrole*	*Industrie métallurgique de base*	*Produits métalliques, machines, etc.*	*Matériel de transport*	*Autres industries manufacturières*
Fecha [2]	Alimentos, bebidas, tabaco	Textiles, vestido, calzado	Papel, imprentas, editoriales	Productos químicos, refinerías de petróleo	Industrias metalúrgicas básicas	Productos metálicos, maquinaria, etc.	Material de transporte	Otras industrias manufactureras
Adult males — Hommes adultes — Hombres adultos								
1970	1.69	1.68	2.02	1.86	1.89	1.77	1.82	1.74
1971	1.92	1.88	2.23	2.17	2.11	2.07	2.10	1.98
1972 [3]	2.10	2.05	2.39	2.41	2.36	2.22	2.18	2.14
1973	2.45	2.44	2.80	2.82	2.76	2.56	2.63	2.51
1974	3.32	3.01	3.72	3.79	3.73	3.42	3.45	3.25
1975	3.73	3.44	4.15	4.28	4.17	3.70	3.82	3.65
1976	4.23	3.91	4.67	4.85	4.77	4.22	4.32	4.11
1977	4.71	4.43	5.19	5.28	5.36	4.62	4.74	4.55
1978	5.03	4.66	5.56	5.68	5.63	4.89	5.00	4.95
1979	5.67	5.17	6.06	6.57	6.17	5.37	5.49	5.53
Adult females — Femmes adultes — Mujeres adultas								
1970	1.12	1.08	1.17	1.19	1.24	1.19	1.23	1.13
1971	1.30	1.26	1.34	1.42	1.49	1.43	1.46	1.31
1972 [3]	1.46	1.37	1.50	1.65	1.64	1.61	1.66	1.48
1973	1.76	1.68	1.78	1.92	1.95	1.87	2.01	1.78
1974	2.55	2.31	2.64	2.80	2.86	2.70	2.76	2.46
1975	3.07	2.83	3.13	3.29	3.36	3.01	3.10	2.93
1976	3.48	3.25	3.46	3.69	3.87	3.41	3.56	3.37
1977	3.91	3.67	3.91	4.14	4.31	3.73	4.00	3.81
1978	4.15	3.92	4.16	4.41	4.62	4.01	4.25	4.01
1979	4.68	4.10	4.57	4.67	5.00	4.35	4.56	4.23

[1] Incl. salaried employees. [2] Oct. of each year. [3] Scope of series enlarged.

[1] *Y compris les employés.* [2] *Oct. de chaque année.* [3] *Portée de la série élargie.*

[1] Incl. los empleados. [2] Oct. de cada año. [3] El alcance de la serie es mayor.

18 Wages in manufacturing / Salaires dans les industries manufacturières / Salarios en las industrias manufactureras

B By industry / Par industrie / Por industria

Fiji

Average weekly earnings *(dollars)*
Gains hebdomadaires moyens *(dollars)*
Promedio de ganancias por semana *(dollars)*

Date [1] / Date [1] / Fecha [1]	311-312 Food / Aliments / Alimentos	313 Beverages / Boissons / Bebidas	322 Clothing / Habillement / Vestido	324 Footwear / Chaussures / Calzado	331 Wood / Bois / Madera	332 Furniture / Ameublement / Mobiliario	341 Paper, paper products / Papier, articles en papier / Papel, artículos de papel	342 Printing, publishing / Imprimerie, édition / Imprentas, editoriales	352 Chemical products / Produits chimiques / Productos químicos
1970	16.98	17.55	11.45	11.00	13.93	14.22	14.26	12.19	13.28
1971	17.49	16.96	10.35	13.27	18.98	14.78	20.93	14.71	14.83
1972	24.46	22.18	13.75	15.31	17.27	17.84	19.14	16.23	17.08
1973	26.03	23.17	13.64	17.38	20.08	19.22	29.06	14.82	19.81
1974	26.40	28.47	15.93	19.88	21.97	26.98	26.86	19.68	24.85
1975	33.44	40.39	17.16	18.03	27.99	28.55	33.06	26.90	32.26
1976	35.45	40.50	23.88	18.56	35.40	33.18	32.89	33.79	35.74
1977	39.90	35.52	31.93	21.28	36.98	35.28	38.56	36.40	43.40
1978 *	42.69	38.00	34.17	22.77	39.57	37.75	41.26	38.95	46.44

Date [1] / Date [1] / Fecha [1]	355 Rubber products / Produits en caoutchouc / Productos de caucho	356 Plastic products / Articles en matière plastique / Productos plásticos	36 Non-metallic mineral products / Produits minéraux non métalliques / Productos minerales no metálicos	381 Metal products / Produits métalliques / Productos metálicos	382 Machinery (non-electrical) / Machines (non électriques) / Maquinaria (no eléctrica)	383 Electrical machinery and apparatus / Machines et appareils électriques / Maquinaria y aparatos eléctricos	384 Transport equipment / Matériel de transport / Material de transporte	390 Other manufacturing industries / Autres industries manufacturières / Otras industrias manufactureras
1970	14.75	10.50	18.28	20.93	17.27	17.75	12.96	10.50
1971	15.70	17.00	20.07	19.50	16.68	16.39	18.13	12.22
1972	22.49	18.79	21.12	22.18	21.60	18.12	19.20	12.04
1973	19.64	20.90	21.72	28.36	23.36	25.58	22.41	17.62
1974	33.79	30.21	31.46	31.60	35.38	28.31	32.52	17.55
1975	39.60	35.99	38.56	38.01	37.87	28.68	35.67	30.61
1976	38.57	28.06	39.15	39.65	36.19	33.59	35.65	23.98
1977	39.89	42.06	43.40	44.30	36.36	38.25	33.61	42.10
1978 *	...	45.00	46.44	47.40	38.91	40.93	35.96	45.04

[1] June of each year.   [1] *Juin de chaque année.*   [1] Junio de cada año.

18 Wages in manufacturing
Salaires dans les industries manufacturières
Salarios en las industrias manufactureras

B By industry
Par industrie
Por industria

New Zealand (1)

Average hourly earnings [1] *(dollars)*
Gains horaires moyens [1] *(dollars)*
Promedio de ganancias por hora [1] *(dollars)*

	311-312	313	314	321	322	323	324	331	332
Date [2]	Food	Beverages	Tobacco		Clothing	Leather, leather products	Footwear	Wood	Furniture
Date [2] Fecha [2]	Aliments	Boissons	Tabac	Textiles	Habillement	Cuir, articles en cuir	Chaussures	Bois	Ameublement
	Alimentos	Bebidas	Tabaco		Vestido	Cuero, artículos de cuero	Calzado	Madera	Mobiliario
1971	1.73	1.54	1.45	1.41	1.03	1.29	1.26	1.53	1.39
1972	1.88	1.63	1.54	1.53	1.15	1.44	1.35	1.65	1.53
1973	2.16	1.98	1.82	1.73	1.37	1.61	1.54	1.87	1.74
1974	2.42	2.19	2.24	2.06	1.62	1.90	1.84	2.15	2.00
1975	2.82	2.48	2.48	2.39	1.93	2.17	2.13	2.44	2.28
1976	3.21	2.79	2.81	2.72	2.24	2.51	2.39	2.78	2.64
1977	3.69	3.18	3.18	3.10	2.64	2.88	2.72	3.17	2.97
1978	4.29	3.67	3.64	3.46	2.98	3.29	3.11	3.60	3.30

	341	342	351	352	353	354	355	356	361	362
Date [2]	Paper, paper products	Printing, publishing	Industrial chemicals	Other chemical products	Petroleum refineries	Products of petroleum and coal	Rubber products	Plastic products	Pottery, china, earthenware	Glass
Date [2] Fecha [2]	Papier, articles en papier	Imprimerie, édition	Chimie industrielle	Autres produits chimiques	Raffineries de pétrole	Dérivés du pétrole et du charbon	Produits en caoutchouc	Articles en matière plastique	Grès, porcelaines, faïences	Verre
	Papel, artículos de papel	Imprentas, editoriales	Química industrial	Otros productos químicos	Refinerías de petróleo	Derivados del petróleo y del carbón	Productos de caucho	Productos plásticos	Barro, loza, porcelana	Vidrio
1971	1.80	1.50	1.75	1.50	2.42	1.56	1.77	1.48	1.46	1.62
1972	1.96	1.65	1.90	1.63	2.74	1.79	1.94	1.63	1.48	1.79
1973	2.23	1.90	2.18	1.87	3.01	2.06	2.26	1.90	1.58	1.87
1974	2.59	2.21	2.55	2.16	3.38	2.26	2.66	2.20	1.85	2.36
1975	3.00	2.50	2.94	2.57	3.81	2.63	2.92	2.49	2.09	2.63
1976	3.53	2.87	3.27	2.99	4.12	2.90	3.35	2.84	2.40	3.12
1977	4.11	3.33	3.65	3.41	4.49	3.36	3.81	3.26	2.78	3.42
1978	4.71	3.80	4.28	3.87	5.86	3.80	4.39	3.66	3.49	4.15

[1] Incl. salaried employees and juveniles. [2] April and Oct. of each year.

[1] *Y compris les employés et les jeunes gens.* [2] *Avril et oct. de chaque unnée.*

[1] Incl. los empleados y los jóvenes. [2] Abril y oct. de cada año.

18 Wages in manufacturing
Salaires dans les industries manufacturières
Salarios en las industrias manufactureras

B By industry
Par industrie
Por industria

New Zealand (2)

Average hourly earnings [1] *(dollars)*
Gains horaires moyens [1] *(dollars)*
Promedio de ganancias por hora [1] *(dollars)*

Date [2] *Date* [2] Fecha [2]	369 Other non-metallic mineral products *Autres produits minéraux non métalliques* Otros productos minerales no metálicos	371 Basic metal industries *Industrie métallurgique de base* Industrias metalúrgicas básicas Iron and steel *Sidérurgie* Hierro y acero	372 Non-ferrous metal *Métaux non ferreux* Metales no ferrosos	381 Metal products *Produits métalliques* Productos metálicos	382 Machinery (non-electrical) *Machines (non électriques)* Maquinaria (no eléctrica)	383 Electrical machinery and apparatus *Machines et appareils électriques* Maquinaria y aparatos eléctricos	384 Transport equipment *Matériel de transport* Material de transporte	385 Scientific, measuring, optical, etc., equipment *Matériel scientifique, de précision, d'optique, etc.* Equipo científico, de medida, de óptica, etc.	390 Other manufacturing industries *Autres industries manufacturières* Otras industrias manufactureras
1971	1.55	1.77	1.79	1.55	1.55	1.43	1.61	1.34	1.27
1972	1.68	2.00	1.94	1.67	1.70	1.54	1.76	1.44	1.38
1973	1.91	2.37	2.28	1.89	1.95	1.76	2.01	1.70	1.61
1974	2.24	2.72	2.66	2.18	2.26	2.02	2.33	1.98	1.89
1975	2.53	3.00	3.14	2.50	2.54	2.29	2.59	2.27	2.19
1976	2.85	3.55	3.49	2.84	2.89	2.67	2.95	2.63	2.53
1977	3.25	3.97	4.02	3.23	3.28	3.09	3.40	3.03	2.92
1978	3.67	4.59	4.64	3.68	3.72	3.57	3.84	3.42	3.30

[1] Incl. salaried employees and juveniles. [2] April and Oct. of each year.

[1] *Y compris les employés et les jeunes gens.* [2] *Avril et oct. de chaque année.*

[1] Incl. los empleados y los jóvenes. [2] Abril y oct. de cada año.

18 Wages in manufacturing
Salaires dans les industries manufacturières
Salarios en las industrias manufactureras

B By industry
Par industrie
Por industria

URSS [1]

Average monthly earnings [2] *(roubles)*
Gains mensuels moyens [2] *(roubles)*
Promedio de ganancias por mes [2] *(roubles)*

Date / Date / Fecha	311-312 Food / Aliments / Alimentos	313 Beverages / Boissons / Bebidas	314 Tobacco / Tabac / Tabaco	321 Textiles	322 Clothing / Habillement / Vestido	323 Leather, leather products / Cuir, articles en cuir / Cuero, artículos de cuero	324 Footwear / Chaussures / Calzado	331 Wood / Bois / Madera	332 Furniture / Ameublement / Mobiliario
1970	115.1	108.2	119.7	108.3	94.8	120.8	110.8	126.4	122.4
1971	118.7	110.3	124.6	112.8	96.6	124.9	112.3	131.4	127.3
1972	122.8	113.0	127.7	115.8	99.4	128.3	113.7	135.4	132.1
1973	127.2	115.4	130.5	120.0	102.8	131.1	118.4	142.1	136.8
1974	136.4	122.9	136.3	125.1	109.7	136.0	126.2	150.6	145.1
1975	142.3	127.8	141.0	130.3	115.5	142.4	132.4	157.7	151.8
1976	148.2	136.1	151.3	140.7	123.3	150.4	141.4	164.0	159.8
1977	153.9	138.2	154.0	144.7	124.5	154.8	145.7	168.2	164.4
1978	156.6	140.3	156.6	151.7	128.0	158.6	151.4	171.2	165.2
1979	159.4	142.5	156.3	155.4	132.1	163.4	156.0	173.8	172.1

Date / Date / Fecha	341 Paper, paper products / Papier, articles en papier / Papel, artículos de papel	351 Industrial chemicals / Chimie industrielle / Química industrial	352 Other chemical products / Autres produits chimiques / Otros productos químicos	355 Rubber products / Produits en caoutchouc / Productos de caucho	356 Plastic products / Articles en matière plastique / Productos plásticos	361 Pottery, china, earthenware / Grès, porcelaines, faïences / Barro, loza, porcelana	362 Glass, and glass products / Verre / Vidrio	369 Other non-metallic mineral products / Autres produits minéraux / Otros productos minerales	371 Iron and steel basic industries / Sidérurgie / Industrias básicas de hierro y acero	383 Electrical machinery and apparatus / Machines et appareils électriques / Maquinaria y aparatos eléctricos
1970	130.8	136.7	134.0	140.1	125.2	125.2	134.2	137.1	153.2	127.8
1971	135.3	140.5	139.3	146.1	130.9	130.0	139.0	142.2	157.7	132.6
1972	139.0	144.5	143.0	150.9	135.7	133.2	142.4	146.3	161.6	136.9
1973	147.5	149.7	147.0	155.3	137.7	136.8	145.6	151.5	166.1	141.8
1974	155.7	158.6	154.5	164.3	141.3	142.4	153.6	158.5	178.4	149.3
1975	163.8	165.2	162.0	169.1	147.4	147.5	160.9	164.4	188.1	152.6
1976	171.5	170.6	171.4	175.4	155.9	153.1	167.1	169.1	191.1	163.4
1977	175.9	172.2	174.5	180.4	161.9	156.4	168.7	171.2	195.8	166.8
1978	180.0	175.3	175.9	183.0	162.2	160.1	172.0	174.3	197.3	170.1
1979	180.9	176.6	178.0	185.1	160.4	161.2	174.1	176.0	201.9	173.7

[1] Socialised sector. Incl. Byelorussian SSR, shown separately in this table. [2] Incl. salaried employees.

[1] *Secteur socialisé. Y compris la RSS de Biélorussie, figurant séparément dans ce tableau.* [2] *Y compris les employés.*

[1] Sector socializado. Incl. la RSS de Bielorrusia, que figura separadamente en este cuadro. [2] Incl. los empleados.

SALAIRES
SALARIOS

18 Wages in manufacturing
Salaires dans les industries manufacturières
Salarios en las industrias manufactureras

B By industry
Par industrie
Por industria

RSS de Biélorussie [1]

Average monthly earnings [2] *(roubles)*
Gains mensuels moyens [2] *(roubles)*
Promedio de ganancias por mes [2] *(roubles)*

Date / Date / Fecha	31 Food, beverages, tobacco *Aliments, boissons, tabac* Alimentos, bebidas, tabaco — Total	Beverages *Boissons* Bebidas	Tobacco *Tabac* Tabaco	321 Textiles	322; 324 Clothing, footwear *Habillement, chaussures* Vestido, calzado	323 Leather, leather products *Cuir, articles en cuir* Cuero, artículos de cuero	324 Footwear *Chaussures* Calzado	331 Wood *Bois* Madera
1972	108.1	102.4	129.3	112.1	103.1	129.3	115.3	117.1
1973	111.5	103.9	131.4	115.9	104.2	130.6	116.6	121.5
1974	114.2	106.8	135.9	119.5	107.1	134.1	121.8	126.0
1975	117.6	111.5	140.0	122.2	110.6	135.0	124.7	130.4

Date / Date / Fecha	332 Furniture *Ameublement* Mobiliario	341 Paper, paper products *Papier, articles en papier* Papel, artículos de papel	355 Rubber products *Industrie du caoutchouc* Productos de caucho	36 Non-metallic mineral products *Produits minéraux non métalliques* Productos minerales no metálicos	37 Basic metal industries *Industrie métallurgique de base* Industrias metalúrgicas básicas	38 Metal products, machinery, etc. *Produits métalliques, machines, etc.* Productos metálicos, maquinaria, etc. — Total	Electrical machinery *Machines électriques* Maquinaria eléctrica
1972	121.8	112.9	134.3	132.3	146.7	138.8	127.9
1973	127.2	117.4	139.1	138.2	150.2	143.6	131.3
1974	133.9	118.3	151.0	143.7	152.5	148.8	136.4
1975	140.6	126.0	153.0	149.0	159.1	153.1	141.8

[1] Socialised sector. [2] Incl. salaried employees.　　[1] *Secteur socialisé.* [2] *Y compris les employés.*　　[1] Sector socializado. [2] Incl. los empleados.

537

WAGES

19 Wages in mining and quarrying
Salaires dans les industries extractives
Salarios en las minas y canteras

Earnings *(E.G.)* or rates *(R.T.)*
per hour *(h.)*, day *(d.j.)*,
week *(w.s.)* or month *(m.)*

Gains *(E.G.)* ou taux *(R.T.)*
par heure *(h.)*, jour *(d.j.)*,
semaine *(w.s.)* ou mois *(m.)*

Ganancias *(E.G.)* o tarifas *(R.T.)*
por hora *(h.)*, día *(d.j.)*,
semana *(w.s.)* o mes *(m.)*

Date / Date / Fecha	AFRICA — AFRIQUE — AFRICA							
	Algérie	Burundi (Bujumbura)	Cameroun Skilled workers *Ouvriers qualifiés* Obreros calificados	Egypt	Kenya	Malawi	Mauritius Salt mining *Mines de sel* Minas de sal	Nigeria
	(E.G./h.) [1]	(E.G./m.) [2,3]	(R.T./h.) [4]	(E.G./w.s.) [5]	(E.G./m.) [3,6]	(E.G./m.) [3]	(E.G./d.j.) [8]	(R.T./d.j.)
	Dinars	Piastres	Francs	Francs (CFA)	Shillings	Kwacha	Rupees	Naira
1970	1.69	.	.	502	549.80	17.43	4.00	.
1971	2.59	.	.	574	580.80	15.23	4.19	.
1972	3.27	.	99.00	608	483.40	16.84	4.46	.
1973	2.68	767	110.00	593	601.40	18.33	4.33	1.42
1974	2.93	1 002	120.43	703	603.20	24.44	5.18	1.75
1975	2.89	1 008	173.28	820	740.60	34.90	7.97	1.78
1976	...		173.28	973	748.20	28.27	8.87	2.17
1977	4.57	1 429	187.11	...	844.60	25.15 [7]	13.14	2.34
1978	...	3 045	187.11	...	912.70	27.58	25.21	2.34
1979	...	3 175	210.15	...	1 013.00	...	13.76	2.57

Date / Date / Fecha	AFRICA — AFRIQUE — AFRICA						AMERICA — AMÉRIQUE — AMÉRICA		
	Sierra Leone	Swaziland Month — *Mois* — Mes Skilled *Qualifiés* Calificados	Unskilled *Non qualifiés* No calificados	Tanzania (Tanganyika)	Zambia Zambians *Zambiens* Zambianos	Others *Autres* Otros	Argentina Stone quarrying *Carrières de pierre* Canteras de piedra	Barbados	Bolivia
	(E.G./w.s.) [9]	(E.G./m.) [10,11]		(E.G./m.) [12]	(E.G./m.) [3,13]		(E.G./h.) [14]	(E.G./w.s.) [15]	(R.T./m.) [3]
	Leones	Emalangeni	Emalangeni	Shillings	Kwacha	Kwacha	Pesos	Dollars	Pesos
1970	8.62	.	.	456	...	...	1.65	47.68	1 033
1971	8.55	.	.	525	...	...	2.33	57.29	1 090
1972	9.06	422	39	548	133	418	3.42	57.50	1 225
1973	9.57	527	37	526	140	450	5.37	62.09	1 345
1974	9.83	511	47	690	142	552	6.93	70.48	1 745
1975	10.58	459	60	...	123	565	10.87	75.55	1 745
1976	11.57	508	78	...	209	859	56.33	89.07	1 745
1977	11.85	530	95	...	219	892	124.37	98.89	2 190
1978	11.96	546	114	...	...	...	...	...	1 569
1979	12.06	...	...	...	...	...	...	...	...

EXPLANATORY NOTES: See p. 423.

[1] April of each year. [2] Incl. family allowances. [3] Incl. salaried employees. [4] Average rates. [5] Oct. of each year. [6] June of each year. Incl. the value of payments in kind. [7] Scope of series enlarged. [8] Sep. of each year. [9] Adults. May and Nov. of each year. [10] June of each year. Prior to 1976: Sep. [11] Males. [12] Adult males; June of each year. [13] Fourth quarter of each year. [14] Unskilled workers. [15] Adults. Prior to 1974: rates per week.

NOTES EXPLICATIVES: Voir p. 426.

[1] *Avril de chaque année.* [2] *Y compris les allocations familiales.* [3] *Y compris les employés.* [4] *Taux moyens.* [5] *Oct. de chaque année.* [6] *Juin de chaque année. Y compris la valeur des paiements en nature.* [7] *Portée de la série élargie.* [8] *Sept. de chaque année.* [9] *Adultes. Mai et nov. de chaque année.* [10] *Juin de chaque année. Avant 1976 : sept.* [11] *Hommes.* [12] *Hommes adultes ; juin de chaque année.* [13] *Quatrième trimestre de chaque année.* [14] *Ouvriers non qualifiés.* [15] *Adultes. Avant 1974 : taux par semaine.*

NOTAS EXPLICATIVAS: Véase pág. 430.

[1] Abril de cada año. [2] Incl. las asignaciones familiares. [3] Incl. los empleados. [4] Tarifas medias. [5] Oct. de cada año. [6] Junio de cada año. Incl. el valor de los pagos en especie. [7] El alcance de la serie es mayor. [8] Sept. de cada año. [9] Adultos. Mayo y nov. de cada año. [10] Junio de cada año. Antes de 1976: sept. [11] Hombres. [12] Hombres adultos; junio de cada año. [13] Cuarto trimestre de cada año. [14] Obreros no calificados. [15] Adultos. Antes de 1974: tarifas por semana.

19 Wages in mining and quarrying
Salaires dans les industries extractives
Salarios en las minas y canteras

Earnings *(E.G.)* or rates *(R.T.)*
per hour *(h.)*, day *(d.j.)*,
week *(w.s.)* or month *(m.)*

Gains *(E.G.)* ou taux *(R.T.)*
par heure *(h.)*, jour *(d.j.)*,
semaine *(w.s.)* ou mois *(m.)*

Ganancias *(E.G.)* o tarifas *(R.T.)*
por hora *(h.)*, día *(d.j.)*,
semana *(w.s.)* o mes *(m.)*

Date / Date / Fecha	AMERICA — AMÉRIQUE — AMÉRICA							
	Canada			Colombia			Chile	República Dominicana
	All mining and quarrying / Ensemble des industries extractives / Todas las minas y canteras	Metal mining / Mines métallifères / Minas metalíferas	Coal mining / Mines de charbon / Minas de carbón	Petroleum / Pétrole / Petróleo	Costa Rica		All mining / Ensemble des mines / Todas las minas	
	(E.G./h.)	*(E.G./w.s.)*	*(E.G./h.)*		*(E.G./h.)* [1]	*(E.G./m.)*	*(E.G./m.)* [2] [3]	*(E.G./m.)* [5]
	Dollars	Dollars	Dollars	Dollars	Pesos	Colones	Pesos	Pesos
1970	3.70	152.10	3.83	3.49	9.96	.	1 835.31	200.27
1971	4.04	163.22	4.17	3.51	9.55	.	2 796.87	212.54
1972	4.34	174.90	4.48	3.92	10.00	.	3 360.48	207.57
1973	4.82	196.89	4.94	4.45	11.80	662	9 993.00	315.67
1974	5.50	222.25	5.65	5.25	13.90	806	68 881.26	349.32
1975	6.51	262.10	6.60	6.38	17.60	998	364.21 [4]	371.28
1976	7.40	...	7.48	6.94	24.20	1 060	1 374.76	423.23
1977	8.11	...	8.18	7.47	26.66	1 122	3 917.29	496.08
1978	8.75	...	8.76	8.07	...	1 300	6 074.15	536.38
1979	9.66	...	9.60	9.02	...	1 506	9 342.94	...

Date / Date / Fecha	AMERICA — AMÉRIQUE — AMÉRICA							
	Ecuador		Guyana	Honduras	México	Netherlands Antilles	Nicaragua	Puerto Rico
	(E.G./h.)	*(E.G./w.s.)*	*(E.G./w.s.)*	*(E.G./w.s.)*	*(E.G./h.)* [6]	*(E.G./m.)* [5]	*(E.G./h.)*	*(E.G./h.)*
	Sucres	Sucres	Dollars	Lempiras	Pesos	Guilders	Córdobas	$
1970	10.50	594	75.24	.	6.51	.	2.55	1.94
1971	11.80	622	75.98	.	7.70	.	2.65	2.07
1972	13.20	702	81.30	.	9.78	.	2.75	2.18
1973	15.80	804	87.25	73.84	11.64	549	3.15	2.26
1974	18.90	890	96.36	45.88	12.36	...	3.76	2.38
1975	20.00	971	93.37	85.76	...	676	3.85	2.60
1976	19.40	986	111.73	120.33	...	703	3.76	2.76
1977	20.90	966	114.92	138.22	...	853	4.09	2.84
1978	...	...	...	178.31	...	853	5.50	3.16
1979	...	...	...	94.56	...	...	...	...

EXPLANATORY NOTES: See p. 423.

[1] Males only. [2] April of each year. [3] Incl. the value of payments in kind. [4] New currency introduced in Sep. 1975: 1 peso = 1,000 old escudos. [5] Incl. salaried employees. [6] Oct. of each year.

NOTES EXPLICATIVES: Voir p. 426.

[1] *Hommes seulement.* [2] *Avril de chaque année.* [3] *Y compris la valeur des paiements en nature.* [4] *Nouvelle monnaie introduite en sept. 1975 : 1 peso = 1 000 anciens escudos.* [5] *Y compris les employés.* [6] *Oct. de chaque année.*

NOTAS EXPLICATIVAS: Véase pág. 430.

[1] Hombres solamente. [2] Abril de cada año. [3] Incl. el valor de los pagos en especie. [4] Nueva moneda adoptada en sept. de 1975: 1 peso = 1 000 antiguos escudos. [5] Incl. los empleados. [6] Oct. de cada año.

WAGES

19 Wages in mining and quarrying
Salaires dans les industries extractives
Salarios en las minas y canteras

Earnings *(E.G.)* or rates *(R.T.)*
per hour *(h.)*, day *(d.j.)*,
week *(w.s.)* or month *(m.)*

Gains *(E.G.)* ou taux *(R.T.)*
par heure *(h.)*, jour *(d.j.)*,
semaine *(w.s.)* ou mois *(m.)*

Ganancias *(E.G.)* o tarifas *(R.T.)*
por hora *(h.)*, día *(d.j.)*,
semana *(w.s.)* o mes *(m.)*

		AMERICA — AMÉRIQUE — AMÉRICA				
		Trinidad and Tobago	United States			
Date / *Date* / Fecha	Suriname	Mining [1] / *Mines* [1] / Minas [1]	All mining and quarrying / *Ensemble des industries extractives* / Todas las minas y canteras	All mining and quarrying / *Ensemble des industries extractives* / Todas las minas y canteras	Bituminous coal mining [4] / *Mines de charbon bitumineux* [4] / Minas de carbón bituminoso [4]	Metal mining / *Mines métallifères* / Minas metalíferas
	(E.G./m.)	*(R.T.)* [2]	*(E.G./h.)*	*(E.G./w.s.)*	*(E.G./h.)*	
	Guilders	(1970 = 100)	$	$	$	$
1970	.	**100.0**	3.85	164.40	4.58	3.88
1971	299	103.5	4.06	172.14	4.83	4.12
1972	313	123.6	4.44	189.14	5.32	4.56
1973	328	131.3	4.75	201.40	5.75	4.84
1974	344	151.1	5.23	219.14	6.26	5.44
1975	...	201.0	5.95	249.31	7.25	6.13
1976	...	246.9	6.46	273.90	7.78	6.76
1977	...	273.4 [3]	6.94	301.20	8.26	7.28
1978	...	292.5	7.67	332.11	9.52	8.23
1979	...	...	8.48	364.64	10.26	9.29

	AMERICA — AMÉRIQUE — AMÉRICA			ASIA — ASIE — ASIA		
	United States	Venezuela		Burma		
Date / *Date* / Fecha	Crude petroleum [5] / *Pétrole brut* [5] / Petróleo crudo [5]	Petroleum / *Pétrole* / Petróleo	Iron / *Fer* / Hierro	Metal mining / *Mines métallifères* / Minas metalíferas		Cyprus
				Males / *Hommes* / Hombres	Females / *Femmes* / Mujeres	
	(E.G./h.)	*(E.G./m.)*		*(E.G./m.)* [6]		*(E.G./w.s.)* [8], [9]
	$	Bolívares	Bolívares	Kyats	Kyats	Pounds
1970	3.83	2 351	1 982	150.94	114.75	11.43
1971	4.15	2 412	1 953	149.28	116.05	13.37
1972	4.52	2 400	2 169	143.19 [7]	99.48 [7]	16.53
1973	4.79	2 310	2 189	155.78	128.43	18.77
1974	5.30	3 025	2 419	171.55	95.44	18.60 [10]
1975	6.01	3 447	2 587	164.73	137.66	19.80
1976	6.61	3 057	2 596	199.14	159.92	21.18
1977	7.16	4 386	3 470	193.40	166.67	25.54
1978	8.06	...	...	226.52	249.94	30.08
1979	8.80	...	...	...	...	38.58

EXPLANATORY NOTES: See p. 423.

[1] Incl. asphalt mining and oil refining. [2] Minimum rates. Adults. May and Nov. of each year. [3] Beginning Nov. 1976: series linked to former series. [4] Eleven months average. [5] Incl. natural gas. [6] Incl. salaried employees. Beginning 1973: March and Sep. of each year. [7] April and Sep. [8] Adults. Oct. of each year. [9] Incl. family allowances and the value of payments in kind. [10] Beginning July 1974: due to a change in the geographical scope of the series, data are not comparable with those for the preceding period.

NOTES EXPLICATIVES: Voir p. 426.

[1] *Y compris les mines d'asphalte et les raffineries de pétrole.* [2] *Taux minima. Adultes. Mai et nov. de chaque année.* [3] *A partir de nov. 1976 : série enchaînée à la précédente.* [4] *Moyenne de onze mois.* [5] *Y compris le gaz naturel.* [6] *Y compris les employés. A partir de 1973: mars et sept. de chaque année.* [7] *Avril et sept.* [8] *Adultes. Oct. de chaque année.* [9] *Y compris les allocations familiales et la valeur des paiements en nature.* [10] *A partir de juillet 1974 : en raison d'un changement de la portée géographique de la série, les données ne sont pas comparables avec celles de la période précédente.*

NOTAS EXPLICATIVAS: Véase pág. 430.

[1] Incl. las minas de asfalto y las refinerías de petróleo. [2] Tarifas mínimas. Adultos. Mayo y nov. de cada año. [3] A partir de nov. de 1976: serie enlazada con la anterior. [4] Promedio de once meses. [5] Incl. el gas natural. [6] Incl. los empleados. A partir de 1973: marzo y sept. de cada año. [7] Abril y sept. [8] Adultos solamente. Oct. de cada año. [9] Incl. las asignaciones familiares y el valor de los pagos en especie. [10] A partir de julio de 1974: en razón de un cambio del alcance geográfico de la serie, los datos no son comparables a los del período precedente.

19 Wages in mining and quarrying
Salaires dans les industries extractives
Salarios en las minas y canteras

Earnings *(E.G.)* or rates *(R.T.)*
per hour *(h.)*, day *(d.j.)*,
week *(w.s.)* or month *(m.)*

Gains *(E.G.)* ou taux *(R.T.)*
par heure *(h.)*, jour *(d.j.)*,
semaine *(w.s.)* ou mois *(m.)*

Ganancias *(E.G.)* o tarifas *(R.T.)*
por hora *(h.)*, día *(d.j.)*,
semana *(w.s.)* o mes *(m.)*

	ASIA — ASIE — ASIA					
	India			Japan		
Date *Date* Fecha	Coal mining *Mines de charbon* Minas de carbón	Other mining and quarrying *Autres industries extractives* Otras minas y canteras	Israel	All mining and quarrying *Ensemble des industries extractives* Todas las minas y canteras	Jordan [2]	Korea, Rep. of
	(E.G./w.s.) [1]	*(E.G./d.j.)* [1]	*(E.G./m.)* [2,3]	*(E.G./m.)* [2,6]	*(E.G./d.j.)* [7,8]	*(E.G./m.)* [2,9]
	Rupees	Rupees	Pounds	Yen	Fils	Won
1970	54.19	5.32	1 029	79 209	.	18 574
1971	56.27	5.78	1 215	90 887	.	22 171
1972	60.17	6.46	1 401	103 679		25 131
1973	72 66	7.88	1 826	123 249 [5]	1 492	30 415
1974	86.60	9.54	2 486	171 810	1 996	41 068
1975	119.87	10.51	3 568 [4]	197 301	2 251	54 650
1976	117.00	10.38	5 069	214 090 [5]	2 726	66 055
1977	126.44	13.21 *	6 821	236 017	2 945	93 851
1978	...	...	9 979	249 217	...	127 685
1979	...	...	22 290 [5]	264 948 [5]	...	166 171

	ASIA — ASIE — ASIA						
	Malaysia				Sri Lanka		République arabe syrienne
	Peninsular Malaysia				Plumbago mining *Mines de plombagine* Minas de plombagina		Phosphate *Phosphate* Fosfato
Date *Date* Fecha	Tin mining *Mines d'étain* Minas de estaño		Philippines	Singapore	Hour *Heure* Hora	Day *Jour* Día	Males [7] *Hommes* [7] Hombres [7]
	10	11					
	(E.G./m.) [2,12]		*(E.G./m.)*	*(E.G./h.)* [13]	*(E.G.)* [14]		*(E.G./w.s.)* [15]
	Ringgits	Ringgits	Pesos	Cents	Cents	Rupees	Pounds
1970	.	176	245	130	.	.	71.15
1971	.	185	276	133	.	.	74.55
1972	275	175	298	127	.	.	80.40
1973	286	182	326	137	.	.	86.95
1974	334	208	367	163	.	.	79.45
1975	366	242	381	169	.	.	103.93
1976	386	248	...	180	204	17.37	127.35
1977	392	258	...	191	257	22.29	131.40
1978	427	285	...	213	316	25.24	...
1979	...	...	...	251	334	28.52	...

EXPLANATORY NOTES: See p. 423.

NOTES EXPLICATIVES: Voir p. 426.

NOTAS EXPLICATIVAS: Véase pág. 430.

[1] Dec. of each year. [2] Incl. salaried employees. [3] Prior to July 1975: incl. family allowances. Beginning July 1975: incl. payments subject to income tax and the value of payments in kind. [4] Scope of series enlarged. [5] Sampling design revised. [6] Incl. family allowances, mid- and end-of-year bonuses. [7] Adults. [8] April of each year. [9] Incl. family allowances and the value of payments in kind. [10] Skilled workers. [11] Semi-skilled workers. [12] July of each year. [13] Aug. of each year. Prior to 1975: July. [14] March and Sep. of each year. [15] May of each year. Prior to 1973: Nov.

[1] *Déc. de chaque année.* [2] *Y compris les employés.* [3] *Avant 1975 : y compris les allocations familiales. A partir de juillet 1975 : y compris les versements soumis à l'impôt sur le revenu et la valeur des paiements en nature.* [4] *Portée de la série élargie.* [5] *Plan d'échantillonnage révisé.* [6] *Y compris les allocations familiales et les primes de mi- et de fin d'année.* [7] *Adultes.* [8] *Avril de chaque année.* [9] *Y compris les allocations familiales et la valeur des paiements en nature.* [10] *Ouvriers qualifiés.* [11] *Ouvriers semi-qualifiés.* [12] *Juillet de chaque année.* [13] *Août de chaque année. Avant 1975: juillet.* [14] *Mars et sept. de chaque année.* [15] *Mai de chaque année. Avant 1973: nov.*

[1] Dic. de cada año. [2] Incl. los empleados. [3] Antes de julio de 1975: incl. las asignaciones familiares. A partir de julio de 1975: incl. los pagos sometidos al impuesto sobre la renta y el valor de los pagos en especie. [4] El alcance de la serie es mayor. [5] Diseño de la muestra revisado. [6] Incl. las asignaciones familiares y las primas de mitad y de fin de año. [7] Adultos. [8] Abril de cada año. [9] Incl. las asignaciones familiares y el valor de los pagos en especie. [10] Obreros calificados. [11] Obreros semicalificados. [12] Julio de cada año. [13] Agosto de cada año. Antes de 1975: julio. [14] Marzo y sept. de cada año. [15] Mayo de cada año. Antes de 1973: nov.

19 Wages in mining and quarrying
Salaires dans les industries extractives
Salarios en las minas y canteras

Earnings *(E.G.)* or rates *(R.T.)*
per hour *(h.)*, day *(d.j.)*,
week *(w.s.)* or month *(m.)*

Gains *(E.G.)* ou taux *(R.T.)*
par heure *(h.)*, jour *(d.j.)*,
semaine *(w.s.)* ou mois *(m.)*

Ganancias *(E.G.)* o tarifas *(R.T.)*
por hora *(h.)*, día *(d.j.)*,
semana *(w.s.)* o mes *(m.)*

EUROPE — EUROPE — EUROPA

Date / Date / Fecha	Austria — All mining / Ensemble des mines / Todas las minas — Hewers underground / Piqueurs du fond / Barreteros bajo la superficie (R.T./h.) [1]	Austria — Other underground workers / Autres ouvriers du fond / Otros obreros bajo la superficie (R.T./h.) [1]	Belgique — Males / Hommes / Hombres (E.G./h.) [2]	Bulgarie [4] (E.G./m.)	Czechoslovakia [5] (E.G./m.) [6]	España (E.G./h.) [6]
	Schilling	Schilling	Francs	Leva	Korunas	Pesetas
1970	17.90	14.00	85.97	165.5	2 680	58.98
1971	21.50	15.60	96.02	171.9	2 827	65.47
1972	24.54	17.34	107.41 [3]	177.5	2 886	76.42
1973	28.00	19.13	123.23	193.5	2 960	89.54
1974	32.00	20.80	150.07	200.0	3 036	117.17
1975	40.00	25.00	183.67	209.3	3 138	157.47
1976	43.66	27.29	199.56	212.7	3 244	203.37
1977	47.33	29.58	217.63	216.3	3 415	...
1978	49.84	31.03	230.81	221.8	3 535	...
1979	52.88	32.83	244.38	...	3 635	...

EUROPE — EUROPE — EUROPA

Date / Date / Fecha	Finland — Metal mining / Mines métallifères / Minas metalíferas (E.G./h.) [7]	Finland — All mining / Ensemble des mines / Todas las minas (E.G./h.) [2]	France — Hard-coal and lignite mining / Mines de houille et de lignite / Minas de hulla y de lignito — All workers / Ensemble des ouvriers / Todos los obreros (E.G./m.)	France — Underground workers / Ouvriers du fond / Obreros bajo la superficie (E.G./m.)	France — Surface workers / Ouvriers du jour / Obreros de la superficie (E.G./m.)	Germany, Fed. Rep. of [10] — Males — Hommes — Hombres — All mining / Ensemble des mines / Todas las minas (E.G./h.)	Germany — Coal mining / Mines de charbon / Minas de carbón (E.G./h.)
	Markkaa	Francs	Francs	Francs	Francs	Mark	Mark
1970	5.95	6.25	47.10	50.43	41.03	6.55	6.64
1971	7.00	6.86	1 286 [9]	1 358 [9]	1 144 [9]	7.26	7.32
1972	8.04	7.99	1 409	1 499	1 244	7.84	7.89
1973	9.26	8.94	1 558	1 659	1 385	8.64 [8]	8.69 [8]
1974	11.15	10.96	1 909	2 027	1 711	9.84	9.92
1975	13.71	13.28	2 352	2 498	2 112	10.81	10.85
1976	15.97	16.35 [8]	2 698	2 890	2 390	11.53	11.50
1977	17.91	18.04	2 992	3 222	2 641	12.20	12.16
1978	19.64	20.06	3 330	3 587	2 951	12.79	12.74
1979	22.03	22.66	3 718	3 308	4 000	13.73	13.69

EXPLANATORY NOTES: See p. 423.

[1] Minimum rates. [2] Oct. of each year. [3] New industrial classification. [4] Socialised sector. [5] State industry. [6] Incl. salaried employees. [7] Males. Incl. the value of payments in kind. [8] Sampling design revised. [9] Series replacing former series; prior to 1971: earnings per day. [10] Incl. family allowances paid directly by the employers.

NOTES EXPLICATIVES: Voir p. 426.

[1] *Taux minima.* [2] *Oct. de chaque année.* [3] *Nouvelle classification industrielle.* [4] *Secteur socialisé.* [5] *Industrie d'Etat.* [6] *Y compris les employés.* [7] *Hommes. Y compris la valeur des paiements en nature.* [8] *Plan d'échantillonnage révisé.* [9] *Série remplaçant la précédente; avant 1971: gains par jour.* [10] *Y compris les allocations familiales payées directement par les employeurs.*

NOTAS EXPLICATIVAS: Véase pág. 430.

[1] Tarifas mínimas. [2] Oct. de cada año. [3] Nueva clasificación industrial. [4] Sector socializado. [5] Industria de Estado. [6] Incl. los empleados. [7] Hombres. Incl. el valor de los pagos en especie. [8] Diseño de la muestra revisado. [9] Serie que substituye a la anterior; antes de 1971: ganancias por día. [10] Incl. las asignaciones familiares pagadas directamente por los empleadores.

19 Wages in mining and quarrying
Salaires dans les industries extractives
Salarios en las minas y canteras

Earnings *(E.G.)* or rates *(R.T.)*
per hour *(h.)*, day *(d.j.)*,
week *(w.s.)* or month *(m.)*

Gains *(E.G.)* ou taux *(R.T.)*
par heure *(h.)*, jour *(d.j.)*,
semaine *(w.s.)* ou mois *(m.)*

Ganancias *(E.G.)* o tarifas *(R.T.)*
por hora *(h.)*, día *(d.j.)*,
semana *(w.s.)* o mes *(m.)*

	Hongrie [1]		Ireland		Luxembourg		Malta
Date / Date / Fecha	All mining and quarrying / Ensemble des industries extractives / Todas las minas y canteras	Coal mining / Mines de charbon / Minas de carbón	Males / Hommes / Hombres	Italie	All mining and quarrying / Ensemble des industries extractives / Todas las minas y canteras	Iron ore mining / Extraction du minerai de fer / Extracción de mineral de hierro	Stone quarrying and clay pits / Carrières de pierre et d'argile / Canteras de piedra y arcilla
	(E.G./m.) [2,3]		*(E.G./h.)* [4]	*(E.G./h.)* [2,6]	*(E.G./h.)* [9,10]		*(E.G./h.)* [11,12]
	Forints	Forints	Pence	Lire	Francs	Francs	Cents
1970	2 945	3 157	51.5	676	98.72	108.39	24.6
1971	3 008	3 220	58.8	783	104.83	113.84	25.8
1972	3 118	3 339	67.7	854	117.15 [5]	128.59 [5]	25.6
1973	3 471	3 724	79.0 [5]	1 051	127.94	142.72	...
1974	3 707	3 975	95.0	1 325	159.36	176.24	31.5
1975	3 992	4 196	121.2	1 890 [7]	171.35	180.22	34.9
1976	4 222	4 443	153.6	2 232	201.37	215.42	42.5
1977	4 572	4 805	163.2	2 763	212.67	230.01	...
1978	5 026	5 284	190.7	3 532 [8]	223.10	240.53	...
1979	5 396	5 689	221.1	...	223.10	242.12	...

	Netherlands	Norway	Pologne [1] Hard-coal mining / Mines de houille / Minas de hulla	Portugal	Suisse Males [11] — Hommes [11] — Hombres [11]		
Date / Date / Fecha					Skilled / Qualifiés / Calificados	Semi-skilled and unskilled / Semi-qualifiés et non qualifiés / Semicalificados y no calificados	Total
	(E.G./h.) [9,11]	*(E.G./h.)* [2,11]	*(E.G./m.)* [2,12]	*(E.G./h.)*	*(E.G./h.)* [9,13]		
	Guilders	Kroner	Zlotys	Escudos	Francs	Francs	Francs
1970	6.00	14.92	3 781	.	8.09	6.98	7.31
1971	6.86	16.50	3 968	11.20	8.95	7.96	8.25
1972	7.70	17.83	4 146	13.20	10.16	8.90	9.27
1973	8.60	19.59	4 478	14.90	11.05	9.80	10.17
1974	9.99	22.85	5 480	23.00	12.37	11.01	11.41
1975	11.80	28.47	6 898	35.10	13.15	11.86	12.24
1976	12.59	33.59	7 201	39.60	13.36	12.08	12.46
1977	14.71	36.79	8 197	48.90	14.78	12.58	13.16
1978	15.41	39.00	8 552	52.94	14.78	13.05	13.50
1979	...	40.40	9 317 *	...	14.71	13.05	13.49

EXPLANATORY NOTES: See p. 423.

NOTES EXPLICATIVES: Voir p. 426.

NOTAS EXPLICATIVAS: Véase pág. 430.

[1] Socialised sector. [2] Incl. the value of payments in kind. [3] Incl. loyalty money. [4] Sep. of each year. Workers on adult rates of pay. [5] New industrial classification. [6] Prior to 1975: excl. payments for annual vacation and public holidays. [7] Series replacing former series. [8] Scope of series revised. [9] Oct. of each year. [10] Males. [11] Adult males. [12] Incl. salaried employees. [13] Statistics of establishments. Incl. family allowances.

[1] *Secteur socialisé.* [2] *Y compris la valeur des paiements en nature.* [3] *Y compris les primes d'assiduité.* [4] *Sept. de chaque année. Travailleurs rémunérés sur la base de taux de salaire pour adultes.* [5] *Nouvelle classification industrielle.* [6] *Avant 1975: non compris les paiements pour congés annuels et jours fériés.* [7] *Série remplaçant la précédente.* [8] *Portée de la série révisée.* [9] *Oct. de chaque année.* [10] *Hommes.* [11] *Hommes adultes.* [12] *Y compris les employés.* [13] *Statistiques d'établissements. Y compris les allocations familiales.*

[1] Sector socializado. [2] Incl. el valor de los pagos en especie. [3] Incl. las primas de asiduidad. [4] Sept. de cada año. Trabajadores pagados sobre la base de tarifas de salarios para adultos. [5] Nueva clasificación industrial [6] Antes de 1975: excl. los pagos por vacaciones anuales y días feriados. [7] Serie que substituye a la anterior. [8] El alcance de la serie es revisado. [9] Oct. de cada año. [10] Hombres. [11] Hombres adultos. [12] Incl. los empleados. [13] Estadísticas de establecimientos. Incl. las asignaciones familiares.

WAGES

19 Wages in mining and quarrying
Salaires dans les industries extractives
Salarios en las minas y canteras

Earnings *(E.G.)* or rates *(R.T.)*
per hour *(h.)*, day *(d.j.)*,
week *(w.s.)* or month *(m.)*

Gains *(E.G.)* ou taux *(R.T.)*
par heure *(h.)*, jour *(d.j.)*,
semaine *(w.s.)* ou mois *(m.)*

Ganancias *(E.G.)* o tarifas *(R.T.)*
por hora *(h.)*, día *(d.j.)*,
semana *(w.s.)* o mes *(m.)*

Date / Date / Fecha	EUROPE — EUROPE — EUROPA						OCEANIA — OCÉANIE — OCEANÍA	
	Sweden[1]		Turquie	United Kingdom[6]		Yugoslavia[9]	Australia[6]	Fiji
	All mining and quarrying / Ensemble des industries extractives / Todas las minas y canteras	Iron mining / Mines de fer / Minas de hierro		Coal mining / Mines de charbon / Minas de carbón	Other mining and quarrying / Autres industries extractives / Otras minas y canteras			Mining / Mines / Minas
	(E.G./h.) 2, 3		(E.G./d.j.) 4, 5	(E.G./w.s.) 7, 8	(E.G./h.) 8	(E.G./m.) 4	(E.G./h.) 1, 4	(R.T./d.j.) 11
	Kronor	Kronor	Liras	£	Pence	Dinars	Dollars	Dollars
1970	.	.	29.12	28.01	55.7	1 044	2.32	2.63
1971	17.59	18.70	35.17	31.65	63.0	1 373	2.68	2.76
1972	19.56	20.83	37.60	38.21	71.7	1 537	2.90 10	3.06
1973	21.09	22.21	52.41	42.43	81.7	1 992	3.28	3.96
1974	23.96	24.96	59.60	58.21	101.0	2 662	4.40	5.06
1975	29.35	32.06	90.19	77.17	126.7	3 241	5.32	5.16
1976	32.85	35.73	112.10	84.13	143.0	3 652	6.11	7.27
1977	36.45	39.31	144.57	89.71	158.8	4 521	6.84	7.01
1978	39.09	43.29	216.47	111.99	179.1	5 382	7.45	7.22
1979	41.46	43.29	334.82	213.30	...	6 626	8.22	7.73 *

Date / Date / Fecha	OCEANIA — OCÉANIE — OCEANÍA					URSS 9, 17	RSS de Biélorussie 9	RSS d'Ukraine 9
	New Zealand				Nouvelle-Calédonie			
	Coal mining / Mines de charbon / Minas de carbón	Other mining and quarrying / Autres industries extractives / Otras minas y canteras	Coal mining — Mines de charbon / Minas de carbón		Labourers[15] / Manœuvres[15] / Obreros no calificados[15]	Month / Mois / Mes	Month / Mois / Mes	Month / Mois / Mes
			Truckers / Wagonniers / Vagoneros	Labourers (surface) / Manœuvres (jour) / Obreros no calif. (superficie)				
	(E.G./h.) 4, 12		(R.T./w.s.) 1, 13		(R.T./h.) 16	(E.G.) 4	(E.G.) 4	(E.G.) 4
	Dollars	Dollars	Dollars	Dollars	Francs (CFP)	Roubles	Roubles	Roubles
1970	1.66	1.46	39.14	38.52	110.42	196.6	.	199.2
1971	1.83	1.63	46.97	44.71	120.10	206.5	.	205.4
1972	2.10	1.76	50.40	47.97	...	209.1	139.0	210.5
1973	2.34	2.01	59.47	54.83	116.74	216.4	141.3	215.2
1974	2.78	2.31	88.39 14	63.61	135.90	228.7	148.8	221.0
1975	3.08	2.72	98.44	73.30	146.41	239.4	150.8	235.1
1976	3.37	3.10	109.58	85.94	155.11	245.2	...	241.8
1977	...	...	123.84	99.62	163.80	250.3	...	...
1978	...	...	141.72	118.99	175.40	256.4	...	...
1979	...	...	...	...	192.80	262.2	...	...

EXPLANATORY NOTES: See p. 423.

1 Adult males. 2 Incl. holiday and sick-leave payments and the value of payments in kind. 3 Beginning 1976: second quarter of each year. 4 Incl. salaried employees. 5 Sep. of each year. 6 Oct. of each year. 7 Excl. Northern Ireland. 8 Full-time adult males. 9 Socialised sector. 10 Scope of series enlarged. 11 June of each year. 12 April and Oct. of each year. Incl. juveniles. 13 Minimum rates. 14 Series replacing former series. 15 First category. Dec. of each year. 16 Prior to 1972: incl. production bonuses. 17 Incl. Byelorussian SSR and Ukrainian SSR, shown separately in this table.

NOTES EXPLICATIVES: Voir p. 426.

1 Hommes adultes. 2 Y compris les versements au titre des vacances et congés de maladie et la valeur des paiements en nature. 3 A partir de 1976 : deuxième trimestre de chaque année. 4 Y compris les employés. 5 Sept. de chaque année. 6 Oct. de chaque année. 7 Non compris l'Irlande du Nord. 8 Hommes adultes à temps complet. 9 Secteur socialisé. 10 Portée de la série élargie. 11 Juin de chaque année. 12 Avril et oct. de chaque année. Y compris les jeunes gens. 13 Taux minima. 14 Série remplaçant la précédente. 15 Première catégorie. Déc. de chaque année. 16 Avant 1972 : y compris les primes de productivité. 17 Y compris les RSS de Biélorussie et d'Ukraine, figurant séparément dans ce tableau.

NOTAS EXPLICATIVAS: Véase pág. 430.

1 Hombres adultos. 2 Incl. los pagos por vacaciones y licencias de enfermedad y el valor de los pagos en especie. 3 A partir de 1976: segundo trimestre de cada año. 4 Incl. los empleados. 5 Sept. de cada año. 6 Oct. de cada año. 7 Excl. Irlanda del Norte. 8 Hombres adultos a tiempo completo. 9 Sector socializado. 10 El alcance de la serie es mayor. 11 Junio de cada año. 12 Abril y oct. de cada año. Incl. los jóvenes. 13 Tarifas mínimas. 14 Serie que substituye a la anterior. 15 Primera categoría. Dic. de cada año. 16 Antes de 1972: incl. las primas de producción. 17 Incl. las RSS de Bielorrusia y de Ucrania, que figuran separadamente en este cuadro.

20 Wages in construction
Salaires dans la construction
Salarios en la construcción

Earnings *(E.G.)* or rates *(R.T.)*
per hour *(h.)*, day *(d.j.)*,
week *(w.s.)* or month *(m.)*

Gains *(E.G.)* ou taux *(R.T.)*
par heure *(h.)*, jour *(d.j.)*,
semaine *(w.s.)* ou mois *(m.)*

Ganancias *(E.G.)* o tarifas *(R.T.)*
por hora *(h.)*, día *(d.j.)*,
semana *(w.s.)* o mes *(m.)*

			Cameroun			
Date *Date* Fecha	Algérie	Burundi (Bujumbura)	Skilled workers *Ouvriers qualifiés* Obreros calificados	Egypt	Kenya	Malawi
	(E.G./h.) [1]	*(E.G./m.)* [2, 3]	*(R.T./h.)* [4]	*(E.G./w.s.)* [5]	*(E.G./m.)* [2, 6]	*(E.G./m.)* [2]
	Dinars	Francs	Francs (CFA)	Piastres	Shillings	Kwacha
1970	2.50	.	85-162	360	521.40	28.27
1971	2.36	2 036	107.39	367	539.40	25.47
1972	2.60	2 170	173.20	378	551.80	25.70
1973	2.77	2 315	187.30	421	573.00	26.60
1974	3.11	2 315	120.43	476	583.40	30.39
1975	3.18	2 342	173.28	535	713.80	33.47
1976	...	...	173.28	624 *	778.20	34.31
1977	3.68	3 594	187.11	...	843.10	35.80 [7]
1978	...	3 831	245.50	...	915.40	38.54
1979	...	4 137	250.70	...	977.80	...

AFRICA — AFRIQUE — AFRICA

				South Africa, Rep. of		Swaziland (1)
Date *Date* Fecha	Mauritius	Nigeria	Sierra Leone	Total	11	Males *Hommes* Hombres
	(E.G./d.j.) [8]	*(R.T./d.j.)*	*(E.G./w.s.)* [9, 10]	*(E.G./m.)*		*(E.G./m.)* [12, 13]
	Rupees	Naira	Leones	Rand	Rand	Emalangeni
1970	9.20	.	7.52	102.30	317.00	.
1971	9.65	.	7.34	109.00	351.90	
1972	9.02	1.00	7.38	117.50	372.40	227
1973	9.78	1.00	6.69	132.80	410.50	178
1974	11.18	2.00	6.87	150.80	446.30	167
1975	16.51	2.00	7.03	172.30	508.70	218
1976	23.85	2.00	8.06	189.30	563.10	264
1977	26.29	2.13	8.75	210.70	642.90	205
1978	28.47	3.00	9.05	231.20	731.20	432
1979	34.02	3.30	10.68	252.37	817.20	...

EXPLANATORY NOTES: See p. 423.

[1] April of each year. [2] Incl. salaried employees. [3] Incl. family allowances. [4] Average rates. [5] Oct. of each year. [6] June of each year. [7] Scope of series enlarged. [8] Sep. of each year. [9] Adults. [10] May and Nov. of each year. [11] White population. [12] June of each year. Prior to 1976: Sep. [13] Skilled workers.

NOTES EXPLICATIVES: Voir p. 426.

[1] *Avril de chaque année.* [2] *Y compris les employés.* [3] *Y compris les allocations familiales.* [4] *Taux moyens.* [5] *Oct. de chaque année.* [6] *Juin de chaque année. Y compris la valeur des paiements en nature.* [7] *Portée de la série élargie.* [8] *Sept. de chaque année.* [9] *Adultes.* [10] *Mai et nov. de chaque année.* [11] *Population blanche.* [12] *Juin de chaque année. Avant 1976 : sept.* [13] *Ouvriers qualifiés.*

NOTAS EXPLICATIVAS: Véase pág. 430.

[1] Abril de cada año. [2] Incl. los empleados. [3] Incl. las asignaciones familiares. [4] Tarifas medias. [5] Oct. de cada año. [6] Junio de cada año. Incl. el valor de los pagos en especie. [7] El alcance de la serie es mayor. [8] Sept. de cada año. [9] Adultos. [10] Mayo y nov. de cada año. [11] Población blanca. [12] Junio de cada año. Antes de 1976: sept. [13] Obreros calificados.

WAGES

20 Wages in construction
Salaires dans la construction
Salarios en la construcción

Earnings *(E.G.)* or rates *(R.T.)*
per hour *(h.)*, day *(d.j.)*,
week *(w.s.)* or month *(m.)*

Gains *(E.G.)* ou taux *(R.T.)*
par heure *(h.)*, jour *(d.j.)*,
semaine *(w.s.)* ou mois *(m.)*

Ganancias *(E.G.)* o tarifas *(R.T.)*
por hora *(h.)*, día *(d.j.)*,
semana *(w.s.)* o mes *(m.)*

Date / Date / Fecha	AFRICA — AFRIQUE — AFRICA				AMERICA — AMÉRIQUE — AMÉRICA			
	Swaziland (2) Males [1] / Hommes [1] / Hombres [1]	Tanzania (Tanganyika)	Zambia Zambians / Zambiens / Zambianos	Zambia Others / Autres / Otros	Argentina Unskilled workers / Ouvriers non qualifiés / Obreros no calificados	Barbados	Bermuda Masons / Maçons / Albañiles	Bolivia
	(E.G./m.) [2]	(E.G./m.) [3]	(E.G./m.) [4],[5]		(E.G./h.)	(E.G./w.s.) [6]	(R.T./h.)	(R.T./m.) [5]
	Emalangeni	Schillings	Kwacha	Kwacha	Pesos	Dollars	Dollars	Pesos
1970	·	231	...	...	1.79	·	·	775
1971	·	247	...	...	2.44	·	3.70	954
1972	25	247	59	365	3.55	·	4.09	1 089
1973	21	247	60	360	6.31	·	4.74	1 209
1974	27	456	60	364	8.32	67.66	5.30	1 209
1975	31	...	64	573	23.38	68.83	5.99	1 609
1976	52	...	76	342	64.43	92.00	6.37	1 609
1977	70	...	74	370	145.62	119.35	6.52	1 609
1978	94	...	...	...	...	...	...	2 053
1979	...	...	...	...	...	...	...	1 687

Date / Date / Fecha	AMERICA — AMÉRIQUE — AMÉRICA							
	Canada	Canada	Costa Rica	Cuba	El Salvador (San Salvador) [7]	El Salvador (San Salvador) [7]	Grenada (St. George's) Semi-skilled workers / Ouvriers semi-qualifiés / Obreros semicalificados	Guyana
	(E.G./h.)	(E.G./w.s.)	(E.G./m.)	(E.G./m.) [5]	(E.G./h.) [8]	(E.G./w.s.) [8]	(R.T./d.j.) [9]	(E.G./w.s.)
	Dollars	Dollars	Colones	Pesos	Colones	Colones	Dollars	Dollars
1970	4.21	165.04	·	·	0.69	30.73	5.00- 7.60	50.92
1971	4.75	186.20	·	141.08	0.71	31.98	8.00-10.00	54.95
1972	5.15	206.52	·	143.92	0.78	34.56	8.00-10.00	53.13
1973	5.66	223.86	616	144.42	0.89	38.36	8.00-10.00	58.39
1974	6.43	250.30	724	150.42	0.93	39.75	8.00-10.00	61.98
1975	7.53	290.95	883	156.90	...	...	...	70.61
1976	8.68	331.02	1 008	150.08	...	...	...	72.23
1977	9.77	369.88	1 166	144.42	...	...	...	81.14
1978	10.28	389.64	1 360	...	...	...	...	...
1979	11.04	422.28	1 561	...	...	...	...	...

EXPLANATORY NOTES: See p. 423.

[1] Unskilled workers. [2] June of each year. Prior to 1976: Sep. [3] Adult males. June of each year. [4] Fourth quarter of each year. [5] Incl. salaried employees. [6] Adults. [7] Metropolitan area. [8] Males. [9] Minimum rates.

NOTES EXPLICATIVES: Voir p. 426.

[1] Ouvriers non qualifiés. [2] Juin de chaque année. Avant 1976 : sept. [3] Hommes adultes. Juin de chaque année. [4] Quatrième trimestre de chaque année. [5] Y compris les employés. [6] Adultes. [7] Région métropolitaine. [8] Hommes. [9] Taux minima.

NOTAS EXPLICATIVAS: Véase pág. 430.

[1] Obreros no calificados. [2] Junio de cada año. Antes de 1976: sept. [3] Hombres adultos. Junio de cada año. [4] Cuarto trimestre de cada año. [5] Incl. los empleados. [6] Adultos. [7] Area metropolitana. [8] Hombres. [9] Tarifas mínimas.

20 Wages in construction
Salaires dans la construction
Salarios en la construcción

Earnings *(E.G.)* or rates *(R.T.)*
per hour *(h.)*, day *(d.j.)*,
week *(w.s.)* or month *(m.)*

Gains *(E.G.)* ou taux *(R.T.)*
par heure *(h.)*, jour *(d.j.)*,
semaine *(w.s.)* ou mois *(m.)*

Ganancias *(E.G.)* o tarifas *(R.T.)*
por hora *(h.)*, día *(d.j.)*,
semana *(w.s.)* o mes *(m.)*

Date / Date / Fecha	AMERICA — AMÉRIQUE — AMÉRICA						
	Honduras	México	Netherlands Antilles	Nicaragua	Perú (Lima-Callao)	Suriname	Trinidad and Tobago
	(E.G./w.s.)	*(E.G./h.)* [1]	*(E.G./m.)* [2]	*(E.G./h.)*	*(E.G./d.j.)* [3]	*(E.G./m.)*	*(R.T.)* [4,5]
	Lempiras	Pesos	Guilders	Córdobas	Soles	Guilders	(1970 = 100)
1970	.	5.31	.	3.39	117.25	.	100.0
1971	.	6.15	.	3.58	135.76	172	105.0
1972	.	5.67	.	3.34	148.72	180	108.3
1973	41.79	7.63	465	3.02	176.00	189	121.5
1974	14.02	10.48	501	4.16	200.23	198	175.1
1975	36.52	11.51	671	4.60	288.86	...	227.9
1976	54.12	15.56	694	4.76	336.66	...	240.6
1977	56.47	18.23	761	4.46	384.39	...	288.6 [6]
1978	74.52	...	835	6.54	516.05	...	361.6
1979	45.36	...	...	...	808.31	...	...

Date / Date / Fecha	AMERICA — AMÉRIQUE — AMÉRICA			ASIA — ASIE — ASIA				
	United States		Uruguay [7]	Bangladesh (Dacca)		Cyprus [1]	Israel	Japan
				Masons / Maçons / Albañiles	Carpenters / Charpentiers / Carpinteros			
	(E.G./h.)	*(E.G./w.s.)*	*(R.T./m.)* [2]	*(R.T./d.j.)* [8]		*(E.G./w.s.)* [9,10]	*(E.G./m.)* [2,12]	*(E.G./m.)* [2,15]
	$	$	(1970 = 100)	Taka	Taka	Pounds	Pounds	Yen
1970	5.24	195.45	100.0	.	.	11.24	637	71 727
1971	5.69	211.67	157.8	8.67	6.67	12.97	705	83 348
1972	6.06	221.19	243.1	9.83	7.83	14.45	807	95 552
1973	6.41	235.89	497.0	12.67	12.00	17.71	986	111 691 [14]
1974	6.81	249.25	897.1	17.62	16.10	20.82 [11]	1 354	138 630
1975	7.31	266.08	1 423.8	20.44	18.11	17.87	1 927 [13]	158 045
1976	7.71	283.73	1 941.5	24.18	20.19	17.43	2 708	177 641 [14]
1977	8.10	295.65	2 658.6	23.92	20.94	21.76	3 585	200 280
1978	8.65	318.32	3 639.8	24.34	22.04	28.80	5 471	218 758
1979	9.26	341.69	5 455.4	31.78	26.49	33.15	10 620 [14]	235 286 [14]

EXPLANATORY NOTES: See p. 423.

[1] Oct. of each year. [2] Incl. salaried employees. [3] June of each year. [4] Minimum rates. [5] Adults. May and Nov. of each year. [6] Beginning Nov. 1976: series linked to former series. [7] Montevideo; private sector only. Average rates. [8] Prior to 1974: May of each year. [9] Adults. [10] Incl. family allowances and the value of payments in kind. [11] Beginning July 1974: due to a change in the geographical scope of the series, data are not comparable with those for the preceding period. [12] Prior to July 1975: incl. family allowances. Beginning July 1975: incl. payments subject to income tax and the value of payments in kind. [13] Scope of series enlarged. [14] Sampling design revised. [15] Incl. family allowances, mid- and end-of-year bonuses.

NOTES EXPLICATIVES: Voir p. 426.

[1] *Oct. de chaque année.* [2] *Y compris les employés.* [3] *Juin de chaque année.* [4] *Taux minima.* [5] *Adultes. Mai et nov. de chaque année.* [6] *A partir de nov. 1976: série enchaînée à la précédente.* [7] *Montevideo; secteur privé seulement. Taux moyens.* [8] *Avant 1974: mai de chaque année.* [9] *Adultes.* [10] *Y compris les allocations familiales et la valeur des paiements en nature.* [11] *A partir de juillet 1974: en raison d'un changement de la portée géographique de la série, les données ne sont pas comparables avec celles de la période précédente.* [12] *Avant juillet 1975: y compris les allocations familiales. A partir de juillet 1975: y compris les versements soumis à l'impôt sur le revenu et la valeur des paiements en nature.* [13] *Portée de la série élargie.* [14] *Plan d'échantillonnage révisé.* [15] *Y compris les allocations familiales et les primes de mi- et de fin d'année.*

NOTAS EXPLICATIVAS: Véase pág. 430.

[1] Oct. de cada año. [2] Incl. los empleados. [3] Junio de cada año. [4] Tarifas mínimas. [5] Adultos. Mayo y nov. de cada año. [6] A partir de nov. de 1976: serie enlazada con la anterior. [7] Montevideo: sector privado solamente. Tarifas medias. [8] Antes de 1974: mayo de cada año. [9] Adultos. [10] Incl. las asignaciones familiares y el valor de los pagos en especie. [11] A partir de julio de 1974: en razón de un cambio del alcance geográfico de la serie, los datos no son comparables a los del período precedente. [12] Antes de julio de 1975: incl. las asignaciones familiares. A partir de julio de 1975: incl. los pagos sometidos al impuesto sobre la renta y el valor de los pagos en especie. [13] El alcance de la serie es mayor. [14] Diseño de la muestra revisado. [15] Incl. las asignaciones familiares y las primas de mitad y de fin de año.

WAGES

20 Wages in construction
Salaires dans la construction
Salarios en la construcción

Earnings *(E.G.)* or rates *(R.T.)*
per hour *(h.)*, day *(d.j.)*,
week *(w.s.)* or month *(m.)*

Gains *(E.G.)* ou taux *(R.T.)*
par heure *(h.)*, jour *(d.j.)*,
semaine *(w.s.)* ou mois *(m.)*

Ganancias *(E.G.)* o tarifas *(R.T.)*
por hora *(h.)*, día *(d.j.)*,
semana *(w.s.)* o mes *(m.)*

	ASIA — ASIE — ASIA					
Date *Date* Fecha	Jordan [1]	Korea, Rep. of	Singapore	Sri Lanka Building *Bâtiment* Edificación		République arabe syrienne [1]
	(E.G./d.j.) [2, 3]	*(E.G./m.)* [1, 4]	*(E.G./h.)* [5]	*(E.G./h.)* [6]	*(E.G./d.j.)* [6]	*(R.T./m.)* [3, 7]
	Fils	Won	Cents	Cents	Rupees	Pounds
1970	.	24 295	108	84.75	6.67	180
1971	.	26 645	114	85.95	6.73	184
1972	.	32 006	124	95.71	7.49	191
1973	1 337	36 740	135	88.97	6.40	191
1974	1 492	43 984	158	112.35	9.71	...
1975	1 631	61 590	164	126.75	10.74	281
1976	2 252	115 274	175	143.00	12.01	...
1977	2 985	154 519	187	148.00	13.02	...
1978	...	222 772	199	161.00	12.40	...
1979	...	247 835	215	170.00	16.96	...

	EUROPE — EUROPE — EUROPA					
Date *Date* Fecha	Austria			Belgique	Bulgarie [10]	Czechoslovakia [11]
	Masons *Maçons* Albañiles	Semi-skilled workers *Ouvriers semi-qualifiés* Obreros semicalificados	Unskilled workers *Ouvriers non qualifiés* Obreros no calificados	Males *Hommes* Hombres		
	(R.T./h.) [7]			*(E.G./h.)* [8]	*(E.G./m.)*	*(E.G./m.)* [1]
	Schilling	Schilling	Schilling	Francs	Leva	Korunas
1970	17.89	16.98	15.54	71.90	146.7	2 195
1971	19.19	18.20	16.67	78.11	149.0	2 269
1972	21.70	20.61	18.79	88.73 [9]	153.8	2 367
1973	24.04	22.78	20.80	103.55	161.3	2 483
1974	27.36	25.85	23.63	130.07	167.5	2 513
1975	32.25	30.48	27.80	150.55	174.1	2 589
1976	36.15	34.17	31.17	172.29	178.4	2 658
1977	39.97	37.80	34.48	190.50	179.2	2 696
1978	43.53	41.15	37.53	202.21	179.5	2 776
1979	45.97	43.46	39.61	217.66	190.3 *	2 835

EXPLANATORY NOTES: See p. 423.

NOTES EXPLICATIVES: Voir p. 426.

NOTAS EXPLICATIVAS: Véase pág. 430.

[1] Incl. salaried employees. [2] April of each year. [3] Adults. [4] Incl. family allowances and the value of payments in kind. [5] August of each year. Prior to 1975: July. [6] March and Sep. of each year. [7] Minimum rates. [8] Oct. of each year. [9] New industrial classification. [10] Socialised sector. [11] State industry.

[1] *Y compris les employés.* [2] *Avril de chaque année.* [3] *Adultes.* [4] *Y compris les allocations familiales et la valeur des paiements en nature.* [5] *Août de chaque année. Avant 1975 : juillet.* [6] *Mars et sept. de chaque année.* [7] *Taux minima.* [8] *Oct. de chaque année.* [9] *Nouvelle classification industrielle.* [10] *Secteur socialisé.* [11] *Industrie d'Etat.*

[1] Incl. los empleados. [2] Abril de cada año. [3] Adultos. [4] Incl. las asignaciones familiares y el valor de los pagos en especie. [5] Agosto de cada año. Antes de 1975: julio. [6] Marzo y sept. de cada año. [7] Tarifas mínimas. [8] Oct. de cada año. [9] Nueva clasificación industrial. [10] Sector socializado. [11] Industria de Estado.

20 Wages in construction
Salaires dans la construction
Salarios en la construcción

Earnings *(E.G.)* or rates *(R.T.)*
per hour *(h.)*, day *(d.j.)*,
week *(w.s.)* or month *(m.)*

Gains *(E.G.)* ou taux *(R.T.)*
par heure *(h.)*, jour *(d.j.)*,
semaine *(w.s.)* ou mois *(m.)*

Ganancias *(E.G.)* o tarifas *(R.T.)*
por hora *(h.)*, día *(d.j.)*,
semana *(w.s.)* o mes *(m.)*

Date / Date / Fecha	Denmark	España	Finland — Building *Bâtiment* Edificación	France	German Democratic Republic [7]	Germany, Fed. Rep. of [9]
	(E.G./h.) [1]	*(E.G./h.)* [2]	*(E.G./h.)* [3]	*(E.G./h.)* [4]	*(E.G./m.)* [8]	*(E.G./h.)* [10]
	Öre	Pesetas	Markkaa	Francs	Mark	Mark
1970	1 812	31.59	6.74	5.72	830	6.67
1971	2 045	36.51	7.82	6.34	843	7.43
1972	2 200	43.06	9.01	7.45 [5]	856	8.12
1973	2 528	51.83	10.63	8.58	871	8.98 [6]
1974	2 917	69.91	13.35	10.08	908	9.68
1975	3 334	89.39	15.67	11.63	937	10.17
1976	3 742	117.67	17.01	13.76 [6]	972	10.75
1977	4 180	...	17.98	15.57	989	11.39
1978	4 644	...	19.01	17.35	1 017	12.14
1979	5 209	...	20.74	19.62	1 021 *	13.00

EUROPE — EUROPE — EUROPA

Date / Date / Fecha	Gibraltar	Hongrie [12]	Ireland [14] — Skilled workers *Ouvriers qualifiés* Obreros calificados	Ireland [14] — Semi-skilled and unskilled workers [15] *Ouvriers semi-qualifiés et non qualifiés* [15] Obreros semicalificados y no calificados [15]	Italie	Luxembourg — Males *Hommes* Hombres
	(E.G./w.s.) [11]	*(E.G./m.)* [3, 13]	*(E.G./h.)*	*(E.G./h.)*	*(E.G./h.)* [3, 16]	*(E.G./h.)* [18]
	£	Forints	Pence	Pence	Lire	Francs
1970	16.78	2 244	53.9	44.9	603	69.73
1971	19.06	2 301	62.1	52.8	673	75 34
1972	19.83	2 392	74.5	64.3	735	82.41 [19]
1973	25.50	2 614	81.1	70.6	898	96.40
1974	26.69	2 830	97.5	86.4	1 114	117.51
1975	31.39	3 006	121.7	107.5	1 552 [5]	139.25
1976	34.81	3 195	139.7	121.9	1 891	157.43
1977	42.51	3 384	167.0	146.8	2 394	169.11
1978	64.69	3 660	185.3	158.5	3 098 [17]	171.19
1979	65.42	3 842	230.7	194.4	...	179.21

EUROPE — EUROPE — EUROPA

EXPLANATORY NOTES: See p. 423.

[1] Adults. Excl. vacation pay July-sep. of each year. [2] Incl. salaried employees. [3] Incl. the value of payments in kind. [4] Oct. of each year, except for 1968-71: Sep. [5] Series replacing former series. [6] Sampling design revised. [7] State sector. [8] Incl. family allowances. [9] Building only. [10] Incl. family allowances paid directly by the employer; males only. [11] Oct. of each year except for 1970-72: April and Oct. and 1974-76: April. [12] Socialised sector. [13] Incl. loyalty money. [14] Sep. of each year. Private sector. [15] Workers on adult rates of pay. [16] Prior to 1975: excl. payments for annual vacation and public holidays. [17] Scope of series revised. [18] Oct. of each year. [19] New industrial classification.

NOTES EXPLICATIVES: Voir p. 426.

[1] *Adultes. Non compris les versements pour congés payés. Juillet-sept. de chaque année.* [2] *Y compris les employés.* [3] *Y compris la valeur des paiements en nature.* [4] *Oct. de chaque année, sauf pour 1968-1971: sept.* [5] *Série remplaçant la précédente.* [6] *Plan d'échantillonnage révisé.* [7] *Secteur d'Etat.* [8] *Y compris les allocations familiales.* [9] *Bâtiment seulement.* [10] *Y compris les allocations familiales payées directement par les employeurs; hommes seulement.* [11] *Oct. de chaque année sauf pour 1970-1972: avril et oct., et 1974-1976: avril.* [12] *Secteur socialisé.* [13] *Y compris les primes d'assiduité.* [14] *Sept. de chaque année. Secteur privé.* [15] *Travailleurs rémunérés sur la base de taux de salaire pour adultes.* [16] *Avant 1975: non compris les paiements pour congés annuels et jours fériés.* [17] *Portée de la série révisée.* [18] *Oct. de chaque année.* [19] *Nouvelle classification industrielle.*

NOTAS EXPLICATIVAS: Véase pág. 430.

[1] Adultos. Excl. los pagos por vacaciones. Julio-sept. de cada año. [2] Incl. los empleados. [3] Incl. el valor de los pagos en especie. [4] Oct. de cada año, salvo para 1968-1971: sept. [5] Serie que substituye a la anterior. [6] Diseño de la muestra revisado. [7] Sector de Estado. [8] Incl. las asignaciones familiares. [9] Edificación solamente. [10] Incl. las asignaciones familiares pagadas directamente por los empleadores; hombres solamente. [11] Oct. de cada año, salvo para 1970-1972: abril y oct., y 1974-1976: abril. [12] Sector socializado. [13] Incl. las primas de asiduidad. [14] Sept. de cada año. Sector privado. [15] Trabajadores pagados sobre la base de tarifas de salarios para adultos. [16] Antes de 1975: excl. los pagos por vacaciones anuales y días feriados. [17] El alcance de la serie es revisado. [18] Oct. de cada año. [19] Nueva clasificación industrial.

20 Wages in construction
Salaires dans la construction
Salarios en la construcción

Earnings *(E.G.)* or rates *(R.T.)*
per hour *(h.)*, day *(d.j.)*,
week *(w.s.)* or month *(m.)*

Gains *(E.G.)* ou taux *(R.T.)*
par heure *(h.)*, jour *(d.j.)*,
semaine *(w.s.)* ou mois *(m.)*

Ganancias *(E.G.)* o tarifas *(R.T.)*
por hora *(h.)*, día *(d.j.)*,
semana *(w.s.)* o mes *(m.)*

	EUROPE — EUROPE — EUROPA						
Date / *Date* / Fecha	Malta	Netherlands	Norway	Pologne [6]	Portugal	Roumanie [6]	Suisse
	Males [1] / *Hommes* [1] / Hombres [1]	Males [1] / *Hommes* [1] / Hombres [1]					
	(E.G./h.) [2]	(E.G./h.) [3]	(E.G./h.) [4, 5]	(E.G./m.) [2, 4]	(E.G./h.)	(E.G./m.) [2]	(E.G./h.) [8]
	Cents	Guilders	Kroner	Zlotys	Escudos	Lei	Francs
1970	21.3	5.56	17.55	2 675	.	1 555	.
1971	24.8	6.59	19.36	2 796	11.60	1 608	.
1972	25.6	7.44	21.04	2 992	12.80	1 648	.
1973	...	8.48	22.64	3 471	14.80	1 734	10.36
1974	28.3	9.70	26.01	3 881	20.10	1 925	11.97
1975	33.8	11.06	30.62	4 511	29.60	2 111	12.68
1976	40.3	11.94	35.29	4 784	34.60	2 203	12.62
1977	...	13.36	39.44	5 063	40.30	2 081 [7]	13.07
1978	...	14.40	43.13	5 296	43.90	2 274	13.22
1979	...	...	44.97	5 678 *	...	2 346	13.58

	EUROPE — EUROPE — EUROPA						
Date / *Date* / Fecha	Suisse [9]			Sweden	Turquie	United Kingdom	
	Males — *Hommes* — Hombres						
	Skilled / *Qualifiés* / Calificados	Semi-skilled and unskilled / *Semi-qualifiés et non qualifiés* / Semicalificados y no calificados	Total	Males [1] / *Hommes* [1] / Hombres [1]		Males [14] / *Hommes* [14] / Hombres [14]	
	(E.G./h.) [1, 3]			(E.G./h.) [10, 11]	(E.G./d.j.) [2, 13]	(E.G./h.) [3]	(E.G./w.s.) [3]
	Francs	Francs	Francs	Kronor	Liras	Pence	£
1970	.	.	.	17.64	33.72	56.5	26.85
1971	.	.	.	18.68 [12]	38.25	63.8	30.11
1972	.	.	.	20.67	41.71	77.9	36.59
1973	.	.	.	22.27	48.10	88.7	41.41
1974	12.30	9.89	10.95	24.03	64.51	104.2	48.75
1975	12.89	10.64	11.63	26.94	77.15	133.6	60.38
1976	12.90	10.61	11.61	31.26	105.54	148.5	65.80
1977	14.08	11.76	12.80	34.71	126.60	163.1	72.91
1978	14.22	11.77	12.87	38.31	188.81	182.1	81.77
1979	14.68	12.13	13.27	41.17	270.36	209.5	94.06

EXPLANATORY NOTES: See p. 423.

NOTES EXPLICATIVES: Voir p. 426.

NOTAS EXPLICATIVAS: Véase pág. 430.

[1] Adults. [2] Incl. salaried employees. [3] Oct. of each year. [4] Incl. the value of payments in kind. [5] Adult males. [6] Socialised sector. [7] Beginning 1977: net earnings after deduction of taxes. [8] Accident insurance statistics. Prior to 1975: incl. family allowance. [9] Statistics of establishments. Incl. family allowances. [10] Incl. holiday and sick-leave payments and the value of payments in kind. [11] Beginning 1976: second quarter of each year. [12] New industrial classification. [13] Sep. of each year. [14] Full-time adult wage earners.

[1] *Adultes.* [2] *Y compris les employés.* [3] *Oct. de chaque année.* [4] *Y compris la valeur des paiements en nature.* [5] *Hommes adultes.* [6] *Secteur socialisé.* [7] *A partir de 1977: gains nets après déduction de l'impôt sur le revenu.* [8] *Statistiques d'assurance-accidents. Avant 1975: y compris les allocations familiales.* [9] *Statistiques d'établissements. Y compris les allocations familiales.* [10] *Y compris les versements au titre de vacances et de congés de maladie et la valeur des paiements en nature.* [11] *A partir de 1976: deuxième trimestre de chaque année.* [12] *Nouvelle classification industrielle.* [13] *Sept. de chaque année.* [14] *Ouvriers adultes à plein temps.*

[1] Adultos. [2] Incl. los empleados. [3] Oct. de cada año. [4] Incl. el valor de los pagos en especie. [5] Hombres adultos. [6] Sector socializado. [7] A partir de 1977: ganancias netas después deducción de los impuestos sobre la renta. [8] Estadísticas del seguro de accidentes. Antes de 1975: incl. las asignaciones familiares. [9] Estadísticas de establecimientos. Incl. las asignaciones familiares. [10] Incl. los pagos por vacaciones y licencias de enfermedad y el valor de los pagos en especie. [11] A partir de 1976: segundo trimestre de cada año. [12] Nueva clasificación industrial. [13] Sept. de cada año. [14] Obreros adultos a tiempo completo.

20 Wages in construction
Salaires dans la construction
Salarios en la construcción

Earnings (E.G.) or rates (R.T.)
per hour (h.), day (d.j.),
week (w.s.) or month (m.)

Gains (E.G.) ou taux (R.T.)
par heure (h.), jour (d.j.),
semaine (w.s.) ou mois (m.)

Ganancias (E.G.) o tarifas (R.T.)
por hora (h.), día (d.j.),
semana (w.s.) o mes (m.)

Date / Date / Fecha	EUROPE EUROPE EUROPA	OCEANIA — OCÉANIE — OCEANÍA					
			Australia		New Zealand (1)		
			Males [4] *Hommes* [4] Hombres [4]	Fiji	Males [4,8] — *Hommes* [4,8] — *Hombres* [4,8]		
	Yugoslavia [1]	American Samoa			Bricklayers *Briqueteurs* Enladrilladores	Carpenters *Charpentiers* Carpinteros	Labourers *Manœuvres* Obreros no calificados
	(E.G./m.) [2]	(R.T./h.) [3]	(E.G./h.) [2,5]	(R.T./d.j.) [7]	(R.T./w.s.) [3]		
	Dinars	Dollars	Dollars	Dollars	Dollars	Dollars	Dollars
1970	1 109	0.88	2.02	2.71	47.23	43.62	36.75
1971	1 342	1.00	2.26	2.88	57.55	58.20	46.10
1972	1 610	1.08	2.27 [6]	3.21	62.58	63.12	49.92
1973	1 848	1.08	2.66	4.11	68.59		54.88
1974	2 340	1.20	3.55	5.01	78.81		63.34
1975	2 968	1.20	3.97	6.37	89.45		76.21
1976	3 464	1.35	4.54	7.16	102.81		87.09
1977	4 090	1.45	4.99	7.70	115.74		98.07
1978	4 927	1.52	5.30	8.21	130.30		109.71
1979	5 911	1.60	5.74	8.78 *	...		...

Date / Date / Fecha	OCEANIA — OCÉANIE — OCEANÍA					
	New Zealand (2) M. + F. [2] H. + F. [2] H. + M. [2]	Nouvelle-Calédonie Labourers [11] *Manœuvres* [11] Obreros no calificados [11]	Samoa (Apia)	URSS [1,13]	RSS de Biélorussie [1]	RSS d'Ukraine [1]
	(E.G./h.) [9,10]	(R.T./h.) [12]	(E.G./w.s.) [2,10]	(E.G./m.) [2]	(E.G./m.) [2]	(E.G./m.) [2]
	Dollars	Francs (CFP)	Sene	Roubles	Roubles	Roubles
1970	1.33	100.32	833	153.0	.	135.0
1971	1.59	109.12	965	157.4	135.3	139.5
1972	1.75	117.04	1 022	162.3	139.3	143.8
1973	1.96	124.00	879	167.2	144.1	146.2
1974	2.25	145.00	1 036	173.7	149.7	150.5
1975	2.55	156.00	...	181.1	154.2	155.9
1976	2.89	166.00	1 302	185.2	157.2	158.6
1977	3.27	175.00	2 046	189.2	160.8	162.1
1978	3.65	188.00	...	191.1	165.8	167.2
1979	...	206.00	...	196.6	169.1	171.6

EXPLANATORY NOTES: See p. 423.

[1] Socialised sector. [2] Incl. salaried employees. [3] Minimum rates. [4] Adults. [5] Oct. of each year. [6] Scope of series enlarged. [7] June of each year. [8] Building only. [9] April and Oct. of each year. [10] Incl. juveniles. [11] First category. Dec. of each year. [12] Prior to Sep. 1972: incl. production bonuses. [13] Incl. Byelorussian SSR and Ukrainian SSR, shown separately in this table.

NOTES EXPLICATIVES: Voir p. 426.

[1] *Secteur socialisé.* [2] *Y compris les employés.* [3] *Taux minima.* [4] *Adultes.* [5] *Oct. de chaque année.* [6] *Portée de la série élargie.* [7] *Juin de chaque année.* [8] *Bâtiment seulement.* [9] *Avril et oct. de chaque année.* [10] *Y compris les jeunes gens.* [11] *Première catégorie. Déc. de chaque année.* [12] *Avant sept. 1972: y compris les primes de productivité.* [13] *Y compris les RSS de Biélorussie et d'Ukraine, figurant séparément dans ce tableau.*

NOTAS EXPLICATIVAS: Véase pág. 430.

[1] Sector socializado. [2] Incl. los empleados. [3] Tarifas mínimas. [4] Adultos. [5] Oct. de cada año. [6] El alcance de la serie es mayor. [7] Junio de cada año. [8] Edificación solamente. [9] Abril y oct. de cada año. [10] Incl. los jóvenes. [11] Primera categoría. Dic. de cada año. [12] Antes de sept. de 1972: incl. las primas de producción. [13] Incl. las RSS de Bielorrusia y de Ucrania, que figuran separadamente en este cuadro.

21 Wages in transport, storage and communication (Excl. sea transport)
Salaires dans les transports, entrepôts et communications (Non compris les transports par mer)
Salarios en los transportes, almacenaje y comunicaciones (Excl. el transporte marítimo)

Earnings *(E.G.)* or rates *(R.T.)*
per hour *(h.)*, day *(d.j.)*,
week *(w.s.)* or month *(m.)*

Gains *(E.G.)* ou taux *(R.T.)*
par heure *(h.)*, jour *(d.j.)*,
semaine *(w.s.)* ou mois *(m.)*

Ganancias *(E.G.)* o tarifas *(R.T.)*
por hora *(h.)*, día *(d.j.)*,
semana *(w.s.)* o mes *(m.)*

AFRICA — AFRIQUE — AFRICA

Date / Date / Fecha	Algérie	Burundi (Bujumbura)	Cameroun — Skilled workers / Ouvriers qualifiés / Obreros calificados	Egypt	Kenya	Malawi
	(E.G./h.) [1]	(E.G./m.) [2,3]	(R.T./h.) [4]	(E.G./w.s.) [5]	(E.G./m.) [2,6]	(E.G./m.) [2]
	Dinars	Francs	Francs (CFA)	Piastres	Shillings	Kwacha
1970	2.10	.	63-173	440	770.40	49.87
1971	2.91	3 925	87-174	425	737.40	51.94
1972	2.43	4 197	90-179	456	785.40	52.91
1973	2.01	4 225	98-197	507	859.40	56.21
1974	2.45	4 096	101-207	479	996.40	58.64
1975	2.82	4 186	120-131	737	1 104.20	62.38
1976	...	...	131-142	682 *	1 176.00	62.00
1977	3.64	9 811	141-153	...	1 238.70	60.80 [7]
1978	...	11 254	162-178	...	1 382.10	65.41
1979	...	11 318	168-190	...	1 606.10	

AFRICA — AFRIQUE — AFRICA

Date / Date / Fecha	Mauritius	Nigeria	Sierra Leone [9,10]	South Africa, Rep. of — Transport [12] / Transports [12] / Transportes [12]		Swaziland — Males / Hommes / Hombres — Skilled / Qualifiés / Calificados	Unskilled / Non qualifiés / No calificados	Tanzania (Tanganyika)
				Total	[13]			
	(E.G./d.j.) [8]	(R.T./d.j.)	(E.G./w.s.) [11]	(E.G./m.)		(E.G./m.) [14]		(E.G./m.) [15]
	Rupees	Naira	Leones	Rand	Rand	Emalangeni	Emalangeni	Shillings
1970	11.43	.	7.90	172.90	295.40	.	.	418
1971	8.27	.	9.96	185.30	318.40	.	.	470
1972	13.13	.	10.63	184.50	320.30	213	42	502
1973	14.79	.	9.51	220.30	283.80	281	39	637
1974	18.27	2.00	9.82	245.50	429.50	224	43	838
1975	18.54	2.00	12.58	283.20	508.10	344	71	...
1976	31.24	2.08	14.68	300.30	542.80	413	89	...
1977	34.44	2.24	14.95	311.40	555.70	238	85	...
1978	38.25	2.24	15.05	332.00	587.30	360	89	...
1979	50.44	2.46	15.60	378.70	667.40	...	...	...

EXPLANATORY NOTES: See p. 423.

[1] April of each year. [2] Incl. salaried employees. [3] Incl. family allowances. [4] Average rates. [5] Oct. of each year. [6] June of each year. Incl. the value of payments in kind. [7] Scope of series enlarged. [8] Sep. of each year. [9] Adults. [10] Incl. sea transport. [11] May and Nov. of each year. [12] Railways and harbours. [13] White population. [14] June of each year. Prior to 1976: Sep. [15] Adult males; June of each year.

NOTES EXPLICATIVES: Voir p. 426.

[1] *Avril de chaque année.* [2] *Y compris les employés.* [3] *Y compris les allocations familiales.* [4] *Taux moyens.* [5] *Oct. de chaque année.* [6] *Juin de chaque année. Y compris la valeur des paiements en nature.* [7] *Portée de la série élargie.* [8] *Sept. de chaque année.* [9] *Adultes.* [10] *Y compris les transports par mer.* [11] *Mai et nov. de chaque année.* [12] *Chemins de fer et ports.* [13] *Population blanche.* [14] *Juin de chaque année. Avant 1976: sept.* [15] *Hommes adultes; juin de chaque année.*

NOTAS EXPLICATIVAS: Véase pág. 430.

[1] Abril de cada año. [2] Incl. los empleados. [3] Incl. las asignaciones familiares. [4] Tarifas medias. [5] Oct. de cada año. [6] Junio de cada año. Incl. el valor de los pagos en especie. [7] El alcance de la serie es mayor. [8] Sept. de cada año. [9] Adultos. [10] Incl. el transporte marítimo. [11] Mayo y nov. de cada año. [12] Ferrocarriles y puertos. [13] Población blanca. [14] Junio de cada año. Antes de 1976: sept. [15] Hombres adultos; junio de cada año.

21 Wages in transport, storage and communication (Excl. sea transport)
Salaires dans les transports, entrepôts et communications (Non compris les transports par mer)
Salarios en los transportes, almacenaje y comunicaciones (Excl. el transporte marítimo)

Earnings *(E.G.)* or rates *(R.T.)* per hour *(h.)*, day *(d.j.)*, week *(w.s.)* or month *(m.)*

Gains *(E.G.)* ou taux *(R.T.)* par heure *(h.)*, jour *(d.j.)*, semaine *(w.s.)* ou mois *(m.)*

Ganancias *(E.G.)* o tarifas *(R.T.)* por hora *(h.)*, día *(d.j.)*, semana *(w.s.)* o mes *(m.)*

	AFRICA — AFRIQUE — AFRICA		AMERICA — AMÉRIQUE — AMÉRICA					
	Zambia		Argentina		Bermuda			
Date / Date / Fecha	Transport and communication / Transports et communications / Transportes y comunicaciones		Road haulage / Camionnage / Camionaje	Barbados	Buses / Autobus / Autobuses — Drivers / Conducteurs / Conductores	Bolivia	Canada	Costa Rica [5]
	Zambians / Zambiens / Zambianos	Others / Autres / Otros						
	(E.G./m.) [1,2]		*(E.G./h.)* [3]	*(E.G./w.s.)* [4]	*(R.T./h.)*	*(R.T./m.)* [2]	*(E.G./w.s.)* [2]	*(E.G./m.)*
	Kwacha	Kwacha	Pesos	Dollars	Dollars	Pesos	Dollars	Colones
1970	...	...	1.67	·	2.64	982	142.35	·
1971	...	...	2.27	·	2.64	1 062	154.14	·
1972	100	345	3.32	·	3.13	1 197	167.94	·
1973	108	365	5.75	·	3.28	1 317	181.89	920
1974	116	388	7.32	114.06	3.66	1 717	204.39	1 076
1975	153	615	22.97	108.54	3.90	1 717	233.98	1 289
1976	152	442	66.65	124.86	4.17	1 717	262.02	1 433
1977	175	530	270.82	148.78	4.74	2 577	291.15	1 591
1978	...	...	...	...	5.00	2 026	313.28	1 788
1979	...	...	...	...	5.36	...	341.45	2 042

	AMERICA — AMÉRIQUE — AMÉRICA								
		Grenada (St. George's)		Guyana		México			Perú (Lima-Callao)
Date / Date / Fecha	Cuba	Transport [6] / Transports [6] / Transportes [6]		Transport and communication / Transports et communications / Transportes y comunicaciones	Honduras	Transport / Transports / Transportes	Netherlands Antilles	Nicaragua	
		Drivers / Conducteurs / Conductores	Conductors / Receveurs / Cobradores						
	(E.G./m.) [2]	*(R.T./m.)* [7]		*(E.G./w.s.)*	*(E.G./w.s.)*	*(E.G./h.)* [8]	*(E.G./m.)* [2]	*(E.G./h.)*	*(E.G./d.j.)* [9,10]
	Pesos	Dollars	Dollars	Dollars	Lempiras	Pesos	Guilders	Córdobas	Soles
1970	·	75.00	50.00	45.01	·	8.09	·	3.80	115.76
1971	150.00	90.00	60.00	50.64	·	9.75	·	3.95	130.97
1972	149.25	90.00	60.00	54.26	·	9.83	·	3.96	159.60
1973	151.25	90.00	60.00	55.22	81.88	11.79	630	4.41	222.00
1974	155.00	90.00	60.00	57.20	67.72	...	640	4.80	183.25
1975	162.08	...	...	56.04	109.10	...	695	4.80	299.06
1976	167.75	...	...	63.30	49.72	...	824	5.26	334.74
1977	173.75	...	...	66.84	58.01	...	896	5.05	403.27
1978	...	...	...	...	81.56	...	1 107	6.71	514.38
1979	...	...	...	...	82.98	...	...	...	834.34

EXPLANATORY NOTES: See p. 423.

1 Fourth quarter of each year. 2 Incl. salaried employees. 3 Unskilled workers. 4 Adults. 5 Incl. sea transport. 6 Public transport. 7 Minimum rates. 8 Oct. of each year. 9 June of each year. 10 Beginning 1975: incl. sea transport.

NOTES EXPLICATIVES: Voir p. 426.

1 *Quatrième trimestre de chaque année.* 2 *Y compris les employés.* 3 *Ouvriers non qualifiés.* 4 *Adultes.* 5 *Y compris les transports par mer.* 6 *Transports publics.* 7 *Taux minima.* 8 *Oct. de chaque année.* 9 *Juin de chaque année.* 10 *A partir de 1975 : y compris les transports par mer.*

NOTAS EXPLICATIVAS: Véase pág. 430.

1 Cuarto trimestre de cada año. 2 Incl. los empleados. 3 Obreros no calificados. 4 Adultos. 5 Incl. el transporte marítimo. 6 Transportes públicos. 7 Tarifas mínimas. 8 Oct. de cada año. 9 Junio de cada año. 10 A partir de 1975: incl. el transporte marítimo.

21 Wages in transport, storage and communication (Excl. sea transport)
Salaires dans les transports, entrepôts et communications (Non compris les transports par mer)
Salarios en los transportes, almacenaje y comunicaciones (Excl. el transporte marítimo)

Earnings (E.G.) or rates (R.T.)
per hour (h.), day (d.j.),
week (w.s.) or month (m.)

Gains (E.G.) ou taux (R.T.)
par heure (h.), jour (d.j.),
semaine (w.s.) ou mois (m.)

Ganancias (E.G.) o tarifas (R.T.)
por hora (h.), día (d.j.),
semana (w.s.) o mes (m.)

Date / Date / Fecha	Suriname	Trinidad and Tobago [1]	United States				Uruguay [5]
			Principal railways / Grandes lignes de chemin de fer / Líneas principales de ferrocarriles	Local railways and buses [4] / Chemins de fer et autobus locaux [4] / Ferrocarriles y autobuses locales [4]	Principal railways / Grandes lignes de chemin de fer / Líneas principales de ferrocarriles	Local railways and buses [4] / Chemins de fer et autobus locaux [4] / Ferrocarriles y autobuses locales [4]	
	(E.G./m.)	(R.T.) [2]	(E.G./h.)		(E.G./w.s.)		(R.T./m.) [6,7]
	Guilders	(1970 = 100)	$	$	$	$	(1970 = 100)
1970	.	100.0	3.89	3.38	171.94	142.30	100.0
1971	105	116.9	4.36	3.61	188.35	150.90	127.5
1972	110	136.5	4.89	3.83	214.67	161.63	187.2
1973	115	143.7	5.40	4.13	240.30	173.05	363.4
1974	120	147.8	5.68	4.58	249.92	190.07	618.0
1975	...	154.4	6.05	5.01	261.97	203.41	1 005.9
1976	...	218.5	6.88	5.53	261.97	227.84	1 381.2
1977	...	269.8 [3]	7.39	6.19	321.47	256.89	1 873.4
1978	...	309.8	7.87	6.84	343.92	282.49	2 564.8
1979	...	...	8.94	6.94	392.47	285.23	3 844.2

Note: The 1976 Principal railways (E.G./w.s.) value reads 261.97; 1975 reads 261.97; the value 300.66 appears for 1976.

ASIA — ASIE — ASIA

Date / Date / Fecha	Burma — Transport [1] / Transports [1] / Transportes [1]		Cyprus	Israel	Japan	Jordan	Korea, Rep. of
	Males / Hommes / Hombres	Females / Femmes / Mujeres					
	(E.G./m.) [6,8]		(E.G./w.s.) [10,11]	(E.G./m.) [6,13]	(E.G./m.) [6,16]	(E.G./d.j.) [6,17]	(E.G./m.) [6,11]
	Kyats	Kyats	Pounds	Pounds	Yen	Fils	Won
1970	(147.48	214.61	11.74	994	84 825	.	18 524
1971	145.85	212.64	12.65	1 158	97 645	.	21 288
1972	149.95 [9]	214.58 [9]	14.07	1 302	113 217	.	27 010
1973	165.58	217.16	16.99	1 676	135 732 [15]	1 680	28 875
1974	167.07	215.90	16.67 [12]	2 262	171 363	1 892	36 497
1975	164.82	215.79	17.96	3 081 [14]	198 669	1 864	45 509
1976	171.49	196.95	20.29	4 016	224 276 [15]	2 253	64 287
1977	208.53	252.60	22.26	6 003	246 194	2 544	89 188
1978	214.03	257.78	25.75	9 504	260 770	...	119 245
1979	...	...	33.32	17 380 [15]	267 414 [15]	...	157 985

EXPLANATORY NOTES: See p. 423.

NOTES EXPLICATIVES: Voir p. 426.

NOTAS EXPLICATIVAS: Véase pág. 430.

[1] Incl. sea transport. [2] Minimum rates. Adults. May and Nov. of each year. [3] Beginning Nov. 1976: series linked to former series. [4] Excl. government-operated transport. [5] Montevideo; private sector. [6] Incl. salaried employees. [7] Average rates. [8] Beginning 1973: March and Sep. of each year. [9] April and Sep. [10] Oct. of each year. Adults. [11] Incl. family allowances and the value of payments in kind. [12] Beginning July 1974: due to a change in the geographical scope of the series, data are not comparable with those for the preceding period. [13] Prior to July 1975: incl. family allowances. Beginning July 1975: incl. payments subject to income tax and the value of payments in kind. [14] Scope of series enlarged. [15] Sampling design revised. [16] Incl. family allowance, mid- and end-of-year bonuses. [17] April of each year. Adults.

[1] Y compris les transports par mer. [2] Taux minima. Adultes. Mai et nov. de chaque année. [3] A partir de nov. 1976 : série enchaînée à la précédente. [4] Non compris les transports gérés par le gouvernement. [5] Montevideo ; secteur privé. [6] Y compris les employés. [7] Taux moyens. [8] A partir de 1973 : mars et sept. de chaque année. [9] Avril et sept. [10] Oct. de chaque année. Adultes. [11] Y compris les allocations familiales et la valeur des paiements en nature. [12] A partir de juillet 1974 : en raison d'un changement de la portée géographique de la série, les données ne sont pas comparables avec celles de la période précédente. [13] Avant juillet 1975 : y compris les allocations familiales. A partir de juillet 1975 : y compris les versements soumis à l'impôt sur le revenu et la valeur des paiements en nature. [14] Portée de la série élargie. [15] Plan d'échantillonnage révisé. [16] Y compris les allocations familiales et les primes de mi- et de fin d'année. [17] Avril de chaque année. Adultes.

[1] Incl. el transporte marítimo. [2] Tarifas mínimas. Adultos. Mayo y nov. de cada año. [3] A partir de nov. de 1976: serie enlazada con la anterior. [4] Excl. los transportes administrados por el Gobierno. [5] Montevideo; sector privado. [6] Incl. los empleados. [7] Tarifas medias. [8] A partir de 1973: marzo y sept. de cada año. [9] Abril y sept. [10] Oct. de cada año. Adultos. [11] Incl. las asignaciones familiares y el valor de los pagos en especie. [12] A partir de julio de 1974: en razón de un cambio del alcance geográfico de la serie, los datos no son comparables a los del período precedente. [13] Antes de julio de 1975: incl. las asignaciones familiares. A partir de julio de 1976: incl. los pagos sometidos al impuesto sobre la renta y el valor de los pagos en especie. [14] El alcance de la serie es mayor. [15] Diseño de la muestra revisado. [16] Incl. las asignaciones familiares y las primas de mitad y de fin de año. [17] Abril de cada año. Adultos.

21 Wages in transport, storage and communication (Excl. sea transport)
Salaires dans les transports, entrepôts et communications (Non compris les transports par mer)
Salarios en los transportes, almacenaje y comunicaciones (Excl. el transporte marítimo)

Earnings *(E.G.)* or rates *(R.T.)*
per hour *(h.)*, day *(d.j.)*,
week *(w.s.)* or month *(m.)*

Gains *(E.G.)* ou taux *(R.T.)*
par heure *(h.)*, jour *(d.j.)*,
semaine *(w.s.)* ou mois *(m.)*

Ganancias *(E.G.)* o tarifas *(R.T.)*
por hora *(h.)*, día *(d.j.)*,
semana *(w.s.)* o mes *(m.)*

	ASIA — ASIE — ASIA					
	Malaysia	**Philippines**		**Sri Lanka**		
Date	**Peninsular Malaysia**					
Date	Road haulage	Transport and communication [3]	Singapore [3,4]	Transport		**République arabe syrienne** [2,6]
Fecha	*Camionnage*	*Transports et communications* [3]		*Transports*		
	Camionaje	Transportes y comunicaciones [3]		Transportes		
	(E.G./m.) [1,2]	*(E.G./m.)*	*(E.G./h.)*	*(E.G./h.)* [5]	*(E.G./d.j.)* [5]	*(R.T./m.)* [7]
	Ringgits	Pesos	Cents	Cents	Rupees	Pounds
1970	.	230	113	137.51	12.28	
1971	236	239	123	148.27	13.85	190
1972	242	276	127	144.23	13.31	190
1973	280	310	153	125.08	11.32	190
1974	320	342	170	158.95	13.91	190
1975	322	361	182	170.41	16.99	...
1976	353	...	199	188.00	18.52	262
1977	373	...	209	252.10	21.47	...
1978	440	...	222	265.44	23.89	...
1979	...	...	249	321.00	29.48	...

	EUROPE — EUROPE — EUROPA						
	Austria		**Belgique**		**Bulgarie** [3,10]		
Date	Transport and storage						
	Transports et entrepôts		Males [8]	Females	Transport and storage	**Czechoslovakia** [11]	**France** [12]
Date	Transportes y almacenaje		*Hommes* [8]	*Femmes*	*Transports et entrepôts*		
Fecha	Road haulage	Miscellaneous activities	Hombres [8]	Mujeres	Transportes y almacenaje		
	Camionnage	*Activités diverses*					
	Camionaje	Actividades diversas					
	(R.T./h.) [7]		*(E.G./d.j.)*		*(E.G./m.)*	*(E.G./m.)* [2]	*(E.G./h.)* [13]
	Schilling	Schilling	Francs	Francs	Leva	Korunas	Francs
1970	20.09	18.28	522.3	364.6	141.1	2 239	6.35
1971	20.09	18.28	580.7	408.0	144.5	2 318	7.05
1972	22.62	20.60	659.1	452.4	147.7	2 432	7.71 [14]
1973	24.83	22.62	744.0 [9]	415.6 [9]	160.5	2 474	8.89
1974	27.20	24.79	909.0	512.3	164.1	2 534	10.26
1975	31.28	28.48	1 071.6	597.6	169.8	2 632	11.96
1976	34.73	31.60	1 219.3	659.4	171.1	2 720	13.97 [15]
1977	37.76	34.35	1 332.5	736.5	176.1	2 819	15.62
1978	39.69	36.13	1 425.3	806.2	180.2	2 936	17.72
1979	41.67	37.95	1 519.3	863.3	189.8	3 026	19.66

EXPLANATORY NOTES: See p. 423.

[1] July of each year. [2] Incl. salaried employees. [3] Incl. sea transport. [4] Aug. of each year. Prior to 1975: July. [5] March and Sep. of each year. [6] Adults. [7] Minimum rates. [8] Excl. dockers, boatmen and temporary railroad workers. [9] New industrial classification. [10] Socialised sector. [11] State industry. Excl. post, telegraph and telephone. [12] Excl. state-operated transport (SNCF and RATP) and communication. [13] Oct. of each year. Prior to 1971: Sep. [14] Series replacing former series. [15] Sampling design revised.

NOTES EXPLICATIVES: Voir p. 426.

[1] *Juillet de chaque année.* [2] *Y compris les employés.* [3] *Y compris les transports par mer.* [4] *Août de chaque année. Avant 1975: juillet.* [5] *Mars et sept. de chaque année.* [6] *Adultes.* [7] *Taux minima.* [8] *Non compris les dockers, bateliers et agents temporaires des chemins de fer.* [9] *Nouvelle classification industrielle.* [10] *Secteur socialisé.* [11] *Industrie d'Etat. Non compris les postes, télégraphes et téléphones.* [12] *Non compris les transports gérés par l'Etat (SNCF et RATP) et les communications.* [13] *Oct. de chaque année. Avant 1971: sept.* [14] *Série remplaçant la précédente.* [15] *Plan d'échantillonnage révisé.*

NOTAS EXPLICATIVAS: Véase pág. 430.

[1] Julio de cada año. [2] Incl. los empleados. [3] Incl. el transporte marítimo. [4] Agosto de cada año. Antes de 1975: julio. [5] Marzo y sept. de cada año. [6] Adultos. [7] Tarifas mínimas. [8] Excl. los obreros de los muelles, los bateleros y los trabajadores ferroviarios temporeros. [9] Nueva clasificación industrial. [10] Sector socializado. [11] Industria de Estado. Excl. correos, telégrafos y teléfonos. [12] Excl. los transportes administrados por el Estado (SNCF y RATP) y las comunicaciones. [13] Oct. de cada año. Antes de 1971: sept. [14] Serie que substituye a la anterior. [15] Diseño de la muestra revisado.

WAGES

21 Wages in transport, storage and communication (Excl. sea transport)
Salaires dans les transports, entrepôts et communications (Non compris les transports par mer)
Salarios en los transportes, almacenaje y comunicaciones (Excl. el transporte marítimo)

Earnings *(E.G.)* or rates *(R.T.)*
per hour *(h.)*, day *(d.j.)*,
week *(w.s.)* or month *(m.)*

Gains *(E.G.)* ou taux *(R.T.)*
par heure *(h.)*, jour *(d.j.)*,
semaine *(w.s.)* ou mois *(m.)*

Ganancias *(E.G.)* o tarifas *(R.T.)*
por hora *(h.)*, día *(d.j.)*,
semana *(w.s.)* o mes *(m.)*

EUROPE — EUROPE — EUROPA

Date / Date / Fecha	German Democratic Republic [1] Transport / Transports / Transportes (E.G./m.) [2]	Gibraltar (E.G./w.s.) [3]	Hongrie [4,5] (E.G./m.) [6]	Italie Transport / Transports / Transportes (R.T./h.)	Malta — Transport and storage / Transports et entrepôts / Transportes y almacenaje — Males [7] / Hommes [7] / Hombres [7] (E.G./h.) [8]	Malta — Females [7] / Femmes [7] / Mujeres [7] (E.G./h.) [8]	Netherlands Males [7] / Hommes [7] / Hombres [7] (E.G./h.) [9]
	Mark	£	Forints	(1970 = 100)	Cents	Cents	Guilders
1970	816	14.18	2 235	**100.0**	24.2	15.8	5.56
1971	821	15.39	2 345	111.8	24.1	15.0	6.42
1972	912	17.42	2 457	120.7	23.4	17.6	7.09
1973	909	23.84	2 620	137.0	…	…	9.31
1974	969	22.37	2 829	173.7	27.1	21.5	9.53
1975	1 006	29.65	3 002	202.0	31.7	31.8	11.25
1976	1 031	34.92	3 159	245.8	46.6	35.3	12.14
1977	1 069	44.03	3 346	310.4	…	…	13.64
1978	1 114	70.16	3 655	361.5	…	…	14.59
1979	1 152 *	82.83	3 910	438.7	…	…	…

EUROPE — EUROPE — EUROPA

Date / Date / Fecha	Norway Private land transport / Transports terrestres privés / Transportes terrestres privados — Males / Hommes / Hombres (E.G./h.) [4,7]	Pologne [5] (E.G./m.) [4,8]	Roumanie [5] Transport / Transports / Transportes (E.G./m.) [8]	Roumanie [5] Communication / Communications / Comunicaciones (E.G./m.) [8]	Suisse [11] Males — Hommes — Hombres — Skilled / Qualifiés / Calificados (E.G./h.) [7,9]	Suisse [11] Semi-skilled and unskilled / Semi-qualifiés et non qualifiés / Semicalificados y no calificados (E.G./h.) [7,9]	Suisse [11] Total (E.G./h.) [7,9]	Sweden [12] Transport / Transports / Transportes — Lorry drivers / Conducteurs de camion / Conductores de camión (E.G./h.) [13]
	Kroner	Zlotys	Lei	Lei	Francs	Francs	Francs	Kronor
1970	12.25	2 281	1 544	1 239	.	.	.	12.70
1971	13.67	2 423	1 568	1 250	.	.	.	12.89 [14]
1972	15.23	2 573	1 599	1 262	.	.	.	16.02
1973	17.11	2 933	1 626	1 332	.	.	.	16.55
1974	19.91	3 332	1 743	1 368	13.04	11.03	11.77	18.10
1975	24.54	3 844	1 870	1 490	14.28	11.87	12.75	21.54
1976	28.35	4 213	2 090	1 737	14.71	12.19	13.12	25.01
1977	31.19	4 516	1 864 [10]	1 551 [10]	15.87	13.44	14.10	28.24
1978	33.40	4 837	2 144	1 775	16.36	13.81	14.50	30.02
1979	35.17	4 297 *	2 208	1 820	16.82	14.36	15.03	31.84

EXPLANATORY NOTES: See p. 423.

NOTES EXPLICATIVES: Voir p. 426.

NOTAS EXPLICATIVAS: Véase pág. 430.

1 State sector. 2 Incl. family allowances. 3 Oct. of each year, except for 1970-72: April and Oct., and 1974-76: April. 4 Incl. the value of payments in kind. 5 Socialised sector. 6 Incl. loyalty money. 7 Adults. 8 Incl. salaried employees. 9 Oct. of each year. 10 Beginning 1977: net earnings after deduction of income taxes. 11 Statistics of establishments. Incl. family allowances. 12 Second quarter of each year. Adult males. 13 Incl. holidays and sick-leave payment and the value of payments in kind. 14 New industrial classification.

1 *Secteur d'Etat.* 2 *Y compris les allocations familiales.* 3 *Oct. de chaque année, sauf pour 1970-1972: avril et oct., et 1974-1976: avril.* 4 *Y compris la valeur des paiements en nature.* 5 *Secteur socialisé.* 6 *Y compris les primes d'assiduité.* 7 *Adultes.* 8 *Y compris les employés.* 9 *Oct. de chaque année.* 10 *A partir de 1977: gains nets après déduction de l'impôt sur le revenu.* 11 *Statistiques d'établissements. Y compris les allocations familiales.* 12 *Deuxième trimestre de chaque année. Hommes adultes.* 13 *Y compris les versements au titre des vacances et la valeur des paiements en nature.* 14 *Nouvelle classification industrielle.*

1 Sector de Estado. 2 Incl. las asignaciones familiares. 3 Oct. de cada año, salvo para 1970-1972: abril y oct., y 1974-1976: abril. 4 Incl. el valor de los pagos en especie. 5 Sector socializado. 6 Incl. las primas de asiduidad. 7 Adultos. 8 Incl. los empleados. 9 Oct. de cada año. 10 A partir de 1977: ganancias netas después deducción de los impuestos sobre la renta. 11 Estadísticas de establecimientos. Incl. las asignaciones familiares. 12 Segundo trimestre de cada año. Hombres adultos. 13 Incl. los pagos por vacaciones y licencias de enfermedad y el valor de los pagos en especie. 14 Nueva clasificación industrial.

21

Wages in transport, storage and communication (Excl. sea transport)
Salaires dans les transports, entrepôts et communications (Non compris les transports par mer)
Salarios en los transportes, almacenaje y comunicaciones (Excl. el transporte marítimo)

Earnings *(E.G.)* or rates *(R.T.)*
per hour *(h.)*, day *(d.j.)*,
week *(w.s.)* or month *(m.)*

Gains *(E.G.)* ou taux *(R.T.)*
par heure *(h.)*, jour *(d.j.)*,
semaine *(w.s.)* ou mois *(m.)*

Ganancias *(E.G.)* o tarifas *(R.T.)*
por hora *(h.)*, día *(d.j.)*,
semana *(w.s.)* o mes *(m.)*

Date / Date / Fecha	EUROPE — EUROPE — EUROPA				
		United Kingdom [3]			
	Turquie	Males / Hommes / Hombres	Females / Femmes / Mujeres	Railways / Chemins de fer / Ferrocarriles	
				Males / Hommes / Hombres	Females / Femmes / Mujeres
	(E.G./d.j.) [1,2]	*(E.G./h.)* [4,5]		*(E.G./w.s.)* [6,7]	
	Liras	Pence	Pence	£	£
1970	40.49	60.3	45.1	29.31	15.92
1971	46.61	70.3	51.6	31.65	18.86
1972	52.54	78.3	58.3	36.15	23.45
1973	62.08	87.3	67.1	39.49	28.17
1974	74.17	105.2	81.6	53.11	32.31
1975	120.15	134.9	106.2	65.64	40.70
1976	117.44	149.9	120.7	69.94	44.31
1977	165.30	160.3	128.9	75.44	48.49
1978	204.47	180.4	146.6	86.53	54.11
1979	311.43	212.6	167.2	103.30	72.38

Date / Date / Fecha	EUROPE — EUROPE — EUROPA	OCEANIA — OCÉANIE — OCEANÍA				
	Yugoslavia [8]	American Samoa	Australia		Fiji	New Zealand (1)
			Males [3,7] / Hommes [3,7] / Hombres [3,7]	Communication / Communications / Comunicaciones	Transport / Transports / Transportes	
	(E.G./m.) [1]	*(R.T./h.)* [9]	*(E.G./h.)* [1,10]	*(R.T./h.)* [9,12]	*(R.T./d.j.)* [13]	*(E.G./h.)* [1,14]
	Dinars	Dollars	Dollars	Cents	Dollars	Dollars
1970	1 263	1.25	1.95	166.8	2.52	1.36
1971	1 539	1.25	2.14	188.4	2.86	1.66
1972	1 797	1.30	2.49 [11]	209.1	3.38	1.87
1973	2 062	1.30	2.89	237.4	4.11	2.06
1974	2 590	1.44	3.86	299.8	5.28	2.40
1975	3 231	1.44	4.27	345.2	6.35	2.74
1976	3 787	1.57	4.79	396.8	7.04	3.04
1977	4 478	1.70	5.38	438.3	7.69	3.40
1978	5 410	1.82	5.70	472.6	8.46	3.83
1979	6 551	1.95	6.07	508.6	9.05 *	...

EXPLANATORY NOTES: See p. 423.

[1] Incl. salaried employees. [2] Sep. of each year. [3] Oct. of each year. [4] Adult full-time wage earners. [5] Excl. railways and London Transport Services. [6] Excl. Northern Ireland. [7] Adults. [8] Socialised sector. Incl. sea transport. [9] Minimum rates. [10] Prior to 1973: excl. communication. [11] Scope of series enlarged. [12] Adult males. [13] June of each year. [14] April and Oct. of each year. Incl. juveniles.

NOTES EXPLICATIVES: Voir p. 426.

[1] *Y compris les employés.* [2] *Sept. de chaque année.* [3] *Oct. de chaque année.* [4] *Ouvriers adultes à temps complet.* [5] *Non compris les chemins de fer et les services de transports londoniens.* [6] *Non compris l'Irlande du Nord.* [7] *Adultes.* [8] *Secteur socialisé. Y compris les transports par mer.* [9] *Taux minima.* [10] *Avant 1973: non compris les communications.* [11] *Portée de la série élargie.* [12] *Hommes adultes.* [13] *Juin de chaque année.* [14] *Avril et oct. de chaque année. Y compris les jeunes gens.*

NOTAS EXPLICATIVAS: Véase pág. 430.

[1] Incl. los empleados. [2] Sept. de cada año. [3] Oct. de cada año. [4] Obreros adultos a tiempo completo. [5] Excl. los ferrocarriles y los transportes londinenses. [6] Excl. Irlanda del Norte. [7] Adultos. [8] Sector socializado. Incl. el transporte marítimo. [9] Tarifas mínimas. [10] Antes de 1973: excl. las comunicaciones. [11] El alcance de la serie es mayor. [12] Hombres adultos. [13] Junio de cada año. [14] Abril y oct. de cada año. Incl. los jóvenes.

WAGES

21 Wages in transport, storage and communication (Excl. sea transport)
Salaires dans les transports, entrepôts et communications (Non compris les transports par mer)
Salarios en los transportes, almacenaje y comunicaciones (Excl. el transporte marítimo)

Earnings *(E.G.)* or rates *(R.T.)* per hour *(h.)*, day *(d.j.)*, week *(w.s.)* or month *(m.)*

Gains *(E.G.)* ou taux *(R.T.)* par heure *(h.)*, jour *(d.j.)*, semaine *(w.s.)* ou mois *(m.)*

Ganancias *(E.G.)* o tarifas *(R.T.)* por hora *(h.)*, día *(d.j.)*, semana *(w.s.)* o mes *(m.)*

Date / Date / Fecha	OCEANIA — OCÉANIE — OCEANÍA				URSS [4,5]	RSS de Biélorussie [4]	RSS d'Ukraine [4]
	New Zealand (2)			Nouvelle-Calédonie			
	Railways / Chemins de fer / Ferrocarriles		Buses / Autobus / Autobuses	Labourers [2] / Manœuvres [2]			
	Engine drivers / Mécaniciens / Maquinistas	Guards / Chefs de train / Jefes de tren	Operators / Conducteurs / Conductores	Obreros no calificados [2]			
	(R.T./w.s.) [1]			(R.T./h.) [3]	(E.G./m.) [6]	(E.G./m.) [6]	(E.G./m.) [6]
	Dollars	Dollars	Dollars	Francs (CFP)	Roubles	Roubles	Roubles
1970	65.68	56.13	48.08	.	131.0	.	117.0
1971	75.90	65.07	51.66	.	137.5	123.9	122.5
1972	83.70	71.74	58.13	.	143.8	128.7	127.7
1973	91.95	79.07	62.83	.	149.6	132.1	130.9
1974	105.30	90.96	73.75	.	159.9	136.7	135.3
1975	119.56	103.77	83.81	.	166.4	140.6	142.3
1976	131.85	115.38	91.21	150.22	175.0	155.3	153.2
1977	155.45	134.60	107.18	160.05	179.2	158.8	156.7
1978	175.50	150.86	121.04	169.87	183.0	161.5	158.9
1979	...	...	...	187.08	185.9	162.9	160.6

EXPLANATORY NOTES: See p. 423.

[1] Minimum rates; adult males. [2] First category. [3] Dec. of each year. [4] Socialised sector. [5] Incl. Byelorussian SSR and Ukrainian SSR, shown separately in this table. [6] Incl. salaried employees.

NOTES EXPLICATIVES: Voir p. 426.

[1] *Taux minima ; hommes adultes.* [2] *Première catégorie.* [3] *Déc. de chaque année.* [4] *Secteur socialisé.* [5] *Y compris les RSS de Biélorussie et d'Ukraine, figurant séparément dans ce tableau.* [6] *Y compris les employés.*

NOTAS EXPLICATIVAS: Véase pág. 430.

[1] Tarifas mínimas; hombres adultos. [2] Primera categoría. [3] Dic. de cada año. [4] Sector socializado. [5] Incl. las RSS de Bielorrusia y de Ucrania, que figuran separadamente en este cuadro. [6] Incl. los empleados.

22 Wages in agriculture
Salaires dans l'agriculture
Salarios en la agricultura

Earnings *(E.G.)* or rates *(R.T.)*
per hour *(h.)*, day *(d.j.)*,
week *(w.s.)* or month *(m.)*

Gains *(E.G.)* ou taux *(R.T.)*
par heure *(h.)*, jour *(d.j.)*,
semaine *(w.s.)* ou mois *(m.)*

Ganancias *(E.G.)* o tarifas *(R.T.)*
por hora *(h.)*, día *(d.j.)*,
semana *(w.s.)* o mes *(m.)*

	Burundi	Cameroun	Kenya	Malawi	Mauritius	Nigeria	Swaziland	Tanzania (Tanganyika)
Date / Date / Fecha	Permanent labourers / *Ouvriers permanents* / Obreros permanentes	Day labourers / *Journaliers* / Jornaleros		All workers / *Ensemble des ouvriers* / Todos los obreros	Sugar cane, tea and tobacco plantations and fishing / *Plantations de canne à sucre, de thé, de tabac et pêche* / Plantaciones de caña de azúcar, de té, de tabaco, y pesca		Unskilled workers / *Ouvriers non qualifiés* / Obreros no calificados	Permanent and seasonal workers / *Ouvriers permanents et saisonniers* / Obreros permanentes y de temporada
	M. + F. / H. + F. / H. + M.	M. + F. / H. + F. / H. + M.	M. + F. / H. + F. / H. + M.	M. + F. / H. + F. / H. + M.	M. + F. / H. + F. / H. + M.	M. + F. / H. + F. / H. + M.	Males / Hommes / Hombres	Males[10] / Hommes[10] / Hombres[10]
	(E.G./m.) [1, 2]	*(R.T./h.)* [3, 4]	*(E.G./m.)* [1, 5]	*(E.G./m.)* [1, 6]	*(E.G./d.j.)* [8]	*(R.T./d.j.)*	*(E.G./m.)* [9]	*(E.G./m.)* [5]
	I	I	II + a + b	I	II + a	I	I	II
	Francs	Francs (CFA)	Shillings	Kwacha	Rupees	Naira	Emalangeni	Shillings
1970	.	29.50	129.20	8.82	6.42	.	.	200
1971	.	29.50	140.00	9.22	6.35	.	.	200
1972	.	29.50	180.60	9.51	8.99	0.88	15	209
1973	3 108	32.50	181.20	9.59	8.24	0.89	20	241
1974	3 306	37.00	194.60	10.90	9.93	1.10	21	368
1975	3 554	...	235.00	10.65	10.80	1.58	30	...
1976	...	...	312.90	10.98	15.67	...	40	...
1977	3 965	...	326.90	12.31 [7]	20.14	...	37	...
1978	4 540	...	376.90	14.39	22.08	...	56	...
1979	5 089	...	411.50	...	26.26	...	...	...

EXPLANATORY NOTES: See p. 423.

NOTES EXPLICATIVES: Voir p. 426.

NOTAS EXPLICATIVAS: Véase pág. 430.

I: Complete wage (workers remunerated wholly in cash).

II: Cash part of remuneration (where received partly in cash and partly in kind). These figures may include the estimated value of payments in kind for:
  a : board;
  b : lodging.

I: *Montant total du salaire (cas des travailleurs entièrement rémunérés en espèces).*

II: *Partie de la rémunération payée en espèces (cas des travailleurs rémunérés partiellement en espèces et partiellement en nature). Ces chiffres peuvent comprendre la valeur estimée des paiements en nature pour :*
  a : les repas ;
  b : le logement.

I: Salario íntegro (trabajadores remunerados enteramente en dinero).

II: Parte de la remuneración en dinero (en los casos en que ésta consiste en una parte en dinero y otra en especie). Estas cifras pueden incluir el valor estimado de los pagos en especie para:
  a : los alimentos;
  b : el alojamiento.

[1] Incl. salaried employees. [2] Incl. family allowances. [3] Minimum rates. [4] Dec. of each year. [5] June of each year. [6] Incl. forestry and fishing. [7] Scope of series enlarged. [8] Sep. of each year. [9] June of each year. Prior to 1975: Sep. [10] Adults.

[1] *Y compris les employés.* [2] *Y compris les allocations familiales.* [3] *Taux minima.* [4] *Déc. de chaque année.* [5] *Juin de chaque année.* [6] *Y compris la sylviculture et la pêche.* [7] *Portée de la série élargie.* [8] *Sept. de chaque année.* [9] *Juin de chaque année. Avant 1975 : sept.* [10] *Adultes.*

[1] Incl. los empleados. [2] Incl. las asignaciones familiares. [3] Tarifas mínimas. [4] Dic. de cada año. [5] Junio de cada año. [6] Incl. la silvicultura y la pesca. [7] El alcance de la serie es mayor. [8] Sept. de cada año. [9] Junio de cada año. Antes de 1975: sept. [10] Adultos.

22 Wages in agriculture
Salaires dans l'agriculture
Salarios en la agricultura

Earnings *(E.G.)* or rates *(R.T.)*
per hour *(h.)*, day *(d.j.)*,
week *(w.s.)* or month *(m.)*

Gains *(E.G.)* ou taux *(R.T.)*
par heure *(h.)*, jour *(d.j.)*,
semaine *(w.s.)* ou mois *(m.)*

Ganancias *(E.G.)* o tarifas *(R.T.)*
por hora *(h.)*, día *(d.j.)*,
semana *(w.s.)* o mes *(m.)*

Date / Date / Fecha	AFRICA — AFRIQUE — AFRICA			AMERICA — AMÉRIQUE — AMÉRICA				
	Tunisie	Zambia [3]		Argentina	Bahamas	Barbados [6]		Bermuda
	Agricultural workers [1] / Ouvriers agricoles [1] / Obreros agrícolas [1]	Zambians / Zambiens / Zambianos	Others / Autres / Otros	Unskilled workers / Ouvriers non qualifiés / Obreros no calificados	Farm workers / Ouvriers agricoles / Obreros agrícolas	Agricultural workers / Ouvriers agricoles / Obreros agrícolas		Agricultural workers / Ouvriers agricoles / Obreros agrícolas
	Males / Hommes / Hombres	M. + F. / H. + F. / H. + M.		Males / Hommes / Hombres	M. + F. / H. + F. / H. + M.	Males [1] / Hommes [1] / Hombres [1]	Females [1] / Femmes [1] / Mujeres [1]	Males / Hommes / Hombres
	(R.T./d.j.) [2]	*(E.G./m.)* [4]		*(E.G./h.)*	*(E.G./w.s.)*	*(E.G./w.s.)*		*(R.T./h.)*
	I	I [5]		I	I	I		I
	Millimes	Kwacha	Kwacha	Pesos	Dollars	Dollars	Dollars	Dollars
1970	550	...	...	1.14	.	26.38	18.56	1.91
1971	600	...	...	1.75	.	31.34	21.67	1.96
1972	600	36	262	2.50	.	39.95	25.58	2.17
1973	600	35	216	4.49	48.77	40.25	23.79	2.80
1974	800	37	217	6.41	44.31	51.42	33.08	3.14
1975	900	38	210	16.83	43.29	61.27	39.08	3.25
1976	900	50	291	50.29	45.12	76.76	48.29	3.47
1977	1 200	53	296	106.32	...	76.81	48.92	3.78
1978	1 332	...	...	...	...	...	...	4.10
1979	1 440	...	...	...	...	...	...	4.90

EXPLANATORY NOTES: See p. 423.　　NOTES EXPLICATIVES: Voir p. 426.　　NOTAS EXPLICATIVAS: Véase pág. 430.

I: Complete wage (workers remunerated wholly in cash).

II: Cash part of remuneration (where received partly in cash and partly in kind). These figures may include the estimated value of payments in kind for:
　a: board;
　b: lodging.

I: *Montant total du salaire (cas des travailleurs entièrement rémunérés en espèces).*

II: *Partie de la rémunération payée en espèces (cas des travailleurs rémunérés partiellement en espèces et partiellement en nature). Ces chiffres peuvent comprendre la valeur estimée des paiements en nature pour :*
　a : les repas ;
　b : le logement.

I: Salario íntegro (trabajadores remunerados enteramente en dinero).

II: Parte de la remuneración en dinero (en los casos en que ésta consiste en una parte en dinero y otra en especie). Estas cifras pueden incluir el valor estimado de los pagos en especie para:
　a: los alimentos;
　b: el alojamiento.

[1] Adults. [2] Minimum rates. [3] Incl. forestry and fishing. [4] Incl. salaried employees. [5] Fourth quarter of each year. [6] Prior to 1974: sugar cane plantations; day labourers.

[1] *Adultes.* [2] *Taux minima.* [3] *Y compris la sylviculture et la pêche.* [4] *Y compris les employés.* [5] *Quatrième trimestre de chaque année.* [6] *Avant 1974 : plantations de canne à sucre ; journaliers.*

[1] Adultos. [2] Tarifas mínimas. [3] Incl. la silvicultura y la pesca. [4] Incl. los empleados. [5] Cuarto trimestre de cada año. [6] Antes de 1974: plantaciones de caña de azúcar; jornaleros.

22 Wages in agriculture
Salaires dans l'agriculture
Salarios en la agricultura

Earnings *(E.G.)* or rates *(R.T.)*
per hour *(h.)*, day *(d.j.)*,
week *(w.s.)* or month *(m.)*

Gains *(E.G.)* ou taux *(R.T.)*
par heure *(h.)*, jour *(d.j.)*,
semaine *(w.s.)* ou mois *(m.)*

Ganancias *(E.G.)* o tarifas *(R.T.)*
por hora *(h.)*, día *(d.j.)*,
semana *(w.s.)* o mes *(m.)*

	AMERICA — AMÉRIQUE — AMÉRICA						
	Canada				Costa Rica		Chile
	General farm hands				General farm hands		Permanent and non-permanent workers [6]
	Domestiques de ferme				*Domestiques de ferme*	Cuba [4]	*Ouvriers permanents et non permanents* [6]
Date *Date* Fecha	Peones agrícolas				Peones agrícolas		Obreros permanentes y no permanentes [6]
					Coffee plantations / *Plantations de caféiers* / Plantaciones de café	Agriculture and livestock production [2] / *Agriculture et élevage* [2] / Agricultura y ganadería [2]	
	Males *Hommes* Hombres				M. + F. / H. + F. / H. + M.	M. + F. / H. + F. / H. + M.	Males *Hommes* Hombres
	(R.T./d.j.) [1]		*(R.T./m.)* [1]		*(R.T./h.)* [3]	*(E.G./m.)* [5]	*(R.T./d.j.)* [3]
	I	II	I	II	II + a + b	I	I
	Dollars	Dollars	Dollars	Dollars	Colones	Colones	Pesos / Pesos
1970	12.50	10.10	288	238	1.34	1.21	. / 12.00
1971	13.10	10.60	300	250	1.50	1.39	110.25 / 20.00
1972	14.03	11.50	323	268	1.61	1.60	108.42 / 30.00 [7]
1973	16.00	13.17	371	315	1.61	1.75	118.00 / 63.33 [8]
1974	18.57	15.63	433	370	2.28	2.26	121.25 / 822.77
1975	22.40	19.06	494	442	2.52	2.52	128.58 / 4.35 [9]
1976	25.64	22.05	578	510	3.00	3.00	135.17 / 17.81
1977	28.40	24.92	632	561	3.39	3.39	112.33 / 41.44
1978	30.11	26.50	668	595	4.00	...	... / 60.45
1979	...	...	...	...	4.50	...	... / 79.97

EXPLANATORY NOTES: See p. 423.   NOTES EXPLICATIVES: Voir p. 426.   NOTAS EXPLICATIVAS: Véase pág. 430.

I: Complete wage (workers remunerated wholly in cash).

II: Cash part of remuneration (where received partly in cash and partly in kind). These figures may include the estimated value of payments in kind for:
   a: board;
   b: lodging.

I: *Montant total du salaire (cas des travailleurs entièrement rémunérés en espèces).*

II: *Partie de la rémunération payée en espèces (cas des travailleurs rémunérés partiellement en espèces et partiellement en nature). Ces chiffres peuvent comprendre la valeur estimée des paiements en nature pour:*
   a: les repas;
   b: le logement.

I: Salario íntegro (trabajadores remunerados enteramente en dinero).

II: Parte de la remuneración en dinero (en los casos en que ésta consiste en una parte en dinero y otra en especie). Estas cifras pueden incluir el valor estimado de los pagos en especie para:
   a: los alimentos;
   b: el alojamiento.

[1] Average rates. Prior to 1975: average of rates on 15 Jan., 15 May and 15 Aug. [2] Excl. plantations. [3] Minimum rates. [4] Incl. forestry and fishing. [5] Incl. salaried employees. [6] Adults. [7] Jan.-Sep. [8] Oct. 1972-Dec. 1973. [9] New currency introduced in Sep. 1975: 1 peso = 1,000 old escudos.

[1] *Taux moyens. Avant 1975: moyenne des taux au 15 janv., 15 mai et 15 août.* [2] *Non compris les plantations.* [3] *Taux minima.* [4] *Y compris la sylviculture et la pêche.* [5] *Y compris les employés.* [6] *Adultes.* [7] *Janv.-sept.* [8] *Oct. 1972-déc. 1973.* [9] *Nouvelle monnaie introduite en sept. 1975: 1 peso = 1 000 anciens escudos.*

[1] Tarifas medias. Antes de 1975: promedio de tarifas al 15 enero, 15 de mayo y 15 de agosto. [2] Excl. las plantaciones. [3] Tarifas mínimas. [4] Incl. la silvicultura y la pesca. [5] Incl. los empleados. [6] Adultos. [7] Enero-sept. [8] Oct. de 1972-dic. de 1973. [9] Nueva moneda adoptada en sept. de 1975: 1 peso = 1 000 antiguos escudos.

561

22 Wages in agriculture
Salaires dans l'agriculture
Salarios en la agricultura

Earnings *(E.G.)* or rates *(R.T.)*
per hour *(h.)*, day *(d.j.)*,
week *(w.s.)* or month *(m.)*

Gains *(E.G.)* ou taux *(R.T.)*
par heure *(h.)*, jour *(d.j.)*,
semaine *(w.s.)* ou mois *(m.)*

Ganancias *(E.G.)* o tarifas *(R.T.)*
por hora *(h.)*, día *(d.j.)*,
semana *(w.s.)* o mes *(m.)*

	AMERICA — AMÉRIQUE — AMÉRICA							
	El Salvador		Grenada		Guyana	México	Suriname
Date *Date* Fecha	Permanent labourers *Ouvriers permanents* Obreros permanentes		Permanent labourers [1] *Ouvriers permanents* [1] Obreros permanentes [1]		Agricultural workers *Ouvriers agricoles* Obreros agrícolas Sugar industry *Industrie sucrière* Industria del azúcar	Regular day labourers *Journaliers stables* Jornaleros estables	Agricultural workers *Ouvriers agricoles* Obreros agrícolas
	Males *Hommes* Hombres	Females *Femmes* Mujeres	Males *Hommes* Hombres	Females *Femmes* Mujeres	M. + F. *H. + F.* H. + M.	Males *Hommes* Hombres	M. + F. *H. + F.* H. + M.
	(E.G./d.j.)		*(E.G./w.s.)* [2]		*(E.G./w.s.)*	*(R.T./d.j.)* [3]	*(E.G./m.)*
	I		I		I	II	I
	Colones	Colones	Dollars	Dollars	Dollars	Pesos	Guilders
1970	2.25	1.75	12.00	10.00	31.48	21.20	.
1971	2.25	1.75	12.00	9.00	32.51	21.20	127
1972	2.25	1.75	12.00	9.00	34.45	24.94	133
1973	2.75	2.25	12.00	9.00	34.04	27.40	139
1974	3.10	2.50	12.00	9.00	39.22	37.79	145
1975	3.10	2.50	...	...	45.73	46.10	...
1976	3.75	3.15	...	...	54.47	63.05	...
1977	3.75	3.15	...	...	53.51	76.48	...
1978	4.25	3.65	...	...	...	88.50	...
1979	5.20	4.60	...	...	...	106.81	...

EXPLANATORY NOTES: See p. 423.

NOTES EXPLICATIVES: Voir p. 426.

NOTAS EXPLICATIVAS: Véase pág. 430.

I: Complete wage (workers remunerated wholly in cash).

II: Cash part of remuneration (where received partly in cash and partly in kind). These figures may include the estimated value of payments in kind for:

    a : board;
    b : lodging.

I: *Montant total du salaire (cas des travailleurs entièrement rémunérés en espèces).*

II: *Partie de la rémunération payée en espèces (cas des travailleurs rémunérés partiellement en espèces et partiellement en nature). Ces chiffres peuvent comprendre la valeur estimée des paiements en nature pour :*

    a : les repas ;
    b : le logement.

I: Salario íntegro (trabajadores remunerados enteramente en dinero).

II: Parte de la remuneración en dinero (en los casos en que ésta consiste en una parte en dinero y otra en especie). Estas cifras pueden incluir el valor estimado de los pagos en especie para:

    a : los alimentos;
    b : el alojamiento.

[1] Adults. [2] Excl. end-of-year bonuses ranging from 1 to 10 days pay. [3] Minimum rates.

[1] *Adultes.* [2] *Non compris les gratifications de fin d'année allant de 1 à 10 jours de paie.* [3] *Taux minima.*

[1] Adultos. [2] Excl. las bonificaciones de fin de año, que varían entre 1 y 10 días de pago. [3] Tarifas mínimas.

22 Wages in agriculture
Salaires dans l'agriculture
Salarios en la agricultura

Earnings *(E.G.)* or rates *(R.T.)*
per hour *(h.)*, day *(d.j.)*,
week *(w.s.)* or month *(m.)*

Gains *(E.G.)* ou taux *(R.T.)*
par heure *(h.)*, jour *(d.j.)*,
semaine *(w.s.)* ou mois *(m.)*

Ganancias *(E.G.)* o tarifas *(R.T.)*
por hora *(h.)*, día *(d.j.)*,
semana *(w.s.)* o mes *(m.)*

	AMERICA — AMÉRIQUE — AMÉRICA						ASIA — ASIE — ASIA	
	United States [1]				Uruguay		Bangladesh (Dacca)	Burma
Date *Date* Fecha	All workers *Ensemble des ouvriers* Todos los obreros	Field and livestock workers *Ouvriers agricoles et éleveurs* Obreros agrícolas y ganaderos	Machine operators *Conducteurs de machines* Conductores de maquinaria	Other agricultural workers *Autres ouvriers agricoles* Otros obreros agrícolas	General farm hands *Domestiques de ferme* Peones agrícolas		Skilled workers *Ouvriers qualifiés* Obreros calificados	Agricultural workers *Ouvriers agricoles* Obreros agrícolas / Hevea plantations *Plantations d'hévéas* Plantaciones de hevea
	Males and females *Hommes et femmes* Hombres y mujeres				Males and females *Hommes et femmes* Hombres y mujeres		Males and females *Hommes et femmes* Hombres y mujeres	Males *Hommes* Hombres
	(R.T./h.)				(E.G./m.) [2]		(R.T./d.j.)	(E.G./m.)
	I; II + a + b				I	II	I	I
	$	$	$	$	Pesos	Pesos	Taka	Kyats
1970	·	·	·	·	17 315	12 070	3.83	218.20
1971	·	·	·	·	22 025	15 355	5.55	228.55
1972	·	·	·	·	31 715	22 110	4.86	230.09
1973	·	·	·	·	56 565	39 500	6.66	188.16
1974	2.25	2.08	2.25	2.40	120 000	73 080	8.80	217.11
1975	2.43	2.26	2.50	2.76	206.25 [3]	140.25 [3]	9.44	226.99
1976	2.66	2.47	2.72	3.11	262.25	178.25	9.81	221.01
1977	2.87	2.65	2.92	3.37	460.00	260.00	10.50	224.88
1978	3.07	2.84	3.11	3.56	661.70	374.00	...	248.79
1979	...	...	...	...	...	...	...	...

EXPLANATORY NOTES: See p. 423.

NOTES EXPLICATIVES: Voir p. 426.

NOTAS EXPLICATIVAS: Véase pág. 430.

I: Complete wage (workers remunerated wholly in cash).

II: Cash part of remuneration (where received partly in cash and partly in kind). These figures may include the estimated value of payments in kind for:

  a : board;
  b : lodging.

I: *Montant total du salaire (cas des travailleurs entièrement rémunérés en espèces).*

II: *Partie de la rémunération payée en espèces (cas des travailleurs rémunérés partiellement en espèces et partiellement en nature). Ces chiffres peuvent comprendre la valeur estimée des paiements en nature pour :*

  a : les repas ;
  b : le logement.

I: Salario íntegro (trabajadores remunerados enteramente en dinero).

II: Parte de la remuneración en dinero (en los casos en que ésta consiste en una parte en dinero y otra en especie). Estas cifras pueden incluir el valor estimado de los pagos en especie para:

  a : los alimentos;
  b : el alojamiento.

[1] Excl. Alaska and Hawaii. [2] Dec. of each year. [3] New currency introduced in July 1975: 1 new peso = 1,000 old pesos.

[1] *Non compris Alaska et Hawaï.* [2] *Déc. de chaque année.* [3] *Nouvelle monnaie introduite en juillet 1975 : 1 nouveau peso = 1 000 anciens pesos.*

[1] Excl. Alaska y Hawai. [2] Dic. de cada año. [3] Nueva moneda adoptada en julio de 1975: 1 nuevo peso = 1 000 antiguos pesos.

22 Wages in agriculture
Salaires dans l'agriculture
Salarios en la agricultura

Earnings *(E.G.)* or rates *(R.T.)*
per hour *(h.)*, day *(d.j.)*,
week *(w.s.)* or month *(m.)*

Gains *(E.G.)* ou taux *(R.T.)*
par heure *(h.)*, jour *(d.j.)*,
semaine *(w.s.)* ou mois *(m.)*

Ganancias *(E.G.)* o tarifas *(R.T.)*
por hora *(h.)*, día *(d.j.)*,
semana *(w.s.)* o mes *(m.)*

	ASIA — ASIE — ASIA							
	Cyprus		India [4]	Israel [6]	Japan [11]		Korea, Rep. of	
Date *Date* Fecha	Agricultural workers [1] *Ouvriers agricoles* [1] Obreros agrícolas [1]		Agricultural workers *Ouvriers agricoles* Obreros agrícolas	Permanent labourers [7] *Ouvriers permanents* [7] Obreros permanentes [7]	Casual day labourers *Journaliers occasionnels* Jornaleros ocasionales		Agricultural workers *Ouvriers agricoles* Obreros agrícolas	
	Males *Hommes* Hombres	Females *Femmes* Mujeres	M. + F. *H. + F.* H. + M.	M. + F. *H. + F.* H. + M.	Males *Hommes* Hombres	Females *Femmes* Mujeres	Males *Hommes* Hombres	Females *Femmes* Mujeres
	(E.G./w.s.) [2]		*(R.T./d.j.)* [5]	*(E.G./m.)* [8]	*(E.G./d.j.)*		*(R.T./d.j.)*	
	II + a + b		II	I	II		II [12]	
	Pounds	Pounds	Rupees	Pounds	Yen	Yen	Won	Won
1970	9.85	4.76	2.87	375	1 509	1 226	579	392
1971	10.46	5.06	2.94	446	1 774	1 389	695	472
1972	10.36	5.34	2.90	521	1 964	1 549	803	552
1973	12.52	7.18	2.93	679	2 300	1 818	886	620
1974	15.05 [3]	8.41 [3]	3.28	970	2 993	2 371	1 141	798
1975	14.41	7.90	3.60	1 523 [9]	3 700	2 926	1 467	1 044
1976	16.63	9.05	3.74	2 018	3 922	3 110	1 903	1 354
1977	16.86	9.34	3.81	2 834	4 324	3 375	2 350	1 695
1978	20.85	11.65	3.95	4 431	4 642	3 569	3 393	2 508
1979	27.35	14.70	4.20	780 [10]	4 815	3 712	5 140	3 815

EXPLANATORY NOTES: See p. 423.

NOTES EXPLICATIVES: Voir p. 426.

NOTAS EXPLICATIVAS: Véase pág. 430.

I: Complete wage (workers remunerated wholly in cash).

II: Cash part of remuneration (where received partly in cash and partly in kind). These figures may include the estimated value of payments in kind for:

    a: board;
    b: lodging.

I: *Montant total du salaire (cas des travailleurs entièrement rémunérés en espèces).*

II: *Partie de la rémunération payée en espèces (cas des travailleurs rémunérés partiellement en espèces et partiellement en nature). Ces chiffres peuvent comprendre la valeur estimée des paiements en nature pour :*

    a: les repas ;
    b: le logement.

I: Salario íntegro (trabajadores remunerados enteramente en dinero).

II: Parte de la remuneración en dinero (en los casos en que ésta consiste en una parte en dinero y otra en especie). Estas cifras pueden incluir el valor estimado de los pagos en especie para:

    a: los alimentos;
    b: el alojamiento.

[1] Adults. [2] Oct. of each year. [3] Beginning July 1974: due to a change in the geographical scope of the series, data are not comparable with those for the preceding period. [4] Maharashtra state. [5] Year beginning in July of year indicated. [6] Incl. forestry and fishing. [7] Incl. salaried employees. [8] Prior to July 1975: incl. family allowances. Beginning July 1975, incl. payments subject to income tax and the value of payments in kind. [9] Scope of series enlarged. [10] Sampling design revised. [11] Prior to 1975: excl. Okinawa Prefecture. [12] Incl. the value of allowances in kind.

[1] *Adultes.* [2] *Oct. de chaque année.* [3] *A partir de juillet 1974 : en raison d'un changement de la portée géographique de la série, les données ne sont pas comparables avec celles de la période précédente.* [4] *Etat de Maharashtra.* [5] *Année commençant en juillet de l'année indiquée.* [6] *Y compris la sylviculture et la pêche.* [7] *Y compris les employés.* [8] *Avant juillet 1975 : y compris les allocations familiales. A partir de juillet 1975 : y compris les versements soumis à l'impôt sur le revenu et la valeur des paiements en nature.* [9] *Portée de la série élargie.* [10] *Plan d'échantillonnage révisé.* [11] *Avant 1975 : non compris la préfecture d'Okinawa.* [12] *Y compris la valeur des prestations en nature.*

[1] Adultos. [2] Oct. de cada año. [3] A partir de julio de 1974: en razón de un cambio del alcance geográfico de la serie, los datos no son comparables a los del período precedente. [4] Estado de Maharashtra. [5] Año que comienza en julio del año indicado. [6] Incl. la silvicultura y la pesca. [7] Incl. los empleados. [8] Antes de julio de 1975: incl. las asignaciones familiares. A partir de julio de 1975: incl. los pagos sometidos al impuesto sobre la renta y el valor de los pagos en especie. [9] El alcance de la serie es mayor. [10] Diseño de la muestra revisado. [11] Antes de 1975: excl. la prefectura de Okinawa. [12] Incl. el valor de las prestaciones en especie.

22 Wages in agriculture
Salaires dans l'agriculture
Salarios en la agricultura

Earnings *(E.G.)* or rates *(R.T.)*
per hour *(h.)*, day *(d.j.)*,
week *(w.s.)* or month *(m.)*

Gains *(E.G.)* ou taux *(R.T.)*
par heure *(h.)*, jour *(d.j.)*,
semaine *(w.s.)* ou mois *(m.)*

Ganancias *(E.G.)* o tarifas *(R.T.)*
por hora *(h.)*, día *(d.j.)*,
semana *(w.s.)* o mes *(m.)*

	ASIA — ASIE — ASIA								
	Malaysia			Pakistan	Philippines	Sri Lanka		République arabe syrienne	
	Peninsular Malaysia								
Date *Date* Fecha	Hevea plantations *Plantations d'hévéas* Plantaciones de hevea			General farm hands *Domestiques de ferme* Peones agrícolas	Agricultural workers *Ouvriers agricoles* Obreros agrícolas	Agricultural workers [1] *Ouvriers agricoles* [1] Obreros agrícolas [1] Tea plantations *Plantations de thé* Plantaciones de té		Seasonal workers [1] *Ouvriers saisonniers* [1] Obreros de temporada [1]	Permanent labourers [1] *Ouvriers permanents* [1] Obreros permanentes [1]
	Agricultural workers [1] *Ouvriers agricoles* [1] Obreros agrícolas [1]	Tappers [1] *Saigneurs* [1] Sangradores [1]							
	Males *Hommes* Hombres	Females *Femmes* Mujeres	M. + F. H. + F. H. + M.	Males *Hommes* Hombres	M. + F. H. + F. H. + M.	Males *Hommes* Hombres	Females *Femmes* Mujeres	M. + F. H. + F. H. + M.	M. + F. H. + F. H. + M.
	(E.G./m.) [2]		*(E.G./m.)* [2]	*(E.G./d.j.)* [3]	*(E.G./d.j.)*	*(E.G./d. j.)* [4]		*(R.T./d. j.)* [5]	
	I		I	I	I + a + b	I		I	
	Ringgits	Ringgits	Ringgits	Rupees	Pesos	Rupees	Rupees	Pounds	Pounds
1970	78	59	113	3.00	.	3.40	2.74	4.45	4.27
1971	75	59	109	3.15	3.55	3.47	3.38	4.49	4.93
1972	76	60	105	3.30	3.72	4.24	3.00	4.49	4.93
1973	82	72	143	5.75	4.40	3.91	3.58	4.61	5.19
1974	108	100	195	7.88	...	4.99	3.80	4.86	5.27
1975	102	86	139	7.53	6.27	6.18	4.72	5.78	5.95
1976	130	129	212	7.69	...	6.84	5.23	6.95	7.24
1977	124	119	197	9.06	...	7.57	5.98	6.95	7.24
1978	136	119	220	10.00	...	8.80	7.61	...	...
1979	...	...	...	13.00	...	...	...	...	...

EXPLANATORY NOTES: See p. 423.

NOTES EXPLICATIVES: Voir p. 426.

NOTAS EXPLICATIVAS: Véase pág. 430.

I: Complete wage (workers remunerated wholly in cash).

II: Cash part of remuneration (where received partly in cash and partly in kind). These figures may include the estimated value of payments in kind for:

    a: board;
    b: lodging.

[1] Adults. [2] July of each year. [3] Incl. the value of payments in kind. [4] March and Sep. of each year. [5] Minimum rates.

I: *Montant total du salaire (cas des travailleurs entièrement rémunérés en espèces).*

II: *Partie de la rémunération payée en espèces (cas des travailleurs rémunérés partiellement en espèces et partiellement en nature). Ces chiffres peuvent comprendre la valeur estimée des paiements en nature pour:*

    a: les repas;
    b: le logement.

[1] *Adultes.* [2] *Juillet de chaque année.* [3] *Y compris la valeur des paiements en nature.* [4] *Mars et sept. de chaque année.* [5] *Taux minima.*

I: Salario íntegro (trabajadores remunerados enteramente en dinero).

II: Parte de la remuneración en dinero (en los casos en que ésta consiste en una parte en dinero y otra en especie). Estas cifras pueden incluir el valor estimado de los pagos en especie para:

    a: los alimentos;
    b: el alojamiento.

[1] Adultos. [2] Julio de cada año. [3] Incl. el valor de los pagos en especie. [4] Marzo y sept. de cada año. [5] Tarifas mínimas.

WAGES

22 Wages in agriculture
Salaires dans l'agriculture
Salarios en la agricultura

Earnings *(E.G.)* or rates *(R.T.)*
per hour *(h.)*, day *(d.j.)*,
week *(w.s.)* or month *(m.)*

Gains *(E.G.)* ou taux *(R.T.)*
par heure *(h.)*, jour *(d.j.)*,
semaine *(w.s.)* ou mois *(m.)*

Ganancias *(E.G.)* o tarifas *(R.T.)*
por hora *(h.)*, día *(d.j.)*,
semana *(w.s.)* o mes *(m.)*

	EUROPE — EUROPE — EUROPA						
Date *Date* Fecha	Austria		Belgique [2]		Bulgarie		Czechoslovakia [5]
	Agricultural workers [1] *Ouvriers agricoles* [1] Obreros agrícolas [1]		Agricultural workers *Ouvriers agricoles* Obreros agrícolas		State agricultural undertakings *Entreprises agricoles d'Etat* Empresas agrícolas del Estado		All workers [4] *Ensemble des ouvriers* [4] Todos los obreros [4]
					Agricultural workers *Ouvriers agricoles* Obreros agrícolas	Total [4]	
	Males *Hommes* Hombres	Females *Femmes* Mujeres	Males *Hommes* Hombres	Females *Femmes* Mujeres	Males and females *Hommes et femmes* Hombres y mujeres		M. + F. H. + F. H. + M.
	(R.T./m.)		*(E.G./d.j.)*		*(E.G./m.)*		*(E.G./m.)*
	II + a + b		I		II		I
	Schilling	Schilling	Francs	Francs	Leva	Leva	Korunas
1970	2 986	2 960	351 9	272.2	102.4	104.2	1 827
1971	3 255	3 310	392.4	297.6	109.9	110.9	1 890
1972	3 582	3 642	436.7	322.7	117.8	118.9	1 978
1973	4 011	4 078	516.1 [3]	127.1 [3]	128.8	129.4	2 090
1974	4 688	4 806	628.6	392.8	128.7	131.6	2 172
1975	5 322	5 504	753.9	470.2	135.2	137.9	2 238
1976	5 833	6 052	852.0	533.8	140.7	143.3	2 310
1977	6 329	6 566	947.9	588.6	141.4	145.7	2 399
1978	6 748	7 001	1 013.6	631.8	152.3	155.1	2 463
1979	7 043	7 308	1 078.2	687.6	151.3 *	156.6 *	2 522

EXPLANATORY NOTES: See p. 423.　　NOTES EXPLICATIVES: Voir p. 426.　　NOTAS EXPLICATIVAS: Véase pág. 430.

I: Complete wage (workers remunerated wholly in cash).

II: Cash part of remuneration (where received partly in cash and partly in kind). These figures may include the estimated value of payments in kind for:

   a: board;
   b: lodging.

I: *Montant total du salaire (cas des travailleurs entièrement rémunérés en espèces).*

II: *Partie de la rémunération payée en espèces (cas des travailleurs rémunérés partiellement en espèces et partiellement en nature). Ces chiffres peuvent comprendre la valeur estimée des paiements en nature pour :*

   a : les repas ;
   b : le logement.

I: Salario íntegro (trabajadores remunerados enteramente en dinero).

II: Parte de la remuneración en dinero (en los casos en que ésta consiste en una parte en dinero y otra en especie). Estas cifras pueden incluir el valor estimado de los pagos en especie para:

   a : los alimentos;
   b : el alojamiento.

[1] Permanent workers. [2] Incl. forestry and fishing. [3] New industrial classification. [4] Incl. salaried employees. [5] Socialised sector (except agricultural cooperatives); incl. forestry.

[1] *Ouvriers permanents.* [2] *Y compris la sylviculture et la pêche.* [3] *Nouvelle classification industrielle.* [4] *Y compris les employés.* [5] *Secteur socialisé (à l'exclusion des coopératives agricoles) ; y compris la sylviculture.*

[1] Obreros permanentes. [2] Incl. la silvicultura y la pesca. [3] Nueva clasificación industrial. [4] Incl. los empleados. [5] Sector socializado (pero excl. las cooperativas agrícolas); incl. la silvicultura.

22 Wages in agriculture
Salaires dans l'agriculture
Salarios en la agricultura

Earnings *(E.G.)* or rates *(R.T.)*
per hour *(h.)*, day *(d.j.)*,
week *(w.s.)* or month *(m.)*

Gains *(E.G.)* ou taux *(R.T.)*
par heure *(h.)*, jour *(d.j.)*,
semaine *(w.s.)* ou mois *(m.)*

Ganancias *(E.G.)* o tarifas *(R.T.)*
por hora *(h.)*, día *(d.j.)*,
semana *(w.s.)* o mes *(m.)*

Date / Date / Fecha	EUROPE — EUROPE — EUROPA							
	Denmark			España	Finland			
	Casual day labourers / Journaliers occasionnels / Jornaleros ocasionales		General farm hands / Domestiques de ferme / Peones agrícolas	Permanent labourers / Ouvriers permanents / Obreros permanentes	General farm hands / Domestiques de ferme / Peones agrícolas		All workers / Ensemble des ouvriers / Todos los obreros	
	Males [1] / Hommes [1] / Hombres [1]	Females [1] / Femmes [1] / Mujeres [1]	M. + F. [1,4] / H. + F. [1,4] / H. + M. [1,4]	Males / Hommes / Hombres	Males / Hommes / Hombres	Females / Femmes / Mujeres	Males / Hommes / Hombres	Females / Femmes / Mujeres
	(E.G./h.) [2]		*(E.G./h.)* [5]	*(E.G./d.j.)*	*(E.G./h.)*		*(E.G./h.)*	
	I		II	I	I; II + a + b			
	Kroner	Kroner	Kroner	Pesetas	Markkaa	Markkaa	Markkaa	Markkaa
1970	8.66	9.59	14 232	174.37	2.89	2.39	3.27	2.65
1971	13.02	11.55	13 860 [3]	187.64	3.36	2.95	3.71	3.14
1972	14.26	13.09	15 300	214.36	3.95	3.51	4.56	3.73
1973	16.58 [3]		16 500	250.80	5.00	4.56	5.64	4.93
1974	19.52		19 920	335.80	6.06	5.82	7.10	6.14
1975	23.59		23 340	392.80	7.49	7.10	9.24	7.61
1976	26.16		26 340	512.30	9.14	8.29	10.98	8.97
1977	30.90		31 200	649.90	10.42	9.33	12.30	9.95
1978	33.17		...	802.70	11.91	10.35	13.53	11.21
1979	...		...	932.70	13.25	11.89	15.20	12.65

EXPLANATORY NOTES: See p. 423.

NOTES EXPLICATIVES: Voir p. 426.

NOTAS EXPLICATIVAS: Véase pág. 430.

I: Complete wage (workers remunerated wholly in cash).

II: Cash part of remuneration (where received partly in cash and partly in kind). These figures may include the estimated value of payments in kind for:
  a: board;
  b: lodging.

I: *Montant total du salaire (cas des travailleurs entièrement rémunérés en espèces).*

II: *Partie de la rémunération payée en espèces (cas des travailleurs rémunérés partiellement en espèces et partiellement en nature). Ces chiffres peuvent comprendre la valeur estimée des paiements en nature pour :*
  a : les repas ;
  b : le logement.

I: Salario íntegro (trabajadores remunerados enteramente en dinero).

II: Parte de la remuneración en dinero (en los casos en que ésta consiste en una parte en dinero y otra en especie). Estas cifras pueden incluir el valor estimado de los pagos en especie para:
  a: los alimentos;
  b: el alojamiento.

[1] Adults. [2] April of each year. [3] Series replacing former series. [4] Prior to 1971: males only. [5] Per year.

[1] *Adultes.* [2] *Avril de chaque année.* [3] *Série remplaçant la précédente.* [4] *Avant 1971 : hommes seulement.* [5] *Par année.*

[1] Adultos. [2] Abril de cada año. [3] Serie que substituye a la anterior. [4] Antes de 1971: hombres solamente. [5] Por año.

WAGES

22 Wages in agriculture
Salaires dans l'agriculture
Salarios en la agricultura

Earnings *(E.G.)* or rates *(R.T.)*
per hour *(h.)*, day *(d.j.)*,
week *(w.s.)* or month *(m.)*

Gains *(E.G.)* ou taux *(R.T.)*
par heure *(h.)*, jour *(d.j.)*,
semaine *(w.s.)* ou mois *(m.)*

Ganancias *(E.G.)* o tarifas *(R.T.)*
por hora *(h.)* día *(d.j.)*,
semana *(w.s.)* o mes *(m.)*

	EUROPE — EUROPE — EUROPA								
	France			German Dem. Rep. [3]	Germany, Fed. Rep. of				
	Permanent labourers *Ouvriers permanents* Obreros permanentes			Agricultural workers [4] *Ouvriers agricoles* [4] Obreros agrícolas [4]	Skilled day labourers *Journaliers qualifiés* Jornaleros calificados	Day labourers *Journaliers* Jornaleros		Farm workers *Ouvriers de ferme* Obreros agrícolas	
Date *Date* Fecha	Males *Hommes* Hombres	Females *Femmes* Mujeres	M. + F. H. + F. H. + M.	M. + F. H. + F. H. + M.	Males *Hommes* Hombres	Males *Hommes* Hombres	Females *Femmes* Mujeres	Males *Hommes* Hombres	Females *Femmes* Mujeres
	(E.G./h.) [1]			*(E.G./m.)* [5]	*(R.T./h.)* [6]			*(R.T./m.)* [6]	
	I; II + *a* + *b*			I	II			II	
	Francs	Francs	Francs	Mark	Mark	Mark	Mark	Mark	Mark
1970	480.00	388.00	.	710	3.80	3.59	2.63	494	390
1971	495.00	465.00	.	765	4.24	4.01	2.95	564	447
1972	520.00	498.00	.	795	4.55	4.29	3.16	613	481
1973	610.00	584.00	.	830	5.02	4.74	3.57	683	540
1974	6.50 [2]	6.17 [2]	6.48	859	5.74	5.42	4.14	611	633
1975	8.93	8.51	8.90	886	6.20	5.85	4.47	874	684
1976	10.48	9.93	10.44	917	6.71	6.33	4.84	946	740
1977	11.93	...	...	939	7.32	6.90	5.28	1 025	803
1978	...	...	...	954	7.78	7.34	5.61	1 078	843
1979	...	...	...	979 *	8.37	7.89	6.04	1 125	878

EXPLANATORY NOTES: See p. 423. NOTES EXPLICATIVES: Voir p. 426. NOTAS EXPLICATIVAS: Véase pág. 430.

I: Complete wage (workers remunerated wholly in cash).

II: Cash part of remuneration (where received partly in cash and partly in kind). These figures may include the estimated value of payments in kind for:

    a: board;
    b: lodging.

I: *Montant total du salaire (cas des travailleurs entièrement rémunérés en espèces).*

II: *Partie de la rémunération payée en espèces (cas des travailleurs rémunérés partiellement en espèces et partiellement en nature). Ces chiffres peuvent comprendre la valeur estimée des paiements en nature pour:*

    a: les repas;
    b: le logement.

I: Salario íntegro (trabajadores remunerados enteramente en dinero).

II: Parte de la remuneración en dinero (en los casos en que ésta consiste en una parte en dinero y otra en especie). Estas cifras pueden incluir el valor estimado de los pagos en especie para:

    a: los alimentos;
    b: el alojamiento.

[1] Oct. of each year, except for 1974: April. [2] Series replacing former series. Prior to 1974: general farm hands, earnings per month (II + *a* + *b*). [3] State sector. [4] Incl. salaried employees. [5] Incl. family allowances. [6] Minimum rates.

[1] *Oct. de chaque année, sauf pour 1974: avril.* [2] *Série remplaçant la précédente. Avant 1974: domestiques de ferme, gains mensuels (II + a + b).* [3] *Secteur d'Etat.* [4] *Y compris les employés.* [5] *Y compris les allocations familiales.* [6] *Taux minima.*

[1] Oct. de cada año, salvo 1974: abril. [2] Serie que substituye a la anterior. Antes de 1974: peones agrícolas, ganancias por mes (II + *a* + *b*). [3] Sector de Estado. [4] Incl. los empleados. [5] Incl. las asignaciones familiares. [6] Tarifas mínimas.

22 Wages in agriculture
Salaires dans l'agriculture
Salarios en la agricultura

Earnings *(E.G.)* or rates *(R.T.)*
per hour *(h.)*, day *(d.j.)*,
week *(w.s.)* or month *(m.)*

Gains *(E.G.)* ou taux *(R.T.)*
par heure *(h.)*, jour *(d.j.)*,
semaine *(w.s.)* ou mois *(m.)*

Ganancias *(E.G.)* o tarifas *(R.T.)*
por hora *(h.)*, día *(d.j.)*,
semana *(w.s.)* o mes *(m.)*

						EUROPE — EUROPE — EUROPA			
Date *Date* Fecha	Hongrie [1]	Ireland	Italie	Netherlands		Norway [6]			
		Permanent labourers [2] *Ouvriers permanents [2]* Obreros permanentes [2]	Agricultural workers *Ouvriers agricoles* Obreros agrícolas	Agricultural workers *Ouvriers agricoles* Obreros agrícolas	All workers [2] *Ensemble des ouvriers [2]* Todos los obreros [2]	General farm hands *Domestiques de ferme* Peones agrícolas			
						Permanent labourers *Ouvriers permanents* Obreros permanentes		Casual day labourers *Journaliers occasionnels* Jornaleros ocasionales	
	M. + F. H. + F. H. + M.	Males *Hommes* Hombres	M. + F. H. + F. H. + M.	Males *Hommes* Hombres	Males *Hommes* Hombres	Males *Hommes* Hombres	Females *Femmes* Mujeres	Males *Hommes* Hombres	Females *Femmes* Mujeres
	(E.G./m.)	*(E.G./w.s.)* [3]	*(R.T./h.)*	*(E.G./h.)* [4]	*(R.T./h.)* [5]	*(E.G./m.)*		*(E.G./h.)*	
	I	I	I	II + a + b	I	II + a + b		II + a + b	
	Forints	Pounds	(1970 = 100)	Guilders	(1970 = 100)	Kroner	Kroner	Kroner	Kroner
1970	2 023	13.07	**100.0**	4.07	**100**	1 684	1 077	10.01	9.54
1971	2 110	16.27	113.7	4.63	111	1 878	1 267	10.93	10.71
1972	2 186	17.17	134.3	5.65	128	2 055	1 504	11.94	11.98
1973	2 292	19.78	166.5	6.39	144	2 386	1 479	13.68	12.97
1974	2 475	24.78	219.5	7.56	164	2 772	...	15.67	14.85
1975	2 444	30.42	291.4	8.83	204	3 182	...	18.10	17.18
1976	2 627	33.07	364.6	9.76	225	3 677	...	21.47	21.09
1977	2 861	38.57	480.0	10.42	243	4 128	...	24.08	23.56
1978	3 071	42.57	567.1	11.25	257	4 452	...	25.78	24.80
1979	3 256	49.93	680.2	...	268	4 495	...	26.83	25.45

EXPLANATORY NOTES: See p. 423.   NOTES EXPLICATIVES: Voir p. 426.   NOTAS EXPLICATIVAS: Véase pág. 430.

I: Complete wage (workers remunerated wholly in cash).

II: Cash part of remuneration (where received partly in cash and partly in kind). These figures may include the estimated value of payments in kind for:

    a : board;
    b : lodging.

I: *Montant total du salaire (cas des travailleurs entièrement rémunérés en espèces).*

II: *Partie de la rémunération payée en espèces (cas des travailleurs rémunérés partiellement en espèces et partiellement en nature). Ces chiffres peuvent comprendre la valeur estimée des paiements en nature pour :*

    a: les repas ;
    b: le logement.

I: Salario íntegro (trabajadores remunerados enteramente en dinero).

II: Parte de la remuneración en dinero (en los casos en que ésta consiste en una parte en dinero y otra en especie). Estas cifras pueden incluir el valor estimado de los pagos en especie para:

    a: los alimentos;
    b: el alojamiento.

[1] Incl. forestry. Socialised sector. Prior to 1975: State sector. [2] Adults. [3] Minimum legal wages. July of each year. [4] Year ending in April of the year indicated. Beginning 1972: Oct. of each year. [5] Incl. vacation pay. [6] Sep. of each year.

[1] *Y compris la sylviculture. Secteur socialisé. Avant 1975 : secteur d'Etat.* [2] *Adultes.* [3] *Salaires légaux minima. Juillet de chaque année.* [4] *Année se terminant en avril de l'année indiquée. A partir de 1972 : oct. de chaque année.* [5] *Y compris les versements pour congés payés.* [6] *Sept. de chaque année.*

[1] Incl. la silvicultura. Sector socializado. Antes de 1975: sector de Estado. [2] Adultos. [3] Salarios legales mínimos. Julio de cada año. [4] Año que termina en abril del año indicado. A partir de 1972: oct. de cada año. [5] Incl. los pagos por vacaciones. [6] Sept. de cada año.

WAGES

22 Wages in agriculture
Salaires dans l'agriculture
Salarios en la agricultura

Earnings *(E.G.)* or rates *(R.T.)*
per hour *(h.)*, day *(d.j.)*,
week *(w.s.)* or month *(m.)*

Gains *(E.G.)* ou taux *(R.T.)*
par heure *(h.)*, jour *(d.j.)*,
semaine *(w.s.)* ou mois *(m.)*

Ganancias *(E.G.)* o tarifas *(R.T.)*
por hora *(h.)*, día *(d.j.)*,
semana *(w.s.)* o mes *(m.)*

	EUROPA — EUROPE — EUROPA								
	Pologne [1]	Portugal				Suisse			
				Roumanie [3]			Horticulture — *Horticulture* — Horticultura		
Date *Date* Fecha	Agricultural workers [2] *Ouvriers agricoles* [2] Obreros agrícolas [2]	Agricultural workers *Ouvriers agricoles* Obreros agrícolas			Horticulture and forestry *Horticulture et sylviculture* Horticultura y silvicultura	Skilled *Qualifiés* Calificados	Semi-skilled and unskilled *Semi-qualifiés et non qualifiés* Semicalificados y no calificados	Total	Total
	M. + F. H. + F. H. + M.	Males *Hommes* Hombres	Females *Femmes* Mujeres	M. + F. [2] H. + F. [2] H. + M. [2]	M. + F. H. + F. H. + M.	Males *Hommes* Hombres			Females *Femmes* Mujeres
	(E.G./m.)	*(E.G./d.j.)*		*(E.G./m.)*	*(E.G./h.)* [5]	*(E.G./h.)* [6]			
	I	I		I	I	I			
	Zlotys	Escudos	Escudos	Lei	Francs	Francs	Francs	Francs	Francs
1970	1 867	66.10	37.30	1 327	.	.	.	.	.
1971	1 988	74.70	43.10	1 372	.	.	.	.	.
1972	2 189	83.90	48.00	1 408	.	.	.	.	.
1973	2 457	94.60	55.60	1 488	.	.	.	.	.
1974	2 822	125.70	78.10	1 543	9.84	.	.	.	.
1975	3 667	156.20	105.20	1 737	10.33	11.31	9.55	10.33	7.47
1976	4 122	178.80	119.40	1 934	10.74	11.51	9.66	10.47	7.48
1977	4 400	205.20	142.20	1 868 [4]	10.94	11.87	9.89	10.87	8.10
1978	4 838	241.20	160.40	1 994	11.37	12.23	10.10	11.16	8.40
1979	5 148	293.10	197.40	2 060	11.87	12.72	10.52	11.61	8.69

EXPLANATORY NOTES: See p. 423.　　　NOTES EXPLICATIVES: Voir p. 426.　　　NOTAS EXPLICATIVAS: Véase pág. 430.

I: Complete wage (workers remunerated wholly in cash).

II: Cash part of remuneration (where received partly in cash and partly in kind). These figures may include the estimated value of payments in kind for:

　a: board;
　b: lodging.

I: *Montant total du salaire (cas des travailleurs entièrement rémunérés en espèces).*

II: *Partie de la rémunération payée en espèces (cas de travailleurs rémunérés partiellement en espèces et partiellement en nature). Ces chiffres peuvent comprendre la valeur estimée des paiements en nature pour :*

　a: *les repas ;*
　b: *le logement.*

I: Salario íntegro (trabajadores remunerados enteramente en dinero).

II: Parte de la remuneración en dinero (en los casos en que ésta consiste en una parte en dinero y otra en especie). Estas cifras pueden incluir el valor estimado de los pagos en especie para:

　a: los alimentos;
　b: el alojamiento.

[1] Socialised sector. Incl. the value of payments in kind. [2] Incl. salaried employees. [3] State sector. [4] Beginning 1977: net earnings after deduction of income taxes. [5] Accident insurance statistics. [6] Statistics of establishments. Oct. of each year. Adults. Incl. family allowances.

[1] *Secteur socialisé. Y compris la valeur des paiements en nature.* [2] *Y compris les employés.* [3] *Secteur d'Etat.* [4] *A partir de 1977 : gains nets après déduction de l'impôt sur le revenu.* [5] *Statistiques d'assurance-accidents.* [6] *Statistiques d'établissements. Oct. de chaque année. Adultes. Y compris les allocations familiales.*

[1] Sector socializado. Incl. el valor de los pagos en especie. [2] Incl. los empleados. [3] Sector de Estado. [4] A partir de 1977: ganancias netas después deducción de los impuestos sobre la renta. [5] Estadísticas del seguro de accidentes. [6] Estadísticas de establecimientos. Oct. de cada año. Adultos. Incl. las asignaciones familiares.

22 Wages in agriculture
Salaires dans l'agriculture
Salarios en la agricultura

Earnings *(E.G.)* or rates *(R.T.)*
per hour *(h.)*, day *(d.j.)*,
week *(w.s.)* or month *(m.)*

Gains *(E.G.)* ou taux *(R.T.)*
par heure *(h.)*, jour *(d.j.)*,
semaine *(w.s.)* ou mois *(m.)*

Ganancias *(E.G.)* o tarifas *(R.T.)*
por hora *(h.)*, día *(d.j.)*,
semana *(w.s.)* o mes *(m.)*

	EUROPE — EUROPE — EUROPA					
	Sweden		Turquie	United Kingdom [5]		Yugoslavia [8]
Date *Date* Fecha	All workers [1] *Ensemble des ouvriers* [1] Todos los obreros [1]		Fishermen *Pêcheurs* Pescadores	Regular workers [6] *Ouvriers stables* [6] Obreros estables [6]		Agricultural workers [9] *Ouvriers agricoles* [9] Obreros agrícolas [9]
	Males *Hommes* Hombres	Females *Femmes* Mujeres	M. + F. H. + F. H. + M.	Males [1] *Hommes* [1] Hombres [1]	Females *Femmes* Mujeres	M. + F. H. + F. H. + M.
	(E.G./h.)		*(E.G./d.j.)*	*(E.G./w.s.)* [7]		*(E.G./m.)*
	I + II [2]		I [4]	I		I
	Kronor	Kronor	Liras	£	£	Dinars
1970	11.21	8.99	35.45	19.18	12.45	1 023
1971	12.15	10.39	44.11	21.42	14.65	1 309
1972	13.35 [3]	11.33 [3]	38.74	24.20	15.49	1 554
1973	14.16	12.92	50.31	29.05	19.28	1 843
1974	15.95	14.58	53.93	36.24	24.52	2 451
1975	19.35	18.25	89.05	45.47	32.31	2 923
1976	22.37	19.52	99.59	51.50	41.18	3 378
1977	24.93	21.48	120.80	56.24	46.73	3 932
1978	26.20	23.57	220.42	63.98	50.42	4 561
1979	28.26	25.53	292.49	…	…	5 458

EXPLANATORY NOTES: See p. 423.

NOTES EXPLICATIVES: Voir p. 426.

NOTAS EXPLICATIVAS: Véase pág. 430.

I: Complete wage (workers remunerated wholly in cash).

II: Cash part of remuneration (where received partly in cash and partly in kind). These figures may include the estimated value of payments in kind for:

    a : board;
    b : lodging.

I: *Montant total du salaire (cas des travailleurs entièrement rémunérés en espèces).*

II: *Partie de la rémunération payée en espèces (cas des travailleurs rémunérés partiellement en espèces et partiellement en nature). Ces chiffres peuvent comprendre la valeur estimée des paiements en nature pour :*

    a : les repas ;
    b : le logement.

I: Salario íntegro (trabajadores remunerados enteramente en dinero).

II: Parte de la remuneración en dinero (en los casos en que ésta consiste en una parte en dinero y otra en especie). Estas cifras pueden incluir el valor estimado de los pagos en especie para:

    a : los alimentos;
    b : el alojamiento.

[1] Adults. [2] Prior to 1972: workers remunerated wholly in cash. [3] Beginning 1972: second quarter of each year. [4] Sep. of each year. [5] Excl. Northern Ireland. [6] Full-time wage earners. [7] Year ending 31 March of following year. Incl. the value of payments in kind. [8] Socialised sector. Incl. forestry and fishing. [9] Incl. salaried employees.

[1] *Adultes.* [2] *Avant 1972: travailleurs entièrement rémunérés en espèces.* [3] *A partir de 1972: deuxième trimestre de chaque année.* [4] *Sept. de chaque année.* [5] *Non compris l'Irlande du Nord.* [6] *Ouvriers à temps complet.* [7] *Année se terminant le 31 mars de l'année suivante. Y compris la valeur des paiements en nature.* [8] *Secteur socialisé. Y compris la sylviculture et la pêche.* [9] *Y compris les employés.*

[1] Adultos. [2] Antes de 1972: trabajadores remunerados enteramente en dinero. [3] A partir de 1972: segundo trimestre de cada año. [4] Sept. de cada año. [5] Excl. Irlanda del Norte. [6] Obreros a tiempo completo. [7] Año que termina el 31 de marzo del año siguiente. Incl. el valor de los pagos en especie. [8] Sector socializado. Incl. la silvicultura y la pesca. [9] Incl. los empleados.

22 Wages in agriculture
Salaires dans l'agriculture
Salarios en la agricultura

Earnings *(E.G.)* or rates *(R.T.)*
per hour *(h.)*, day *(d.j.)*,
week *(w.s.)* or month *(m.)*

Gains *(E.G.)* ou taux *(R.T.)*
par heure *(h.)*, jour *(d.j.)*,
semaine *(w.s.)* ou mois *(m.)*

Ganancias *(E.G.)* o tarifas *(R.T.)*
por hora *(h.)*, día *(d.j.)*,
semana *(w.s.)* o mes *(m.)*

Date / Date / Fecha	OCEANIA — OCÉANIE — OCEANÍA				Polynésie française — Workers / Ouvriers / Obreros				
	Fiji	New Zealand		Nouvelle-Calédonie	Copra harvest and preparation / Ramassage et préparation du coprah / Recogida y preparación de la copra	URSS [5, 6]	RSS de Biélorussie [5]	RSS d'Ukraine [5]
	Agricultural workers / Ouvriers agricoles / Obreros agrícolas	Farm workers / Ouvriers agricoles / Obreros agrícolas	Dairy farms / Fermes laitières / Granjas lecheras					
	M. + F.	Males		M. + F.	M. + F.	M. + F. [7]	M. + F. [7]	M. + F. [7]
	H. + F.	Hommes		H. + F.	H. + F.	H. + F. [7]	H. + F. [7]	H. + F. [7]
	H. + M.	Hombres		H. + M.	H. + M.	H. + M. [7]	H. + M. [7]	H. + M. [7]
	(R.T./d.j.) [1]	*(R.T./w.s.)* [2]		*(R.T./h.)*	*(R.T./h.)* [2, 3]	*(E.G./m.)*	*(E.G./m.)* [8]	*(E.G./m.)*
	I	I		II + a + b	I	I	I	I
	Dollars	Dollars	Dollars	Francs (CFP)	Francs (CFP)	Roubles	Roubles	Roubles
1970	1.97	26.00		.	43.20	100.9	76.1	95.7
1971	2.13	26.75		.	45.00	106.3	81.4	101.5
1972	2.39	27.00		.	45.00	111.8	85.9	104.6
1973	3.12	39.18		.	45.00 [4]	117.5	91.0	112.2
1974	4.49	50.25		100.94	63.95	124.2	93.7	116.1
1975	4.98	58.22		129.98	71.25	126.7	95.8	116.4
1976	5.02	72.03		141.48	76.00	134.7	110.6	124.2
1977	5.76	78.23		149.26	101.00	139.1	114.7	128.7
1978	6.67	94.31	98.06	160.10	153.30	143.1	120.0	133.4
1979	7.14 *	...	...	169.80	171.00	146.0	121.6	134.1

EXPLANATORY NOTES: See p. 423.   NOTES EXPLICATIVES: Voir p. 426.   NOTAS EXPLICATIVAS: Véase pág. 430.

I: Complete wage (workers remunerated wholly in cash).

II: Cash part of remuneration (where received partly in cash and partly in kind). These figures may include the estimated value of payments in kind for:
   a: board;
   b: lodging.

I: *Montant total du salaire (cas des travailleurs entièrement rémunérés en espèces).*

II: *Partie de la rémunération payée en espèces (cas des travailleurs rémunérés partiellement en espèces et partiellement en nature). Ces chiffres peuvent comprendre la valeur estimée des paiements en nature pour :*
   a : les repas ;
   b : le logement.

I: Salario íntegro (trabajadores remunerados enteramente en dinero).

II: Parte de la remuneración en dinero (en los casos en que ésta consiste en una parte en dinero y otra en especie). Estas cifras pueden incluir el valor estimado de los pagos en especie para:
   a : los alimentos;
   b : el alojamiento.

[1] June of each year. [2] Minimum rates. [3] Dec. of each year. [4] Sep. [5] State sector. [6] Incl. Byelorussian SSR and Ukrainian SSR, shown separately in this table. [7] Incl. salaried employees. [8] Inc. forestry.

[1] *Juin de chaque année.* [2] *Taux minima.* [3] *Déc. de chaque année.* [4] *Sept.* [5] *Secteur d'Etat.* [6] *Y compris les RSS de Biélorussie et d'Ukraine, figurant séparément dans ce tableau.* [7] *Y compris les employés.* [8] *Y compris la sylviculture.*

[1] Junio de cada año. [2] Tarifas mínimas. [3] Dic. de cada año. [4] Sept. [5] Sector de Estado. [6] Incl. las RSS de Bielorrusia y de Ucrania, que figuran separadamente en este cuadro. [7] Incl. los empleados. [8] Incl. la silvicultura.

Consumer prices

Prix à la consommation

Precios del consumo

Consumer prices

Table 23

Consumer prices

Part A of this table contains general consumer price indices for all groups of consumption items combined. Parts B through E contain group indices respectively for " Food " (incl. drinks), " Fuel and light ", " Clothing " and " Rent ".

The consumer price indices are designed to show changes over time in the price level of certain goods and services which are selected as representative of the consumption patterns of the population concerned. Prices of items included in the index are collected at regular intervals in shops and markets and from service establishments in the area covered. The method employed in calculating the indices varies somewhat from one country to another. Usually the indices are calculated in the form of weighted arithmetic averages of price ratios between the base period and the period of reference (price relatives), using fixed weights corresponding to the base period (Laspeyres formula). The weights, which represent the relative importance of each item, are usually derived from family expenditure surveys conducted to obtain the pattern of consumer expenditure and the relative importance of each item for a particular population group.[1] Where data on family expenditures are not available, or are insufficient for a system of weights, supplementary calculations are commonly made for the purpose of establishing theoretical budgets; in a few cases weights are based on estimated total consumption, in the country, of the items considered.

Owing to differences in scope and in methods used for the compilation of the indices, the statistics for the different countries shown in the table are not uniformly representative of changes in price levels and vary in reliability from one country to another.[2]

As the original base period of the series also varies, a uniform base period (1970) has been adopted for the presentation of the data and as many as possible of the series have been recalculated by dividing the index for each date shown by the index for the year 1970 and multiplying the quotient by 100. Where data are available only for periods subsequent to 1970, the indices are generally presented with the first available calendar year as base. This operation does not involve any change in the weighting systems, etc., used by the countries.

In several cases, indicated by footnotes, where a series has been discontinued and has been replaced by a new series sufficiently comparable with the former, the two have been spliced.

The general consumer price index (Part A of this table) covers, in most cases, all the main categories of expenditure such as food (incl. drinks), fuel and light, clothing, rent and miscellaneous. Indices relating to this latter group are not shown separately in the *Year Book*, on account of the important variations in the composition of such group from one country to another.[3]

The consumer price indices are often used as deflators of nominal wage indices in the calculation of crude indicators of trends of real wages. Although such a deflation of nominal wages by consumer prices provides a useful measure of the relative purchasing power (with regard to consumer goods and services), the results may be misleading, in particular when the wage data correspond to a population group whose social and economic characteristics are very different from the population group to which the consumer price index corresponds.[4]

---

[1] In addition to the series presented in this table, readers will find in national publications of various countries (see Appendix, " References and Sources ") series referring to other localities, regions or population groups.

[2] For a detailed discussion of consumer price indices and techniques used in their compilation, see ILO: *Cost-of-living Statistics*, Studies and Reports, New Series, No. 7 (Part 2) (Geneva, 1948), and *Computation of Consumer Price Indices* (Special Problems), Tenth International Conference of Labour Statisticians, Report IV (Geneva, 1970) (mimeographed).

[3] For the descriptions of the various national series, their scope, methods of compilation and definitions used, etc., see ILO: *Technical Guide 1980* (descriptions of general series published in the *Bulletin* and the *Year Book of Labour Statistics*), Vol. I, " Consumer Prices " (Geneva, 1980).

[4] For an analysis of some of the problems involved, see ILO: *International Comparisons of Real Wages*, Studies and Reports, New Series, No. 45 (Geneva, 1956).

Prix à la consommation

Prix à la consommation

La partie A de ce tableau présente les indices généraux des prix à la consommation pour tous les groupes d'articles de consommation combinés. Les parties B à E présentent les indices concernant respectivement les groupes suivants: « Alimentation » (y compris les boissons), « Combustible et éclairage », « Habillement » et « Loyer ».

Les indices des prix à la consommation ont pour objet de mettre en évidence les variations, au cours du temps, des prix de certains biens et services choisis de façon à représenter les habitudes de consommation de la population considérée. Les prix des articles retenus dans l'indice sont relevés à intervalles réguliers dans des magasins, des marchés et auprès de prestataires de services situés dans la zone à laquelle se rapporte la série. Les méthodes suivies lors du calcul des indices varient d'un pays à un autre. En général, les indices sont calculés sous forme de moyennes arithmétiques pondérées des rapports de prix entre la période de base et la période considérée (formule de Laspeyres). Les coefficients de pondération, qui permettent de tenir compte de l'importance relative des dépenses de consommation, sont généralement fondés sur les résultats d'enquêtes sur les dépenses familiales reflétant la structure des dépenses de consommation et leur importance relative pour un groupe de population donné [1]. Si l'on ne dispose pas de données sur les dépenses des familles ou si ces données sont insuffisantes pour qu'on puisse établir un système de coefficients de pondération, on effectue généralement des calculs supplémentaires en vue d'établir des budgets théoriques; dans quelques cas, les coefficients de pondération sont fondés sur une estimation de la consommation totale, dans le pays, des articles considérés.

Vu les différences existant dans la portée des indices et dans les méthodes utilisées pour les établir, les statistiques figurant dans le tableau pour les différents pays ne sont pas uniformément représentatives des variations des niveaux de prix et elles n'ont pas la même précision d'un pays à un autre [2].

Comme la période de base originale des séries varie elle aussi, on a adopté une période de base uniforme (1970) pour la présentation des données et le plus grand nombre possible des séries ont été recalculées en divisant l'indice se rapportant à chacune des dates indiquées par l'indice pour l'année 1970 et en multipliant le quotient par 100. Lorsqu'on ne dispose de données que pour des périodes postérieures à 1970, les indices sont généralement présentés en prenant pour période de base la première année civile pour laquelle existent des données. Ces opérations n'impliquent aucune modification des systèmes de pondération utilisés par les pays intéressés.

Dans plusieurs cas, indiqués en note, lorsqu'une série a été interrompue et remplacée par une nouvelle série suffisamment comparable à la première, les deux séries ont été raccordées.

L'indice général des prix à la consommation (partie A) couvre, dans la majeure partie des cas, toutes les catégories importantes de dépenses telles que l'alimentation (y compris les boissons), le combustible et l'éclairage, l'habillement, le loyer et les dépenses diverses. Des indices relatifs à ce dernier groupe ne sont pas présentés séparément dans l'*Annuaire*, en raison des variations importantes dans la composition de ce groupe d'un pays à un autre [3].

---

[1] En plus des séries figurant dans ce tableau, le lecteur trouvera dans les publications nationales des différents pays des séries concernant d'autres localités, d'autres régions ou d'autres groupes de population (voir annexe, « Références et sources »).

[2] Pour une étude détaillée des indices des prix à la consommation et des méthodes utilisées pour établir ces indices, voir BIT: *Statistiques du coût de la vie*, Etudes et documents, nouvelle série, n° 7 (partie 2) (Genève, 1948), et *Calcul des indices des prix à la consommation* (Problèmes particuliers), dixième Conférence internationale des statisticiens du travail, rapport IV (Genève, 1970) (document polycopié).

[3] Pour la description des diverses séries nationales, de leur portée, des méthodes de calcul et des définitions utilisées, etc., voir BIT: *Guide technique 1980* (descriptions des séries générales publiées dans le *Bulletin* et l'*Annuaire des statistiques du travail*), vol. I, « Prix à la consommation » (Genève, 1980).

On se sert fréquemment des indices des prix à la consommation pour corriger les indices des salaires nominaux lorsqu'on calcule les indicateurs approximatifs des tendances des salaires réels. Bien que cette correction des salaires nominaux au moyen des prix à la consommation permette de mesurer utilement le pouvoir d'achat relatif (en ce qui concerne les biens de consommation et les services), les résultats peuvent prêter à des interprétations erronées, notamment lorsque les données relatives aux salaires se rapportent à un groupe de population dont les caractéristiques sociales et économiques sont très différentes de celles du groupe de population auquel se rapporte l'indice des prix à la consommation [1].

---

[1] Pour une analyse de certains des problèmes relatifs à cette question, voir BIT: *Les comparaisons internationales des salaires réels*, Etudes et documents, nouvelle série, n° 45 (Genève, 1956).

Precios del consumo

Precios del consumo

La parte A de este cuadro presenta los índices generales de los precios del consumo de todos los grupos de artículos de consumo en su conjunto. Las partes B a E presentan los índices para los grupos siguientes: « Alimentación » (inclusive las bebidas), « Combustible y alumbrado », « Vestido » y « Alquiler ».

Los índices de los precios del consumo tienen por objeto medir los cambios que sufre, con el transcurso del tiempo, el nivel de los precios de un conjunto de bienes y servicios que se considera representativo de los hábitos del consumo de una población determinada. Los precios de los artículos incluidos en el índice se obtienen a intervalos regulares en almacenes, mercados y establecimientos de suministro de servicios ubicados en la zona abarcada por la serie. Los métodos utilizados para calcular los índices varían de un país a otro. Por lo general, dichos índices se calculan en forma de promedios aritméticos ponderados de los relativos de precios entre el período de base y el período considerado (fórmula de Laspeyres). Los coeficientes de ponderación, que permiten tener en cuenta la importancia relativa de los gastos del consumo, se basan generalmente en los resultados de encuestas sobre los gastos de las familias que reflejan la estructura de los gastos del consumo y su importancia relativa para un grupo dado de población [1]. Cuando no se dispone de informaciones sobre gastos de las familias, o cuando son insuficientes para establecer un sistema de ponderaciones, se efectúan ordinariamente cálculos adicionales con el fin de establecer presupuestos teóricos; en unos pocos casos, las ponderaciones se basan en el consumo total estimado de los artículos que se consideran en un determinado país.

Dadas las diferencias en el alcance de los índices y en los métodos que se utilizan para calcularlos, las estadísticas que se presentan en este cuadro para los diferentes países no representan de modo uniforme las variaciones de los niveles de los precios, y la exactitud de los datos varía de un país a otro [2].

En vista de que también varía el período escogido como base en las diferentes series, se ha adoptado un período de base uniforme (1970) para la presentación de los datos, y, en la medida de lo posible, se han calculado nuevamente en su mayor parte estas series dividiendo el índice de cada fecha indicada por el índice del año 1970 y multiplicando el cociente por 100. Cuando se dispone de datos sólo para los años posteriores a 1970, generalmente se presentan los índices escogiendo como base el primer año civil accesible. Esta operación no implica ninguna modificación en el procedimiento de ponderación, etc., utilizado por los distintos países.

En algunos casos que se indican en las notas de pie de página, cuando ha habido interrupción en una serie, y ha sido reemplazada por otra serie que puede compararse satisfactoriamente con la primera, se ha procedido a enlazar las dos series.

El índice general de los precios del consumo (parte A de este cuadro) comprende, en la mayoría de los casos, todas las principales categorías de gastos, a saber, la alimentación (inclusive las bebidas), el combustible y el alumbrado, el vestido, el alquiler y los gastos varios. Los índices relativos a este último grupo no se presentan por separado en el *Anuario*, a causa de las variaciones importantes, en la composición de este grupo, de un país a otro [3].

---

[1] Además de las series que se presentan en este cuadro, el lector encontrará en las publicaciones nacionales de los diversos países series que se refieren a otras localidades, zonas y grupos de población (véase anexo, « Referencias y fuentes »).

[2] Para un estudio detallado de los índices de precios del consumo y de los métodos que se utilizan en su cálculo, véanse OIT: *Estadísticas del costo de la vida*, nueva serie, núm. 7 (parte 2) (Ginebra, 1948), y *Cálculo de los índices de los precios del consumo* (Problemas especiales), décima Conferencia Internacional de Estadígrafos del Trabajo, Informe IV (Ginebra, 1970) (mimeografiado).

[3] Para las descripciones de las diversas series nacionales, su alcance, métodos de compilación y definiciones utilizados, etc., véase OIT: *Guía Técnica 1980* (descripciones de las series generales publicadas en el *Boletín* y el *Anuario de Estadísticas del Trabajo*), vol. I, « Precios del consumo » (Ginebra, 1980).

Los índices de los precios del consumo se utilizan a menudo para corregir los índices de salarios nominales cuando se calculan los indicadores aproximados de las tendencias de los salarios reales. Aunque esta corrección de los salarios nominales mediante los precios del consumo proporciona una medida del poder de compra relativo (con respecto a los bienes de consumo y a los servicios), los resultados pueden inducir en error, sobre todo cuando las informaciones sobre salarios corresponden a un grupo de población cuyas características económicas y sociales son muy diferentes de las del grupo de población a que corresponde el índice de los precios del consumo [1].

---

[1] Para el estudio de algunos de los problemas conexos, véase OIT: *Les comparaisons internationales des salaires réels*, Etudes et documents, nouvelle série, núm. 45 (Ginebra, 1956; en inglés y francés solamente).

23 Consumer prices / Prix à la consommation / Precios del consumo — A General indices / Indices généraux / Indices generales

(1970 = 100)

Country — Pays — País	1970	1971	1972	1973	1974	1975	1976	1977	1978	1979	1980 (VI)
AFRICA — AFRIQUE AFRICA											
Algérie (Alger)	100.0	102.6	106.4	112.9	118.2	128.6	140.1	156.8	183.8	...	...
Botswana [1, 2]	100.0	.		119.7 [3]	135.7	▌111.7 [4]	125.6	141.7	154.4	172.6	189.8 [25]
Burundi (Bujumbura) [1, 5]	100.0	103.9	107.8	114.2	132.2	153.1	163.5	174.0	235.5	294.5	329.8 [25]
Cameroun (Yaoundé) . . . . . . Afric.	100.0	104.2	112.5	124.3	145.7	165.4	181.8	208.2	234.6	249.9	271.0 [26]
» » [6] . . . . . Europ.	100.0	103.8	110.2	117.5	137.1	157.6	170.8	187.4	202.0	218.3	236.2 [26]
Cap-Vert (Praia) [7]	100.0	115.1	126.7	144.5	219.2	280.1	283.6	303.4	437.0	...	...
République centrafricaine (Bangui) [6] . Europ.	100.0	106.8	114.5	120.9	132.4	153.7	169.8	188.4 [8]	210.3	...	...
Congo (Brazzaville) [6] . Europ.	100.0	104.1	114.2	118.2	124.8	146.3	156.9	...	197.7	213.7	224.5 [27]
Côte-d'Ivoire (Abidjan) . . . . Afric.	100.0	99.2	99.5	110.2	129.8	144.6	162.0	206.4	233.3	272.1	323.2
» » » [6] . Europ.	100.0	104.1	107.9	112.3	130.5	155.2	174.9	198.2	237.0	258.1	278.6
Egypt	100.0	103.1	105.3	109.8	121.7	133.5	147.3	166.0	184.4	202.7	246.1
Ethiopia (Addis Ababa) [6]	100.0	100.5	94.4	102.8	111.7	119.0	152.9	178.4	203.9	236.6	251.3
Gabon (Libreville) [9] . . . . Afric.	96.7 [10]	100.0	104.8	110.0	123.2	▌158.2 [11]	190.1 [28]	216.3 [28]	239.6	258.7	291.5 [26]
» » [6] . 12	100.0	103.8	111.2	▌123.7 [11]	138.3	156.8	185.3	207.4	225.0	239.5	261.4 [26]
Gambia (Banjul-Kombo, St. Mary)	100.0	103.1	112.0	119.8	130.9	164.8	192.9	216.9	236.0	250.4	257.3
Ghana (Accra)	100.0	104.9	114.8	127.9	163.3	230.5	351.5	634.9	▌169.9 [13]	276.4	371.2
Kenya (Nairobi) 14	100.0	101.9 [15]	▌100.0 [16]	108.2	124.3	147.2	▌159.4 [11]	177.7	196.0	210.1	233.2
Lesotho 17	.	.	93.5 [18]	100.0	114.6	131.6	145.4	171.2	193.5	...	...
Liberia (Monrovia)	100.0	100.2	104.2	124.6	148.9	169.1	178.6	189.7	203.6	226.8	257.7 [25]
Libyan Arab Jamahiriya (Tripoli) . . .	100.0	97.3	97.0	104.5	112.5	122.9	129.6	137.6	178.2	...	...
Madagascar (Tananarive) [6] 19	100.0	105.4	111.4	▌118.2 [11]	144.2	156.1	163.9	168.9	180.0	205.3	235.0
» » [6] . Europ.	100.0	106.2	113.0	▌115.5 [11]	127.7	145.2	160.3	174.5	187.6	207.9	231.3
Malawi (Blantyre) [6] 17	100.0	108.2	112.1	117.8	135.9	157.0	163.8	170.7	185.2	206.1	242.5
» » [6] . 12	100.0	108.3	112.5	119.7	140.0	167.5	187.7	212.0	240.8	278.3	364.4 [27]
Maroc [20]	100.0	104.2	108.1	112.5	▌100.0 [16]	107.9	117.1	131.8	144.6	156.6	168.1
Mauritanie (Nouakchott) [6] . . . . Europ.	100.0	107.6	116.4	124.8	140.4 [21]	▌100.0 [16]	114.4	126.2	135.3	...	...
Mauritius	100.0	100.3	105.7	120.0	154.9	177.7	▌201.6 [11]	220.2	238.9	273.6	379.4
Mozambique (Maputo)	100.0	115.7	123.9	130.6	159.0	164 2	171.6	.	.		
Niger (Niamey) [6] . . . . . Afric.	100.0	104.3	114.4	127.8	132.2	144.2	178.2	219.7	241.8	...	...
» » [6] . Europ.	100.0	103.6	105.6	108.2	116.4	128.7	141.3	154.7	171.1	...	...
Nigeria (Lagos) 17	100.0	113.5	116.8	121.0 [22]	141.4	186.3	226.7	285.4	.	.	.
» » 23	.	.	.	.	.	100.0	124.3	141.5	176.0	195.6	...
» » 24	.	.	.	.	.	100.0	123.9	143.0	166.7	186.3	...
Réunion (Saint-Denis)	100.0	106.4	▌114.6 [11]	127.9	146.5	165.6	180.0	197.3	210.3	230.4	262.4

EXPLANATORY NOTES AND CODES: See p. 575.

NOTES EXPLICATIVES ET CODES: Voir p. 576.

NOTAS EXPLICATIVAS Y CLAVES: Véase pág. 578.

[1] Incl. income taxes. [2] Prior to 1975: Gaborone only. [3] June-Dec. [4] Series (base 1974 = 100) replacing former series. [5] Government officials. [6] Excl." Rent ". [7] Excl. " Clothing " and " Rent ". [8] Jan.-June and Sep.-Dec. [9] Prior to 1975: excl. " Rent ". [10] Jan.-June and Aug.-Dec. [11] Series linked to former series. [12] High income group. [13] Series (base 1977 = 100) replacing former series. [14] Middle income group; prior to 1972: low income group; excl. " Rent ". [15] Jan.-Aug. [16] Series replacing former series. [17] Low income group. [18] Oct. [19] Madagascans. [20] Prior to 1974: Casablanca only. [21] Jan.-July and Sep.-Dec. [22] Jan.-Sep. and Dec. [23] Urban areas. [24] Rural and urban areas. [25] March. [26] May. [27] April. [28] Official estimates.

[1] Y compris les impôts sur le revenu. [2] Avant 1975: Gaborone seulement. [3] Juin-déc. [4] Série (base 100 en 1974) remplaçant la précédente. [5] Fonctionnaires. [6] Non compris le groupe « Loyer ». [7] Non compris les groupes « Habillement » et « Loyer ». [8] Janv.-juin et sept.-déc. [9] Avant 1975: non compris le groupe « Loyer ». [10] Janv.-juin et août-déc. [11] Série enchaînée à la précédente. [12] Familles à revenu élevé. [13] Série (base 100 en 1977) remplaçant la précédente. [14] Familles à revenu moyen; avant 1972: familles à revenu modique; non compris le groupe « Loyer ». [15] Janv.-août. [16] Série remplaçant la précédente. [17] Familles à revenu modique. [18] Oct. [19] Malgaches. [20] Avant 1974: Casablanca seulement. [21] Janv.-juillet et sept.-déc. [22] Janv.-sept. et déc. [23] Régions urbaines. [24] Régions rurales et urbaines. [25] Mars. [26] Mai. [27] Avril. [28] Estimations officielles.

[1] Incl. los impuestos sobre los ingresos. [2] Antes de 1975: Gaborone solamente. [3] Junio-dic. [4] Serie (base 1974 = 100) que substituye a la anterior. [5] Funcionarios. [6] Excl. el grupo « Alquiler ». [7] Excl. los grupos « Vestido » y « Alquiler ». [8] Enero-junio y sept.-dic. [9] Antes de 1975: excl. el grupo « Alquiler ». [10] Enero-junio y agosto-dic. [11] Serie enlazada con la anterior. [12] Familias de ingresos elevados. [13] Serie (base 1977 = 100) que substituye a la anterior. [14] Familias de ingresos medios; antes de 1972: familias de ingresos módicos; excl. el grupo « Alquiler ». [15] Enero-agosto. [16] Serie que substituye a la anterior. [17] Familias de ingresos módicos. [18] Oct. [19] Malgaches. [20] Antes de 1974: Casablanca solamente. [21] Enero-julio y sept.-dic. [22] Enero-sept. y dic. [23] Areas urbanas. [24] Areas rurales y urbanas. [25] Marzo. [26] Mayo. [27] Abril. [28] Estimaciones oficiales.

580

23 Consumer prices / Prix à la consommation / Precios del consumo

A General indices / Indices généraux / Indices generales

(1970 = 100)

Country — Pays — País	1970	1971	1972	1973	1974	1975	1976	1977	1978	1979	1980 (VI)
Rwanda (Kigali) [1]	100	103	106	114	152	199	199	202	...	...	.
Sénégal (Dakar)	100.0	103.9	110.3	122.7	143.1	188.4	190.5	212.0	219.3	240.7	260.3 [19]
Seychelles [2]	100.0	114.9	139.1	164.4	204.5 [3]	242.6	278.8	100.0 [4]	111.9	125.4	...
Sierra Leone (Freetown)	100.0	98.3	103.8	109.6	125.4	150.4	176.2	190.9	211.7	256.7	281.2 [20]
Somalia (Mogadishu)	100.0	99.4	96.5	102.7	121.5	145.0	165.4	182.9	204.7	...	...
South Africa, Rep. of [5]	100.0	106.1	113.0	123.7	138.1	156.7	174.1	193.9	215.0	243.4	...
Sudan	100.0	101.3	113.3	132.6	167.2	207.3	210.8	246.2	294.9	385.9	455.2 [21]
Swaziland (Mbabane-Manzini) [1] [6]	100.0	103.2	106.0	118.6	141.2	160.0	171.2	200.7	217.8	253.6	277.5 [19]
Tanzania	100.0	104.7	112.8	124.5	148.9	187.7	200.6	223.9	249.7	283.7	...
Tchad (N'djamena) [1] [6]	.	.	.	.	100.5 [7]	100.0	102.5 [8]	134.0	144.8	...	...
» » [1] [9]	100.0	106.0	109.1	115.0	127.9 [3]	147.9	152.9	165.7	186.0	...	...
Togo (Lomé)	100.0	108.9	113.6	119.5	134.6	158.7	179.0	215.1	216.8	...	...
Tunisie [10]	100.0	106.0	108.2	113.1	117.7	128.9	135.8	144.9	105.4 [11]	113.5	122.7
Uganda (Kampala) [1] [6]	100.0	115.8	112.3	139.7	233.6	280.8	434.2	730.3 [12]	...	...	...
Zaïre (Kinshasa)	100	106	122	142	182 [3]	233	438	715	1 132	...	...
Zambia [6]	100.0	104.9	110.2	117.3	126.8	139.7	165.9	198.7	231.2	253.8	...
Zimbabwe [18] [6]	100.0	103.0	106.0	109.3	116.5	128.1	142.9	160.0	175.6	198.8	206.2
AMERICA — AMÉRIQUE AMÉRICA											
Antigua	100.0	108.6	118.3	134.2	167.6	186.8	207.5	236.0	250.5	288.9 [13]	340.3 [22]
Argentina (Buenos Aires) [14]	100	135	213	342	425	1 202	6 539	18 050 [3]	49 729	129 051	252 694
Bahamas (Nassau)	100.0	104.6	100.0 [4]	105.3	119.1	131.4	137.0	141.3	150.0	163.7	181.3
Barbados	100.0	107.5	120.2	140.5	195.1	234.7	246.4	267.0	292.3	330.8	387.7 [22]
Bermuda	100.0	108.2	116.4	131.4	153.0	162.9	165.5	171.2	100.0 [4]	110.5	122.2 [21]
Bolivia (La Paz)	100.0	103.7	110.4	145.2	236.5	255.3	266.8	288.4	318.3	381.1	569.1
Brasil (São Paulo)	100.0	121.1	100.0 [4]	115.5	144.3	187.9	254.3	357.3	494.3	742.5	...
Canada	100.0	102.9	107.8	115.9	128.6	142.5	153.2	165.4	180.2	196.7	215.9
Colombia (Bogotá)	100.0	109.0	124.6	152.9	190.3	239.2	280.8	365.1	428.5	532.4 [3]	690.9
Costa Rica (San José) [14]	100.0	103.1	107.8	124.2 [15]	161.6 [16]	189.5	196.2 [3]	204.4	216.6	236.5	280.1
Chile (Santiago)	100	120	213	967	5 846	27 752	86 564	166 163	232 773	310 499 [3]	413 669
Dominica	100.0	103.7	107.6	120.6	164.2	194.3	215.4	235.9	254.2	299.8 [17]	392.9

EXPLANATORY NOTES AND CODES: See p. 575.

[1] Excl. "Rent". [2] Prior to 1977: Victoria only. [3] Series linked to former series. [4] Series replacing former series. [5] White population. [6] Low income group. [7] April-Dec. [8] Jan.-Nov. [9] High income group. [10] Prior to 1978: Tunis metropolitan area only. [11] Series (base 1977 = 100) replacing former series. [12] Jan.-March and July-Dec. [13] Jan.-Nov. [14] Metropolitan area. [15] June and Dec. [16] June, Aug. and Oct.-Dec. [17] Jan.-Aug. and Nov.-Dec. [18] Former Southern Rhodesia. [19] April. [20] Second quarter. [21] March. [22] May.

NOTES EXPLICATIVES ET CODES: Voir p. 576.

[1] Non compris le groupe « Loyer ». [2] Avant 1977: Victoria seulement. [3] Série enchaînée à la précédente. [4] Série remplaçant la précédente. [5] Population blanche. [6] Familles à revenu modique. [7] Avril-déc. [8] Janv.-nov. [9] Familles à revenu élevé. [10] Avant 1978: région métropolitaine de Tunis seulement. [11] Série (base 100 en 1977) remplaçant la précédente. [12] Janv.-mars et juillet-déc. [13] Janv.-nov. [14] Région métropolitaine. [15] Juin et déc. [16] Juin, août et oct.-déc. [17] Janv.-août et nov.-déc. [18] Précédemment Rhodésie du Sud. [19] Avril. [20] Deuxième trimestre. [21] Mars. [22] Mai.

NOTAS EXPLICATIVAS Y CLAVES: Véase pág. 578.

[1] Excl. el grupo « Alquiler ». [2] Antes de 1977: Victoria solamente. [3] Serie enlazada con la anterior. [4] Serie que substituye a la anterior. [5] Población blanca. [6] Familias de ingresos módicos. [7] Abril-dic. [8] Enero-nov. [9] Familias de ingresos elevados. [10] Antes de 1978: área metropolitana de Túnez solamente. [11] Serie (base 1977 = 100) que substituye a la anterior. [12] Enero-marzo y julio-dic. [13] Enero-nov. [14] Area metropolitana. [15] Junio y dic. [16] Junio, agosto y oct.-dic. [17] Enero-agosto y nov.-dic. [18] Anteriormente Rhodesia del Sur. [19] Abril. [20] Segundo trimestre. [21] Marzo. [22] Mayo.

23

Consumer prices
Prix à la consommation
Precios del consumo

A

General indices
Indices généraux
Indices generales

(1970 = 100)

Country — Pays — País	1970	1971	1972	1973	1974	1975	1976	1977	1978	1979	1980 (VI)
República Dominicana (Santo Domingo) [1] . .	*97.1* [2]	**100.0**	*107.8*	*124.1*	*140.4*	*160.8*	*173.4*	*195.6*	*202.5*	*221.1*	*251.0* [24]
Ecuador (Quito)	100.0	108.4	117.0	132.1	163.0	188.0	208.1	235.2	262.6	289.6	326.4 [25]
El Salvador [3]	100.0	100.3 [4]	102.0	108.5	126.8	151.1	161.7	180.8	204.8	**100.0** [5]	*117.8*
Falkland Is. (Malvinas) (Stanley) [6]	100.0	108.1	*83.4* [7]	**100.0**	*119.4*	*147.2*	*163.3*	*191.1*	*207.0*	226.7	246.5 [24]
Greenland	.	**100.0**	*106.0*	*116.4*	*135.1*	*156.0*	*174.0*	*187.1*	*204.0*	*221.7*	*254.1* [26]
Guadeloupe [3]	100.0	106.4	114.9	122.7	142.3	166.4	180.7 [8]	197.5 [9]	213.1	**232.1** [10]	267.0
Guatemala [3]	100.0	99.5	100.1	114.4	132.7	**100.0** [5]	*110.6*	*124.6*	*134.5*	*149.9*	*166.6*
Guyana [3]	100.0	101.0	106.0	114.0	133.9	144.6	157.6	170.5	196.5	231.4	261.2 [25]
Guyane française (Cayenne)	100.0	106.9 [11]	112.7	120.6	140.4	160.3 [12]	176.1	194.3	210.1 [13]	232.7	257.7
Haïti (Port-au-Prince) [14]	100.0	110.4	113.9	139.8	161.5	188.3	200.0	213.9	208.3	235.4	268.5
Honduras (Tegucigalpa)	100.0	103.1	108.7	113.2	127.5	135.4	142.3	154.3	163.8	178.5	210.2 [25]
Jamaica	100.0	105.3	111.0	130.5	166.0	195.1	214.1	238.0	321.0	414.4	...
Martinique (Fort-de-France)	100.0	106.6	112.8	121.5	144.4	165.7	184.3	202.8	224.1	246.7	.
México	100.0	105.4	110.7	**112.0** [15]	*138.7*	*159.7*	*184.9*	*238.4*	*280.1*	*331.1*	412.6
Montserrat	.	.	.	.	77.2 [16]	**100.0**	108.5	127.5	139.5	161.9	207.7 [24]
Netherlands Antilles [17, 18]	.	**100.0**	*104.0*	*112.5*	*134.5*	**155.3** [10]	163.5	172.4	186.4	*207.8*	236.8
Nicaragua (Managua) [19]	.	.	.	89.3 [20]	**100.0**	107.5	110.6	*123.2*	*128.7*	*190.8*	...
Panamá (Panamá)	100.0	102.0	107.4	114.8	134.1	141.5	**104.2** [21]	*109.1*	*113.3*	*122.3*	*139.7*
Paraguay (Asunción)	100.0	105.0	114.7	129.3	161.9	172.8	180.5	197.4	218.4	279.9	345.1
Perú (Lima) [19]	100.0	106.8	114.5	**125.4** [10]	146.5	181.2	241.8	333.9	527.0	883.7	1257 [25]
Puerto Rico	100.0	104.3	107.6	115.5	138.4	150.3	153.3	160.0	167.8	178.7	197.4
St. Kitts	100.0	98.4	104.5	115.2	148.0	163.8	185.2	218.1	**100.0** [5]	*111.2*	*130.8* [25]
St. Lucia	100.0	108.4	116.9	132.7	178.0	209.6	229.9	250.3	277.4	303.6	356.2
St. Vincent	100.0	106.5	109.3	127.1	172.3	196.8	219.0	241.3	261.6	302.4	343.3 [24]
Suriname (Paramaribo)	100.0	100.2	103.4	116.9	136.6	148.0	162.9	178.9	194.6	223.6	247.5 [24]
Trinidad and Tobago	100.0	103.5	113.1	129.9	158.5	185.5	**204.6** [10]	228.7	252.0	289.1	333.9
United States	100.0	104.3	107.7	114.4	127.0	138.6	146.6	156.1	**167.9** [10]	187.2	213.1
Uruguay (Montevideo)	100	124	219	**431** [10]	763	1 384	2 086	3 299	4 769	7 957	11 544 [24]
Venezuela (Caracas) [19]	100.0	103.2	106.2	110.6	119.7	131.9	142.0	153.0	164.0	184.2	223.4
Virgin Is. (Brit.) [22]	100.0	*104.3*	**94.4** [23]	**100.0**	*115.8*	*127.1*	*133.8*	...	...	...	.
Virgin Is. (US)	100.0	106.5	118.8	132.2	148.7	160.9	163.0	170.9	182.6	...	.

EXPLANATORY NOTES AND CODES: See p. 575.

NOTES EXPLICATIVES ET CODES: Voir p. 576.

NOTAS EXPLICATIVAS Y CLAVES: Véase pág. 578.

1 Incl. direct taxes. 2 Nov. 3 Urban areas (Guadeloupe: prior to 1979: Basse-Terre only; Guatemala: prior to 1975: Guatemala City only.) 4 Jan.-May and Aug.-Dec. 5 Series replacing former series. 6 Beginning 1972: excl. "Rent". 7 June-Dec.; series replacing former series. 8 Jan.-July. 9 Feb.-Dec. 10 Series linked to former series. 11 Jan.-July and Sep.-Dec. 12 Jan.-May and Sep.-Dec. 13 Jan.-June and Sep.-Dec. 14 Excl. "Miscellaneous". 15 Series (base 1972 = 100) replacing former series. 16 March. 17 Curaçao, Aruba and Bonaire; prior to 1975: excl. Bonaire and Windward Is. 18 Excl. compulsory social security. 19 Metropolitan area. 20 Dec. 21 Series (base 1975 = 100) replacing former series. 22 Prior to 1972: Dec. of each year. 23 May-Dec.; series replacing former series. 24 March. 25 May. 26 July.

1 Y compris les impôts directs. 2 Nov. 3 Régions urbaines (Guadeloupe : avant 1979 : Basse-Terre seulement ; Guatemala : avant 1975 : ville de Guatemala seulement). 4 Janv.-mai et août-déc. 5 Série remplaçant la précédente. 6 A partir de 1972 : non compris le groupe « Loyer ». 7 Juin-déc ; série remplaçant la précédente. 8 Janv.-juillet. 9 Fév.-déc. 10 Série enchaînée à la précédente. 11 Janv.-juillet et sept.-déc. 12 Janv.-mai et sept.-déc. 13 Janv.-juin et sept.-déc. 14 Non compris le groupe « Divers ». 15 Série (base 100 en 1972) remplaçant la précédente. 16 Mars. 17 Curaçao, Aruba et Bonaire ; avant 1975 : non compris Bonaire et les îles Windward. 18 Non compris la sécurité sociale obligatoire. 19 Région métropolitaine. 20 Déc. 21 Série (base 100 en 1975) remplaçant la précédente. 22 Avant 1972 : déc. de chaque année. 23 Mai-déc. ; série remplaçant la précédente. 24 Mars. 25 Mai. 26 Juillet.

1 Incl. los impuestos directos. 2 Nov. 3 Areas urbanas (Guadalupe: antes de 1979: Basse-Terre solamente; Guatemala: antes de 1975: ciudad de Guatemala solamente). 4 Enero-mayo y agosto-dic. 5 Serie que substituye a la anterior. 6 A partir de 1972: excl. el grupo "Alquiler". 7 Junio-dic.; serie que substituye a la anterior. 8 Enero-julio. 9 Febr.-dic. 10 Serie enlazada con la anterior. 11 Enero-julio y sept.-dic. 12 Enero-mayo y sept.-dic. 13 Enero-junio y sept.-dic. 14 Excl. el grupo "Varios". 15 Serie (base 1972 = 100) que substituye a la anterior. 16 Marzo. 17 Curazao, Aruba y Bonaire; antes de 1975: excl. Bonaire y las islas Windward. 18 Excl. la seguridad social obligatoria. 19 Area metropolitana. 20 Dic. 21 Serie (base 1975 = 100) que substituye a la anterior. 22 Antes de 1972: dic. de cada año. 23 Mayo-dic.; serie que substituye a la anterior. 24 Marzo. 25 Mayo. 26 Julio.

23 Consumer prices / Prix à la consommation / Precios del consumo — A General indices / Indices généraux / Indices generales

(1970 = 100)

Country — Pays — País	1970	1971	1972	1973	1974	1975	1976	1977	1978	1979	1980 (VI)
ASIA — ASIE / ASIA											
Afghanistan (Kabul)[1]	100.0	125.6	109.9	98.7	110.0	121.0	121.6	133.2	142.1	|109.9[2]	...
Bahrain						85.4[3]	100.0	117.8	136.3	139.3	...
Bangladesh (Dacca)[4]	100.0	112.4[5]	144.5	|145.1[6]	224.1	278.8	252.1	278.2	314.9	354.8	398.5
Brunei (Bandar Seri Begawan)[7]	100.0	101.0	97.4	108.9	132.2	137.4	145.5	161.7	165.3	168.6	...
Burma (Rangoon)	100.0	102.2	109.9	135.8	172.4	226.9	285.4	274.5	257.9	272.5	276.3[27]
Cyprus	100.0	104.1	109.2	117.7	|136.8[8]	143.1	148.5	|100.0[9]	107.4	117.6	131.7
Hong Kong	100.0	103.1	109.4	129.1	148.0	|108[10]	112	118	125	139	157
India	100.0	103.3	109.8	128.3	165.2	174.5	160.9	174.5	178.8	190.2	209.8
» (Bombay)	100.0	104.4	110.0	124.4	152.8	168.3	163.3	175.0	179.4	192.8	208.3[28]
» (Delhi)	100.0	107.2	111.8	128.2	166.2	172.3	168.2	181.5	187.2	195.9	204.1[28]
» (Jamshedpur)	100.0	102.2	108.8	128.2	169.1	165.2	155.8	173.5	176.2	187.3	219.9[28]
Indonesia[11]	100.0	104.3	111.1	145.6	204.8	243.8	292.2	324.4	351.3	|132.4[12]	156.6
Iran	100.0	104.2	110.9	121.9	139.2	157.0	174.8	222.4	247.5[13]	.	.
Iraq[14]	100.0	103.6	109.0	114.3	|107.7[15]	118.0	133.1	145.3	151.9	.	.
Israel	100	112	126	152	212	295	388	|522[16]	786	1 401	3 020
Japan	100.0	106.0	110.9	124.0	154.1	172.4	188.4	203.6	211.4	219.0	237.6
Jordan[17]	100.0	104.4	112.6	124.5	149.4	167.3	|111.5[18]	127.7	136.6	156.0	172.9
Kampuchea dém. (Phnom-Penh)[19]	100.0	171.3	214.9	554.2	1 818.9[20]	.	.	.	.	.	.
Korea, Rep. of	100.0	113.4	126.7	130.8	162.5	203.7	234.8	258.7	295.9	350.1	447.7
Kuwait	.	.	100.0	108.4	122.7	133.7	141.0	153.9	166.0	175.0	...
République lao (Vientiane)	100.0	101.3	126.8	167.5	248.1	457.3	.	.	.	.	.
Liban (Beyrouth)	100.0	101.6	106.6	113.0	125.5	130.4[21]	.	.	.	.	.
Malaysia:											
Peninsular Malaysia	100.0	101.6	104.8	115.9	136.0	142.2	145.9	152.8	160.3	166.1	176.0
Sabah	100.0	102.2	104.7	111.6	127.7	136.2	139.1	144.0	147.3	152.3	163.0
Sarawak	100.0	99.4	102.9	111.2	127.1	134.0	139.7	147.6	150.8	156.6	167.2
Nepal[22]	102.0[3]	100.0	106.2	115.3	|100.0[9]	107.0	103.6	115.2	122.5	127.8	137.9[28]
Pakistan[23]	100.0	104.7	|105.2[24]	126.9	164.0	198.2	212.4	233.9	249.6	273.1	296.5
Philippines[25]	100.0	123.3	142.7	|116.5[6]	156.3	166.9	182.3	200.4	215.0	250.5	286.8[27]
Singapore	100.0	101.9	104.0	127.9	|122.3[15]	125.5	123.1	127.0	133.1	|104.0[26]	112.5

EXPLANATORY NOTES AND CODES: See p. 575.

1 Excl "Rent"; prior to 1979: excl. "Rent" and "Miscellaneous". 2 March-Dec.; series (base April 1978-March 1979 = 100) replacing former series. 3 July-Dec. 4 Government officials. 5 Jan., Feb. and April-Dec. 6 Series (base 1972 = 100) replacing former series. 7 Excl. "Rent". 8 Jan.-July and Sep.-Dec.; series linked to former series. 9 Series replacing former series. 10 Series (base July 1973-June 1974 = 100) replacing former series. 11 Prior to 1979: Djakarta only. 12 Series (base April 1977-March 1978 = 100) replacing former series. 13 Jan.-Nov. 14 Prior to 1974: Baghdad only. 15 Series (base 1973 = 100) replacing former series. 16 Series linked to former series. 17 Prior to 1976: Amman only. 18 Series (base 1975 = 100) replacing former series. 19 Working class. 20 Jan.-Oct. 21 Jan.-July. 22 Prior to 1974: Katmandu only. 23 Prior to 1972: Karachi only: industrial workers. 24 Series (base 1971 = 100) replacing former series. 25 Prior to 1973: Manila only; middle income group. 26 Series (base 1978 = 100) replacing former series. 27 April. 28 March.

NOTES EXPLICATIVES ET CODES: Voir p. 576.

1 Non compris le groupe « Loyer » ; avant 1979 : non compris les groupes « Loyer » et « Divers ». 2 Mars-déc. ; série (base avril 1978-mars 1979 = 100) remplaçant la précédente. 3 Juillet-déc. 4 Fonctionnaires. 5 Janv., fév. et avril-déc. 6 Série (base 100 en 1972) remplaçant la précédente. 7 Non compris le groupe « Loyer ». 8 Janv.-juillet et sept.-déc. ; série enchaînée à la précédente. 9 Série remplaçant la précédente. 10 Série (base juillet 1973-juin 1974 = 100) remplaçant la précédente. 11 Avant 1979 : Djakarta seulement. 12 Série (base avril 1977-mars 1978 = 100) remplaçant la précédente. 13 Janv.-nov. 14 Avant 1974 : Bagdad seulement. 15 Série (base 100 en 1973) remplaçant la précédente. 16 Série enchaînée à la précédente. 17 Avant 1976 : Amman seulement. 18 Série (base 100 en 1975) remplaçant la précédente. 19 Classe ouvrière. 20 Janv.-oct. 21 Janv.-juillet. 22 Avant 1974 : Katmandou seulement. 23 Avant 1972 : Karachi seulement ; travailleurs de l'industrie. 24 Série (base 100 en 1971) remplaçant la précédente. 25 Avant 1974 : Manille seulement ; familles à revenu moyen. 26 Série (base 100 en 1978) remplaçant la précédente. 27 Avril. 28 Mars.

NOTAS EXPLICATIVAS Y CLAVES: Véase pág. 578.

1 Excl. el grupo « Alquiler »; antes de 1979; excl. los grupos « Alquiler ». y « Varios ». 2 Marzo-dic.; serie (base abril de 1978-marzo de 1979 = 100) que substituye a la anterior. 3 Julio-dic. 4 Funcionarios. 5 Enero, febr. y abril-dic. 6 Serie (base 1972 = 100) que substituye a la anterior. 7 Excl. el grupo « Alquiler ». 8 Enero-julio y sept.-dic.; serie enlazada con la anterior. 9 Serie que substituye a la anterior. 10 Serie (base julio de 1973-junio de 1974 = 100) que substituye a la anterior. 11 Antes de 1979: Djakarta solamente. 12 Serie (base abril de 1977-marzo de 1978 = 100) que substituye a la anterior. 13 Enero-nov. 14 Antes de 1974: Bagdad solamente. 15 Serie (base 1973 = 100) que substituye a la anterior. 16 Serie enlazada con la anterior. 17 Antes de 1976: Amman solamente. 18 Serie (base 1975 = 100) que substituye a la anterior. 19 Serie obrera. 20 Enero-oct. 21 Enero-julio. 22 Antes de 1974: Katmandú solamente. 23 Antes de 1972: Karachi solamente; trabajadores de la industria. 24 Serie (base 1971 = 100) que substituye a la anterior. 25 Antes de 1973: Manila solamente; familias de ingresos medios. 26 Serie (base 1978 = 100) que substituye a la anterior. 27 Abril. 28 Marzo.

23 Consumer prices / Prix à la consommation / Precios del consumo — A General indices / Indices généraux / Indices generales

(1970 = 100)

Country — Pays — País	1970	1971	1972	1973	1974	1975	1976	1977	1978	1979	1980 (VI)
Sri Lanka (Colombo)	100.0	102.7	109.2	119.7	134.4	143.5	145.2	147.0	164.8	182.6	231.8
République arabe syrienne (Damas)	100.0	104.9	105.7	126.8	146.3	169.9	195.1	▌218 [1]	229	239	287
Thailand (Bangkok-Metropolis)	100.0	102.0	106.1	118.5	146.1	152.1	159.6	173.1	▌188.2 [2]	207.5	251.8
Viet Nam (Ho Chi Minh) [3]	100.0	118.2	▌148.1 [2]	213.9	331.7	.	.	.	.	.	.
Yemen (Sanaa)	.	.	100	143	181	224	...	...	...	...	.
Yemen, Democratic (Aden)	100.0	105.7	110.5	128.6	159.0	178.1	184.8	194.3	...	...	.
EUROPE — EUROPE EUROPA											
Austria	100.0	104.7	111.3	119.7	131.1	142.2	152.6	▌161.0 [2]	166.8	172.9	184.4
Belgique [4]	100.0	104.3	▌110.0 [2]	117.7	132.6	149.5	▌163.2 [2]	174.8	182.6	190.8	201.4
Bulgarie	100.0	99.9	99.9	100.1	100.6	100.9	101.2	101.6	103.2	107.7	.
Czechoslovakia	100.0	99.7	99.5	99.7	100.2	100.8	101.6	103.0	104.6	108.6	112.0 [11]
Denmark	100.0	105.8	112.8	123.3	142.1	155.8	169.8	188.7	207.6	▌227.6 [2]	254.1
España	100.0	108.3	117.3	130.8	151.1	176.7	207.9	258.8	310.0	358.6	411.0
Faeroe Is.	100.0	107.3	117.5	129.2	150.7	164.6 [5]	▌100.0 [1]	105.6	113.1	123.5	...
Finland	100.0	106.5	114.1	127.5	▌149.6 [2]	176.3	201.7	227.1	244.3	▌262.2 [2]	291.0
France	100.0	105.5	112.0	120.2	136.7	152.8	167.5	183.2	199.8	221.3	248.7
German Democratic Republic	100.0	99.8	99.3	▌97.8 [1]	96.6	96.6	96.6	96.4	96.3	...	.
Germany, Fed. Rep. of	100.0	105.2	111.1	118.8	127.1	134.7	140.4	145.6	149.6	155.8	164.9
Gibraltar	100.0	109.9	121.7	▌135.2 [2]	157.4	187.6	211.1	245.9	277.2	322.3	365.6 [12]
Grèce	100.0	103.0	107.4	124.1	157.5	178.6	202 4	226.9	255.4	303.9	383.0
Hongrie	100.0	102.0	104.9	108.4	110.4	114.6	120.3	125.0	130.8	142.4	157.3
Iceland (Reykjavik)	100.0	106.4	117.4	143.5	205.2	305.6	403.9	527.0	759.2	1104.3	1 623.9 [13]
Ireland	100.0	108.9	118.4	131.8	154.2	186.4	▌219.9 [2]	249.9	269.0	304.5	358.1 [13]
Isle of Man	.	.	.	.	.	.	89.0 [6]	100.0	109.2	124.4	146.5 [13]
Italie	100.0	104.8	110.8	122.8	146.3	171.1	199.8	▌236.6 [2]	265.3	304.5	363.2
Luxembourg [7]	100.0	104.7	110.1	116.8	128.0	141.7	155.6	166.0	171.1	178.9	189.7
Malta	100.0	102.3	105.7	113.9	122.2	129.7	▌133.7 [2]	147.0	154.0	165.0	191.1
Netherlands	100.0	▌107.6 [2]	116.0	125.2	137.3	151.3	164.6	175.6	▌182.7 [2]	190.5	201.8
Norway	100.0	106.2	113.9	122.4	▌133.9 [2]	149.5	163.2	178.0	192.5	201.7	221.7
Pologne	100.0	99.9	99.9	102.7	110.0	113.3	118.3	124.1	134.2	143.6	.
Portugal [7, 8]	100.0	112.0	124.0	140.0	175.1	201.8	244.2	▌127.4 [9]	155.4	193.0 [10]	223.5
Roumanie	100.0	100.6	100.6	101.3	102.4	102.6	103.2	103.8	105.5	107.6	.
Suisse	100.0	106.6	113.7	123.6	135.7	144.8	147.3	149.2	▌150.8 [2]	156.2	162.3

EXPLANATORY NOTES AND CODES: See p. 575.

[1] Series replacing former series. [2] Series linked to former series. [3] Working class. [4] 1972-1975: excl. "Rent" and "Miscellaneous"; prior to 1972: excl. "Rent" only. [5] Jan., April and July. [6] March-Dec. [7] Excl. "Rent" (Portugal: beginning 1977). [8] Prior to 1977: Lisbon only. [9] Series (base 1976 = 100) replacing former series. [10] Jan.-Aug. and Oct.-Dec. [11] First quarter. [12] July. [13] May.

NOTES EXPLICATIVES ET CODES: Voir p. 576.

[1] Série remplaçant la précédente. [2] Série enchaînée à la précédente. [3] Classe ouvrière. [4] 1972-1975: non compris les groupes « Loyer » et « Divers »; avant 1972: non compris le groupe « Loyer » seulement. [5] Janv., avril et juillet. [6] Mars-déc. [7] Non compris le groupe « Loyer » (Portugal: à partir de 1977). [8] Avant 1977: Lisbonne seulement. [9] Série (base 100 en 1976) remplaçant la précédente. [10] Janv.-août et oct.-déc. [11] Premier trimestre. [12] Juillet. [13] Mai.

NOTAS EXPLICATIVAS Y CLAVES: Véase pág. 578.

[1] Serie que substituye a la anterior. [2] Serie enlazada con la anterior. [3] Clase obrera. [4] 1972-1975: excl. los grupos « Alquiler » y « Varios »; antes de 1972: excl. el grupo « Alquiler » solamente. [5] Enero, abril y julio. [6] Marzo-dic. [7] Excl. el grupo « Alquiler » (Portugal: a partir de 1977). [8] Antes de 1977: Lisboa solamente. [9] Serie (base 1976 = 100) que substituye a la anterior. [10] Enero-agosto y oct.-dic. [11] Primer trimestre. [12] Julio. [13] Mayo.

23 Consumer prices / Prix à la consommation / Precios del consumo — A — General indices / Indices généraux / Indices generales

(1970 = 100)

Country — Pays — País	1970	1971	1972	1973	1974	1975	1976	1977	1978	1979	1980 (VI)
Sweden	100.0	107.4	113.8	121.5	133.5	146.6	161.7	180.1	198.1	212.4	237.8
Turquie (Ankara)[1]	100.0	116.3	131.4	153.2	181.8	218.3	251.7	323.3	483.3	756.6	1 632.8[16]
United Kingdom	100.0	109.4	117.2	128.0	148.4	184.4	214.9	249.0	269.6	305.8	363.5
Yugoslavia	100.0	115.6	134.8	161.3	195.3	242.7	271.0	311.6	356.1	428.5	563
OCEANIA — OCÉANIE OCEANÍA											
American Samoa (Pago-Pago)	.	.	.	.	100.0	119.1	119.9	125.7	132.9	156.2	179.9[17]
Australia	100.0	106.1	112.3	122.9	141.5	162.8	184.9	207.6	224.0	244.3	267.2[17]
Cook Is. (Rarotonga)	100.0	110.6	123.2	135.1	152.6	176.5	217.1	261.6	292.2	...	...
Fiji	100.0	106.5	116.2	129.2	147.9[2]	167.2	186.3	199.3	211.5	227.8	257.5[18]
Guam	.	.	.	100.0	115.1	126.2	129.3	133.6	150.8	169.1	197.6[17]
Kiribati (Tarawa)	95.5[3]	100.0	104.6	118.0	133.6	151.9	100.0[4]	108.6	121.5	...	...
New Zealand	100.0	110.6	118.2	127.8	142.1	162.8	190.3	217.7	243.7	277.2	319.1[17]
Niue Is.	.	.	100.0	115.3	135.2	164.3	232.1[2]	275.7	317.1	...	...
Nouvelle-Calédonie (Nouméa)	100.0	108.2	116.6	124.0	139.8	156.9	165.9	175.8	188.6	200.5	225.3
Papua New Guinea	100.0	106.5	106.1[5]	114.9	141.6	156.4	168.6[2]	176.0	186.2	196.9	216.8[17]
Polynésie française (Tahiti) (Papeete)	100.0	103.5	108.8	117.6[2]	138.8	161.5	171.5	187.1	198.2	217.2	240.2[16]
Samoa (Apia)[1,6]	100.0	104.6	112.6	100.0[4]	124.9	135.9	142.7	163.3	166.8	185.3	214.5
Solomon Is. (Honiara)[1]	.	100.0	107.0	110.4	131.2	144.4	150.6	163.3	106.3[7]	114.8	127.4
Tonga[1]	100.0	102.1	108.8	131.4	150.6	165.8	177.6	208.7	228.7	241.2	269.8[19]
Vanuatu[8,9,10] ... [11]	93.9[12]	100.0	118.8	115.7	149.4	155.0[12]	100.0[4]	104.2[13]	113.0[14]	116.8	120.1[19]
URSS[15]	100.0	99.9	99.7	99.7	99.6	99.7	99.7	100.0	100.7	101.8	.
RSS de Biélorussie	100.0	99.6	99.4	99.4	99.3	99.4	99.5	...	...	...	.
RSS d'Ukraine	100.0	99.8	99.7	99.7	99.8	99.9	99.9	100.3	101.1	102.2	.

EXPLANATORY NOTES AND CODES: See p. 575.

1 Excl. " Rent " (Samoa: beginning 1973; Solomon Is: prior to 1978). 2 Series linked to former series. 3 Oct.-Dec. 4 Series replacing former series. 5 Series (base 1971 = 100) replacing former series. 6 Urban area; prior to 1973: Apia only. 7 Series (base Oct.-Dec. 1977 = 100) replacing former series. 8 Former New Hebrides. 9 Urban areas; prior to 1976: Vila only; excl. " Rent ". 10 Indices based on prices paid in francs. 11 Low income group. 12 Jan.-Sep. 13 Jan.-June. 14 April-Dec. 15 Incl. Byelorussian SSR and Ukrainian SSR, shown separately in this table. 16 May. 17 Second quarter. 18 April. 19 First quarter.

NOTES EXPLICATIVES ET CODES: Voir p. 576.

1 Non compris le groupe « Loyer » (Samoa : à partir de 1973; Iles Salomon : avant 1978). 2 Série enchaînée à la précédente. 3 Oct.-déc. 4 Série remplaçant la précédente. 5 Série (base 100 en 1971) remplaçant la précédente. 6 Région urbaine ; avant 1973 : Apia seulement. 7 Série (base oct.-déc. 1977 = 100) remplaçant la précédente. 8 Précédemment Nouvelles-Hébrides. 9 Régions urbaines ; avant 1976 : Vila seulement ; non compris le groupe « Loyer ». 10 Indices fondés sur des prix payés en francs. 11 Familles à revenu modique. 12 Janv.-sept. 13 Janv.-juin. 14 Avril-déc. 15 Y compris les RSS de Biélorussie et d'Ukraine, figurant séparément dans ce tableau. 16 Mai. 17 Deuxième trimestre. 18 Avril. 19 Premier trimestre.

NOTAS EXPLICATIVAS Y CLAVES: Véase pág. 578.

1 Excl. el grupo « Alquiler » (Samoa: a partir de 1973; Islas Salomón: antes de 1978). 2 Serie enlazada con la anterior. 3 Oct.-dic. 4 Serie que substituye a la anterior. 5 Serie (base 1971 = 100) que substituye a la anterior. 6 Area urbana; antes de 1973: Apia solamente. 7 Serie (base oct.-dic. 1977 = 100) que substituye a la anterior. 8 Anteriormente Nuevas Hébridas. 9 Areas urbanas; antes de 1976: Vila solamente; excl. el grupo « Alquiler ». 10 Indices basados en los precios pagados en francos. 11 Familias de ingresos módicos. 12 Enero-sept. 13 Enero-junio. 14 Abril-dic. 15 Incl. las RSS de Bielorrusia y de Ucrania, que figuran separadamente en este cuadro. 16 Mayo. 17 Segundo trimestre. 18 Abril. 19 Primero trimestre.

23 Consumer prices / Prix à la consommation / Precios del consumo

B Food indices / Indices de l'alimentation / Indices de la alimentación

(1970 = 100)

Country — Pays — País	1970	1971	1972	1973	1974	1975	1976	1977	1978	1979	1980 (VI)
AFRICA — AFRIQUE AFRICA											
Algérie (Alger)	100.0	102.7	106.7	118.7	127.1	141.7	162.1	186.9	222.6	...	...
Botswana [1]	100.0	99.4	105.5	121.7	142.8	❘ 111.0 [2]	120.7	137.8	153.4	170.9	193.6 [21]
Burundi (Bujumbura) [3]	100.0	104.9	106.9	113.2	135.5	161.1	171.2	199.5	225.4	295.5	319.8 [21]
Cameroun (Yaoundé) . . . . *Afric.*	100.0	106.3	119.1	129.9	148.2	172.1	191.3	236.3	263.5	276.1	288.3 [21]
» » . . . . . . *Europ.*	100.0	106.1	114.5	122.8	146.1	171.2	186.8	213.4	231.8	252.4	267.7 [22]
Cap-Vert (Praya)	100.0	121.0	135.8	154.9	236.4	300.6	304.3	342.0	435.8	...	...
République centrafricaine (Bangui) . *Europ.*	100.0	108.1	118.4	125.3	137.4	158.0	172.1	193.0 [4]	215.0	...	...
Congo (Brazzaville) . . . . *Europ.*	100.0	104.9	115.7	121.4	128.4	150.7	158.0	...	...	...	...
Côte-d'Ivoire (Abidjan) . . . . . *Afric.*	100.0	98.2	97.1	114.3	135.0	149.0	159.8	223.7	249.0	303.4	381.9
» » . . . . . *Europ.*	100.0	105.3	110.5	114.7	134.6	169.0	192.5	215.8	234.1	257.6	283.4
Egypt	100.0	105.4	108.3	115.6	135.2	151.6	174.0	198.9	218.0	234.2	298.7
Ethiopia (Addis Ababa)	100.0	99.9	87.9	99.2	107.7	112.5	159.6	186.4	218.2	257.5	277.2
Gabon (Libreville) . . . . *Afric.*	94.0 [5]	100.0	106.1	113.3	121.8	❘ 106.6 [6]	.	.	156.9	...	...
» . . . . [7]	100.0	103.6	111.1	❘ 125.2 [8]	143.7	162.5	.	.	235.9	...	...
Gambia (Banjul-Kombo, St. Mary)	100.0	103.1	113.2	120.0	135.9	182.6	217.9	245.1	260.6	275.8	275.1
Ghana (Accra)	100.0	106.2	118.9	141.9	184.7	252.4	414.1	886.8	❘ 163.5 [9]	283.7	376.0
Kenya (Nairobi) . . . . [10]	100.0	102.5 [11]	100.0 [12]	104.8	123.6	149.5	❘ 159.6 [8]	179.9	201.0	212.3	239.4
Lesotho . . . . [13]	.	.	91.6 [14]	100.0	114.5	135.6	149.4	188.7	217.6	...	...
Liberia (Monrovia)	100.0	90.8	90.8	118.2	149.4	172.4	171.4	188.3	209.6	233.9	253.4 [21]
Libyan Arab Jamahiriya (Tripoli)	100.0	88.9	80.9	74.1	79.3	85.0	95.9	107.4	120.0	...	...
Madagascar (Tananarive) . . . . [15]	100.0	105.3	111.9	❘ 122.3 [8]	159.1	169.9	176.3	178.8	192.5	220.2	251.0
» » . . . . . *Europ.*	100.0	107.1	114.4	❘ 119.9 [8]	138.6	157.6	171.7	187.8	201.6	224.0	255.2
Malawi (Blantyre) . . . . [13]	100.0	111.2	115.9	123.8	144.2	171.8	175.7	178.7	190.0	216.4	264.0
» » . . . . [7]	100.0	110.6	115.2	125.3	134.6	153.2	158.2	176.9	197.5	206.7	248.6 [22]
Mali (Bamako)	100.0	120.7	130.0	168.0	171.5	181.6	196.2	245.3	326.7	...	...
Maroc [16]	100.0	106.3	111.7	117.7	❘ 100.0 [12]	107.6	118.6	135.0	146.3	155.7	162.4
Mauritanie (Nouakchott) . . . . . . *Europ.*	100.0	109.6	119.2	132.4	153.8 [17]	❘ 100.0 [12]	119.5	128.4	139.8	...	...
Mauritius	100.0	100.1	106.3	123.0	162.9	189.0	❘ 200.9 [8]	218.2	232.7	266.1	385.5
Mozambique (Maputo)	100.0	113.6	129.5	127.3	155.3	173.5	187.9	.	.	.	.
Niger (Niamey) . . . . *Afric.*	100.0	105.5	122.7	143.8	147.8	159.9	201.3	255.1	273.0	...	...
» » . . . . *Europ.*	100.0	104.6	108.6	113.2	124.2	141.4	163.1	182.7	205.0	...	...
Nigeria (Lagos) . . . . [13]	100.0	126.2	128.1	125.1 [18]	150.0	214.4	268.4	358.2	.	.	.
» » [19]	.	.	.	.	.	100.0	128.1	155.2	196.3	210.2	...
» » [20]	.	.	.	.	.	100.0	122.0	144.7	171.9	185.7	...
Réunion (Saint-Denis)	100.0	103.1	❘ 111.7 [8]	132.8	156.3	175.4	187.9	217.9	232.4	258.1	304.2

EXPLANATORY NOTES AND CODES: See p. 575.

NOTES EXPLICATIVES ET CODES: Voir p. 576.

NOTAS EXPLICATIVAS Y CLAVES: Véase pág. 578.

[1] Prior to 1975: Gaborone only. [2] Series (base 1974 = 100) replacing former series. [3] Government officials. [4] Jan.-June and Sep.-Dec. [5] Jan.-June and Aug.-Dec. [6] June-Dec.; series (base June 1975 = 100) replacing former series. [7] High income group. [8] Series linked to former series. [9] Series (base 1977 = 100) replacing former series. [10] Middle income group; prior to 1972: low income group. [11] Jan.-Aug. [12] Series replacing former series. [13] Low income group. [14] Oct. [15] Madagascans. [16] Prior to 1974: Casablanca only. [17] Jan.-July and Sep.-Dec. [18] Jan.-Sep. and Dec. [19] Urban areas. [20] Rural and urban areas. [21] March. [22] April.

[1] Avant 1975 : Gaborone seulement. [2] Série (base 100 en 1974) remplaçant la précédente. [3] Fonctionnaires. [4] Janv.-juin et sept.-déc. [5] Janv.-juin et août-déc. [6] Juin-déc.; série (base 100 en juin 1975) remplaçant la précédente. [7] Familles à revenu élevé. [8] Série enchaînée à la précédente. [9] Série (base 100 en 1977) remplaçant la précédente. [10] Familles à revenu moyen; avant 1972: familles à revenu modique. [11] Janv.-août. [12] Série remplaçant la précédente. [13] Familles à revenu modique. [14] Oct. [15] Malgaches. [16] Avant 1974: Casablanca seulement. [17] Janv.-juillet et sept.-déc. [18] Janv.-sept. et déc. [19] Régions urbaines. [20] Régions rurales et urbaines. [21] Mars. [22] Avril.

[1] Antes de 1975: Gaborone solamente. [2] Serie (base 1974 = 100) que substituye a la anterior. [3] Funcionarios. [4] Enero-junio y sept.-dic. [5] Enero-junio y agosto-dic. [6] Junio-dic.; serie (base junio de 1975 = 100) que substituye a la anterior. [7] Familias de ingresos elevados. [8] Serie enlazada con la anterior. [9] Serie (base 1977 = 100) que substituye a la anterior. [10] Familias de ingresos medios; antes de 1972: familias de ingresos módicos. [11] Enero-agosto. [12] Serie que substituye a la anterior. [13] Familias de ingresos módicos. [14] Oct. [15] Malgaches. [16] Antes de 1974: Casablanca solamente. [17] Enero-julio y sept.-dic. [18] Enero-sept. y dic. [19] Areas urbanas. [20] Areas rurales y urbanas. [21] Marzo. [22] Abril.

23 B Consumer prices / Prix à la consommation / Precios del consumo — Food indices / Indices de l'alimentation / Indices de la alimentación

(1970 = 100)

Country — Pays — País	1970	1971	1972	1973	1974	1975	1976	1977	1978	1979	1980 (VI)
Rwanda (Kigali)	100	105	110	117	151	204	200	208	...	...	.
Sénégal (Dakar)	100.0	105.0	111.8	134.2	152.1	213.2	209.9	239.0	247.6	268.8	292.2 [18]
Seychelles [1]	100.0	118.4	152.3	188.3	❙100.0 [2]	122.1	142.5	❙100.0 [2]	109.8	114.6	...
Sierra Leone (Freetown)	100.0	96.2	104.6	114.0	135.2	166.5	195.4	209.7	226.9	280.3	297.7
Somalia (Mogadishu)	100.0	99.3	96.9	107.2	127.9	154.5	182.9	207.0	236.2	...	...
South Africa, Rep. of . . . . [3]	100.0	104.8	112.1	129.4	148.7	170.9	183.6	202.4	228.5	264.4	...
Sudan	100.0	99.2	109.5	127.4	159.9	204.9	201.2	239.0	302.2	398.3	466.2 [19]
Swaziland (Mbabane-Manzini) . . . . . . [4]	100.0	102.3	103.8	120.0	143.9	160.8	169.9	201.7	218.5	249.2	282.6 [18]
Tanzania	100.0	105.8	115.4	128.5	173.8	227.0	226.5	257.9	297.7	334.3	...
Tchad (N'djamena) . . . . [4]	.	.	.	.	111.3 [5]	100.0	98.1 [6]	144.2	155.0	...	...
» » . . . . . [7]	100.0	106.0	108.6	115.8	❙128.6 [8]	148.0	144.6	163.9	182.2	...	...
Togo (Lomé)	100.0	110.4	119.0	121.4	136.4	169.0	198.8	252.1	230.4	...	
Tunisie [9]	100.0	110.3	113.0	120.5	121.5	133.0	141.5	148.1	❙106.2 [10]	116.1	128.2
Uganda (Kampala) . . . . [4]	100.0	124.7	117.8	139.7	245.2	302.7	490.4	880.0 [11]	...	...	...
Zaïre (Kinshasa)	100	110	133	155	❙200 [8]	261	515	863	1 423	...	...
Zambia . . . . [4]	100.0	105.9	110.9	118.7	129.0	143.7	176.0	208.0	243.4	265.1	...
Zimbabwe [17] . . . . [4]	100.0	102.3	105.2	109.6	117.3	132.0	143.6	159.9	176.0	197.3	198.2

AMERICA — AMÉRIQUE
AMÉRICA

Country — Pays — País	1970	1971	1972	1973	1974	1975	1976	1977	1978	1979	1980 (VI)
Antigua	100.0	110.1	121.2	146.2	192.0	223.6	246.1	277.8	295.0	337.6 [6]	390.8 [20]
Argentina (Buenos Aires) [12]	100	142	231	359	413	1 187	6 632	❙4 506 [13]	11 860	31 865	61 999
Bahamas (Nassau)	100.0	104.8	❙100.0 [2]	105.4	125.1	139.7	143.8	146.4	158.4	175.6	197.4
Barbados	100.0	108.2	126.3	148.7	214.6	262.5	273.7	297.0	326.9	363.2	415.0 [20]
Bermuda	100.0	107.9	119.2	143.6	175.9	182.0	176.4	179.7	❙100.0 [2]	121.5	135.8 [19]
Bolivia (La Paz)	100.0	104.0	110.6	149.3	271.2	285.6	292.5	316.5	348.2	413.1	624.7
Brasil (São Paulo)	100.0	123.9	❙100.0 [2]	120.1	153.7	198.6	267.1	371.6	522.5	820.0	...
Canada	100.0	101.1	108.8	124.7	145.0	163.7	168.0	182.1	210.3	238.0	262.4
Colombia (Bogotá)	100.0	107.5	128.1	168.9	214.6	281.2	328.6	447.9	508.0	❙627.4 [8]	976.0
Costa Rica (San José) [12]	100.0	103.7	104.9	127.6 [14]	165.0 [15]	191.9	❙191.6 [8]	201.1	221.7	249.7	308.3
Chile (Santiago)	100	124	267	1 270	7 793	35 821	112 040	208 672	280 924	❙368 167 [8]	481 806
Dominica	100.0	102.0	104.6	118.5	163.2	192.6	213.1	228.1	239.8	289.7 [16]	387.7

EXPLANATORY NOTES AND CODES: See p. 575. NOTES EXPLICATIVES ET CODES: Voir p. 576. NOTAS EXPLICATIVAS Y CLAVES: Véase pág. 578.

[1] Prior to 1977: Victoria only. [2] Series replacing former series. [3] White population. [4] Low income group. [5] Jan., Feb. and April-Dec. [6] Jan.-Nov. [7] High income group. [8] Series linked to former series. [9] Prior to 1978: Tunis metropolitan area only. [10] Series (base 1977 = 100) replacing former series. [11] Jan.-March and July-Dec. [12] Metropolitan area. [13] Series (base 1974 = 100) replacing former series. [14] June and Dec. [15] June, Aug. and Oct.-Dec. [16] Jan.-Aug. and Nov.-Dec. [17] Former Southern Rhodesia. [18] April. [19] March. [20] May.

[1] Avant 1977 : Victoria seulement. [2] Série remplaçant la précédente. [3] Population blanche. [4] Familles à revenu modique. [5] Janv., fév. et avril-déc. [6] Janv.-nov. [7] Familles à revenu élevé. [8] Série enchaînée à la précédente. [9] Avant 1978 : région métropolitaine de Tunis seulement. [10] Série (base 100 en 1977) remplaçant la précédente. [11] Janv.-mars et juillet-déc. [12] Région métropolitaine. [13] Série (base 100 en 1974) remplaçant la précédente. [14] Juin et déc. [15] Juin, août et oct.-déc. [16] Janv.-août et nov.-déc. [17] Précédemment Rhodésie du Sud. [18] Avril. [19] Mars. [20] Mai.

[1] Antes de 1977: Victoria solamente. [2] Serie que substituye a la anterior. [3] Población blanca. [4] Familias de ingresos módicos. [5] Enero, febr. y abril-dic. [6] Enero-nov. [7] Familias de ingresos elevados. [8] Serie enlazada con la anterior. [9] Antes de 1978: área metropolitana de Túnez solamente. [10] Serie (base 1977 = 100) que substituye a la anterior. [11] Enero-marzo y julio-dic. [12] Area metropolitana. [13] Serie (base 1974 = 100) que substituye a la anterior. [14] Junio y dic. [15] Junio, agosto y oct.-dic. [16] Enero-agosto y nov.-dic. [17] Anteriormente Rhodesia del Sur. [18] Abril. [19] Marzo. [20] Mayo.

23 Consumer prices / Prix à la consommation / Precios del consumo

B Food indices / Indices de l'alimentation / Indices de la alimentación

(1970 = 100)

Country — Pays — País	1970	1971	1972	1973	1974	1975	1976	1977	1978	1979	1980 (VI)
República Dominicana (Santo Domingo) . . .	95.1[1]	100.0	106.0	125.5	147.7	173.9	169.0	184.8	179.2	205.2	227.2[20]
Ecuador (Quito)	100.0	106.5	118.3	142.3	188.4	223.4	244.7	283.0	312.1	343.2	386.6[21]
El Salvador[2]	100.0	100.2[3]	101.3	108.9	127.8	154.1	164.8	179.1	198.3	|100.0[4]	121.1
Falkland Is. (Malvinas) (Stanley)	100.0	105.4	|94.5[5]	100.0	110.1	127.1	131.2	149.9	158.0	165.5	174.8[20]
Greenland	.	100.0	106.8	122.3	144.7	166.0	185.4	203.9	223.3	244.7	274.8[22]
Guadeloupe[2]	100.0	107.8	117.0	126.2	149.9	174.3	188.6[6]	206.7[7]	223.3	|246.2[8]	292.2
Guatemala[2]	100.0	98.1	98.2	117.1	135.7	|100.0[4]	109.5	121.7	127.3	140.3	157.5
Guyana[2]	100.0	101.2	110.1	123.3	155.9	169.0	192.3	208.7	244.7	291.0	321.1[21]
Guyane française (Cayenne)	100.0	107.8[9]	113.1	121.7	144.6	162.4[10]	174.6	197.8	212.6[11]	228.9	250.5
Haïti (Port-au-Prince)	100.0	107.2	117.9	150.2	169.1	200.5	213.2	229.7	213.7	247.1	299.0
Honduras (Tegucigalpa)	100.0	103.9	112.3	116.6	134.6	145.3	154.0	170.8	182.1	195.9	232.9[21]
Jamaica	100.0	106.6	111.7	139.3	179.9	211.7	230.7	252.3	344.9	459.4	...
Martinique (Fort-de-France)	100.0	107.8	112.4	121.3	148.4	165.8	181.4	199.6	215.0	234.4	...
México	100.0	104.7	108.9	|115.7[12]	150.3	169.1	190.6	245.4	285.7	338.3	418.3
Montserrat	.	.	.	.	73.6[13]	100.0	109.1	125.3	137.9	168.0	205.4[20]
Netherlands Antilles[14]	.	100.0	106.8	123.2	168.5	|207.5[8]	219.4	232.6	275.3	291.3	329.2
Nicaragua (Managua)[15]	.	.	.	88.4[16]	100.0	107.8	109.0	125.1	129.6	211.7	...
Panamá (Panamá)	100.0	102.4	107.1	117.7	144.5	154.3	|101.8[17]	104.5	110.9	122.2	138.2
Paraguay (Asunción)	100.0	108.6	120.7	146.8	183.2	191.6	199.7	222.2	251.1	324.9	386.9
Perú (Lima)[15]	100.0	106.8	114.7	|126.3[8]	150.0	199.2	263.2	369.2	589.5	1 027.0	1 495.5
Puerto Rico	100.0	105.7	109.5	123.3	160.2	174.4	173.3	182.9	193.7	207.6	230.2
St. Kitts	100.0	101.3	118.6	138.8	181.8	197.9	221.6	268.7	|100.0[4]	111.0	127.0[21]
St. Lucia	100.0	111.8	121.6	144.1	202.4	237.1	260.7	281.8	311.8	341.2	386.9
St. Vincent	100.0	104.0	108.6	131.9	184.1	210.4	215.7	259.4	276.9	310.9	342.9[20]
Suriname (Paramaribo)	100.0	98.8	102.3	125.8	147.0	157.8	173.5	186.2	195.4	220.5	235.8[20]
Trinidad and Tobago	100.0	104.6	116.6	138.8	180.4	210.6	|226.1[8]	241.6	263.6	300.1	350.3
United States	100.0	103.0	107.5	123.1	140.7	152.7	157.4	167.3	|179.5[8]	199.0	214.4
Uruguay (Montevideo)	100	124	241	|489[8]	844	1 441	2 128	3 491	5 045	8 624	11 990[20]
Venezuela (Caracas)[15]	100.0	103.5	108.5	116.8	131.6	151.0	164.3	184.7	201.8	235.4	309.3
Virgin Is. (Brit.)[18]	100.0	108.3	|90.7[19]	100.0	126.4	144.8	144.6	...	...	...	.
Virgin Is. (US)	100.0	107.9	117.5	144.2	189.7	192.0	194.4	209.9	222.3	...	.

EXPLANATORY NOTES AND CODES: See p. 575.

NOTES EXPLICATIVES ET CODES: Voir p. 576.

NOTAS EXPLICATIVAS Y CLAVES: Véase pág. 578.

[1] Nov. [2] Urban areas (Guadeloupe: prior to 1979: Basse-Terre only; Guatemala: prior to 1975: Guatemala City only). [3] Jan.-May and Aug.-Dec. [4] Series replacing former series. [5] June-Dec.; series replacing former series. [6] Jan.-July. [7] Feb.-Dec. [8] Series linked to former series. [9] Jan.-July and Sep.-Dec. [10] Jan.-May and Sep.-Dec. [11] Jan.-June and Sep.-Dec. [12] Series (base 1972 = 100) replacing former series. [13] March. [14] Curaçao, Aruba and Bonaire; prior to 1975: excl. Bonaire and Windward Is. [15] Metropolitan area. [16] Dec. [17] Series (base 1975 = 100) replacing former series. [18] Prior to 1972: Dec. of each year. [19] May-Dec.; series replacing former series. [20] March. [21] May. [22] July.

[1] Nov. [2] Régions urbaines (Guadeloupe : avant 1979 : Basse-Terre seulement ; Guatemala : avant 1975 : ville de Guatemala seulement). [3] Janv.-mai et août-déc. [4] Série remplaçant la précédente. [5] Juin-déc. ; série remplaçant la précédente. [6] Janv.-juillet. [7] Fév.-déc. [8] Série enchaînée à la précédente. [9] Janv.-juillet et sept.-déc. [10] Janv.-mai et sept.-déc. [11] Janv.-juin et sept.-déc. [12] Série (base 100 en 1972) remplaçant la précédente. [13] Mars. [14] Curaçao, Aruba et Bonaire ; avant 1975 : non compris Bonaire et les Iles Windward. [15] Région métropolitaine. [16] Déc. [17] Série (base 100 en 1975) remplaçant la précédente. [18] Avant 1972 : déc. de chaque année. [19] Mai-déc. : série remplaçant la précédente. [20] Mars. [21] Mai. [22] Juillet.

[1] Nov. [2] Areas urbanas (Guadalupe: antes de 1979: Basse-Terre solamente; Guatemala: antes de 1975: ciudad de Guatemala solamente). [3] Enero-mayo y agosto-dic. [4] Serie que substituye a la anterior. [5] Junio-dic.; serie que substituye a la anterior. [6] Enero-julio. [7] Febr.-dic. [8] Serie enlazada con la anterior. [9] Enero-julio y sept.-dic. [10] Enero-mayo y sept.-dic. [11] Enero-junio y sept.-dic. [12] Serie (base 1972 = 100) que substituye a la anterior. [13] Marzo. [14] Curazao, Aruba y Bonaire; antes de 1975: excl. Bonaire y las islas Windward. [15] Area metropolitana. [16] Dic. [17] Serie (base 1975 = 100) que substituye a la anterior. [18] Antes de 1972: dic. de cada año. [19] Mayo-dic.; serie que substituye a la anterior. [20] Marzo. [21] Mayo. [22] Julio.

23 Consumer prices / Prix à la consommation / Precios del consumo

B Food indices / Indices de l'alimentation / Indices de la alimentación

(1970 = 100)

Country — Pays — País	1970	1971	1972	1973	1974	1975	1976	1977	1978	1979	1980 (VI)
ASIA — ASIE ASIA											
Bangladesh (Dacca) [1]	100.0	110.1 [2]	147.6	147.3 [3]	248.4	300.1	241.7	266.1	302.0	340.5	381.3
Brunei (Bandar Seri Begawan)	.	.	100.0	112.4	134.9	139.6	150.1	170.6	175.2	178.8	...
Burma (Rangoon)	100.0	102.4	114.8	150.0	187.4	254.4	299.7	290.7	269.3	284.4	292.4 [24]
Cyprus	100.0	104.9	111.9	121.4	145.9 [4]	159.3	163.5	100.0 [5]	105.7	112.8	126.3
Hong Kong	100.0	103.4	111.0	137.9	160.0	104 [6]	107	114	122	136	152
India	100.0	101.5	108.0	131.0	171.0	178.5	156.0	171.5	173.0	181.0	198.5 [25]
» (Bombay)	100.0	102.0	107.1	126.3	156.1	170.7	158.6	172.7	174.7	186.4	201.5 [26]
» (Delhi)	100.0	103.3	107.9	129.0	164.0	163.1	153.3	165.9	171.5	176.6	181.8 [26]
» (Jamshedpur)	100.0	100.0	107.6	130.0	177.6	164.8	148.1	167.1	167.1	179.0	190.5 [26]
Indonesia [7]	100.0	102.6	113.2	162.4	229.4	276.5	337.5	373.5	402.6	133.2 [8]	151.3
Iran	100.0	106.6	115.9	123.9	143.5	161.0	172.1	204.5	242.0 [9]	.	.
Iraq [10]	100.0	104.2	109.5	115.7	110.1 [11]	120.8	134.3	145.3	153.4	...	...
Israel	100.0	113.6	123.4	149.0	215.2	314.5	401.5	569.8 [12]	833.6	1 486.5	3 645.7
Japan	100.0	105.9	110.1	124.4	158.9	179.5	195.9	209.0	216.3	221.0	230.7
Jordan [13]	100.0	106.2	118.0	140.3	189.1	218.7	114.6 [14]	131.0	135.7	143.6	157.5
Kampuchea dém. (Phnom-Penh) [15]	100.0	194.5	249.6	714.9	2 277.7 [16]	.	.	.	.	.	.
Korea, Rep. of	100.0	118.8	134.7	138.1	176.3	232.6	274.0	305.8	356.7	406.0	497.7
Kuwait	.	.	100.0	115.3	135.9	153.7	163.7	175.4	181.3	186.5	...
République lao (Vientiane)	100.0	100.6	135.8	190.7	289.9	544.9	.	.	.	.	.
Liban (Beyrouth)	100.0	102.6	111.5	122.3	142.7	148.4 [17]	.	.	.	.	.
Malaysia:											
Peninsular Malaysia	100.0	101.5	104.7	121.4	153.1	158.8	162.0	170.8	179.3	183.4	189.9
Sabah	100.0	103.3	106.2	119.1	147.4	158.0	159.2	164.6	167.6	174.7	190.1
Sarawak	100.0	98.4	103.4	119.0	146.4	152.6	160.1	170.2	170.4	177.8	189.4
Nepal [18]	104.2 [19]	100.0	109.9	122.8	100.0 [5]	104.9	96.4	110.5	117.7	121.1	131.7 [26]
Pakistan [20]	100.0	105.2	104.5 [21]	131.4	171.1	209.1	221.6	246.6	260.4	279.0	293.9
Philippines [22]	100.0	133.4	157.4	115.6 [3]	155.3	163.4	178.5	195.6	207.9	239.2	267.0 [24]
Singapore	100.0	102.5	105.3	142.7	125.6 [11]	127.0	119.3	125.1	132.6	102.8 [23]	110.2

EXPLANATORY NOTES AND CODES: See p. 575.

[1] Government officials. [2] Jan., Feb. and April-Dec. [3] Series (base 1972 = 100) replacing former series. [4] Jan.-July and Sep.-Dec.; series linked to former series. [5] Series replacing former series. [6] Series (base July 1973-June 1974 = 100) replacing former series. [7] Prior to 1979: Djakarta only. [8] March-Dec.; series (base April 1977-March 1978 = 100) replacing former series. [9] Jan.-Nov. [10] Prior to 1974: Baghdad only. [11] Series (base 1973 = 100) replacing former series. [12] Series linked to former series. [13] Prior to 1976: Amman only. [14] Series (base 1975 = 100) replacing former series. [15] Working class. [16] Jan.-Oct. [17] Jan.-July. [18] Prior to 1974: Katmandu only. [19] July-Dec. [20] Prior to 1972; Karachi only; industrial workers. [21] Series (base 1971 = 100) replacing former series. [22] Prior to 1973: Manila only; middle income group. [23] Series (base 1978 = 100) replacing former series. [24] April. [25] May. [26] March.

NOTES EXPLICATIVES ET CODES: Voir p. 576.

[1] Fonctionnaires. [2] Janv., fév. et avril-déc. [3] Série (base 100 en 1972) remplaçant la précédente. [4] Janv.-juillet et sept.-déc.; série enchaînée à la précédente. [5] Série remplaçant la précédente. [6] Série (base juillet 1973-juin 1974 = 100) remplaçant la précédente. [7] Avant 1979: Djakarta seulement. [8] Mars-déc.; série (base avril 1977-mars 1978 = 100) remplaçant la précédente. [9] Janv.-nov. [10] Avant 1974: Bagdad seulement. [11] Série (base 100 en 1973) remplaçant la précédente. [12] Série enchaînée à la précédente. [13] Avant 1976: Amman seulement. [14] Série (base 100 en 1975) remplaçant la précédente. [15] Classe ouvrière. [16] Janv.-oct. [17] Janv.-juillet. [18] Avant 1974: Katmandu seulement. [19] Juillet-déc. [20] Avant 1972: Karachi seulement; travailleurs de l'industrie. [21] Série (base 100 en 1971) remplaçant la précédente. [22] Avant 1973: Manille seulement; familles à revenu moyen. [23] Série (base 100 en 1978) remplaçant la précédente. [24] Avril. [25] Mai. [26] Mars.

NOTAS EXPLICATIVAS Y CLAVES: Véase pág. 578.

[1] Funcionarios. [2] Enero, febr. y abril-dic. [3] Serie (base 1972 = 100) que substituye a la anterior. [4] Enero-julio y sept.-dic.; serie enlazada con la anterior. [5] Serie que substituye a la anterior. [6] Serie (base julio de 1973-junio de 1974 = 100) que substituye a la anterior. [7] Antes de 1979: Djakarta solamente. [8] Marzo-dic.; serie (base abril de 1977-marzo de 1978 = 100) que substituye a la anterior. [9] Enero-nov. [10] Antes de 1974: Bagdad solamente. [11] Serie (base 1973 = 100) que substituye a la anterior. [12] Serie enlazada con la anterior. [13] Antes de 1976: Amman solamente. [14] Serie (base 1975 = 100) que substituye a la anterior. [15] Clase obrera. [16] Enero-oct. [17] Enero-julio. [18] Antes de 1974: Katmandú solamente. [19] Julio-dic. [20] Antes de 1972: Karachi solamente; trabajadores de la industria. [21] Serie (base 1971 = 100) que substituye a la anterior. [22] Antes de 1973: Manila solamente; familias de ingresos medios. [23] Serie (base 1978 = 100) que substituye a la anterior. [24] Abril. [25] Mayo. [26] Marzo.

23 Consumer prices / Prix à la consommation / Precios del consumo

B Food indices / Indices de l'alimentation / Indices de la alimentación

(1970 = 100)

Country — Pays — País	1970	1971	1972	1973	1974	1975	1976	1977	1978	1979	1980 (VI)
Sri Lanka (Colombo)	100.0	101.9	108.0	121.7	138.9	149.6	148.0	148.9	174.0	192.8	254.1
République arabe syrienne (Damas)	100.0	103.8	103.8	126.7	145.8	173.3	197.7	▎234 [1]	246	260	316
Thailand (Bangkok-Metropolis)	100.0	100.6	107.1	122.5	157.4	163.8	172.8	192.7	▎209.0 [2]	228.2	277.6
Viet Nam (Ho Chi Minh) [3]	100.0	113.8	▎146.9 [2]	216.0	321.3	.	.	.	.	.	.
Yemen (Sanaa)	.	.	100	142	166	203	...	...	...	...	.
Yemen, Democratic (Aden)	100.0	107.5	112.3	139.6	171.7	184.9	189.6	191.5	...	...	.
EUROPE — EUROPE / EUROPA											
Austria	100.0	103.8	109.8	118.4	128.3	136.4	144.4	▎153.5 [2]	158.7	162.9	171.9
Belgique	100.0	101.9	▎108.6 [2]	117.3	128.3	142.7	▎159.6 [2]	169.3	171.7	172.6	175.0
Bulgarie	100.0	100.2	100.2	101.1	102.2	102.8	103.3	103.5	104.7	...	.
Czechoslovakia	100.0	99.6	99.4	99.5	99.7	99.6	100.8	102.2	104.1	105.6	105.8 [8]
Denmark	100.0	105.9	115.7	131.4	147.1	163.4	181.0	202.0	221.6	▎148 [4]	161
España	100.0	107.8	117.7	129.1	151.6	177.3	210.5	260.2	310.1	341.7	365.5
Faeroe Is.	.	.	.	.	.	.	100.0	103.2	108.3	118.6	...
Finland	100.0	104.4	114.1	128.3	▎148.8 [2]	179.5	208.8	247.7	257.5	▎265.9 [2]	299.6
France	100.0	106.4	114.8	125.6	141.4	157.5	174.5	196.5	212.5	231.5	249.4
German Democratic Republic	100.0	100.6	99.6	▎98.2 [1]	98.6	99.7	99.7	99.7	99.7	99.7	.
Germany, Fed. Rep. of	100.0	103.8	109.8	117.9	123.5	130.0	136.0	142.7	144.7	147.2	154.4
Gibraltar	100.0	110.5	124.0	▎150.2 [2]	186.6	224.4	251.7	299.4	324.0	352.9	382.9
Grèce	100.0	105.1	109.3	132.5	169.2	189.2	215.4	245.5	280.5	333.3	432.1
Hongrie	100.0	102.0	103.1	107.9	108.4	109.7	120.9	127.5	132.1	145.4	170.5
Iceland (Reykjavik)	100.0	101.9	118.8	154.5	224.3	338.2	459.9	609.5	876.5	1162.4	1 737.4 [9]
Ireland	100.0	107.4	120.1	139.8	160.3	194.7	▎226.9 [2]	264.2	290.4	333.4	364.9 [9]
Isle of Man	.	.	.	.	.	.	86.4 [5]	100.0	108.9	122.3	141.9 [9]
Italie	100.0	104.0	110.6	123.9	145.9	172.2	201.6	▎240.5 [2]	271.6	307.6	350.6
Luxembourg	100.0	103.5	110.5	118.3	129.0	143.5	160.9	167.4	170.0	174.5	179.4
Malta	100.0	100.7	105.0	119.6	128.6	137.2	▎136.6 [2]	162.5	174.8	183.8	215.9 [10]
Netherlands	100.0	104.2	111.1	119.9	128.5	138.8	152.5	162.8	▎116.3 [4]	118.8	123.5
Norway	100.0	106.1	113.7	121.6	▎131.8 [2]	151.6	167.1	181.0	191.0	199.3	215.8
Pologne	100.0	101.9	101.8	102.8	113.1	114.1	118.0	124.0	136.8	147.9	.
Portugal [6]	100.0	108.8	119.6	130.5	173.0	213.9	263.8	▎131.9 [7]	161.5	206.8	228.2
Roumanie	100.0	101.5	102.1	103.3	105.1	105.5	106.1	107.1	108.1	109.0	.
Suisse	100.0	106.5	113.4	120.2	133.2	141.4	139.3	141.2	▎146.8 [2]	152.2	163.5

EXPLANATORY NOTES AND CODES: See p. 575.

[1] Series replacing former series. [2] Series linked to former series. [3] Working class. [4] Series (base 1975 = 100) replacing former series. [5] March-Dec. [6] Prior to 1977: Lisbon only. [7] Series (base 1976 = 100) replacing former series. [8] First quarter. [9] May. [10] March.

NOTES EXPLICATIVES ET CODES: Voir p. 576.

[1] Série remplaçant la précédente. [2] Série enchaînée à la précédente. [3] Classe ouvrière. [4] Série (base 100 en 1975) remplaçant la précédente. [5] Mars-déc. [6] Avant 1977 : Lisbonne seulement. [7] Série (base 100 en 1976) remplaçant la précédente. [8] Premier trimestre. [9] Mai. [10] Mars.

NOTAS EXPLICATIVAS Y CLAVES: Véase pág. 578.

[1] Serie que substituye a la anterior. [2] Serie enlazada con la anterior. [3] Clase obrera. [4] Serie (base 1975 = 100) que substituye a la anterior. [5] Marzo-dic. [6] Antes de 1977: Lisboa solamente. [7] Serie (base 1976 = 100) que substituye a la anterior. [8] Primer trimestre. [9] Mayo. [10] Marzo.

23 Consumer prices
Prix à la consommation
Precios del consumo

B Food indices
Indices de l'alimentation
Indices de la alimentación

(1970 = 100)

Country — Pays — País	1970	1971	1972	1973	1974	1975	1976	1977	1978	1979	1980 (VI)
Sweden	100.0	109.2	119.1	126.0	133.8	149.5	168.8	193.4	211.9	223.2	243.9
Turquie (Ankara)	100.0	114.0	126.5	151.8	180.8	235.1	277.2	362.0	523.7	792.6	1 655.7 [15]
United Kingdom	100.0	111.1	120.9	139.1	164.1	206.2	247.3	294.3	315.2	353.1	398.9
Yugoslavia	100.0	116.6	138.8	169.1	195.9	243.9	278.3	329.5	380.2	449.8	623
OCEANIA — OCÉANIE OCEANÍA											
American Samoa (Pago-Pago)	.	.	.	.	100.0	113.9	111.5	113.7	122.1	140.7	159.6 [16]
Australia	100.0	103.9	107.9	124.3	143.3	154.1	173.0	193.0	211.4	240.9	268.2 [16]
Cook Is. (Rarotonga)	100.0	114.1	127.0	140.5	156.3	181.8	227.1	272.9	301.1	...	...
Fiji	100.0	109.1	121.8	146.4	169.3 [1]	190.2	196.2	211.0	222.0	235.4	273.7 [17]
Guam	.	.	.	100.0	118.3	131.4	137.3	138.8	164.5	192.1	223.0 [16]
Kiribati (Tarawa)	94.9 [2]	100.0	106.2	124.0	145.0	168.7	100.0 [3]	108.3	122.5	...	...
New Zealand	100.0	108.9	114.2	127.1	141.7	156.7	185.8	217.4	240.7	282.3	337.4
Niue Is.	.	.	100.0	118.8	145.0	178.0	268.8 [1]	335.1	388.9	...	...
Nouvelle-Calédonie (Nouméa)	100.0	108.1	117.0	124.8	150.5	168.3	174.3	183.2	195.2	204.1	227.7
Papua New Guinea	100.0	107.7	106.8 [4]	117.4	155.9	167.1	174.8 [1]	181.3	188.7	197.3	225.9 [16]
Polynésie française (Tahiti) (Papeete)	100.0	103.2	104.8	117.9 [1]	143.5	162.8	163.8	178.4	189.9	209.4	224.3 [15]
Samoa (Apia) [5]	100.0	105.8	117.5	100.0 [3]	131.0	142.3	149.0	166.7	166.7	189.7	225.2
Solomon Is. (Honiara)	.	100.0	108.8	112.7	141.9	157.4	160.4	171.3	106.4 [6]	116.0	129.7
Tonga	100.0	100.9	110.5	144.7	169.0	181.6	187.6	221.4	250.1	256.5	277.2 [18]
Vanuatu [7, 8, 9] .... [10]	92.6 [11]	100.0	110.8	119.2	161.7	165.0 [11]	100.0 [3]	102.8 [12]	113.0 [13]	114.8	116.9 [18]
URSS [14]	100.0	100.3	100.3	100.5	100.8	100.9	100.9	100.9	101.9	102.4	.
RSS de Biélorussie	100.0	100.0	100.1	100.2	100.5	100.6	100.8	...	...	...	.
RSS d'Ukraine	100.0	100.4	100.6	100.7	101.2	101.3	101.2	101.2	102.3	...	

EXPLANATORY NOTES AND CODES: See p. 575.

1 Series linked to former series. 2 Oct.-Dec. 3 Series replacing former series. 4 Series (base 1971 = 100) replacing former series. 5 Urban area: prior to 1973: Apia only. 6 Series (base Oct.-Dec. 1977 = 100) replacing former series. 7 Urban areas; prior to 1976: Vila only. 8 Indices based on prices paid in francs. 9 Former New Hebrides. 10 Low income group. 11 Jan.-Sep. 12 Jan.-June. 13 April-Dec. 14 Incl. Byelorussian SSR and Ukranian SSR, shown separately in this table. 15 May. 16 Second quarter. 17 April. 18 First quarter.

NOTES EXPLICATIVES ET CODES: Voir p. 576.

1 Série enchaînée à la précédente. 2 Oct.-déc. 3 Série remplaçant la précédente. 4 Série (base 100 en 1971) remplaçant la précédente. 5 Région urbaine : avant 1973 : Apia seulement. 6 Série (base oct.-déc. 1977 = 100) remplaçant la précédente. 7 Régions urbaines ; avant 1976 : Vila seulement. 8 Indices fondés sur des prix payés en francs. 9 Précédemment Nouvelles-Hébrides. 10 Familles à revenu modique. 11 Janv.-sept. 12 Janv.-juin. 13 Avril-déc. 14 Y compris les RSS de Biélorussie et d'Ukraine, figurant séparément dans ce tableau. 15 Mai. 16 Deuxième trimestre. 17 Avril. 18 Premier trimestre.

NOTAS EXPLICATIVAS Y CLAVES: Véase pág. 578.

1 Serie enlazada con la anterior. 2 Oct.-dic. 3 Serie que substituye a la anterior. 4 Serie (base 1971 = 100) que substituye a la anterior. 5 Area urbana: antes de 1973: Apia solamente. 6 Serie (base oct.-dic. 1977 = 100) que substituye a la anterior. 7 Areas urbanas; antes de 1976: Vila solamente. 8 Indices basados en los precios pagados en francos. 9 Anteriormente Nuevas Hébridas. 10 Familias de ingresos módicos. 11 Enero-sept. 12 Enero-junio. 13 Abril-dic. 14 Incl. las RSS de Bielorrusia y de Ucrania, que figuran separadamente en este cuadro. 15 Mayo. 16 Segundo trimestre. 17 Abril. 18 Primer trimestre.

23 Consumer prices / Prix à la consommation / Precios del consumo

C Fuel and light indices / Indices du combustible et éclairage / Indices del combustible y alumbrado

(1970 = 100)

Country — Pays — País	1970	1971	1972	1973	1974	1975	1976	1977	1978	1979
AFRICA — AFRIQUE AFRICA										
Algérie (Alger)	100.0	100.0	100.0	100.0	100.4	101.6	...	...	...	...
Botswana [1,2,3]	100.0	.	.	124.6 [4]	145.3	❙116.6 [5]	135.4	150.0	160.6	188.9
Cap-Vert (Praya) [2,6]	100.0	100.0	100.9	116.8	170.8	224.8	226.5	...	...	
République centrafricaine (Bangui) [2,7] . Europ.	100.0	107.7	113.4	113.4	111.7	147.6	159.2	...		
Congo (Brazzaville) [2] . . . . Europ.	100.0	104.5	106.1	106.1	105.5	106.1	106.1	...	...	...
Côte-d'Ivoire (Abidjan) [2,6] . . . . Afric.	100.0	104.4	109.2	116.2	139.1	156.9	183.7	212.5	253.8	280.1
» » » . . . Europ.	100.0	101.3	106.9	106.7	120.8	136.8	148.5	156.3	158.3	161.4
Egypt	100.0	98.2	93.3	88.6	90.5	93.8	99.1	99.4	101.0	102.4
Ethiopia (Addis Ababa) [8]	100.0	101.3	107.2	108.3	119.1	136.4	155.9	198.0	212.7	244.5
Gabon (Libreville) . . . . Afric.	97.4 [9]	100.0	106.7	108.1	111.3	...	...	...	...	...
Gambia (Banjul-Kombo, St. Mary)	.	.	.	.	100.0	125.6	160.4	163.0	186.7	200.0
Ghana (Accra)	100.0	98.0	111.3	127.6	170.9	237.8	294.7	409.4	.	.
Kenya (Nairobi) . . . . [10]	.	.	100.0	105.7	117.7	132.3	❙164.6 [11]	171.5	174.1	199.5
Lesotho . . . . [12]	.	.	96.5 [13]	100.0	144.6	169.6	211.6	241.9	267.3	...
Liberia (Monrovia)	100.0	104.3	103.1	115.7	151.5	160.9	183.7	203.4	232.1	...
Libyan Arab Jamahiriya (Tripoli)	100.0	97.0	76.9	79.8	83.2	89.1	93.8	94.3	95.4	...
Madagascar (Tananarive) . . . . [14]	100.0	100.9	101.3	❙103.6 [11]	115.0	129.2	131.1	141.1	148.4	170.5
» » . . . . Europ.	100.0	100.4	102.3	❙104.5 [11]	114.5	121.5	119.4	123.6	128.0	157.2
Malawi (Blantyre) [15] . . . . [12]	100.0	107.0	110.3	113.0	137.8	158.1	171.0	190.6	223.8	245.4
» » [15] . . . . [16]	100.0	108.0	111.4	117.2	131.0	171.1	192.5	204.2	230.9	263.3
Maroc	.	.	.	.	.	100.0	114.0	138.7	146.6	...
Mauritanie (Nouakchott) [2,7] . . . . Europ.	100.0	109.6	119.8	123.8	134.8 [17]	❙100.0 [18]	112.1	125.5	131.4	...
Mauritius	100.0	99.9	99.9	106.9	125.2	138.0	❙177.9 [11]	202.6	202.7	274.5
Mozambique (Maputo)	100.0	108.4	114.7	115.8	144.2	149.5	174.7	.	.	.
Niger (Niamey) [2] . . . . Europ.	100.0	100.0	97.8	97.1	103.9	116.9	116.9	117.1	117.1	...
Nigeria (Lagos) . . . . [12]	100.0	96.5	99.4	87.1 [19]	88.1	159.4	151.4	176.0	.	.
Réunion (Saint-Denis)	.	.	100.0	101.3	121.0	125.6	126.6	125.3	123.0	133.8
Sénégal (Dakar)	100.0	100.4	103.3	105.9	142.2	161.1	165.2	163.7	163.1	
Seychelles (Victoria)	100.0	137.0	144.1	150.6	❙100.0 [18]	117.1	138.8	173.1	.	

EXPLANATORY NOTES AND CODES: See p. 575.

[1] Prior to 1975: Gaborone only. [2] Incl. water. [3] Incl. certain household equipment. [4] June-Dec. [5] Series (base 1974 = 100) replacing former series. [6] Incl. soap. [7] Incl. cleaning products. [8] Incl. soap and certain kitchen utensils. [9] Jan.-June and Aug.-Dec. [10] Middle income group. [11] Series linked to former series. [12] Low income group. [13] Oct. [14] Madagascans. [15] Incl. certain household items. [16] High income group. [17] Jan.-July and Sep.-Dec. [18] Series replacing former series. [19] Jan.-Sep. and Dec.

NOTES EXPLICATIVES ET CODES: Voir p. 576.

[1] Avant 1975 : Gaborone seulement. [2] Y compris l'eau. [3] Y compris certains biens d'équipement de ménage. [4] Juin.-déc. [5] Série (base 100 en 1974) remplaçant la précédente. [6] Y compris le savon. [7] Y compris les produits d'entretien. [8] Y compris le savon et certains ustensiles de cuisine. [9] Janv.-juin et août-déc. [10] Familles à revenu moyen. [11] Série enchaînée à la précédente. [12] Familles à revenu modique. [13] Oct. [14] Malgaches. [15] Y compris certains articles de ménage. [16] Familles à revenu élevé. [17] Janv.-juillet et sept.-déc. [18] Série remplaçant la précédente. [19] Janv.-sept. et déc.

NOTAS EXPLICATIVAS Y CLAVES: Véase pág. 578.

[1] Antes de 1975: Gaborone solamente. [2] Incl. el agua. [3] Incl. ciertos enseres domésticos. [4] Junio-dic. [5] Serie (base 1974 = 100) que substituye a la anterior. [6] Incl. el jabón. [7] Incl. los productos de limpieza. [8] Incl. el jabón y ciertos utensilios de cocina. [9] Enero-junio y agosto-dic. [10] Familias de ingresos medios. [11] Serie enlazada con la anterior. [12] Familias de ingresos módicos. [13] Oct. [14] Malgaches. [15] Incl. ciertos artículos domésticos. [16] Familias de ingresos elevados. [17] Enero-julio y sept.-dic. [18] Serie que substituye a la anterior. [19] Enero-sept. y dic.

23 Consumer prices
Prix à la consommation
Precios del consumo

C Fuel and light indices
Indices du combustible et éclairage
Indices del combustible y alumbrado

(1970 = 100)

Country — Pays — País	1970	1971	1972	1973	1974	1975	1976	1977	1978	1979
Sierra Leone (Freetown)	100.0	100.0	103.7	104.7	116.9	128.9	153.2	172.6	196.8	173.5
Somalia (Mogadishu)	100.0	102.8	101.0	74.1	78.3	84.0	79.1	92.4	117.8	...
South Africa, Rep. of . . . . [1]	100.0	103.2	111.0	122.7	132.4	151.9	181.8	227.5	263.5	...
Swaziland (Mbabane-Manzini) . . . . . [2]	100.0	108.9	112.8	117.7	171.8	212.2	241.6	279.9	318.0	463.2
Tanzania [3] . . . . [5]	100.0	103.8	104.5	117.6	115.5	156.4	172.2	232.0	244.7	...
Tchad (Ndjamena) [4] . . . . [5]	100.0	99.2	100.3	108.0	|135.2 [6]	172.5	172.5	171.7	181.2	...
Togo (Lomé) [7]	100.0	111.1	112.8	119.6	147.2	168.2	172.6	203.2	234.3	...
Tunisie [3, 8]	100.0	101.9	103.9	105.1	106.7	111.1	113.4	117.8	|101.4 [9]	106.4
AMERICA — AMÉRIQUE AMÉRICA										
Argentina (Buenos Aires) [10, 11]	100	139	220	345	461	1 499	9 143 }	|4 709 [15]	12 456	30 999
» » » [10, 12]	100	126	134	188	206	256	1 563 }			
Bermuda	100.0	105.9	112.3	125.5	192.2	224.0	235.5	234.4	|100.0 [14]	129.7
Canada	100.0	106.0	110.2	120.9	137.4	155.5	183.6	211.3	273.3	259.4
Costa Rica (San José) [10]	100.0	100.3	102.5	109.4 [15]	206.0 [16]	248.3	|269.2 [6]	290.8	294.9	329.8
Dominica	100.0	101.6	105.0	112.6	152.4	166.8	175.3	184.0	225.0	278.6 [17]
República Dominicana (Santo Domingo) . . .	96.4 [18]	100.0	107.0	110.8	149.4	156.2	161.6	160.7	162.7	172.2
Ecuador (Quito)	100.0	107.6	113.2	113.2	114.3	116.2	118.5	124.6	138.6	144.9
El Salvador [19, 20]	100.0	90.2 [21]	98.7	118.7	148.5	216.1	269.7	360.3	472.9	.
Falkland Is. (Malvinas) (Stanley)	100.0	99.3	|99.5 [22]	100.0	102.6	105.3	105.4	105.8	106.6	107.6
Greenland	.	100.0	108.8	113.7	149.0	191.2	217.6	222.5	232.4	264.7
Guatemala (Guatemala)	100.0	101.4	103.0	114.1	175.5	180.6	.	.		
Honduras (Tegucigalpa)	100.0	98.4	113.3	125.7	187.5	203.3	206.1	200.6	200.6	254.0
Jamaica [19]	100.0	106.9	116.2	130.5	194.1	203.4	222.8	233.7	...	...
Montserrat [3]	.	.	.	.	61.7 [23]	100.0	109.6	152.7	161.0	180.0
Netherlands Antilles [24]	99.4 [25]	100.0	100.9	101.0	112.2	|115.5 [6]	122.4	138.7	142.4	169.8
Panamá (Panamá)	100.0	102.6	104.4	105.9	142.7	152.3	|112.0 [26]	127.6	162.9	172.3

23 Consumer prices / Prix à la consommation / Precios del consumo — C Fuel and light indices / Indices du combustible et éclairage / Indices del combustible y alumbrado

(1970 = 100)

Country — *Pays* — País	1970	1971	1972	1973	1974	1975	1976	1977	1978	1979
Perú (Lima) [1]	100.0	100.0	100.3	❘ 105.0 [2]	106.9	117.1	166.7	211.5	358.2	572.1
Puerto Rico	100.0	104.8	108.7	110.7	134.5	119.9	121.2	125.6	125.5	130.9
St. Kitts	100.0	99.8	103.7	109.2	176.0	186.5	213.8	238.1	❘ 100.0 [3]	114.9
St. Lucia	100.0	101.6	105.3	109.6	177.9	190.5	217.9	236.2	261.8	338.2
St. Vincent	100.0	112.1	110.9	135.5	221.0	231.8	222.4	262.1	321.7	419.2
Suriname (Paramaribo) [4]	100.0	100.8	101.0	103.9	146.0	161.9	156.0	165.9	152.4	172.7
Trinidad and Tobago	100.0	102.8	109.4	116.2	133.1	160.7	❘ 165.4 [2]	168.2	169.6	172.1
United States [5]	100.0	106.7	107.6	123.5	194.9	213.7	227.8	257.4 }		
» » [6]	100.0	106.9	112.3	117.8	135.9	158.1	176.1	198.9 }	❘ 108.2 [7]	125.2
Uruguay (Montevideo) [8]	.	.	.	.	.	.	100.0	154.7	204.1	317.4
Venezuela (Caracas) [1]	100.0	100.0	100.0	100.0	100.0	100.7	101.3	101.9	102.3	102.7
Virgin Is. (US)	100.0	100.0	111.9	125.5	130.5	155.4	173.0	180.8	184.1	...
ASIA — ASIE / ASIA										
Bangladesh (Dacca) [9]	100.0	108.4 [10]	158.2	❘ 133.5 [11]	191.8	227.6	233.9	244.2	252.8	...
Burma (Rangoon)	100.0	101.1	102.2	108.9	175.5	196.3	292.1	304.1	298.5	336.3
Cyprus	100.0	99.8	100.3	101.0	❘ 133.7 [12]	149.4	156.4	❘ 100.0 [3]	106.6	121.2
Hong Kong	100.0	103.0	104.0	111.0	160.0	❘ 129 [13]	132	134	134	169
India	100.0	106.6	115.0	126.9	170.1	187.4	195.2	201.2	215.0	253.3
» (Bombay)	100.0	103.4	113.5	120.2	174.2	204.5	212.9	212.4	218.0	248.9
» (Delhi)	100.0	119.7	121.3	127.3	165.0	186.3	192.9	193.4	200.5	231.7
» (Jamshedpur)	100.0	103.5	102.9	122.7	156.4	168.6	176.2	187.8	201.7	243.0
Iran	100.0	99.4	101.8	104.5	109.9	114.6	116.6	126.4	...	...
Iraq [4, 14]	100.0	91.3	92.3	90.4	❘ 94.4 [15]	95.1	106.2	110.9	105.4	...
Israel	100	110	123	136	247	405	543	❘ 721 [2]	1 099	1 910
Japan	100.0	103.7	105.3	111.1	142.1	161.3	172.9	189.4	186.8	194.0
Jordan [16]	100.0	104.3	105.8	109.0	109.8	109.8	❘ 106.7 [17]	107.1	115.3	...
Korea, Rep. of	100.0	108.2	119.2	125.9	173.7	199.6	208.0	243.7	306.8	383.8
Liban (Beyrouth)	100.0	100.2	100.5	100.7	101.0	.	.	.	.	.
Nepal [18]	98.9 [19]	100.0	96.7	94.1	❘ 100.0 [3]	119.6	131.3	139.5	141.2	165.8
Philippines [20]	100.0	107.7	111.3	❘ 112.4 [11]	153.7	170.5	189.2	205.2	230.5	291.2
Singapore	100.0	101.4	101.8	107.0	❘ 141.2 [15]	142.2	144.2	147.0	❘ 100.0 [3]	113.9
Sri Lanka (Colombo)	100.0	103.5	107.2	120.8	162.4	174.2	194.9	189.2	192.6	241.4
République arabe syrienne (Damas)	100.0	101.9	102.8	106.6	105.7	109.4	129.2	❘ 130 [3]	141	150
Yemen (Sanaa)	.	.	100	212	318	421	...	...	...	...
Yemen, Democratic (Aden)	100.0	102	108	111	156	202	207	216	...	...

EXPLANATORY NOTES AND CODES: See p. 575.

1 Metropolitan area. 2 Series linked to former series. 3 Series replacing former series. 4 Fuel only (Iraq: beginning 1974). 5 Fuel oil and coal. 6 Gas and electricity. 7 Series (base 1977 = 100) replacing former series. 8 Electricity only. 9 Government officials. 10 Jan., Feb. and April-Dec. 11 Series (base 1972 = 100) replacing former series. 12 Jan.-July and Sep.-Dec., series linked to former series. 13 Series (base July 1973-June 1974 = 100) replacing former series. 14 Prior to 1974: Baghdad only. 15 Series (base 1973 = 100) replacing former series. 16 Prior to 1976: Amman only. 17 Series (base 1975 = 100) replacing former series. 18 Prior to 1974: Katmandu only. 19 June-Dec. 20 Prior to 1973: Manila only; middle income group.

NOTES EXPLICATIVES ET CODES: Voir p. 576.

1 *Région métropolitaine.* 2 *Série enchaînée à la précédente.* 3 *Série remplaçant la précédente.* 4 *Combustible seulement (Iraq: à partir de 1974).* 5 *Combustibles solides et mazout.* 6 *Gaz et électricité.* 7 *Série (base 100 en 1977) remplaçant la précédente.* 8 *Électricité seulement.* 9 *Fonctionnaires.* 10 *Janv., fév. et avril-déc.* 11 *Série (base 100 en 1972) remplaçant la précédente.* 12 *Janv.-juillet et sept.-déc., série enchaînée à la précédente.* 13 *Série (base juillet 1973-juin 1974 = 100) remplaçant la précédente.* 14 *Avant 1974 : Bagdad seulement.* 15 *Série (base 100 en 1975) remplaçant la précédente.* 16 *Avant 1976 : Amman seulement.* 17 *Série (base 100 en 1975) remplaçant la précédente.* 18 *Avant 1974 : Katmandu seulement.* 19 *Juin-déc.* 20 *Avant 1973 : Manille seulement ; familles à revenu moyen.*

NOTAS EXPLICATIVAS Y CLAVES: Véase pág. 578.

1 Area metropolitana. 2 Serie enlazada con la anterior. 3 Serie que substituye a la anterior. 4 Combustible solamente (Iraq: a partir de 1974). 5 Combustibles sólidos y líquidos. 6 Gas y electricidad. 7 Serie (base 1977 = 100) que substituye a la anterior. 8 Electricidad solamente. 9 Funcionarios. 10 Enero, febr. y abril-dic. 11 Serie (base 1972 = 100) que substituye a la anterior. 12 Enero-julio y sept.-dic.; serie enlazada con la anterior. 13 Serie (base julio de 1973-junio de 1974 = 100) que substituye a la anterior. 14 Antes de 1974: Bagdad solamente. 15 Serie (base 1973 = 100) que substituye a la anterior. 16 Antes de 1976: Amman solamente. 17 Serie (base 1975 = 100) que substituye a la anterior. 18 Antes de 1974: Katmandú solamente. 19 Junio-dic. 20 Antes de 1973: Manila solamente; familias de ingresos medios.

23 Consumer prices / Prix à la consommation / Precios del consumo

C Fuel and light indices / Indices du combustible et éclairage / Indices del combustible y alumbrado

(1970 = 100)

Country — Pays — País	1969	1970	1971	1972	1973	1974	1975	1976	1977	1978
EUROPE — EUROPE EUROPA										
Austria	100.0	106.7	111.0	117.5	135.7	156.6	165.7	173.7 [1]	177.8	189.8
Belgique	100.0	104.9	106.8 [1]	109.2	142.0	164.0	174.9 [1]	182.9	184.2	220.1
Denmark	100.0	113.6	114.3	130.6	206.1	220.4	238.1	259.2	285.7	220.1
España [3]	100.0	107.5	114.0	122.6	146.9	173.1	205.2	104.5 [4]	108.9	181 [2]
										125.2
Faeroe Is.	.	.			.		100.0	104.1	107.3	127.7
Finland	100.0	116.8	121.8	132.7	193.9 [1]	220.7	239.9	265.4	283.4	304.9 [1]
France	100.0	106.7	109.7	114.1	156.8	169.2	187.3	209.2	227.3	263.6
German Democratic Republic [5]	100.0	100.0	100.0	100.0 [6]	100.0	100.0	100.0	100.0	100.0	...
Germany, Fed. Rep. of	100.0	105.5	110.3	128.3	149.9	165.7	177.0	178.6	182.8	220.9
Grèce	100.0	99.7	100.6	107.3	158.0	184.2	196.7	217.4	226.1	288.9
Hongrie	100.0	99.1	97.0	95.1	100.4	108.2	107.2	106.4	106.7	116.1
Iceland (Reykjavik)	100.0	106.6	107.2	127.6	196.0	312.5	385.9	468.3	636.9	1 005.8
Ireland	100.0	111.7	122.8	131.6	198.7	231.2	262.0 [1]	313.9	325.1	371.6
Isle of Man	.	.	.	.	.			100.0	105.1	125.4
Italie	100.0	103.9	103.9	104.7	149.2	158.8	179.1	230.0 [1]	256.2	303.7
Luxembourg	100.0	104.6	106.7	109.2	120.5	141.0	150.8	163.6	165.9	188.9
Malta	100.0	100.0	100.6	100.9	142.8	127.5	124.1 [1]	173.3	173.3	211.8
Netherlands	100.0	107.1	111.6	116.7	133.8	159.4	178.5	185.1	135.0 [2]	144.5
Norway	100.0	105.2	111.1	118.2	137.6 [1]	156.3	172.4	193.0	231.9	256.4
Portugal [7]	100.0	103.5	103.5	110.4	132.3	144.8	170.3	130.0 [4]	178.5	214.5
Roumanie	100.0	100.0	100.0	100.2	100.2	110.9	120.8	121.3	122.0	137.8
Suisse	100.0	109.7	106.8	137.8	160.4	159.7	164.9	168.2	155.4 [1]	235.4
Sweden	100.0	110.6	111.4	136.0	194.6	206.6	239.5	264.8	302.6	365.6
United Kingdom	100.0	110.4	119.0	122.4	143.3	190.8	236.1	273.5	294.5	324.3
Yugoslavia	100.0	125.8	150.6	182.2	252.6	332.8	382.7	433.7	485.7	605.8
OCEANIA — OCÉANIE OCEANÍA										
Australia	100.0	102.6	106.3	109.4	122.3	147.6	161.3	176.3	192.0	216.5
Fiji [3, 8]	100.0	105.2	109.0	109.6	133.0 [1]	152.2	168.6	179.9	194.7	212.0
Guam	.	.	.	100.0	114.0	164.4	154.8	155.8	168.6	182.3
New Zealand	100.0	102.9	106.0	109.9	116.9	125.8	165.5	226.1	250.5	316.4
Nouvelle-Calédonie (Nouméa)	100.0	101.4	104.4	114.4	140.6	152.9	159.3	173.1	184.3	204.1
Solomon Is. (Honiara) [5]	95.1 [9]	100.0	100.2	101.8	106.2	116.8	128.1	140.5	.	.
Tonga	.	.	.	.	.	100.0	112.0	126.3	127.4	148.6
Vanuatu (Vila) [10, 11] .... [12]	96.7 [13]	100.0	110.5	115.7	137.5	140.8 [13]	.	.	.	.

PRICES

23 Consumer prices / Prix à la consommation / Precios del consumo

D Clothing indices / Indices de l'habillement / Indices del vestido

(1970 = 100)

Country — Pays — País	1970	1971	1972	1973	1974	1975	1976	1977	1978	1979
AFRICA — AFRIQUE AFRICA										
Algérie (Alger)	**100.0**	102.9	106.5	107.1	112.6	114.3	122.0	...	...	...
Botswana [1]	**100.0**	.	.	124.5 [2]	142.9	115.0 [3]	129.0	146.3	152.3	171.8
Burundi (Bujumbura) [4]	**100.0**	105.5	108.6	111.5	123.9	138.3	152.7	172.9	297.0	352.4
Cameroun (Yaoundé) . . . . . . *Afric.*	**100.0**	100.4	110.4	122.4	134.8	146.5	176.6	193.7	211.2	267.6
» » . . . . . *Europ.*	**100.0**	100.8	107.3	120.3	141.1	165.4	190.8	212.5	236.1	241.1
République centrafricaine (Bangui) . *Europ.*	**100.0**	101.8	107.0	116.6	125.9	135.1	139.3	...	...	...
Congo (Brazzaville) . . . . *Europ.*	**100.0**	98.8	141.2	137.3	133.1	152.7	159.6	...	...	...
Côte-d'Ivoire (Abidjan) . . . . . *Afric.*	**100.0**	96.6	96.7	97.6	114.2	131.9	162.0	179.2	208.7	242.7
» » » [5,6] . . . . . *Europ.*	**100.0**	102.2	102.4	107.8	121.3	134.7	158.4	168.7	179.1	204.2
Egypt	**100.0**	99.9	104.1	110.8	121.4	133.6	142.0	168.8	249.5	240.7
Ethiopia (Addis Ababa)	**100.0**	103.3	107.1	119.8	128.1	139.5	149.8	163.5	179.2	192.9
Gabon (Libreville) [5] . . . . *Afric.*	*102.6* [7]	**100.0**	*102.7*	*101.6*	*126.6*	...	...	...	...	...
» » [8] [9]	**100.0**	100.5	106.1	117.9 [10]	139.5	172.3	...	...	...	...
Gambia (Banjul-Kombo, St. Mary) [5]	.	.	.	.	**100.0**	*105.1*	107.2	124.7	148.5	160.6
Ghana (Accra)	**100.0**	107.4	111.8	127.1	160.4	224.8	323.2	450.1	165.3 [11]	266.7
Kenya (Nairobi) . . . . [12]	.	.	**100.0**	*115.5*	*149.5*	*171.8*	190.3 [10]	204.0	226.9	241.0
Lesotho . . . . [13]	.	.	*95.7* [14]	**100.0**	*109.9*	*119.0*	128.4	134.3	142.7	...
Liberia (Monrovia)	**100.0**	96.4	104.4	117.5	143.1	172.4	199.8	210.1	213.7	...
Libyan Arab Jamahiriya (Tripoli)	**100.0**	95.6	92.9	92.1	95.4	102.0	119.6	144.6	194.7	...
Madagascar (Tananarive) . . . . [15]	.	.	.	**100.0**	*107.6*	*124.6*	*142.0*	150.8	160.6	171.6
» » . . . . *Europ.*	.	.	.	**100.0**	*109.1*	*125.0*	*147.3*	167.8	176.2	181.7
Malawi (Blantyre) . . . . [13]	**100.0**	100.3	103.2	109.4	120.8	132.2	137.2	141.5	151.4	...
» » . . . . . . [9]	**100.0**	108.9	111.6	118.5	143.5	179.7	198.9	201.3	200.5	211.1
Maroc [16]	**100.0**	101.6	102.0	105.5	100.0 [17]	108.5	*112.2*	*125.6*	*143.9*	*154.9*
Mauritanie (Nouakchott) . . . . . *Europ.*	**100.0**	103.7	118.2	124.7	137.3 [18]	100.0 [17]	115.6	122.3	141.3	...
Mauritius	**100.0**	100.8	103.3	120.6	161.7	173.1	180.8 [10]	195.8	213.4	239.3
Mozambique (Maputo)	**100.0**	121.8	135.5	146.0	193.5	225.8	222.6	.	.	.
Niger (Niamey) . . . . *Afric.*	**100.0**	99.3	89.5	89.5	90.9	107.7	126.4	145.7	176.0	.
» » [5] . . . . . *Europ.*	**100.0**	109.2	107.0	107.0	109.5	131.9	144.4	184.7	197.2	...
Nigeria (Lagos) . . . . [13]	**100.0**	107.0	110.5	135.1 [19]	167.1	192.0	257.5	333.1	.	.
» » [20]	.	.	.	.	.	**100.0**	126.6	135.1	158.5	180.6
» » [21]	.	.	.	.	.	**100.0**	128.1	141.4	176.3	219.1
Réunion (Saint-Denis) [5]	**100.0**	107.7	122.1 [10]	128.8	141.5	158.3	175.8	178.4	187.7	193.5

EXPLANATORY NOTES AND CODES: See p. 575.

NOTES EXPLICATIVES ET CODES: Voir p. 576.

NOTAS EXPLICATIVAS Y CLAVES: Véase pág. 578.

[1] Prior to 1975: Gaborone only. [2] June-Dec. [3] Series (base 1974 = 100) replacing former series. [4] Government officials. [5] Incl. household linen (Réunion: beginning 1972). [6] Incl. certain household items. [7] Jan.-June and Aug.-Dec. [8] Prior to 1973: incl. household linen. [9] High income group. [10] Series linked to former series. [11] Series (base 1977 = 100) replacing former series. [12] Middle income group. [13] Low income group. [14] Oct. [15] Madagascans. [16] Prior to 1974: Casablanca only. [17] Series replacing former series. [18] Jan.-July and Sep.-Dec. [19] Jan.-Sep. and Dec. [20] Urban areas. [21] Rural and urban areas.

[1] Avant 1975: Gaborone seulement. [2] Juin-déc. [3] Série (base 100 en 1974) remplaçant la précédente. [4] Fonctionnaires. [5] Y compris le linge de maison (Réunion: à partir de 1972). [6] Y compris certains articles de ménage. [7] Janv.-juin et août-déc. [8] Avant 1973: y compris le linge de maison. [9] Familles à revenu élevé. [10] Série enchaînée à la précédente. [11] Série (base 100 en 1977) remplaçant la précédente. [12] Familles à revenu moyen. [13] Familles à revenu modique. [14] Oct. [15] Malgaches. [16] Avant 1974: Casablanca seulement. [17] Série remplaçant la précédente. [18] Janv.-juillet et sept.-déc. [19] Janv.-sept. et déc. [20] Régions urbaines. [21] Régions rurales et urbaines.

[1] Antes de 1975: Gaborone solamente. [2] Junio-dic. [3] Serie (base 1974 = 100) que substituye a la anterior. [4] Funcionarios. [5] Incl. la ropa de casa (Reunión: a partir de 1972). [6] Incl. ciertos artículos domésticos. [7] Enero-junio y agosto-dic. [8] Antes de 1973: incl. la ropa de casa. [9] Familias de ingresos elevados. [10] Serie enlazada con la anterior. [11] Serie (base 1977 = 100) que substituye a la anterior. [12] Familias de ingresos medios. [13] Familias de ingresos módicos. [14] Oct. [15] Malgaches. [16] Antes de 1974: Casablanca solamente. [17] Serie que substituye a la anterior. [18] Enero-julio y sept.-dic. [19] Enero-sept. y dic. [20] Areas urbanas. [21] Areas rurales y urbanas.

23 Consumer prices
Prix à la consommation
Precios del consumo

D Clothing indices
Indices de l'habillement
Indices del vestido

(1970 = 100)

Country — Pays — País	1970	1971	1972	1973	1974	1975	1976	1977	1978	1979
Rwanda (Kigali)	100	102	104	118	181	196	197	215	...	...
Sénégal (Dakar)	100.0	102.4	106.4	111.5	120.8	140.6	165.6	175.5	180.9	...
Seychelles (Victoria)	100.0	104.5	114.3	140.3	| 100.0 [1]	114.5	135.9	155.1	.	.
Sierra Leone (Freetown)	100.0	100.6	100.6	100.6	105.3	113.0	141 0	168.6	228.6	326.1
Somalia (Mogadishu)	100.0	103.7	104.9	110.1	126.5	145.3	179.6	195.2	195.0	...
South Africa, Rep. of . . . . [2]	100.0	102.3	107.6	116.3	133.2	147.7	161.8	176.7	195.1	...
Sudan	100.0	100.0	100.0	129.9	183.4	216.7	219.4	260.9	292.1	316.0
Swaziland (Mbabane-Manzini) . . . . . [3]	100.0	100.6	101.1	109.0	136.2	151.6	165.7	185.6	202.0	210.0
Tanzania	100.0	104.7	116.3	132.5	147.5	175.7	212.1	231.8	258.7	...
Tchad (Ndjamena) . . . . [4]	100.0	110.4	111.5	126.6	| 155.2 [5]	183.6	207.7	224.7	234.1	...
Togo (Lomé)	100.0	108.2	113.3	113.9	132.4	153.3	162.8	215.7	245.1	...
Tunisie [6]	100.0	101.1	102.7	105.3	115.2	125.2	132.2	140.4	| 103.6 [7]	109.1
Zaïre (Kinshasa)	100.0	100.6	118.9	136.3	| 159.0 [5]	206.7	316.5	507.1	795.8	...
Zambia . . . . [3]	100.0	105.8	114.5	122.8	133.5	145.1	168.9	226.1	280.7	328.9
Zimbabwe [18] . . . . [3]	100.0	100.6	103.6	107.7	120.8	126.0	136.6	153.3	159.5	185.1
AMERICA — AMÉRIQUE AMÉRICA										
Antigua	100.0	108.0	125.8	142.9	162.3	182.6	213.2	183.2	261.0	285.1 [8]
Argentina (Buenos Aires) [9]	100	118	183	288	445	1 293	6 785	| 2 404 [10]	5 989	14 974
Bahamas (Nassau)	100.0	103.6	| 100.0 [1]	106.0	119.2	134.0	143.1	147.1	156.3	175.8
Barbados	100.0	107.0	116.7	132.9	165.3	212.9	232.7	246.3	254.0	283.2
Bermuda	100.0	105.0	109.2	118.0	130.8	146.7	157.7	171.1	| 100.0 [1]	118.9
Bolivia (La Paz)	100.0	104.7	114.1	158.1	230.9	267.3	296.7	308.9	336.3	389.7
Brasil (São Paulo)	100.0	117.5	| 100.0 [1]	108.1	125.3	157.1	212.3	303.8	392.5	574.7
Canada	100.0	101.7	104.4	109.6	120.0	127.3	134.3	143.4	148.9	162.7
Colombia (Bogotá)	100.0	111.6	126.3	158.6	203.3	238.9	285.4	356.5	487.1	| 617.6 [5]
Costa Rica (San José) [9]	100.0	101.1	103.6	117.7 [11]	145.9 [12]	164.2	| 169.2 [5]	159.6	150.8	145.3
Chile (Santiago)	100	126	200	1 074	3 927	14 974	47 418	94 232	132 873	| 175 394 [5]
Dominica	100.0	104.1	105.4	107.6	153.8	182.8	204.6	220.8	259.1	310.8 [13]
República Dominicana (Santo Domingo) . . .	98.3 [14]	100.0	116.6	137.0	154.3	184.5	207.4	241.0	272.3	297.7
Ecuador (Quito)	100.0	111.2	118.3	127.6	155.4	182.9	206.3	227.8	248.6	270.2
El Salvador [15]	100.0	102.1 [16]	105.4	108.6	118.4	152.7	170.5	185.8	202.6	.
Falkland Is. (Malvinas) (Stanley)	100.0	101.1	| 97.3 [17]	100.0	101.8	104.9	108.8	112.4	113.6	116.5

EXPLANATORY NOTES AND CODES: See p. 575.

[1] Series replacing former series. [2] White population. [3] Low income group. [4] High income group. [5] Series linked to former series. [6] Prior to 1978: Tunis metropolitan area only. [7] Series (base 1977 = 100) replacing former series. [8] Jan.-Nov. [9] Metropolitan area. [10] Series (base 1974 = 100) replacing former series. [11] June and Dec. [12] June, August and Oct.-Dec. [13] Jan.-Aug. and Nov.-Dec. [14] Nov. [15] San Salvador, Mejicanos and Villa Delgado. [16] Jan.-May and Aug.-Dec. [17] June-Dec.; series replacing former series. [18] Former Southern Rhodesia.

NOTES EXPLICATIVES ET CODES: Voir p. 576.

[1] Série remplaçant la précédente. [2] Population blanche. [3] Familles à revenu modique. [4] Familles à revenu élevé. [5] Série enchaînée à la précédente. [6] Avant 1978 : région métropolitaine de Tunis seulement. [7] Série (base 100 en 1977) remplaçant la précédente. [8] Janv.-nov. [9] Région métropolitaine. [10] Série (base 100 en 1974) remplaçant la précédente. [11] Juin et déc. [12] Juin, août et oct.-déc. [13] Janv.-août et nov.-déc. [14] Nov. [15] San Salvador, Mejicanos et Villa Delgado. [16] Janv.-mai et août-déc. [17] Juin-déc.; série remplaçant la précédente. [18] Précédemment Rhodésie du Sud.

NOTAS EXPLICATIVAS Y CLAVES: Véase pág. 578.

[1] Serie que substituye a la anterior. [2] Población blanca. [3] Familias de ingresos módicos. [4] Familias de ingresos elevados. [5] Serie enlazada con la anterior. [6] Antes de 1978: área metropolitana de Túnez solamente. [7] Serie (base 1977 = 100) que substituye a la anterior. [8] Enero-nov. [9] Area metropolitana. [10] Serie (base 1974 = 100) que substituye a la anterior. [11] Junio y dic. [12] Junio, agosto y oct.-dic. [13] Enero-agosto y nov.-dic. [14] Nov. [15] San Salvador, Mejicanos y Villa Delgado. [16] Enero-mayo y agosto-dic. [17] Junio-dic.; serie que substituye a la anterior. [18] Anteriormente Rhodesia del Sur.

23 Consumer prices / Prix à la consommation / Precios del consumo

D Clothing indices / Indices de l'habillement / Indices del vestido

(1970 = 100)

Country — Pays — País	1970	1971	1972	1973	1974	1975	1976	1977	1978	1979
Greenland	.	100.0	105.9	118.8	136.6	162.4	177.2	180.1	211.9	232.7
Guadeloupe [1]	100.0	104.9	111.6	116.8	125.3	139.7	149.9 [2]	160.2 [3]	172.0	|184.7 [4]
Guatemala [1]	100.0	101.3	105.0	121.7	135.4	|100.0 [5]	124.7	147.1	163.2	181.9
Guyana [1]	100.0	104.8	107.2	119.9	138.8	153.4	162.5	185.9	235.8	313.0
Guyane française (Cayenne)	100.0	108.7 [6]	119.6	127.6	163.2	197.8 [7]	232.4	260.2	301.7 [8]	338.0
Haïti (Port-au-Prince)	100.0	100.1	99.4	101.7	140.9	175.8	178.3	175.5	179.2	182.6
Honduras (Tegucigalpa)	100.0	101.9	107.1	117.9	129.4	135.5	140.5	151.0	157.3	176.7
Jamaica	100.0	107.2	116.1	125.5	149.8	174.7	194.5	213.4	...	...
Martinique (Fort-de-France)	100.0	102.3	106.5	113.4	128.7	152.3	181.5	207.5	238.6	258.7
México	100.0	106.0	113.0	|117.1 [9]	137.9	157.8	189.8	255.0	310.6	386.6
Montserrat	.	.	.	.	.	100.0	120.8	168.6	188.7	236.7
Netherlands Antilles [10]	.	100.0	102.1	107.0	116.2	|126.8 [4]	133.0	139.9	140.7	159.9
Nicaragua (Managua) [11]	.	.	.	91.4 [12]	100.0	109.0	109.6	112.8	116.4	147.0
Panamá (Panamá)	100.0	102.6	106.4	110.9	121.9	130.5	|103.4 [13]	109.4	112.0	118.2
Paraguay (Asunción)	100.0	101.0	104.5	110.4	133.3	150.7	159.6	171.5	191.5	235.9
Perú (Lima) [11]	100.0	109.5	121.7	|133.5 [4]	155.8	184.6	232.1	305.6	465.3	834.1
Puerto Rico	100.0	102.0	103.9	106.0	111.1	116.3	120.1	122.9	125.9	129.4
St. Kitts	100.0	116.2	135.8	132.9	148.8	169.5	191.5	239.2	|100.0 [5]	107.3
St. Lucia	100.0 [14]	111.6	123.0	128.7	148.2	172.3	184.1	215.6	232.9	257.1
St. Vincent	100.0	107.2	102.7	116.4	168.0	194.0	212.9	233.2	261.1	349.8
Suriname (Paramaribo)	100.0	98.3	98.7	109.4	123.1	138.9	163.9	198.4	227.7	283.2
Trinidad and Tobago	100.0	101.9	108.6	120.1	136.4	156.2	|175.1 [4]	200.7	217.5	236.6
United States	100.0	103.2	105.3	109.2	117.3	122.6	127.1	132.8	|137.4 [4]	143.3
Uruguay (Montevideo)	100	130	209	|393 [4]	640	1 072	1 582	2 323	3 243	3 918
Venezuela (Caracas) [11]	100.0	100.4	102.8	111.3	133.8	156.4	182.3	200.5	217.5	272.4
Virgin Is. (Brit.) [15]	100.0	108.7	110.5	121.8	123.2	.	.	.	.	.
Virgin Is. (US)	100.0	111.4	123.2	138.7	160.3	194.2	166.6	175.5	180.6	...
ASIA — ASIE / ASIA										
Bangladesh (Dacca) [16]	100.0	103.6 [17]	160.0	|186.2 [9]	244.0	250.7	228.6	265.2	307.8	...
Burma (Rangoon)	100.0	102.3	100.0	108.1	132.7	157.4	226.8	237.8	203.1	190.3
Cyprus	100.0	102.7	107.0	115.2	|127.1 [18]	131.4	135.0	|100.0 [5]	108.6	119.4
Hong Kong	100.0	101.0	104.9	115.5	126.2	|98 [19]	98	100	102	109
India	100.0	113.2	122.6	140.9	189.3	198.7	198.7	217.0	234.0	248.4
» (Bombay)	100.0	115.3	122.9	136.3	166.9	177.1	184.7	202.5	216.6	232.5
» (Delhi)	100.0	114.5	117.3	131.8	187.3	206.4	207.5	237.0	243.4	250.3
» (Jamshedpur)	100.0	111.8	120.8	146.5	196.5	202.1	204.2	230.6	255.6	274.3

EXPLANATORY NOTES AND CODES: See p. 575.

[1] Urban areas (Guadeloupe: prior to 1979: Basse-Terre only; Guatemala: prior to 1975: Guatemala City only). [2] Jan.-July. [3] Feb.-Dec. [4] Series linked to former series. [5] Series replacing former series. [6] Jan.-July and Sep.-Dec. [7] Jan.-May and Sep.-Dec. [8] Jan.-June and Sep.-Dec. [9] Series (base 1972 = 100) replacing former series. [10] Curaçao, Aruba and Bonaire; prior to 1975: excl. Bonaire and Windward Is. [11] Metropolitan area. [12] Dec. [13] Series (base 1975 = 100) replacing former series. [14] Jan.-April and June-Dec. [15] Dec. of each year. [16] Government officials. [17] Jan., Feb. and April-Dec. [18] Jan.-July and Sep.-Dec.; series linked to former series. [19] Series (base July 1973-June 1974 = 100) replacing former series.

NOTES EXPLICATIVES ET CODES: Voir p. 576.

[1] Régions urbaines (Guadeloupe : avant 1979 : Basse-Terre seulement ; Guatemala : avant 1975 : ville de Guatemala seulement). [2] Janv.-juillet. [3] Fév.-déc. [4] Série enchaînée à la précédente. [5] Série remplaçant la précédente. [6] Janv.-juillet et sept.-déc. [7] Janv.-mai et sept.-déc. [8] Janv.-juin et sept.-déc. [9] Série (base 100 en 1972) remplaçant la précédente. [10] Curaçao, Aruba et Bonaire ; avant 1975 : non compris Bonaire et les îles Windward. [11] Région métropolitaine. [12] Déc. [13] Série (base 100 en 1975) remplaçant la précédente. [14] Janv.-avril et juin-déc. [15] Déc. de chaque année. [16] Fonctionnaires. [17] Janv., fév. et avril-déc. [18] Janv.-juillet et sept.-déc. ; série enchaînée à la précédente. [19] Série (base juillet 1973-juin 1974 = 100) remplaçant la précédente.

NOTAS EXPLICATIVAS Y CLAVES: Véase pág. 578.

[1] Areas urbanas (Guadalupe: antes de 1979: Basse-Terre solamente; Guatemala: antes de 1975: ciudad de Guatemala solamente). [2] Enero-julio. [3] Febr.-dic. [4] Serie enlazada con la anterior. [5] Serie que substituye a la anterior. [6] Enero-julio y sept.-dic. [7] Enero-mayo y sept.-dic. [8] Enero-junio y sept.-dic. [9] Serie (base 1972 = 100) que substituye a la anterior. [10] Curazao, Aruba y Bonaire; antes de 1975: excl. Bonaire y las islas Windward. [11] Area metropolitana. [12] Dic. [13] Serie (base 1975 = 100) que substituye a la anterior. [14] Enero-abril y junio-dic. [15] Dic. de cada año. [16] Funcionarios. [17] Enero, febr. y abril-dic. [18] Enero-julio y sept.-dic.; serie enlazada con la anterior. [19] Serie (base julio de 1973-junio de 1974 = 100) que substituye a la anterior.

23 D Consumer prices / Prix à la consommation / Precios del consumo — Clothing indices / Indices de l'habillement / Indices del vestido

(1970 = 100)

Country — Pays — País	1970	1971	1972	1973	1974	1975	1976	1977	1978	1979
Indonesia (Djakarta)	100.0	109.5	109.5	128.4	175.7	201.4	226.9	247.1	262.0	...
Iran	100.0	103.3	107.3	122.8	138.8	154.2	164.8	202.4	...	...
Iraq [1,2]	100.0	108.4	114.2	122.9	|115.3[3]	125.1	137.3	152.8	155.9	...
Israel	100.0	109.3	125.0	146.3	187.9	236.3	324.7	|421.1[4]	632.4	1 037.9
Japan	100.0	109.1	115.0	139.9	172.4	182.8	196.5	208.4	215.7	226.1
Jordan [5]	100.0	104.4	111.5	124.2	140.3	149.7	|107.6[6]	139.3	146.1	180.5
Korea, Rep. of	100.0	106.4	115.6	129.8	158.6	181.5	205.3	227.6	255.0	320.1
Kuwait	.	.	100.0	105.5	116.7	124.4	135.6	151.8	159.8	178.0
République lao (Vientiane)	100.0	101.4	121.9	146.5	228.4	333.8[7]	.	.	.	.
Liban (Beyrouth) [8]	100.0	108.2	115.0	126.3	143.8	.	.	.	.	.
Malaysia:										
Peninsular Malaysia	100.0	100.7	103.4	126.1	140.9	140.1	143.6	149.2	154.3	164.3
Sabah	100.0	102.9	105.7	115.6	132.9	134.6	134.3	138.2	139.6	148.5
Sarawak	100.0	99.8	103.4	120.7	133.2	131.8	132.4	135.0	137.3	144.9
Nepal [9]	99.4[10]	100.0	100.8	118.7	|100.0[11]	105.0	108.8	114.6	119.0	128.5
Pakistan [12]	100.0	105.7	|104.2[13]	137.3	185.0	214.8	224.8	241.2	253.8	272.3
Philippines [14] ...[13]	100.0	117.9	138.3	|115.9[15]	172.2	186.5	195.2	215.5	235.6	275.6
Singapore	100.0	102.7	104.6	124.9	|110.1[3]	108.7	109.4	111.1	|100.0[11]	103.5
Sri Lanka (Colombo)	100.0	105.6	119.1	135.5	149.0	151.6	154.2	163.0	164.8	168.4
République arabe syrienne (Damas)	100.0	101.8	104.4	138.1	150.4	158.4	180.5	|249[11]	255	256
Thailand (Bangkok-Metropolis)	100.0	100.8	101.8	116.3	137.1	144.0	146.9	150.5	|160.2[4]	188.7
Yemen (Sanaa)	.	.	100	126	210	249	...	...	...	...
Yemen, Democratic (Aden)	100.0	100.9	123.9	131.2	216.5	283.5	320.2	356.9	...	...
EUROPE — EUROPE EUROPA										
Austria	100.0	103.4	108.5	116.6	127.4	135.2	142.3	|148.8[4]	153.8	159.1
Belgique	100.0	105.2	|109.8[4]	116.4	130.4	143.1	|151.3[4]	160.7	171.0	177.7
Denmark	100.0	102.5	107.4	117.4	131.4	141.3	148.8	162.0	178.5	|136[6]
España	100.0	108.5	118.0	131.9	159.2	182.5	211.4	273.4	335.9	411.4
Faeroe Is.	.	.	.	.	.	.	100.0	107.0	116.3	122.5
Finland	100.0	102.5	108.2	118.6	|136.7[4]	159.5	176.8	192.5	205.4	|226.5[4]
France [8]	100.0	104.3	109.8	118.1	134.3	151.4	164.2	177.4	195.5	216.7
German Democratic Republic [2,8]	100.0	95.6	94.1	|89.0[11]	83.0	81.2	81.2	80.3	79.7	...
Germany, Fed. Rep. of	100.0	105.9	112.3	120.7	129.8	136.4	141.0	147.8	154.3	161.1
Gibraltar	100.0	108.0	121.9	|130.0[4]	145.8	169.9	184.9	208.3	250.5	293.7

EXPLANATORY NOTES AND CODES: See p. 575.

[1] Prior to 1974: Baghdad only. [2] Excl. footwear (Iraq: beginning 1974). [3] Series (base 1973 = 100) replacing former series. [4] Series linked to former series. [5] Prior to 1976: Amman only. [6] Series (base 1975 = 100) replacing former series. [7] Jan.-Aug. [8] Incl. household linen. [9] Prior to 1974: Katmandu only; excl. footwear. [10] June-Dec. [11] Series replacing former series. [12] Prior to 1972: Karachi only; industrial workers. [13] Series (base 1971 = 100) replacing former series. [14] Prior to 1973: Manila only; middle income group. [15] Series (base 1972 = 100) replacing former series.

NOTES EXPLICATIVES ET CODES: Voir p. 576.

[1] Avant 1974 : Bagdad seulement. [2] Non compris la chaussure (Iraq : à partir de 1974). [3] Série (base 100 en 1973) remplaçant la précédente. [4] Série enchaînée à la précédente. [5] Avant 1976 : Amman seulement. [6] Série (base 100 en 1975) remplaçant la précédente. [7] Janv.-août. [8] Y compris le linge de maison. [9] Avant 1974 : Katmandu seulement ; non compris la chaussure. [10] Juin-déc. [11] Série remplaçant la précédente. [12] Avant 1972 : Karachi seulement ; travailleurs de l'industrie. [13] Série (base 100 en 1971) remplaçant la précédente. [14] Avant 1973 : Manille seulement ; familles à revenu moyen. [15] Série (base 100 en 1972) remplaçant la précédente.

NOTAS EXPLICATIVAS Y CLAVES: Véase pág. 578.

[1] Antes de 1974: Bagdad solamente. [2] Excl. el calzado (Irak: a partir de 1974). [3] Serie (base 1973 = 100) que substituye a la anterior. [4] Serie enlazada con la anterior. [5] Antes de 1976: Amman solamente. [6] Serie (base 1975 = 100) que substituye a la anterior. [7] Enero-agosto. [8] Incl. la ropa de casa. [9] Antes de 1974: Katmandú solamente; excl. el calzado. [10] Junio-dic. [11] Serie que substituye a la anterior. [12] Antes de 1972: Karachi solamente; trabajadores de la industria. [13] Serie (base 1971 = 100) que substituye a la anterior. [14] Antes de 1973: Manila solamente; familias de ingresos medios. [15] Serie (base 1972 = 100) que substituye a la anterior.

PRICES

23 Consumer prices / Prix à la consommation / Precios del consumo
D Clothing indices / Indices de l'habillement / Indices del vestido

(1970 = 100)

Country — Pays — País	1970	1971	1972	1973	1974	1975	1976	1977	1978	1979
Grèce	100.0	101.2	105.3	120.1	146.4	162.8	184.8	208.3	237.8	290.9
Hongrie	100.0	102.5	106.5	108.4	110.6	115.8	121.8	127.3	133.7	145.7
Iceland (Reykjavik)	100.0	110.1	121.1	144.2	191.0	297.2	420.0	515.9	728.5	1 096.8
Ireland	100.0	109.5	120.3	139.4	167.9	193.7	|214.3[1]	245.7	274.2	302.0
Isle of Man	.	.	.	.	.	.	.	100.0	116.0	135.9
Italie	100.0	106.2	112.7	126.3	151.7	175.9	204.1	|250.3[1]	287.4	327.5
Luxembourg	100.0	105.5	111.0	119.4	130.8	140.7	147.8	159.4	174.0	184.9
Malta	100.0	101.7	103 6	106.5	109.7	114.4	|117.7[1]	118.0	121.0	127.4
Netherlands	100.0	110.7	118.9	130.8	148.0	164.8	175.3	189.1	|121.1[2]	127.6
Norway	100.0	105.3	114.1	124.1	|137.0[1]	147.0	158.1	174.5	189.9	200.0
Portugal[3]	100.0	106.1	115.7	145.4	191.8	208.0	211 9	|118.7[4]	141.8	177.4
Roumanie	100.0	99.8	99.8	99.8	99.6	100.0	100.0	100.5	100.9	100.8
Suisse	100.0	105.9	114.2	125.9	138.2	146.9	147.8	149.4	|151.3[1]	152.7
Sweden	100.0	108.8	114.7	118.0	125.7	138.7	150.2	160.3	170.9	'179.2
Turquie (Ankara)	100.0	118.4	139.0	174.3	218.6	239.8	272.8	358.4	551.0	919.7
United Kingdom	100.0	106.8	114.5	125.3	147.2	169.2	187.6	211.8	230.1	251.9
Yugoslavia	100.0	113.0	129.9	157.1	193.7	236.2	261.5	291.1	339.5	410.5

OCEANIA — OCÉANIE / OCEANÍA

Country — Pays — País	1970	1971	1972	1973	1974	1975	1976	1977	1978	1979
American Samoa (Pago-Pago)	.	.	.	.	100.0	114.5	120.9	127.7	129.5	153.2
Australia	100.0	105.5	111.3	121.8	144.4	170.5	198.5	225.3	244.6	261.5
Cook Is. (Rarotonga)	100.0	105.7	118.8	137.0	173.8	197.6	233.6	296.6	345.8	...
Fiji	100.0	103.3	110.3	120.2	|138.0[1]	171.2	193.0	206.9	221.9	234.2
Guam	.	.	96.3[5]	100.0	108.4	126.6	135.8	153.5	162.1	171.3
Kiribati (Tarawa)	89.6[6]	100.0	107.8	106.5	125.3	134.6	|100.0[7]	110.5	135.9	...
New Zealand	100.0	113.1	120.3	128.6	143.9	165.2	189.2	221.5	255.1	284.0
Niue Is.	.	.	100.0	108.5	118.7	150.4	|187.9[1]	218.1	248.1	...
Nouvelle-Calédonie (Nouméa)[8]	100.0	105.6	109.9	115.8	120.6	135.1	148.3	162.2	181.4	199.8
Papua New Guinea[8]	.	100.0	104.2	108.6	124.9	149.1	|167.4[1]	174.2	188.0	195.6
Polynésie française (Tahiti) (Papeete)	100.0	101.9	110.6	|111.2[1]	120.7	130.3	161.4	180.9	197.8	216.7
Samoa (Apia)[9]	100.0	104.9	111.1	|100.0[7]	127.8	150.2	158.7	166.1	166.1	203.2
Solomon Is. (Honiara)	.	100.0	101.4	107.0	121.6	136.6	144.7	162.0	|101.9[10]	104.0
Tonga	100.0	102.7	105.6	109.0	113.4	135.2	162.7	186.3	208.9	225.7
Vanuatu[11,12,13] [14]	95.3[15]	100.0	103.0	109.4	124.7	133.2[15]	|100.0[7]	103.1[16]	118.1[17]	111.4
URSS[18]	100.0	99.7	99.6	99.3	98.6	98.6	98.6	99.2	98.6	98.9
RSS de Biélorussie	100.0	99.6	99.6	99.2	98.0	98.0	98.0	...	...	...
RSS d'Ukraine	100.0	99.7	99.9	99.7	99.3	99.3	99.3	100.4	99.9	100.2

23 Consumer prices / Prix à la consommation / Precios del consumo — E Rent indices / Indices du loyer / Indices del alquiler

(1970 = 100)

Country — Pays — País	1970	1971	1972	1973	1974	1975	1976	1977	1978	1979
AFRICA — AFRIQUE AFRICA										
Algérie (Alger)	100.0	100.0	100.0	102.8	103.1	109.6	...	...	...	...
Burundi (Bujumbura) [1,2,3]	100.0	102.3	103.8	107.7	123.1	139.1	125.7	135.6	161.4	207.6
Cameroun (Yaoundé) [1] *Afric.*	100.0	103.1	114.2	121.7	137.9	166.3	144.0	148.3	157.3	195.7
Côte-d'Ivoire (Abidjan) *Afric.*	100.0	95.8	95.9	96.2	103.0	114.2	151.7	153.1	165.5	169.2
Egypt	100.0	100.0	100.0	100.0	100.0	100.0	100.0	100.0	100.0	100.0
Gambia (Banjul-Kombo, St. Mary)					100.0	105.2	115.8	130.0	141.2	149.6
Ghana (Accra) [1]	100.0	100.0	100.0	100.0	100.0	100.0	100.0	95.1	134.6 [4]	167.9
Kenya (Nairobi) [5]			100.0	116.4	127.8	136.9	151.4 [6]	178.4	200.8	215.2
Lesotho [7] [8]			93.5 [9]	100.0	105.8	122.2	129.1	138.1	167.4	...
Liberia (Monrovia)	100.0	100.9	110.3	140.3	140.8	152.4	162.5	173.3	193.3	...
Libyan Arab Jamahiriya (Tripoli)	100.0	108.0	124.8	172.4	192.1	220.9	220.6	208.5	343.2	...
Maroc [10]	100.0	101.1	105.8	108.3	113.5	100.0 [11]	105.8	114.5	124.4	134.7
Mauritius	100.0	100.0	100.0	100.0	100.0	100.0	100.0 [6]	100.0	100.0	100.0
Mozambique (Maputo)	100.0	114.5	124.2	132.7	135.2	113.3	107.9			
Nigeria (Lagos) [7] [8]	100.0	103.0	105.8	108.0 [12]	110.0	113.6	118.4	121.5		
» » [1,13]						100.0	112.0	129.0	139.3	172.7
» » [1,14]						100.0	108.6	127.3	131.4	166.9
Réunion (Saint-Denis) [15]	100.0	111.6	107.9 [16]	123.0	135.7	156.2	169.0	173.5	186.6	197.0
Sénégal (Dakar) [7]	100.0	106.6	115.9	117.3	125.0	127.5	127.5	132.9	142.0	...
Seychelles (Victoria)	100.0	109.3	130.0	138.4	100.0 [11]	107.3	124.5	135.6		...
Sierra Leone (Freetown)	100.0	100.3	100.4	101.1	101.0	123.3	131.5	132.7	137.0	137.6
Somalia (Mogadishu) [17]	100.0	89.1	74.9	76.3	74.7	82.8	85.3	87.1	87.2	...
South Africa, Rep. of [7] [18]	100.0	107.2	113.7	122.1	133.4	149.4	164.0	175.4	187.5	...
Sudan [1]	100.0	115.5	130.9	153.7	199.1	252.5	289.4	300.9	311.9	390.4
Tanzania	100.0	103.9	103.9	105.0	100.0 [11]	103.6	104.9	106.6	114.0	...
Togo (Lomé)	100.0	108.0	116.1	117.9	131.8	143.8	142.3	147.3	205.6	...
Tunisie [19]	100.0	103.6	102.0	104.6	107.4	111.3	111.4	111.4	105.6 [4]	110.9
Zaïre (Kinshasa) [1,17,20]	100.0	90.1	90.5	100.2	123.5 [6]	141.6	209.0	298.7	331.4	...
Zambia [1] [8]	100.0	98.4	101.0	104.9	108.9	114.5	116.2	125.3	132.8	136.8
Zimbabwe [1,21] [8]	100.0	105.6	107.6	107.7	110.6	120.8	144.0	160.4	183.9	204.7

EXPLANATORY NOTES AND CODES: See p. 575.

[1] Incl. "Fuel and light" (Ghana: beginning 1978; Zaire: beginning 1974). [2] Incl. certain household items. [3] Government officials. [4] Series (base 1977 = 100) replacing former series. [5] Middle income group. [6] Series linked to former series. [7] Incl. expenditure on maintenance and repairs of dwelling. [8] Low income group. [9] Oct. [10] Prior to 1975: Casablanca only; incl. "Fuel and light" and kitchen utensils. [11] Series replacing former series. [12] Jan.-Sep. and Dec. [13] Urban areas. [14] Rural and urban areas. [15] Incl. "Fuel and light" and certain household equipment (Réunion: prior to 1972; Bahamas: beginning 1972). [16] Series (base 1971 = 100) replacing former series. [17] Incl. water. [18] White population. [19] Prior to 1978: Tunis metropolitan area only. [20] Prior to 1974: incl. electricity. [21] Former Southern Rhodesia.

NOTES EXPLICATIVES ET CODES: Voir p. 576.

[1] Y compris le groupe « Combustible et éclairage » (Ghana: à partir de 1978; Zaire: à partir de 1974). [2] Y compris certains articles de ménage. [3] Fonctionnaires. [4] Série (base 100 en 1977) remplaçant la précédente. [5] Familles à revenu moyen. [6] Série enchaînée à la précédente. [7] Y compris les dépenses pour l'entretien et la réparation du logement. [8] Familles à revenu modique. [9] Oct. [10] Avant 1975: Casablanca seulement; y compris le groupe « Combustible et éclairage » et les ustensiles de cuisine. [11] Série remplaçant la précédente. [12] Janv.-sept. et déc. [13] Régions urbaines. [14] Régions rurales et urbaines. [15] Y compris le groupe « Combustible et éclairage » et certains biens d'équipement de ménage (Réunion: avant 1972; Bahamas: à partir de 1972). [16] Série (base 100 en 1971) remplaçant la précédente. [17] Y compris l'eau. [18] Population blanche. [19] Avant 1978: région métropolitaine de Tunis seulement. [20] Avant 1974: y compris l'électricité. [21] Précédemment Rhodésie du Sud.

NOTAS EXPLICATIVAS Y CLAVES: Véase pág. 578.

[1] Incl. el grupo « Combustible y alumbrado » (Ghana: a partir de 1978; Zaire: a partir de 1974). [2] Incl. ciertos artículos domésticos. [3] Funcionarios. [4] Serie (base 1977 = 100) que substituye a la anterior. [5] Familias de ingresos medios. [6] Serie enlazada con la anterior. [7] Incl. los gastos de conservación y reparación de la vivienda. [8] Familias de ingresos módicos. [9] Oct. [10] Antes de 1975: Casablanca solamente; incl. el grupo « Combustible y alumbrado » y los utensilios de cocina. [11] Serie que substituye a la anterior. [12] Enero-sept. y dic. [13] Areas urbanas. [14] Areas rurales y urbanas. [15] Incl. el grupo « Combustible y alumbrado » y ciertos enseres domésticos (Reunión: antes de 1972; Bahamas: a partir de 1972). [16] Serie (base 1971 = 100) que substituye a la anterior. [17] Incl. el agua. [18] Población blanca. [19] Antes de 1978: área metropolitana de Túnez solamente. [20] Antes de 1974: incl. la electricidad. [21] Anteriormente Rhodesia del Sur.

601

23	Consumer prices Prix à la consommation Precios del consumo	E	Rent indices Indices du loyer Indices del alquiler

(1970 = 100)

Country — *Pays* — País	1970	1971	1972	1973	1974	1975	1976	1977	1978	1979
AMERICA — AMÉRIQUE AMÉRICA										
Antigua [1]	**100.0**	107.3	114.1	119.7	137.3	139.6	151.4	168.7	172.7	195.8 [2]
Argentina (Buenos Aires) [3] .	**100**	156	210	673	751	1 430	5 029	❘ 4 261 [4]	10 794	27 244
Bahamas (Nassau) [1, 5]	**100.0**	104.6	❘ 100.0 [6]	103.4	111.6	118.8	123.3	127.3	131.3	139.8
Barbados [3]	**100.0**	102.8	106.1	126.5	167.1	182.2	193.2	217.7	234.6	269.8
Bermuda	**100.0**	107.1	113.1	118.0	121.6	125.8	129.2	132.8	❘ 100.0 [6]	113.4
Brasil (São Paulo) [1, 7] . .	**100.0**	113.7	.	❘ 100.0 [6]	120.9	154.4	211.3	294.9	405.8	569.5
Canada	**100.0**	101.6	102.8	104.3	107.1	112.9	120.8	128.4	135.1	141.2
Colombia (Bogotá) [1, 5] . .	**100.0**	111.6	121.9	136.5	163.2	186.3	198.8	262.2	313.4	❘ 395.5 [8]
Costa Rica (San José) [9] . .	**100.0**	102.7	105.6	110.9 [10]	136.7 [11]	177.8	❘ 185.3 [8]	200.2	210.4	227.5
Chile (Santiago) [1, 5] . .	**100**	116	148	471	2 989	15 763	49 461	96 690	147 004	227.5
Dominica	**100.0**	104.2	117.6	132.7	170.4	210.0	229.3	253.4	276.1	❘ 207 094 [8]
República Dominicana (Santo Domingo) . . .	*97.0* [13]	**100.0**	*110 7*	*118.4*	*122.2*	*137.0*	*151.0*	*169.8*	*169.8*	*174.5*
Ecuador (Quito)	**100.0**	104.4	108.2	112.2	124.7	141.0	167.9	198.0	220.7	248.3
El Salvador [14, 15, 16] . .	**100.0**	101.3 [17]	102.7	108.7	128.2	144.0	147.3	156.4	187.5	248.3
Greenland	.	**100.0**	*110*	*141*	*176*	*183*	*187*	*201*	*218*	*221*
Guadeloupe (Basse-Terre) [1, 5, 7]	**100.0**	105.1	111.9	118.7	135.4	159.3	172.5 [18]	188.7 [19]	201.0	❘ 213.8 [8]
Guatemala [1, 20]	**100.0**	100.0	100.0	100.0	100.0	❘ 100.0 [6]	109.7	131.1	147.3	171.4
Guyana [1, 20]	**100.0**	100.4	100.5	100.8	107.3	113.2	113.4	115.3	116.6	125.3
Guyane française (Cayenne) [1, 15] .	**100.0**	106.6 [21]	109.7	112.6	123.1	140.8 [22]	153.9	161.5	170.7 [23]	197.6
Haïti (Port-au-Prince) . .	**100.0**	125.5	110.9	135.7	150.8	157.6	173.5	192.2	210.0	237.2
Honduras (Tegucigalpa) . .	**100.0**	113.2	116.4	118.8	121.5	124.3	131.0	140.5	161.1	189.5
Jamaica	**100.0**	107.1	114.7	135.2	171.7	207.5	237.9	249.3	161.1	189.5
Martinique (Fort-de-France) [1, 5, 7]	**100.0**	107.2	112.9	120.4	141.8	166.9	183.6	199.7	...	...
México [1]	**100.0**	105.0	110.8	❘ 108.9 [24]	121.2	138.5	163.2	197.8	218.0	241.9
									240.4	280.0
Montserrat	.	.	.	.	.	**100.0**	*100.0*	*102.9*	*118.7*	*110.5*
Netherlands Antilles [25] .	.	**100.0**	*102.4*	*104.7*	*107.1*	❘ *109.5* [8]	*112.1*	*115.0*	*118.4*	*122.0*
Nicaragua (Managua) [1, 3, 5, 9]	.	.	.	*86.8* [26]	**100.0**	*107.7*	*112.1*	*119.9*	*127.5*	*165.6*
Panamá (Panamá)	**100.0**	102.0	106.6	109.5	111.6	113.1	❘ 103.2 [27]	107.2	*112.1*	*115.5*
Paraguay (Asunción) [1, 3, 5, 7, 15]	**100.0**	101.6	104.2	111.4	139.2	152.0	156.7	169.2	180.2	220.2

EXPLANATORY NOTES AND CODES: See p. 575.

[1] Incl. " Fuel and light " (Bahamas: beginning 1972; Brazil: beginning 1973; Guatemala: beginning 1975). [2] Jan.-Nov. [3] Incl. expenditure on maintenance and repairs of dwelling (Argentina: beginning 1977). [4] April-Dec.; series (base 1974 = 100) replacing former series. [5] Incl. certain household equipment (Bahamas: beginning 1972. [6] Series replacing former series. [7] Incl. cleaning products (Brazil: beginning 1973). [8] Series linked to former series. [9] Metropolitan area. [10] June and Dec. [11] June, Aug. and Oct.-Dec. [12] Jan.-Aug. and Nov.-Dec. [13] Nov. [14] San Salvador, Mejicanos and Villa Delgado. [15] Incl. water. [16] Incl. electricity. [17] Jan.-May and Aug.-Dec. [18] Jan.-July. [19] Feb.-Dec. [20] Urban areas (Guatemala: prior to 1975: Guatemala City only). [21] Jan.-July and Sep.-Dec. [22] Jan.-May and Sep.-Dec. [23] Jan.-June and Sep.-Dec. [24] Series (base 1972 = 100) replacing former series. [25] Curaçao, Aruba and Bonaire; prior to 1975: excl. Bonaire and Windward Is. [26] Dec. [27] Series (base 1975 = 100) replacing former series.

NOTES EXPLICATIVES ET CODES: Voir p. 576.

[1] *Y compris le groupe « Combustible et éclairage » (Bahamas : à partir de 1972 ; Brésil : à partir de 1973 ; Guatemala : à partir de 1975).* [2] *Janv.-nov.* [3] *Y compris les dépenses pour l'entretien et la réparation du logement (Argentine : à partir de 1977).* [4] *Avril-déc. ; série (base 100 en 1974) remplaçant la précédente.* [5] *Y compris certains biens d'équipement de ménage (Bahamas : à partir de 1972).* [6] *Série remplaçant la précédente.* [7] *Y compris les produits d'entretien (Brésil : à partir de 1973).* [8] *Série enchaînée à la précédente.* [9] *Région métropolitaine.* [10] *Juin et déc.* [11] *Juin, août et oct.-déc.* [12] *Janv.-août et nov.-déc.* [13] *Nov.* [14] *San Salvador, Mejicanos et Villa Delgado.* [15] *Y compris l'eau.* [16] *Y compris l'électricité.* [17] *Janv.-mai et août-déc.* [18] *Janv.-juillet.* [19] *Fév.-déc.* [20] *Régions urbaines (Guatemala : avant 1975 : ville de Guatemala seulement).* [21] *Janv.-juillet et sep.-déc.* [22] *Janv.-mai et sept.-déc.* [23] *Janv.-juin et sept.-déc.* [24] *Série (base 100 en 1972) remplaçant la précédente.* [25] *Curaçao, Aruba et Bonaire ; avant 1975 : non compris Bonaire et les îles Windward.* [26] *Déc.* [27] *Série (base 100 en 1975) remplaçant la précédente.*

NOTAS EXPLICATIVAS Y CLAVES: Véase pág. 578.

[1] Incl. el grupo « Combustible y alumbrado » (Bahamas: a partir de 1972; Brasil: a partir de 1973; Guatemala: a partir de 1975). [2] Enero-nov. [3] Incl. los gastos de conservación y reparación de la vivienda (Argentina: a partir de 1977). [4] Abril-dic., serie (base 1974 = 100) que substituye a la anterior. [5] Incl. ciertos enseres domésticos (Bahamas: a partir de 1972). [6] Serie que substituye a la anterior. [7] Incl. los productos de limpieza (Brasil: a partir de 1973). [8] Serie enlazada con la anterior. [9] Area metropolitana. [10] Junio y dic. [11] Junio, agosto y oct.-dic. [12] Enero-agosto y nov.-dic. [13] Nov. [14] San Salvador, Mejicanos y Villa Delgado. [15] Incl. el agua. [16] Incl. la electricidad. [17] Enero-mayo y agosto-dic. [18] Enero-julio. [19] Febr.-dic. [20] Areas urbanas (Guatemala: antes de 1975: ciudad de Guatemala solamente). [21] Enero-julio y sept.-dic. [22] Enero-mayo y sept.-dic. [23] Enero-junio y sept.-dic. [24] Serie (base 1972 = 100) que substituye a la anterior. [25] Curazao, Aruba y Bonaire; antes de 1975: excl. Bonaire y las islas Windward. [26] Dic. [27] Serie (base 1975 = 100) que substituye a la anterior.

23 Consumer prices / Prix à la consommation / Precios del consumo

E Rent indices / Indices du loyer / Indices del alquiler

(1970 = 100)

Country — Pays — País	1970	1971	1972	1973	1974	1975	1976	1977	1978	1979
Perú (Lima) [1]	100.0	108.3	118.0	▎132.8 [2]	154.4	175.0	187.9	215.5	278.3	350.6
Puerto Rico	100.0	100.3	100.5	100.7	101.5	103.0	104.1	105.0	106.7	107.7
St. Lucia [3]	100.0	102.1	111.5	119.9	150.0	198.9	218.2	225.3	265.5	273.6
St. Vincent	100.0	109.2	110.6	121.3	138.1	158.0	189.5	199.6	208.6	239.8
Suriname (Paramaribo) [4, 5]	100.0	100.4	100.4	101.6	123.6	118.2	126.3	136.2	142.5	145.4
Trinidad and Tobago	100.0	101.8	105.4	116.3	119.5	127.0	▎131.3 [2]	147.6	171.3	203.6
United States	100.0	104.6	108.3	112.9	118.6	124.7	131.4	139.4	▎148.9 [2]	159.8
Uruguay (Montevideo) [5]	100	121	173	▎303 [2]	536	1 449	2 541	4 606	8 015	12 794
Venezuela (Caracas) [1]	100.0	100.9	101.7	103.1	105.2	107.0	109.6	110.4	112.1	114.8
Virgin Is. (US)	100.0	108.2	115.9	123.0	123.5	132.9	132.9	132.9	144.6	...
ASIA — ASIE ASIA										
Bangladesh (Dacca) [6, 7]	100.0	103.1 [8]	118.5	147.3	▎100.0 [9]	201.0	241.7	282.6	337.3	...
Burma (Rangoon) [3]	100.0	104.0	90.1	102.0	124.8	155.7	188.7	194.5	179.6	174.4
Cyprus	100.0	105.0	112.9	119.6	▎123.7 [10]	120.9	121.1	▎100.0 [9]	108.4	120.1
Hong Kong	100.0	102.9	107.7	116.3	128.8	▎110 [11]	115	123	129	142
India	100.0	101.5	104.5	109.1	113.6	122.7	129.5	137.1	143.9	150.0
» (Bombay)	100.0	104.5	105.4	106.3	108.1	113.5	120.7	129.7	133.3	140.5
» (Delhi)	100.0	103.2	107.7	111.0	116.1	127.1	139.4	142.6	146.5	158.7
» (Jamshedpur)	100.0	100.0	102.8	104.7	107.5	119.6	123.4	135.5	135.5	139.3
Indonesia (Djakarta) [4, 12]	100.0	107.2	108.0	121.7	147.5	185.0	231.9	272.0	292.2	...
Iran	100.0	105.0	112.5	122.7	135.8	153.5	177.3	219.1	...	...
Iraq [13, 14]	100.0	101.7	102.3	103.8	▎102.1 [15]	115.2	127.5	139.8	154.7	...
Israel	100.0	112.9	136.6	180.4	258.4	338.2	417.0	▎507.9 [2]	746.0	1 652.9
Japan	100.0	108.4	117.1	127.1	136.7	149.7	164.8	181.7	196.7	335.1
Jordan [16]	100.0	106.0	118.1	122.0	126.7	132.2	▎106.5 [17]	114.7	128.7	...
Korea, Rep. of	100.0	110.2	119.3	123.4	135.5	151.7	172.8	198.5	231.1	287.3
Kuwait [12]	.	.	100.0	100.3	102.2	106.0	113.4	130.7	164.3	174.7
République lao (Vientiane) [12]	100.0	102.5	108.6	128.6	185.4	246.1 [18]	.	.	.	.
Liban (Beyrouth)	100.0	100.0-	100.0	100.0	100.0	.	.	.	.	.

23 Consumer prices / Prix à la consommation / Precios del consumo

E Rent indices / Indices du loyer / Indices del alquiler

(1970 = 100)

Country — Pays — País	1970	1971	1972	1973	1974	1975	1976	1977	1978	1979
Malaysia:										
Peninsular Malaysia [1]	**100.0**	100.9	101.7	103.2	110.3	117.6	124.2	131.8	138.4	147.5
Sabah [1]	**100.0**	102.3	103.8	105.4	108.6	116.4	120.9	125.0	127.9	130.8
Sarawak [1]	**100.0**	99.6	102.0	102.2	105.6	114.0	119.5	128.3	135.6	140.0
Nepal [2]	*100.0* [3]	**100.0**	*100.0*	*103.5*	|*100.0* [4]	*115.0*	*131.0*	*148.2*	*163.7*	*176.1*
Pakistan [1,5,6]	**100.0**	102.3	|*105.7* [7]	*118.9*	*149.6*	*180.4*	*200.6*	*217.0*	*233.3*	*254.9*
Philippines [8,9] [8]	**100.0**	112.6	136.8	|*127.2* [10]	*155.0*	*162.7*	*181.2*	*205.2*	*225.0*	*262.7*
Singapore	**100.0**	101.8	103.7	109.5	|*104.7* [11]	*115.1*	*125.4*	*126.4*	|**100.0** [4]	*104.3*
Sri Lanka (Colombo)	**100.0**	100.0	100.0	100.0	100.0	100.0	100.0	100.0	100.0	100.0
République arabe syrienne (Damas)	**100.0**				176	185	185	196	198	208
Thailand (Bangkok-Metropolis) [8]	**100.0**	102.0	102.7	105.6	117.2	123.5	135.2	138.1	|*138.8* [12]	...
Yemen (Sanaa)	.	.	100	*128*	*185*	*256*	...	...	...	...
Yemen, Democratic (Aden)	100	100	90	75	75	75	75	75	...	...
EUROPE — EUROPE — EUROPA										
Austria [8]	**100.0**	112.3	124.5	141.7	155.4	176.5	204.9	|*218.6* [12]	229.9	241.2
Belgique	.	.	.	.	.	.	.	**100.0**	*107.2*	*113.6*
Denmark	**100.0**	109.6	117.5	126.3	137.2	151.0	171.1	190.8	207.1	|*147* [13]
España	**100.0**	106.0	111.4	121.6	138.6	157.9	175.4	198.4	223.3	253.5
Faeroe Is.	.	.	.	.	.	.	**100.0**	*110.1*	*118.6*	128.8
Finland	**100.0**	108.0	113.2	132.8	|*165.3* [12]	185.9	196.0	210.3	223.5	|*238.0* [12]
France [8]	**100.0**	105.4	110.3	118.9	127.3	139.7	153.9	167.2	180.2	199.0
German Democratic Republic	**100.0**	100.0	100.0	|*100.0* [14]	100.0	100.0	100.0	100.0	100.0	...
Germany, Fed. Rep. of	**100.0**	106.2	112.6	119.2	125.2	133.1	138.9	143.6	147.8	152.5
Gibraltar [1,8,14]	**100.0**	103.2	103.2	.	.	|**100.0** [4]	*115.5*	*127.5*	*154.0*	*207.9*
Grèce	**100.0**	101.5	103.5	110.1	123.6	134.9	146.5	164.2	192.7	216.8
Hongrie	**100.0**	157.5	215.0	215.0	215.0	215.0	215.0	215.0	215.0	215.0
Iceland (Reykjavik)	**100.0**	105.5	119.5	137.7	172.1	226.3	304.7	387.4	540.8	788.6
Ireland [8]	**100.0**	110.4	123.2	131.6	143.3	159.3	|*181.8* [12]	197.5	175.4	191.9
Isle of Man	.	.	.	.	.	.	**100.0**	*109.8*	*129.8*	
Italie	**100.0**	103.6	107.8	115.4	121.8	138.8	155.5	|*165.0* [12]	176.8	225.0
Malta [8,14]	**100.0**	101.2	102.1	103.1	105.1	110.0	|*109.3* [12]	111.2	114.6	118.9
Netherlands [8]	**100.0**	109.4	119.3	130.6	141.4	151.8	169.4	182.8	|*127.0* [13]	*136.4*
Norway [8]	**100.0**	106.2	112.2	120.8	|*131.6* [12]	142.6	152.8	164.5	175.3	182.9

EXPLANATORY NOTES AND CODES: See p. 575.

[1] Incl. "Fuel and light" (Gibraltar: beginning 1975). [2] Prior to 1974: Katmandu only. [3] June-Dec. [4] Series replacing former series. [5] Prior to 1972: Karachi only; industrial workers. [6] Beginning 1972: incl. certain household equipment. [7] Series (base 1971 = 100) replacing former series. [8] Incl. expenditure on maintenance and repairs of dwelling (Netherlands: prior to 1978; Gibraltar: beginning 1975). [9] Prior to 1973: Manila only; middle income group. [10] Series (base 1972 = 100) replacing former series. [11] Series (base 1973 = 100) replacing former series. [12] Series linked to former series. [13] Series (base 1975 = 100) replacing former series. [14] Incl. water (Gibraltar: beginning 1975).

NOTES EXPLICATIVES ET CODES: Voir p. 576.

[1] Y compris le groupe « Combustible et éclairage » (Gibraltar : à partir de 1975). [2] Avant 1974 : Katmandu seulement. [3] Juin-déc. [4] Série remplaçant la précédente. [5] Avant 1972 : Karachi seulement ; travailleurs de l'industrie. [6] A partir de 1972 : y compris certains biens d'équipement de ménage. [7] Série (base 100 en 1971) remplaçant la précédente. [8] Y compris les dépenses pour l'entretien et la réparation du logement (Pays-Bas : avant 1978 ; Gibraltar : à partir de 1975). [9] Avant 1973 : Manille seulement ; familles à revenu moyen. [10] Série (base 100 en 1972) remplaçant la précédente. [11] Série (base 100 en 1973) remplaçant la précédente. [12] Série enchaînée à la précédente. [13] Série (base 100 en 1975) remplaçant la précédente. [14] Y compris l'eau (Gibraltar : à partir de 1975).

NOTAS EXPLICATIVAS Y CLAVES: Véase pág. 578.

[1] Incl. el grupo « Combustible y alumbrado » (Gibraltar: a partir de 1975). [2] Antes de 1974: Katmandú solamente. [3] Junio-dic. [4] Serie que substituye a la anterior. [5] Antes de 1972: Karachi solamente; trabajadores de la industria. [6] A partir de 1972: incl. ciertos enseres domésticos. [7] Serie (base 1971 = 100) que substituye a la anterior. [8] Incl. los gastos de conservación y reparación de la vivienda (Paises Bajos: antes de 1978; Gibraltar: a partir de 1975). [9] Antes de 1973: Manila solamente; familias de ingresos medios. [10] Serie (base 1972 = 100) que substituye a la anterior. [11] Serie (base 1973 = 100) que substituye a la anterior. [12] Serie enlazada con la anterior. [13] Serie (base 1975 = 100) que substituye a la anterior. [14] Incl. el agua (Gibraltar; a partir de 1975).

23 Consumer prices / Prix à la consommation / Precios del consumo
E Rent indices / Indices du loyer / Indices del alquiler

(1970 = 100)

Country — Pays — País	1970	1971	1972	1973	1974	1975	1976	1977	1978	1979
Portugal (Lisbonne)	100.0	130.8	156.4	185.0	202.8	187.1	247.1	277.1	264.8	.
Roumanie	100.0	100.0	100.0	100.0	100.0	108.3	111.1	112.2	114.9	116.6
Suisse	100.0	108.6	117.7	125.5	134.9	148.2	154.6	156.5	❙157.0 [1]	156.9
Sweden [2]	100.0	101.8	106.7	114.0	125.5	135.7	146.1	164.6	177.4	191.0
United Kingdom [2]	100.0	109.2	120.6	134.8	150.6	178.7	203.9	230.4	246.9	297.4
Yugoslavia	100.0	103.7	112.4	129.6	151.8	184.8	207.8	236.4	279.7	320.0
OCEANIA — OCÉANIE **OCEANÍA**										
American Samoa (Pago-Pago) [3]	.	.	.	.	*100.0*	*125.0*	*123.3*	*143.1*	*137.3*	*175.6*
Australia [2]	100.0	107.3	115.3	124.7	143.5	171.0	198.8	221.2	237.6	253.4
Cook Is. (Rarotonga) [2, 4]	100.0	106.6	118.9	127.8	141.5	166.2	188.7	214.1	233.3	...
Fiji [4]	100.0	106.4	120.5	129.5	❙140.4 [1]	155.4	189.1	204.7	220.0	236.8
Guam	.	.	.	100.0	*101.0*	97.5	*88.1*	123.3	*86.1*	*87.3*
Kiribati (Tarawa) [2, 5, 6]	98.5 [7]	100.0	102.7	105.9	117.5	130.5	❙*100.0* [8]	130.8	*156.4*	...
New Zealand [2]	100.0	107.6	117.5	130.7	149.3	174.9	193.0	214.3	233.9	252.7
Nouvelle-Calédonie (Nouméa)	100.0	111.6	123.9	138.1	137.4	140.1	144.7	146.2	148.4	151.6
Papua New Guinea [3]	.	.	.	.	.	.	*97.4*	100.0	*106.6*	*127.4*
Polynésie française (Tahiti) (Papeete) [6]	100.0	106.5	121.0	❙*100.0* [8]	*112.6*	*148.9*	*163.2* [9]	*173.9*	*181.5*	*194.4*
Solomon Is. (Honiara) [3, 4]	100.0	102.6	74.6	75.4	77.7	83.3	.	.	❙*102.3* [10]	*108.4*
Vanuatu [3, 4, 11, 12, 13] . . . . [14]	.	.	.	.	.	.	100.0	*103.1* [15]	*112.0* [16]	*127.5*
URSS [17]	100.0	100.0	100.0	100.0	100.0	100.0	100.0	100.0	100.0	100.0
RSS d'Ukraine	100.0	100.0	100.0	100.0	100.0	100.0	100.0	100.0	100.0	...

EXPLANATORY NOTES AND CODES: See p. 575.

[1] Series linked to former series. [2] Incl. expenditure on maintenance and repairs of dwelling (Kiribati: beginning 1976). [3] Incl. " Fuel and light ". [4] Incl. water. [5] Prior to 1976: incl. " Fuel " and water. [6] Incl. " Fuel and light " and certain household items (Kiribati: beginning 1976; French Polynesia: beginning 1973). [7] Oct.-Dec. [8] Series replacing former series. [9] March-Nov. [10] Series (base Oct.-Dec. 1977 = 100) replacing former series. [11] Urban areas. [12] Indices based on prices paid in francs. [13] Former New Hebrides. [14] Low income group. [15] Jan.-June. [16] April-Dec. [17] Incl. Ukrainian SSR, shown separately in this table.

NOTES EXPLICATIVES ET CODES: Voir p. 576.

[1] *Série enchaînée à la précédente.* [2] *Y compris les dépenses pour l'entretien et la réparation du logement (Kiribati : à partir de 1976).* [3] *Y compris le groupe « Combustible et éclairage ».* [4] *Y compris l'eau.* [5] *Avant 1976 : y compris le groupe « Combustible » et l'eau.* [6] *Y compris le groupe « Combustible et éclairage » et certains articles de ménage (Kiribati : à partir de 1976 ; Polynésie française : à partir de 1973).* [7] *Oct.-déc.* [8] *Série remplaçant la précédente.* [9] *Mars-nov.* [10] *Série (base oct.-déc. 1977 = 100) remplaçant la précédente.* [11] *Régions urbaines.* [12] *Indices fondés sur des prix payés en francs.* [13] *Précédemment Nouvelles-Hébrides.* [14] *Familles à revenu modique.* [15] *Janv.-juin.* [16] *Avril-déc.* [17] *Y compris la RSS d'Ukraine, figurant séparément dans ce tableau.*

NOTAS EXPLICATIVAS Y CLAVES: Véase pág. 578.

[1] Serie enlazada con la anterior. [2] Incl. los gastos de conservación y reparación de la vivienda (Kiribati: a partir de 1976). [3] Incl. el grupo « Combustible y alumbrado ». [4] Incl. el agua. [5] Antes de 1976: incl. el grupo « Combustible » y el agua. [6] Incl. el grupo « Combustible y alumbrado » y ciertos artículos domésticos (Kiribati: a partir de 1976; Polinesia Francesa: a partir de 1973). [7] Oct.-dic. [8] Serie que substituye a la anterior. [9] Marzo-nov. [10] Serie (base oct.-dic. 1977 = 100) que substituye a la anterior. [11] Areas urbanas. [12] Indices basados en los precios pagados en francos. [13] Anteriormente Nuevas Hébridas. [14] Familias de ingresos módicos. [15] Enero-junio. [16] Abril-dic. [17] Incl. la RSS de Ucrania, que figura separadamente en este cuadro.

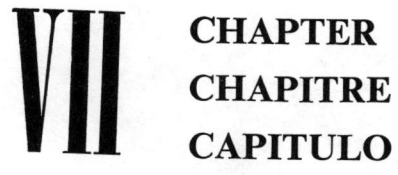

VII

CHAPTER
CHAPITRE
CAPITULO

Industrial accidents

Accidents du travail

Accidentes del trabajo

Industrial accidents

Table 24 (Parts A to E) gives industrial accident *frequency* or *incidence rates* for a number of divisions of economic activities. In each case only *fatal* accident rates are given. As a rule deaths resulting from occupational diseases or commuting accidents (accidents on the way to or from work) are not included. The minimum duration of incapacity to which an accident must give rise in order to be included in the statistics varies greatly from one country to another; bearing in mind that the number of minor accidents is relatively high, data on non-fatal accidents do not lend themselves easily to international comparison and have therefore been excluded from these tables.

An accident frequency or incidence rate is the ratio of the number of cases of accident occurring during a given period to a number representing " exposure to risk " during the same period.

The number of cases of accident is generally based on industrial accident compensation data or on a compulsory accident reporting system. To indicate the basis of the rate for each country a series of symbols is used in the table headings and explained beneath each table.

The " exposure to risk " may be expressed in terms of the number of full-time workers, of persons insured or of hours of work. The industrial accident *frequency rate* is computed on the basis of hours worked, by dividing the number of accidents (multiplied by 1,000,000) occurring during the period covered by the statistics by the number of hours worked by all persons exposed to risk during the same period. Where the number of hours worked is unknown it may be estimated from the number of persons exposed to risk and average hours of work. The frequency rate is the best way of measuring accident risk as it is not affected by differences in working hours from one industry to another or from one country to another. In practice, however, such data are available in only a few countries. The majority of countries calculate the *incidence rate* of industrial accidents, which is the ratio of the number of industrial accidents (multiplied by 1,000) occurring during the period covered by the statistics to the average number of workers exposed to risk during that

same period. As a rule information on the average number of workers may be obtained from returns of undertakings or from accident or other insurance data.

In an international comparison of industrial accident frequency and incidence rates full account must be taken of the effect on the figures of differences in the economic scope of the data or lack of uniformity in the definitions used or the methods of computation and estimation.

Variations in a series of accident frequency or incidence rates for a single country over a period of time will, in general, reflect changes in the conditions of accident risk within that country, though they may on occasion be affected by alterations in methods of reporting or computation. [1]

Table 24 A

Fatal accident rates for mining and quarrying

In so far as data are available, this table gives the rates for fatal accidents occurring in the mining industry in general, including quarrying. In comparing these rates from one country to another account must be taken of differences in the relative importance of the various types of mining covered (coal mining, iron mining, gold mining, etc.).

Table 24 B

Fatal accident rates for coal mining

This table shows separately the rates for coal mining, in view of the importance of this industry and the relatively high risk of accident involved. As with mining in general, the accident risk varies from country to country and from mine to mine, depending on the type of coal

---

[1] For further information on accident statistics, definitions, sources and methods of classification and with respect to Resolution No. II of the Tenth International Conference of Labour Statisticians concerning statistics of employment injuries, see ILO: *Statistics of Industrial Injuries* (Geneva, 1970), document D.17.1970/X.CIST/ II/SAT.

extracted (anthracite, bituminous or lignite), the mineral formation, the depth, and the presence of water or fire-damp.

Table 24 C

Fatal accident rates for manufacturing

This table indicates the fatal industrial accident rates for all manufacturing industries. In comparing these figures from one country to another it should be borne in mind that the accident risk is not the same in every industry and that the predominant divisions of economic activities in a given country may be those with a high accident risk (such as woodworking or iron and steel) or those with a low accident risk (such as textiles, printing or tobacco); differences in rates from one country to another are thus influenced by differences in the industrial structure of the countries compared.

Table 24 D

Fatal accident rates for construction

In so far as data are available, this table shows the rates for fatal accidents occurring to construction workers.

Table 24 E

Fatal accident rates for railways

This table gives the fatal accident frequency or incidence rates among railway workers. Unless otherwise indicated, the figures shown exclude railway construction and railway workshops.

Accidents du travail

Les données présentées dans le tableau 24 (parties A à E) se rapportent aux *taux de fréquence* ou *d'incidence* des accidents du travail dans plusieurs branches d'activité économique. Pour chacune de ces branches, les taux de fréquence ou d'incidence ne sont donnés que pour les accidents *mortels* du travail. En règle générale, les cas mortels résultant de maladies professionnelles ou d'accidents de trajet (accidents survenus sur le chemin que parcourt le travailleur pour se rendre à son lieu de travail et en revenir) ne sont pas compris. La durée minimum de l'incapacité que doit entraîner un accident pour que celui-ci soit compté dans les statistiques varie beaucoup d'un pays à un autre; compte tenu du fait que le nombre des accidents peu graves est relativement élevé, les données se rapportant aux accidents non mortels ne se prêtent donc guère aux comparaisons sur le plan international. En conséquence les taux de ces accidents ne figurent pas dans les tableaux.

Le taux de fréquence ou le taux d'incidence des accidents du travail traduit le rapport du nombre des cas d'accidents survenus au cours d'une certaine période à un autre nombre représentant l'« exposition au risque » durant la même période.

Le nombre des cas d'accidents est généralement tiré des données du régime d'indemnisation ou d'un système de déclaration obligatoire. Pour préciser la méthode utilisée par chaque pays, on s'est servi, dans les en-têtes des tableaux, d'un certain nombre de symboles dont la signification est donnée en dessous de chaque tableau.

L'« exposition au risque » peut être mesurée par le nombre de travailleurs occupés à plein temps, par le nombre de personnes assurées ou par le nombre d'heures de travail. Le *taux de fréquence* des accidents du travail est calculé sur la base des heures de travail. Il est obtenu en divisant le nombre des accidents (multiplié par 1 000 000) survenus au cours de la période couverte par les statistiques par le nombre des heures de travail effectuées par toutes les personnes exposées au risque pendant la même période. Lorsque le nombre d'heures de travail est inconnu, il peut être évalué à partir du nombre de personnes exposées au risque et de la durée moyenne du travail. Le taux de fréquence est la meilleure mesure du risque d'accident, car il n'est pas influencé par les différences de la durée du travail d'une industrie à une autre ou d'un pays à un autre. En pratique, cependant, on ne dispose de ces données que pour un petit nombre de pays. La majorité des pays calcule le *taux d'incidence* des accidents du travail, qui est le rapport entre le nombre des accidents du travail (multiplié par 1 000) survenus au cours de la période couverte par les statistiques et le nombre moyen des travailleurs exposés au risque pendant la même période. Les informations relatives au nombre moyen des travailleurs proviennent généralement des rapports d'établissements ou sont obtenus à partir des données de l'assurance-accident ou d'une autre assurance.

Lors de la comparaison internationale des taux de fréquence et d'incidence des accidents du travail, il faut tenir pleinement compte de l'influence qu'exercent sur les chiffres les différences dans la portée économique des données ainsi que le manque d'uniformité des définitions utilisées et des méthodes d'élaboration et d'estimation.

Pour un pays donné, les variations des taux de fréquence ou d'incidence des accidents du travail durant une certaine période reflètent en général les changements dans les risques d'accidents dans ce pays, mais peuvent à l'occasion être influencés par des modifications des méthodes de rassemblement et de calcul des données [1].

Tableau 24 A

Taux des accidents mortels dans les industries extractives

Ce tableau fournit les taux des accidents mortels survenus dans les industries extractives

---

[1] Pour de plus amples détails sur les statistiques des accidents du travail, les définitions, les sources et les méthodes de classification, et pour la résolution II sur les statistiques des lésions professionnelles adoptée par la dixième Conférence internationale des statisticiens du travail, voir BIT: *Statistiques des accidents du travail* (Genève, 1970), document D.17.1970/X.CIST/II/SAT.

en général, y compris les carrières. Il faut tenir compte, lors de la comparaison de ces taux d'un pays à un autre, des différences dans l'importance respective des divers genres de mines (de charbon, de fer, d'or, etc.) couvertes par ces statistiques.

Tableau 24 B

Taux des accidents mortels dans les mines de charbon

Ce tableau présente séparément les taux pour les mines de charbon, étant donné l'importance de cette industrie et les risques d'accidents relativement élevés qu'elle comporte. Comme c'est le cas pour les industries extractives en général, les risques d'accidents ne sont pas identiques de pays à pays; ils varient d'un charbonnage à un autre en fonction de la qualité du charbon extrait (anthracite, charbon bitumineux ou lignite), de la structure minéralogique, de la profondeur, de la présence d'eau ou de grisou.

Tableau 24 C

Taux des accidents mortels dans les industries manufacturières

Ce tableau indique les taux des accidents mortels du travail dans l'ensemble des industries manufacturières. Dans la comparaison de ces chiffres d'un pays à un autre, il y a lieu de tenir compte de ce que les différentes industries ne présentent pas toutes les mêmes risques d'accidents et que les branches d'activité économique qui dominent dans un pays donné peuvent être celles à risques d'accidents élevés, comme l'industrie du bois ou l'industrie du fer et de l'acier, ou au contraire des secteurs à risques faibles comme l'industrie textile, les arts graphiques ou l'industrie du tabac; les différences de taux observées d'un pays à un autre sont donc influencées par les différences dans la structure industrielle des pays comparés.

Tableau 24 D

Taux des accidents mortels dans la construction

Ce tableau présente, dans la mesure où elles sont disponibles, les données se rapportant aux taux des accidents mortels survenus aux travailleurs du bâtiment et des travaux publics.

Tableau 24 E

Taux des accidents mortels dans les chemins de fer

Ce tableau donne les taux de fréquence ou d'incidence des accidents mortels survenus aux travailleurs des chemins de fer. Sauf indication contraire, les chiffres présentés excluent les accidents survenus dans la construction des lignes de chemin de fer et dans les ateliers de réparation.

Accidentes del trabajo

Los datos que se presentan en las partes A a E del cuadro 24 se refieren a las *tasas de frecuencia* o de *incidencia* de los accidentes del trabajo en varias ramas de actividades económicas. En cada una de estas ramas, las tasas de frecuencia o de incidencia se presentan sólo para los accidentes *mortales* del trabajo. Por regla general, no se incluyen los casos mortales que provienen de las enfermedades profesionales o de los accidentes ocurridos en el trayecto que efectúa el trabajador para ir a su sitio de trabajo o para regresar. La duración mínima de la incapacidad que debe ocasionar un accidente para que pueda incluirse en las estadísticas varía mucho de un país a otro; puesto que el número de accidentes poco graves es relativamente alto, los datos referentes a accidentes no mortales no se prestan a comparaciones internacionales. Por ello, las tasas de estos accidentes no figuran en los cuadros.

La tasa de frecuencia o de incidencia de los accidentes del trabajo indica la razón entre el número de los casos de accidentes ocurridos durante un período determinado y un número que representa la « exposición al riesgo » durante el mismo período.

El número de los casos de accidentes se obtiene generalmente de las informaciones sobre el régimen de indemnización o de un sistema de notificación obligatoria de los accidentes. A fin de precisar el método utilizado en cada país, en los encabezamientos del cuadro se ha empleado una serie de símbolos cuya explicación aparece al pie de cada cuadro.

La « exposición al riesgo » puede medirse ya sea por el número de trabajadores ocupados a tiempo completo o por el número de personas aseguradas, o por el número de horas de trabajo. La *tasa de frecuencia* de los accidentes del trabajo se calcula sobre la base de las horas de trabajo. Se la obtiene dividiendo el número de los accidentes (multiplicado por 1 000 000) ocurridos durante el período comprendido en las estadísticas por el número de las horas de trabajo efectuadas por todas las personas expuestas al riesgo durante el mismo período. Cuando se desconoce el número de horas de trabajo, la tasa de frecuencia puede ser calculada sobre la base del número de personas expuestas al riesgo y de la duración

media del trabajo. La tasa de frecuencia es la mejor medida del riesgo del accidente, ya que no se halla influida por las diferencias en la duración del trabajo de una industria a otra o de un país a otro. Sin embargo, en la práctica se dispone de estos datos sólo para un reducido número de países. La mayor parte de los países calculan la *tasa de incidencia* de los accidentes del trabajo, que es la razón entre el número de los accidentes del trabajo (multiplicado por 1 000) ocurridos durante el período comprendido en las estadísticas y el promedio de los trabajadores expuestos al riesgo durante dicho período. Las informaciones relativas al promedio de los trabajadores proceden generalmente de los informes de los establecimientos o se las obtiene a partir de los datos de los seguros de accidentes o de otras clases de seguros.

Al efectuar comparaciones internacionales de las tasas de frecuencia y de incidencia de los accidentes del trabajo hay que tener plenamente en cuenta la influencia que ejerce sobre las cifras la diferencia del alcance económico de los datos, así como la falta de uniformidad de las definiciones y de los métodos de elaboración y de estimación que se utilizan.

En un país dado, las variaciones de las tasas de frecuencia o de incidencia de los accidentes del trabajo durante un período determinado reflejan de ordinario los cambios de los riesgos de accidentes en dicho país, pero pueden hallarse influidas a veces por las modificaciones en los métodos de recolección y de cálculo de los datos [1].

Cuadro 24 A

Tasas de los accidentes mortales en minas y canteras

Este cuadro proporciona, en la medida en que se dispone de datos, las tasas de los accidentes

---

[1] Para mayores detalles sobre las estadísticas de los accidentes del trabajo, definiciones, fuentes y métodos de clasificación, véase OIT: *Estadísticas de los accidentes del trabajo*, décima Conferencia Internacional de Estadígrafos del Trabajo, Informe II (Ginebra, 1962). Respecto de la resolución II sobre las estadísticas de las lesiones profesionales, adoptada por la décima Conferencia Internacional de Estadígrafos del Trabajo, véase OIT: *Recomendaciones internacionales sobre estadísticas del trabajo* (Ginebra, 1975).

mortales ocurridos en las minas y canteras en general. Al efectuar comparaciones de estas tasas de un país a otro, hay que tener en cuenta las diferencias de la respectiva importancia de los diversos tipos de minas (de carbón, de hierro, de oro, etc.) comprendidas por estas estadísticas.

Cuadro 24 B

Tasas de los accidentes mortales en las minas de carbón

Este cuadro presenta por separado las tasas en las minas de carbón, considerando la importancia de esta industria y los riesgos de accidentes relativamente elevados que ella comporta. Como ocurre en las minas y canteras en general, los riesgos de accidentes en las minas de carbón varían según los países, y aun de una mina a otra, en función del tipo de carbón extraído (antracita, carbón bituminoso o lignito), la estructura mineralógica, la profundidad, la presencia de agua o de grisú.

Cuadro 24 C

Tasas de los accidentes mortales en las industrias manufactureras

Este cuadro presenta las tasas de los accidentes mortales del trabajo para el conjunto de las industrias manufactureras. Al efectuar la comparación de estas cifras de un país a otro hay que tener en cuenta que las diversas industrias no tienen todas el mismo riesgo de accidentes, y que las ramas de actividades económicas que predominan en un país determinado pueden ser aquellas que comportan riesgos de accidentes elevados, tal como sucede en la industria de la madera, del hierro o del acero, o, al contrario, pueden existir sectores de riesgos bajos, como ocurre en la industria textil, las artes gráficas o la industria del tabaco. Las diferencias de las tasas que se observan en los distintos países se hallan, pues, influidas por las diferencias en la estructura industrial de los países que se comparan.

Cuadro 24 D

Tasas de los accidentes mortales en la construcción

Este cuadro proporciona, en la medida en que se dispone de datos, las tasas de los accidentes mortales ocurridos entre los trabajadores de la construcción.

Cuadro 24 E

Tasas de los accidentes mortales en los ferrocarriles

Este cuadro proporciona las tasas de frecuencia o de incidencia de los accidentes ocurridos entre los trabajadores ferroviarios. Salvo indicación en contrario, las cifras que se presentan excluyen los accidentes que se producen en la construcción de las líneas de ferrocarriles y en los talleres de reparación.

24

Industrial accident rates
(Fatal accidents)

Taux des accidents du travail
(Accidents mortels)

Tasas de frecuencia de los accidentes del trabajo
(Accidentes mortales)

A

Mining and quarrying
Industries extractives
Minas y canteras

Country — Pays — País	Code Code Clave	1970	1971	1972	1973	1974	1975	1976	1977	1978	1979
AFRICA — AFRIQUE AFRICA											
Egypt [1]	I/c	0.35	0.49	—	0.51	0.55	1.10	0.28	0.64	1.07	0.47
Kenya	II/c	…	…	…	0.80	…	…	…	…	…	…
Libyan Arab Jamahiriya	II/c	0.42	0.42	…	…	…	…	…	…	…	…
Mali	I/c	—	—	…	…	…	…	…	…	…	…
Maroc	I/b	0.79	1.01	…	…	…	…	…	0.85	1.31	0.85
Niger	II/b	2.60	0.95	—	0.62	…	…	…	…	…	…
Tanzania (Tanganyika)	II/b	0.74	0.54	…	…	…	…	…	…	…	…
Tunisie	I/d	0.96	1.16	1.03	0.73	0.16	0.38	0.57	0.61	0.31	0.39
Uganda	I/c	0.76	1.08	1.74	1.40 *	…	…	…	…	…	…
Zambia	I/c	2.92	0.91	0.45	0.71	0.53 *	…	…	…	…	…
AMERICA — AMÉRIQUE AMÉRICA											
Canada [2]	I/b	1.96	2.07	2.20	2.26	2.44	2.02	1.99	1.44	1.50	1.59 *
El Salvador	I/c	—	—	0.74	—	—	2.23	2.23	—	1.80	1.85
Guatemala	I/b	1.17	1.73	2.97	3.64	1.38	0.98	0.90	0.80	1.56	2.27
Haïti [3]	II/a	—	—	—	0.03	—	—	—	—	—	0.02
Jamaica	I/c	0.04	0.05	—	0.04	0.02	—	0.08	…	…	…
México	II/c	1.67	1.38	0.07	1.97	1.06	…	1.48 *	…	…	…
Perú	II/ [4]	.	.	.	.	0.63	1.05	0.78	0.69	…	…
Suriname	II/a	0.20	0.10	—	0.10	0.02	0.01	0.02	0.01	0.38	…
United States	I/d	0.53	0.42	0.53	0.42	0.38	0.33	0.28	0.30	0.26	0.27 *

EXPLANATORY NOTES: See p. 609.

NOTES EXPLICATIVES: Voir p. 611.

NOTAS EXPLICATIVAS: Véase pág. 613.

I: Reported accidents.
II: Compensated accidents.

a: Rates per 1 000 man-years of 300 days each.
b: Rates per 1 000 wage earners (average numbers).
c: Rates per 1 000 persons employed (average numbers).
d: Rates per 1 000 000 man-hours worked.

I: *Accidents signalés.*
II: *Accidents indemnisés.*

a: *Taux pour 1 000 années-homme de 300 jours.*
b: *Taux pour 1 000 ouvriers (effectif moyen).*
c: *Taux pour 1 000 personnes occupées (effectif moyen).*
d: *Taux pour 1 000 000 d'heures-homme effectuées.*

I: Accidentes declarados.
II: Accidentes indemnizados.

a: Tasas por 1 000 años-hombre de 300 días cada uno.
b: Tasas por 1 000 obreros (ocupació media).
c: Tasas por 1 000 personas ocupadas (ocupación media).
d: Tasas por 1 000 000 de horas-hombre efectuadas.

[1] Year ending in June of the following year. [2] Incl. accidents on the way to and from work and deaths arising from occupational illnesses. [3] Year ending in Sep. of the year indicated. [4] Rates per 1 000 insured persons.

[1] *Année se terminant en juin de l'année suivante.* [2] *Y compris les accidents de trajet et les décès dus à des maladies professionnelles.* [3] *Année se terminant en sept. de l'année indiquée.* [4] *Taux pour 1 000 personnes assurées.*

[1] Año que termina en junio del año siguiente. [2] Incl. los accidentes del trayecto y las defunciones debidas a enfermedades profesionales. [3] Año que termina en sept. del año indicado. [4] Tasas por cada 1 000 asegurados.

24 Industrial accident rates
(Fatal accidents)
Taux des accidents du travail
(Accidents mortels)
Tasas de frecuencia de los accidentes del trabajo
(Accidentes mortales)

A Mining and quarrying
Industries extractives
Minas y canteras

Country — *Pays* — País	Code *Code* Clave	1970	1971	1972	1973	1974	1975	1976	1977	1978	1979
ASIA — ASIE ASIA											
Cyprus	I/c	—	0.24	—	0.28	0.59	—	—	0.42	0.50	—
Hong Kong	I/c	3.70	0.77	4.30	4.65	1.07	—	2.11	1.71	1.56	4.14
India	I/c	0.43	0.48	0.44	0.44	0.40	0.95	0.51	0.40	...	...
Israel	II/b [1]	0.53	0.86	0.44	0.74	0.25	0.06	...	...	...	...
Japan	I/d [2]	0.69	0.43	0.69	0.51	0.62	0.61	0.33	0.51	0.30	0.48
Korea, Rep. of	II/c [3]	4.72	4.41	3.64	5.98	4.50	4.43	3.65	3.68	3.22	3.70
Malaysia:											
Peninsular Malaysia [4]	II/c	0.94	0.87	1.19	0.92	0.75	1.13	1.60	...	...	...
Sarawak	I/c	1.48	1.40	2.41	1.45	4.75	1.73	—	0.97	—	—
Pakistan	I/b	1.07	0.93	0.78	0.08	0.12	1.55	1.14	...	...	...
Singapore	I/d	0.27	1.08	0.55	0.44	2.10	...	...	...	...	—
République arabe syrienne	II/c	—	1.43	1.01	4.20	0.90	1.49	1.95	2.20	...	1.48
EUROPE — EUROPE EUROPA											
Austria	I/c [5]	0.61	0.99	0.58	0.87	0.51	0.52	0.47	0.40	0.57	...
Belgique	II/a	0.73	0.39	0.82	0.38	0.24	0.38	...	...	...	...
Czechoslovakia	I/b	0.43	0.35	0.47	0.35	0.31	0.36	0.54	0.56	0.34	0.26
España	I/a	0.50	1.20	0.49	0.57	0.62	1.07	1.11	0.60	0.86	0.20
Finland	II/b [6]	0.63	0.33	0.52	0.15	0.46	0.85	0.35	0.69	0.46	...
France [7]	I/a	0.78	0.74	0.51	0.69	1.05	0.39	0.91	0.37	0.43	...
Germany, Fed. Rep. of	II/a	0.68	0.71	0.62	0.69	0.56	0.46	0.49	0.52	0.56	0.52
Grèce	I/b	1.00	1.13	0.42	0.47	0.71	0.81	0.40	...	...	...
Hongrie [8]	I/b [9]	0.32	0.45	0.45	0.44	0.36	0.33	0.36	0.30	0.62	0.33
Ireland	I/b	0.67	0.65	0.65	0.85	0.43	0.45	0.65	...	...	...
Italie	II/a	0.43	0.33	0.35	0.26	0.41	0.34	0.31	...	...	...

EXPLANATORY NOTES: See p. 609. NOTES EXPLICATIVES: Voir p. 611. NOTAS EXPLICATIVAS: Véase pág. 613.

I: Reported accidents.
II: Compensated accidents.

a: Rates per 1 000 man-years of 300 days each.
b: Rates per 1 000 wage earners (average numbers).
c: Rates per 1 000 persons employed (average numbers).
d: Rates per 1 000 000 man-hours worked.

I: *Accidents signalés.*
II: *Accidents indemnisés.*

a: *Taux pour 1 000 années-homme de 300 jours.*
b: *Taux pour 1 000 ouvriers (effectif moyen).*
c: *Taux pour 1 000 personnes occupées (effectif moyen).*
d: *Taux pour 1 000 000 d'heures-homme effectuées.*

I: Accidentes declarados.
II: Accidentes indemnizados.

a: Tasas por 1 000 años-hombre de 300 días cada uno.
b: Tasas por 1 000 obreros (ocupación media).
c: Tasas por 1 000 personas ocupadas (ocupación media).
d: Tasas por 1 000 000 de horas-hombre efectuadas.

[1] Incl. accidents on the way to and from work. Year ending in March of the following year. [2] Establishments employing 100 or more workers. [3] Establishments employing 50 or more workers. [4] Former West Malaysia. [5] Insured persons only. [6] Prior to 1973: code II/a. [7] Excl. quarrying. [8] State industry. [9] Prior to 1977: code I/a.

[1] *Y compris les accidents de trajet. Année se terminant en mars de l'année suivante.* [2] *Etablissements employant 100 ouvriers et plus.* [3] *Etablissements employant 50 ouvriers et plus.* [4] *Précédemment Malaisie occidentale.* [5] *Personnes assurées seulement.* [6] *Avant 1973 : code II/a.* [7] *Non compris les carrières.* [8] *Industrie d'Etat.* [9] *Avant 1977 : code I/a.*

[1] Incl. accidentes en el trayecto de ida al trabajo o vuelta del mismo. Año que termina en marzo del año siguiente. [2] Establecimientos que emplean 100 obreros y más. [3] Establecimientos que emplean 50 obreros y más. [4] Anteriormente Malasia Occidental. [5] Sólo las personas aseguradas. [6] Antes de 1973: clave II/a. [7] Excl. las canteras. [8] Industria de Estado. [9] Antes de 1977: clave I/a.

24 Industrial accident rates
(Fatal accidents)

Taux des accidents du travail
(Accidents mortels)

Tasas de frecuencia de los accidentes del trabajo
(Accidentes mortales)

A Mining and quarrying
Industries extractives
Minas y canteras

Country — Pays — País	Code Code Clave	1970	1971	1972	1973	1974	1975	1976	1977	1978	1979
Luxembourg	II/d	—	—	1.67	0.65	—	0.82	—	0.92	—	...
Malta	II/c	—	—	0.10	0.20	0.10	0.20	0.40	0.20	—	—
Netherlands	I/a	0.37	0.15	0.29	—	0.10	—	—	0.14	...	...
Norway	I/b[1]	0.64	0.67	1.33	0.51	0.56	0.39	0.47	0.10	0.24	...
Sweden [2]	II/d	0.24	0.40	0.28	0.28	0.20	0.03	0.31	0.22	...	...
Turquie	II/a	3.20	2.40	3.10	4.10	3.10	2.60	3.00	3.43	4.12	4.29
United Kingdom [3]	I/a	0.45	0.36	0.39	0.45	0.33	0.37	0.35	0.26	0.41	0.29 *
Yugoslavia [4]	I/c	0.50	0.39	0.19	0.18	0.20	0.19	0.32	0.22	0.35	0.20
OCEANIA — OCÉANIE OCEANÍA											
Australia [5]	I/c	1.34	0.96	0.90	1.11	0.64	0.62	0.68	0.59	0.42	...
New Zealand	I/c	0.78	0.91	1.13	0.90	...	...	...	...	...	...
Nouvelle-Calédonie	I/b	0.12	0.12	0.33	0.34	1.02	1.70	2.26	0.11	0.06	...
Papua New Guinea	I/c	3.60	1.50	...	...	1.90 *	...	...	...	...	...

EXPLANATORY NOTES: See p. 609.　　　　NOTES EXPLICATIVES: Voir p. 611.　　　　NOTAS EXPLICATIVAS: Véase pág. 613.

I: Reported accidents.
II: Compensated accidents.

a: Rates per 1 000 man-years of 300 days each.
b: Rates per 1 000 wage earners (average numbers).
c: Rates per 1 000 persons employed (average numbers).
d: Rates per 1 000 000 man-hours worked.

[1] Excl. coal mining. Prior to 1973: code I/a. [2] Year ending in June. [3] Excl. Northern Ireland. Excl. quarrying. [4] Incl. processing of minerals and basic metal industries. 1978: Excl. province of Kosovo [5] Year ending in June of the year indicated. Excl. uranium mining.

I: Accidents signalés.
II: Accidents indemnisés.

a: Taux pour 1 000 années-homme de 300 jours.
b: Taux pour 1 000 ouvriers (effectif moyen).
c: Taux pour 1 000 personnes occupées (effectif moyen).
d: Taux pour 1 000 000 d'heures-homme effectuées.

[1] Non compris les mines de charbon. Avant 1973 : code I/a. [2] Année se terminant en juin. [3] Non compris l'Irlande du Nord. Non compris les carrières. [4] Y compris le traitement des minéraux et les industries métallurgiques de base. 1978 : Non compris province de Kosovo. [5] Année se terminant en juin de l'année indiquée. Non compris l'extraction d'uranium.

I: Accidentes declarados.
II: Accidentes indemnizados.

a: Tasas por 1 000 años-hombre de 300 días cada uno.
b: Tasas por 1 000 obreros (ocupación media).
c: Tasas por 1 000 personas ocupadas (ocupación media).
d: Tasas por 1 000 000 de horas-hombre efectuadas.

[1] Excl. las minas de carbón. Antes de 1973: clave I/a. [2] Año que termina en junio. [3] Excl. Irlanda del Norte. Excl. las canteras. [4] Incl. el tratamiento de los minerales y las industrias metalúrgicas básicas. 1978: excl. provincia de Kosovo. [5] Año que termina en junio del año indicado. Excl. la extracción de uranio.

ACCIDENTS

24

Industrial accident rates
(Fatal accidents)

Taux des accidents du travail
(Accidents mortels)

Tasas de frecuencia de los accidentes del trabajo
(Accidentes mortales)

B

Coal mining
Mines de charbon
Minas de carbón

Country — *Pays* — País	Code *Code* Clave	1970	1971	1972	1973	1974	1975	1976	1977	1978	1979
AFRICA — AFRIQUE AFRICA											
Maroc	I/b	0.69	1.38	0.32	0.49	0.45	0.47	0.60	1.70	2.05	0.53
AMERICA — AMÉRIQUE AMÉRICA											
Canada [1]	I/b	2.03	2.01	1.93	2.03	1.69	1.14	1.77	1.06	1.40	1.65 *
Perú	I/d	—	0.84	...	...	...	...	...	...	...	...
United States	I/d	0.98	0.69	0.57	0.46	0.43	0.41	0.36	0.34	0.26	0.32 *
ASIA — ASIE ASIA											
India	I/c	0.54	0.60	0.53	0.50	0.46	1.26	0.58	0.47	...	...
Japan	I/d [2]	0.85	0.45	0.87	0.59	0.72	0.77	0.34	0.72	0.32	0.58
Pakistan	I/b	2.12	0.95	0.92	0.13	0.20	2.42	1.51	...	...	...
EUROPE — EUROPE EUROPA											
Czechoslovakia	I/b	0.43	0.36	0.54	0.38	0.32	0.39	0.64	0.60	0.34	0.27
France	I/a	0.76	0.70	0.41	0.64	1.31	0.34	0.84	0.28	0.36	...
Hongrie [3]	I/b [4]	0.34	0.47	0.40	0.54	0.36	0.34	0.37	0.30	0.73	0.37
Pologne [5]	I/c	0.47	0.45	...	...	...	...	...	...	...	...
Turquie	II/a	4.00	3.00	3.70	5.50	4.40	3.70	4.20	3.17	4.73	6.08
United Kingdom [6]	I/a	0.43	0.34	0.36	0.43	0.30	0.35	0.29	0.23	0.38	0.27
Yugoslavia	I/c	1.21	0.69	0.28	0.25	0.38	0.27	0.63	0.20	0.48	0.13
OCEANIA — OCÉANIE OCEANÍA											
Australia [7]	I/c	1.40	0.87	0.97	1.69	0.51	0.69	0.86	0.56	0.26	...
New Zealand	I/c	0.38	1.03	1.21	0.64	...	...	...	...	...	...

EXPLANATORY NOTES: See p. 609. NOTES EXPLICATIVES: Voir p. 611. NOTAS EXPLICATIVAS: Véase pág. 613.

I: Reported accidents.
II: Compensated accidents.

a: Rates per 1 000 man-years of 300 days each.
b: Rates per 1 000 wage earners (average numbers).
c: Rates per 1 000 persons employed (average numbers).
d: Rates per 1 000 000 man-hours worked.

I: *Accidents signalés.*
II: *Accidents indemnisés.*

a: *Taux pour 1 000 années-homme de 300 jours.*
b: *Taux pour 1 000 ouvriers (effectif moyen).*
c: *Taux pour 1 000 personnes occupées (effectif moyen).*
d: *Taux pour 1 000 000 d'heures-homme effectuées.*

I: Accidentes declarados.
II: Accidentes indemnizados.

a: Tasas por 1 000 años-hombre de 300 días cada uno.
b: Tasas por 1 000 obreros (ocupación media).
c: Tasas por 1 000 personas ocupadas (ocupación media).
d: Tasas por 1 000 000 de horas-hombre efectuadas.

[1] Incl. accidents on the way to and from work and deaths arising from occupational illnesses. [2] Establishments employing 100 or more workers. [3] State industry. [4] Prior to 1977: code I/a. [5] Incl. auxiliary enterprises. [6] Excl. Northern Ireland. [7] Year ending in June of the year indicated. Incl. extraction of crude oil and natural gas.

[1] *Y compris les accidents de trajet et les décès dus à des maladies professionnelles.* [2] *Etablissements employant 100 ouvriers et plus.* [3] *Industrie d'Etat.* [4] *Avant 1977: code I/a.* [5] *Y compris les entreprises auxiliaires.* [6] *Non compris l'Irlande du Nord.* [7] *Année se terminant en juin de l'année indiquée. Y compris l'extraction de pétrole brut et de gaz naturel.*

[1] Incl. los accidentes del trayecto y las defunciones debidas a enfermedades profesionales. [2] Establecimientos que emplean 100 obreros y más. [3] Industria de Estado. [4] Antes de 1977: clave I/a. [5] Incl. las empresas auxiliares. [6] Excl. Irlanda del Norte. [7] Año que termina en junio del año indicado. Incl. la extracción de petróleo crudo y gas natural.

24 Industrial accident rates
(Fatal accidents)
Taux des accidents du travail
(Accidents mortels)
Tasas de frecuencia de los accidentes del trabajo
(Accidentes mortales)

C Manufacturing
Industries manufacturières
Industrias manufactureras

Country — *Pays* — País	Code *Code* Clave	1970	1971	1972	1973	1974	1975	1976	1977	1978	1979
AFRICA — AFRIQUE AFRICA											
Burundi	I/c	.	1.02	0.49	0.96	0.59	—	0.90	—	—	0.66
Cameroun	II/c	0.16	0.34	—	—	—	—	0.01	—	0.05	...
Egypt [1]	I/c	0.09	0.08	0.02	| 0.20	0.22	0.19	0.24	0.28	0.23	0.16
Ghana	I/c	0.64	0.02	0.13	0.02	0.02	—	—	—	...	...
Kenya	II/c	...	...	...	0.20	...	0.04	0.05	0.18	0.49	...
Libyan Arab Jamahiriya	II/c	0.07	0.07	...	...	...	...	...	...	...	...
Malawi	I/b	0.05	0.05	0.09	0.05	0.26	0.03	0.19	0.22	0.17 *	...
Mali	I/c	—	0.30	—	...	...	...	...	...	...	...
Maroc	I/b	2.20	2.88	3.29	1.70	...	0.84	...	2.89	—	—
Mauritius	I/d	.	.	0.13	—	0.06	0.13	0.08	—	0.05	—
Nigeria [2]	I/c	0.12	1.00	0.21	0.06	0.18	0.24	0.07	0.07	0.13	...
Tanzania (Tanganyika)	II/b	0.13	0.15	...	...	...	...	...	...	...	...
Tunisie	I/d	0.05	0.05	0.08	0.07	0.07	0.05	0.06	0.07	0.01	0.01
Uganda	I/c	0.09	0.05	0.09	0.10 *	...	...	...	...	...	...
Zambia	I/c	0.03	0.92	0.12 *	0.08 *	...	...	...	...	...	...
AMERICA — AMÉRIQUE AMÉRICA											
Barbados	I/c	...	...	...	...	0.10	0.11	—	—	—	—
Canada [3]	I/c	0.11	0.11	0.16	0.15	0.17	0.13	0.11	0.10	0.11	0.09 *
El Salvador	I/c	0.13	0.08	0.15	0.13	0.20	0.18	0.24	0.27	0.27	0.25
Guadeloupe	I/b	0.28	—	0.33	0.25	0.25	0.23	0.25	...	...	...
Guatemala	I/b	0.17	0.23	0.23	0.30	0.31	0.21	0.17	0.23	0.21	0.23
Haïti [4]	II/a	0.15	0.03	0.06	0.03	0.20	0.15	0.05	0.10	0.10	0.02
Jamaica	I/c	—	0.04	0.15	0.09	—	—	—	...	...	...
México	II/c	0.19	0.34	0.05	0.33	0.26	...	0.01 *	...	...	...
Panamá	II/c	0.14	0.74	0.14	0.07	0.22	0.23	0.18	0.02	0.06 *	0.14 *

EXPLANATORY NOTES: See p. 609. NOTES EXPLICATIVES: Voir p. 611. NOTAS EXPLICATIVAS: Véase pág. 613.

I: Reported accidents.
II: Compensated accidents.

a: Rates per 1 000 man-years of 300 days each.
b: Rates per 1 000 wage earners (average numbers).
c: Rates per 1 000 persons employed (average numbers).
d: Rates per 1 000 000 man-hours worked.

I: *Accidents signalés.*
II: *Accidents indemnisés.*

a: *Taux pour 1 000 années-homme de 300 jours.*
b: *Taux pour 1 000 ouvriers (effectif moyen).*
c: *Taux pour 1 000 personnes occupées (effectif moyen).*
d: *Taux pour 1 000 000 d'heures-homme effectuées.*

I: Accidentes declarados.
II: Accidentes indemnizados.

a: Tasas por 1 000 años-hombre de 300 días cada uno.
b: Tasas por 1 000 obreros (ocupación media).
c: Tasas por 1 000 personas ocupadas (ocupación media).
d: Tasas por 1 000 000 de horas-hombre efectuadas.

[1] Year ending in June of the following year. [2] Year ending in March of the following year. [3] Incl. accidents on the way to and from work and deaths arising from occupational illnesses. [4] Year ending in Sep. of the year indicated.

[1] *Année se terminant en juin de l'année suivante.* [2] *Année se terminant en mars de l'année suivante.* [3] *Y compris les accidents de trajet et les décès dus à des maladies professionnelles.* [4] *Année se terminant en sept. de l'année indiquée.*

[1] Año que termina en junio del año siguiente. [2] Año que termina en marzo del año siguiente. [3] Incl. los accidentes del trayecto y las defunciones debidas a enfermedades profesionales. [4] Año que termina en sept. del año indicado.

24 Industrial accident rates
(Fatal accidents)

Taux des accidents du travail
(Accidents mortels)

Tasas de frecuencia de los accidentes del trabajo
(Accidentes mortales)

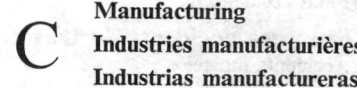

C Manufacturing
Industries manufacturières
Industrias manufactureras

Country — Pays — País	Code / Code / Clave	1970	1971	1972	1973	1974	1975	1976	1977	1978	1979
Perú	II/ [1]	.	.	.	.	0.08	0.06	0.06	0.06	...	...
Puerto Rico [2]	II/a	0.16	0.10	0.13	0.54	0.17	0.13	0.09	0.08	0.11	...
Suriname	II/a	0.10	0.20	—	0.10	...	...	0.01	0.20	0.62	0.12
Trinidad and Tobago	I/c	0.20	0.02	—	0.04	—	0.05	...	0.03	0.05	0.02
United States	I/d [3]	0.03	0.04	0.04	0.03	0.03	0.03	0.03	0.03	0.03	...
ASIA — ASIE / ASIA											
Bangladesh	I/b	0.07	0.13	0.06	0.02	0.02	0.04	0.04	0.04	0.03	0.03
Burma	I/c	0.08	0.11	0.02	0.05	0.04	0.04	0.11	0.11	0.07	0.08
Cyprus [4]	I/c	0.03	0.05	0.10	0.05	0.06	—	0.04	0.03	0.02	—
Hong Kong	I/c	0.06	0.12	0.07	0.07	0.09	0.08	0.11	0.10	0.08	0.09
India [5]	I/c	0.14	0.15	0.15	0.15	0.14	0.14	0.16 *	0.13 *	...	...
Israel	II/b [6]	0.14	0.18	0.15	0.25	0.13	0.16	...	...	...	...
Japan	I/d [7]	0.04	0.03	0.03	0.03	0.02	0.02	0.01	0.02	0.01	0.02
Jordan	I/c	—	—	0.01	0.02	0.22	0.17	0.20	0.12	0.13	...
Korea, Rep. of	II/c [8]	0.26	0.25	0.24	0.19	0.25	0.22	0.15	0.19	0.23	0.21
Malaysia:											
Peninsular Malaysia [9]	II/c	0.45	0.23	0.29	0.25	0.21	...	...	...	...	...
Sarawak	I/c	0.79	0.83	0.25	0.93	0.48	0.37	0.70	0.23	0.75	0.22
Pakistan	I/b	0.16	0.28	0.25	0.29	0.17	0.48	0.39	...	...	...
Singapore	I/d	0.07	0.05	0.08	0.09	0.11	0.07	0.07	0.04	0.15	0.04
Sri Lanka	II/c	1.68	1.67	1.65	1.66	1.68	1.67	1.68	1.66	1.69	...
République arabe syrienne	II/b	0.17	0.15	0.18	0.35	0.32	0.18	0.38	0.62	...	0.44
Thailand	II/c	0.03	0.02	0.03	0.04	0.04	...	...	...	—	...
Viet Nam [10]	I/c	0.66	0.46	0.23	0.41	...	...	...	...	...	...

EXPLANATORY NOTES: See p. 609.　　　NOTES EXPLICATIVES: Voir p. 611.　　　NOTAS EXPLICATIVAS: Véase pág. 613.

I: Reported accidents.
II: Compensated accidents.

a: Rates per 1 000 man-years of 300 days each.
b: Rates per 1 000 wage earners (average numbers).
c: Rates per 1 000 persons employed (average numbers).
d: Rates per 1 000 000 man-hours worked.

I: *Accidents signalés.*
II: *Accidents indemnisés.*

a: *Taux pour 1 000 années-homme de 300 jours.*
b: *Taux pour 1 000 ouvriers (effectif moyen).*
c: *Taux pour 1 000 personnes occupées (effectif moyen).*
d: *Taux pour 1 000 000 d'heures-homme effectuées.*

I: Accidentes declarados.
II: Accidentes indemnizados.

a: Tasas por 1 000 años-hombre de 300 días cada uno.
b: Tasas por 1 000 obreros (ocupación media).
c: Tasas por 1 000 personas ocupadas (ocupación media).
d: Tasas por 1 000 000 de horas-hombre efectuadas.

[1] Rates per 1 000 insured persons. [2] Year ending in Feb. of the following year. [3] Based on sample surveys. [4] Incl. electricity, gas, water and sanitary services. [5] Prior to 1973: Incl. electricity, gas, water and sanitary services. [6] Incl. accidents on the way to and from work. Year ending in March of the following year. [7] Establishments employing 100 or more workers. [8] Establishments employing 50 or more workers. [9] Former West Malaysia. [10] Data refer to the former Rep. of South Viet-Nam only.

[1] *Taux pour 1 000 personnes assurées.* [2] *Année se terminant en fév. de l'année suivante.* [3] *Fondé sur des enquêtes par sondage.* [4] *Y compris l'électricité, le gaz, l'eau et les services sanitaires.* [5] *Avant 1973 : y compris l'électricité, le gaz, l'eau et les services sanitaires.* [6] *Y compris les accidents de trajet. Année se terminant en mars de l'année suivante.* [7] *Etablissements employant 100 ouvriers et plus.* [8] *Etablissements employant 50 ouvriers et plus.* [9] *Précédemment Malaisie occidentale.* [10] *Les données se rapportent à l'ancienne Rép. du Sud Viet-Nam seulement.*

[1] Tasas por cada 1 000 asegurados. [2] Año que termina en febr. del año siguiente. [3] Basado en encuestas por muestra. [4] Incl. la electricidad, el gas, el agua y los servicios sanitarios. [5] Antes de 1973: Incl. la electricidad, el gas, el agua y los servicios sanitarios. [6] Incl. accidentes en el trayecto de ida al trabajo o vuelta del mismo. Año que termina en marzo del año siguiente. [7] Establecimientos que emplean 100 obreros y más. [8] Establecimientos que emplean 50 obreros y más. [9] Anteriormente Malasia Occidental. [10] Los datos se refieren a la antigua Rep. de Viet-Nam del Sur solamente.

24 Industrial accident rates
(Fatal accidents)

Taux des accidents du travail
(Accidents mortels)

Tasas de frecuencia de los accidentes del trabajo
(Accidentes mortales)

C Manufacturing
Industries manufacturières
Industrias manufactureras

Country — Pays — País	Code Code Clave	1970	1971	1972	1973	1974	1975	1976	1977	1978	1979
EUROPE — EUROPE EUROPA											
Austria [1]	I/c [2]	0.29	0.23	0.20	0.20	0.17	0.18	0.17	0.18	0.19	...
Belgique	II/a	0.12	0.11	0.10	0.11	0.10	0.11	...	...	...	...
Czechoslovakia	I/b	0.09	0.10	0.08	0.08	0.08	0.07	0.08	0.08	0.08	0.07
España	I/a	0.07	0.12	0.05	0.10	0.11	0.08	0.12	0.12	0.12	0.12
Finland	II/b [3]	0.10	0.07	0.04	0.07	0.08	0.08	0.13	0.06	0.06	...
France	II/c [4]	0.12	0.12	0.12	0.10	0.10	0.10	0.08	0.09	0.08	...
German Democratic Republic [5]	./c	0.06	0.06	0.06	0.05	0.05	0.05	0.05	0.05	0.05	0.04
Germany, Fed. Rep. of	II/a	0.18	0.19	0.18	0.17	0.16	0.16	0.14	0.13	0.14	0.13
Hongrie [6,7]	I/b [8]	0.10	0.13	0.09	0.10	0.08	0.09	0.10	0.08	0.09	0.10
Ireland	I/b	0.06	0.09	0.07	0.10	0.08	0.09	0.05	...	...	...
Italie	II/a	0.11	0.09	0.08	0.08	0.08	0.08	0.07	...	...	...
Luxembourg [9]	II/d	0.14	0.15	0.08	0.15	0.33	0.20	0.18	0.07	0.19	...
Malta	II/c	0.13	—	0.11	1.20	1.10	1.20	1.40	1.36	0.03	—
Netherlands	I/a	0.03	0.04	0.04	0.04	0.04	0.04	0.03	0.03	0.02	...
Norway	I/b [10]	0.11	0.06	0.09	0.08	0.05	0.06	0.07	0.03	0.05	...
Roumanie [4]	I/c	0.22	0.18	...	...	...	...	...	...	...	...
Suisse	II/b	.	0.17	0.12	0.12	0.13	0.12	0.11	0.10	0.10	...
Sweden [11]	II/d	0.05	0.04	0.04	0.03	0.03	0.03	0.02	0.03	...	...
Turquie	II/a	0.16	0.17	0.17	0.19	0.23	0.19	0.18	0.11	0.14	0.24
United Kingdom [12]	I/c	0.04	0.04	0.04	0.04	0.04	0.04	0.03	0.03 *	0.03	0.03
Yugoslavia	I/c	0.12	0.11	0.10	0.09	0.07	0.07	0.07	0.07	0.09	0.07
OCEANIA — OCÉANIE OCEANÍA											
Fiji	I/b	—	0.23	...	...	...	...	...	0.40	0.50	0.10
Nouvelle-Calédonie [13]	I/b	0.02	0.03	0.36	1.36	0.19	—	—	...	...	...
Papua New Guinea	I/c	0.10	0.50	...	...	0.90 *	...	...	...	...	...
Polynésie française	I/c	...	...	...	...	0.14	...	1.78	—	...	...

EXPLANATORY NOTES: See p. 609.   NOTES EXPLICATIVES: Voir p. 611.   NOTAS EXPLICATIVAS: Véase pág. 613.

I: Reported accidents.
II: Compensated accidents.

a: Rates per 1 000 man-years of 300 days each.
b: Rates per 1 000 wage earners (average numbers).
c: Rates per 1 000 persons employed (average numbers).
d: Rates per 1 000 000 man-hours worked.

I: *Accidents signalés.*
II: *Accidents indemnisés.*

a: *Taux pour 1 000 années-homme de 300 jours.*
b: *Taux pour 1 000 ouvriers (effectif moyen).*
c: *Taux pour 1 000 personnes occupées (effectif moyen).*
d: *Taux pour 1 000 000 d'heures-homme effectuées.*

I: Accidentes declarados.
II: Accidentes indemnizados.

a: Tasas por 1 000 años-hombre de 300 días cada uno.
b: Tasas por 1 000 obreros (ocupación media).
c: Tasas por 1 000 personas ocupadas (ocupación media).
d: Tasas por 1 000 000 de horas-hombre efectuadas.

[1] Prior to 1971: Incl. construction. [2] Insured persons only. [3] Prior to 1973: code II/a. [4] Incl. mining and quarrying. Excl. food industry. [5] Incl. mining electricity and gas. [6] State industry. Incl. electricity and gas. [7] Beginning 1971: Excl. railway workshops. [8] Prior to 1977: code I/a. [9] Iron and steel industries only. [10] Prior to 1973: code I/a. [11] Year ending in June. [12] Excl. Northern Ireland. [13] Nickel basic industries only.

[1] *Avant 1971 : y compris la construction.* [2] *Personnes assurées seulement.* [3] *Avant 1973 : code I/a.* [4] *Y compris les industries extractives. Non compris les industries de l'alimentation.* [5] *Y compris les mines, l'électricité et le gaz.* [6] *Industrie d'Etat. Y compris l'électricité et le gaz.* [7] *A partir de 1971 : non compris les ateliers de réparation des chemins de fer.* [8] *Avant 1977 : code I/a.* [9] *Industrie sidérurgique seulement.* [10] *Avant 1973 : code I/a.* [11] *Année se terminant en juin.* [12] *Non compris l'Irlande du Nord.* [13] *Industries de transformation du minerai de nickel seulement.*

[1] Antes de 1971: Incl. la construcción. [2] Sólo las personas aseguradas. [3] Antes de 1973: clave II/a. [4] Incl. las minas y canteras. Excl. la industria de la alimentación. [5] Incl. las minas, la electricidad y el gas. [6] Industria de Estado. Incl. la electricidad y el gas. [7] A partir de 1971: excl. los talleres de ferrocarriles. [8] Antes de 1977: clave I/a. [9] Sólo industrias del hierro y del acero. [10] Antes de 1973: clave I/a. [11] Año que termina en junio. [12] Excl. Irlanda del Norte. [13] Industrias básicas de níquel solamente.

24 Industrial accident rates
(Fatal accidents)

Taux des accidents du travail
(Accidents mortels)

Tasas de frecuencia de los accidentes del trabajo
(Accidentes mortales)

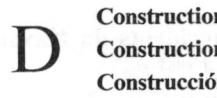

D Construction
Construction
Construcción

Country — *Pays* — País	Code *Code* Clave	1970	1971	1972	1973	1974	1975	1976	1977	1978	1979
AFRICA — AFRIQUE AFRICA											
Burundi	I/c	.	0.80	—	0.39	1.05	3.60	1.59	0.21	1.64	0.97
Cameroun	II/c	1.07	0.89	0.24	1.04	1.01	1.05	1.01	1.08	1.10	...
Egypt [1]	I/c	0.50	0.18	0.03	0.44	0.40	0.33	0.49	0.52	0.44	0.46
Libyan Arab Jamahiriya	II/c	0.38	0.35	...	...	...	...	...	...	...	...
Malawi	I/b	0.38	0.23	0.16	0.23	0.26	0.25	0.25	0.31	0.44 *	...
Mali	I/c	0.10	0.40	0.20	...	...	...	...	...	...	...
Maroc	I/b	1.89	0.92	1.23	2.55	...	0.40	...	3.83	—	—
Mauritius	II/d	.	.	—	1.50	0.47	0.23	0.21	0.25	0.26	0.09
Niger	II/b	4.33	4.00	1.71	2.13	...	...	...	...	...	...
Tanzania (Tanganyika)	II/b	0.12	0.10	...	...	...	...	...	...	...	...
Tunisie	I/d	0.16	0.13	0.26	0.18	0.21	0.26	0.26	0.28	0.08	0.06
Uganda	I/c	0.02	0.14	0.16	0.08	...	...	...	...	...	...
Zambia	I/c	0.19	0.13	0.10	0.10	...	...	...	...	...	...
AMERICA — AMÉRIQUE AMÉRICA											
Canada [2]	I/c	0.54	0.58	0.52	0.53	0.52	0.48	0.41	0.37	0.39	0.39 *
El Salvador	I/c	0.22	0.22	0.11	0.14	0.07	0.14	0.58	0.57	0.63	0.59
Guadeloupe	I/b	0.50	0.40	0.66	0.40	0.35	0.45	0.37	...	...	...
Guatemala	I/b	2.78	3.47	3.47	4.31	3.67	2.75	2.54	3.03	2.05	2.13
Guyane française	II/c	.	0.14	0.13	...	1.00	1.04	0.82	—	—	0.74
Haïti [3]	II/a	0.07	—	0.03	0.06	0.14	0.08	—	—	0.10	0.05
México	II/c	2.64	2.46	0.49	4.60	3.59	...	0.03 *	...	...	...
Panamá	II/c	0.21	0.42	0.47	0.26	1.38	0.36	0.48	0.20	0.08 *	0.11 *
Puerto Rico [4]	II/a	1.15	1.09	1.42	0.07	0.86	0.55	0.71	0.55	0.43	...
Suriname	II/a	—	—	0.10	0.20	0.01	0.04	...	0.30	...	0.20
Trinidad and Tobago	I/c	—	.	.	0.06	0.03	0.06	...	0.06	0.02	0.03
United States	I/d [5]	0.20	0.25	0.23	0.13	0.16	0.16	0.12	0.18	0.14	...
Virgin Is. (U.S.)	I/c	.	.	0.34	0.47	—	—	...	...	...	...
ASIA — ASIE ASIA											
Cyprus	I/c	0.16	0.15	0.19	0.20	0.05	—	0.11	0.09	0.17	0.05
Israel	II/b [6]	0.24	0.31	0.36	0.37	0.33	0.36	...	...	...	...
Japan	I/d [7]	0.23	0.17	0.19	0.21	0.16	0.13	0.06	0.13	0.07	0.03
Jordan	I/c	0.03	0.01	0.01	0.05	0.31	0.39	0.18	0.66	0.20	...

EXPLANATORY NOTES: See p. 609.

I: Reported accidents.
II: Compensated accidents.

a: Rates per 1 000 man-years of 300 days each.
b: Rates per 1 000 wage earners (average numbers).
c: Rates per 1 000 persons employed (average numbers).
d: Rates per 1 000 000 man-hours worked.

[1] Year ending in June of the following year. [2] Incl. accidents on the way to and from work and deaths arising from occupational illnesses. [3] Year ending in Sep. of the year indicated. [4] Year ending in Feb. of the following year. [5] Based on sample surveys. [6] Incl. accidents on the way to and from work. Year ending in March of the following year. [7] Establishments employing 100 or more workers.

NOTES EXPLICATIVES: Voir p. 611.

I: *Accidents signalés.*
II: *Accidents indemnisés.*

a: *Taux pour 1 000 années-homme de 300 jours.*
b: *Taux pour 1 000 ouvriers (effectif moyen).*
c: *Taux pour 1 000 personnes occupées (effectif moyen).*
d: *Taux pour 1 000 000 d'heures-homme effectuées.*

[1] *Année se terminant en juin de l'année suivante.* [2] *Y compris les accidents de trajet et les décès dus à des maladies professionnelles.* [3] *Année se terminant en sept. de l'année indiquée.* [4] *Année se terminant en fév. de l'année suivante.* [5] *Fondé sur des enquêtes par sondage.* [6] *Y compris les accidents de trajet. Année se terminant en mars de l'année suivante.* [7] *Etablissements employant 100 ouvriers et plus.*

NOTAS EXPLICATIVAS: Véase pág. 613.

I: Accidentes declarados.
II Accidentes indemnizados.

a: Tasas por 1 000 años-hombre de 300 días cada uno.
b: Tasas por 1 000 obreros (ocupación media).
c: Tasas por 1 000 personas ocupadas (ocupación media).
d: Tasas por 1 000 000 de horas-hombre efectuadas.

[1] Año que termina en junio del año siguiente. [2] Incl. los accidentes del trayecto y las defunciones debidas a enfermedades profesionales. [3] Año que termina en sept. del año indicado. [4] Año que termina en febr. del año siguiente. [5] Basado en encuestas por muestra. [6] Incl. accidentes en el trayecto de ida al trabajo o vuelta del mismo. Año que termina en marzo del año siguiente. [7] Establecimientos que emplean 100 obreros y más.

24 Industrial accident rates
(Fatal accidents)
Taux des accidents du travail
(Accidents mortels)
Tasas de frecuencia de los accidentes del trabajo
(Accidentes mortales)

D Construction
Construction
Construcción

Country — Pays — País	Code Code Clave	1970	1971	1972	1973	1974	1975	1976	1977	1978	1979
Korea, Rep. of	II/c[1]	3.07	1.36	3.73	0.82	0.72	0.68	0.53	0.53	0.53	0.50
Malaysia:											
Sarawak	I/c	1.78	1.89	0.93	3.30	4.46	1.02	2.02	1.81	2.08	0.50
Singapore	I/d	0.40	0.53	0.43	0.59	0.28	0.26	0.33	0.20	0.11	0.23
République arabe syrienne	II/b	0.84	0.52	0.42	0.57	0.76	0.76	0.86	0.97	...	1.07
Thailand	II/c	0.01	0.02	0.01	0.02	0.02	...	...	...	...	...
EUROPE — EUROPE EUROPA											
Austria	I/c	.	0.77	0.84	0.76	0.61	0.62	0.59	0.54	0.60	...
Czechoslovakia	I/b	0.20	0.23	0.31	0.23	0.16	0.19	0.22	0.20	0.20	0.19
España	I/a	0.24	0.44	0.33	0.35	0.34	0.30	0.39	0.33	0.31	0.28
Finland	II/b[2]	0.54	0.31	0.29	0.25	0.24	0.22	0.28	0.15	0.19	...
France	II/c	0.49	0.50	0.47	0.45	0.46	0.43	0.42	0.34	0.31	...
German Democratic Republic[3]	./c	0.19	0.19	0.13	0.15	0.14	0.10	0.10	0.09	0.11	0.09
Germany, Fed. Rep. of	II/a	0.40	0.44	0.39	0.37	0.33	0.35	0.39	0.38	0.33	0.35
Hongrie[4]	I/b[5]	0.37	0.28	0.27	0.24	0.26	0.23	0.19	0.29	0.24	0.26
Ireland	I/b	0.16	0.25	0.14	0.15	0.15	0.08	0.09	...	...	...
Italie	II/a	0.65	0.53	0.55	0.53	0.62	0.56	0.54	...	...	...
Malta	II/c	0.08	0.09	0.09	0.10	0.09	0.08	0.10	0.36	0.22	0.20
Netherlands	I/a	0.07	0.13	0.13	0.12	0.08	0.10	0.10	0.10	0.08	...
Norway	I/b[6]	0.41	0.20	0.15	0.11	0.18	0.17	0.20	0.15	0.12	...
Pologne	I/c	0.20	0.22	...	...	...	...	...	...	...	...
Roumanie	I/c	0.26	0.27	...	...	...	...	...	...	...	...
Suisse[7]	II/b	.	0.53	0.63	0.58	0.61	0.48	0.63	0.64	0.62	...
Sweden[8]	II/d	0.07	0.06	0.08	0.06	0.08	0.08	0.05	0.05	...	...
Turquie	II/a	0.86	0.93	0.89	0.94	0.97	0.90	0.91	0.97	0.86	0.93
United Kingdom[9]	I/c	0.19	0.20	0.19	0.22	0.16	0.18	0.15	0.13	0.12 *	0.14
Yugoslavia	I/c	0.24	0.22	0.26	0.20	0.18	0.23	0.26	0.19	0.16	0.16
OCEANIA — OCÉANIE OCEANÍA											
Fiji	I/b	0.44	0.26	0.40	0.20	0.30	0.40	0.10	—	—	...
Nouvelle-Calédonie	I/b	0.03	0.03	0.83	0.34	1.01	1.10	—	0.05	—	...
Papua New Guinea	I/c	0.50	0.50	...	...	0.40 *	...	...	...	...	...
Polynésie française	I/c	...	...	...	...	0.13	...	0.40	—	...	...

EXPLANATORY NOTES: See p. 609.   NOTES EXPLICATIVES: Voir p. 611.   NOTAS EXPLICATIVAS: Véase pág. 613.

I: Reported accidents.
II: Compensated accidents.

a: Rates per 1 000 man-years of 300 days each.
b: Rates per 1 000 wage earners (average numbers).
c: Rates per 1 000 persons employed (average numbers).
d: Rates per 1 000 000 man-hours worked.

I: *Accidents signalés.*
II: *Accidents indemnisés.*

a: *Taux pour 1 000 années-homme de 300 jours.*
b: *Taux pour 1 000 ouvriers (effectif moyen).*
c: *Taux pour 1 000 personnes occupées (effectif moyen).*
d: *Taux pour 1 000 000 d'heures-homme effectuées.*

I: Accidentes declarados.
II: Accidentes indemnizados.

a: Tasas por 1 000 años-hombre de 300 días cada uno.
b: Tasas por 1 000 obreros (ocupación media).
c: Tasas por 1 000 personas ocupadas (ocupación media).
d: Tasas por 1 000 000 de horas-hombre efectuadas.

[1] Establishments employing 50 or more workers. [2] Prior to 1973: code II/a. [3] Incl. quarrying. [4] State industry. Beginning 1969: excl. construction of railway lines. [5] Prior to 1977: code I/a. [6] Prior to 1973: code I/a. [7] Beginning 1972: incl. quarrying. [8] Year ending in June. [9] Excl. Northern Ireland.

[1] *Etablissements employant 50 ouvriers et plus.* [2] *Avant 1973 : code II/a.* [3] *Y compris les carrières.* [4] *Industrie d'Etat. A partir de 1969 : non compris la construction de lignes de chemin de fer.* [5] *Avant 1977 : code I/a.* [6] *Avant 1973 : code I/a.* [7] *A partir de 1972 : y compris les carrières.* [8] *Année se terminant en juin.* [9] *Non compris l'Irlande du Nord.*

[1] Establecimientos que emplean 50 obreros y más. [2] Antes de 1973: clave II/a. [3] Incl. las canteras. [4] Industria de Estado. A partir de 1969: excl. la construcción de vías férreas. [5] Antes de 1977: clave I/a. [6] Antes de 1973: clave I/a. [7] A partir de 1972: incl. las canteras. [8] Año que termina en junio. [9] Excl. Irlanda del Norte.

ACCIDENTS

24
Industrial accident rates
(Fatal accidents)
Taux des accidents du travail
(Accidents mortels)
Tasas de frecuencia de los accidentes del trabajo
(Accidentes mortales)

E
Railways
Chemins de fer
Ferrocarriles

Country — Pays — País	Code Code Clave	1970	1971	1972	1973	1974	1975	1976	1977	1978	1979
AFRICA — AFRIQUE AFRICA											
Cameroun	II/c	—	—	—	0.35	0.78	0.51	—	0.97	1.07	...
Egypt [1,2]	I/c	0.34	0.23	—	0.22	0.26	0.49	0.55	0.43	0.43	0.57
Kenya [3]	II/c	...	...	—	0.05	...	...	...	0.05	...	...
Malawi [1]	I/b	0.59	0.55	1.02	0.29	1.05	1.10	0.40	0.64	0.46 *	...
Mali	I/c	0.30	—	...	...	...	...	...	...	...	...
Maroc [3]	I/b	0.63	0.86	...	...	...	...	...	0.46	0.38	0.58
Tanzania (Tanganyika) [4]	II/b	0.15	0.12	...	...	...	...	...	...	...	...
Tunisie [3]	I/d	0.06	0.06	0.06	0.50	0.56	—	0.05	0.05	...	...
Zambia [5]	I/c	0.12	0.35	0.12	2.98	...	...	...	...	...	...
AMERICA — AMÉRIQUE AMÉRICA											
Canada [6]	I/c	0.25	0.28	0.36	0.40	0.44	0.28	0.30	0.25	0.25	0.27
El Salvador	I/c	0.09	—	—	—	0.28	—	0.09	0.51	2.08	1.06
Guatemala	I/b	2.38	1.83	1.83	2.38	2.28	1.88	1.43	1.82	1.75	1.79
Haïti [7]	II/a	0.03	—	0.06	0.06	0.38	0.02	—	0.02	—	0.02
Jamaica [3]	I/c	—	—	...	...	...	...	...	...	...	...
México	II/c	0.58	0.66	0.17	0.83	0.71	...	1.03 *	...	...	...
Perú [5]	II/ [8]	.	.	.	.	0.18	0.14	0.13	0.12	...	...
Puerto Rico [3,9]	II/a	—	...	...	...	—	...	...	...	...	...
United States [4]	I/d	0.16	0.13	0.12	0.14	0.11	0.10	0.11	0.10	0.10	...
ASIA — ASIE ASIA											
India [10]	I/c	0.28	0.24	0.25	0.20	0.19	0.21	0.24	0.21	0.22	...
Japan [4]	I/d [11]	0.04	0.04	0.04	0.02	0.04	0.03	0.02	0.02	0.01	—
Malaysia:											
Peninsular Malaysia [12,3]	II/c	...	1.30	0.86	1.10	0.92	0.60	—	0.20	—	...
Sarawak [13]	I/c	3.50	1.08	0.53	0.45	2.02	1.36	1.90	1.54	—	—
Sri Lanka [3]	II/c	0.27	0.26	0.25	0.26	0.28	0.27	0.28	0.26	0.27	...
République arabe syrienne	II/c	0.60	1.27	0.48	0.80	2.84	—	1.32	1.06	...	...
Thailand [1]	II/c	—	—	—	0.01	0.03	...	...	...	...	...
Viet Nam [14]	I/c	0.61	0.63	0.22	2.52	...	...	...	...	...	...

EXPLANATORY NOTES: See p. 609.　　NOTES EXPLICATIVES: Voir p. 611.　　NOTAS EXPLICATIVAS: Véase pág. 613.

I: Reported accidents.
II: Compensated accidents.

a: Rates per 1 000 man-years of 300 days each.
b: Rates per 1 000 wage earners (average numbers).
c: Rates per 1 000 persons employed (average numbers).
d: Rates per 1 000 000 man-hours worked.

I: *Accidents signalés.*
II: *Accidents indemnisés.*

a: *Taux pour 1 000 années-homme de 300 jours.*
b: *Taux pour 1 000 ouvriers (effectif moyen).*
c: *Taux pour 1 000 personnes occupées (effectif moyen).*
d: *Taux pour 1 000 000 d'heures-homme effectuées*

I: Accidentes declarados.
II: Accidentes indemnizados.

a: Tasas por 1 000 años-hombre de 300 días cada uno.
b: Tasas por 1 000 obreros (ocupación media).
c: Tasas por 1 000 personas ocupadas (ocupación media).
d: Tasas por 1 000 000 de horas-hombre efectuadas.

[1] Transport and communications. [2] Year ending in June of the following year. [3] Incl. railway workshops and construction of railway lines. [4] Incl. railway workshops. [5] Transport, storage and communications. [6] Incl. accidents on the way to and from work and deaths arising from occupational illnesses. [7] Year ending in Sep. of the year indicated. [8] Rates per 1 000 insured persons. [9] Year ending in Feb. of the following year. [10] Year ending in March of the year indicated. [11] Establishments employing 100 or more workers. [12] Former West Malaysia. [13] Road transport. [14] Data refer to the former Rep. of South Viet-Nam only.

[1] *Transports et communications.* [2] *Année se terminant en juin de l'année suivante.* [3] *Y compris les ateliers de réparation des chemins de fer et la construction de lignes de chemin de fer.* [4] *Y compris les ateliers de réparation des chemins de fer.* [5] *Transports, entrepôts et communications.* [6] *Y compris les accidents de trajet et les décès dus à des maladies professionnelles.* [7] *Année se terminant en sept. de l'année indiquée.* [8] *Taux pour 1 000 personnes assurées.* [9] *Année se terminant en fév. de l'année suivante.* [10] *Année se terminant en mars de l'année indiquée.* [11] *Etablissements employant 100 ouvriers et plus.* [12] *Précédemment Malaisie occidentale.* [13] *Transport routier.* [14] *Les données se rapportent à l'ancienne Rép. du Sud Viet-Nam seulement.*

[1] Transportes y comunicaciones. [2] Año que termina en junio del año siguiente. [3] Incl. los talleres de ferrocarriles y la construcción de vías férreas. [4] Incl. los talleres de ferrocarriles. [5] Transportes, almacenaje y comunicaciones. [6] Incl. los accidentes del trayecto y las defunciones debidas a enfermedades profesionales. [7] Año que termina en sept. del año indicado. [8] Tasas por cada 1 000 asegurados. [9] Año que termina en febr. del año siguiente. [10] Año que termina en marzo del año indicado. [11] Establecimientos que emplean 100 obreros y más. [12] Anteriormente Malasia Occidental. [13] Transporte por carretera. [14] Los datos se refieren a la antigua Rep. de Viet-Nam del Sur solamente.

24

Industrial accident rates
(Fatal accidents)

Taux des accidents du travail
(Accidents mortels)

Tasas de frecuencia de los accidentes del trabajo
(Accidentes mortales)

E

Railways
Chemins de fer
Ferrocarriles

Country — Pays — País	Code / Code / Clave	1970	1971	1972	1973	1974	1975	1976	1977	1978	1979
EUROPE — EUROPE / EUROPA											
Austria [1]	I/c [2]	0.39	0.39	0.43	0.33	0.26	0.31	0.34	0.31	0.26	...
Belgique [3]	II/b	0.24	0.20	0.23	0.17	0.13	...	...	...	...	...
Czechoslovakia	I/b	0.41	0.28	0.27	0.36	0.23	0.20	0.25	0.20	0.25	...
Finland	I/b [4]	—	—	0.06	|0.16	0.16	0.08	0.23	0.17	0.17	0.26
France	II/c	...	0.20	0.23	0.19	0.22	0.21	0.20	0.13	0.21	...
German Democratic Republic [5]	./c	0.17	0.16	0.17	0.15	0.15	0.14	0.20	0.12	0.12	0.11
Germany, Fed. Rep. of [6]	II/a	0.31	0.33	0.38	0.26	0.26	0.26	0.30	0.25	0.14	0.20
Hongrie [7, 8]	I/b [9]	0.32	0.32	0.30	0.23	0.22	0.26	0.21	|0.29	0.28	0.31
Ireland	I/c	0.40	0.22	—	—	0.43	0.43	—	—	0.24	—
Italie [10]	II/c	0.20	0.18	0.10	0.18	0.14	0.12	0.15	0.09	...	...
Malta [11]	II/c	—	—	0.24	0.30	0.20	0.30	0.40	0.28	0.18	—
Netherlands	I/a	0.44	0.11	—	0.15	0.07	0.22	0.15	0.07	—	...
Norway	I/c	0.30	0.06	0.18	0.12	0.19	0.38	0.19	0.32	0.06	0.06
Pologne [8]	I/c	0.33	0.41	...	...	...	...	...	...	...	...
Roumanie [11]	I/c	0.26	0.17	...	...	...	...	...	...	...	...
Suisse [1]	II/b	.	0.60	0.34	0.36	0.36	0.32	0.36	0.52	0.24	...
Sweden [7, 12]	II/d	0.10	0.06	0.14	0.07	0.18	0.06	0.14	0.12	...	...
Turquie [11]	II/a	1.35	0.97	1.15	1.30	1.56	1.16	0.95	0.36	0.25	1.33
United Kingdom [13]	I/b	0.28	0.27	0.22	0.18	0.15	0.19	0.19	0.17	0.20	0.18 *
Yugoslavia [7, 14]	I/c	0.49	0.41	0.36	0.31	0.34	0.15	0.32	0.24	0.17	0.27
OCEANIA — OCÉANIE / OCEANÍA											
New Zealand	I/a	0.69	0.51	0.17	0.42	...	...	...	...	...	...

EXPLANATORY NOTES: See p. 609. — NOTES EXPLICATIVES: Voir p. 611. — NOTAS EXPLICATIVAS: Véase pág. 613.

I: Reported accidents.
II: Compensated accidents.

a: Rates per 1 000 man-years of 300 days each.
b: Rates per 1 000 wage earners (average numbers).
c: Rates per 1 000 persons employed (average numbers).
d: Rates per 1 000 000 man-hours worked.

I: *Accidents signalés.*
II: *Accidents indemnisés.*

a: *Taux pour 1 000 années-homme de 300 jours.*
b: *Taux pour 1 000 ouvriers (effectif moyen).*
c: *Taux pour 1 000 personnes occupées (effectif moyen).*
d: *Taux pour 1 000 000 d'heures-homme effectuées.*

I: Accidentes declarados.
II: Accidentes indemnizados.

a: Tasas por 1 000 años-hombre de 300 días cada uno.
b: Tasas por 1 000 obreros (ocupación media).
c: Tasas por 1 000 personas ocupadas (ocupación media).
d: Tasas por 1 000 000 de horas-hombre efectuadas.

[1] Incl. railway workshops. [2] Insured persons only. [3] State railways; incl. daily workers. [4] Prior to 1973: code II/a. [5] Transport and communications. [6] Incl. railway workshops and accidents involving road vehicles operated by federal railways. [7] Incl. railway workshops and construction of railway lines. [8] State industry. [9] Prior to 1977: code I/a. [10] Regular staff only: incl. railway workshops. [11] Transport. [12] Year ending in June. [13] Excl. Northern Ireland. [14] 1978: Excl. province of Kosovo.

[1] Y compris les ateliers de réparation des chemins de fer. [2] Personnes assurées seulement. [3] Chemins de fer de l'Etat, y compris les travailleurs à la journée. [4] Avant 1973 : code II/a. [5] Transports et communications. [6] Y compris les ateliers de réparation des chemins de fer et les accidents survenus à des véhicules routiers des chemins de fer fédéraux. [7] Y compris les ateliers de réparation des chemins de fer et la construction de lignes de chemin de fer. [8] Industrie d'Etat. [9] Avant 1977 : code I/a. [10] Personnel permanent seulement ; y compris les ateliers de réparation des chemins de fer. [11] Transports. [12] Année se terminant en juin. [13] Non compris l'Irlande du Nord. [14] 1978 : Non compris la province de Kosovo.

[1] Incl. los talleres de ferrocarriles. [2] Sólo las personas aseguradas. [3] Ferrocarriles del Estado; incl. los jornaleros. [4] Antes de 1973: clave II/a. [5] Transportes y comunicaciones. [6] Incl. los talleres de ferrocarriles y los accidentes sufridos por vehículos de carretera de los ferrocarriles federales. [7] Incl. los talleres de ferrocarriles y la construcción de vías férreas. [8] Industria de Estado. [9] Antes de 1977: clave I/a. [10] Sólo personal de plantilla; incl. los talleres de ferrocarriles. [11] Transportes. [12] Año que termina en junio. [13] Excl. Irlanda del Norte. [14] 1978: excl. provincia de Kosovo.

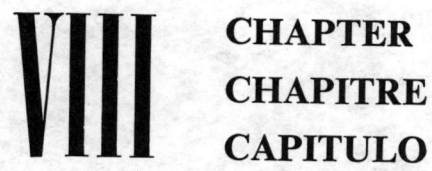

VIII

**CHAPTER
CHAPITRE
CAPITULO**

Industrial disputes

Conflits du travail

Conflictos del trabajo

Industrial disputes

Table 25

Industrial disputes

This table shows the total number of *industrial disputes (wilfully effected by a group of workers or by one or more employers with a view to enforcing a demand) which resulted in a stoppage of work, and the numbers of workers involved and working days lost.* No differentiation between strikes and lockouts has been possible, since in most countries the distinction is not observed in the compilations. In a few cases, however, the data relate to strikes only. Disputes of small importance and political strikes are frequently not included in the statistics. In some cases the data do not cover workers " indirectly affected ". i.e. workers who, though not parties in the dispute, are thrown out of work *within* the establishment directly affected by the stoppage of work. As far as possible, such cases are indicated by footnotes.

Various methods are used for calculating the number of working days lost, and these data, as well as the statistics of workers involved, are often approximations only. Because of this variation between countries in definitions, sources, scope and statistical treatment of data at country level, any comparison of the magnitude and relative importance of industrial disputes should be made with extreme care.[1]

An additional table, providing a breakdown by major divisions of economic activity of the data on industrial disputes published in Table 25, is released, generally every three years, in the *Year Book* (see 1979 edition, Table 25 B).

---

[1] For references concerning the methods on statistics of industrial disputes, see ILO: *International Recommendations on Labour Statistics* (Geneva, 1976).

Conflits du travail

Tableau 25

Conflits du travail

Ce tableau fournit le nombre total des *conflits du travail (volontairement provoqués par un groupement de travailleurs ou par un ou plusieurs employeurs en vue d'imposer une revendication) ayant entraîné un arrêt du travail, le nombre des travailleurs impliqués et le nombre des journées de travail perdues* dans ces conflits. Il n'a pas été possible de distinguer entre les grèves et les lock-out, la plupart des pays n'établissant pas de statistiques séparées pour ces deux groupes. Toutefois, dans quelques cas, les données ne se réfèrent qu'aux grèves. Les conflits de peu d'importance et les grèves ayant un caractère politique sont fréquemment exclus des statistiques. Dans certains cas, les données ne couvrent pas les travailleurs « indirectement atteints », c'est-à-dire ceux qui, sans être partie au conflit, sont mis par celui-ci dans l'impossibilité de travailler *dans* l'établissement directement atteint par l'arrêt du travail. Dans la mesure du possible, ces cas sont indiqués dans les notes de bas de page.

Les méthodes utilisées pour le calcul du nombre des journées perdues varient aussi selon les pays. Ces chiffres, ainsi que le nombre des travailleurs impliqués, ne sont souvent que des approximations. C'est, précisément, à cause de cette hétérogénité des définitions, des sources, de la portée et des méthodes de traitement des statistiques pratiquées par les différents pays, que toute comparaison de l'ampleur et de l'importance relative des conflits du travail doit être faite avec une extrême prudence.[1]

Un tableau complémentaire, fournissant la ventilation par branches principales d'activité économique des données sur les conflits du travail présentées au tableau 25, est publié en général tous les trois ans dans l'*Annuaire* (voir édition de 1979, tableau 25 B).

---

[1] Pour des références concernant les méthodes relatives aux statistiques des conflits du travail, voir BIT: *Recommandations internationales sur les statistiques du travail* (Genève, 1975).

Conflictos del trabajo

Cuadro 25

Conflictos del trabajo

Este cuadro presenta el número total de *conflictos del trabajo (efectuados voluntariamente por un grupo de trabajadores o por uno o más empleadores con objeto de imponer una reivindicación) que provocaron interrupciones de labores, el número de trabajadores afectados y los días de trabajo perdidos.* No ha sido posible distinguir entre huelgas y cierres a causa de que la mayoría de los países no hacen esa distinción en sus compilaciones. En unos pocos casos, las informaciones se refieren a huelgas solamente. Los conflictos de poca importancia y las huelgas políticas frecuentemente no se incluyen en las estadísticas. En algunos casos, las informaciones no se aplican a los trabajadores « indirectamente afectados », es decir, a los que, sin tomar parte en el conflicto, deben cesar en sus labores ante la imposibilidad de trabajar *dentro* del establecimiento directamente afectado por el conflicto. En la medida de lo posible, estos casos se indican en notas de pie de página.

El cálculo del número de días de trabajo perdidos se hace utilizando varios métodos, y este dato, así como las estadísticas del número de trabajadores afectados, es sólo aproximado. Precisamente, es a causa de esta diversidad de definiciones, fuentes, alcance y métodos de elaboración de las estadísticas, en la práctica de los diferentes países, que toda comparación de la amplitud e importancia relativa de los conflictos del trabajo debe emprenderse con gran prudencia.[1]

Un cuadro complementario, en que los datos sobre conflictos del trabajo presentados en el cuadro 25 aparecen clasificados según divisiones mayores de la actividad económica, se publica por lo general cada tres años en el *Anuario* (véase edición de 1979, cuadro 25 B).

---

[1] Para referencias relativas a los métodos sobre las estadísticas de los conflictos del trabajo, véase OIT: *Recomendaciones internacionales sobre estadísticas del trabajo* (Ginebra, 1975).

25 Industrial disputes
Conflits du travail
Conflictos del trabajo

Country — *Pays* — País	Code *Code* Clave	1970	1971	1972	1973	1974	1975	1976	1977	1978	1979
AFRICA — AFRIQUE AFRICA											
Algérie	D/C	57	70	100	99	...	...	...	...	...	...
	W/T	6 363	12 276	10 706	12 079	...	...	...	...	...	...
	D/J	25 771	52 161	40 588	5 321	...	...	...	...	...	...
Burundi	D/C	1	9	10	11	11	18	5	2	17	13
	W/T	110	2 498	3 712	2 382	3 395	5 539	8 440	2 600	519	2 325
	D/J	330	7 148	10 585	7 690	7 419	15 622	27 674	5 200	7 446	5 906
Cameroun	D/C	4	32	5	7	10	12	3	—	6	1
	W/T	1 857	2 530	3 901	8 124	6 313	3 861	1 377	—	5 965	745
	D/J	999	17 810	...	...	231 746	122 068	13 778	—	23 617	745
Côte-d'Ivoire.	D/C	...	...	...	...	...	30	43	35	28	31
	W/T	...	...	...	...	...	6 381	15 404	9 437	7 406	6 785
	D/J	...	...	...	...	...	52 164	40 179	13 778	14 751	20 362
Egypt	D/C	45	90	537	13	6	7	10	5	3	7
	W/T	1 311	11 425	11 864	4 222	13 172	40 527	793	1 042	3 900	5 235
	D/J	...	...	22 275	4 907	71 321	200 528	921	2 541	1 450	3 933
Ghana	D/C	56	79	10	13	43	33	45	61	65	50
	W/T	21 376	41 053	2 336	3 917	32 371	15 301	32 360	47 304	42 913	40 606
	D/J	123 050	116 041	3 198	3 109	64 408	39 410	114 259	205 170	196 167	170 598
Haute-Volta	D/C	3	2	2	7	10	...	4	...	3	...
	W/T	287	252	42	...	...	...	6 679	...	245	...
	D/J	674	328	1 890	...	...	...	18 967	...	1 665	...
Kenya	D/C	84	74	94	83	123	26	44	45	43	...
	W/T	18 941	14 398	28 006	14 125	22 144	4 148	12 964	7 288	9 459	...
	D/J	49 517	32 681	42 462	42 267	127 951	8 755	26 248	...	18 726	...
Malawi	D/C	7	16	18	6	13	4	13	8	10	6
	W/T	475	3 543	2 544	1 387	981	272	787	596	850	596
	D/J	393	3 202	1 228	4 890	1 081	643	865	437	515	283
Mali	D/C	—	—	—	—	—	...	...	...	...	...
	W/T	—	—	—	—	—	...	...	...	...	...
	D/J	—	—	—	—	—	...	...	...	...	...
Maroc	D/C	97	259	479	462	367	267	521	421	490	779
	W/T	17 211	82 027	100 767	52 320	65 463	35 768	83 061	60 433	73 672	88 087
	D/J	81 274	589 334	785 860	353 499	320 631	228 523	479 863	375 802	335 722	429 397

EXPLANATORY NOTES: See p. 629.   NOTES EXPLICATIVES: Voir p. 630.   NOTAS EXPLICATIVAS: Véase pág. 631.

D/C : Number of disputes — *Nombre de conflits* — Número de conflictos.
W/T : Workers involved — *Travailleurs impliqués* — Trabajadores afectados.
D/J : Working days lost — *Journées de travail perdues* — Días de trabajo perdidos.

25 **Industrial disputes**
Conflits du travail
Conflictos del trabajo

Country — *Pays* — País	Code *Code* Clave	1970	1971	1972	1973	1974	1975	1976	1977	1978	1979
Mauritius [1]	D/C	8	19	1	9	26	69	86	41	33	29
	W/T	2 073	25 845	150	29 738	8 449	70 075	67 841	9 629	42 813	64 698
	D/J	5 214	142 916	150	88 588	17 847	123 930	114 716	11 644	46 591	373 058
Nigeria [1,2]	D/C	34	118	85	69	163	394	107	165*	105*	132
	W/T	20 015	79 598	29 656	43 504	62 693	214 560	55 273	73 385*	129 858*	173 309
	D/J	52 630	233 863	65 254	106 387	159 613	469 186	160 822	208 623*	1 012 413*	1 309 361
Réunion	D/C	...	...	...	...	...	...	19	23	27	...
	W/T	...	...	...	...	...	...	1 015	2 064	1 654	...
	D/J	...	...	...	...	...	...	10 050	20 660	17 538	...
Seychelles	D/C	—	3	2	2	2	1	—	—	...	...
	W/T	—	117	2 150	100	159	40	—	—	...	...
	D/J	—	2 392	12 446	100	195	120	—	—	...	...
Sierra Leone	D/C	7	5	4	3	4	8	3	4	12	18
	W/T	903	2 711	860	612	438	1 195	800	1 050	4 792	4 665
	D/J	474	5 708	965	4 851	1 026	9 770	1 300	2 100	15 531	13 791
South Africa, Rep. of . .	D/C	76	69	71	370	384	276	248	90	...	...
	W/T	4 168	4 451	9 224	98 378	59 114	23 488	28 098	15 335	...	...
	D/J	5 158	3 485	14 959	246 071	102 119	19 209	73 585	16 153	...	...
Sudan	D/C	—	—	...	...	...	...	...	...	...	...
	W/T	—	—	...	...	...	...	...	...	...	...
	D/J	—	—	...	...	...	...	...	...	...	...
Tanzania (Tanganyika) [3] .	D/C	3	3	...	...	...	...	...	...	...	...
	W/T	357	654	...	...	...	...	...	...	...	...
	D/J	726	3 026	...	...	...	...	...	...	...	...
Tunisie	D/C	25	32	150	49	131	363	372	452	178	240
	W/T	5 887	2 623	18 458	18 473	21 000	40 671	67 386	88 335	21 433	22 430
	D/J	6 104	3 587	31 589	49 653	8 197[4]	11 750[4]	27 500[4]	140 201[4]	36 938[4]	35 287[4]
Uganda	D/C	...	44	64	34	...	...	...	...	...	...
	W/T	...	23 245	23 301	5 834	...	...	...	...	...	...
	D/J	...	55 162	56 896	15 031	...	...	...	...	...	...
Zambia	D/C	128	127	74	68	60	78	59	51	50	...
	W/T	17 040	14 964	10 453	9 892	7 725	17 121	5 619	9 166	42 067	...
	D/J	122 951	18 894	20 874	6 453	38 334	51 003	6 527	15 990	297 331	...

EXPLANATORY NOTES: See p. 629.   NOTES EXPLICATIVES: Voir p. 630.   NOTAS EXPLICATIVAS: Véase pág. 631.

D/C : Number of disputes — *Nombre de conflits* — Número de conflictos.
W/T : Workers involved — *Travailleurs impliqués* — Trabajadores afectados.
D/J : Working days lost — *Journées de travail perdues* — Días de trabajo perdidos.

[1] Excl. workers indirectly affected. [2] Year ending in March of the year indicated. [3] Excl. disputes lasting less than one day. [4] Computed on the basis of eight-hour working days.

[1] *Non compris les travailleurs indirectement atteints.* [2] *Année se terminant en mars de l'année indiquée.* [3] *Non compris les conflits dont la durée est inférieure à une journée.* [4] *Calculées sur la base de journées de travail de huit heures.*

[1] Excl. los trabajadores indirectamente afectados. [2] Año que termina en marzo del año indicado. [3] Excl. los conflictos de menos de un día de duración. [4] Calculados a base de días de trabajo de ocho horas.

DISPUTES

25 Industrial disputes
Conflits du travail
Conflictos del trabajo

Country — Pays — País	Code / Code / Clave	1970	1971	1972	1973	1974	1975	1976	1977	1978	1979
AMERICA — AMÉRIQUE / AMÉRICA											
Antigua	D/C	2	3	5	4	102	...	...	...	6	12
	W/T	25	218	...	574	149	...	...	...	199	1 503
	D/J	87	272	2 612	1 322	188	...	...	...	1 237	12 339
Argentina [1]	D/C	5	16	12	.	| 543*	1 266	...	...	...	...
	W/T	2 912	68 632	61 259	.	| 271 697*	...	...	...	...	...
	D/J	32 849	159 277	153 047	.	| 651 555*	...	...	...	...	...
Bahamas	D/C	1	—	—	...	...	...	...	...		
	W/T	153	—	—	...	...	...	...			
	D/J	1 224	—	—	...	...	...				
Barbados	D/C	—	3 [2]	7	71	2	3	2	—		...
	W/T	—	415	1 353	2 549	550	823	282	—		...
	D/J	—	54 065	1 450	4 147	2 400	3 431	129	—		...
Belize	D/C	2	...	2	4	...	...	...	...	...	...
	W/T	44	...	700	128	...	...	...	...	...	...
	D/J	439	...	17 700	240	...	...	...	...	...	...
Bermuda	D/C	5	6	13	1	5	2	1	6	3	2
	W/T	518	672	1 485	494	556	807	20	3 006	360	12
	D/J	6 098	6 107	36 006	3 613	8 444	9 545	1 260	11 986	2 270	30
Canada [3]	D/C	542	569	598	724	1 218	1 171	1 039	803	1 058	1 050
	W/T	261 706	239 631	706 474	348 470	580 912	506 443	1 570 921	217 557	401 688	462 504
	D/J	6 539 560	2 866 590	7 753 530	5 776 080	9 221 890	10 908 810	11 609 890	3 307 880	7 392 820	7 834 230
Costa Rica	D/C	...	...	...	14	8	18	14	9	15	...
	W/T	...	...	...	8 303	15 300	11 500		10 482	20 278	...
	D/J	...	...	...	17 913	328 922	47 252	...	...	...	...
Chile [4]	D/C	1 819	2 696	3 325	2 050	...	...	...	...	...	...
	W/T	656 170	298 677	393 954	711 028	...	...	...	...	...	...
	D/J	2 804 517	1 387 505	1 678 124	2 503 356	...	...	...	...	...	...
Ecuador	D/C	...	...	...	...	61	61	58	9	7	...
	W/T	...	...	...	...	5 948	11 913	7 016	802	538	...
	D/J	...	...	...	...	105 380	418 226	265 107	43 282	17 394	...
El Salvador	D/C	.	12	23	6	6*	14	2	19	29	103
	W/T	.	10 614	3 919	618	37 406*	2 902	25 300	84 879	7 169	29 432
	D/J	.	196 595	42 021	7 118	...	39 059	601 800	154 792	72 962	292 276

EXPLANATORY NOTES: See p. 629. NOTES EXPLICATIVES: Voir p. 630. NOTAS EXPLICATIVAS: Véase pág. 631.

D/C : Number of disputes — *Nombre de conflits* — Número de conflictos.
W/T : Workers involved — *Travailleurs impliqués* — Trabajadores afectados.
D/J : Working days lost — *Journées de travail perdues* — Días de trabajo perdidos.

[1] Prior to 1973: Buenos Aires City. Strikes only; excl. strikes lasting less than one day. Excl. workers indirectly affected. Beginning 1974: new series covering Great Buenos Aires. Excl. general strikes. [2] Excl. a general strike in the distributive trade, for which no information is available on the number of workers involved and working days lost. [3] Excl. disputes in which the time lost is less than ten man-days. Excl. workers indirectly affected. [4] Strikes only.

[1] *Avant 1973 : ville de Buenos Aires. Grèves seulement ; non compris les grèves dont la durée est inférieure à une journée. Non compris les travailleurs indirectement atteints. A partir de 1974 : nouvelle série couvrant le grand Buenos Aires. Non compris les grèves générales.* [2] *Non compris une grève générale dans le commerce, pour laquelle il n'y a pas d'informations sur le nombre des travailleurs impliqués et des journées de travail perdues.* [3] *Non compris les conflits pour lesquels moins de dix journées-homme sont perdues. Non compris les travailleurs indirectement atteints.* [4] *Grèves seulement.*

[1] Antes de 1973: Buenos Aires. Huelgas solamente; excl. las huelgas de menos de un día de duración. Excl. los trabajadores indirectamente afectados. A partir de 1974: nueva serie que abarca el Gran Buenos Aires. Excl. las huelgas generales. [2] Excl. una huelga general en el comercio, por no disponerse del número de trabajadores afectados y días de trabajo perdidos. [3] Excl. los conflictos en los que se pierden menos de diez días-hombre. Excl. los trabajadores indirectamente afectados. [4] Huelgas solamente.

25 Industrial disputes
Conflits du travail
Conflictos del trabajo

Country — *Pays* — País	Code *Code* Clave	1970	1971	1972	1973	1974	1975	1976	1977	1978	1979
Guadeloupe	D/C	4	6	8	8	3	4	4	51	48	35
	W/T	121	12 818	1 485	4 277	249	267	267	5 021	5 847	...
	D/J	866	145 557[1]	66 567	16 589	466	1 770	20 295	19 458	17 485	21 860*
Guatemala [2]	D/C	36	1	4	16	53	7	16	9	229	...
	W/T	27 067	92	4 868	22 711	43 934	8 336	5 757	8 670	144 956	...
	D/J	50 934	460	33 238	257 089	562 593	53 476	167 831	60 641	1 479 246	...
Guyana [2]	D/C	159	198	175	186	151	129*	400*	383	300	219
	W/T	84 056	41 447	44 597	34 692	61 932	68 616*	82 142*	89 687	52 060	106 366
	D/J	453 928	141 816	135 199	93 109	155 277	551 100*	229 480*	964 282	75 791	324 473
Guyane française	D/C	—	20	24	3	—	6	11	10	5	14
	W/T	—	1 288	1 485	89	—	765	758	1 173	79	676
	D/J	—	14 480	28 305	4 136	—	8 354	5 666	12 120	432	3 031
Jamaica [3]	D/C	70	77	55	90	137	205	142	163*	...	...
	W/T	23 181	18 623	30 286	18 726	21 194	10 993	12 169	12 557*	...	...
	D/J	335 432	76 079	266 369	236 805	769 139	112 584	139 619	81 688*	...	...
Martinique	D/C	4	9	8	5	2	5	15	...	...	...
	W/T	2 332	3 968	7 710	656	6 150	5 725	7 664	...	...	...
	D/J	16 162	32 320	268 450	9 980	48 450	131 375	24 645	...	...	...
México [2,4]	D/C	206	204	207	211	742	236	547	476	...	...
	W/T	14 329	9 299	2 684	8 395	17 863	9 680	23 684	13 411	...	...
Panamá	D/C	6	280	...	11	3	6	15	8	7	10
	W/T	7 510	15 606	...	1 414	232	...	2 080	229	1 479	1 217
	D/J [5]	13 148	...	...	...	1 063	...	18 939	8 002	4 719	18 193
Paraguay	D/C	—	—	...	...	...	...	...	...	...	...
	W/T	—	—	...	...	...	...	...	...	...	...
	D/J	—	—	...	...	...	...	...	...	...	...
Perú	D/C	345	377	409	788	570	779	440	234	364	577*
	W/T	110 990	161 415	130 643	416 251	362 737	617 120	258 101	406 461	1 398 387	703 483*
	D/J [5]	722 732	1 360 244	791 377	1 961 086	1 676 630	2 533 676	852 778	817 919	4 518 092	1 318 919*
Puerto Rico [2,6]	D/C	93	77	107	76	95	65	37	35	33	27*
	W/T	19 454	14 296	23 779	17 757	22 109	19 961	8 580	14 788	11 401	3 611*
	D/J	191 293	232 106	222 624	140 703	289 397	365 380	331 859	325 626	698 757	49 253*
St. Lucia	D/C	5	5	6	4	6	1	6	3	12	...
	W/T	583	720	490	560	1 271	600	...	...	1 308	...
	D/J	1 339	1 020	674	1 432	9 651	600	10 885	18 800	1 288	...

EXPLANATORY NOTES: See p. 629.   NOTES EXPLICATIVES: Voir p. 630.   NOTAS EXPLICATIVAS: Véase pág. 631.

D/C : Number of disputes — *Nombre de conflits* — Número de conflictos.
W/T : Workers involved — *Travailleurs impliqués* — Trabajadores afectados.
D/J : Working days lost — *Journées de travail perdues* — Días de trabajo perdidos.

[1] Excl. working days lost in agriculture. [2] Excl. workers indirectly affected. [3] Prior to 1973: excl. disputes for which data relating to workers involved and working days lost are not available. Excl. disputes concerning less than ten workers and those for which less than 100 working days have been lost. [4] Strikes only. [5] Computed on the basis of eight-hour working days. [6] Year ending in June of the year indicated.

[1] *Non compris les journées de travail perdues dans l'agriculture.* [2] *Non compris les travailleurs indirectement atteints.* [3] *Avant 1973: non compris les conflits pour lesquels les données concernant les travailleurs impliqués et les journées de travail perdues ne sont pas disponibles. Non compris les conflits touchant moins de dix travailleurs ni ceux pour lesquels moins de 100 journées de travail sont perdues.* [4] *Grèves seulement.* [5] *Calculées sur la base de journées de travail de huit heures.* [6] *Année se terminant en juin de l'année indiquée.*

[1] Excl. los días de trabajo perdidos en la agricultura. [2] Excl. los trabajadores indirectamente afectados. [3] Antes de 1973: excl. los conflictos en los cuales los datos concernientes a los trabajadores afectados y los días de trabajo perdidos no están disponibles. Excl. los conflictos que implican a menos de diez trabajadores y aquellos para los cuales se han perdido menos de 100 días de trabajo. [4] Huelgas solamente. [5] Calculados a base de días de trabajo de ocho horas. [6] Año que termina en junio del año indicado.

DISPUTES

25 Industrial disputes
Conflits du travail
Conflictos del trabajo

Country — Pays — País	Code Code Clave	1970	1971	1972	1973	1974	1975	1976	1977	1978	1979
Saint-Pierre-et-Miquelon .	D/C	—	—	...	...	...	...	...	8	6	5
	W/T	—	—	...	...	...	...	...	680	585	440
	D/J	—	—	...	...	...	...	...	1 180	2 925	880
Suriname	D/C	7	49	15	30	12	8	24	12	11	8
	W/T	420	6 641	2 826	5 073	3 438	1 999	2 044	2 845	772	2 186
	D/J	1 469	21 774	43 701	31 840	27 383	16 728	9 091	6 517	3 197	10 583
Trinidad and Tobago . . .	D/C	64	71	32	84	78	88	44	16	38	40
	W/T	11 280	18 022	8 486	18 741	55 555	35 679	26 729	5 413	10 921	10 134
	D/J	99 600	139 794	24 139	113 305	253 220	777 389	140 711	104 149	112 478	215 931
United States [1]	D/C	5 716	5 138	5 010	5 353	6 074	5 031	5 648	5 506	4 230	4 780*
	W/T	3 305 200	3 279 600	1 713 600	2 250 700	2 778 100	1 746 000	2 420 000	2 040 100	1 623 600	1 720 100*
	D/J	66 413 800	47 589 100	27 066 400	27 948 400	47 990 900	31 237 000	37 859 900	35 821 800	36 921 500	35 467 300*
Venezuela	D/C	64	106	172[3]	250	116	100	171	214	...	145
	W/T	23 934	39 094	24 654	45 508	17 463	25 752	33 932	63 923	...	23 268
	D/J [2]	234 349	519 919	146 186	144 671	129 978	100 662	91 267	687 975	...	400 126
ASIA — ASIE ASIA											
Bangladesh	D/C	.	9	39	58	32	2	5	22	89	92
	W/T	.	35 324	43 615	35 027	57 387	28 327	14 517	76 675	113 209	99 193
	D/J	.	70 333	126 000	285 177	231 736	162 000	25 618	81 715	662 332	542 244
Burma	D/C	—	—	—	—	37	—	—	...	...	...
	W/T	—	—	—	—	15 251	—	—	...	...	...
	D/J	—	—	—	—	76 364	—	—	...	...	...
Cyprus [4]	D/C	35	28	46	26	36	9	9	7	14	27
	W/T	4 725	6 867	21 431	2 790	8 498	1 132	1 007	670	7 735	7 185
	D/J	5 938	23 629	142 427	12 874	14 349	7 808	2 683	2 469	9 169	22 243
Hong Kong	D/C	47	42	46	54	19	17	16	38	51	46
	W/T	9 119	10 981	13 039	19 788	4 462	4 786	3 383	4 460	8 185	12 194
	D/J	47 243	25 600	41 834	56 691	10 708	17 600	4 977	10 814	30 927	39 743
India [5]	D/C	2 889	2 752	3 243	3 370	2 938	1 943	1 459	3 117	3 187	2 829*
	W/T	1 827 752	1 615 140	1 736 737	2 545 602	2 854 623	1 143 426	736 974	2 193 215	1 915 603	2 741 321*
	D/J	20 563 381	16 545 636	20 543 916	20 626 253	40 262 417	21 900 931	12 745 735	25 320 072	28 340 199	37 100 751*

EXPLANATORY NOTES: See p. 629.   NOTES EXPLICATIVES: Voir p. 630.   NOTAS EXPLICATIVAS: Véase pág. 631.

D/C : Number of disputes — *Nombre de conflits* — Número de conflictos.
W/T : Workers involved — *Travailleurs impliqués* — Trabajadores afectados.
D/J : Working days lost — *Journées de travail perdues* — Días de trabajo perdidos.

[1] Excl. disputes involving less than six workers and those lasting less than a full day or shift. [2] Computed on the basis of eight-hour working days. [3] Incl. 57 disputes for which data relating to workers involved and working days lost are not available. [4] Beginning July 1974: due to a change in the geographical scope of the series, data are not comparable with those for previous years. [5] Disputes involving ten or more workers; excl. political strikes.

[1] *Non compris les conflits touchant moins de six travailleurs et ceux dont la durée est inférieure à une journée ou à un poste de travail.* [2] *Calculées sur la base de journées de travail de huit heures.* [3] *Y compris 57 conflits pour lesquels les données concernant les travailleurs impliqués et les journées de travail perdues ne sont pas disponibles.* [4] *A partir de juillet 1974 : en raison d'un changement de la portée géographique de la série, les données ne sont pas comparables avec celles de la période précédente.* [5] *Conflits dans lesquels dix travailleurs ou plus sont impliqués ; non compris les grèves de caractère politique.*

[1] Excl. los conflictos que afectan a menos de seis trabajadores y los de una duración menor de un día o turno completo. [2] Calculados a base de días de trabajo de ocho horas. [3] Incl. 57 conflictos en los cuales los datos concernientes a los trabajadores afectados y los días de trabajo perdidos no están disponibles. [4] A partir de julio de 1974: en razón de un cambio del alcance geográfico de la serie, los datos no son comparables a los del período precedente. [5] Se refiere a conflictos que afectan a diez o más trabajadores; excl. las huelgas políticas.

25 Industrial disputes
Conflits du travail
Conflictos del trabajo

Country — *Pays* — País	Code *Code* Clave	1970	1971	1972	1973	1974	1975	1976	1977	1978	1979
Indonesia	D/C	—	1	1	3	6	13	6	32	20	72
	W/T	—	27	70	624	672	5 636	1 420	10 209	3 772	18 940
	D/J [1]	—	56	70	282	426	2 952	1 148	45 433	36 572	19 680
Iraq	D/C	7	—	—	—	—	—	—	—	...	...
	W/T	1 124	—	—	—	—	—	—	—	...	...
	D/J	14 000	—	—	—	—	—	—	—	...	...
Israel [2]	D/C	163	169	168	96	71	117	123	126	85	117
	W/T	114 941	88 265	87 309	122 338	27 141	114 091	114 970	194 297	224 354	250 420
	D/J	390 344	178 612	235 058	375 020	51 333	164 509	308 214	416 526	1 071 961	539 162
Japan [3]	D/C	2 260	2 527	2 498	3 326	5 211	3 391	2 720	1 712	1 517	1 153
	W/T	1 720 135	1 896 252	1 543 557	2 236 119	3 621 049	2 732 184	1 356 025	691 908	659 966	449 504
	D/J	3 914 807	6 028 746	5 146 668	4 603 821	9 662 945	8 015 772	3 253 715	1 518 476	1 357 502	930 304
Jordan	D/C	2	—	—	2	5	...	...	...	...	...
	W/T	700	—	—	240	215	...	...	...	...	...
	D/J	2 600	—	—	240	...	...	...	...	...	...
Korea, Rep. of [4]	D/C	4	10	—	—	58	52	49	58	102	105
	W/T	541	832	—	—	22 609	10 256	6 570	7 975	10 598	14 258
	D/J	9 013	11 323	—	—	16 831	13 557	17 046	8 294	13 230	16 366
Malaysia:											
Peninsular Malaysia . .	D/C	17	45	66	66	85	64	70	40	36	...
	W/T	1 216	5 311	9 701	14 003	21 830	12 124	20 040	7 783	6 792	...
	D/J	1 867	20 265	33 455	40 866	103 884	45 749	108 562	73 729	35 032	...
Sabah	D/C	8	7	7	4	7	8	5	2	5	4
	W/T	302	361	532	823	658	399	242	131	441	1 034
	D/J	446	564	567	1 530	1 459	925	695	2 011	1 766	1 112
Sarawak	D/C	1	—	1	4	3	1	6	1	7	2
	W/T	80	—	28	864	61	25	276	80	329	852
	D/J	30	—	28	1 038	214	75	410	...	518	13 872
Pakistan [5]	D/C	356	141	341	229	370	260	171	81	85	65
	W/T	272 387	107 962	125 588	126 930	301 753	129 385	77 502	49 093	58 565	38 733
	D/J	3 114 850	815 211	611 908	399 317	1 433 553	798 183	514 891	200 865	107 627	247 867
Philippines [4, 6]	D/C	104	157	69	...	...	...	91	30	47	39
	W/T	36 852	62 138	33 396	...	...	...	72 689	30 183	33 731	16 728
	D/J	994 689	1 429 195	1 003 646	...	...	...	218 067	34 198	156 203	71 246

EXPLANATORY NOTES: See p. 629.   NOTES EXPLICATIVES: Voir p. 630.   NOTAS EXPLICATIVAS: Véase pág. 631.

D/C : Number of disputes — *Nombre de conflits* — Número de conflictos.
W/T : Workers involved — *Travailleurs impliqués* — Trabajadores afectados.
D/J : Working days lost — *Journées de travail perdues* — Días de trabajo perdidos.

[1] Computed on the basis of seven-hour working days. [2] Excl. disputes where less than ten working days were lost. Prior to 1972: excl. disputes lasting two hours or less. [3] Excl. workers indirectly affected and disputes lasting less than four hours. [4] Excl. workers indirectly affected. [5] Disputes involving ten or more workers; excl. political strikes. Beginning 1971: geographical scope revised. 1973: excl. data relating to Sind province. [6] Excl. disputes involving less than six workers and those lasting less than a full day or shift.

[1] *Calculées sur la base de journées de travail de sept heures.* [2] *Non compris les conflits dans lesquels moins de dix journées de travail ont été perdues. Avant 1972 : non compris les conflits d'une durée de deux heures ou moins.* [3] *Non compris les travailleurs indirectement atteints et les conflits dont la durée est inférieure à quatre heures.* [4] *Non compris les travailleurs indirectement atteints.* [5] *Conflits dans lesquels dix ouvriers ou plus sont impliqués ; non compris les grèves de caractère politique. A partir de 1971 : portée géographique révisée. 1973 : non compris les données relatives à la province de Sind.* [6] *Non compris les conflits touchant moins de six travailleurs et ceux dont la durée est inférieure à une journée ou à un poste de travail.*

[1] Calculados a base de días de trabajo de siete horas. [2] Excl. los conflictos que causaron una pérdida menor de diez días de trabajo. Antes de 1972: excl. los conflictos de una duración de dos horas o menos. [3] Excl. los trabajadores indirectamente afectados y los conflictos de menos de cuatro horas de duración. [4] Excl. los trabajadores indirectamente afectados. [5] Se refiere a conflictos que afectan a diez o más trabajadores; excl. las huelgas políticas. A partir de 1971: alcance geográfico revisado. 1973: excl. los datos relativos a la provincia de Sind. [6] Excl. los conflictos que afectan a menos de seis trabajadores y los de una duración menor de un día o turno completo.

DISPUTES

25 Industrial disputes
Conflits du travail
Conflictos del trabajo

Country — Pays — País	Code / Code / Clave	1970	1971	1972	1973	1974	1975	1976	1977	1978	1979
Singapore	D/C	5	2	10	5	10	7	4	1	—	—
	W/T	1 749	1 380	3 168	1 312	1 901	1 865	1 576	406	—	—
	D/J	2 514	5 449	18 233	2 295	5 380	4 853	3 193	1 011	—	—
Sri Lanka [1]	D/C	340	165	187	448	91	70	157	124	134	...
	W/T	149 018	91 619	55 037	260 602	27 073	19 081	55 995	44 874	62 657	...
	D/J	1 314 563	568 161	298 898	1 179 042	105 744	66 476	161 092	222 047	265 069	...
Thailand	D/C	22	27	34	501	357	241	133	7	21	64
	W/T	2 482	5 153	7 803	177 896	105 883	94 747	65 342	4 868	6 842	16 203
	D/J	7 670	12 646	19 903	296 887	507 607	722 946	495 619	12 331	8 600	33 838
Viet Nam [2]	D/C	94	79	27	8	...	...	...	...	...	...
	W/T	60 653	35 623	9 138	2 927	...	...	...	...	...	...
	D/J	230 415	374 877	25 001	2 893	...	...	...	...	...	...
Yemen, Democratic (Aden)	D/C	4	—	—	—	—	...	...	...	...	...
	W/T	594	—	—	—	—	...	...	...	...	...
	D/J	5 589	—	—	—	—	...	...	...	...	...
EUROPE — EUROPE EUROPA											
Austria	W/T	7 547	2 431	7 096	78 251	7 295	3 783	2 352	43	699	786
	D/J	26 616	3 702	15 104	160 138	7 243	5 512	589	11	10 222	764
Belgique [3]	D/C	151	184	191	172	235	243	281	220	195	215
	W/T	107 670	86 979	66 622	62 281	55 747	85 801	106 654	65 761	90 813	55 722
	D/J	1 432 274	1 240 472	354 086	871 872	580 032	607 809	896 805	664 236	1 002 489	615 484
Denmark [4]	D/C	77	31	35	205	134	147	204	228	314	218
	W/T	55 585	6 379	7 601	337 100	142 352	59 128	87 224	36 305	59 340	156 589
	D/J	102 000	20 600	21 800	3 901 200	184 200	100 100	210 300	229 700	128 800	173 000
España	D/C	1 547	549	710	731	2 009	2 807	3 662	1 194	1 128	2 680
	W/T	440 114	196 665	236 421	303 132	557 318	504 250	2 556 373	2 955 000	3 863 855	5 713 193
	D/J [5]	1 092 364	859 693	586 616	1 081 158	1 748 695	1 815 237	12 593 100	16 641 700	11 550 911	18 916 984 [5]

EXPLANATORY NOTES: See p. 629.   NOTES EXPLICATIVES: Voir p. 630.   NOTAS EXPLICATIVAS: Véase pág. 631.

D/C : Number of disputes — *Nombre de conflits* — Número de conflictos.
W/T : Workers involved — *Travailleurs impliqués* — Trabajadores afectados.
D/J : Working days lost — *Journées de travail perdues* — Días de trabajo perdidos.

[1] Strikes only. Excl. political strikes and workers indirectly affected as well as strikes involving less than five workers or lasting less than one day except in cases where the aggregate number of man-days lost exceeds 50. [2] Data refer to the former Rep. of South Viet-Nam only. [3] Excl. workers indirectly affected. [4] Excl. political strikes. Excl. disputes where less than 100 working days were lost. [5] 1970-78: Computed on the basis of eight-hour working days. 1979: Computed on the basis of 7.35-hour working days.

[1] *Grèves seulement. Non compris les grèves de caractère politique et les travailleurs indirectement atteints, ni les grèves touchant moins de cinq travailleurs ou durant moins d'une journée, sauf dans les cas où plus de 50 journées-homme sont perdues. [2] Les données se rapportent à l'ancienne Rép. du Sud Viet-Nam seulement. [3] Non compris les travailleurs indirectement atteints. [4] Non compris les grèves de caractère politique. Non compris les conflits dans lesquels moins de 100 journées de travail sont perdues. [5] 1970-1978 : calculées sur la base de journées de travail de huit heures. 1979 : Calculées sur la base de journées de travail de 7,35 heures.*

[1] Huelgas solamente. Excl. las huelgas políticas y los trabajadores indirectamente afectados, así como las huelgas que afectan a menos de cinco trabajadores o las de duración menor de un día, salvo los casos en que el total de días-hombre perdidos exceda de 50. [2] Los datos se refieren a la antigua Rep. de Viet-Nam del Sur solamente. [3] Excl. los trabajadores indirectamente afectados. [4] Excl. las huelgas políticas. Excl. los conflictos que causaron una pérdida menor de 100 días de trabajo. [5] 1970-1978: calculados a base de días de trabajo de ocho horas. 1979: calculados a base de días de trabajo de 7,35 horas.

25 Industrial disputes
Conflits du travail
Conflictos del trabajo

Country — _Pays_ — País	Code _Code_ Clave	1970	1971	1972	1973	1974	1975	1976	1977	1978	1979
Finland [1]	D/C	240	838	849	1 010	1 795	1 530	3 199	1 633	1 207	1 715
	W/T	201 556	403 297	239 732	678 193	370 700	215 140	496 830	738 630	161 290	225 170
	D/J	233 173	2 711 100	473 100	2 496 929	434 790	284 200	1 237 830	2 374 700	132 400	243 400
France [2]	D/C	2 942	4 318	3 464	3 731	3 381	3 888	4 348	3 302	3 206	...
	W/T	1 079 800	3 234 500	2 721 348	2 245 973	1 563 540	1 827 142	2 022 500	1 919 900	704 800	...
	D/J	1 742 175	4 387 781	3 755 343	3 914 598	3 379 977	3 868 926	5 010 687	3 665 940	2 200 400	...
Germany, Fed. Rep. of [3]	W/T	184 269	536 303	22 908	185 010	250 352	35 814	169 312	34 437	487 050	77 326
	D/J	93 203	4 483 740	66 045	563 051	1 051 290	68 680	533 696	23 681	4 281 284	483 083
Gibraltar	D/C	3	2	1	10	7	8	...	...	...	...
	W/T	1 500	118	20	252	4 960	1 014	...	...	...	...
	D/J	4 500	314	2	1 873	7 800	3 040	17 000*	...	...	...
Iceland [4]	D/C	66	7	5	5	94	122	123	292	7	13
	W/T	15 855	1 790	1 100	729	30 948	20 843	35 219	48 043	29 910	805
	D/J	298 242	31 985	12 061	14 320	93 289	62 531	309 950	189 598	51 270	15 970
Ireland	D/C	134	133	131	182	219	151	134	175	152	140
	W/T	28 752	43 783	22 274	31 761	43 459	29 124	42 281	33 805	32 558	63 612
	D/J	1 007 714	273 770	206 955	206 725	551 833	295 716	776 949	442 145	624 266	1 548 322
Italie [4, 5]	D/C	4 162	5 598	4 765	3 769	5 174	3 601	2 706	3 308	2 479	2 000
	W/T	3 721 919	3 891 253	4 405 251	6 132 747	7 824 397	14 109 732	11 897 819	13 802 955	8 774 193	16 237 444
	D/J	20 887 459	14 798 589	19 497 143	23 419 286	19 466 714	27 189 142	25 377 571	16 566 143	10 177 033	27 530 428
Malta	D/C	35	23	42	60	36	30	17	62	11	14
	W/T	23 794	2 103	11 999	12 513	8 573	5 262	3 724	10 980	5 133	3 398
	D/J	148 499	24 070	14 677	42 300	15 068	14 136	6 971	75 894	28 400	33 679
Netherlands	D/C	99	15	31	7	14	5	11	19	10	30
	W/T	52 233	35 560	19 548	58 113	2 979	268	15 255	35 945	2 548	31 844
	D/J	262 810	96 846	134 187	583 783	6 854	480	13 984	236 090	2 834	306 730
Norway [6]	D/C	15	10	9	12	13	22	35	15	14	10
	W/T	3 133	2 519	1 185	2 380	22 149	3 282	21 586	2 429	4 459	2 773
	D/J	47 204	9 105	12 402	11 382	318 433	12 473	137 651	25 049	62 888	7 010

EXPLANATORY NOTES: See p. 629.   NOTES EXPLICATIVES: Voir p. 630.   NOTAS EXPLICATIVAS: Véase pág. 631.

D/C : Number of disputes — _Nombre de conflits_ — Número de conflictos.
W/T : Workers involved — _Travailleurs impliqués_ — Trabajadores afectados.
D/J : Working days lost — _Journées de travail perdues_ — Días de trabajo perdidos.

[1] Prior to 1971: excl. workers indirectly affected but incl. working days lost by these workers. Excl. disputes lasting less than four hours, except when a loss of more than 100 working days is involved. [2] Excl. agriculture and public administration. [3] Excl. disputes lasting less than one day except when a loss of more than 100 working days is involved. [4] Excl. workers indirectly affected. [5] 1969-74: excl. political strikes. [6] Excl. workers indirectly affected and disputes lasting less than one day.

[1] _Avant 1971 : non compris les travailleurs indirectement atteints, mais y compris les journées de travail perdues par ces travailleurs. Non compris les conflits dont la durée est inférieure à quatre heures, sauf dans les cas où plus de 100 journées de travail sont perdues._ [2] _Non compris l'agriculture et l'administration publique._ [3] _Non compris les conflits dont la durée est inférieure à une journée, sauf dans les cas où plus de 100 journées de travail sont perdues._ [4] _Non compris les travailleurs indirectement atteints._ [5] _1969-1974 : non compris les grèves de caractère politique._ [6] _Non compris les travailleurs indirectement atteints et les conflits dont la durée est inférieure à une journée._

[1] Antes de 1971: excl. los trabajadores indirectamente afectados, pero incl. los días de trabajo perdidos por éstos. Excl. los conflictos de menos de cuatro horas de duración, salvo los casos que implican una pérdida de más de 100 días de trabajo. [2] Excl. agricultura y administración pública. [3] Excl. los conflictos de menos de un día de duración, salvo los casos que implican una pérdida de más de 100 días de trabajo. [4] Excl. los trabajadores indirectamente afectados. [5] 1969-1974: excl. las huelgas políticas. [6] Excl. los conflictos indirectamente afectados y los conflictos de menos de un día de duración.

DISPUTES

25 Industrial disputes
Conflits du travail
Conflictos del trabajo

Country — *Pays* — País	Code *Code* Clave	1970	1971	1972	1973	1974	1975	1976	1977	1978	1979
Suisse	D/C	3	11	5	—	3	6	19	9	10	8
	W/T	320	2 267	526	—	299	323	2 395	1 380	1 240	463
	D/J	2 623	7 491	2 002	—	2 777	1 733	19 586	4 649	5 317	2 331
Sweden	D/C	134	60	44	48	85	86	73	35	99	207
	W/T	26 669	62 919	7 145	4 252	17 470	23 631	8 715	13 101	8 319	32 315
	D/J	155 700	839 000	10 507	11 802	57 604	365 507	24 744	87 151	37 135	28 664
Turquie	D/C	112	96	121	55	105	113	56	...	...	...
	W/T	21 150	10 916	13 437	12 286	22 922	13 848	7 256	...	...	...
	D/J	241 226	475 456	628 246	677 345	741 397	664 576	395 245	...	...	...
United Kingdom[1]	D/C	3 906	2 228	2 497	2 873	2 922	2 282	2 016	2 703	2 471	2 145
	W/T	1 800 700	1 178 200	1 734 400	1 527 600	1 626 400	808 900	668 000	1 165 800	1 041 500	4 607 800
	D/J	10 980 000	13 551 000	23 909 000	7 197 000	14 750 000	6 012 000	3 284 000	10 143 000	9 405 000	29 474 000
OCEANIA — OCÉANIE OCEANÍA											
Australia[2]	D/C	2 738	2 404	2 298	2 538	2 809	2 432	2 055	2 090	2 277	2 042
	W/T	1 367 400	1 326 500	1 113 800	803 000	2 004 800	1 398 000	2 189 900	596 200	1 075 700	1 862 900
	D/J	2 393 700	3 068 600	2 010 300	2 634 700	6 292 500	3 509 900	3 799 200	1 654 800	2 130 800	3 964 400
Fiji[3]	D/C	8	28	47	69	83	46	46	64	33	65
	W/T	887	5 163	5 104	13 737	7 974	12 180	5 990	10 045	4 408	4 686
	D/J	752	13 312	21 679	116 998	83 332	57 373	15 669	77 615	32 803	36 754
New Zealand[4]	D/C	323	313	266	394	380	428	487	562	411	...
	W/T	110 096	86 009	60 429	115 865	70 904	74 820	201 085	159 407	157 903	...
	D/J	277 348	162 563	134 505	271 706	183 688	214 632	488 441	436 808	380 606	...
Nouvelle-Calédonie	D/C	23	25	...	9	21	4	3	13	3	3
	W/T	4 708	5 846	...	4 064	3 811	529	358	4 733	2 670	1 214
	D/J	18 263	129 874	...	2 597	14 817	1 439	466	10 560	120 875	1 214
Polynésie Française	D/C	...	...	...	...	1	1	2	—	2	4
	W/T	...	...	...	...	400	400	600	—	52	419
	D/J	...	...	...	...	2 400	1 200	1 200	—	92	950
Solomon Is.	D/C	2	10	9	3	5	56	2	6	...	...
	W/T	381	600	425	145	317	1 264	55	278	...	...
	D/J	2 149	8 301	2 601	292	192	6 973	26	953	...	...

EXPLANATORY NOTES: See p. 629. NOTES EXPLICATIVES: Voir p. 630. NOTAS EXPLICATIVAS: Véase pág. 631.

D/C: Number of disputes — *Nombre de conflits* — Número de conflictos.
W/T: Workers involved — *Travailleurs impliqués* — Trabajadores afectados.
D/J : Working days lost — *Journées de travail perdues* — Días de trabajo perdidos.

[1] Excl. disputes not connected with terms of employment or conditions of labour. Disputes involving less than ten workers or lasting less than one day are not included unless a loss of more than 100 working days is involved. [2] Excl. disputes where less than ten working days were lost. [3] Excl. workers indirectly affected. [4] Excl. political protest stoppages.

[1] *Non compris les conflits dus à des causes autres que les conditions d'emploi ou les conditions de travail. Les conflits touchant moins de dix travailleurs ou durant moins d'une journée ne sont pas compris, sauf dans les cas ou plus de 100 journées de travail sont perdues.* [2] *Non compris les conflits dans lesquels moins de dix journées de travail sont perdues.* [3] *Non compris les travailleurs indirectement atteints.* [4] *Non compris les grèves de caractère politique.*

[1] Excl. los conflictos que no resulten del contrato de empleo o de las condiciones de trabajo. Excl. los conflictos que afectan a menos de diez trabajadores o aquellos cuya duración es menor de un día, salvo cuando implican una pérdida de más de 100 días de trabajo. [2] Excl. los conflictos que causaron una pérdida de menos de diez días de trabajo. [3] Excl. los trabajadores indirectamente afectados. [4] Excl. las huelgas políticas.

APPENDIX
ANNEXE
APENDICE

Classifications used in the " Year Book "
Classifications utilisées dans l'« Annuaire »
Clasificaciones empleadas en el « Anuario »

References and sources
Références et sources
Referencias y fuentes

International standard industrial classification of all economic activities (ISIC–1968)[1]

Major Division 1. — Agriculture, hunting, forestry and fishing:

11. Agriculture and hunting.
12. Forestry and logging.
13. Fishing.

Major Division 2. — Mining and quarrying:

21. Coal mining.
22. Crude petroleum and natural gas production.
23. Metal ore mining.
29. Other mining.

Major Division 3. — Manufacturing:

31. Manufacture of food, beverages and tobacco.
   - 311-12. Food manufacturing.
   - 313. Beverage industries.
   - 314. Tobacco manufactures.

32. Textile, wearing apparel and leather industries.
   - 321. Manufacture of textiles.
   - 322. Manufacture of wearing apparel, except footwear.
   - 323. Manufacture of leather and products of leather, leather substitutes and fur, except footwear and wearing apparel.
   - 324. Manufacture of footwear, except vulcanized or moulded rubber or plastic footwear.

33. Manufacture of wood and wood products, including furniture.
   - 331. Manufacture of wood and wood and cork products, except furniture.
   - 332. Manufacture of furniture and fixtures, except primarily of metal.

34. Manufacture of paper and paper products, printing and publishing.
   - 341. Manufacture of paper and paper products.
   - 342. Printing, publishing and allied industries.

35. Manufacture of chemicals and chemical, petroleum, coal, rubber and plastic products.
   - 351. Manufacture of industrial chemicals.
   - 352. Manufacture of other chemical products.
   - 353. Petroleum refineries.
   - 354. Manufacture of miscellaneous products of petroleum and coal.
   - 355. Manufacture of rubber products.
   - 356. Manufacture of plastic products not elsewhere classified.

36. Manufacture of non-metallic mineral products, except products of petroleum and coal.
   - 361. Manufacture of pottery, china and earthenware.
   - 362. Manufacture of glass and glass products.
   - 369. Manufacture of other non-metallic mineral products.

[1] For full details see United Nations: *Statistical Papers*, Series M, No. 4, rev. 2 (New York, 1968).

37. Basic metal industries.
    - 371. Iron and steel basic industries.
    - 372. Non-ferrous metal basic industries.

38. Manufacture of fabricated metal products, machinery and equipment.
    - 381. Manufacture of fabricated metal products, except machinery and equipment.
    - 382. Manufacture of machinery except electrical.
    - 383. Manufacture of electrical machinery apparatus, appliances and supplies.
    - 384. Manufacture of transport equipment.
    - 385. Manufacture of professional and scientific and measuring and controlling equipment not elsewhere classified, and of photographic and optical goods.

39. Other manufacturing industries.

Major Division 4. — Electricity, gas and water:

41. Electricity, gas and steam.
42. Water works and supply.

Major Division 5. — Construction:

50. Construction.

Major Division 6. — Wholesale and retail trade, restaurants and hotels:

61. Wholesale trade.
62. Retail trade.
63. Restaurants and hotels.

Major Division 7. — Transport, storage and communication:

71. Transport and storage.
72. Communication.

Major Division 8. — Financing, insurance, real estate and business services:

81. Financial institutions.
82. Insurance.
83. Real estate and business services.

Major Division 9. — Community, social and personal services:

91. Public administration and defence.
92. Sanitary and similar services.
93. Social and related community services.
94. Recreational and cultural services.
95. Personal and household services.
96. International and other extra-territorial bodies.

Major Division 0. — Activities not adequately defined:

00. Activities not adequately defined.

Classification internationale type, par industrie, de toutes les branches d'activité économique (CITI–1968) [1]

Branche 1. — Agriculture, chasse, sylviculture et pêche:

11. Agriculture et chasse.
12. Sylviculture et exploitation forestière.
13. Pêche.

Branche 2. — Industries extractives:

21. Extraction du charbon.
22. Production de pétrole brut et de gaz naturel.
23. Extraction des minerais métalliques.
29. Extraction d'autres minéraux.

Branche 3. — Industries manufacturières:

31. Fabrication de produits alimentaires, boissons et tabacs.

   311-12. Industries alimentaires.
     313. Fabrication des boissons.
     314. Industrie du tabac.

32. Industries des textiles, de l'habillement et du cuir.

     321. Industrie textile.
     322. Fabrication d'articles d'habillement, à l'exclusion des chaussures
     323. Industrie du cuir, des articles en cuir et en succédanés du cuir, et de la fourrure, à l'exclusion des chaussures et des articles d'habillement.
     324. Fabrication des chaussures, à l'exclusion des chaussures en caoutchouc vulcanisé ou moulé et des chaussures en matière plastique.

33. Industrie du bois et fabrication d'ouvrages en bois, y compris les meubles.

     331. Industrie du bois et fabrication d'ouvrages en bois et en liège, à l'exclusion des meubles.
     332. Fabrication de meubles et d'accessoires, à l'exclusion des meubles et accessoires faits principalement en métal.

34. Fabrication de papier et d'articles en papier; imprimerie et édition.

     341. Fabrication de papier et d'articles en papier.
     342. Imprimerie, édition et industries annexes.

35. Industrie chimique et fabrication de produits chimiques, de dérivés du pétrole et du charbon, et d'ouvrages en caoutchouc et en matière plastique.

     351. Industrie chimique.
     352. Fabrication d'autres produits chimiques.
     353. Raffineries de pétrole.
     354. Fabrication de divers dérivés du pétrole et du charbon.
     355. Industrie du caoutchouc.
     356. Fabrication d'ouvrages en matière plastique non classés ailleurs.

---

[1] Pour de plus amples détails, voir Nations Unies: *Etudes statistiques*, série M, n° 4, rév. 2 (New York, 1969).

Classification internationale type, par industrie, de toutes les branches d'activité économique (CITI — 1968) *(suite)*

36. Fabrication de produits minéraux non métalliques, à l'exclusion des dérivés du pétrole et du charbon.

    361. Fabrication des grès, porcelaines et faïences.
    362. Industrie du verre.
    369. Fabrication d'autres produits minéraux non métalliques.

37. Industrie métallurgique de base.

    371. Sidérurgie et première transformation de la fonte, du fer et de l'acier.
    372. Production et première transformation des métaux non ferreux.

38. Fabrication d'ouvrages en métaux, de machines et de matériel.

    381. Fabrication d'ouvrages en métaux, à l'exclusion des machines et du matériel.
    382. Construction de machines, à l'exclusion des machines électriques.
    383. Fabrication de machines, appareils et fournitures électriques.
    384. Construction de matériel de transport.
    385. Fabrication de matériel médico-chirurgical, d'instruments de précision, d'appareils de mesure et de contrôle, non classés ailleurs, de matériel photographique et d'instruments d'optique.

39. Autres industries manufacturières.

Branche 4. — Electricité, gaz et eau:

41. Electricité, gaz et vapeur.
42. Installations de distribution d'eau et distribution publique de l'eau.

Branche 5. — Bâtiment et travaux publics [1]:

50. Bâtiment et travaux publics.

Branche 6. — Commerce de gros et de détail; restaurants et hôtels:

61. Commerce de gros.
62. Commerce de détail.
63. Restaurants et hôtels.

Branche 7. — Transports, entrepôts et communications:

71. Transports et entrepôts.
72. Communications.

Branche 8. — Banque, assurances, affaires immobilières et services fournis aux entreprises:

81. Etablissements financiers.
82. Assurances.
83. Affaires immobilières et services fournis aux entreprises.

---

[1] Dans le but de faciliter la présentation des tableaux du présent *Annuaire*, les données relatives à cette branche figurent sous la dénomination « Construction ».

Branche 9. — Services fournis à la collectivité, services sociaux et services personnels:

91. Administration publique et défense nationale.
92. Services sanitaires et services analogues.
93. Services sociaux et services connexes fournis à la collectivité.
94. Services récréatifs et services culturels annexes.
95. Services fournis aux particuliers et aux ménages.
96. Organisations internationales et autres organismes extra-territoriaux.

Branche 0. — Activités mal désignées:

00. Activités mal désignées.

Clasificación industrial internacional uniforme de todas las actividades económicas (CIIU–1968) [1]

Gran división 1. — Agricultura, caza, silvicultura y pesca:

11. Agricultura y caza.
12. Silvicultura y extracción de madera.
13. Pesca.

Gran división 2. — Explotación de minas y canteras:

21. Explotación de minas de carbón.
22. Producción de petróleo crudo y gas natural.
23. Extracción de minerales metálicos.
29. Extracción de otros minerales.

Gran división 3. — Industrias manufactureras:

31. Productos alimenticios, bebidas y tabaco.

  311-12. Fabricación de productos alimenticios.
    313. Industrias de bebidas.
    314. Industria del tabaco.

32. Textiles, prendas de vestir e industrias del cuero.

    321. Fabricación de textiles.
    322. Fabricación de prendas de vestir, excepto calzado.
    323. Industria del cuero y productos de cuero y sucedáneos de cuero y pieles, excepto el calzado y otras prendas de vestir.
    324. Fabricación de calzado, excepto el de caucho vulcanizado o moldeado o de plástico.

33. Industria de la madera y productos de la madera, incluidos muebles.

    331. Industria de la madera y productos de madera y de corcho, excepto muebles.
    332. Fabricación de muebles y accesorios, excepto los que son principalmente metálicos.

34. Fabricación de papel y productos de papel; imprentas y editoriales.

    341. Fabricación de papel y productos de papel.
    342. Imprentas, editoriales e industrias conexas.

35. Fabricación de sustancias químicas y de productos químicos, derivados del petróleo y del carbón, de caucho y plásticos.

    351. Fabricación de substancias químicas industriales.
    352. Fabricación de otros productos químicos.
    353. Refinerías de petróleo.
    354. Fabricación de productos diversos derivados del petróleo y del carbón.
    355. Fabricación de productos de caucho.
    356. Fabricación de productos plásticos, n.e.p.

---

[1] Para más amplios detalles, véase Naciones Unidas: *Informes estadísticos*, serie M, núm. 4, rev. 2 (Nueva York, 1969).

Clasificación industrial internacional uniforme de todas las actividades económicas (CIIU — 1968) *(cont.)*

36. Fabricación de productos minerales no metálicos, exceptuando los derivados del petróleo y del carbón.

    361. Fabricación de objetos de barro, loza y porcelana.
    362. Fabricación de vidrio y productos de vidrio.
    369. Fabricación de otros productos minerales no metálicos.

37. Industrias metálicas básicas.

    371. Industrias básicas de hierro y acero.
    372. Industrias básicas de metales no ferrosos.

38. Fabricación de productos metálicos, maquinaria y equipo.

    381. Fabricación de productos metálicos, exceptuando maquinaria y equipo.
    382. Construcción de maquinaria, exceptuando la eléctrica.
    383. Construcción de maquinaria, aparatos, accesorios y suministros eléctricos.
    384. Construcción de material de transporte.
    385. Fabricación de equipo profesional y científico, instrumentos de medida y de control n.e.p., y de aparatos fotográficos e instrumentos de óptica.

39. Otras industrias manufactureras.

Gran división 4. — Electricidad, gas y agua:

41. Electricidad, gas y vapor.
42. Obras hidráulicas y suministro de agua.

Gran división 5. — Construcción:

50. Construcción.

Gran división 6. — Comercio al por mayor y al por menor y restaurantes y hoteles:

61. Comercio al por mayor.
62. Comercio al por menor.
63. Restaurantes y hoteles.

Gran división 7. — Transportes, almacenamiento y comunicaciones:

71. Transporte y almacenamiento.
72. Comunicaciones.

Gran división 8. — Establecimientos financieros, seguros, bienes inmuebles y servicios prestados a las empresas:

81. Establecimientos financieros.
82. Seguros.
83. Bienes inmuebles y servicios prestados a las empresas.

Clasificación industrial internacional uniforme de todas las actividades
económicas (CIIU – 1968) *(fin)*

Gran división 9. — Servicios comunales, sociales y personales:

91. Administración pública y defensa.
92. Servicios de saneamiento y similares.
93. Servicios sociales y otros servicios comunales conexos.
94. Servicios de diversión y esparcimiento y servicios culturales.
95. Servicios personales y de los hogares.
96. Organizaciones internacionales y otros organismos extraterritoriales.

Gran división 0. — Actividades no bien especificadas:

00. Actividades no bien especificadas.

International standard classification of occupations (ISCO–1968)[1]

Major Group 0/1. — Professional, technical and related workers:

0-1.   Physical scientists and related technicians.
0-2/3. Architects, engineers and related technicians.
0-4.   Aircraft and ships' officers.
0-5.   Life scientists and related technicians.
0-6/7. Medical, dental, veterinary and related workers.
0-8.   Statisticians, mathematicians, systems analysts and related technicians.
0-9.   Economists.
1-1.   Accountants.
1-2.   Jurists.
1-3.   Teachers.
1-4.   Workers in religion.
1-5.   Authors, journalists and related writers.
1-6.   Sculptors, painters, photographers and related creative artists.
1-7.   Composers and performing artists.
1-8.   Athletes, sportsmen and related workers.
1-9.   Professional, technical and related workers not elsewhere classified.

Major Group 2. — Administrative and managerial workers:

2-0.   Legislative officials and government administrators.
2-1.   Managers.

Major Group 3. — Clerical and related workers:

3-0.   Clerical supervisors.
3-1.   Government executive officials.
3-2.   Stenographers, typists and card- and tape-punching machine operators.
3-3.   Bookkeepers, cashiers and related workers.
3-4.   Computing machine operators.
3-5.   Transport and communications supervisors.
3-6.   Transport conductors.
3-7.   Mail distribution clerks.
3-8.   Telephone and telegraph operators.
3-9.   Clerical related workers not elsewhere classified.

Major Group 4. — Sales workers:

4-0.   Managers (wholesale and retail trade).
4-1.   Working proprietors (wholesale and retail trade).
4-2.   Sales supervisors and buyers.
4-3.   Technical salesmen, commercial travellers and manufacturers' agents.
4-4.   Insurance, real estate, securities and business services salesman and auctioneers.
4-5.   Salesmen, shop assistants and related workers.
4-9.   Sales workers not elsewhere classified.

---

[1] Major and minor groups only; for full details see ILO: *International Standard Classification of Occupations, revised edition 1968* (Geneva, 1969).

Major Group 5. — Service workers:

5-0. Managers (catering and lodging services).
5-1. Working proprietors (catering and lodging services).
5-2. Housekeeping and related service supervisors.
5-3. Cooks, waiters, bartenders and related workers.
5-4. Maids and related housekeeping service workers not elsewhere classified.
5-5. Building caretakers, charworkers, cleaners and related workers.
5-6. Launderers, dry-cleaners and pressers.
5-7. Hairdressers, barbers, beauticians and related workers.
5-8. Protective service workers.
5-9. Service workers not elsewhere classified.

Major Group 6. — Agriculture, animal husbandry and forestry workers, fishermen and hunters:

6-0. Farm managers and supervisors.
6-1. Farmers.
6-2. Agriculture and animal husbandry workers.
6-3. Forestry workers.
6-4. Fishermen, hunters and related workers.

Major Group 7/8/9. — Production and related workers, transport equipment operators and labourers:

7-0. Production supervisors and general foremen.
7-1. Miners, quarrymen, well drillers and related workers.
7-2. Metal processers.
7-3. Wood preparation workers and paper makers.
7-4. Chemical processers and related workers.
7-5. Spinners, weavers, knitters, dyers and related workers.
7-6. Tanners, fellmongers and pelt dressers.
7-7. Food and beverage processers.
7-8. Tobacco preparers and tobacco product makers.
7-9. Tailors, dressmakers, sewers, upholsterers and related workers.

8-0. Shoemakers and leather goods makers.
8-1. Cabinetmakers and related woodworkers.
8-2. Stone cutters and carvers.
8-3. Blacksmiths, toolmakers and machine-tool operators.
8-4. Machinery fitters, machine assemblers and precision instrument makers (except electrical).
8-5. Electrical fitters and related electrical and electronics workers.
8-6. Broadcasting station and sound equipment operators and cinema projectionists.
8-7. Plumbers, welders, sheet metal and structural metal preparers and erectors.
8-8. Jewellery and precious metal workers.
8-9. Glass formers, potters and related workers.

9-0. Rubber and plastics product makers.
9-1. Paper and paperboard products makers.
9-2. Printers and related workers.

9-3. Painters.
9-4. Production and related workers not elsewhere classified.
9-5. Bricklayers, carpenters and other construction workers.
9-6. Stationary engine and related equipment operators.
9-7. Material-handling and related equipment operators, dockers and freight handlers.
9-8. Transport equipment operators.
9-9. Labourers not elsewhere classified.

Major Group X. — Workers not classifiable by occupation:

X-1. New workers seeking employment.
X-2. Workers reporting occupations unidentifiable or inadequately described.
X-3. Workers not reporting any occupation.

Armed Forces. — Members of the armed forces.

Classification internationale type des professions (CITP–1968)[1]

Grand groupe 0/1. — Personnel des professions scientifiques, techniques, libérales et assimilées:

0-1.   Spécialistes des sciences physico-chimiques et techniciens assimilés.
0-2/3. Architectes, ingénieurs et techniciens assimilés.
0-4.   Pilotes, officiers de pont et officiers mécaniciens (marine et aviation).
0-5.   Biologistes, agronomes et techniciens assimilés.
0-6/7. Médecins, dentistes, vétérinaires et travailleurs assimilés.
0-8.   Statisticiens, mathématiciens, analystes de systèmes et techniciens assimilés.
0-9.   Economistes.
1-1.   Comptables.
1-2.   Juristes.
1-3.   Personnel enseignant.
1-4.   Membres du clergé et assimilés.
1-5.   Auteurs, journalistes et écrivains assimilés.
1-6.   Sculpteurs, peintres, photographes et artistes créateurs assimilés.
1-7.   Musiciens, acteurs, danseurs et artistes assimilés.
1-8.   Athlètes, sportifs et assimilés.
1-9.   Personnel des professions scientifiques, techniques, libérales et assimilés non classé ailleurs.

Grand groupe 2. — Directeurs et cadres administratifs supérieurs:

2-0.   Membres des corps législatifs et cadres supérieurs de l'administration publique.
2-1.   Directeurs et cadres dirigeants.

Grand groupe 3. — Personnel administratif et travailleurs assimilés:

3-0.   Chefs de groupe d'employés de bureau.
3-1.   Agents administratifs (administration publique).
3-2.   Sténographes dactylographes et opérateurs sur machines perforatrices de cartes et de rubans.
3-3.   Employés de comptabilité, caissiers et travailleurs assimilés.
3-4.   Opérateurs sur machines à traiter l'information.
3-5.   Chefs de services de transports et de communications.
3-6.   Chefs de train et receveurs.
3-7.   Facteurs et messagers.
3-8.   Opérateurs des téléphones et télégraphes.
3-9.   Personnel administratif et travailleurs assimilés non classés ailleurs.

Grand groupe 4. — Personnel commercial et vendeurs:

4-0.   Directeurs (commerces de gros et de détail).
4-1.   Propriétaires-gérants de commerces de gros et de détail.
4-2.   Chefs des ventes et acheteurs.
4-3.   Agents commerciaux techniciens et voyageurs de commerce.
4-4.   Agents d'assurances, agents immobiliers, courriers en valeurs, agents de vente de services aux entreprises et vendeurs aux enchères.
4-5.   Commis vendeurs, employés de commerce et travailleurs assimilés.
4-9.   Personnel commercial et vendeurs non classés ailleurs.

---

[1] Grands et sous-groupes seulement; pour de plus amples détails, voir BIT: *Classification internationale type des professions, édition révisée, 1968* (Genève, 1969).

Grand groupe 5. — Travailleurs spécialisés dans les services:

5-0. Directeurs d'hôtels, de cafés ou de restaurants.
5-1. Propriétaires-gérants d'hôtels, de cafés ou de restaurants.
5-2. Chefs de groupe d'employés de maison et travailleurs assimilés.
5-3. Cuisiniers, serveurs, barmen et travailleurs assimilés.
5-4. Employés de maison et travailleurs assimilés non classés ailleurs.
5-5. Gardiens d'immeubles, nettoyeurs et travailleurs assimilés.
5-6. Blanchisseurs, dégraisseurs et presseurs.
5-7. Coiffeurs, spécialistes des soins de beauté et travailleurs assimilés.
5-8. Personnel des services de protection et de sécurité.
5-9. Travailleurs spécialisés dans les services non classés ailleurs.

Grand groupe 6. — Agriculteurs, éleveurs, forestiers, pêcheurs et chasseurs:

6-0. Directeurs et chefs d'exploitations agricoles.
6-1. Exploitants agricoles.
6-2. Travailleurs agricoles.
6-3. Travailleurs forestiers.
6-4. Pêcheurs, chasseurs et travailleurs assimilés.

Grand groupe 7/8/9. — Ouvriers et manœuvres non agricoles et conducteurs d'engins de transport:

7-0. Agents de maîtrise et assimilés.
7-1. Mineurs, carriers, foreurs de puits et travailleurs assimilés.
7-2. Ouvriers de la production et du traitement des métaux.
7-3. Ouvriers de la première préparation des bois et de la fabrication du papier.
7-4. Conducteurs de fours et d'appareils chimiques.
7-5. Ouvriers du textile.
7-6. Tanneurs, peaussiers, mégissiers et ouvriers de la pelleterie.
7-7. Ouvriers de l'alimentation et des boissons.
7-8. Ouvriers des tabacs.
7-9. Tailleurs, couturiers, couseurs, tapissiers et ouvriers assimilés.

8-0. Bottiers, ouvriers de la chaussure et du cuir.
8-1. Ebénistes, menuisiers et travailleurs assimilés.
8-2. Tailleurs et graveurs de pierres.
8-3. Ouvriers du façonnage et de l'usinage des métaux.
8-4. Ajusteurs-monteurs, installateurs de machines et mécaniciens de précision (électriciens exceptés).
8-5. Electriciens, électroniciens et travailleurs assimilés.
8-6. Opérateurs de stations d'émissions de radio et de télévision, opérateurs d'appareils de sonorisation et projectionnistes de cinéma.
8-7. Plombiers soudeurs, tôliers-chaudronniers, monteurs de charpentes et de structures métalliques.
8-8. Joailliers et orfèvres.
8-9. Verriers, potiers et travailleurs assimilés.

9-0. Ouvriers de la fabrication d'articles en caoutchouc et en matières plastiques.
9-1. Confectionneurs d'articles en papier et en carton.
9-2. Compositeurs typographes et travailleurs assimilés.
9-3. Peintres.
9-4. Ouvriers à la production et assimilés non classés ailleurs.
9-5. Maçons, charpentiers et autres travailleurs de la construction.
9-6. Conducteurs de machines et d'installations fixes.
9-7. Conducteurs d'engins de manutention et de terrassement, dockers et manutentionnaires.
9-8. Conducteurs d'engins de transport.
9-9. Manœuvres non classés ailleurs.

Grand groupe X. — Travailleurs ne pouvant être classés selon la profession:

X-1. Personnes en quête de leur premier emploi.
X-2. Travailleurs ayant fait au sujet de leur profession une déclaration imprécise ou insuffisante.
X-3. Travailleurs n'ayant déclaré aucune profession.

Forces armées: Membres des forces armées.

Clasificación internacional uniforme de ocupaciones (CIUO–1968) [1]

Gran grupo 0/1. — Profesionales, técnicos y trabajadores asimilados:

0-1.   Especialistas en ciencias físico-químicas y técnicos asimilados.
0-2/3. Arquitectos, ingenieros y técnicos asimilados.
0-4.   Pilotos y oficiales de cubierta y oficiales maquinistas (aviación y marina).
0-5.   Biólogos, agrónomos y técnicos asimilados.
0-6/7. Médicos, odontólogos, veterinarios y trabajadores asimilados.
0-8.   Estadígrafos, matemáticos, analistas de sistemas y técnicos asimilados.
0-9.   Economistas.
1-1.   Contadores.
1-2.   Juristas.
1-3.   Profesores.
1-4.   Miembros del clero y asimilados.
1-5.   Autores, periodistas y escritores asimilados.
1-6.   Escultores, pintores, fotógrafos y artistas asimilados.
1-7.   Músicos, artistas, empresarios y productores de espectáculos.
1-8.   Atletas, deportistas y trabajadores asimilados.
1-9.   Profesionales, técnicos y trabajadores asimilados no clasificados bajo otros epígrafes.

Gran grupo 2. — Directores y funcionarios públicos superiores:

2-0.   Miembros de los cuerpos legislativos y personal directivo de la administración pública.
2-1.   Directores y personal directivo.

Gran grupo 3. — Personal administrativo y trabajadores asimilados:

3-0.   Jefes de empleados de oficinas.
3-1.   Agentes administrativos (administración pública).
3-2.   Taquígrafos, mecanógrafos y operadores de máquinas perforadoras de tarjetas y cintas.
3-3.   Empleados de contabilidad, cajeros y trabajadores asimilados.
3-4.   Operadores de máquinas para cálculos contables y estadísticos.
3-5.   Jefes de servicios de transportes y de comunicaciones.
3-6.   Jefes de tren, controladores de coches-cama y cobradores.
3-7.   Carteros y mensajeros.
3-8.   Telefonistas y telegrafistas.
3-9.   Personal administrativo y trabajadores asimilados no clasificados bajo otros epígrafes.

Gran grupo 4. — Comerciantes y vendedores:

4-0.   Directores (comercio al por mayor y al por menor).
4-1.   Comerciantes propietarios (comercio al por mayor y al por menor).
4-2.   Jefes de ventas y compradores.
4-3.   Agentes técnicos de ventas, viajantes de comercio y representantes de fábrica.
4-4.   Agentes de seguros, agentes inmobiliarios, agentes de cambio y bolsa, agentes de venta de servicios a las empresas y subastadores.
4-5.   Vendedores, empleados de comercio y trabajadores asimilados.
4-9.   Comerciantes y vendedores no clasificados bajo otros epígrafes.

---

[1] Grandes grupos y subgrupos solamente; para más amplios detalles, véase OIT: *Clasificación internacional uniforme de ocupaciones, edición revisada, 1968* (Ginebra, 1970).

Gran grupo 5. — Trabajadores de los servicios:

5-0. Directores (servicios de hostelería, bares y similares).
5-1. Gerentes propietarios (servicios de hostelería, bares y similares).
5-2. Jefes de personal de servidumbre.
5-3. Cocineros, camareros, bármanes y trabajadores asimilados.
5-4. Personal de servidumbre no clasificado bajo otros epígrafes.
5-5. Guardianes de edificios, personal de limpieza y trabajadores asimilados.
5-6. Lavanderos, limpiadores en seco y planchadores.
5-7. Peluqueros, especialistas en tratamientos de belleza y trabajadores asimilados.
5-8. Personal de los servicios de protección y de seguridad.
5-9. Trabajadores de los servicios no clasificados bajo otros epígrafes.

Gran grupo 6. — Trabajadores agrícolas y forestales, pescadores y cazadores:

6-0. Directores y jefes de explotaciones agrícolas.
6-1. Explotadores agrícolas.
6-2. Obreros agrícolas.
6-3. Trabajadores forestales.
6-4. Pescadores, cazadores y trabajadores asimilados.

Gran grupo 7/8/9. — Obreros no agrícolas, conductores de máquinas y vehículos de transporte y trabajadores asimilados:

7-0. Contramaestres y capataces mayores.
7-1. Mineros, canteros, sondistas y trabajadores asimilados.
7-2. Obreros metalúrgicos.
7-3. Obreros del tratamiento de la madera y de la fabricación de papel.
7-4. Obreros de los tratamientos químicos y trabajadores asimilados.
7-5. Hilanderos, tejedores, tintoreros y trabajadores asimilados.
7-6. Obreros de la preparación, curtido y tratamiento de pieles.
7-7. Obreros de la preparación de alimentos y bebidas.
7-8. Obreros del tabaco.
7-9. Sastres, modistos, peleteros, tapiceros y trabajadores asimilados.

8-0. Zapateros y guarnicioneros.
8-1. Ebanistas, operadores de máquinas de labrar madera y trabajadores asimilados.
8-2. Labrantes y adornistas.
8-3. Obreros de la labra de metales.
8-4. Ajustadores-montadores e instaladores de maquinaria e instrumentos de precisión, relojeros y mecánicos (excepto electricistas).
8-5. Electricistas, electronicistas y trabajadores asimilados.
8-6. Operadores de estaciones emisoras de radio y televisión y de equipos de sonorización y de proyecciones cinematográficas.
8-7. Fontaneros, soldadores, chapistas, caldereros y preparadores y montadores de estructuras metálicas.
8-8. Joyeros y plateros.
8-9. Vidrieros, ceramistas y trabajadores asimilados.

9-0. Obreros de la fabricación de productos de caucho y plástico.
9-1. Confeccionadores de productos de papel y cartón.
9-2. Obreros de las artes gráficas.
9-3. Pintores.
9-4. Obreros manufactureros y trabajadores asimilados no clasificados bajo otros epígrafes.
9-5. Obreros de la construcción.
9-6. Operadores de máquinas fijas y de instalaciones similares.
9-7. Obreros de la manipulación de mercancías y materiales y de movimiento de tierras.
9-8. Conductores de vehículos de transporte.
9-9. Peones no clasificados bajo otros epígrafes.

Gran grupo X. — Trabajadores que no pueden ser clasificados según la ocupación:

X-1. Personas en busca de su primer empleo.
X-2. Trabajadores que han declarado ocupaciones no identificables o insuficientemente descritas.
X-3. Trabajadores que no han declarado ninguna ocupación.

Fuerzas armadas. — Miembros de las fuerzas armadas.

References and sources
Références et sources
Referencias y fuentes

The references given in **Part A** are a selected list of International Labour Office publications on methodology and practice in the field of labour statistics.

Part B lists the *principal* sources of current national statistics on labour topics, generally those cited by governments forwarding data for the *Year Book of Labour Statistics*. They often contain more detailed statistics than the Office has been able to use in the *Year Book*. Readers making investigations covering an extended period should also refer to previous issues of the *Year Book* and the sources listed therein.

Countries are grouped by continents in the alphabetical order, as presented in page xix. So far as possible the title of each publication is given in the respective national language. Where a publication contains translations into English (or French) the official English (or French) title is given in parentheses.

Les références présentées dans la **partie A** fournissent une liste sélectionnée de publications du Bureau international du Travail traitant des pratiques et des méthodes utilisées en matière de statistiques du travail.

La **partie B** contient les sources *principales* dans lesquelles sont publiées les statistiques nationales courantes sur les divers aspects du travail; en général, ces sources sont celles qui ont été transmises par les gouvernements en annexe aux données fournies pour l'*Annuaire des statistiques du travail*. On y trouvera souvent des statistiques plus détaillées que celles que le Bureau a pu utiliser dans l'*Annuaire*. Il est recommandé aux lecteurs qui se livrent à des recherches portant sur une période assez longue de consulter les éditions précédentes de l'*Annuaire* et les sources qui y sont indiquées.

Les pays sont groupés par continents, suivant l'ordre alphabétique tel qu'il est présenté à la page xix. Dans la mesure du possible, le titre de chaque publication est donné dans la langue nationale respective. Lorsque la publication contient des traductions en français (ou en anglais), le titre officiel français (ou anglais) est indiqué entre parenthèses.

Las referencias dadas en la **parte A** comprenden una selección de publicaciones de la Oficina Internacional del Trabajo sobre la metodología y la práctica en materia de estadísticas del trabajo.

La **parte B** contiene las *principales* fuentes de las estadísticas nacionales de la actualidad sobre temas del trabajo; en general, aquellas que los propios gobiernos citan al proporcionar los datos para el *Anuario de Estadísticas del Trabajo*. A menudo contienen estadísticas más detalladas que las que la Oficina ha podido usar en el *Anuario*. Los lectores que deseen practicar investigaciones que abarquen un período más extenso deben consultar, además, las ediciones anteriores del *Anuario* y las fuentes allí indicadas.

Los países se agrupan por continentes, en el orden alfabético tal como se presenta en la página xx. En la medida de lo posible, el título de cada publicación aparece en el idioma nacional respectivo. Cuando una publicación contiene traducciones al francés (o al inglés), su título oficial en francés (o en inglés) se indica entre paréntesis.

References and sources Références et sources Referencias y fuentes	A	References Références Referencias

Subject — *Sujet* — Sujeto	Publications — *Publications* — Publicaciones
General **Général** **General**	*International Recommendations on Labour Statistics* (Geneva, 1976) *Recommandations internationales sur les statistiques du travail* (Genève, 1975) *Recomendaciones internacionales sobre estadísticas del trabajo* (Ginebra, 1975) *International Standard Classification of Occupations (Revised 1968)* (Geneva, 1969) *Classification internationale type des professions (révisée 1968)* (Genève, 1969) *Clasificación internacional uniforme de ocupaciones (revisada, 1968)* (Ginebra, 1970) *Revision of the International Standard Classification of Occupations*, Eleventh International Conference of Labour Statisticians, Report III (Geneva, 1966) *Révision de la Classification internationale type des professions*, onzième Conférence internationale des statisticiens du travail, rapport III (Genève, 1966) *Revisión de la Clasificación internacional uniforme de ocupaciones*, undécima Conferencia Internacional de Estadígrafos del Trabajo, Informe III (Ginebra, 1966)

Employment and unemployment
Emploi et chômage
Empleo y desempleo
	Employment, Unemployment and Labour Force Statistics, A Study of Methods, Studies and Reports, New Series, No. 7, Part 1 (Geneva, 1948)
	Statistiques de l'emploi, du chômage et de la main-d'œuvre, Etude méthodologique, Etudes et documents, nouvelle série, nº 7, partie 1 (Genève, 1948)
	Estadísticas del empleo, del desempleo y de la mano de obra, Estudio metodológico, Estudios y documentos, nueva serie, núm. 7, parte 1 (Ginebra, 1948)
	
	Employment and Unemployment Statistics, Eighth International Conference of Labour Statisticians, Report IV (Geneva, 1954)
	Statistiques de l'emploi et du chômage, huitième Conférence internationale des statisticiens du travail, rapport IV (Genève, 1954)
	Estadísticas del empleo y del desempleo, octava Conferencia Internacional de Estadígrafos del Trabajo, Informe IV (Ginebra, 1954)
	
	Measurement of Underemployment, Ninth International Conference of Labour Statisticians, Report IV (Geneva, 1957)
	Mesure du sous-emploi, neuvième Conférence internationale des statisticiens du travail, rapport IV (Genève, 1957)
	Medición del subempleo, novena Conferencia Internacional de Estadígrafos del Trabajo, Informe IV (Ginebra, 1957)
	
	Measurement of Underemployment, Concepts and Methods, Eleventh International Conference of Labour Statisticians, Report IV (Geneva, 1966)
	Mesure du sous-emploi, concepts et méthodes, onzième Conférence internationale des statisticiens du travail, rapport IV (Genève, 1966)
	Medición del subempleo, conceptos y métodos, undécima Conferencia Internacional de Estadígrafos del Trabajo, Informe IV (Ginebra, 1966)
	
	Labour Force Estimates and Projections, 1950-2000 (Geneva, 1977)
	    Vol. I: Asia—Vol. II: Africa—Vol. III: Latin America—Vol. IV: Europe, Northern America, Oceania and USSR—Vol. V: World Summary—Vol. VI: Methodological Supplement
	Evaluations et projections de la main-d'œuvre, 1950-2000 (Genève, 1977)
	    Vol. I: Asie — Vol. II: Afrique — Vol. III: Amérique latine — Vol. IV: Europe, Amérique du Nord, Océanie et URSS — Vol. V: Monde (résumé) — Vol. VI: Supplément méthodologique
	Estimaciones y proyecciones de la fuerza de trabajo, 1950-2000 (Ginebra, 1977)
	    Vol. I: Asia — Vol. II: Africa — Vol. III: América latina — Vol. IV: Europa, América del Norte, Oceanía y URSS — Vol. V: Mundo (resumen) — Vol. VI: Suplemento metodológico

REFERENCES

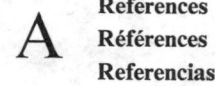
Subject — *Sujet* — Sujeto	Publications — *Publications* — Publicaciones
Employment and unemployment (concl.) **Emploi et chomage** (fin) **Empleo y desempleo** (fin)	*Technical Guide 1980*, Descriptions of general series published in both the *Bulletin* and the *Year Book of Labour Statistics*, Vol. II, Employment—Unemployment—Hours of work—Wages (Geneva, 1980) *Guide technique 1980*, descriptions des séries générales publiées à la fois dans le *Bulletin* et l'*Annuaire des statistiques du travail*, vol. II, Emploi — Chômage — Durée du travail — Salaires (Genève, 1980) *Guía Técnica 1980*, descripciones de las series generales publicadas al mismo tiempo en el *Boletín* y el *Anuario de Estadísticas del Trabajo*, vol. II, Empleo — Desempleo — Horas de trabajo — Salarios (Ginebra, 1980)
Hours of work **Durée du travail** **Horas de trabajo**	*Statistics of Hours of Work*, Tenth International Conference of Labour Statisticians, Report III (Geneva, 1962) *Statistiques de la durée du travail*, dixième Conférence internationale des statisticiens du travail, rapport III (Genève, 1962) *Estadísticas de la duración del trabajo*, décima Conferencia Internacional de Estadígrafos del Trabajo, Informe III (Ginebra, 1962) *Technical Guide 1980*, Descriptions of general series published in both the *Bulletin* and the *Year Book of Labour Statistics*, Vol. II, Employment—Unemployment—Hours of work—Wages (Geneva, 1980) *Guide technique 1980*, descriptions des séries générales publiées à la fois dans le *Bulletin* et l'*Annuaire des statistiques du travail*, vol. II, Emploi — Chômage — Durée du travail — Salaires (Genève, 1980) *Guía Técnica 1980*, descripciones de las series generales publicadas al mismo tiempo en el *Boletín* y el *Anuario de Estadísticas del Trabajo*, vol. II, Empleo — Desempleo — Horas de trabajo — Salarios (Ginebra, 1980)
Wages **Salaires** **Salarios**	*Wages and Payroll Statistics*, Studies and Reports, New Series, No. 16 (Geneva, 1949) *Statistiques des bordereaux des salaires et des gains*, Etudes et documents, nouvelle série, nº 16 (Genève, 1949) *Estadísticas de nóminas de salarios y de ganancias*, Estudios y documentos, nueva serie, núm. 16 (Ginebra, 1949) *International Comparisons of Real Wages*, Studies and Reports, New Series, No. 45 (Geneva, 1956) *Les comparaisons internationales des salaires réels*, Etudes et documents, nouvelle série, nº 45 (Genève, 1956) *Statistics of Labour Cost*, Eleventh International Conference of Labour Statisticians, Report II (Geneva, 1966) *Statistiques du coût de la main-d'œuvre*, onzième Conférence internationale des statisticiens du travail, rapport II (Genève, 1966) *Estadísticas del costo de la mano de obra*, undécima Conferencia Internacional de Estadígrafos del Trabajo, Informe II (Ginebra, 1966) *Statistics of Wages and Employee Income*, Twelfth International Conference of Labour Statisticians, Report II (Geneva, 1973) *Statistiques des salaires et du revenu salarial*, douzième Conférence internationale des statisticiens du travail, rapport II (Genève, 1973) *Estadísticas de salarios e ingresos de los trabajadores*, duodécima Conferencia Internacional de Estadígrafos del Trabajo, Informe II (Ginebra, 1973) *An integrated system of wages statistics : a manual on methods* (Geneva, 1979) *Un système intégré des statistiques des salaires — Manuel de méthodologie* (Genève, 1980) (edición española en preparación) *Technical Guide 1980*, Descriptions of general series published in both the *Bulletin* and the *Year Book of Labour Statistics*, Vol. II, Employment—Unemployment—Hours of work—Wages (Geneva, 1980) *Guide technique 1980*, descriptions des séries générales publiées à la fois dans le *Bulletin* et l'*Annuaire des statistiques du travail*, vol. II, Emploi — Chômage — Durée du travail — Salaires (Genève, 1980) *Guía Técnica 1980*, descripciones de las series generales publicadas al mismo tiempo en el *Boletín* y el *Anuario de Estadísticas del Trabajo*, vol. II, Empleo — Desempleo — Horas de trabajo — Salarios (Ginebra, 1980)

References and sources
Références et sources
Referencias y fuentes

A
References
Références
Referencias

Subject — *Sujet* — Sujeto	Publications — *Publications* — Publicaciones
Consumer prices **Prix à la consommation** **Precios del consumo**	*A Contribution to the Study of International Comparisons of Cost of Living*, Studies and Reports, Series N, No. 17 (Geneva, 1932) *Contribution à l'étude de la comparaison internationale du coût de la vie*, Etudes et documents, série N, nº 17 (Genève, 1932)
	International Comparisons of Cost of Living, Studies and Reports, Series N, No. 20 (Geneva, 1934) *La comparaison internationale du coût de la vie*, Etudes et documents, série N, nº 20 (Genève, 1934)
	Cost-of-Living Statistics, Studies and Reports, New Series, No. 7, Part 2 (Geneva, 1948) *Statistiques du coût de la vie*, Etudes et documents, nouvelle série, nº 7, partie 2 (Genève, 1948) *Estadísticas del costo de la vida*, Estudios y documentos, nueva serie, núm. 7, parte 2 (Ginebra, 1948)
	Computation of Consumer Price Indices (Special Problems), Tenth International Conference of Labour Statisticians, Report IV (Geneva, 1970) *Calcul des indices des prix à la consommation (Problèmes particuliers)*, dixième Conférence internationale des statisticiens du travail, rapport IV (Genève, 1970) *Cálculo de los índices de los precios del consumo (Problemas especiales)*, décima Conferencia Internacional de Estadígrafos del Trabajo, Informe IV (Ginebra, 1970)
	Technical Guide 1980, Descriptions of general series published in both the *Bulletin* and the *Year Book of Labour Statistics*, Vol. I, Consumer Prices (Geneva, 1980) *Guide technique 1980*, descriptions des séries générales publiées à la fois dans le *Bulletin* et l'*Annuaire des statistiques du travail*, vol. I, Prix à la consommation (Genève, 1980) *Guía Técnica 1980*, descripciones de las series generales publicadas al mismo tiempo en el *Boletín* y el *Anuario de Estadísticas del Trabajo*, vol. I, Precios del consumo (Ginebra, 1980)
Household budgets **Budgets de ménage** **Presupuestos del hogar**	*Methods of Family Living Studies*, Studies and Reports, Series N, No. 23 (Geneva, 1940) *Méthodes d'enquête sur les conditions de vie des familles*, Etudes et documents, série N, nº 23 (Genève, 1941) *Métodos de encuesta sobre las condiciones de vida de las familias*, Estudios y documentos, serie N, núm. 23 (Montreal, 1942)
	Methods of Family Living Studies, Studies and Reports, New Series, No. 17 (Geneva, 1949) *Méthodes d'enquête sur les conditions de vie des familles*, Etudes et documents, nouvelle série, nº 17 (Genève, 1949) *Métodos de encuesta sobre las condiciones de vida de las familias*, Estudios y documentos, nueva serie, núm. 17 (Ginebra, 1949)
	Family Living Studies—A Symposium, Studies and Reports, New Series, No. 63 (Geneva, 1961) *Enquêtes sur les conditions de vie des familles : Recueil de monographies*, Etudes et documents, nouvelle série, nº 63 (Genève, 1961) *Encuestas sobre las condiciones de vida de las familias : Recopilación de monografías*, Estudios y documentos, nueva serie, núm. 63 (Ginebra, 1961)

REFERENCES

References and sources
Références et sources
Referencias y fuentes

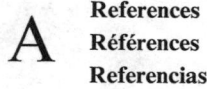

References
Références
Referencias

Subject — *Sujet* — Sujeto	Publications — *Publications* — Publicaciones
Household budgets (concl.) **Budgets de ménage** (fin) **Presupuestos del hogar** (fin)	*Scope, Methods and Uses of Family Expenditure Surveys*, Twelth International Conference of Labour Statisticians, Report III (Geneva, 1971) *Portée, méthodes et utilisation des enquêtes sur les dépenses des familles*, douzième Conférence internationale des statisticiens du travail, rapport III (Genève, 1973) *Alcance, métodos y utilización de las encuestas sobre gastos familiares*, duodécima Conferencia Internacional de Estadígrafos del Trabajo, Informe III (Ginebra, 1971) *Household Income and Expenditure Statistics* No. 3 — 1968-1976 (Geneva, 1979) *Statistiques des revenus et des dépenses des ménages* nº 3 — 1968-1976 (Genève, 1979) *Estadísticas de ingresos y gastos de los hogares* núm. 3 — 1968-1976 (Ginebra, 1979)
Industrial accidents **Accidents du travail** **Accidentes del trabajo**	*Statistics of Industrial Injuries*, Geneva 1970 (document D17/1970/XCIST/II/SAT) *Statistiques des accidents du travail*, Genève, 1970 (document D17/1970/XCIST/II/SAT) *Estadísticas de los accidentes del trabajo*, décima Conferencia Internacional de Estadígrafos del Trabajo, Informe II (Ginebra, 1962) (documento mimeografiado)

References and sources
Références et sources
Referencias y fuentes

B

Sources
Sources
Fuentes

Country — *Pays* — País	Author — *Auteur* — Autor	Publications — *Publications* — Publicaciones
Africa — Afrique Africa		
Algérie	Secrétariat d'Etat au Plan Direction des statistiques	*Bulletin de statistiques générales*
Angola	Direcção dos Serviços de Estatística Banco de Angola	*Boletim mensal* *Boletim trimestrial*
Botswana	Central Statistics Office	*Statistical Bulletin* *Statistical Abstract*
Burundi	Département des études et statistiques	*Bulletin de statistique* (trimestriel)
Rép.-Unie du Cameroun	Direction de la statistique et de la comptabilité nationale	*Bulletin mensuel de statistique* *Note trimestrielle de statistique, série B*
Cap-Vert	Direcção Geral de Estadística	*Boletim trimestral de estatística (Bulletin trimestriel de statistique)*
République centrafricaine	Direction de la statistique générale et des études économiques	*Bulletin mensuel de statistique*
Congo	Ministère du Plan. Commissariat général du Plan	*Bulletin mensuel de statistique*
Côte-d'Ivoire	Ministère de l'Economie et des Finances. Direction de la statistique Chambre d'industrie de Côte-d'Ivoire	*Bulletin mensuel de statistique* *Bulletin mensuel*
Egypt	Central Agency for Public Mobilisation and Statistics	*Statistical Abstract of the UAR* *Monthly Bulletin of Consumer Price Index* *Statistical Handbook*
Ethiopia	Central Statistical Office National Bank of Ethiopia	*Statistical Abstract* *Quarterly Bulletin*
Gabon	Direction générale de la statistique et des études économiques	*Bulletin mensuel de statistique*
Gambia	Central Statistics Division	*Consumer Price Index* *Quarterly Survey of Employment and Earnings*
Ghana	Central Bureau of Statistics Ministry of Labour. National Employment Service Ghana Commercial Bank	*Quarterly Digest of Statistics* *Labour Statistics* *Statistical Year Book* *Employment Market Report* *Monthly Economic Bulletin*
Haute-Volta	Ministère du Plan. Institut national de la statistique et de la démographie	*Bulletin mensuel d'information statistique et économique*
Kenya	Central Bureau of Statistics. Ministry of Finance and Planning	*Kenya Statistical Digest (Quarterly Economic Report)* *Statistical Abstract* *Employment and Earnings in the Modern Sector*
Lesotho	Bureau of Statistics	*Retail Price Indices for Lesotho's Towns*
Liberia	Bureau of Statistics. National Planning Agency	*Statistical Newsletter*
Libyan Arab Jamahiriya	Technical Planning Body. Census and Statistical Department Central Bank of Libya. Economic Research and Statistics Division	*Monthly Cost-of-Living Index for Tripoli Town* *Quarterly Bulletin of Statistics* *Economic Bulletin*
Madagascar	Ministère des Finances et du Plan. Direction de l'Institut national de la statistique et de la recherche économique	*Bulletin mensuel de statistique* *Situation économique*
Malawi	National Statistical Office Ministry of Labour	*Monthly Statistical Bulletin* *Malawi Statistical Year Book* *Reported Employment and Earnings, Annual Report* *Labour Statistics*

SOURCES

References and sources
Références et sources
Referencias y fuentes

B Sources
Sources
Fuentes

Country — *Pays* — País	Author — *Auteur* — Autor	Publications — *Publications* — Publicaciones
Mali	Ministère du Plan. Direction nationale de la statistique et de l'informatique	*Bulletin mensuel de statistique*
Maroc	Premier ministre. Secrétariat d'Etat au plan et au développement régional. Direction de la statistique	*Bulletin mensuel de statistiques* *Indice du coût de la vie* *Annuaire statistique du Maroc*
Mauritanie	Ministère de la Planification et de la Recherche. Direction de la statistique	*Bulletin mensuel de statistique* *Annuaire statistique*
Mauritius	Ministry of Labour Government Central Statistical Office Bank of Mauritius	*Annual Report* *The Government Gazette of Mauritius* *Survey of Employment and Earnings in Large Establishments* *Bi-annual Digest of Statistics* *Quarterly Review*
Mozambique	Direcção Nacional de Estatística	*Boletim mensal de estatística*
Niger	Commissariat général au développement. Service de la statistique	*Bulletin de statistique*
Nigeria	Ministry of Labour Federal Office of Statistics	*Quarterly Review* *Annual Abstract of Statistics* *Digest of Statistics* *Retail Prices in Selected Centres and Consumer Price Indices* *Economic Indicators*
Réunion	Institut national de la statistique et des études économiques (INSEE) INSEE. Service départemental de la Réunion	*Mémento statistique* *Bulletin de statistique des départements et territoires d'outre-mer* *Bulletin de statistiques* *Informations statistiques rapides*
Sénégal	Ministère des Finances et des Affaires économiques. Direction de la statistique	*Bulletin statistique et économique mensuel*
Seychelles	Office of the Statistics	*Seychelles Statistical Bulletin (quarterly)* *Statistical Abstract*
Sierra Leone	Labour Division Government Central Statistics Office	*Annual Report* *The Sierra Leone Gazette* *Statistical Bulletin* *Cost of Living*
Somalia	General Directorate of Planning Co-ordination and Statistics. Central Statistical Department	*Monthly Statistical Bulletin*
South Africa, Rep. of	Department of Labour Department of Statistics	*Annual Report* *South African Statistics* *Bulletin van Statistiek (Bulletin of Statistics)* *Short-Term Economic Indicators*
Sudan	National Commission for Planning. Department of Statistics Manpower Administration. Labour Market Information Unit	*Statistical Year Book* *Survey of Employment Earnings and Hours of Work in establishments employing five employees and more*
Swaziland	Central Statistical Office	*Annual Statistical Bulletin* *Employment and Wages* *Quarterly Digest of Statistics* *Swaziland Statistical News*
Tanzania (Tanganyika)	Department of Labour Ministry of Finance and Planning. Bureau of Statistics	*Annual Report* *Survey of Employment and Earnings* *Statistical Abstract* *Survey of Industrial Production*
Tchad	Ministère de l'Economie, du Plan et des Transports. Sous-direction de la statistique	*Bulletin de statistique*
Togo	Ministère du Plan, du Développement industriel et de la Réforme administrative. Direction de la statistique	*Bulletin mensuel de statistique*

References and sources		Sources
Références et sources	B	Sources
Referencias y fuentes		Fuentes

Country — *Pays* — País	Author — *Auteur* — Autor	Publications — *Publications* — Publicaciones
Tunisie	Ministère du Plan. Institut national de la statistique	*Bulletin mensuel de statistique* *L'économie de la Tunisie en chiffres*
	Banque centrale de Tunisie	*Statistiques financières*
Uganda	Labour Department	*Annual Report*
	East African Statistical Department	*Economic and Statistical Review*
	Ministry of Planning and Economic Development. Statistics Division	*Statistical Abstract* *Quarterly Economic and Statistical Bulletin*
Zaïre	Office national de la recherche et du développement. Institut national de la statistique	*Bulletin trimestriel des statistiques générales* *Prix et indice des prix à la consommation familiale*
	Banque du Zaïre	*Bulletin trimestriel*
Zambia	Department of Labour	*Annual Report*
	Central Statistical Office	*Monthly Digest of Statistics*
	Ministry of Rural Development. Statistics Section	*Statistical Bulletin*
AMERICA — AMÉRIQUE AMÉRICA		
Argentina	Ministerio de Economía. Secretaría de Estado, de Programación y Coordinación Económica. Instituto Nacional de Estadística y Censos	*Boletín estadístico trimestral* *Indices de precios al consumidor y salarios industriales*
Bahamas	Ministry of Labour	*Annual Report*
	Department of Statistics	*Quarterly Statistical Summary* *Annual Review of Prices Report* *Retail Price Index*
Barbados	Department of Labour	*Annual Report*
	Statistical Service	*Monthly Digest of Statistics* *Abstract of Statistics*
Belize	The Labour Department	*Annual Report* *Manpower Report*
	Government	*Government Gazette*
Bolivia	Banco Central. Gerencia Técnica	*Boletín Estadístico*
Brasil	Fundação IBGE. Secretaria de Planejamento da Presidencia da República	*Boletim estatístico* *Anuário estatístico do Brasil*
	Instituto Brasileiro de Economía. Fundação Getulio Vargas	*Conjuntura económica*
	Banco Central do Brasil	*Boletim*
	Instituto de Pesquisas Econômicas, Universidade de São Paulo	*Indices de Preços ao Consumidor*
Canada	Statistics Canada	*Employment Earnings and Hours* *The Labour Force* *Canada Yearbook* *Consumer Prices and Price Indexes* *The Consumer Price Index* *Canadian Statistical Review*
	Department of Labour	*Labour Gazette (Gazette du travail)*
Colombia	Departamento Administrativo Nacional de Estadística	*Anuario general de estadística* *Indicadores socioeconómicos* *Boletín mensual de estadística*
	Banco de la República	*Revista*
Costa Rica	Ministerio de Economía, Industria y Comercio. Dirección General de Estadística y Censos	*Anuario estadístico* *Indice de precios para los consumidores de ingresos medios y bajos del área metropolitana de San José*
	Banco Central de Costa Rica	*Boletín estadístico*

SOURCES

References and sources   **Sources**
Références et sources   **B**   **Sources**
Referencias y fuentes   **Fuentes**

Country — *Pays* — País	Author — *Auteur* — Autor	Publications — *Publications* — Publicaciones
Cuba	Junta Central de Planificación. Dirección Central de Estadística	*Anuario Estadístico de Cuba*
	State Committee of Statistics	*Statistical Year Book Compendium of the Republic of Cuba*
Chile	Instituto Nacional de Estadísticas	*Boletín*
		Indice de precios al consumidor
		Informativo Estadística (trimestral)
		Anuario Estadístico (anual)
		Anuario Laboral (bianual)
		Encuesta Nacional del Empleo
		Gran Santiago : trimestral
		Total país : anual
		Indice de Remuneraciones
	Oficina Nacional de Estadística	*Estadística Industrial*
República Dominicana	Banco Central de la República Dominicana	*Boletín mensual*
Ecuador	Junta Nacional de Planificación y Coordinación. Departamento técnico. División de Estadística y Censos	*Estadísticas de precios. Indice de precios al consumidor de las familias de ingresos bajos y medios de Quito*
	Instituto Nacional de Estadística y Censos	*Indice de precios al consumidor*
		Estadísticas del trabajo : Indices de empleo y remuneraciones
	Banco Central del Ecuador	*Boletín*
El Salvador	Ministerio de Economía. Dirección General de Estadística y Censos	*Boletín estadístico*
		Indice de precios al consumidor obrero para San Salvador, Mejicanos y Villa Delgado
	Ministerio de Trabajo y Previsión Social. Departamento de Planificación	*Estadísticas del trabajo*
	Ministerio de Planificación y Coordinación del Desarrollo Económico y Social Casa Presidencial	*Indicadores económicos y sociales*
Falkland Is. (Malvinas)	Government Printing Office	*The Falkland Islands Gazette*
Greenland	Danmarks Statistik	*Statistiske Efterretninger*
		Statistisk Aarbog (Statistical Yearbook)
Guadeloupe	Institut national de la statistique et des études économiques	*Bulletin de statistique des départements et territoires d'outre-mer*
Guatemala	Banco de Guatemala	*Boletín estadístico*
	Ministerio de Economía. Dirección General de Estadística	*Informador estadístico*
Guyana	Ministry of Economic Development. The Statistical Bureau	*Quarterly Statistical Digest*
	Department of Labour	*Annual Report*
	Government	*The Official Gazette*
Guyane française	Institut national de la statistique et des études économiques	*Bulletin de statistique des départements et territoires d'outre-mer*
	INSEE — Service interrégional Antilles-Guyane	*Bulletin de statistique, Guyane (trimestriel)*
		Bulletin de statistique (sélection mensuelle)
Haïti	Département du Travail	*Revue du travail*
	Département des Finances et des Affaires économiques. Institut haïtien de statistique	*Bulletin trimestriel de statistique*
Honduras	Ministerio de Economía. Dirección General de Estadística y Censos	*Investigación industrial*
		Honduras en cifras
		Anuario estadístico
	Secretaría de Trabajo y Previsión Social. Departamento Nacional de Investigaciones y Estudios Sociales	*Estadísticas del trabajo*
	Banco Central. Departamento de Estudio Económico	*Boletín Estadístico*
Jamaica	Department of Statistics	*Quarterly Abstract of Statistics*
		Consumer Prices Indices, Urban and Rural
		The Labour Force
Martinique	Institut national de la statistique et des études économiques	*Bulletin de statistique des départements et territoires d'outre-mer*
	INSEE (Martinique)	*Bulletin de statistique*

References and sources
Références et sources
Referencias y fuentes

B
Sources
Sources
Fuentes

Country — *Pays* — País	Author — *Auteur* — Autor	Publications — *Publications* — Publicaciones
México	Secretaría de Industria y Comercio. Dirección General de Estadística	*Revista de estadística* *Anuario estadístico compendiado* *Trabajo y Salarios Industriales*
	Banco de México	*Indicadores económicos*
	Secretaría de Programación y Presupuesto	*Anuario estadístico* *Encuesta continua sobre ocupación*
Netherlands Antilles	Departement Economische Zaken. Bureau voor de Statistiek	*Statistische Mededelingen*
Nicaragua	Banco Central de Nicaragua	*Boletín trimestral*
Panamá	Contraloría General de la República. Dirección de Estadística y Censo	*Estadística del trabajo (Mano de obra)* *Panamá en cifras*
Paraguay	Ministerio de Hacienda. Dirección General de Estadística y Censos	*Boletín estadístico del Paraguay*
	Banco Central del Paraguay. Departamento de Estudios Económicos	*Boletín estadístico*
Perú	Ministerio de Justicia y Trabajo. Dirección General del Trabajo. Sección Estadística	*Estadística de Trabajo*
	Instituto Nacional de Estadística	*Indices de precios al consumidor*
	Banco Central de Reserva del Perú	*Boletín*
	Ministerio del Trabajo	*Anuario Estadístico del Sector Trabajo*
Puerto Rico	Department of Labor. Bureau of Labor Statistics	*Employment, Hours and Earnings in the Manufacturing Industries in Puerto Rico* *Employment and Unemployment in Puerto Rico* *Consumer Price Index for Wage Earners' Families in Puerto Rico*
	Puerto Rico Planning Board	*Monthly Economic Indicators of Puerto Rico*
	Banco Central	*Boletín*
St. Lucia	Government	*St. Lucia Gazette*
Suriname	Algemeen Bureau voor de Statistiek	*Prijsindexcijfers van de Gezinsconsumptie (Consumer Price Index)*
Trinidad and Tobago	Central Statistical Office	*Quarterly Economic Report* *CSSP Labour Force* *Economic Indicators* *Annual Statistical Digest*
	Government	*Trinidad and Tobago Gazette (extraordinary)*
United States	Department of Labor. Bureau of Labor Statistics	*News* *Employment and Earnings* *Handbook of Labor Statistics* *Monthly Labor Review*
	Department of Agriculture. Statistical Reporting Service	*Farm Labor*
	Department of Commerce. Bureau of the Census	*Annual Report on the Labor Force* *Statistical Abstract of the United States*
	Economic Statistics Bureau	*The Handbook of Basic Economic Statistics*
Uruguay	Dirección General de Estadística y Censos	*Indice medio de salarios* *Indice de los precios del consumo*
	Banco Central del Uruguay	*Boletín Estadística mensual*
Venezuela	Ministerio de Fomento. Dirección General de Estadística y Censos Nacionales	*Boletín mensual* *Anuario Estadístico*
	Banco Central de Venezuela	*Revista*
	Ministerio del Trabajo. Dirección de Estadística Laboral	*Anuario de estadísticas del trabajo*
	Presidencia de la República. Oficina Central de Estadística e Informática	*Encuesta de hogares por muestreo*

SOURCES

References and sources
Références et sources
Referencias y fuentes

B Sources
Sources
Fuentes

Country — *Pays* — País	Author — *Auteur* — Autor	Publications — *Publications* — Publicaciones
ASIA — ASIE ASIA		
Bangladesh	Bangladesh Bureau of Statistics	*Monthly Statistical Bulletin* *Economic Indicators of Bangladesh*
Brunei	State and Labour Department	*Annual Report*
Burma	Department of Labour Socialist Republic of the Union of Burma. Central Statistical Organization	*People's Workers' Gazette* *Quarterly Bulletin of Statistics* *Statistical Year Book*
Cyprus	Ministry of Finance. Statistics and Research Department	*Statistical Summary* *Statistical Abstract* *Statistics of Wages, Salaries and Hours of Work* *Monthly Economic Indicators* *Economic Report (Annual)*
	Ministry of Labour and Social Insurance	*Annual Report* *Report on the unemployment situation*
Hong Kong	Commisioner for Labour Census and Statistiks Department	*Annual Departmental Report* *Hong Kong Monthly Digest of Statistics* *Wage statistics* *Statistics of Establishments and Employment* *Hong Kong Annual Digest of Statistics*
India	Central Statistical Organisation. Department of Statistics Ministry of Planning	*Monthly Abstract of Statistics* *Indian Labour Journal* *Indian Labour Statistics*
	Directorate General of Employment and Training. Ministry of Labour	*Employment Review (Annual)*
Indonesia	Biro Pusat Statistik	*Buletin Statistik Bulanan. Indikator Ekonomi (Monthly Statistical Bulletin)* *Statistik Indonesia (Statistical Pocketbook of Indonesia)* *Statistik Indonesia (Statistical Year Book of Indonesia)*
Iran	Bank Markazi. Economic Research Department	*Bulletin*
Iraq	Ministry of Planning. Central Statistical Organization. Publication and Public Relations	*Annual Abstract of Statistics* *Quarterly Bulletin of Statistics* *Price and Index Numbers*
Israel	Central Bureau of Statistics	*Monthly Bulletin of Statistics* *Statistical Abstract of Israel*
	Bank of Israel National Insurance Institute. Bureau of Research and Planning	*Economic Review* *Quarterly Statistics*
Japan	Minister's Secretariat. Ministry of Labour. Statistics and Information Department	*Monthly Labour Statistics and Research Bulletin* *Year Book of Labour Statistics*
	Economic Planning Agency	*Economic Statistics* *Japanese Economic Indicators*
	Statistics Bureau. Prime Minister's Office	*Monthly Report on the Labour Force Survey* *Annual Report on the Labour Force Survey* *Annual Report on the Consumer Price Index* *Consumer Price Index (Monthly)* *Statistical Yearbook* *Monthly Statistics of Japan*
	The Bank of Japan. Statistics Department Japan Productivity Center	*Monthly Economic Statistics*
Jordan	The Hashemite Kingdom of Jordan. Department of Statistics Central Bank of Jordan	*The cost of living index* *Monthly Statistical Bulletin*

References and sources
Références et sources
Referencias y fuentes

B Sources
Sources
Fuentes

Country — *Pays* — País	Author — *Auteur* — Autor	Publications — *Publications* — Publicaciones
Kampuchea démocratique	Ministère du Plan. Institut national de la statistique et des recherches économiques.	*Bulletin statistique*
Korea, Rep. of	Economic Planning Board. Bureau of Statistics	*Monthly Statistics of Korea* *Annual Report on the Economically Active Population Survey* *Korea Statistical Yearbook*
	Bank of Korea	*Monthly Economic Statistics* *Monthly Economic Review*
Kuwait	Central Statistical Office. Ministry of Planning	*Annual Statistical Abstract* *Quarterly Statistical Bulletin* *Monthly Bulletin of Price Index Numbers*
République lao	Ministère du Plan et de la Coopération. Service national de la statistique	*Bulletin de statistiques*
Liban	Ministère du Plan. Direction centrale de la statistique	*Bulletin statistique mensuel*
Malaysia	Department of Statistics	*Monthly Statistical Bulletin of West Malaysia* *Consumer Price Index (Peninsular Malaysia-Sabah-Sarawak)*
	Manpower Department	*Monthly Bulletin*
	Ministry of Labour and Manpower	*Handbook of Labour Statistics (Peninsular Malaysia)*
Nepal	Nepal Rasha Bank, Research Department	*Main Economic Indicators*
Pakistan	Ministry of Labour, Manpower, Health and Population Planning (Labour Division)	*Pakistan Labour Gazette*
	Statistics Division	*Monthly Statistical Bulletin* *Key Economic Indicators* *Newsletter*
	State Bank of Pakistan. Department of Public Relations	*Bulletin*
Philippines	Department of Labor	*Selected Labor Indicators*
	National Economic and Development Authority. Bureau of the Census and Statistics	*Monthly Bulletin of Statistics* *Statistical Year Book* *Journal of Philippine Statistics* *Consumers' Price Index for all income households* *The BCS Survey of Households Bulletin—Labour Force*
	Office of Statistical Coordination and Standards. National Economic Council	*The Statistical Reporter* *Philippines Financial Statistics*
	Central Bank of the Philippines. Department of Economic Research	*Statistical Bulletin* *Central Bank New Digest*
	Bureau of Employment Service	*The Employment Situation (Annual)*
Saudi Arabia	Ministry of Finance and National Economy. Central Department of Statistics	*The Statistical Indicator*
Singapore	Department of Statistics	*Monthly Digest of Statistics* *Yearbook of Statistics*
	Ministry of Labour and National Statistical Commission	*Report on the Labour Force Survey of Singapore* *Singapore Yearbook of Labour Statistics*
Sri Lanka	Department of Labour	*Sri Lanka Labour Gazette* *Employment Survey*
	Department of Census and Statistics	*Statistical Abstract of Sri Lanka*
	Central Bank of Ceylon	*Bulletin*
République arabe syrienne	Office of the Prime Minister. Central Bureau of Statistics	*Statistical Abstract*
	Centre d'études et de documentations économiques, financières et sociales	*Etude mensuelle sur l'économie et les finances des pays arabes*
	Central Bank of Syria	*Quarterly Bulletin*
	Ministry of Social Affairs and Labour. Statistics Division	*The Annual Statistical Bulletin of the Ministry of Social Affairs and Labour*

SOURCES

References and sources
Références et sources
Referencias y fuentes

B

Sources
Sources
Fuentes

Country — *Pays* — País	Author — *Auteur* — Autor	Publications — *Publications* — Publicaciones
Thailand	National Statistical Office. Office of the Prime Minister	*Quarterly Bulletin of Statistics*
		Final Report of the Labor Force Survey
	Bank of Thailand	*Monthly Bulletin*
	Department of Labour	*Yearbook of Labour Statistics*
Viet Nam [1]	Bô Ké-Hoach Và Phât-Triên Quôc-Gia. Viên Quôc-Gia Thóng-Kê (National Institute of Statistics. Ministry of National Planning and Development)	*Niên giám Thong-Kê Viet-Nam (Statistical Yearbook/Annuaire statistique)* [2]
		Thong-kê Nguyêt-San (Monthly Bulletin of Statistics/Bulletin mensuel de statistique) [2]
Yemen, Democratic	Department of Labour and Welfare	*Annual Report*
	Government	*People's Republic, Official Gazette*
EUROPE — EUROPE EUROPA		
Austria	Österreichisches Statistisches Zentralamt	*Statistisches Handbuch für die Republik Österreich*
		Statistische Nachrichten
	Österreichisches Institut für Wirtschaftsforschung	*Monatsberichte*
		Statistische Übersichten
	Bundesministerium für Soziale Verwaltung	*Amtliche Nachrichten des Bundesministeriums für Soziale Verwaltung*
	Bundeskammer der gewerblichen Wirtschaft. Sektion Industrie (Bundessektion Industrie)	*Monatliche Beschäftigtenstatistik*
Belgique	Banque nationale de Belgique	*Bulletin*
	Ministère des Affaires économiques. Institut national de statistique	*Bulletin de statistique*
		Communiqué hebdomadaire
		Statistiques sociales
		Annuaire statistique de la Belgique
	Ministère de l'Emploi et du Travail	*Revue du travail*
		Informations statistiques. Etudes
	Ministère de l'Emploi et du Travail. Office national de l'emploi	*Bulletin mensuel*
		Rapport annuel
	Office national de sécurité sociale	*Les gains des travailleurs assujettis à la Sécurité sociale*
	Ministère des Affaires économiques. Direction générale des études et de la documentation	*Aperçu de l'évolution économique*
Bulgarie	Комитет ло единна система за сочиална информация лри Министерския съвет	*Статистически годишник на НР България (Annuaire statistique)*
	Comité de système unifié d'information sociale auprès du Conseil des ministres	*Статистически известия (Bulletin statistique trimestriel)*
		Статистически справочник (Manuel statistique)
Czechoslovakia	Office fédéral de la statistique	*Statistická ročenka Československé socialistické republiky (Annuaire statistique de la République socialiste tchécoslovaque)*
	Federálni Statistický Úřad	*Statistické Přehledy*
Denmark	Danmarks Statistiks	*Statistiske Efterretninger*
		Statistisk Aarbog (Statistical Yearbook)
		Arbejds Løsheden
		Nyt fra Danmarks Statistik
	Dansk Arbejdsgiverforenings Lønstatistik	*Statistikken "Arbejderløn"*
España	Ministerio de Economía. Instituto Nacional de Estadística	*Boletín mensual de estadística*
		Anuario estadístico
		Salarios
		Encuesta de población activa
	Servicio nacional de colocación de la Organización sindical española. Departamento de Estadística	*Estadísticas de demandas y ofertas de trabajo, colocaciones y desempleo*
	Ministerio de Agricultura	*Boletín mensual de estadística agraria*

[1] Former Democratic Rep. of Viet-Nam and Rep. of South Viet-Nam. [2] Data refer to the former Rep. of South Viet-Nam only.

[1] *Précédemment Rép. démocratique du Viet-Nam et Rép. du Sud Viet-Nam.* [2] *Les données se rapportent à l'ancienne Rép. du Sud Viet-Nam seulement.*

[1] Anteriormente Rep. Democrática de Viet-Nam y Rep. de Viet-Nam del Sur. [2] Los datos se refieren a la antigua Rep. de Viet-Nam del Sur solamente.

References and sources
Références et sources   **B**   Sources
Referencias y fuentes   Sources
                                  Fuentes

Country — *Pays* — País	Author — *Auteur* — Autor	Publications — *Publications* — Publicaciones
Finland	Tilastokeskus Statistikcentralen (Central Statistical Office)	*Suomen Tilastollinen Vuosikirja — Statistisk Årsbok för Finland (Statistical Yearbook of Finland)* *Tilastokatsauksia (Bulletin of Statistics)* *Työvoimatiedustelu (Labour Force Survey)* *Tilastotiedotus PA (Statistical reports, subseries PA wage statistics)* *Tilastollisia tiedonantoja (Statistical surveys) No 61, Työvoimatiedustelun tuloksia vuosilta 1959-1975 (Results of the labour force survey from the years 1959-1975)*
	Sosiaaliministeriö — Socialministeriet	*Sosiaalinen Aikakauskirja — Social Tidskrift (Social Review)*
	Bank of Finland	*Monthly Bulletin*
	Työvoimaministeriö (Ministry of Labour)	*Työvoimakatsaus (Labour Reports)*
	Suomen Virallinen Tilasto (Official Statistics of Finland)	*Teollisuustilasto (Industrial Statistics) Osa 1, Vol. 1*
	Työsuojeluhallitus (National Board of Labour)	*Suomen virallinen tilasto (Official statistics of Finland) XXVI A, Työtapaturmat (Industrial accidents)*
France	Ministère du Travail et de la Participation	*Statistiques du travail (Bulletin mensuel)* *Supplément : Enquête trimestrielle sur l'activité et les conditions d'emploi de la main-d'œuvre* *Données mensuelles sur le marché du travail* *Revue française des affaires sociales*
	Ministère de l'Economie et des Finances. Institut national de la statistique et des études économiques	*Bulletin mensuel de statistique* *Annuaire statistique de la France* *Economie et statistique* *Informations rapides*
German Democratic Republic	Staatlichen Zentralverwaltung für Statistik	*Statistisches Jahrbuch der Deutschen Demokratischen Republik*
Germany, Fed. Rep. of	Statistisches Bundesamt, Wiesbaden	*Wirtschaft und Statistik* *Statistischer Wochendienst* *Statistisches Jahrbuch für die Bundesrepublik Deutschland* *Preise* *Beruf, Ausbildung und Arbeitsbedingungen der Erwerbstätigen 1975 bis 1976, Fachserie 1, Reihe 4.1.2.* *Industrie und Handwerk (Beschäftigung, Umsatz und Energieversorgung der Unternehmen und Betriebe), Fachserie 4, Reihe 4.1.* *Löhne und Gehälter (Arbeiterverdienste in der Industrie), Fachserie 16, Reihe 2.1.*
	Bundesanstalt für Arbeit	*Amtliche Nachrichten der Bundesanstalt für Arbeit*
	Bundesminister für Arbeit und Sozialordnung	*Arbeits- und Sozialstatistik* *Hauptergebnisse der Arbeits- und Sozialstatistik*
Gibraltar	Government	*Gibraltar Gazette*
Grèce	National Statistical Service	*Monthly Statistical Bulletin* *Statistical Yearbook of Greece*
	Bank of Greece. Economic Research Department	*Monthly Statistical Bulletin*
Hongrie	Központi statisztikai hivatal (Central Statistical Office)	*Statisztikai havi közlemények (Monthly Bulletin of Statistics)* *Statisztikai Zsebkönyv (Manuel statistique)* *Statisztikai Évkönyv (Statistical Yearbook)*
Iceland	The Statistical Bureau of Iceland and the Central Bank of Iceland	*Statistical Bulletin*
	Gefin út af Hagstofu Islands	*Hagtídindi*
Ireland	Central Statistics Office	*Irish Statistical Bulletin (Quarterly)* *Statistical Abstract of Ireland* *The Trend of Employment and Unemployment* *Industrial Inquiries*
	Central Bank of Ireland	*Quarterly Bulletin*

SOURCES

References and sources
Références et sources
Referencias y fuentes

B

Sources
Sources
Fuentes

Country — *Pays* — País	Author — *Auteur* — Autor	Publications — *Publications* — Publicaciones
Italie	Ministero del Lavoro e della Previdenza Sociale	*Statistiche del lavoro* *Annuario di statistiche del lavoro* *Supplemento al Bollettino statistiche del lavoro*
	Istituto Centrale di Statistica	*Annuario statistico italiano* *Bollettino mensile di statistica* *Supplemento al Bolletino mensile di statistica* *Indicatori mensili* *Compendio statistico italiano* *Rilevazione delle forze di lavoro*
	Servizio Italiano Pubblicazioni Internazionali	*Rassegna di statistiche del lavoro*
Luxembourg	Service central de la statistique et des études économiques	*Bulletin du Statec* *Annuaire statistique* *Indicateurs rapides* *Cahiers économiques* *Notes trimestrielles de conjoncture*
Malta	Government Central Office of Statistics	*The Malta Government Gazette* *Annual Abstract of Statistics* *Quarterly Digest of Statistics*
Netherlands	Centraal Bureau voor de Statistiek (Central Bureau of Statistics)	*Maandschrift* *Sociale Maandstatistiek* *Statistisch bulletin* *Jaarcijfers voor Nederland (Statistical Yearbook of the Netherlands)* *Maandstatistiek van de industrie (Monthly Statistical Bulletin of Manufacturing)*
Norway	Statistisk Sentralbyrå (Central Bureau of Statistics)	*Statistisk Månedshefte (Monthly Bulletin of Statistics)* *Statistik Årbok (Statistical Yearbook)* *Statistisk Ukehefte (Weekly Bulletin of Statistics)* *Historisk Statistikk 1978 (Historical Statistics 1978)* *Arbeidsmarkedstatistikk (Labour Market Statistics)*
	Arbeidsdirektoratet (The Directorate of Labour)	*Lønnsstatistikk (Wage Statistics)* *Månedsrapport om utviklingen på arbeidsmarkedet*
	Norges Bank (Bank of Norway)	*Economic Bulletin*
Pologne	Główny Urzad Statystyczny. Central Statistical Office	*Biuletyn statystyczny* *Rocznik Statystyczny (Statistical Yearbook)*
Portugal	Instituto Nacional de Estatística. Serviços Centrais	*Boletim mensal de estatística (Bulletin mensuel de statistique)* *Anuário estatístico (Annuaire statistique)* *Estatísticas industriais (Statistiques industrielles)* *Estatísticas agrícolas* *Inquérito permanente do emprego (Enquête permanente sur l'emploi)*
	Serviço de Estatística, Ministério do Trabalho	*Estatísticas do Trabalho*
Roumanie	Directia Centralá de Statisticá	*Buletin Statistic Trimestrial* *Anuarul Statistic al RSR*
Suisse	Département fédéral de l'Economie publique Bureau fédéral de statistique Banque nationale suisse	*La Vie économique* *Annuaire statistique de la Suisse* *Bulletin mensuel*
Sweden	Kommerskollegium	*Sveriges Officiella Statistik, Olycksfall i arbete (Industrial Accidents)*
	Statistiska Centralbyrán (National Central Bureau of Statistics)	*Statistisk Årsbok för Sverige (Statistical Abstract of Sweden)* *Sveriges Officiella Statistik (Official Statistics of Sweden), Industri (Manufacturing)* *Allmän Månadsstatistik (Monthly Digest of Swedish Statistics)* *Statistiska Meddelanden (Statistical Reports)* *Arbetmarknadsstatistik*

References and sources
Références et sources
Referencias y fuentes

B

Sources
Sources
Fuentes

Country — *Pays* — País	Author — *Auteur* — Autor	Publications — *Publications* — Publicaciones
Turquie	Türkiye Cumhuriyet Merkez Bankasi (Banque centrale de la République de Turquie)	*Aylik Bülten (Bulletin mensuel)*
	Basbakanlik Devlet İstatístík Enstitüsu (State Institute of Statistics)	*Aylik İstatístik Bülteni (Monthly Bulletin of Statistics)* *İstatistik Yilligi (Annuaire statistique)* *Aylik Fiyat Indeksleri Bülteni*
	Tícaret Bakanligi (Ministère du Commerce)	*Konjonktür (Conjoncture)*
United Kingdom	Board of Trade	*Board of Trade Journal*
	Central Statistical Office	*Monthly Digest of Statistics* *Annual Abstract of Statistics* *Economic Trends*
	Department of Employment	*Department of Employment Gazette* *British Labour Statistics, Year Book* *British Labour Statistics, Historical Abstract*
Yugoslavia	Savezni Zavod za Statistiku	*Statistički Godišnjak SFRJ (Annuaire statistique de la République socialiste fédérative de Yougoslavie)* *Indeks, Mesečni Pregled Privredne Statistike SFR Jugoslavije (L'Indice, revue mensuelle des statistiques économiques de la RSF de Yougoslavie)*
	Gradski Zavod za Statistiku	*Statistički bitten (Bulletin statistique)*
OCEANIA — OCÉANIE OCEANÍA		
Australia	Australian Bureau of Statistics	*Digest of Current Economic Statistics* *Monthly Review of Business Statistics* *Employment and Unemployment* *Wage Rates and Earnings* *Labour Report* *Year Book of the Commonwealth of Australia* *Labour Statistics* *Consumer Price Index* *Average weekly earnings* *Civilian employees*
Fiji	Department of Labour	*Annual Report*
	Government	*Fiji Royal Gazette*
	Bureau of Statistics	*Current Economic Statistics* *Quarterly Survey on Employment* *Annual Report on Employment Survey*
Guam	Office of Business and Economic Statistics, Economic Research Center	*Quarterly Economic and Social Indicators*
	Department of Commerce, Economic Research Center	*Statistical Abstract (Annual)*
New Zealand	Department of Statistics	*Monthly Abstract of Statistics* *Industrial Injuries* *Prices, Wages, Labour* *New Zealand Official Year Book* *Social Trends in New Zealand*
	Department of Labour	*Monthly Statistics of Employment* *Labour and Employment Gazette*
	Social Security Department	*Annual Reports*
Nouvelle-Calédonie	Institut national de la statistique et des études économiques	*Bulletin de statistique des départements et territoires d'outre-mer*
	Service de la statistique (Nouméa)	*Informations statistiques rapides* *Annuaire statistique de la Nouvelle-Calédonie*

SOURCES

| References and sources
Références et sources
Referencias y fuentes | **B** | Sources
Sources
Fuentes |

Country — *Pays* — País	Author — *Auteur* — Autor	Publications — *Publications* — Publicaciones
Papua New Guinea	Bureau of Statistics	*Statistical Bulletin* *Abstract of Statistics* *Economic Indicators*
Polynésie française	Institut national de la statistique et des études économiques	*Bulletin de statistique des départements et territoires d'outre-mer*
Samoa	Department of Statistics	*Quarterly Statistical Bulletin* *Annual Statistical Abstract*
Solomon Is.	Statistics Division. Ministry of Finance	*Quarterly Digest of Statistics* *Statistical Bulletin*
Tonga	Department of Statistics	*Consumer Price Index* *Annual Statistical Abstract*
Vanuatu [1]	Condominium Bureau of Statistics	*Statistical Bulletin*
URSS	Центральное статистическое управление при Совете Министров СССР (Central Statistical Board under the Council of Ministers of the USSR; Office central de statistique près le Conseil des ministres de l'URSS)	*Вестник статистики* *Народное хозяйство СССР, статистический ежегодник* *Страна Советов за 60 лет, статистический сборник,* Москва, 1978 (*Soviet Union, 60 years: Statistical returns,* Moscow, 1978; *L'Union soviétique en 60 ans: Recueil de statistiques,* Moscou, 1978) *Труд в СССР, статистический сборник,* Москва, 1968
RSS de Biélorussie	Центральное статистическое управление при Совете Министров Белорусской ССР	*Народное хозяйство Белорусской ССР. Статистический сборник*
RSS d'Ukraine	Центральне статистичне управління при Раді Міністрів УРСР	*Народне господарство Української РСР*

[1] Former New Hebrides.   [1] *Précédemment Nouvelles Hébrides.*   [1] Anteriormente Nuevas Hébridas.